AMERICAN CONSTITUTIONAL INTERPRETATION

SECOND EDITION

By

WALTER F. MURPHY
Princeton University

JAMES E. FLEMING
Fordham University

SOTIRIOS A. BARBER
University of Notre Dame

Westbury, New York
THE FOUNDATION PRESS, INC.
1995

Library of Congress Cataloging-in-Publication Data

Murphy, Walter F., 1929–
    American constitutional interpretation / by Walter F. Murphy,
James E. Fleming, Sotirios A. Barber. — 2nd ed.
      p.   cm.
    Includes index.
    ISBN 1–56662–240–9 (hardcover)
    1. United States—Constitutional law—Interpretation and
construction—Cases. I. Fleming, James E. II. Barber, Sotirios A.
III. Title.
KF4549.M87   1995
342.73'02—dc20
[347.3022]   95–5575

TEXT IS PRINTED ON 10% POST
CONSUMER RECYCLED PAPER

PRINTED WITH
SOY INK™

*To the past and future of Princeton's tradition of
constitutional scholarship, begun by*

*Woodrow Wilson and nurtured by
W. F. Willoughby,
Edward S. Corwin, and
Alpheus Thomas Mason*

*

PREFACE

The goal of both editions of this book has been to meet a need for teaching materials that directly confront the core problems of the enterprise of *constitutional interpretation*. To learn about politics in a constitutional democracy, to teach students about politics in such a polity, and to share ideas with colleagues with similar interests, we must teach about a political system as a whole. And, for the United States and most industrialized nations, that "whole" includes a constitutional text. Relationships between those texts and the socio-political entities that Aristotle called "constitutions" remain problematic, even for the United States, as many of the readings in this volume demonstrate.

How authoritative interpreters construe a nation's constitutional text and broader constitution will always have a significant, and sometimes a critical, effect on the future of that polity as well as on specific public policies. We try to highlight those broader systemic effects by stressing the dual nature of the American political system: It is a constitutional democracy, not a democracy or even a representative democracy. It rests on a pair of political theories,[1] constitutionalism as well as democracy.

We have organized this volume around a set of basic interrogatives: WHAT is the constitution that is to be interpreted? WHO are its authoritative interpreters? And HOW do (and should) they go about their interpretive tasks? Although we do not harbor any illusions that constitutional interpretation can ever be a science in the sense of chemistry or physics, it need not, indeed, should not, be mere partisan responses to particular practical problems. In sum, while we believe that constitutional interpretation is an art, we also believe that it is an art that can be disciplined. This view is not universally shared among political scientists, practicing lawyers, elected public officials, or even members of the U.S. Supreme Court. But it is a belief that is hardly unique to us. We hope to convince others to think about and even test its validity for the United States and other nations as well.[2]

We have tried to accomplish these tasks not by focusing exclusively on legal doctrines, but by showing students how constitutional interpretation connects with both political theory and public policy. Constitutional interpretation is, perhaps inevitably, informed by political theory, usually produces legal doctrine, and always interacts with, and sometimes changes, other forces in the political system. In turn, those forces act on the interpretive enterprise, sometimes changing the decisions it yields, sometimes modifying the nature of that enterprise, and occasionally reshaping the polity itself.

[1] Later we make the obvious point that there is no single democratic theory any more than there is a single theory of constitutionalism, a fact that complicates constitutional interpretation not only in the United States but also in Australia, Canada, India, Japan, most nations of Europe, and some in Latin America.

[2] One of us did co-produce a volume of essays, cases, and materials that cut across national lines: Walter F. Murphy and Joseph Tanenhaus, *Comparative Constitutional Law* (New York: St. Martin's, 1977).

Answers to the WHAT, WHO, and HOW of constitutional interpretation are difficult and controversial, but no intellectually serious effort to understand or engage in constitutional interpretation can avoid them. And answers, as we have indicated, may have enormous consequences for the entire polity. A public official who believes "the Constitution" is totally contained within the plain words of the document of 1787–88 and its amendments is very apt to see the rules of the political system, its distributions of decision-making authority, and its values and goals very differently from an official who believes that "the Constitution" includes traditions, practices, and perhaps even political theories that bind and loose as authoritatively as does the document. So, too, a response to the interrogative WHO that Congress or the President has interpretive authority equal or superior to that of the judiciary has massive implications not only for public policy, but also for the nature of the political system. Similarly significant consequences follow from responses about HOW to interpret.

We recognize that, if students are to explore these basic questions intelligently, they need to understand some of the substance of constitutional law. We have therefore organized analyses of these interrogatives around customary categories of constitutional law and theory. For example, we discuss questions of HOW to interpret in connection with approaches to interpretation such as *textualism, structuralism*, and *reinforcing representative democracy*. To some extent, all of the materials illustrate *textualism*, for the American constitutional document has such sanctity that, even when going against its terms, public officials find it necessary to rationalize their actions by "interpreting" those words.[3] To illustrate *structuralism*, we look at sharings of power among the presidency, Congress, and the national judiciary as well as sharings generated by federalism. To illustrate how interpreters approach "the Constitution" as a device to *reinforce representative democracy*, we deal with problems involving freedom of communication and political participation. And to analyze an approach that views "the Constitution" as a scheme to *protect fundamental rights*, we examine writings concerned with property, religious liberty, privacy, and personhood. In sum, we have designed this book so that no one who uses it can avoid learning a great deal of constitutional law. We intend, however, that users will also learn much more.

Instructors will thus find much in these pages that is familiar from other casebooks, but those materials are organized here in ways that, we believe, will enlighten students about the nature and relevance of constitutional interpretation. We should caution, however, that our editings of materials often include sections omitted by editors who are more concerned to present legal doctrines than to link political theory, public policy, and constitutional interpretation.

[3] Thomas Jefferson's refusal to engage in constitutional interpretation to rationalize what he thought was his own unconstitutional action in purchasing the Louisiana Territory is the great exception.

To guide students, we have begun Parts and Chapters with introductory essays and included bibliographies there as well as after some of the cases. Because we know that many instructors will not assign all pages of this book, we have deliberately built in some redundancy. We fear that a neat, economical presentation of questions, arguments, evidence, and bibliography will cause many important points to be lost. After most of the readings we have also appended additional notes and queries. Some of this apparatus may be of use to busy instructors as well as to beginning students.

To allow students to savor the rhetoric as well as the reasoning that judges deploy to justify their work—something of the *doctrinal approach* judges so often follow—we have retained many (though not all) of their references to previous decisions. To make the book more legible, we have eliminated the citations to those cases. At the end of the volume a Table of Cases, with full citations, enables readers to pursue further research.

This book is large. It provides more than enough readings—and we hope ideas—to energize a two-semester course, though the editors themselves have used this volume only for one-semester courses. In any event, if we take democratic theory seriously, having a choice is not a bad thing.

We would make a pair of additional points. None of us pretends to be indifferent about either the three basic interrogatives around which we have structured this book or the enterprise of constitutional interpretation itself. Each of us thinks of himself as a defender of constitutional democracy. On the other hand, we do not completely agree about some aspects of the American version of free government. We disagree among ourselves, for instance, on precisely WHAT it is "the Constitution" includes, the limits on how it may be legitimately changed, and HOW it should be interpreted. We also disagree about some of the substantive results of constitutional interpretation.

We hope our disagreements are functional for users of this book. Rather than present a party line about "correct" answers to the basic interrogatives or specific issues of constitutional interpretation and law, we have tried to offer readers a range of arguments for differing responses. As Gerald Graff, the noted literary critic, has said, "the surest way to protect students from being bullied by their teachers' political views is to expose them to the debates between those views."[4]

Efforts to present several sides of disputes do not, we think, reflect moral or constitutional relativism or even pragmatic compromise, for none of us subscribes to the equality of all moral or constitutional answers. Rather, our editorial decision represents a collective faith in reasoned argument, a belief that offering readers options that require them to think long and hard gives them the best chance of reaching justifiable conclusions. Faith in constitutional democracy, after all, rests on belief in human dignity and, therefore, on the capacity of free men and

[4] Letter to the Editor, *New York Review of Books*, May 16, 1991, p. 62.

women to solve moral and constitutional problems in ways that preserve and enhance that dignity.

———

William F. Harris II, one of the three editors/authors of the first edition, did not take part in preparing this second edition. We appreciate his contributions to the first edition and have missed his wisdom on this version. Sotirios A. Barber has joined us. During the years when the first edition was gestating as a set of photocopied materials, he twice taught at Princeton as a visitor and used those readings both there and at the University of South Florida. Later, he read and criticized the manuscript of the first edition for us and used the published book at Notre Dame.

We are grateful to many other people for years of assistance, some of it unwitting. We first used a photocopied form of this volume at Princeton in "Constitutional Interpretation," a course begun by Edward S. Corwin during World War I, continued by Alpheus Thomas Mason after Corwin's retirement in 1946, and later carried on by each of us. Early versions of these pages travelled to the University of Michigan (where Corwin had been President of the class of 1900) when Harris joined that faculty in 1982.[5] As a result, several generations of undergraduates at these institutions, as well as at South Florida, put up with some of what is here. Their sharp criticisms of those materials and later students' equally pointed comments about the first edition helped make this a better book. We are grateful to them, though they might believe otherwise. We are also indebted to faculty at other institutions, including Christopher L. Eisgruber of New York University School of Law, Peter Fish of Duke, John E. Finn of Wesleyan, Ronald Kahn of Oberlin, and Stephen Wasby of SUNY at Albany for commenting on either or both editions. Karen Flax, Esq., read portions of the manuscript of both editions and gently, though firmly, corrected some of our errors; Prof. Linda C. McClain of Hofstra University School of Law gave similar and much needed advice on the second edition and also helped in examining the Papers of Justice Thurgood Marshall in the Library of Congress. People who taught with us at Princeton, Notre Dame, and Michigan, some as visiting faculty, some as teaching fellows, also liberally offered time and ideas:

Mark E. Brandon, University of Michigan

Donald Drakeman, Princeton, NJ

Judith Lynn Failer, Indiana University

Robert P. George, Princeton University

Benjamin Gregg, University of Texas

Suzette Marie Hemberger, Johns Hopkins University

Gregory C. Keating, University of Southern California

Andrew M. M. Koppelman, Princeton University

Wayne D. Moore, Virginia Polytechnic Institute

[5] After moving in 1986 to the University of Pennsylvania, where Corwin had obtained his Ph.D. in 1905, Harris used the published version there.

Ethan Nadelmann, Lindesmith Center
Jennifer Nedelsky, University of Toronto
Anthony J. Sebok, Brooklyn Law School
Jeffrey Tulis, University of Texas
The late Clement E. Vose, Wesleyan University
Paul K. Warr, Texas A & M University
Peter Widulski, Columbia University
Thomas H. Wright, Princeton University

Stephanie Jinks and Kelly Murphy of Princeton and Denise Stauber of Chicago translated some of our marginal scribblings into machine-readable language. Kelly Murphy also undertook the tedious task of cross-referencing much of the material reprinted here. James Sigmund of the Princeton Class of 1995 and Lynda Bazarian and J. Kyle Hudson, both graduate students at Princeton, performed ably as research assistants for this edition, as did Lawrence McGabe, Steven Shaw, and Sabrena Silver of Fordham Law School. The Cromwell Fund of Princeton University provided funds for research. For this book as well as for most other work in political science done at Princeton during the past thirty-three years, Rosemary Allen Little cheerfully and efficiently opened the resources of Firestone Library.

We must also thank two publishers: Harold Eriv, who, when this book existed as a concept rather than a conception, was President of Foundation Press and had the courage to support it; and his successor, Richard T. Fenton, who had the good judgment to ask us to continue its life. Dr. Charles ViVona of Foundation has been a continuing source of encouragement, generally relying on the carrot of meals at good restaurants to urge us on but occasionally brandishing a stick when we seemed to lag. For both editions, James Coates skillfully shepherded the manuscript through that labyrinth euphemistically called production.

We acknowledge responsibility for all errors that remain, including those that "Spellcheck" missed. Yet, as we said in the Preface to the first edition, if there were a way of graciously sharing blame with those commentators, judges, and other public officials who have so often misinterpreted the constitutional text as well as the broader constitution, we would most eagerly seize it.

WFM
Princeton, NJ

JEF
New York, NY

SAB
Notre Dame, IN

April 24, 1995

*

SUMMARY OF CONTENTS

Section D: Treating Equals Equally

Section E: Maintaining Constitutional Democracy: Protecting Fundamental Rights

PART V

CONSTITUTIONAL DEMOCRACY IN THE CRUCIBLE OF CRISIS

EPILOGUE

APPENDICES

TABLE OF CONTENTS

PART I

THE CONTEXT OF CONSTITUTIONAL INTERPRETATION

PART II

WHAT IS THE CONSTITUTION?

PART III

WHO MAY AUTHORITATIVELY INTERPRET THE CONSTITUTION?

Section D: Treating Equals Equally

PART V

CONSTITUTIONAL DEMOCRACY IN THE CRUCIBLE OF CRISIS

AMERICAN CONSTITUTIONAL INTERPRETATION

*

1

Interpreting a Constitution

The initial question anyone interested in constitutional interpretation must ask is: What is "the constitution" that is to be interpreted? Any answer to this most basic of interpretive questions requires that we be clear about several terms, *constitution, constitutional text*, and *constitutionalism*.[1] Every country has a *constitution*; but not all have a formal document so labelled, and not all that have a constitutional document endorse *constitutionalism*. (To facilitate distinction, we shall, but only in this chapter, put *constitution* and *constitutionalism* in italics.)

In its narrowest sense, the term *constitution* refers to the ways in which a government is organized: the reach of public authority, methods of selecting public officials and making policy, as well as divisions (if any) of power among institutions. In its broadest sense, as Aristotle came to use the word, a *constitution* reaches far beyond government and designates a people's way of life. Thus it is accurate not only to describe the American form of government as belonging to the category of constitutional democracy, but also to say that the United States is a constitutional democracy.

Although most nations now have a document that calls itself a *constitution*, a few, even some that like to refer to themselves constitutional democracies, such as Britain, Israel, and New Zealand, lack such a central text. Instead, they have "understandings" and/or traditions about fundamental political arrangements.[2] Even in countries that have a constitutional text, the *constitution* may or may not be completely encapsulated in that document. Indeed, the *constitution* and the constitutional text may bear little or no relation to each other. The words of Josef Stalin's or Mao Tse Tung's constitutional texts gave only misleading clues about how political

---

1. For a more detailed analysis, see Walter F. Murphy, "Constitutions, Constitutionalism, and Democracy," in Douglas Greenberg, Stanley N. Katz, Melanie Beth Oliviero, and Steven C. Wheatley, eds., *Constitutionalism and Democracy* (New York: Oxford University Press, 1993).

2. A nation that does not have a formal *constitutional text* may codify, as the British have done, some of its fundamental political orderings through statutes. These laws do not of themselves provide standards for the validity of later legislative or executive action. They may express those standards but do not, by their own authority, control the legitimacy of later statutes. It is the "understandings" and/or traditions that are authoritative.

power was distributed and exercised in the Soviet Union or China. To understand the real *constitution* of either nation, one had to look elsewhere.

In contrast, so Americans like to believe, their constitutional text, "the Constitution" with a capital C, not only *pre*scribes their system of government but also *de*scribes it. This belief, however, does not fully comport with reality. Some significant aspects of the American political system, such as judicial review, executive privilege, a right to privacy, and a presumption of innocence for those accused of crime[3] nowhere appear in the constitutional text. Furthermore, although the document proclaims itself the "supreme law of the land," some clauses—that which commands Congress to publish "from time to time" a "regular Statement and Account of the Receipts and Expenditures of all public Money," is among the more notable—speak only to the wind.

What a *constitution* includes is a problem, not a datum. Thus the first and in many ways the most important issue this book addresses is the relationship among (1) the constitutional text adopted in 1787–88 and periodically amended, (2) a broader *constitution*, and (3) a normative theory of politics called *constitutionalism*.[4] The issues here are difficult and highly controversial. They are also crucial to constitutional interpretation. For, if interpreters are confused about what it is they are interpreting, the odds of their producing incoherence are enormous. As a sign on the door of Prof. Marion J. Levy's office says: "People who can't define their terms don't know what they're talking about."

To reduce confusion, our introductory essays will refer to the constitutional document ratified in 1787–88 and later amended as the constitutional text or the constitutional document. Alas, the three of us who put this book together have no control over the terminology employed by other commentators and public officials, most especially justices of the Supreme Court. Therefore, when others whose writings are reproduced in this book use the term "the Constitution," readers should ask whether those people are referring only to the text itself or including additional materials, whether putative "original understandings," supplementary documents like the Declaration of Independence, earlier interpretations, long practices, political theories, or other elements. Where we quote others or reproduce documents, we cannot, of course, change what was written. In our essays and notes, however, we

---

3. For discussions of the presumption of innocence and the closely related obligation of government in a criminal trial to prove guilt beyond a reasonable doubt, see: In re Winship (1970), Estelle v. Williams (1976), Sandstrom v. Montana (1979), Jackson v. Virginia (1979), and Francis v. Franklin (1985).

4. For elaborations, see William F. Harris II, *The Interpretable Constitution* (Baltimore: Johns Hopkins University Press, 1993), espec. chs. 2–3; and Walter F. Murphy, "The Nature of the American Constitution: The James Lecture, 1987," (Urbana: Department Political Science, University of Illinois, 1988).

shall put "the Constitution" within quotation marks either where we are either referring to others' comments about it and those people have not been clear what they mean or where, in the case of our own writing, we want to minimize use of such phrases as: "the Constitution, whether simply the text or the text plus other elements."

The third necessary distinction is between the concept *constitutionalism*, on the one hand, and, on the other, both a *constitution* and a constitutional text. As Chapter 3 will explain, the United States was founded on and continues to operate under versions of two normative political theories, democracy and *constitutionalism*. There is no universally agreed of definition of either, but we can briefly define *constitutionalism* as a theory that accepts the necessity of both government and limited government. It contends that all power, even that of the people, must be limited.

Absence of official definitions of democracy and *constitutionalism* creates severe problems for analysts. Even more bedeviling for those beginning to study constitutional interpretation is the linguistic proximity of *constitutionalism* to the words *constitution* and constitutional text. English is a marvelously flexible language with an enormous vocabulary, but here it serves us ill; and we caution readers to be on their guard not to confuse these words and the concepts they express. Any particular *constitution* and/or constitutional text, such as Stalin's for the old Soviet Union, James Madison's for the United States, or Pierre Trudeau's for Canada, may or may not reflect *constitutionalism's* values; and those *constitutions* and constitutional texts that do reflect those values may do so to widely varying extents and in quite different ways.

I. THE FUNCTIONS OF A CONSTITUTIONAL TEXT

Those who frame and try to maintain constitutional texts do not necessarily share the same goals. A dictator may be only arranging fig leaves to conceal naked tyranny. On the other hand, a Madison or a Trudeau may be trying to constitute a people, to structure a polity, to use words to control power. Even in a constitutional democracy, a constitutional text may perform many functions. The most obvious, and for that reason often overlooked, is to confer legitimacy on certain kinds of public action: to empower a government.

Another function may be to serve as a deposit for some of the society's fundamental political values. A constitutional document can reflect these values in substantive ways, as in recognizing certain rights, such freedom of religion, and in procedural ways, as in allowing government to punish people for criminal actions only after trial by jury at which the defendant has been represented by counsel. Similarly, a constitutional text may reflect society's fundamental values in "allocative" ways. It may try to constrain government by structuring a system in which power is shared among various institutions[5] whose officials are chosen in different ways.

In addition to authorizing, structuring, allocating, and limiting power, a constitutional text may perform an "aspirational" function. Through its institutional arrangements and commandments about rights, duties, and prohibitions, it might try to shape as well as reflect a people's values by hallowing a particular vision of a good and achievable life—not a wispy hope or utopian dream, but a picture of the best sort of community a people can attain given the restrictions of the very real world in which they struggle to exist. The Preamble to the American constitutional document, for instance, lists the overarching goals of the founding generation:

> to form a more perfect Union, establish Justice, insure domestic Tranquility, provide for the common defense, promote the general Welfare, and secure the blessings of liberty to ourselves and our Posterity. . . .

Thus a constitutional text can be more than a set of statements about relations to be protected, regulated, or left alone; it may also provide a declaration of what some people hope will become the society's fundamental purposes. The "only way to make complete sense of the Constitution," one commentator has argued about the American constitutional document, "is to understand it in light of what our best thinking shows Americans do and ought to stand for as a people—past, present, and future." [6]

To perform these functions a constitutional text must include, or, implicitly or explicitly, refer interpreters to a political theory or a set of political theories. For a *constitution's* operations concern politics not merely in the earthy sense of shaping "Who gets what, when, and how," [7] but also in the more abstract sense of expressing a society's general aspirations and more specific goals, and how it may, consistently with those aspirations and goals, utilize its resources and distribute costs, benefits, rewards, and punishments among its members.[8]

The complexities of these functions make constitutional interpretation an intricate, arduous, and inherently controversial pro-

---

5. The term "separation of powers" is misleadingly simple here. See the discussions in Chapters 7 and 10.

6. Sotirios A. Barber, *On What the Constitution Means* (Baltimore: Johns Hopkins University Press, 1984), p. 9; see also Gary J. Jacobsohn, *The Supreme Court and the Decline of Constitutional Aspiration* (Totowa, NJ: Rowman & Littlefield, 1986); and Hendrik Hartog, "The Constitution of Aspiration and 'The Rights that Belong to Us All,' " 74 *Jo. of Am. Hist.* 1013 (1987).

7. Harold Lasswell, *Politics: Who Gets What, When, and How* (New York: McGraw–Hill, 1936).

8. See Michael N. Danielson and Walter F. Murphy, *American Democracy* (10th ed.; New York: Holmes–Meier, 1983), ch. 1.

cess. It involves much more than translating the general principles and more particular rules of a document so they can be applied to concrete problems of public policy. It also requires finding and justifying one's understanding of the fundamental values and aspirations the constitutional text may reflect, then explaining how they, along with the principles and rules contained in the text, fit current problems. As in theology,[9] music,[10] and literature,[11] constitutional interpretation often requires creativity as well as analysis. This sort of enterprise is typically political in the highest sense of that word, that is, concerned with society's goals and values. In trying to understand constitutional interpretation, readers should never permit those stark facts of creativeness and "politicalness" to move far from the center of their focus.

Moreover, a constitutional text may be quite different after interpretation from what it was before. By explaining what the document means in the context of a particular problem, an interpreter can shape what that text and even the larger *constitution* will

9. For attempts to link interpretation of religious and legal texts, see, for example: H. Jefferson Powell, *The Moral Tradition of American Constitutionalism: A Theological Interpretation* (Durham: Duke University Press, 1993); Milner S. Ball, *The Promise of American Law* (Athens: University of Georgia Press, 1981); Ball, *Lying Down Together: Law Metaphor, and Theology* (Madison: University of Wisconsin Press, 1985); Ball, *The Word and the Law* (Chicago: University of Chicago Press, 1993); Ronald R. Garet, "Comparative Normative Hermeneutics: Scripture, Literature, Constitution," 58 *So.Cal. L.Rev.* 35 (1985); Sanford V. Levinson, " 'The Constitution' in American Civil Religion," 1979 *Sup.Ct.Rev.* 123; Levinson, "The Confrontation of Religious Faith and Civil Religion: Catholics Becoming Justices," 39 *De Paul L.Rev.* 1047 (1990); Levinson, "Religious Language and the Public Square," 105 *Harv.L.Rev.* 2061 (1992); Levinson, "Identifying the Jewish Lawyer: Reflections on the Construction of Professional Identity," 14 *Cardozo L.Rev.* 1577 (1993); Michael J. Perry, *Morality, Politics, and Law* (New York: Oxford University Press, 1988); Perry, *Love and Power: The Role of Religion and Morality in American Politics* (New York: Oxford University Press, 1991); and Graham Walker, *Foundations of Constitutional Thought* (Princeton: Princeton University Press, 1990). For a more general analysis linking biblical with other forms of interpretation, see Raymond F. Collins, *Introduction to the New Testament* (New York: Doubleday, 1983).

10. For an effort to draw analogies between musical and legal interpretation, see Jerome Frank, "Words and Music," 47 *Colum.L.Rev.* 1259 (1947); a slightly revised version appears in his *Courts on Trial* (Princeton: Princeton University Press, 1949), ch. 21. See also Sanford V. Levinson and J. M. Balkin, "Law, Music, and Other Performing Arts," 139 *U.Pa.L.Rev.* 1597 (1991); and Lief H. Carter, "*Die Meistersinger von Nürnberg*' and the United States Supreme Court: Aesthetic Theory in Constitutional Jurisprudence," 18 *Polity* 272 (1985).

11. There is a growing literature on the similarities and differences between legal and literary interpretation; see, for example, John Brigham, *Constitutional Language* (Westport, CN: Greenwood Press, 1978); Lief H. Carter, *Contemporary Constitutional Lawmaking* (New York: Pergamon Press, 1985), ch. 6; Robert M. Cover, "Nomos and Narrative," 97 *Harv.L.Rev.* 4 (1984); William F. Harris, II, *op. cit.*, supra note 4; Gregory Leyh, ed., *Legal Hermeneutics* (Berkeley: University of California Press, 1992); Sanford Levinson and Steven Mailloux, eds., *Interpreting Law and Literature: A Hermeneutic Reader* (Evanston: Northwestern University Press, 1988); Richard A. Posner, *Law and Literature: A Misunderstood Relation* (Cambridge: Harvard University Press, 1988); Symposium: Law and Literature, 60 *Tex.L.Rev.* 373 (1982); Interpretation Symposium, 58 *So.Cal.L.Rev.* 1 (1985); James Boyd White, *When Words Lose Their Meaning* (Chicago: University of Chicago Press, 1984); White, "The Judicial Opinion and the Poem," 82 *Mich.L.Rev.* 1669 (1984); White, *Justice as Translation: An Essay in Cultural and Legal Criticism* (Chicago: University of Chicago Press, 1990). White, "What Can Lawyers Learn from Literature?" 101 *Harv.L.Rev.* 2014 (1989) (a critical review of Posner's *Law and Literature*).

mean in the future—what fundamental values they will enshrine, what aspirations they will encourage, and what concrete policies their rules, principles, and aspirations will nourish or starve.

In the United States, the impact of these and other aspects of constitutional interpretation on collective and individual lives can be profound. Boundaries between the President's power as commander in chief of the armed forces and Congress' power to declare war, or between the power of the state and federal governments to regulate commerce, depend on interpretations of "the Constitution" no less than do questions about whether a woman has a right to an abortion, a pacifist to a draft exemption, a city dweller to a vote equal in weight to that of a farmer, a person to marry someone of a different race, one homosexual to cohabit with another, or any citizen to travel freely across state lines.

For twentieth-century America, Brown v. Board of Education (reprinted below, pp. 912 and 919) provides the most dramatic example of constitutional interpretation's impact on society. In 1896, the Court had ruled that states could segregate citizens by race,[12] validating a public policy that was becoming widespread in the South and border states. But in 1954, after almost two decades of chipping away at the old formula of "separate but equal," the justices reversed themselves. They held, in effect, that governmentally imposed segregation in public schools stigmatized African–American children and therefore violated the general value of equality that supposedly infuses "the Constitution" as well as the specific prohibition of the Fourteenth Amendment against a state's denying "to any person within its jurisdiction the equal protection of the laws." Spurred by the Court and aided by a powerful coalition of white liberals and blacks, Congress and the President agreed in the Civil Rights Act of 1964 that government's requiring or even supporting separation by race was constitutionally anathema not only in schools but in most other phases of life. That statute went even further and outlawed some forms of racial discrimination by private citizens.[13]

---

12. Plessy v. Ferguson (1896).

13. Gerald Rosenberg, *The Hollow Hope: Can Courts Bring About Social Change?* (Chicago: University of Chicago Press, 1991) believes that *Brown* was far less important than we do. We agree that, without strong action by Congress and the President, school desegregation would have been long delayed (it is still not a full reality) and the caste system would have continued. The strangulation of every civil rights bill, including those proposals that would have only made lynching a federal crime, between Reconstruction and *Brown* indicates, however, that, without Court's removing the halo of legitimacy from Jim Crow, Congress would not have acted. On the Court's creation of a new awareness among African Americans of their constitutional rights, see the book by a leader of the Black Panthers: Eldridge Cleaver, *Soul on Ice* (New York: McGraw–Hill, 1968), espec. pp. 3–4. The obvious lesson here, it seems to us, is that effective public policy almost always requires the cooperation of at least two branches of government, and, especially where the policy's goal is significant social and/or economic change, probably the cooperation of all three branches. That sort of interaction is, after all, what James Madison talked about before, during, and after the Constitutional Convention. (For Madison's views, see Chapter 3.)

The importance of this new constitutional understanding was not merely that it eventually allowed many African Americans to attend "white" schools, ride in the front seats of buses, sit at lunch counters beside whites, and have equal opportunity for all public and some private jobs. More deeply significant was the fact that *Brown's* message rippled throughout the United States, teaching whites as well as blacks, Native Americans, and citizens of other races that caste was unconstitutional. And, in American political culture, "unconstitutionality" carries moral as well as legal taint. Furthermore, there has been a contagion: Public acknowledgement of the evil of racial discrimination has cast a moral shadow over discrimination based on religion, ethnic origin, sex, and to a lesser extent wealth. The point is not that discrimination has ended. Certainly it has not. But now American society is more likely to stigmatize the discriminators than their victims.

In sum, constitutional interpretation links the political theories and ideals on which the nation is founded—the vision reflected in the constitutional text of a good society—to the legitimacy of public policies. And American constitutional interpretation performs this function through the medium of a document that points to, without precisely defining, the content of underlying political theories and ideals. The process, moreover, does not occur once and then harden forever. The changing nature of the problems the nation faces demands that interpreters frequently reexamine the constitutional text in light of their own and their perceptions of the country's values and traditions, thus producing a dynamic process that will end only when the political system itself ends.

II. WHY INTERPRET THE CONSTITUTIONAL TEXT?

But why do we need constitutional interpretation? After all, the document the Philadelphia Convention produced is supposedly a model of clear, concise prose. Its sentences are crisp, its words carefully chosen. The skeleton of its "architectural scheme" provides strong support for the muscle of its words. All public officials and many private citizens take an oath to support it, and the overwhelming majority of them seem to think they faithfully do so.

These claims for clarity and dutiful compliance are not mere pious myths. The document's words are often precise; and most that are have been followed precisely. Free elections take place at regular intervals, every two years for representatives, every four for presidents, every six for senators. No party has ever nominated for the presidency a person who was less than thirty-five or not a native-born citizen. More important, no candidate whom the electorate rejected has ever tried to seize the White House or a seat in

Congress.[14] Other constitutional provisions seem equally exact and have been as uniformly followed. Congress, for example, has never conferred a title of nobility or declared an official religion. In these respects, though hardly in all others, the federal government has been true not only to the document's explicit terms but also to an underlying concern for equal citizenship.

Without a doubt, then, the constitutional document settles many potentially dangerous issues so that they seldom rise to the level of public consciousness. Nevertheless, with this much said and emphasized, serious problems remain, problems of clarity, of conflict, of omission, and of developments not "foreseen by the most gifted of [the Constitution's] begetters." [15]

A. Clarity

Although many clauses of the constitutional text are models of specificity, some admit of several meanings.[16] James Madison conceded as much in *Federalist* No. 37 and noted that the problem was unique neither to the proposed constitutional document nor even to politics:

> When the Almighty himself condescends to address mankind in their own language, his meaning, luminous as it must be, is rendered dim and doubtful by the cloudy medium through which it is communicated.

For human affairs, Madison identified three sources of the difficulty: the complexity of the relations to be regulated, the imperfections of human notions about politics, and the inadequacy of words to convey complex ideas with precision and accuracy.

For the constitutional document of 1787 and its amendments, he might have added several other sources of difficulty. Not only has the English language changed over time,[17] but also the framers:

---

14. Losers at the polls, of course, often contest the validity of particular elections; but, with a few exceptions in state politics, most notably Rhode Island and Georgia, losers do so in the courts or before boards of election commissioners, not in the streets. There have also been controversies about whether the federal or state governments have violated the First Amendment's ban against establishing a religion. But, though serious, questions whether such legislation as those providing for free textbooks for religious as well as public schools, tax exemptions for contributions to any religious organization, or even starting the school day off with a prayer seem minor compared to what an "establishment of religion" meant in the eighteenth century.

15. Missouri v. Holland (1920; reprinted below, p. 206).

16. Even the most seemingly obvious textual clauses may permit several equally defensible meanings. See, for instance, Mark V. Tushnet's discussion of the constitutional provision specifying 35 as the minimum age for presidents: "A Note on the Revival of Textualism in Constitutional Theory," 58 *So.Cal.L.Rev.* 683, 686–687 (1985).

17. See below Chapter 9 for a fuller discussion of "originalism" in constitutional interpretation. The problem of recapturing original understanding is complicated by the fact that, although American and British English had diverged prior to the Revolution, the first comprehensive dictionary of American English did not appear until 1828, forty years after ratification. Noah Webster, *An American Dictionary of the English Language*, 2 vols.

(1) frequently found it necessary to compromise among themselves as well as between what they wanted and what they believed the larger community would accept; (2) were sometimes unsure in their own minds exactly what it was they wished to establish, either because their vision was cloudy or because some of the values they shared were not easily adjusted to each other; and, (3) like the men who sat in the ratifying conventions and their successors who have proposed and approved constitutional amendments—indeed, like most of us—lacked both the time and capacity to arrange their competing values in a systematic, hierarchical order.

Either because of these difficulties, because they believed that the language of a workable constitutional document would have to be flexible, or for both reasons, the framers often adopted abstract principles rather than detailed rules. They frequently spoke, as Ronald Dworkin says, in general concepts rather than in specific conceptions.[18] The Eighth Amendment, for instance, forbids "cruel and unusual punishments"; it does not offer a word of explanation or even a single example of what might be either "cruel" or "unusual." The Fourth Amendment prohibits "unreasonable searches and seizures," but does not define or illustrate what is reasonable. Moreover, the framers expressly conferred general powers, such as "to regulate Commerce with foreign Nations, and among the several States and with the Indian Tribes," leaving it to governmental institutions to work out specifics.

It is hardly a mechanical task to determine what these and similar phrases import for specific political problems such as capital punishment, "stop and frisk" laws, or congressional requirements that state governments pay their employees at least wages the federal government deems to be "minimum." A great deal of thought, adjustment, compromise, and explanation must come first. Many clauses of the document, Felix Frankfurter wrote when he was still a professor, "leave the individual [interpreter] free, if indeed they do not compel him, to gather meaning not from reading the

---

Earlier there had been an occasional, more modest effort; see, for example, Caleb Alexander, *The Columbian Dictionary of the English Language* (1800); and, generally, David Simpson, *The Politics of American English* (New York: Oxford University Press, 1986).

For an effort to reconstruct an eighteenth century legal dictionary as *the* tool for constitutional interpretation, see William W. Crosskey, *Politics and the Constitution* (Chicago: University of Chicago Press, 1953), 2 vols. In 1980, after Crosskey's death, Chicago published a third volume, co-authored by William Jeffrey, Jr. The first two volumes created a seismic tremor in academic circles. For citations to many of these reactions, see David Fellman, "Constitutional Law in 1952–1953," 48 *Am.Pol.Sci.Rev.* 63, 63n (1954); and Fellman, "Constitutional Law in 1953–1954," 49 *Am.Pol.Sci.Rev.* 63, 64n (1955). Among the reviewers who engaged Crosskey on the accuracy of his definitions was Henry M. Hart, Jr., "Professor Crosskey and Judicial Review," 67 *Harv.L.Rev.* 1456 (1954).

18. *Taking Rights Seriously* (Cambridge: Harvard University Press, 1977), ch. 5.

Constitution, but from reading life." [19]   He might have put it
another way: Not from reading specific clauses of the constitutional
document, but from reading the *constitution* understood more
broadly.

B. Conflict

Some clauses in the document stand in potential conflict with
each other. In clashes between the states and the national government, the so called "sweeping clause" may be pitted against the
Tenth Amendment. After listing specific powers delegated to Congress, Article I, § 8 adds a very broad grant:

> To make all Laws which shall be necessary and proper for carrying
> into Execution the foregoing Powers, and all other Powers vested
> by this Constitution in the Government of the United States, or in
> any Department or Officer thereof.

The Tenth Amendment, however, reads:

> The powers not delegated to the United States by the Constitu-
> tion, nor prohibited by it to the States, are reserved to the States
> respectively, or to the people.

This intratextual conflict need not only be between nation and state;
the last four words of the Tenth Amendment also speak of powers
reserved "to the people." So, too, a claim for congressional power
under the sweeping clause may conflict with the Ninth Amendment's protection of individual rights:

> The enumeration in the Constitution, of certain rights, shall
> not be construed to deny or disparage others retained by the
> people.

In addition, some parts of the document read as if they take
away what other parts give. Article I § 8 empowers Congress "to
raise and support armies" and so appears to authorize a draft. But
the Thirteenth Amendment forbids not only slavery but also "involuntary servitude, except as punishment for crime whereof the party
shall have been duly convicted." The *U.S. Code* does not list being
a healthy young male as a crime, and no court has yet "duly
convicted" anyone for enduring such a condition; yet from time to
time Congress, at the urging of the President and with the approval
of the Supreme Court,[20] has forced young men to serve in the
armed forces.

The collection of clauses lumped under the term "war powers"
(see Chapter 19) exemplifies how the document lays the groundwork for further disputes. Article I allocates to Congress power to
declare war, to make regulations for the armed forces, to appropri-

---

19. *Law and Politics*, eds. E.F. Pritchard and A. MacLeish (New York: Harcourt,
Brace, 1939), p. 30.

20. Selective Draft Law Cases (1918). See also the cases on conscientious objection in
Chapter 17.

ate (or not appropriate) money to carry on the government's operations, and to organize federal agencies; and to the Senate authority to "advise and consent" to the President's nominations of executive officials, including those who deal with defense and diplomacy. On the other hand, Article II vests "the executive power" in the President and designates him commander in chief of the armed forces and chief diplomat. This sharing of authority creates an arena for bitterly self-righteous and self-serving disputes between the President and Congress over the constitutional legitimacy as well as the wisdom of foreign policies. (See the War Powers Resolution of 1973, reprinted below, p. 455.)

Reconciling implied powers in the national government either with a reservoir of retained state authority or with unlisted individual rights may not be impossible. After all, the country has been living with and formulating solutions, however delicate, to those problems for most of two centuries. The same thing could be said about finding allocations of power between Congress and the President that the two institutions—and the nation—can live with, at least for a time. None of these efforts, however, is any more likely to be a mechanical task than is divining the meaning of the document's general concepts. And four years of Civil War remind us that the bill for failure may be payable in blood.

C. Omissions

The American constitutional text, Justice William O. Douglas once observed, "is a compendium, not a code; a declaration of articles of faith, not a compilation of laws." [21] Although in many ways the document's succinctness is a blessing, this brevity means that much is left unsaid or only hinted at. Because it is a declaration of faith rather than an elaborate treatise, it is more like "a system of signs" [22] than a detailed map. Nowhere in the document, for instance, is there specific authorization for Congress to found anything like the Federal Reserve System or even a bank to enable it to discharge its fiscal responsibilities, create a national police force like the Federal Bureau of Investigation, or establish an agency like the Federal Communications Commission to regulate use of airwaves by the mass media. Nor, as we have seen, are there references to many kinds of intragovernmental authority, such as executive privilege, senatorial courtesy, or judicial review. Neither does the text mention some rights that most of us consider basic, such as to enjoy privacy, to marry, or to move our place of residence. There is not even a positive declaration of a right to vote, only prohibitions against denials of the ballot because of race, sex, age (for those over 18), or failure to pay a tax.

---

21. *We, the Judges* (New York: Doubleday, 1956), p. 429.
22. Harris, supra note 4, espec. ch. 3.

If the system is to survive, some person or persons will have to do a lot of filling in; and, one can argue, the Preamble, the sweeping clause, the Ninth Amendment, and the "empowerment clauses" of the Thirteenth, Fourteenth, Fifteenth, and Nineteenth amendments[23] provide textual mandates for such work.[24] But, even accepting that claim—and not all constitutional interpreters do accept it—does little to lessen the complexity of determining what powers are "necessary and proper," what rights, though unlisted, are fundamental, the reach of rights that are listed, or settle whose institutional task it is to make such decisions.

D. Unforeseen Developments

Among the more remarkable aspects of the American constitutional document are its durability and flexibility. It was drafted in an age when people and their goods travelled on sea by ships powered by sail and on land by horse and buggy, when farming, with ploughs pulled by oxen, by farmers' wives, or by the farmers themselves, was the main occupation. Nevertheless, most of the document's language fits an industrialized world of television, microchips, antibiotics, organ transplants, supersonic transports, and explorations of outer space. No one in the founding generation foresaw a polyglot society like ours, which would bring together people of all races and religions of the world—and not to work the land, but to live in sprawling metropolises, earn wages, luxuriate in dividends from multinational corporations, or exist off welfare. Nor did the people of 1787–88 imagine a culture that would provide twelve or more years of free public schooling, the safety net of inoculations against disease, the convenience of no-fault divorce, the uplifting effects of parades of tawdry sex and violence on television, the flourishing of "clinics" for abortion, or the importuning of telephones and fax machines.

But at a higher level of abstraction, the founders did foresee as constants in a changing universe struggles for money, power, peace, and justice among fallible, sinful men and women who are also capable of rational thought and decent deeds. Madison and his colleagues built a political system to cope with the perennial problems of people who are, as Hamilton asserted in *Federalist* No. 6, "ambitious, vindictive, and rapacious," and yet, as he claimed in *Federalist* No. 1, also open to "philanthropy and patriotism."

Despite the founders' collective genius for political engineering, we sometimes encounter grave difficulties in inferring from their specific conceptions and even general concepts solutions to our

---

23. With minor stylistic variations, these clauses state: "The Congress shall have power to enforce this article by appropriate legislation."

24. But, again, the limitations of the plain words are not always plain. See Tushnet, *supra* note 16; and Sanford V. Levinson, "On Interpretation: The Adultery Clause of the Ten Commandments," 58 *So.Cal.L.Rev.* 719 (1985).

problems. How does America's commitment to peacekeeping through the United Nations affect Congress' power to declare war? Electronic surveillance the Fourth Amendment's protection against "unreasonable searches and seizures"? Does the complexity of modern social and economic problems compel Congress to delegate some of its power to expert but unelected bureaucrats who have the technical knowledge necessary for intelligent decision making? If so, can Congress exercise a "legislative veto" over their actions, lest experts, intentionally or unintentionally, negate public policy made by elected officials?

One may answer these and similar problems, but those answers require thought, research, and analysis; and the resulting "interpretations" may well be closer to "adaptations." Moreover, any answer to these sorts of questions will be controversial in the sense that, even after careful study within the framework of imposed by the constitutional text, reasonable people can reasonably disagree. But any procedure less sophisticated is likely to divorce the constitutional text from the *constitution* or turn that text into a suicide pact.

E. Reaffirmation

These are all good and important reasons for constitutional interpretation. There is, however, another critically significant justification: to reaffirm commitment to "the Constitution." That the constitutional document of 1787–88 constitutes Americans as a people is a common claim. It is also easy to respond that " 'the Constitution' constituted *them*, the people of 1787–88, as a people, not us, 'the people' of today. We cannot be ruled by the dead." The problem is that of consent.[25] How do citizens agree to live under this system and owe allegiance to it and its "Constitution"?

Some answers are obvious. First, we do not choose to move out of the country, though we are all, if not in jail, indicted for a crime, or subject to some extraordinary judicial decree, legally free to expatriate ourselves. Second, at some time in our lives, most of us take oaths to support and defend "the Constitution"—when we enter the armed forces, serve as jurors or as one of millions of minor and not so minor governmental officials or party officers, or even play some professional roles in private life. Third, through the electoral processes we may take part in amending the constitutional text by voting for officials who will—or will not—try to change it.

There is yet another way of affirming commitment to "the Constitution": by interpreting it, by discovering, translating, justify-

---

25. Acceptance of the premise that government derives "its just powers from the consent of the governed" neither implies that the people will consent to a democracy nor that their consent can validate all governmental policies. For a discussion, see Walter F. Murphy, "Consent and Constitutional Change," in James O'Reilly, ed., *Human Rights and Constitutional Law* (Dublin: Round Hall Press, 1992).

ing, and applying its values and principles to our public problems. Only a few citizens perform those acts directly, but all citizens can do so indirectly by communicating with public officials, holding them or their superiors responsible at elections for their interpretations, filing lawsuits, or even by writing books or articles on the subject.

III. THE ENTERPRISE CALLED CON-
STITUTIONAL INTERPRETATION

We have made some important distinctions among a *constitutional text*, a *constitution,* and *constitutionalism*. We have said that constitutional interpretation, even if limited to the document so labelled, is likely to have enormous consequences for citizens' lives and is also likely to be, in part, a creative act. We have also explained why interpretation, even if "the Constitution" includes only the text, is necessary. But what is that enterprise all about? There can be no simple answer, perhaps there cannot even be a complete answer. Nevertheless, we can make a start, at least for interpretation within a constitutional democracy.

First of all, because constitutional interpretation involves discovering a nation's fundamental political principles and values, the enterprise is quintessentially normative. As students of, commentators on, or participants in interpretation, we can try to put aside personal biases and ambitions and make dispassionate judgments; but the work itself is about what certain, and at times uncertain, norms have to say about the legitimacy of political actions. Constitutional texts, like *constitutions* and *constitutionalism* itself, are concerned with the relation of abstract principles and more specific rules to human conduct: What a people and their officials can and cannot legitimately do and how they can validly act within their prescribed fields of competence. Thus, as Miller and Howell once said, constitutional principles are not "neutral." [26] They proscribe certain kinds of actions, such as taking "life, liberty, or property without due process of law." One may believe, as we do, that a people and their officials should discover and then apply constitutional principles and rules in an even-handed way, to disregard the sex, race, religion, and financial status of particular persons whom those principles and rules touch. The principles and rules themselves, however, are not neutral.

A second aspect of constitutional interpretation is that, for a viable constitutional democracy, the core message of the constitutional text must be both clear and authoritative. When a nation

---

26. Arthur S. Miller and Ronald F. Howell, "The Myth of Neutrality in Constitutional Adjudication," 27 *U.Chi.L.Rev.* 661 (1960).

reaches a stage at which "words lose their meaning,"[27] a constitutional text becomes no more than a cultural artifact, a piece of literature and not necessarily very good literature at that. And, when there cannot be at least general understanding of that text, it cannot be authoritative. Then, the *constitution* is likely to become no more than the whim of men and women in power.

A third aspect of constitutional interpretation in a constitutional democracy is that around that core of meaning probably lurks a mass of contestable and contested issues. Principles and even rules seldom offer only one clear ("correct"?) answer to complex questions of constitutional meaning. When all the problems of language of which Madison spoke combine with the difficulties of distinguishing what is history and tradition from what is mere myth, there will be ample room for reasonable men and women to differ. Moreover, the stakes of constitutional interpretation provide rich incentives for disagreement.

A fourth aspect of constitutional interpretation is that it is a *public* enterprise in a double sense. In one sense, it is concerned with what the Preamble calls "the general Welfare." The text and the larger *constitution* direct interpreters not merely toward what benefits particular persons or groups, though inevitably some interpretations will profit some people more than others, but the long-range good of the nation as a whole.[28]

Interpretation is public in another sense. Because it concerns the fundamental principles and rules around which a society organizes itself, because it is based on a core of accepted values, and because at critically important places that core becomes fuzzy and its boundaries contestable and contested, constitutional interpretation necessarily involves debate that must be carried on, at least in large part, in public forums. It is probable that only a minority, possibly only a small minority, of that society has a sophisticated comprehension of the debate. Nevertheless, because that debate affects all citizens and, insofar as the polity is a constitutional democracy, they have a right to participate, if they choose. Thus, critical decisions must be publicly justified. Democratic theory demands that, in the end, "the people shall judge"; constitutionalism adds the requirement that "the people shall judge within certain generals norms"; and prudence insists those who judge for the people not only do so honestly but be seen to do so honestly.

---

27. See James Boyd White, *When Words Lose Their Meaning: Constitutions and Reconstitutions of Language, Character, and Community* (Chicago: University of Chicago Press, 1984).

28. As sophisticated readers know, there has been a long debate on whether, or the extent to which, one can intelligently speak of a "common good." For a critical analysis of the literature, see Bernard Groffman, "Public Choice, Civic Republicanism, and American Politics," 71 *Tex.L.Rev.* 1541 (1993).

IV. THE PLAN OF THIS BOOK

We think the most effective, though surely not the quickest, way to help readers to understand constitutional interpretation is to invite them to share in that process by confronting the central problems with which constitutional interpreters inevitably, if not always consciously, grapple. Accordingly, we have structured this book around three interrelated interrogatives:

    1. WHAT is "the Constitution" that is to be interpreted?

    2. WHO are "the Constitution's" authoritative interpreters?

    3. HOW can/should/do those interpreters accomplish their tasks?

A. WHAT is "the Constitution?"

We have said enough to indicate that this question is more tangled than it seemed a dozen or so pages ago. For Americans one set of concerns involves the nature of the amended constitutional text of 1787–88: Was it a compact among sovereign states or among a larger community of private citizens who styled themselves "the people of the United States"? Or was it merely a hortatory resolution that those people and perhaps succeeding generations hoped to follow? Or was it a solemn charter that constituted a people and continues to constitute a people, stating their purposes and values, distributing powers, rights, and duties to achieve those goals? Did it and does it continue to bind us together with strong moral and legal chains?

For most Americans approaching the end of the twentieth century, the answers may seem obvious. We should not forget, however, that our ancestors fought a bloody civil war over whether the constitutional agreement was a treaty among states or a solemn charter of a people. We should also be aware that, as a practical matter, the issue of "the Constitution's" binding power will always be with us. "What's the Constitution between friends?" is sometimes more than a bad joke. As Chapter 19 shows, both Thomas Jefferson and Abraham Lincoln thought that, in some circumstances, supporting "the Constitution" took second place among their political duties. Furthermore, the degree to which the people of the United States form a "community" for any purpose other than vulnerability to muggers, terrorist bombs, and income taxes remains an open question.[29]

A second concern involves what the term "the Constitution" includes. We have questioned whether the amended constitutional text of 1787–88 is identical to the American *constitution*. We have said enough to indicate our own position: The text forms the nucleus of the larger *constitution*, but the two are not identical.

---

    29. See Sanford V. Levinson, *Constitutional Faith* (Princeton: Princeton University Press, 1988).

We are not interested in persuading others than we are right. Rather, we want to stress that any answer is contestable, including our own. A conscientious constitutional interpreter cannot simply assume the correctness of the easy response of high school civics books, one that even justices of the Supreme Court sometimes repeat: "The Constitution" is the document of 1787–88 as amended. On the contrary, one must worry about the problem, gnaw at it, and justify an answer by hard evidence and toughly reasoned argument.

A closely related query involves change: Is the meaning of "the Constitution" permanent except insofar as the text is formally amended? If the document's meaning can change without formal amendment, and if the *constitution* is not the same as that text, what, if anything, does an oath to support "the Constitution" imply? If a society's credo of fundamental values and aspirations fluctuates, does "the Constitution" constitute a community or simply mark a collection of individuals bound together by force and fear? On the other hand, if "the Constitution's" meaning were frozen in time, could it or the nation survive? Must a "constitution intended to endure for ages to come," as John Marshall claimed, be "adapted to the various *crises* of human affairs"?

The cases and materials in Part II of this book confront these fascinating and complicated problems.

B. WHO Shall Interpret?

"[U]nder the Constitution," Chief Justice William H. Rehnquist once remarked, "the first question to be answered is not whose plan is best, but in what branch of the Government is lodged the authority initially to devise the plan." [30] Most Americans who have taken courses in civics or the government of the United States are likely to respond that, regardless of who has initial authority, the Supreme Court has the final word on constitutional interpretation. And, without doubt, in practice the justices are the most conspicuous interpreters. Yet every public official, state or federal, takes an oath to support "the Constitution"; none, as President Andrew Jackson once observed (see below, p. 313), takes an oath to support the Supreme Court's interpretations of it. And the text itself is wondrously profligate in designating authoritative interpreters. Article I hints at Congress, Article II at the President, and Article III at judges. Appeals to a long established tradition of judicial review, of an authority in courts to invalidate executive and legislative actions that judges believe violate "the Constitution's" terms, are themselves appeals to something outside the document. Even more so is a claim that the Supreme Court's interpretations take precedence over those of Congress and the President.

---

30. Bell v. Wolfish (1979). When he wrote this sentence, Rehnquist was still an associate justice.

At times, presidents, senators, representatives, and state officials have asserted interpretive authority at least equal if not superior to that of judges. Thomas Jefferson, for example, formulated a coherent theory of American politics around a claim of coordinate authority that later commentators have labeled "departmentalism." (See his arguments reprinted below, pp. 263 and 306.) And, the Supreme Court itself has usually been reluctant to make explicit claims to bind the President and Congress by its interpretations. On the other hand, the justices have frequently and flatly insisted on their authority to obligate state officials and have implied more authority over other branches of the federal government than they have openly proclaimed.

Questions of WHO shall interpret have had and will continue to have obvious and critical implications for the country. From time to time, visions of the content and functions of "the Constitution" have varied from institution to institution. And differences in institutional competence, perspective, and procedure may make important differences in the values and policies various branches of government accept as more or as less fundamental and the capacity of one branch to persuade the others to agree to that ranking.

We feel a strong obligation to warn readers: That most of the materials reprinted in this book are excerpts from opinions of the Supreme Court, does not mean that judges are the ultimate constitutional interpreters. James Madison, Thomas Jefferson, Andrew Jackson, Abraham Lincoln, and Franklin D. Roosevelt, among others, denied that judges have that status. As with "WHAT does 'the Constitution' include?" any answer to the interrogative WHO is controversial and must be supported by reason and evidence. Nevertheless, an adequate understanding of constitutional interpretation must be able to justify an answer to the interrogative WHO shall interpret and do so consistently with solutions to other basic interrogatives. Part III of this volume addresses several facets of this basic problem.

C. HOW to Interpret?

Any serious attempt to answer the question of HOW to interpret will be complex. Part IV, by far the largest share of this book, takes up that interrogative. It opens in Chapter 9 with a general essay discussing some of the basic approaches to interpretation. Subsequent sets of chapters analyze several broad interpretative approaches and do so in the context of substantive problems. Chapters 10 and 11 deal with a structural approach by examining, first, sharings of power among the branches of the federal government and, next, sharings of power between state and nation. In discussing the purposive approach of reinforcing representative democracy, one set of chapters (12 and 13) deals with problems of free speech, press, voting, and other forms of political participation. The ensuing section takes up a purposive approach of insuring that government treats equals equally in the setting of a system that has historically discriminated on many grounds including race and sex. The last section of Part IV looks at a purposive approach that tries to protect certain fundamental rights, in our examples, to own and use property, to free exercise of religion, and to privacy and bodily integrity.

D. Putting It Back Together

The fifth and final Part of this volume tries to put the basic interrogatives constitutional interpretation together in an even more open manner than the previous Parts. Chapter 19 examines the problems of a constitution in crisis, which forces us to ask all three basic interrogatives simultaneously. Chapter 20 offers a reprise of the book's themes.

We hope that readers will emerge from this volume knowing something substantive about constitutional law in such doctrinal areas as speech, equal protection, property, religion, and privacy. Even more, however, we hope readers will learn a great deal about the nature of constitutional interpretation and understand not merely what rights and powers it has delineated and what doctrines it has produced, but also how the enterprise operates and what are its relations to political theory, to a long history, and to current public policy. In sum, we hope readers will appreciate more than the "output" of constitutional interpretation and come to understand how that enterprise helps discover, articulate, and translate abstract principles into viable public policy and how validation or invalidation of public policy, in turn, influences the system's abstract principles.

SELECTED BIBLIOGRAPHY

Ackerman, Bruce. "Discovering the Constitution," 93 *Yale L.J.* 1013 (1984).

————. *We the People: Foundations* (Cambridge: Harvard University Press, 1991).

————. "Liberating Abstraction," 59 *U.Chi.L.Rev.* 317 (1992).

Arkes, Hadley. *Beyond the Constitution* (Princeton: Princeton University Press, 1990).

Barber, Sotirios A. *On What the Constitution Means* (Baltimore: Johns Hopkins University Press, 1984).

_____. "The Ninth Amendment: Ink Blot or Another Hard Nut to Crack?" 64 *Chi.-Kent L.Rev.* 67 (1988).

_____. *The Constitution of Judicial Power* (Baltimore: Johns Hopkins University Press, 1993).

Berns, Walter. *Taking the Constitution Seriously* (New York: Simon & Schuster, 1987).

Bobbitt, Philip. *Constitutional Interpretation* (Cambridge, MA: Basil Blackwell, 1991).

Bork, Robert H. *The Tempting of America: The Political Seduction of the Law* (New York: The Free Press, 1990).

Brigham, John. *Constitutional Language* (Westport, CN: Greenwood Press, 1978).

Carter, Lief H. *Contemporary Constitutional Lawmaking* (New York: Pergamon Press, 1985).

Chemerinsky, Erwin. *Interpreting the Constitution* (New York: Praeger, 1987).

Corwin, Edward S. *Liberty Against Government* (Baton Rouge: Louisiana State University Press, 1948). (See also the entry under Loss, Richard.)

Dahl, Robert A. "Decision–Making in a Democracy: The Supreme Court as a National Policy–Maker," 6 *Jo. of Pub.L.* 279 (1957).

Dworkin, Ronald M. *Taking Rights Seriously* (Cambridge: Harvard University Press, 1977), ch. 5.

_____. *Law's Empire* (Cambridge: Harvard University Press, 1986).

_____. *Life's Dominion* (New York: Knopf, 1993).

Ely, John Hart. *Democracy and Distrust* (Cambridge: Harvard University Press, 1980). (See the critiques, listed below, by Fleming and Murphy.)

Fleming, James E. "A Critique of John Hart Ely's Quest for the Ultimate Constitutional Interpretivism of Representative Democracy," 80 *Mich.L.Rev.* 634 (1982).

_____. "Constructing the Substantive Constitution," 72 *Tex. L.Rev.* 211 (1993).

Garvey, John H., and T. Alexander Aleinikoff (eds.). *Modern Constitutional Theory: A Reader* (3d ed.; St. Paul: West Publishing Co., 1994).

Gerhardt, Michael J., and Thomas D. Rowe, Jr. *Constitutional Theory: Arguments and Perspectives* (Charlottesville, VA: Michie, 1993).

Graber, Mark A. "Why Interpret? Political Justification and American Constitutionalism," 56 *Rev. of Pols.* 415 (1994).

Grey, Thomas. "Do We Have an Unwritten Constitution?" 27 *Stan.L.Rev.* 703 (1975).

_____. "The Constitution as Scripture," 37 *Stan.L.Rev.* 1 (1984).

Harris, William F. II. *The Interpretable Constitution*. (Baltimore: Johns Hopkins University Press, 1993).

Hartog, Hendrik. "The Constitution of Aspiration and 'The Rights that Belong to Us All,' " 74 *Jo.Am.Hist.* 1013 (1987).

Kahn, Ronald. *The Supreme Court & Constitutional Theory, 1953– 1993* (Lawrence: University of Kansas Press, 1994).

Levinson, Sanford V. *Constitutional Faith* (Princeton: Princeton University Press, 1988).

_____. "Some Reflections on the Posnerian Constitution," 56 *Geo.Wash.U.L.Rev.* 39 (1987). (See the entry under "Posner," below.)

Loss, Richard, ed. *Corwin on the Constitution* (Ithaca: Cornell University Press, 1981–88), 3 vols.

Mason, Alpheus Thomas. *The Supreme Court: Palladium of Freedom* (Ann Arbor: University of Michigan Press, 1962).

Monaghan, Henry P. "Foreword: Constitutional Common Law," 89 *Harv.L.Rev.* 1 (1975).

Murphy, Walter F. "The Art of Constitutional Interpretation," in M. Judd Harmon, ed., *Essays on the Constitution of the United States* (Port Washington, NY: Kennikat Press, 1978).

_____. "Constitutional Interpretation: The Art of the Historian, Magician, or Statesman?" 87 *Yale L.J.* 1752 (1978).

_____. "An Ordering of Constitutional Values," 53 *So.Cal.L.Rev.* 703 (1980).

_____. "Constitutional Interpretation: Text, Values, and Processes," 9 *Revs. in Am. Hist.* 7 (1981). (See also the entry under "Ely," listed above.)

_____. "Staggering Toward the New Jerusalem of Constitutional Theory," 37 *Am.Jo.Juris.* 337 (1992).

_____. "Constitutions, Constitutionalism, and Democracy," in Douglas Greenberg et al., eds., *Constitutionalism and Democracy: Transitions in the Contemporary World* (New York: Oxford University Press, 1993).

Nelson, William E. "History and Neutrality in Constitutional Adjudication," 72 *Va.L.Rev.* 1237 (1986).

Powell, Thomas Reed. "The Logic and Rhetoric of Constitutional Law," 15 *Jo. of Phil., Psych., and Sc'fc Method* 654 (1918); reprinted in Robert G. McCloskey, ed., *Essays in American Constitutional Law* (New York: Knopf, 1957).

_____. *Vagaries and Varieties in Constitutional Interpretation* (New York: Columbia University Press, 1956).

Posner, Richard A. "The Constitution as an Economic Document," 56 *Geo.Wash.U.L.Rev.* 4 (1987). (See also Levinson's critique, listed above.)

Schauer, Frederick. "An Essay on Constitutional Language," 29 *UCLA L.Rev.* 797 (1982).

_____. *Playing by the Rules* (Oxford: Clarendon Press, 1990).

Schrock, Thomas S., and Robert C. Welsh. "Reconsidering the Constitutional Common Law," 91 *Harv.L.Rev.* 1117 (1978).

Sunstein, Cass R. *The Partial Constitution* (Cambridge: Harvard University Press, 1993).

Symposium on Interpretation. 58 *So.Cal.L.Rev.* 1 (1985).

Tribe, Laurence H. *American Constitutional Law* (2d ed.; Mineola, NY: Foundation Press, 1988).

_____ and Michael C. Dorf. *On Reading the Constitution* (Cambridge: Harvard University Press, 1991).

Wechsler, Herbert. "Toward Neutral Principles of Constitutional Law," 73 *Harv.L.Rev.* 1 (1959).

2

Constitutional Literacy

The document that calls itself "the Constitution of the United States" prescribes a political order for America. People who would engage in or criticize constitutional interpretation must understand that text. They must also understand the order that text would impose, the resulting system, and how that system—which some might dub the larger constitution—changes interpretations of the text. Each of these activities is highly complex and involves many controversies. For example, many jurists and scholars would deny that the system can legitimately change the meaning of the text. Once again, we urge readers to be aware of this sort of controversy and to sit in critical judgment on what judges, senators, representatives, presidents, state officials, and, not least, professors say.

Yet as novices in constitutional interpretation attempt critical judgments, they may have trouble coping with a strange language. Intelligent people can easily understand presidential addresses and legislative debates. Although elected officials may use more than their fair share of blather and blarney and be adept at evasion and circumlocution, they generally use terms familiar to ordinary citizens. The same is largely true of the constitutional document itself. Although that text has a few terms of art, such as "bill of attainder" [1] and *"ex post facto law*," [2] its prose seems, by and large, straightforward. But when a reader moves from the text to the theories, practices, traditions, values, and interpretive encrustations that lawyers, judges, and academics have developed in the name of "the Constitution," he or she encounters strange jargon. Indeed, an experienced federal judge has written wistfully about the scarcity of "oases in the vast desert of our law libraries." [3] To acquire the camel-like capacity to travel that desert safely, beginners must acquire a new literacy.

---

1. A bill of attainder is a legislative act that convicts a person of a crime and imposes a punishment, both without benefit of a judicial trial.

2. As defined in Calder v. Bull (1798; reprinted below, p. 121), an ex post facto law is essentially a retroactive criminal statute that makes an act, lawful when done, a crime, or, again after the deed was done, lowers the standards of proof for a crime or increases punishment for a crime.

3. Marvin E. Frankel, "A Matter of Opinions," *New York Times*, May 15, 1994. (This was an "Op Ed" piece.)

I. PURPOSES OF READING JUDICIAL OPINIONS

In at least one important respect, judicial opinions are like presidential addresses and legislative speeches: None of them is basically an explanation of how the speakers or authors arrived at a decision, though it may purport to be. Rather, each offers reasons for a decision and tries to persuade readers that the solution proffered is constitutionally correct.

But judges' message is often lost. Beginning students who have examined—even conscientiously studied—the raw materials of constitutional interpretation frequently feel lost when asked to analyze cases. We offer neither tricks nor easy solutions: There are no substitutes for a great deal of sweat, a lot of tears, and even perhaps a bit of blood. We can, however, offer some advice. First: Readers must decide why they are reading the material, for how (and how accurately) we read something, whether it be a poem, a novel, a comic strip, a political speech, a constitutional text, or a judicial opinion, is strongly dependent on the purposes for which we read it. If one is not looking for something, he or she is not apt to find it. As Yogi Berra once put it, "If you don't know where you're going, you're liable to end up somewhere else." Some of the most common reasons people have for reading a judicial opinion include searches for:

1. LEGAL SUBSTANCE. What are (a) the question(s) a case poses and (b) the answer(s) judges offer? The latter we call "the *holding*" of the case. How does it fit into or change legal doctrine on this subject matter, such as free speech or federalism? Here one is concerned with the principles or rules that the case stands for. This preoccupation is the main focus of courses in constitutional *law*.

2. METHOD OF ARGUMENTATION. What is the intellectual power and persuasiveness of the justification(s) for an interpretation? On what points do opinion writers' logic turn? Where do they get the authoritative material they use? What factors do they incorporate in their reasoning to ground the next stage of argument? Where do they leave gaps? To what extent do they address real problems of the real world? How cogently do they do so? How convincing is their reasoning?

3. HISTORY. One might see judicial opinions as "period pieces"—evidence of policies and underlying values long cherished, long repudiated, or moving toward public acceptance. Here one might ask how constitutional interpretation affects and is affected by the course of history. To accomplish these aims, it is necessary to know something of the general context, economic, social, as well as political, of constitutional problems and proffered solutions.

4. JUDICIAL STRATEGY. Here one is concerned not merely with the reasoning that judges offer for public consumption but

also with what the case indicates about how the justices are consciously or unconsciously shaping public policy. As do most public officials and private citizens, the justices want to convince various audiences of the correctness of their interpretations. Their colleagues form the first audience, for to speak for "the Court" requires five votes. This victory may require cautious compromises that shape the justifications an opinion offers and even, on occasion, do considerable damage to the logical flow of argument, further complicating difficulties of making full sense of opinions. Close analyses may also reveal efforts to win the votes of other justices or to convince other public officials and groups of citizens outside the Court. Again like a presidential or legislative speech, a judicial opinion may also evade some issues. The opinion writer may not have been able to muster a majority of the Court on some points; the justices may have believed that those who must live with and enforce the decision would not provide adequate support for the ruling the Court thinks best; or the justices may have thought that, for a variety of reasons, the time was not yet right for them to present their full justifications. Thus one might look at judicial opinions as sharing with other forms of political rhetoric the goal of building coalitions and unifying majorities within and outside an institution.[4]

5. PROPER INSTITUTIONAL ROLES. In construing "the Constitution," interpreters often confront important problems of political theory.[5] Not only do these issues involve critical substantive issues such as freedom, equality, and dignity, they also deal with allocative questions. For instance: WHO shall make decisions about the existence and/or extent of a constitutional right to an abortion, public officials' protection against libel and slander, or the power of communities to ban movies or live performances that feature explicit sexual activity? Citizens? State legislators? Congress? Federal judges? Thus, readers should ask themselves what each case implies about proper divisions of functions among private citizens, judges, and other public officials.

6. POLITICAL IMPACT. This aspect of constitutional interpretation is much like the bottom line in business. One of the more obvious facts of American political life, to which we often allude, is that constitutional interpretation can have a deep impact on society. Thus neither conscientious public officials nor responsible citizens can be indifferent to the possible effects, long and short range, anticipated and unanticipated, of an interpretation. We lack space fully to explore such concerns;[6] but the

---

4. See Walter F. Murphy, *Elements of Judicial Strategy* (Chicago: University of Chicago Press, 1964).

5. Whether interpreters will address those questions directly or indirectly is, of course, another matter.

6. For studies of the impact of judicial decisions, see espec. Charles A. Johnson and Bradley C. Cannon, *Judicial Policies: Implementation and Impact* (Washington, DC: Congressional Quarterly Press, 1984); John T. Noonan, *The Antelope* (Berkeley: University of California Press, 1977); and the discussion and bibliography in Walter F. Murphy, C.

reader might gain perspective by looking at judicial opinions as parables, moral fables, efforts to reshape the polity by appeals to abstract principles may at first seem to have little relation to the world of day-to-day politics.

It will help readers, we believe, to be attentive to these six sets of concerns and the ways in which they interact with one another. This advice is not easy to follow, but keeping in mind that the objective of opinion writers is to persuade and that the goals of readers are to understand and assess the arguments will, over the long haul, bring some order into an admittedly arduous process. And, because constitutional interpretation is characterized by complexity not simplicity, by interrelationships not isolation, it will soon be apparent that dissenting and concurring opinions may be as enlightening as majority opinions. Furthermore, protests against what the Court has said, such as those by Thomas Jefferson or John C. Calhoun (reprinted below, p. 306 and p. 365) or more modern critics, can offer valuable insights into what the Court us saying about—and perhaps doing to—"the Constitution."

II. BRIEFING A CASE

If the first step is to decide why one wants to read cases, the next must be to decide how to read cases for those purposes. Whatever readers' objectives, it is necessary to take the opinion apart and put it together again. Most students have found it helpful in this process to prepare a "brief" of each case, a written summary of a page or two to deepen understanding at the time and refresh memories later. We shall use the School Segregation Cases, Brown v. Board of Education (1954), to illustrate a standard form:

(1) The facts (the context). What is the case all about? What governmental policy has conflicted with what asserted individual right, or what public policies have clashed with each other, or what rights are in opposition? What are the terms of the statutes, executive orders, or constitutional clauses involved? What is/are the shape(s) of the alleged right(s) and/or powers? In four separate cases from Delaware, Kansas, South Carolina, and Virginia (generally cited simply as *Brown*, the first of the four), state law required separate public schools for children of different races. In each state, those schools were either physically equal or were in the process of being made so. African Americans claimed that such segregation ran afoul of the Fourteenth Amendment's prohibition: "No State shall ... deny to any person within its jurisdiction the equal protection of the laws."

(2) The fundamental question or questions of constitutional meaning the case presents, in *Brown* the meaning of "equal protection." Does that phrase allow states to provide "separate"

Herman Pritchett, and Sotirios A. Barber, *Courts, Judges, & Politics* (5th ed.; Boston: McGraw–Hill, 1995), ch. 8.

educational facilities for children of both races if, in fact, those facilities are essentially equal physically?

(3) The holding of the case—i.e., the answer(s) to the constitutional question(s) posed by the controversy. If one has neatly phrased (2) the answer(s) will be simply "yes" or "no." In *Brown*, the answer was emphatically no.

(4) A summary of the reasoning behind the decision. How does the opinion writer get from the question(s) to the answer(s)? In *Brown*, the Court reasoned that judges must look beyond tangible, physical facilities; for a state to shunt children of a minority race into a different educational system was to label them as inferior to whites and so to deny them "equal protection" in a critically important aspect of their present and future lives.

(5) An analysis of dissenting and concurring opinions, much like those in (4). In *Brown*, all the justices joined the Chief Justice's opinion.

(6) The general constitutional principle(s) or rule(s) for which the case stands. In *Brown*, the general principle was that "Separate [public] educational facilities are inherently unequal." (Later cases would apply this principle to other public facilities such as parks and buses.)

This standard form of briefing helps readers achieve two of the basic purposes for which we read cases: to learn about legal substance and to judge the quality of reasoning. It also helps provides raw material for other objectives, such as understanding the strategy the justices were pursuing and the historical significance of a case and its political impact.

We suggest yet a seventh step that a brief might take, that is, analyzing:

(7) The answers that various opinions give or imply to any (or all) of the three central interrogatives of WHAT, WHO, and HOW as well as the ways in which these opinions orchestrate these answers.

We shall not repeat our arguments about the centrality of these interrogatives for constitutional interpretation. We merely note (again) that, even when interpreters do not directly or even consciously address them, they do so indirectly and no less importantly.

To understand a case, it is necessary both to grasp the crux of the competing arguments and to make a more abstract assessment. The first five steps in the standard brief push readers to examine carefully the words and organizational details of the opinions. To some extent the sixth step and to an even greater extent the seventh require the analyst to move back and ask "What else is going on here?" In the beginning, this sort of work may well seem extraordinarily difficult—probably because it often is. Within a few weeks, however, it will become easier; soon it will become a natural and valuable part of one's intellectual style, and not only for constitutional interpretation.

III. STARE DECISIS[7]

In reading and briefing judicial opinions, students encounter copious references to previous decisions. These references spawn two kinds of confusion among beginners. First, they clutter an opinion, making it more difficult to understand its sentences. And, second, they may leave a misleading impression of the legal model they illustrate, stare decisis. Like most else in constitutional interpretation, those problems interact, but we shall try to treat them separately.

A. Cluttered Style

Usually judges splatter their opinions with quotations from and splice citations to previous cases right into the text. The following sort of sentence, taken from Justice John Marshall Harlan's opinion in Cohen v. California (1971; reprinted below, p. 705), is common:

> That is why "[w]holly neutral futilities ... come under the protection of free speech as fully as do Keats' poems or Donne's sermons." Winters v. New York, 333 U.S. 507, 528 (1948) (Frankfurter, J., dissenting), and why "so long as the means are peaceful, the communication need not meet standards of acceptability." Organization for a Better Austin v. Keefe, 402 U.S. 415, 419 (1971).

By "wholly neutral futilities" Harlan referred to speech or writing that expresses emotion without threatening social harm, and it would have made better sense to have used precisely those words rather than arcane legal phraseology. Running in quotations from, names of, and, worse, citations to previous cases further disrupts a reader's train of thought. One simply has to get accustomed to this style. Felicitous it is not, yet, as we shall explain, it may be an effective means of communication—and at several different levels. As we edited the materials for this volume, we eased the problem by eliminating all the numbers that located cases in the *U.S. Reports* except those noting the year in which cases were decided. To replace the strings of numbers in the text, we created a Table of Cases at the end of the book so that interested readers can find the full citations if they wish. (An Appendix to this chapter will explain what those numbers, which refer to a very logical system of citation, mean.) Other difficulties remain, however.

---

7. Edward H. Levi, *An Introduction to Legal Reasoning* (Chicago: University of Chicago Press, 1948), espec. ch. 1 offers one of the best analyses of stare decisis; for a general discussion and bibliography, see Murphy, Pritchett, and Barber, *op. cit.* supra note 6, ch. 10.

Let us back up a few paces, explain why Harlan's sentence follows the form it does, and then show how such a style communicates several messages. What we see is an example of stare decisis—literally, "the [previous] decision stands." This term refers to a mode of legal reasoning that most prominently distinguishes the common law from other legal systems. Judges in late medieval England, when few statutes regulated social conflict, proceeded inductively to develop one law for the whole kingdom (a "common law") by trying to decide similar disputes similarly. Gradually, though often reluctantly, judges linked together their reasons for deciding these cases to formulate guidelines to shape the behavior of citizens and to handle future disputes. Rarely, however, did judges sit down and weave these rules into a coherent jurisprudence. As Chapter 1 pointed out, the common law's style has tended to be cautious, even timid, preferring gradual accretion or erosion to sudden avulsion or systematic codification.

In the early decades of American government under the constitutional text of 1787–88, there were, of course, few precedents to follow; but almost immediately, judges began to claim and exercise interpretive authority; thus, reading judicial opinions became necessary to an understanding of what "the Constitution" *really* meant. John Marshall, however, refused to punctuate his opinions with references to previous decisions. Conceiving his task as elucidating "the Constitution" rather than refining judicial doctrines, he preferred a grand style of reasoning. He saw the text of 1787–88 as pretty much expressing John Locke's political philosophy as filtered through the thinking of Federalists like himself, George Washington, Alexander Hamilton, and Gouverneur Morris, and he construed it accordingly. But, as precedents multiplied, Marshall's magisterial style became the exception. As readers will become painfully aware, citation-studded sentences like those of Justice Harlan have become typical. Indeed, judges often argue more about what other judges have said "the Constitution" means than about what the text itself means.

B. Style and Substance

One must distinguish a modern style of profusely citing precedents from stare decisis itself. Anticipated in theological treatises and aped in law reviews, that style lists, with near neurotic obsession, cases as authorities for almost every statement and heaps quotation upon quotation. The "string citation"—a listing of six or even a dozen cases that may be, though only tangentially, relevant—epitomizes the modern style. In this book, we have left many (but not all) of these strings in the opinions because they represent yet another kind form of communication: They attempt to convey a message through deliberate redundancy,[8] among the most venerable ways of teaching. The string is the message: The Court is being true to its previous announced doctrine on the particular problem at bar and also to its heritage as a common-law tribunal.

Moreover, a citation can symbolize a whole jurisprudence. Thus the single word *Griswold* is shorthand for the Court's acceptance in Griswold v. Connecticut (1965; reprinted below, p. 147) of constitutionally protected but textually unspecified rights, such as that to privacy. Further, that single citation also communicates the justices' acceptance of a view of "the Constitution" as consisting of more than the text and being adaptable, through interpretation, rather than fixed in meaning.

One should not infer, however, that stare decisis ever provides *the* answer, at least *the* answer that judges will provide. One reason is that the sheer number of judicial decisions and various changes in doctrine during more than two centuries make it possible for attorneys to find and judges to rely on *dicta*[9] if not actual holdings to bolster a broad, though not unrestricted, range of possible decisions on many constitutional issues. After all, as this book goes to press, the *U.S. Reports* take up 513 volumes, and that number will probably rise by three, four, or even five each year.

A second, related, reason for stare decisis' limited capacity to predict outcomes is that judges must often choose which among several previous rulings is truly relevant to the problem at hand, leaving room for conscious and unconscious play of judicial preferences among policies and values. In its ideal form, stare decisis proceeds by means of analogy.[10] The reasoning supposedly moves in three steps. First, judges see a likeness between the problems now presented and those of earlier cases. Next, judges determine the factors that settled earlier cases and, then, decide how those factors pertain to the dispute at hand. But reasonable people often reasonably differ about how apt an analogy is. "The problem," Prof. Steven Pinker claims with only a trace of literary exaggeration, "is that similarity is in the mind of the beholder ... not in the world." [11]

Take a policy of inviting a member of the clergy to offer a benediction at graduation ceremonies of public schools. Is that

---

8. See Martin Shapiro, "Toward a Theory of Stare Decisis," 2 *Jo. of Legal Studies* 125 (1972).

9. Dicta—literally "words," in the singular, dictum—refer to statements in a judicial opinion not necessary to justify the decision. What are and are not dicta is often difficult even for the opinion writer to say. Indeed, it is the distinction that later courts make between the two that is crucial. See Levi, supra note 7, p. 2, and materials reprinted and literature cited in Murphy, Pritchett, and Barber, *op. cit.* supra note 6, ch. 10.

10. The noted philosopher Richard Rorty argues that philosophy also proceeds more by analogy than most of his colleagues would like to believe: *Philosophy and the Mirror of Nature* (Princeton: Princeton University Press, 1979).

11. *The Language Instinct* (New York: Morrow, 1994), p. 416.

policy more like one that requires each session of the Supreme Court to open with the Crier's invocation, "God save the United States and this Honorable Court," [12] or is it more like a compulsory recitation of prayers in public schools? Choice of the first analogy would mean the policy fits a series a decisions holding such practices constitutional, while choice of the second would mean that it fits another stream of cases holding that compulsory prayer in public schools violates the First Amendment's ban on establishment of a religion, which the Fourteenth Amendment, so the Supreme Court has said, makes binding on the states. Later, in Lee v. Weisman (1992; reprinted below, p. 167), we shall see the justices sharply divide on precisely this issue.

A third cause of stare decisis' limitations as a predictor lies in the trait to which we have already alluded: It not merely winks at but encourages *incremental* change. Fourth, the American version of stare decisis requires lower courts to follow higher courts, but higher courts may change their minds. And the Supreme Court has repeatedly said that it is not rigidly bound by precedent in constitutional interpretation,[13] often citing Chief Justice Taney's remark in the Passenger Cases (1849) that the justices are always willing to re-examine their constitutional decisions.[14] And sometimes they carry through on that promise. On many occasions, however, they have become quite cross when a litigant has suggested they should reconsider earlier interpretations. We see specific examples of such grumpiness in Cooper v. Aaron (1958; reprinted below, p. 375), when Arkansas challenged the correctness of the School Segregation Cases (1954; reprinted below, p. 912), and Planned Parenthood v. Casey (1992; reprinted below, p. 1281) when Pennsylvania, supported by the Bush administration, challenged Roe v. Wade (1973; reprinted below, p. 1258).

Furthermore, judges often play fast and loose with stare decisis, as when they cite cases for rules they did not embody or wrench sentences out of context to make decisions seem to stand for something quite new.[15] Moreover, judicial attachment to stare decisis differs from issue to issue and time to time. In Planned

---

12. During the mid–1930s, when the justices were wreaking havoc with Franklin D. Roosevelt's efforts at economic reform, a pro-New Deal wag suggested changing the chant to "God save the United States *from* this Honorable Court."

13. The justification is that, although Congress can rather easily correct judicial errors in statutory interpretation by passing a new statute, amending the constitutional document requires an awkward, tedious, and extraordinarily difficult process; thus judges should undo their own constitutional mistakes.

14. Thus, with a nice touch of irony, the Court relies on stare decisis to justify overruling precedents.

15. See, for example, the Supreme Court's systematic misuse of its decisions validating the abuse of constitutional rights of Japanese–Americans during World War II (discussed below in Chapter 4, pp. 87-99). Time and again, the Court has plucked sentences out of context and cited these rulings as justifications for *protecting* civil rights. The first dozen years of this strange history are analyzed in Walter F. Murphy, "Civil Liberties and the Japanese American Cases: A Study in the Uses of Stare Decisis," 11 *West.Pol.Q.* 3 (1958).

Parenthood v. Casey, for example, three justices who co-authored
what has become famous as "the joint opinion" offered a hymn of
praise to the stability stare decisis brings. Yet one week earlier, two
of the three had joined Justice Antonin Scalia's opinion for the
Court in R.A.V. v. St. Paul (1992; reprinted below, p. 686) that
gutted much of the Court's previous jurisprudence on freedom of
speech. Ten days earlier, one of the three wrote the opinion for
the Court in New York v. United States (1992), an opinion in which
the other two joined, cutting back on a recent ruling, Garcia v.
SAMTA (1985).

The point is not that stare decisis is no more than a charade,
though it sometimes seems so and on occasion may be. Usually,
stare decisis is a complex device that plays several roles. It preserves continuity while effecting change, signals change or stability
by the ways in which previous rulings are cited, explained, or not
cited, and, as noted above, affirms faith in an historic system of
judicial decision making.

Sophisticated commentators understand these functions of preserving while changing, though critics may become incensed when
the Court mangles a particular earlier ruling or when it often
reverses itself. In fact, of course, a tribunal that frequently twisted
its own previous opinions or regularly performed interpretive flip
flops could not expect others to respect, much less follow, its
decisions. Overrulings and misuse seem to occur more often than
they actually do because the justices usually refuse to review appeals
from lower courts that followed earlier rulings or, where a lower
court has not followed those prior decisions, to reverse it summarily. When the Supreme Court takes a case, it is usually either
because the issues are novel, different lower courts have interpreted
a precedent differently, or it appears that a lower court has misinterpreted what the justices meant to say. To meet these sorts of
situations, the Court may ignore a prior ruling or, more likely,
expand or contract the reasons justifying earlier decisions. To
cushion the shock of change, the justices may copiously quote from
previous *dicta* now transformed, if only temporarily, into dogma.

With that much said, there are periods in American history
when reversals come fast and often. These are times when political
forces throughout the country have shifted and are being reflected
in changed minds and/or membership among judges. For example,
the period after 1937 that followed the New Deal's war with the
Supreme Court saw the new justices abandon several dozen older
rulings for fresh constitutional doctrines. Less dramatically but still
significantly, the politically conservative men and women Ronald
Reagan and George Bush nominated to the bench turned away from
some earlier doctrines that more liberal justices had endorsed.
And, William J. Clinton's early nominations indicate that he will try
to undo at least some of his predecessors' work.

We can also observe reliance on precedent, though that specific term may not be used, when Congress or the President engages in constitutional interpretation. To lend respectability to their reasoning, they, too, may call the roll of history and muster previous practices and constructions. President Andrew Jackson's message justifying his veto of the renewal of the Bank of the United States in 1832 (reprinted below, p. ___) precisely fits this sort of model. And the Supreme Court itself may perform such a function for Congress or the President by citing as an authority, as in McCulloch v. Maryland (1819; reprinted below, p. 530), how another branch of government has construed "the Constitution."

C.   Continuity and Change

To recapitulate, stare decisis is more than the past's grip on the present. For issues often thrashed over, it can provide speedy solutions. It also cautions judges to value continuity with old rules while formulating new rules, and it provides a means of affirming fidelity to the past while adapting that past to fit the needs of the present. This dual role is important, but it is also limited. It offers little help in deciding whether to expand or contract a substantive doctrine or even whether to abandon it.

IV.   PROBLEMS OF OMNICOMPETENCE AND OBJECTIVITY

People beginning constitutional interpretation often feel overwhelmed. Not only do judges often use jargon and awkward syntax,[16] often they also simultaneously address several questions, each of them highly technical. These are facts of life that we are powerless to change. The situation, however, is not hopeless. As editors, we have tried to help by excluding much excess verbiage from opinions, by writing introductory essays to highlight the principal problems, and pursuing issues in headnotes and hindnotes to cases. Some of these notes are explanatory, some interrogatory. We intend the first kind to soothe by providing additional information, the second kind to irritate by goading readers toward deeper understanding.

Because problems of constitutional interpretation, like all significant problems of life, are interrelated, because it often seems that one must understand everything at once, we have liberally, even lavishly, cross referenced material. The phrase "reprinted above, p. ___" will become familiar. Its purpose is to allow readers immediately to turn to other matter that is relevant to what they are now analyzing.

---

16. For a critical assessment of judicial prose (and logic) by an attorney who has a doctorate in linguistics, see Lawrence M. Solan, *The Language of Judges* (Chicago: University of Chicago Press, 1993).

Nevertheless, no editorial effort, however industrious and imaginative, can change the hard fact that constitutional interpretation is intellectually demanding. It requires careful reading and rereading, close analysis, concentrated thought, and a willingness to imagine other worlds. For those who make those efforts, few enterprises are more challenging, important, or rewarding.

APPENDIX:

Deciphering the Numbers

The first thing a reader should notice about a case is, of course, its title, indicating who is taking legal action against whom. Somebody against (versus, abbreviated as v.) somebody else is the typical form, though very famous cases may acquire a descriptive title— Brown v. Board of Education is often referred to as the School Segregation Cases.

The next and possibly confusing item is a string of numbers and abbreviations following the title. These are the "citations," references to where the case can be found in its original form. The Government Printing Office publishes the official reports of opinions by the Supreme Court. These are called the *United States Reports* and are cited simply as U.S. The number that precedes U.S. is the volume and the number that follows is the page at which the case begins in that volume. The date in parentheses is the year in which the Court announced its decision. Thus the citation to the School Segregation Cases, Brown v. Board of Education, is 347 U.S. 483 (1954), meaning the cases can be found in volume 347 of the *United States Reports*, beginning at p. 483, and the decisions were announced in 1954.

Several commercial publishers also print the Supreme Court's opinions. The *United States Law Week*, distributed by the Bureau of National Affairs, Washington, D.C., puts out a loose leaf copy within a week or ten days of the decision, as does the Commerce Clearing House. Slower but more widely used are volumes compiled by the West Publishing Co. of St. Paul, MN, and the Lawyers Cooperative Publishing Co. of Rochester, NY. West's volumes are called the *Supreme Court Reporter* and are abbreviated as S.Ct. *Brown*'s citation is 74 S.Ct. 686, meaning that it appears in volume 74 of the *Supreme Court Reporter*, beginning at p. 686. The Lawyers Cooperative version is called the *Lawyers' Edition* and is cited as L.Ed. *Brown*'s citation is 98 L.Ed. 873, meaning it appears in volume 98, beginning at p. 873. (After volume 100 came out, the *Lawyers' Edition* went into a second series, so that cases decided after November, 1956 appear in volumes with a "2d"; for example, 6 L.Ed.2d means that the case appears in the sixth volume of the second series of the *Lawyers' Edition*.)

Both West and the Lawyers Cooperative put additional material into their volumes. The latter, for example, reprints precis of the briefs for each side and for any amici curiae ("friends of the court" whom the justices invite or allow to file briefs or even offer oral argument) in each case and often includes "annotations," that is, summaries and analyses of earlier rulings on the same point and perhaps discussions of where the Court seems to be heading. Both publishers have copious references to multi-volume encyclopedias they publish that collate summaries of the Court's opinions on particular points of law.

West also selects for publication many opinions of federal district courts and courts of appeal. The first are now contained in either the *Federal Supplement* (cited as F.Supp.) or the *Federal Rules Decisions* (cited as F.R.D.) and the latter in the *Federal Reporter*, now in its third series, cited as F.3d. The first two series are cited as Fed and F.2d. Early decisions of lower federal courts are collected in a set of volumes called Federal Cases, cited as Fed. Cases. Most states publish some of the rulings by their own tribunals, and West puts out a series of regional reporters that reprint most of the opinions by the highest courts and occasionally lower courts in states in the region.

Before 1816, we have unofficial and incomplete reports of the U.S. Supreme Court's opinions, first under the name of A. J. Dallas (cited as Dall.) then William Cranch (cited as Cr.). In 1816 Congress created the office of Reporter for the Court;[17] and from then until 1875, opinions were published under his name:

Dates	Reporter	Citation
1816–1827	Wheaton	Wh.
1828–1843	Peters	Pet.
1843–1860	Howard	How.
1861–1862	Black	Bl.
1863–1874	Wallace	Wall.

Thus the citation to Marbury v. Madison is 1 Cranch 137 (1803), meaning it appears in the first volume of Cranch's Reports, beginning at p. 137. (Early on, there might be several years' opinions in one volume.) In 1875, the Court's reporter began to use the current system, titling the volumes *United States Reports*, and renumbered earlier cases, so that, for instance, *Marbury* can be cited as 1 Cr. 137 (1803) or as 5 U.S. 137 (1803). Some scholarly writers use both forms of citation.

In recent years, several commercial houses have provided services that allow, via computers and modems, electronic retrieval of much legal material, including opinions of the principal courts

---

17. See Charles Warren, *The Supreme Court in United States History* (Rev. ed.; Boston: Little, Brown, 1926), I, 454–455.

around the United States as well as in some other political systems. The two chief providers are WestLaw, a subsidiary of the West Publishing Co., and Lexis/Nexis, owned by Mead Data Central, Inc. of Dayton, Ohio. Both open treasure troves of material relevant to political and legal analyses.

SELECTED BIBLIOGRAPHY

Atiyah, P. S., and Robert S. Summers. *Form and Substance in Anglo–American Law: A Comparative Study of Legal Reasoning, Legal Theory, and Legal Institutions* (Oxford: Clarendon Press, 1987).

Burton, Steven J. *An Introduction to Law and Legal Reasoning* (Boston: Little, Brown, 1985).

Cardozo, Benjamin N. *The Nature of the Judicial Process* (New Haven: Yale University Press, 1921).

————. *Law and Literature* (Littleton, CO: Rothman, 1986) (first published, 1931).

————. *The Growth of the Law* (New Haven: Yale University Press, 1924).

Carter, Lief H. *An Introduction to Constitutional Interpretation* (New York: Longmans, 1991).

————. *Reason in Law* (4th ed.; New York: HarperCollins, 1993).

Cover, Robert M. "Foreward: Nomos and Narrative," 97 *Harv. L.Rev.* 4 (1984).

Harris, William F. II. *The Interpretable Constitution* (Baltimore: Johns Hopkins University Press, 1993).

Levi, Edward H. *An Introduction to Legal Reasoning* (Chicago: University of Chicago Press, 1948).

Levinson, Sanford V. "Law as Literature," 60 *Tex.L.Rev.* 373 (1982).

————, and Steven Mailloux, eds. *Interpreting Law and Literature: A Hermeneutic Reader* (Evanston: Northwestern University Press, 1988)

Murphy, Walter F. *Elements of Judicial Strategy* (Chicago: University of Chicago Press, 1964).

————, C. Herman Pritchett, and Sotirios A. Barber. *Courts, Judges, & Politics* (5th ed.; Boston: McGraw–Hill, 1995), espec. chs. 1, 10–14.

Posner, Richard A. *Law and Literature: A Misunderstood Relation* (Cambridge: Harvard University Press, 1988); (see also the review by James Boyd White, listed below).

Schauer, Frederick. "An Essay on Constitutional Language," 34 *UCLA L.Rev.* 797 (1982).

Shapiro, Martin. "Toward a Theory of Stare Decisis," 2 *Jo. of Legal Studies* 125 (1972).

Solan, Lawrence M. *The Language of Judges* (Chicago: University of Chicago Press, 1993).

White, James Boyd. *When Words Lose Their Meaning: Constitutions and Reconstitutions of Language, Character, and Community* (Chicago: University of Chicago Press, 1984).

_____. *Heracles' Bow: Essays on the Rhetoric and Poetics of the Law* (Madison: University of Wisconsin Press, 1985).

_____. "What Can Lawyers Learn from Literature?" 101 *Harv. L.Rev.* 2014 (1989) (a critical review of Posner's *Law and Literature*).

*

I

The Context of Constitutional Interpretation

At the end of the great battle over constitutional interpretation between the Supreme Court and President Franklin D. Roosevelt, Max Lerner quipped that "judicial decisions are not babies brought by judicial storks, but are born out of the travail of economic circumstance." [1] He might have added that all constitutional interpretation is born out of travail, not merely economic but also political. It is also the product of the intellectual travail of trying to solve an immediate problem of public policy while remaining true to overarching principles—or perhaps even while creating new general principles.

How interpreters face these sorts of problems depends on many factors. This Part looks first, in Chapter 3, at the theoretical context of constitutional interpretation. Here we examine the sometimes reinforcing, sometimes competing, and sometimes conflicting theories of democracy and constitutionalism that underpin the American political system. Their implications for constitutional interpretation are individually important; how an interpreter combines their elements or chooses between them may be profoundly significant.

Chapter 4 analyzes the institutional setting in which governmental agencies interact. It provides a brief overview of the structure of the political system and looks at the implications for constitutional interpretation of relations between the federal and state governments and, at the national level, among the presidency, Congress, and the judiciary. More particularly, it focuses on decision making and persuasion within the Supreme Court.

These two chapters provide a basis for understanding much of the controversy about constitutional interpretation that the rest of the book develops. They also help further understanding of the nature of the solutions interpreters offer and provide a partial explanation of why so many of those solutions seem less than logically complete.

---

1. *Ideas for the Ice Age* (New York: Viking, 1941), p. 259.

3

The Theoretical Context
of Constitutional
Interpretation

American government does not fit a simple model of representative democracy in which elected officials rule in the name of the people. The political system of the United States—like those of Australia, Canada, India, Japan, western Europe, and to an increasing extent eastern Europe as well—is a constitutional democracy, a political hybrid of constitutionalism and democracy. Its formal political structures and the political theories on which they are based combine government by popularly chosen representatives with limited government.

The two kinds of political theory on which the American system rests, democracy and constitutionalism, coexist sometimes in harmony, often in competition, and occasionally in conflict. The notion that the people should govern through those whom they elect sometimes blends lumpily with the notion that there are critical limitations on both what government—however democratically chosen—may validly do and on how it may carry out its legitimate powers.

I. COMPETING POLITICAL THEORIES

A. Representative Democracy

Although the social and economic prerequisites for a successful representative democracy are complex and the actual functioning of a democratic system wonderfully elaborate, only six formal, institutional conditions need obtain: (1) Popular election for limited terms of most of the important policy makers to governmental institutions that allow the majority's representatives to govern in fact and not merely in name; (2) Universal adult suffrage with only minimal restrictions to protect against fraud; (3) Electoral districts of approximately equal population that are not skewed to give disproportionate advantage to particular areas, interests, or persons; (4) Free entry of citizens to candidacy for elective office, with only minimal restrictions to prevent overcrowding the ballot with frivolous candidates; (5) Freedom of political communication—written and oral—so that private citizens, public officials, and candidates can be as informed as they care to be about politics, can discuss issues and personalities with each other, can try to persuade each other, and can join with each to form coalitions; and (6) A right to political privacy so that discussion, persuasion, and association can have effective meaning for those who advocate unpopular causes as well as for those who float in the political mainstream.[1]

These six conditions, if operative, create a free market place of political ideas and encourage civic participation. As Justice Hugo L. Black said for the Supreme Court in 1964:

> No right is more precious in a free country than that of having a voice in the election of those who make the laws under which, as good citizens, we must live. Other rights, even the most basic, are illusory if the right to vote is undermined.[2]

But even more, these conditions allow citizens to act together to form groups to express shared economic and social interests and so increase their political influence. As Alexis de Tocqueville noted in 1835: "The most natural privilege of man, next to the right of acting for himself, is that of combining his exertions with those of his fellow creatures and of acting in common with them."[3]

Most modern democratic theorists stress the value of political participation and the centrality of the political processes to community life—in sum, the right to participate politically is a, if not the, fundamental right. Open discussion, the ability to associate with others, and the right to vote mean that, for democratic theorists, the ballot box supplies legitimacy to decisions of public officials. Judge Hans Linde of the Oregon Supreme Court has extolled

> the primacy of process over product in a free society, the knowledge that no ends can be better than the means of their achievement. "The highest morality is almost always the morality of process," Professor [Alexander] Bickel wrote. ... If this republic is remembered in the distant history of law, it is likely to be for its enduring adherence to legitimate institutions and processes, not for its perfection of unique principles of justice and certainly not for the rationality of its laws.[4]

For most democratic theorists, what obliges citizens to obey "the law" is the fact that officials chosen under an open system operating under the six conditions made the decisions. Democratic theorists tend toward legal positivism, the view that law has no

---

1. See espec. NAACP v. Alabama (1958) and Walter F. Murphy, "The Right to Privacy and Legitimate Constitutional Change," in Shlomo Shlonim, *The Constitutional Bases of Political and Social Change in the United States* (New York: Praeger, 1990).

2. Wesberry v. Sanders (1964).

3. *Democracy in America*, Philips Bradley, ed. (New York: Vintage Books, 1959), I, 203.

4. "Due Process of Lawmaking," 55 *Neb.L.Rev.* 197, 255 (1976).

necessary connection with principles of morality or justice, but is grounded in specific enactments of the "sovereign" or its representatives. And for democratic theorists, the people are sovereign and therefore their representatives partake of that sovereign legitimacy.

Most democratic theorists do not assume that the citizenry as a whole is politically infallible or that all people have equal capacities to understand and choose among the options open to them. "The claim is most persuasively put," Michael Walzer says, "not in terms of what the people know, but in terms of who they are. They are the subjects of the law, and if the law is to bind them as free men and women, they must also be its makers." [5]

Although one can hear occasional echoes of Aristotle's argument that the people's collective wisdom and morality may exceed those of any individual or small group of individuals, the basic assumptions of democratic theory need only be that, with some education: (1) All sane adults can cope with political problems to the extent of being able to recognize their own self interests, join with others who share those interests, and choose among candidates; and (2) a large portion of citizens are willing to be persuaded that they should, much of the time, look beyond their own selfish interests to those shared by the community.

Democrats realize, of course, that political issues are often complex, thus their qualification "with some education" and their insistence on large amounts of equal and public education.[6] "At its core," Professor Joseph Tussman has written about democratic theory,

> is the significance it gives to universal (normal adult) participation in the political process, and the faith that men can, if encouraged and given the opportunity, develop the arts, the skills and habits necessary for a life of responsible deliberation and decision making. Democracy seeks to universalize the parliamentary state of mind.[7]

The chief check that most democratic theorists posit against tyranny is that the people will not tyrannize themselves. Therefore they will vote out of office officials who try to enact oppressive measures. The "mass of citizens," Jefferson once claimed, is "the safest depository for their own rights." [8] Foreknowledge of the likelihood of defeat for reelection will keep most officials from infringing civil rights.

Many theorists find an effective second check in what they perceive to be the way in which democratic politics operates.

---

5. "Philosophy and Democracy," 9 *Political Theory* 379, 383 (1981).

6. See Justice Thurgood Marshall's dissent in San Antonio v. Rodriguez (1973; reprinted below, p. 1002).

7. *Government and the Mind* (New York: Oxford University Press, 1977), p. 143.

8. To John Taylor, May 28, 1816; Paul L. Ford, ed., *The Works of Thomas Jefferson* (New York: Putnam's Sons, 1905), XI, 527.

Echoing Madison in *Federalist* No. 10, they argue that, in a large and diverse nation, the population will seldom be divided between those who fervently favor a particular policy and those who adamantly oppose it. Rather, more typically, coalitions of minority groups form and reform as different issues arise. On a particular matter, some group or groups care very deeply, while others are more or less indifferent but are willing to trade their support in exchange for backing on different issues that they deem critical.

These theorists stress the claim that political cleavages are seldom cumulative.[9] That is, alliances of groups organize and dissolve as issues change, rather than the same interests always finding themselves in coalition with and opposition to the same other groups. On this view, democratic politics is characterized by shifting coalitions of minorities rather than by a more or less constant division between an equally passionate majority and minority. In addition, the existence of open political processes makes it difficult if not impossible for one set of groups to coalesce without alerting others with conflicting interests to form an opposing alliance. As a result, public officials who wish to be reelected will be forced, or at very least strongly pushed, to mediate interests, to act as brokers and compromise clashes rather than adjudicate winner-take-all struggles.

Some theorists add a third check. In a representative democracy, they assert, professional politicians develop and internalize a political subculture that constrains them from trying to tyrannize their constituents. Fear of being voted out of office is not a trivial restraint, nor are crosspressures from competing alliances, actual and latent; but also quite effective is acceptance of rules of the political game that "some things are not done." [10] And it is difficult to argue with the claim that for American presidents, if not other leading public officials, the "judgment of history" has been a strong factor in decision making.

Some proponents of democracy add a limitation that may link it with constitutionalism: To be legitimate, the popular will must will generally; that is, valid laws may not merely reflect prejudices against minorities by imposing burdens only or principally on them.[11] Such a limiting principle may flow from the premise that the people *as a whole* are sovereign, but it is problematic how

9. Robert A. Dahl has done much theoretical and empirical work here. Most important in his *Democracy and Its Critics* (New Haven: Yale University Press, 1989); see also his *A Preface to Democratic Theory* (Chicago: University of Chicago Press, 1956); "Decision-Making in a Democracy: The Supreme Court as a National Policy-Maker," 6 *J. of Pub.L.* 279 (1957); and *Democracy in the United States* (4th ed.; Boston: Houghton–Mifflin, 1981), espec. ch. 18.

10. See again the various writings of Robert A. Dahl, espec. *Who Governs?* (New Haven: Yale University Press, 1961), chs. 27–28; *Dilemmas of Pluralist Democracy* (New Haven: Yale University Press, 1982); and *Democracy and Its Critics*, supra note 9, Part V.

11. See espec. Walzer, supra note 5, and John Hart Ely, *Democracy and Distrust* (Cambridge: Harvard University Press, 1980).

much it is compatible with majority rule. And this potential incompatibility raises fascinating questions about the relationship between democracy and majority rule.[12]

B. Constitutionalism

Democratic theory focuses on how the system chooses decision makers and makes public policy. No less than constitutionalists, proponents of democracy see government as a necessity. Left alone, individuals are quite likely to oppress one another and even more likely to fear such oppression from their fellow humans. To devise public policy to protect civil rights both against private citizens and public officials, democracy relies mainly on process. Constitutionalists share these concerns about threats from individuals and government; they also share many of the values, such as protection of human dignity, that most democratic theorists believe open political processes protect. There are, however, significant differences between several thrusts of the two theories.

First, at a psychological level, constitutionalists tend to be more pessimistic about human nature and the efficacy of the checks of democratic political processes as protectors of fundamental rights: People are often sufficiently clever to oppress others without hurting themselves. Constitutionalism is thus constantly concerned with the human penchant to act selfishly and abuse power. On an empirical level, it is also less optimistic about the claim that cleavages within a polity will not be cumulative. Indeed, constitutionalism fears that divisions between a majority and a minority may be quite long lived and that the shifting alliances of interests that do occur will not protect the fundamental rights of those who lack both political savvy and clout. As John Rawls put it:

> [T]he democratic political process is at best regulated rivalry; it does not even ... have the desirable properties that price theory ascribes to truly competitive markets. Moreover, the effects of injustices in the political system are much more grave and long lasting than market imperfections. Political power rapidly accumulates and becomes unequal; making use of the coercive apparatus of the state and its law, those who gain the advantage can often assure themselves of a favored position. ... Universal suffrage is an insufficient counterpoise; for when parties and elections are financed not by public funds but by private contributions, the political forum is so constrained by the wishes of the dominant interests that the basic measures needed to establish just constitutional rule are seldom seriously presented.[13]

---

12. Madison was concerned in *Federalist* No. 10 with the possibility that in a democratic system a majority could oppress the whole society as well as minorities: "When a majority is included in a faction, the form of popular government ... enables it to sacrifice to its ruling passion or interest, both the *public good* and *the rights of other citizens*." (Italics supplied.)

13. *A Theory of Justice* (Cambridge: Harvard University Press, 1971), p. 226.

Most basic, perhaps, is that constitutionalism rejects the primacy of process. Where individual rights are concerned, the legitimacy of public policy depends, constitutionalism contends, not merely on the authenticity of decision makers' credentials but also on the substance of their work. There are some fundamental rights that government may not trample on, even with the active support of the overwhelming majority of the population, whether aggregated individually or by groups. For a constitutionalist, a law unanimously enacted by a Congress chosen after long, open public debate and free elections and signed by a President similarly chosen would have no legitimacy if that statute violated human dignity.

Each individual has, constitutionalism claims, a zone of physical and psychological space that should be largely immune from governmental regulation, even regulation that an overwhelming majority of society considers wise and just. At the heart of constitutionalism, as of democratic theory, is a belief in the intrinsic moral worth of each person. That belief, to be sure, is the result of a value judgment, but so is the belief that the people *should* govern. The "core objective" of constitutionalism, Professor Carl J. Friedrich once wrote,

> is that of safeguarding each member of the political community as a political person, possessing a sphere of genuine autonomy. The constitution is meant to protect the *self* in its dignity and worth. ... The prime function of a constitutional political order has been and is being accomplished by means of a system of regularized restraints imposed upon those who exercise political power.[14]

Lord Byron expressed the constitutionalist's fear of unlimited popular sovereignty when he wrote:

> What from this barren being do we reap?
>
> Our senses narrow, and our reason frail,
>
> Life short, and truth a gem which loves the deep,
>
> And all things weigh'd in custom's falsest scale;
>
> Opinion an omnipotence,—whose veil
>
> Mantles the earth with darkness, until right
>
> And wrong are accidents, and men grow pale
>
> Lest their own judgments should become too bright,

And their free thoughts be crimes, and earth have too much light.[15]

For the constitutionalist, political morality cannot be weighed on a scale in which "opinion is an omnipotence," but only against the moral criteria of individual rights. And the constitutionalist

---

14. *Transcendent Justice* (Durham: Duke University Press, 1964), pp. 16–17.

15. "Childe Harold's Pilgrimmage," Canto IV, xciii; Frederick Page, ed., *Byron's Poetical Works* (London: Oxford University Press, 1970), p. 239.

insists on institutional limitations beyond those of open political processes to curb government. After all, a constitutionalist would argue, semi-totalitarian democracy[16] in which a government, elected by, responsible to, and responsive to a majority, controls all aspects of behavior except those relating to the six conditions for representative democracy is a logical possibility. Further, oppressive popular government is a practical as well as logical possibility. As James Madison wrote to Jefferson:

> In our Governments the real power lies in the majority of the Community, and the invasion of private rights is *chiefly* to be apprehended, not from acts of Government contrary to the sense of its constituents, but from acts in which Government is the mere instrument of the major number of its constituents.[17]

On the other hand, totalitarian or even semi-totalitarian constitutionalism is a contradiction in terms, though a constitutionalist regime might, like any other government, betray its fundamental principles and become tyrannical. A constitutional democracy, blending popular government with limited government, may require some logical legerdemain; but, in many countries in the world, it has become a practical, if fragile and imperfect, reality.

One must be very careful in defining the differences between constitutionalism and democratic theory. Constitutionalism does not reject democratic processes, it treats them as a means—necessary, but insufficient—to achieve what it considers the ultimate civic purpose of protecting individual liberty against both private citizens and public officials. Nor does constitutionalism reject the notion of community or the importance of civil society; it is merely suspicious of the claims of these concepts when pitted against those of individual autonomy. Moreover, constitutionalism is committed to its own kind of process: When government acts within its proper sphere, it must respect certain procedural rights—for example, to a fair trial—again even when the people and their representatives wish otherwise. In short, by limiting government, constitutionalism attempts to limit the risks of being a member of civil society.

The basic difference between constitutionalism and democratic theory lies not in a dispute over the importance of human dignity but on how best to protect that value. Because of its distrust of human nature, constitutionalism cannot accept the workings of political processes, even if they are open, as *sufficient* criteria of legitimate public policy. Because of its belief in the primacy of self-government, democratic theory can accept no other standard as of more or even equal importance.

---

16. We say "semi-totalitarian" because of the sixth condition of representative democracy, the existence of a strong enough right to privacy that participatory rights can be effective.

17. October 17, 1788. A convenient source for this letter is Marvin Meyers, ed., *The Mind of the Framer* (Indianapolis: Bobbs–Merrill, 1973), pp. 205–209.

II. THE "PURE CONSTITUTIONALIST" v. THE "PURE REPRESENTATIVE DEMOCRAT"

One can visualize the attitudes of constitutionalism and democratic theory toward a system's basic law as falling along a spectrum ranging from an imaginary Pure Constitutionalist at one end to an equally imaginary Pure Representative Democrat at the other:

+ ———————————————————————————————————— +
Pure Constitutionalist   Pure Representative Democrat

The Pure Constitutionalist would see a constitutional document as surrounded by "an ocean of rights." The fundamental assumption would be that people are by nature free and only to protect their rights do they give limited authority to society. Government, as Tom Paine said, "has of itself no rights; they are altogether duties." [18] To legitimate its action, government would have to point to language in the constitutional document granting the power it asserts. Individual liberty, on the other hand, would need no justification. As Edward S. Corwin put it:

> From this point of view ... governmental authority ... is a trust which, save for the grant of it effected by the written constitution, was non-existent, and private rights, since they precede the constitution, gain nothing of authoritativeness from being enumerated in it, though possibly something of security. *These rights are not, in other words, fundamental because they find mention in the written instrument; they find mention there because [they are] fundamental.* ... The written constitution is, in short, but a nucleus or core of a much wider region of private rights, which, though not reduced to black and white, are as fully entitled to the protection of government as if defined in the minutest detail.[19]

Madison used similar language when he introduced what became the Bill of Rights in the first session of Congress:

> It has been objected also against a bill of rights, that, by enumerating particular exceptions to the grant of power, it would disparage those rights which were not placed in that enumeration; and it might follow by implication, that those rights which were not singled out, were intended to be assigned into the hands of the General Government, and were consequently insecure. This is one of the most plausible arguments I have ever heard urged against the admission of a bill of rights into this system; but, I conceive, that it may be guarded against. I have

---

18. *The Rights of Man*, Part II, ch. 4; Henry Collins, ed. (Baltimore: Pelican Books, 1969), p. 187.

19. "The Basic Doctrine of American Constitutional Law," 12 *Mich.L.Rev.* 247, 247–248 (1914). (Italics supplied.)

attempted it, as gentlemen may see by turning to the last clause of the fourth resolution.[20]

That clause of the fourth resolution ultimately became the Ninth Amendment:

> The enumeration in the Constitution, of certain rights, shall not be construed to deny or disparage others retained by the people.

In contrast, the Pure Representative Democrat would see all power as vested in the people and, through the ballot, in their representatives. Whatever those representatives would do, provided they remained within the six conditions specified earlier, would be legitimate. At most, a constitutional document would express national ideals and codify general provisions of the formal rules for democratic government discussed above. For the Pure Representative Democrat, no document, no matter how solemn or ancient, could define rights and duties beyond free political participation and its cognates; only the people's will, as expressed through their elected representatives, could perform those functions.

In the modern world, the Pure Constitutionalist's attitude might well cripple government and so bring about one of the evils constitutionalism aims to prevent, tyranny by private citizens. On the other hand, the Pure Representative Democrat's attitude might create the other evil, tyranny by public officials who would express the wishes of most of the people. Neither result would be acceptable to a nation that endorsed values like religious freedom, private property, or a right to "equal concern and respect."[21] Even the British qualify parliamentary sovereignty by placing it within a political culture in which some things are supposedly not done.

Most American public officials and private citizens who have thought about the matter would probably align themselves at various points near the center of the spectrum. Those people somewhat closer to the democratic pole would view a constitutional text as a plenary grant of power to government, although they might differ widely among themselves about which level or branch of government possessed which power. The only exclusions would be those explicitly listed or clearly implicit in those listed by the democratic authority of the ratifiers of the document. The relevant credo might read: "The voice of the people's elected representatives is sovereign except when speaking either on an issue or in a manner explicitly forbidden by the constitutional document." Chief Justice William H. Rehnquist put it succinctly:

> If such a [democratic] society adopts a constitution and incorporates in that constitution safeguards for individual liberty, these safeguards indeed do take on a generalized moral rightness or goodness. They assume a general social acceptance neither because of any intrinsic worth nor because of unique origins in

---

20. *Annals*, 1st Cong., 1st sess., I, 456.

21. Ronald Dworkin, *Taking Rights Seriously* (Cambridge: Harvard University Press, 1977), p. 180; see also Ely, supra note 11, p. 82.

someone's idea of natural justice but instead simply because they have been incorporated in the constitution by the people.[22]

As we have noted, scholars and jurists who hold these views have faith in open political processes as both protecting fundamental rights and creating viable public policies. For people near the democratic end of the spectrum, constitutional interpretation consists of reading the terms of the actual document and its amendments, ascertaining the meaning of its words, and applying them to the factual matrix of the current problem. To be legitimate, a public policy must meet several sets of criteria that relate mainly to process. It must:

> 1) Be enacted by the people's representatives, chosen according to the rules of representative democracy listed above, and operating in conformity with the processes established in the constitutional text; *and*
>
> 2) Be authorized *either* by:
>
>> a) the explicit powers delegated by that document, *or*
>>
>> b) the powers reasonably implied by that document's terms; *or*
>>
>> c) the residuum of inherent power on which government may call to preserve the polity; *and*
>
> 3) Violate *neither*:
>
>> a) any of the specific prohibitions of the constitutional document, *nor*
>>
>> b) any of the rights clearly implied in the constitutional document.

Testing a policy's legitimacy by the first set of criteria might appear a simple task. In fact, of course, numerous problems swiftly arise, not least of which are how to determine who is qualified to vote and how to apportion electoral districts fairly.

Testing under 2(a) and 3(a) is even more difficult. As the cases reprinted in this book will demonstrate, understanding the American constitutional text is far less easy than it initially might seem. The basic document is now more than two centuries old. Does an interpreter try to discover the original meanings such words had or the meanings those words have taken on as the American version of the English language has developed? Whatever the answer to that question, whose usage does the interpreter adopt, that of lawyers or ordinary people on whose authority the document claims to speak? Assuming a satisfactory answer to that query, how does the interpreter choose among popular dictionaries or among expert inter-

---

22. "Observation: The Notion of a Living Constitution," 54 *Tex.L.Rev.* 693, 704 (1976) reprinted below, p. 243. (When Rehnquist wrote this piece, he was still an associate justice; he became Chief Justice in 1986.)

pretations of such words?   What if, as was the case for the American
founding generation, there was no comprehensive dictionary?

Such questions only begin to chart the difficulties.   The "plain
words" of the constitutional text are often not very plain.   The
Fourth Amendment forbids only "unreasonable" searches and seizures; the Fifth Amendment orders the federal government to pay
"just compensation" if it takes private property for public use; the
Eighth bans "cruel and unusual punishments."   What is "reasonable," "just," "cruel," "unusual," or "public use" is often controversial.   The Fourteenth Amendment forbids states to deny any
person "the equal protection of the laws."   But laws frequently
must discriminate among people.   No one would contend that a
state must, or even should, permit the blind to drive automobiles or
pedophiles to teach in kindergartens.

Testing under 2(b) (that the document implies as well as lists
powers) or 3(b) (that government may draw on a residuum of
inherent power to preserve the nation) opens a new universe of
problems.   Still taking only the text's own words, an interpreter
must confront, sooner or later, the "sweeping clause" of Article I,
which authorizes Congress to enact "all Laws which shall be necessary and proper for carrying into Execution" powers delegated to
Congress itself or to any other branch of the federal government.
Then, too, there is the problem what to do about the Ninth
Amendment, which, as we saw, specifies protection of unspecified
rights.   These clauses are such stuff as legal positivists' nightmares
are made of.

Interpreters somewhat closer to the Pure Constitutionalist's end
of the spectrum also face great difficulties.   In general, they insist
on testing a public policy by its conformity to constitutionalist
values of individual rights, values that may well go beyond the
words of the constitutional document—precisely what Chief Justice
Rehnquist rejects.   They accept the notion of implied governmental
powers, but they also embrace the idea that a constitution is
surrounded by "an ocean of rights" and that, as the Ninth Amendment explicitly says, these rights need not be mentioned in the
document to be worthy of, even demanding of, protection by all
branches of government, including a non-elected judiciary.

For such people—"constitutionalists" as distinguished from
Pure Constitutionalists—a legitimate public policy must meet all the
criteria just listed plus one other:

> 3) Not violate . . .
>
>> c) any of "the ocean of rights" that surround the
>> constitutional text and so are part of the larger
>> constitution and equally as binding as the docu-
>> ment's plain words.

It is this position of the moderate "constitutionalist," with all
its complexities and uncertainties, that the U.S. Supreme Court has

typically taken. The justices' visions of the size and depth of that "ocean of rights" have varied; sometimes that ocean has seemed a vast sea, at other times a lake, at still others a mere puddle. But it has been a rare Court that has not seen "the Constitution" as being girded by at least a moat of some unlisted rights, whether to "freedom of contract" or privacy.

For all those who find themselves near the center of the spectrum, whether somewhat more constitutionalist or somewhat more democratic, political life is not a matter of clear-cut choices. On the one hand, there must an operative government to protect citizens from each other and the people must control that government. The right to participate in one's government is a mark of human dignity, a fundamental claim that all sane adults can make against their society. On the other hand, to have a life worth living, citizens must retain their dignity as human beings, which means they must retain some sphere of privacy and autonomy. The authority of the people to govern must be limited if society is to fulfill its purpose of making it possible for men and women to live as free human beings. "What," a constitutionalist might ask, "doth it profit a nation to survive if it suffers the loss of what it holds most dear?"

On many of the abstract and concrete issues here, the demands of constitutionalism and those of democracy may sometimes point in different directions. And solutions are likely to be neither obvious nor easy. With that much said, there are also ways in which the two philosophies, if joined in a given polity, can reinforce one another. Both, for instance, look to the dignity and freedom of the individual person as the great public good; both preach the equal worth of citizens; and both try to legitimize certain exercises of governmental power as well as to limit exercises of governmental power—democracy by requiring open political processes, constitutionalism by other institutional checks, and both through a political culture that both empowers and limits government. At minimum, this mutual nurturing of values should discourage many potentially oppressive demands from ever being voiced.

Indeed, there are some constitutional theorists who maintain that democracy needs constitutionalism to prevent self-destruction and that analyses, such as ours, are misleading. Stephen Holmes, for example, claims that the alleged tension between constitutionalism and democracy is "one of the core myths of modern political thought." [23] He stresses, as we do, that a constitutional text that rests on constitutionalism enables and organizes governmental au-

---

23. "Precommitment and the Paradox of Democracy," in Jon Elster and Rune Slagstad, eds., *Constitutionalism and Democracy* (Chicago: University of Chicago Press, 1988), p. 197. See also his "Gag Rules and the Politics of Omission," *ibid.*, pp. 19–58, and Jon Elster, *Ulysses and the Sirens* (Chicago: University of Chicago Press, 1979). For a critique of Holmes's arguments, see Cass R. Sunstein, "Constitutions and Democracies: An Epilogue," in Elster and Slagstad.

thority as well as limits it. "[W]ithout tying their hands, the people will have no hands."[24] To work, democracy must function as popular government operating according to rules that transform what would otherwise be an emotional mob into a deliberating people.

Holmes's argument, which we have only barely outlined here, is rich and presents a powerful case for the democratic nature of constitutionalist restraints that protect free, open political processes. In that sense, claims of tension, at least long-run tension, between constitutionalism and democracy may well be exaggerated. But Holmes's argument, we believe, is less successful in demonstrating an absence of hard tension between, on the one hand, democracy's according to the people pretty much free rein over substantive matters that do not touch on rights of political participation and, on the other hand, constitutionalism's protecting substantive rights against the wishes of public officials chosen through free and open elections and representing the will of the overwhelming majority of the nation. If one wishes to play down the tensions of which we have spoken, one must do so by arguing that without restricting the stakes of politics—one of constitutionalism's principal goals—open political processes might put too much at risk, that losers would be quite likely to resort to violence, and thus stability would be frequently and seriously threatened. Such an argument, of course, is not at all incompatible with Holmes's, and he hints at such reasoning.

This controversy is another of those disputes that readers should carefully ponder and about which they should make up their own minds. To facilitate understanding, we turn to a discussion of how the American system blends constitutionalism and democracy and begin by looking at the general scheme of government the framers in Philadelphia proposed; then we examine the ways in which the system has developed.

III. FREE GOVERNMENT: THE FOUNDING GENERATION

A. The Critical Problems of 1787

Almost all the delegates to the Philadelphia Convention of 1787 were largely members of what journalists today would call "the establishment"; some enjoyed wealth, all but one had social status and power. Despite their constitutional prohibition of titles of nobility, it would not be unfair to say that they considered themselves a natural aristocracy. Partly because of their social and economic position, most were deeply troubled by government under the Articles of Confederation. More in name than in fact was

---

24. "Precommitment," supra note 23, p. 230.

the "national" government either "national" or a "government." It could neither command the respect of foreign nations necessary to negotiate treaties to assist international trade, nor could it enforce uniform rules of commerce across state boundaries.

Lacking central direction, the separate states went their own ways. Many of them had democratic political systems that responded to the wishes of the majority to favor debtors over creditors and so eased contractual obligations and printed bales of paper money, called those bills legal tender, and thus enabled debtors to pay off their obligations in greatly depreciated currency. Some states were also erecting barriers against the products and people of sister states. As men of means and vision, the delegates saw this bundle of policies as menacing the institution of private property[25] and ideals of national unity, threatening the prosperity of the whole nation and turning the country into the "DisUnited States."

To minimize these difficulties, the framers strove for two objectives. First, they tried to construct a national government that was much stronger than that which existed under the Articles, a government that would take over many important functions from the states. The delegates' second objective complemented the first. As men of wealth and property, they knew that they and people like them were apt to remain a minority. Furthermore, not only were the excesses of democratically elected state governments causing immediate distress, but so had, only a few years earlier, the rule of a British monarch. Thus the framers' second fundamental objective was not merely to limit the states, but also to organize national power in a manner that would protect property rights at all levels and so prevent the most likely form of tyranny.

Before the Convention, James Madison published a booklet in which he explained the dual objective in constructing a constitution:

> The great desideratum of Government is such a modification of the sovereignty as will render it sufficiently neutral between the different interests and factions, to controul one part of the society from invading the rights of another, and at the same time sufficiently controuled itself from setting up an interest adverse to that of the whole Society.[26]

After the Convention, he described these objectives in similar terms, "combining the requisite stability and energy in government, with the inviolable attention due to liberty and the republican form."[27]

---

25. On the framers' primary devotion to rights of property over those of political participation, see Jennifer Nedelsky, *Private Property and the Limits of American Constitutionalism: The Madisonian Framework and Its Legacy* (Chicago: University of Chicago Press, 1990).

26. "Vices of the Political System of the United States," (1787), reprinted in Meyers, supra note 17, pp. 83–92.

27. *The Federalist*, No. 37, Benjamin F. Wright, ed. (Cambridge: The Belknap Press of Harvard University Press, 1961), p. 267.

And, without being troubled by false modesty, he boasted that the delegates at Philadelphia had improved on the efforts of the leaders of the revolt against England to carry out "a revolution which has no parallel in the annals of human society. They reared the fabrics of governments which have no model on the face of the globe."[28]

There was some truth in Madison's bravado. The new constitutional text did outline a much more powerful central government than the Articles of Confederation had allowed. At the same time, however, the terms of the new document and the frictions it would generate might well keep political power at all levels of government faithful to its appointed, and limited, tasks, especially protecting, as Madison said in *Federalist* No. 10, "diversity in the faculties of men" to acquire property.

Unlike the old government, which lacked an effective executive and a judiciary and could really only recommend action to the states, the new national government had its own executive and judicial systems and would operate directly on the people of the United States. New powers included those to tax and spend; to regulate commerce among the several states, with foreign nations, and with the Indian tribes; to coin and borrow money, establish postal services and post roads, and enact uniform rules of bankruptcy; to conduct foreign relations, raise armies and navies, wage war, and conclude treaties; and, under the so-called "sweeping clause," to make all laws "necessary and proper" to carry out any or all enumerated powers.

The new constitutional document also expressly denied many powers to the states, such as authority to enter into a treaty or alliance, enact ex post facto laws[29] or bills of attainder,[30] or grant titles of nobility. More directly related to the policies that had aroused the framers were prohibitions against states' impairing the obligations of contracts, issuing bills of credit, making anything but gold or silver legal tender, or taxing (without congressional approval) exports or imports. Further, the supremacy clause proclaimed "this Constitution," along with "the laws of the United States which shall be made in Pursuance thereof, and all Treaties made, or which shall be made, under the authority of the United States" to be the "supreme Law of the Land" and decreed that "Judges in every State shall be bound thereby, any Thing in the Constitution or Laws of any State to the Contrary notwithstanding."

---

28. *The Federalist,* No. 14, p. 154.

29. As construed by Calder v. Bull (1798; reprinted below, p. 121), a statute that makes an act that was lawful when committed a crime, retroactively increases the penalty for a crime, or, again retroactively, lowers the conditions of proof to establish guilt.

30. A legislative act that convicts a named or easily identified person of a crime and punishes that person without benefit of a judicial trial.

B. The Grand Strategy of Checks and Counter-checks[31]

When the framers undertook to limit power, they did not deem elections to be the sole means. Making public officials responsible to their constituencies was by no means insignificant; but it was not enough. The injustice of recent state laws regarding property, Madison wrote before the Convention, was alarming because it brought into question whether "the majority ... are the safest Guardians both of public Good and private rights." Like a good constitutionalist, he went on to speculate:

> A succeeding election it might be supposed, would displace the offenders, and repair the mischief. But how easily are base and selfish measures, masked by pretexts of public good and apparent expediency? How frequently will a repetition of the same arts and industry which succeeded in the first instance, again prevail on the unwary to misplace their confidence?[32]

Madison saw the source of the evil in human nature, in the propensity of all men, individually and collectively, to act selfishly, a flaw that neither philosophy nor religion could eradicate. As a result, the gravest danger of oppression in a society that allowed wide popular participation would come not from a government that ignored or violated the will of the majority, but from one that followed the majority will.[33] As he wrote in *Federalist* No. 51:

> It is of great importance in a republic, not only to guard against the oppression of its rulers; but to guard one part of society against the injustice of the other part. ... If a majority be united by a common interest, the rights of the minority will be insecure.

Initially, the framers chose not to rely on a bill of rights to protect against governmental abuse of power. They included some taboos, especially, as we have just seen, where the states were concerned as well as a few against national action, such as bans against ex post facto laws, bills of attainder, taxes on exports, and prohibition of the slave trade before 1808. On the whole, however, the framers believed, as John Randolph later expressed it: "You

---

31. We are especially indebted in this section to Paul Eidelberg, *The Philosophy of the American Constitution* (New York: The Free Press, 1968). For important studies of *The Federalist* and its explanation of the new political system, see espec: George W. Carey, *The Federalist: Design for a Constitutional Republic* (Urbana: University of Illinois Press, 1989); David F. Epstein, *The Political Theory of* The Federalist (Chicago: University of Chicago Press, 1984); Gottfried Dietze, *The Federalist: A Classic of Federalism and Free Government* (Baltimore: Johns Hopkins University Press, 1960); and Morton White, *Philosophy*, The Federalist, *and the Constitution* (New York: Oxford University Press, 1987). Chapter 2 of Sotirios A. Barber, *The Constitution of Judicial Power* (Baltimore: Johns Hopkins University Press, 1993), analyzes *The Federalist* 's views on judicial power and judicial review.

32. "Vices of the Political System," in Meyers, supra note 17, p. 89.

33. See his letter to Jefferson, October 17, 1788; Meyers, supra note 17, p. 206.

may cover whole skins of parchment with limitations but power alone can limit power." [34]

Madison explained to Jefferson that there were many reasons not to include a Bill of Rights against the national government:

1. Because I conceive that in a certain degree, though not to the extent argued by Mr. [James] Wilson [of Pennsylvania], the rights in question are reserved by the manner in which the federal powers are granted.

2. Because there is great reason to fear that a positive declaration of some of the most essential rights could not be obtained in the requisite latitude. I am sure that the rights of conscience in particular, if submitted to public definition, would be narrowed much more than they are likely ever to be by an assumed power. One of the objections in New England was, that the Constitution, by prohibiting religious tests, opened a door for Jews, Turks, and infidels.

3. Because the limited power of the federal Government, and the jealousy of the subordinate Governments, afford a security which has not existed in the case of the State Governments, and exists in no other.

4. Because experience proves the inefficacy of a bill of rights on those occasions when its controul is most needed. Repeated violations of these parchment barriers have been committed by overbearing majorities in every State.[35]

Later, in 1789, partly because of Jefferson's arguments and partly because of concerns expressed in state ratifying conventions, Madison changed his mind about a bill of rights. But in 1787 most of the framers put their main reliance for limiting governmental power on geographic, social, and institutional strategies that recognized human selfishness and sinfulness and tried to play groups of selfish sinners off against each other.

1. Geographic Strategy

The geographic strategy was to widen the scope of the political unit and so the number of citizens as well as the diversity of their interests—in sum, to make the entire nation a meaningful political arena of widely diverse interest groups. In *Federalist* No. 10, Madison argued that a large as contrasted with a small republic would make it easier for the people to choose men of character as their representatives and more difficult for a majority to coalesce to oppress smaller groups.

The smaller the society, the fewer probably will be the distinct parties and interests composing it; the fewer the distinct parties and interests, the more frequently will a majority be found of the same party; and the smaller the number of individuals composing

---

34. Quoted in William Bruce, *John Randolph of Roanoke* (New York: Putnam's, 1922), II, 211.

35. To Jefferson, October 17, 1788; Meyers, supra note 17, p. 206.

a majority, the more easily will they concert and execute their plan of oppression. Extend the sphere, and you take in a greater variety of parties and interests; you make it less probable that a majority of the whole will have a common motive to invade the rights of other citizens; or if such a common motive exists, it will be more difficult for all who feel it to discover their own strength, and to act in unison with each other. ...

2. Socio–Economic Strategy

In a related fashion, the framers devised a socio-economic strategy to divide power among economic interests in society by providing different constituencies for various federal offices. Membership in the House of Representatives would be apportioned among the states according to population, terms would run for only two years, and all persons eligible to vote for the more numerous house of the state's legislature could vote for candidates for the House.

"Here, sir," Hamilton claimed, "the people govern"[36]—though more in a negative than a positive sense because, acting alone, the House cannot enact legislation. The broad nature of its electorate and the requirement of frequent elections could mean, however, that the House would represent the policies of the less affluent and require the more affluent, represented in the Senate, to compromise if they wished to enact legislation.

Senators—two from each state, originally chosen by its legislature—would be more insulated from the popular will. Their over-representing the smaller states, indirect election, relatively long terms of office (six years), and the fact that only one-third of them would come up for election in the same year in which the entire House or the House and the President were chosen further detached senators from the popular will. And many of the framers were quite candid in their image of the Senate as an institution that would represent the policies of the more affluent and stable elements in society. Edmund Randolph of Virginia told his fellow delegates that the Senate was needed to restrain "the turbulence

---

36. Speech in New York's ratifying convention, in Jonathan Elliot, ed., *Debates in The Several State Conventions on the Adoption of the Federal Constitution* (Philadelphia: Lippincott, 1901), II, 348. (Orig. published, 1836.) One should treat Elliot's "reports" of the debates with some skepticism. Not only was he himself an active partisan in politics, but he relied heavily on newspaper accounts and notes taken by "secretaries," themselves sometimes partisans of one side or the other, who did not know shorthand. For problems here, see James H. Hutson, "The Creation of the Constitution: The Integrity of the Documentary Record," 65 *Tex.L.Rev.* 1 (1986); and Leonard W. Levy, *Original Intent and the Framers' Constitution* (New York: Macmillan, 1988), ch. 1. Several decades ago, Prof. Merrill Jensen of the University of Wisconsin formed a team of scholars to undertake the heroic task of recapturing the documents of the debate over ratification. Prof. John P. Kaminski has now long succeeded Jensen as editor-in-chief, and, as of 1994, the team has produced 10 volumes, all published by the University of Wisconsin Press: *The Documentary History of the Ratification of the Constitution* (1976ff). For an excellent collection of essays, examining ratification state by state, see Michael Allen Gillespie and Michael Lienesch, eds., *Ratifying the Constitution* (Lawrence: University Press of Kansas Press, 1989).

and follies of democracy." [37] John Dickenson of Delaware made a more extreme argument: "In the formation of the Senate we ought to carry it through such a refining process as will assimilate it as near as may be to the House of Lords of England." [38] Few other delegates wanted to adopt a British model, but Madison apparently agreed that the "Senate shd. come from, and represent, the wealth of the Nation. ..." [39]

The President was also to be indirectly chosen through the Electoral College. Each state would have a number of electors equal to its combined representation in the House and Senate (and so smaller states would have a relative advantage over the more populous), and every state could decide how it would choose its electors. The people so selected would meet in their own state capitals, cast their ballots, then send them to Congress to be counted. (Some framers seem to have expected this process to be more one of nomination than election, for political parties as we have them were unknown and communications slow). If no candidate received an absolute majority of electoral votes, the House would choose (initially among the five leading candidates, but since adoption of the Twelfth Amendment in 1804, the top three), with each state having one vote regardless of the size of its congressional delegation.

Federal judges, nominated by an indirectly elected President and confirmed by an indirectly elected Senate, would serve for "good Behaviour"—a term that in practice has usually meant until the judge decides to retire or is overtaken by death. In the political context of the last dozen years of the eighteenth century, only the most naive populist would have expected that men so chosen

---

37. "Debates in the Federal Convention of 1787 as Reported by James Madison," reprinted in Max Farrand, ed., *The Records of the Federal Convention of 1787* (New Haven: Yale University Press, 1911; reprinted 1966), I, 51. At least seven of the framers took more or less extensive notes of the debates. Farrand reprints in their entirety those of Alexander Hamilton, Rufus King, George Mason, James McHenry, James Madison, William Paterson, William Pierce, James Wilson, and Robert Yates. Robert Lansing also kept a set of notes, first published in 1939 and republished in 1967: Joseph R. Strayer, ed., *The Delegate from New York* (Port Washington, NY: Kennikat Press, 1967). None of these is a "record" in any formal sense or even an informal shorthand transcript, but notes written in longhand by participants during and sometimes well after the debates. Not only are they individually and collectively incomplete, they also sometimes disagree with each other on what was said. Madison, for example, accused Yates, who published his notes during Madison's lifetime, of perverting the historical record for partisan political purposes. A recent scholar, James H. Hutson, "The Creation of the Constitution," supra note 36, goes further and claims that what we have of Yates's "notes" are very likely forgeries, manufactured or at least grossly edited by his son-in-law. Madison's own notes were published in 1840, four years after his death. In sum, one should treat these notes of debates with the same caution that one treats the notes that justices of the Supreme Court take of the secret conferences in which they discuss cases. See below, Chapter 4.

38. Farrand, supra note 37, I, 136. 163.

39. "Notes of Rufus King in the Federal Convention of 1787," Farrand, supra note 37, I, 158. Madison's "Notes" report no such remark, but that omission proves little, for Madison never claimed to have made a full transcript of the proceedings.

would support the economic policies of state legislatures under the Articles of Confederation.

In this network of competing constituencies, the more affluent could anticipate great advantages. They could reasonably expect to control the executive, the judiciary, and the Senate—expectations that alarmed and angered Anti–Federalists. Even that avid defender of the new constitutional order, Alexander Hamilton, conceded that, through "the natural operation of the different interests and views of the various classes of the community," federal legislators would "consist almost entirely of proprietors of land, of merchants, and of members of the learned professions"; but, he insisted, such men would represent different interests and views.[40]

Nevertheless, even if one could not accept Hamilton's hope for "virtual representation" of most interests, control of the House with its exclusive authority to initiate tax bills would allow the common people's actual representatives to block any positive policy their "betters" wished to enact into law—always providing, of course, that the common people could in fact exercise their potential power to choose their legislators and hold them to account.

3. Institutional Strategy

The institutional web the framers spun fit the same strategy as the geographic and social arrangements—playing off sets of officials and interests against each other. Basically, the constitutional text tried to fracture governmental power and give overlapping pieces to different officials. The constitutional structure explicitly provided for the states to continue as important political entities. The document required the federal government to guarantee to every state "a Republican Form of Government," to protect each against invasion and insurrection, and to insure that none lost any of its territory without its consent. Furthermore, grants of power to the national government were seldom exclusive, leaving it open to negotiation and interpretation how much authority states retained.

Some of the founders, such as James Madison and James Wilson, thought that specific references to state/federal relations would be less consequential than the supposed fact that the federal government was to be one of delegated powers. "The Powers not delegated to the United States by the Constitution," as the Tenth Amendment later said, "nor prohibited by it to the States, are reserved to the States respectively, or to the people." Like the rest of the document, however, that provision offers a general guide rather than a precise formula for federal-state relations. For, in proposing the Tenth Amendment, Congress three times rejected the wording "expressly delegated" and thus left intact Article I's grant of implied powers in its conferring on Congress all powers "neces-

---

40. *The Federalist*, No. 36, p. 259.

sary and proper" to carry out powers expressly delegated to the national government.

By drawing only vague verbal boundaries and leaving both national and state officials with tracts of apparently overlapping powers, the framers insured enduring rivalry and constant friction among the representatives of various geographic and socio-economic interests. That same pattern reappears in the fabric of the federal government itself. What we see is less a system of separated than of shared powers.[41] Article I begins: "All legislative Powers herein granted shall be vested in a Congress of the United States"; then Article II makes the President part of the legislative process by allowing him, among other things, to recommend and veto legislation. So, too, that Article allows the Senate a share in executive power by confirming the President's nominees to all important offices, including his own cabinet; and Article I confers on Congress authority to organize the entire executive branch and makes all federal programs dependent on congressional appropriations of money. Similarly, Article II's grant of executive power to the President includes quasi-judicial authority to nominate judges and to pardon people convicted of crimes.

Article III establishes a Supreme Court and empowers Congress to institute a system of lower federal courts and to make exceptions to the appellate jurisdiction of the Supreme Court. On these tribunals Article III conferred but did not define "the judicial power of the United States."

If, as seems probable, the founders thought that judges would share in constitutional interpretation, they left wide room for judicial discretion; indeed, they required judicial discretion. Many clauses are couched in broad language that demands creative interpretation. What powers are "necessary and proper" to carry out those specifically delegated to the national government is far from obvious, and many of the expressly delegated powers are hardly specific. What is "commerce" is no easier to define than it is in an interdependent society to distinguish commerce "among the several states" from local businesses.

C. Sentinels Over Public Rights

The system that the Convention produced seems chaotic and devoid of any master plan. But that assessment would be wrong. Many of the framers, most especially Madison, consciously tried to knit networks of tensions and jealousies among competing public officials, whose inexact grants of power would make them insecure and thus zealous watchdogs against efforts of rivals to aggrandize power. "Ambition," Madison explained, "must be made to coun-

---

41. Richard E. Neustadt, *Presidential Power* (New York: Wiley, 1960), p. 33.

teract ambition. The interest of the man must be connected with the constitutional rights of the place." He continued:

> the constant aim is to divide and arrange the several offices in such a manner as that each may be a check on the other—that the private interest of every individual may be a sentinel over the public rights.[42]

IV. THE DEVELOPING SYSTEM

We have been careful not to speak of the "intent" or "understanding" of the framers and ratifiers—the founders. Instead, we have offered the views of individual delegates and have spoken about the larger architectural scheme they created. We can discuss the founders' broad "purposes" with some confidence, but if we try to determine the exact meaning those men collectively intended or understood to be in specific clauses—what, for instance, most of them had precisely in mind when they proposed and approved congressional authority to regulate "commerce among the several states"—difficulties multiply. In the first place, we lack a complete and accurate "record" of debates either at Philadelphia or in the state ratifying conventions. More fundamentally, it is open to doubt whether future generations are bound by the founders' specific intentions and understandings, even if we knew what they were, rather than by the document and the constitutional order to which it gave birth.

That order has developed in ways the founders could not have foreseen. The most dramatic political changes have involved democratization not merely of government but of the entire society. The political and social cultures of the nation have become far more egalitarian; the right to vote has been broadened; slavery has been abolished; and the notion of the equal moral and legal worth of every human being has come closer to being a fully accepted political value.

Formal amendments to the constitutional text have at times recognized these changes, at other times precipitated them. The Thirteenth Amendment's outlawing of slavery culminated a long campaign for freedom; it owes as much to constitutionalist as to democratic theory and most of all to military victory in the Civil War. The Fourteenth Amendment's prohibition of denials of equal protection of the laws and the Fifteenth's ban on denials of suffrage based on race did not become effective until more than another century had elapsed. More recent voting amendments have reflected growing democratic sentiment: The Nineteenth Amendment forbids denying a person the ballot because of his or her sex, the Twenty–Fourth because of failure to pay a tax, the Twenty–Sixth because of age, for those over 18; the Seventeenth made senators

---

42. *The Federalist.*, No. 51, p. 356.

directly elected by popular vote; and the Twenty–Third gave citizens of the District of Columbia the franchise in presidential elections. In addition, without amendment to the document that labels itself "the Constitution of the United States," every state now chooses its presidential electors by popular vote, and none retains a property qualification for general elections.

Even the least democratic among the founders believed that a free and stable government must rest on the consent of the governed. And, they explicitly provided that the fate of the proposed constitutional document was to be determined by *conventions* chosen in the states (qualifications of electors for the conventions were not specified), not by state legislatures. Furthermore, as already noted, the House was to be chosen by a broad constituency.

Madison expressed a common sentiment when he wrote that it was a "fundamental principle that men cannot be justly bound by laws in [the] making of which they have no part." [43] But, believing in government by consent is not equivalent to believing in representative as distinguished from constitutional democracy. And, as we have seen, the formal and informal structures proposed at Philadelphia in 1787 hedged all political power within mazes of checks and counterchecks. "One person, one vote" was not a value originally embodied in the letter or spirit of the constitutional document; even "one vote for each white, male, adult citizen" did not find strong support among the delegates.

Part of the opposition to democracy was undoubtedly due to fear that elected representatives would govern at the national level as they had in the states and further endanger property and progress. Another part of the opposition came from a more deeply rooted distrust, a doubt that people without property could be sufficiently autonomous to vote in their own self interest. As John Dickinson remarked, "No one could be considered as having an interest in the government unless he possessed some of the soil." [44] Gouverneur Morris added a similar objection:

> If the suffrage was to be open to all *freemen*—the government would indubitably be an aristocracy. . . . It [would] put in the power of opulent men whose business created numerous dependents to rule at all elections. Hence so soon as we erected large manufactories and our towns became more populous—wealthy merchants and manufacturers would elect the house of representatives. This was an aristocracy. This could only be avoided by confining the suffrage to *free holders.* [45]

---

43. Madison appended these words in a "Note" to his speech of August 7, 1787; reprinted in Farrand, supra note 37, II, 204n.

44. "Papers of Dr. James McHenry on the Federal Convention of 1787," Farrand, supra note 37, II, 209.

45. *Ibid.*, II, 209–210. McHenry added: "Mr. Maddison [sic] supported similar sentiments." Madison recorded himself as saying that "in its merits alone, the freeholders of the Country would be the safest depositories of Republican liberty." *Ibid.*, II, 203. He left

(Morris's remarks make more sense when one realizes that at the time voting was typically both public and oral. The secret ballot as we know it did not come into widespread use in the United States until almost a century had passed.)

Despite dramatic democratization, the American system is still deeply implanted in constitutionalism. Industrialization has helped multiply the number and kinds of interest groups, but development of instant mass communications and democratization of political processes have weakened the grand strategy of geographic, socio-economic, and institutional checks. And, today, federal judges, especially justices of the Supreme Court, have had thrust on them or have taken on themselves the duty of defending constitutionalism.

It was Jefferson, who was to become the foe of the federal judiciary led by John Marshall, who planted some of the most intellectually fruitful seeds for the growth of judicial authority. After the Revolution, he complained about the almost unlimited power Virginia's constitutional document gave the legislature: "One hundred and seventy-three despots would surely be as oppressive as one. . . . An elective despotism was not the government we fought for. . . ." [46] After the Convention, he urged Madison to fight for a national bill of rights. It was, Jefferson claimed, "what the people are entitled to against every government on earth, general or particular, and what no just government should refuse, or rest on inference." [47]

For the reasons noted above, Madison at first resisted, though he conceded that a bill of rights might "acquire by degrees the character of fundamental maxims of *free* governments, and as they become incorporated with the national sentiment"—modern scholars would say become part of the "political culture"—"counteract the impulses of interest and passion." He also admitted that such a bill would be useful to the extent that tyranny sprang from government alone, rather than from government's obeying a popular mandate.

In response, Jefferson said he approved of Madison's arguments *for* a bill of rights, but:

---

no record of broader agreement with Morris's description of the harm that broadening the franchise might engender.

46. "Notes on Virginia," (1784), Andrew A. Lipscomb, ed., *The Writings of Thomas Jefferson* (Washington, DC: Thomas Jefferson Memorial Association, 1903), II, 163. Compare Tom Paine, *The Rights of Man* (New York: Dutton, 1951), Part II, p. 192: "It is not because a part of the Government is elective that makes it less a despotism, if the persons so elected possess afterwards, as a Parliament, unlimited powers."

47. The exchange of letters is reprinted in Julian P. Boyd, ed., *The Papers of Thomas Jefferson* (Princeton: Princeton University Press, 1955) XII, 439–442; *ibid.* (1958), XIV, 18–21, 656–661. A more convenient source for these and many other documents in American constitutional history is Alpheus T. Mason and Gordon E. Baker, eds., *Free Government in the Making* (4th ed.; New York: Oxford University Press, 1985), pp. 285–294.

you omit one which has great weight with me, the legal check
which it puts into the hands of the judiciary. This is a body,
which if rendered independent, and kept strictly to their own
department merits great confidence for their learning and integrity.

When he introduced in the House of Representatives the
amendments that became the Bill of Rights, Madison polished
Jefferson's reasoning:

If they are incorporated into the constitution, independent tribunals of justice will consider themselves in a peculiar manner the
guardians of those rights; they will be an impenetrable bulwark
against every assumption of power in the legislative or executive;
they will be naturally led to resist every encroachment upon the
rights expressly stipulated for in the constitution by the declaration of rights.[48]

Judicial protection against legislative or executive tyranny was quite
compatible with the other checks that Madison had persuaded the
Convention to adopt, but it was not an arrangement that he had
earlier stressed. To show that he saw a bill of rights as also fitting
into his strategic scheme, he quickly added:

Besides this security, there is a great probability that such a
declaration in the federal system would be enforced; because the
State Legislatures will jealously and closely watch the operations
of this Government, and be able to resist with more effect every
assumption of power, than any other power on earth can do; and
the greatest opponents to a Federal Government admit the State
Legislatures to be sure guardians of the people's liberty.[49]

The proposition that federal judges, appointed for what
amounts to life terms, should sometimes stand with, and at other
times stand against, elected legislators as bulwarks of individual
liberty against the will of the people underscores the potential
conflict between constitutionalism and democracy. And it is important to understand the precise nature of that conflict. It is undemocratic for a group of appointed officials to declare invalid decisions reached by the people's elected representatives. But federalism is similarly undemocratic. The democratic ideal of equal electoral districts is incompatible with giving 25 million people in
California the same number of senators as fewer than a half million
in Alaska, or for the Electoral College to overweight small states in
presidential elections. Neither is it democratic for the people to be
unable to elect a majority of senators in any given election, or for
the Electoral College to be able to frustrate the popular will in
choosing a President—or, when no candidate receives a majority of
electoral votes, for the House, voting by states with Alaska having
the same single vote as California, to select the chief executive.

---

48. *Annals*, 1st Cong., 1st sess., I, 457.
49. *Idem.*

These sorts of potential conflict have occasionally become very real. They indicate the differing demands that constitutionalism and democracy may make on the political system and the differing ways in which the system accommodates those competing demands. The relationship between the two is conceptually as well as practically difficult. Yet the system has survived its inner tensions and perhaps prospered because of those tensions.

V. CONCLUSION

It is highly probable that most of the delegates at Philadelphia would have arrayed themselves much closer to the Pure Constitutionalist's end of the spectrum than to the Pure Representative Democrat's. It is not at all clear where "the people" of 1787–88, in whose name the text purports to speak, would have placed themselves. In any event, the system has become more democratic, eroding some geographic, socio-economic, and institutional checks. At the same time, the sheer size of government has increased enormously along with its reach into once private affairs. These changes have heightened concern for some check on the huge, faceless power of government. In the place of these eroded checks, judges have blossomed as the most visible, if not the most important, protectors of individual rights in particular and constitutionalism in general, so much so that most Americans probably look on the justices of the U.S. Supreme Court as the true guardians of constitutional chastity.

Because American legislators and executives have often shunted off on judges the duties of constitutional interpretation and the task of reconciling democracy and constitutionalism, the study of constitutional interpretation has largely become the study of what the U.S. Supreme Court says and does. But, as we have already noted and Chapters 7 and 8 will detail, Congress, the President, state officials, and private citizens are frequently obliged to engage in constitutional interpretation. And the occasions on which public officials challenge the Court's role as ultimate constitutional interpreter provide magnificent debates on political fundamentals.

By deciding what "the Constitution" allows and forbids—defining unplain plain words and imparting a blessing on claims to implied powers and/or implied rights—all interpreters may have a great impact on public policy. In determining who may vote, what restrictions any level of government may put on political communications, or what differences in population among electoral districts are permissible, judicial decisions affect who will be elected to office, what demands will be given favorable hearings, and what policies will be enacted into law. More immediate are the policy effects of decisions like those regarding the authority of the President to seize vital industries that have been crippled by strikes[50] or to contract with a foreign government to suspend lawsuits by American citizens against that government; [51] or the authority of Congress to command, as part of its power to "regulate commerce among the several states," hotels and restaurants to serve all customers without regard to race; [52] or state authority to regulate abortions[53] or impose capital punishment.[54]

Public officials and private citizens who lose such cases often cry foul and complain that judges are acting "undemocratically" in overturning decisions of the people's representatives. The charge may be basically correct—although it is not always correct that elections have been truly free, that debate on a particular policy has been full and open, or that "the people," or at times even their representatives, have understood what the legislature did. Further, as we have just seen, a cluster of institutional arrangements including federalism, staggered elections, and the staffing of the Senate limits the capacity of the people to choose officials who can actually govern at the national level.

Despite these qualifications, there can be no doubt that judicial decisions have often frustrated the popular will. But that statement says very little. Indeed, to focus on a conflict between judicial review and democratic government is to miss much of what is interesting and important about the American political system: The tension is between democracy and constitutionalism. Judicial review, like each of the other institutional restraints on popular rule, is only one aspect of constitutionalism's larger efforts to simultaneously empower and limit government.

SELECTED BIBLIOGRAPHY

Arkes, Hadley. *Beyond the Constitution* (Princeton: Princeton University Press, 1990).

Barber, Benjamin. *Strong Democracy: Participatory Politics for a New Age* (Berkeley: University of California Press, 1984).

Barber, Sotirios A. *On What the Constitution Means* (Baltimore: Johns Hopkins Press, 1984).

---

50. Youngstown Sheet & Tube Co. v. Sawyer (1952).

51. Dames & Moore v. Regan (1981).

52. Heart of Atlanta Motel v. United States (1964).

53. Roe v. Wade (1973); reprinted below, p. 1258; and Planned Parenthood v. Casey (1992); reprinted below, p. 1281.

54. Compare Furman v. Georgia (1972), with Gregg v. Georgia (1976).

———. *The Constitution of Judicial Power* (Baltimore: Johns Hopkins University Press, 1993).

Berns, Walter F. *Taking the Constitution Seriously* (New York: Simon & Schuster, 1987).

Bork, Robert H. *The Tempting of America: The Political Seduction of the Law* (New York: The Free Press, 1990).

Brest, Paul. "The Fundamental Rights Controversy," 90 *Yale L.J.* 1063 (1981).

Carter, Lief H. *Contemporary Constitutional Lawmaking* (New York: Pergamon Press, 1985).

Corwin, Edward S. "The Basic Doctrine of American Constitutional Law," 12 *Mich.L.Rev.* 247 (1914); reprinted in Richard Loss, ed., *Corwin on the Constitution* (Ithaca: Cornell University Press, 1988), III.

———. *The "Higher Law" Background of American Constitutional Law* (Ithaca: Cornell University Press, 1928, 1955).

———. *Liberty Against Government* (Baton Rouge: Louisiana State University Press, 1948).

Dahl, Robert A. *A Preface to Democratic Theory* (Chicago: University of Chicago Press, 1956).

———. *Polyarchy: Participation and Opposition* (New Haven: Yale University Press, 1971).

———. *Dilemmas of Pluralist Democracy: Autonomy vs. Control* (New Haven: Yale University Press, 1982).

———. *Democracy and Its Critics* (New Haven: Yale University Press, 1989).

———. "A Democratic Dilemma: System Effectiveness versus Citizen Participation," 109 *Pol.Sci.Q.* 23 (1994).

Dworkin, Ronald. *Taking Rights Seriously* (Cambridge: Harvard University Press, 1977), ch. 5.

———. *A Matter of Principle* (Cambridge: Harvard University Press, 1985).

———. *Life's Dominion* (New York: Knopf, 1993).

Edelman, Martin. *Democratic Theories and the Constitution* (Albany: State University of New York Press, 1984).

Eidelberg, Paul. *The Philosophy of the American Constitution* (New York: The Free Press, 1968).

Elkin, Stephen L., and Karol Edward Soltan, eds. *A New Constitutionalism: Designing Political Institutions for a Good Society* (Chicago: University of Chicago Press, 1993).

Elkin, Stanley, and Eric McKitrick. *The Age of Federalism* (New York: Oxford University Press, 1993).

Elster, Jon, and Rune Slagstad, eds. *Constitutionalism and Democracy* (New York: Cambridge University Press, 1988).

Ely, John Hart. *Democracy and Distrust* (Cambridge: Harvard University Press, 1980).

Fleming James E. "Constructing the Substantive Constitution," 72 *Tex.L.Rev.* 211 (1993).

————. "Securing Deliberative Autonomy," 48 *Stan.L.Rev.*— (forthcoming 1995).

Friedrich, Carl J. *Constitutional Reason of State* (Providence, RI: Brown University Press, 1957).

————. *Transcendent Justice: The Religious Dimension of Constitutionalism* (Durham: Duke University Press, 1964).

————. *Constitutional Government and Democracy* 4th ed.; (Waltham, MA: Blaisdell, 1968), espec. chs. 1, 7–11, 13, 25.

Hallowell, John H. *The Moral Foundations of Democracy* (Chicago: University of Chicago Press, 1954).

Harris, William F. II. *The Interpretable Constitution* (Baltimore: Johns Hopkins University Press, 1993).

Hirschman, Albert O. *The Passions and the Interests: Political Arguments for Capitalism before Its Triumph* (Princeton: Princeton University Press, 1977).

Holmes, Stephen. "Gag Rules or the Politics of Omission," in Jon Elster and Rune Slagstad, eds., *Constitutionalism and Democracy* (New York: Cambridge University Press, 1988).

————. "Precommitment and the Paradox of Democracy," in Jon Elster and Rune Slagstad, eds., *Constitutionalism and Democracy* (New York: Cambridge University Press, 1988).

Kahn, Ronald. *The Supreme Court in Constitutional Theory, 1953–1993* (Lawrence: University of Kansas Press, 1994).

Kammen, Michael G. *Sovereignty and Liberty: Constitutional Discourse in American Culture* (Madison: University of Wisconsin Press, 1988).

Keller, Morton. "Powers and Rights: Two Centuries of American Constitutionalism," 74 *Jo.Am.Hist.* 675 (1987).

Levinson, Sanford V. *Constitutional Faith* (Princeton: Princeton University Press, 1988).

Lijpjart, Arend. *Democracies: Patterns of Majoritarian and Consensus Government in Twenty–One Countries* (New Haven: Yale University Press, 1984).

McIlwain, Charles H. *Constitutionalism: Ancient & Modern* (Ithaca: Cornell University Press, 1947).

Maddox, Graham. "A Note on the Meaning of 'Constitution,'" 76 *Am.Pol.Sci.Rev.* 805 (1982).

McDowell, Gary L. "Coke, Corwin, and the Constitution: The 'Higher Law Background' Reconsidered," 55 *Rev. of Pols.* 393 (1993).

Muller, James W., ed. *The Revival of Constitutionalism* (Lincoln: University of Nebraska Press, 1988).

Murphy, Walter F. "Constitutions, Constitutionalism, and Democracy," in Douglas Greenberg, Stanley N. Katz, Melanie Beth Oliviero, and Stephen C. Wheatley, eds. *Constitutionalism and Democracy: Transitions in the Contemporary World* (New York: Oxford University Press, 1993).

Pennock, J. Roland. *Democratic Political Theory* (Princeton: Princeton University Press, 1979).

_____ and John W. Chapman, eds. *Constitutionalism* (New York: New York University Press, 1979).

_____. *Liberal Democracy* (New York: New York University Press, 1983).

Powell, H. Jefferson. *The Moral Tradition of American Constitutionalism* (Durham: Duke University Press, 1993).

Richards, David A. J. *Foundations of American Constitutionalism* (New York: Oxford University Press, 1989).

Sartori, Giovanni. *The Theory of Democracy Revisited* (Chatham, NJ: Chatham House, 1987), 2 vols., espec. chs. 11–13, 15.

Shapiro, Ian, ed. *The Rule of Law* (New York: New York University Press, 1994).

Smith, Rogers M. *Liberalism and American Constitutional Law* (Cambridge: Harvard University Press, 1985).

Stoner, James R. *Constitutional Law and Liberal Theory: Coke, Hobbes, and the Origins of American Constitutionalism* (Lawrence: University of Kansas Press, 1992).

Storing, Herbert J. *What the Anti–Federalists Were For* (Chicago: University of Chicago Press, 1981).

Sunstein, Cass R. *The Partial Constitution* (Cambridge: Harvard University Press, 1993).

Tribe, Laurence H. "The Puzzling Persistence of Process–Based Constitutional Theories," 89 *Yale L.J.* 1063 (1980); reprinted as ch. 2 in his *Constitutional Choices* (Cambridge: Harvard University Press, 1985).

Wheeler, Harvey. "Constitutionalism," in Fred I. Greenstein and Nelson W. Polsby, eds., *Handbook of Political Science* (Reading, Mass.: Addison–Wesley, 1975), vol. V.

4

The Political and Institutional Contexts of Constitutional Interpretation

"Jurisprudence" is a compound word linking the notion of "right" or "justice" on the one hand, with "practical wisdom" on the other. That verbal union symbolizes the dual role of constitutional interpretation in keeping the political system both true to its ideals and practically viable. Thus, to understand constitutional interpretation, one needs to understand not only the theoretical but also the political and institutional contexts in which it takes place.

This Chapter looks at these latter contexts mainly from the perspective of the Supreme Court. We adopt that perspective not because the Court is the exclusive constitutional interpreter, but, as we have already noted, because it has become the most visible of constitutional interpreters. We do not prejudge Part III's interrogative of WHO are the authoritative interpreters of "the Constitution."

I. THE POLITICAL SYSTEM

The framers at Philadelphia did not design a scheme of government to transform selfish human beings into saints, but to allow people to survive in liberty by pitting power against power and ambition against ambition. The system has developed in many ways the Framers could not have foreseen, but it continues to function as a network of checks and counterchecks restraining power and ambition. The official who thinks that he or she has a monopoly of any form of political power, including constitutional interpretation, is doomed to frustration.

A. Sharing Powers Within the National System of Government

The widely repeated term "separation of powers" is misleading. The structure of the constitutional document has combined with long usage to produce a system that Richard E. Neustadt has far more accurately described as one of "separated institutions *sharing* powers." [1]   Article I begins "All legislative power herein granted shall be vested in a Congress of the United States"; but both Article I and II make the President a critical part of the legislative process. He can propose legislation and veto bills, call Congress into special session and adjourn the two houses when they cannot agree on a date.   Presidents have used those formal powers in expansive ways to create a long tradition that has become part of the system. Executive agencies write the initial drafts of many, at times most, public laws;   executive officials are among the most numerous lobbyists on Capitol Hill;   and the President can be the most influential lobbyist of all, if he chooses to prod Congress by using his position as leader of his party, his nominating power, his authority "to take care that the laws be faithfully executed," and his capacity to shape general public opinion.   In short, he is as much "chief legislator" as he is "chief executive." [2]

Article II vests "the executive power" in the President, but Articles I and II also give Congress some of that power.   Together, the two houses create every executive office and agency, including the President's staff;   establish lines of authority among those institutions;   enact rules for selecting, promoting, and firing officials; and appropriate (or refuse to appropriate) money to pay salaries and carry out policies.   The Senate can refuse to consent to presidential choices of people for the more important executive positions.   The President also finds himself forced to share power by unwritten constitutional rules.   For instance, "senatorial courtesy"—the custom that the Senate will not confirm a nominee over the disapproval of a senator from the President's party in whose state the nominee is to serve—often allows senators to share in the power to select as well as to confirm federal officials.   And not infrequently officials so chosen feel stronger loyalty to a senator than to a President.

Control over the budget gives legislators an even greater share of executive power.   The President often confronts an iron triangle: a tight alliance among an interest group, a congressional subcommittee, and an executive agency.   In such situations, bureaucrats are as likely to follow the wishes of the chair of a subcommittee (who in turn may be following the wishes of the interest group) as of the President, lest their operating funds be drastically reduced. [3]

Both Congress and the President exercise some judicial powers. Most European countries pretty much allow judges to determine who may join their ranks.   In the United States, however, the President nominates federal judges and the Senate confirms or

---

1. *Presidential Power* (rev. ed.; New York: Wiley, 1976), p. 101.

2. See Michael N. Danielson and Walter F. Murphy, *American Democracy* (10th ed.; New York: Holmes & Meier, 1983), espec. ch. 11.

3. The classic study is Arthur Maass, *Muddy Waters* (Cambridge: Harvard University Press, 1951).

rejects appointments. At least that is the formula the constitutional document presents. In fact, under the tradition of senatorial courtesy, senators from the President's party play a very active role in selecting federal district judges who will serve in their states and a smaller, though not necessarily insignificant role in choosing judges of the U.S. courts of appeals, whose jurisdiction includes several states. Here as elsewhere in selecting federal officials, the process tends to be one of negotiation, with the President typically getting more than the senators, but not always all that he would like.

The President is also formally responsible for initiating law suits—civil or criminal—in the name of the United States and for carrying out judicial decisions. His discretion in these areas is wide. Moreover, he may pardon anyone convicted of a federal crime, including criminal contempt of court. Perhaps even more significant is the fact that the President may be able to persuade Congress to use (or not use) its quasi-judicial powers.

And Congress's potential to affect the federal judiciary is vast. First is the matter of jurisdiction, the authority of a court to hear and decide cases. Questions of jurisdiction are always issues of power; without jurisdiction a court is impotent. Article III, § 2, ¶ 1—as modified by the Eleventh Amendment's withdrawal of authority to hear suits brought against a state by foreigners or out-of-state citizens[4]—details the sorts of issues and parties to which federal jurisdiction "shall extend."[5] It was not, however, until after the Civil War that Congress conferred on federal courts the bulk of this jurisdiction; and it has never seen fit to give federal courts exclusive jurisdiction over all these matters. In sum, Congress has defied the rules of English grammar and claimed that "shall extend" is permissive rather than mandatory, allowing it discretion to grant, not grant, and even remove jurisdiction from federal courts. Two centuries of practice, accepted by federal judges[6] no less than by presidents, have probably—but not certainly—validated that interpretation. As the Supreme Court said in 1938: "There can be no

---

4. Hans v. Louisiana (1890) held that the framers of the Eleventh Amendment erred: They had meant to deprive federal courts of jurisdiction to hear cases brought either by in—or by out-of-state citizens as well as by foreigners. And, the Court ruled, what the framers had meant to ask the states to ratify took precedence over what they actually asked the states to ratify. Green v. Mansour (1985) affirmed this rule, but four justices dissented and would have overturned *Hans*.

5. "The judicial power shall extend to all cases, in law and equity, arising under this Constitution, the laws of the United States, and treaties made, or which shall be made, under their authority;—to all cases affecting ambassadors, other public ministers and consuls;—to all cases of admiralty and maritime jurisdiction;—to controversies to which the United States shall be a party;—to controversies between two or more states;— . . . between citizens of different states;—between citizens of the same state claiming lands under grant of different states;—and between a state, or the citizens thereof, and foreign states, citizens or subjects."

6. See espec. Durousseau v. United States (1810) and Martin v. Hunter's Lessee (1816; reprinted below, p. 359).

question of the power of Congress thus to define and limit the jurisdiction of the inferior courts of the United States."[7]

The language of Article II, § 2, ¶ 2 regarding congressional power to make "exceptions" to and "regulations" for the appellate jurisdiction of the Supreme Court is even more problematic. ("Original" jurisdiction refers to the authority of a court to hear a case in the first instance, "appellate" to the authority of one court to review rulings of a court further down the judicial hierarchy.) The crucial disputes revolve around when an "exception" becomes so wide or a "regulation" so restrictive as to deprive the Court of its fundamental character as the head of the branch of government entrusted with "the judicial power."

Chapter 6 discusses these issues in some detail. Here we note only that, after the Civil War, Congress used this authority to prevent the Court's deciding a critical issue regarding the constitutionality of the centerpiece of Reconstruction, military rule in the South. With only Justice Grier dissenting, the Court meekly acquiesced,[8] setting a precedent that has haunted the justices, when opponents of decisions—such as those defending free speech during the McCarthy era or, more recently, defining a woman's right to abortion—have generated bills in Congress to remove the Court's jurisdiction to hear controversial matters.

Congress also has authority to determine the organization of lower federal courts, the number of Supreme Court justices—which has varied over American history from five to ten—the compensation that federal judges shall receive, as well as the rules under which all federal courts operate.[9] And the content of the criminal law that federal judges interpret and apply is contained in acts of Congress, just as is most federal civil law.

What should not be lost in a discussion of specific checks is that any time Congress passes a bill it at least implicitly—and often explicitly after lengthy, heated, and learned debate—engages in constitutional interpretation, for, in effect, it says: "We think that making this kind of public policy falls within our authority and the means we have chosen to carry out that policy meet constitutional standards." In addition, Congress may propose amendments to the constitutional text. Four of these—the Eleventh, Fourteenth, Sixteenth, and Twenty-sixth—changed the Supreme Court's interpreta-

---

7. Lauf v. Shinner & Co.

8. Ex parte McCardle (1868 and 1869). The Court's reporter did not publish Justice Grier's bitter dissenting opinion, though several newspapers printed excerpts. See Charles Warren, *The Supreme Court in United States History* (Rev. ed.; Boston: Little, Brown, 1926), II, 482.

9. Congress has chosen to delegate its rule-making authority to the Supreme Court, subject to congressional approval; but INS v. Chadha (1983; reprinted below, p. 485) casts a constitutional pall over this delegation. In any event, Congress may revoke that delegation by passing a new statute, which, like all statutes including those relating to jurisdiction and organization, is subject to a presidential veto.

tions[10]; and one of these, the Eleventh, did so by striking directly at federal judicial authority.[11]

The veto not only makes the President a part of the legislative process in the sense of shaping (or aborting) statutes, the power to refuse to sign bills into law also gives him authority to interpret "the Constitution" and formally justify his interpretations. Indeed, until after the Civil War, Presidents explained most of their vetoes on constitutional grounds and sometimes still publicly announce such reasons.

Further, the money to carry out the Supreme Court's decisions—indeed to operate the entire judicial system—comes only from congressional appropriations, subject to presidential vetoes. In a much more constitutionally problematic fashion, congressional investigations may also exercise a form of judicial power. Committees have often paraded witnesses' sins before television cameras and so punished them in a very real sense. As a final judicial power, the House may impeach any federal judge for "treason, bribery, or other high crimes and misdemeanors," and he or she will be removed if the Senate convicts.

For their part, judges exercise some legislative and executive as well as judicial authority. Most basically, interpreting "the law," especially "the law of the Constitution" with its references in the Ninth Amendment, for example, to unlisted rights and (in the necessary and proper clause) to unenumerated powers, may require creating that law. We need not repeat what Chapter 1 argued about the inevitability of discretion and creativity in interpreting "the Constitution."

Statutes are often even more difficult to decipher, requiring judges to rethink thoughts legislators were trying or should have been trying to think. Congressional and presidential efforts to placate assorted interest groups while grappling with difficult practical problems typically result in obtuse language and even incompatible provisions that force judges, if they are to make sense of what Congress has done, to become part of the legislative process.[12]

---

10. The Eleventh changed the interpretation in Chisholm v. Georgia (1793) that citizens of one state could sue another state in a federal court; the Fourteenth reversed the holding of Dred Scott v. Sandford (1857; reprinted below, p. 195), that a black person could not be a citizen of the United States; the Sixteenth displaced the decision in the Income Tax Cases (1895) that a federal income tax was a direct tax and so had, by the terms of Art. I, § 2, to be apportioned among the states by population; and the Twenty-sixth changed the interpretation of Oregon v. Mitchell (1970) that Congress could not set 18 as the minimum voting age for state elections.

11. For an argument that the Eleventh Amendment "merely requires a narrow construction of constitutional language affirmatively authorizing federal jurisdiction and ... did nothing to prohibit federal court jurisdiction," see William A. Fletcher, "A Historical Interpretation of the Eleventh Amendment," 35 *Stan.L.Rev.* 1033 (1983).

12. For analyses of and cases and bibliography on the arcane world of statutory construction, see Walter F. Murphy, C. Herman Pritchett, and Sotirios A. Barber, eds., *Courts, Judges, & Politics* (5th ed.; Boston: McGraw–Hill, 1995), ch. 11.

Much the same sort of thing can happen with executive orders, which frequently qualify as grammarians' nightmares.

B.   Sharing Powers Within the Federal System

As Chapter 3 pointed out, the constitutional document looks to a federal system in which the national government is supreme within a sphere only inexactly sketched, and in which states also function as important political units, retaining broad, though unde-fined, residual powers.   The result is additional sharings of power and pittings of ambitions against ambitions.

For our purposes three points are critical.   First, states may compete with federal power, even in the field of constitutional interpretation.   (See Chapter 8 for a detailed discussion.)   Second, as the ratifiers of proposed constitutional amendments, states may participate directly in changing the document's provisions and indirectly the system's traditions.   Third, and perhaps most impor-tant, state officials may influence senators, congressmen, and presi-dents, all of whom are to some extent dependent for reelection on the good will of officials in their home states and completely dependent on the approval of local voters.   This influence may affect not only the ways in which elected officials interpret "the Constitution" but also the kinds of men and women they will select to become federal judges.

C.   The Checking of Sharing

The result of these "separated institutions sharing powers" is a messy, rather than a neat political system.   Not only do governmen-tal institutions compete, but they check and countercheck each other.   Each can use its own power as well as the power it shares with another branch to thwart another branch's action.   This net-work of restraints often deadlocks government; and were each branch to unleash its weapons against the others, the system would self-destruct.   Recognizing these dangers, most politicians who be-come national leaders have the good sense to use their power with caution.   Friction is continual and conflict frequent, but all-out-war is rare.   The norm is a process of accommodation, negotiation, and compromise with the resulting public policy, including constitution-al interpretation, often being fuzzily rather than sharply defined.

Yet, even when conflict stops short of war, it can change, at least temporarily, the balance of power within the system.   The scandals of Watergate and an imminent threat of impeachment led to Richard Nixon's resignation in 1974 from an "imperial presiden-cy"; his next two successors inherited a much weaker office.   It was not until Ronald Reagan that the White House regained much of its former power.   Similarly, in 1937, the likelihood of some form of curb on its power nudged the Supreme Court to change its constitutional interpretation and to demote "freedom of contract" from its former status as a fundamental right. That shift, which Edward S. Corwin termed a "constitutional revolution," [13] was dramatic; but, each time a President nominates a new justice, he tries to affect the Court's constitutional interpretation. And similar hopes have usually fired representatives and senators when they have deployed Congress's quasi-judicial powers.

D. The Capacity of Interest Groups and Officials to Trigger Checks

The very nature of a constitution means that almost every piece of constitutional interpretation is likely, in the long run, to have some impact on a wide spectrum of values, people, and very tangible interests. Even in the short run, the effects may be broad. Statutes and administrative orders are aimed at large audiences. And, though a judicial decision formally binds only the parties to a case, its reasoning is likely to ripple across the community. A decision about the validity of governmental regulations of economic affairs will encourage business, labor, and consumers to bring fresh lawsuits and/or pressure legislative and executive officials to enact new laws or regulations; rulings about reapportionment immediately shape the electoral structure in the state involved and flash omens to other states; constitutional standards concerning the rights of the criminally accused may not only change the treatment accorded those people, but may also influence the degree of liberty as well as "domestic tranquility" the entire population can enjoy. Any controversial ruling in any field is likely to move some groups to try to persuade elected officials to select new judges who think in different constitutional terms.

Thus whenever any governmental institution interprets "the Constitution," some interests are likely to be furthered and others injured.[14] And these interests include not only those of segments of the general public but also of public officials. To the extent, for instance, that Congress claims a substantial share of authority to make foreign policy, it is probably infringing on what the President considers to be his prerogatives. The "interests of the man," as Madison put it in *Federalist* 51, are connected to "the constitutional rights of the place," and ambition clashes with ambition.

Because of the open nature of the political processes, individuals and groups aggrieved by a piece of constitutional interpretation

---

13. *Constitutional Revolution, Ltd.* (Claremont, CA: The Claremont Press, 1941). Bruce Ackerman makes a similar assessment: *We the People: Foundations* (Cambridge: Harvard University Press, 1991).

14. It is worth mentioning here that the same people—the general public, for instance, in matters of criminal justice—may find a particular constitutional interpretation enhances some of their rights at the same time as it diminishes others.

may utilize their access to one or another governmental institution to frustrate or reverse policies they do not like or to reinforce those they like. Public officials may strike directly at interpretations that threaten their peculiar interests as officials.

Not only can individuals and groups lobby senators, representatives, federal executive officials, or state legislators and administrators to counter judicial decisions, but they can also go to court—again as individuals or as members of a group—to block (or, under some circumstances, to validate) legislative or executive action, state or federal. So, too, can governmental officials. It is unusual, but hardly rare, to see one set of officials suing another. The Buckley who was the leading litigant in Buckley v. Valeo (1976; reprinted below, p. 828), which attacked the constitutionality of the Federal Election Campaign Act of 1974, was James Buckley, U.S. Senator from New York.

Litigation designed to affect public policy, the Supreme Court has said, is "a form of political expression." As such, it is fully protected from federal or state interference by the First and Fourteenth amendments. This right can be especially important to people who lack the numbers, organization, or prestige to influence popularly elected officials, or popularly elected officials whose views have been rejected by a majority of their colleagues. "[U]nder the conditions of modern government," the Court has added, "litigation may well be the sole practical avenue open to a minority to petition for redress of grievances." [15]

Because public officials, interest groups, and private citizens can so readily challenge the validity of governmental action, constitutional interpretation is often unsettled. But, if the system's open nature offers many routes to governmental power, it does not guarantee success in effecting substantive change. For, just as any particular constitutional interpretation will anger some groups, that same interpretation is likely to please others who are not apt to watch passively while their opponents try to rechange it. Open access insures only the availability of additional arenas for peaceful struggle. It is also important to keep in mind that open access does not insure that all groups will have an equal chance in each arena. Money, education, organization, prestige, and particular skills, whether in obtaining publicity, mustering blocs of voters, bargaining, or legal reasoning, confer great advantages; and none of these is evenly distributed among the population.

---

15. NAACP v. Button (1963). See also Bounds v. Smith (1977), which spoke of "the fundamental constitutional right of access to the courts" in the context of a duty on the part of prison officials to provide inmates with adequate law libraries or professional assistance to help them appeal their convictions or seek habeas corpus.

E. An Open System of Checks and Counterchecks

In sum, when a judge, a President, a senator, a representative, or state official interprets "the Constitution," writ small or large, he or she must realize that other officials may also be engaged in that enterprise. Moreover, constitutional interpretation affects the short and long term interests of human beings who have needs and rights and wants and demands and ambitions and access to other political institutions. Thus, not only is any interpretation to some extent subject to frustration, modification, or even reversal by other interpreters, but the institution making an interpretation is also vulnerable to being curbed by other branches. That an interpreter may ride out any particular storm is very possible, indeed likely, especially if his or her institution is willing to make corrections in its course; but the threat of shipwreck is always present.

The reality of the political system does not force justices continually to look over their shoulders to see what Congress and the President are doing, nor do they need to hire a polling agency to keep them in touch with public opinion. The justices have a much more extensive area of interpretive autonomy than do other officials. As a practical matter, however, judges are not free to construe "the Constitution" as they wish. That reality also means that, however much they want what they honestly believe to be the most justifiable constitutional interpretation to prevail, they may have to settle for less than the best. Constitutionalism does not prescribe total judicial freedom; democratic theory emphatically denies it; and the institutional webs of the political system limit both the good and evil that any set of public officials can accomplish—one important objective of constitutional democracy.

In essence, constitutional interpretation is a theoretical process both in the sense of explaining what has been developing and trying to place that maturation in a normative context. The enterprise is thus a search for the best in the past to guide the present and shape the future; but it is more than an abstract intellectual process. It also forms a critically important aspect of the practical processes of governing a nation, an integral part of the art of politics—the art of defining fundamental principles and adapting them to changing needs, of obtaining as much good as possible while staving off as much evil as possible. And in such controversial undertakings, interpreters' values, personal as well as institutional, are bound to play important roles.

II. THE JUDICIAL PROCESS: PROCEDURAL DIFFERENCES

In their operations courts differ from other branches of government in several constitutionally consequential ways.[16] First, judges have "no self-starting capacity." [17] When legislators or executive officials perceive a problem, they can attack it directly by passing new legislation, prosecuting, investigating, or merely generating publicity to embarrass wrongdoers. Judges, however, cannot initiate action. They must wait until someone formally brings a lawsuit before them.

Second, that lawsuit must display certain characteristics. It must present a "case or controversy," that is, a real dispute between genuinely adverse parties involving injury, or immediate threat of injury, to a legally protected right. Furthermore, that person must show that this case raises a legal issue over which the court has jurisdiction, that is, authority to decide. The litigant must also meet technical rules relating to "standing." Essentially, these require a person bringing suit to show that: (a) the legally protected right involved is a personal one, not someone else's right or a right shared by the public generally; [18] (b) the dispute is "justiciable," that is, a matter, *judges have determined*, "the Constitution" assigns to them; (c) if governmental action is challenged, the action is sufficiently "final" to be "ripe" for judicial determination, and sufficiently "live" not to be dead (moot); and (d) the judicial decision will be binding between the parties to the case, that is, it will not merely be advice the litigants are legally free to ignore.[19] A moment's reflection shows that these judge-made rules allow judges enormous discretion.

A third peculiarity of judicial operations relates to the limited number and kinds of remedies that a judge can fashion. More of these are negative than positive. A court can hold a particular criminal statute constitutional, but it cannot force the attorney general to prosecute those who violate that law. It may invalidate a statute for failing to protect the rights of minorities, but it cannot directly compel either Congress or the states to enact a law that protects rights.

Fourth, although the influence of an opinion as a precedent may be far flung, a formal judicial decree is quite limited in its

---

16. For a normative argument supporting these differences, see John Hart Ely, "Another Such Victory: Constitutional Theory and Practice in a World Where Courts are No Different from Legislatures," 77 *Va.L.Rev.* 833 (1991).

17. Robert H. Jackson, *The Supreme Court in the American System of Government* (Cambridge: Harvard University Press, 1955), p. 24. But see Abram Chayes, "The Role of the Judge in Public Law Litigation," 89 *Harv.L.Rev.* 1281 (1976), for a model of the judicial role as declaring law rather than merely as resolving disputes.

18. There are some notable exceptions; see espec.: Truax v. Raich (1915), Pierce v. Society of Sisters (1925), Barrows v. Jackson (1953), and Flast v. Cohen (1968). R.A.V. v. St. Paul (1992, reprinted below, p. 686) contains dicta to the effect that, where statutes affecting the First Amendment may sweep too broadly (be guilty of "overbreadth"), the Court will relax its standards for standing.

19. For a fuller discussion of standing, see Murphy, Pritchett, and Barber, supra note 12, ch. 5 and literature cited.

reach. Unlike a statute, which may obligate everyone in the United States and its possessions, an order of a court binds only the parties to the case, their employees, agents, successors in office, and those who, knowing an order is in force, conspire with the litigants to violate that order. Thus the School Segregation Cases (1954; reprinted below, p. 912) technically bound only the four school districts and did not legally compel officials anywhere else to end racially segregated schools, at least not until someone brought and won a new law suit against them.

The fifth and perhaps the most obvious difference between courts and other institutions lies in procedure. In court, each side is entitled to be represented by an attorney, to present full evidence and argument to support its position, to compel witnesses to testify about what they know, to hear all opposing evidence and have an opportunity to rebut it, including a right to cross examine opposing witnesses. The proceeding takes place in public before a judge, who must be neutral between the litigants, and sometimes before a jury, whose members are also chosen to maximize the chances of impartiality. If the matter is criminal in nature, the government must prove guilt "beyond a reasonable doubt" and must not only respect all of the accused's constitutional rights at the trial but must be further prepared to show it also did so during the period before the trial.

After the verdict, the loser normally has a right to appeal to a higher court to correct any alleged errors at the trial. (Because of the Fifth Amendment's protection against double jeopardy, of course, the government may not appeal an acquittal in a criminal case.) The loser also has a right to expect that the trial judge and any appellate judges who have reviewed the case will justify their decisions by legal principles, not merely by expediency or wise public policy. In sum, "a day in court" has become another way of saying "fair play." Other institutions may also operate fairly, but they do not do so with such fastidious regard for formal procedures as do courts.

III. PROCEDURES WITHIN THE SUPREME COURT

The Supreme Court's procedures can effect the substance of its decisions. Appendix A to this book, pp. 1403-11, explains in detail how litigants bring cases to the justices. For our immediate purposes, it is sufficient to understand that most cases come up as "petitions for certiorari," that is, as requests that the Court review decisions of lower federal courts or state judicial rulings on federal questions. The person asking for the writ (the petitioner) must succinctly set out the pertinent facts of the dispute, the questions of law, and a justification for the Court's hearing the case. The other party (the respondent) has 30 days in which to file counterargument.

The justices have complete discretion to grant or deny these petitions. In fact, they deny more than 95 per cent of them and seldom offer any reason whatsoever. That statistic does not mean the justices treat petitions cavalierly, though their sheer number—more than 4,000 a year—demands efficiency. When a petition arrives, the Clerk of the Court assigns the case a docket number and sends a copy of all papers to every justice. The next step varies among the justices. Some read all or most of these petitions themselves; others divide them among their law clerks;[20] and several have agreed to share their clerks' recommendations.

The following memorandum, written by Justice Hugo L. Black for his own use, is typical of these recommendations:

NO. 788

HARRY BRIDGES V.I.F. WIXON, AS DISTRICT DIRECTOR, IMMIGRATION AND NATURALIZATION SERVICE

Cert. to CCA 9th

In this case Harry Bridges has been ordered deported by the Attorney General after hearings before an appointed Commissioner. Hearings before a previous Commissioner, Dean Landis, had decided that the evidence failed to show that Bridges was a member of the Communist Party. Thereafter Congress amended the law, expressly intending to hit Bridges, so that deportation could be brought about for past membership in the Communist Party. It is under this new legislation that the deportation was ordered here.

Questions are raised with reference to the absence of evidence to support the finding and which involved freedom of speech and association. They are of sufficient importance that I think we should grant certiorari on all the points requested.

GRANT.

H.L.B.

Every week or so the chief justice circulates a "discuss list," the petitions for certiorari that he recommends for debate at the Court's next conference. All other petitions received during the period covered by the list are automatically denied unless any other justice objects. That objection, even if it comes from a single justice, automatically adds a case to the "discuss list."

The Supreme Court's term begins on the first Monday in October and, until 1981, ran until early summer. The Court still recesses then, but the term does not end until the following

---

20. Each justice has four clerks, typically young men or women who recently graduated at or near the top of their classes at the most prestigious law schools. Because of his heavy administrative burdens, the chief justice also has a more senior lawyer and an experienced judicial administrator as assistants.

October, just before the new one begins. During vacations as well as term time, petitions for certiorari roll endlessly in. Oliver Wendell Holmes, who called them the "bloody certs," used to greet new members of the Court with a cheery "Welcome to our chain gang."

During term, the Court usually is in session for two weeks, hearing oral arguments on Mondays, Tuesdays, and Wednesdays from 10 a.m. until noon, and from 1 until 3 p.m. Then the justices recess for two weeks to continue arguing among themselves and to write opinions. During the weeks when the Court is sitting, the justices meet in conference late on Wednesday afternoons and all day Friday. It is here that they debate petitions on the "discuss list" and decide cases just argued. It takes a vote of four, one less than a majority, to grant certiorari.

When the Court grants that writ, it agrees only to hear the case (though it is somewhat more likely that the justices will reverse than affirm cases it has agreed to hear). Each side may then submit a brief on the merits, more fully stating its arguments, and a reply brief, responding to the other's arguments. Either at this stage or when the petition for certiorari is filed, other parties may also present briefs to the Court as *amici curiae*, friends of the court. Such individuals or organizations must show that they, too, have interests at stake in the litigation and wish to present arguments different from those of either side. On occasion, the Court will invite someone to appear as an *amicus*, usually the Solicitor General of the United States or an attorney general of a state.

If the justices grant certiorari, the Clerk of the Supreme Court sets a date for oral argument. Each side is allowed 30 minutes, although in cases whose impact is likely to be especially far reaching, the Court may grant additional time. Normally, *amici* are not allowed to participate in oral argument, though the Court often allows the solicitor general or sometimes state attorneys general to do so.

Counsel stands at a lectern facing the bench and begins "Chief Justice, may it please the Court. ..." Frequently, these are his or her last prepared words. In italics the Court's rules say: *"The Court looks with disfavor on any oral argument that is read from a prepared text."* Instead of a lecture, the justices want a discussion, in which they can sate their appetites for information. Most lawyers who argue before the Court do not do so on a regular basis and wrongly assume the justices want explanations of their own previous decisions. Counsel find themselves constantly interrupted, as two or three justices simultaneously push for responses to questions that range in sweep from a decision's potential effects on public policy to more details about the factual background of the case.

When an attorney has five minutes remaining, a white light flashes on the lectern. When time is up, a red light goes on. Argument must immediately stop. There is a story that Chief Justice Charles Evans Hughes once cut a famous lawyer off in the middle of the word "if."

Later that week when the justices meet in conference, no one except the nine members of the Court is allowed into the room. Messengers are met at the door by the junior justice in time of service on the Court. The only outsider to get as much as a foot inside is the man who pushes a coffee cart, and he seldom makes it farther than the threshold before the justices wheel his wagon from him.

The chief justice opens discussion by summarizing the case and explaining his views. Then the justices speak in order of seniority. The Court keeps no formal record of these debates, but some justices scribble notes either to refresh their memories or to enlighten history. We have used in this book some of the notes that Harold Burton, William O. Douglas, Felix Frankfurter, Robert H. Jackson, Thurgood Marshall, and Frank Murphy left. We urge readers to treat these with caution because the people who took them were usually hotly engaged in discussion themselves. Still, all these papers sketch the same general picture of intense, informed, often heated, and sometimes wide-ranging debate.

Justices use the conference either to try to persuade their colleagues or, if they are undecided, to learn from them. At times tempers flash. "We do take our jobs seriously," one justice has said in private, "and we do get angry. Any judge who didn't get angry when he saw the Constitution misinterpreted ought to be impeached."

The style of conferences has varied with the personality of the chief justice. Charles Evans Hughes (1930–41) and Harlan Fiske Stone (1941–46) represent opposite extremes. Hughes disciplined himself to speak only a few minutes, and he expected similar self control from his colleagues. He would cut off a speech with a curt "thank you" and nod to the justice next in seniority to begin. He preferred rapid disposition of cases to debate. Stone, a former professor, rankled under Hughes's management; and, when he became chief, he tried to turn the conference into a seminar. His colleagues sometimes turned it into a shouting match. Business that took several hours under Hughes often took several days under Stone, but no one complained that issues were not thoroughly aired.

When the chief believes that further discussion would be fruitless, he calls for a vote. From John Marshall to Earl Warren, the justices voted in reverse order of seniority, increasing the power of the more senior members, especially of the chief since by voting last he could always be in the majority. Warren felt that procedure was unfair and persuaded the justices to vote in the same order as they had spoken.

Being in the majority is important, for the chief has the prerogative of assigning the task of writing the opinion of the Court unless he votes with the minority. If the chief is in the minority, the senior associate justice in the majority makes the assignment. The person who assigns the opinion may, of course, keep it him-or herself or give it to the justice whom he or she thinks most likely to reflect the views he or she wants to prevail. Some chief justices—Marshall, Taft, and Hughes, for instance—almost never dissented; others— such as Earl Warren and Warren Burger—frequently did so. William H. Rehnquist has followed the latter tradition.

Being assigned the task of writing the Court's opinion does not guarantee that the opinion written will be that of the Court. To be so labelled and carry the institutional authority of the Supreme Court rather than merely be an expression of personal views, an opinion must have the approval of at least five justices; and all justices are free to write their own opinions, either concurring or dissenting, to join in whichever other opinion(s) suit(s) them, and to change their votes up to the minute the Court announces its decision. Even afterward, if the losing party asks for a rehearing, justices can change their minds.

The opinion writer prepares a manuscript and, when he or she thinks it ready, circulates it in the form of a printed "slip opinion" to the rest of the Court, usually referred to as "the Conference." Each justice is supposed to give such drafts immediate attention, and few have been bashful about suggesting changes. Sometimes these are minor; sometimes they involve recasting the entire reasoning; and sometimes suggestions from different justices are mutually incompatible. If the last is true, the opinion writer has to convert others or decide which colleague's vote to lose.

At the same time, the dissenters, acting alone or together, may circulate their opinion(s), although they may wait until the majority's opinion is approaching final form. Dissents are also circulated to every member of the Court, and sometimes they persuade justices to change their votes. It is uncommon but not unheard of for what began as a dissent to end up as the opinion of the Court. It is more common for the Court's opinion writer to try to accommodate some of the dissenters' views and win them over. Indeed, circulation of a dissent can be a means of tacit negotiation, one that Louis D. Brandeis used with great effectiveness.[21]

---

21. See Alexander M. Bickel, *The Unpublished Opinions of Mr. Justice Brandeis* (Cambridge: The Belknap Press of Harvard University Press, 1957). For more general discussions of judicial strategy, see Walter F. Murphy, *Elements of Judicial Strategy* (Chicago: University of Chicago Press, 1964), and David M. O'Brien, *Storm Center: The Supreme Court in American Politics* (New York: Norton, 1986).

Like the larger political system of which it is a part, the intra-Court process encourages compromise, even bargaining of a sort. First, there is the magic goal of five votes. The justice who refuses to compromise seldom writes for the Court in important cases. Sometimes the price of compromise is high. Holmes complained that "the boys generally cut one of the genitals" out of his opinions.[22] Some of the cases reprinted in this book contain incompatible, incomplete, and at times even illogical arguments. On occasion, the opinion writer has erred; but more often, to achieve a majority, the justice has incorporated differing views.

Second, the justices realize that they will be working together over a long period. The average tenure on the Court is almost 20 years. The person who graciously concedes a point today can hope for similar treatment tomorrow; just as the person who refuses to compromise when in the majority may face a similar stonewall the next week when in the minority. Thus, as Felix Frankfurter once said, an opinion for the Court involves "an orchestral and not a solo performance." [23]

IV. THE INFLUENCE OF PERSONAL VALUES

In a post-Freudian world, there can be no serious doubt that a judge's—or a senator's, representative's, governor's, President's, police officer's, professor's, or student's—personal values influence the way in which he or she interprets "the Constitution," indeed, how an interpreter answers the basic interrogative, WHAT is the Constitution? Society can require that judges be neutral between parties to a case; but no one can ask a mature adult to be neutral between ideas that go to the heart of political philosophy. Not only do we all carry our peculiar DNA Code and bear the effects of early childhood, religious and moral instruction, family relations, and social class, but we are also affected by our more formal education and experiences through life. These factors shape the values that we apply to choices; they also influence the ways we selectively perceive the "facts" from which we make choices.

The political system puts one set of limitations on judicial choices, the rules of the judicial process impose another, and the internal operating procedures of the Supreme Court yet a third set. Of comparable significance are the restraints implanted by political culture, especially as transmitted through training in law school, law practice, and practical political experience. Still, these are limitations, not iron fetters. The American political system is flexible, allowing for what Holmes termed "play in the joints"; rules of law—in particular of constitutional law—are often open-ended; and

---

22. Holmes to Sir Frederick Pollock, Jan. 24, 1918; Mark DeWolf Howe, ed., *Holmes-Pollock Letters* (Cambridge: Harvard University Press, 1942), II, 258.

23. *The Commerce Clause under Marshall, Taney and Waite* (Chapel Hill: University of North Carolina Press, 1937), p. 43.

political culture is a variegated and complex force that is felt rather than read in black letters. There is, in short, much room for the play of individual values, not only among judges but among other public officials as well. It does make a difference whether Earl Warren or William H. Rehnquist is Chief Justice, whether the Court is composed of William J. Brennans or Antonin Scalias, just as it matters whether James Earl Carter, Ronald Reagan, George Bush, or William Clinton is President.

The procedures of the Court also make it probable that the justices will influence each other—and not always positively. Feuds and friendships sometimes develop on the Court. Felix Frankfurter and William O. Douglas detested each other, as did Hugo Black and Robert Jackson. James C. McReynolds, a blatant anti-semite, refused to speak "with the Orient"—Louis D. Brandeis or Benjamin N. Cardozo—unless absolutely necessary. On the other hand, Oliver Wendell Holmes and Brandeis enjoyed a close relationship and later brought Harlan Fiske Stone along as the third musketeer.

All such human interactions influence opinions. It is normal to listen more sympathetically to arguments of friends than to those of foes. With some justification, Chief Justice William H. Taft complained that Brandeis's friendship with Holmes often gave him two votes; and Stone freely conceded that the warmth of Holmes and Brandeis helped move him away from Taft's conservative views of "the Constitution's" content and meaning. Justice William J. Brennan's genial nature allowed him to play the role of an intellectual bridge between the more and less libertarian justices on the Warren Court and later among quite different factions when quite differently minded justices were in the majority. Conversely, Brandeis and McReynolds could never negotiate except through intermediaries; Black and Jackson and Douglas and Frankfurter found negotiation almost, though not quite, as difficult.

It is important to keep in mind, however, that affection or animosity seldom *causes* agreement or disagreement on matters of jurisprudence. Douglas and Rehnquist had great mutual respect, but they voted against each other in almost every non-unanimous decision in which they both participated. So, too, Douglas and his dear friend Sherman Minton seldom agreed on constitutional issues. On the other hand, jurisprudential agreement or disagreement can form the basis of friendship or enmity. Because justices feel so deeply about their work, it is sometimes difficult for them to leave their battles in the conference room.

V. *KOREMATSU:* A CASE STUDY

We have been speaking of the contexts in which constitutional interpretation, as performed by justices of the Supreme Court, takes place. In this section, we shall go through one case, Korematsu v.

United States (1944), to illustrate how various political and institutional factors interact with personal values to produce decisions. (We reprint the opinions in that case, below at p. 1383.)

A. General Background

On December 7, 1941, while their special emissaries were in Washington supposedly negotiating, the Japanese attacked Pearl Harbor and wiped out a large part of the American fleet. They then swept across the western Pacific, quickly conquering Wake, Guam, the Philippines, Malaya, Singapore, and the Dutch East Indies; invaded New Guinea, the Solomon Islands, Burma, and even the westernmost of the Aleutian Islands, threatening Australia to the south, India to the west, and, so some panicked American civilian and military leaders thought, the American west coast as well.

Agitation for action against both alien Japanese and American citizens of Japanese descent (Nisei) began within weeks of the attack on Pearl Harbor. Some military leaders, most notably General John L. DeWitt, commanding the west coast area, wanted to intern these people. (He was also worried about the large number of "colored troops" under his command.) Others, such as the Office of Naval Intelligence, thought that the Nisei posed no danger to national safety—a view in which the FBI concurred. But more was involved than a dispute about national security. Racism, evidenced on the west coast by anti-oriental more than by anti-black prejudice, was hardly unknown in the United States. The Japanese government's treachery and their troops' systematic raping, torturing, and murdering civilians and prisoners of war provided a license for Americans to hate. Some public officials honestly, if incorrectly, feared mass violence against people of Japanese extraction and raised the argument that the Nisei as well as enemy aliens should be locked up for their own good.

Economic self interests encouraged radical governmental action against Japanese Americans. Their work ethic had made them tough competitors in farming, fishing, and small businesses. It did not escape notice that, if they were forcibly removed, competition from the Nisei would be destroyed—and their homes and businesses would have to be offered at fire-sale prices. Legislators, especially from the west coast, were soon swamped with demands from individuals and interest groups for action against all people of Japanese ancestry. Other groups, the American Civil Liberties Union and the Japanese American Citizens League, for example, fought back; but their prestige was low, their numbers few, and their influence small. Even the doubts publicly expressed by the ONI and the FBI about need for a restrictive program and the misgivings of some officials about the constitutionality of incarcerating people because their ancestors had emigrated from a country with whom we later were at war could not stop a juggernaut fed by fear, hate, and economic self interest.[24]

On March 27, 1942, Franklin Roosevelt signed into law a bill which made it a crime to remain in a "military zone" designated by a commander acting under authority of the Secretary of War or, for those allowed to remain in such a zone, to disobey the commander's regulations. This statute legitimated an earlier executive order authorizing the Secretary of War to designate military zones "from which any and all persons" might be excluded. The statute also retroactively validated the curfew that General DeWitt had imposed on enemy aliens and Nisei living in the Pacific states.

Pursuant to this new authority, the Army required all persons of Japanese ancestry to report to designated centers for transportation to and imprisonment in concentration camps.[25] General DeWitt explained that it was legitimate to put the Nisei behind barbed wire while allowing German and Italian aliens to remain free because "a Jap is a Jap" and World War II was "a war of the white race against the yellow race."

B. Hirabayashi v. United States (1943)

Gordon Hirabayashi, a student at the University of Washington, disobeyed both the curfew and the order to report for evacuation and provided the first judicial test of the statute as applied to an American citizen. A federal district court convicted him on both counts. He lost in the court of appeals and obtained certiorari from the U.S. Supreme Court. The justices held oral argument in May, 1943, and discussed and voted on the case a few days later.

Chief Justice Stone opened the conference. According to Justice Frank Murphy's notes, the Chief stressed that, although Hirabayashi had been convicted on counts of violating both the curfew and evacuation, the trial judge had imposed concurrent sentences. Thus affirming a conviction on either count would mean that Hirabayashi would have to serve the full sentence, and, therefore, the Chief contended, there was no need for the Court to go beyond the validity of the curfew.

---

24. The ugly story is most fully told in Morton Grodzins, *Americans Betrayed: Politics and the Japanese Evacuation* (Chicago: University of Chicago Press, 1949); Commission on the Wartime Relocation and Internment of Civilians, *Personal Justice Denied* (Washington, DC: Government Printing Office, 1982); Peter Irons, *Justice at War* (New York: Oxford University Press, 1983); Richard Drinnon, *Keeper of Concentration Camps* (Berkeley: University of California Press, 1987); and Roger Daniels, *Prisoners Without Trial: Japanese–Americans in World War II* (New York: Hill & Wang, 1993).

25. Some Americans confuse the term "concentration camps" with "death camps" like Auschwitz, where the Germans systematically murdered millions of people, and object to labelling as "concentration camps" the tent cities surrounded by barbed wire and armed guards in which we confined Japanese–Americans. The Germans also operated concentration camps, like those the United States used, in which people were "concentrated" and imprisoned, usually, as were the Nisei in this country, without trial or even formal charges, for long periods of time.

Stone saw three major constitutional problems: 1. Had Congress unconstitutionally delegated legislative power to executive officials? He believed not. Congress had known what action the executive would take and approved it. The debate went on:

CHIEF JUSTICE STONE: "2. So you come to whether it was within [the] constitutional power of Congress and [the] President together. 3. Then you come to discrimination against Japanese. All this depends [on] whether there was a reasonable basis at the time government took action. It is jarring to me that U.S. citizens were subjected to this treatment, but I can't say ... it was unconstitutional. They [the military] conducted a war under peculiar danger and great treachery. ... Our safety was involved. They could draw [a] distinction between an Italian and [a] Japanese. You cannot say that it was an unconstitutional measure during wartime. It is a power about which I am abhorrent and mistrustful. [But] we can't walk through fire lines even at misconvenience. ... [W]e should not deal with second count."

ROBERTS: "I take the narrow ground that you do, if we can pass the destruction of citizens' rights in camp."

BLACK: "I want it done on narrowest possible points."

REED: "The curfew is the same as concentration camp. The difficulty is [that] it is applied to certain types of citizens."

FRANKFURTER: "I am for deciding this case on narrow grounds. ..."

JACKSON: "I don't think [a] military commander is bound by due process. [But] can you make as simple a test as who is [an] ancestor?"

ROBERTS: "If applied to all citizens, it would be all right."

Murphy did not record Douglas as speaking. It is quite possible, given that justice's taciturn nature, that he said little, for he was nursing serious doubts. Murphy noted that he himself was concerned about racial discrimination.

Fear of dividing a nation at war reinforced the normal desire of a chief justice to mass the Court in an important case. Thus Stone assumed the task of writing the Court's opinion and sought to mute conflict by considering only the validity of the curfew. He wrote that the Court would not in 1943 say that in 1942, only months after the disaster at Pearl Harbor, it had been unreasonable for the military to fear espionage and sabotage and to doubt there was time to separate the loyal from the disloyal among groups most likely to contain enemy sympathizers. It had been legitimate, therefore, to require such people to remain in their homes after dark.

The Chief insisted that "it is not for any court to sit in review" of the wisdom of the military's choices. And, toward the close of his opinion, he re-emphasized the limited nature of the Court's holding: "it is unnecessary to consider whether or to what extent such findings [of military peril] would support orders differing from the curfew order."

Hugo Black and Felix Frankfurter were generally satisfied with the draft, and three others, Owen Roberts, Stanley Reed, and Robert H. Jackson, swallowed their doubts. Reed remarked to Stone that his task had been "thankless," but he had "done it well."

On the other hand, Wiley Rutledge, Frank Murphy, and William O. Douglas still had serious reservations. Murphy was the most outspoken. Not only did General DeWitt's crass racism anger the justice, he was also worried that Stone's opinion undercut judicial authority by requiring the military to meet only a test of "reasonableness" to justify its actions, rather than the stricter test that Stone himself had suggested for "insular minorities" in United States v. Carolene Products (1938; reprinted below, p. 609) and the Court had strengthened in Skinner v. Oklahoma (1942; reprinted below, p. 1014). "While this Court sits," Murphy said, "it has the inescapable duty of seeing that the mandates of the Constitution are obeyed."

Learning of Murphy's plans to dissent, Frankfurter urged him to negotiate with Stone:

> Please, Frank, with your eagerness for the austere functions of the Court and your desire to do all that is humanly possible to maintain and enhance the corporate reputation of the Court, why don't you take the initiative with the Chief Justice in getting him to take out everything that either offends you or that you would want to express more irenically?

Even after an exchange of several notes, Stone and Murphy remained far apart, and the latter circulated a blistering opinion branding the army's program as "utterly inconsistent with our ideals and traditions" and "at variance with the principles for which we are fighting." Frankfurter read Murphy's draft in horror and immediately wrote another plea:

> Of course I shan't try to dissuade you from filing a dissent . . . not because I do not think it highly unwise but because I think you are immovable. But I would like to say two things to you about the dissent: (1) it has internal contradictions which you ought not to allow to stand, and (2) do you really think it is conducive to the things you care about, including the great reputation of this Court, to suggest that everybody is out of step except Johnny, and more particularly that the Chief Justice and seven other Justices of this Court are behaving like the enemy and thereby playing into the hands of the enemy?

Murphy had second thoughts. Within a few days he modified his dissent into a concurrence. Still, he felt obliged to say publicly:

> We give great deference to the judgment of the Congress and of the military authorities as to what is necessary in the effective prosecution of the war, but we can never forget that there are

constitutional boundaries which it is our duty to uphold.   . . .
Under the curfew order . . . no less than 70,000 American citizens
have been placed under a special ban and deprived of their liberty
because of their particular racial inheritance.   In this sense, it
bears a melancholy resemblance to the treatment accorded to
members of the Jewish race in Germany and in other parts of
Europe.

Douglas also tried to negotiate with Stone. He had some
success in persuading the Chief to remove a reference to the
"ethnic solidarity" of the Nisei that smacked to Douglas of racism
and, for a brief time, to include a hint that the Court would require
individual judicial hearings before allowing internment. But several
other members of the majority complained; Justice Black went so
far as to state that, if he were the commanding general, he would
refuse to allow the Nisei to return to the West Coast even if a court
so ordered. Stone then explained to Douglas he feared that "if I
accepted your suggestions very little of the structure of my opinion
would be left, and that I should lose most of my adherents. It
seems to me, therefore, that it would be wiser for me to stand by
the substance of my opinion and for you to express your views in
your concurring opinion."

As published, Douglas' concurrence noted that he agreed "substantially" with the opinion of the Court that, in 1942, the curfew
had not been unreasonable. He insisted, however, that "[l]oyalty is
a matter of mind and of heart not race."

Wiley Rutledge confessed to Stone that "I have had more
anguish over this case than any I have ever decided, save possibly
one death case in the Court of Appeals." And in an early draft of a
concurring opinion he wrote:

> I have very strong sympathies with Mr. Justice Murphy's views.
> Next to totalitarian power, sheer racial discrimination goes to the
> heart of the Nazi–Fascist political policy that we now fight.[26]

Eventually, however, Rutledge removed this statement and contented himself with a notation that he did not join in the suggestion,

> if that is intended, that the courts have no power to review any
> action a military officer may "in his discretion" find it necessary to
> take with respect to civilian citizens. . . . [It] does not follow that
> there may not be bounds beyond which he cannot go and, if he
> oversteps them, that courts may not have power to protect the
> civilian citizen.

C. *Korematsu* and *Endo* (1944) Reach the Court

The Court announced its decision in *Hirabayashi* in June,
1943. In the fall of 1944, Fred Korematsu, a young Nisei who had

---

26. Quoted in Fowler V. Harper, *Justice Rutledge and the Bright Constellation* (Indianapolis: Bobbs–Merrill, 1965), p. 176.

been unwilling to leave his sweetheart, brought the issue of concentration camps before the Court. He had been convicted on the single count of not reporting for evacuation, and the circuit court of appeals had sustained his conviction. Korematsu then petitioned the Supreme Court for certiorari. According to Justice Douglas's notes, Stone did not vote at all on the question of granting the writ. Black voted against, but the others agreed to take the case.

On the same day the Court heard argument in both *Korematsu* and Ex parte Endo. The latter was a challenge by a Nisei to her continued detention in a camp after a governmental board had found that she was not even suspected of disloyalty. Logically—and, it turned out, tactically—her suit was closely tied to Korematsu's. The government argued that danger to the Nisei from other American citizens made it necessary to keep them imprisoned until some "orderly" way of resettling them could be found.

Murphy's notes on the conference for *Korematsu* are sparse, perhaps because he himself was heavily engaged in the debate. The way in which the justices spoke out of turn indicates something of the heat.

JACKSON: "I would limit this to sabotage. It was a state of war. I don't think [DeWitt] could exclude [people of] Japanese ancestry. I stop with H[irabayashi] last year and [go] no further. They say the courts have got to become a part of it. I don't accept [a] military order as something we have got to accept without any inquiry into [its] reasonableness."

CHIEF JUSTICE: "You are saying that the Congress and President acting together are unable to create zones to protect us against military espionage and sabotage. If you can do it for curfew you can do it for exclusion."

RUTLEDGE: "I had to swallow H[irabayashi]. I didn't like it. At that time I knew if I went along with that order I had to go along with detention for [a] reasonably necessary time. Nothing but necessity would justify it. ... And so I vote to affirm."

CHIEF JUSTICE: "I affirm on this record."

Douglas recalled that Black "was very much on Stone's side, very eloquent in defense of the power of the military to do what they did. And he had no doubts, no reservations." [27]

The initial vote was 5–4. Black, Reed, Frankfurter, and, sadly, Rutledge, agreed with Stone that *Hirabayashi*, despite all its careful disclaimers of upholding no more than the curfew, disposed of *Korematsu*. On the other hand, Roberts, never before known as a crusader for civil liberty, voted with Douglas, Murphy, and Jackson to reverse. Stone assigned the opinion to Black, a staunch libertari-

---

27. "Transcriptions of Conversations between William O. Douglas and Walter F. Murphy," (Tape recorded during 1961–63), Mudd Library, Princeton University, pp. 165–66.

an who was on close personal terms with two of the dissenters, Douglas and Murphy.

Discussion at conference focused rather than ended wrangling. *Korematsu* "was very much discussed, very much considered," Douglas remembered, "very much debated up and down the halls of the, the corridors of the Court." Pens cut eloquent phrases; and tempers—of clerks as well as justices—flared.

As in *Hirabayashi*, Black, like Stone, wanted a very narrow opinion, and he tried to stick to this plan, despite prodding by some of his other colleagues. Probably at Stone's suggestion, he asserted that the charge against Korematsu had only been failing to report to a relocation center. Thus Black hoped to avoid the issue of the camps altogether and simply say that the Court could not know that Korematsu would have been imprisoned. No one, however, except Stone and Black took this disclaimer seriously. Even the government's brief conceded that if Korematsu had reported to the center he would have been interned.

Jackson, who detested Black, quickly wrote another dissent. His law clerk, however, read it with a very critical eye and urged the justice to revise it. The next draft, this one circulated to the Conference, in effect, charged the majority with bad faith and shoddy logic in relying on *Hirabayashi*. Quoting copiously from Stone's restrictive sentences in the earlier opinion, Jackson pointed out: "The Court is now saying that in *Hirabayashi* we did decide the very things we there said we were not deciding." On the merits, his tone was no less scathing, alleging that the decision violated the fundamental constitutional principle that guilt was personal and distorted the constitutional system to rationalize racism.[28]

The military, Jackson added, might be faced with dire emergencies and have to take action it thought appropriate, action that might, on more careful examination, be seen to violate constitutional commands. That was a fact of life. But, by allowing violations of the military order to be prosecuted in federal courts, Congress was requiring the judiciary to examine the military action; when judges so acted, they had to apply *their* standards, for the decision of a court set a precedent for future cases. And in this instance, Jackson wrote, the majority had ignored its own doctrine that invasions of basic rights had to be subjected to "the strictest scrutiny." Instead, the justices had refused to examine the reasons behind the military's decision. Thus the Court "for all time has validated the principle of racial discrimination in criminal procedure and of transplanting American citizens. The principle . . . lies about like a loaded weapon ready for the hand of any authority that can bring forward a plausible claim of urgent need."

---

28. Perhaps Jackson knew that General DeWitt and Black were old friends and was, for a select audience, tarring Black with the same brush as DeWitt.

Murphy had been busy with his law clerk preparing his own dissent, an opinion that made heavy use of the *amicus curiae* brief of the Japanese American Citizens League. He gleefully read Jackson's draft and sent it to his clerk, Eugene Gressman, with a brief note:

Gene—

Read this and perish!

The Court has blown up over the Jap case—just as I expected it would.

Murphy's own dissent was even more impassioned than Jackson's. He opened by asserting that "exclusion goes over 'the very brink of constitutional power' "—a phrase he had used in *Hirabayashi*— "and falls into the ugly abyss of racism." His closing paragraph stated his personal ideals, earlier versions of which had earned him Felix Frankfurter's sarcastic rebaptism as "St. Francis":

> I dissent . . . from this legalization of racism. Racial discrimination in any form and in any degree has no justifiable part whatever in our democratic way of life. It is unattractive in any setting but it is utterly revolting among a free people who have embraced the principles set forth in the Constitution of the United States.

Meanwhile, Roberts circulated a short dissent, arguing that Korematsu had been caught in a trap. Had he left his home to report to the center, he would have violated the curfew; had he not reported to the center, he would have violated the exclusion order.

Despite despising Black, Frankfurter wrote several memoranda to inform and stiffen him. Their essential reasoning was: "To find that the Constitution does not forbid the military measures now complained of does not carry with it approval of that which Congress and the Executive did. That is their business not mine." Circulation of the dissents, however, especially Jackson's, led Frankfurter to write a full scale concurrence.

Stone was concerned that Black, despite his initial resolve, was not sufficiently emphasizing the narrowness of the Court's decision. The Chief followed his usual practice of writing a draft of a concurrence and sending it to the author of the Court's opinion for his enlightenment.

Mr. Chief Justice **STONE** concurring.

> I concur in the opinion of the Court and add a word only because it seems desirable, and a matter of some importance, to state explicitly the reasons why we are not free to decide petitioner's main contention that a relocation order applied to him would be unconstitutional.

> Petitioner has not been convicted of violating a relocation order and in fact has never been subjected to such an order. He has been convicted of violating an Act of Congress which penal-

izes his disobedience of an order which in effect required him, pending further orders, to enter and remain in an assembly center. ... The conviction is plainly sustained by the reasoning of the opinion in the *Hirabayashi* case. ...

It was no necessary consequence of obedience to enter the assembly center that petitioner would ever be subjected to a relocation order. For it does not follow, either as a matter of fact or of law, that his presence in the assembly center would result in his detention under a relocation order. Many who were sent to the assembly center were not sent to relocation centers, but instead were released and sent out of the military area. We cannot say that petitioner would not have been released, as others were. We do not and cannot know the terms of any relocation order to which he might be but has not been subjected. For there is nothing to preclude the radical modification or complete abandonment of the relocation scheme at any time before petitioner could have been subjected to it.

This Court does not decide moot cases or give advisory opinions. It will be time enough to decide the serious constitutional issue which petitioner seeks to raise here when a relocation order is in fact applied or is certain to be applied to him, and we are advised of its terms.

Douglas circulated a dissent, based on statutory rather than constitutional interpretation. Given his strong antipathy to racism, it was a surprisingly mild document. But he was not only a civil libertarian, he also deeply loved his country and, as a close friend of President Roosevelt, trusted its leaders. As a former executive official, Douglas could also sympathize with the sense of urgency that decent and patriotic military officers might have felt in early 1942, as the United States and its allies suffered disaster after disaster. While he could recognize and despise the racism of DeWitt and the leaders of interest groups who had lobbied against the Nisei, Douglas was hesitant to ascribe that racism to the political system as a whole.

D. Negotiations Within the Court

A unanimous Court would have made such a shaky constitutional decision seem less tortured, but that possibility did not exist. Next best would be to pick off several of the dissenters, but the majority had no real hope of winning over anyone except Douglas. He accepted the difficulties that the military faced in 1942, as they confronted a victorious enemy. Moreover, he and Black were friends and, more important, jurisprudential allies. Each thought of the other as an ardent defender of civil liberties.

By nature a self-contained and independent man, Douglas usually resented efforts to persuade him to change his vote. Ex parte Endo, however, presented a potential avenue of indirect communication. The Court had voted in conference to hold that the government was obliged to release Miss Endo; and Stone, perhaps sensing early that there were grounds for negotiating with Douglas, had assigned him the task of writing the opinion of the Court. Douglas wanted, he later said, "to put it [*Endo*] on the constitutional grounds, but I couldn't get a court [a majority] to do that. Black, Frankfurter, [and] Stone were very clear that that [keeping Nisei imprisoned even after the government's own processes had shown them to be loyal] was not unconstitutional, but that this would have to turn, *Endo* would have to turn, upon the construction of the regulations."

Now, even while *Korematsu* was churning up the Court, Douglas, who always wrote swiftly and was typically impatient to secure agreement, was getting anxious about when *Endo* could come down. Black was delaying the case, even though Douglas had reluctantly agreed to restrict the opinion to holding that Congress had not authorized detention of any citizen whom the government conceded to be loyal.

Stone tried to persuade Douglas that *Endo*, not *Korematsu*, was the critical case, at least if the latter ruling clearly stated that the Court's sustaining exclusion did not legitimate detention. So restricted, Stone reasoned, *Korematsu* would uphold only authority to exclude potentially dangerous people from a war zone during a state of emergency. *Endo*, on the other hand, would compel the government to release all Nisei who were not charged with disloyalty—and, of course, almost no Nisei was so charged. *Endo* would be the great ruling; *Korematsu*, a narrow, technical decision.

Black had also been talking to Douglas. Eventually, they sat down in Black's chambers with Black's clerk to seek accommodation. To meet many of Douglas' objections, Black heavily edited the draft of his opinion for the Court. But the changes, though numerous, were largely in tone—for instance, stressing the Court's rejection of racism as a justification for evacuation. He did not retreat from his position that the power to evacuate the Nisei fell within Congress' power to wage war.

Frankfurter, who loved to debate and negotiate with his colleagues, was working on Jackson, with whom he had developed a close personal relationship, trying to nudge him into the fold. In a brief memo beginning "Dear Bob," Frankfurter asked: "If ... Congress in the exercise of its war power could constitutionally authorize the military to do what General DeWitt did in California without giving a Japanese[-American] citizen ground for applying to a federal court for [a writ of] *habeas corpus*, what is the constitutional restriction upon Congress to authorize enforcement of that order in the usual way—*i.e.*, penal sanctions in civil[ian] courts—in which a constitutional command is vindicated?"[29]   If Jackson responded, he left no record of having done so and stuck to his dissent.

But if Jackson was still out, Douglas was now a member of the majority.   After only minor changes, the Conference approved Black's amended opinion.   The vote had become 6–3 to place the mantle of constitutionality on forced evacuation of the Nisei—and despite what Stone pretended to believe—imprisonment, without charge or trial, in concentration camps.   For his part, Black withdrew whatever reservations he had about *Endo*, and the Court announced the two decisions on the same Monday, a week before Christmas, 1944.

E. Aftermath

Korematsu quickly became and remains an important case in American constitutional law, indicating just how far the Court may be willing to shrink the constitutional text as well as the broader constitution to rationalize governmental power in time of war.   As Douglas ruefully mused in 1963, "I think that those cases, like *Korematsu* and *Hirabayashi*, probably would have been decided the same way by any Court that I have sat on in the twenty-three years [I've been a justice]."[30]   In contrast to *Korematsu*'s notoriety, Ex Parte Endo belongs in the domain of esoteric historians.

Shortly before his death in 1971, Hugo Black still stoutly maintained that his opinion in *Korematsu* had been constitutionally correct and that he would make the same choice if faced with the problem again.   Douglas, on the other hand, came to regard *Korematsu* as a tragic, even shameful, mistake.   "I caved in," he remarked as he expressed bitter regret at having suppressed his dissent.   *Endo*, too, continued to gnaw at his conscience.

> I think perhaps the biggest disappointment to me was the fact that they couldn't, the Court wouldn't, in *Endo*, go to the constitutional ground but just stick to the conventional way of deciding the case, strain to construe a regulation to avoid a constitutional question.   I'm the author of that, but I did it under the necessities of the situation.   But it seemed to me to be a much more wholesome thing, from the point of view of the Court as an educating influence, just to say what you can and can't do.

During the war, others were even more insensitive.   As attorney general of California, Earl Warren, whose tenure as Chief Justice would become synonymous with civil liberty, strongly urged evacuation of the Nisei in 1942 and, the following year, adamantly opposed release and resettlement in the state of even those Japanese–

---

29.   Frankfurter to Jackson, Oct. 27, 1944; the Papers of Robert H. Jackson, The Library of Congress, Box 132.

30.   Douglas–Murphy Conversations, supra note 27, p. 172.

Americans who had been cleared by loyalty-security programs. Later, he confessed profound regret at denying

> our American concept of freedom and the rights of citizens. . . .
> It was wrong to react so impulsively, without positive evidence of
> disloyalty, even though we felt we had a good motive in the
> security of our state.[31]

Among the sharpest contemporary critics was a combat-weary Air Corps lieutenant, who had been a lawyer in civilian life. In a letter to Justice Jackson written from the Philippines during the war, the lieutenant described some of his experiences. "In short," he noted, "I can be said to have no love for the Japanese." Moreover, it was in his "selfish interests" to "support that which help us defeat the enemy." But, he added, *Korematsu* "is the type of blow from which we cannot recover so easily. It introduces racialism, the very racialism we are fighting so strenuously to eliminate. . . . [Through that decision] the Court has . . . deprived an American citizen of his rights, utterly devitalizing the constitutional principles which are included within the word 'citizen.' "[32]

The economic harm the Nisei suffered was staggering. They were forced to abandon their homes and businesses, and, to sell for whatever they could immediately get, almost everything they had worked all their lives to accumulate. Far worse was the psychological injury of being denied the most basic rights of citizenship. They were herded like criminals behind barbed wire enclosures and deprived of liberty and dignity without any process of law whatsoever other than General DeWitt's savage scream, "A Jap is a Jap," and Hugo Black's pious nostrum that "hardships are part of war, and war is an aggregation of hardships."

VI. CONCLUSION

Writing in *Federalist* No. 72, Alexander Hamilton asserted that "the best security for the fidelity of mankind is to make their interest coincide with their duty." That hard-headed psychology underlies the American constitutional structure. To a large extent the political processes are open, though money, education, and experience confer great advantages on some people and interests over others. And as Chapter 3 pointed out, democracy in the United States is also curtailed in other consequential ways. National public policy is made in arenas subject to pressures, crosspressures, checks, and counterchecks—some more democratic in character, some more constitutionalist.

---

31. *The Memoirs of Chief Justice Earl Warren* (New York: Doubleday, 1977), p. 149.

32. Lt. Felix F. Stumpf to Robert H. Jackson, April 18, 1945; Jackson Papers, Box 132. Jackson may have appreciated even more the terse note he received from Jerome Frank, former professor at Yale, one of the leading "Legal Realists," former member of Roosevelt's "Brain Trust," and later a distinguished judge on the U.S. Court of Appeals for the Second Circuit: "I want to let you know how much I admire your opinion in the *Korematsu* case."

In one important sense, *Korematsu* highlights the constitution-alist's fear of representative democracy. Here there can be little doubt that an overwhelming majority of the nation approved the decision to fill up concentration camps with American citizens of Japanese descent. Open political processes, institutional access, crosspressures, political culture, and the potential judgment of history did nothing to sway Congress, the President, the War Department, or General DeWitt from violating the right of the Nisei to be treated by their government with equal dignity and respect.

In another important sense, however, *Korematsu* also high-lights the democrat's fear of the futility, if not the undesirability, of extra-democratic checks on popular government. For even federal judges, those people whom James Wilson thought would be "the noble guards" of "the Constitution," caved in. Their reason may have been respect for military judgment at a time of crisis rather than fear of defeat at the polls, but the result was still surrender. For the Nisei, the Bill of Rights was no more than the parchment barrier many Federalists of 1787–91 had feared it would be. Madison would have understood, even if he would have wept.

Yet, as *Korematsu* illustrates a failure of the system, it also illustrates the way the system works. Freely elected officials approved the underlying policy, though they did not initiate it. The Nisei found a few allies and they had access to the congressional phase of decision making as well as to the courts. Curiously, however, negotiation and compromise—the supposed hallmarks of the legislative process—occurred mostly in the judicial process, and on issues that were of little help to the Nisei. And for all the shame that the evacuation policy earned, even *Korematsu* did not end the matter. (See Eds.' Notes to the text of the opinions in *Korematsu*, below, p. 1383.) First, in 1948 Congress enacted a reparations bill that, in token form, acknowledged guilt and offered small economic recompense. Second, in the 1980s, Fred Korematsu and Gordon Hirabayashi, old men but still proud of their American citizenship, returned to court. Korematsu had his conviction vacated, but Hirabayashi was only partially successful. The trial judge vacated the conviction for failing to report for "relocation" but left intact the conviction for disobeying the curfew.

Third, at about the same time that Korematsu and Hirabayashi were reopening their cases, a group of Nisei sued the U.S. government for damages under federal Torts Claims Acts. They lost in the district court but won on appeal. Eventually, the case reached the Supreme Court, and the justices unanimously decided against the Nisei on jurisdictional grounds and remanded the case to the Federal Circuit,[33] which, in 1988, ruled that the statute of limitations had run. Congress, however, responded to a suggestion in Justice Harry Blackmun's concurring opinion, the recommendations of a

---

33. United States v. Hohri (1987).

commission Congress had established to recommend remedies for what the government had done to the Nisei,[34] the lobbying of the Japanese–American Citizens League, and the prodding of conscience by acknowledging "the fundamental injustice of the evacuation, relocation, and internment." As an additional token of remorse, Congress also authorized payment of approximately $20,000 (worth less than $1,500 in 1942 dollars) to each survivor of the camps.[35]

Fourth, and with marvelous irony, the Supreme Court took a different kind of action. Early in his opinion in *Hirabayashi*, Stone had written that "Distinctions between citizens solely because of their ancestry are by their very nature odious to a free people whose institutions are founded upon the doctrine of equality." Similarly, Black had begun his opinion *Korematsu*, by stating, then promptly ignoring, a principle constitutional law: "[A]ll legal restrictions which curtail the civil rights of a single racial group are immediately suspect." The justices, of course, have never again faced the spectacle of American concentration camps, but time after time they have plucked Stone's and Black's sentences out of context and used them to justify striking down various sorts of racial and ethnic discrimination. (See below, Chapters 14 and 15, for the development of the doctrine of "suspect classifications," for which the Court often cites *Hirabayashi* and *Korematsu* as authorities.) If one had not read the actual opinions and decisions in these two cases but only looked at the way the Court has used them, it would be quite reasonable to conclude that they must have been ringing affirmations of the right of all Americans to equal justice under law.[36]

SELECTED BIBLIOGRAPHY

Abraham, Henry. *Justices & Presidents* (3d ed.; New York: Oxford University Press, 1991).

---

34. *Report of the Commission on Wartime Relocation and Internment of Civilians*, supra note 24.

35. P.L. 100–38, 102 Stat. 903 (1988). When the Japanese invaded the Aleutian Islands off the coast of Alaska, the United States evacuated many Aleuts. The reasons were largely humanitarian, to get them out of an area of combat. Still, the Commission on Wartime Relocation described as "deplorable" the conditions in the camps to which they were taken. Disease was rampant and the death rate high, though lower than among those who remained behind and were captured. Only half of the latter group survived captivity under the Japanese. In any event, the 1988 Act included Aleuts among those entitled to reparations.

36. For an analysis of the Court's use of these cases through 1957, see Walter F. Murphy, "Civil Liberty and the Japanese American Cases: A Study in the Uses of *Stare Decisis*," 11 *West.Pol.Q.* 3 (1958). In the intervening decades, the justices have continued to "miscite" these rulings. For a more general discussion of stare decisis, see above, Chapter 2.

————. *The Judicial Process* (6th ed.; New York: Oxford University Press, 1993).

Barber, Sotirios A. *The Constitution of Judicial Power* (Baltimore: Johns Hopkins University Press, 1993).

Bessette, Joseph M., and Jeffrey Tulis, eds. *The Presidency in the Constitutional Order* (Baton Rouge: Louisiana State University Press, 1981).

Beveridge, Albert J. *The Life of John Marshall* (Boston: Houghton Mifflin, 1916), 4 vols.

Bork, Robert H. *The Tempting of America: The Political Seduction of the Law* (New York: The Free Press, 1990).

Brigham, John. *The Cult of the Court* (Philadelphia: Temple University Press, 1987).

Commission on Wartime Relocation and Internment of Civilians. *Report: Personal Justice Denied* (Washington, DC: Government Printing Office, 1982).

Dahl, Robert A. "Decision–Making in a Democracy: The Role of the Supreme Court as a National Policy–Maker," 6 *Jo. of Pub.Law* 279 (1957).

Danelski, David J. *A Supreme Court Justice Is Appointed* (New York: Random House, 1964).

Elkins, Stanley, and Eric McKitrick. *The Age of Federalism* (New York: Oxford University Press, 1994).

Ely, John Hart. "Another Such Victory: Constitutional Theory and Practice in a World Where Courts are No Different from Legislatures," 77 *Va.L.Rev.* 833 (1991).

Fish, Peter G. *The Office of Chief Justice* (Charlottesville, VA: White Burkett Miller Center of Public Affairs, 1984).

Fisher, Louis. *Constitutional Conflicts Between Congress and the President* (Princeton: Princeton University Press, 1985).

————. *The Politics of Shared Power: Congress and the Executive* (3rd ed.; Washington, DC: Congressional Quarterly Press, 1993).

Fleming James E. "Constructing the Substantive Constitution," 72 *Tex.L.Rev.* 211 (1993).

Grodzins, Morton. *Americans Betrayed: Politics and the Japanese Evacuation* (Chicago: University of Chicago Press, 1949).

Hodder–Williams, Richard. "Six Notions of 'Political' and the U.S. Supreme Court," 22 *Br. J. Pol. Sci.* 1 (1991).

Howard, J. Woodford. *Mr. Justice Murphy* (Princeton: Princeton University Press, 1968).

Jackson, Robert H. *The Supreme Court in the American System of Government* (Cambridge: Harvard University Press, 1955).

Irons, Peter. *Justice at War: The Story of the Japanese American Internment Cases* (New York: Oxford University Press, 1983).

Kluger, Richard. *Simple Justice: The History of Brown v. Board of Education and Black America's Struggle for Equality* (New York: Knopf, 1976).

Lasser William. *The Limits of Judicial Power: The Supreme Court in American Politics* (Chapel Hill: University of North Carolina Press, 1988).

McCloskey, Robert. *The American Supreme Court* (rev. by Sanford V. Levinson) (2d ed.; Chicago: University of Chicago Press, 1994).

Mason, Alpheus Thomas. *Harlan Fiske Stone* (New York: Viking, 1956).

_____. *The Supreme Court from Taft to Burger* (3d ed.; Baton Rouge: Louisiana State University Press, 1979).

Murphy, Walter F. *Congress and the Court* (Chicago: University of Chicago Press, 1962).

_____. *Elements of Judicial Strategy* (Chicago: University of Chicago Press, 1964).

_____ and Joseph Tanenhaus. *The Study of Public Law* (New York: Random House, 1972).

_____, C. Herman Pritchett, and Sotirios A. Barber. *Courts, Judges, & Politics* (5th ed.; New York: Random House, 1995).

O'Brien, David M. *Storm Center: The Supreme Court in American Politics* (New York: Norton, 1986).

Pritchett, C. Herman. *The Roosevelt Court* (Chicago: Quadrangle Books, 1969; originally published, 1948).

_____. *Congress versus the Supreme Court* (Minneapolis: University of Minnesota Press, 1961).

Schubert, Glendon A. *The Judicial Mind* (Evanston: Northwestern University Press, 1965).

_____. *The Judicial Mind Revisited* (New York: Oxford University Press, 1974).

Schwartz, Bernard. *Super Chief: Earl Warren and His Supreme Court* (New York: New York University Press, 1983).

_____. *The Unpublished Opinions of the Warren Court* (New York: Oxford University Press, 1985).

Stumpf, Harry P. *American Judicial Politics* (New York: Harcourt, Brace, & Jovanovich, 1988).

Tribe, Lawrence H. *God Save This Honorable Court* (New York: Random House, 1985).

Ulmer, S. Sidney. *Courts, Law, and Judicial Processes* (New York: The Free Press, 1981).

Woodward, Bob, and Scott Armstrong. *The Brethren: Inside the Supreme Court* (New York: Simon & Schuster, 1979).

*

II

What Is "the Constitution"?

Part I sketched the intellectual, institutional, and political frameworks within which American constitutional interpretation operates. We now turn to the most basic problem of that enterprise: What is the "it" to be interpreted?

Chapter 1 distinguished among several terms, constitution, constitutional text, and constitutionalism. We shall not repeat what we said there, but merely remind readers that: In its narrowest sense, the term constitution connotes governmental organization and processes and, in its broadest sense, a people's way of life; a constitutional text refers to a document or set of documents that claims to describe as well as prescribe the political order; and constitutionalism is a normative political theory that would impose limits on all governments, even those by, of, and for the people. Chapter 3 developed this theory in more detail and linked it to democratic theory as well as to the American political system.

Earlier we said the question "WHAT is 'the Constitution'?" posed the most important problem in constitutional interpretation, for if interpreters are confused about what it is they are interpreting, their work will inevitably be confused. Chapter 1 discussed several segments of the basic interrogative: What is the character of "the Constitution"? Is it a compact among states or an effort to constitute a people? What is the authority of the text? What are the functions of the constitutional text and the larger constitution? What does the "Constitution" include? How does it validly change over time? All of these subquestions, of course, are interrelated with each other as well as with questions of HOW to interpret and WHO are the authoritative interpreters. Nevertheless, the chapters in this Part try to focus on problems of inclusion and change.

Chapter 5 shows interpreters grappling—not always self-consciously and certainly never systematically—with such issues as: Does "the Constitution" encompass only the text of 1787–88 and its amendments? Does it include other documents—for instance, the Declaration of Independence? Does it, also or alternatively, include various "original understandings," other documents, interpretations, practices, traditions, and/or political theories? In sum, in the United States, are the constitution and the constitutional text the same? If not, how do they differ and how do interpreters decide which principles and rules belong within the constitutional canon even if omitted from the constitutional text?

In reading these materials, one must also be alert for the dimensions of character, authority, and function. They frequently flicker across the background, influencing, perhaps subliminally, both the work that interpreters do and the ways the rest of us evaluate that work.

Chapter 6 addresses yet another aspect of the character of the American constitution that includes but moves beyond the relationships between constitution and constitutional text: the system's rigidity and flexibility, and thus its stability. No political order could "endure for ages to come" if it could not adjust to cope with unforeseen problems. Thus "the American Constitution," like all constitutions and most constitutional texts, includes procedures for change. But are Article V's procedures sufficient? Can any constitutional text remain authoritative if its terms are so rigid as to be incapable of being "adapted to the various *crises* of human affairs" by other than cumbersome formal amendment? Alternatively, if constitutional change is easy, will that text's prescription of fundamental principles and rules be taken seriously?

In short, to what extent can the meaning of the constitutional document and relationships between that text and the larger constitution be legitimately changed by interpretation, practice, or tradition? Who has authority to recognize or effect such changes? Immediately we find ourselves facing questions not only about WHAT but also about the second basic interpretive interrogative, WHO shall interpret? And, although these latter kinds of questions form the focus of Part III of this book, we cannot avoid raising them here.

Underlying these inquires is yet another problem: If the compact of 1787–88 constituted the American people as a political community, have subsequent changes in that compact, either in the narrow sense of constitutional text or the broader sense of constitution, "reconstituted" that people? If, indeed, valid constitutional change may come about through interpretation, is the process of "constituting" the American people a continuous one? Justices Scalia and Brennan debate these issues, both in Michael H. v. Gerald D. (1989; reprinted below, p. 158) and in their lectures at law schools (reprinted below, pp. 231-43).

In reading materials dealing with constitutional interpretation, it is easy to miss a critical point: Implicit in most of these analyses is a vision of an attainable good society. This sort of vision, we emphasized in Chapter 1, is not a mystic out-of-body experience or a feathery dream of utopia; rather, it is a mental sketch of what sort of people Americans can and should become, given the hard and sometimes grubby facts of their existence. Some such vision is probably necessary if constitutional interpretation is to make sense as a logical whole.[1] One of the principal difficulties in constitutional interpretation—indeed, of all politics—is that the men and women making the critical decisions seldom have (or take) the time to reflect systematically on their aspirations for the nation. President

---

1. For discussions of constitutional "aspiration," see: Sotirios A. Barber, *On What the Constitution Means* (Baltimore: Johns Hopkins University Press, 1984), chs. 3–5; William J. Brennan, Jr., "The Constitution of the United States: Contemporary Ratification," (1985; reprinted below, p. 236); Gary J. Jacobsohn, *The Supreme Court and the Decline of Constitutional Aspiration* (Totowa, NJ: Rowman & Littlefield, 1986); and Hendrik Hartog, "The Constitution of Aspiration and 'The Rights That Belong to Us All,'" 74 *Jo. of Am. Hist.* 1013 (1987).

George Bush's disclaimer that "I'm not into the vision thing" triggered derision, but he was probably typical of public officials and their academic critics.

Most versions of theories of democracy and constitutionalism offer such visions, and here the two differ more in means than in objectives. Each sees an achievable good society as consisting of free, self-governing men and women enjoying not only specific liberties but, more basically, the status of human beings equal in worth and dignity, able to choose, without interference from government, society, or other individuals, their lives and life styles, as long as they respect the equal rights and dignity of others in making the same sorts of choices. What is evident is an aspiration for a constitution to become an integral part of a way of life; and both a constitutional text and constitutional interpretation represent efforts to shape that way.

5

What Is "the Constitution"? Problems of Inclusion

Professor Sanford V. Levinson has likened various views of WHAT "the Constitution" includes to the differences between Fundamentalist Protestant and Roman Catholic theologians. The archetypal Fundamentalist Protestant sees the revealed word of God as fully contained in collection of writings called the Bible.[1] So, too, some American interpreters have viewed "the Constitution" as including only the document produced at Philadelphia in 1787 together with its amendments.[2] Thus, it is tempting to think of Justice Hugo L. Black as a "Fundamentalist Protestant." He often spoke as if "the Constitution" were the text, the whole text, and nothing but the text. He would angrily dissent when he thought the Court was adding to or subtracting from the document's plain words, even when his own values would have led him to agree with the majority's decision had he been drafting a new constitutional text. (See, for example, his dissent in Griswold v. Connecticut [1965; reprinted below, p. 147].)

In sharp contrast, Catholic theologians believe that the Bible is only one source, though a very important one, of revelation. God's truth, they argue, is also found in a tradition and in "authoritative" interpretations of that tradition as well as of the text. In this sense, if no other, most American constitutional commentators and interpreters have followed the Roman model.

Several generations ago, the noted scholar Thomas Reed Powell would begin his course on constitutional law at the Harvard Law School by warning students not to read the constitutional text. "It will only confuse you," he would say. What mattered was what interpreters, most especially judges, had said, not what James Madison, Gouverneur Morris, and company had written. Powell's

---

1. What "the Bible" includes poses its own set of problems, even for Christians. It took the early Church almost three centuries to narrow down hundreds of writings that various local communities thought authoritative to the handful now in the canon. Furthermore, even today Catholics and most Protestant sects differ about whether several books are inspired, and many scholars believe that the so-called Pastoral Letters attributed to St. Paul and the two letters allegedly written by St. Peter were composed long after their deaths.

2. *Constitutional Faith* (Princeton: Princeton University Press, 1988), ch. 1.

109

even more famous colleague at Columbia, Karl Llewellyn, went further: "Wherever there are today established practices 'under' or 'in accordance with' the Document, *it is only the practice which can legitimize the words as still being part of our going Constitution.* It is *not* the words which legitimaize the practice." [3]

There was (and remains) a great deal of truth in Powell's and Llewellyn's efforts to shock their students. The truth of their claims, however, does not settle the issue whether such practices and interpretive additions and subtractions are legitimate. Certainly no one would pretend that all such "emendations" have been correct; such an assertion would be self-refuting, for most individual interpreters and institutions have managed to contradict themselves as often as have commentators. Moreover, even if interpreters could agree on standards and "correctly" sort out constitutional wheat from unconstitutional chaff, the question would still remain whether *any* addition or subtraction from the constitutional text, other than by formal amendment, was valid.

I.   INCLUSION: INTERPRETATIONS? USAGES? TRADITIONS? POLITICAL THEORIES?

Whether not commentators, judges, and other public officials have acted properly, Powell was clearly right in saying they had commonly regarded as "authoritative" some previous interpretations of "the Constitution." Those offered by judges tend to achieve a higher status. Still, Justice Felix Frankfurter noted in the Steel Seizure Case (1952; reprinted below, p. 443) that long and unchallenged usages of other branches of government should also qualify for constitutional status. Twenty-two years later, United States v. Nixon (1974; reprinted below, p. 323) presented the Supreme Court with perhaps was the most dramatic example of Frankfurter's contention: a clash between, on the one hand, "executive privilege," the President's authority to maintain the confidentiality of conversations and papers relating to the inner workings of the executive department, and, on the other, judicial review, the authority of judges to declare unconstitutional acts of coordinate officials. Although interpreters could reasonably read both concepts into the constitutional document, that text did not explicitly mention either of these terms or use words remotely like them. Moreover, Presidents since George Washington had invoked executive privilege, and judges since that time had invalidated acts of coordinate officials.[4] Thus a decision for either side required the

---

3. "The Constitution as an Institution," 34 *Colum.L.Rev.* 1, 12 (1934).

4. Several cases antedated Marbury v. Madison (1803; reprinted below, p. 298): In Hylton v. United States (1796), the justices asserted authority to invalidate an act of Congress, but actually upheld it. Probably in Hayburn's Case (1792) and certainly in Yale Todd's Case (1794), the justices did invalidate provisions of federal statutes.

Court to move outside the text.[5]

Dissenting in Poe v. Ullman (1961; reprinted below p. 141), Justice John Marshall Harlan, II, envisioned an even more extensive constitutional canon[6] than had Frankfurter:

> Due process has not been reduced to any formula; its content cannot be determined by reference to any code. The best that can be said is that through the course of this Court's decisions it has represented the balance which our Nation, built upon postulates of respect for the liberty of the individual, has struck between that liberty and the demands of organized society. . . . The balance of which I speak is the balance struck by this country, having regard to what history teaches are the traditions from which it broke. That tradition is a living thing.

Although judges seldom admit it, they, like other interpreters, also often read political theory into as well as out of the document. Chief Justice Earl Warren used a theory of representative democracy to hold that "the Constitution" required electoral districts to conform to the principle of "one person, one vote." (Reynolds v. Sims [1964; reprinted below, p. 777].) So, too, Justice Antonin Scalia unsuccessfully urged his colleagues to leave the validity of state laws regulating abortion to democratic settlement, thus importing democratic theory in "the Constitution." (Planned Parenthood v. Casey [1992; reprinted below, p. 1287].) And many of the Court's rulings about the substance of such "fundamental rights" as those to marry, travel, and enjoy privacy depend at least as heavily on a theory of constitutionalism as on the plain words of the text. (See especially *Griswold* reprinted below, p. 147, and the cases reprinted in Chapter 18.)

Almost as frequently as a majority of justices find a "tradition," hallow a practice, or rely on a political theory, dissenting justices will question the legitimacy of including such material. Michael H. v. Gerald D. (1989; reprinted below p. 158) provided the occasion for a wonderful argument between Justices Scalia and William J. Brennan, Jr., over the scope of "tradition" and its relevance for constitutional interpretation. Lee v. Weisman (1992; reprinted below, p. 167) renewed the debate, with Scalia taking on Justices Kennedy and Souter.

On the other hand, when the Court sticks to the plain words of the text, dissenters will protest against "mechanical interpretation" that ignores "the living Constitution." This disagreement over

---

5. That Chief Justice Warren Earl Burger would write the opinion of the Court heightened the irony, for, when Nixon nominated Burger to become chief justice, the President had said that he was a strict constructionist who would stick to "the Constitution."

6. Historically, "canon" referred to an authoritative body of writing—originally a collection of Greek poetry amassed at Alexandria. The word has also come to mean a basic principle or rule, usually regarding interpretation; thus legal commentators and literary critics often speak of "canons of construction." In its first meaning, canon often has an ecclesiastical connotation. We use the word in its historic, secular sense.

WHAT "the Constitution" includes began shortly after ratification, as illustrated by the debate between Justices Samuel Chase and James Iredell in Calder v. Bull (1798; reprinted below, p. 121), the very first case in this book. That debate echoes through the more than 500 volumes of the United States Reports that come after *Calder*.

II. "THE CONSTITUTION": WRITTEN? LIVING? OR BOTH?

The notion of a "living Constitution" or an unwritten constitution supplementing the official document is open-ended. Thus we prefer to use the terms, defined above at pp. 1–3, constitutional text (or "the Constitution") for the document of 1787–88 as amended, and the *constitution*, italicized this once, to refer to elements that, although not mentioned in the text, have taken on constitutional authority. Not only is there doubt, even confusion, about WHAT interpreters mean to include when they speak of "the Constitution," but American constitutional interpretation also lacks "rules of recognition,"[7] standards to determine when and how a practice, tradition, political theory, or document which the amended text of 1787–88 does not mention becomes part of the constitutional canon. These are serious deficiencies, for it may be a long and widely accepted practice—segregation by race, for example, or different legal treatment of women and men—that generates the very problem constitutional interpretation confronts. Moreover, any possibility of constitutional change raises grave questions of WHO has authority to add to or subtract from the nation's fundamental political principles.

Strict textualists respond that constitutional interpretation does have a rule of recognition, the one and only one needed: Inclusion in the words of the amended text makes a practice, tradition, theory, or other document part of the canon; exclusion makes any or all of these illegitimate, unless part of the usual definition of the text's own words.

At first glance, those who would restrict the constitution to the amended document of 1787–88 have the tidier argument. That text is tangible, bounded, set in hard print, and reproduced on pages that can be read, analyzed, and explained. And the single "rule of recognition" seems to provide a clear standard. Yet textualists have problems of their own. As we saw in Chapter 1, some clauses of the document cry out for interpretations that go beyond parsing sentences and looking up definitions in a dictionary. The words of the Preamble setting such goals as justice, liberty, and domestic tranquility no more lend themselves to rigid application than do the

---

7. See H.L.A. Hart, *The Concept of Law* (2d ed.; Oxford: Clarendon Press, 1994), ch. 6; and Richard S. Kay, "Preconstitutional Rules," 42 2d; *Ohio St.L.J.* 187 (1981).

terms of the "sweeping clause" of Article I authorizing Congress "to make all Laws which shall be necessary and proper" to carry out delegated powers.

Thus even textualists concede that sometimes it is necessary to go behind the document to find the meaning of its words. Hugo Black, the greatest of the textualists, sought help when plain words failed by trying to reconstruct the "intent of the framers." He was fond of quoting from Ex parte Bain (1887): [8]

> It is never to be forgotten that, in the construction of the language of the Constitution ... as indeed in all other instances where construction becomes necessary, we are to place ourselves as nearly as possible in the condition of the men who framed the instrument.

But "intent" adds something to the words of the document. And, as Chapter 9 will develop in detail, questing for the "intent of the framers" or the "original understanding" of the founding generation is usually as open-ended as foraging for the contents of the "unwritten constitution." (Indeed, the two may be only different aspects of the same search.) What the framers, whether of 1787–88 or of later amendments had in mind, is seldom crystal clear. Moreover, as Frankfurter noted when Black claimed to have discovered the intent of the Fourteenth Amendment in the speeches of one of the resolution's managers in Congress: "What was submitted for ratification was his proposal, not his speech." [9]

Furthermore, although the constitutional text in several places instructs interpreters about how to go about their work,[10] nowhere does it tell them to seek the intent of the framers or their "original understanding." Thus, to justify utilizing such intent and/or understanding, assuming either could be found, interpreters must employ interpretive principles that are external to the text. They face the difficult task of justifying the use of principles outside the text to demonstrate that it is wrong to go outside the text.[11]

More generally, as we have already seen, the constitutional text is riddled with language that, in Ronald Dworkin's phrase expresses broad "concepts" rather than specific "conceptions." [12] These terms make sense, one might argue, only when understood as

8. He quoted this passage, for instance, in his *A Constitutional Faith* (New York: Knopf, 1969), p. 8; and in his dissent in Adamson v. California (1947).

9. Adamson v. California, concur. op. (1947).

10. The Ninth Amendment, reprinted on the next page, issues one such interpretive command; the Eleventh Amendment issues another: "The Judicial power of the United States shall not be construed to extend to any suit in law or equity, commenced or prosecuted against one of the United States by Citizens of another State, or by Citizens or Subjects of any Foreign State."

11. For a discussion of the use of interpretive principles located outside the constitutional text, see Cass R. Sunstein, *The Partial Constitution* (Cambridge: Harvard University Press, 1993), chs. 4–5.

12. *Taking Rights Seriously* (Cambridge: Harvard University Press, 1977), ch. 5.

products of a political theory or set of political theories, with constitutionalism and representative democracy being the most serious contenders for canonical honors.

As we have mentioned earlier, for an interpreter who believes only in following the black letter of the law the Ninth Amendment presents the most troublesome problem of broad language. That amendment's exact terms directs interpreters to read "the Constitution" as including more than the words of the document: "The enumeration in the Constitution, of certain rights, shall not be construed to deny or disparage others retained by the people." The amendment does not say "the Constitution need not be construed" or "might not be construed" to exclude unlisted rights. Rather, the mood of the verb "construe" is imperative, its tense is future, and its allusion Biblical. Thus this sentence *commands* later interpreters: The "Constitution . . . shall not be construed." One might try to dismiss these words as not being cognizable by judges, but that reasoning seems circular, at least if the speaker believes that judicial review is legitimate.[13] In essence, the argument says:

> "The Constitution" consists only in the text. Thus when the words of that text say "the Constitution" includes more than the text's words, judges must ignore the text's words.

In addition, the document presents, as Chief Justice Marshall asserted in McCulloch v. Maryland (1819; reprinted below, p. 530), only the framework of a political system, one that must be filled in by interpretation and practice. As we have already seen, some of the most important parts of the constitutional system are not found in the text.

The apparent ratification of the Twenty-seventh Amendment has posed an additional problem: Has that amendment, which requires that congressional pay raises not take effect until after the next election, become part of the constitutional text? It was the second item of the original Bill of Rights that James Madison introduced in the First Congress. But it lay dormant for 203 years until resentment against legislators' increasing their own salaries led to its approval by the thirty-eighth state in 1992.

The problem for constitutional inclusion revolves around whether that prolonged coma constituted legal death. In Dillon v. Gloss (1921), the Supreme Court had said "it is quite untenable" that long dormant amendments from 1789 could become part of "the Constitution." Because "ratification is but the expression of the approbation of the people and is to be effective when had in three-fourths of the States," the justices reasoned, "there is a fair

---

13. The Canadian Supreme Court has made a useful distinction here. Admitting that the constitution includes more than the constitutional text, the justices have said they have authority only to interpret the latter. In Re the Matter of § 6 of the Judicature Act, [1981] S.C.R. 753. Applied to constitutional interpretation in the United States, this distinction would narrow judges' tasks. It would not, however, eliminate interpretive the problems the Ninth Amendment raises, for that amendment is part of the text.

implication that it must be sufficiently contemporaneous in that number of States to reflect the will of the people in all sections at relatively the same period. ...."

Eighteen years later, however, four justices, speaking through Hugo Black, said in Coleman v. Miller (1939), that *Dillon's* comment about more or less contemporary ratification was no more than an "advisory opinion." "Congress has sole and complete control" over the question "whether ratification has occurred within a reasonable period of time." The plurality, in effect, responded to a question of WHAT by offering a response to WHO: The legislature not the judiciary shall determine when an amendment enters the canon. In fact, in recent decades Congress has written into its proposals for constitutional amendments that they would die if not ratified within a specified number of years. But Black could not muster a fifth vote for his opinion; and a plurality doth not a court make. Thus, as far as judges are concerned, the general question of the shelf-life of proposed amendments is still open.[14]

Congress, smarting under a series of scandals and harsh public criticism, quickly declared in 1992 that the Twenty-seventh Amendment was "valid ... as part of the Constitution of the United States." The vote was 414–3 in the House, 99–0 in the Senate. Commentators, however, are divided; *Dillon's* reasoning about an implicit time limit is still convincing to many.[15] And, if limitations on the life of an amendment must be explicitly stated in the proposal itself, some fascinating difficulties might arise. Among the proposals that could be resurrected is the so-called "Corwin Amendment," which Congress approved and sent to the states in 1861 in a desperate effort to persuade the South to remain in the Union:

> No amendment shall be made to the Constitution which will authorize or give to Congress the power to abolish or interfere, within any State, with the domestic institutions thereof, including that of persons held to labor or service by the laws of said State.

III. RESPECT FOR THE TEXT

A small minority of constitutional commentators are "deconstructionists."[16] They believe that words can never convey a writ-

---

14. For a general debate, which occurred before the validity of the Twenty-seventh Amendment had become a live issue, about the proper roles of Congress and the Court in deciding when an amendment had become canonized, see Walter Dellinger, "The Legitimacy of Constitutional Change: Rethinking the Amendment Process," 97 *Harv.L.Rev.* 386 (1983); Laurence H. Tribe, "A *Constitution* We Are Amending: In Defense of a Restrained Judicial Role," 97 *ibid.* 433 (1983); Dellinger, "Constitutional politics: A Rejoinder," 97 *ibid.* 446 (1983); and John R. Vile, *The Constitutional Amending Process in American Political Thought* (New York: Praeger, 1992). See also Chapter 6, below.

15. For an excellent analysis, see Sanford V. Levinson, "Authorizing the Constitutional Text: On the (So-Called) Twenty-seventh Amendment," 10 *Con'l Comm.* 101 (1994).

16. If any justice of the Supreme Court is a deconstructionist, he or she has yet to come out of the closet.

er's real thoughts to a reader. No document has meaning other than what the reader puts into it; the reader is the author. Therefore, deconstructionists contend, the notion of a constitutional text authoritative for an entire people makes no sense. Deconstructionists' claims have a delightfully ironic twist: If words can never convey writers' real thoughts to readers, readers cannot understand writings that say words can never convey writers' real thoughts—if, indeed, a claim that words can never convey writers' real thoughts to readers conveys writers' real thoughts. If, on the other hand, words can convey writers' thoughts to readers, writers of such sentences are deceiving us—and themselves.

Most commentators and interpreters who see "the American Constitution" as including more than the amended document of 1787–88 are not deconstructionists and do not believe they are belittling that text. Their contention is twofold: First, textualists have oversimplified the real work of interpretation; and, second, deconstructionists have pointed to, but exaggerated, a serious problem: Language, whether written or spoken, is an inexact mode of transmitting complex ideas. Words can have a variety of meanings, and readers do not always impose the writer's framework of understanding on a text. This problem, however, does not destroy the possibility of a text's conveying meaning, though it often does cause significant difficulty.

Recognition of this interpretive problem is hardly recent in constitutional interpretation. As we saw in Chapter 1, James Madison mused in *Federalist* No. 37: "When the Almighty himself condescends to address mankind in their own language, his meaning, luminous as it must be, is rendered dim and doubtful by the cloudy medium through which it is communicated." Words often distort thoughts. On a more mundane plane, Chief Justice John Marshall noted that "Such is the character of human language, that no word conveys to the mind, in all situations, one single definite idea; and nothing is more common than to use words in a figurative sense." (McCulloch v. Maryland [1819; reprinted below, p. 530].)

Thus, most constitutional commentators and even the more sophisticated among constitutional interpreters argue that the constitutional text does, in fact, settle many problems about the legitimacy of governmental action and inaction, and the principles it announces restrict the range of legitimate answers to many other problems. To restrict, however, is not to determine. A constitutional text must itself be based on concepts of what is proper, prudent, and good, improper, imprudent, and bad for a political system. To sum up much of the discussion so far, such a document must inevitably leave gaps and contain words and phrases that need clarification for those who share, are ignorant of, or opposed to those basic values. Even the constitutional text of India, which runs to more than 300 pages, has required in its first for years more than 50 amendments and at least as much judicial interpretation as has the American document.

Other constitutional democracies have encountered similar difficulties in turning constitutional texts into instruments of governance. Constitutional interpretation is a heavy industry in countries such as Australia, Canada, the Federal Republic of Germany, Ireland, and Italy as well as in India and the United States. Finding underlying theories and judging the compatibility of earlier interpretations, traditions, and usages with a not always crystal clear text and its formative principles is no less central to that enterprise than defining the document's explicit terms.

American proponents of a constitution more inclusive than the amended document of 1787–88 assert that open acknowledgement that WHAT "the Constitution" contains poses a problem shows more respect for the text than do efforts to conceal what interpreters are actually doing. Interpretive candor, these people argue, better enables the people and their representatives to amend the text to clarify its meaning or to narrow or broaden its scope in a way that will make real, not merely formal, changes in the political system.

These sorts of debates about constitutional inclusion, textual meaning, and deconstruction remain debates. All claims here are contestable; and commentators and interpreters, including judges, have sometimes changed their minds. Moreover, as we have seen, disagreement may not only concern "the Constitution's" content but also WHO has authority to speak definitively about that content. Once again, we are not advancing a version of constitutional relativism but stressing the necessity of reason and evidence in discovering and, equally important in a constitutional democracy, the meaning of "the Constitution." Constitutional interpretation is fundamentally different from constitutional pontification.

IV. THE OBJECTIVES OF THIS CHAPTER

The preceding chapters have consisted of essays introducing readers to the enterprise of constitutional interpretation and its intellectual and political setting in American politics. This chapter continues to pursue those purposes, but our methodology changes dramatically. Each of the chapters that follow will begin with an essay, but all except Chapter 9 will, after a few pages, mainly reprint clauses of the constitutional document, texts of statutes and executive decrees, legislative debates, and judicial opinions—the basic elements of constitutional interpretation. At this point, readers might want to look back at Chapter 2 to refresh their memories about its discussion of constitutional literacy, for these elements are sometimes as elusive as quarks and as translucent as bones.

The elusiveness and/or opacity of these raw materials causes most beginning readers to experience difficulty in interpreting constitutional interpreters. And, in addition to the difficulties Chapter 2 sketched, readers will encounter substantive problems of constitutional law—for example, the meaning of such terms as *ex post facto* law or "self-incrimination," the existence of a right to privacy, and some of the wide-ranging implications of the phrase "due process of law" in the Fourteenth Amendment, such as the extent to which it "incorporates" the Bill of Rights and makes them applicable against state governments. These are interesting issues in themselves, and they form important dimensions of WHAT the constitutional text and the constitution include, as well as HOW to find meaning from those materials.

This Chapter, however, has two fundamental objectives that go beyond the substance of constitutional doctrine. The first is to push readers into the pit of constitutional interpretation, to mix their minds with the raw materials about which the essays have been speaking, to let readers see and judge for themselves. The second objective is to help readers start hacking a path through that pit, if not to impose order, to tame its chaos, by confronting the basic interrogative WHAT. As they read these materials, they will, we hope, be learning something about substantive constitutional law, but they should keep asking themselves WHAT it is that the interpreters think they are interpreting.

This task is hardly easy, for often judges, commentators, and other interpreters do not convincingly justify their answers. Indeed, they sometimes fail to ask the question, even of themselves. Still, how they try to solve the problem of WHAT and other times ignore it, may be useful. For we can learn from failures as well as from successes. And learn we must, for this elemental question is not about to disappear or to become less central to constitutional interpretation or the political system.

SELECTED BIBLIOGRAPHY

Ackerman, Bruce. "Discovering the Constitution," 93 *Yale L.J.* 1013 (1984).

_____. *We the People: Foundations* (Cambridge: Harvard University Press, 1991).

Barber, Sotirios A. *On What the Constitution Means* (Baltimore: The Johns Hopkins University Press, 1984).

Belz, Herman. "History, Theory, and the Constitution," 11 *Const. Comm.* 45 (1994).

Black, Hugo L. *A Constitutional Faith* (New York: Knopf, 1969).

Cortner, Richard C. *The Supreme Court and the Second Bill of Rights* (Madison: University of Wisconsin Press, 1981).

Corwin, Edward S. "The Constitution *versus* Constitutional Theory," 19 *Am.Pol.Sci.Rev.* 290 (1925); reprinted in Alpheus Thomas Mason and Gerald Garvey, eds., *American Constitutional History* (New York: Harper & Row, 1964).

_____. *The "Higher Law" Background of American Constitutional Law* (Ithaca: Cornell University Press, 1928, 1955).

_____. "The Constitution as Instrument and Symbol," 30 *Am. Pol.Sci.Rev.* 1071 (1936); reprinted in Richard Loss, ed., *Corwin on the Constitution* (Ithaca: Cornell University Press, 1981), vol. I.

Douglas, William O. *We, the Judges* (New York: Doubleday, 1956), especially chs. 1 & 12.

Elazar, Daniel J., and John Kinkaid, eds. *Covenant, Polity, and Constitution* (Lanham, MD: University Press of America, 1980). (This collection of essays also appeared in 10 *Publius* 1 [1980].)

Ely, John Hart. *Democracy and Distrust* (Cambridge: Harvard University Press, 1980), chs. 1–4.

Fleming, James E. "Constructing the Substantive Constitution," 72 *Tex.L.Rev.* 211 (1993).

Grey, Thomas. "Do We Have an Unwritten Constitution?" 27 *Stan.L.Rev.* 703 (1975).

_____. "The Constitution as Scripture," 37 *Stan.L.Rev.* 1 (1984).

Harris, William F. II. *The Interpretable Constitution* (Baltimore: Johns Hopkins University Press, 1993).

Horwill, Herbert A. *The Usages of the American Constitution* (Port Washington, NY: Kennikat Press, 1969) (first published 1925), ch. 1.

Kay, Richard S. "Preconstitutional Rules," 42 *Ohio St.L.J.* 187 (1982).

Levinson, Sanford V. *Constitutional Faith* (Princeton: Princeton University Press, 1988).

Maddox, Graham. "A Note on the Meaning of 'Constitution,' " 76 *Am.Pol.Sci.Rev.* 805 (1982).

Monaghan, Henry P. "Our Perfect Constitution," 56 *N.Y.U.L. Rev.* 353 (1981).

Moore, Michael S. "Do We have an Unwritten Constitution?" 63 *So. Cal. L.Rev.* 107 (1989).

Murphy, Walter F. "The Nature of the American Constitution: The James Lecture," (Urbana: Department of Political Science, University of Illinois, 1989).

————. "The Right to Privacy and Legitimate Constitutional Change," in Shlomo Slonim, ed., *The Constitutional Bases of Political and Social Change in the United States* (New York: Praeger, 1990).

————. "Constitutions, Constitutionalism, and Democracy," in Douglas Greenberg, Stanley N. Katz, Melanie Beth Oliviero, and Steven C. Wheatley, eds., *Constitutionalism and Democracy* (New York: Oxford University Press, 1993).

Perry, Michael J. "The Authority of Text, Tradition, and Reason: A Theory of Constitutional 'Interpretation,' " 58 *So. Cal.L. Rev.* 551 (1985).

Powell, H. Jefferson. "Parchment Matters: A Meditation on the Constitution as Text," 71 *Iowa L.Rev.* 1427 (1986).

————. *The Moral Tradition of American Constitutionalism: A Theological Interpretation* (Durham: Duke University Press, 1993).

Schauer, Frederick. "An Essay on Constitutional Language," 29 *UCLA L.Rev.* 797 (1982).

Story, Joseph. *Commentaries on the Constitution of the United States* (Boston: Hilliard, Grey & Co., 1833) Book III, ch. 3.

Sunstein, Cass R. *The Partial Constitution* (Cambridge: Harvard University Press, 1993).

Tiedeman, Christopher G. *The Unwritten Constitution of the United States* (New York: Putnam's Sons, 1890).

Tribe, Laurence H. *Constitutional Choices* (Cambridge: Harvard University Press, 1985), ch. 2.

Tushnet, Mark V. "A Note on the Revival of Textualism in Constitutional Theory," 58 *So.Cal.L.Rev.* 683 (1985).

"There are certain vital principles in our free republican governments which will determine and overrule an apparent and flagrant abuse of legislative power. . . . "— Justice CHASE

"If . . . the legislature of the Union, or the legislature of any member of the Union, shall pass a law, within the general scope of their constitutional power, the court cannot pronounce it void, merely because it is, in their

judgment, contrary to the principles of natural justice."—Justice IREDELL

CALDER v. BULL

3 U.S. (Dall.) 386, 1 L.Ed. 648 (1798).

Connecticut's legislature passed a law setting aside a decree of a probate court disapproving and refusing to record a will. The statute granted a new hearing, after which the probate court approved and recorded the will. Calder, who would have inherited the property had the probate court disapproved the will, contended that the statute granting a new hearing was an ex post facto law, prohibited by Article I, § 10 of the constitutional document. The state superior court rejected the argument, as did the Connecticut Supreme Court of Errors. Calder obtained a writ of error from the U.S. Supreme Court.

CHASE, Justice. . . .

It appears to me a self-evident proposition, that the several state legislatures retain all the powers of legislation, delegated to them by the state constitutions; which are not expressly taken away by the constitution of the United States. . . . All the powers delegated by the people of the United States to the federal government are defined, and NO CONSTRUCTIVE powers can be exercised by it, and all the powers that remain in the state governments are indefinite. . . . The sole inquiry is, whether this resolution or law of Connecticut . . . is an ex post facto law, within the prohibition of the federal constitution?

. . . I cannot subscribe to the omnipotence of a state legislature, or that it is absolute and without controul; although its authority should not be expressly restrained by the constitution, or fundamental law of the state. The people of the United States erected their constitutions or forms of government, to establish justice, to promote the general welfare, to secure the blessings of liberty, and to protect their persons and property from violence. The purposes for which men enter into society will determine the nature and terms of the social compact; and as they are the foundation of the legislative power, they will decide what are the proper objects of it. This fundamental principle flows from the very nature of our free republican governments, that no man should be compelled to do what the laws do not require, nor to refrain from acts which the laws permit. There are acts which the federal or state legislatures cannot do, without exceeding their authority. There are certain vital principles in our free republican governments which will determine and overrule an apparent and flagrant abuse of legislative power; as to authorize manifest injustice by positive law; or to take away that security for personal liberty, or private property, for the protection whereof government was established. An act of the legislature (for I cannot call it a law), contrary to the great first principles of the social compact, cannot be considered a rightful exercise of legislative authority. The obligation of a law in governments established on express compact, and on republican principles, must be determined by the nature of the power on which it is founded.

A few instances will suffice to explain what I mean. A law that punished a citizen for an innocent action, or, in other words, for an act which, when done, was in violation of no existing law; a law that destroys, or impairs, the lawful private contracts of citizens; a law that makes a man a judge in his own cause; or a law that takes property from A, and gives it to B. It is against all reason and justice for a people to intrust a legislature with such powers; and, therefore, it cannot be presumed that they have done it. The genius, the nature, and the spirit of our state governments amount to a prohibition of such acts of legislation; and the general principles of law and reason forbid them. The legislature may enjoin, permit, forbid and punish; they may declare new crimes, and establish rules of conduct for all its citizens in future cases; they may command what is right, and prohibit what is wrong; but they cannot change innocence into guilt, or punish innocence as a crime; or violate the right of an antecedent lawful private contract; or the right of private property. To maintain that our federal or state legislature possesses such powers, if they had not been expressly restrained, would, in my opinion, be a political heresy altogether inadmissible in our free republican governments. ...

The Constitution of the United States ... lays several restrictions on the legislatures of the several states; and among them, "that no state shall pass any *ex post facto* law." ...

I will state what laws I consider *ex post facto* laws, within the words and the intent of the prohibition. 1st. Every law that makes an action done before the passing of the law, and which was innocent when done, criminal; and punishes such action. 2d. Every law that aggravates a crime, or makes it greater than it was, when committed. 3d. Every law that changes the punishment, and inflicts a greater punishment, than the law annexed to the crime, when committed. 4th. Every law that alters the legal rules of evidence, and receives less, or different testimony, than the law required at the time of the commission of the offense, in order to convict the offender. All these, and similar laws, are manifestly unjust and oppressive. In my opinion, the true distinction is between *ex post facto* laws, and retrospective laws. Every *ex post facto* law must necessarily be retrospective; but every retrospective law is not an *ex post facto* law; the former only are prohibited. Every law that takes away or impairs rights vested, agreeably to existing laws, is retrospective, and is generally unjust, and may be oppressive. ... But I do not consider any law *ex post facto*, within the prohibition, that mollifies the rigor of the criminal law; but only those that create or aggravate the crime; or increase the punishment, or change the rules of evidence, for the purpose of conviction. ... There is a great and apparent difference between making an unlawful act lawful; and the making an innocent action criminal, and punishing it as a crime. The expressions "*ex post facto* laws" are technical, they had been in use long before the revolution, and had acquired an appropriate meaning by legislators, lawyers and authors. The celebrated and judicious Sir William Blackstone, in his *Commentaries,* considers an *ex post facto* law precisely in the same light I have done. His opinion is confirmed by his successor, Mr. Wooddeson; and by the author of *The Federalist,* who I esteem superior to both, for his extensive and accurate knowledge of the true principles of government. ....

... The restraint against making any *ex post facto* laws was not considered, by the framers of the constitution, as extending to prohibit the depriving a citizen even of a vested right to property; or the provision, "that private property should not be taken for public use, without just compensation," was unnecessary. ...

It seems to me, that the *right* of property, in its origin, could only arise from *compact express,* or *implied,* and I think it the better opinion, that the *right,* as well as the *mode,* or *manner,* of acquiring property, and of alienating or transferring, inheriting, or transmitting it, is conferred by society ... and is always subject to the rules prescribed by *positive* law. ...

I am of opinion that the decree of the supreme court of errors of Connecticut be affirmed, with costs.

PATERSON, Justice. ...

IREDELL, Justice. ...

If ... a government composed of legislative, executive and judicial departments, were established by a constitution which imposed no limits on the legislative power, the consequence would inevitably be, that whatever the legislative power chose to enact, would be lawfully enacted, and the judicial power could never interpose to pronounce it void. It is true, that some speculative jurists have held, that a legislative act against natural justice must, in itself, be void; but I cannot think that, under such a government any court of justice would possess a power to declare it so. Sir William Blackstone, having put the strong case of an act of parliament, which authorizes a man to try his own cause, explicitly adds, that even in that case, "there is no court that has power to defeat the intent of the legislature, when couched in such evident and express words, as leave no doubt whether it was the intent of the legislature or no." 1 *Bl.Com.* 91.

In order, therefore, to guard against so great an evil, it has been the policy of all the American states, which have, individually, framed their state constitutions, since the revolution, and of the people of the United States, when they framed the federal constitution, to define with precision the objects of legislative power, and to restrain its exercise within marked and settled boundaries. If any act of congress, or of the legislature of a state, violates those constitutional provisions, it is unquestionably void; though, I admit, that as the authority to declare it void is of a delicate and awful nature, the court will never resort to that authority, but in a clear and urgent case. If, on the other hand, the legislature of the Union, or the legislature of any member of the Union, shall pass a law within the general scope of their constitutional power, the court cannot pronounce it to be void, merely because it is, in their judgment, contrary to the principles of natural justice. The ideas of natural justice are regulated by no fixed standard; the ablest and purest men have differed upon the subject; and all that the court could properly say, in such an event, would be that the legislature (possessed of an equal right of opinion) had passed an act which, in the opinion of the judges, was inconsistent with the abstract principles of natural justice. There are then but two lights, in which the subject can be viewed: 1st. If the legislature pursue the authority delegated to them, their acts are valid. 2d. If they transgress the boundaries of that authority, their acts are invalid. In the former case, they exercise the discretion vested in them by the people, to whom alone they are responsible for the faithful discharge of their trust: but in the latter case, they violate a fundamental law, which must be our guide, whenever we are called upon as judges, to determine the validity of a legislative act.

Still, however, in the present instance, the act or resolution of the legislature of Connecticut, cannot be regarded as an *ex post facto* law; for the true construction of the prohibition extends to criminal, not to civil issues. ...

... It is not sufficient to urge, that the power may be abused, for such is the nature of all power—such is the tendency of every human institution. ... We must be content to limit power, where we can, and where we cannot, consistently with its use, we must be content to repose a salutary confidence. It is our consolation, that there never existed a government, in ancient or modern times, more free from danger in this respect, than the governments of America. ...

CUSHING, Justice. The case appears to me to be clear of difficulty, taken either way. If the act is a judicial act, it is not touched by the Federal Constitution; and, if it is a legislative act, it is maintained and justified by the ancient and uniform practice of the state of Connecticut.

JUDGMENT *affirmed.*

Editors' Notes

(1) The definition of an *ex post facto* law is not the central point of this case for constitutional interpretation, but it is still important, for Chase's definition remains good law to this day. Where does he find that definition?

(2) For the purposes of this Chapter, the critical issues concern what "the Constitution" encompasses. To what extent does Chase contend that "the Constitution" includes a political theory? Does Iredell deny such a claim?

(3) Iredell attacks the notion that federal judges can apply standards of natural justice or law to constitutional interpretation. Does Chase claim that

judges can use such criteria? What precisely is the political theory that Chase uses here?

(4) Until the early years of John Marshall's tenure as chief justice (1801–1835), each member of the Court usually wrote his own opinion or joined in one of the several opinions filed by colleagues. In 1798 there were six justices. Apparently two, Chief Justice Oliver Ellsworth and Justice James Wilson, did not participate in this case.

(5) In 1804 the House of Representatives impeached Samuel Chase for abusing his powers as a trial judge (until near the end of the nineteenth century, Supreme Court justices "rode circuit" and sat as trial as well as appellate judges) to launch partisan attacks against Jeffersonians. In 1805, the Senate failed to convict by the required two-thirds. There was little doubt of Chase's guilt, however. He was saved by a combination of sympathy for an old man who had signed the Declaration of Independence, antipathy toward the arrogant John Randolph of Roanoke, who managed the case for the House, and, of course, by partisan Federalists. Chase remains the only justice of the Supreme Court ever to be impeached, though threats have been frequent.

"There are manifold restraints to which every person is necessarily subject for the common good."

JACOBSON v. MASSACHUSETTS

197 U.S. 11, 25 S.Ct. 358, 49 L.Ed. 643 (1905).

The Massachusetts legislature authorized localities to require vaccinations when they thought it necessary for public health. After an increase in smallpox, Cambridge in 1902 ordered all residents to be vaccinated. Jacobson refused and was prosecuted. At the trial he attacked the law's constitutionality and tried unsuccessfully to introduce evidence that such vaccinations often had injurious and sometimes fatal side effects and that both he and one of his sons had earlier become seriously ill after being vaccinated. The trial court found him guilty, a decision that state appellate courts affirmed. Jacobson then appealed to the U.S. Supreme Court.

Mr. Justice **HARLAN*** delivered the opinion of the Court.

We pass without extended discussion the suggestion that the particular section of the statute of Massachusetts . . . is in derogation of rights secured by the Preamble of the Constitution of the United States. Although that Preamble indicates the general purposes for which the people ordained and established the Constitution, it has never been regarded as the source of any substantive power conferred on the Government of the United States or on any of its Departments. . . .

We also pass without discussion the suggestion that the above section of the statute is opposed to the spirit of the Constitution.

---

* John Marshall Harlan (1833–1911), the grandfather of Justice John Marshall Harlan [II] (1899–1971)—**Eds.**

Undoubtedly, as observed by Chief Justice Marshall, speaking for the court in Sturges v. Crowninshield, [1819] "the spirit of an instrument, especially of a constitution, is to be respected not less than its letter, yet the spirit is to be collected chiefly from its words." We have no need in this case to go beyond the plain, obvious meaning of the words in those provisions of the Constitution which, it is contended, must control our decision. ...

The authority of the State to enact this statute is to be referred to what is commonly called the police power—a power which the State did not surrender when becoming a member of the Union under the Constitution. ... According to settled principles the police power of a State must be held to embrace, at least, such reasonable regulations established directly by legislative enactment as will protect the public health and the public safety. ...

... The defendant insists that his liberty is invaded when the State subjects him to fine or imprisonment for neglecting or refusing to submit to vaccination; that a compulsory vaccination law is unreasonable, arbitrary, and oppressive, and, therefore, hostile to the inherent right of every freeman to care for his own body and health in such way as to him seems best; and that the execution of such a law against one who objects to vaccination, no matter for what reason, is nothing short of an assault upon his person. But the liberty secured by the Constitution ... does not import an absolute right in each person to be, at all times and in all circumstances, wholly freed from restraint. There are manifold restraints to which every person is necessarily subject for the common good. On any other basis organized society could not exist with safety to its members. Society based on the rule that each one is a law unto himself would soon be confronted with disorder and anarchy. ... This court has more than once recognized it as a fundamental principle that "persons and property are subjected to all kinds of restraints and burdens in order to secure the general comfort, health, and prosperity of the State. ..." In Crowley v. Christensen [1890] we said: "The possession and enjoyment of all rights are subject to such reasonable conditions as may be deemed by the governing authority of the country, essential to the safety, health, peace, good order and morals of the community. Even liberty itself, the greatest of all rights, is not unrestricted license to act according to one's own will. It is only freedom from restraint under conditions essential to the equal enjoyment of the same right by others. It is then liberty regulated by law." ...

... Upon the principle of self-defense, of paramount necessity, a community has the right to protect itself against an epidemic of disease which threatens the safety of its members. ... Smallpox being prevalent and increasing at Cambridge, the court would usurp the functions of another branch of government if it adjudged, as matter of law, that the mode adopted under the sanction of the State, to protect the people at large, was arbitrary and not justified by the necessities of the case. We say necessities of the case, because it might be that an acknowledged power of a local community to protect itself against an epidemic threatening the safety of all, might be exercised in particular circumstances and in reference to particular persons in such an arbitrary, unreasonable manner, or might go so far beyond what was reasonably required for the safety of the public, as to authorize or compel the courts to interfere for the protection of such persons. ... There is, of course, a sphere within which the individual may assert the supremacy of his own will and rightfully dispute the authority of any human government, especially of any free government existing under a written constitution, to interfere with the exercise of that will. But it is equally true that in every well-ordered society ... the rights of the individual in respect of his liberty may at times, under the pressure of great dangers, be subjected to such restraint, to be enforced by reasonable regulations, as the safety of the general public may demand. ... The liberty secured by the Fourteenth Amendment, this court has said, consists, in part, in the right of a person "to live and work where he will," Allgeyer v. Louisiana [1897] and yet he may be compelled, by force if need be, against his will and without regard to his personal wishes or his pecuniary interests, or even his religious or political convictions, to take his place in the ranks of the army of his country and risk the chance of being shot down in its defense. ...

[The Court then discussed Jacobson's effort to present medical evidence attacking the effectiveness of vaccination in preventing smallpox.]

... We must assume that when the statute in question was passed, the legislature of Massachusetts was not unaware of these opposing theories, and was compelled ... to choose between them. ... It is no part of the function of a court or a jury to determine which one of two modes was likely to be the most effective for the protection of the public against disease. That was for the legislative department to determine in the light of all the information it had or could obtain. ... If there is any such power in the judiciary to review legislative action in respect of a matter affecting the general welfare, it can only be when that which the legislature has done comes within the rule that if a statute purporting to have been enacted to protect the public health, the public morals or the public safety, has no real or substantial relation to those objects, or is, beyond all question, a plain, palpable invasion of rights secured by the fundamental law, it is the duty of the courts to so adjudge, and thereby give effect to the Constitution. ...

... While this court should guard with firmness every right appertaining to life, liberty or property as secured to the individual by the Supreme Law of the Land, it is of the last importance that it should not invade the domain of local authority except when it is plainly necessary to do so in order to enforce that law. ...

The judgment of the court below must be affirmed. ...

Mr. Justice **BREWER** and Mr. Justice **PECKHAM** dissent.

Editors' Notes

(1) Note how smoothly Harlan dismissed the Preamble to the constitutional text. To what extent did that dismissal thereby eliminate that paragraph from "the Constitution" the Court interprets? It is worth remembering that judges rarely refer to the Preamble—an interesting phenomenon given that the Preamble announces the political system's purposes and judges often claim that any textual interpretation must take into account the document's purposes.

(2) Note also the equal smoothness with which Harlan dismissed "the spirit of the Constitution," to which the Court under Chief Justice Marshall had several times alluded.

(3) Apply Harlan's mode of reasoning about the Preamble to other clauses, the First Amendment, for example. Does that part of the text confer any power on federal courts? Would it follow, then, that courts could not invalidate an effort to establish a national church? If not, why not? How does determining the meaning of such phrases in the Preamble as "the blessings of liberty" differ from determining the scope of the "liberty" the Fifth and Fourteenth amendments purport to protect?

(4) Regarding the substantive issue in dispute: Would Harlan's logic sustain the constitutionality of compulsory tests for AIDS?

(5) By the mid–1970s most U.S. public health officials believed that smallpox had become so rare that the danger of an adverse reaction to the vaccination—something the Court in *Jacobson* weighed lightly—was many times greater than that of contracting the disease. As a result, it has become difficult in the United States to be vaccinated against smallpox.

"If the Fourteenth Amendment has absorbed them [portions of the Bill of Rights], the process of absorption has had its source in the belief that neither liberty nor justice would exist if they were sacrificed."

PALKO v. CONNECTICUT
302 U.S. 319, 58 S.Ct. 149, 82 L.Ed. 288 (1937).

For several generations, a majority of the Supreme Court held that the Fourteenth Amendment did not make the Bill of Rights binding on the states. Hurtado v. California (1884) ruled that the Fifth Amendment's requirement of indictment by grand jury did not apply to the states; In re Kemmler (1890) held that a state's use of electrocution as a method of execution was not a "cruel and unusual" punishment, thus implying that the Eighth Amendment applied to the states; Maxwell v. Dow (1900) reaffirmed *Hurtado*; and Twining v. New Jersey (1908) said the Fourteenth Amendment did not extend to the states the Fifth's ban against compulsory self-incrimination.

On the other hand, after 1890 the Court not only extended the Fourteenth Amendment's protection of property but also held that protection included the

Fifth Amendment's prohibition against government's taking private property without "just compensation." Chicago, Burlington & Quincy R.R. v. Chicago (1897). In addition, a series of cases decided that "liberty of contract" was included under the general term "liberty" in the due process clause. See espec. Lochner v. New York (1905; reprinted below, p. 1110). Then, without further warning, in 1925 Gitlow v. New York held that the First Amendment's protection of freedom of speech restricted the states. This ruling was followed by others that included in the Fourteenth Amendment freedom of the press, Near v. Minnesota (1931); under certain circumstances, the Sixth Amendment's guarantee of the right to counsel, Powell v. Alabama (1932); and, the Sixth Amendment's requirement of a trial by "an impartial jury," at least where a state chose to use juries, Norris v. Alabama (1935).

By the mid–1930s the whole question of which of the Bill of Rights were included in the Fourteenth was thoroughly confused. Palko v. Connecticut presented the Court with an opportunity to clarify the situation. A state statute allowed a prosecutor in a criminal case to appeal rulings of law and so seek to retry a defendant who had been acquitted under a mistaken interpretation of the law. Palko was tried for first degree murder, but the jury returned a verdict of guilty only of second degree murder. The prosecutor appealed, and the state supreme court ordered a new trial, holding that the trial judge had erred in excluding certain testimony as well in instructing the jury. At the second trial, the jury found Palko guilty of murder in the first degree, and he was sentenced to death. He lost in the state appellate courts and appealed to the U.S. Supreme Court.

Mr. Justice **CARDOZO** delivered the opinion of the Court. . . .

1. The execution of the sentence will not deprive appellant of his life without the process of law assured to him by the Fourteenth Amendment of the Federal Constitution.

The argument for appellant is that whatever is forbidden by the Fifth Amendment is forbidden by the Fourteenth also. The Fifth Amendment, which is not directed to the states, but solely to the federal government, creates immunity from double jeopardy. No person shall be "subject for the same offense to be twice put in jeopardy of life or limb." The Fourteenth Amendment ordains, "nor shall any State deprive any person of life, liberty, or property, without due process of law." To retry a defendant, though under one indictment and only one, subjects him, it is said, to double jeopardy in violation of the Fifth Amendment, if the prosecution is one on behalf of the United States. From this the consequence is said to follow that there is a denial of life or liberty without due process of law, if the prosecution is one on behalf of the People of a State. . . .

. . . Is double jeopardy in such circumstances [as those of this case], if double jeopardy it must be called, a denial of due process forbidden to the states? The tyranny of labels, Snyder v. Massachusetts [1934], must not lead us to leap to a conclusion that a word which in one set of facts may stand for oppression or enormity is of like effect in every other.

. . . [I]n appellant's view the Fourteenth Amendment is to be taken as embodying the prohibitions of the Fifth. His thesis is even broader. Whatever would be a violation of the original bill of rights (Amendments I to VIII)* if done by the federal government is now equally unlawful by force of the Fourteenth Amendment if done by a state. There is no such general rule.

The Fifth Amendment provides, among other things, that no person shall be held to answer for a capital or otherwise infamous crime unless on presentment or indictment of a grand jury. This court has held that, in prosecutions by a state, presentment or indictment by a grand jury may give way to informations at the instance of a public officer. Hurtado v. California [1884]. The Fifth Amendment provides also that no person shall be compelled in any criminal case to be a witness against himself. This court has said that, in prosecutions by a state, the exemption will fail if the state elects to end it. Twining v. New Jersey [1908]. The Sixth Amendment calls for a jury trial in criminal cases and the Seventh for a jury trial in civil cases at common law where the value in controversy shall exceed twenty dollars. This court has ruled that consistently with those amendments trial by jury may be modified by a state or abolished altogether.

On the other hand, the due process clause of the Fourteenth Amendment may make it unlawful for a state to abridge by its statutes the freedom of speech which the First Amendment safeguards against encroachment by the Congress, De Jonge v. Oregon [1937]; Herndon v. Lowry [1937]; or the like freedom of the press, Grosjean v. American Press Co. [1936]; Near v. Minnesota [1931]; or the free exercise of religion, Pierce v. Society of Sisters [1925]; or the right of peaceable assembly, without which speech would be unduly trammeled, De Jonge; Herndon; or the right of one accused of crime to the benefit of counsel, Powell v. Alabama [1932]. In these and other situations immunities that are valid as against the federal government by force of the specific pledges of particular amendments have been found to be implicit in the concept of ordered liberty, and thus, through the Fourteenth Amendment, become valid as against the states.

The line of division may seem to be wavering and broken if there is a hasty catalogue of the cases on the one side and the other. Reflection and analysis will induce a different view. There emerges the perception of a rationalizing principle which gives to discrete instances a proper order and coherence. The right to trial by jury and the immunity from prosecution except as the result of an indictment may have value and importance. Even so, they are not of the very essence of a scheme of ordered liberty. To abolish them is not to violate a "principle of justice so rooted in the traditions and conscience of our people as to be ranked as fundamental." Snyder. Few would be so narrow or provincial as to

---

* **Eds.' Query:** Why only amendments 1–8? Why not the Ninth Amendment as well? Or even the Ninth and the Tenth? The Tenth relates only in part to powers reserved to the states; it also speaks of powers reserved "to the people."

maintain that a fair and enlightened system of justice would be impossible without them. What is true of jury trials and indictments is true also, as the cases show, of the immunity from compulsory self-incrimination. This too might be lost, and justice still be done. Indeed, today as in the past there are students of our penal system who look upon the immunity as a mischief rather than a benefit, and who would limit its scope, or destroy it altogether. ... No doubt there would remain the need to give protection against torture, physical or mental. ... Justice, however, would not perish if the accused were subject to a duty to respond to orderly inquiry. The exclusion of these immunities and privileges from the privileges and immunities protected against the action of the states has not been arbitrary or casual. It has been dictated by a study and appreciation of the meaning, the essential implications, of liberty itself.

We reach a different plane of social and moral values when we pass to the privileges and immunities that have been taken over from the earlier articles of the federal bill of rights and brought within the Fourteenth Amendment by a process of absorption. ... If the Fourteenth Amendment has absorbed them, the process of absorption has had its source in the belief that neither liberty nor justice would exist if they were sacrificed. *Twining*. This is true, for illustration, of freedom of thought, and speech. Of that freedom one may say that it is the matrix, the indispensable condition, of nearly every other form of freedom. With rare aberrations a pervasive recognition of that truth can be traced in our history, political and legal. So it has come about that the domain of liberty, withdrawn by the Fourteenth Amendment from encroachment by the states, has been enlarged by latter-day judgments to include liberty of the mind as well as liberty of action. The extension became, indeed, a logical imperative when once it was recognized, as long ago it was, that liberty is something more than exemption from physical restraint, and that even in the field of substantive rights and duties the legislative judgment, if oppressive and arbitrary, may be overridden by the courts. Fundamental too in the concept of due process, and so in that of liberty, is the thought that condemnation shall be rendered only after trial. The hearing, moreover, must be a real one, not a sham or a pretense. For that reason, ignorant defendants in a capital case were held to have been condemned unlawfully when in truth, though not in form, they were refused the aid of counsel. *Powell*. The decision did not turn upon the fact that the benefit of counsel would have been guaranteed to the defendants by the provisions of the Sixth Amendment if they had been prosecuted in a federal court. The decision turned upon the fact that in the particular situation laid before us in the evidence the benefit of counsel was essential to the substance of a hearing.

Our survey of the cases serves, we think, to justify the statement that the dividing line between them, if not unfaltering throughout its course, has been true for the most part to a unifying principle. On which side of the line the case made out by the appellant has appropriate location must be the next inquiry and the final one. Is that kind of double jeopardy to which the statute has subjected him a hardship so acute and shocking that our polity will not endure it? Does it violate those "fundamental principles of liberty and justice which lie at the base of all our civil and political institutions"? Hebert v. Louisiana [1926]. The answer surely must be "no." What the answer would have to be if the state were permitted after a trial free from error to try the accused over again or to bring another case against him, we have no occasion to consider. We deal with the statute before us and no other. The state is not attempting to wear the accused out by a multitude of cases with accumulated trials. It asks no more than this, that the case against him shall go on until there shall be a trial free from the corrosion of substantial legal error. This is not cruelty at all, nor even vexation in any immoderate degree. If the trial had been infected with error adverse to the accused, there might have been review at his instance, and as often as necessary to purge the vicious taint. A reciprocal privilege, subject at all times to the discretion of the presiding judge[,] ... has now been granted to the state. There is here no seismic innovation. The edifice of justice stands, its symmetry, to many, greater than before.

2. The conviction of appellant is not in derogation of any privileges or immunities that belong to him as a citizen of the United States. ...

The judgment is *affirmed.*

Mr. Justice **BUTLER** dissents.

Editors' Notes

(1) **Query:** To what extent were Cardozo and the justices who joined him and went before him adding to the constitutional document in explaining the meaning of "due process of law"? Or were the justices not adding but merely explaining? More specifically, Cardozo, quoting himself speaking for the Court in Snyder v. Massachusetts (1934), referred to a "principle of justice so rooted in the traditions and conscience of our people as to be ranked as fundamental" as the proper gauge to determine if the Fourteenth Amendment included a particular right. What did he mean by "tradition" in this context? How does an interpreter discover it? What about the "conscience of our people"? For efforts to answer the question about tradition, see the various opinions in Michael H. v. Gerald D. (1989; reprinted below, p. 158), and Lee v. Weisman (1992; reprinted below, p. 167).

(2) **Query:** To what extent did Cardozo read a version of democratic theory into the text when he wrote that "freedom of thought and speech" formed "the matrix, the indispensable condition, of nearly every form of freedom"? Did he also thereby import into the text a theory of constitutionalism, as we defined that term in Chapter 3? If he did not import either, where, in the constitutional document, did he find the standard(s) to determine what rights are "fundamental"?

(3) **Query:** Look back at the opinions in Calder v. Bull (1798; reprinted above, p. 121): What would Justice Chase have said about Cardozo's reasoning? Justice Iredell?

Editors' Note
"INCORPORATION" OF THE BILL OF RIGHTS

The plain words of the Fourteenth Amendment indicate that, if any of its clauses "incorporates" some or all of the Bill of Rights so as to make them applicable against the states, it is the so-called "privileges or immunities clause": "No State shall make or enforce any law which shall abridge the privileges or immunities of citizens of the United States. . . ." The amendment's legislative history, though complex and confused, gives far stronger support to such a claim for this clause than for the so-called "due process clause," which forbids states to "deprive any person of life, liberty, or property without due process of law. . . ."

But in The Slaughter–House Cases (1873; reprinted below, p. 550), the very first judicial interpretation of the amendment, the Supreme Court gutted the privileges or immunities clause. Thus, to make any part of the Bill of Rights applicable to the states, the Court either had to overrule much of *Slaughter-House*, find another clause to bear the burden, or look beyond the constitutional document for justification. Despite occasional protests, the justices have opted to use the due process clause as the instrument of incorporation.

The opinion for the Court in *Slaughter-House*, as did the debate in Congress on the Fourteenth Amendment, utilized an opinion by Justice Bushrod Washington, while sitting as a circuit judge, in Corfield v. Coryell (1823), in which he discussed the meaning of the very similar clause in Article IV. Crandall v. Nevada (1868; reprinted below p. 543), *Slaughter-House*, and Twining v. New Jersey (1908) listed as among the privileges and immunities of citizens of the United States rights to: travel interstate, petition Congress, vote for national officials, enter public lands, inform federal officials of crimes, and be protected against violence when in federal custody. During the great battle between the Court and the New Deal, Colgate v. Harvey (1935) tried to resurrect privileges and immunities for use as a defense against governmental regulation of business, but the attempt was short-lived. Only five years later Madden v. Kentucky (1940) overruled *Colgate*.

The Court has now held that the due process clause of the Fourteenth Amendment incorporates most of the Bill of Rights:

1) First Amendment: Free speech—Gitlow v. New York (1925); freedom of the press—Near v. Minnesota (1931); free exercise of religion—Hamilton v. Regents (1934), Cantwell v. Connecticut (1940); ban against establishment of religion—Everson v. Ewing Township (1947); freedom of assembly—De Jonge v. Oregon (1937); right to petition government for redress of grievances—NAACP v. Button (1963).

2) Fourth Amendment: General protection of a right to privacy: Griswold v. Connecticut (1965; reprinted below, p. 147); protection against "unreasonable searches and seizures"—Wolf v. Colorado (1949); exclusion of unconstitutionally seized evidence—Mapp v. Ohio (1961); exclusion of illegally seized

evidence—Berger v. New York (1967), Terry v. Ohio (1968); requirement of probable cause to arrest a suspect—Terry v. Ohio (1968).

3) Fifth Amendment: Protection against taking private property without "just compensation"—Chicago, Burlington & Quincy R.R. v. Chicago (1897); protection against self-incrimination—Malloy v. Hogan (1964), overruling Twining v. New Jersey (1908) and Adamson v. California (1947); protection against double jeopardy—Benton v. Maryland (1969), overruling the specific holding of Palko v. Connecticut (1937), but not Palko's general approach to the problem of incorporation.

4) Sixth Amendment: Gideon v. Wainwright (1963), Miranda v. Arizona (1966), and Argersinger v. Hamlin (1972); trial by jury for serious offenses—Duncan v. Louisiana (1968); right to a speedy trial—Klopfer v. North Carolina (1967); right to be informed of the nature of the charge—Connally v. General Construction Co. (1926), Lanzetta v. New Jersey (1939), and Winters v. New York (1948) (Actually the Court has often decided such cases on the basis of the "void for vagueness rule," that is, to be valid a criminal statute must be sufficiently clear and specific to give fair warning of what it outlaws.); right to confront and cross examine witnesses—Pointer v. Texas (1965); right to compulsory processes (subpoenas) to require attendance of witnesses at a criminal trial—Washington v. Texas (1967).

5) Eighth Amendment: Protection against "cruel and unusual" punishment—Louisiana ex rel. Francis v. Resweber (1947) and Robinson v. California (1962). (See also our comment in the headnote to Palko about In re Kemmler [1890].)

6) Ninth Amendment: Protection of unlisted fundamental rights—Griswold v. Connecticut (1965) and Roe v. Wade (1973; reprinted below, p. 1258.

Not included have been the Fifth Amendment's right to indictment by grand jury and the Seventh's right to a jury trial in civil cases where the amount in controversy exceeds $20. There has been no specific ruling on the Third Amendment's protection against quartering of troops in civilian homes in time of peace, but Griswold, a case involving state action, cited this guarantee as part of the general right to privacy. So, too, the Court has not specifically held that the Eighth Amendment's ban against excessive bail binds the states, but the logic of recent criminal justice decisions indicates that the Court would so rule. The Second Amendment's guarantee of "the right of the people to keep and bear Arms" is preceded by the words: "A well regulated militia, being necessary to the security of a free State"; and to date the Court has treated this right as that of a state to maintain a militia, not of individual citizens to own or carry weapons. See United States v. Cruikshank (1875); United States v. Miller (1939); Lewis v. United States (1980); and the discussion in C. Herman Pritchett, Constitutional Civil Liberties (Englewood Cliffs, NJ: Prentice–Hall, 1984), p. 3n; and Laurence H. Tribe, American Constitutional Law (2d. ed.; Mineola, NY: Foundation, 1988), p. 299n. For questioning of this interpretation, see Paul Brest and Sanford V. Levinson, Processes of Constitutional Decisionmaking (3rd ed.; Boston: Little, Brown, 1992), pp. 550–54. For arguments against the prevailing interpretation, see Nelson Lund, "The Second Amendment, Political Liberty, and the Right to Self–Preservation," 39 Ala.L.Rev. 103 (1987); and Levinson, "The Embarrassing Second Amendment," 99 Yale L.J. 637 (1989).

There have been at least four approaches to the general problem of the Bill of Rights and the due process clause of the Fourteenth Amendment: (1) Due process incorporates all of the Bill of Rights, at least all of the first eight (though why not the Ninth and Tenth as well?)—Hugo Black; (2) Due process incorporates all of the Bill of Rights plus some other "fundamental" rights not listed there—Frank Murphy and Wiley Rutledge, dissenting in Adamson v. California (1947); William O. Douglas, dissenting in Poe v. Ullman (1961) and speaking for the Court in Griswold v. Connecticut (1965); (3) Due process "selectively" incorporates only those parts of the Bill of Rights that are "of the very essence of a scheme of ordered liberty"—Cardozo in *Palko* and, generally, the Court since; (4) Due process includes none of the Bill of Rights, and so the states are pretty much free from the *particular* restraints of the Bill of Rights—a view, not altogether unfairly, Black attributed to the Court in Hurtado v. California (1884) and Twining v. New Jersey (1908).

John Marshall Harlan, II, offered a variation on the fourth theme: The Fourteenth Amendment "incorporates" none of the Bill of Rights; rather, "due process" includes restrictions very much like those contained in some of the clauses of the Bill of Rights. Thus it is "due process" the Court must interpret, not the Bill of Rights. See his dissent in Poe v. Ullman (1961; reprinted below, p. 141) and his concurring opinion in Griswold v. Connecticut (1965; reprinted below, p. 147). See also Sanford Kadish, "Methodology and Criteria in Due Process Analysis—A Survey and Criticism," 66 *Yale L.J.* 319 (1957):

> The consequence of requiring due process to be measured precisely by the provisions of the Bill of Rights is not to eliminate broad judicial inquiry, but rather to change its focus from due process to freedom of speech or freedom from double jeopardy and the rest, and to disguise its essential character.

———

"The vague contours of the Due Process Clause do not leave judges at large. ... [Its] limits are derived from considerations that are fused in the whole nature of our judicial process ... considerations deeply rooted in reason and in the compelling traditions of the legal profession."—Justice FRANKFURTER

"I long ago concluded that the accordion-like qualities of this philosophy must inevitably imperil all the individual liberty safeguards enumerated in the Bill of Rights."—Justice BLACK

ROCHIN v. CALIFORNIA

342 U.S. 165, 72 S.Ct. 205, 96 L.Ed. 183 (1952).

Suspecting Antonio Rochin of dealing in narcotics, Los Angeles police forcibly entered his room. Before they could seize the two capsules they spotted, Rochin swallowed them. After failing to extract this evidence from Rochin's mouth, the officers took him to a hospital and, against Rochin's will, directed a physician to pump the suspect's stomach. The vomited matter contained the remains of the capsules, which the state used to convict Rochin of possessing morphine. The California supreme court refused review, and the U.S. Supreme Court granted certiorari.

Mr. Justice **FRANKFURTER** delivered the opinion of the Court. ...

In our federal system the administration of criminal justice is predominantly committed to the care of the States. ... Accordingly, in reviewing a State criminal conviction under a claim of right guaranteed by the Due Process Clause of the Fourteenth Amendment[,] ... "we must be deeply mindful of the responsibilities of the States for the enforcement of criminal laws, and exercise with due humility our merely negative function in subjecting convictions from state courts to the very narrow scrutiny which the Due Process Clause of the Fourteenth Amendment authorizes." Malinski v. New York [1945]. ...

However, this Court too has its responsibility. Regard for the requirements of the Due Process Clause "inescapably imposes upon this Court an exercise of judgment upon the whole course of the proceedings [resulting in a conviction] in order to ascertain whether they offend those canons of decency and fairness which express the notions of justice of English-speaking peoples. ..." *Ibid.* These standards of justice are not authoritatively formulated anywhere as though they were specifics. Due process of law is a summarized constitutional guarantee of respect for those personal immunities which, as Mr. Justice Cardozo twice wrote for the Court, are "so rooted in the traditions and conscience of our people as to be ranked as fundamental," Snyder v. Massachusetts [1934], or are "implicit in the concept of ordered liberty." Palko v. Connecticut [1937].

The Court's function in the observance of this settled conception of the Due Process Clause does not leave us without adequate guides in subjecting State criminal procedures to constitutional judgment. In dealing not with the machinery of government but with human rights, the absence of formal exactitude, or want of fixity of meaning, is not an unusual or even regrettable attribute of constitutional provisions. Words being symbols do not speak without a gloss. On the one hand the gloss may be the deposit of history, whereby a term gains technical content. ... On the other hand, the gloss of some of the verbal symbols of the Constitution does not give them a fixed technical content. It exacts a continuing process of application.

When the gloss has thus not been fixed but is a function of the process of judgment, the judgment is bound to fall differently at different times and differently at the same time through different judges. Even more specific provisions, such as the guaranty of freedom of speech and the detailed protection against unreasonable searches and seizures, have inevitably evoked as sharp divisions in this Court as the least specific and most comprehensive protection of liberties, the Due Process Clause.

The vague contours of the Due Process Clause do not leave judges at large. We may not draw on our merely personal and private notions and disregard the limits that bind judges in their judicial function. Even though the concept of due process of law is not final and fixed, these limits are derived from considerations that are fused in the whole nature of our judicial process. See Cardozo, *The Nature of the Judicial Process.* These are considerations deeply rooted in reason and in the compelling traditions of the legal profession. The Due Process Clause places upon this Court the duty of exercising a judgment, within the narrow confines of judicial power in reviewing State convictions, upon interests of society pushing in opposite directions.

Due process of law thus conceived is not to be derided as resort to a revival of "natural law." To believe that this judicial exercise of judgment could be avoided by freezing "due process of law" at some fixed stage of time or thought is to suggest that the most important aspect of constitutional adjudication is a function for inanimate machines and not for judges. ... Even cybernetics has not yet made that haughty claim. To practice the requisite detachment and to achieve sufficient objectivity no doubt demands [*sic*] of judges the habit of self-discipline and self-criticism, incertitude that one's own views are incontestable and alert tolerance toward views not shared. But these are precisely ... the qualities society has a right to expect from those entrusted with ultimate judicial power.

Restraints on our jurisdiction are self-imposed only in the sense that there is from our decisions no immediate appeal short of impeachment or constitutional amendment. But that does not make due process of law a matter of judicial caprice. The faculties of the Due Process Clause may be indefinite and vague, but the mode of their ascertainment is not self-willed. In each case "due process of law" requires an evaluation based on a disinterested inquiry pursued in the spirit of science, on a balanced order of facts exactly and fairly stated, on the detached consideration of conflicting claims, on a judgment not ad hoc and episodic but duly mindful of reconciling the needs both of continuity and of change in a progressive society.

Applying these general considerations to the circumstances of the present case, we are compelled to conclude that the proceedings by which this conviction was obtained do more than offend some fastidious squeamishness or private sentimentalism about combatting crime too energetically. This is conduct that shocks the conscience. Illegally breaking into the privacy of the petitioner, the struggle to open his mouth and remove what was there, the forcible extraction of his stomach's contents—this course of proceeding by agents of government to obtain evidence is bound to offend even hardened sensibilities. They are methods too close to the rack and the screw to permit of constitutional differentiation.

... Due process of law, as a historic and generative principle, precludes defining, and thereby confining, these standards of conduct more precisely than to say that convictions cannot be brought about by methods that offend "a sense of justice." ...

... Use of involuntary verbal confessions in State criminal trials is constitutionally obnoxious not only because of their unreliability. They are inadmissible under the Due Process Clause even though statements contained in them may be independently established as true. Coerced confessions offend the community's sense of fair play and decency. So here, to sanction the brutal conduct which naturally enough was condemned by the court whose judgment is before us, would be to afford brutality the cloak of the law. Nothing would be more calculated to discredit law and thereby to brutalize the temper of a society. ...

Reversed.

Mr. Justice **MINTON** took no part in the consideration or decision of this case.

Mr. Justice **BLACK**, concurring.

Adamson v. California [1947] sets out reasons for my belief that state as well as federal courts and law enforcement officers must obey the Fifth Amendment's command that "No person ... shall be compelled in any criminal case to be a witness against himself." I think a person is compelled to be a witness against himself not only when he is compelled to testify, but also when as here, incriminating evidence is forcibly taken from him by a contrivance of modern science. ... I believe that faithful adherence to the specific guarantees in the Bill of Rights insures a more permanent protection of individual liberty than that which can be afforded by the nebulous standards stated by the majority.

What the majority hold is that the Due Process Clause empowers this Court to nullify any state law if its application "shocks the conscience," offends "a sense of justice" or runs counter to the "decencies of civilized conduct." The majority emphasize that these statements do not refer to their own consciences or to their senses of justice and decency. For we are told that "we may not draw on our merely personal and private notions"; our judgment must be grounded on "considerations deeply rooted in reason, and in the compelling traditions of the legal profession." We are further admonished to measure the validity of state practices, not by our reason, or by the traditions of the legal profession, but by "the community's sense of fair play and decency"; by the "traditions and conscience of our people"; or by "those canons of decency and fairness which express the notions of justice of English-speaking peoples." These canons are made necessary, it is said, because of "interests of society pushing in opposite directions."

If the Due Process Clause does vest this Court with such unlimited power to invalidate laws, I am still in doubt as to why we should consider only the notions of English-speaking peoples to determine what are immutable and fundamental principles of justice. Moreover, one may well ask what avenues of investigation are open to discover "canons" of conduct so universally favored that this Court should write them into the Constitution? All we are told is that the discovery must be made by an "evaluation based on a disinterested inquiry pursued in the spirit of science on a balanced order of facts."

Some constitutional provisions are stated in absolute and unqualified language such ... as the First Amendment stating that no law shall be passed prohibiting the free exercise of religion or abridging the freedom of speech or press. Other constitutional provisions do require courts to choose between competing policies, such as the Fourth Amendment which, by its terms, necessitates a judicial decision as to what is an "unreasonable" search or seizure. There is, however, no express constitutional language granting judicial power to invalidate *every* state law of *every* kind deemed "unreasonable" or contrary to the Court's notion of civilized decencies; yet the constitutional philosophy used by the majority has, in the past, been used ... to nullify state legislative programs passed to suppress evil economic practices. ... Of even graver concern ... is the use of the philosophy to nullify the Bill of Rights. I long ago concluded that the accordion-like qualities of this philosophy must inevitably imperil all the individual liberty safeguards specifically enumerated in the Bill of Rights. ...

Mr. Justice **DOUGLAS,** concurring. ...

As an original matter it might be debatable whether the provision in the Fifth Amendment that no person "shall be compelled in any criminal case to be a witness against himself" serves the ends of justice. Not all civilized legal procedures recognize it. But the choice was made by the Framers, a choice which sets a standard for legal trials in this country. ... I think that words taken from [an accused's] lips, capsules taken from his stomach, blood taken from his veins are all inadmissible provided they are taken from him without his consent. They are inadmissible because of the command of the Fifth Amendment.

That is an unequivocal, definite and workable rule of evidence for state and federal courts. But we cannot in fairness free the state courts from that command and yet excoriate them for flouting the "decencies of civilized conduct" when they admit the evidence. That is to make the rule turn not on the Constitution but on the idiosyncrasies of the judges who sit here. ...

Editors' Notes

(1) **Query:** "Words being symbols do not speak without a gloss," Frankfurter wrote on p. 136. Does this sentence merely state the obvious or does it significantly affect an answer to the problem of WHAT "the Constitution" includes? Did Black disagree with Frankfurter about the validity of this sentence? If Black agreed, how does his conception of WHAT "the Constitution" includes differ from Frankfurter's?

(2) **Query:** To what extent is *Rochin* compatible with Jacobson v. Massachusetts (1905), reprinted above, p. 125. To put the question another way, was the Court in *Rochin* finding that a right to bodily integrity was protected by the "whole nature of the judicial process" and/or "the compelling traditions of

the legal profession"? Or was the Court merely setting outer limits to such terms in the constitutional document as "self-incrimination" and "unreasonable searches and seizures"? Whatever one believes the majority to have been doing in *Rochin*, the concurring opinions of Black and Douglas were much more limited and positivistic in their reasoning. The reasoning of several more recent opinions of the Court dealing with efforts to obtain evidence from the bodies' of suspects have also tended to be more positivistic than that of the Court in *Rochin*, but Black and Douglas dissented against those results, while they were still on the Court:

(i) Breithaupt v. Abram (1957) sustained a conviction for drunken driving based on a test done on a sample of blood taken from a suspect while he was unconscious. The majority found nothing "brutal" or "offensive" in such procedures: "As against the right of an individual that his person be held inviolable even against so slight an intrusion as is involved in applying a blood test of the kind to which millions of Americans submit as a matter of course nearly every day, must be set the interests of society in the scientific determination of intoxication, one of the great causes of the mortal hazards of the road."

(ii) Schmerber v. California (1966) upheld a conviction based on a similar test, even though conducted on a conscious and protesting suspect. The majority conceded that the basic reason underlying constitutional protection against self-incrimination and unreasonable searches was concern for human dignity: "If the scope of the privilege [against self-incrimination] coincided with the complex of values it helps to protect, we might be obliged to conclude that the privilege was violated." The majority, however, found the privilege more limited and chose to follow *Breithaupt.* Nevertheless, the Court added: "The integrity of the individual is a cherished value of our society. That we today hold that the Constitution does not forbid the State's minor intrusion into an individual's body under stringently limited conditions in no way indicates that it permits more substantial intrusions or intrusions under other conditions."

(iii) South Dakota v. Neville (1983) allowed use in evidence of a defendant's refusal to take a blood test to determine sobriety.

(iv) Bell v. Wolfish (1979) ruled that defendants being detained in jail awaiting trial could be subjected to routine searches of bodily cavities to detect smuggling of contraband.

(v) Skinner v. R'way Lbr Executives (1989) held that the Fourth Amendment does not bar compulsory testing, without a warrant, of railroad workers for drugs and alcohol.

(vi) Nat'l Treasury Union v. Von Raab (1989) sustained similar testing of federal officers whose work involves enforcement of laws against drugs, carrying a firearm, or handling classified material. See also:

(i) Mills v. Rogers (1982), which involved a challenge by patients in a Massachusetts mental institution protesting against being compelled to take certain kinds of drugs. The Supreme Court remanded (sent back) the case to the U.S. court of appeals for reconsideration in light of a ruling by the Massachusetts supreme court that non-institutionalized mental patients have a right to refuse such treatment.

(ii) Youngberg v. Romeo (1982), which held that patients involuntarily institutionalized for mental illness have rights to safe conditions, to freedom from restraints except as necessary to protect them or others, and to such training as may be necessary to ensure their safety or to enable them to live safely without restraints.

(3) For general efforts by the justices to explain how they discover rights not listed in the constitutional document as well as attacks on such efforts, see not only the various opinions in *Griswold* but also the dissenting opinions of Douglas and Harlan in Poe v. Ullman (1961; reprinted as the next case), the opinions of White and Blackmun in Bowers v. Hardwick (1986; reprinted below, p. 1322), and Scalia and Brennan in Michael H. v. Gerald D. (1989; reprinted below, p. 158).

"[We must approach] the text which is the only commission for our power not in a literalistic way, as if we had a tax statute before us, but as the basic charter of our society, setting out in spare but meaningful terms the principles of government."—Justice HARLAN

"The notion of privacy ... emanates from the totality of the constitutional scheme under which we live."—Justice DOUGLAS

POE v. ULLMAN
367 U.S. 497, 81 S.Ct. 1752, 6 L.Ed.2d 989 (1961).

In 1879 Connecticut adopted a statute making it a crime to use or aid in using contraceptives. As technology and notions about sexual morality changed, so did the composition of the state's population. In the nineteenth century, a heavily Protestant majority had apparently supported the law; by the middle of the twentieth century, it was the large Catholic population who were, at least according to their bishops, in favor of the statute. Thus repeal was politically unlikely.

In the 1940s a group advocating birth control went to court to attack the law as violating the Fourteenth Amendment. A doctor challenged the statute as depriving his patients of life and liberty without due process by preventing his giving them medical advice that might save their lives. State courts sustained the law, and the U.S. Supreme Court dismissed the action on the ground that the doctor lacked standing to assert his patients' rights. Tileston v. Ullman (1943). In the late 1950s, the group tried again. This time the plaintiffs were married couples and a physician. They, too, lost in state courts, and once more the Supreme Court dismissed the suit. For four justices, Felix Frankfurter concluded that there was no imminent threat to any putative right: In the 82 years the statute had been on the books, Connecticut had only once tried to enforce it. Brennan concurred separately on similar grounds, while Black and Stewart dissented for procedural reasons. Douglas and Harlan also dissented.

We reprint here only that part of Harlan's opinion dealing with substantive issues.

Mr. Justice **HARLAN,** dissenting. ...

... I believe that a statute making it a criminal offense for *married* couples to use contraceptives is an intolerable and unjustifiable invasion of privacy in the conduct of the most intimate concerns of an individual's personal life. ...

I

In reviewing state legislation ... in provision for the health, safety, morals or welfare of its people, it is clear that what is concerned are "the powers of government inherent in every sovereignty." License Cases [1847]. Only to the extent that the Constitution so requires may this Court interfere with the exercise of this plenary power of government. Barron v. Baltimore [1833]. But precisely because it is the Constitution alone which warrants judicial interference in sovereign operations of the State, the basis of judgment as to the Constitutionality of state action must be a rational one, approaching the text which is the only commission for our power not in a literalistic way, as if we had a tax statute before us, but as the basic charter of our society, setting out in spare but meaningful terms the principles of government. McCulloch v. Maryland [1819]. But as inescapable as is the rational process in Constitutional adjudication in general, nowhere is it more so than in giving meaning to the prohibitions of the Fourteenth Amendment and, where the Federal Government is involved, the Fifth Amendment, against the deprivation of life, liberty or property without due process of law.

It is but a truism to say that this provision of both Amendments is not self-explanatory. As to the Fourteenth, which is involved here, the history of the Amendment also sheds little light on the meaning of the provision. It is important to note, however, that two views of the Amendment have not been accepted by this Court. ... One view ... sought to limit the provision to a guarantee of procedural fairness. The other view ... would have it that the Fourteenth Amendment ... applied against the States only and precisely those restraints which had prior to the Amendment been applicable merely to federal action. However, "due process" in the consistent view of this Court has ever been a broader concept than the first view and more flexible than the second. ...

... [I]t is not the particular enumeration of rights in the first eight Amendments which spells out the reach of Fourteenth Amendment due process, but rather ... those concepts which are considered to embrace those rights "which are ... *fundamental*; which belong ... to the citizens of all free governments." Corfield v. Coryell [1823], for "the purposes [of securing] which men enter into society," Calder v. Bull [1798]. Again and again this Court has resisted the notion that the Fourteenth Amendment is no more than a shorthand reference to what is explicitly set out elsewhere in the Bill of Rights. Indeed the fact that an identical provision limiting federal action is found among the first eight Amendments, applying to the Federal Government, suggests that due process is a discrete concept which subsists as an independent guaranty of liberty and procedural fairness, more general and inclusive than the specific prohibitions.

Due process has not been reduced to any formula; its content cannot be determined by reference to any code. The best that can be said is that through the course of this Court's decisions it has represented the balance which our Nation, built upon postulates of respect for the liberty of the individual, has struck between that liberty and the demands of organized society. If the supplying of content to this Constitutional concept has of necessity been a rational process, it certainly has not been one where judges have felt free to roam where unguided speculation might take them. The balance of which I speak is the balance struck by this country, having regard to what history teaches are the traditions from which it developed as well as the traditions from which it broke. That tradition is a living thing. A decision of this Court which radically departs from it could not long survive, while a decision which builds on what has survived is likely to be sound. No formula could serve as a substitute, in this area, for judgment and restraint.

It is this outlook which has led the Court continuingly to perceive distinctions in the imperative character of Constitutional provisions, since that character must be discerned from a particular provision's larger context. And inasmuch as this context is one not of words, but of history and purposes, the full scope of the liberty guaranteed by the Due Process Clause cannot be found in or limited by the precise terms of the specific guarantees elsewhere provided in the Constitution. This "liberty" is not a series of isolated points pricked out in terms of the taking of property; the freedom of speech, press, and religion; the right to keep and bear arms; the freedom from unreasonable searches and seizures; and so on. It is a rational continuum which, broadly speaking, includes a freedom from all substantial arbitrary impositions and purposeless restraints and which also recognizes, what a reasonable and sensitive judgment must, that certain interests require particularly careful scrutiny of the state needs asserted to justify their abridgment. Cf. Skinner v. Oklahoma [1942]; Bolling v. Sharpe [1954].

As was said in *Meyer*, "this Court has not attempted to define with exactness the liberty thus guaranteed. ... Without doubt, it denotes not merely freedom from bodily restraint. ..." Thus, for instance, when in that case and in Pierce v. Society of Sisters [1925] the Court struck down laws which sought not to require what children must learn in schools, but to prescribe, in the first case, what they must *not* learn, and in the second, *where* they must acquire their learning, I do not think

it was wrong to put those decisions on "the right of the individual to ...
establish a home and bring up children," or on the basis that "The
fundamental theory of liberty upon which all governments in this Union
repose excludes any general power of the State to standardize its
children by forcing them to accept instruction from public teachers
only." I consider this so, even though today those decisions would
probably have gone by reference to the concepts of freedom of expression
and conscience assured against state action by the Fourteenth Amendment, concepts that are derived from the explicit guarantees of the First
Amendment against federal encroachment upon freedom of speech and
belief.* For it is the purposes of those guarantees and not their text, the
reasons for their statement by the Framers and not the statement itself,
see Palko v. Connecticut [1037]; United States v. Carolene Products Co.
[1938], which have led to their present status in the compendious notion
of "liberty" embraced in the Fourteenth Amendment.

Each new claim to Constitutional protection must be considered
against a background of Constitutional purposes, as they have been
rationally perceived and historically developed. Though we exercise
limited and sharply restrained judgment, yet there is no "mechanical
yardstick," no "mechanical answer." The decision of an apparently
novel claim must depend on grounds which follow closely on well-
accepted principles and criteria. ...

III

Precisely what is involved here is this: the State is asserting the
right to enforce its moral judgment by intruding upon the most intimate
details of the marital relation with the full power of the criminal law.
...

... The statute must pass a more rigorous Constitutional test than
that going merely to the plausibility of its underlying rationale. This
enactment involves what, by common understanding throughout the
English-speaking world, must be granted to be a most fundamental
aspect of "liberty," the privacy of the home in its most basic sense, and
it is this which requires that the statute be subjected to "strict scrutiny." *Skinner.*

That aspect of liberty which embraces the concept of the privacy of
the home receives explicit Constitutional protection at two places only.
These are the Third Amendment, relating to the quartering of soldiers,
and the Fourth Amendment, prohibiting unreasonable searches and
seizures. While these Amendments reach only the Federal Government,
this Court has held ... that the concept of "privacy" embodied in the
Fourth Amendment is part of the "ordered liberty" assured against state
action by the Fourteenth Amendment. See Wolf v. Colorado [1949];
Mapp v. Ohio [1961]. ...

---

* Compare Douglas's opinion for the Court in Griswold v. Connecticut (1965; reprinted
below, p. 147), interpreting *Meyer* and *Pierce* in light of the First Amendment rather than
"substantive due process."—**Eds.**

Perhaps the most comprehensive statement of the principle of liberty underlying these aspects of the Constitution was given by Mr. Justice Brandeis, dissenting in Olmstead v. United States [1928]:

> The makers of our Constitution undertook to secure conditions favorable to the pursuit of happiness. ... They conferred, as against the Government, the right to be let alone—the most comprehensive of rights and the right most valued by civilized men. To protect that right, every unjustifiable intrusion by the Government upon the privacy of the individual, whatever the means employed, must be deemed a violation of the Fourth Amendment. ...

I think the sweep of the Court's decisions ... amply shows that the Constitution protects the privacy of the home against all unreasonable intrusion of whatever character. "[These] principles ... affect the very essence of constitutional liberty and security. They ... apply to all invasions on the part of the government and its employees of the sanctity of a man's home and the privacies of life. ..." Boyd v. United States [1886]. "The security of one's privacy against arbitrary intrusion by the police—which is at the core of the Fourth Amendment—is basic to a free society." *Wolf.*

It would surely be an extreme instance of sacrificing substance to form were it to be held that the Constitutional principle of privacy against arbitrary official intrusion comprehends only physical invasions by the police. To be sure, the times presented the Framers with two particular threats to that principle, the general warrant and the quartering of soldiers in private homes. But ... "a principle to be vital must be capable of wider application than the mischief which gave it birth." Weems v. United States [1910].

... [T]here is another sense in which it could be argued that this intrusion on privacy differs from what the Fourth Amendment, and the similar concept of the Fourteenth, were intended to protect: here we have not an intrusion into the home so much as on the life which characteristically has its place in the home. But to my mind such a distinction is so insubstantial as to be captious. ... Certainly the safeguarding of the home does not follow merely from the sanctity of property rights. The home derives its preeminence as the seat of family life. And the integrity of that life is something so fundamental that it has been found to draw to its protection the principles of more than one explicitly granted Constitutional right. ...

Of this whole "private realm of family life" [Prince v. Massachusetts (1944)] it is difficult to imagine what is more private or more intimate than a husband and wife's marital relations. ...

Of course, just as the requirement of a warrant is not inflexible in carrying out searches and seizures, so there are countervailing considerations at this more fundamental aspect of the right involved. "[T]he family ... is not beyond regulation," *Prince*, and it would be an absurdity to suggest either that offenses may not be committed in the bosom of the family or that the home can be made a sanctuary for crime.

The right of privacy most manifestly is not an absolute. Thus, I would not suggest that adultery, homosexuality, fornication and incest are immune from criminal enquiry, however privately practiced. ...

Adultery, homosexuality and the like are sexual intimacies which the State forbids altogether, but the intimacy of husband and wife is necessarily an essential and accepted feature of the institution of marriage, an institution which the State ... always ... has fostered and protected. ...

Editors' Notes

(1) **Query:** How consistent with Chase's opinion in Calder v. Bull (1798; reprinted above, p. 121) is Harlan's opinion? How would Iredell have responded to Harlan?

(2) **Query:** What, in Harlan's judgment, does "the Constitution" include?

(3) **Query:** Why, according to Harlan, must the Court subject legislation touching on a right to privacy not mentioned in the constitutional text to a more rigorous test than laws impinging on some rights actually listed in the text? What textual basis is there for such reasoning?

(4) **Query:** Harlan said, with only a hint of explanation, he would have allowed states to regulate homosexual relations. How, given his view of WHAT "the Constitution" includes, could he make a reasonable argument for this distinction? For a discussion of the constitutional inclusion of certain traditions and how interpreters can discover those traditions, see Michael H. v. Gerald D. (1989; reprinted below, p. 158).

(5) Harlan's comment about regulating homosexual sex is known as a *dictum* (plural *dicta*), discussed in Chapter 2, and, even when found in an opinion of the Supreme Court, is not binding on judges of lower courts. Of course, deciding what in an opinion was *dicta* and what was dogma is a trying business. For further discussion in the context of a case that presented directly the issue of the rights of homosexuals to privacy in their sexual relations, see Bowers v. Hardwick (1986; reprinted below, p. 1322).

"[S]pecific guarantees in the Bill of Rights have penumbras, formed by emanations from those guarantees that help give them life and substance."—Justice DOUGLAS

"[T]he Ninth Amendment ... simply shows the intent of the Constitution's authors that other fundamental personal rights should not be denied ... simply because they are not specifically listed in the first eight constitutional amendments."—Justice GOLDBERG

"I get nowhere in this case by talk about a constitutional 'right to privacy' as an emanation from one or more constitutional provisions. I like my privacy as well as the next one, but I am nevertheless compelled to admit that government has a right to invade it unless prohibit-

ed by some specific constitutional provision."—Justice
BLACK

GRISWOLD v. CONNECTICUT
381 U.S. 479, 85 S.Ct. 1678, 14 L.Ed.2d 510 (1965).

This case marked a further stage in the long struggle against the Connecticut law of 1879 that made it a crime to use or to aid, abet, or counsel use of "any drug, medicinal article or instrument for the purpose of preventing conception." After the decision in Poe v. Ullman (1961; reprinted above, p. 141), dismissing a suit against the constitutionality of this statute on grounds that the plaintiffs had not shown that the state was likely to enforce it against them, the Director of the Planned Parenthood League of Connecticut and a physician flouted the law by publicly advising married persons about the use of contraceptives. They were arrested, tried, convicted, and fined $100 each. State courts sustained the convictions, and the two men appealed to the U.S. Supreme Court.

Mr. Justice **DOUGLAS** delivered the opinion of the Court. ...

[W]e are met with a wide range of questions that implicate the Due Process Clause of the Fourteenth Amendment. Overtones of some arguments suggest that Lochner v. New York [1905] * should be our guide. But we decline that invitation as we did in West Coast Hotel Co. v. Parrish [1937].** We do not sit as a super-legislature to determine the wisdom, need, and propriety of laws that touch economic problems, business affairs, or social conditions. This law, however, operates directly on an intimate relation of husband and wife and their physician's role in one aspect of that relation.

The association of people is not mentioned in the Constitution nor in the Bill of Rights. The right to educate a child in a school of the parents' choice—whether public or private or parochial—is also not mentioned. Nor is the right to study any particular subject or any foreign language. Yet the First Amendment has been construed to include certain of those rights.

By Pierce v. Society of Sisters [1925], the right to educate one's children as one chooses is made applicable to the States by the force of the First and Fourteenth Amendments. By Meyer v. Nebraska [1923], the same dignity is given the right to study the German language in a private school. In other words, the State may not, consistently with the spirit of the First Amendment, contract the spectrum of available knowledge. The right of freedom of speech and press includes not only the right to utter or to print, but the right to distribute, the right to receive, the right to read (Martin v. Struthers [1943]) and freedom of inquiry, freedom of thought, and freedom to teach (see Wieman v. Updegraff [1952])—indeed the freedom of the entire university commu-

---

* Reprinted below, p. 1110—**Eds.**

** Reprinted below, p. 1123—**Eds.**

nity. Sweezy v. New Hampshire [1957]; Barenblatt v. United States [1959]. Without those peripheral rights the specific rights would be less secure. And so we reaffirm the principle of the Pierce and the Meyer cases.

In NAACP v. Alabama [1958], we protected the "freedom to associate and privacy in one's associations," noting that freedom of association was a peripheral First Amendment right. ... In other words, the First Amendment has a penumbra where privacy is protected from governmental intrusion. In like context, we have protected forms of "association" that are not political in the customary sense but pertain to the social, legal, and economic benefit of the members. NAACP v. Button [1963]. ...

Those cases involved more than the "right of assembly"—a right that extends to all irrespective of their race or ideology. De Jonge v. Oregon [1937]. The right of "association," like the right of belief (Board of Education v. Barnette [1943]), is more than the right to attend a meeting; it includes the right to express one's attitudes or philosophies by membership in a group or by affiliation with it or by other lawful means. Association in that context is a form of expression of opinion; and while it is not expressly included in the First Amendment its existence is necessary in making the express guarantees fully meaningful.

The foregoing cases suggest that specific guarantees in the Bill of Rights have penumbras, formed by emanations from those guarantees that help give them life and substance. See Poe v. Ullman [1961] (dissenting opinion [by Douglas, J.]). Various guarantees create zones of privacy. The right of association contained in the penumbra of the First Amendment is one, as we have seen. The Third Amendment in its prohibition against the quartering of soldiers "in any house" in time of peace without the consent of the owner is another facet of that privacy. The Fourth Amendment explicitly affirms the "right of the people to be secure in their persons, houses, papers, and effects, against unreasonable searches and seizures." The Fifth Amendment in its Self–Incrimination Clause enables the citizen to create a zone of privacy which government may not force him to surrender to his detriment. The Ninth Amendment provides: "The enumeration in the Constitution, of certain rights, shall not be construed to deny or disparage others retained by the people."

The Fourth and Fifth Amendments were described in Boyd v. United States [1886] as protection against all governmental invasions "of the sanctity of a man's home and the privacies of life." We recently referred in Mapp v. Ohio [1961] to the Fourth Amendment as creating a "right to privacy, no less important than any other right carefully and particularly reserved to the people." See Beaney, The Constitutional Right to Privacy, 1962 Sup.Ct. Rev. 212; Griswold, The Right to be Let Alone, 55 Nw.U.L.Rev. 216 (1960).

We have had many controversies over these penumbral rights of "privacy and repose." See, e.g., Public Utilities Com. v. Pollak [1952]; Skinner v. Oklahoma [1942]. These cases bear witness that the right of privacy which presses for recognition here is a legitimate one.

The present case, then, concerns a relationship lying within the zone of privacy created by several fundamental constitutional guarantees. And it concerns a law which, in forbidding the *use of* contraceptives rather than regulating their manufacture or sale, seeks to achieve its goals by means having a maximum destructive impact upon that relationship. Such a law cannot stand in light of the familiar principle ... that a "governmental purpose to control or prevent activities constitutionally subject to state regulation may not be achieved by means which sweep unnecessarily broadly and thereby invade the area of protected freedoms." NAACP v. Alabama. Would we allow the police to search the sacred precincts of marital bedrooms for telltale signs of the use of contraceptives? The very idea is repulsive to the notions of privacy surrounding the marriage relationship.

We deal with a right of privacy older than the Bill of Rights—older than our political parties, older than our school system. Marriage is a coming together for better or for worse, hopefully enduring, and intimate to the degree of being sacred. It is an association that promotes a way of life, not causes; a harmony in living, not political faiths; a bilateral loyalty, not commercial or social projects. Yet it is an association for as noble a purpose as any involved in our prior decisions.

Reversed.

Mr. Justice **GOLDBERG**, whom the Chief Justice [**WARREN**] and Mr. Justice **BRENNAN** join, concurring.

... Although I have not accepted the view that "due process" as used in the Fourteenth Amendment incorporates all of the first eight Amendments, I do agree that the concept of liberty protects those personal rights that are fundamental, and is not confined to the specific terms of the Bill of Rights. My conclusion that the concept of liberty is not so restricted and that it embraces the right of marital privacy though that right is not mentioned explicitly in the Constitution is supported both by numerous decisions of this Court, referred to in the Court's opinion, and by the language and history of the Ninth Amendment. ... I add these words to emphasize the relevance of that Amendment to the Court's holding. ...

This Court, in a series of decisions, has held that the Fourteenth Amendment absorbs and applies to the States those specifics of the first eight amendments which express fundamental personal rights. The language and history of the Ninth Amendment reveal that the Framers of the Constitution believed that there are additional fundamental rights, protected from governmental infringement, which exist alongside

those fundamental rights specifically mentioned in the first eight constitutional amendments. . . .

In presenting the proposed Amendment, Madison said:

It has been objected also against a bill of rights, that, by enumerating particular exceptions to the grant of power, it would disparage those
rights which were not placed in that enumeration; and it might follow
by implication, that those rights which were not singled out, were
intended to be assigned into the hands of the General Government, and
were consequently insecure. This is one of the most plausible arguments I have ever heard urged against the admission of a bill of rights
into this system; but, I conceive, that it may be guarded against. I have
attempted it, as gentlemen may see by turning to the last clause of the
fourth resolution [the Ninth Amendment]. . . .

While this Court has had little occasion to interpret the Ninth
Amendment, "[i]t cannot be presumed that any clause in the constitution is intended to be without effect." Marbury v. Madison [1803]. . . .
The Ninth Amendment to the Constitution may be regarded by some as
a recent discovery and may be forgotten by others, but since 1791 it has
been a basic part of the Constitution which we are sworn to uphold. To
hold that a right so basic and fundamental and so deep-rooted in our
society as the right of privacy in marriage may be infringed because that
right is not guaranteed in so many words by the first eight amendments
to the Constitution is to ignore the Ninth Amendment and to give it no
effect whatsoever. Moreover, a judicial construction that this fundamental right is not protected by the Constitution because it is not mentioned
in explicit terms by one of the first eight amendments or elsewhere in
the Constitution would violate the Ninth Amendment, which specifically
states that "[t]he enumeration in the Constitution, of certain rights,
shall not be *construed* to deny or disparage others retained by the
people." (Emphasis added.)

A dissenting opinion suggests that my interpretation of the Ninth
Amendment somehow "broaden[s] the powers of this Court." . . . With
all due respect, I believe that it misses the import of what I am saying.
. . . [I do not mean] to state that the Ninth Amendment constitutes an
independent source of rights protected from infringement by either the
States or the Federal Government. Rather, the Ninth Amendment . . .
simply shows the intent of the Constitution's authors that other fundamental personal rights should not be denied such protection or disparaged in any other way simply because they are not specifically listed in
the first eight constitutional amendments. I do not see how this
broadens the authority of the Court; rather it serves to support what
this Court has been doing in protecting fundamental rights.

Nor am I turning somersaults with history in arguing that the
Ninth Amendment is relevant in a case dealing with a *State's* infringement of a fundamental right. While the Ninth Amendment—and indeed
the entire Bill of Rights—originally concerned restrictions upon *federal*
power, the subsequently enacted Fourteenth Amendment prohibits the
States as well from abridging fundamental personal liberties. And, the

Ninth Amendment, in indicating that not all such liberties are specifically mentioned in the first eight amendments, is surely relevant in showing the existence of other fundamental personal rights, now protected from state, as well as federal, infringement. In sum, the Ninth Amendment simply lends strong support to the view that the "liberty" protected by the Fifth and Fourteenth Amendments from infringement by the Federal Government or the States is not restricted to rights specifically mentioned in the first eight amendments.

In determining which rights are fundamental, judges are not left at large to decide cases in light of their personal and private notions. Rather, they must look to the "traditions and [collective] conscience of our people" to determine whether a principle is "so rooted [there] ... as to be ranked as fundamental." Snyder v. Massachusetts [1934]. The inquiry is whether a right involved "is of such a character that it cannot be denied without violating those 'fundamental principles of liberty and justice which lie at the base of all our civil and political institutions'. ..." Powell v. Alabama [1932]. "Liberty" also "gains content from the emanations of ... specific [constitutional] guarantees" and "from experience with the requirements of a free society." *Poe* (dissenting opinion of Mr. Justice Douglas).

I agree fully with the Court that, applying these tests, the right of privacy is a fundamental personal right, emanating "from the totality of the constitutional scheme under which we live." *Ibid.* ...

The entire fabric of the Constitution and the purposes that clearly underlie its specific guarantees demonstrate that the rights to marital privacy and to marry and raise a family are of similar order and magnitude as the fundamental rights specifically protected. ...

In a long series of cases this Court has held that ... fundamental personal liberties ... may not be abridged by the States simply on a showing that a regulatory statute has some rational relationship to the effectuation of a proper state purpose. "Where there is a significant encroachment upon personal liberty, the State may prevail only upon showing a subordinating interest which is compelling." Bates v. Little Rock [1960]. The law must be shown "necessary, and not merely rationally related, to the accomplishment of a permissible state policy." McLaughlin v. Florida [1964].

... Here, as elsewhere, "[p]recision of regulation must be the touchstone in an area so closely touching our most precious freedoms." NAACP v. Button. The State of Connecticut does have statutes, the constitutionality of which is beyond doubt, which prohibit adultery and fornication. These statutes demonstrate that means for achieving the same basic purpose of protecting marital fidelity are available to Connecticut without the need to "invade the area of protected freedoms." NAACP v. Alabama.

Finally, it should be said of the Court's holding today that it in no way interferes with a State's proper regulation of sexual promiscuity or misconduct [e.g., homosexuality and extra-marital sexuality]. ...

Mr. Justice **HARLAN**, concurring in the judgment.

I fully agree with the judgment of reversal, but find myself unable to join the Court's opinion. The reason is that it seems to me to evince an approach to this case very much like that taken by my Brothers Black and Stewart in dissent, namely: the Due Process Clause of the Fourteenth Amendment does not touch this Connecticut statute unless the enactment is found to violate some right assured by the letter or penumbra of the Bill of Rights.

In other words, what I find implicit in the Court's opinion is that the "incorporation" doctrine may be used to *restrict* the reach of Fourteenth Amendment Due Process. For me this is just as unacceptable constitutional doctrine as is the use of the "incorporation" approach to *impose* upon the States all the requirements of the Bill of Rights as found in the provisions of the first eight amendments and in the decisions of this Court interpreting them.

In my view, the proper constitutional inquiry in this case is whether this Connecticut statute infringes the Due Process Clause of the Fourteenth Amendment because the enactment violates basic values "implicit in the concept of ordered liberty," Palko v. Connecticut [1937]. For reasons stated at length in my dissenting opinion in *Poe*, I believe that it does. While the relevant inquiry may be aided by resort to one or more of the provisions of the Bill of Rights, it is not dependent on them or any of their radiations. The Due Process Clause of the Fourteenth Amendment stands, in my opinion, on its own bottom.

A further observation seems in order respecting the justification of my Brothers Black and Stewart for their "incorporation" approach to this case. Their approach does not rest on historical reasons, which are of course wholly lacking, but on the thesis that by limiting the content of the Due Process Clause of the Fourteenth Amendment to the protection of rights which can be found elsewhere in the Constitution, in this instance in the Bill of Rights, judges will thus be confined to "interpretation" of specific constitutional provisions, and will thereby be restrained from introducing their own notions of constitutional right and wrong into the "vague contours of the Due Process Clause." Rochin v. California [1952].

While I could not more heartily agree that judicial "self restraint" is an indispensable ingredient of sound constitutional adjudication, I do submit that the formula suggested for achieving it is more hollow than real. "Specific" provisions of the Constitution, no less than "due process," lend themselves as readily to "personal" interpretations by judges whose constitutional outlook is simply to keep the Constitution in supposed "tune with the times". ...

Judicial self-restraint will not, I suggest, be brought about in the "due process" area by the historically unfounded incorporation formula. ... It will be achieved in this area, as in other constitutional areas, only by continual insistence upon respect for the teachings of history, solid recognition of the basic values that underlie our society, and wise appreciation of the great roles that the doctrines of federalism and separation of powers have played in establishing and preserving American freedoms. See Adamson v. California [1947] (Mr. Justice Frankfurter, concurring). Adherence to these principles will not, of course, obviate all constitutional differences of opinion among judges, nor should it. Their continued recognition will, however, go farther toward keeping most judges from roaming at large in the constitutional field than will the interpolation into the Constitution of an artificial and largely illusory restriction on the content of the Due Process Clause.

Mr. Justice **WHITE**, concurring in the judgment. ...

Mr. Justice **BLACK**, with whom Mr. Justice **STEWART** joins, dissenting.

... I do not to any extent whatever base my view that this Connecticut law is constitutional on a belief that the law is wise or that its policy is a good one. ... There is no single one of the graphic and eloquent strictures and criticisms fired at the policy of this Connecticut law either by the Court's opinion or by those of my concurring Brethren to which I cannot subscribe—except their conclusion that the evil qualities they see in the law make it unconstitutional. ...

The Court talks about a constitutional "right of privacy" as though there is some constitutional provision or provisions forbidding any law ever to be passed which might abridge the "privacy" of individuals. But there is not. There are, of course, guarantees in certain specific constitutional provisions which are designed in part to protect privacy at certain times and places with respect to certain activities. Such, for example, is the Fourth Amendment's guarantee against "unreasonable searches and seizures." But I think it belittles that Amendment to talk about it as though it protects nothing but "privacy." To treat it that way is to give it a niggardly interpretation, not the kind of liberal reading I think any Bill of Rights provision should be given. ...

One of the most effective ways of diluting or expanding a constitutionally guaranteed right is to substitute for the crucial word or words of a constitutional guarantee another word or words more or less flexible and more or less restricted in meaning. ... "Privacy" is a broad, abstract and ambiguous concept which can easily be shrunken in meaning but which can also, on the other hand, easily be interpreted as a constitutional ban against many things other than searches and seizures. ... I get nowhere in this case by talk about a constitutional "right of privacy" as an emanation from one or more constitutional provisions. I like my privacy as well as the next one, but I am nevertheless compelled to admit that government has a right to invade it unless prohibited by some specific constitutional provision. ...

This brings me to the arguments made by my Brothers Harlan, White and Goldberg. ... I discuss the due process and Ninth Amendment arguments together because on analysis they turn out to be the same thing. ...

The due process argument which my Brothers Harlan and White adopt here is based ... on the premise that this Court is vested with power to invalidate all state laws that it considers to be arbitrary, capricious, unreasonable, or oppressive, or this Court's belief that a particular state law under scrutiny has no "rational or justifying" purpose, or is offensive to a "sense of fairness and justice." If these formulas based on "natural justice," or others which mean the same thing are to prevail, they require judges to determine what is or is not constitutional on the basis of their own appraisal of what laws are unwise or unnecessary. ... [P]erhaps it is not too much to say that no legislative body ever does pass laws without believing that they will accomplish a sane, rational, wise and justifiable purpose. ... Such an appraisal of the wisdom of legislation is an attribute of the power to make laws, not of the power to interpret them. The use by federal courts of such a formula or doctrine or whatnot to veto federal or state laws simply takes away from Congress and States the power to make laws based on their own judgment of fairness and wisdom and transfers that power to this Court for ultimate determination—a power which was specifically denied to federal courts by the convention that framed the Constitution.

Of the cases on which my Brothers White and Goldberg rely so heavily, undoubtedly the reasoning of two of them supports their result here—as would that of a number of others which they do not bother to name, e.g., *Lochner* and Adkins v. Children's Hospital [1923]. The two they do cite and quote from, *Meyer* and *Pierce*, were both decided in opinions by Mr. Justice McReynolds which elaborated the same natural law due process philosophy found in *Lochner* ... which many later opinions repudiated, and which I cannot accept.

My Brother Goldberg has adopted the recent discovery that the Ninth Amendment as well as the Due Process Clause can be used by this Court as authority to strike down all state legislation which this Court thinks violates "fundamental principles of liberty and justice," or is contrary to the "traditions and [collective] conscience of our people." He also states, without proof satisfactory to me, that in making decisions on this basis judges will not consider "their personal and private notions." One may ask how they can avoid considering them. Our Court certainly has no machinery with which to take a Gallup Poll. And the scientific miracles of this age have not yet produced a gadget which the Court can use to determine what traditions are rooted in the "[collective] conscience of our people." Moreover, one would certainly have to look far beyond the language of the Ninth Amendment to find that the Framers vested in this Court any such awesome veto powers over law-making, either by the States or by the Congress. Nor does anything in the history of the Amendment offer any support for such a shocking doctrine. The whole history of the adoption of the Constitution and Bill of Rights points the other way, and the very material quoted by my Brother Goldberg shows that the Ninth Amendment was intended to protect against the idea that "by enumerating particular exceptions to the grant of power" to the Federal Government, "those rights which were not singled out, were intended to be assigned into the hands of the General Government [the United States], and were consequently insecure." That Amendment was passed, not to broaden the powers of this Court or any other department of "the General Government," but, as every student of history knows, to assure the people that the Constitution in all its provisions was intended to limit the Federal Government to the powers granted expressly or by necessary implication. If any broad, unlimited power to hold laws unconstitutional because they offend what this Court conceives to be the "[collective] conscience of our people" is vested in this Court by the Ninth Amendment, the Fourteenth Amendment, or any other provision of the Constitution, it was not given by the Framers, but rather has been bestowed on the Court by the Court. ... Use of any such broad, unbounded judicial authority would make of this Court's members a day-to-day constitutional convention. ...

I realize that many good and able men have eloquently spoken and written, sometimes in rhapsodical strains, about the duty of this Court to keep the Constitution in tune with the times. The idea is that the Constitution must be changed from time to time and that this Court is charged with a duty to make those changes. For myself, I must with all deference reject that philosophy. The Constitution makers knew the need for change and provided for it. Amendments suggested by the people's elected representatives can be submitted to the people or their selected agents for ratification. That method of change was good for our Fathers, and being somewhat old-fashioned I must add it is good enough for me. And so, I cannot rely on the Due Process Clause or the Ninth Amendment or any mysterious and uncertain natural law concept as a reason for striking down this state law. The Due Process Clause with an "arbitrary and capricious" or "shocking to the conscience" formula was liberally used by this Court to strike down economic legislation in the early decades of this century, threatening, many people thought, the tranquility and stability of the Nation. See, e.g., *Lochner*. That formula, based on subjective considerations of "natural justice," is no less dangerous when used to enforce this Court's views about personal rights than those about economic rights. I had thought that we had laid that formula, as a means for striking down state legislation, to rest once and for all in cases like *West Coast Hotel*. ...

[Black quoted from Iredell's opinion in Calder v. Bull (1798) and from his own dissenting opinion in *Adamson*.]

So far as I am concerned, Connecticut's law as applied here is not forbidden by any provision of the Federal Constitution as that Constitution was written, and I would therefore affirm.

Mr. Justice **STEWART**, whom Mr. Justice **BLACK** joins, dissenting.
. . .

Editors' Notes

(1) **Query:** Implicitly each justice who wrote in *Griswold* offered a conception of "the Constitution" that he was interpreting. How do those conceptions differ from one another? Did those three members of the majority who wrote opinions—Douglas, Harlan, and Goldberg—agree on a conception, or did they differ among themselves as well as with Black and Stewart?

(2) **Query:** "I like my privacy as well as the next one," Black wrote, "but I am nevertheless compelled to admit that government has a right to invade it unless prohibited by some specific constitutional provision." Was Black turning constitutionalism, as defined in Chapter 3, on its head?

(3) Chapter 9 will analyze in detail various approaches to constitutional interpretation, but even before reading that chapter it should be apparent that the justices who wrote in *Griswold* looked at constitutional interpretation quite differently. Their opinions show the complex ways in which the question of WHAT "the Constitution" includes interrelates with the question of HOW one interprets "the Constitution." It is not unfair to say that Black's principal concern was to preserve individual constitutional clauses as watertight compartments. On the other hand, Douglas looked to what might be called "the structure" of "the Constitution," or as he phrased it in a different context, its "architectural scheme." ("Stare Decisis," 4 *Rec. of the Assn. of the Bar of the City of New York* 152 [1949].)

Structural analysis examines the thing to be interpreted as a whole rather than as a series of particular clauses. (See espec. Charles L. Black, *Structure and Relationship in Constitutional Law* [Baton Rouge: Louisiana State University Press, 1969]; William F. Harris II, *The Interpretable Constitution* [Baltimore: Johns Hopkins University Press, 1993], espec. ch. 3; and James E. Fleming, "Constructing the Substantive Constitution," 72 *Tex.L.Rev.* 211 [1993].) In constitutional interpretation, structuralism may limit itself to the document, to the document plus the larger political system, or to these plus the political theories on which the interpreter believes they are based. At which of these levels did Douglas operate?

(4) *Griswold* represents, as Black noted, the first time the Court had cited the Ninth Amendment as a basis for striking down a statute, state or federal. Black, it will be recalled, had often argued—see especially Adamson v. California (1947)—that the Fourteenth Amendment "incorporates" the first eight amendments. By what logic could he, an avowed textualist, have excluded the Ninth?

(5) **Query:** How did Douglas and Goldberg differ on their uses of the Ninth Amendment?

(6) The first draft of his opinion that Douglas circulated to the Court laid greater stress on the sacredness of the marital relationship, constitutionally

protected as a form of association, and much less on the right of privacy. In a long memorandum Brennan urged Douglas to shift the emphasis to "an expansive interpretation" of privacy: "where fundamentals are concerned, the Bill of Rights guarantees are but expression or examples of those rights, and do not preclude applications or extensions of those rights to situations unanticipated by the framers." For a general discussion of the path of *Griswold* through the Court, see Bernard Schwartz, *The Unpublished Opinions of the Warren Court* (New York: Oxford University Press, 1985), pp. 227–239.

In an article Douglas cited, Prof. William M. Beaney had suggested such an approach three years earlier ("The Constitutional Right to Privacy," 1962 *Sup.Ct.Rev.* 212, 214):

> Why should one assume that the right to privacy is protected by fundamental law? ... The answer in a few words must be that our Constitution and our system of constitutional government reflect a decision that government is limited in the powers and in the methods it may use. ... "Liberty against government," a phrase used by Professor Corwin, expresses this idea forcefully. In this sense, virtually all enumerated rights in the Constitution can be described as contributing to the right of privacy, if by the term is meant the integrity and freedom of the individual person and personality.

(7) Even as amended, Douglas' opinion for the Court (and also Harlan's concurrence) emphasized that *Griswold* involved advice given to married couples. In 1972 Eisenstadt v. Baird invalidated, as a violation of equal protection of the laws, Massachusetts' ban against distributing information about birth control to unmarried persons. For the Court, Brennan wrote: "If the right of privacy means anything, it is the right of the *individual*, married or single, to be free from unwarranted governmental intrusion into matters so fundamentally affecting a person as the decision whether to bear or beget a child." Concurring, Douglas said he would strike the law down as interfering with freedom of speech.

Carey v. Population Services (1977) held unconstitutional a New York statute making it criminal for anyone: (i) To sell contraceptives to minors under 16; (ii) Except a licensed pharmacist to sell contraceptives to a person over 16; or (iii) To advertise or display contraceptives.

(8) The Court's decisions holding that the right to privacy includes a woman's right, at least during the first trimester of pregnancy, to obtain an abortion—see, espec. Roe v. Wade (1973; reprinted below, p. 1258); modified by Planned Parenthood v. Casey (1992; reprinted below, p. 1281)—build on *Griswold*. On the other hand, Bowers v. Hardwick (1986; reprinted below, p. 1322), citing Harlan in *Poe* and *Griswold*, rejected a homosexual's challenge to a state statute punishing sodomy, even in private between consenting adults. Earlier, in denying a prison inmate's claim that he had a right to be protected against "shakedowns" designed merely to harass or humiliate and to keep such "noncontraband items" as a picture of his family, Chief Justice Burger said for five members of the Court in Hudson v. Palmer (1984): "We hold that society is not prepared to recognize as legitimate any subjective expectation of privacy that a prisoner might have in his jail cell." See also Bell v. Wolfish (1979).

(9) For more detailed discussion of the source(s) and reach of the right to privacy, see the materials reprinted and cited in Chapter 18, below.

(10) Stephen G. Breyer was one of Justice Goldberg's clerks the year that *Griswold* came down. Reportedly Breyer wrote the first draft of Goldberg's concurrence. Nevertheless, as a self-styled "constitutional pragmatist," Breyer has never since published a general theory of the Ninth Amendment or of constitutional interpretation—except insofar as a decision not to formulate a general theory is itself a general theory. See Jeffrey Rosen, "Breyer Restraint," *The New Republic*, July 11, 1994, p. 19.

"Though the dissent has no basis for the level of generality it would select, we do: We refer to the most specific level at which a relevant tradition protecting, or denying protection to, the asserted right can be identified."— Justice SCALIA

"In a community such as ours, 'liberty' must include the freedom not to conform. The plurality today squashes this freedom by requiring specific approval from history before protecting anything in the name of liberty."— Justice BRENNAN

MICHAEL H. v. GERALD D.

491 U.S. 110, 109 S.Ct. 2333, 105 L.Ed.2d 91 (1989).

In 1981, Gerald's wife, Carole, who had been having an affair with Michael, gave birth to a daughter, Victoria. Blood tests showed a 98.07 per cent probability that Michael was the father. During Victoria's first three years, she and her mother lived part of the time with Michael and part of the time with yet a third man. During that period Victoria called Michael daddy, and Carole admitted in a legal document that Michael was the father. Later Carole and Gerald were reconciled and denied Michael the right to visit Victoria. Michael then sued in a state court asking to be declared Victoria's father and allowed to visit her. The trial judge dismissed the case *without a hearing*, saying § 621 of California's Evidence Code established a presumption that a baby born in wedlock was the husband's child. This presumption was rebuttable only in very limited circumstances, none of which obtained in this case. California's appellate courts affirmed, and Michael appealed to the U.S. Supreme Court.

The reader should note that this case presents two very different sets of issues. The first concerns rights of unwed fathers. We are principally interested in the second set: What is the content of the due process clause of the constitutional text? Does it encompass a "tradition"? And if due process does include a "tradition," how do interpreters discover it? The reader should also note that important parts of Justice Scalia's debate with Justice Brennan take place in footnotes. We have not included all of these but have retained the justices' numbering because of cross-references to them.

Justice **SCALIA** announced the judgment of the Court and delivered an opinion in which the Chief Justice [**REHNQUIST**] joins, and in all but note 6 of which Justice **O'CONNOR** and Justice **KENNEDY** join. ...

III

... California law, like nature itself, makes no provision for dual fatherhood. ...

Michael contends as a matter of substantive due process that because he has established a parental relationship with Victoria, protection of Gerald's and Carole's marital union is an insufficient state interest to support termination of that relationship. This argument is, of course, predicated on the assertion that Michael has a constitutionally protected liberty interest in his relationship with Victoria.

It is an established part of our constitutional jurisprudence that the term "liberty" in the Due Process Clause extends beyond freedom from physical restraint. See, e.g., Pierce v. Society of Sisters (1925); Meyer v. Nebraska (1923). Without that core textual meaning as a limitation, defining the scope of the due Process Clause "has at times been a treacherous field for this Court," giving "reason for concern lest the only limits to ... judicial intervention become the predilections of those who happen at the time to be Members of this Court." Moore v. East Cleveland (1977). The need for restraint has been cogently expressed by Justice White:

> "... The Judiciary ... is the most vulnerable and comes nearest to illegitimacy when it deals with judge-made constitutional law having little or no cognizable roots in the language or even the design of the Constitution. Realizing that the present construction of the Due Process Clause represents a major judicial gloss on its terms, as well as on the anticipation of the Framers ... the Court should be extremely reluctant to breathe still further substantive content into the Due Process Clause so as to strike down legislation adopted by a State or city to promote its welfare. Whenever the Judiciary does so, it unavoidably preempts for itself another part of the governance of the country without express constitutional authority." (Moore, dis. op.).

In an attempt to limit and guide interpretation of the Clause, we have insisted not merely that the interest denominated as a "liberty" be "fundamental" (a concept that, in isolation, is hard to objectify), but also that it be an interest traditionally protected by our society.[2]

---

2. We do not understand what Justice Brennan has in mind by an interest "that society traditionally has thought important ... without protecting it." The protection need not take the form of an explicit constitutional provision or statutory guarantee, but it must at least exclude (all that is necessary to decide the present case) a societal tradition of enacting laws *denying* the interest. Nor do we understand why our practice of limiting the Due Process Clause to traditionally protected interests turns the clause "into a redundancy." Its purpose is to prevent future generations from lightly casting aside important traditional values—not to enable this Court to invent new ones. [Footnote by Justice Scalia.]

This insistence that the asserted liberty interest be rooted in history and tradition is evident ... in our cases according constitutional protection to certain parental rights. Michael reads the landmark case of Stanley v. Illinois (1972), and the subsequent cases of Quilloin v. Walcott (1978), Caban v. Mohammed (1979), and Lehr v. Robertson (1983), as establishing that a liberty interest is created by biological fatherhood plus an established parental relationship—factors that exist in the present case as well. We think that distorts the rationale of those cases. As we view them, they rest not upon such isolated factors but upon the historic respect—indeed, sanctity would not be too strong a term—traditionally accorded to the relationships that develop within the unitary family.[3] In *Stanley*, for example, we forbade the destruction of such a family when, upon the death of the mother, the state had sought to remove children from the custody of a father who had lived with and supported them and their mother for 18 years. As Justice Powell stated for the plurality in Moore v. East Cleveland: "Our decisions establish that the Constitution protects the sanctity of the family precisely because the institution of the family is deeply rooted in this Nation's history and tradition."

Thus, the legal issue in the present case reduces to whether the relationship between persons in the situation of Michael and Victoria has been treated as a protected family unit under the historic practices of our society, or whether on any other basis it has been accorded special protection We think it impossible to find that it has. In fact, quite to the contrary, our traditions have protected the marital family ... against the sort of claim Michael asserts.

The presumption of legitimacy was a fundamental principle of the common law. H. Nicholas, *Adulterine Bastardy* 1 (1836). Traditionally that presumption could be rebutted only by proof that a husband was incapable of procreation or had had no access to his wife during the relevant period. *Id.*, at 9–10 (citing Bracton, *De Legibus et Consuetudinibus Angliae*). As explained by Blackstone, nonaccess could only be proved "if the husband be out of the kingdom of England ... for above nine months. ..." And, under the common law both in England and here, "neither husband nor wife [could] be a witness to prove access or nonaccess." The primary policy rationale underlying the common law[ ] ... appears to have been an aversion to declaring children illegitimate, thereby depriving them of rights of inheritance and succession, and likely making them wards of the state. A secondary policy concern was the interest in promoting the "peace and tranquility of States and

---

3. Justice Brennan asserts that only "a pinched conception of 'the family' would exclude Michael, Carole and Victoria from protection." We disagree. The family unit accorded traditional respect in our society, which we have referred to as the "unitary family," is typified, of course, by the marital family, but also includes the household of unmarried parents and their children. Perhaps the concept can be expanded even beyond this, but it will bear no resemblance to traditionally respected relationships—and will thus cease to have any constitutional significance—if it is stretched so far as to include the relationship established between [sic] a married woman, her lover and their child. ... [Footnote by Justice Scalia.]

families." ... [A]s bastardy laws became less harsh ... "the law [still] retained a strong bias against ruling the children of married women illegitimate."

We have found nothing in the older sources, nor in the older cases, addressing specifically the power of the natural father to assert parental rights over a child born into a woman's existing marriage with another man. Since it is Michael's burden to establish that such a power (at least where the natural father has established a relationship with the child) is so deeply embedded within our traditions as to be a fundamental right, the lack of evidence alone might defeat his case. But the evidence shows that even in modern times ... the ability of a person in Michael's position to claim paternity has not been generally acknowledged.

... What Michael asserts here is a right to have himself declared the natural father *and* thereby to obtain parental prerogatives. What he must establish, therefore, is not that our society has traditionally allowed a natural father in his circumstances to establish paternity, but that it has traditionally accorded such a father parental rights, or at least has not traditionally denied them. ... Thus, it is ultimately irrelevant, even for purposes of determining *current* social attitudes towards the alleged substantive right Michael asserts, that the present law in a number of States appears to allow the natural father—including the natural father who has not established a relationship with the child—the theoretical power to rebut the marital presumption. What counts is whether the States in fact award substantive parental rights to the natural father of a child conceived within and born into an extant marital union that wishes to embrace the child. We are not aware of a single case, old or new, that has done so. This is not the stuff of which fundamental rights qualifying as liberty interests are made.[6]

---

6. Justice Brennan criticizes our methodology in using historical traditions specifically relating to the rights of an adulterous natural father, rather than inquiring more generally "whether parenthood is an interest that historically has received our attention and protection." There seems to us no basis for the contention that this methodology is "novel[l]". For example, in Bowers v. Hardwick (1986), we noted that at the time the Fourteenth Amendment was ratified all but 5 of the 37 States had criminal sodomy laws, that all 50 of the States had such laws prior to 1961, and that 24 States and the District of Columbia continued to have them; and we concluded from that record, regarding that very specific aspect of sexual conduct, that "to claim that right to engage in such conduct is 'deeply rooted in this Nation's history and tradition' or 'implicit in the concept of ordered liberty' is, at best, facetious." In Roe v. Wade (1973), we spent about a fifth of our opinion negating the proposition that there was a longstanding tradition of laws proscribing abortion.

We do not understand why, having rejected our focus upon the societal tradition regarding the natural father's rights vis-à-vis a child whose mother is married to another man, Justice Brennan would choose to focus instead upon "parenthood." Why should the relevant category not be even more general—perhaps "family relationships"; or "personal relationships"; or even "emotional attachments in general"? Though the dissent has no basis for the level of generality it would select, we do: We refer to the most specific level at which a relevant tradition protecting, or denying protection to, the asserted right can be identified. If, for example, there were no societal tradition, either way, regarding the rights of the natural father of child adulterously conceived, we would have to consult, and

In *Lehr*, a case involving a natural father's attempt to block his child's adoption by the unwed mother's new husband, we observed that "[t]he significance of the biological connection is that it offers the natural father an opportunity that no other male possesses to develop a relationship with his offspring," and we assumed that the Constitution might require some protection of that opportunity. Where, however, the child is born into an extant marital family, the natural father's unique opportunity conflicts with the similarly unique opportunity of the husband of the marriage; and it is not unconstitutional for the State to give categorical preference to the latter. ... In accord with our traditions, a limit is also imposed by the circumstance that the mother is, at the time of the child's conception and birth, married to and cohabitating with another man, both of whom wish to raise the child as the offspring of their union.[7] It is a question of legislative policy and not constitutional law whether California will allow the presumed parenthood of a couple desiring to retain a child conceived within and born into their marriage to be rebutted.

We do not accept Justice Brennan's criticism that this result "squashes" the liberty that consists of "the freedom not to conform." It ... reflects the erroneous view that there is only one side to this controversy—that one disposition can expand a "liberty" of sorts without contracting an equivalent "liberty" on the other side. Such a happy choice is rarely available. Here, to *provide* protection to an adulterous

---

(if possible) reason from, the traditions regarding natural fathers in general. But there is such a more specific tradition, and it unqualifiedly denies protection to such a parent.

One would think that Justice Brennan would appreciate the value of consulting the most specific tradition available, since he acknowledges that "[e]ven if we can agree ... that 'family' and 'parenthood' are part of the good life, it is absurd to assume that we can agree on the content of those terms and destructive to pretend that we do." Because such general traditions provide such imprecise guidance, they permit judges to dictate rather than discern the society's views. The need, if arbitrary decision-making is to be avoided, to adopt the most specific tradition as the point of reference—or at least to announce, as Justice Brennan declines to do, some other criterion for selecting among the innumerable relevant traditions that could be consulted—is well enough exemplified by the fact that in the present case Justice Brennan's opinion and Justice O'Connor's opinion, which disapproves this footnote, *both* appeal to tradition, but on the basis of the tradition they select reach opposite results. Although assuredly having the virtue (if it be that) of leaving judges free to decide as they think best when the unanticipated occurs, a rule of law that binds neither by text nor by any particular, identifiable tradition, is no rule of law at all.

Finally, we may note that this analysis is not inconsistent with the result in cases such as Griswold v. Connecticut or Eisenstadt v. Baird (1972). None of those cases acknowledged a longstanding and still extant societal tradition withholding the very right pronounced to be the subject of a liberty interest and then rejected it. Justice Brennan must do so here. In this case, the existence of such a tradition, continuing to the present day, refutes any possible contention that the alleged right is "so rooted in the traditions and conscience of our people as to be ranked as fundamental," or "implicit in the concept of ordered liberty," Palko v. Connecticut (1937). [Footnote by Justice Scalia.]

7. ... [W]e rest our decision not upon our independent "balancing" of such interests, but upon the absence of any constitutionally protected right to legal parentage on the part of an adulterous natural father in Michael's situation, as evidenced by long tradition. That tradition reflects a "balancing" that has already been made by society itself. We limit our pronouncement to the relevant facts of this case because it is at least possible that our traditions lead to a different conclusion with regard to adulterous fathering of a child whom the marital parents do not wish to raise as their own. ... [Footnote by Justice Scalia.]

natural father is to *deny* protection to a marital father. ... If Michael has a "freedom not to conform" (whatever that means), Gerald must equivalently have a "freedom to conform." One of them will pay a price for asserting that "freedom"—Michael by being unable to act as father of the child he has adulterously begotten, or Gerald by being unable to preserve the integrity of the traditional family unit he and Victoria have established. Our disposition does not choose between these two "freedoms," but leaves that to the people of California. Justice Brennan's approach chooses one of them as the constitutional imperative, on no apparent basis except that the unconventional is to be preferred. ...

The judgment of the California Court of Appeal is *affirmed.*

Justice **O'CONNOR**, with whom Justice **KENNEDY** joins, concurring in part.

I concur in all but footnote 6 of Justice Scalia's opinion. This footnote sketches a mode of historical analysis to be used when identifying liberty interests protected by the Due Process Clause of the Fourteenth Amendment that may be somewhat inconsistent with our past decisions in this area. See Griswold v. Connecticut (1965); Eisenstadt v. Baird (1972). On occasion the Court has characterized relevant traditions protecting asserted rights at levels of generality that might not be "the most specific level" available. See Loving v. Virginia (1967); Turner v. Safley (1987); cf. United States v. Stanley (1987) (opinion concurring in part and dissenting in part). I would not foreclose the unanticipated by the prior imposition of a single mode of historical analysis. Poe v. Ullman (1961) (Harlan, J., dissenting).

Justice **STEVENS**, concurring in the judgment.

... I do not agree with Justice Scalia's ... [seeming rejection of] the possibility that a natural father might ever have a constitutionally protected interest in his relationship with a child whose mother was married to and cohabiting with another man at the time of the child's conception and birth. ... I am satisfied, however, that the California statute, as applied in this case, gave him that opportunity.

Justice **BRENNAN**, with whom Justice **MARSHALL** and Justice **BLACKMUN** join, dissenting. ...

I

Once we recognized that the "liberty" protected by the Due Process Clause of the Fourteenth Amendment encompasses more than freedom from bodily restraint ... the concept was cut loose from one natural limitation on its meaning. This innovation paved the way, so the plurality hints, for judges to substitute their own preferences for those of elected officials. Dissatisfied with this supposedly unbridled and uncertain state of affairs, the plurality casts about for another limitation on the concept of liberty.

It finds this limitation in "tradition." Apparently oblivious to the fact that this concept can be as malleable and as elusive as "liberty" itself, the plurality pretends that tradition places a discernible border around the Constitution. The pretense is seductive; it would be comforting to believe that a search for "tradition" involves nothing more idiosyncratic or complicated than poring through dusty volumes on American history. Yet, as Justice White observed in his dissent in Moore v. East Cleveland (1977): "What the deeply rooted traditions of the country are is arguable." Indeed, wherever I would begin to look for an interest "deeply rooted in the country's traditions," one thing is certain; I would not stop (as does the plurality) at Bracton, or Blackstone, or Kent, or even the American Law Reports in conducting my search. Because reasonable people can disagree about the content of particular traditions, and because they can disagree even about which traditions are relevant to the definition of "liberty," the plurality has not found the objective boundary that it seeks.

Even if we could agree, moreover, on the content and significance of particular traditions, we still would be forced to identify the point at which a tradition becomes firm enough to be relevant to our definition of liberty and the moment at which it becomes too obsolete to be relevant to our definition of liberty any longer. The plurality supplies no objective means by which we might make these determinations. Indeed, as soon as the plurality sees signs that the tradition upon which it bases its decision (the laws denying putative fathers like Michael standing to assert paternity) is crumbling, it shifts ground and says that the case has nothing to do with that tradition, after all.

It is ironic that an approach so utterly dependent on tradition is so indifferent to our precedents. Citing barely a handful of this Court's numerous decisions defining the scope of the liberty protected by the Due Process Clause to support its reliance on tradition, the plurality acts as though English legal treatises and the American Law Reports always have provided the sole source for our constitutional principles. They have not. Just as common-law notions no longer define the "property" that the Constitution protects, see Goldberg v. Kelly (1970), neither do they circumscribe the "liberty" that it guarantees. On the contrary, " '[l]iberty' and 'property' are broad and majestic terms. They are among the '[g]reat [constitutional] concepts ... purposely left to gather meaning from experience. ... [T]hey relate to the whole domain of social and economic fact, and the statesmen who founded this Nation knew too well that only a stagnant society remains unchanged.' " Board of Regents v. Roth (1972), quoting National Ins. v. Tidewater (1949) (Frankfurter, J., dissenting).

It is not that tradition has been irrelevant to our prior decisions. Throughout our decisionmaking in this important area runs the theme that certain interests and practices—freedom from physical restraint, marriage, childbearing, childrearing, and others—form the core of our definition of "liberty." Our solicitude for these interests is partly the result of the fact that the Due Process Clause would seem an empty promise if it did not protect them, and partly the result of the historical and traditional importance of these interests in our society. ...

Today's plurality, however, does not ask whether parenthood is an interest that historically has received our attention and protection; the answer to that question is too clear for dispute. Instead, the plurality asks whether the specific variety of parenthood under consideration—a natural father's relationship with a child whose mother is married to another man—has enjoyed such protection.

If we had looked to tradition with such specificity in past cases, many a decision would have reached a different result. Surely the use of contraceptives by unmarried couples, Eisenstadt v. Baird (1972) or even by married couples, Griswold v. Connecticut (1965); the freedom from corporal punishment in schools, Ingraham v. Wright (1977); the freedom from an arbitrary transfer from a prison to a psychiatric institution, Vitek v. Jones (1980); and even the right to raise one's natural but illegitimate children, Stanley v. Illinois (1972), were not "interest[s] traditionally protected by our society," at the time of their consideration by this Court. ...

The plurality's interpretive method is more than novel; it is misguided. It ignores the good reasons for limiting the role of "tradition" in interpreting the Constitutions's deliberately capacious language. In the plurality's constitutional universe, we may not take notice of the fact that the original reasons for the conclusive presumption of paternity are out of place in a world in which blood tests can prove virtually beyond a shadow of a doubt who sired a particular child and in which the fact of illegitimacy no longer plays the burdensome and stigmatizing role it once did. Nor, in the plurality's world, may we deny "tradition" its full scope by pointing out that the rationale for the conventional rule has changed over the years, as has the rationale for § 621; [1] instead, our task is simply to identify a rule denying the asserted interest and not to ask whether the basis for that rule ... has changed too often or too recently to call the rule embodying that rationale a "tradition." Moreover, by describing the decisive question as whether Michael['s] ... interest is one that has been "traditionally *protected* by our society," rather than one that society traditionally has thought important (with or without protecting it), and by suggesting that our sole function is to "*discern* the society's views," (emphasis added), the plurality acts as if the only purpose of the Due Process Clause is to confirm the importance of interests already protected by a majority of the States. Transforming the protection afforded by the Due Process Clause into a redundancy mocks those who, with care and purpose, wrote the Fourteenth Amendment.

---

1. See In re Marriage of Sharyne B. and Stephen (Cal., 1981) (noting that California courts initially justified conclusive presumption of paternity on the ground that biological paternity was impossible to prove, but that the preservation of family integrity became the rule's paramount justification when paternity tests became reliable). [Footnote by Justice Brennan.]

In construing the Fourteenth Amendment to offer shelter only to those interests specifically protected by historical practice, moreover, the plurality ignores the kind of society in which our Constitution exists. We are not an assimilative, homogenous society, but a facilitative pluralistic one, in which we must be willing to abide someone else's unfamiliar or even repellant practice because the same tolerant impulse protects our own idiosyncracies. Even if we can agree, therefore, that "family" and "parenthood" are part of the good life, it is absurd to assume that we can agree on the content of those terms and destructive to pretend that we do. In a community such as ours, "liberty" must include the freedom not to conform. The plurality today squashes this freedom by requiring specific approval from history before protecting anything in the name of liberty.

The document that the plurality construes today is unfamiliar to me. It is not the living charter that I have taken to be our Constitution; it is instead a stagnant, archaic, hide-bound document steeped in the prejudices and superstitions of a time long past. *This* Constitution does not recognize that times change, does not see that sometimes a practice or rule outlives its foundations. I cannot accept an interpretive method that does such violence to the charter that I am bound by oath to uphold.
. . .

[Justice Brennan went on to explain that he was not claiming Michael would prevail on the merits, only that he was entitled to a hearing on the merits.]

Justice **WHITE**, with whom Justice **BRENNAN** joins, dissenting.

. . . Because I believe that Michael H. has a liberty interest that cannot be denied without due process of the law, I must dissent. . . .

Editors' Notes

(1) For other debates between Justices Brennan and Scalia on similar issues of constitutional inclusion and change, see Burnham v. Superior Court of California (1990) and the article by each we have excerpted in Chapter 6.

(2) **Query:** What was Scalia's conception of "tradition"? What was Brennan's? On Scalia's understanding would, in 1954, a southern white child have had a constitutionally protected "liberty interest" to attend a public school solely with other children of her own race? If so, why so? If not, why not? If Justice Harlan had accepted Brennan's conception of tradition, would Harlan have been obliged to vote the other way in Poe v. Ullman (1961) and Griswold v. Connecticut (1965)? If so, why so? If not, why not?

(3) **Query:** How does "tradition," as defined by either Brennan or Scalia, become embedded in the constitutional canon? WHO does the embedding? WHO discovers whether some persons, institution(s), or processes have done so? What were the criteria that Brennan and Scalia suggested for determining when a tradition, however it is defined, enters the constitutional canon?

(4) **Query:** Assuming Justice Hugo Black had been alive in 1990 and stood by his opinions in Rochin v. California (1952; reprinted above p. 135)

and Griswold v. Connecticut (1965; reprinted above p. 147), how would he have responded to Scalia's opinion? To Brennan's?

(5) **Query:** To what extent did either Scalia or Brennan (or do both) conflate "tradition" and "history"? Two of us have proposed distinctions between tradition as reflecting historical practices and tradition as reflecting aspirational principles or the "normative theory of what we stand for as a people." Sotirios A. Barber, *On What the Constitution Means* (Baltimore: Johns Hopkins Univesity Press, 1984), p. 84, and James E. Fleming, "Constructing the Substantive Constitution," 72 *Tex.L.Rev.* 211, 268–273 (1993). To what extent would this distinction clarify the issues that *Michael H.* presents?

(6) For further discussion about the proper "level of generality" in constitutional interpretation, see: Paul Brest, "The Fundamental Rights Controversy: The Essential Contradictions of Normative Constitutional Scholarship," 90 *Yale L.J.* 1063 (1981); Laurence H. Tribe and Michael C. Dorf, "Levels of Generality in the Definition of Rights," 57 *U.Chi.L.Rev.* 1057 (1990); Frank H. Easterbrook, "Abstraction and Authority," 59 *U.Chi.L.Rev.* 349 (1992); and Bruce Ackerman, "Liberating Abstraction," 59 *ibid.* 317 (1992).

"In religious debate or expression the government is not a prime participant, for the Framers deemed religious establishment antithetical to the freedom of all."—Justice KENNEDY

"A government cannot be premised on the belief that all persons are created equal when it asserts that God prefers some."—Justice BLACKMUN

"... those [early] practices prove, at best, that the Framers simply did not share a common understanding of the Establishment Clause, and, at worst, that they, like other politicians, could raise constitutional ideals one day and turn their backs on them the next."—Justice SOUTER

"Today's opinion shows more forcefully than volumes of argumentation why our Nation's protection, that fortress which is our Constitution, cannot possibly rest upon the changeable philosophical predilections of the Justices of this Court, but must have deep foundations in the historic practices of our people."—Justice SCALIA

LEE v. WEISMAN

505 U.S. 577, 112 S.Ct. 2649, 120 L.Ed.2d 467 (1992).

The school board of Providence, R.I., allowed principals to invite members of the clergy to offer non-denominational prayers at graduations. Graduating students were not, however, required either to attend the ceremonies or to participate in prayer. In 1989, Daniel Weisman, the father of Deborah Weisman, who was graduating from a public middle school, asked a federal district court to enjoin the practice as a violation of the "establishment clause" of the First Amendment, which the Fourteenth Amendment, so the Supreme Court has said, makes binding on the states. The district court granted the injunction and the Court of Appeals for the First Circuit affirmed. The principal obtained certiorari.

Justice **KENNEDY** delivered the opinion of the Court. ...

I

A. ...

The school board (and the United States, which supports it as *amicus curiae*) argued that these short prayers and others like them at graduation exercises are of profound meaning to many students and parents throughout this country who consider that due respect and acknowledgement for divine guidance and for the deepest spiritual aspirations of our people ought to be expressed at an event as important in life as a graduation. We assume this to be so ... for the significance of the prayers lies also at the heart of Daniel and Deborah Weisman's case.

B ...

... The District Court ... applied the three-part Establishment Clause test set forth in Lemon v. Kurtzman (1971). Under that test as described in our past cases, to satisfy the Establishment Clause a governmental practice must (1) reflect a clearly secular purpose; (2) have a primary effect that neither advances nor inhibits religion; and (3) avoid excessive government entanglement with religion. ... The District Court held that petitioners' actions violated the second part of the test, and so did not address either the first or the third. ...

II

... State officials direct the performance of a formal religious exercise at promotional and graduation ceremonies for secondary schools. Even for those students who object to the religious exercise, their attendance and participation in the state-sponsored religious activity are in a fair and real sense obligatory, though the school district does not require attendance. ...

... The government involvement with religious activity in this case is pervasive, to the point of creating a state-sponsored and state-directed religious exercise in a public school. Conducting this formal religious observance conflicts with settled rules pertaining to prayer exercises for students, and that suffices to determine the question before us.

The principle that government may accommodate the free exercise of religion does not supersede the fundamental limitations imposed by the Establishment Clause. It is beyond dispute that, at a minimum, the Constitution guarantees that government may not coerce anyone to support or participate in religion or its exercise, or otherwise act in a way which "establishes a [state] religion or religious faith, or tends to do so." Lynch v. Donnelly (1984). ... The State's involvement in the school prayers challenged today violates these central principles. ...

Divisiveness, of course, can attend any state decision respecting religions, and neither its existence nor its potential necessarily invalidates the State's attempts to accommodate religion in all cases. The potential for divisiveness is of particular relevance here though, because it centers around an overt religious exercise in a secondary school environment where ... subtle coercive pressures exist and where the student had no real alternative which would have allowed her to avoid the fact or appearance of participation.

The State's role did not end with the decision to include a prayer and with the choice of clergyman. Principal Lee provided Rabbi Gutterman with a copy of the "Guidelines for Civic Occasions," and advised him that his prayers should be nonsectarian. Through these means the principal directed and controlled the content of the prayer. Even if the only sanction for ignoring the instructions were that the rabbi would not be invited back, we think no religious representative who valued his or her continued reputation and effectiveness in the community would incur the State's displeasure in this regard. ...

The First Amendment's Religion Clauses mean that religious beliefs and religious expression are too precious to be either proscribed or prescribed by the State. The design of the Constitution is that preservation and transmission of religious beliefs and worship is a responsibility and a choice committed to the private sphere. ... James Madison, the principal author of the Bill of Rights, did not rest his opposition to a religious establishment on the sole ground of its effect on the minority. A principal ground for his view was: "[E]xperience witnesseth that ecclesiastical establishments, instead of maintaining the purity and efficacy of Religion, have had a contrary operation." *Memorial and Remonstrance Against Religious Assessments* (1785). ...

The lessons of the First Amendment are as urgent in the modern world as in the 18th Century when it was written. One timeless lesson is that if citizens are subjected to state-sponsored religious exercises, the State disavows its own duty to guard and respect that sphere of inviolable conscience and belief which is the mark of a free people. To compromise that principle today would be to deny our own tradition and forfeit our standing to urge others to secure the protections of that tradition for themselves.

... [T]here are heightened concerns with protecting freedom of conscience from subtle coercive pressure in the elementary and secondary public schools. See, e.g., Abington School District v. Schempp (1963) (Goldberg, J., concurring). ... Our decisions in Engel v. Vitale (1962) and *Abington* ... recognize ... that prayer exercises in public schools carry a particular risk of indirect coercion. ... What to most believers may seem nothing more than a reasonable request that the nonbeliever respect their religious practices, in a school context may appear to the nonbeliever or dissenter to be an attempt to employ the machinery of the State to enforce a religious orthodoxy.

We need not look beyond the circumstances of this case to see the phenomenon at work. The undeniable fact is that the school district's supervision and control of a high school * graduation ceremony places public pressure, as well as peer pressure, on attending students to stand as a group or, at least, maintain respectful silence during the Invocation and Benediction. This pressure, though subtle and indirect, can be as real as any overt compulsion. Of course, in our culture standing or remaining silent can signify adherence to a view or simple respect for the views of others. And no doubt some persons who have no desire to join a prayer have little objection to standing as a sign of respect for those who do. But for the dissenter of high school age, who has a reasonable perception that she is being forced by the State to pray in a manner her conscience will not allow, the injury is no less real. There can be no doubt that for many, if not most, of the students at the graduation, the act of standing or remaining silent was an expression of participation in the Rabbi's prayer. That was the very point of the religious exercise. It is of little comfort to a dissenter, then, to be told that for her the act of standing or remaining in silence signifies mere respect, rather than participation. What matters is that, given our social conventions, a reasonable dissenter in this milieu could believe that the group exercise signified her own participation or approval of it.

... We do not address whether that choice is acceptable if the affected citizens are mature adults, but we think the State may not, consistent with the Establishment Clause, place primary and secondary school children in this position. Research in psychology supports the common assumption that adolescents are often susceptible to pressure from their peers towards conformity, and that the influence is strongest in matters of social convention.** To recognize that the choice imposed by the State constitutes an unacceptable constraint only acknowledges that the government may no more use social pressure to enforce orthodoxy than it may use more direct means. ...

There was a stipulation in the District Court that attendance at graduation and promotional ceremonies is voluntary. ... Petitioners and the United States, as amicus, made this a center point of the case, arguing that the option of not attending the graduation excuses any inducement or coercion in the ceremony itself. The argument lacks all persuasion. Law reaches past formalism. And to say a teenage student has a real choice not to attend her high school graduation is formalistic

---

* Kennedy several times referred to "high school" ceremonies; this case, however, involved a pupil in a middle school.—**Eds.**

** At this point Kennedy inserted citations to: Brittain, "Adolescent Choices and Parent–Peer Cross-pressures," 28 *Am. Socio. Rev.* 385 (1963); Clasen and Brown, "The Multidimensionality of Peer Pressure in Adolescence," 14 *J. of Youth and Adolescence* 451 (1985); and Brown, Clasen, and Eicher, "Perceptions of Peer Pressure, Peer Conformity Dispositions, and and Self-Reported Behavior Among Adolescents," 22 *Develop'l Psych.* 521 (1986).—**Eds.**

in the extreme. ... Everyone knows that in our society and in our culture high school graduation is one of life's most significant occasions. ... Attendance may not be required by official decree, yet it is apparent that a student is not free to absent herself from the graduation exercise in any real sense of the term "voluntary," for absence would require forfeiture of those intangible benefits which have motivated the student through youth and all her high school years. ...

... [W]hat for many of Deborah's classmates and their parents was a spiritual imperative was for Daniel and Deborah Weisman religious conformance compelled by the State. While in some societies the wishes of the majority might prevail, the Establishment Clause of the First Amendment is addressed to this contingency and rejects the balance urged upon us. The Constitution forbids the State to exact religious conformity from a student as the price of attending her own high school graduation. ...

Our society would be less than true to its heritage if it lacked abiding concern for the values of its young people, and we acknowledge the profound belief of adherents to many faiths that there must be a place in the student's life for precepts of a morality higher even than the law we today enforce. We express no hostility to those aspirations, nor would our oath permit us to do so. ... We recognize that, at graduation time and throughout the course of the educational process, there will be instances when religious values, religious practices, and religious persons will have some interaction with the public schools and their students. ... But these matters, often questions of accommodation of religion, are not before us. The sole question presented is whether a religious exercise may be conducted at a graduation ceremony in circumstances where, as we have found, young graduates who object are induced to conform. No holding by this Court suggests that a school can persuade or compel a student to participate in a religious exercise. That is being done here, and it is forbidden by the Establishment Clause of the First Amendment.

Justice **BLACKMUN**, with whom Justices **STEVENS** and **O'CONNOR** join, concurring.

Nearly half a century of review and refinement of Establishment Clause jurisprudence has distilled one clear understanding: Government may neither promote nor affiliate itself with any religious doctrine or organization, nor may it obtrude itself in the internal affairs of any religious institution. The application of these principles to the present case mandates the decision reached today by the Court. ...

The mixing of government and religion can be a threat to free government, even if no one is forced to participate. When the government puts its imprimatur on a particular religion, it conveys a message of exclusion to those who do not adhere to the favored beliefs. A government cannot be premised on the belief that all persons are created equal when it asserts that God prefers some. ...

When the government arrogates to itself a role in religious affairs, it abandons its obligation as guarantor of democracy. Democracy requires the nourishment of dialogue and dissent, while religious faith puts its trust in an ultimate divine authority above all human deliberation. When the government appropriates religious truth, it "transforms rational debate into theological decree." ... Those who disagree no longer are questioning the policy judgment of the elected but the rules of a higher authority who is beyond reproach. ...

Justice **SOUTER**, with whom Justice **STEVENS** and Justice **O'CON-NOR** join, concurring. ...

[Souter offered a long analysis of the doctrine the Court had built up over the past decades, then addressed the issues of original understanding and early practice that Justice **SCALIA** raised in his dissent (below, pp. 175–77.]

Petitioners argue from the political setting in which the Establishment Clause was framed, and from the Framers' own political practices following ratification, that government may constitutionally endorse religion so long as it does not coerce religious conformity. The setting and the practices warrant canvassing, but while they yield some evidence for petitioners' argument, they do not reveal the degree of consensus in early constitutional thought that would raise a threat to stare decisis by challenging the presumption that the Establishment Clause adds something to the Free Exercise Clause that follows it.

The Framers adopted the Religion Clauses in response to a long tradition of coercive state support for religion, particularly in the form of tax assessments, but their special antipathy to religious coercion did not exhaust their hostility to the features and incidents of establishment. Indeed, Jefferson and Madison opposed any political appropriation of religion, and, even when challenging the hated assessments, they did not always temper their rhetoric with distinctions between coercive and noncoercive state action. When, for example, Madison criticized Virginia's general assessment bill, he invoked principles antithetical to all state efforts to promote religion. An assessment, he wrote, is improper not simply because it forces people to donate "three pence" to religion, but, more broadly, because "it is itself a signal of persecution. It degrades from the equal rank of Citizens all those whose opinions in Religion do not bend to those of the Legislative authority." J. Madison, *Memorial and Remonstrance Against Religious Assessments* (1785). ...

Petitioners contend that because the early Presidents included religious messages in their inaugural and Thanksgiving Day addresses, the Framers could not have meant the Establishment Clause to forbid noncoercive state endorsement of religion. The argument ignores the fact, however, that Americans today find such proclamations less controversial than did the founding generation, whose published thoughts on the matter belie petitioners' claim. President Jefferson, for example, steadfastly refused to issue Thanksgiving proclamations of any kind, in part because he thought they violated the Religion Clauses. Letter from Thomas Jefferson to Rev. S. Miller (Jan. 23, 1808). ... Jefferson effectively anticipated, and rejected, petitioners' position:

> "It is only proposed that I should *recommend*, not prescribe a day of fasting & prayer. That is, that I should *indirectly* assume to the U.S. an authority over religious exercises which the Constitution has directly precluded from them. It must be meant too that this recommendation is to carry some authority, and to be sanctioned by some penalty on those who disregard it; not indeed of fine and imprisonment, but of some degree of proscription perhaps in public opinion." (Emphasis in original.)

... [Jefferson] construed the Establishment Clause to forbid not simply state coercion, but also state endorsement, of religious belief and observance. And if he opposed impersonal presidential addresses for inflicting "proscription in public opinion," all the more would he have condemned less diffuse expressions of official endorsement.[1] ...

Petitioners also seek comfort in a different passage of the same letter. Jefferson argued that presidential religious proclamations violate not just the Establishment Clause, but also the Tenth Amendment, for "what might be a right in a state government, was a violation of that right when assumed by another." Jefferson did not, however, restrict himself to the Tenth Amendment in condemning such proclamations by a national officer. ...

During his first three years in office, James Madison also refused to call for days of thanksgiving and prayer, though later, amid the political turmoil of the War of 1812, he did so on four separate occasions. Upon retirement, in an essay condemning as an unconstitutional "establishment" the use of public money to support congressional and military chaplains,[2] he concluded that "religious proclamations by the Executive recommending thanksgivings & fasts are shoots from the same root with the legislative acts reviewed. Altho' recommendations only, they imply a religious agency, making no part of the trust delegated to political rulers." Explaining that "the members of a Govt ... can in no sense, be regarded as possessing an advisory trust from their Constituents in their religious capacities," he further observed that the state necessarily freights all of its religious messages with political ones: "the idea of policy [is] associated with religion, whatever be the mode or the occasion, when a function of the latter is assumed by those in power."

Madison's failure to keep pace with his principles in the face of congressional pressure cannot erase the principles. He admitted to

---

1. ... Jefferson's practice, like Madison's, sometimes diverged from principle, for he did include religious references in his inaugural speeches. Homer nodded. [Footnote by Justice Souter.]

2. Madison found this practice "a palpable violation of ... Constitutional principles." Although he sat on the committee recommending the congressional chaplainship, he later insisted that "it was not with my approbation, that the deviation from [the immunity of Religion from civil jurisdiction] took place in Congs., when they appointed Chaplains, to be paid from the Natl. Treasury." Letter from J. Madison to E. Livingston (July 10, 1822). [Footnote by Justice Souter.]

backsliding, and explained that he had made the content of his wartime proclamations inconsequential enough to mitigate much of their impropriety. While his writings suggest mild variations in his interpretation of the Establishment Clause, Madison was no different in that respect from the rest of his political generation. That he expressed so much doubt about the constitutionality of religious proclamations, however, suggests a brand of separationism stronger even than that embodied in our traditional jurisprudence. So too does his characterization of public subsidies for legislative and military chaplains as unconstitutional "establishments," for the federal courts, however expansive their general view of the Establishment Clause, have upheld both practices. See Marsh v. Chambers (1983) (legislative chaplains); Katcoff v. Marsh (CA2 1985) (military chaplains).

To be sure, the leaders of the young Republic engaged in some of the practices that separationists like Jefferson and Madison criticized. The First Congress did hire institutional chaplains, and Presidents Washington and Adams unapologetically marked days of "public thanksgiving and prayer." Yet in the face of the separationist dissent, those practices prove, at best, that the Framers simply did not share a common understanding of the Establishment Clause, and, at worst, that they, like other politicians, could raise constitutional ideals one day and turn their backs on them the next. ... Ten years after proposing the First Amendment, Congress passed the Alien and Sedition Acts, measures patently unconstitutional by modern standards. If the early Congress's political actions were determinative, and not merely relevant, evidence of constitutional meaning, we would have to gut our current First Amendment doctrine to make room for political censorship.

While we may be unable to know for certain what the Framers meant by the Clause, we do know that, around the time of its ratification, a respectable body of opinion supported a considerably broader reading than petitioners urge upon us. ... [Souter went on to argue that the prayer violated the First and Fourteenth amendments.—**Eds.**]

Justice **SCALIA**, with whom the Chief Justice [**REHNQUIST**] and
    Justice **WHITE** and Justice **THOMAS** join, dissenting.

Three Terms ago, I joined an opinion recognizing that the Establishment Clause must be construed in light of the "government policies of accommodation, acknowledgment, and support for religion [that] are an accepted part of our political and cultural heritage." That opinion affirmed that "the meaning of the Clause is to be determined by reference to historical practices and understandings." It said that "[a] test for implementing the protections of the Establishment Clause that, if applied with consistency, would invalidate longstanding traditions cannot be a proper reading of the Clause." Allegheny County v. Greater Pittsburgh ACLU (1989) (Kennedy, J., concurring ... in part and dissenting in part).

These views of course prevent me from joining today's opinion, which is conspicuously bereft of any reference to history. In holding that the Establishment Clause prohibits invocations and benedictions at public-school graduation ceremonies, the Court—with nary a mention that it that it is doing so—lays waste a tradition that is as old as public-school graduation ceremonies themselves, and that is a component of an even more longstanding American tradition of nonsectarian prayer to God at public celebrations generally. As its instrument of destruction, the bulldozer of its social engineering, the Court invents a boundless, and boundlessly manipulable, test of psychological coercion. ... Today's opinion shows more forcefully than volumes of argumentation why our Nation's protection, that fortress which is our Constitution, cannot possibly rest upon the changeable philosophical predilections of the Justices of this Court, but must have deep foundations in the historic practices of our people.

I ...

The history and tradition of our Nation are replete with public ceremonies featuring prayers of thanksgiving and petition. Illustrations of this point have been amply provided in our prior opinions, see, e.g., *Lynch*, *Marsh*, but since the Court is so oblivious to our history as to suggest that the Constitution restricts "preservation and transmission of religious beliefs ... to the private sphere" ... it appears necessary to provide another brief account.

From our Nation's origin, prayer has been a prominent part of governmental ceremonies and proclamations. The Declaration of Independence, the document marking our birth as a separate people, "appealed to the Supreme Judge of the world for the rectitude of our intentions" and avowed "a firm reliance on the protection of divine Providence." In his first inaugural address, after swearing his oath of office on a Bible, George Washington deliberately made a prayer a part of his first official act as President:

> "it would be peculiarly improper to omit in this first official act my fervent supplications to that Almighty Being who rules over the universe, who presides in the councils of nations, and whose providential aids can supply every human defect, that His benediction may consecrate to the liberties and happiness of the people of the United States a Government instituted by themselves for these essential purposes." ...

Such supplications have been a characteristic feature of inaugural addresses ever since. Thomas Jefferson, for example, prayed in his first inaugural address: "may that Infinite Power which rules the destinies of the universe lead our councils to what is best, and give them a favorable issue for your peace and prosperity." ... In his second inaugural address, Jefferson acknowledged his need for divine guidance and invited his audience to join his prayer:

> "I shall need, too, the favor of that Being in whose hands we are, who led our fathers, as Israel of old, from their native land and planted them in a country flowing with all the necessaries and comforts of life; who

has covered our infancy with His providence and our riper years with His wisdom and power, and to whose goodness I ask you to join in supplications with me. ...."

Similarly, James Madison, in his first inaugural address, placed his confidence

"in the guardianship and guidance of that Almighty Being whose power regulates the destiny of nations, whose blessings have been so conspicuously dispensed to this rising Republic, and to whom we are bound to address our devout gratitude for the past, as well as our fervent supplications and best hopes for the future." ...

Most recently, President [George] Bush, continuing the tradition established by President Washington, asked those attending his inauguration to bow their heads, and made a prayer his first official act as President. ...

The other two branches of the Federal Government also have a long-established practice of prayer at public events. As we detailed in *Marsh*, Congressional sessions have opened with a chaplain's prayer ever since the First Congress. ... And this Court's own sessions have opened with the invocation "God save the United States and this Honorable Court" since the days of Chief Justice Marshall. ...

In addition to this general tradition of prayer at public ceremonies, there exists a more specific tradition of invocations and benedictions at public-school graduation exercises. ... As the Court obliquely acknowledges ... graduations ... and as respondents do not contest, the invocation and benediction have long been recognized to be "as traditional as any other parts of the [school] graduation program and are widely established." ...

II ...

[Scalia proceeded to attack the Court's finding of "psychological coercion" and its "few citations" to "research in psychology" that, he asserted, "have no particular bearing upon the precise issues here." He found such claims of coercion to be as "absurd" as the assertion that simply standing out of respect to others signified acceptance of the beliefs of others. He also denied that the principal's giving the Rabbi a two-page flyer prepared by the National Conference of Christians and Jews on non-sectarian prayers in any way indicated the state controlled the content of the Rabbi's prayer.—**Eds.**]

III

The deeper flaw in the Court's opinion ... lies ... in the Court's making violation of the Establishment Clause hinge on such a precious question [as psychological coercion]. The coercion that was a hallmark of historical establishments of religion was coercion of religious orthodoxy and of financial support by force of law and threat of penalty. Typically, attendance at the state church was required; only clergy of the official church could lawfully perform sacraments: and dissenters, if tolerated, faced an array of civil disabilities. L. Levy, *The Establishment Clause* 4 (1986). Thus, for example, in the colony of Virginia, where the Church of England had been established, ministers were required by law to conform to the doctrine and rites of the Church of England; and all persons were required to attend church and observe the Sabbath, were tithed for the public support of Anglican ministers, and were taxed for the costs of building and repairing churches. . . .

The Establishment Clause was adopted to prohibit such an establishment of religion at the federal level (and to protect state establishments of religion from federal interference). I will further acknowledge for the sake of argument that, as some scholars have argued, by 1790 the term "establishment" had acquired an additional meaning—"financial support of religion generally, by public taxation"—that reflected the development of "general or multiple" establishments, not limited to a single church. . . . But that would still be an establishment coerced by force of law. And I will further concede that our constitutional tradition, from the Declaration of Independence and the first inaugural address of Washington down to the present day, has, with a few aberrations . . . ruled out of order government-sponsored endorsement of religion—even when no legal coercion is present, and indeed even when no ersatz, "peer-pressure" psycho-coercion is present—where the endorsement is sectarian. . . . But there is simply no support for the proposition that the officially sponsored nondenominational invocation and benediction read by Rabbi Gutterman . . . violated the Constitution. . . . To the contrary, they are so characteristically American they could have come from the pen of George Washington or Abraham Lincoln himself.

Thus, while I have no quarrel with the Court's general proposition that the Establishment Clause "guarantees that government may not coerce anyone to support or participate in religion or its exercise," . . . I see no warrant for expanding the concept of coercion beyond acts backed by threat of penalty—a brand of coercion that, happily, is readily discernible to those of us who have made a career of reading the disciples of Blackstone rather than of Freud. . . .

IV . . .

The reader has been told much in this case about the personal interest of Mr. Weisman and his daughter, and very little about the personal interests on the other side. They are not inconsequential. Church and state would not be such a difficult subject if religion were, as the Court apparently thinks it to be, some purely personal avocation that can be indulged entirely in secret, like pornography, in the privacy of one's room. For most believers it is not that, and has never been. Religious men and women of almost all denominations have felt it necessary to acknowledge and beseech the blessing of God as a people, and not just as individuals, because they believe in the "protection of divine Providence," as the Declaration of Independence put it, not just for individuals but for societies; because they believe God to be, as

Washington's first Thanksgiving Proclamation put it, the "Great Lord and Ruler of Nations." One can believe in the effectiveness of such public worship, or one can deprecate and deride it. But the longstanding American tradition of prayer at official ceremonies displays with unmistakable clarity that the Establishment Clause does not forbid the government to accommodate it.

I must add one final observation: The founders of our Republic knew the fearsome potential of sectarian religious belief to generate civil dissension and civil strife. And they also knew that nothing, absolutely nothing, is so inclined to foster among religious believers of various faiths a toleration—no, an affection—for one another than voluntarily joining in prayer together, to the God whom they all worship and seek. Needless to say, no one should be compelled to do that, but it is a shame to deprive our public culture of the opportunity, and indeed the encouragement, for people to do it voluntarily. The Baptist or Catholic who heard and joined in the simple and inspiring prayers of Rabbi Gutterman on this official and patriotic occasion was inoculated from religious bigotry and prejudice in a manner that can not be replicated. To deprive our society of that important unifying mechanism, in order to spare the nonbeliever what seems to me the minimal inconvenience of standing or even sitting in respectful nonparticipation, is as senseless in policy as it is unsupported in law.

Editors' Notes

(1) **Query:** Both Kennedy for the Court and Scalia in dissent mentioned the *Lemon* test. What is that test's relation to the constitutional text?

(2) **Query:** Kennedy, Souter, and Scalia each supported their conclusions with appeals to "tradition," but Scalia sharply disagreed with the other two. They must have had different conceptions or theories of tradition. What were the differences among the justices? Did they principally disagree about the content of tradition? In the ways in which interpreters should discover tradition? In the weight that tradition should carry in constitutional interpretation and the function(s) it should perform? By what test could an interpreter determine which theory of tradition is best? In any event, to what extent is "tradition" a part of "the Constitution"? Whose tradition? Did any justice address this critical issue? If so, who and how? If not, why not?

(3) **Query:** To what extent did Scalia's concept of tradition change in the intervening three years since *Michael H.*, reprinted above p. 158?

(4) **Query:** The justices were unanimous that public schools may not coerce students to pray; they disagreed over what constitutes coercion. Kennedy believed a rule against coercion should cover heavy psychological pressure (Scalia called it "psycho-coercion"), and Scalia contended that for constitutional purposes coercion must be accompanied by threats of legal or physical penalties. He added that the meaning of coercion depends on the beliefs of Blackstone and the American founding generation, not Freud and his followers. Did Scalia suggest that the law does not accommodate scientific advances in our understanding of the things to which it refers? Can some

other proposition justify Scalia's view of the constitutional meaning of coercion?

(5) **Query:** Scalia claimed that the "original understanding" of "the Constitution" provides the safest guide for judges. (See also his article, "Originalism: The Lesser Evil," reprinted below, p. 231.) What about Souter? Who made the better argument? What does their disagreement imply for the worth of "original understanding" as an *approach* to constitutional interpretation? (Chapter 9 defines an *approach* to constitutional interpretation in a rather specific way; but for purposes of this query, one can use it in its common-sense meaning.) For scholarship that would have supported Scalia's substantive argument, see Gary D. Glenn, "Forgotten Purposes of the First Amendment Religion Clauses," 49 *Rev. of Pols.* 340 (1987), which contends that the amendment's objectives included righting what many Anti–Federalists saw as the constitutional text's tilt against religion. Thus, Glenn claims, one goal of the amendment was to make the new system more friendly toward religion. The matter, however, remains controversial, subject to all the difficulties that a quest for original understanding raises.

(6) **Query:** "A government," Blackmun said, "cannot be premised on the belief that all persons are created equal when it asserts that God prefers some." The official constitutional text does not speak of people as being "created equal": that language is found in the Declaration of Independence. To what extent did Blackmun treat the Declaration as part of the larger constitution? He went on to talk about the danger of government's abandoning its task of a "guarantor of democracy," yet the word "democracy" nowhere appears in the constitutional text. To what extent did Blackmun assume that democratic theory is part of "the Constitution"? Did he or any other justice address this question in *Lee*? If so, how? If not, why not?

6

What Is "the Constitution"?
Problems of Continuity
and Change

Among the myriad of difficulties facing the founding generation in America was how to achieve stability while permitting change. Too much of either might destroy the infant political system, and neither contemporary Europe nor earlier history presented a model for the framers to copy. A few of the collections of customs and usages that nations in the eighteenth century called constitutions were so difficult to adapt to meet unforeseen crises as to encourage officials to ignore them. Most were constitutions without constitutionalism and so easy to recast (even to re-invent) as to allow officials unfettered discretion. The typical result of either sort of constitutional arrangement was uncontrolled power.

The American colonists wanted a different kind of constitution, one that would constrain as well as legitimate power. Having had recent unpleasant experiences with their "mother country," they saw a need for more tangible restraints than those the "customs and usages" the British system so vaguely imposed. That words can control power might seem a strange notion to most people, but the revolutionists' long experience living under colonial charters made constitutional covenants, embossed in a document, seem a "natural" way of simultaneously empowering and curbing government. Yet this alternative posed its own risks. Reducing a constitutional scheme to a document binding on public officials citizens might narrow discretion and control power; but the price could well be a government unable to cope with crises the document's authors had not foreseen. Such a system might soon lead either to national suicide, to a *coup d'etat*, or to the text's becoming a mere "parchment barrier" against tyranny.

Some considerations of justice also argued against trying to control the future by the words of the present. What one generation thought fair might seem unjust to its grandchildren. The likely alternatives were tyranny by the past or revolution by the future. This issue of fairness deeply troubled Jefferson. His solution was to

180

allow each generation to write a new constitutional text.[1] During the midst of debates on ratification, Noah Webster, the father of the first systematic dictionary of American English, cut to the core of the matter: "[T]he very attempt to make *perpetual* constitutions is the assumption of a right to controul the opinions of future generations; and to legislate for those over whom we have as little authority as we have over a nation in Asia."[2]

It seems obvious to us that the solution to this problem is to incorporate into the text itself procedures for amendment. But we have had more than two centuries of living under such an arrangement; for those who lacked our long experience, it was not so obvious. Indeed, the noted historian Gordon Wood has labelled this idea "a totally new contribution to politics."[3]

The formula contained in Article V of the document of 1787–88 stipulates that Congress can either: (a) at the request of two-thirds of the state legislatures, call a national convention; or (b) on its own motion propose an amendment approved by a two-thirds vote of each house. A would-be amendment birthed in either fashion then would go to the states, where it would have to be ratified by three-quarters of the states acting, as Congress has designated, either through the legislatures or conventions specially chosen for this purpose. The difficulty of securing such extraordinary majorities protects stability; the possibility of amendment when there is something close to consensus allows change.

It is not clear, however, that Article V avoids the dangers a constitutional text poses for coping with crises. The amending process may not be as slow as it is sometimes pictured;[4] but, at

---

1. This theme ran through much of Jefferson's writings. See, for example, his letter to Madison, Sept. 6, 1789; William T. Hutchinson and William M. E. Rachal, eds., *The Papers of James Madison* (Chicago: University of Chicago Press, 1979), XII, 382ff.

2. "Bills of Rights" (1788), reprinted in Noah Webster, *Collection of Essays and Fugitive Writings on Moral, Historical, Political and Literary Subjects* (Boston: Thomas & Andrews, 1790), p. 47 (italics in original).

3. *The Creation of the American Republic, 1776–1787* (New York: Norton, 1969), p. 613. Wood went further and claimed that, via the amending clause, Americans had "institutionalized and legitimized revolution." *Ibid.*, p. 614. This more extended claim conflates three concepts that are important to constitutional interpretation: (1) "amendment," a change within an existing political framework; (2) "revision," a change that may even reshape, without necessarily destroying, an existing political framework; and (3) "revolution," a change that substitutes a radically new political framework for the old. In Raven v. Deukmejian (1990), California's Supreme Court invalidated a supposed amendment to the state constitutional text on the ground that it was, in fact, a revision of that document not an amendment.

4. If one counts the Bill of Rights, submitted together and ratified together, as one amendment, the average length of time required for ratification, *before the Twenty-seventh Amendment*, was only about fifteen months. The longest time had been for the Twenty-second, setting a two-term limit on the presidency (three years and eleven months); and only the Bill of Rights (two years, three months) and the Fourteenth (two years, one month) had taken longer than two years. The median time for ratification had been slightly more than eleven months. These figures, however, do not count the time the amendments spent in Congress. See Clement E. Vose, *Constitutional Change: Amendment Politics and Supreme Court Litigation Since 1900* (Lexington, MA: Heath, 1972). The 203

minimum, it does take many months—a very long time when the country is facing a crisis, especially one involving national security. As Chapter 19 will illustrate, from the earliest days of the Republic, presidents have believed it necessary sometimes to operate outside the textual boundaries of their authority. And members of the founding generation as politically far apart as Alexander Hamilton and Thomas Jefferson agreed with James Madison that a higher law of necessity could justify such actions. One might make a cogent argument that some of these presidential usages have become part of the larger constitution and even that we now interpret the constitutional text as authorizing many such practices—and thus have amended the text through practice and interpretation.

In fact, Americans may have deceived themselves about the centrality of Article V to constitutional change. Its elaborate procedures do help explain why, since the Bill of Rights was ratified in 1791, the United States has formally amended its text only 17 times, two of which cancel each other out. But even close analysis of the other 15 amendments would yield only a partial picture of the evolution of the constitutional system. On the one hand, several amendments that might appear to effect important changes, such as the Seventeenth providing for direct election of senators, the Twentieth acknowledging the right of women to vote, and the Twenty-fourth eliminating the poll tax, only recognized and made more or less permanent what was becoming or had already become political reality. Before these amendments were ratified, most states were, in effect, electing senators directly, 30 were permitting women to vote (though only 17 in all elections), and 46 had repealed the poll tax.

On the other hand, the post-Civil War amendments, which prescribed enormous changes in the citizenry and nature of the Union, were slow to have the sorts of effects to which their words committed the United States. The Thirteenth formally abolished slavery in 1865, yet legally enforced racial segregation, "a badge of servitude," continued for most of a century and still slinks in the shadows of American life. In 1868, the Fourteenth restricted state power in many ways, but for decades those who benefitted were large corporations, not former slaves and their children. Worse, the amendment's principal promise of "the equal protection of the laws" is not yet a reality 125 years after its adoption. The Fifteenth admitted African American males to full citizenship by forbidding states to deny them the right to vote because of their race; but that promise was not fulfilled until after 1965, when Congress passed a tough voting rights law.

---

years between the time Congress proposed and enough states finally ratified the Twenty-seventh presents a statistical outlier. For a discussion of the problems ratification after such a time presents for the question of WHAT "the Constitution" includes, see Chapter 5, pp. 114-15.

For white males, the democratization of the United States came largely in the 1830s and was far more a product of politics in the states than of formal amendments. Even today the constitutional text does not recognize a right to vote. It is silent about who can cast a ballot for the President—the electoral college still officially chooses the Chief Executive—and only designates as having a right to vote for senators and representatives those people who are eligible to vote for the more numerous house of the state legislature. And the document does not contain any other positive instructions about who should be able to participate in those state contests. The remaining textual references to voting are largely negative; [5] that is, they forbid states to deny the ballot in state or federal elections because of race, sex, failure to pay a tax, or age (if a citizen is over 18). More recent insistence on fair districting through the rule of "one person, one vote" came as a result of the Supreme Court's interpretations after 1962, applying the equal protection clause of the Fourteenth Amendment to voting. [6] This construction would have amazed many of that amendment's supporters. They thought the Fifteenth Amendment was needed to protect voting rights.

So, too, the growth of modern judicial, congressional, and, even more strikingly, presidential power has largely come from practice and interpretation. The unfolding of specific civil liberties and the development of operational concepts of "fundamental rights" also owes more to judicial interpretations than to amendment. In effect, practice and interpretation have expanded the constitution considerably beyond the constitutional text. It is not that the two point in opposite directions; rather the document allows but does not determine the exact shape the constitution has taken on. Here the problems of constitutional change and constitutional inclusion collide, perhaps even merge.

No intelligent person would deny the statement that the constitutional text and the broader constitution have changed and have had to change over time. No group of founders can be omniscient. Any constitutional document has gaps, contains technical phrases, and must be written in a language whose syntax and vocabulary will evolve. In handling new problems, therefore, interpreters frequently need to decide on the legitimacy of others' efforts to fill in those lacunae or even to fill them in themselves, to explain the text's specialized wording, and to translate its old language into the current idiom. These sorts of processes necessarily require creativi-

---

5. The Twenty-third Amendment allows the District of Columbia to choose members of the Electoral College, but the selection of those delegates, the amendment says, shall be "in such manner as the Congress may direct"—hardly a ringing affirmation of citizens' right to vote in presidential elections.

6. For the judicial creation of this right, see Baker v. Carr (1962; reprinted below, p. 769 and Reynolds v. Sims (1964; reprinted below, p. 777). For an interpretation of the views of framers of the Fourteenth Amendment on voting rights, see Justice John Marshall Harlan's dissent in *Reynolds*.

ty, imagination, and judgment. Whether judges or other public officials are doing the interpretation, that work is likely to generate change and beget anxiety and opposition as well as relief and support.

There are three separable sets of issues here. First is the question of what sorts of changes, if any, are necessary—whether, that is, the interpreters' imagination is skewed and/or judgment faulty. Second is the question of how such changes as may be necessary should be brought about. Is it unreasonable to contend that interpreters who see themselves confronting the necessity of constitutional change should stop their process and allow the procedures of Article V to operate? The third issue comes into play if the response to the second is that formal amendment is unnecessary: WHO, which interpreters, make whatever changes are necessary?

At root, the first question focuses on matters of prudence, which will always divide the electorate as well as public officials. While not devoid of prudential dimensions, the second and third questions point to fundamental problems for constitutional interpretation. This chapter, therefore, focuses on the extent, if any, it is legitimate for constitutional interpreters, especially interpreters who are federal judges appointed for what amounts to life terms, to change "the Constitution" through construction.

As anyone who has read this far would predict, this question is and continues to be hotly contested. One long tradition holds that, in the drama of constitutional change, the judge has only a walk-on part. Justice Joseph Story, John Marshall's colleague and the most noted constitutional commentator of that era, wrote that "the Constitution" should "have a fixed, uniform, permanent construction." [7] Judge Thomas Cooley, the great commentator of the next generation, expressed the same thought: "The meaning of the constitution is fixed when it is adopted, and it is not different at any subsequent time when a court has occasion to pass upon it." [8] A century later, Justice Hugo Black wrote that the notion of a "living Constitution" was "an attack not only on the great value of the Constitution itself, but also on the concept of a written constitution which is to survive through the years as originally written unless changed through the amendment process which the Framers wisely provided." (Harper v. Virginia, dis. op. [1966]; reprinted below, p. 225.) Thus although Chief Justice William H. Rehnquist [9] and Justice Antonin Scalia ("Originalism: The Lesser Evil," reprinted below, p. 231) stop short of accepting the absolute ban

---

7. *Commentaries on the Constitution of the United States* (Boston: Hilliard, Gray & Co., 1833), I, § 426.

8. *A Treatise on Constitutional Limitations* (Boston: Little, Brown, 1868), p. 55.

9. "The Notion of a Living Constitution," (1976; reprinted below, p. 243). (When Rehnquist wrote this article, he was still an associate justice. He became Chief Justice of the United States in 1986.)

on interpretive change that Story and Cooley espouse, they stand in a venerable tradition when they argue for a tightly restricted judicial role in effecting constitutional change.

It is important to keep in mind, however, that the modern debate is not between those who see judges as having no valid role in adapting "the Constitution" and those who contend that judges may freely interpret the text to facilitate whatever changes they deem desirable. Disputes are far more subtle and not between two groups but among several, reflecting differences about precisely how limited is the role that judges can legitimately play in bringing about constitutional change. We can intelligently speak only of arguments for "more restricted" and "less restricted" roles for judges in effecting change-through-interpretation. Everyone admits that judges, like other interpreters, have to apply the words of an old text to new problems and such an application inevitably entails *some* legitimate range of change. As Justice George Sutherland, who would have found Hugo Black a blood brother on this issue, wrote in his dissent in the Minnesota Moratorium Case (1934; reprinted below, p. 210, applications of constitutional principles can change, it is only the principles themselves that are permanent.

Furthermore, most modern interpreters and commentators would admit that it might be appropriate for judges to correct and so change *their* branch's constitutional interpretation. That is to say, while there may be a presumption that a Court composed of justices who lived at or very near the time of the adoption of the text or one of its amendments would have better understood it than would later generations, any such presumption is rebuttable. That presumption may even not be very useful because there may have been no contemporaneous or near-contemporaneous exegesis. We have, for instance, very little interpretation of the free speech clause of the First Amendment until World War I, more than a dozen decades after the amendment was ratified.

Equally important for judicial reexamination is the plain fact that, like Homer, judges sometimes nod. And, although other institutions might correct those interpretive errors, the system works more smoothly if judges repair their own mistakes. And, as Chapter 2 pointed out, the Supreme Court has frequently said it will do so, *providing* the justices reckon that reversal will not beget greater harm than will adhering to an earlier opinion. When the justices agree their former selves erred, differences among them mostly center on evaluations of the harm likely to flow from emending the older construction.

Judges like Benjamin N. Cardozo, William O. Douglas, and William J. Brennan, Jr., agree with Story, Black, Scalia, et al. that judges' roles in effecting constitutional change should be limited; but these other judges think the situation is more complicated. The most fundamental differences concern judgments about the capacity of interpreters to recover the intent of the framers about or the original understanding of a clause in the body of the text of 1787–88 or an amendment. For reasons like those Chapter 9 discusses, some judges (and many more commentators) deny that we can put ourselves back into the original position, either of 1787–88 or of the adoption of most amendments. We know what the founders wrote into the document; and sometimes, but only sometimes, what they did or said elsewhere gives us a general idea of what they thought were the implications of their words. But, "non-originalists" insist, in most situations interpreters who make a "finding" about intent or understanding are deluding themselves if they think they are simply reporting the views of the authors and ratifiers of the text. Originalist interpreters are often exercising their creative imaginations, not reporting historical "facts."

There is a closely related dispute about the weight such an original understanding should carry in those instances it might be recovered. Where the political system has developed in ways the framers did not and could not have foreseen, judges, like all other interpreters, may have to decide which of these ways are legitimate and which are illegitimate. In so doing, most judges acknowledge, they inevitably help shape constitutional change. As Oliver Wendell Holmes explained for the Court in 1920:

> [W]hen we are dealing with words that are also a constituent act, like the Constitution of the United States, we must realize that they have called into life a being the development of which could not have been foreseen completely by the most gifted of its begetters. It was enough for them to realize or to hope that they had created an organism; it has taken a century and cost their successors much sweat and blood to prove that they created a nation. The case before us must be considered in the light of our whole experience and not merely in that of what was said a hundred years ago. [Missouri v. Holland (reprinted below, p. 206).]

But agreement on Holmes's general proposition may provide the occasion for war rather than peace. Precisely what light "our whole experience" sheds is a matter open to heady dispute. And the stakes for future constitutional interpretation as well as for immediate public policies may be immense.

It may also happen that circumstances have changed so much that the solution the founders prescribed for a particular problem would destroy their underlying goal. The reasoning of some justices runs along lines that Ronald Dworkin has spelled out:[10] The constitutional text often speaks in broad "concepts" not in particularized "conceptions"—when it talks of "due process of law" or "equal protection," for instance, it lays down general principles rather than offers a catalogue of specific do's and don'ts. It might

---

10. *Taking Rights Seriously* (Cambridge: Harvard University Press, 1977), ch. 5.

well pervert the founders' purposes to carry out those general principles as if they represented no more than the concrete examples they had in mind.

The School Segregation Cases (1954; reprinted below, p. 912) might provide an illustration. The same Congress that proposed the Fourteenth Amendment also established segregated public schools in the District of Columbia. *Assuming* such an establishment is convincing proof of the understanding of Congress and the ratifying state legislatures in 1868 that enforced segregation did not violate equal protection, would that understanding have required judges in 1954 to uphold compulsory segregation?[11] One might well say no, reasoning that: (1) the overriding purpose of the Amendment had been to help the newly freed slaves to achieve legal equality; (2) because before the Civil War it had been a crime in most southern states to teach a slave to read and write, very few African Americans could read or write; (3) therefore, it made some sense in 1868 to believe that school segregation would actually help the children of newly freed (and almost totally illiterate) slaves achieve an education and so be better able to assume their rightful role in society;[12] (4) but, whatever value that argument had three years after emancipation, the subsequent history of segregation demonstrated that it had been a means of preventing African Americans from enjoying equality before the law; (5) thus the general concept of equality that infused the Fourteenth Amendment justified the Supreme Court's invalidating the framers' historically conditioned conceptions of equality.

Stated in Ronald Dworkin's terminology, this rationale for change-through-interpretation might sharply divide the justices. But Judge Robert H. Bork, an opponent of Dworkin who advocates a very limited judicial role in constitutional change and forcefully presses the view that judges should find and scrupulously apply original intent, makes very much this sort of argument about segregation.[13] Moreover, Scalia adopts similar reasoning, as did Hugo Black. Each of these jurists, however, has been extremely reluctant to extend this reasoning to other constitutional problems. For them, governmental efforts to impose and maintain a caste

---

11. It is true that the equal protection clause of the Fourteenth Amendment does not, by its own terms, restrict Congress—see, however, the cases and discussion in Chapters 14 and 15 in which the Supreme Court has ruled that the due process clause of the Fifth Amendment contains "an equal protection component." The second assumption of the example is that, if the state legislatures and Congress had understood equal protection to forbid segregation, Congress would not have deliberately deprived the newly free slaves of constitutional rights that it had required the states to protect.

12. Of course, a majority of Congress might have thought that it was wrong for white children to have to go to school with black children. Many Radical Republicans who hated slavery were still racists by our standards. Besides, many of them were as much, or more, concerned with punishing white southerners as in helping the newly freed slaves.

13. *The Tempting of America: The Political Seduction of the Law* (New York: The Free Press, 1990), pp. 74–84.

system present a highly unusual, perhaps a unique, cause for judges' playing a broad role in fomenting constitutional change.

For Hugo Black, we have an eloquent case in point for his refusing to extend something like the concept-conception distinction beyond race. In 1966 Justice Douglas persuaded a majority of his colleagues to invalidate a state's requiring payment of a poll tax as a prerequisite for voting. Such a regulation, Douglas said, discriminated on the basis of wealth and so violated the equal protection clause. This reading of the clause was new, he admitted, then added: "[T]he Equal Protection Clause is not shackled to the political theory of a particular era. . . . Notions of what constitutes equal treatment for purposes of the Equal Protection clause *do* change." Black, who had consistently voted against segregation, now protested bitterly against what he claimed was the Court's "consulting its own notions rather than following the original meaning" of the Fourteenth Amendment. (Harper v. Virginia, italics in original [1966; reprinted below, p. 225].)

In an *unpublished* slip opinion circulated within the Court while the justices were deliberating the Minnesota Moratorium Case (1934; reprinted below, p. 210), Justice Benjamin N. Cardozo went as far as any justice has in arguing against giving much authority to the founders' views. The time was the middle of the Great Depression and banks were foreclosing on thousands of loans on homes, businesses, and farms. In response, Minnesota enacted a law delaying for as long as two years the capacity of a creditor to seize the property of a defaulting debtor. This statute ran afoul not only of Article I's explicit prohibition against a state's "impairing the obligation of contracts," but also the framers' broader goal of protecting property against democratically elected legislators. But even in the face of the plain words of the document and considerable evidence about purpose if not intent, Cardozo would have interpreted the constitutional text to sustain such legislation. He was candid in his reasoning:

> To hold this may be inconsistent with things that men said in 1787 when expounding to compatriots the newly written constitution. They did not see the changes in the relation between states and nation or in the play of social forces that lay hidden in the womb of time. It may be inconsistent with things they believed or took for granted. [But t]heir beliefs to be significant must be adjusted to the world they knew. It is not in my judgment inconsistent with what they would say today nor with what today they would believe, if they were called upon to interpret "in the light of our whole experience" the constitution they framed for the needs of an expanding future.

That Cardozo did not publish this opinion might say something about how extreme were its views of the judicial role in constitutional change. Still, Chief Justice Charles Evans Hughes did incorporate, in a much toned down fashion, some of his colleague's reasoning.

Arguments about the legitimacy of change through interpretation rely heavily on answers to questions with which we are already familiar: WHAT does "the Constitution" include? WHAT are its functions? And WHO are its authoritative interpreters? Thus for most of those who believe they are prescribing a very narrow role for judges' engaging in creative interpretation, "the Constitution" includes the text of 1787–88, its amendments, and the original intent or understanding of the founders. Interpretation merely involves examining the document's specific words and clauses, discovering their initial meanings, and applying those meanings without regard either to intervening national development or to the consequences of departing from the original conception. Such broader issues fall under the jurisdiction of elected officials; they can enact statutes or amend the constitutional document to meet changing circumstances.

In contrast, those who see a less restricted for judges commonly reject originalism, conceive of "the Constitution" as more than a concise code, and look on constitutional interpretation as an effort, always struggling and often unsuccessful, to apply imperfectly stated general principles, such as those contained in the Preamble, the "sweeping clause" of Article I, and the Ninth and Fourteenth amendments, to changing circumstances. For them, then, constitutional interpretation is a proper part of statesmanship; they find the notion of constitutional change through judicial interpretation less bothersome than do their opponents.

Those officials and commentators who approve a less restricted role also tend to see the constitutional text as announcing aspirations of and for the American people. Justice Brennan has made one such claim: "[T]he Constitution embodies the aspiration to social justice, brotherhood, and human dignity that brought this nation into being." ("The Constitution of the United States: Contemporary Ratification," reprinted below, p. 236.) This specific list might not be shared by all who agree with him about the valid scope of change through judicial interpretation, but once one conceptualizes "the Constitution" as having aspirational functions— once one takes the document's Preamble seriously, such people might say—then the legitimate reach of adaptive interpretation becomes wonderfully (or frighteningly) capacious.

Proponents of a more restricted judicial role in constitutional change, like Hugo Black and Antonin Scalia, would respond that Brennan's speech illustrates why they are concerned. Enlarging "the Constitution" to include more than the text (and original understanding) and reading the Preamble as directed at judges turns a charter for practical government into a disquisition on moral and social philosophy. "Aspirational interpretation" performed by judges will destroy a complex democratic system and replace it with government by wooly-minded do-gooders who wear black robes.

It should be clear that democratic theory is a critical element in this opposition. "If the Constitution were a[n] ... invitation to apply current societal values," Justice Scalia asks, "what reason would there be to believe that the invitation was addressed to the courts rather than to the legislature?" ("Originalism: The Lesser Evil," reprinted below, p. 231.) Dissenting in *Griswold* (reprinted above, p. 147), Justice Black summed up the reasoning of those opposed to adaption by judicial interpretation:

> [M]any good and able men have eloquently spoken and written ... about the duty of this Court to keep the Constitution in tune with the times. ... I must with all deference reject that philosophy. The Constitution makers knew the need for change and provided for it. Amendments suggested by the people's elected representatives can be submitted to the people or their selected agents for ratification. That method of change was good for our Fathers, and ... it is good enough for me.

There is constitutionalist as well as democratic wariness of adaption through judicial interpretation. If judges create the principles they interpret, they transform themselves into both makers of law and interpreters of law. The political system would degenerate into a judicial oligarchy, and liberty would become dependent on judges' wisdom and benevolence. Either we have, one commentator asserts, "a fixed Constitution," or we "convert the chains of the Constitution to ropes of sand." [14] Interpreters and commentators who believe in a less restricted judicial role reply that neither the constitutional text nor the constitution grants judges anything approaching plenary power. They operate within a network of "separated institutions *sharing* powers." [15] And, within this network, judges are obliged to interpret "the Constitution" to keep it from becoming a "whited sepulcher."

As the lectures by Justices Scalia and Brennan show, the debate goes on. And as we have tried to emphasize, these disputes center on the legitimate reach of judges' creative and aspirational roles. What about other interpreters? Most of the debaters all along the spectrum would, in the abstract, agree that attempting to adapt "the Constitution" to changing events is not only within the authority of Congress and the President but even an obligation that rests on the members of both institutions. Whether, however, any particular effort at adaption would be valid is not a question that can be answered apart from a concrete situation. Furthermore, any democratic objection would not run against aspirational interpretation by elected officials—insofar as an interpretation did not interfere with

---

14. Raoul Berger, *Government by Judiciary* (Cambridge: Harvard University Press, 1977), p. 371.

15. Richard E. Neustadt, *Presidential Power: The Politics of Leadership* (rev. ed.; New York: Wiley, 1976), p. 101.

the conditions necessary for the system to remain democratic—for these people should soon have to face the electorate's judgment.

There are two other important questions that this chapter raises only implicitly. Because of their importance, readers should keep them in mind as they read the materials that follow. First, is it possible *formally* to amend the constitutional text outside of Article V? That is, is it possible that an amendment not approved by the procedures specified there can become a valid part of the text?

Before rejecting this possibility out of hand, one should recall that constitutional text of 1787–88 was proposed and ratified by procedures that, beyond doubt, violated the explicit terms of Article XIII of the Articles of Confederation, the then existing constitutional text. Moreover, the pedigree of the Fourteenth Amendment under the constitutional text of 1787–88 is, at best, dubious. Congress required southern states to ratify it as a condition of re-admission to the Union; and without their approval it would not have gained the consent of three-quarters of the states. The problem is that: *If* the southern states were not in the Union, their ratification was worthless; and, *if* they had never lost their status as states, that is, if they had never dissolved the Union—and Lincoln had justified fighting the Civil War on the constitutional theory that the southern states could not leave the Union—then Congress could not have constitutionally required them to ratify. There is some provocative literature on this point.[16]

A second important question sounds almost foolish on first reading: Are there substantive limits on the amending power? Can there be such a thing as an "unconstitutional constitutional amendment"? Are there differences, as footnote 3 above suggested, among "amending," "revising," and "replacing" a constitutional document? Does the nature of "the constitutional text" as resting on both democratic and constitutionalist theory restrict the sorts of changes that even the most rigorously observed procedures can bring about? The Constitutional Court of the Federal Republic of Germany has answered yes, as has the Supreme Court of India on several occasions. What is the answer for the American political system? Even Jefferson, who advocated each generation's adopting a fresh constitutional text, did not condone all revisions: "Nothing is unchangeable," he said, "but the inherent and unalienable rights

---

16. On the historical background of the adoption of the Fourteenth Amendment, see, for example: Walter Southon, "The Dubious Origin of the Fourteenth Amendment," 28 *Tul.L.Rev.* 22 (1953); and Ferdinand F. Fernandez, "The Constitutionality of the Fourteenth Amendment," 39 *So.Cal.L.Rev.* 378 (1966). On the fascinating question of ratification outside of the formal procedures of Article V, see: Akhil Reed Amar, "Philadelphia Revisited: Amending the Constitution Outside Article V," 55 *U.Chi.L.Rev.* 1043 (1988); Amar, "Consent of the Governed: Constitutional Amendment Outside Article V," 94 *Colum.L.Rev.* 457 (1994); and Bruce Ackerman, *We the People: Foundations* (Cambridge: Harvard University Press, 1991).

of man" [17]—a massive limitation on amendment. Was Jefferson wrong? Can Article V's elaborate procedures validate all changes? Would they legitimate abolishing the principle (which does not appear in the text) of "one person, one vote"? What about an amendment that would make the federal government totalitarian? Re-impose slavery on African Americans? One might hope that such questions will never arise, for neither the answers nor the remedies are self-evident.[18]

SELECTED BIBLIOGRAPHY

Ackerman, Bruce. "Discovering the Constitution," 93 *Yale L.J.* 1013 (1984).

————. "Constitutional Politics/Constitutional Law," 99 *Yale L.J.* 453 (1989).

————. *We the People: Foundations* (Cambridge: Harvard University Press, 1991).

Amar, Akhil Reed. "Philadelphia Revisited: Amending the Constitution Outside Article V," 55 *U.Chi.L.Rev.* 1043 (1988).

————. "Consent of the Governed: Constitutional Amendment Outside Article V," 94 *Colum.L.Rev.* 457 (1994).

Ball, Terence, and J.G.A. Pocock, eds. *Conceptual Change and the Constitution* (Lawrence: University of Kansas Press, 1988).

Barber, Sotirios A. *On What the Constitution Means* (Baltimore: John Hopkins University Press, 1984).

————. *The Constitution of Judicial Power* (Baltimore: Johns Hopkins University Press, 1993).

Berger, Raoul. *Government by Judiciary* (Cambridge: Harvard University Press, 1977).

Black, Hugo L. *A Constitutional Faith* (New York: Knopf, 1968).

---

17. To Major John Cartwright, June 5, 1824; Andrew A. Lipscomb, ed., *The Writings of Thomas Jefferson* (Washington, DC: The Jefferson Memorial Association, 1903), XVI, 48.

18. See, for example, Edward S. Corwin, "The Constitutional Law of Constitutional Amendment," 26 *Notre Dame Lawyer* 185 (1951); Amar, *loc. cit.* supra note 16; Jeff Rosen, "Was the Flag Burning Amendment Unconstitutional?" 100 *Yale L.J.* 1073 (1991); and the articles by Walter F. Murphy: "The Right to Privacy and Legitimate Constitutional Change," in Shlomo Slonim, ed., *The Constitutional Bases of Political and Social Change in the United States* (New York: Praeger, 1990); "Consent and Constitutional Change," in James O'Reilly, ed., *Human Rights and Constitutional Law* (Dublin: Round Hall Press, 1992); "Staggering Toward the New Jerusalem of Constitutional Theory," 37 *Am.J.Jurisp.* 337 (1992); and "Merlin's Memory: The Past and Future Imperfect of the Once and Future Polity," in Sanford V. Levinson, ed., *Responding to Imperfection* (Princeton: Princeton University Press, 1995).

Brest, Paul. "The Misconceived Quest for Original Understanding," 60 *Bost.U.L.Rev.* 204 (1980).

Cooley, Thomas M. *A Treatise on Constitutional Limitations* (Boston: Little, Brown, 1868).

Crosskey, William W. *Politics and the Constitution* (Chicago: University of Chicago Press, vols. 1 & 2, 1953; vol. 3 [with William Jeffrey, Jr.], 1980). (See also entry under Hart, below.)

Dellinger, Walter. See the Tribe–Dellinger Debate, under Tribe, below.

Dworkin, Ronald. *Taking Rights Seriously* (Cambridge: Harvard University Press, 1977), ch. 5.

Elliott, William Y. "The Constitution as the American Social Myth," in Conyers Read, ed., *The Constitution Reconsidered* (New York: Columbia University Press, 1938).

Fleming, James E. "We the Exceptional American People," 11 *Const. Comm.* 355 (1994).

Grey, Thomas C. "Do We Have an Unwritten Constitution?" 27 *Stan.L.Rev.* 703 (1975).

————. "The Constitution as Scripture," 37 *Stan.L.Rev.* 1 (1984).

Hall, Kermit L., Harold M. Hyman, and Leon V. Sigal, eds. *The Constitutional Convention as an Amending Device* (Washington, DC: The American Historical Association and The American Political Science Association, 1981).

Harris, William F. II. *The Interpretable Constitution* (Baltimore: Johns Hopkins University Press, 1993), ch. 4.

Hart, Henry M. "Professor Crosskey and Judicial Review," 67 *Harv.L.Rev.* 1456 (1954).

Levinson, Sanford V. "The Constitution's Text: The Problem of the (So–Called) Twenty-seventh Amendment," 10 *Const. Comm.* 101 (1993).

————, ed. *Responding to Imperfection* (Princeton: Princeton University Press, 1995).

Miller, Charles A. *The Supreme Court and the Uses of History* (Cambridge: The Belknap Press of Harvard University Press, 1969).

Munzer, Stephen R., and James W. Nickel. "Does the Constitution Mean What It Always Meant?" 77 *Colum.L.Rev.* 1029 (1977).

Murphy, Walter F. "Constitutional Interpretation: The Art of the Historian, Magician, or Statesman?" 87 *Yale L.J.* 1752 (1978).

————. "An Ordering of Constitutional Values," 53 *So.Cal.L.Rev.* 703 (1980).

————. *"Slaughter–House, Civil Rights*, and Limits on Constitutional Change," 21 *Am.J.Jurisp.* 1 (1986).

————. "The Right to Privacy and Legitimate Constitutional Change," in Shlomo Slonim, ed., *The Constitutional Bases of Political and Social Change in the United States* (New York: Praeger, 1990).

————. "Consent and Constitutional Change," in James O'Reilly, ed., *Human Rights and Constitutional Law* (Dublin: Round Hall Press, 1992).

————. "Staggering Toward the New Jerusalem of Constitutional Theory," 37 *Am.J.Jurisp.* 337 (1992).

————. "Excluding Political Parties," in Paul Kirchhof and Donald P. Kommers, eds., *Germany and Its Basic Law* (Baden–Baden: Nomos, 1993).

Perry, Michael J. "The Authority of Text, Tradition, and Reason: A Theory of Constitutional 'Interpretation,' " 58 *So.Cal.L.Rev.* 551 (1985).

Rosen, Jeff. "Was the Flag Burning Amendment Unconstitutional?" 100 *Yale L.J.* 1073 (1991).

Story, Justice Joseph. *Commentaries on the Constitution of the United States* (Boston: Hilliard, Gray & Co., 1833). 2 vols.

Tribe–Dellinger Debate:

   Walter Dellinger. "The Legitimacy of Constitutional Change: Rethinking the Amendment Process," 97 *Harv.L.Rev.* 386 (1983);

   Laurence H. Tribe. "A Constitution We Are Amending: In Defense of a Restrained Judicial Role," 97 *ibid.* 433 (1983);

   Walter Dellinger. "Constitutional Politics: A Rejoinder," 97 *ibid.* 446 (1983).

Vile, John R. *Rewriting the United States Constitution: An Examination of Proposals from Reconstruction to the Present* (New York: Praeger, 1991).

————. *The Constitutional Amending Process in American Political Thought* (New York: Praeger, 1992).

————. "Three Kinds of Constitutional Founding and Change: The Convention Model and Its Alternatives," 46 *Pol.Res.Q.* 881 (1993)

Vose, Clement E. *Constitutional Change: Amendment Politics and Supreme Court Litigation Since 1900* (Lexington, MA: Heath, 1972).

"[W]hile [the Constitution] remains unaltered, it must be construed now as it was understood at the time of its adoption. It is not only the same in words, but the same in meaning. ..."—Chief Justice TANEY

"I prefer the lights of Madison, Hamilton, and Jay, as a means of construing the Constitution in all its bearings, rather than to look behind that period, into a traffic which is now declared to be piracy, and punished with death by Christian nations."—Justice McLEAN

"To engraft on any instrument a substantive exception not found in it, must be admitted to be a matter attended with great difficulty."—Justice CURTIS

DRED SCOTT v. SANDFORD

60 U.S. (19 How.) 393, 15 L.Ed. 691 (1857).

In 1820, Congress adopted the Missouri Compromise, admitting Missouri as a slave state but prohibiting slavery in other parts of the Louisiana Territory north of 36 degrees, 30 minutes north latitude. In 1833, Dr. John Emerson, a citizen of Missouri, took his slave Dred Scott to Illinois (a free state) and in 1836 to (what later became) Minnesota, part of the Louisiana Territory north of the compromise line. Later Emerson took Scott back to Missouri.

After the doctor's death, his wife conveyed Scott (and his family) to her brother, John F.A. Sanford, a citizen of New York. (Because of an error by the Reporter of the Supreme Court's decisions, he would go down in history as Sandford.) In the following year, 1853, Scott, claiming to be a citizen of Missouri, brought suit against Sanford in federal court in Missouri, alleging federal jurisdiction based on diversity of citizenship and claiming that Sanford had assaulted him and falsely imprisoned him as a slave. Scott contended that residence in a free state and territory had made him a free man. Sanford contested the court's jurisdiction on the ground that Scott, as a "negro of African descent," was not a citizen of Missouri or of the United States but was, rather, a slave, the lawful property of a white man. The court agreed that Scott was still a slave, and he appealed to the Supreme Court.

The justices first heard argument in 1856 but put the case over for reargument until after the presidential election. much to the annoyance of Justice John McLean, who had his own agenda: He had been trying to obtain the Republican nomination for the presidency in 1856 (earlier he had several times tried to woo other parties while on the Court) and had planned a strident dissent to endear him to anti-slavery forces. James Buchanan, a Democrat, won the election of 1856 and took a deep interest in the case. It was duly re-argued and bitterly debated among the justices.

The presidential inauguration came two days before the decision was announced. In his address, Buchanan gently touched on the question of the constitutionality of federal control over slavery in the territories: "[I]t is a judicial question, which legitimately belongs to the Supreme Court of the United States. ... To their decision, in common with all good citizens, I shall cheerfully submit, whatever this may be." These words were grossly disingenuous, for he already knew what the Court's decision would be. He had been corresponding with his old friend Justice John Catron (who drafted the portion of the inaugural address just quoted) as well as with Justice Robert Grier, and indeed had written Grier urging him to rule on the constitutionality of the Missouri Compromise. Grier, in turn, showed the letter to the Chief Justice and another associate justice. The initial draft of the opinion of the Court, written by Justice Samuel Nelson, would have upheld the decision of the lower court on very narrow grounds. For details, see: Don E. Fehren-bacher, *The Dred Scott Case* (New York: Oxford University Press, 1978), pp. 305–314; and Carl Brent Swisher, *Roger Brooke Taney* (New York: Macmillan, 1935), ch. 24.

Mr. Chief Justice **TANEY** delivered the opinion of the court. ...

The question is simply this: Can a negro, whose ancestors were imported into this country, and sold as slaves, become a member of the political community formed and brought into existence by the Constitution of the United States, and as such become entitled to all the rights, and privileges, and immunities, guarantied by that instrument to the citizen? One of which rights is the privilege of suing in a court of the United States in the cases specified in the Constitution. ...

The words "people of the United States" and "citizens" are synonymous terms. ... They both describe the political body who, according to our republican institutions, form the sovereignty, and who hold the power and conduct the Government through their representatives. ... The question before us is, whether ... [negroes] compose a portion of this people, and are constituent members of this sovereignty? We think they are not, and that they are not included, and were not intended to be included, under the word "citizens" in the Constitution. ... On the contrary, they were at that time considered as a subordinate and inferior class of beings, who had been subjugated by the dominant race, and, whether emancipated or not, yet remained subject to their authority, and had no rights or privileges but such as those who held the power and the Government might choose to grant them.

It is not the province of the court to decide upon the justice or injustice, the policy or impolicy, of these laws.* The decision of that question belonged to the political or law-making power; to those who formed the sovereignty and framed the Constitution. The duty of the court is, to interpret the instrument they have framed, with the best lights we can obtain on the subject, and to administer it as we find it, according to its true intent and meaning when it was adopted.

... [W]e must not confound the rights of citizenship which a State may confer within its own limits, and the rights of citizenship as a member of the Union. It does not by any means follow, because he has

---

* More than three decades earlier, in serving as defense attorney for an abolitionist minister, Taney had attacked slavery as an evil that must be "gradually wiped away," freed his own slaves and supported colonizing free slaves in what is now Liberia (an idea that John Marshall, in private life an adamant opponent of slavery, had also publicly endorsed). On the bench, however, Taney's attitude was consistently even "fiercely anti-antislavery." See Fehrenbacher, p. 560.—**Eds.**

all the rights and privileges of a citizen of a State, that he must be a citizen of the United States. ... Each State may still confer them upon an alien, or any one it thinks proper, or upon any class or description of persons; yet he would not be a citizen in the sense in which that word is used in the Constitution of the United States. ...

It becomes necessary, therefore, to determine who were citizens of the several States when the Constitution was adopted. ... In the opinion of the court, the legislation and histories of the times, and the language used in the Declaration of Independence, show, that neither the class of persons who had been imported as slaves, nor their descendants, whether they had become free or not, were then acknowledged as a part of the people, nor intended to be included in the general words used in that memorable instrument.

It is difficult at this day to realize the state of public opinion in relation to that unfortunate race, which prevailed in the civilized and enlightened portions of the world at the time of the Declaration of Independence, and when the Constitution of the United States was framed and adopted. ... They had for more than a century before been regarded as beings of an inferior order ... and so far inferior, that they had no rights which the white man was bound to respect; and that the negro might justly and lawfully be reduced to slavery for his benefit. He was bought and sold, and treated as an ordinary article of merchandise and traffic, whenever a profit could be made by it. This opinion was at that time fixed and universal in the civilized portion of the white race. It was regarded as an axiom in morals as well as in politics. ...

The legislation of the different colonies furnishes positive and indisputable proof of this fact. ... [These laws] show that a perpetual and impassable barrier was intended to be erected between the white race and the one which they had reduced to slavery, and governed as subjects with absolute and despotic power, and which they then looked upon as so far below them in the scale of created beings, that intermarriages between white persons and negroes or mulattoes were regarded as unnatural and immoral, and punished as crimes, not only in the parties, but in the person who joined them in marriage. And no distinction in this respect was made between the free negro or mulatto and the slave, but this stigma, of the deepest degradation, was fixed upon the whole race. ...

The language of the Declaration of Independence is equally conclusive: ... "We hold these truths to be self-evident: that all men are created equal; that they are endowed by their Creator with certain unalienable rights; that among them is life, liberty, and the pursuit of happiness; that to secure these rights, Governments are instituted, deriving their just powers from the consent of the governed."

The general words above quoted would seem to embrace the whole human family, and if they were used in a similar instrument at this day would be so understood. But it is too clear for dispute, that the enslaved African race were not intended to be included, and formed no part of the people who framed and adopted this declaration; for if the language, as understood in that day, would embrace them, the conduct of the distinguished men who framed the Declaration of Independence would have been utterly and flagrantly inconsistent with the principles they asserted; and instead of the sympathy of mankind, to which they so confidently appealed, they would have deserved and received universal rebuke and reprobation.

Yet the men who framed this declaration were great men—high in literary acquirements—high in their sense of honor, and incapable of asserting principles inconsistent with those on which they were acting. They perfectly understood the meaning of the language they used, and how it would be understood by others; and they knew that it would not in any part of the civilized world be supposed to embrace the negro race, which, by common consent, had been excluded from civilized Governments and the family of nations, and doomed to slavery. They spoke and acted according to the then established doctrines and principles, and in the ordinary language of the day, no one misunderstood them. ...

This state of public opinion had undergone no change when the Constitution was adopted, as is equally evident from its provisions and language. The brief preamble sets forth by whom it was formed, for what purposes, and for whose benefit and protection. It declares that it is formed by the people of the United States; that is to say, by those who were members of the different political communities in the several States; and its great object is declared to be to secure the blessings of liberty to themselves and their posterity. It speaks in general terms of the people of the United States, and of citizens of the several States, when it is providing for the exercise of the powers granted or the privileges secured to the citizen. It does not define what description of persons are intended to be included under these terms, or who shall be regarded as a citizen and one of the people. It uses them as terms so well understood, that no further description or definition was necessary.

But there are two clauses in the Constitution which point directly and specifically to the negro race as a separate class of persons, and show clearly that they were not regarded as a portion of the people or citizens of the Government then formed. One of these clauses reserves to each of the thirteen States the right to import slaves until the year 1808. ... And by the other provision the States pledge themselves to each other to maintain the right of property of the master, by delivering up to him any slave who may have escaped from his service, and be found within their respective territories. ... And these two provisions show, conclusively, that neither the description of persons therein referred to, nor their descendants, were embraced in any of the other provisions of the Constitution; for certainly these two clauses were not intended to confer on them or their posterity the blessings of liberty, or any of the personal rights so carefully provided for the citizen. ...

No one, we presume, supposes that any change in public opinion or feeling, in relation to this unfortunate race, in the civilized nations of

Europe or in this country, should induce the court to give to the words of the Constitution a more liberal construction in their favor than they were intended to bear when the instrument was framed and adopted. Such an argument would be altogether inadmissible in any tribunal called on to interpret it. If any of its provisions are deemed unjust, there is a mode prescribed in the instrument itself by which it may be amended; but while it remains unaltered, it must be construed now as it was understood at the time of its adoption. It is not only the same in words, but the same in meaning, and delegates the same powers to the Government, and reserves and secures the same rights and privileges to the citizen; and as long as it continues to exist in its present form, it speaks not only in the same words, but with the same meaning and intent with which it spoke when it came from the hands of its framers, and was voted on and adopted by the people of the United States. Any other rule of construction would abrogate the judicial character of this court, and make it the mere reflex of the popular opinion or passion of the day. ...

What the construction was at that time, we think can hardly admit of doubt. ... And upon a full and careful consideration of the subject, the court is of opinion, that ... Dred Scott was not a citizen of Missouri within the meaning of the Constitution of the United States, and not entitled as such to sue in its courts; and, consequently, that the Circuit Court had no jurisdiction of the case, and that the judgment on the plea in abatement is erroneous. ...

... [T]he difficulty which meets us at the threshold of [the next] part of the inquiry [regarding the constitutionality of the Missouri Compromise] is, whether Congress was authorized to pass this law under any of the powers granted to it by the Constitution; for if the authority is not given by that instrument, it is the duty of this court to declare it void and inoperative, and incapable of conferring freedom upon any one who is held as a slave under the laws of any one of the States.

The counsel for the plaintiff has laid much stress upon that article in the Constitution which confers on Congress the power "to dispose of and make all needful rules and regulations respecting the territory or other property belonging to the United States;" but, in the judgment of the court, that provision had no bearing on the present controversy, and the power there given ... is confined, and was intended to be confined, to the territory which at that time belonged to, or was claimed by, the United States, and was within their boundaries as settled by the treaty with Great Britain, and can have no influence upon a territory afterwards acquired from a foreign Government. It was a special provision for a known and particular territory, and to meet a present emergency, and nothing more. ...

... [T]he power of Congress over the person or property of a citizen can never be a mere discretionary power under our Constitution. ... The powers of the Government and the rights and privileges of the citizen are regulated and plainly defined by the Constitution itself. And

when the Territory becomes a part of the United States, the Federal
Government enters into possession in the character impressed upon it by
those who created it. ... [I]t cannot, when it enters a Territory of the
United States, put off its character, and assume discretionary or despotic
powers which the Constitution has denied to it. ... For example, no
one ... will contend that Congress can make any law in a Territory
respecting that establishment of religion, or the free exercise thereof, or
abridging the freedom of speech or of the press, or the right of the people
of the Territory peaceably to assemble, and to petition the Government
for the redress of grievances. ...

These powers, and others, in relation to rights of person, ... are in
express and positive terms, denied to the General Government; and the
rights of private property have been guarded with equal care. Thus the
rights of property are united with the rights of person, and placed on the
same ground by the fifth amendment to the Constitution, which provides
that no person shall be deprived of life, liberty, and property, without
due process of law. And an act of Congress which deprives a citizen of
the United States of his liberty or property, merely because he came
himself or brought his property into a particular Territory of the United
States, and who had committed no offence against the laws, could hardly
be dignified with the name of due process of law.

... [T]he right of property in a slave is distinctly and expressly
affirmed in the Constitution. The right to traffic in it, like an ordinary
article of merchandise and property, was guarantied to the citizens of
the United States, in every State that might desire it, for twenty years.
And the Government in express terms is pledged to protect it in all
future time, if the slave escapes from his owner. This is done in plain
words—too plain to be misunderstood. ... The only power conferred
[on Congress] is the power coupled with the duty of guarding and
protecting the owner in his rights.

Upon these considerations, it is the opinion of the court that the act
of Congress which prohibited a citizen from holding and owning property
of this kind in the territory of the United States north of the line therein
mentioned, is not warranted by the Constitution, and is therefore void;
and that neither Dred Scott himself, nor any of his family, were made
free by being carried into this territory; even if they had been carried
there by the owner, with the intention of becoming a permanent resident. ...

[Justices **WAYNE**, **NELSON**, **GRIER**, **DANIEL**, **CAMPBELL**, and
CATRON each filed a separate concurring opinion.]

Mr. Justice **McLEAN** dissenting. ...

Being born under our Constitution and laws, no naturalization is
required, as one of foreign birth, to make [the plaintiff] a citizen. The
most general and appropriate definition of the term citizen is "a freeman." Being a freeman, and having his domicil in a State different from

that of the defendant, he is a citizen within the act of Congress, and the courts of the Union are open to him. ...

In ... Prigg v. Pennsylvania [1842], this court says that, by the general law of nations, no nation is bound to recognize the state of slavery ... in favor of the subjects of other nations where slavery is organized. If it does it, it is as a matter of comity, and not as a matter of international right. The state of slavery is deemed to be a mere municipal regulation, founded upon and limited to the range of the territorial laws. This was fully recognized in Somersett's case [1772], which was decided before the American Revolution. There was some contrariety of opinion among the judges on certain points ruled in Prigg's case, but there was none in regard to the great principle, that slavery is limited to the range of the laws under which it is sanctioned. ...

I will now consider the relation which the Federal Government bears to slavery in the States: Slavery is emphatically a State institution. ... The only connection which the Federal Government holds with slaves in a State, arises from that provision of the Constitution which declares that "No person held to service or labor in one State, under the laws thereof, escaping into another, shall, in consequence of any law or regulation therein, be discharged from such service or labor, but shall be delivered up, on claim of the party to whom such service or labor may be due." This being a fundamental law of the Federal Government, it rests mainly for its execution, as has been held, on the judicial power of the Union; and so far as the rendition of fugitives from labor has become a subject of judicial action, the Federal obligation has been faithfully discharged.

In the formation of the Federal Constitution, care was taken to confer no power on the Federal Government to interfere with this institution in the States. In the provision respecting the slave trade, in fixing the ratio of representation, and providing for the reclamation of fugitives from labor, slaves were referred to as persons, and in no other respect are they considered in the Constitution.

We need not refer to the mercenary spirit which introduced the infamous traffic in slaves, to show the degradation of negro slavery in our country. This system was imposed upon our colonial settlements by the mother country, and it is due to truth to say that the commercial colonies and States were chiefly engaged in the traffic. But we know as a historical fact, that James Madison, that great and good man, a leading member in the Federal Convention, was solicitous to guard the language of that instrument so as not to convey the idea that there could be property in man.

I prefer the lights of Madison, Hamilton, and Jay, as a means of construing the Constitution in all its bearings, rather than to look behind that period, into a traffic which is now declared to be piracy, and punished with death by Christian nations. I do not like to draw the sources of our domestic relations from so dark a ground. Our independence was a great epoch in the history of freedom; and while I admit the Government was not made especially for the colored race, yet many of them were citizens of the New England States, and exercised the rights of suffrage when the Constitution was adopted, and it was not doubted by any intelligent person that its tendencies would greatly ameliorate their condition.

Many of the States, on the adoption of the Constitution, or shortly afterward, took measures to abolish slavery within their respective jurisdictions; and it is a well-known fact that a belief was cherished by the leading men, South as well as North, that the institution of slavery would gradually decline, until it would become extinct. The increased value of slave labor, in the culture of cotton and sugar, prevented the realization of this expectation. Like all other communities and States, the South were influenced by what they considered to be their own interests.

But if we are to turn our attention to the dark ages of the world, why confine our view to colored slavery? On the same principles, white men were made slaves. All slavery has its origin in power, and is against right. . . .

I will now consider . . . [t]he effect of taking slaves into a State or Territory, and so holding them, where slavery is prohibited. If the principle laid down in [*Prigg*] is to be maintained . . . there can be no difficulty on this point. In that case, the court says: "The state of slavery is deemed to be a mere municipal regulation, founded upon and limited to the range of the territorial laws." If this be so, slavery can exist nowhere except under the authority of law. . . .

Now, if a slave abscond, he may be reclaimed; but if he accompany his master into a State or Territory where slavery is prohibited, such slave cannot be said to have left the service of his master where his services were legalized. And if slavery be limited to the range of the territorial laws, how can the slave be coerced to serve in a State or Territory, not only without the authority of law, but against its express provisions? What gives the master the right to control the will of his slave? The local law, which exists in some form. But where there is no such law, can the master control the will of the slave by force? Where no slavery exists, the presumption, without regard to color, is in favor of freedom. . . .

Mr. Justice **CURTIS** dissenting. . . .

. . . When . . . the Constitution speaks of citizenship of the United States, existing at the time of the adoption of the Constitution, it must necessarily refer to citizenship under the Government which existed prior to and at the time of such adoption. . . . That Government was simply a confederacy of the several States, possessing a few defined powers over subjects of general concern, each State retaining every power, jurisdiction, and right, not expressly delegated to the United States in Congress assembled. And no power was thus delegated to the

Government of the Confederation, to act on any question of citizenship, or to make any rules in respect thereto. The whole matter was left to stand upon the action of the several States, and to the natural consequence of such action, that the citizens of each State should be citizens of that Confederacy into which that State had entered, the style whereof was, "The United States of America."

To determine whether any free persons, descended from Africans held in slavery, were citizens of the United States under the Confederation, and consequently at the time of the adoption of the Constitution of the United States, it is only necessary to know whether any such persons were citizens of either of the States under the Confederation, at the time of the adoption of the Constitution. Of this there can be no doubt. At the time of the ratification of the Articles of Confederation, all free native-born inhabitants of the States of New Hampshire, Massachusetts, New York, New Jersey, and North Carolina, though descended from African slaves, were not only citizens of those States, but such of them as had the other necessary qualifications possessed the franchise of electors, on equal terms with other citizens.

. . . I shall not enter into an examination of the existing opinions of that period respecting the African race, nor into any discussion concerning the meaning of those who asserted, in the Declaration of Independence, that all men are created equal; that they are endowed by their Creator with certain inalienable rights; that among these are life, liberty, and the pursuit of happiness. My own opinion is, that a calm comparison of these assertions of universal abstract truths, and of their own individual opinions and acts, would not leave these men under any reproach of inconsistency; that the great truths they asserted on that solemn occasion, they were ready and anxious to make effectual, wherever a necessary regard to circumstances, which no statesman can disregard without producing more evil than good, would allow; and that it would not be just to them, nor true in itself, to allege that they intended to say that the Creator of all men had endowed the white race, exclusively, with the great natural rights which the Declaration of Independence asserts. . . .

Did the Constitution of the United States deprive [negroes] or their descendants of citizenship?

That Constitution was ordained and established by the people of the United States, through the action, in each State, of those persons who were qualified by its laws to act thereon, in behalf of themselves and all other citizens of that State. In some of the States, as we have seen, colored persons were among those qualified by law to act on this subject. These colored persons were not only included in the body of "the people of the United States," by whom the Constitution was ordained and established, but in at least five of the States they had the power to act, and doubtless did act, by their suffrages, upon the question of its adoption. It would be strange, if we were to find in that instrument anything which deprived of their citizenship any part of the people of the United States who were among those by whom it was established.

I can find nothing in the Constitution which, *proprio vigore*, deprives of their citizenship any class of persons who were citizens of the United States at the time of its adoption, or who should be native-born citizens of any State after its adoption; nor any power enabling Congress to disfranchise persons born on the soil of any State, and entitled to citizenship of such State by its Constitution and laws. And my opinion is, that, under the Constitution of the United States, every free person born on the soil of a State, who is a citizen of that State by force of its Constitution or laws, is also a citizen of the United States. ...

The Constitution declares that Congress shall have power to make "*all* needful rules and regulations" respecting the territory belonging to the United States. ...

It appears, however, ... that notwithstanding the language of the Constitution, and the long line of legislative and executive precedents under it, three different and opposite views are taken of the power of Congress respecting slavery in the Territories. One is, that though Congress can make a regulation prohibiting slavery in a Territory, they cannot make a regulation allowing it; another is, that it can neither be established nor prohibited by Congress, but that the people of a Territory, when organized by Congress, can establish or prohibit slavery; while the third is, that the Constitution itself secures to every citizen who holds slaves, under the laws of any State, the indefeasible right to carry them into any Territory, and there hold them as property.

No particular clause of the Constitution has been referred to ... in support of either of these views. The first seems to be rested upon general considerations concerning the social and moral evils of slavery, its relations to republican Governments, its inconsistency with the Declaration of Independence and with natural right. The second is drawn from considerations equally general, concerning the right of self-government, and the nature of the political institutions which have been established by the people of the United States.

While the third is said to rest upon the equal right of all citizens to go with their property upon the public domain, and the inequality of a regulation which would admit the property of some and exclude the property of other citizens; and, inasmuch as slaves are chiefly held by citizens of those particular States where slavery is established, it is insisted that a regulation excluding slavery from a Territory operates, practically, to make an unjust discrimination between citizens of different States, in respect to their use and enjoyment of the territory of the United States.

With the weight of either of these considerations ... this court has no concern. ... The question here is, whether they are sufficient to authorize this court to insert into this clause of the Constitution an exception of the exclusion or allowance of slavery, not found therein, nor in any other part of that instrument. To engraft on any instrument a substantive exception not found in it, must be admitted to be a matter attended with great difficulty. And the difficulty increases with the importance of the instrument, and the magnitude and complexity of the interests involved in its construction. To allow this to be done with the Constitution, upon reasons purely political, renders its judicial interpretation impossible—because judicial tribunals, as such, cannot decide upon political considerations. Political reasons have not the requisite certainty to afford rules of juridical interpretation. They are different in different men. They are different in the same men at different times. And when a strict interpretation of the Constitution, according to the fixed rules which govern the interpretation of laws, is abandoned, and the theoretical opinions of individuals are allowed to control its meaning, we have no longer a Constitution; we are under the government of individual men, who for the time being have power to declare what the Constitution is, according to their own views of what it ought to mean. When such a method of interpretation of the Constitution obtains, in place of a republican Government, with limited and defined powers, we have a Government which is merely an exponent of the will of Congress; or what, in my opinion, would not be preferable, an exponent of the individual political opinions of the members of this court.

If it can be shown, by anything in the Constitution itself, that when it confers on Congress the power to make *all* needful rules and regulations respecting the territory belonging to the United States, the exclusion or the allowance of slavery was excepted; or if anything in the history of this provision tends to show that such an exception was intended by those who framed and adopted the Constitution to be introduced into it, I hold it to be my duty carefully to consider, and to allow just weight to such considerations in interpreting the positive text of the Constitution. But where the Constitution has said *all* needful rules and regulations, I must find something more than theoretical reasoning to induce me to say it did not mean *all*. ...

Editors' Notes

(1) What was Taney's conception of WHAT "the Constitution" included? Did his view of valid constitutional change leave any room for development other than by formal amendment? What about Curtis's view? McLean's?

(2) For a discussion of *Dred Scott* with respect to the interrogative WHO shall interpret, see Abraham Lincoln's First Inaugural Address (1861; reprinted below, p. 314.

(3) *Dred Scott* is the most infamous case in American history. It brought scorn and ridicule on the Court and deepened the divisions between North and South. Its specter, even more than that of Lochner v. New York (1905; reprinted below, p. 1110), has haunted constitutional interpretation. See, for example, Justice Scalia's partial dissent in Planned Parenthood v. Casey (1992; reprinted below, p. 1281). Granting that Chief Justice Taney's opinion was morally callous and politically disastrous, what is wrong with his *approach* to constitutional interpretation? Proponents of an *approach* that looks on

constitutional interpretation as having the basic purpose of protecting certain "fundamental rights" typically contend that *Dred Scott* shows the perils of an *originalist approach*, that is, approaching constitutional interpretation as if its basic goal were to divine what the founding generation intended or understood the document's words to mean. Advocates of *originalism*, by contrast, commonly claim that *Dred Scott* illustrates the dangers of a *fundamental-rights approach*. (Here the "fundamental right" was to own property, even in other human beings, not the right to liberty that we might think far more fundamental.) See Christopher L. Eisgruber, "*Dred* Again: Originalism's Forgotten Past," 10 *Con'l Comm.* 37 (1993). Which view is more persuasive? Assuming for the sake of argument, that *originalism* offers the better approach, how persuasive was Taney's evidence of original understanding?

(4) *Dred Scott* also had some positive effects,. Congress took Taney's invitation to change the text and proposed the Fourteenth Amendment. It opening clause erases part of his interpretation: "All persons born or naturalized in the United States and subject to the jurisdiction thereof, are citizens of the United States and of the State wherein they reside."

(5) Our headnote to this case treats it as if it had been a bona fide suit between two private parties. But some contemporary observers as well as later historians have claimed that Sanford was an abolitionist who was conspiring, via a feigned case, to force the Court to settle the issue of the constitutionality of congressional regulation of slavery in the territories. In the definitive book on the case, however, Don E. Fehrenbacher concludes: "Unless more positive documentary evidence is discovered, the suspicion of a political plot should probably be laid aside." *The Dred Scott Case*, pp. 275–76. Carl Brent Swisher, Taney's biographer, reached the same conclusion: "It does not seem probable that the Dred Scott case was deliberately initiated for the purpose of getting a Supreme Court decision on the constitutional status of slavery in the territories." *History of the Supreme Court of the United States*, vol. 5, *The Taney Period, 1836–64* (New York: Macmillan, 1974), p. 599.

(6) *Dred Scott* was the next occasion after Marbury v. Madison (1803; reprinted below, p. 298) on which the Supreme Court declared an act of Congress unconstitutional. The ironic fact is that, by the time *Dred Scott* was decided, Congress had repealed the Missouri Compromise. Its replacement, however, also forbade slavery in some of the territories.

———

"[W]hen we are dealing with words that also are a constituent act, like the Constitution of the United States, we must realize that they have called into life a being the development of which could not have been foreseen completely by the most gifted of its begetters."

MISSOURI v. HOLLAND

252 U.S. 416, 40 S.Ct. 382, 64 L.Ed. 641 (1920).

As a conservation measure, Congress in 1913 enacted a law limiting the season during which migratory birds could be shot and the number of birds any hunter could kill. Today this sort of federal law would seem unexceptional, but it was unusual for the time. During this period, the Supreme Court had been largely, though not altogether consistently, following a doctrine known as "dual federalism": State and nation were co-equals, each supreme within its own sphere; thus all national powers, even those specifically delegated, had to be interpreted against the Tenth Amendment's reservation of authority to the states. More specifically, in Geer v. Connecticut (1896) the Court had upheld a state law regulating hunting of wild game, ruling that such power had inhered in colonial governments and had been passed on to the states upon independence, "insofar as its exercise may not be incompatible with, or restrained by, the rights conveyed to the Federal government by the Constitution." Following *Geer* a federal district judge held the 1913 act unconstitutional, and the Department of Justice was unwilling to press the case before the Supreme Court.*

Even the act's proponents had had some doubts about constitutionality, and Senator Elihu Root had suggested that the United States first sign a treaty protecting migratory birds. Shortly before the district court's decision, the Senate passed a resolution urging the administration to negotiate just such an agreement. The district court's decision made a treaty appear a more prudent route, and Woodrow Wilson's diplomats began several years of negotiations with Britain, acting for Canada. The final treaty went into effect in 1916. Citing the value of migratory birds, including wild ducks, as both a direct source of food and effective in keeping down insects that attacked crops, Congress then passed a new statute to enforce the treaty by providing for, among other things, closed seasons on hunting.

Lobbied by hunters and concerned about state sovereignty, some state officials prepared to resist enforcement. In 1919, Missouri's legislature directed the state attorney general to "investigate the matter of enjoining the Federal game inspectors . . . from further interfering with or molesting any or all of our citizens in the exercise of their privileges" to hunt birds. Frank W. McAllister, Missouri's attorney general, added a note of personal drama. He was an avid duck hunter who opposed a long closed season on his sport. After being caught poaching by Ray Holland, the U.S. game warden, McAllister tried to get a state court to enjoin enforcement of the federal law, but local officials persuaded him to challenge the act's constitutionality in a U.S. district court. That tribunal sustained the statute, and McAllister appealed to the U.S. Supreme Court, arguing:

> If the Act of Congress now in question would have been unconstitutional when the Constitution and the first [ten] amendments were framed and ratified, it is unconstitutional now. The Constitution does not change.

Mr. Justice **HOLMES** delivered the opinion of the Court. . . .

---

* The "facts" offered in the U.S. Reports are sparse. In this headnote we summarize the account of Clement E. Vose, "State Against Nation: The Conservation Case of *Missouri v. Holland*," *Prologue* (Winter, 1984), *233.*

... [T]he question raised is the general one whether the treaty and statute are void as an interference with the rights reserved to the states.

To answer this question it is not enough to refer to the Tenth Amendment, reserving the powers not delegated to the United States, because by Article II, § 2, the power to make treaties is delegated expressly, and by Article VI treaties made under the authority of the United States, along with the Constitution and laws of the United States made in pursuance thereof, are declared the supreme law of the land. If the treaty is valid there can be no dispute about the validity of the statute under Article I, § 8, as a necessary and proper means to execute the powers of the Government. ...

It is said that a treaty cannot be valid if it infringes the Constitution; that there are limits, therefore, to the treaty-making power; and that one such limit is that which an act of Congress could not do unaided, in derogation of the powers reserved to the States, a treaty cannot do. An earlier act of Congress that attempted by itself and not in pursuance of a treaty to regulate the killing of migratory birds within the states had been held bad in [two decisions of] the district court. These decisions were supported by the arguments that migratory birds were owned by the States in their sovereign capacity for the benefit of their people, and that under cases like Geer v. Connecticut [1896] this control was one that Congress had no power to displace. The same argument is supposed to apply now with equal force.

Whether the two cases ... were decided rightly or not, they cannot be accepted as a test of the treaty power. Acts of Congress are the supreme law of the land only when made in pursuance of the Constitution, while treaties are declared to be so when made under the authority of the United States. It is open to question whether the authority of the United States means more than the formal acts prescribed to make the convention. We do not mean to imply that there are no qualifications to the treaty-making power; but they must be ascertained in a different way. It is obvious that there may be matters of the sharpest exigency for the national well being that an act of Congress could not deal with, but that a treaty followed by such an act could, and it is not lightly to be assumed that, in matters requiring national action, "a power which must belong to and somewhere reside in every civilized government" is not to be found. Andrews v. Andrews [1903]. ...

We are not yet discussing the particular case before us but only are considering the validity of the test proposed. With regard to that we may add that when we are dealing with words that are also a constituent act, like the Constitution of the United States, we must realize that they have called into life a being the development of which could not have been foreseen completely by the most gifted of its begetters. It was enough for them to realize or to hope that they had created an organism; it has taken a century and has cost their successors much sweat and blood to prove that they created a nation. The case before us must be considered in the light of our whole experience and not merely in that of what was said a hundred years ago. The treaty in question does not contravene any prohibitory words to be found in the Constitution. The only question is whether it is forbidden by some invisible radiation from the general terms of the Tenth Amendment. We must consider what this country has become in deciding what that Amendment has reserved.

The State ... founds its claim of exclusive authority upon an assertion of title to migratory birds. ... No doubt it is true that as between a State and its inhabitants the State may regulate the killing and sale of such birds, but it does not follow that its authority is exclusive of paramount powers. To put the claim of the State upon title is to lean upon a slender reed. Wild birds are not in the possession of anyone; and possession is the beginning of ownership. The whole foundation of the State's rights is the presence within their jurisdiction of birds that yesterday had not arrived, tomorrow may be in another State and in a week a thousand miles away. ...

As most of the laws of the United States are carried out within the States, and as many of them deal with matters which in the silence of such laws the State might regulate, such general grounds are not enough to support Missouri's claim. Valid treaties of course "are as binding within the territorial limits of the States as they are elsewhere through-out the dominion of the United States." No doubt the great body of private relations usually fall within the control of the State, but a treaty may override its power. ...

Here a national interest of very nearly first magnitude is involved. It can be protected only by national action in concert with that of another power. The subject-matter is only transitorily within the State and has no permanent habitat therein. But for the treaty and the statute there soon might be no birds for any powers to deal with. We see nothing in the Constitution that compels the Government to sit by while a food supply is cut off and the protectors of our forests and our crops are destroyed. ... We are of the opinion that the treaty and statute must be upheld.

Decree affirmed.

Mr. Justice **VAN DEVANTER** and Mr. Justice **PITNEY** dissent.

Editors' Notes

(1) To what extent did Holmes address Missouri's argument about the unchanging nature of "the Constitution"? What line of reasoning did he use to support his claim that the Court must look to "our whole experience" to interpret "the Constitution"? What authority, textual or otherwise, did he use to support his conclusion?

(2) In addition to the article by Vose, cited in the headnote, see Charles A. Lofgren, "Missouri v. Holland in Historical Perspective," 1975 *Sup.Ct.Rev.* 77.

(3) Among the justices of his time, Holmes stands out as the most ardent supporter of national supremacy. But did his opinion waver between a broad assertion of federal power and a much more particularistic discussion of why

federal power is valid under the peculiar circumstances of this case? If so, what could account for this ambivalence?

(4) "We do not mean to imply that there are no qualifications to the treaty-making power; but they must be ascertained in a different way," Holmes said here. That statement is less than precise, and the Court has not yet offered much clearer guidance. See, for example, Reid v. Covert (1957), and, more generally, Louis Henkin, *Foreign Affairs and the Constitution* (Mineola, NY: Foundation Press, 1972); and Henkin, *Constitutionalism, Democracy, and Foreign Affairs* (New York: Columbia University Press, 1990). States-righters have frequently voiced fears about the havoc that power could wreak on federalism, and occasionally civil libertarians have speculated about the peril a treaty could present to the Bill of Rights as a bar to governmental action. During the late 1940s and early 1950s, there was a concerted effort to amend the constitutional document to provide: "A treaty shall become effective as internal law in the United States only through legislation which would be valid in the absence of the treaty." In 1954, after a great debate, this so-called Bricker Amendment, named after its principal sponsor Senator John Bricker of Ohio, was decisively defeated in the Senate.

"It is no answer to say that this public need was not apprehended a century ago, or to insist that what the provision of the Constitution meant to the vision of that day it must mean to the vision of our time."—Chief Justice HUGHES

"The whole aim of construction, as applied to a provision of the Constitution, is to discover the meaning, to ascertain and give effect to the intent, of its framers and the people who adopted it."—Justice SUTHERLAND

HOME BUILDING & LOAN ASSOCIATION v. BLAISDELL

(The Minnesota Moratorium Case) 290 U.S. 398, 54 S.Ct. 231, 78 L.Ed. 413 (1934).

During the Great Depression, tumbling prices and tidal waves of unemployment led to a massive inability to pay debts. Farmers, many of whom had large mortgages on their crops, animals, and equipment as well as on their homes, were especially hard hit. In the Midwest, sporadic violence broke out against bankers' trying to foreclose. Under pressure from the governor and thousands of angry farmers demonstrating outside the capitol, the Minnesota legislature adopted an emergency measure that allowed a judicial proceeding to place a moratorium on a foreclosure for as long as two years, with the debtor paying the creditor the functional equivalent of rent during that period. Bankers quickly challenged the constitutionality of the new statute, alleging it violated the contract clause of Art. I, § 10. After losing in state courts, the bankers appealed to the U.S. Supreme Court.

The vote among the justices at conference was 5–4 to uphold the statute. Chief Justice Charles Evans Hughes assigned himself the task of writing the opinion of the Court and promptly circulated a draft that evaded the central difficulty of the case: On the one hand, Article I, § 10 of the constitutional text reads: "No State shall . . . pass any . . . Law impairing the Obligation of Contracts"; and, as Chapter 3 pointed out, the framers had most wanted to stop states from interfering with debtors' obligations to creditors by issuing paper money and passing laws making it easier to avoid payment of contractual obligations.* On the other hand, in late 1929 the country had plummeted into a depression that was threatening to become a bottomless economic chasm; and refusal to permit some relief to debtors would insure chaos. Instead of confronting this dilemma, the Chief Justice tried to distinguish the *obligation* of a contract from the *remedy* for enforcement of a contract. Minnesota, Hughes reasoned, recognized the obligation of contracts and so did not violate Art. I, § 10. It had merely changed the remedy open to creditors to enforce those obligations.

This reasoning had some basis in earlier opinions, but Justice Benjamin N. Cardozo thought it more clever than sound. He preferred a direct attack the underlying problem of continuity and change in constitutional interpretation. He circulated within the Court the following draft of a concurring opinion.

Mr. Justice **CARDOZO** concurring.

"We must never forget that it is a *constitution* we are expounding." Marshall, C.J., in McCulloch v. Maryland [1819]. "A constitution [is] intended to endure for ages to come, and, consequently, to be adapted to the various *crises* of human affairs." *Ibid.*

"The case before us must be considered in the light of our whole experience and not merely in that of what was said a hundred years ago" Holmes, J. in Missouri v. Holland [1920].

A hundred years ago . . . property might be taken without due process of law through the legislation of the states, and the courts of the nation were powerless to give redress, unless indeed they could find that a contract had been broken. Dartmouth College v. Woodward [1819]; Fletcher v. Peck [1810]. The judges of those courts had not yet begun to speak of the police power except in an off hand way or in expounding the effect of the commerce clause upon local regulations. The License Cases [1847]. Due process in the states was whatever the states ordained. In

---

* Luther Martin, a brilliant, hard-drinking lawyer who was a delegate at the Constitutional Convention, was among the more vocal opponents of § 10's restrictions on the states. Its inclusion was one of the reasons he refused to sign the final document. As he explained to Maryland's legislature: "[T]here might be times of such *great public calamities and distress* . . . as should render it the *duty* of a government, for the *preservation* of even the *most valuable part* of its citizens in some measure to interfere in their favour, by passing laws *totally or partially stopping* the courts of justices, or authorizing the debtor to pay by *installments,* or by delivering up his property to his creditors at a *reasonable and honest* valuation. The times have been such as to render regulations of this kind necessary in most, or all of the States, to prevent the *wealthy creditor* and the *monied man* from *totally* destroying the *poor* though even *industrious* debtor—*Such times* may *again* arrive." "The Genuine Information Delivered to the Legislature of the State of Maryland Relative to the Proceedings of the General Convention Lately Held at Philadelphia," reprinted in Herbert J. Storing, ed., *The Complete Anti–Federalist* (Chicago: University of Chicago Press, 1981), II, 64. After ratification, Martin became a staunch defender of the new constitutional order.

such circumstances there was jeopardy, or the threat of it, in encroachment, however slight, upon the obligation to adhere to the letter of a
contract. Once reject that test, and no other was available, or so it
might well have seemed. The states could not be kept within the limits
of reason and fair dealing for such restraints were then unknown as
curbs upon their power. It was either all or nothing.*

The Fourteenth Amendment came, and with it a profound change in
the relation between the federal government and the governments of the
states. No longer were the states invested with arbitrary power. Their
statutes affecting property or liberty were brought within supervision of
independent courts and subjected to the rule of reason. The dilemma of
"all or nothing" no longer stared us in the face.

Upon the basis of that amendment, a vast body of law unknown to
the fathers has been built in treatise and decision. The economic and
social changes wrought by the industrial revolution and by the growth of
population have made it necessary for government at this day to do a
thousand things that were beyond the experience or the thought of a
century ago. With the growing recognition of this need, courts have
awakened to the truth that the contract clause is perverted from its
proper meaning when it throttles the capacity of the states to exert their
governmental power in response to crying needs. The early cases dealt
with the problem as one affecting the conflicting rights and interests of
individuals and classes. This was the attitude of the courts up to the
Fourteenth Amendment; and the tendency to some extent persisted
even later. The rights and interests of the state itself were involved, as
it seemed, only indirectly and remotely, if they were thought to be
involved at all. We know better in these days, with the passing of the
frontier and of the unpeopled spaces of the west. With these and other
changes, the welfare of the social organism in any of its parts is bound
up more inseparably than ever with the welfare of the whole. A gospel
of *laissez-faire*—of individual initiative—of thrift and industry and sacrifice—may be inadequate in that great society we live in to point the way
to salvation, at least for economic life. The state when it acts today by
statutes like the one before us is not furthering the selfish good of
individuals or classes as ends of ultimate validity. It is furthering its
own good by maintaining the economic structure on which the good of
all depends. Such at least is its endeavor, however much it miss the
mark. The attainment of that end, so august and impersonal, will not
be barred and thwarted by the obstruction of a contract set up along the
way.

* **Eds.' Query:** Was Cardozo correct on this point? See Justice Chase's opinion in
Calder v. Bull (1798; reprinted above, p. 121). and Chief Justice Marshall's opinion for
the Court in Fletcher v. Peck (1810; reprinted below, p. 1091, holding that a Georgia law
voiding sale of land by the state to a private company would have been invalid as violating
"general principles which are common to our free institutions" even had the contract
clause not been included in the constitutional text. (See also Justice Johnson's concurring
opinion, claiming that such principles bound even the Deity.)

Looking back over the century, one perceives a process of evolution too strong to be set back. The decisions brought together by the Chief Justice [Hughes] show with impressive force how the court in its interpretation of the contract clause has been feeling its way toward a rational compromise between private rights and public welfare. From the beginning it was seen that something must be subtracted from the words of the Constitution in all their literal and stark significance. This was forcefully pointed out by Johnson, J., in Ogden v. Saunders [1827]. At first refuge was found in the distinction between right and remedy with all its bewildering refinements. Gradually the distinction was perceived to be inadequate. The search was for a broader base, for a division that would separate the lawful and the forbidden by lines more closely in correspondence with the necessities of government. The Fourteenth Amendment was seen to point the way. Contracts were still to be preserved. There was to be no arbitrary destruction of their binding force, nor any arbitrary impairment. There was to be no impairment, even though not arbitrary, except with the limits of fairness, of moderation, and of pressing an emergent need. But a promise exchanged between individuals was not to paralyze the state in its endeavor in times of direful crisis to keep its life-blood flowing.

To hold this may be inconsistent with things that men said in 1787 when expounding to compatriots the newly written constitution. They did not see the changes in the relation between states and nation or in the play of social forces that lay hidden in the womb of time. It may be inconsistent with things that they believed or took for granted. Their beliefs to be significant must be adjusted to the world they knew. It is not in my judgment inconsistent with what they would say today nor with what today they would believe, if they were called upon to interpret "in the light of our whole experience" the constitution that they framed for the needs of an expanding future. ...

As the last sentence of Cardozo's draft says, he was not threatening to reject Hughes's opinion. Had he not been willing to join, Hughes could not have spoken for the Court, since there were only five justices in the majority. The closeness of the vote, however, gave added weight to Cardozo's views. (Justice Harlan Fiske Stone was sympathetically revising and strengthening Cardozo's concurrence—a fact the Chief Justice may not have known.) So Hughes decided to placate Cardozo and incorporated paragraphs from the draft concurrence into his own opinion, though still retaining the distinction between obligation and remedy. Cardozo did not wish to press his argument further and withdrew his concurrence. It was never published until many years after his death, when Prof. Alpheus Thomas Mason found a copy in Stone's private papers, now located in the Library of Congress.

Mr. Chief Justice **HUGHES** delivered the opinion of the Court.   ...

[We must determine] whether the provision for this temporary and conditional relief exceeds the power of the State by reason of the clause in the Federal Constitution prohibiting impairment of the obligations of contracts.   ...

Emergency does not create power.   Emergency does not increase granted power or remove or diminish the restrictions imposed upon power granted or reserved.   The Constitution was adopted in a period of grave emergency.   Its grants of power to the Federal Government and its limitations of the power of the States were determined in the light of emergency and they are not altered by emergency.   ...

While emergency does not create power, emergency may furnish the occasion for the exercise of power.   ...   The constitutional question presented in the light of an emergency is whether the power possessed embraces the particular exercise of it in response to particular conditions.   ...   When the provisions of the Constitution, in grant or restriction, are specific, so particularized as not to admit of construction, no question is presented.   ...   But where constitutional grants and limitations of power are set forth in general clauses, which afford a broad outline, the process of construction is essential to fill in the details.   That is true of the contract clause.   The necessity of construction is not obviated by the fact that the contract clause is associated in the same section with other and more specific prohibitions.   Even the grouping of subjects in the same clause may not require the same application to each of the subjects, regardless of differences in their nature.

In the construction of the contract clause, the debates in the Constitutional Convention are of little aid.   But the reasons which led to the adoption of that clause, and of the other prohibitions of Section 10 of Article 1, are not left in doubt and have frequently been described.   ...
The widespread distress following the revolutionary period and the plight of debtors had called forth in the States an ignoble array of legislative schemes for the defeat of creditors and the invasion of contractual obligations.   Legislative interferences had been so numerous and extreme that the confidence essential to prosperous trade had been undermined and the utter destruction of credit was threatened.   ...   It was necessary to interpose the restraining power of a central authority in order to secure the foundations even of "private faith."   ...

But full recognition of the occasion and general purpose of the clause does not suffice to fix its precise scope.   Nor does an examination of the details of prior legislation in the States yield criteria which can be considered controlling.   To ascertain the scope of the constitutional prohibition we examine the course of judicial decisions in its application. These put it beyond question that the prohibition is not an absolute one and is not to be read with literal exactness like a mathematical formula. ...   [Chief Justice Hughes then reviewed decisions interpreting the contract clause].

... Chief Justice Marshall pointed out the distinction between obligation and remedy. Sturges v. Crowninshield [1819]: "The distinction between the obligation of a contract, and the remedy given by the legislature to enforce that obligation, has been taken at the bar, and exists in the nature of things. Without impairing the obligation of the contract, the remedy may certainly be modified as the wisdom of the nation shall direct." And in Von Hoffman v. Quincy [1867], ... [the Court observed that:]

> It is competent for the States to change the form of the remedy, or to modify it otherwise, as they may see fit, provided no substantial right secured by the contract is thereby impaired. No attempt has been made to fix definitely the line between alterations of the remedy, which are to be deemed legitimate, and those which, under the form of modifying the remedy, impair substantial rights. Every case must be determined upon its own circumstances.

And Chief Justice Waite, quoting this language in Antoni v. Greenhow [1883], added: "In all such cases the question becomes therefore, one of reasonableness, and of that the legislature is primarily the judge." ...

Not only is the constitutional provision qualified by the measure of control which the State retains over remedial processes, but the State also continues to possess authority to safeguard the vital interests of its people. It does not matter that legislation appropriate to that end "has the result of modifying or abrogating contracts already in effect." Stephenson v. Binford [1932]. Not only are existing laws read into contracts in order to fix obligations as between the parties, but the reservation of essential attributes of sovereign power is also read into contracts as a postulate of the legal order. The policy of protecting contracts against impairment presupposes the maintenance of a government by virtue of which contractual relations are worth while—a government which retains adequate authority to secure the peace and good order of society. This principle of harmonizing the constitutional prohibition with the necessary residuum of state power has had progressive recognition in the decisions of this Court. ...

Undoubtedly, whatever is reserved of state power must be consistent with the fair intent of the constitutional limitation of that power. ... They must be construed in harmony with each other. This principle precludes a construction which would permit the State to adopt as its policy the repudiation of debts or the destruction of contracts or the denial of means to enforce them. But it does not follow that conditions may not arise in which a temporary restraint of enforcement may be consistent with the spirit and purpose of the constitutional provision and thus be found to be within the range of the reserved power of the State to protect the vital interests of the community. ...

It is manifest from [a] review of our decisions that there has been a growing appreciation of public needs and of the necessity of finding ground for a rational compromise between individual rights and public welfare. The settlement and consequent contraction of the public domain, the pressure of a constantly increasing density of population, the interrelation of the activities of our people and the complexity of our economic interests, have inevitably led to an increased use of the organization of society in order to protect the very bases of individual opportunity. Where, in earlier days, it was thought that only the concerns of individuals or of classes were involved, and that those of the State itself were touched only remotely, it has later been found that the fundamental interests of the State are directly affected; and that the question is no longer merely that of one party to a contract as against another, but of the use of reasonable means to safeguard the economic structure upon which the good of all depends.

It is no answer to say that this public need was not apprehended a century ago, or to insist that what the provision of the Constitution meant to the vision of that day it must mean to the vision of our time. If by the statement that what the Constitution meant at the time of its adoption it means to-day, it is intended to say that the great clauses of the Constitution must be confined to the interpretation which the framers, with the conditions and outlook of their time, would have placed upon them, the statement carries its own refutation. It was to guard against such a narrow conception that Chief Justice Marshall uttered the memorable warning—"We must never forget that it is a *constitution* we are expounding" (McCulloch v. Maryland [1819])—"a constitution intended to endure for ages to come, and, consequently, to be adapted to the various *crises* of human affairs." When we are dealing with the words of the Constitution, said this Court in Missouri v. Holland [1920], "we must realize that they have called into life a being the development of which could not have been foreseen completely by the most gifted of its begetters. ... The case before us must be considered in the light of our whole experience and not merely in that of what was said a hundred years ago."

Nor is it helpful to attempt to draw a fine distinction between the intended meaning of the words of the Constitution and their intended application. ... The vast body of [contract clause] law which has been developed was unknown to the fathers but it is believed to have preserved the essential content and the spirit of the Constitution. With a growing recognition of public needs and the relation of individual right to public security, the court has sought to prevent the perversion of the clause through its use as an instrument to throttle the capacity of the States to protect their fundamental interests. This development is a growth from the seeds which the fathers planted. ...

We are of the opinion that the Minnesota statute as here applied does not violate the contract clause of the Federal Constitution. Whether the legislation is wise or unwise as a matter of policy is a question with which we are not concerned. ...

Judgment affirmed.

Mr. Justice **SUTHERLAND** dissenting.   . . .

A provision of the Constitution, it is hardly necessary to say, does not admit of two distinctly opposite interpretations. It does not mean one thing at one time and an entirely different thing at another time. If the contract impairment clause, when framed and adopted, meant that the terms of a contract for the payment of money could not be altered *in invitum* by a state statute enacted for the relief of hardly pressed debtors to the end and with the effect of postponing payment or enforcement during and because of an economic or financial emergency, it is but to state the obvious to say that it means the same now.   . . .

The provisions of the federal Constitution, undoubtedly, are pliable in the sense that in appropriate cases they have the capacity of bringing within their grasp every new condition which falls within their meaning. But, their *meaning* is changeless; it is only their *application* which is extensible. Constitutional grants of power and restrictions upon the exercise of power are not flexible as the doctrines of the common law are flexible. These doctrines, upon the principles of the common law itself, modify or abrogate themselves whenever they are or whenever they become plainly unsuited to different or changed conditions.   . . .

The whole aim of construction, as applied to a provision of the Constitution, is to discover the meaning, to ascertain and give effect to the intent, of its framers and the people who adopted it. The necessities which gave rise to the provision, the controversies which preceded, as well as the conflicts of opinion which were settled by its adoption, are matters to be considered to enable us to arrive at a correct result.   . . . As nearly as possible we should place ourselves in the condition of those who framed and adopted it. And if the meaning be at all doubtful, the doubt should be resolved, wherever reasonably possible to do so, in a way to forward the evident purpose with which the provision was adopted.

An application of these principles to the question under review removes any doubt, if otherwise there would be any, that the contract impairment clause denies to the several states the power to mitigate hard consequences resulting to debtors from financial or economic exigencies by an impairment of the obligation of contracts of indebtedness. A candid consideration of the history and circumstances which led up to and accompanied the framing and adoption of this clause will demonstrate conclusively that it was framed and adopted with the specific and studied purpose of preventing legislation designed to relieve debtors *especially* in time of financial distress.   . . .

The present exigency is nothing new. From the beginning of our existence as a nation, periods of depression, of industrial failure, of financial distress, of unpaid and unpayable indebtedness, have alternated with years of plenty.   . . .

The defense of the Minnesota law is made upon grounds which were discountenanced by the makers of the Constitution and have many times been rejected by this court. That defense should not now succeed because it constitutes an effort to overthrow the constitutional provision by an appeal to facts and circumstances identical with those which brought it into existence. With due regard for the processes of logical thinking, it legitimately cannot be urged that conditions which produced the rule may now be invoked to destroy it. ...

The Minnesota statute either impairs the obligation of contracts or it does not. If it does not, the occasion to which it relates becomes immaterial, since then the passage of the statute is the exercise of a normal, unrestricted, state power and requires no special occasion to render it effective. If it does, the emergency no more furnishes a proper occasion for its exercise than if the emergency were non-existent. ...

I quite agree with the opinion of the court that whether the legislation under review is wise or unwise is a matter with which we have nothing to do. ... The only legitimate inquiry we can make is whether it is constitutional. If it is not, its virtues, if it have any, cannot save it; if it is, its faults cannot be invoked to accomplish its destruction. If the provisions of the Constitution be not upheld when they pinch as well as when they comfort, they may as well be abandoned. Being unable to reach any other conclusion than that the Minnesota statute infringes the constitutional restriction under review, I have no choice but to say so.

I am authorized to say that Mr. Justice **VAN DEVANTER,** Mr. Justice **McREYNOLDS** and Mr. Justice **BUTLER** concur in this opinion.

Editors' Notes

(1) **Query:** Cardozo's (unpublished) dissent frankly talks about interpreters adding and subtracting from the constitutional text. What do such claims tell us about the nature of "the Constitution"?

(2) **Query:** To what extent did Hughes modify Cardozo's theory of constitutional change? How effectively did Sutherland argue against Cardozo? Hughes? Is it self-evident that, as Sutherland claimed, "The whole aim of construction, as applied to a provision of the Constitution, is to discover the meaning, to ascertain and give effect to the intent, of its framers and the people who adopted it"? How effectively does Sutherland defend this conclusion?

(3) **Query:** To what extent does Sutherland's statement that the "*meaning* [of constitutional principles] is changeless; it is only their *application* which is extensible" vitiate his own theory of legitimate constitutional change?

(4) **Query:** To what extent was Sutherland also attacking Holmes's opinion in Missouri v. Holland?

(5) To appreciate the collegial nature of the Court's decision—and opinion-writing processes, one might re-read Cardozo's draft and then re-read

Hughes's opinion to identify the points at which the Chief Justice integrated Cardozo's reasoning into his own.

———

"The [Eighth] Amendment must draw its meaning from the evolving standards of a maturing society."—Chief Justice WARREN.

"The awesome power of this Court to invalidate such legislation, because in practice it is bounded only by our own prudence in discerning the limits of the Court's constitutional function, must be exercised with the utmost restraint."—Justice FRANKFURTER.

TROP v. DULLES
356 U.S. 86, 78 S.Ct. 590, 2 L.Ed.2d 630 (1958).

During World War II, Albert L. Trop served in the U.S. Army in North Africa. In 1944 a court martial sentenced him to a term in a stockade in Casablanca. Shortly after, he and a companion escaped. They were recaptured the next day and tried for desertion. The second court martial convicted Trop and sentenced him to three years at hard labor and ordered him dishonorably discharged from the armed forces. In 1952 he applied for a passport, but the Department of State refused the request because § 401q of the Nationality Act of 1940 explicitly provided that persons convicted by courts martial for desertion in time of war and dishonorably discharged lost their American citizenship. Trop sued in a federal district court, asking for a declaratory judgment that he was still a citizen of the United States. The district court decided against him; the court of appeals affirmed that decision; and the Supreme Court granted certiorari.

Mr. Chief Justice **WARREN** announced the judgment of the Court and
    delivered an opinion in which Mr. Justice **BLACK**, Mr. Justice
    DOUGLAS, and Mr. Justice **WHITTAKER** join. . . .

In Perez v. Brownell [1958] I expressed the principles that I believe govern the constitutional status of United States citizenship. It is my conviction that citizenship is not subject to the general powers of the National Government and therefore cannot be divested in the exercise of those powers. The right may be voluntarily relinquished or abandoned either by express language or by language and conduct that show a renunciation of citizenship.

Under these principles, this petitioner has not lost his citizenship. Desertion in wartime, though it may merit the ultimate penalty, does not necessarily signify allegiance to a foreign state. Section 401(g) is not limited to cases of desertion to the enemy, and there is no such element in this case. This soldier committed a crime for which he should be and was punished, but he did not involve himself in any way with a foreign state. There was no dilution of his allegiance to this country. The fact that the desertion occurred on foreign soil is of no consequence. The Solicitor General acknowledged that forfeiture of citizenship would have occurred if the entire incident had transpired in this country.

Citizenship is not a license that expires upon misbehavior. The duties of citizenship are numerous, and the discharge of many of these obligations is essential to the security and well-being of the Nation. The citizen who fails to pay his taxes or to abide by the laws safeguarding the integrity of elections deals a dangerous blow to his country. But could a citizen be deprived of his nationality for evading these basic responsibilities of citizenship? . . . [T]he punishing power is available to deal with derelictions of duty. But citizenship is not lost every time a duty of citizenship is shirked. And the deprivation of citizenship is not a weapon that the Government may use to express its displeasure at a citizen's conduct, however reprehensible that conduct may be. . . .

. . . [W]e must face the question whether the Constitution permits the Congress to take away citizenship as a punishment for crime. . . . The question is whether this penalty subjects the individual to a fate forbidden by the principle of civilized treatment guaranteed by the Eighth Amendment. At the outset, let us put to one side the death penalty as an index of the constitutional limit on punishment. . . . [T]he existence of the death penalty is not a license to the Government to devise any punishment short of death within the limit of its imagination.

The exact scope of the constitutional phrase "cruel and unusual" has not been detailed by this Court. But the basic policy reflected in these words is firmly established in the Anglo–American tradition of criminal justice. The phrase in our Constitution was taken directly from the English Declaration of Rights of 1688, and the principle it represents can be traced back to the Magna Carta. The basic concept underlying the Eighth Amendment is nothing less than the dignity of man. While the State has the power to punish, the Amendment stands to assure that this power be exercised within the limits of civilized standards. Fines, imprisonment and even execution may be imposed depending upon the enormity of the crime, but any technique outside the bounds of these traditional penalties is constitutionally suspect. This Court has had little occasion to give precise content to the Eighth Amendment, and, in an enlightened democracy such as ours, this is not surprising. But when the Court was confronted with a punishment of 12 years in irons at hard and painful labor imposed for the crime of falsifying public records, it did not hesitate to declare that the penalty was cruel in its excessiveness and unusual in its character. Weems v. United States [1910]. The Court recognized in that case that the words of the Amendment are not precise, and that their scope is not static. The Amendment must draw its meaning from the evolving standards of decency that mark the progress of a maturing society. . . .

. . . [D]enationalization as a punishment is barred by the Eighth Amendment. There may be involved no physical mistreatment, no primitive torture. There is instead the total destruction of the individual's status in organized society. It is a form of punishment more primitive than torture, for it destroys for the individual the political existence that was centuries in the development. The punishment strips the citizen of his status in the national and international political community. His very existence is at the sufferance of the country in which he happens to find himself. While any one country may accord him some rights, and presumably as long as he remained in this country he would enjoy the limited rights of an alien, no country need do so because he is stateless. Furthermore, his enjoyment of even the limited rights of an alien might be subject to termination at any time by reason of deportation. In short, the expatriate has lost the right to have rights.

This punishment is offensive to cardinal principles for which the Constitution stands. It subjects the individual to a fate of ever-increasing fear and distress. He knows not what discriminations may be established against him, what proscriptions may be directed against him, and when and for what cause his existence in his native land may be terminated. He may be subject to banishment, a fate universally decried by civilized people. He is stateless, a condition deplored in the international community of democracies. It is no answer to suggest that all the disastrous consequences of this fate may not be brought to bear on a stateless person. The threat makes the punishment obnoxious. ...

In concluding as we do that the Eighth Amendment forbids Congress to punish by taking away citizenship, we are mindful of the gravity of the issue inevitably raised whenever the constitutionality of an Act of the National Legislature is challenged. No member of the Court believes that in this case the statute before us can be construed to avoid the issue of constitutionality. That issue confronts us, and the task of resolving it is inescapably ours. This task requires the exercise of judgment, not the reliance upon personal preferences. Courts must not consider the wisdom of statutes but neither can they sanction as being merely unwise that which the Constitution forbids.

We are oath-bound to defend the Constitution. This obligation requires that congressional enactments be judged by the standards of the Constitution. The Judiciary has the duty of implementing the constitutional safeguards that protect individual rights. When the Government acts to take away the fundamental right of citizenship, the safeguards of the Constitution should be examined with special diligence.

The provisions of the Constitution are not time-worn adages or hollow shibboleths. They are vital, living principles that authorize and limit governmental powers in our Nation. They are the rules of government. When the constitutionality of an Act of Congress is challenged in this Court, we must apply those rules. If we do not, the words of the Constitution become little more than good advice.

When it appears that an Act of Congress conflicts with one of these provisions, we have no choice but to enforce the paramount commands of the Constitution. We are sworn to do no less. We cannot push back the limits of the Constitution merely to accommodate challenged legislation.

We must apply those limits as the Constitution prescribes them, bearing in mind both the broad scope of legislative discretion and the ultimate responsibility of constitutional adjudication. We do well to approach this task cautiously, as all our predecessors have counseled. But the ordeal of judgment cannot be shirked. In some 81 instances since this Court was established it has determined that congressional action exceeded the bounds of the Constitution. It is so in this case. ...

Reversed and remanded.

Mr. Justice **BLACK**, whom Mr. Justice **DOUGLAS** joins, concurring.

While I concur in the opinion of The Chief Justice there is one additional thing that needs to be said. Even if citizenship could be involuntarily divested, I do not believe that the power to denationalize may be placed in the hands of military authorities. ...

Mr. Justice **BRENNAN**, concurring. ...

... I can only conclude that the requisite rational relation between this statute and the war power does not appear—for in this relation the statute is not "really calculated to effect any of the objects entrusted to the government. ..." McCulloch v. Maryland—[1819]—and therefore that § 401(g) falls beyond the domain of Congress.

Mr. Justice **FRANKFURTER**, whom Mr. Justice **BURTON**, Mr. Justice **CLARK**, and Mr. Justice **HARLAN** join, dissenting. ...

... What is always basic when the power of Congress to enact legislation is challenged is the appropriate approach to judicial review of congressional legislation. All power is, in Madison's phrase, "of an encroaching nature." *Federalist*, No. 48. Judicial power is not immune against this human weakness. It also must be on guard against encroaching beyond its proper bounds, and not the less so since the only restraint upon it is self-restraint. When the power of Congress to pass a statute is challenged, the function of this Court is to determine whether legislative action lies clearly outside the constitutional grant of power to which it has been, or may fairly be, referred. In making this determination, the Court sits in judgment on the action of a co-ordinate branch of the Government while keeping unto itself—as it must under our constitutional system—the final determination of its own power to act. No wonder such a function is deemed "the gravest and most delicate duty that this Court is called on to perform." ...

Rigorous observance of the difference between limits of power and wise exercise of power—between questions of authority and questions of prudence—requires the most alert appreciation of this decisive but subtle relationship of two concepts that too easily coalesce. No less does it require a disciplined will to adhere to the difference. It is not easy to stand aloof and allow want of wisdom to prevail, to disregard one's own strongly held view of what is wise in the conduct of affairs. But it is not the business of this Court to pronounce policy. It must observe a fastidious regard for limitations on its own power, and this precludes the Court's giving effect to its own notions of what is wise or politic. That self-restraint is of the essence in the observance of the judicial oath, for the Constitution has not authorized the judges to sit in judgment on the wisdom of what Congress and the Executive Branch do.

One of the principal purposes in establishing the Constitution was to "provide for the common defence." To that end the States granted to Congress the several powers of Article 1, Section 8, clauses 11 to 14 and 18, compendiously described as the "war power." Although these specific grants of power do not specifically enumerate every factor relevant to the power to conduct war, there is no limitation upon it (other than what the Due Process Clause commands). . . .

Probably the most important governmental action contemplated by the war power is the building up and maintenance of an armed force for the common defense. Just as Congress may be convinced of the necessity for conscription for the effective conduct of war . . ., Congress may justifiably be of the view that stern measures—what to some may seem overly stern—are needed in order that control may be had over evasions of military duty when the armed forces are committed to the Nation's defense, and that the deleterious effects of those evasions may be kept to the minimum. Clearly Congress may deal severely with the problem of desertion from the armed forces in wartime; it is equally clear—from the face of the legislation and from the circumstances in which it was passed—that Congress was calling upon its war powers when it made such desertion an act of expatriation. . . .

Possession by an American citizen of the rights and privileges that constitute citizenship imposes correlative obligations, of which the most indispensable may well be "to take his place in the ranks of the army of his country and risk the chance of being shot down in its defense," Jacobson v. Massachusetts [1905]. Harsh as this may sound, it is no more so than the actualities to which it responds. Can it be said that there is no rational nexus between refusal to perform this ultimate duty of American citizenship and legislative withdrawal of that citizenship? . . . It is not for us to deny that Congress might reasonably have believed the morale and fighting efficiency of our troops would be impaired if our soldiers knew that their fellows who had abandoned them in their time of greatest need were to remain in the communion of our citizens. . . .

This legislation is the result of an exercise by Congress of the legislative power vested in it by the Constitution and of an exercise by the President of his constitutional power in approving a bill and thereby making it "a law." To sustain it is to respect the actions of the two branches of our Government directly responsive to the will of the people and empowered under the Constitution to determine the wisdom of legislation. The awesome power of this Court to invalidate such legislation, because in practice it is bounded only by our own prudence in discerning the limits of the Court's constitutional function, must be exercised with the utmost restraint. Mr. Justice Holmes . . . expressed the conviction that "I do not think the United States would come to an end if we lost our power to declare an Act of Congress void. I do think the Union would be imperiled if we could not make that declaration as to the laws of the several States." ... He did not, of course, deny that the power existed to strike down congressional legislation, nor did he shrink from its exercise. But the whole of his work during his thirty years of service on this Court should be a constant reminder that the power to invalidate legislation must not be exercised as if, either in constitutional theory or in the art of government, it stood as the sole bulwark against unwisdom or excesses of the moment.

Editors' Notes

(1) **Query:** What are the textual bases of the debate between Warren and Frankfurter? Where does the text speak, directly or indirectly, about "the dignity of man" or about judicial "prudence"? To what extent did either justice meet the other on his own textual grounds? Were textual grounds critical for either's argument?

(2) **Query:** Warren said the Eighth Amendment drew "its meaning from the evolving standards of decency that mark the progress of a maturing society." How (or where) does he suggest that an interpreter find those standards? How parallel is the debate in Michael H. v. Gerald D. (1989; reprinted above, p. 158) between Justices Scalia and Brennan about how to find "tradition"? For an earlier effort to cope with the problem of "evolving standards," see the dissenting opinion of Judge Jerome Frank of the U.S. Court of Appeals for the 2d Circuit in Repouille v. United States (1947).

(3) **Query:** To what extent can one argue that the terms of the Eighth Amendment are different from most other parts of the constitutional text in that the word "unusual" in "cruel and unusual" requires interpreters to apply contemporary standards?

(4) **Query:** To what extent is the debate between Warren and Frankfurter really about the basic interrogative, WHO shall interpret?

(5) Warren and Frankfurter sharply disagreed on the merits of the substantive issue before the Court. They did not basically disagree on the notion of the constitutional clauses meaning different things at different times. In a internal memorandum written during the Court's deliberation of the School Segregation Cases (1954), Frankfurter said:

> [T]he equality of laws enshrined in a constitution which was "made for an undefined and expanding future, and for a people gathered and to be gathered from many nations and many tongues," Hurtado v. California, is not a fixed formula defined with finality at a particular time. It does not reflect, as a congealed summary, the social arrangements and beliefs of a particular epoch. It is addressed to the changes wrought by time and not merely the changes that are the consequences of physical development. Law must respond to transformation of views as well as to that of outward circumstances. The effect of changes in men's feelings for what is right and just is equally relevant in determining whether a discrimination denies the equal

protection of the laws. [Quoted in Richard Kluger, *Simple Justice* (New York: Knopf, 1976), p. 685.]

It was, of course, in the School Segregation Cases (Brown v. Board; reprinted below, p. 912) that Warren wrote for the Court: "[W]e cannot turn back the clock to 1868 when the [Fourteenth] Amendment was adopted. . . . We must consider public education in the light of its full development and its present place in American life throughout the Nation."

(6) *Trop* involved a substantive problem that was very painful to people who had lived through the years when the Nazis ruled Germany. One of the standard techniques the Nazis used against dissenters, when they did not imprison or kill them, was to remove their citizenship and forcibly deport them. The USSR used, and the Chinese still use, similar tactics, but most nations of the West have welcomed exiles from Marxist regimes. During the 1930s, however, Europeans were usually hostile to these outcasts, who were very often Jews, typically imprisoning them for illegal entry and then re-deporting them to Germany or to a third nation, where they suffered the same fate over again and again. Erich Maria Remarque brilliantly captured the sufferings of these people in his novel *Arch of Triumph*, W. Sorrell & D. Lindley, trans., (New York: Appleton–Century, 1945), later made into a movie starring Ingrid Bergman and Charles Boyer.

(7) In *Trop* a majority of the justices could not agree on a single opinion. Thus Warren spoke for only four justices, not for the Court. It was not until 1967, in Afroyim v. Rusk, that a full majority held that government could not for any reason whatsoever take away an American's citizenship, though a citizen could voluntarily renounce that status.

———

"[T]he Equal Protection Clause is not shackled to the political theory of a particular era."—Justice DOUGLAS

"[W]hen a 'political theory' embodied in our Constitution becomes outdated . . . a majority of the nine members of this Court are not only without constitutional power but are far less qualified to choose a new constitutional political theory than the people of the country proceeding in the manner provided by Article V."—Justice BLACK

HARPER v. VIRGINIA STATE BOARD OF ELECTIONS
383 U.S. 663, 86 S.Ct. 1079, 16 L.Ed.2d 169 (1966).

The Twenty–Fourth Amendment, adopted in 1964, outlawed a poll tax as a requirement for voting for *federal* officials, but made no mention of such taxes as prerequisites for voting for *state* officials. Virginia continued to demand payment of an annual poll tax of $1.50 before voting in state elections. A group of citizens of Virginia filed suit in a federal district court, claiming the tax violated the equal protection clause of the Fourteenth Amendment. That court dismissed the case, saying it was bound by Breedlove v.

Suttles (1937), in which the Supreme Court had unanimously sustained Georgia's poll tax against a similar attack. The litigants then appealed directly to the Supreme Court, as federal statutes permitted.

Mr. Justice **DOUGLAS** delivered the opinion of the Court. ...

While the right to vote in federal elections is conferred by Art I, § 2, of the Constitution, the right to vote in state elections is nowhere expressly mentioned. It is argued that the right to vote in state elections is implicit, particularly by reason of the First Amendment and that it may not constitutionally be conditioned upon the payment of a tax or fee. We do not stop to canvass the relation between voting and political expression. For it is enough to say that once the franchise is granted to the electorate, lines may not be drawn which are inconsistent with the Equal Protection Clause of the Fourteenth Amendment. That is to say, the right of suffrage "is subject to the imposition of state standards which are not discriminatory and which do not contravene any restriction that Congress, acting pursuant to its constitutional powers, has imposed." Lassiter v. Northampton Election Board [1959]. We were speaking there of a state literacy test which we sustained, warning that the result would be different if a literacy test, fair on its face, were used to discriminate against a class. But *Lassiter* does not govern the result here, because, unlike a poll tax, the "ability to read and write ... has some relation to standards designed to promote intelligent use of the ballot."

We conclude that a State violates the Equal Protection Clause of the Fourteenth Amendment whenever it makes the affluence of the voter or payment of any fee an electoral standard. Voter qualifications have no relation to wealth nor to paying this or any other tax. Our cases demonstrate that the Equal Protection Clause ... restrains the States from fixing voter qualifications which invidiously discriminate. Thus without questioning the power of a State to impose reasonable residence restrictions on the availability of the ballot, we held in Carrington v. Rash [1965] that a State may not deny the opportunity to vote to a bona fide resident merely because he is a member of the armed services. ... Previously we had said that neither homesite nor occupation "affords a permissible basis for distinguishing between qualified voters within the State." Gray v. Sanders [1963]. We think the same must be true of requirements of wealth or affluence or payment of a fee.

Long ago in Yick Wo v. Hopkins [1886] the Court referred to "the political franchise of voting" as a "fundamental political right, because preservative of all rights." Recently in Reynolds v. Sims [1964], we said, "Undoubtedly, the right of suffrage is a fundamental matter in a free and democratic society. Especially since the right to exercise the franchise in a free and unimpaired manner is preservative of other basic civil and political rights, any alleged infringement of the right of citizens to vote must be carefully and meticulously scrutinized." There we were considering charges that voters in one part of the State had greater representation per person in the State Legislature than voters in another part of the State. We concluded: "A citizen, a qualified voter, is no more nor no less so because he lives in the city or on the farm. This is the clear and strong command of our Constitution's Equal Protection Clause. ..."

We say the same whether the citizen, otherwise qualified to vote, has $1.50 in his pocket or nothing at all, pays the fee or fails to pay it. The principle that denies the State the right to dilute a citizen's vote on account of his economic status or other such factors by analogy bars a system which excludes those unable to pay a fee to vote or who fail to pay. ...

... In this context—that is, as a condition of obtaining a ballot—the requirement of fee paying causes an "invidious" discrimination (Skinner v. Oklahoma [1942]). ... Breedlove v. Suttles sanctioned its use as "a prerequisite of voting." To that extent *Breedlove* is overruled.

We agree, of course, with Mr. Justice Holmes that the Due Process Clause of the Fourteenth Amendment "does not enact Mr. Herbert Spencer's *Social Statics* " (Lochner v. New York [1905]). Likewise, the Equal Protection Clause is not shackled to the political theory of a particular era. In determining what lines are unconstitutionally discriminatory, we have never been confined to historic notions of equality, any more than we have restricted due process to a fixed catalogue of what was at a given time deemed to be the limits of fundamental rights. See Malloy v. Hogan [1964]. Notions of what constitutes equal treatment for purposes of the Equal Protection Clause *do* change. This Court in 1896 held that laws providing for separate public facilities for white and Negro citizens did not deprive the latter of the equal protection and treatment that the Fourteenth Amendment commands. Plessy v. Ferguson. ... When, in 1954 ... we repudiated the "separate-but-equal" doctrine of *Plessy* as respects public education we stated: "In approaching this problem, we cannot turn the clock back to 1868 when the Amendment was adopted, or even to 1896 when *Plessy* was written." Brown v. Board of Education.

In [*Reynolds*], we held ... that "the opportunity for equal participation by all voters in the election of state legislators" is required. We decline to qualify that principle by sustaining this poll tax. ...

Reversed.

Mr. Justice **BLACK,** dissenting. ...

... [T]he Court's decision is to no extent based on a finding that the Virginia law as written or as applied is being used as a device or mechanism to deny Negro citizens of Virginia the right to vote on account of their color. ... If the record could support [such] a finding, the law would of course be unconstitutional as a violation of the Fourteenth and Fifteenth Amendments and also 42 USC § 1971(a). ...

(1) ... The mere fact that a law results in treating some groups differently from others does not, of course, automatically amount to a

violation of the Equal Protection Clause. To bar a State from drawing any distinctions in the application of its laws would practically paralyze the regulatory power of legislative bodies. ... Voting laws are no exception to this principle. All voting laws treat some persons differently from others in some respects. ... Some bar convicted felons or the insane, and some have attached a freehold or other property qualification for voting. *Breedlove* upheld a poll tax which was imposed on men but was not equally imposed on women and minors, and the Court today does not overrule that part of *Breedlove* which approved those discriminatory provisions. And in *Lassiter,* this Court held that state laws which disqualified the illiterate from voting did not violate the Equal Protection Clause. From these cases ... it is clear that some discriminatory voting qualifications can be imposed without violating the Equal Protection Clause.

... The equal protection cases carefully analyzed boil down to the principle that distinctions drawn and even discriminations imposed by state laws do not violate the Equal Protection Clause so long as these distinctions and discriminations are not "irrational," "irrelevant," "unreasonable," "arbitrary," or "invidious." These vague and indefinite terms do not, of course, provide a precise formula or an automatic mechanism for deciding cases. ... The restrictive connotations of these terms, however[,] ... are a plain recognition of the fact that under a proper interpretation of the Equal Protection Clause States are to have the broadest kind of leeway in areas where they have a general constitutional competence to act. In view of the purpose of the terms to restrain the courts from a wholesale invalidation of state laws under the Equal Protection Clause it would be difficult to say that the poll tax requirement is "irrational" or "arbitrary" or works "invidious discriminations." State poll tax legislation can "reasonably," "rationally" and without an "invidious" or evil purpose to injure anyone be found to rest on a number of state policies including (1) the State's desire to collect its revenue, and (2) its belief that voters [who] pay a poll tax will be interested in furthering the State's welfare when they vote. Certainly it is rational to believe that people may be more likely to pay taxes if payment is a prerequisite to voting. And if history can be a factor in determining the "rationality" of discrimination in a state law[,] ... then ... history is on the side of "rationality" of the State's poll tax policy. Property qualifications existed in the Colonies and were continued by many States after the Constitution was adopted. Although I join the Court in disliking the policy of the poll tax, this is not in my judgment a justifiable reason for holding this poll tax law unconstitutional. ...

(2) Another reason for my dissent ... is that [the Court] seems to be using the old "natural-law-due-process formula" to justify striking down state laws as violations of the Equal Protection Clause. I have heretofore had many occasions to express my strong belief that there is no constitutional support whatever for this Court to use the Due Process Clause as though it provided a blank check to alter the meaning of the Constitution as written so as to add to it substantive constitutional

changes which a majority of the Court at any given time believes are needed to meet present-day problems. Nor is there in my opinion any more constitutional support for this Court to use the Equal Protection Clause, as it has today, to write into the Constitution its notions of what it thinks is good governmental policy. ...

The Court denies that it is using the "natural-law-due-process formula." It says that its invalidation of the Virginia law "is founded not on what we think governmental policy should be, but on what the Equal Protection Clause requires." I find no statement in the Court's opinion, however, which advances even a plausible argument as to why the alleged discriminations which might possibly be effected by Virginia's poll tax law are "irrational," "unreasonable," "arbitrary," or "invidious" or have no relevance to a legitimate policy which the State wishes to adopt. ... The Court's failure to give any reasons ... is a pretty clear indication to me that none exist. I can only conclude that the primary, controlling, predominate, if not the exclusive reason for declaring the Virginia law unconstitutional is the Court's deep-seated hostility and antagonism, which I share, to making payment of a tax a prerequisite to voting.

The Court's justification for consulting its own notions rather than following the original meaning of the Constitution, as I would, apparently is based on the belief of the majority of the Court that for this Court to be bound by the original meaning of the Constitution is an intolerable and debilitating evil; that our Constitution should not be "shackled to the political theory of a particular era," and that to save the country from the original Constitution the Court must have constant power to renew it and keep it abreast of this Court's more enlightened theories of what is best for our society. It seems to me that this is an attack not only on the great value of our Constitution itself but also on the concept of a written constitution which is to survive through the years as originally written unless changed through the amendment process which the Framers wisely provided. Moreover, when a "political theory" embodied in our Constitution becomes outdated, it seems to me that a majority of the nine members of this Court are not only without constitutional power but are far less qualified to choose a new constitutional political theory than the people of this country proceeding in the manner provided by Article V.

The people have not found it impossible to amend their Constitution to meet new conditions. ... Moreover, the people, in § 5 of the Fourteenth Amendment, designated the governmental tribunal they wanted to provide additional rules to enforce the guarantees of that Amendment. The branch of Government they chose was not the Judicial Branch but the Legislative. I have no doubt at all that Congress has the power under § 5 to pass legislation to abolish the poll tax. ... This Court had occasion to discuss this very subject in Ex parte Virginia (1880). There this Court said, referring to the first section of the Amendment:

It is not said the *judicial power* of the general government shall extend to enforcing the prohibitions and to protecting the rights and immunities guaranteed. It is not said that branch of the government shall be authorized to declare void any action of a State in violation of the prohibitions. *It is the power of Congress which has been enlarged.* Congress is authorized *to enforce* the prohibitions by appropriate legislation. ... (Emphasis partially supplied.)

. . .

Mr. Justice **HARLAN**, whom Mr. Justice **STEWART** joins, dissenting.
. . .

Editors' Notes

(1) **Query:** Justice Douglas claimed that Art. I, § 2 of the constitutional document confers a right to vote in federal elections. Does the text say so, explicitly or implicitly?

(2) **Query:** How similar is the debate between Black and Douglas similar to that between Chase and Iredell in Calder v. Bull (1798; reprinted above, p. 121)?

(3) **Query:** In this debate, is Black or Douglas the true defender of democratic theory? Why?

(4) Compare Black's theory of legitimate constitutional change with that of Justice Sutherland in *Blaisdell* (1934; reprinted above, p. 210).

(5) **Query:** To what extent is the Black–Douglas debate really about WHO shall interpret?

(6) **Query:** See Note (5) to Trop v. Dulles (1958), above, at p. 219. Justice Black joined Warren's opinion for the Court in the School Segregation Cases (1954; reprinted below, p. 912). How does that choice square with Black's dissent in *Harper*?

(7) **Query:** To what extent can one say that "equal protection" is, like the ban against "cruel and unusual punishments," in a different category from most constitutional clauses in that its very terms require interpreters to impose current—and hence possibly changing—standards? What about "due process of law"?

(8) The four states that, when *Harper* was decided, still required payment of poll taxes for state elections were: Alabama, Mississippi, Texas, and Virginia.

(9) See also the Editors' Notes concerning *Harper* on p. 787.

———

"If the Constitution were ... a novel invitation to apply current societal values, what reason would there be to believe that the invitation was addressed to the courts rather than to the legislature?"

ORIGINALISM: THE LESSER EVIL*

Antonin Scalia.

... It may surprise the layman ... to learn that originalism is not, and had perhaps never been, the sole method of constitutional exegesis. It would be hard to count on the fingers of both hands and the toes of both feet, yea, even on the hairs of one's youthful head, the opinions that have in fact been rendered not on the basis of what the Constitution originally meant, but on the basis of what the judges currently thought it desirable for it to mean. ... But in the past, nonoriginalist opinions have almost always had the decency to lie, or at least to dissemble, about what they were doing—either ignoring strong evidence of original intent that contradicted the minimal recited evidence of an original intent congenial to the court's desires, or else not discussing original intent at all, speaking in terms of broad constitutional generalities with no pretense of historical support. ... It is only in relatively recent years ... that nonoriginalist exegesis has ... come out of the closet, and put itself forward overtly as an intellectually legitimate device. To be sure, in support of its venerability as a legitimate interpretive theory there is often trotted out John Marshall's statement in *McCulloch v. Maryland* [1819] that "we must never forget it is a constitution we are expounding"—as though the implication of that statement was that our interpretation must change from age to age. But that is a canard. The real implication was quite the opposite: Marshall was saying that the Constitution had to be interpreted generously because the powers conferred upon Congress under it had to be broad enough to serve not only the needs of the federal government originally discerned but also the needs that might arise in the future. If constitutional interpretation could be adjusted as changing circumstances required, a broad initial interpretation would have been unnecessary. ...

The principal theoretical defect of nonoriginalism ... is its incompatibility with the very principle that legitimizes judicial review of constitutionality. Nothing in the text of the Constitution confers upon the courts the power to inquire into, rather than passively assume, the constitutionality of federal statutes. That power is, however, reasonably implicit because, as Marshall said in Marbury v. Madison, (1) "[i]t is emphatically the province and duty of the judicial department to say what the law is," (2) "[i]f two laws conflict with each other, the courts must decide on the operation of each," and (3) "the constitution is to be considered, in court, as a paramount law." Central to that analysis, it seems to me, is the perception that the Constitution, though it has an effect superior to other laws, is in its nature the sort of "law" that is the business of the courts—an enactment that has a fixed meaning ascertainable through the usual devices familiar to those learned in the law.

* Published originally in 57 *U.Cinn.L.Rev.* 849 (1989). Copyright © 1989 by Antonin Scalia. Reprinted by permission.

Antonin Scalia has been an Associate Justice of the U.S. Supreme Court since 1986.

If the Constitution were not that sort of a "law," but a novel invitation to apply current societal values, what reason would there be to believe that the invitation was addressed to the courts rather than to the legislature? One simply cannot say, regarding that sort of novel enactment, that "[i]t is emphatically the province and duty of the judicial department" to determine its content. Quite to the contrary, the legislature would seem a much more appropriate expositor of social values, and its determination that a statute is compatible with the Constitution should, as in England, prevail.

Apart from the frailty of its theoretical underpinning, nonoriginalism confronts a practical difficulty reminiscent of the truism of elective politics that "You can't beat somebody with nobody." It is not enough to demonstrate that the other fellow's candidate (originalism) is no good; one must also agree upon another candidate to replace him. ... If the law is to make any attempt at consistency and predictability, surely there must be general agreement not only that judges reject one exegetical approach (originalism), but that they adopt another. And it is hard to discern any emerging consensus among the nonoriginalists as to what this might be. Are the "fundamental values" that replace original meaning to be derived from the philosophy of Plato, or of Locke, or [John Stuart] Mill, or [John] Rawls, or perhaps from the latest Gallup poll? This is not to say that originalists are in entire agreement as to what the nature of their methodology is. ... But as its name suggests, it by and large represents a coherent approach, or at least an agreed-upon point of departure. As the name "nonoriginalism" suggests (and I know no other, more precise term by which this school of exegesis can be described), it represents agreement on nothing except what is the wrong approach.

Finally, I want to mention what is not a defect of nonoriginalism, but one of its supposed benefits that seems to me illusory. ... [O]ne of the most prominent nonoriginalists, Professor [Laurence] Tribe ... [wrote] that the Constitution "invites us, and our judges, to expand on the ... freedoms that are uniquely our heritage." I think it fair to say that that is a common theme of nonoriginalists in general. But why, one may reasonably ask—once the original import of the Constitution is cast aside to be replaced by the "fundamental values" of the current society—why are we invited only to "expand on" freedoms, and not to contract them as well? ... Nonoriginalism, in other words, is a two-way street that handles traffic both to and from individual rights.

Let me turn next to originalism, which is also not without its warts. Its greatest defect, in my view, is the difficulty of applying it correctly. Not that I agree with, or even take very seriously, the intricately elaborated scholarly criticisms to the effect that (believe it or not) words have no meaning. They have meaning enough, as the scholarly critics themselves must surely believe when they choose to express their views in text rather than music. But what is true is that it is often exceedingly difficult to plumb the original understanding of an ancient text.

Properly done, the task requires the consideration of an enormous mass of material—in the case of the Constitution and its Amendments, for example ... the records of the ratifying debates in all the states. Even beyond that, it requires an evaluation of the reliability of that material— many of the reports of the ratifying debates, for example, are thought to be quite unreliable. And further still, it requires immersing oneself in the political and intellectual atmosphere of the time—somehow placing out of mind knowledge that we have which an earlier age did not, and putting on beliefs, attitudes, philosophies, prejudices and loyalties that are not those of our day. It is, in short, a task sometimes better suited to the historian than the lawyer. ...

... [T]he second most serious objection to originalism: In its undiluted form, at least, it is medicine that seems too strong to swallow. Thus, almost every originalist would adulterate it with the doctrine of stare decisis—so that Marbury v. Madison would stand even if Professor Raoul Berger should demonstrate unassailably that it got the meaning of the Constitution wrong. (Of course recognizing stare decisis is seemingly even more incompatible with nonoriginalist theory: If the most solemnly and democratically adopted text of the Constitution and its Amendments can be ignored on the basis of current values, what possible basis could there be for enforced adherence to a legal decision of the Supreme Court?) But stare decisis alone is not enough to prevent originalism from being what many would consider too bitter a pill. What if some state should enact a new law providing public lashing, or branding of the right hand, as punishment for certain criminal offenses? Even if it could be demonstrated unequivocally that these were not cruel and unusual measures in 1791, and even though no prior Supreme Court decision has specifically disapproved them, I doubt whether any federal judge—even among the many who consider themselves originalists— would sustain them against an eighth amendment challenge. ... [A]ny espousal of originalism as a practical theory of exegesis must somehow come to terms with that reality.

One way of doing so, of course, would be to say that it was originally intended that the cruel and unusual punishment clause would have an evolving content—that "cruel and unusual" originally meant "cruel and unusual for the age in question" and not "cruel and unusual in 1791." But to be faithful to originalist philosophy, one must not only say this but demonstrate it to be so on the basis of some textual or historical evidence. Perhaps the mere words "cruel and unusual" suggest an evolutionary intent more than other provisions of the Constitution, but that is far from clear; and I know of no historical evidence for that meaning. And if the faint-hearted originalist is willing simply to posit such an intent for the "cruel and unusual punishment" clause, why not for the due process clause, the equal protection clause, the privileges and immunity clause, etc.? When one goes down that road, there is really no difference between the faint-hearted originalist and the moderate non-originalist, except that the former finds it comforting to make up (out of whole cloth) an original evolutionary intent, and the latter thinks that superfluous. It is, I think, the fact that most originalists are faint-hearted and most nonoriginalists are moderate (that is, would not ascribe evolving content to such clear provisions as the requirement that the President be no less than thirty-five years of age) which accounts for the fact that the sharp divergence between the two philosophies does not produce an equivalently sharp divergence in judicial opinions.

Having described what I consider the principal difficulties with the originalist and nonoriginalist approaches ... I owe it to the listener to say which of the two evils I prefer. It is originalism. I take the need for theoretical legitimacy seriously, and even if one assumes (as many nonoriginalists do not even bother to do) that the Constitution was originally meant to expound evolving rather than permanent values[,] ... I see no basis for believing that supervision of the evolution would have been committed to the courts. At an even more general theoretical level, originalism seems to me more compatible with the nature and purpose of a Constitution in a democratic system. A democratic society does not, by and large, need constitutional guarantees to insure that its laws will reflect "current values." Elections take care of that quite well. The purpose of constitutional guarantees—and in particular those constitutional guarantees of individual rights ...—is precisely to prevent the law from reflecting certain changes in original values that the society adopting the Constitution thinks fundamentally undesirable. Or, more precisely, to require the society to devote to the subject the long and hard consideration required for a constitutional amendment before those particular values can be cast aside.

I also think that the central practical defect of nonoriginalism is fundamental and irreparable: the impossibility of achieving any consensus on what, precisely, is to replace original meaning, once that is abandoned. The practical defects of originalism, on the other hand, while genuine enough, seem to me less severe. While it may indeed be unrealistic to have substantial confidence that judges and lawyers will find the correct historical answer to such refined questions of original intent as the precise content of "the executive Power," for the vast majority of questions the answer is clear. The death penalty, for example, was not cruel and unusual punishment because it is referred to in the Constitution itself; and the right of confrontation by its plain language meant, at least, being face-to-face with the person testifying against one at trial. For the nonoriginalist, even these are open questions.

As for the fact that originalism is strong medicine, and that one cannot realistically expect judges (probably myself included) to apply it without a trace of constitutional perfectionism: I suppose I must respond that this is a world in which nothing is flawless, and fall back upon G. K. Chesterton's observation that a thing worth doing is worth doing badly. It seems to me, moreover, that the practical defects of originalism are defects more appropriate for the task at hand—that is, less likely to aggravate the most significant weakness of the system of judicial review and more likely to produce results acceptable to all. ...

Now the main danger in judicial interpretation of the Constitution— or, for that matter, in judicial interpretation of any law—is that the judges will mistake their own predilections for the law. Avoiding this error is the hardest part of being a conscientious judge; perhaps no conscientious judge ever succeeds entirely. Nonoriginalism, which under one or another formulation invokes "fundamental values" as the touchstone of constitutionality, plays precisely to this weakness. It is very difficult for a person to discern a difference between those political values that he personally thinks most important, and those political values that are "fundamental to our society." Thus, by the adoption of such a criterion judicial personalization of the law is enormously facilitated. (One might reduce this danger by insisting that the new "fundamental values" invoked to replace original meaning be clearly and objectively manifested in the laws of the society. But among all the varying tests suggested by nonoriginalist theoreticians, I am unaware that that one ever appears. Most if not all nonoriginalists, for example, would strike down the death penalty, though it continues to be widely adopted in both state and federal legislation.)

Originalism does not aggravate the principal weakness of the system, for it establishes a historical criterion that is conceptually quite separate from the preferences of the judge himself. And the principal defect of that approach—that historical research is always difficult and sometimes inconclusive—will, unlike nonoriginalism, lead to a more moderate rather than a more extreme result. The inevitable tendency of judges to think that the law is what they would like it to be will, I have no doubt, cause most errors in judicial historiography to be made in the direction of projecting upon the age of 1789 current, modern values—so that as applied, even as applied in the best of faith, originalism will (as the historical record shows) end up as something of a compromise. Perhaps not a bad characteristic for a constitutional theory. ...

Having made that endorsement, I hasten to confess that in a crunch I may prove a faint-hearted originalist. I cannot imagine myself, any more than any other federal judge, upholding a statute that imposes the punishment of flogging. But then I cannot imagine such a case's arising either. In any event, in deciding the cases before me I expect I will rarely be confronted with making the stark choice between giving evolutionary content (not yet required by stare decisis) and not giving evolutionary content to particular constitutional provisions. The vast majority of my dissents from nonoriginalist thinking (and I hope at least some of those dissents will be majorities) will, I am sure, be able to be framed in the terms that, even if the provision in question has an evolutionary content, there is inadequate indication that any evolution in social attitudes has occurred. That ... is the real dispute that appears in the case: not between nonoriginalists on the one hand and pure originalists on the other, concerning the validity of looking at all to current values; but rather between, on the one hand, nonoriginalists, fainthearted originalists and pure-originalists-accepting-for-the-sake-of-argument-evolutionary-content, and, on the other hand, other adherents of the same three approaches, concerning the nature and degree of evidence necessary to demonstrate that constitutional evolution has occurred.

I am left with a sense of dissatisfaction, as I am sure you are, that a discourse concerning what one would suppose to be a rather fundamental—indeed, the most fundamental—aspect of constitutional theory and practice should end so inconclusively. But it should come as no surprise. We do not yet have an agreed-upon theory for interpreting statutes, either. I find it perhaps too laudatory to say that this is the genius of the common law system; but it is at least its nature.

Editors' Note

Because we believe that Justices Scalia's and Brennan's lectures should be read as a debate, as a unit, we have placed the Editors' Notes at the end of Brennan's lecture, at p. 242.

––––––

"We current Justices read the Constitution in the only way we can: as Twentieth–Century Americans. . . . [T]he ultimate question must be, what do the words of the text mean in our time?"

THE CONSTITUTION OF THE UNITED STATES: CONTEMPORARY RATIFICATION*

William J. Brennan, Jr.

. . . [T]he Constitution embodies the aspiration to social justice, brotherhood, and human dignity that brought this nation into being. The Declaration of Independence, the Constitution, and the Bill of Rights solemnly committed the United States to be a country where the dignity and rights of all persons were equal before all authority. In all candor we must concede that part of this egalitarianism in America has been more pretension than realized fact. But we are an aspiring people, a people with faith in progress. Our amended Constitution is the lodestar for our aspirations. Like every text worth reading, it is not crystalline. The phrasing is broad and the limitations of its provisions are not clearly marked. Its majestic generalities and ennobling pronouncements are both luminous and obscure. This ambiguity, of course, calls forth interpretation, the interaction of reader and text. . . .

––––––

* Lecture delivered at Georgetown University, Oct. 12, 1985; also published at 27 *S.Tex.L.J.* 433 (1986). Copyright© by William J. Brennan, Jr. Reprinted by permission.

William J. Brennan, Jr., was an Associate Justice of the U.S. Supreme Court from 1956 until 1990.

... The Constitution is fundamentally a public text—the monumental charter of a government and a people—and a Justice of the Supreme Court must apply it to resolve public controversies. ... Not infrequently, these are the issues upon which contemporary society is most deeply divided. ... The main burden of my twenty-nine Terms on the Supreme Court has thus been to wrestle with the Constitution in this heightened public context, to draw meaning from the text in order to resolve public controversies.

Two other aspects of my relation to this text warrant mention. First, constitutional interpretation for a federal judge is, for the most part, obligatory. ... Judges cannot avoid a definitive interpretation because they feel unable to, or would prefer not to, penetrate to the full meaning of the Constitution's provisions. Unlike literary critics, judges cannot merely savor the tensions or revel in the ambiguities inhering in the text—judges must resolve them.

Second, consequences flow from a Justice's interpretation in a direct and immediate way. A judicial decision respecting the incompatibility of Jim Crow with a constitutional guarantee of equality is not simply a contemplative exercise in defining the shape of a just society. It is an order—supported by the full coercive power of the State—that the present society change in a fundamental aspect. Under such circumstances the process of deciding can be a lonely, troubling experience for fallible human beings conscious that their best may not be adequate to the challenge. ...

... When Justices interpret the Constitution they speak for their community, not for themselves alone. The act of interpretation must be undertaken with full consciousness that it is, in a very real sense, the community's interpretation that is sought. Justices are not Platonic guardians appointed to wield authority according to their personal moral predilections. Precisely because coercive force must attend any judicial decision to countermand the will of a contemporary majority, the Justices must render constitutional interpretations that are received as legitimate. The source of legitimacy is, of course, a wellspring of controversy in legal and political circles. At the core of the debate is what the late Yale Law School professor Alexander Bickel labeled "the counter-majoritarian difficulty." Our commitment to self-governance in a representative democracy must be reconciled with vesting in electorally unaccountable Justices the power to invalidate the expressed desires of representative bodies on the ground of inconsistency with higher law. Because judicial power resides in the authority to give meaning to the Constitution, the debate is really a debate about how to read a text, about constraints on what is legitimate interpretation.

There are those who find legitimacy in fidelity to what they call "the intentions of the Framers." In its most doctrinaire incarnation, this view demands that Justices discern exactly what the Framers thought about the question under consideration and simply follow that intention in resolving the case before them. It is a view that feigns self-effacing deference to the specific judgments of those who forged our original social compact. But in truth it is little more than arrogance cloaked as humility. It is arrogant to pretend that from our vantage point we can gauge accurately the intent of the Framers on application of principle to specific, contemporary questions. All too often, sources of potential enlightenment such as records of the ratification debates provide sparse or ambiguous evidence of the original intention. Typically, all that can be gleaned is that the Framers themselves did not agree about the application or meaning of particular constitutional provisions, and hid their differences in cloaks of generality. Indeed, it is far from clear whose intention is relevant—that of the drafters, the congressional disputants, or the ratifiers in the states?—or even whether the idea of an original intention is a coherent way of thinking about a jointly drafted document drawing its authority from a general assent of the states. And apart from the problematic nature of the sources, our distance of two centuries cannot but work as a prism refracting all we perceive. One cannot help but speculate that the chorus of lamentations calling for interpretation faithful to 'original intention' ... must come from persons who have no familiarity with the historical record.

Perhaps most importantly, while proponents of this facile historicism justify it as a depoliticization of the judiciary, the political underpinnings of such a choice should not escape notice. A position that upholds constitutional claims only if they were within the specific contemplation of the Framers in effect establishes a presumption of resolving textual ambiguities against the claim of constitutional right. It is far from clear what justifies such a presumption against claims of right. Nothing intrinsic in the nature of interpretation—if there is such a thing as the 'nature' of interpretation—commands such a passive approach to ambiguity. This is a choice no less political than any other; it expresses antipathy to claims of the minority to rights against the majority. Those who would restrict claims of right to the values of 1789 specifically articulated in the Constitution turn a blind eye to social progress and eschew adaptation of overarching principles to changes of social circumstances.

Another, perhaps more sophisticated, response to the potent power of judicial interpretation stresses democratic theory: because ours is a government of the people's elected representatives, substantive value choices should by and large be left to them. This view emphasizes not the transcendent historical authority of the framers but the predominant contemporary authority of the elected branches of government. Yet it has similar consequences for the nature of proper judicial interpretation. . . .

The view that all matters of substantive policy should be resolved through the majoritarian process has appeal under some circumstances, but I think it ultimately will not do. Unabashed enshrinement of majority will would permit the imposition of a social caste system or wholesale confiscation of property so long as a majority of the authorized legislative body, fairly elected, approved. Our Constitution could not abide such a situation. It is the very purpose of a Constitution—and particularly of the Bill of Rights—to declare certain values transcendent, beyond the reach of temporary political majorities. The majoritarian process cannot be expected to rectify claims of minority right that arise as a response to the outcomes of that very majoritarian process. As James Madison put it: "The prescriptions in favor of liberty ought to be levelled against that quarter where the greatest danger lies, namely, that which possesses the highest prerogative of power. But this is not found in either the Executive or Legislative departments of Government, but in the body of the people, operating by the majority against the minority." [1]

Faith in democracy is one thing, blind faith quite another. Those who drafted our Constitution understood the difference. One cannot read the text without admitting that it embodies substantive value choices; it places certain values beyond the power of any legislature. Obvious are the separation of powers; the privilege of the Writ of Habeas Corpus; prohibition of Bills of Attainder and ex post facto laws; prohibition of cruel and unusual punishments; the requirement of just compensation for official taking of property; the prohibition of laws tending to establish religion or enjoining the free exercise of religion; and, since the Civil War, the banishment of slavery and official race discrimination. With respect to at least such principles, we simply have not constituted ourselves as strict utilitarians. While the Constitution may be amended, such amendments require an immense effort by the People as a whole.

To remain faithful to the content of the Constitution, therefore, an approach to interpreting the text must account for the existence of these substantive value choices, and must accept the ambiguity inherent in the effort to apply them to modern circumstances. The Framers discerned fundamental principles through struggles against particular contours of the articulated principles. But our acceptance of the fundamental principles has not and should not bind us to those precise, at times anachronistic, contours. Successive generations of Americans have continued to respect these fundamental choices and adopt them as their own guide to evaluating quite different historical practices. Each generation has the choice to overrule or add to the fundamental principles enunciated by the Framers; the Constitution can be amended or it can be ignored. Yet with respect to its fundamental principles, the text has suffered neither fate. Thus, if I may borrow the words of an esteemed predecessor, Justice Robert Jackson, the burden of judicial interpretation is to translate "the majestic generalities of the Bill of Rights, conceived as part of the pattern of liberal government in the eighteenth century, into concrete restraints on officials dealing with the problems of the twentieth century." [2]

---

1. 1 *Annals of Congress* 437.

2. West Virginia v. Barnette (1943). [**Eds.:** Reprinted below, p. 1174.]

We current Justices read the Constitution in the only way we can: as Twentieth-Century Americans. We look to the history of the time of framing and to the intervening history of interpretation. But the ultimate question must be, what do the words of the text mean in our time? For the genius of the Constitution rests not in any static meaning it might have had in a world that is dead and gone, but in the adaptability of its great principles to cope with current problems and current needs. What the constitutional fundamentals meant to the wisdom of other times cannot be their measure to the vision of our time. Similarly, what those fundamentals mean for us, our descendants will learn, cannot be the measure to the vision of their time. ... Interpretation must account for the transformative purpose of the text. Our Constitution was not intended to preserve a preexisting society but to make a new one, to put in place new principles that the prior political community had not sufficiently recognized. Thus, for example, when we interpret the Civil War Amendments to the charter—abolishing slavery, guaranteeing blacks equality under law, and guaranteeing blacks the right to vote—we must remember that those who put them in place had no desire to enshrine the status quo. Their goal was to make over their world, to eliminate all vestige of the slave caste. ...

The Constitution on its face is, in large measure, a structuring text, a blueprint for government. And when the text is not prescribing the form of government it is limiting the power of that government. ... As augmented by the Bill of Rights and the Civil War Amendments, this text is a sparkling vision of the supremacy of the human dignity of every individual. This vision is reflected in the very choice of democratic self-governance: the supreme value of a democracy is the presumed worth of each individual. And this vision manifests itself most dramatically in the specific prohibitions of the Bills of Rights, a term which I henceforth will apply to describe not only the original first eight amendments, but the Civil War amendments as well. ...

Until the end of the nineteenth century, freedom and dignity in our country found meaningful protection in the institution of real property. In a society still largely agricultural, a piece of land provided men not just with sustenance but with the means of economic independence, a necessary precondition of political independence and expression. ...

But the days when common law property relationships dominated litigation and legal practice are past. To a growing extent economic existence now depends on less certain relationships with government—licenses, employment, contracts, subsidies, unemployment benefits, tax exemptions, welfare, and the like. ... We turn to government and to the law for controls which would never have been expected or tolerated before this century, when a man's answer to economic oppression or difficulty was to move two hundred miles west. Now hundreds of thousands of Americans live entire lives without any real prospect of the dignity and autonomy that ownership of real property could confer.

Protection of the human dignity of such citizens requires a much modified view of the proper relationship of individual and state.

... As government acts ever more deeply upon those areas of our lives once marked "private," there is an even greater need to see that individual rights are not curtailed or cheapened in the interest of what may temporarily appear to be the "public good." And as government continues in its role of provider for so many of our disadvantaged citizens, there is an even greater need to ensure that government act with integrity and consistency in its dealings with these citizens. ... The modern activist state is a concomitant of the complexity of modern society; it is inevitably with us. We must meet the challenge rather than wish it were not before us.

The challenge is essentially, of course, one to the capacity of our constitutional structure to foster and protect the freedom, the dignity, and the rights of all persons within our borders, which it is the great design of the Constitution to secure. ... There is no worse injustice than wrongly to strip a man of his dignity. And our adherence to the constitutional vision of human dignity is so strict that even after convicting a person according to these stringent standards, we demand that his dignity be infringed only to the extent appropriate to the crime and never by means of wanton infliction of pain or deprivation. ...

Of course, the constitutional vision of human dignity has ... infused far more than our decisions about the criminal process. Recognition of the principle of "one person, one vote" as a constitutional one redeems the promise of self-governance by affirming the essential dignity of every citizen in the right to equal participation in the democratic process. Recognition of so-called "new property" rights in those receiving government entitlements affirms the essential dignity of the least fortunate among us by demanding that government treat with decency, integrity, and consistency those dependent on its benefits for their very survival. ... [D]ue process rights prohibit government from imposing the devil's bargain of bartering away human dignity in exchange for human sustenance. Likewise, recognition of full equality for women—equal protection of the laws—ensures that gender has no bearing on claims to human dignity.

Recognition of broad and deep rights of expression and of conscience reaffirm the vision of human dignity in many ways. They too redeem the promise of self-governance by facilitating—indeed demanding—robust, uninhibited, and wide-open debate on issues of public importance. Such public debate is, of course, vital to the development and dissemination of political ideas. As importantly, robust public discussion is the crucible in which personal political convictions are forged. In our democracy, such discussion is a political duty; it is the essence of self government. The constitutional vision of human dignity rejects the possibility of political orthodoxy imposed from above. ...

I do not mean to suggest that we have ... achieved a comprehensive definition of the constitutional ideal of human dignity. We are still striving toward that goal, and doubtless it will be an eternal quest. For if the interaction of this Justice and the constitutional text over the years confirms any single proposition, it is that the demands of human dignity will never cease to evolve.

Indeed, I cannot in good conscience refrain from mention of one grave and crucial respect in which we continue, in my judgment, to fall short of the constitutional vision of human dignity. It is in our continued tolerance of State-administered execution as a form of punishment.
. . .

If we are to be as a shining city upon a hill, it will be because of our ceaseless pursuit of the constitutional ideal of human dignity. For the political and legal ideals that form the foundation of much that is best in American institutions—ideals jealously preserved and guarded throughout our history—still form the vital force in creative political thought and activity within the nation today. . . .

Editors' Notes

(1) **Query:** In these two lectures, Justices Scalia and Brennan agreed that American judges should not act as "Platonic guardians" in preserving stability of facilitating constitutional change. How, then, did these two justices—see, for example, Michael H. v. Gerald D. (1989; reprinted above, p. 158—disagree so sharply? What conceptions of "the Constitution" did they hold? How did these differences affect their arguments about what role(s) judges should play in constitutional interpretation?

(2) **Query:** Scalia acknowledged the difficulties in discovering "original understanding" but still claimed judges can do a quite decent job in this search; and, by thus focusing their analysis, they will reduce their discretion. Brennan asserted that such a search is likely to be sterile and will do little, if anything, to reduce judicial discretion. Who had the better of the argument? What are "the records" of the debates at Philadelphia and in the state ratifying campaigns and conventions of which Scalia speaks? Do we have such "records"? Even if accurate records exist, would reliance on them be more likely to increase or decrease judicial discretion? Why?

(3) **Query:** What limitations on judicial discretion would Brennan's "aspirational approach" to constitutional interpretation impose? How effective are these likely to be? What limitations on the authority of popularly elected officials would Scalia's approach impose? (One might look at his opinion in Lee v. Weisman [1992; reprinted above, p. 167] before answering.)

(4) **Query:** Did Scalia here and/or in *Michael H.* implicitly adopt an aspirational approach? If so, what was his vision of the good American society?

(5) **Query:** Justice Brennan said: "It is the very purpose of a Constitution—particularly of the Bill of Rights—to declare certain values transcendent, beyond the reach of temporary political majorities." Two paragraphs later, he added that constitutional amendment was possible but would "require an immense effort by the People as a whole." Now, think about the issue raised

at the close of the introductory essay to this chapter (at pp. 191–92) about possible limitations on legitimate constitutional amendments: Given what you have read of Brennan's work, how do you think he would address that issue? What sort of response would he make to an amendment, adopted in perfect accord with the terms of Article V, that declared women (or African Americans or any other group) were entitled to lesser protection of laws than white males? How about Scalia?

(6) **Query:** See Editors' Note 3 to *Dred Scott* (1857; at p. 195). How would Scalia's *originalism* fit Taney's argument? Brennan's interpretive approach of *protecting fundamental rights*?

"Once we have abandoned the idea that the authority of the courts to declare laws unconstitutional is somehow tied to the language of the Constitution ... [judges obtain] a roving commission to second-guess Congress, state legislatures, and state and federal administrative officers concerning what is best for the country."

THE NOTION OF A LIVING CONSTITUTION *

William H. Rehnquist.

At least one of the more than half-dozen persons nominated during the past decade [1965–75] to be an Associate Justice of the Supreme Court of the United States has been asked by the Senate Judiciary Committee at his confirmation hearings whether he believed in a living Constitution. It is not an easy question to answer; the phrase "living Constitution" has about it a teasing imprecision that makes it a coat of many colors....

... The phrase is really a shorthand expression that is susceptible of at least two quite different meanings.

The first meaning was expressed ... by Mr. Justice Holmes in Missouri v. Holland [1920] ...:

When we are dealing with words that also are a constituent act, like the Constitution of the United States, we must realize that they have called into life a being the development of which could not have been foreseen completely by the most gifted of its begetters. It was enough for them to realize or to hope that they had created an organism; it has taken a century and has cost their successors much sweat and blood to prove that they created a nation.

... The framers of the Constitution wisely spoke in general language and left to succeeding generations the task of applying that

---

* Published originally in 54 *Tex.L.Rev.* 693 (1976). Copyright © 1976 by the *Texas Law Review*. Reprinted by permission.

William H. Rehnquist was an Associate Justice of the U.S. Supreme Court from 1971 to 1986 and has been Chief Justice of the United States since 1986.

language to the unceasingly changing environment in which they would live.... Merely because a particular activity may not have existed when the Constitution was adopted, or because the framers could not have conceived of a particular method of transacting affairs, cannot mean that general language in the Constitution may not be applied to such a course of conduct....

... I have sensed a second connotation of the phrase "living Constitution." ... Embodied in its most naked form, it recently came to my attention in some language from a brief ... on behalf of state prisoners asserting that the conditions of their confinement offended the United States Constitution ...:

> We are asking a great deal of the Court because other branches of government have abdicated their responsibility.... Prisoners are like other "discrete and insular" minorities for whom the Court must spread its protective umbrella because no other branch of government will do so.... This Court, as the voice and conscience of contemporary society, as the measure of the modern conception of human dignity, must declare that the [named prison] and all it represents offends the Constitution of the United States and will not be tolerated.

Here we have a living Constitution with a vengeance. Although the substitution of some other set of values for those which may be derived from the language and intent of the framers is not urged in so many words, that is surely the thrust of the message. Under this brief writer's version of the living Constitution, nonelected members of the federal judiciary may address themselves to a social problem simply because other branches of government have failed or refused to do so. These same judges, responsible to no constituency whatever, are nonetheless acclaimed as "the voice and conscience of contemporary society."

... [T]hose who have pondered the matter have always recognized that ... judicial review has basically antidemocratic and antimajoritarian facets that require some justification in this Nation, which prides itself on being a self-governing representative democracy....

... John Marshall's classic defense of judicial review [is] in Marbury v. Madison [1803].... [W]hile it supports the Holmes version of the phrase "living Constitution," it also suggests some outer limits for the brief writer's version. The ultimate source of authority in this Nation, Marshall said, is not Congress, not the states, not for that matter the Supreme Court.... The people are the ultimate source of authority; they have parceled out the authority that originally resided entirely with them by adopting the original Constitution and by later amending it....

In addition, Marshall said that if the popular branches of government ... are operating within the authority granted to them by the Constitution, their judgment and not that of the Court must obviously prevail. When these branches overstep the authority given them by the Constitution ... or invade protected individual rights, and a constitutional challenge to their action is raised in a lawsuit brought in federal court, the Court must prefer the Constitution to the government acts.

John Marshall's justification for judicial review makes the provision for an independent federal judiciary not only understandable but also thoroughly desirable. Since the judges will be merely interpreting an instrument framed by the people, they should be detached and objective. A mere change in public opinion since the adoption of the Constitution, unaccompanied by a constitutional amendment, should not change the meaning of the Constitution....

Clearly Marshall's explanation contains certain elements of either ingenuousness or ingeniousness.... The Constitution is in many of its parts obviously not a specifically worded document but one couched in general phraseology. There is obviously wide room for honest difference of opinion over the meaning of general phrases in the Constitution; any particular Justice's decision when a question arises under one of these general phrases will depend to some extent on his own philosophy of constitutional law. One may nevertheless concede all of these problems ... yet feel that [Marshall's] justification for nonelected judges exercising the power of judicial review is the only one consistent with democratic philosophy of representative government....

One senses no ... connection with a popularly adopted constituent act in ... the brief writer's version of the living Constitution. [It] seems instead to be based upon the proposition that federal judges, perhaps judges as a whole, have a role[,] ... quite independent of popular will, to play in solving society's problems. Once we have abandoned the idea that the authority of the courts to declare laws unconstitutional is somehow tied to the language of the Constitution that the people adopted, a judiciary exercising the power of judicial review appears in a quite different light. Judges then are no longer the keepers of the covenant; instead they are a small group of fortunately situated people with a roving commission to second-guess Congress, state legislatures, and state and federal administrative officers concerning what is best for the country. Surely there is no justification for a third legislative branch in the federal government, and there is even less justification for a federal legislative branch's reviewing on a policy basis the laws enacted by the legislatures of the fifty states.... If there is going to be a council of revision, it ought to have at least some connection with popular feeling. Its members either ought to stand for reelection on occasion, or their terms should expire and they should be allowed to continue serving only if reappointed by a popularly elected Chief Executive and confirmed by a popularly elected Senate.

The brief writer's version of the living Constitution is seldom presented in its most naked form, but is instead usually dressed in more attractive garb. The argument in favor of this approach generally begins with a sophisticated wink—why pretend that there is any ascertainable content to the general phrases of the Constitution as they are written since, after all, judges constantly disagree about their meaning? ... We all know the basis of Marshall's justification for judicial review, the argument runs, but it is necessary only to keep the window dressing in place. Any sophisticated student of the subject knows that judges need not limit themselves to the intent of the framers, which is very difficult to determine in any event. Because of the general language used in the Constitution, judges should not hesitate to use their authority to make the Constitution relevant and useful in solving the problems of modern society....

At least three serious difficulties flaw the brief writer's version of the living Constitution. First, it misconceives the nature of the Constitution, which was designed to enable the popularly elected branches of government, not the judicial branch, to keep the country abreast of the times. Second, the brief writer's version ignores the Supreme Court's disastrous experiences when in the past it embraced contemporary, fashionable notions of what a living Constitution should contain. Third, however socially desirable the goals sought to be advanced by the brief writer's version, advancing them through a free-wheeling, nonelected judiciary is quite unacceptable in a democratic society.

It seems to me that it is almost impossible, after reading the record of the Founding Fathers' debates in Philadelphia, to conclude that they intended the Constitution itself to suggest answers to the manifold problems that they knew would confront succeeding generations. The Constitution that they drafted was indeed intended to endure indefinitely, but the reason for this very well-founded hope was the general language by which national authority was granted to Congress and the Presidency. These two branches were to furnish the motive power within the federal system, which was in turn to coexist with the state governments.... Limitations were indeed placed upon both federal and state governments.... These limitations, however, were not themselves designed to solve the problems of the future, but were instead designed to make certain that the constituent branches, when they attempted to solve those problems, should not transgress these fundamental limitations.

... [T]he Civil War Amendments [XIII–XV] were designed more as broad limitations on the authority of state governments.... To the extent that the language of these amendments is general, the courts are of course warranted in giving them an application coextensive with their language. Nevertheless, I greatly doubt that even ... leaders of the radical Republicans in Congress would have thought any portion of the Civil War Amendments, except section five of the fourteenth amendment,[1] was designed to solve problems that society might confront a century later. I think they would have said that those amendments were designed to prevent from ever recurring abuses in which the states had engaged prior to that time.

The brief writer's version of the living Constitution, however, suggests that if the states' legislatures and governors, or Congress and the President, have not solved a particular social problem, then the federal

---

1. "The Congress shall have power to enforce, by appropriate legislation, the provisions of this article." U.S. Const. amend. XIV, § 5. [Footnote by Justice Rehnquist.]

court may act. I do not believe that this argument will withstand rational analysis. Even in the face of a conceded social evil, a reasonably competent and reasonably representative legislature may decide to do nothing. It may decide that the evil is not of sufficient magnitude to warrant any governmental intervention. It may decide that the financial cost of eliminating the evil is not worth the benefit which would result from its elimination. It may decide that the evils which might ensue from the proposed solution are worse than the evils which the solution would eliminate....

The second difficulty with the brief writer's version of the living Constitution lies in its inattention to or rejection of the Supreme Court's historical experience gleaned from similar forays into problem solving ... [e.g., Dred Scott v. Sandford (1857) and Lochner v. New York (1905)].

... [Such] experimentation with [this] expansive notion of a living Constitution has done the Court little credit.... [Some] appear to cleave nevertheless to the view that [these] experiments ... ended in failure not because they sought to bring into the Constitution a principle that ... was not there but because they sought to bring into the Constitution the *wrong* extraconstitutional principle. This school of thought appears to feel that while added protection for slave owners ... and safeguards for businessmen ... were not desirable, expansion of the protection accorded to individual liberties against the state or to the interests of "discrete and insular" minorities, such as prisoners, must stand on a quite different, more favored footing. To the extent, of course, that such a distinction may legitimately be derived from the Constitution itself, these latter principles do indeed stand on an entirely different footing. To the extent that one must, however, go beyond even a generously fair reading of the language and intent of that document in order to subsume these principles, ... they are not really distinguishable from those espoused in *Dred Scott* and *Lochner*.

The third difficulty with the brief writer's notion of the living Constitution is that it seems to ignore totally the nature of political value judgments in a democratic society. If such a society adopts a constitution and incorporates in that constitution safeguards for individual liberty, these safeguards indeed do take on a generalized moral rightness or goodness. They assume a general social acceptance neither because of any intrinsic worth nor because of any unique origins in someone's idea of natural justice but instead simply because they have been incorporated in a constitution by the people. Within the limits of our Constitution, the representatives of the people in the legislative branches of the state and national governments enact laws. The laws that emerge after a typical political struggle in which various individual value judgments are debated likewise take on a form of moral goodness.... It is the fact of their enactment that gives them whatever moral claim they have upon us as a society, however, and not any independent virtue they may have in any particular citizen's own scale of values.

Beyond the Constitution and the laws in our society, there simply is no basis other than the individual conscience of the citizen that may serve as a platform for the launching of moral judgments. There is no conceivable way in which I can logically demonstrate to you that the judgments of my conscience are superior to the judgments of your conscience, and vice versa. Many of us necessarily feel strongly and deeply about our own moral judgments, but they remain only personal moral judgments until in some way given the sanction of law....

... Representative government is predicated upon the idea that one who feels deeply upon a question as a matter of conscience will seek out others of like view or will attempt to persuade others who do not initially share that view. When adherents to the belief become sufficiently numerous, he will have the necessary armaments required in a democratic society to press his views upon the elected representatives of the people, and to have them embodied into positive law.

Should a person fail to persuade the legislature, or should he feel that a legislative victory would be insufficient because of its potential for future reversal, he may seek to run the more difficult gauntlet of amending the Constitution....

I know of no other method compatible with political theory basic to democratic society by which one's own conscientious belief may be translated into positive law and thereby obtain the only general moral imprimatur permissible in a pluralistic, democratic society. It is always time consuming, frequently difficult, and not infrequently impossible to run successfully the legislative gauntlet.... It is even more difficult ... to succeed in having such a value judgment embodied in the Constitution. All of these burdens and difficulties are entirely consistent with the notion of a democratic society. It should not be easy for any one individual or group of individuals to impose by law their value judgments upon fellow citizens who may disagree with those judgments. Indeed, it should not be easier just because the individual in question is a judge....

The brief writer's version of the living Constitution, in the last analysis, is a formula for an end run around popular government. To the extent that it makes possible an individual's persuading one or more appointed federal judges to impose on other individuals a rule of conduct that the popularly elected branches of government would not have enacted and the voters have not and would not have embodied in the Constitution, the brief writer's version of the living Constitution is genuinely corrosive of the fundamental values of our democratic society.

————————

"The constitutional theory on which our government rests is not a simple majoritarian theory. The Constitu-

tion ... is designed to protect individual citizens and groups against certain decisions that a majority of citizens might want to make."

TAKING RIGHTS SERIOUSLY: CONSTITUTIONAL CASES *
Ronald Dworkin.

1

... [I]n what follows I shall use the name "Nixon" to refer, not to [the late President Richard] Nixon, but to any politician holding the set of attitudes about the Supreme Court that he made explicit in his political campaigns. There ... are, in the special sense in which I use the name, many Nixons.

What can be the basis of this composite Nixon's opposition to the controversial decisions of the Warren Court? He cannot object to these decisions simply because they went beyond prior law, or say that the Supreme Court must never change its mind. Indeed the Burger Court itself seems intent on limiting the liberal decisions of the Warren Court.... The Constitution's guarantee of "equal protection of the laws," it is true, does not in plain words determine that "separate but equal" school facilities are unconstitutional, or that segregation was so unjust that heroic measures are required to undo its effects. But neither does it provide that as a matter of constitutional law the Court would be wrong to reach these conclusions. It leaves these issues to the Court's judgment, and the Court would have made law just as much if it had, for example, refused to hold [segregation] unconstitutional....

So we must search further to find a theoretical basis for Nixon's position....

2

The constitutional theory on which our government rests is not a simple majoritarian theory. The Constitution, and particularly the Bill of Rights, is designed to protect individual citizens and groups against certain decisions that a majority of citizens might want to make, even when that majority acts in what it takes to be the general or common interest. Some of these constitutional restraints take the form of fairly precise rules.... But other constraints take the form of what are often called "vague" standards, for example, the provision that the government shall not deny men due process of law, or equal protection of the laws.

This interference with democratic practice requires a justification. The draftsmen of the Constitution assumed that these restraints could be justified by appeal to moral rights which individuals possess against

---

* Abridged by permission of the author and publishers from *Taking Rights Seriously* by Ronald Dworkin, Cambridge: Harvard University Press, Copyright © 1972, 1977 by Ronald Dworkin. He is University Professor of Jurisprudence, Oxford University, and Professor of Law, New York University.

the majority, and which the constitutional provisions, both "vague" and precise, might be said to recognize and protect.

The "vague" standards were chosen deliberately ... in place of the more specific and limited rules that they might have enacted. But their decision ... has caused a great deal of legal and political controversy, because even reasonable men of good will differ when they try to elaborate, for example, the moral rights that the due process clause or the equal protection clause brings into the law. They also differ when they try to apply these rights, however defined, to complex matters of political administration....

The practice has developed of referring to a "strict" and a "liberal" side to these controversies, so that the Supreme Court might be said to have taken the "liberal" side in the segregation cases and its critics the "strict" side. Nixon has this distinction in mind when he calls himself a "strict constructionist." But the distinction is in fact confusing, because it runs together two different issues that must be separated. Any case that arises under the "vague" constitutional guarantees can be seen as posing two questions: (1) Which decision is required by strict, that is to say faithful, adherence to the text of the Constitution or to the intention of those who adopted that text? (2) Which decision is required by a political philosophy that takes a strict, that is to say narrow, view of the moral rights that individuals have against society? Once these questions are distinguished, it is plain that they may have different answers. The text of the First Amendment, for example, says that Congress shall make *no* law abridging the freedom of speech, but a narrow view of individual rights would permit many such laws....

In the case of the "vague" provisions, however, like the due process and equal protection clauses, lawyers have run the two questions together because they have relied, largely without recognizing it, on a theory of meaning that might be put this way: If the framers of the Constitution used vague language[,] ... then what they "said" or "meant" is limited to the instances of official action that they had in mind as violations, or, at least, to those instances that they would have thought were violations if they had had them in mind....

This theory makes a strict interpretation of the text yield a narrow view of constitutional rights, because it limits such rights to those recognized by a limited group of people at a fixed date of history. It forces those who favor a more liberal set of rights to concede that they are departing from strict legal authority, a departure they must then seek to justify by appealing only to the desirability of the results they reach.

But the theory of meaning on which this argument depends is far too crude; it ignores a distinction that philosophers have made but lawyers have not yet appreciated. Suppose I tell my children simply that I expect them not to treat others unfairly. I no doubt have in mind examples of the conduct I mean to discourage, but I would not accept that my "meaning" was limited to these examples, for two reasons.

First, I would expect my children to apply my instructions to situations I had not and could not have thought about. Second, I stand ready to admit that some particular act I had thought was fair when I spoke was in fact unfair, or vice versa, if one of my children is able to convince me of that later; in that case I should want to say that my instructions covered the case he cited, not that I had changed my instructions. I might say that I meant the family to be guided by the *concept* of fairness, not by any specific *conception* of fairness I might have had in mind.

This is a crucial distinction.... Suppose a group believes in common that acts may suffer from a special moral defect which they call unfairness, and which consists in a wrongful division of benefits and burdens, or a wrongful attribution of praise or blame. Suppose also that they agree on a great number of standard cases of unfairness and use these as benchmarks against which to test other, more controversial cases. In that case, the group has a concept of unfairness, and its members may appeal to that concept in moral instruction or argument. But members of that group may nevertheless differ over a large number of these controversial cases, in a way that suggests that each either has or acts on a different theory of *why* the standard cases are acts of unfairness. They may differ, that is, on which more fundamental principles must be relied upon to show that a particular division or attribution is unfair. In that case, the members have different conceptions of fairness.

If so, then members of this community who give instructions or set standards in the name of fairness may be doing two different things. First they may be appealing to the concept of fairness, simply by instructing others to act fairly; in this case they charge those whom they instruct with the responsibility of developing and applying their own conception of fairness as controversial cases arise. That is not the same thing, of course, as granting them a discretion to act as they like; it sets a standard which they must try—and may fail—to meet....

On the other hand, the members may be laying down a particular conception of fairness; I would have done this, for example, if I had listed my wishes with respect to controversial examples or if, even less likely, I had specified some controversial and explicit theory of fairness.... The difference is a difference not just in the *detail* of the instructions given but in the *kind* of instructions given. When I appeal to the concept of fairness I appeal to what fairness means, and I give my views on that issue no special standing. When I lay down a conception of fairness, I lay down what I mean by fairness, and my view is therefore the heart of the matter....

Once this distinction is made it seems obvious that we must take what I have been calling "vague" constitutional clauses as representing appeals to the concepts they employ, like legality, equality, and cruelty....

Those who ignore the distinction between concepts and conceptions ... are forced to argue in a vulnerable way. They say that ideas of cruelty change over time, and that the Court must be free to reject out-of-date conceptions; this suggests that the Court must change what the Constitution enacted. But in fact the Court can enforce what the Constitution says only by making up its own mind about what is cruel. . . . If those who enacted the broad clauses had meant to lay down particular conceptions, they would have found the sort of language conventionally used to do this, that is, they would have offered particular theories of the concepts in question.

Indeed the very practice of calling these clauses "vague" . . . can now be seen to involve a mistake. The clauses are vague only if we take them to be botched or incomplete or schematic attempts to lay down particular conceptions. If we take them as appeals to moral concepts they could not be made more precise by being more detailed.

The confusion I mentioned between the two senses of "strict" construction is therefore very misleading indeed. If courts try to be faithful to the text of the Constitution, they will for that very reason be forced to decide between competing conceptions of political morality. So it is wrong to attack the Warren Court, for example, on the ground that it failed to treat the Constitution as a binding text. On the contrary, if we wish to treat fidelity to that text as an overriding requirement of constitutional interpretation, then it is the conservative critics of the Warren Court who are at fault, because their philosophy ignores the direction to face issues of moral principle that the logic of the text demands.

I put the matter in a guarded way because we may not want to accept fidelity to the spirit of the text as an overriding principle of constitutional adjudication. It may be more important for courts to decide constitutional cases in a manner that respects the judgments of other institutions of government, for example. Or it may be more important for courts to protect established legal doctrines, so that citizens and the government can have confidence that the courts will hold to what they have said before. But it is crucial to recognize that these other policies compete with the principle that the Constitution is the fundamental and imperative source of constitutional law. They are not, as the "strict constructionists" suppose, simply consequences of that principle.

3

Once the matter is put in this light . . . we are able to assess these competing claims of policy, free from the confusion imposed by the popular notion of "strict construction." For this purpose I want now to compare and contrast two very general philosophies of how the courts should decide difficult or controversial constitutional issues. I shall call these two philosophies by the names they are given in the legal litera-ture—the programs of "judicial activism" and "judicial restraint"—though it will be plain that these names are in certain ways misleading.

The program of judicial activism holds that courts should accept the directions of the so-called vague constitutional provisions in the spirit I described.... They should work out principles of legality, equality, and the rest, revise these principles from time to time in the light of what seems to the Court fresh moral insight, and judge the acts of Congress, the states, and the President accordingly....

The program of judicial restraint, on the contrary, argues that courts should allow the decisions of other branches of government to stand, even when they offend the judges' own sense of the principles required by the broad constitutional doctrines, except when these decisions are so offensive to political morality that they would violate the provisions on any plausible interpretation, or, perhaps, when a contrary decision is required by clear precedent....

The Supreme Court followed the policy of activism rather than restraint in cases like the segregation cases because the words of the equal protection clause left it open whether the various educational practices of the states concerned should be taken to violate the Constitution, no clear precedent held that they did, and reasonable men might differ on the moral issues involved.... But the program of restraint would not always act to provide decisions that would please political conservatives. In the early days of the New Deal ... it was the liberals who objected to Court decisions that struck down acts of Congress in the name of the due process clause.

It may seem, therefore, that if Nixon has a legal theory it depends crucially on some theory of judicial restraint. We must now, however, notice a distinction between two forms of judicial restraint, for there are two different, and indeed incompatible, grounds on which that policy might be based.

The first is a theory of political skepticism that might be described in this way. The policy of judicial activism presupposes a certain objectivity of moral principle; in particular it presupposes that citizens do have certain moral rights against the state, like a moral right to equality of public education or to fair treatment by the police. Only if such moral rights exist in some sense can activism be justified as a program based on something beyond the judge's personal preferences. The skeptical theory attacks activism at its roots; it argues that in fact individuals have no such moral rights against the state. They have only such legal rights as the Constitution grants them, and these are limited to the plain and uncontroversial violations of public morality that the framers must have had actually in mind, or that have since been established in a line of precedent.

The alternative ground of a program of restraint is a theory of judicial deference. Contrary to the skeptical theory, this assumes that citizens do have moral rights against the state beyond what the law expressly grants them, but it points out that the character and strength of these rights are debatable and argues that political institutions other than courts are responsible for deciding which rights are to be recognized.

This is an important distinction, even though the literature of constitutional law does not draw it with any clarity. The skeptical theory and the theory of deference differ dramatically in the kind of justification they assume, and in their implications for the more general moral theories of the men who profess to hold them. These theories are so different that most American politicians can consistently accept the second, but not the first.

A skeptic takes the view ... that men have no moral rights against the state and only such legal rights as the law expressly provides. But what does this mean, and what sort of argument might the skeptic make for his view? ... I shall rely, in trying to answer these questions, on a low-keyed theory of moral rights against the state.... Under that theory, a man has a moral right against the state if for some reason the state would do wrong to treat him in a certain way, even though it would be in the general interest to do so....

I want to say a word about the virtues of this way of looking at moral rights against the state.... [I]t simply shows a claim of right to be a special, in the sense of a restricted, sort of judgment about what is right or wrong for governments to do.

Moreover, this way of looking at rights avoids some of the notorious puzzles associated with the concept. It allows us to say, with no sense of strangeness, that rights may vary in strength and character from case to case, and from point to point in history. If we think of rights as things, these metamorphoses seem strange, but we are used to the idea that moral judgments about what it is right or wrong to do are complex and are affected by considerations that are relative and that change.

The skeptic who wants to argue against the very possibility of rights against the state of this sort has a difficult brief. He must rely, I think, on one of three general positions: (a) He might display a more pervasive moral skepticism, which holds that even to speak of an act being morally right or wrong makes no sense.... (b) He might hold a stark form of utilitarianism, which assumes that the only reason we ever have for regarding an act as right or wrong is its impact on the general interest. Under that theory, to say that busing may be morally required even though it does not benefit the community generally would be inconsistent. (c) He might accept some form of totalitarian theory, which merges the interest of the individual in the good of the general community, and so denies that the two can conflict.

Very few American politicians would be able to accept any of these three grounds....

I do not want to suggest, however, that no one would in fact argue for judicial restraint on grounds of skepticism; on the contrary, some of the best known advocates of restraint have pitched their arguments entirely on skeptical grounds. In 1957, for example, the great judge

Learned Hand ... argued for judicial restraint, and said that the
Supreme Court had done wrong to declare school segregation illegal....
It is wrong to suppose, he said, that claims about moral rights express
anything more than the speakers' preferences. If the Supreme Court
justifies its decisions by making such claims, rather than by relying on
positive law, it is usurping the place of the legislature, for the job of the
legislature, representing the majority, is to decide whose preferences
shall govern.

This simple appeal to democracy is successful if one accepts the
skeptical premise.... But a very different, and much more vulnerable,
argument from democracy is needed to support judicial restraint if it is
based not on skepticism but on deference, as I shall try to show.

4

... [A] theory of restraint based ... on deference [holds] that courts
ought not to decide controversial issues of political morality because they
ought to leave such decisions to other departments of government....

There is one very popular argument in favor of the policy of
deference, which might be called the argument from democracy....
Who ought to decide these debatable issues of moral and political theory?
Should it be a majority of a court in Washington, whose members are
appointed for life and are not politically responsible to the public whose
lives will be affected by the decision? Or should it be the elected and
responsible state or national legislators? A democrat, so this argument
supposes, can accept only the second answer.

But the argument from democracy is weaker than it might first
appear. The argument assumes, for one thing, that state legislatures
are in fact responsible to the people in the way that democratic theory
assumes. But in all the states, though in different degrees and for
different reasons, that is not the case.... I want to pass that point,
however, because it does not so much undermine the argument from
democracy as call for more democracy.... I want to fix attention on the
issue of whether the appeal to democracy in this respect is even right in
principle.

The argument assumes that in a democracy all unsettled issues,
including issues of moral and political principle, must be resolved only by
institutions that are politically responsible in the way that courts are
not. Why should we accept that view of democracy? To say that is
what democracy means does no good, because it is wrong to suppose that
the word, as a word, has anything like so precise a meaning. Even if it
did, we should then have to rephrase our question to ask why we should
have democracy, if we assume that is what it means. Nor is it better to
say that view of democracy is established in the American Constitution,
or so entrenched in our political tradition that we are committed to it.
We cannot argue that the Constitution, which provides no rule limiting
judicial review to clear cases, establishes a theory of democracy that

excludes wider review, nor can we say that our courts have in fact
consistently accepted such a restriction. . . .

So the argument from democracy is not an argument to which we
are committed either by our words or our past. We must accept it, if at
all, on the strength of its own logic. In order to examine the arguments
more closely, however, we must make a further distinction. The argument . . . might be continued in two different ways: one might argue
that judicial deference is required because democratic institutions, like
legislatures, are in fact likely to make *sounder* decisions than courts . . .
about the nature of an individual's moral right against the state.

Or one might argue that it is for some reason *fairer* that a democratic institution rather than a court should decide such issues. . . . The
distinction between these two arguments would make no sense to a
skeptic, who would not admit that someone could do a better or worse
job at identifying moral rights against the state, any more than someone
could do a better or worse job of identifying ghosts. But a lawyer who
believes in judicial deference rather than skepticism must acknowledge
the distinction. . . .

I shall start with the second argument, that legislatures and other
democratic institutions have some special title to make constitutional
decisions. . . . One might say that the nature of this title is obvious,
because it is always fairer to allow a majority to decide any issue than a
minority. But that . . . ignores the fact that decisions about rights
against the majority are not issues that in fairness ought to be left to the
majority. Constitutionalism—the theory that the majority must be
restrained to protect individual rights—may be a good or bad political
theory, but the United States has adopted that theory, and to make the
majority judge in its own cause seems inconsistent and unjust. So
principles of fairness seem to speak against, not for, the argument from
democracy.

Chief Justice Marshall recognized this . . . in Marbury v. Madison. . . . He argued that since the Constitution provides that the Constitution shall be the supreme law of the land, the courts . . . must have
power to declare statutes void that offend that Constitution. Many legal
scholars regard his argument as a *non sequitur,* because, they say,
although constitutional constraints are part of the law, the courts, rather
than the legislature itself, have not necessarily been given authority to
decide whether in particular cases that law has been violated. But the
argument is not a *non sequitur* if we take the principle that no man
should be judge in his own cause to be so fundamental a part of the ideal
of legality that Marshall would have been entitled to disregard it only if
the Constitution had expressly denied judicial review.

Some might object that it is simple-minded to say that a policy of
deference leaves the majority to judge its own cause. Political decisions
are made, in the United States, not by one stable majority but by many
different political institutions each representing a different constituency
which itself changes its composition over time. The decision of one

branch of government may well be reviewed by another branch that is also politically responsible, but to a larger or different constituency....

But this objection is itself too glib, because it ignores the special character of disputes about individual moral rights as distinct from other kinds of political disputes. Different institutions do have different constituencies when, for example, labor or trade or welfare issues are involved.... But this is not generally the case when individual constitutional rights, like the rights of accused criminals, are at issue. It has been typical of these disputes that the interests of those in political control of the various institutions of the government have been both homogeneous and hostile. Indeed that is why political theorists have conceived of constitutional rights as rights against the 'state' or the 'majority' as such....

It does seem fair to say, therefore, that the argument from democracy asks that those in political power be invited to be the sole judge of their own decisions.... That is not a final proof that a policy of judicial activism is superior to a program of deference.... But the point does undermine the argument that the majority, in fairness, must be allowed to decide the limits of its own power.

We must therefore turn to the other continuation of the argument from democracy, which holds that democratic institutions, like legislatures, are likely to reach *sounder* results about the moral rights of individuals than would courts....

... On this view, the rights of blacks, suspects, and atheists will emerge through the process of political institutions responding to political pressures in the normal way. If a claim of right cannot succeed in this way, then for that reason it is, or in any event it is likely to be, an improper claim or right. But this bizarre proposition is only a disguised form of the skeptical point that there are in fact no rights against the state.

Perhaps, as Burke and his modern followers argue, a society will produce the institutions that best suit it only by evolution and never by radical reform. But rights against the state are claims that, if accepted, require society to settle for institutions that may not suit it so comfortably. The nerve of a claim of right ... is that an individual is entitled to protection against the majority even at the cost of the general interest. Of course the comfort of the majority will require some accommodation for minorities but only to the extent necessary to preserve order; and that is usually an accommodation that falls short of recognizing their rights....

5

This has been a complex argument, and I want to summarize it. Our constitutional system rests on a particular moral theory, namely, that men have moral rights against the state. The difficult clauses of the Bill of Rights, like the due process and equal protection clauses, must be understood as appealing to moral concepts rather than laying down particular conceptions; therefore a court that undertakes the burden of applying these clauses fully as law must be an activist court, in the sense that it must be prepared to frame and answer questions of political morality.

It may be necessary to compromise that activist posture to some extent, either for practical reasons or for competing reasons of principle. But Nixon's public statements about the Supreme Court suggest that the activist policy must be abandoned altogether, and not merely compromised, for powerful reasons of principle. If we try to state these reasons of principle, we find that they are inconsistent with the assumption of a constitutional system, either because they leave the majority to judge its own cause, or because they rest on a skepticism about moral rights that neither Nixon nor most American politicians can consistently embrace.

So Nixon's jurisprudence is a pretense and no genuine theory at all....

Constitutional law can make no genuine advance until it isolates the problem of rights against the state and makes that problem part of its own agenda. That argues for a fusion of constitutional law and moral theory, a connection that, incredibly, has yet to take place....

III

Who May Authoritatively Interpret the Constitution?

The materials in this Part focus on the interrogative "WHO shall interpret the Constitution?" This basic inquiry and its subqueries are both more subtle and complex than they may at first appear. At one level, it is a plain, if sometimes painful, fact of American political life that all public officials, state and federal, from presidents, senators, and representatives, to governors, state legislators, local district attorneys and police, may often have to engage in constitutional interpretation. Deciding what policies government may legitimately pursue, how—or whether—to enforce a law, when to arrest and search a suspect, all create problems of constitutional interpretation.

Even if one were to concede what is not at all self-evident, that judges are the ultimate constitutional interpreters, if government had to stop and await a judicial decision every time a constitutional problem arose, we would have only grand anarchy. Every public official, after all, takes an oath to support "the Constitution of the United States," to guide his or her actions by the commands of that "Constitution." And, as we have already time and again seen, not only are those commands sometimes so general as to cry out for interpretation, but what "the Constitution" includes and what it is supposed to do present serious problems.

That oath is also one that millions of private citizens have taken. Moreover, the Preamble lodges responsibility for "the Constitution" in "the people of the United States." Thus, it is not far fetched to argue that, as its ultimate source of authority, "the people" are themselves not only authoritative constitutional interpreters but also that, collectively, they are the ultimate interpreters. One could go further and plausibly argue that "the people," individually as well as collectively have the duty to interpret "the Constitution," to consider carefully, when they cast their ballots, candidates' records and promises about how they will interpret "the Constitution." Private citizens also have the same right and obligation when they speak out on political issues, lobby elected representatives, or utilize other means of advocating or opposing public policies.

Thus the central problem we face in this Part is not simply WHO shall interpret, for the answer to that question is obvious: "Some of us most of the time, most of us some of the time." Rather, here we confront questions about the extent to which—as well as the circumstances under which—some governmental institutions should defer to the judgment of other institutions (and/or to those other institutions' claims to speak "for the people"), and, in cases of conflict, which institution's interpretation should prevail. In effect, this Part of the book searches not only for authoritative constitutional interpreters, but also for relationships among those interpreters.

How an interpreter views the political system affects the direction he or she takes in that search. One who sees "the Constitution" as a compact among the states is likely to find answers at the state level; for, logically, it would be the parties to the compact who should determine its meaning.   On the other hand, one who sees the constitutional text or the larger constitution as an agreement among the entire American people is likely to search at the national level, for the national government would be the direct creature of the people as a whole rather than of separate, sovereign states.

So, too, one who looks on "the Constitution" as establishing a representative democracy is apt to be more sympathetic toward elected officials as the ultimate interpreters.   Conversely, as one puts more stress on constitutionalism, one is more likely to prefer the ultimate interpreters to be more removed from direct popular influences.

We have divided this Part into two chapters.   Chapter 7 addresses the question of WHO should provide authoritative constitutional interpretation *within* the national system of government. Chapter 8 examines the question of an ultimate interpreter *between* the states and the national government.   Cases and other materials in these two chapters also underline the additional and ever-present tensions between democracy and constitutionalism.   And always part of any effort to answer the question of WHO must be the equally vexing question of WHAT is "the Constitution" that must be interpreted.   The variety of responses to these inquiries points to continuing debates rather than to neatly packaged answers.

7

Who May Authoritatively Interpret the Constitution for the National Government?

A person who had read the chapters thus far, one would have to have been deliberately inattentive not to have noticed that the question WHAT is "the Constitution" often, if not inevitably, bleeds into the question of WHO are its authoritative interpreters; and, in addressing either or both questions, interpreters typically find themselves confronting issues of HOW to interpret. This chapter and the one that follows try to focus on the question of WHO. We do not, however, attempt to isolate it, for such an effort would not only be doomed to eventual failure but what apparent success it might enjoy would come at the cost of conjuring up a deceptive illusion of the enterprise called constitutional interpretation.

The plain words of the amended text of 1787–88 convey indirect but important messages about WHO shall be its authoritative interpreters. In conferring on Congress authority to make "all laws necessary and proper" to carry out powers delegated to the national government, Article I, § 8 clearly implies that Congress (with the participation of the President since he is part of the legislative process) shall make judgments about constitutional meaning, for what laws are "proper" under "the Constitution" may be far from obvious. There are similar terms in the Thirteenth, Fourteenth, Fifteenth, Nineteenth, Twenty-fourth, and Twenty-sixth amendments, authorizing Congress to enact "appropriate legislation" to carry out the amendments' provisions.

In specifying the exact wording of the oath the President shall take to "preserve, protect, and defend the Constitution," Article II imposes on the chief executive additional responsibility for constitutional interpretation. He could hardly be expected to "preserve, protect, and defend" that "Constitution" without interpreting it to determine how or if it was being threatened. By extending "the judicial power" "to all cases, in law and equity, arising under this Constitution," Article III brings the courts into the processes of constitutional interpretation, as judges before and since Chief Justice John Marshall have modestly admitted.

These clauses implicitly acknowledge that the three branches of national government share authority. There is not, however, a single word about whose views should prevail in case of disagreement. Thomas Jefferson's response was that the people should judge: They could express their will by means of a national convention. As he explained to Justice William Johnson, John Marshall's colleague on the Court: "The ultimate arbiter is the people of the Union, assembled by their deputies in convention, at the call of Congress, or of two-thirds of the States." [1] But what happened in Philadelphia in 1787, when the convention the Continental Congress summoned to propose amendments to the Articles of Confederation drafted an entirely new constitutional document, has not encouraged Congress to call such a body back into session.

Moreover, it would take some time and much deliberation to choose delegates to a national convention; additional time for them to debate and propose amendments, if, indeed, those were all the convention proposed, to the states; and yet more time for the states to vote on the proposals. For some crises, this solution would be too slow and cumbersome, even assuming senators and representatives were willing to accept the risks to their own careers and to the larger political system such a convention would present.

The ballot box provides a periodic, institutional means for direct popular interpretation of "the Constitution." As the Introduction to this set of chapters observed, one could argue that citizens are obliged to judge candidates by the way they have or indicate they will interpret "the Constitution." The election of 1936 might be seen as a sort of constitutional referendum: During the previous year and a half the Supreme Court had held unconstitutional most of Franklin Roosevelt's efforts to regulate the economy; but the people of 46 of the then 48 states voted to continue him and his New Deal. That landslide had an effect on the justices, for, six weeks after the election, the Court began to change its constitutional interpretation to conform to that of the President, Congress, and the people. One justice who quickly reconceptualized "the Constitution" in a new electoral light later said: "Looking back, it is difficult to see how the Court could have resisted the popular urge for uniform standards throughout the country—for what in effect was a unified economy." [2]

---

1. June 12, 1823; Andrew A. Lipscomb, ed., *Writings of Thomas Jefferson* (Washington, D.C.: Thomas Jefferson Memorial Association, 1903), XV, 451. See also Jefferson's letter to Madison, Sept. 6, 1789; cited above at p. 181, n. 1.

2. Owen J. Roberts, *The Court and the Constitution* (Cambridge: Harvard University Press, 1951), p. 61. This "switch in time that saved nine" has often been attributed to Roosevelt's "Court-packing plan," his effort to persuade Congress to increase the number of justices to 15, which he announced in February, 1937. The first "switching" vote within the Court had occurred, however, in early December, 1936. As usual, it took months for the justices to write out their arguments and agree on an opinion for the Court. Publication of the decision came shortly after FDR had announced his plan and made it appear as if some justices had caved in to his pressure and not to the electorate's judgment.

This example is dramatic, but one searches in vain for a close parallel. The most likely candidate would be the presidential election of 1940, in which the electorate decided that the tradition against a third term was no longer valid. In 1944 the voters reaffirmed that change in the constitution when they elected Roosevelt to yet a fourth term. But those changes were short-lived, for the Twenty-second Amendment, adopted in 1951, imbedded into the constitutional text the old two-term limit of the pre–1940 constitution. Distant analogues have occurred when voters in a state or region push their senators and representatives to adopt a specific line of constitutional interpretation: after 1954, for example, when the mass of white southern voters (and most voters in the South before the Voting Rights Act of 1965 were white) pushed their legislators (and were often urged by their legislators to push) to argue that the School Segregation Cases represented gross constitutional misinterpretation.

Nevertheless, such events do not fall within the normal patterns of American voting behavior. Not many private citizens often, consciously, or systematically utilize their ballots to express constitutional interpretations; and there is precious little evidence that many even take the trouble to formulate such views. This failure in civic duty leaves officials a wide range of freedom to engage in constitutional interpretation.

I.   WHO IS THE ULTIMATE INTERPRETER?

Three theories compete for the honor of answering the question of WHO is the ultimate interpreter: judicial supremacy, legislative supremacy, and departmentalism. All, however, even judicial supremacy, draw heavily on democratic theory; and, in a sense, much of the debate rests on the possibility of an appeal to "the people," though seldom is that basis so clear as it was in Jefferson's plan for calling national conventions.

Even Alexander Hamilton in *Federalist* No. 78 (reprinted below, p. 285) rested his argument for judicial review—which, though not the same as judicial supremacy, forms a necessary basis for such a thesis—on democratic theory: Where "the will of the legislature, declared in its statutes, stands in opposition to that of the people, declared in the Constitution, the judges ought to be governed by the latter rather than the former." Such a power, he added, does not imply that judges are superior to legislators but that "the power of the people is superior to both."

A.   Judicial Supremacy

Judicial supremacy is the theory most familiar to Americans. Many Anti–Federalists—who on the whole tended to be much more deeply committed to democratic theory than were the Federalists—feared that the new "Constitution" would ram a government by judiciary down the throats of a free people. Brutus (see his essay reprinted below, p. 281) was only one of such critics, though perhaps the most eloquent. It was to answer his arguments that Hamilton wrote *Federalist* No. 78.

Despite the Federalists' explanations, the doctrine of judicial supremacy lives on. One justification for it rests on the sort of textual and functional grounds John Marshall used in Marbury v. Madison (1803; reprinted below, p. 298) for judicial review. The essential argument is: (1) Article VI says the Constitution is law; (2) "it is emphatically the province and duty of the judicial department to say what the law is"; and thus (3) judicial review must be an integral part of the political system. Then follows a smooth, though long, stride from judicial review—the authority of a court, when deciding cases, to refuse to give force to an act of a coordinate branch of government—to judicial supremacy, the obligation of coordinate officials not only to obey that particular ruling but to follow its reasoning in future deliberations. Justice Joseph Story gladly took this step, but in his role as commentator and not as judge:

> Now, it is the proper function of the judicial department to interpret laws, and by the very terms of the constitution to interpret the supreme law. Its interpretation, then, becomes obligatory and conclusive upon all the departments of the federal government, and upon the whole people, so far as their rights and duties are derived from, or affected by that constitution.[3]

Story reinforced his conclusion with the claim that "[w]e find the power to construe the constitution expressly confined to the judicial department, without any limitation or qualification, as to its conclusiveness."[4]

Before accepting Story's conclusion, one should recognize that: (1) he did not point to any words through which constitutional text "expressly confined" constitutional interpretation to the judiciary—indeed, as we just saw, the document's wording contradicts such a claim; (2) judicial review says nothing about the obligation of other branches of government either to obey that decision or to follow its reasoning in the future; and (3) Marshall himself did not draw Story's conclusion, though one might well argue that he approved of it and it is implicit in *Marbury*. Ironically, Brutus's argument against the new "Constitution" provides the strongest support for Story's claim.

The practical need for an umpire provides a second and quite different justification for judicial supremacy. If there is a constitu-

---

3. *Commentaries on the Constitution of the United States* (Boston: Hilliard, Gray, 1833), I, Bk. III, § 383.

4. *Ibid.* § 385.

tional dispute among the branches of government, there must exist somewhere, so the argument goes, a final decision maker. As Story put it, "to produce uniformity of interpretation, and to preserve the constitution, as a perpetual bond of union, a supreme arbiter or authority of construing is, if not absolutely indispensable, at least of the highest practical utility and importance."[5]   One might agree on the need for an umpire but disagree, as Jefferson did, that the judiciary best fulfills that function.   One might also take the position that Madison's architectural strategy to design a system of fractured, separated, and shared powers is, at root, incongruent with the notion of a final umpire.[6]

The matter of institutional competence provides a third justification for judicial supremacy.   Administrative and legislative processes, the argument runs, do not provide time for interpreters to research and engage in intellectual debate about underlying constitutional issues or settings that encourage dispassionate investigation and coherent, consistent, and systematic analysis.[7]   Nor, the argument continues, does the President's and legislators' world of representing constituents' immediate interests provide an hospitable forum for principled constitutional interpretation.   This sort of premise permeates Story's *Commentaries on the Constitution*. Charles Evans Hughes put it more bluntly a century later: "It is only from the Supreme Court that we can obtain a sane, well-ordered interpretation of the Constitution."[8]

There is ample room for reasonable doubt here.   Many debates in Congress—see eswrcially that on the Judiciary Act of 1802, reprinted below, pp. 289ff—stand up well against the justices' most sophisticated analyses.   And, as for consistency and coherence, Chapter 2 indicated the Court has modified and reversed its interpretations sufficiently often that studying the malleable and sometimes swiftly changing substance of judge-made constitutional law is a full time profession.

There is a fourth, constitutionalist, justification for judicial supremacy.   Partly it relies on need, function, and competence, and, of course, it claims support in the text; but basically it rests on constitutionalism.   In the debates on the Judiciary Act of 1802, Gouverneur Morris, who had chaired the Committee on Style at

---

5. *Ibid.*

6. For an argument that courts should not act as constitutional judges between Congress and the President or between the nation and the states, see Jesse H. Choper, *Judicial Review and the National Political Process* (Chicago: University of Chicago Press, 1980).

7. See the attack on congressional interpretation by Circuit Judge (and former Congressman and later presidential counsellor) Abner J. Mikva, "How Well Does Congress Support and Defend the Constitution?" 61 *No.Car.L.Rev.* 587 (1983), and the defense of congressional interpretation by Louis Fisher, "Constitutional Interpretation by Members of Congress," 63 *ibid.* 707 (1985).

8. Quoted in Carl Brent Swisher, *American Constitutional Development* (Boston: Houghton Mifflin, 1943), p. 773.

Philadelphia and had written much of the final draft of the document, made an unambiguous claim for judicial supremacy. Judges derive that power, he said, "from authority higher than this Constitution. They derive it from the constitution of man, from the nature of things, from the necessary progress of human affairs." He was arguing that human nature required that, if government were to be limited, some institution, removed from popular control, would have to check the people and their representatives—the core of the constitutionalist position.

However convincing this sort of reasoning would be to the "pure constitutionalist" described in Chapter 3, it causes problems that increase in seriousness as one moves across the spectrum toward the "pure democrat." Even an interpreter who falls near the center, a constitutional democrat, could accept such an argument only with important qualifications relating to such matters as the nature of the substantive issue in dispute.

In sum, whether acceptance of judicial review necessarily carries acceptance of judicial supremacy is a matter about which public officials and commentators heatedly disagree. Certainly Jefferson, Jackson, Lincoln, and Franklin D. Roosevelt did not believe that they or Congress were bound by the Supreme Court's constitutional interpretations. And, soon after the Convention, Madison emphatically denied the correctness of judicial supremacy. (See his letter to John Brown, 1788, reprinted below, p. 279, as well his comments quoted below, pp. 279–81.)

The Court itself has seldom explicitly claimed judicial supremacy and has never articulated a full argument for it vis-à-vis Congress or the President. In Ableman v. Booth (1859; reprinted below, p. 367), a unanimous Court claimed:

> [N]o power is more clearly conferred by the Constitution and laws of the United States, than the power of this court to decide, ultimately and finally, all cases arising under such Constitution and laws. . . .

To "decide, ultimately and finally, all cases arising under such Constitution" is not quite the same as to interpret that "Constitution" in a manner that all other public officials must follow in situations other than the particular cases. Moreover, in *Ableman* the justices were asserting their interpretive superiority over state officials, not their superiority over Congress or the President. The first modern, general claim by the Court to supremacy came in Cooper v. Aaron (1958; reprinted below, p. 375), where the justices said that "the federal judiciary is supreme in the exposition of the law of the Constitution." Obviously, the phrase "exposition of the Constitution" has far more sweeping implications than merely deciding cases under "the Constitution." If one takes the justices at their word, Brown v. Board (1954) became "the supreme law of the land," an addition to the amended text of 1787–88. And we find ourselves once more enmeshed in problems of constitutional inclusion and change.

Although *Cooper* spoke in broad terms, that case, like *Ableman*, involved only the authority of state versus federal officials. Similarly, only state officials were parties to Baker v. Carr (1962), where the Court first referred to itself as the "ultimate interpreter of the Constitution." It was not until Powell v. McCormack (1969) that the Court so designated itself in a dispute pertaining to its authority over Congress, an assertion the justices repeated about their relations to the President in United States v. Nixon (1974; reprinted below, p. 323) and reiterated about both in the Legislative Veto case, INS v. Chadha, (1983; reprinted below, p. 485). *Powell*, however, addressed only the authority of the House of Representatives to exclude a duly elected member and did not require that he be readmitted (his term had expired before the decision) or that he be given back pay. *Nixon* upheld a subpoena to a President whose political situation was desperate, and the fate of the Legislative Veto remains in doubt. (See the notes to that case, INS v. Chadha [1983], at p. 485.)

B. Legislative Supremacy

Serious assertions of legislative supremacy in constitutional interpretation have been infrequent, although they have at times been vigorously pushed, as after the Civil War when the Radical Republicans dominated Congress, impeached the President, and curbed the Court. Early on, some Jeffersonians had also pressed for congressional supremacy. (See the debate on the Judiciary Act of 1802, reprinted below, p. 289.) As Caesar Rodney of Delaware wrote in 1803: "Judicial supremacy may be made to bow before the strong arm of Legislative authority. We shall discover who is master of the ship." [9] John Marshall was sufficiently frightened by Jeffersonians' threats to impeach and remove Federalist judges that he was willing even to modify judicial review. As he wrote a colleague:

> [T]he modern doctrine of impeachment should yield to an appellate jurisdiction in the legislature. A reversal of those legal opinions deemed unsound by the legislature would certainly better comport with the mildness of our character than [would] a removal of the Judge who has rendered them unknowing of his fault.[10]

This notion has been several times revived—usually with the proposed appellate jurisdiction resting in the Senate alone—but, of course, has never become part of the text.

---

9. Quoted in Charles Warren, *The Supreme Court in United States History* (rev. ed.; Boston: Little, Brown, 1926), I, 228–229.

10. Quoted in Albert J. Beveridge, *The Life of John Marshall* (Boston: Houghton Mifflin, 1919), III, 177.

Even without appellate review, the basis of any claim that Congress' constitutional interpretation should prevail over that of judges rests on legislators' connections to the people through the ballot. As Justice Gibson of the Pennsylvania Supreme Court, dissenting in Eakin v. Raub (1825; reprinted below, p. 308) wrote: "It may be said, the power of the legislature . . . is limited by prescribed rules. It is so. But it is nevertheless, the power of the people, and sovereign as far as it extends. . . ." Therefore, he concluded:

> it rests with the people, in whom full and absolute sovereign power resides, to correct abuses in legislation, by instructing their representatives to repeal the obnoxious act. What is wanting to plenary power in the government, is reserved to the people for their own immediate use; and to redress an infringement of their rights in this respect, would seem to be an accessory to the power thus reserved.

On the other hand, constitutionalism emphatically rejects any argument that popularly elected officials should have the final word in determining fundamental relations within the polity. Those officials, a constitutionalist would say, will be responsible to the people, who are themselves a potent source of danger to civil liberty. One does not, as the Italian proverb goes, make the goat one's gardener.

C. Departmentalism

No President has ever pressed a claim to supremacy in constitutional interpretation; but like many legislators, some presidents have asserted equality, at least where the issue involves their own authority. (See the opinions of Jefferson, Jackson, Lincoln, and Roosevelt, reprinted below, pp. 306-23.) Madison's position fluctuated as he faced various crises, but in the early days of the Republic he was clearly a departmentalist. His strategy of allowing different social interests to dominate particular institutions and of pitting ambition against ambition and power against power pushes toward stalemate that can only be overcome by compromise, not by legal formulae. He was opposed to judicial supremacy, as he explained in 1788 (reprinted below, p. 279), just as he feared legislative supremacy.

Furthermore, Madison told the First Congress that the American constitutional system was departmentalist:

> There is not one Government . . . in the United States, in which provision is made for a particular authority to determine the limits of the constitutional division of power between the branches of the Government. In all systems, there are points which must be adjusted by the departments themselves, to which no

one of them is competent.[11]

Jefferson was more consistent in his departmentalism. When he became President, he pardoned many people who had been convicted under the Sedition Act for libelling John Adams. Upset, John's wife Abigail wrote Jefferson and asked for an explanation. He replied:

> You seem to think it devolved on the judges to decide on the validity of the sedition law. But nothing in the Constitution has given them a right to decide for the Executive, more than the Executive to decide for them. Both magistrates are equally independent in the sphere of action assigned to them. The judges, believing the law constitutional, had a right to pass a sentence. ... But the executive, believing the law to be unconstitutional, were bound to remit the execution of it because that power had been confined to them by the Constitution. That instrument meant that its coordinate branches should be checks on each other. But the opinion which gives to the judges the right to decide what laws are constitutional and what are not, not only for themselves in their own sphere of action, but for the legislature and executive also in their spheres, would make the judiciary a despotic branch.[12]

Two decades later, Jefferson chided his friend William Jarvis for considering "judges as the ultimate arbiters of all constitutional questions." The former President would agree only that they "have more frequent occasion to act on constitutional questions." That power, however, was neither exclusively nor finally theirs:

> The constitution has erected no such single tribunal, knowing that to whatever hands confided, with the corruptions of time and party, its members would become despots. It has more wisely made all the departments co-equal and co-sovereign within themselves.[13]

D. Resolution?

As for many of the basic questions in constitutional interpretation, the plain words of the text do not prescribe a single answer to the question of whose interpretation should prevail. "pure constitutionalists" might argue, however, that whatever the ambiguities of the document, the constitution, considered as including many of the political system's interpretations, practices, traditions, and the underlying political theory of constitutionalism, endorses judicial supremacy. The system accepts not only judicial review but also the obligation of Congress and the President to conform their

---

11. *Annals of Congress* (1789), I, 521.

12. Lipscomb, supra note 1, XI, 50–51.

13. September 28, 1820; Paul L. Ford, ed., *The Works of Thomas Jefferson* (New York: Putnam's, 1905), XII, 161–164; see also Jefferson's letter to Torrance, June 11, 1815; Lipscomb, supra note 1, XIV, 303–306.

actions to the Court's constitutional interpretations. The primary
option open to Congress and the President when fundamentally
disagreeing with the Court is to amend the constitutional text. And
the "pure constitutionalist" would remind us that early and often
elected leaders have followed precisely this route in reversing the
Court's constitutional interpretation.

The practice of amending the document began in 1793, when,
after Chisholm v. Georgia interpreted Article III as giving federal
courts jurisdiction over suits for money against a state government,
Congress proposed and the states quickly ratified the Eleventh
Amendment. This practice continued in 1866–68 with the Fourteenth Amendment's erasing *Dred Scott's* reading of the text as
precluding citizenship for African Americans,[14] in the Sixteenth
Amendment's specifically delegating to Congress the power to tax
incomes, which the Court had denied, and in the Twenty-sixth
Amendment's modifying the text to give eighteen year olds a right
to vote after the Court had said a state might deny the franchise to
those under 21. This long litany, the "pure constitutionalist"
would assert, testifies to a tradition that the Court's constitutional
interpretation is so definitive as to require explicit, formal expung-
ing to lose its validity.

We have said enough to indicate, however, that matters are not
so clear as the "pure constitutionalist" would like to believe. It is
true that the American system usually accepts the Court's constitutional interpretations. But, reasoning from this pattern raises at
least three difficulties. Many constitutional problems, such as those
involving foreign policy, do not lend themselves to judicial resolution. Second, if practice is to the guide, then we should recall that
judges often defer to Congress. The normal rule, subject to important exceptions as when a fundamental individual right is at stake or
the government has used a "suspect" classification like race (see
below, Chapters 14–15), is that courts "presume" an act of Congress is constitutional. In almost two centuries, the Supreme Court
has invalidated only about a hundred provisions of federal law, few
of them of great significance to the political system.

The readings in this Chapter illustrate a third difficulty with the
"pure constitutionalist's" argument: Even where problems have
amenable to judicial resolution and the issues have been significant,
the general pattern of acceptance of the Court's interpretations has
been broken often enough to further shake the case for judicial
supremacy on the basis of legislative and presidential deference.
Not only have presidents openly defied the Court, and not only did
the election of 1936 constitute a sort of constitutional referendum
that rejected the Court's constitutional jurisprudence, but Congress
has on occasion merely repassed, in slightly modified form, a statute
the Court has invalidated and watched the justices change their

---

14. Dred Scott v. Sandford (1857) is reprinted above, p. 195.

minds.[15]   Furthermore, presidents have frequently nominated for judgeships men and women who, they thought, would speed the process of reshaping the judicial mind.

Nor does political theory supply *the* answer; instead, it provides several answers.   Democratic theory favors legislative supremacy, constitutionalism judicial supremacy.   A mixed theory of constitutional democracy would tilt one way or the other, depending on the specific issue involved and whether the theoretical mix was more constitutionalist or more democratic.   Departmentalism might form a logical compromise.   But accepting departmentalism might merely recognize the problem rather than solve it, especially given the impracticality of using Jefferson's suggestion for frequent national conventions.

Perhaps the most fruitful way of beginning to solve the problem is to break it down into several subproblems.   First would be the nature of the substantive issue.   If the dispute concerned, for example, procedures that a judge must follow in conducting a criminal trial, the argument for judicial supremacy would be stronger than if the issue concerned the President's conduct of foreign relations.   The question would become: Is there anything in the document's words, the larger system's structure, interpretations, practices, traditions, and/or underlying political theories as well as the practicalities of political life that indicates a particular agency of government should have the final word on specific sets of issues?

The vague and oft-maligned "doctrine of political questions," [16] that certain constitutional matters lie beyond the judiciary's institu-

---

15.   For discussions, see Walter F. Murphy, *Congress and the Court* (Chicago: University of Chicago Press, 1962); William Lasser, *The Limits of Judicial Power: The Supreme Court in American Politics* (Chapel Hill: University of North Carolina Press, 1988), and the literature cited in each.

16.   Marbury v. Madison (1803) hinted at the doctrine: "The province of the court is, solely, to decide on the rights of individuals, not to inquire how the executive, or executive officers, perform duties in which they have a discretion.   Questions in their nature political, or which are, by the constitution and laws, submitted to the executive, can never be made in this court."   Luther v. Borden (1849) is the classic, if murky, case.   The Court has since made several heroic, if ultimately unsuccessful, efforts to distinguish "political" from "justiciable" questions.   Perhaps the most useful was Justice Brennan's in Baker v. Carr (1962):

(i) "Prominent on the surface of any case held to involve a political question is found a textually demonstrable constitutional commitment of the issue to a coordinate political department; or"

(ii) "a lack of judicially discoverable and manageable standards for resolving it; or"

(iii) "the impossibility of deciding without an initial policy determination of a kind clearly for non-judicial discretion; or"

(iv) "the impossibility of a court's undertaking independent resolution without expressing a lack of the respect due coordinate branches of government; or"

(v) "an unusual need for unquestioning adherence to a political decision already made; or"

(vi) "the potentiality of embarrassment from multifarious pronouncements by various departments on one question."

tional authority and competence, makes some sense in this context. Take, for example, the tragic incident at Kent State University in 1970, when Ohio National Guardsmen fired on students demonstrating against the war in Vietnam, killing and wounding a number of people. Later, a group of students filed suit in a federal district court, asking the judge to restrain the governor from future "premature" use of the National Guard to cope with situations that could be handled by nonlethal force. The district court dismissed the case, but the court of appeals ordered the trial judge to determine if the National Guard's pattern of training made inevitable the use of lethal force. When the case reached the Supreme Court, the majority noted that Article I, § 8 vested *in Congress* the authority "to provide for organizing, arming, and disciplining, the militia. ..." Thus:

> It would be difficult to think of a clearer example of the type of governmental action that was intended by the Constitution to be left to the political branches. ... Moreover, it is difficult to conceive of an area of governmental activity in which the courts have less competence. The complex, subtle, and professional decisions as to the composition, training, equipping, and control of a military force are essentially professional military judgments, subject *always* to civilian control of the Legislative and Executive Branches. The ultimate responsibility for these decisions is appropriately vested in branches of the government subject to electoral accountability.[17]

Another series of questions would deal with the range of judicial authority. Is there a difference in the obligation of other officials to obey a judicial decision in a specific case and their obligation to follow its reasoning in making future policy? Is there a difference in officials' obligations to obey a judicial decision when they themselves brought the lawsuit and when someone else sued them?

This sort of analysis transforms the question of WHO from one that might be expected to yield a universally applicable response, into a more complex set of queries for which one could provide replies about degrees of deference one institution owes another under varying circumstances.

See Fritz W. Scharf, "Judicial Review and the Political Question," 75 *Yale L.J.* 517 (1966), and Louis Henkin, "Is There a 'Political Question' Doctrine?" 85 *ibid.* 597 (1976).

17. Gilligan v. Morgan (1973). See also Dalton v. Specter (1994), which held that presidential discretion, exercised under the Defense Base Closure Act of 1990, to close military bases was not subject to judicial review. For the Court, Rehnquist said:

> Respondents tell us that failure to allow judicial review here would virtually repudiate Marbury v. Madison (1803) and nearly two centuries of constitutional adjudication. ... [But t]he judicial power of the United States conferred by Article III of the Constitution is upheld just as surely by withholding judicial relief where Congress has permissibly foreclosed it, as it is by granting such relief where authorized by the Constitution or by statute.

II. DEFERENCE AND THE FOURTEENTH AMENDMENT

Among the more difficult contexts in which the question of deference arises concerns the Fourteenth Amendment. Section 5 reads: "The Congress shall have power to enforce, by appropriate legislation, the provisions of this article." Those provisions ban, among other things, state denials of "due process of law" and "the equal protection of the laws." And for the second half of the twentieth century, the most persistent and serious problems of domestic politics have been caused by a long history of discrimination based race, ethnicity, sex, and poverty. Thus those problems all raise questions about the meaning and application of equal protection.

For several decades after the mid–1930s, federal judges, with institutional help only from President Harry S Truman, fought for the ideal of "equal justice under law." Since the late 1950s, however, Congress has become more sensitive to such problems and has passed more than a dozen civil rights statutes that penalize various forms of discrimination by state and federal agencies as well as by private corporations and individual citizens. Furthermore, some of these statutes have gone beyond judicial interpretations about the reach of the Fourteenth Amendment. Given § 5, what deference, beyond the usual presumption of constitutionality, should judges accord to Congress, composed of people elected from all the states, when it interprets state obligations more stringently than have judges? When Congress interprets state obligations less stringently than have judges? Katzenbach v. Morgan (1966; reprinted below, p. 327) raises some of these questions.

Issues of equal protection do not exhaust the possibilities here. There are other clauses in the Fourteenth Amendment. In holding that that amendment acknowledged a woman's right to an abortion, at least during her first trimester of pregnancy, the Court said that a fetus was not a "person" and therefore not protected by the amendment. Might Congress, under § 5, validly define the term "person," which after all judges have said does include corporations and ships, to encompass fetuses and entitle them to governmental protection of a right to life and liberty? How much deference should Congress give to the Court's holding that a fetus is not a person? The Court to a congressional determination that a fetus is a person, at least for the purposes of the Fourteenth Amendment? The debate over the Right to Life Bill (reprinted below, p. 336) explored those questions.

SELECTED BIBLIOGRAPHY

Agresto, John. *The Supreme Court and Constitutional Democracy* (Ithaca, NY: Cornell University Press, 1984).

Arkes, Hadley. "On the Moral Standing of the President as an Interpreter of the Constitution," 20 *PS: Pol. Sci. & Pols.* 637 (1987).

Barber, Sotirios A. *On What the Constitution Means* (Baltimore.: Johns Hopkins University Press, 1984), Chap. 6.

_____. *The Constitution of Judicial Power* (Baltimore: Johns Hopkins University Press, 1993).

Brest, Paul. "Who Decides?" 58 *So.Cal.L.Rev.* 661 (1985).

_____. "The Conscientious Legislator's Guide to Constitutional Interpretation," 27 *Stan.L.Rev.* 585 (1975).

Burgess, Susan R. *Contest for Constitutional Authority: The Abortion and War Powers Debates* (Lawrence: University of Kansas Press, 1992).

Burt, Robert A. *The Constitution in Conflict* (Cambridge: Harvard University Press, 1992).

Choper, Jesse H. *Judicial Review and the National Political Process* (Chicago: University of Chicago Press, 1980).

Clinton, Robert L. *Marbury v. Madison and Judicial Review* (Lawrence: University of Kansas Press, 1989).

Corwin, Edward S. "Marbury v. Madison and the Doctrine of Judicial Review," 12 *Mich.L.Rev.* 538 (1914).

Cox, Archibald. "Foreward: Constitutional Adjudication and the Protection of Human Rights," 80 *Harv.L.Rev.* 91 (1966).

_____. "The Role of Congress in Constitutional Determinations," 40 *U. of Cinn.L.Rev.* 199 (1971).

_____. *The Role of the Supreme Court in American Government* (New York: Oxford University Press, 1976).

Ely, John Hart. *Democracy and Distrust* (Cambridge: Harvard University Press, 1980).

Fisher, Louis. "Constitutional Interpretation by Members of Congress," 63 *No.Car.L.Rev.* 701 (1985).

_____. *Constitutional Dialogues: Interpretation as a Political Process* (Princeton: Princeton University Press, 1988).

Franck, Thomas M. *Political Questions, Judicial Answers: Does the Constitution Apply to Foreign Affairs?* (Princeton: Princeton University Press, 1992).

Glennon, Michael J. *Constitutional Diplomacy* (Princeton: Princeton University Press, 1990), chs. 2, 8.

Henkin, Louis, *Foreign Affairs and the Constitution* (Mineola, NY: Foundation Press, 1972), chs. 2–4, 8, 10.

―――――. *Constitutionalism, Democracy, and Foreign Affairs* (New York: Columbia University Press, 1992).

Keynes, Edward, with Randall K. Miller. *The Court vs. Congress: Prayer, Busing, and Abortion* (Durham: Duke University Press, 1989).

Lasser, William. *The Limits of Judicial Power: The Supreme Court in American Politics* (Chapel Hill: University of North Carolina Press, 1988).

Mikva, Abner J. "How Well Does Congress Support and Defend the Constitution?" 61 *No.Car.L.Rev.* 587 (1983).

Monaghan, Henry P. "Constitutional Adjudication: The Who and the When," 82 *Yale L.J.* 1361 (1973).

Morgan, Donald G. *Congress and the Constitution* (Cambridge: Harvard University Press, 1966).

Murphy, Walter F. *Congress and the Court* (Chicago: University of Chicago Press, 1962).

―――――. "Who Shall Interpret the Constitution?" 48 *Rev. of Pols.* 401 (1986).

Note. "Congressional Reversal of Supreme Court Decisions: 1945–57," 71 *Harv.L.Rev.* 1324 (1958).

Pritchett, C. Herman. *Congress versus the Supreme Court, 1957–1960* (Minneapolis: University of Minnesota Press, 1961).

Sager, Lawrence G. "Fair Measure: The Legal Status of Under-enforced Constitutional Norms," 91 *Harv.L.Rev.* 1212 (1978).

Schmidhauser, John R., and Larry L. Berg. *The Supreme Court and Congress: Conflict and Interaction, 1945–1968* (New York: The Free Press, 1972).

Sunstein, Cass R. *The Partial Constitution* (Cambridge: Harvard University Press, 1993).

Warren, Charles. *Congress, the Constitution and the Supreme Court* (Boston: Little, Brown, 1925).

"A law violating a constitution established by the people themselves, would be considered by the Judges as null & void."—MADISON at the Philadelphia Convention (1787)

> **"This makes the Judiciary Department paramount in fact to the Legislature, which was never intended and can never be proper."—MADISON to John Brown (1788)**

> **"In all systems there are points which must be adjusted by the departments themselves. ..."—MADISON in U.S. House of Representatives (1789)**

JAMES MADISON ON JUDICIAL REVIEW AND JUDICIAL SUPREMACY

On July 23, 1787, at the Constitutional Convention, Oliver Ellsworth of Connecticut moved that the delegates reconsider their decision to have final ratification made by conventions in the several states and instead have state legislatures have the last word on accepting or rejecting the new constitution. According to Madison's notes of the debates:

Mr. **MADISON** thought it clear that the Legislatures were incompetent to the proposed changes. These changes would make essential inroads on the State Constitutions, and it would be a novel & dangerous doctrine that a Legislature could change the constitution under which it held its existence. ... He considered the difference between a system founded on the Legislatures only, and one founded on the people, to be the true difference between a *league* or *treaty*, and a *Constitution*. The former in point of *moral obligation* might be as inviolable as the latter. In point of *political operation,* there were two important distinctions in favor of the latter. 1. A law violating a treaty ratified by a pre-existing law, might be respected by the Judges as a law, though an unwise or perfidious one. A law violating a constitution established by the people themselves, would be considered by the Judges to be null & void. 2. The doctrine laid down by the law of Nations in the case of treaties is that a breach of any one article by any of the parties, frees the other parties from their engagements. In the case of a union of people under one Constitution, the nature of the pact has always been understood to exclude such an interpretation. ... [1]

Ellsworth's motion failed by a wide margin.

On August 27, the Convention took up William S. Johnson's proposal, now contained in broader form in Art. III, § 1, § 2, that the Supreme Court's jurisdiction should extend to cases arising under the Constitution. According to Madison's notes:

---

1. Max Farrand, ed., *The Records of the Federal Convention of 1787* (Rev. ed.; New Haven: Yale University Press, 1937), II, 92–93.

Mr. **MADISON** doubted whether it was not going too far to extend the jurisdiction of the [Supreme] Court generally to cases arising under the Constitution & whether it ought not to be limited to cases of a Judiciary Nature. The right of expounding the Constitution in cases not of this nature ought not to be given to that Department.

The motion of Docr. Johnson was agreed to nem: con [no one dissenting] it being generally supposed that the jurisdiction given was constructively limited to cases of a Judiciary nature.[2]

It is not altogether clear what "cases of a Judiciary Nature" means, but it implies that the Court could only interpret "the Constitution" in actual disputes between litigants that presented a problem of constitutional meaning. One cannot help but wonder whether in fact the delegates "generally supposed" that the clause in Art. III conveyed such a restricted message. None of the other delegates whose notes we have reports anything about this debate.

During the long debates on ratification of the new "Constitution," Madison, as co-author of *The Federalist*, published several tracts that touched on judicial review. In Number 39 (reprinted below, p. 526), he indicated the Supreme Court would play a critical role in settling disputes between nation and state. "Some such tribunal," he wrote, "is clearly essential to prevent an appeal to the sword and a dissolution of the compact. ..." Madison, however, was either less impressed with the role the Court would play to control Congress or was less candid in his evaluations. In *Federalist* No. 44, he said:

It might be asked what is to be the consequence, in case the Congress shall misconstrue this part of the Constitution,* and exercise powers not warranted by its true meaning. I answer, the same as if they should misconstrue or enlarge any other power vested in them ... the same, in short, as if the State legislatures should violate their respective constitutional authorities. In the first instance, the success of the usurpation will depend on the executive and judiciary departments, which are to expound and give effect to the legislative acts; and in the last resort a remedy must be obtained from the people, who can, by the election of more faithful representatives, annul the acts of the usurpers. The truth is, that this ultimate redress may be more confided in against unconstitutional acts of the federal than the State legislatures, for the plain reason, that as every such act of the former will be an invasion of the rights of the latter, these will be ever ready to mark the innovation, to sound the alarm to the

---

2. Farrand, supra note 1, II, 430.

* Art. I, § 8: "Congress shall have power ... To make all Laws which shall be necessary and proper for carrying into execution the foregoing Powers, and all other Powers vested by this Constitution in the Government of the United States, or in any Department or Officer thereof."

people, and to exert their local influence in effecting a change of federal representatives.

Shortly after "the Constitution" had been ratified, however, Madison seemed to take judicial review more seriously. John Brown, an old friend from Madison's days at Princeton, wrote to ask his views about proposals for a constitution for Kentucky, which was preparing for statehood. Brown enclosed a draft of a constitution that Jefferson had suggested for Virginia in 1783. Madison replied at length. We reprint here only his remarks dealing with constitutional interpretation:

A revisionary power is meant as a check to precipitate, to unjust, and to unconstitutional laws. These important ends would it is conceded be more effectually secured, without disarming the Legislature of its authority, by requiring bills to be separately communicated to the Exec: & Judic^y dep^{ts} If either of these object, let ⅔, if both ¾ of each House be necessary to overrule the objection; and if either or both protest agst a bill as violating the Constitution, let it moreover be suspended notwithstanding the overruling proportion of the Assembly, until there shall have been a subsequent election of the H[ouse] of D[elegates] and a re-passage of the bill by ⅔ or ¾ of both Houses, as the case may be. It s[houl]^d not be allowed the Judges or y^e, Executive to pronounce a law thus enacted unconstitu^l & invalid.

In the State Constitutions & indeed in the Fed^1 one also, no provision is made for the case of a disagreement in expounding them; and as the Courts are generally the last in making ye decision, it results to them by refusing or not refusing to execute a law, to stamp it with its final character. This makes the Judiciary Dep^t paramount in fact to the Legislature, which was never intended and can never be proper.[3]

In June, 1789, during the first session of the First Congress, the House of Representatives debated a proposal to give (or acknowledge) in the President alone authority to remove officials whom he had appointed with the advice and consent of the Senate. Madison, now a congressman from Virginia, believed that the constitutional document vested the removal power solely in the President, but he also wanted the House to address this issue.

Mr. **MADISON**— ...

Another species of argument has been urged against this clause. It is said, that it is improper, or at least unnecessary, to come to any decision on this subject. It has been said by one gentleman, that it

3. Madison to John Brown, October 12, 1788, "Observations on the 'Draught of a Constitution for Virginia,'" Gaillard Hunt, ed., *The Writings of James Madison* (New York: Putnam's Sons, 1904), V, 292–294.

would be officious in this branch of the Legislature to expound the constitution, so far as it relates to the division of power between the President and Senate; it is incontrovertibly of as much importance to this branch of the Government as to any other, that the constitution should be preserved entire. It is our duty, so far as it depends upon us, to take care that the powers of the constitution be preserved entire to every department of Government; the breach of the constitution in one point, will facilitate the breach in another; a breach in this point may destroy that equilibrium by which the House retains its consequence and share of power; therefore we are not chargeable with an officious interference. Besides, the bill, before it can have effect, must be submitted to both those branches who are particularly interested in it; the Senate may negative, or the President may object, if he thinks it unconstitutional.

But the great objection drawn from the source to which the last arguments would lead us is, that the Legislature itself has no right to expound the constitution; that wherever its meaning is doubtful, you must leave it to take its course, until the Judiciary is called upon to declare its meaning. I acknowledge, in the ordinary course of Government, that the exposition of the laws and constitution devolves upon the Judiciary. But, I beg to know, upon what principle it can be contended, that any one department draws from the constitution greater powers than another, in marking out the limits of the powers of the several departments? The constitution is the charter of the people to the Government; it specifies certain great powers as absolutely granted, and marks out the departments to exercise them. If the constitutional boundary of either be brought into question, I do not see that any one of these independent departments has more right than another to declare their sentiments on that point.

Perhaps this is an omitted case. There is not one Government on the face of the earth, so far as I recollect, there is not one in the United States, in which provision is made for a particular authority to determine the limits of the constitutional division of power between the branches of the Government. In all systems there are points which must be adjusted by the departments themselves, to which no one of them is competent. If it cannot be determined in this way, there is no resource left but the will of the community, to be collected in some mode to be provided by the constitution, or one dictated by the necessity of the case. It is therefore a fair question, whether this great point may not as well be decided, at least by the whole Legislature as by a part, by us as well as by the Executive or Judiciary? As I think it will be equally constitutional, I cannot imagine it will be less safe, that the exposition should issue from the legislative authority than any other; and the more so, because it involves in the decision the opinions of both those departments, whose powers are supposed to be affected by it. Besides, I do not see in what way this question could come before the judges, to obtain a fair and solemn decision; but even if it were the case that it could, I should suppose, at least while the Government is not led by passion, disturbed by faction, or deceived by any discolored medium of sight, but while there is a desire in all to see and be guided by the benignant ray of truth, that the decision may be made with the most advantage by the Legislature itself.

My conclusion from these reflections is, that it will be constitutional to retain the clause; that it expresses the meaning of the constitution as must be established by fair construction, and a construction which, upon the whole, not only consists with liberty, but is more favorable to it than any one of the interpretations that have been proposed.[4]

Editors' Note

Query: How can one reconcile these varying opinions of Madison about the WHO of constitutional interpretation? Is there any consistent theory about the nature of "the Constitution" or of constitutional interpretation running through his various pronouncements? Or was he merely offering ad hoc reactions to specific problems?

"The opinions of the supreme court, whatever they may be, will have the force of law; because there is no power provided in the constitution, that can correct their errors, or controul their adjudications."—BRUTUS

"A constitution is, in fact, and must be regarded by the judges, as a fundamental law. It therefore belongs to them to ascertain its meaning. ..."—Alexander HAMILTON

THE LETTERS OF BRUTUS, NO. 11 (JANUARY 31, 1788)

Whatever views Madison have had during the convention and the fight over ratification on judges' authority to interpret the new "Constitution," many Anti–Federalists glimpsed the specter of judicial review, indeed judicial supremacy, lurking in the shadows of the text. Among the most persistent opponents of ratification in New York was a writer who labelled himself Brutus. In a series of newspaper articles, he doggedly debated Madison and Hamilton and urged voters to reject the document the Philadelphia Convention had presented. The author may have been Judge Robert Yates, a delegate to the convention who had refused to sign the proposed constitutional text. Whoev-

---

4. *Annals of Congress,* I, 519–521 (June 17, 1789). As we have noted before and shall again, these "records" of congressional debates are not what we today would call stenographic transcripts. Modern forms of shorthand had not yet been developed; typically, several secretaries would take turns writing down what they thought legislators were saying. Sometimes these scribes fell behind and would paraphrase remarks. It is difficult, two centuries later, to distinguish summaries from quotations, unless, as often happened, a secretary used the third person.

er he was, Brutus focused several of his attacks on judicial power.*

The nature and extent of the judicial power of the United States, proposed to be granted by this constitution, claims our particular attention.

This government is a complete system, not only for making, but for executing laws. And the courts of law, which will be constituted by it, are not only to decide upon the constitution and the laws made in pursuance of it, but by officers subordinate to them to execute all their decision. The real effect of this system of government, will therefore be brought home to the feelings of the people, through the medium of the judicial power. It is, moreover, of great importance, to examine with care the nature and extent of the judicial power, because those who are to be vested with it, are to be placed in a situation altogether unprecedented in a free country. They are to be rendered totally independent, both of the people and the legislature, both with respect to their offices and salaries. No errors they may commit can be corrected by any power above them, if any such power there be, nor can they be removed from office for making ever so many erroneous adjudications.

The only causes for which they can be displaced, is, conviction of treason, bribery, and high crimes and misdemeanors.

This part of the plan is so modelled, as to authorize the courts, not only to carry into execution the powers expressly given, but where these are wanting or ambiguously expressed, to supply what is wanting by their own decisions.

That we may be enabled to form a just opinion on this subject, I shall, in considering it,

1st. Examine the nature and extent of the judicial powers—and 2d. Inquire, whether the courts who are to exercise them, are so constituted as to afford reasonable ground of confidence, that they will exercise them for the general good. . . .

In article 3d, sect. 2d, it is said, "The judicial power shall extend to all cases in law and equity arising under this constitution, the laws of the United States, and treaties made, or which shall be made, under their authority, & c."

The first article to which this power extends, is, all cases in law and equity arising under this constitution.

What latitude of construction this clause should receive, it is not easy to say. At first view, one would suppose, that it meant no more than this, that the courts under the general government should exercise,

---

* These articles appeared a weekly newspaper, *The New York Journal and Weekly Register*, beginning in October, 1787 through April, 1788. Number 11 appeared on January 31, 1788, and Brutus continued hammering at the proposed federal judiciary through March 20, 1788. Herbert A. Storing has reprinted all of Brutus's tracts (as well as the attacks of most of the other Anti–Federalists): *The Complete Anti–Federalist* (Chicago: University of Chicago Press, 1981), II, 358–446.

not only the powers of courts of law, but also that of courts of equity, in the manner in which those powers are usually exercised in the different states. But this cannot be the meaning, because the next clause authorizes the courts to take cognizance of all cases in law and equity arising under the laws of the United States; this last article, I conceive, conveys as much power to the general [federal] judicial as any of the state courts possess.

The cases arising under the constitution must be different from those arising under the laws, or else the two clauses mean exactly the same thing.

The cases arising under the constitution must include such, as bring into question its meaning, and will require an explanation of the nature and extent of the powers of the different departments under it.

This article, therefore, vests the judicial with a power to resolve all questions that may arise on any case on the construction of the constitution, either in law or in equity.

1st. They are authorized to determine all questions that may arise upon the meaning of the constitution in law. This article vests the courts with authority to give the constitution a legal construction, or to explain it according to the rules laid down for construing a law.—These rules give a certain degree of latitude of explanation. According to this mode of construction, the courts are to give such meaning to the constitution as comports best with the common, and generally received acceptation of the words in which it is expressed, regarding their ordinary and popular use, rather than their grammatical propriety. Where words are dubious, they will be explained by the context. The end of the clause will be attended to, and the words will be understood, as having a view to it; and the words will not be so understood as to bear no meaning or a very absurd one.

2d. The judicial are not only to decide questions arising upon the meaning of the constitution in law, but also in equity.

By this they are empowered, to explain the constitution according to the reasoning spirit of it, without being confined to the words or letter.

"From this method of interpreting laws (says Blackstone) by the reason of them, arises what we call equity;" which is thus defined by Grotius, "the correction of that, wherein the law, by reason of its universality, is deficient.["]   . . .

The same learned author observes, "That equity, thus depending essentially upon each individual case, there can be no established rules and fixed principles of equity laid down, without destroying its very essence, and reducing it to a positive law."   . . .

They [federal judges] will give the sense of every article of the constitution, that may from time to time come before them. And in their decisions they will not confine themselves to any fixed or established rules, but will determine, according to what appears to them, the reason and spirit of the constitution. The opinions of the supreme court, whatever they may be, will have the force of law; because there is no power provided in the constitution, that can correct their errors, or control their adjudications. From this court there is no appeal. And I conceive the legislature themselves, cannot set aside a judgment of this court, because they are authorized by the constitution to decide in the last resort. The legislature must be controlled by the constitution, and not the constitution by them. They have therefore no more right to set aside any judgment pronounced upon the construction of the constitution, than they have to take from the president, the chief command of the army and navy, and commit it to some other person. The reason is plain; the judicial and executive derive their authority from the same source, that the legislature do theirs; and therefore in all cases, where the constitution does not make the one responsible to, or controllable by the other, they are altogether independent of each other.

The judicial power will operate to effect, in the most certain, but yet silent and imperceptible manner, what is evidently the tendency of the constitution:—I mean, an entire subversion of the legislative, executive and judicial powers of the individual states. Every adjudication of the supreme court, on any question that may arise upon the nature and extent of the general government, will affect the limits of the state jurisdiction. In proportion as the former enlarge the exercise of their powers, will that of the latter be restricted.

That the judicial power of the United States, will lean strongly favor of the general government, and will give such an explanation to the constitution, as will favor an extension of its jurisdiction, is very evident from a variety of considerations.

1st. The constitution itself strongly countenances such a mode of construction. Most of the articles in this system, which convey powers of any considerable importance, are conceived in general and indefinite terms, which are either equivocal, ambiguous, or which require long definitions to unfold the extent of their meaning. The two most important powers committed to any government, those of raising money, and of raising and keeping up troops, have already been considered, and shown to be unlimited by any thing but the discretion of the legislature. The clause which vests the power to pass all laws which are proper and necessary, to carry the powers given into execution, it has been shown, leaves the legislature at liberty, to do everything, which in their judgment is best. It is said, I know, that this clause confers no power on the legislature, which they would not have had without it—though I believe this is not the fact, yet, admitting it to be, it implies that the constitution is not to receive an explanation strictly, according to its letter; but more power is implied than is expressed. And this clause, if it is to be considered, as explanatory of the extent of the powers given, rather than giving a new power, is to be understood as declaring, that in construing any of the articles conveying power, the spirit, intent and design of the clause, should be attended to, as well as the words in their common acceptation.

This constitution gives sufficient color for adopting an equitable construction, if we consider the great end and design it professedly has in view—these appear from its preamble to be, "to form a more perfect union, establish justice, insure domestic tranquility, provide for the common defence, promote the general welfare, and secure the blessings of liberty to ourselves and posterity." The design of this system is here expressed, and it is proper to give such a meaning to the various parts, as will best promote the accomplishment of the end; this idea suggests itself naturally upon reading the preamble, and will countenance the court in giving the several articles such a sense, as will the most effectually promote the ends the constitution had in view—how this manner of explaining the constitution will operate in practice, shall be the subject of future enquiry.

2d. Not only will the constitution justify the courts in inclining to this mode of explaining it, but they will be interested in using this latitude of interpretation. Every body of men invested with office are tenacious of power; they feel interested, and hence it has become a kind of maxim, to hand down their offices, with all its rights and privileges, unimpaired to their successors; the same principle will influence them to extend their power, and increase their rights; this of itself will operate strongly upon the courts to give such a meaning to the constitution in all cases where it can possibly be done, as will enlarge the sphere of their own authority. Every extension of the power of the general legislature, as well as of the judicial powers, will increase the powers of the courts; and the dignity and importance of the judges, will be in proportion to the extent and magnitude of the powers they exercise. I add, it is highly probable the emolument of the judges will be increased, with the increase of the business they will have to transact and its importance. From these considerations the judges will be interested to extend the powers of the courts, and to construe the constitution as much as possible, in such a way as to favor it; and that they will do it, appears probable. ...

When the courts will have a precedent before them of a court which extended its jurisdiction in opposition to an act of the legislature, is it not to be expected that they will extend theirs, especially when there is nothing in the constitution expressly against it? and they are authorized to construe its meaning, and are not under any control?

This power in the judicial, will enable them to mould the government, into almost any shape they please.

———

FEDERALIST NO. 78 (MAY 28, 1788)

Alexander Hamilton.

Brutus's challenge, echoed by other prominent Anti–Federalists, was one that the Federalists could ignore only at their peril. Two months after his final broadside against the Federalists' judicial system, and as the campaign for ratification was reaching its climax in New York, Hamilton took up the cudgels in defense of judges and judicial review.

... Whoever attentively considers the different departments of power must perceive that, in a government in which they are separated from each other, the judiciary, from the nature of its functions, will always be the least dangerous to the political rights of the Constitution; because it will be least in capacity to annoy or injure them. The Executive not only dispenses honors, but holds the sword of the community. The legislature not only commands the purse, but prescribes the rules by which the duties and rights of every citizen are to be regulated. The judiciary, on the contrary, has no influence over either the sword or the purse; no direction either of the strength or of the wealth of the society; and can take no active resolution whatever. It may truly be said to have neither FORCE nor WILL, but merely judgment; and must ultimately depend upon the aid of the executive arm even for the efficacy of its judgment. ...

Some perplexity respecting the rights of the courts to pronounce legislative acts void, because contrary to the constitution, has arisen from an imagination that the doctrine would imply a superiority of the judiciary to the legislative power. It is urged that the authority which can declare the acts of another void, must necessarily be superior to the one whose acts may be declared void. As this doctrine is of great importance in all the American constitutions, a brief discussion of the ground on which it rests cannot be unacceptable.

There is no position which depends on clearer principles, than that every act of a delegated authority, contrary to the tenor of the commission under which it is exercised, is void. No legislative act, therefore, contrary to the Constitution, can be valid. To deny this, would be to affirm that the deputy is greater than his principal; that the servant is above his master; that the representatives of the people are superior to the people themselves; that men acting by virtue of powers may do not only what their powers do not authorize, but what they forbid.

If it be said that the legislative body are themselves the constitutional judges of their own powers, and that the construction put on them is conclusive upon the other departments, it may be answered, that this cannot be the natural presumption, where it is not to be collected from any particular provisions in the Constitution. It is not otherwise to be supposed, that the Constitution could intend to enable the representatives of the people to substitute their *will* to that of their constituents. It is far more rational to suppose, that the courts were designed to be an intermediate body between the people and the legislature, in order, among other things, to keep the latter within the limits assigned to their authority. The interpretation of the laws is the proper and peculiar province of the courts. A constitution is, in fact, and must be regarded by the judges, as a fundamental law. It therefore belongs to them to ascertain its meaning, as well as the meaning of any particular act proceeding from the legislative body. If there should happen to be an irreconcilable variance between the two, that which has the superior obligation and validity ought, of course, to be preferred; or, in other words, the Constitution ought to be preferred to the statute, the intention of the people to the intention of their agents.

Nor does this conclusion by any means suppose a superiority of the judicial to the legislative power. It only supposes that the power of the people is superior to both; and that where the will of the legislature, declared in its statutes, stands in opposition to that of the people, declared in the Constitution, the judges ought to be governed by the latter rather than the former. They ought to regulate their decisions by the fundamental laws, rather than by those which are not fundamental.
. . .

It can be of no weight to say that the courts, on the pretence of a repugnancy, may substitute their own pleasure to the constitutional intentions of the legislature. This might as well happen in the case of two contradictory statutes; or it might as well happen in every adjudication upon any single statute. The courts must declare the sense of the law; and if they should be disposed to exercise WILL instead of JUDGMENT, the consequence would equally be the substitution of their pleasure to that of the legislative body. The observation, if it prove any thing, would prove that there ought to be no judges distinct from that body.

If, then, the courts of justice are to be considered as the bulwarks of a limited Constitution against legislative encroachments, this consideration will afford a strong argument for the permanent tenure of judicial offices, since nothing will contribute so much as this to that independent spirit in the judges which must be essential to the faithful performance of so arduous a duty.

This independence of the judges is equally requisite to guard the Constitution and the rights of individuals from the effects of those ill humors, which the arts of designing men, or the influence of particular conjunctures, sometimes disseminate among the people themselves, and which, though they speedily give place to better information, and more deliberate reflection, have a tendency, in the meantime, to occasion dangerous innovations in the government, and serious oppressions of the minor party in the community. Though I trust the friends of the proposed Constitution will never concur with its enemies, in questioning that fundamental principle of republican government, which admits the right of the people to alter or abolish the established Constitution, whenever they find it inconsistent with their happiness, yet it is not to be inferred from this principle, that the representatives of the people, whenever a momentary inclination happens to lay hold of a majority of their constituents, incompatible with the provisions in the existing Constitution, would, on that account, be justifiable in a violation of those provisions; or that the courts would be under a greater obligation to connive at infractions in this shape, than when they had proceeded wholly from the cabals of the representative body. Until the people have, by some solemn and authoritative act, annulled or changed the established form, it is binding upon themselves collectively, as well as individually; and no presumption, or even knowledge, of their sentiments, can warrant their representatives in a departure from it, prior to such an act. But it is easy to see, that it would require an uncommon portion of fortitude in the judges to do their duty as faithful guardians of the Constitution, where legislative invasions of it had been instigated by the major voice of the community. ...

There is yet a further and a weightier reason for the permanency of the judicial offices. ... To avoid an arbitrary discretion in the courts, it is indispensable that they should be bound down by strict rules and precedents, which serve to define and point out their duty in every particular case that comes before them; and it will readily be conceived from the variety of controversies which grow out of the folly and wickedness of mankind, that the records of those precedents must unavoidably swell to a very considerable bulk, and must demand long and laborious study to acquire a competent knowledge of them. Hence it is, that there can be but few men in the society who will have sufficient skill in the laws to qualify them for the stations of judges. And making the proper deductions for the ordinary depravity of human nature, the number must be still smaller of those who unite the requisite integrity with the requisite knowledge. These considerations apprise us, that the government can have no great option between fit character; and that a temporary duration in office, which would naturally discourage such characters from quitting a lucrative line of practice to accept a seat on the bench, would have a tendency to throw the administration of justice into hands less able, and less well qualified, to conduct it with utility and dignity. ...

Editors' Notes

(1) **Query:** Brutus and Hamilton agreed that, if adopted, the new constitutional text would authorize judges to exercise judicial review. What is the disagreement between them and, more important, the basis of that disagreement?

(2) **Query:** How did Madison's theory of WHO, as reflected in his speech in the First Congress, differ from that of Brutus? From Hamilton?

(3) **Query:** The introductory essay to this chapter suggested that answers to WHO might be classified as advocating judicial supremacy, legislative supremacy, or departmentalism. In which category would Madison fall? Brutus? Hamilton?

(4) **Query:** To some extent, Hamilton makes a democratic argument for a strong judicial role in constitutional interpretation. How would Brutus have responded? Madison?

(5) **Query:** If we consider "original understanding" as part of the larger constitution to be interpreted, what weight should we accord to Brutus's understanding?

(6) **Query:** Reflect on the readings in Chapters 5 and 6 regarding WHAT: Who offers the most realistic description of the way judges have interpreted "the Constitution," Madison, Brutus, or Hamilton?

———

"[T]he Legislature have the exclusive right to interpret the Constitution, in what regards the law-making power, and the judges are bound to execute the laws they make."—Senator John BRECKENRIDGE

"Why does a judge swear to discharge his duties agreeably to the constitution of the United States, if that constitution forms no rule for his government?"—Chief Justice John MARSHALL

THE GREAT DEBATE OF 1802–1803

Until adoption in 1933 of the Twentieth Amendment, the terms of incumbent presidents, senators, and congressmen did not expire until March of the year following an election, allowing the possibility of almost four months of rule by lame ducks. In the critical election of 1800, the Jeffersonians routed the Federalists under John Adams. The Federalists, however, took advantage of their period of grace to adopt the Judiciary Act of 1801, a law that, on the one hand, created sixteen circuit judgeships and, on the other hand, provided that, upon the next death or resignation on the Supreme Court, the number of justices would be reduced from six to five, thereby depriving Thomas Jefferson of an opportunity to choose a justice.

There were sound reasons for creating circuit judgeships. Earlier statutes had required justices of the Supreme Court to go around the country singly or in pairs to preside at trials. Not only was travel during that period always slow, often difficult, and sometimes perilous, the arrangement also caused awkward problems when a litigant appealed to the Supreme Court, for at least one of the justices had already heard the case and registered opinions about it. Nevertheless, coupled as it was with the reduction of the number of justices and recent experience under the Sedition Act of 1798—which many Federalist judges had gleefully used to fine and imprison men who dared to criticize John Adams and support Thomas Jefferson—the Act of 1801 smacked of a crude power play. As Jefferson wrote to a confidante, the Federalists

> have retired into the judiciary as a stronghold. There the remains of federalism are to be preserved and fed from the treasury, and from that battery all the works of republicanism are to be beaten down and erased. By a fraudulent use of the Constitution, which has made judges irremovable, they have multiplied useless judges merely to strengthen their phalanx.

Not unexpectedly, repeal was one of the primary objectives of the administration when the new Congress met in December, 1801.

Meanwhile, the judiciary was also providing the stage for other scenes in the drama. After Jefferson's electoral victory, the Federalists persuaded the ailing Oliver Ellsworth to resign as Chief Justice while Adams was still in office and so deprive Jefferson of another opportunity to put one of his own men on the bench. For Ellsworth's place, Adams nominated and the Senate quickly confirmed his Secretary of State, John Marshall, a very healthy man not quite 46 years old.

On the evening before leaving office, Adams had signed commissions for 42 justices of the peace in the District of Columbia—the so-called "midnight judges." As required by law, the Secretary of State—still John Marshall, who had not thought it necessary to resign when accepting the chief justiceship— affixed the official seal and gave the commissions to his assistant, his brother James, to deliver. James, however, neglected to deliver them. When he assumed office the next day, Jefferson instructed his Secretary of State, James Madison, to withhold 17 of the commissions.

After some initial hesitation, William Marbury and three other men who had not received their commissions filed suit in the U.S. Supreme Court, asking for a mandamus—an order from a court to a public official commanding him to perform a non-discretionary act—directing James Madison to deliver the commissions. In December, 1801, just as the congressional session had begun, the Court ordered Madison to "show cause" why the justices should not grant Marbury's request.

The lawsuit and the Court's "show cause" order alarmed the Jeffersonians. On Christmas Eve, Senator John Breckenridge,* one of Jefferson's staunchest supporters in Congress, wrote a friend that the Court's "show cause" order was "the most daring attack which the annals of Federalism have yet exhibited. I wish the subject of the Courts to be brought forward in the Senate next week. ..." Breckenridge had his way. Repeal of the Judiciary Act of 1801 soon became the Senate's first order of business.

As drafted, the bill that became the Judiciary Act of 1802 would not only have abolished the circuit courts but would also have turned out of office the sixteen circuit judges, all of whom had been serving for at least nine months on the federal bench. Immediately at issue was whether such dismissals without impeachment and trial violated the plain words of Article III of the Constitution that "judges shall hold their offices during good behavior." Jefferson's private comments indicate that, however angry he was at the Federalists' slickness, he thought removal unconstitutional. Nevertheless, he allowed Senator Breckenridge and other friends on Capitol Hill to pit their interpretive ingenuity against that of the Federalists. Almost inevitably, discussion of judicial independence raised the more complex issue of the legitimacy of judicial interpretation of "the Constitution."

"... I ask gentlemen to point out the clause [in the constitutional text] which grants it [judicial review]. ...

---

* In keeping with some of the loose standards of spelling of the times, he sometimes wrote his name "Breckinridge," at other times—and apparently more often—as "Breckenridge."—**Eds**.

Is it not extraordinary, that if this high power was intended, it should nowhere appear?"—Senator BRECK-ENRIDGE

"I answer, they [judges] derived that power from authority higher than this Constitution. They derive it from the constitution of man, from the nature of things, from the necessary progress of human affairs."—Senator MORRIS

A. THE SENATE DEBATES*

(1801–1802)

Mr. BRECKENRIDGE. ...

... [T]here is little doubt indeed, in my mind, as to the power of Congress on this law. The first section of the third article [of the constitutional text] vests the judicial power of the United States in one Supreme Court and such inferior courts as Congress may, from time to time, ordain and establish. By this clause Congress *may*, from time to time, establish inferior courts; but it is clearly a discretionary power, and they *may not* establish them. The language of the Constitution is very different when regulations are not left discretional. For example, "The trial," says the Constitution, "of all crimes (except in cases of impeachment) shall be by jury: representatives and direct taxes shall be apportioned according to numbers. All revenue bills shall originate in the House of Representatives," & c. It would, therefore, in my opinion, be a perversion, not only of language, but of intellect, to say, that although Congress may, from time to time, establish inferior courts, yet, when established, that they shall not be abolished by a subsequent Congress possessing equal powers. ...

2d. As to the judges. The Judiciary department is so constructed as to be sufficiently secured against the improper influence of either the Executive or Legislative departments. The courts are organized and established by the Legislature, and the Executive creates the judges. Being thus organized, the Constitution affords the proper checks to secure their honesty and independence in office. It declares they shall not be removed from office during good behaviour; nor their salaries diminished during their continuance in office. From this it results, that a judge, after his appointment, is totally out of the power of the President, and his salary secured against legislative diminution, during his continuance in office. ...

But because the Constitution declares that a judge shall hold his office during good behaviour, can it be tortured to mean, that he shall hold his office after it is abolished? ...

---

* *Annals of Congress,* 7th Cong., 1st sess., pp. 27–183 (1802).

The construction obviously is, that a judge should hold an existing office, so long as he did his duty in that office. ... Had the construction which I contend against been contemplated by those who framed the Constitution, it would have been necessary to have declared, explicitly that the judges should hold their offices and their salaries during good behaviour.

Such a construction is not only irreconcilable with reason and propriety, but is repugnant to the principles of the Constitution. It is a principle of our Constitution, as well as of common honesty, that no man shall receive public money but in consideration of public services. ...

Upon this construction, also, an infallibility is predicated. ... On all other subjects of legislation we are allowed, it seems, to change our minds, except on judiciary subjects, which, of all others, is the most complex and difficult. I appeal to our own statute book to prove this difficulty; for in ten years Congress have passed no less than twenty-six laws on this subject.

I conceive, sir, that the tenure by which a judge holds his office, is evidently bottomed on the idea of securing his honesty and independence. ... [I]f the construction now contended for shall prevail, we shall [establish] a judicial oligarchy. ...

... [A]s we have undeniable evidence before us that the creation of the courts now under consideration was totally unnecessary; and as no Government can ... seriously deny that this Legislature has a right to repeal a law enacted by a preceding one, we will, in any event, discharge our duty by repealing this law; and thereby doing all in our power to correct the evil. If the judges are entitled to their salaries under the Constitution, our repeal will not affect them; and they will, no doubt, resort to their proper remedy. For where there is a Constitutional right, there must be a Constitutional remedy.

Mr. J. MASON of Massachusetts. ...

... [T]he people, in forming their Constitution, meant to make the judges as independent of the Legislature as of the Executive. Because the duties which they have to perform, call upon them to expound not only the laws, but the Constitution also; in which is involved the power of checking the Legislature in case it should pass any laws in violation of the Constitution. For this reason it was more important that the judges in this country should be placed beyond the control of the Legislature, than in other countries where no such power attaches to them. ...

Thus [the Constitution] says "the judges *shall* hold their offices during good behaviour." How can this direction of the Constitution be complied with, if the Legislature shall, from session to session, repeal the law under which the office is held, and *remove the office?* He* did not

---

* See our earlier note on p. 281, The switch to the third person here illustrates difficulties stenographers had before the invention of modern shorthand. They sometimes fell behind in recording the debates and had to summarize what had been said. We can only hope that both the purported quotations and the summaries are accurate, though

conceive that any words, which human ingenuity could devise, could more completely get over the remarks that had been made by the gentleman from Kentucky. ...

Besides, if Congress have the right to repeal the whole of the law, they must possess the right to repeal a section of it. If so, they may repeal the law so far as it applies to a particular district, and thus get rid of an obnoxious judge. ... Would it not be absurd still to say, that the removed judge held his office during good behaviour? ...

Mr. MORRIS,** of New York. ...

... What will be the effect of the desired repeal? Will it not be a declaration to the remaining judges that they hold their offices subject to your will and pleasure? And what will be the result of this? It will be, that the check established by the Constitution, wished for by the people, and necessary in every contemplation of common sense, is destroyed. It had been said, and truly, too, that Governments are made to provide against the follies and vices of men. For to suppose that Governments rest upon reason is a pitiful solecism. If mankind were reasonable, they would want no Government. Hence, checks are required in the distribution of power among those who are to exercise it for the benefit of the people. Did the people of America vest all powers in the Legislature? No; they had vested in the judges a check intended to be efficient—a check of the first necessity, to prevent an invasion of the Constitution by unconstitutional laws—a check which might prevent any faction from intimidating or annihilating the tribunals themselves. ...

Let us then, secondly, consider whether we have constitutionally a power to repeal this law. [Here Mr. Morris quoted the third article and first section of the Constitution.] I have heard a verbal criticism about the words *shall* and *may*, which appeared the more unnecessary to me, as the same word, *shall*, is applied to both members of the section. For it says "the judicial power, & c. *shall* be vested in one Supreme Court and such inferior courts as the Congress *may*, from time to time, ordain and establish." The Legislature, therefore, had, without doubt, the right of determining, in the first instance, what inferior courts should be established; but when established, the words are imperative, a part of the judicial power shall vest in them. And "the judges shall hold their offices during good behaviour." They shall receive a compensation which shall not be diminished during their continuance in office. Therefore, whether the remarks be applied to the tenure of office, or the quantum of compensation, the Constitution is equally imperative. ...

---

there is evidence that such was not always the case. See, for example, the analysis in James H. Hutson, "The Creation of the Constitution: The Integrity of the Documentary Record," 65 *Tex. L. Rev.* 1 (1986).—**Eds**.

** Gouverneur Morris had been one of the more influential delegates at the Philadelphia Convention in 1787. He had chaired the Committee on Style and had written much of the final document. He remained a staunch Federalist and was a bitter foe of Thomas Jefferson.—**Eds**.

But another criticism ... has been made: ... you shall not take the man from the office, but you may take the office from the man. ... The Constitution secures to a judge his office ... during good behaviour; the Legislature shall not diminish, though their bounty may increase, his salary; the Constitution provides perfectly for the inviolability of his tenure; but yet we may destroy the office which we cannot take away. ... Is not this absurd? ...

Mr. JACKSON, of Georgia. ...

We have been asked, if we are afraid of having an army of judges? For myself, I am more afraid of an army of judges, under the patronage of the President, than of an army of soldiers. The former can do us more harm. ... Have we not seen sedition laws? Have we not heard judges crying out through the land, sedition! ...

Here then, said he, are two tribunals. First, the Supreme Court, the creature of the Constitution, the creature of the people; the other, the inferior jurisdictions, the creature of the Legislature. ... The word *shall,* applied to the Supreme Court, is imperative and commanding, while the word *may,* applied to the inferior courts, is discretionary, and leaves to the Legislature a volition to act, or not to act, as it sees fit.

Again, why are the peculiar and exclusive powers of the Supreme Court designated in the following section of the Constitution, but because the Constitution considered that tribunal as absolutely established; while it viewed the inferior tribunals as dependent upon the will of the Legislature? And that this was the case was evident from the conduct of the Supreme Court on the pension act, which that court had some time since declared unconstitutional; and which declaration, he was convinced, would not have been hazarded by an inferior tribunal. ... *

... Do not the observations of gentlemen, who insist upon the permanent tenure of the Judicial office, place the creature above its creator, man above his God, the model above its mechanic? ...

... What is the implication of this doctrine? To alter or amend what may greatly require alteration or amendment, it is necessary to return to the creator, and to inquire what this creator is. My principle

---

* The reference is probably either to Hayburn's Case (1792) or to United States v. Todd (decided in 1794 but not reported until 1851). The Invalid Pension Act of 1792 in effect authorized U.S. circuit courts—at that time the principal federal trial courts, staffed by two justices of the Supreme Court and one district judge—to act as commissioners and recommend to the Secretary of War awards for pensions to veterans of the Revolution. On circuit, four justices wrote to the President, protesting that such duties were nonjudicial, and declined to perform them. One of these suits—Hayburn's Case—reached the Supreme Court, but before the Court reached a decision on the merits, Congress amended the statute. *Todd* questioned whether a recommendation actually given by a circuit court under the Act of 1792 was a legal judgment. The Supreme Court held, apparently unanimously, that that statute had attempted to confer nonjudicial duties on judges and was therefore unconstitutional. (One should note that *Todd* was brought under the Court's original jurisdiction, according to the terms of an Act of 1793. Cf. Marbury v. Madison [1803], which held that Congress could not add to the Court's original jurisdiction as spelled out in Article III of the Constitution.)—**Eds**.

is, that the creator is the people themselves; that very people of the
United States whom the gentleman from New York [Sen. Morris] had
declared ourselves to be the guardians of, to save the people themselves
from their greatest enemies; and to save whom from destroying themselves he had invoked this House. Good God! is it possible that I have
heard such a sentiment in this body? ...

   ... Look to the Constitution, and see how it is to be amended.

   There is required first, then, two-thirds of both Houses of Congress.
Can this two-thirds be found now, or is there any probability of its being
found for twenty years to come, who will concur in making the necessary
alterations in the Judiciary system that are now, or may hereafter, be
required? On this subject there are as many opinions as there are
persons on this floor. ... How, then, can we expect three-fourths of the
Legislatures of the several States to agree when we cannot agree among
ourselves. ...

   I am clearly, therefore, of opinion, that if the power to alter the
Judiciary system vests not here, it vests no where. ...

Mr. MORRIS, of New York. ...

   It is said, the judicial institution is intended for the benefit of the
people, and not of the judge. ... But the question remains, how will it
be rendered most beneficial? Is it by making the judge independent, by
making it *his* office, or is it by placing him in a state of abject
dependence, so that the office shall be his to-day and belong to another
to-morrow? Let the gentleman hear the words of the Constitution: It
speaks of *their* offices; consequently, as applied to a single judge, of *his*
office, to be exercised by him for the benefit of the people of America, to
which exercise his independence is as necessary as his office. ...

   ... In so far as they [judges] may be busied with the great mischief
of checking the Legislative or Executive departments in any wanton
invasion of our rights, I shall rejoice in that mischief. I hope, indeed,
they will not be so busied, because I hope we shall give them no cause.
But I also hope they will keep an eagle eye upon us lest we should. It
was partly for this purpose they were established, and, I trust, that when
properly called on, they will dare to act. I know this doctrine is
unpleasant; I know it is more popular to appeal to public opinion—that
equivocal, transient being, which exists nowhere and everywhere. But if
ever the occasion calls for it, I trust the Supreme Court will not neglect
doing the great mischief of saving this Constitution, which can be done
much better by their deliberations, than by resorting to what are called
revolutionary measures. ...

   ... The Judicial power, that fortress of the Constitution, is now to
be overturned. ... I am too weak to defend the rampart against the
host of assailants. I must call to my assistance their good sense, their
patriotism, and their virtue. ... Do not rely on that popular will, which
has brought us frail beings into political existence. That opinion is but a
changeable thing. ... Do not, I beseech you, in reliance on a foundation

so frail, commit the dignity, the harmony, the existence of our nation to the wild wind. Trust not your treasure to the waves. Throw not your compass and your charts into the ocean. ... Cast not away this only anchor of our safety. I have seen its progress. I know the difficulties through which it was obtained. I stand in the presence of Almighty God, and of the world; and I declare to you, that if you lose this charter, never, no, never will you get another! We are now, perhaps, arrived at the parting point. Here, even here, we stand on the brink of fate. Pause—pause! For Heaven's sake, pause!

Mr. BRECKENRIDGE. ...

I did not expect, sir, to find the doctrine of the power of the courts to annul the laws of Congress as unconstitutional, so seriously insisted on. ... It is said that the different departments of Government are to be checks on each other, and that the courts are to check the Legislature. If this be true I would ask where they got that power, and who checks the courts when they violate the Constitution? Would they not, by this doctrine, have the absolute direction of the Government? To whom are they responsible? But I deny the power which is so pretended. If it is derived from the Constitution, I ask gentlemen to point out the clause which grants it. I can find no such grant. Is it not extraordinary, that if this high power was intended, it should nowhere appear? Is it not truly astonishing that the Constitution, in its abundant care to define the powers of each department, should have omitted so important a power as that of the courts to nullify all the acts of Congress, which, in their opinion, were contrary to the Constitution?

Never were such high and transcendent powers in any Government ... claimed or exercised by construction only. The doctrine of constructions, not warranted by the letter of an instrument, is dangerous in the extreme. ... Once admit the doctrine, that judges are to be indulged in these astute and wire-drawn constructions, to enlarge their own power, and control that of others, and I will join gentlemen of the opposition, in declaring that the Constitution is in danger.

To make the Constitution a practical system, this pretended power of the courts to annul the laws of Congress cannot possibly exist. My idea of the subject ... is, that the Constitution intended a separation of the powers vested in the three great departments, giving to each exclusive authority on the subjects committed to it. That these departments are co-ordinate, to revolve each within the sphere of their own orbits, without being responsible for their own motion, and are not to direct or control the course of others. That those who made the laws are presumed to have an equal attachment to, and interest in the Constitution; are equally bound by oath to support it, and have an equal right to give a construction to it. That the construction of one department of the powers vested in it, is of higher authority than the construction of any other department; and that, in fact, it is competent to that department to which powers are confided exclusively to decide upon the proper exercise of those powers: that therefore the Legislature have the exclusive right to interpret the Constitution, in what regards the law—making power, and the judges are bound to execute the laws they make. For the Legislature would have at least an equal right to annul the decisions of the courts, founded on their construction of the Constitution, as the courts would have to annul the acts of the Legislature, founded on their construction.

Although, therefore, the courts may take upon them to give decisions which impeach the constitutionality of a law, and thereby, for a time, obstruct its operations, yet I contend that such a law is not the less obligatory because the organ through which it is to be executed, has refused its aid. A pertinacious adherence of both departments to their opinions, would soon bring the question to issue, in whom the sovereign power of legislation resided, and whose construction of the law-making power should prevail.

If the courts have a right to examine into, and decide upon the constitutionality of laws, their decision ought to be final and effectual. I ask then, if gentlemen are prepared to admit, that in case the courts were to declare your revenue, impost and appropriation laws unconstitutional, that they would thereby be blotted out of your statute book and the operations of Government be arrested? It is making, in my opinion, a mockery of the high powers of legislation. ... Let gentlemen consider well before they insist on a power in the Judiciary which places the Legislature at their feet. ...

Mr. MORRIS, of New York. ...

... The honorable member tells us the Legislature have the supreme and exclusive right to interpret the Constitution, so far as regards the making of laws; which, being made, the judges are bound to execute. And he asks where the judges got their pretended power of deciding on the constitutionality of laws? ... I answer, they derived that power from authority higher than this Constitution. They derive it from the constitution of man, from the nature of things, from the necessary progress of human affairs. When you have enacted a law, when process thereon has been issued, and suit brought it becomes eventually necessary that the judges decide on the case before them, and declare what the law is. They must, of course, determine whether that which is produced and relied on, has indeed the binding force of law. The decision of the Supreme Court is, and, of necessity, must be final. This, Sir, is the principle and the source of the right for which we contend. But it is denied and the supremacy of the Legislature insisted on. Mark, then, I pray, the result: The Constitution says, no bill of attainder, or *ex post facto* law shall be passed, no capitation or other direct tax shall be laid, unless in proportion to the census or enumeration to be taxed; no tax or duty shall be laid on articles exported from any State. ... Suppose that, notwithstanding these prohibitions, a majority of the two Houses should (with the President) pass such laws. Suppose, for instance, that a capitation tax (not warranted by the Constitution) or a duty on exports were imposed. The citizen refuses to pay; but courts dependent on the will and pleasure of the Legislature are compelled to enforce the collection. Shall it be said, that there is an appeal to the Supreme Court? Sir, that appeal is subject to such exceptions and regulations as Congress shall make. Congress can, therefore, defeat the appeal, and render final the judgment of inferior tribunals, subjected to their absolute control. Nay, sir, to avoid all possible doubt or question, the honorable member last up has told us in so many words, that the Legislature may decide exclusively on the Constitution, and that the judges are bound to execute the laws which the Legislature enact. Examine then the state to which we are brought. If this doctrine be sustained . . . what possible mode is there to avoid the conclusion that the moment the Legislature of the Union declare themselves supreme, they become so? The analogies so often assumed to the British Parliament, will then be complete. The sovereignty of America will no longer reside in the people, but in the Congress, and the Constitution is whatever they choose to make it. . . .

Editors' Notes

(1) The bill to repeal passed the Senate 16–15 and the House 59–32. It became law on March 31, 1802. The sixteen circuit judges lost their offices and their salaries. Although John Marshall thought that Congress could not constitutionally require justices of the Supreme Court to function also as trial judges, he acquiesced in the views of his colleagues and resumed circuit riding. A short time later, when a private litigant raised Marshall's point, the Court curtly and unanimously dismissed the issue as settled by long practice. Stuart v. Laird (1803).

(2) **Query:** To some extent, of course, Morris and Breckenridge were engaged in a partisan debate about how to exercise raw political power and each was trying to advance the cause of his party. But underlying this disagreement were also more substantial differences. To what extent did their arguments depend on disputes about the meaning of the plain words of the constitutional text? To what extent did they depend on different political theories?

(3) **Query:** With whom would Brutus's logic have compelled him to agree, Morris or Breckenridge?

(4) **Query:** Was Breckenridge an advocate of legislative supremacy or departmentalism?

"It is emphatically the province and duty of the judicial department to say what the law is."

B. MARBURY v. MADISON
5 U.S. (1 Cranch) 137, 2 L.Ed. 60 (1803).

Against the backdrop of debate and repeal, Marbury v. Madison continued its way through the Court's processes. It was scheduled to come up again in June, 1802; but, soon after repeal of the Judiciary Act of 1801, the Jeffersonians pushed through Congress a statute postponing the next sitting of the Supreme Court until February, 1803. The additional fourteen months were supposed to allow the justices to reflect on the distrust in which they were held by the new President and his Congress and dissuade the Court from issuing a mandamus to the Secretary of State. Indeed, rumors were rife in Washington that, were the justices to issue the writ, Jefferson would instruct Madison to ignore it; the question of the relative authority of judges and elected officials to interpret "the Constitution" would then have been determined on the scales of political power.

Mr. Chief Justice **MARSHALL** delivered the opinion of the Court. . . .

In the order in which the court has viewed this subject, the following questions have been considered and decided.

1st. Has the applicant a right to the commission he demands?

2d. If he has a right, and that right has been violated, do the laws of his country afford him a remedy?

3d. If they do afford him a remedy, is it a mandamus issuing from this court?

The first object of inquiry is,

1st. Has the applicant a right to the commission he demands? . . .

It is . . . decidedly the opinion of the court, that when a commission has been signed by the President, the appointment is made; and that the commission is complete when the seal of the United States has been affixed to it by the Secretary of State. . . .

The discretion of the executive is to be exercised until the appointment has been made. But having once made the appointment, his power over the office is terminated in all cases, where by law the officer is not removable by him. The right to the office is then in the person appointed, and he has the absolute, unconditional power of accepting or rejecting it.

Mr. Marbury, then, since his commission was signed by the President, and sealed by the Secretary of State, was appointed; and as the law creating the office, gave the officer a right to hold for five years, independent of the executive, the appointment was not revocable, but vested in the officer legal rights, which are protected by the laws of his country.

To withhold his commission, therefore, is an act deemed by the court not warranted by law, but violative of a vested legal right.

This brings us to the second inquiry; which is,

2d. If he has a right, and that right has been violated, do the laws of his country afford him a remedy?

The very essence of civil liberty certainly consists in the right of every individual to claim the protection of the laws, whenever he receives an injury. One of the first duties of government is to afford that protection. In Great Britain the king himself is sued in the respectful form of a petition, and he never fails to comply with the judgment of his court.

In ... his *Commentaries* Blackstone states two cases in which a remedy is afforded by mere operation of law.

"In all other cases," he says, "it is a general and indisputable rule, that where there is a legal right, there is also a legal remedy by suit, or action at law, whenever that right is invaded." ...

The government of the United States has been emphatically termed a government of laws, and not of men. It will certainly cease to deserve this high appellation, if the laws furnish no remedy for the violation of a vested legal right.

If this obloquy is to be cast on the jurisprudence of our country, it must arise from the peculiar character of the case. ...

[Marshall then analyzed the "peculiar character" of the case and found nothing that exempted it from the usual rules of law.]

It is, then, the opinion of the Court,

1st. That by signing the commission of Mr. Marbury, the President of the United States appointed him a justice of peace for the county of Washington, in the District of Columbia; and that the seal of the United States, affixed thereto by the Secretary of State, is conclusive testimony of the verity of the signature, and of the completion of the appointment; and that the appointment conferred on him a legal right to the office for the space of five years.

2d. That, having this legal title to the office, he has a consequent right to the commission; a refusal to deliver which is a plain violation of that right, for which the laws of his country afford him a remedy.

It remains to be inquired whether,

3d. He is entitled to the remedy for which he applies. This depends on,

1st. The nature of the writ applied for; and,

2d. The power of this court.

1st. The nature of the writ. ...

This writ [of mandamus], if awarded, would be directed to an officer of government [the Secretary of State], and its mandate to him would be, to use the words of Blackstone, "to do a particular thing therein specified, which appertains to his office and duty, and which the court has previously determined, or at least supposes, to be consonant to right and justice." ...

These circumstances certainly concur in this case. ...

... The intimate political relation subsisting between the President of the United States and the heads of departments, necessarily renders any legal investigation of the acts of one of those high officers peculiarly irksome, as well as delicate; and excites some hesitation with respect to the propriety of entering into such investigation. ...

It is scarcely necessary for the court to disclaim all pretensions to such jurisdiction. An extravagance, so absurd and excessive, could not have been entertained for a moment. The province of the court is, solely, to decide on the rights of individuals, not to inquire how the executive, or executive officers, perform duties in which they have a discretion. Questions in their nature political, or which are, by the constitution and laws, submitted to the executive, can never be made in this court. ...

[But i]f one of the heads of departments commits an illegal act, under colour of his office, by which an individual sustains an injury, it cannot be pretended that his office alone exempts him from being sued in the ordinary mode of proceeding, and being compelled to obey the judgment of the law. ...

The act to establish the judicial courts of the United States authorizes the Supreme Court "to issue writs of mandamus in cases warranted by the principles and usages of law, to any courts appointed, or persons holding office, under the authority of the United States."

The Secretary of State, being a person holding an office under the authority of the United States, is precisely within the letter of the description, and if this court is not authorized to issue a writ of mandamus to such an officer, it must be because the law is unconstitutional, and therefore absolutely incapable of conferring the authority, and assigning the duties which its words purport to confer and assign.

The constitution vests the whole judicial power of the United States in one Supreme Court, and such inferior courts as congress shall, from time to time, ordain and establish. This power is expressly extended to all cases arising under the laws of the United States; and, consequently, in some form, may be exercised over the present case; because the right claimed is given by a law of the United States.

In the distribution of this power it is declared that "the Supreme Court shall have original jurisdiction in all cases affecting ambassadors, other public ministers and consuls, and those in which a state shall be a party. In all other cases, the Supreme Court shall have appellate jurisdiction." ...

If it had been intended to leave it in the discretion of the legislature to apportion the judicial power between the supreme and inferior courts according to the will of that body, it would certainly have been useless to have proceeded further than to have defined the judicial power, and the tribunals in which it should be vested. ... If congress remains at liberty to give this court appellate jurisdiction, where the constitution has declared their jurisdiction shall be original; and original jurisdiction where the constitution has declared it shall be appellate; the distribution of jurisdiction, made in the constitution, is form without substance.

Affirmative words are often, in their operation, negative of other objects than those affirmed; and in this case, a negative or exclusive sense must be given to them, or they have no operation at all.

It cannot be presumed that any clause in the constitution is intended to be without effect; and, therefore, such a construction is inadmissible, unless the words require it. . . .

To enable this court, then, to issue a mandamus, it must be shown to be an exercise of appellate jurisdiction, or to be necessary to enable them to exercise appellate jurisdiction. . . .

It is the essential criterion of appellate jurisdiction, that it revises and corrects the proceedings in a cause already instituted, and does not create that cause. Although, therefore, a mandamus may be directed to courts, yet to issue such a writ to an officer for the delivery of a paper, is in effect the same as to sustain an original action for that paper, and, therefore, seems not to belong to appellate, but to original jurisdiction. . . .

The authority, therefore, given to the Supreme Court, by the act establishing the judicial courts of the United States, to issue writs of mandamus to public officers, appears not to be warranted by the constitution; * and it becomes necessary to inquire whether a jurisdiction so conferred can be exercised.

The question, whether an act, repugnant to the constitution, can become the law of the land, is a question deeply interesting to the United States; but, happily, not of an intricacy proportioned to its interest. It seems only necessary to recognize certain principles, supposed to have been long and well established, to decide it.

That the people have an original right to establish, for their future government, such principles, as, in their opinion, shall most conduce to their own happiness is the basis on which the whole American fabric has been erected. The exercise of this original right is a very great exertion; nor can it, nor ought it, to be frequently repeated. The principles, therefore, so established, are deemed fundamental. And as the authority from which they proceed is supreme, and can seldom act, they are designed to be permanent.

This original and supreme will organizes the government, and assigns to different departments their respective powers. It may either

---

* **Eds.' Note**—Section 13 of the Judiciary Act of 1789, which Marbury was claiming conferred authority on the Supreme Court to hear his case under the Court's original jurisdiction, read:

The Supreme Court shall also have appellate jurisdiction from the circuit courts [of the United States] and courts of the several states, in the cases herein after specifically provided for; and shall have power to issue writs of prohibition to the district courts [of the United States], when proceeding as courts of admiralty and maritime jurisdiction, and writs of mandamus, in cases warranted by the principles and usages of law, to any courts appointed, or persons holding office, under the authority of the United States.

Query: Is Marshall's contention that Section 13 attempted to confer additional original jurisdiction on the Supreme Court based on a fair reading of the plain words of the statute?

stop here, or establish certain limits not to be transcended by those departments.

The government of the United States is of the latter description. The powers of the legislature are defined and limited; and that those limits may not be mistaken, or forgotten, the constitution is written. To what purpose are powers limited, and to what purpose is that limitation committed to writing, if these limits may, at any time, be passed by those intended to be restrained? The distinction between a government with limited and unlimited powers is abolished, if those limits do not confine the persons on whom they are imposed, and if acts prohibited and acts allowed, are of equal obligation. It is a proposition too plain to be contested, [either] that the constitution controls any legislative act repugnant to it; or, that the legislature may alter the constitution by an ordinary act.

Between these alternatives there is no middle ground. The constitution is either a superior paramount law, unchangeable by ordinary means, or it is on a level with ordinary legislative acts, and, like other acts, is alterable when the legislature shall please to alter it.

If the former part of the alternative be true, then a legislative act contrary to the constitution is not law: if the latter part be true, then written constitutions are absurd attempts, on the part of the people, to limit a power in its own nature illimitable.

Certainly all those who have framed written constitutions contemplate them as forming the fundamental and paramount law of the nation, and, consequently, the theory of every such government must be, that an act of the legislature, repugnant to the constitution, is void.

This theory is essentially attached to a written constitution, and, is consequently, to be considered, by this court, as one of the fundamental principles of our society. ...

If an act of the legislature, repugnant to the constitution, is void, does it, notwithstanding its invalidity, bind the courts, and oblige them to give it effect? ... This would be to overthrow in fact what was established in theory; and would seem, at first view, an absurdity too gross to be insisted on. It shall, however, receive a more attentive consideration.

It is emphatically the province and duty of the judicial department to say what the law is. Those who apply the rule to particular cases, must of necessity expound and interpret that rule. If two laws conflict with each other, the courts must decide on the operation of each.

So if a law be in opposition to the constitution; if both the law and the constitution apply to a particular case, so that the court must either decide that case conformably to the law, disregarding the constitution; or conformably to the constitution, disregarding the law; the court must determine which of these conflicting rules governs the case. This is of the very essence of judicial duty.

If, then, the courts are to regard the constitution, and the constitution is superior to any ordinary act of the legislature, the constitution, and not such ordinary act, must govern the case to which they both apply.

Those then who controvert the principle that the constitution is to be considered, in court, as a paramount law, are reduced to the necessity of maintaining that courts must close their eyes on the constitution, and see only the law.

This doctrine would subvert the very foundation of all written constitutions. It would declare that an act which, according to the principles and theory of our government, is entirely void, is yet, in practice, completely obligatory. It would declare that if the legislature shall do what is expressly forbidden, such act, notwithstanding the express prohibition, is in reality effectual. It would be giving to the legislature a practical and real omnipotence, with the same breath which professes to restrict their powers within narrow limits. ...

That it thus reduces to nothing what we have deemed the greatest improvement on political institutions, a written constitution, would of itself be sufficient, in America, where written constitutions have been viewed with so much reverence, for rejecting the construction. But the peculiar expressions of the constitution of the United States furnish additional arguments in favour of its rejection.

The judicial power of the United States is extended to all cases arising under the constitution.

Could it be the intention of those who gave this power, to say that in using it the constitution should not be looked into? That a case arising under the constitution should be decided without examining the instrument under which it arises?

This is too extravagant to be maintained.

In some cases, then, the constitution must be looked into by the judges. And if they can open it at all, what part of it are they forbidden to read or to obey?

There are many other parts of the constitution which serve to illustrate this subject. ...

The constitution declares "that no bill of attainder or ex post facto law shall be passed."

If, however, such a bill should be passed, and a person should be prosecuted under it; must the court condemn to death those victims whom the constitution endeavours to preserve?

"No person," says the constitution, "shall be convicted of treason unless on the testimony of two witnesses to the same overt act, or on confession in open court."

Here the language of the constitution is addressed especially to the courts. It prescribes, directly for them, a rule of evidence not to be departed from. If the legislature should change that rule, and declare one witness, or a confession out of court, sufficient for conviction, must the constitutional principle yield to the legislative act?

From these, and many other selections which might be made, it is apparent, that the framers of the constitution contemplated that instrument as a rule for the government of courts, as well as of the legislature.

Why otherwise does it direct the judges to take an oath to support it? This oath certainly applies, in an especial manner, to their conduct in their official character. How immoral to impose it on them, if they were to be used as the instruments, and the knowing instruments, for violating what they swear to support!

The oath of office, too, imposed by the legislature, is completely demonstrative of the legislative opinion on this subject. It is in these words: "I do solemnly swear that I will administer justice without respect to persons, and do equal right to the poor and to the rich; and that I will faithfully and impartially discharge all the duties incumbent on me as according to the best of my abilities and understanding, agreeably to the constitution and laws of the United States."

Why does a judge swear to discharge his duties agreeably to the constitution of the United States, if that constitution forms no rule for his government? ...

If such be the real state of things, this is worse than solemn mockery. To prescribe, or to take this oath, becomes equally a crime.*

It is also not entirely unworthy of observation, that in declaring what shall be the supreme law of the land, the constitution itself is first mentioned; and not the laws of the United States generally, but those only which shall be made in pursuance of the constitution, have that rank.

Thus, the particular phraseology of the constitution of the United States confirms and strengthens the principle, supposed to be essential to all written constitutions, that a law repugnant to the constitution is void; and that courts, as well as other departments, are bound by that instrument.

The rule must be *discharged.*

Editors' Notes

(1) **Query**: Does Marshall assert that the judiciary has an exclusive or even primary authority in constitutional interpretation? Does he claim that other branches of government, in their operations, are bound by judicial interpretations of "the Constitution"? Compare the reach of Marshall's reasoning with that of the Court in Cooper v. Aaron (1958), reprinted below, p. 375.

---

* See Justice John Gibson's response to Marshall's claim that the judicial oath requires judicial review: Eakin v. Raub (1825; reprinted below, p. 308).—**Eds.**

(2) **Query**: How does Marshall's reasoning about the Court's authority in constitutional interpretation differ from that of Brutus? Hamilton? Morris?

(3) On p. 301 Marshall spoke of questions involving presidential discretion as "in their nature political" and beyond the purview of courts. Here we have the origins of the so-called doctrine of political questions, to which the introductory essay alluded and later readings will illustrate. See espec. Baker v. Carr (1962; reprinted below, p. 769).

(4) For important analyses of *Marbury,* see espec.: Albert J. Beveridge, *The Life of John Marshall* (Boston: Houghton Mifflin Co., 1919), III, ch. 3; Charles Warren, *The Supreme Court in United States History* (Rev. ed.; Boston: Little, Brown, and Co., 1926), I, chs. 4–5; Robert K. Faulkner, *The Jurisprudence of John Marshall* (Princeton: Princeton University Press, 1968), pp. 192–223; William Van Alstyne, "A Critical Guide to Marbury v. Madison," 1969 *Duke L.J.* 1; George L. Haskins and Herbert A. Johnson, *History of the Supreme Court of the United States,* Vol. II: *Foundations of Power: John Marshall, 1801–1815* (New York: Macmillan, 1981), chs. 5–6.

"The Constitution intended that the three great branches of government should be co-ordinate, & independent of each other. As to acts, therefore, which are to be done by either, it has given no controul to another branch."

JEFFERSON INSTRUCTS A FEDERAL PROSECUTOR
(1807).

Marshall's cunning handling of Marbury v. Madison was a masterpiece of political strategy. He had, more firmly than the justices' letters to President Washington in Hayburn's Case (1792) or the judgment in United States v. Todd (1794), proclaimed the doctrine of judicial review and had done so without issuing an order that Jefferson could flout. The reaction of the President's followers to *Marbury* was one of outrage; but, curiously, attention focused less on Marshall's assertion of judicial power to annul acts of Congress than on the opening sections of the opinion in which the Chief Justice had ruled that Jefferson, that ardent civil libertarian, had violated Marbury's legal right to his commission.

Marbury chose not to seek redress in a lower court, and so the case quietly died. The Jeffersonians turned their energies to further cleansing the bench of Federalists. The House impeached and the Senate convicted and removed a district judge from New Hampshire. The House then impeached one of Marshall's colleagues, Justice Samuel Chase. In addressing grand and trial juries proceeding under the Sedition Act, he had flagrantly abused his power so as to ensure that Jeffersonians would be punished for their political views. Nevertheless, the President's men could not muster the necessary two-thirds vote in the Senate for conviction.

That same year, 1804, Marshall deftly advanced judicial power another long step by asserting authority to sit in constitutional judgment over presidential acts. In Little v. Barreme (reprinted below, p. 435), he held for the Court that President Adams had exceeded his lawful authority in carrying out the quasi-naval war with France in the late 1790s. The justices affirmed a district court order to a naval captain to return to its owners a ship seized in a blockade of French ports in the West Indies. Jefferson might have commanded the navy to ignore the order had it not been for the fact that, at the time Adams had ordered the blockade, Jefferson had openly opposed the policy. Thus Marshall neatly skewered the President again.

In 1807, Jefferson's decision to prosecute Aaron Burr, his former vice president, for treason provided another battlefield. The federal court that had jurisdiction to conduct the trial was located in Virginia; and, because of the repeal of the Act of 1801, Supreme Court justices were again riding circuit, and Burr's tribunal was presided over by the Chief Justice. Anticipating that Marshall would issue a subpoena to the White House to forward various papers relating to earlier reports of a key witness for the government, Jefferson informed the prosecutor that he would "voluntarily" provide "whatever the purposes of justice may require," at the same time reserving "the necessary right of the President of the U S to decide, independently of all other authority, what papers, coming to him as President, the public interests permit to be communicated, & to whom. ..." In addition, the President gave special instructions regarding the government's position about Marbury v. Madison:

Washington, June 2, 07.

DEAR SIR,—While Burr's case is depending before the court, I will trouble you, from time to time, with what occurs to me. I observe that the case of Marbury v. Madison has been cited, and I think it material to stop at the threshold the citing that case as authority, and to have it denied to be law. 1. Because the judges, in the outset, disclaimed all cognizance of the case, altho' they then went on to say what would have been their opinion, had they had cognizance of it. This, then, was confessedly an extrajudicial opinion, and, as such, of no authority. 2. Because, had it been judicially pronounced, it would have been against law; for to a commission, a deed, a bond, *delivery* is essential to give validity. Until, therefore, the commission is delivered out of the hands of the Executive & his agents, it is not his deed. He may withhold or cancel it at pleasure, as he might his private deed in the same situation. The Constitution intended that the three great branches of the government should be co-ordinate, & independent of each other. As to acts, therefore, which are to be done by either, it has given no controul to another branch. A judge, I presume, cannot sit on a bench without a commission, or a record of a commission; & the Constitution having given to the judiciary branch no means of compelling the executive either to *deliver* a commission, or to make a record of it, shews it did not intend to give the judiciary that controul over the executive, but that it should remain in the power of the latter to do it or not. Where different branches have to act in their respective lines, finally & without appeal, under any law, they may give to it different and opposite constructions. ... In the cases of Callendar & some others, the judges determined the sedition act was valid under the Constitution, and exercised their regular powers of sentencing them to fine & imprisonment.   But the executive determined that the sedition act was a nullity under the Constitution, and exercised his regular power of prohibiting the execution of the sentence.   ...

On this construction I have hitherto acted; on this I shall ever act, and maintain it with the powers of the government, against any control which may be attempted by the judges, in subversion of the independence of the executive & Senate within their peculiar department.   I presume, therefore, that in a case where our decision is by the Constitution the supreme one, & that which can be carried into effect, it is the constitutionally authoritative one, and that by the judges was *coram non judice,* & unauthoritative, because it cannot be carried into effect.   I have long wished for a proper occasion to have the gratuitous opinion in Marbury v. Madison brought before the public, & denounced as not law; & I think the present a fortunate one, because it occupies such a place in the public attention.   I should be glad, therefore, if, in noticing that case, you could take occasion to express the determination of the executive, that the doctrines of that case were given extrajudicially & against law, and that their reverse will be the rule of action with the executive.   ...

Marshall did issue the subpoena.   Not out of recognition of the court's authority but to promote justice, Jefferson complied with most of its terms.   He also drafted a letter to the federal marshal of the circuit court instructing him not to try to enforce the subpoena.   The Chief Justice did not press the matter, though Burr's attorneys asked the court to enforce full compliance with the writ.

"The grant of a power so extraordinary ought to appear so plain, that he who should run might read."

EAKIN v. RAUB

12 Sergeant & Rawle 330 (Supreme Court of Pennsylvania) (1825).

Measured by substantive standards, this case from the Supreme Court of Pennsylvania was trivial.   It is important for constitutional interpretation because Justice John Gibson wrote a dissenting opinion that made a straightforward attack on Marshall's reasoning in *Marbury*.

GIBSON, J. ...

... I begin, then, by observing that in this country, the powers of the judiciary are divisible into those that are POLITICAL and those that are purely CIVIL. Every power by which one organ of the government is enabled to control another, or to exert an influence over its acts, is a political power. ... [The judiciary's] civil, are its *ordinary* and *appropriate* powers; being part of its essence, and existing independently of any supposed grant in the constitution. But where the government exists by virtue of a *written* constitution, the judiciary does not necessarily derive from that circumstance, any other than its ordinary and appropriate powers. Our judiciary is constructed on the principles of the common law, which enters so essentially into the composition of our social institutions as to be inseparable from them, and to be, in fact, the basis of the whole scheme of our civil and political liberty. In adopting any organ or instrument of the common law, we take it with just such powers and capacities as were incident to it at the common law, except where these are expressly, or by necessary implication, abridged or enlarged in the act of adoption; and, that such act is a written instrument, cannot vary its consequences or construction. ... Now, what are the powers of the judiciary at the common law? They are those that necessarily arise out of its immediate business; and they are therefore commensurate only with the judicial execution of the municipal law, or, in other words, with the administration of distributive justice, without extending to anything of a political cast whatever. ... With us, although the legislature be the depository of only so much of the sovereignty as the people have thought fit to impart, it is nevertheless sovereign within the limit of its powers, and may relatively claim the same pre-eminence here that it may claim elsewhere. It will be conceded, then, that the ordinary and essential powers of the judiciary do not extend to the annulling of an act of the legislature. ...

The constitution of *Pennsylvania* [like that of the United States] contains no express grant of political powers to the judiciary. But, to establish a grant by implication, the constitution is said to be a law of superior obligation; and, consequently, that if it were to come into collision with an act of the legislature, the latter would have to give way. This is conceded. But it is a fallacy, to suppose that they can come into collision *before the judiciary*. ...

The constitution and the right of the legislature to pass the act, may be in collision. But is that a legitimate subject for judicial determination? If it be, the judiciary must be a peculiar organ, to revise the proceedings of the legislature, and to correct its mistakes; and in what part of the constitution are we to look for this proud pre-eminence? Viewing the matter in the opposite direction, what would be thought of an act of assembly in which it should be declared that the Supreme Court had, in a particular case, put a wrong construction on the constitution of the United States, and that the judgment should therefore be reversed? It would doubtless be thought a usurpation of judicial power. But it is by no means clear, that to declare a law void which has been enacted according to the forms prescribed in the constitution, is not a usurpation of legislative power. ...

But it has been said to be emphatically the business of the judiciary, to ascertain and pronounce what the law is; and that this necessarily involves a consideration of the constitution. It does so: but how far? If the judiciary will inquire into anything besides the form of enactment, where shall it stop? There must be some point of limitation to such an inquiry; for no one will pretend that a judge would be justifiable in calling for the election returns, or scrutinizing the qualifications of those who composed the legislature. ...

... In theory, all the organs of the government are of equal capacity; or, if not equal, each must be supposed to have superior capacity only for those things which peculiarly belong to it; and, as legislation peculiarly involves the consideration of those limitations which are put on the law-making power, and the interpretation of the laws when made, involves only the construction of the laws themselves, it follows that the construction of the constitution in this particular belongs to the legislature, which ought therefore to be taken to have superior capacity to judge of the constitutionality of its own acts. But suppose all to be of equal capacity in every respect, why should one exercise a controlling power over the rest? That the judiciary is of superior rank, has never been pretended, although it has been said to be coordinate. It is not easy, however, to comprehend how the power which gives law to all the rest, can be of no more than equal rank with one which receives it, and is answerable to the former for the observance of its statutes. Legislation is essentially an act of sovereign power; but the execution of the laws by instruments that are governed by prescribed rules and exercise no power of volition, is essentially otherwise. ... It may be said, the power of the legislature, also, is limited by prescribed rules. It is so. But it is, nevertheless, the power of the people, and sovereign as far as it extends. It cannot be said, that the judiciary is co-ordinate merely because it is established by the constitution. ... Inequality of rank arises not from the manner in which the organ has been constituted, but from its essence and the nature of its functions; and the legislative organ is superior to every other, inasmuch as the power to will and to command, is essentially superior to the power to act and to obey. ...

... [H]ad it been intended to interpose the judiciary as an additional barrier, the matter would surely not have been left in doubt. The judges would not have been left to stand on the insecure and ever shifting ground of public opinion as to constructive powers; they would have been placed on the impregnable ground of an express grant. They would not have been compelled to resort to the debates in the convention, or the opinion that was generally entertained at the time. ... The grant of a power so extraordinary ought to appear so plain, that he who should run might read. ...

What I have in view in this inquiry, is the supposed right of the judiciary to interfere, in cases where the constitution is to be carried into effect through the instrumentality of the legislature, and where that organ must necessarily first decide on the constitutionality of its own act. The oath to support the constitution is not peculiar to the judges, but is taken indiscriminately by every officer of the government, and is designed rather as a test of the political principles of the man, than to bind the officer in the discharge of his duty: otherwise it is difficult to determine what operation it is to have in the case of a recorder of deeds, for instance, who, in the execution of his office, has nothing to do with the constitution. But granting it to relate to the official conduct of the judge, as well as every other officer, and not to his political principles, still it must be understood in reference to supporting the constitution, *only as far as that may be involved in his official duty;* and, consequently, if his official duty does not comprehend an inquiry into the authority of the legislature, neither does his oath. ...

But do not the judges do a positive act in violation of the constitution, when they give effect to an unconstitutional law? Not if the law has been passed according to the forms established in the constitution. The fallacy of the question is, in supposing that the judiciary adopts the acts of the legislature as its own; whereas the enactment of a law and the interpretation of it are not concurrent acts, and as the judiciary is not required to concur in the enactment, neither is it in the breach of the constitution which may be the consequence of the enactment. The fault is imputable to the legislature, and on it the responsibility exclusively rests. ...

But it has been said, that this construction would deprive the citizen of the advantages which are peculiar to a written constitution, by at once declaring the power of the legislature in practice to be illimitable. ... But there is no magic or inherent power in parchment and ink, to command respect and protect principles from violation. In the business of government a recurrence to first principles answers the end of an observation at sea with a view to correct the dead reckoning; and for this purpose, a written constitution is an instrument of inestimable value. It is of inestimable value, also, in rendering its first principles familiar to the mass of people; for, after all, there is no effectual guard against legislative usurpation but public opinion, the force of which, in this country is inconceivably great. ... Once let public opinion be so corrupt as to sanction every misconstruction of the constitution and abuse of power which the temptation of the moment may dictate, and the party which may happen to be predominant, will laugh at the puny efforts of a dependent power to arrest it in its course.

For these reasons, I am of opinion that it rests with the people, in whom full and absolute sovereign power resides, to correct abuses in legislation, by instructing their representatives to repeal the obnoxious act. ... On the other hand, the judiciary is not infallible; and an error by it would admit of no remedy but a more distinct expression of the public will, through the extraordinary medium of a convention; whereas, an error by the legislature admits of a remedy by an exertion of the same will, in the ordinary exercise of the right of suffrage,—a mode better calculated to attain the end, without popular excitement. ...

But in regard to an act of [a state] assembly, which is found to be in collision with the constitution, laws, or treaties of the *United States,* I take the duty of the judiciary to be exactly the reverse. By becoming parties to the federal constitution, the states have agreed to several limitations of their individual sovereignty, to enforce which, it was thought to be absolutely necessary to prevent them from giving effect to laws in violation of those limitations, through the instrumentality of their own judges. Accordingly, it is declared in the sixth article and second section of the federal constitution, that "This constitution, and the laws of the *United States* which shall be made in pursuance thereof, and all treaties made, or which shall be made under the authority of the *United States,* shall be the *supreme* law of the land; and the *judges* in every *state* shall be BOUND thereby: anything in the *laws* or *constitution* of any *state* to the contrary notwithstanding."

This is an express grant of a political power, and it is conclusive to show that no law of inferior obligation, as every state law must necessarily be, can be executed at the expense of the constitution, laws, or treaties of the *United States.* ...

Editors' Notes

(1) **Query:** How effectively did Gibson rebut Marshall's reasoning in *Marbury*? To what extent did Gibson's argument (and Marshall's) depend on a normative political theory outside the constitutional text?

(2) **Query:** To what extent did Gibson's reasoning about the problem of WHO coincide with that of Senator Breckenridge during the debate on the Judiciary Act of 1802?

(3) In 1830 Gibson, who by then was chief justice of Pennsylvania, was touted by the states-rights faction led by John C. Calhoun for a vacancy on the U.S. Supreme Court. President Jackson, however, nominated Henry Baldwin. **Query:** Does the logic of Gibson's dissent in *Eakin* support a states—rights position?

(4) Gibson later changed his mind regarding the authority of Pennsylvania courts to declare acts of the state legislature unconstitutional. He explained the shift as due to the failure of the state constitutional convention that met after *Eakin* to change the clauses that a majority of the court had interpreted to imply that power. Norris v. Clymer, 2 Pa.St. 277 (1845). See Charles Warren, *The Supreme Court in United States History* (Rev. ed.; Boston: Little, Brown, 1926), I, 711–713. Does that change logically affect his argument about authority of courts to declare acts of Congress unconstitutional?

**"The Congress, the Executive, and the Court must each
... be guided by its own opinion of the Constitution."**

ANDREW JACKSON'S VETO OF THE BANK BILL*
(1832).

On July 4, 1832, Congress passed an act to continue the Bank of the United States. On July 10, 1832, President Andrew Jackson vetoed the bank bill as unwise, unfair, and unconstitutional. We reprint the portion of his veto message dealing with the argument that the constitutionality of the Bank had been definitively settled by the decision of the United States Supreme Court in McCulloch v. Maryland (1819). This part of the message was largely drafted by Roger Brooke Taney, who was soon to succeed John Marshall as Chief Justice of the United States and found himself somewhat embarrassed by the common knowledge of his authorship.

It is maintained by the advocates of the bank that its constitutionality in all its features ought to be considered as settled by precedent and by the decision of the Supreme Court. To this conclusion I can not assent. Mere precedent is a dangerous source of authority, and should not be regarded as deciding questions of constitutional power except where the acquiescence of the people and the States can be considered as well settled. So far from this being the case on the subject, an argument against the bank might be based on precedent. One Congress, in 1791, decided in favor of a bank; another, in 1811, decided against. One Congress, in 1815, decided against a bank; another, in 1816, decided in its favor. Prior to the present Congress, therefore, the precedents drawn from that source were equal. If we resort to the States, the expressions of legislative, judicial, and executive opinions against the bank have been probably to those in its favor as 4 to 1. There is nothing in precedent, therefore, which, if its authority were admitted, ought to weigh in favor of the act before me.

If the opinion of the Supreme Court covered the whole ground of this act, it ought not to control the coordinate authorities of this Government. The Congress, the Executive, and the Court must each for itself be guided by its own opinion of the Constitution. Each public officer who takes an oath to support the Constitution swears that he will support it as he understands it, and not as it is understood by others. It is as much the duty of the House of Representatives, of the Senate, and of the President to decide upon the constitutionality of any bill or resolution which may be presented to them for passage or approval as it is of the supreme judges when it may be brought before them for judicial decision. The opinion of the judges has no more authority over Congress than the opinion of Congress has over the judges, and on that point the President is independent of both. The authority of the Supreme

---

*From James D. Richardson (ed.), *A Compilation of the Messages and Papers of the Presidents* (Washington, DC: Bureau of National Literature and Art, 1908), II, 581–582.

Court must not, therefore, be permitted to control the Congress or the Executive when acting in their legislative capacities, but to have only such influence as the force of their reasoning may deserve.

"[I]f the policy ... is to be irrevocably fixed by decisions of the Supreme Court ... the people will have ceased, to be their own rulers. ..."

ABRAHAM LINCOLN'S FIRST INAUGURAL ADDRESS*
(March 4, 1861).

Believing Lincoln's election marked the start of a federal effort to end slavery, southern state legislatures began adopting resolutions of secession and setting about the business of establishing the Confederate States of America. A divided nation was becoming a reality.

Hovering in the background was the specter of the Supreme Court's decision in Dred Scott v. Sandford (1857; reprinted above, p. 195), which had helped polarize the country on the issue of slavery. The Court had ruled: (1) The Framers of the Constitution had meant to exclude blacks from citizenship; (2) Slaves were property; (3) The Fifth Amendment forbade Congress to take a person's property without due process of law, and "due process" had a substantive as well as a procedural aspect; thus Congress could not forbid a man to take his slave into any federal territory or free a slave if he travelled in federal territory; (4) Therefore, the Missouri Compromise and by implication all other political compromises, past and future, to control slavery in the territories were unconstitutional.

If Congress and the president accepted the authority of the Supreme Court to interpret "the Constitution" definitively for them, slavery could spread through the territories as the slaveholders themselves willed, something many if not most northern state officials were not willing to tolerate. It was widely expected, then, that Lincoln would have to attack the Court's authority, since he was on public record as saying that Dred Scott had been wrongly decided.

In addition to the tremendous practical problems of preventing disunion, Lincoln faced a difficult double problem of constitutional interpretation: Defining the nature of the Union and its distribution of authority between state and nation and, at the same time, defining the distribution of authority among the three branches of the federal government.

Fellow citizens of the United States. ...

Apprehension seems to exist among the people of the Southern States, that by the accession of a Republican Administration, their property, and their peace, and personal security, are to be endangered. There has never been any reasonable cause for such apprehension.

Indeed, the most ample evidence to the contrary has all the while existed. ... It is found in nearly all the published speeches of him who now addresses you. I do but quote from one of those speeches when I declare that "I have no purpose, directly or indirectly, to interfere with the institution of slavery in the States where it exists. I believe I have no lawful right to do so, and I have no inclination to do so." Those who nominated and elected me did so with full knowledge that I had made this, and many similar declarations, and had never recanted them. ...

There is much controversy about the delivering up of fugitives from service or labor. The clause I now read is as plainly written in the Constitution as any other of its provisions:

"No person held to service or labor in one State, under the laws thereof, escaping into another, shall, in consequence of any law or regulation therein, be discharged from such service or labor, but shall be delivered up on claim of the party to whom such service or labor may be due."

It is scarcely questioned that this provision was intended by those who made it, for the reclaiming of what we call fugitive slaves; and the intention of the law-giver is the law. All members of Congress swear their support to the whole Constitution—to this provision as much as to any other. To the proposition, then, that slaves whose cases come within the terms of this clause, "shall be delivered up," their oaths are unanimous. Now, if they would make the effort in good temper, could they not, with nearly equal unanimity, frame and pass a law, by means of which to keep good that unanimous oath?

There is some difference of opinion whether this clause should be enforced by national or by state authority; * but surely that difference is not a very material one. ...

Again, in any law upon this subject, ought not all the safeguards of liberty known in civilized and humane jurisprudence to be introduced, so that a free man be not, in any case, surrendered as a slave? And might it not be well, at the same time, to provide by law for the enforcement of that clause in the Constitution which guarranties [sic] that "The citizens of each State shall be entitled to all previleges [sic] and immunities of citizens in the several States?"

I take the official oath to-day, with no mental reservations, and with no purpose to construe the Constitution or laws, by any hypercritical rules. And while I do not choose now to specify particular acts of Congress as proper to be enforced, I do suggest that it will be much safer for all, both in official and private stations, to conform to, and abide by, all those acts which stand unrepealed, than to violate any of them, trusting to find impunity in having them held to be unconstitutional. ...

---

* Lincoln was referring to the Supreme Court's controversial decision in Prigg v. Pennsylvania (1842), which, though upholding the constitutionality of the federal Fugitive Slave Act of 1793, indicated that the national government could not require state officers to assist in the execution of that statute.—**Eds.**

I hold, that in contemplation of universal law, and of the Constitution, the Union of these States is perpetual. Perpetuity is implied, if not expressed, in the fundamental law of all national governments. ...

Descending from these general principles, we find the proposition that, in legal contemplation, the Union is perpetual, confirmed by the history of the Union itself. The Union is much older than the Constitution. It was formed in fact, by the Articles of Association in 1774. It was matured and continued by the Declaration of Independence in 1776. It was further matured and the faith of all the then thirteen States expressly plighted and engaged that it should be perpetual, by the Articles of Confederation in 1778. And finally, in 1787, one of the declared objects for ordaining and establishing the Constitution, was "*to form a more perfect union.*"

But if destruction of the Union, by one, or by a part only, of the States, be lawfully possible, the Union is *less* perfect than before the Constitution, having lost the vital element of perpetuity.

It follows from these views that no State, upon its own mere motion, can lawfully get out of the Union,—that *resolves* and *ordinances* to that effect are legally void; and that acts of violence, within any State or States, against the authority of the United States, are insurrectionary or revolutionary, according to circumstances.

I therefore consider that, in view of the Constitution and the laws, the Union is unbroken; and, to the extent of my ability, I shall take care, as the Constitution itself expressly enjoins upon me, that the laws of the Union be faithfully executed in all the States. Doing this I deem to be only a simple duty on my part; and I shall perform it, so far as practicable, unless my rightful masters, the American people, shall withhold the requisite means, or, in some authoritative manner, direct the contrary. I trust this will not be regarded as a menace, but only as the declared purpose of the Union that it *will* constitutionally defend, and maintain itself.

In doing this there needs to be no bloodshed or violence; and there shall be none, unless it be forced upon the national authority. The power confided to me, will be used to hold, occupy, and possess the property, and places belonging to the government, and to collect the duties and imposts; but beyond what may be necessary for these objects, there will be no invasion—no using of force against, or among the people anywhere. ...

All profess to be content in the Union, if all constitutional rights can be maintained. Is it true, then, that any right, plainly written in the Constitution, has been denied? I think not. ... Think, if you can, of a single instance in which a plainly written provision of the Constitution has ever been denied. If, by the mere force of numbers, a majority should deprive a minority of any clearly written constitutional right, it might, in a moral point of view, justify revolution—certainly would, if such right were a vital one. But such is not our case. All the vital rights of minorities, and of individuals, are so plainly assured to them, by affirmations and negations, guarranties and prohibitions, in the Constitution, that controversies never arise concerning them. But no organic law can ever be framed with a provision specifically applicable to every question which may occur in practical administration. No foresight can anticipate, nor any document of reasonable length contain express provisions for all possible questions. Shall fugitives from labor be surrendered by national or by State authority? The Constitution does not expressly say. *May* Congress prohibit slavery in the territories? The Constitution does not expressly say. *Must* Congress protect slavery in the territories? The Constitution does not expressly say.

From questions of this class spring all our constitutional controversies, and we divide upon them into majorities and minorities. If the minority will not acquiesce, the majority must, or the government must cease. There is no other alternative; for continuing the government, is acquiescence on one side or the other. If a minority, in such case, will secede rather than acquiesce, they make a precedent which, in turn, will divide and ruin them; for a minority of their own will secede from them, whenever a majority refuses to be controlled by such minority. ...

Plainly, the central idea of secession, is the essence of anarchy. A majority, held in restraint by constitutional checks, and limitations, and always changing easily, with deliberate changes of popular opinions and sentiments, is the only true sovereign of a free people. Whoever rejects it, does, of necessity, fly to anarchy or to despotism. Unanimity is impossible; the rule of a minority, as a permanent arrangement, is wholly inadmissible; so that, rejecting the majority principle, anarchy, or despotism in some form, is all that is left.

I do not forget the position assumed by some, that constitutional questions are to be decided by the Supreme Court; nor do I deny that such decisions must be binding in any case, upon the parties to a suit, as to the object of that suit, while they are also entitled to very high respect and consideration, in all parallel cases, by all other departments of the government. And while it is obviously possible that such decision may be erroneous in any given case, still the evil effect following it, being limited to that particular case, with the chance that it may be over-ruled, and never become a precedent for other cases, can better be borne than could the evils of a different practice. At the same time the candid citizen must confess that if the policy of the government, upon vital questions, affecting the whole people, is to be irrevocably fixed by decisions of the Supreme Court, the instant they are made, in ordinary litigation between parties, in personal actions, the people will have ceased, to be their own rulers, having, to that extent, practically resigned their government, into the hands of that eminent tribunal. Nor is there, in this view, any assault upon the court, or the judges. It is a duty, from which they may not shrink, to decide cases properly brought before them; and it is no fault of theirs, if others seek to turn their decisions to political purposes. ...

The Chief Magistrate derives all his authority from the people, and they have conferred none upon him to fix terms for the separation of the States. The people themselves can do this also if they choose; but the executive, as such, has nothing to do with it. His duty is to administer the present government, as it came to his hands, and to transmit it, unimpaired by him, to his successor.

Why should there not be a patient confidence in the ultimate justice of the people? Is there any better, or equal hope, in the world? In our present differences, is either party without faith of being in the right? If the Almighty Ruler of nations, with his eternal truth and justice, be on your side of the North, or on yours of the South, that truth, and that justice, will surely prevail, by the judgment of this great tribunal, the American people. ...

In *your* hands, my dissatisfied fellow countrymen, and not in *mine,* is the momentous issue of civil war. The government will not assail *you.* You can have no conflict, without being yourselves the aggressors. *You* have no oath registered in Heaven to destroy the government, while *I* shall have the most solemn one to "preserve, protect and defend" it.

I am loth to close. We are not enemies, but friends. We must not be enemies. Though passion may have strained, it must not break our bonds of affection. The mystic chords of memory, stretching from every battle-field, and patriot grave, to every living heart and hearthstone, all over this broad land, will yet swell the chorus of the Union, when again touched, as surely they will be, by the better angels of our nature.

Editors' Note

Query: To what extent is Lincoln's argument about the WHO of constitutional interpretation that of a departmentalist? A believer in executive supremacy? Who or what institution is the authority for his claim that under "the Constitution" the "Union of these States is perpetual"?

"We must find a way to take an appeal from the Supreme Court to the Constitution itself."

FRANKLIN D. ROOSEVELT'S SPEECH ON REORGANIZING THE FEDERAL JUDICIARY*
(1937).

During 1935 and 1936, a majority of the Supreme Court waged what was, in effect, a constitutional war against the economic programs that FDR's administration in Washington and some state governments had enacted to cope with the Great Depression. As a result of these decisions, lower federal judges issued 1,600 injunctions against enforcement of federal statutes. Writing to his sister in June, 1936, Justice Harlan Stone commented sadly that

---

* Speech of March 9, 1937. Senate Report No. 711, 75th Cong., 1st Sess., pp. 41–44.

"We seem to have tied Uncle Sam up in a hard knot." During the presidential campaign of 1936, Roosevelt was silent about the justices, but shortly after his second inauguration he announced a plan to authorize the President, with the advice and consent of the Senate, to appoint an additional member of the Supreme Court every time a sitting justice reached the age of 70 and did not retire; the maximum number of justices would be 16—a proposal, which, if enacted into law, would have immediately given FDR six nominations.

Roosevelt's plan encountered heavy and unexpected opposition in Congress; and, as was his custom, he took his case to the people.

In 1933 you and I knew that we must never let our economic system get completely out of joint again—that we could not afford to take the risk of another great depression.

We also became convinced that the only way to avoid a repetition of those dark days was to have a government with power to prevent and to cure the abuses and the inequalities which had thrown that system out of joint.

We then began a program of remedying those abuses and inequalities—to give balance and stability to our economic system—to make it bombproof against the causes of 1929.

Today we are only part way through that program—and recovery is speeding up to a point where the dangers of 1929 are again becoming possible, not this week or month perhaps, but within a year or two.

National laws are needed to complete that program. Individual or local or State effort alone cannot protect us in 1937 any better than 10 years ago. ... The American people have learned from the depression. For in the last three national elections an overwhelming majority of them voted a mandate that the Congress and the President begin the task of providing that protection—not after long years of debate, but now.

The courts, however, have cast doubts on the ability of the elected Congress to protect us against catastrophe by meeting squarely our modern social and economic conditions.

We are at a crisis in our ability to proceed with that protection. ...

I want to talk with you very simply about the need for present action in this crisis—the need to meet the unanswered challenge of one-third of a nation ill-nourished, ill-clad, ill-housed.

Last Thursday I described the American form of government as a three-horse team provided by the Constitution to the American people so that their field might be plowed. The three horses are, of course, the three branches of government—the Congress, the executive, and the courts. Two of the horses are pulling in unison today; the third is not. Those who have intimated that the President of the United States is trying to drive that team overlook the simple fact that the President, as Chief Executive, is himself one of the three horses.

It is the American people themselves who are in the driver's seat.

It is the American people themselves who want the furrow plowed.

It is the American people themselves who expect the third horse to pull in unison with the other two.

I hope that you have reread the Constitution of the United States. Like the Bible, it ought to be read again and again.

It is an easy document to understand when you remember that it was called into being because the Articles of Confederation under which the Original Thirteen States tried to operate after the Revolution showed the need of a National Government with power enough to handle national problems. In its preamble the Constitution states that it was intended to form a more perfect Union and promote the general welfare; and the powers given to the Congress to carry out those purposes can be best described by saying that they were all the powers needed to meet each and every problem which then had a national character and which could not be met by merely local action.

But the framers went further. Having in mind that in succeeding generations many other problems then undreamed of would become national problems, they gave to the Congress the ample broad powers "to levy taxes ... and provide for the common defense and general welfare of the United States."

That, my friends, is what I honestly believe to have been the clear and underlying purpose of the patriots who wrote a Federal Constitution to create a National Government with national power, intended as they said, "to form a more perfect union ... for ourselves and our posterity." . . .

But since the rise of the modern movement for social and economic progress through legislation, the Court has more and more often and more and more boldly asserted a power to veto laws passed by the Congress and State legislatures in complete disregard of this original limitation.

In the last four years the sound rule of giving statutes the benefit of all reasonable doubt has been cast aside. The Court has been acting not as a judicial body, but as a policy-making body.

When the Congress has sought to stabilize national agriculture, to improve the conditions of labor, to safeguard business against unfair competition, to protect our national resources, and in many other ways to serve our clearly national needs, the majority of the Court has been assuming the power to pass on the wisdom of these acts of the Congress—and to approve or disapprove the public policy written into these laws.

That is not only my accusation. It is the accusation of the most distinguished justices of the present Supreme Court. I have not the time to quote to you all the language used by dissenting justices in many of these cases. But in the case holding the Railroad Retirement Act unconstitutional, for instance, Chief Justice Hughes said in a dissenting opinion that the majority opinion was "a departure from sound principles," and placed "an unwarranted limitation upon the commerce clause." And three other justices agreed with him.

In the case holding the A[gricultural] A[djustment] A[ct] unconstitutional, Justice Stone said of the majority opinion that it was a "tortured construction of the Constitution." And two other justices agreed with him.

In the case holding the New York Minimum Wage Law unconstitutional, Justice Stone said that the majority were actually reading into the Constitution their own "personal economic predilections," and that if the legislative power is not left free to choose the methods of solving the problems of poverty, subsistence, and health of large numbers in the community, then "government is to be rendered impotent." And two other justices agreed with him. ...

In the face of such dissenting opinions, it is perfectly clear that as Chief Justice Hughes has said, "We are under a Constitution, but the Constitution is what the judges say it is."

The Court in addition to the proper use of its judicial functions has improperly set itself up as a third House of the Congress—a superlegislature, as one of the justices has called it—reading into the Constitution words and implications which are not there, and which were never intended to be there.

We have, therefore, reached the point as a Nation where we must take action to save the Constitution from the Court and the Court from itself. We must find a way to take an appeal from the Supreme Court to the Constitution itself. We want a Supreme Court which will do justice under the Constitution—not over it. In our courts we want a government of laws and not of men.

I want—as all Americans want—an independent judiciary as proposed by the framers of the Constitution. That means a Supreme Court that will enforce the Constitution as written—that will refuse to amend the Constitution by the arbitrary exercise of judicial power—amendment by judicial say-so. It does not mean a judiciary so independent that it can deny the existence of facts universally recognized. ...

What is my proposal? It is simply this: Whenever a judge or justice of any federal court has reached the age of seventy and does not avail himself of the opportunity to retire on a pension, a new member shall be appointed by the President then in office, with the approval, as required by the Constitution, of the Senate of the United States.

That plan has two chief purposes: By bringing into the judicial system a steady and continuing stream of new and younger blood, I hope, first, to make the administration of all federal justice speedier and therefore less costly; secondly, to bring to the decision of social and economic problems younger men who have had personal experience and contact with modern facts and circumstances under which average men have to live and work. This plan will save our National Constitution from hardening of the judicial arteries. . . .

Those opposing this plan have sought to arouse prejudice and fear by crying that I am seeking to "pack" the Supreme Court and that a baneful precedent will be established.

What do they mean by the words "packing the Court"?

Let me answer this question with a bluntness that will end all honest misunderstanding of my purposes.

If by that phrase "packing the Court" it is charged that I wish to place on the bench spineless puppets who would disregard the law and would decide specific cases as I wished them to be decided, I make this answer: That no President fit for his office would appoint, and no Senate of honorable men fit for their office would confirm, that kind of appointees to the Supreme Court.

But if by that phrase the charge is made that I would appoint and the Senate would confirm justices worthy to sit beside present members of the Court who understand those modern conditions; that I will appoint justices who will not undertake to override the judgment of the Congress on legislative policy; that I will appoint justices who will act as justices and not as legislators—if the appointment of such justices can be called "packing the Courts"—then I say that I, and with me the vast majority of the American people, favor doing just that thing—now. . . . Our difficulty with the Court today rises not from the Court as an institution but from human beings within it. But we cannot yield our constitutional destiny to the personal judgment of a few men who, being fearful of the future, would deny us the necessary means of dealing with the present.

This plan of mine is no attack on the Court; it seeks to restore the Court to its rightful and historic place in our system of constitutional government and to have it resume its high task of building anew on the Constitution "a system of living law." . . .

Editors' Notes

(1) **Query:** Roosevelt was implicitly making a kind of departmentalist argument. How did it differ from Jefferson's departmentalism? Was FDR, again implicitly, invoking a normative political theory to support his proposal?

(2) The Senate mangled Roosevelt's plan to increase the number of justices. The bill that eventually passed left that number at nine, but Congress liberalized pensions for judges, making retirement more attractive. Very soon thereafter, Justice Willis Van Devanter, one of the dreaded "Four Horseman" who had voted against the validity of almost every New Deal measure that had come before the Court, announced his retirement, part of a compromise worked out among senators. Within the next seven years Roosevelt was able to name the replacements for eight of the justices sitting in 1937. Moreover, as observed earlier, some of the older justices had begun to change their

minds shortly after the election of 1936 and before FDR announced his plan—though unfortunately for the Court's reputation that change did not become public until after the President had launched his attack. The result was, as the saying went, that Roosevelt lost the battle but won the war against the Supreme Court.

"[W]e must weigh the importance of the general privilege of confidentiality of presidential communications . . . against the inroads of such a privilege on the fair administration of criminal justice."

UNITED STATES v. NIXON

418 U.S. 683, 94 S.Ct. 3090, 41 L.Ed.2d 1039 (1974).

Following the indictment of seven high-ranking White House officials—including former special presidential assistants H.R. Haldeman and John Ehrlichman and former attorney general John Mitchell—for conspiracy to defraud the U.S. government and obstruction of justice, the special prosecutor obtained a subpoena directing President Richard M. Nixon to deliver to the trial judge certain tape recordings and memoranda of conversations held in the White House. The trial judge would then examine those tapes and documents and give to the prosecution and defense those portions relevant to the issues at the trial. The remainder would be returned to the President. Nixon produced some of the subpoenaed material but withheld other portions, invoking executive privilege, which, he claimed, placed confidential presidential documents beyond judicial control. The trial judge denied the President's claim, and he appealed to the court of appeals. The special prosecutor asked the Supreme Court to review the case before the court of appeals had passed judgment, and the justices agreed.

Mr. Chief Justice **BURGER** delivered the opinion of the Court. . . .

A

. . . [W]e turn to the claim that the subpoena should be quashed because it demands "confidential conversations between a President and his close advisors that it would be inconsistent with the public interest to produce." . . . The first contention is a broad claim that the separation of powers doctrine precludes judicial review of a President's claim of privilege. The second contention is that if he does not prevail on the claim of absolute privilege, the court should hold as a matter of constitutional law that the privilege prevails over the subpoena *duces tecum*.

In the performance of assigned constitutional duties each branch of the Government must initially interpret the Constitution, and the interpretation of its powers by any branch is due great respect from the others. The President's counsel . . . reads the Constitution as providing an absolute privilege of confidentiality for all presidential communications. Many decisions of this Court, however, have unequivocally reaffirmed the holding of Marbury v. Madison [1803] . . . that "it is emphatically the province and duty of the judicial department to say what the law is." . . .

No holding of the Court has defined the scope of judicial power specifically relating to the enforcement of a subpoena for confidential presidential communications for use in a criminal prosecution, but other exercises of powers by the Executive Branch and the Legislative Branch have been found invalid as in conflict with the Constitution. Powell v. McCormack [1969] . . . Youngstown [Sheet & Tube Co. v. Sawyer (1952)]. . . . Since this Court has consistently exercised the power to construe and delineate claims arising under express powers, it must follow that the Court has authority to interpret claims with respect to powers alleged to derive from enumerated powers. . . .

B

In support of his claim of absolute privilege, the President's counsel urges two grounds one of which is common to all governments and one of which is peculiar to our system of separation of powers. The first ground is the valid need for protection of communications between high government officials and those who advise and assist them in the performance of their manifold duties; the importance of this confidentiality is too plain to require further discussion. . . . Whatever the nature of the privilege of confidentiality of presidential communications in the exercise of Art. II powers, the privilege can be said to derive from the supremacy of each branch within its own assigned area of constitutional duties. Certain powers and privileges flow from the nature of enumerated powers; the protection of the confidentiality of presidential communications has similar constitutional underpinnings.

The second ground asserted by the President's counsel in support of the claim of absolute privilege rests on the doctrine of separation of powers. Here it is argued that the independence of the Executive Branch within its own sphere . . . insulates a President from a judicial subpoena in an ongoing criminal prosecution. . . .

However, neither the doctrine of separation of powers, nor the need for confidentiality of high level communications, without more, can sustain an absolute, unqualified presidential privilege of immunity from judicial process under all circumstances. The President's need for complete candor and objectivity from advisers calls for great deference from the courts. However, when the privilege depends solely on the broad, undifferentiated claim of public interest in the confidentiality of such conversations, a confrontation with other values arises. Absent a claim of need to protect military, diplomatic or sensitive national security secrets, we find it difficult to accept the argument that even the very important interest in confidentiality of presidential communications is significantly diminished by production of such material for *in camera* inspection with all the protection that a district court will be obliged to provide.

The impediment that an absolute, unqualified privilege would place in the way of the primary constitutional duty of the Judicial Branch to do justice in criminal prosecutions would plainly conflict with the function of the courts under Art. III. In designing the structure of our Government and dividing and allocating the sovereign power among three coequal branches, the Framers of the Constitution sought to provide a comprehensive system, but the separate powers were not intended to operate with absolute independence.

> While the Constitution diffuses power the better to secure liberty, it also contemplates that practice will integrate the dispersed powers into a workable government. It enjoins upon its branches separateness but interdependence, autonomy but reciprocity. *Youngstown* (Jackson, J., concurring). ...

C

Since we conclude that the legitimate needs of the judicial process may outweigh presidential privilege, it is necessary to resolve those competing interests in a manner that preserves the essential functions of each branch. The right and indeed the duty to resolve that question does not free the judiciary from according high respect to the representations made on behalf of the President. United States v. Burr (1807).

The expectation of a President to the confidentiality of his conversations and correspondence, like the claim of confidentiality of judicial deliberations, for example, has all the values to which we accord deference for the privacy of all citizens and added to those values the necessity for protection of the public interest in candid, objective, and even blunt or harsh opinions in presidential decision-making. ... These are the considerations justifying a presumptive privilege for presidential communications. The privilege is fundamental to the operation of government and inextricably rooted in the separation of powers under the Constitution. In Nixon v. Sirica (1973), the Court of Appeals held that such presidential communications are "presumptively privileged," and this position is accepted by both parties in the present litigation. We agree with Mr. Chief Justice Marshall's observation, therefore, that "in no case of this kind would a court be required to proceed against the President as against an ordinary individual." *Burr.*

But this presumptive privilege must be considered in light of our historic commitment to the rule of law. This is nowhere more profoundly manifest than in our view that "the twofold aim [of criminal justice] is that guilt shall not escape or innocence suffer." Berger v. United States [1935]. We have elected to employ an adversary system of criminal justice in which the parties contest all issues before a court of law. The need to develop all relevant facts in the adversary system is both fundamental and comprehensive. ... The very integrity of the judicial system and public confidence in the system depend on full disclosure of all the facts, within the framework of the rules of evidence. To ensure that justice is done, it is imperative to the function of courts that compulsory process be available for the production of evidence needed either by the prosecution or by the defense. ...

In this case the President ... does not place his claim of privilege on the ground they are military or diplomatic secrets. As to these areas of Art. II duties the courts have traditionally shown the utmost deference to presidential responsibilities. ... No case of the Court ... has extended this high degree of deference to a President's generalized interest in confidentiality. Nowhere in the Constitution ... is there any explicit reference to a privilege of confidentiality, yet to the extent this interest relates to the effective discharge of a President's powers, it is constitutionally based.

The right to the production of all evidence at a criminal trial similarly has constitutional dimensions. The Sixth Amendment explicitly confers upon every defendant in a criminal trial the right "to be confronted with the witnesses against him" and "to have compulsory process for obtaining witnesses in his favor." Moreover, the Fifth Amendment also guarantees that no person shall be deprived of liberty without due process of law. It is the manifest duty of the courts to vindicate those guarantees and to accomplish that it is essential that all relevant and admissible evidence be produced.

In this case we must weigh the importance of the general privilege of confidentiality of presidential communications ... against the inroads of such a privilege on the fair administration of criminal justice. The interest in preserving confidentiality is weighty indeed and entitled to great respect. However, we cannot conclude that advisers will be moved to temper the candor of their remarks by the infrequent occasions of disclosure because of the possibility that such conversations will be called for in the context of a criminal prosecution.

On the other hand, the allowance of the privilege to withhold evidence that is demonstrably relevant in a criminal trial would cut deeply into the guarantee of due process of law and gravely impair the basic function of the courts. A President's acknowledged need for confidentiality in the communications of his office is general in nature, whereas the constitutional need for production of relevant evidence in a criminal proceeding is specific and central to the fair adjudication of a particular criminal case in the administration of justice. Without access to specific facts a criminal prosecution may be totally frustrated. ...

We conclude that when the ground for asserting privilege as to subpoenaed materials sought for use in a criminal trial is based only on the generalized interest in confidentiality, it cannot prevail over the fundamental demands of due process of law in the fair administration of criminal justice. The generalized assertion of privilege must yield to the demonstrated, specific need for evidence in a pending criminal trial. ...

D

Enforcement of the subpoena *duces tecum* was stayed pending this Court's resolution of the issues raised by the petitions for certiorari.

Those issues now having been disposed of, the matter of implementation will rest with the District Court. ... Statements that meet the test of admissibility and relevance must be isolated; all other material must be excised. ... We have no doubt that the District Judge will at all times accord to presidential records that high degree of deference suggested in *Burr*. ...

Affirmed.

Mr. Justice **REHNQUIST** took no part in the consideration or decision of these cases.

Editors' Notes

(1) **Query:** Earlier we saw critics of judicial review like Senator Breckenridge and Justice Gibson protest that such authority did not appear in the constitutional text. Where does that text mention "executive privilege"? How did Burger justify its inclusion in "the Constitution"?

(2) **Query:** To what extent was Burger asserting judicial supremacy in constitutional interpretation? To what extent was he putting forth a modified form of departmentalism?

(3) **Query:** Practical political considerations aside, would Nixon have been constitutionally justified in refusing to comply with the Court's mandate? Why or why not? What would Jefferson have said? Jackson? Lincoln? Franklin Roosevelt? James Madison?

(4) Because the subpoenaed tapes revealed that Nixon had publicly lied about his knowledge of and participation in felonious acts to obstruct justice, he seriously considered disobeying the Court's ruling. Shortly after the decision, however, the House Judiciary Committee favorably reported a bill of impeachment, and defiance of the Court would have probably meant even worse catastrophe. Release of the tapes was quickly followed by Nixon's resignation on August 9, 1974, seventeen days after the Court's decision. One of Gerald Ford's first acts as President was to pardon Nixon for all the crimes he had committed while President.

"**It is not for us to review the congressional resolution of these factors.**"—Justice **BRENNAN**

"**[I]t is a judicial question whether the condition with which Congress has ... sought to deal is in truth an infringement of the Constitution. ...**"—Justice **HARLAN**

KATZENBACH v. MORGAN

384 U.S. 641, 86 S.Ct. 1717, 16 L.Ed.2d 828 (1966).

In 1959, in Lassiter v. Northampton County, the Supreme Court unanimously sustained the constitutionality under the Fourteenth Amendment of a state requirement that voters be able to read and write English. Congress, however, included as § 4(e) of the Voting Rights Act of 1965 a ban against any state's denying the right to vote to any person who had completed the sixth grade in the United States or Puerto Rico, regardless of the language in which the school was taught and regardless of whether that person could read or write English. A group of registered voters in New York sued in a U.S. district court and obtained an injunction against enforcement of § 4(e) as a violation of the Tenth Amendment. The United States appealed directly to the Supreme Court.

Mr. Justice **BRENNAN** delivered the opinion of the Court. ...

... We hold that, in the application challenged in these cases, § 4(e) is a proper exercise of the powers granted to Congress by § 5 of the Fourteenth Amendment and that by force of the Supremacy Clause, Article VI, the New York English literacy requirement cannot be enforced to the extent that it is inconsistent with § 4(e).

Under the distribution of powers effected by the Constitution, the States establish qualifications for voting for state officers, and the qualifications established by the States for voting for members of the most numerous branch of the state legislature also determine who may vote for United States Representatives and Senators, Art I, § 2; Seventeenth Amendment; Ex parte Yarbrough [1884]. But, of course, the States have no power to grant or withhold the franchise on conditions that are forbidden by the Fourteenth Amendment, or any other provision of the Constitution. ...

... As was said with regard to § 5 [of the Fourteenth Amendment] in Ex parte Virginia [1880]:

> It is the power of Congress which has been enlarged. Congress is authorized to *enforce* the prohibitions by appropriate legislation. Some legislation is contemplated to make the amendments fully effective.

A construction of § 5 that would require a judicial determination that the enforcement of the state law precluded by Congress violated the Amendment, as a condition of sustaining the congressional enactment, would depreciate both congressional resourcefulness and congressional responsibility for implementing the Amendment. It would confine the legislative power in this context to the insignificant role of abrogating only those state laws that the judicial branch was prepared to adjudge unconstitutional, or of merely informing the judgment of the judiciary by particularizing the "majestic generalities" of § 1 of the Amendment. See Fay v. New York [1947].

Thus our task in this case is not to determine whether the New York English literacy requirement as applied to deny the right to vote to a person who successfully completed the sixth grade in a Puerto Rican school violates the Equal Protection Clause. Accordingly, our decision in Lassiter v. Northampton Election Bd. [1959] sustaining the North Carolina English literacy requirement as not in all circumstances prohibited by the first sections of the Fourteenth and Fifteenth Amendments, is inapposite. *Lassiter* did not present the question before us here: Without regard to whether the judiciary would find that the Equal Protection

Clause itself nullifies New York's English literacy requirement as so applied, could Congress prohibit the enforcement of the state law by legislating under § 5 of the Fourteenth Amendment? In answering this question, our task is limited to determining whether such legislation is, as required by § 5, appropriate legislation to enforce the Equal Protection Clause.

By including § 5 the draftsmen sought to grant to Congress, by a specific provision applicable to the Fourteenth Amendment, the same broad powers expressed in the Necessary and Proper Clause, Art. I, § 8, cl. 18. The classic formulation of the reach of those two powers was established by Chief Justice Marshall in McCulloch v. Maryland [1819].

> Let the end be legitimate, let it be within the scope of the constitution, and all means which are appropriate, which are plainly adapted to that end, which are not prohibited, but consist with the letter and spirit of the constitution, are constitutional. ...

... Section 2 of the Fifteenth Amendment grants Congress a similar power to enforce by "appropriate legislation" the provisions of that amendment; and we recently held in South Carolina v. Katzenbach [1966] that "[t]he basic test to be applied in a case involving § 2 of the Fifteenth Amendment is the same as in all cases concerning the express powers of Congress with relation to the reserved powers of the States." That test was identified as the one formulated in *McCulloch*.

We therefore proceed to the consideration whether § 4(e) is "appropriate legislation" to enforce the Equal Protection Clause, that is, ... whether it is "plainly adapted to that end" and whether it is not prohibited by but is consistent with "the letter and spirit of the constitution." [1]

There can be no doubt that § 4(e) may be regarded as an enactment to enforce the Equal Protection Clause. Congress explicitly declared that it enacted § 4(e) "to secure the rights under the fourteenth amendment of persons educated in American—flag schools in which the predominant classroom language was other than English." The persons referred to include those who have migrated from the Commonwealth of Puerto Rico to New York and who have been denied the right to vote because of their inability to read and write English, and the Fourteenth Amendment rights referred to include those emanating from the Equal Protection Clause. More specifically, § 4(e) may be viewed as a measure to secure for the Puerto Rican community residing in New York nondiscriminatory treatment by government—both in the imposition of voting qualifications and the provision or administration of governmental services, such as public schools, public housing and law enforcement.

Section 4(e) may be readily seen as "plainly adapted" to furthering these aims of the Equal Protection Clause. The practical effect of § 4(e)

---

1. Contrary to the suggestion of the dissent, § 5 does not grant Congress power to exercise discretion in the other direction and to enact "statutes so as in effect to dilute equal protection and due process decisions of this Court." We emphasize that Congress' power under § 5 is limited to adopting measures to enforce the guarantees of the Amendment; § 5 grants Congress no power to restrict, abrogate, or dilute these guarantees. ... [Footnote by the Court.]

is to prohibit New York from denying the right to vote to large segments of its Puerto Rican community. Congress has thus prohibited the State from denying to that community the right that is "preservative of all rights." Yick Wo v. Hopkins [1886]. This enhanced political power will be helpful in gaining nondiscriminatory treatment in public services for the entire Puerto Rican community. ... It was for Congress, as the branch that made this judgment, to assess and weigh the various conflicting considerations. ... It is not for us to review the congressional resolution of these factors. It is enough that we be able to perceive a basis upon which the Congress might resolve the conflict as it did. There plainly was such a basis to support § 4(e) in the application in question in this case. Any contrary conclusion would require us to be blind to the realities familiar to the legislators.

The result is no different if we confine our inquiry to the question whether § 4(e) was merely legislation aimed at the elimination of an invidious discrimination in establishing voter qualifications. ...

There remains the question whether the congressional remedies adopted in § 4(e) constitute means which are not prohibited by, but are consistent "with the letter and spirit of the constitution." ...

Section 4(e) does not restrict or deny the franchise but in effect extends the franchise to persons who otherwise would be denied it by state law. Thus we need ... only decide whether the challenged limitation on the relief effected in § 4(e) was permissible. In deciding that question, the principle that calls for the closest scrutiny of distinctions in laws *denying* fundamental rights ... is inapplicable. ... Rather ... we are guided by the familiar principles that a "statute is not invalid under the Constitution because it might have gone farther than it did," Roschen v. Ward [1929], that a legislature need not "strike at all evils at the same time," Semler v. Dental Examiners [1935], and that "reform may take one step at a time, addressing itself to the phase of the problem which seems most acute to the legislative mind," Williamson v. Lee Optical Co. [1955].

Guided by these principles, we are satisfied that appellees' challenge to this limitation in § 4(e) is without merit. ...

Reversed.

Mr. Justice **DOUGLAS** joins the Court's opinion except for the discussion ... of the question whether the congressional remedies adopted in § 4(e) constitute means which are not prohibited by, but are consistent with "the letter and spirit of the constitution." On that question he reserves judgment until such time as it is presented by a member of the class against which that particular discrimination is directed.

Mr. Justice **HARLAN**, whom Mr. Justice **STEWART** joins, dissenting.

Worthy as its purposes may be, I do not see how § 4(e) of the Voting Rights Act of 1965 can be sustained except at the sacrifice of fundamentals in the American constitutional system—the separation between the legislative and judicial function and the boundaries between federal and state political authority. ...

When recognized state violations of federal constitutional standards have occurred, Congress is of course empowered by § 5 [of the Fourteenth Amendment] to take appropriate remedial measures to redress and prevent the wrongs. See Strauder v. West Virginia [1880]. But it is a judicial question whether the condition with which Congress has thus sought to deal is in truth an infringement of the Constitution, something that is the necessary prerequisite to bringing the § 5 power into play at all. Thus, in Ex parte Virginia [1880] involving a federal statute making it a federal crime to disqualify anyone from jury service because of race, the Court first held as a matter of constitutional law that "the Fourteenth Amendment secures, among other civil rights, to colored men, when charged with criminal offences against a State, an impartial jury trial, by jurors indifferently selected or chosen without discrimination against such jurors because of their color." Only then did the Court hold that to enforce this prohibition upon state discrimination, Congress could enact a criminal statute of the type under consideration.

A more recent Fifteenth Amendment case also serves to illustrate this distinction. In South Carolina v. Katzenbach [1966], we held certain remedial sections of this Voting Rights Act of 1965 constitutional under the Fifteenth Amendment, which is directed against deprivations of the right to vote on account of race. In enacting those sections of the Voting Rights Act the Congress made a detailed investigation of various state practices that had been used to deprive Negroes of the franchise. In passing upon the remedial provisions, we reviewed first the "voluminous legislative history" as well as judicial precedents supporting the basic congressional finding that the clear commands of the Fifteenth Amendment had been infringed by various state subterfuges. Given the existence of the evil, we held the remedial steps taken by the legislature under the Enforcement Clause of the Fifteenth Amendment to be a justifiable exercise of congressional initiative.

Section 4(e), however, presents a significantly different type of congressional enactment. The question here is not whether the statute is appropriate remedial legislation to cure an established violation of a constitutional command, but whether there has in fact been an infringement of that constitutional command. ... That question is one for the judicial branch ultimately to determine. Were the rule otherwise, Congress would be able to qualify this Court's constitutional decisions under the Fourteenth and Fifteenth Amendments, let alone those under other provisions of the Constitution, by resorting to congressional power under the Necessary and Proper Clause. In view of this Court's holding in *Lassiter* that an English literacy test is a permissible exercise of state supervision over its franchise, I do not think it is open to Congress to limit the effect of that decision as it has undertaken to do by § 4(e). In effect the Court reads § 5 of the Fourteenth Amendment as giving

Congress the power to define the *substantive* scope of the Amendment. If that indeed be the true reach of § 5, then I do not see why Congress should not be able as well to exercise its § 5 "discretion" by enacting statutes so as in effect to dilute equal protection and due process decisions of this Court. In all such cases there is room for reasonable men to differ as to whether or not a denial of equal protection or due process has occurred, and the final decision is one of judgment. Until today this judgment has always been one for the judiciary to resolve.

I do not mean to suggest ... that a legislative judgment of the type incorporated in § 4(e) is without any force whatsoever. Decisions on questions of equal protection and due process are based not on abstract logic, but on empirical foundations. To the extent "legislative facts" are relevant to a judicial determination, Congress is well equipped to investigate them, and such determinations are of course entitled to due respect. . . .

But no such factual data provide a legislative record supporting § 4(e) by way of showing that Spanish-speaking citizens are fully as capable of making informed decisions in a New York election as are English-speaking citizens. Nor was there any showing whatever to support the Court's alternative argument that § 4(e) should be viewed as but a remedial measure designed to cure or assure against unconstitutional discrimination of other varieties. . . .

Thus, we have here not a matter of giving deference to a congressional estimate, based on its determination of legislative facts, bearing upon the validity *vel non* of a statute, but rather what can at most be called a legislative announcement that Congress believes a state law to entail an unconstitutional deprivation of equal protection. Although this kind of declaration is of course entitled to the most respectful consideration, coming as it does from a concurrent branch and one that is knowledgeable in matters of popular political participation, I do not believe it lessens our responsibility to decide the fundamental issue of whether in fact the state enactment violates federal constitutional rights.

In assessing the deference we should give to this kind of congressional expression of policy, it is relevant that the judiciary has always given to congressional enactments a presumption of validity. The Propeller Genesee Chief v. Fitzhugh [1851]. However, it is also a canon of judicial review that state statutes are given a similar presumption, Butler v. Commonwealth [1850]. Whichever way this case is decided, one statute will be rendered inoperative in whole or in part, and although it has been suggested that this Court should give somewhat more deference to Congress than to a state legislature, such a simple weighing of presumptions is hardly a satisfying way of resolving a matter that touches the distribution of state and federal power in an area so sensitive as that of the regulation of the franchise. Rather it should be recognized that while the Fourteenth Amendment is a "brooding omnipresence" over all state legislation, the substantive matters which it touches are all within the primary legislative competence of the States.

Federal authority, legislative no less than judicial, does not intrude unless there has been a denial by state action of Fourteenth Amendment limitations. ... At least in the area of primary state concern a state statute that passes constitutional muster under the judicial standard of rationality should not be permitted to be set at naught by a mere contrary congressional pronouncement unsupported by a legislative record justifying that conclusion.

To deny the effectiveness of this congressional enactment is not of course to disparage Congress' exertion of authority in the field of civil rights; it is simply to recognize that the Legislative Branch like the other branches of federal authority is subject to the governmental boundaries set by the Constitution. ...

Editors' Notes

(1) What is the core of the difference between the answers that Brennan and Harlan give to the question of WHO? To what extent was Brennan arguing for legislative supremacy, at least insofar as the Fourteenth Amendment is concerned? Was Harlan arguing for judicial supremacy? To what extent was either a departmentalist?

(2) A standard analysis of Brennan's opinion holds hat he applied a "ratchet theory" of constitutional interpretation to the Fourteenth Amendment—under § 5 Congress can add to but not take away from the liberties protected by the Fourteenth Amendment. (See: William Cohen, "Congressional Power to Interpret Due Process and Equal Protection," 27 *Stan.L.Rev.* 603 [1975]; and Jesse H. Choper, "Congressional Power to Expand Judicial Definitions of the Substantive Terms of the Civil War Amendments," 67 *Minn.L.Rev.* 299 [1982].) How does this explanation fit, if at all, within the triple categories of judicial supremacy, legislative supremacy, and departmentalism?

(3) On p. 329 Brennan wrote: "By including § 5 the draftsmen sought to grant to Congress ... the same broad powers expressed in the Necessary and Proper Clause, Art. 6, § 8, cl. 18." Was he trying to smuggle in a form of "originalism" or was he really referring to "purpose" rather "intent"? Assuming he actually meant "purpose," does that usage constitute a form of originalism?

(4) The history of *Katzenbach* is checkered:

(a) *Oregon v. Mitchell (1970)*. Here the Court sustained amendments to the Voting Rights Act of 1965 that allowed 18–year–olds to vote for federal officials, suspended all literacy tests for federal and state elections, and regulated residency and absentee registration in presidential elections. By a 5–4 vote, however, the Court held that authorizing 18–year–olds to vote in *state* elections exceeded congressional power both under Article I of the original text and § 5 of the Fourteenth Amendment.

There was no opinion for the Court, but five separate opinions that consumed 185 pages of the U.S. Reports. Justice Black announced the judgment of the Court but wrote only for himself. He did not acknowledge that Congress had the sweeping interpretive power that Brennan's opinion for the Court had in *Katzenbach*. In particular, Black doubted congressional authority to regulate elections under the Fourteenth and Fifteenth amendments where there was no issue of racial discrimination. More generally, he wrote:

> As broad as the congressional enforcement power is, it is not unlimited. Specifically, there are at least three limitations upon Congress' power to enforce the guarantees of the Civil War Amendments. First, Congress may not by legislation repeal other provisions of the Constitution. Second, the power granted to Congress was not intended to strip the States of their power to govern themselves or to convert our national government of enumerated powers into a central government of unrestrained authority. . . . Third, Congress may only "enforce" the provisions of the amendments and may do so only by "appropriate legislation." Congress has no power under the enforcement sections to undercut the amendments' guarantees of personal equality and freedom from discrimination, or to undermine those protections of the Bill of Rights which we have held the Fourteenth Amendment made applicable to the States.

Douglas, Brennan, White, and Marshall adhered to *Katzenbach's* broad views of congressional interpretive power and would have sustained all the amendments to the Voting Rights Act. Justice Harlan reiterated and amplified his previous dissent:

> As the Court is not justified in substituting its own views of wise policy for the commands of the Constitution, still less is it justified in allowing Congress to disregard those commands as the Court understands them. . . . The reason for this goes beyond Marshall's assertion that: "It is emphatically the province and duty of the judicial department to say what the law is." Marbury v. Madison (1803). It inheres in the structure of the constitutional system itself. Congress is subject to none of the institutional restraints imposed on judicial decisionmaking. In Article V, the Framers expressed the view that the political restraints on Congress alone were an insufficient control over the process of constitution making. The concurrence of two-thirds of each House and of three-fourths of the States was needed for the political check to be adequate. To allow a simple majority of Congress to have final say on matters of constitutional interpretation is therefore fundamentally out of keeping with the constitutional structure. Nor is that structure adequately protected by a requirement that the judiciary be able to perceive a basis for the interpretation. . . .

Justice Potter Stewart, joined by Chief Justice Burger and Justice Blackmun, concurred in part and dissented in part. They thought it would stretch *Katzenbach's* reasoning to sustain those amendments to the Voting Rights Act relating to age requirements for either federal or state elections.

(The Twenty–Sixth Amendment, ratified in 1971, disposed of the substantive issue of voting age: "The right of citizens of the United States, who are eighteen years of age or older, to vote shall not be denied or abridged by the United States or by any State on account of age." Sec. 2 repeats the formula of § 5 of the Fourteenth Amendment, "The Congress shall have power to enforce this article by appropriate legislation.")

(b) *Rome v. United States (1980).* If *Mitchell* seemed to signal a retreat from *Katzenbach, Rome* appeared to move a step forward. In upholding another provision of the Voting Rights Act of 1965, Justice Thurgood Marshall's opinion for the Court reasoned along lines that closely paralleled Brennan's in *Katzenbach:*

> It is clear, then, that under § 2 of the Fifteenth Amendment Congress may prohibit practices that in and of themselves do not violate § 1 of the Amendment, so long as the prohibitions attacking racial discrimination in voting are "appropriate" as that term is defined in McCulloch v. Maryland [1819] and Ex parte Virginia (1880).

(5) Critical to any analysis of *Katzenbach, Mitchell,* and *Rome* is the question whether the phrase "prohibitions attacking racial discrimination" merely reflects the fact that it was the Fifteenth Amendment that was before the Court in *Rome* and not the Fourteenth, as in *Katzenbach,* or whether the Court was adopting Black's doubts about congressional authority to regulate elections under the Fourteenth and Fifteenth amendments where no racial discrimination was present.

Whatever the answer to that question, Justice William H. Rehnquist, who had joined the Court five years after *Katzenbach* and a year after Oregon v. Mitchell, thought his brethren were going too far in *Rome:*

> While the presumption of constitutionality is due to any act of a coordinate branch of the Federal Government or of one of the States, it is this Court which is ultimately responsible for deciding challenges to the exercise of power by those entities. Marbury v. Madison (1803). United States v. Nixon (1974). Today's decision is nothing less than a total abdication of that authority, rather than an exercise of the deference due to a coordinate branch of the government.

Stewart joined Rehnquist's dissent. Justice Lewis Powell, who had also not been on the Court when *Katzenbach* or *Mitchell* was decided, dissented separately, reasoning that the challenged section of the statute exceeded Congress' powers. He did not, however, directly address the extent of deference the Court owed congressional interpretations of the Civil War amendments.

(6) In 1975 Congress further amended the Voting Rights Act to outlaw permanently all literacy tests as prerequisites for voting. 42 U.S.C. § 1971(a)(2)(c).

————

"[I]f ... Congress can redefine terms in this one area so as to entrust to a majority vote ... a matter that the Supreme Court has held individual women entitled to resolve for themselves, then Congress has equal power to effectuate such a divestment of personal rights in other areas as well. ..."—Professor Laurence H. TRIBE

"A decision of the Supreme Court interpreting the Constitution is neither infallible nor eternal nor unchangeable. ..."—Professor John T. NOONAN

ABORTION, THE SUPREME COURT, AND CONGRESSIONAL AUTHORITY UNDER THE FOURTEENTH AMENDMENT TO DEFINE "PERSON"

Roe v. Wade (1973; reprinted below, p. 1258) held that, at least during the first three months of pregnancy, a woman had a constitutional right to an abortion. In reaching its decision, the Court held that a fetus was not a "person" protected by the Fourteenth Amendment, but conceded that if a fetus were a "person" much state regulation of abortion would be valid. Popular reactions ranged from effusive praise for recognizing women's rights to bitter condemnation for legalizing murder. As any reader would have guessed from Chapters 5 and 6, constitutional scholars were equally acerbic in their debates about the legitimacy of the Court's discovering such a right in the due process clause and/or in the Ninth Amendment. And, like others, commentators also sharply divided about the correctness of the substantive ruling. Additional state and federal legislation tried to counter Roe, but with the notable exception of withholding federal funding for abortions (see Harris v. McRae [1980; reprinted below, p. 1271] and Planned Parenthood v. Casey [1992; reprinted below, p. 1281]), judges struck down most of these proposals. Among the efforts to disarm Roe was S. 158, introduced by Senator Jesse A. Helms (Rep., N.C.) in 1981. This bill tried to take advantage of Katzenbach v. Morgan and define "person" in the Fourteenth Amendment to include a fetus.

A. SENATE BILL 158

97th Congress, First Session.

To provide that human life shall be deemed to exist from conception

Be it enacted by the Senate and House of Representatives of the United States of America in Congress assembled, That title 42 of the United States Code shall be amended at the end thereof by adding the following new chapter:

CHAPTER 101

Sec. 1. The Congress finds that present day scientific evidence indicates a significant likelihood that actual human life exists from conception.

The Congress further finds that the fourteenth amendment to the Constitution of the United States was intended to protect all human beings.

Upon the basis of these findings, and in the exercise of the powers of the Congress, including its power under section 5 of the fourteenth amendment to the Constitution of the United States, the Congress hereby declares that for the purpose of enforcing the obligation of the

States under the fourteenth amendment not to deprive persons of life without due process of law, human life shall be deemed to exist from conception, without regard to race, sex, age, health, defect, or condition of dependency; and for this purpose "person" shall include all human life as defined herein.

Sec. 2. Notwithstanding any other provision of law, no inferior Federal court ordained and established by Congress under article III of the Constitution of the United States shall have jurisdiction to issue any restraining order, temporary or permanent injunction, or declaratory judgment in any case involving or arising from any State law or municipal ordinance that (1) protects the rights of human persons between conception and birth, or (2) prohibits, limits, or regulates (a) the performance of abortions or (b) the provision at public expense of funds, facilities, personnel, or other assistance for the performance of abortions.

Sec. 3. If any provision of this Act or the application thereof to any person or circumstance is judicially determined to be invalid, the validity of the remainder of the Act and the application of such provision to other persons and circumstances shall not be affected by such determination.

———

In the spring of 1981, the Senate's Subcommittee on Separation of Powers began holding hearings on the bill.

B. PREPARED STATEMENT OF LAURENCE H. TRIBE ON S. 158*

... In substance, § 1 attempts to enshrine a congressional "theory of life" so as to "override the rights of the pregnant woman" under Roe v. Wade (1973)—precisely what the Supreme Court in *Roe* held a *state* powerless to do.

The fact that § 1 might operate merely as an authorization for the *states* to restrict the rights of pregnant women rather than as a direct restriction mandated by Congress itself is immaterial, since the Due Process Clause of the Fifth Amendment forbids Congress *either* to do by itself what the Fourteenth Amendment would prohibit states from doing *or* to license the states to do what, absent congressional permission, they would be prohibited by the Fourteenth Amendment from doing.

The only possible argument supporting the constitutionality of S. 158, § 1, is that Katzenbach v. Morgan somehow empowered Congress to restrict the rights of women, or to authorize states to do so, in circumstances where states would otherwise be constitutionally forbidden to

* U.S. Senate, Subcommittee on Separation of Powers, *The Human Life Bill: Hearings on S. 158,* 97th Cong., 1st Sess., I, 249–252.

Laurence H. Tribe is Tyler Professor of Constitutional Law, Harvard Law School.

take such action. Even if *Morgan* had not been considerably restricted by Oregon v. Mitchell ... that decision obviously would *not* endow Congress with blank-check authority to restrict one set of judicially-declared rights upon Congress' decision, by majority vote, to proclaim another set of "rights" into existence.

This is so for three reasons. *First,* however expansive may be Congress' power, under § 5 of the Fourteenth Amendment, to make empirical determinations that might have eluded the courts or to create remedial structures that the courts may have been unprepared to require on their own, no corresponding power exists simply to reject, as a legislative matter, a legal conclusion reached by the Supreme Court as to the proper interpretation of constitutional language:

> It is emphatically the province and duty of the judicial department to say what the law is,

Marbury v. Madison (1803), a duty in which "the federal judiciary is supreme," Cooper v. Aaron (1958), see also United States v. Nixon (1974), not least because:

> Congress is subject to none of the institutional restraints imposed on judicial decisionmaking; it is controlled only by the political process. In Article V, the Framers expressed the view that the political restraints on Congress alone were an insufficient control over the process of constitution making. The concurrence of two-thirds of each House and of three-fourths of the States was needed for the political check to be adequate. To allow a simple majority of Congress to have final say on matters of constitutional interpretation is therefore fundamentally out of keeping with the constitutional structure.

Oregon v. Mitchell (Harlan, J., concurring in part and dissenting in part).

Second, the premise of S. 158, § 1 ... is the extraordinary proposition that the identification of human life or personhood, as a basis for justifying restraints upon the freedom, equality, and bodily integrity of a pregnant woman, is an empirical matter—one which "present-day scientific evidence" might somehow resolve. Suffice it to say, however, that such questions as when "human life" exists, or what is a "person," call at bottom for normative judgments no less profound than those involved in defining "liberty" or "equality." In this context, therefore, one cannot escape the conclusion that identifying "human life" and defining "person" entail "question[s] to which science can provide no answer," as the National Academy of Sciences itself acknowledged in a Resolution passed on April 28, 1981, during its 118th Annual Meeting. Congress cannot transform an issue of religion, morality, and law into one of fact by waving the magic wand of § 5. The section empowering Congress "to enforce, by appropriate legislation, the provisions of" the Fourteenth Amendment no more authorizes Congress to transmute a matter of values into a matter of scientific observation than it authorizes Congress to announce a mathematical formula for human freedom.

Third, even if S. 158, § 1, were deemed to fall within the ambit of Congress' affirmative authority—under § 5 of the Fourteenth Amendment or otherwise—it would still be subject to judicial invalidation as a clear violation of the Liberty Clause of the Fifth Amendment, a clause that restricts Congress in precisely the same manner that, and to precisely the same degree as, its counterpart clause in the Fourteenth Amendment restricts the states. Any other approach would simultaneously denigrate the place of each state as "a coordinate element in the system established by the Framers for governing our Federal Union," National League of Cities v. Usery (1976), and jeopardize the personal rights and liberties whose fate the Framers wisely declined to leave entirely to a Congress unchecked by judicial review. . . .

Nor could the delegation of judicially unchecked power to Congress over such rights and liberties be confined to cases in which the judiciary has candidly confessed, as it did in Roe v. Wade its inability to give determinate meaning to constitutional terms like "life." For when Congress acts to override, or to invite states to override, the "liberty" of pregnant women, it does not merely "inform the judiciary" . . . of its legislative findings and views. Congress is empowered only to *make laws,* not to lobby or advise the courts. And if a law made by Congress can redefine terms in this one area so as to entrust to majority vote or other governmental determination a matter that the Supreme Court has held individual women entitled to resolve for themselves, then Congress has equal power to effectuate such a divestment of personal rights in other areas as well—regardless of the Supreme Court's degree of confidence or perplexity.

The only way to avoid that radical and profoundly threatening conclusion is to insist that *any* Act of Congress, even if that Act constitutes otherwise "appropriate legislation," be subject to judicial review for its consistency with the liberties secured by the Bill of Rights, under criteria no less demanding than those under which state legislation of similar effect would be scrutinized. . . .

C. PREPARED STATEMENT OF JOHN T. NOONAN, JR., ON S. 158*

II

THE FACT-FINDING AND DEFINITIONAL PROVISIONS OF THE ACT

The Act does four things. It finds "a significant likelihood that actual human life exists from conception." It finds that the Fourteenth

---

* U.S. Senate, Subcommittee on Separation of Powers, *The Human Life Bill: Hearings on S. 158,* 97th Cong., 1st Sess., I, 263–271.

John T. Noonan, Jr., was then Professor of Law, University of California at Berkeley; later he became a judge on the U.S. Court of Appeals for the Ninth Circuit.

Amendment was "intended to protect all human beings." It declares that for the purpose of enforcing the obligation of the States "not to deprive persons of life without due process of law," human life "shall be deemed to exist from conception." For the same purpose it declares that "person" shall include all human life as so defined. Are these findings and declarations within the power of Congress?

1. *The Source of Congressional Power.* The Fourteenth Amendment, § 5 declares, "The Congress shall have power to enforce, by appropriate legislation, the provisions of this article." The key terms of this constitutional grant of power are "appropriate legislation" and "enforce." In general, there must be said of this part of the Constitution what Chief Justice Marshall said in McCulloch v. Maryland of congressional power under the "Necessary and Proper Clause of Article I": "1st. The clause is placed among the powers of Congress, not among the limitations on those powers. Its terms purport to enlarge, not to diminish the powers vested in the government. It purports to be an additional power, not a restriction on those already granted."

The parallel in interpretation of Congress' power under § 5 and Congress' power under Article I has very recently been affirmed by Chief Justice Warren Burger in Fullilove v. Klutznick. The Court, he declared, had "equated the scope of this authority with the broad powers expressed in the Necessary and Proper Clause, U.S. Const., Act. 1, § 8, cl. 18." In the light of this interpretation, Congress has the power under § 5 to find facts, to adopt remedies, and to enact legislation it finds appropriate to secure the rights guaranteed by the Fourteenth Amendment.

It should be added that the enforcement of the Fourteenth Amendment by *congressional* action has solid historical roots. As the Supreme Court said unanimously in 1879 in Ex parte Virginia . . .: "It is not said that the *judicial power* of the government shall extend to enforcing the prohibitions and to protecting the rights and immunities guaranteed. . . . It is the power of Congress which has been enlarged." Even if today the judicial branch has taken to itself a more active part in enforcing the Amendments, surely its more assertive role cannot deprive Congress of the power which the framers of the Amendment intended to confer, as the 1879 Court acknowledged, and which the Court in 1980 has recognized to be as broad as Article I's fundamental grant of power to make "all laws which shall be necessary and proper for carrying into Execution the foregoing Powers."

2. *The Power of Congress Where the Supreme Court is in Doubt.* In Roe v. Wade the Supreme Court declared, "We need not resolve the difficult question of where life begins. When those trained in the respective disciplines of medicine, philosophy, and theology are unable to arrive at any consensus, the judiciary at this point in the development of man's knowledge, is not in a position to speculate as to the answer." . . .

Congress, as a coordinate branch of the national government, is of course in a position very different from any State vis-à-vis the Supreme

Court. In this area it is acting within the terms of power expressly conferred by the Fourteenth Amendment and expressly recognized by the Court itself. It is acting with better sources of information than the Court. ... It is acting with a better ability than the Court to balance competing value considerations that go to the assessment of the facts. Further, Congress is performing an essential function in the enforcement of the Fourteenth Amendment; for if the judiciary is not "in a position to speculate" when life begins, the Fourteenth Amendment must fail, in a significant way, to be implemented, unless Congress draws on its power to supply an answer.

3. *The Power of Congress When the Supreme Court Has Made a Contrary Determination.* The objection will be raised, however, that the ... Court in Roe v. Wade has formally held that "the word 'person' as used in the Fourteenth Amendment, does not include the unborn." Does not the proposed statute squarely conflict with this holding of the Court and, if it does so, is not the statute void?

It is clear that Congress will reach, if the proposed statute is enacted, a conclusion different from the Court's in Roe v. Wade on the meaning of person in the Fourteenth Amendment. It does not follow that the statute is void. It follows, rather, that the Court may, and should, change its mind, give deference to the congressional findings and declarations, and overrule Roe v. Wade.

In the area of the Fourteenth Amendment the Court has already provided just such an example of retreating from its own announced understanding of the Constitution in deference to congressional action taken after, and contrary to, the Court's announcement of what it found the Constitution to mean. In Lassiter v. Northampton Election Board (1959) the plaintiff complained that a literacy test for voting was unconstitutional. The Supreme Court, unanimously, held that Article 1, § 2 of the Constitution expressly reserves to the States the power to determine the qualifications of electors. Seven years later in Katzenbach v. Morgan (1966), the Court considered an Act of Congress eliminating literacy in English as a condition for voting. ...

The Court ... found *Lassiter* "inapposite." Speaking through Justice Brennan and quoting Ex parte Virginia of 1879, the Court held the congressional action a proper exercise of congressional power under § 5 of the Fourteenth Amendment. ... The action of Congress, directly contrary to the interpretation of the Constitution by a unanimous Supreme Court, was upheld by the Court. In Oregon v. Mitchell (1970), while splitting on other issues, the Court unanimously upheld Congress' total elimination of literacy tests. ...

4. *Congressional Action Affecting Personal Liberties.* In Shapiro v. Thompson, a case involving the welfare residency requirement of California, it was said by way of dictum that even if Congress had consented to the residency requirement—which the Court held it had not—the requirement was invalid, because "Congress may not authorize the States to violate the Equal Protection Clause." Similarly in a footnote to

Katzenbach v. Morgan, Justice Brennan declared that § 5 "grants Congress no power to restrict, abrogate or dilute" the guarantees of the Fourteenth Amendment. . . . The question is thus presented whether the proposed Act authorizes states to violate the Equal Protection Clause, dilutes or abrogates Fourteenth Amendment guarantees, or is based on the same evidence on which state legislatures acted unreasonably.

In recognizing the unborn as persons, so far as protection of their lives is concerned, the proposed Act treats no one unequally but gives equal protection to one class of humanity now unequally treated. It does not dilute a Fourteenth Amendment guarantee, but expands the rights of a whole class. It is based not on evidence before the state legislatures—what that evidence was we do not know—but on evidence freshly taken from leading geneticists and physicians.

Yet the question will be pressed, "Does not the Act dilute or abrogate the right to an abortion?" Necessarily, the expression of the rights of one class of human beings has an impact on the rights of others. The elimination of literacy tests in this way "diluted" the voting rights of the literate. It is inescapable that congressional expression of the right to life will have an impact on the abortion right; but in the eyes of Congress, if it enacts this law, there will be a net gain for Fourteenth Amendment rights by the expansion and the attendant diminution. . . .

5. *Section 5 and Marbury v. Madison.* The cornerstone of the judicial power, Chief Justice Marshall's opinion in Marbury v. Madison, announces that the Constitution "controls any legislative act repugnant to it" and imposes on the judges the duty to determine this repugnancy. Does the proposed Act defy or subvert these fundamental principles?

Not in the least. Congress is not ousting the Court of jurisdiction, "overruling" the Court, or declaring its will superior to Constitution or Court. On the basis of hearings and fresh evidence, Congress is taking a position which in one important particular disagrees with the Court's interpretation of the Constitution in Roe v. Wade. Under the principles of Marbury v. Madison, it will be for the Court to decide whether, following such precedents as Katzenbach v. Morgan, it should now defer to Congress' interpretation.

To suppose that the statute proposed is a challenge to judicial review assumes a radical—I am inclined to say willful—misunderstanding of the functions of Court and Congress. A decision of the Supreme Court interpreting the Constitution is neither infallible nor eternal nor unchangeable. The Court has often been wrong. The Court has often corrected itself. There is nothing in our constitutional theory that says the Court must remain forever in a mistaken position, and much contrary example to its so doing. The proposed Act is an invitation to the Court to correct its error itself. . . .

The story is an old one, frequently retold. The Supreme Court is not immune to reason and to instruction. It reverses itself. It listens to Congress. Those who want an institution immovable and beyond the reach of popular instruction must look elsewhere.

6. *Further Reasons for Congress to Exercise Its Section 5 Power Here.* "The *Morgan* case," Archibald Cox has written, "is soundly rooted in constitutional principles, yet it clears the way for a vast expansion of congressional legislation promoting human rights." This expansion, as Cox observes, can be achieved by any law which "may be viewed" as having a relation to an end specified by the Fourteenth Amendment. In the present context, the Fourteenth Amendment guarantees life to persons. But no one can enjoy adult life unless he or she is born. To protect the life guaranteed by the Amendment, Congress has the power under § 5 to protect the path to that life. The proposed legislation is readily seen as a way of protecting the means necessary to have life after birth.

Further, it is sometimes forgotten that the Court in Roe v. Wade, acknowledging that "the Constitution does not explicitly mention any right of privacy," finally located that right with some uncertainty in the Fourteenth Amendment "or, as the District Court determined, in the Ninth Amendment's reservation of rights to the people." To this point in this presentation, focus has been upon the Fourteenth Amendment. But if Justice Blackmun's other basis be accepted, Congress is better suited than the Court to make the determination as to the balance struck between the rights of the States and reserved Ninth Amendment rights. Such a determination requires political discretion. As Archibald Cox has written generally of why the Court should defer to Congress in its exercise of § 5 power, such judicial following of a congressional lead "rests upon application of the fact that the fundamental basis for legislative action is the knowledge, experience, and judgment of the people's representatives, only a small part, or even none of which may come from the hearings and reports of committees or debates upon the floor." As Ninth Amendment rights are reserved to the people, the people through its elected representatives can determine, better than a nonelected elite, where the line limiting governmental power should be drawn. ...

Editors' Notes

(1) S. 158 died in committee.

(2) **Query:** Think back to *Katzenbach*: If Congress can expand the rights protected by the Fourteenth Amendment, why may it not define who is a "person" entitled to that amendment's protection? In defining a fetus as a person, would not Congress expand the rights of a certain class, fetuses, beyond the minimum the Court set in *Roe*, just as the Voting Rights Act extended the rights of those not literate in English beyond the definition that Court offered in Lassiter v. Northampton County? To use a different example, if *Katzenbach* correctly interpreted "the Constitution," why could Congress not

legislate that women had an absolute legal right to abortion at any stage whatever in pregnancy, rather than during the first trimester as *Roe* held?

(3) **Query:** Does the "ratchet theory" not contain a self-destructive difficulty in that any expansion of the rights of one class of "persons" may well constrict the rights of another class?   To the extent that the ratchet theory is so flawed, what sort of answer does it offer to the basic interrogative WHO?

8

Who May Authoritatively Interpret the Constitution for the Federal System?

Article VI of the constitutional text explicitly declares its supremacy over all forms of state law:

> This Constitution, and the Laws of the United States which shall be made in Pursuance thereof; and all Treaties made, or which shall be made, under the Authority of the United States, shall be the supreme Law of the Land; and the Judges in every State shall be bound thereby, any Thing in the Constitution or Laws of any State to the Contrary notwithstanding.

Yet, as plainly as these words proclaim national supremacy, they leave open important questions of WHO should authoritatively determine constitutional meaning. By specifically singling out judges and instructing them to prefer the "Constitution," laws, and treaties of the United States over state laws and constitutions, Article VI certainly acknowledges that the judiciary has an important and legitimate role in constitutional interpretation, at least where questions of federalism occur. But Article VI does *not* say that "when state and federal judges disagree, the interpretation of federal judges shall prevail."

More than two centuries of experience, including a civil war and the adoption of that great centralizer, the Fourteenth Amendment, may make it obvious that the ultimate constitutional interpreters must be people acting in the name of the nation, whether as judges, legislators, executives, or simply as voters. Here, it seems to us at the end of the twentieth century, the arguments of men like Justice Joseph Story and Charles Evans Hughes, quoted in the introduction to Chapter 7, take on compelling power. If, within its own borders, every state were the authoritative interpreter of "the Constitution of the United States," we would soon have several dozen such constitutions, even as many as fifty-one, if federal judges shared interpretive power.

The first Congress adopted such reasoning. Section 25 of the Judiciary Act of 1789 (reprinted below, p. 352) gave the United States Supreme Court appellate jurisdiction over state judges on constitutional issues. But such a fundamental issue of federalism as interpretive supremacy could not be put to rest by congressional fiat. Until the eve of the Civil War, states righters from the North and Midwest as well as from the South heatedly and repeatedly contested the validity of § 25.[1] As Virginia's Supreme Court of Appeals said in 1815:

> The court is unanimously of the opinion that the appellate power of the Supreme Court of the United States does not extend to this court, under a sound construction of the constitution of the United States; that so much of the 25th section of the act of congress to establish the judicial courts of the United States, as extends the appellate jurisdiction of the Supreme Court to this court is not in pursuance of the constitution of the United States. (Hunter v. Martin; reversed in Martin v. Hunter's Lessee [1816], reprinted below, p. 359.)

The Supreme Court's decision in Brown v. Board of Ed. (1954; reprinted below, p. 912) declaring unconstitutional mandatory segregation in public education provoked similar reactions from many southern governors and legislators as well as judges. Echoing Virginia's arguments in Hunter's Case, eight states "nullified" *Brown*. (See Alabama's "nullification," reprinted below, p. 374.) One might dismiss those legislators, as did Alabama's governor, as "just a bunch of hound dogs bayin' at the moon"; but they reflected and strengthened resistance to the Supreme Court's insistence on racial equality in public schools—a resistance that still lives within and without the South.

Moreover, these resolutions were grounded, as was the interpretation of Virginia's judges in 1815, on a claim that "the Constitution" is a compact among the several states rather than a covenant among the American people. If that statement is correct, then nullification follows a constitutional course. Surely state officials would possess interpretive authority at least equal to that of federal officers—perhaps, superior, for the states would be the principals to an agreement and the federal government would be only the product of that agreement. Here again we see questions of WHAT "the Constitution" is intersect with questions about WHO its authoritative interpreters are.

We should not be misled into thinking that these battles over federal-state interpretive authority are merely quaint academic disputes about constitutional theory or even petty squabbles among competing officials over public "turf." As with most conflicts about the relative interpretive authority among branches of the federal government, the usual stakes in federal-state clashes have been possession of power and concern about public policies that affect

---

1. For the long chronology of opposition to § 25, see the two-part article by Charles Warren, "Legislative and Judicial Attacks on the Supreme Court of the United States—A History of the Twenty-Fifth Section of the Judiciary Act," 47 *Am.L.Rev.* 1; 47 *ibid.* 161 (1913).

basic economic, social, and political interests. The dispute in Hunter's Case, for instance, was over ownership of large tracts of land. Federal and state courts had disagreed, putting, for private citizens, huge sums of money at risk and, for public officials, issues of power over public policy. In 1954 the School Segregation Cases put much more at risk: a caste system that shaped an entire way of life and the authority of state officials to preserve that society.

As befits such high-stakes games, the rhetoric has always been loud and has sometimes accompanied by violence. If, however, we step back from the verbal bombast and the smoke of battle, we can see that the debate has assumed a shape similar to the pattern that Chapter 7 described for those who have offered principles for determining the ultimate interpreter among the branches of the federal government. Here again, three theories compete: state supremacy, confederational departmentalism, and national supremacy.

I. STATE SUPREMACY

Probably because of the plain words of Article VI, a defense of state supremacy in constitutional interpretation was seldom systematically articulated. Nevertheless, for almost three-quarters of a century its rationale infused much of the political debate surrounding problems of federalism. The document produced by the Philadelphia Convention was not greeted with universal enthusiasm. Persuading the country to ratify the new text was a difficult task that barely succeeded. Whatever else its opponents had in common, they shared a deep-seated distrust of strong central government and an equally marked desire for local autonomy. In 1793, this mood moved the lower house of the Georgia legislature to threaten with death anyone who tried to take advantage of the Supreme Court's ruling in Chisholm v. Georgia that a state could be sued without its consent in a federal court. The actual resolution was peaceful: adoption of the Eleventh Amendment, denying the jurisdiction of federal courts to hear suits against a state brought by citizens of other states or foreign nations.[2]

---

2. Curiously, the wording of the amendment did not deny federal jurisdiction over suits brought against a state by its own citizens. Providing a marvelous example of interpretation's adding to the constitutional text, the Supreme Court repaired that "omission" in Hans v. Louisiana (1890) by declaring it a mere oversight. The Fourteenth Amendment's prohibitions against certain kinds of state action, however, certainly seem to modify the Eleventh, for, if citizens could not go into federal courts for remedies against a state's denial of "due process" or "equal protection," those prohibitions might well have little impact. The Supreme Court, however, has used circular reasoning to justify bringing state officials back under federal jurisdiction. Essentially, the Court held in a line of decisions culminating in Ex parte Young (1908) that when state officials take life, liberty, or property without due process of law or deny equal protection of the laws, they cannot claim to act in the name of the state. Thus, federal courts have jurisdiction under the Fourteenth Amendment because these officials act in the name of state, the target of the amendment. But those officials cannot claim immunity under the Eleventh Amendment because insofar

II. CONFEDERATIONAL DEPARTMENTALISM

The term "confederational departmentalism" is awkward, but it is descriptive and points to parallels with the departmental doctrine that Thomas Jefferson and others espoused for constitutional interpretation among the three branches of the national government. The basis of this theory is much like that on which Virginia's Supreme Court of Appeals had operated in Hunter's Case and many southern states after 1954: "The Constitution" is a compact among sovereign states. Thus, as a party to this compact, an individual state is equal in interpretive authority[3] to any other state and *at least* equal to the national government. Jefferson put the argument succinctly in the Kentucky Resolutions of 1798 (reprinted below, p. 354):

> Resolved, . . . That the Government created by this compact was not made the exclusive or final judge of the extent of the powers delegated to itself; since that would have made its discretion, and not the Constitution, the measure of its powers; but that as in all other cases of compact among parties having no common Judge, *each party has an equal right to judge for itself, as well of infractions as of the mode and measure of redress.* (Italics in original.)

From then until the eve of the Civil War at least seven states, including Pennsylvania and Wisconsin, repeated this sort of argument. Even James Madison, who at the Constitutional Convention had fought vehemently for national supremacy and in *Federalist* No. 39 (reprinted below, p. 526) had gone on public record as believing that the U.S. Supreme Court was the authoritative constitutional interpreter in disputes between state and nation, used language similar to that of Jefferson when writing the Virginia Resolutions of 1799. That Madison in 1799 contradicted his earlier claims and then in later years changed again and valiantly tried to explain away his endorsement of confederational departmentalism only highlights the doctrine's attractiveness to those who have lost at the national level on important policy questions.

It was John C. Calhoun, of course, who most elaborately and systematically developed Jefferson's argument in the Kentucky Reso-

---

as their actions violate the Fourteenth, they are not truly state officers. "Logic," Justice William O. Douglas once remarked,

> cannot justify the rule of *Ex parte Young*. I have never thought it was in full harmony with the Eleventh Amendment. *Ex parte Young* and its offspring do, however, reflect perhaps an even higher policy: the belief that courts must be allowed in the interest of justice to police unruly, lawless government officials who seek to impose oppressive laws on the citizen. *We, the Judges* (Garden City, NY: Doubleday, 1956), p. 75.

3. This logic would seem to lead to the conclusion that the state's interpretive authority was superior to the federal government's, though many states righters did not push the argument this far. John C. Calhoun did: If a majority of states agreed with the nullifying state, their collective interpretation took precedence over that of federal officials.

lutions. Calhoun's writings provided the theoretical basis for much of southern sectionalism in the years 1828–1861, reshaped nullification (or "interposition," as he preferred) into a powerful threat to the federal government, and eventually sought to justify secession. (See his the selections from his *Discourse on the Constitution of the United States*, reprinted below, p. 365.)

III. NATIONAL SUPREMACY

Congress, presidents (including Madison when he was in the White House), and the Supreme Court have all consistently rejected both state supremacy and confederational departmentalism, at least insofar as constitutional interpretation is concerned. These institutions have opted for and acted on a theory that not only is "the Constitution" the "supreme Law of the Land," but also that national officials are its authoritative interpreters. As we saw in Chapter 7, however, federal officials have been less than unanimous in deciding which of the three national branches is the ultimate interpreter. And, as Chapter 11 will point out, these officials have differed among each other when dividing substantive authority between state and nation.

The most decisive congressional action came, as we have seen, in its very first session in enactment of § 25 of the Judiciary Act of 1789. Its post-Civil War action in proposing the Fourteenth Amendment and asserting more extensive federal jurisdiction over state courts pushed well beyond § 25. The Supreme Court has been even more constant. Martin v. Hunter's Lessee (1816; reprinted below, p. 359), McCulloch v. Maryland (1819; reprinted below, p. 530),[4] and Ableman v. Booth (1859; reprinted below p. 367), not only upheld the constitutionality of § 25 but also stressed the Court's own role as ultimate arbiter of the federal system. Cooper v. Aaron (1958; reprinted below, p. 375) followed ineluctably in that tradition.

The most significant decisions, however, were by executive officials: Lincoln's first inaugural (reprinted above, p. 314) ranks among the most important pieces of constitutional interpretation in American history. For, on his own authority as chief executive and commander in chief of the armed forces, he determined that "the Constitution" forbade secession. Although he was a skilled lawyer, he did not rely on or even cite any of the several Supreme Court rulings or acts of Congress that supported his argument. "I hold," he said, "that in contemplation of universal law, and of the Constitution, the Union of these States is perpetual." And on Lincoln's decision the continuation of the United States as a nation turned. The next and only somewhat less crucial decision to use force to prevent disunion took final form when Ulysses S. Grant sat at

---

4. See also Cohens v. Virginia (1821).

Appomattox Courthouse, as an executive rather than a judicial officer.

Yet, like the question of the relative interpretive authority of the branches of the federal government, that between the nation and the states is more subtle and complex than legal rules might make it seem. Every senator and representative is elected from a constituency no broader than an individual state. To return to Washington for another term, those legislators have to persuade their local constituencies—among whose most influential members are typically state officials—that they are protecting local interests, including as much freedom from "outside interference" as is feasible. Although less parochially bound than senators and representatives, presidents can seldom afford to alienate state officials en masse. Thus these people have significant opportunities to persuade elected federal officials to lend a sympathetic ear, as well as their own interpretive authority, to arguments for "states rights."

Recognizing that the United States is "an indestructible union of indestructible states"[5] and not a unitary political system, the Supreme Court has managed to assert its interpretive supremacy while according state interpreters considerable deference. The justices take as definitive a state supreme court's interpretation of its own laws or constitution, and they often claim to accord state laws a presumption of constitutionality.[6] This presumption is subject to the same exceptions for fundamental rights and suspect classifications as are acts of Congress; and it is highly doubtful that, whatever the degree of presumption the justices do in fact and not merely in rhetoric accord state legislation, that presumption is nearly so strong as that which they give to federal acts. Still, the Court usually does go out of its way to express respect for the dignity and authority of state judges.

The justices have also developed an elaborate set of rules that they sometimes but not always deploy to avoid conflict with state constitutional interpretation. Among the most important of these is the doctrine of "equitable abstention," which instructs federal judges not to decide the constitutionality of an unclearly worded state statute until state courts have had a chance to determine the law's validity or to interpret it so as to avoid a constitutional question. (See, example, NAACP v. Button [1963; reprinted below, p. 811]).

In short, even at times when federal supremacy is secure and federal judicial supremacy over state constitutional interpretation

---

5. Texas v. White (1869; reprinted below, p. 546).

6. The rhetoric goes back to the very early cases. See, for example, the Court's claim in Fletcher v. Peck (1810; reprinted below, p. 1091) and the Dartmouth College Case (1819) that it would never declare a doubtful state law invalid, only one that clearly violated "the Constitution." For more recent claims regarding economic regulation, see Williamson v. Lee Optical (1955; reprinted below, p. 908); for a more general statement of presumption of the validity of state laws, see Parham v. Hughes (1979).

equally firmly anchored in accepted norms, the Supreme Court has usually been respectful of the pride of state officials, especially state judges. Considerations of raw power encourage that attitude, but so do democratic and constitutionalist theory. State legislators, after all, are popularly, if very locally, elected officials. And constitutionalism recognizes federalism's potential to check oppressive national power. Both these theories reinforce the attractiveness of a policy of diplomacy rather than domination.

SELECTED BIBLIOGRAPHY

Barber, Sotirios A. *On What the Constitution Means* (Baltimore: Johns Hopkins University Press, 1984), ch. 4.

Corwin, Edward S. "National Power and State Interposition, 1787–1861," 10 *Mich.L.Rev.* 535 (1912).

Davis, Sue. *Justice Rehnquist and the Constitution* (Princeton: Princeton University Press, 1989).

Douglas, William O. "Interposition and the Peters Case," 9 *Stan. L.Rev.* 3 (1956).

Koch, Adrienne, and Harry Ammon. "The Virginia and Kentucky Resolutions," 5 *Wm. & Mary Q.* (3rd Series) 145 (1948).

McKay, Robert B. "Georgia versus the United States Supreme Court," 4 *Jo. of Pub.L.* 285 (1955).

Madison, James. "On Nullification," originally published as a letter to the editor of the *North American Review* (1830). Reprinted in Marvin Meyers, ed., *The Mind of the Founder* (Indianapolis: Bobbs–Merrill, 1973).

Mason, Alpheus Thomas, ed. *The States Rights Debate* (2d ed.; New York: Oxford University Press, 1972).

Mathis, Doyle. "*Chisholm v. Georgia*: Background and Settlement," 54 *Jo. of Am. Hist.* 19 (1967).

Murphy, Walter F. *Elements of Judicial Strategy* (Chicago: University of Chicago Press, 1964), chaps. 4–6.

Note. "Judge Spencer Roane of Virginia: Champion of States' Rights—Foe of John Marshall," 66 *Harv.L.Rev.* 1242 (1953).

Note. "Interposition v. Judicial Power," 1 *Race Rel.L.Rep.* 464 (1956).

Peltason, Jack W. *Fifty-Eight Lonely Men: Southern Federal Judges and School Desegregation* (New York: Harcourt, Brace & World, 1961).

Storing, Herbert. *What the Anti–Federalists Were For* (Chicago: University of Chicago Press, 1981).

Warren, Charles. "Legislative and Judicial Attacks on the Supreme Court of the United States," 47 *Am.L.Rev.* 1, and 47 *ibid.* 161 (1913).

Wasby, Stephen L. *The Supreme Court in the Federal Judicial System* (4th ed.; Chicago: Nelson Hall, 1993).

"[A state decision] may be re-examined and reversed or affirmed in the Supreme Court of the United States."

JUDICIARY ACT OF 1789, SECTION 25

Article III of the constitutional text outlines the general jurisdiction of federal courts. Among the initial pieces of legislation adopted by the First Congress was the Judiciary Act of 1789, organizing and spelling out in detail the jurisdictions of various federal tribunals. Section 25 pertained to the authority of the Supreme Court to review decisions of state courts.

Sec. 1. *Be it enacted.* ...

Sec. 25. That a final judgment or decree in any suit, in the highest court of law or equity of a State in which a decision in the suit could be had, where is drawn in question the validity of a treaty or statute of, or an authority exercised under the United States, and the decision is against their validity; or where is drawn in question the validity of a statute of, or an authority exercised under any State, on the ground of their being repugnant to the constitution, treaties or laws of the United States, and the decision is in favour of their validity, or where is drawn in question the construction of any clause of the constitution, or of a treaty, or statute of, or commission held under the United States, and the decision is against the title, right, privilege or exemption specifically set up or claimed by either party, under such clause of the said constitution, treaty, statute or commission, may be re-examined and reversed or affirmed in the Supreme Court of the United States. ...

Editors' Note

Reread Articles III and VI of the constitutional text. Does it follow that, because state judges are obliged to give preference to the "Constitution" of the United States, they are bound to accept that the U.S. Supreme Court says that "the Constitution" means? Does not the answer depend on the definition of WHAT is "the Constitution"?

"[E]ach party [to the Constitution] has an equal right to judge for itself, as well of infractions as of mode and measure of redress."—Thomas Jefferson

"It belongs not to state legislatures to decide on the constitutionality of laws made by the general government; this power being exclusively vested in the judiciary courts of the Union."—Vermont's House of Representatives

THE DEBATE OF 1798-99

In 1798, the Federalist majority in Congress, fearful of the spread of "radical" ideas, enacted the Alien and Sedition Acts. The first of the Alien Acts—there were two such statutes—authorized the President to deport "all such *aliens* as he shall judge dangerous to the peace and safety of the United States"; the second provided that all citizens of a nation with whom the United States might go to war "shall be liable to be apprehended, restrained, secured and removed" from this country.

The Sedition Act not only punished efforts to use violence to oppose or overthrow the federal government, but also put into statutory form the traditional British ban against "seditious libel." The law made it a crime to write or speak anything "false, scandalous and malicious" about the federal government in general, either house of Congress, or the President "with intent to defame . . . or to bring them, or either of them, into contempt or disrepute. . . ." In sum, the Act made it a crime to criticize in any but the most polite forms the national government or its officials. Federalist prosecutors promptly began cases against Jeffersonians, and many Federalist judges—and during this period justices of the Supreme Court spent most of their time as circuit judges, presiding with district judges over important federal trials around the country—delighted in delivering charges to juries about the evils of Jeffersonianism and the malignant spirit of the French Revolution.[1]

Almost as promptly, Jefferson began drafting a series of resolutions attacking the constitutionality of the new statutes. Initially, he argued that protection against libel and slander fell under the jurisdiction of state legislatures, not Congress. The notion that freedom of speech and press as protected by the First Amendment forbade Congress to enact such legislation did not develop until the debate was well underway,[2] but it did find its way into a set of resolutions Jefferson prepared for state legislatures. He asked a friend to introduce his resolutions in North Carolina's legislature; but John Breckenridge, who would later lead efforts in the Senate to repeal the Judiciary Act of 1801 (see above, pp. 291ff), persuaded Jefferson to let him present the document to the Kentucky legislature. Breckenridge, however, made a change of major importance, one that the Kentucky legislature

---

1. See J.C. Miller, *Crisis in Freedom: The Alien and Sedition Acts* (Boston: Little, Brown, 1951); and James Morton Smith, *Freedom's Fetters: The Alien and Sedition Laws and American Civil Liberties* (Ithaca: Cornell University Press, 1956).

2. See Leonard W. Levy, *Legacy of Suppression: Freedom of Speech and Press in Early American History* (Cambridge: The Belknap Press of Harvard University Press, 1960), espec. chs. 1 and 6; see also Levy's somewhat revised thoughts: *"The Legacy* Reexamined," 37 *Stan.L.Rev.* 767 (1985).

adopted: He omitted Jefferson's claim that "every State has a natural right in cases not within the compact ... to nullify of their own authority all assumptions of power by others within their limitations. ..."

"In questions of power then let no more be heard of confidence in man, but bind him down from mischief by the chains of the Constitution."—Thomas Jefferson

A. THE KENTUCKY RESOLUTIONS OF 1798*

I. *Resolved,* that the several States composing the United States of America, are not united on the principle of unlimited submission to their general government; but that by compact under the style and title of a Constitution for the United States and of amendments thereto, they constituted a general government for special purposes, delegated to that government certain definite powers, reserving each State to itself, the residuary mass of right to their own self-government; and that whensoever the general government assumes undelegated powers, its acts are unauthoritative, void, and of no force: That to this compact each State acceded as a State, and is an integral party, its co-States forming, as to itself, the other party: That the government created by this compact was not made the exclusive or final judge of the extent of the powers delegated to itself; since that would have made its discretion, and not the Constitution, the measure of its powers; but that as in all other cases of compact among parties having no common Judge, *each party has an equal right to judge for itself, as well of infractions as of the mode and measure of redress.*

II. *Resolved,* that the Constitution of the United States having delegated to Congress a power to punish treason, counterfeiting the securities and current coin of the United States, piracies and felonies committed on the high seas, and offenses against the laws of nations, and no other crimes whatever, and it being true as a general principle, and one of the amendments to the Constitution having also declared "that the powers not delegated to the United States by the Constitution, nor prohibited by it to the States, are reserved to the States respectively, or to the people," therefore also ... [the Sedition Act of July 14, 1798]; as also the act ... entitled "An act to punish frauds committed on the Bank of the United States" (and all other their acts which assume to create, define, or punish crimes other than those enumerated in the Constitution), are altogether void and of no force, and that the power to create, define, and punish such other crimes is reserved, and of right appertains solely and exclusively to the respective States, each within its own Territory.

---

* Jonathan Elliot, ed., *The Debates in the Several State Conventions on the Adoption of the Federal Constitution* (2d ed.; Philadelphia: Lippincott, 1861), IV, 540–544.

III. *Resolved,* that it is true as a general principle, and is also expressly declared by one of the amendments to the Constitution that "the powers not delegated to the United States by the Constitution, nor prohibited by it to the States, are reserved to the States respectively or to the people;" and that no power over the freedom of religion, freedom of speech, or freedom of the press being delegated to the United States by the Constitution, nor prohibited by it to the States, all lawful powers respecting the same did of right remain, and were reserved to the States, or to the people: That thus was manifested their determination to retain to themselves the right of judging how far the licentiousness of speech and of the press may be abridged without lessening their useful freedom, and how far those abuses which cannot be separated from their use should be tolerated rather than the use be destroyed; and thus also they guarded against all abridgment by the United States of the freedom of religious opinions and exercises, and retained to themselves the right of protecting the same, as this State, by a law passed on the general demand of its citizens, had already protected them from all human restraint or interference: And that in addition to this general principle and express declaration, another and more special provision has been made by one of the amendments to the Constitution which expressly declares, that "Congress shall make no law respecting an establishment of religion, or prohibiting the free exercise thereof, or abridging the freedom of speech, or of the press" ... and that libels, falsehoods, defamation equally with heresy and false religion, are withheld from the cognizance of Federal tribunals. That therefore ... [the Sedition Act], which does abridge the freedom of the press, is not law, but is altogether void and of no effect. ...

[Resolutions IV–VII detailed arguments against the constitutionality of the Alien Acts and the statute punishing fraud against the Bank of the United States.]

VIII. *Resolved,* that the preceding Resolutions be transmitted to the Senators and Representatives in Congress from this Commonwealth, who are hereby enjoined to present the same to their respective Houses, and to use their best endeavors to procure, at the next session of Congress, a repeal of the aforesaid unconstitutional and obnoxious acts.

IX. *Resolved,* lastly, that the Governor of this Commonwealth be, and is hereby authorized and requested to communicate the preceding Resolutions to the Legislatures of the several States, to assure them that this Commonwealth considers Union for specified National purposes, and particularly for those specified in their late Federal Compact, to be friendly to the peace, happiness, and prosperity of all the States; that faithful to that compact according to the plain intent and meaning in which it was understood and acceded to by the several parties, it is sincerely anxious for its preservation: that it does also believe, that to take from the States all the powers of self-government, and transfer them to a general and consolidated government, without regard to the special delegations and reservations solemnly agreed to in that compact, is not for the peace, happiness, or prosperity of these States ... that it would be a dangerous delusion were a confidence in the men of our choice to silence our fears for the safety of our rights; that confidence is everywhere the parent of despotism—free government is founded in jealousy, not in confidence; it is jealousy and not confidence which prescribes limited constitutions, to bind down those whom we are obliged to trust with power: that our Constitution has accordingly fixed the limit to which, and no further, our confidence may go. ... In questions of power, then, let no more be heard of confidence in man, but bind him down from mischief by the chains of the Constitution.   That this commonwealth does therefore call on its co-States for an expression of their sentiments on the acts concerning aliens, and for the punishment of certain crimes herein before specified, plainly declaring whether these acts are or are not authorized by the Federal Compact. ...

Madison drafted another set of resolutions for the Virginia legislature. Although similar to Jefferson's in proclaiming the unconstitutionality of the Alien and Sedition Acts, Madison's resolutions were more moderate in tone and substance, for, unlike Jefferson, Madison rejected the notion that a state legislature could nullify a federal statute.[4] The Virginia legislature "solemnly," if vaguely, appealed "to the like dispositions of the other states, in confidence that they will concur with this Commonwealth in declaring ... that the acts aforesaid are unconstitutional; and that the necessary and proper measures will be taken by each for co-operating with this state, in maintaining unimpaired the authorities, rights, and liberties reserved to the states respectively, or to the people. ..."

---

4. Jefferson was displeased with what he thought was Madison's mincing on this issue. In response, Madison wrote to his mentor: "Have you ever considered thoroughly the distinction between the power of the *State,* & that of the *Legislature,* on questions relating to the federal pact. On the supposition that the former is clearly the ultimate Judge of infractions, it does not follow that the latter is the legitimate organ, especially as a convention was the organ by which the compact was made." Quoted in Nathan Schachner, *Thomas Jefferson: A Biography* (New York: Thomas Yoseloff, 1951), p. 617. During the Constitutional Convention, Madison had been in favor of a very strong central government, one stronger than the structure that took shape. During the debates on ratification, he had taken a less nationalistic line and had attempted to quiet states' fears. And, in introducing the Bill of Rights in the First Congress, he had stressed that such a listing would help state legislatures "jealously and closely watch the operations of this Government, and be able to resist with more effect every assumption of power, than any other power on earth can do"—pretty much the course he took in the Virginia Resolutions. Later, when President, Madison faced an effort by Pennsylvania to nullify the Supreme Court's decision in United States v. Peters (1809). He not only refused to accept the state's assertion of authority, he also insisted on his duty as President to use force, if necessary, to ensure compliance with the Court's ruling. His firmness caused the governor, who had called out the militia to prevent execution of the Court's mandate, to beat a hasty retreat. For details, see Charles Warren, *The Supreme Court in U.S. History* (Rev. ed.; Boston: Little, Brown, 1926), I, 366ff.

"[T]he Constitution . . . vests in the Federal Courts, exclusively, and in the Supreme Court of the United States, ultimately, the authority of deciding on the constitutionality of any act or law of the Congress of the United States."—Rhode Island

B. THE STATES RESPOND TO KENTUCKY AND VIRGINIA*

Seven state legislatures replied directly to the resolutions, three indirectly. All were negative. The other state legislatures were silent.

State of Rhode Island and Providence Plantations.

In General Assembly, *February, A.D.* 1799

Certain resolutions of the legislature of Virginia, passed on 21st of December last, being communicated to this Assembly,—

1. *Resolved,* That, in the opinion of this legislature, the second section of third article of the Constitution of the United States, in these words, to wit,—"The judicial power shall extend to all cases arising under the laws of the United States,"—vests in the federal courts, exclusively, and in the Supreme Court of the United States, ultimately, the authority of deciding on the constitutionality of any act or law of the Congress of the United States.

2. *Resolved,* That for any state legislature to assume that authority would be—

1st. Blending together legislative and judicial powers;

2d. Hazarding an interruption of the peace of the states by civil discord, in case of a diversity of opinions among the state legislatures; each state having, in that case, no resort, for vindicating its own opinions, but the strength of its own arm;—

3d. Submitting most important questions of law to less competent tribunals; and,

4th. An infraction of the Constitution of the United States, expressed in plain terms.

3. *Resolved,* That, although, for the above reasons, this legislature, in their public capacity, do not feel themselves authorized to consider and decide on the constitutionality of the Sedition and Alien laws, (so called,) yet they are called upon, by the exigency of this occasion, to declare that, in their private opinions, these laws are within the powers delegated to Congress, and promotive of the welfare of the United States.

. . .

---

* Jonathan Elliot, *The Debates in the Several State Conventions on the Adoption of the Federal Constitution* (2d ed.; Philadelphia: Lippincott, 1861), IV, 533–539.

Commonwealth of Massachusetts

In Senate, February 9, 1799.

The legislature of Massachusetts, having taken into serious consideration the resolutions of the state of Virginia, ... deem it their duty solemnly to declare that, while they hold sacred the principle, that consent of the people is the only pure source of just and legitimate power, they cannot admit the right of the state legislatures to denounce the administration of that government to which the people themselves, by a solemn compact, have exclusively committed their national concerns. That, although a liberal and enlightened vigilance among the people is always to be cherished, yet an unreasonable jealousy of the men of their choice, and a recurrence to measures of extremity upon groundless or trivial pretexts, have a strong tendency to destroy all rational liberty at home, and to deprive the United States of the most essential advantages in relations abroad. That this legislature are persuaded that the decision of all cases in law and equity arising under the Constitution of the United States, and the construction of all laws made in pursuance thereof, are exclusively vested by the people in the judicial courts of the United States. ...

State of Vermont

In the House of Representatives, October 30, A.D. 1799.

The house proceeded to take under their consideration the resolutions of the General Assembly of Virginia, relative to certain measures of the general government, transmitted to the legislature of this state, for their consideration: Whereupon,—

Resolved, That the General Assembly of the state of Vermont do highly disapprove of the resolutions of the General Assembly of Virginia, as being unconstitutional in their nature, and dangerous in their tendency. It belongs not to state legislatures to decide on the constitutionality of laws made by the general government; this power being exclusively vested in the judiciary courts of the Union. ... And that the same be sent to the governor and council for their concurrence.

In Council, October 30, 1799. Read and concurred unanimously.

Editors' Notes

(1) **Query:** What light does the constitutional text shed on this aspect of the debate about WHO?

(2) **Query:** To what extent does Jefferson's reasoning follow from his claim that "the Constitution" was a compact among the states? What textual basis did he have for such an assertion?

(3) **Query:** Would the logic of Brutus's argument (reprinted above, p. 281) have compelled him to agree with Jefferson or with the responding state legislatures?

(4) The strongly negative character of these responses pushed John Breckenridge and other political leaders in Kentucky to publish a counter-

response. In 1799, after a bitter debate, the state legislature repeated its condemnation of the federal legislation and added to its earlier resolution the sort of clause that Breckenridge had removed from Jefferson's draft:

> That the several states who formed that instrument [the Constitution] being sovereign and independent, have the unquestionable right to judge of the infraction; and, That a nullification of those sovereign-ties, of all unauthorized acts done under color of that instrument is the rightful remedy.

Madison managed to cool Jefferson down and persuade him that caution was wiser than confronting Federalist (and federal) power. The Alien and Sedition Acts expired before Jefferson took office after winning the election of 1800. He pardoned three people still in prison under the acts, and Congress later remitted all the fines. (Jefferson was less opposed to state prosecutions for seditious libel when he himself was the target of the alleged libel.) After 1828, when John C. Calhoun began to trumpet a new doctrine of nullification, Madison called it "a colossal heresy" and claimed it was false to associate Jefferson's name with such an "inlet to anarchy." [5]

"It is a mistake [to contend], that the constitution was not designed to operate upon states, in their corporate capacities."

MARTIN v. HUNTER'S LESSEE

14 U.S. (1 Wheat.) 304, 4 L.Ed. 97 (1816).

In 1813 the Supreme Court had reversed a decision of the Virginia Court of Appeals regarding the protection afforded land rights of British citizens by Jay's Treaty (1794). The Virginia Court of Appeals, however, responded by defying the U.S. Supreme Court:

> The court is unanimously of opinion that the appellate power of the Supreme Court of the United States does not extend to this court, under a sound construction of the constitution of the United States; that so much of the 25th section of the act of congress to establish the judicial courts of the United States, as extends the appellate jurisdiction of the supreme court to this court is not in pursuance of the constitution of the United States; that the writ of error, in this cause, was improvidently allowed under the authority of that act; that the proceedings thereon in the supreme court were coram non judice [in the presence of a person not a judge of competent jurisdiction], in relation to this court, and that obedience to its mandate be declined by the court.

Martin, who had won in the U.S. Supreme Court the first time, brought his case back to Washington.

---

5. See vol. 4 of W. C. Rives and P. R. Fendall, eds., *Letters and Other Writings of James Madison* (Philadelphia: Lippincott, 1865), which collects a number of his letters and essays opposing nullification.

STORY, J., delivered the opinion of the court.   . . .

The constitution of the United States was ordained and established, not by the states in their sovereign capacities, but emphatically, as the preamble of the constitution declares, by "the People of the United States." There can be no doubt, that it was competent to the people to invest the general government with all the powers which they might deem proper and necessary; to extend or restrain these powers according to their own good pleasure, and to give them a paramount and supreme authority. As little doubt can there be, that the people had a right to prohibit to the states the exercise of any powers which were, in their judgment, incompatible with the objects of the general compact; to make the powers of the state governments, in given cases, subordinate to those of the nation, or to reserve to themselves those sovereign authorities which they might not choose to delegate to either. The constitution was not, therefore, necessarily carved out of existing state sovereignties, nor a surrender of powers already existing in state institutions, for the powers of the states depend upon their own constitutions. . . . On the other hand, it is perfectly clear, that the sovereign powers vested in the state governments, by their respective constitutions, remained unaltered and unimpaired, except so far as they were granted to the government of the United States. These deductions do not rest upon general reasoning, plain and obvious as they seem to be. They have been positively recognised by one of the articles in amendment of the constitution, which declares, that "the powers not delegated to the United States by the constitution, nor prohibited by it to the states, are reserved to the states respectively, or to the people."

The government, then, of the United States can claim no powers which are not granted to it by the constitution, and the powers actually granted, must be such as are expressly given, or given by necessary implication. On the other hand, this instrument, like every other grant, is to have a reasonable construction, according to the import of its terms; and where a power is expressly given, in general terms, it is not to be restrained to particular cases, unless that construction grow out of the context, expressly, or by necessary implication. The words are to be taken in their natural and obvious sense, and not in a sense unreasonably restricted or enlarged.

The constitution unavoidably deals in general language. . . . Hence, its powers are expressed in general terms, leaving to the legislature, from time to time, to adopt its own means to effectuate legitimate objects, and to mould and model the exercise of its powers, as its own wisdom, and the public interests, should require. . . .

The third article of the constitution is that which must principally attract our attention. The 1st section declares, "the judicial power of the United States shall be vested in one supreme court, and in such other inferior courts as the congress may, from time to time, ordain and establish." The 2d section declares, that "the judicial power shall extend to all cases in law or equity, arising under this constitution, the laws of the United States, and the treaties made, or which shall be made, under their authority. ..."

Such is the language of the article creating and defining the judicial power of the United States. It is the voice of the whole American people, solemnly declared, in establishing one great department of that government which was, in many respects, national, and in all, supreme. It is a part of the very same instrument which was to act, not merely upon individuals, but upon states; and to deprive them altogether of the exercise of some powers of sovereignty, and to restrain and regulate them in the exercise of others.

Let this article be carefully weighed and considered. The language of the article throughout is manifestly designed to be mandatory upon the legislature. Its obligatory force is so imperative, that congress could not, without a violation of its duty, have refused to carry it into operation. The judicial power of the United States *shall* be vested (not *may* be vested) in one supreme court, and in such inferior courts as congress may, from time to time, ordain and establish. Could congress have lawfully refused to create a supreme court, or to vest in it the constitutional jurisdiction? "The judges, both of the supreme and inferior courts, shall hold their offices during good behavior, and shall, at stated times, receive, for their services, a compensation which shall not be diminished during their continuance in office." Could congress create or limit any other tenure of the judicial office? Could they refuse to pay, at stated times, the stipulated salary, or diminish it during the continuance in office? But one answer can be given to these questions: it must be in the negative. ...

The same expression, "shall be vested," occurs in other parts of the constitution, in defining the powers of the other co-ordinate branches of the government. The first article declares that "all legislative powers herein granted shall be vested in a congress of the United States." Will it be contended that the legislative power is not absolutely vested? ... The second article declares that "the executive power shall be vested in a president of the United States of America." Could congress vest it in any other person ...? It is apparent, that such a construction, in either case, would be utterly inadmissible. Why, then, is it entitled to a better support, in reference to the judicial department?

If, then, it is a duty of congress to vest the judicial power of the United States, it is a duty to vest the whole judicial power. The language, if imperative as to one part, is imperative as to all. ...

The next consideration is, as to the courts in which the judicial power shall be vested. It is manifest, that a supreme court must be established; but whether it be equally obligatory to establish inferior courts, is a question of some difficulty. If congress may lawfully omit to establish inferior courts, it might follow, that in some of the enumerated cases, the judicial power could nowhere exist. ...

This construction will be fortified by an attentive examination of the second section of the third article. The words are "the judicial power shall extend," & c. . . . For the reasons which have been already stated, we are of opinion, that the words are used in an imperative sense; they import an absolute grant of judicial power. . . .

It being, then, established, that the language of this clause is imperative, the question is, as to the cases to which it shall apply. The answer is found in the constitution itself "the judicial power shall extend to all the cases enumerated in the constitution." . . .

This leads us to the consideration of the great question, as to the nature and extent of the appellate jurisdiction of the United States. . . . [A]ppellate jurisdiction is given by the constitution to the supreme court, in all cases where it has not original jurisdiction; subject, however, to such exceptions and regulations as congress may prescribe. It is, therefore, capable of embracing every case enumerated in the constitution, which is not exclusively to be decided by way of original jurisdiction. . . . The appellate power is not limited by the terms of the third article to any particular courts. The words are, "the judicial power (which includes appellate power) shall extend to all cases," & c., and "in all other cases before mentioned the supreme court shall have appellate jurisdiction." It is the case, then, and not the court, that gives the jurisdiction. If the judicial power extends to the case, it will be in vain to search in the letter of the constitution for any qualification as to the tribunal where it depends. It is incumbent, then, upon those who assert such a qualification, to show its existence, by necessary implication. If the text be clear and distinct, no restriction upon its plain and obvious import ought to be admitted, unless the inference be irresistible.

If the constitution meant to limit the appellate jurisdiction to cases pending in the courts of the United States, it would necessarily follow, that the jurisdiction of these courts would, in all the cases enumerated in the constitution, be exclusive of state tribunals. . . .

But it is plain, that the framers of the constitution did contemplate that cases within the judicial cognisance of the United States, not only might, but would, arise in the state courts, in the exercise of their ordinary jurisdiction. With this view, the sixth article declares, that "this constitution, and the laws of the United States which shall be made in pursuance thereof, and all treaties made, or which shall be made, under the authority of the United States, shall be the supreme law of the land, and the judges in every state shall be bound thereby, anything in the constitution or laws of any state to the contrary notwithstanding." It is obvious, that this obligation is imperative upon the state judges, in their official, and not merely in their private, capacities. . . . They were not to decide merely according to the laws or constitution of the state, but according to the constitution, laws and treaties of the United States—"the supreme law of the land." . . .

It must, therefore, be conceded, that the constitution not only contemplated, but meant to provide for cases within the scope of the judicial power of the United States, which might yet depend before state tribunals.

It has been argued, that such an appellate jurisdiction over state courts is inconsistent with the genius of our governments, and the spirit of the constitution. That the latter was never designed to act upon state sovereignties. ... We cannot yield to the force of this reasoning; it assumes principles which we cannot admit, and draws conclusions to which we do not yield our assent.

It is a mistake, that the constitution was not designed to operate upon states, in their corporate capacities. It is crowded with provisions which restrain or annul the sovereignty of the states, in some of the highest branches of their prerogatives. The tenth section of the first article contains a long list of disabilities and prohibitions imposed upon the states. Surely, when such essential portions of state sovereignty are taken away, or prohibited to be exercised, it cannot be correctly asserted, that the constitution does not act upon the states. The language of the constitution is also imperative upon the states, as to the performance of many duties. It is imperative upon the state legislatures, to make laws prescribing the time, places and manner of holding elections for senators and representatives, and for electors of president and vice-president. And in these, as well as some other cases, congress have a right to revise, amend or supersede the laws which may be passed by state legislatures. When, therefore, the states are stripped of some of the highest attributes of sovereignty, and the same are given to the United States; when the legislatures of the states are, in some respects, under the control of congress, and in every case are, under the constitution, bound by the paramount authority of the United States; it is certainly difficult to support the argument, that the appellate power over the decisions of state courts is contrary to the genius of our institutions. ...

Nor can such a right be deemed to impair the independence of state judges. It is assuming the very ground in controversy, to assert that they possess an absolute independence of the United States. In respect to the powers granted to the United States, they are not independent; they are expressly bound to obedience, by the letter of the constitution; and if they should unintentionally transcend their authority, or misconstrue the constitution, there is no more reason for giving their judgments an absolute and irresistible force, than for giving it to the acts of the other co-ordinate departments of state sovereignty. ...

This is not all. A motive of another kind, perfectly compatible with the most sincere respect for state tribunals, might induce the grant of appellate power over the decisions. That motive is the importance, and even necessity of uniformity of decisions throughout the whole United States, upon all subjects within the purview of the constitution. Judges of equal learning and integrity, in different states, might differently interpret the statute, or a treaty of the United States, or even the constitution itself: if there were no revising authority to control these jarring and discordant judgments, and harmonize them into uniformity, the laws, the treaties and the constitution of the United States would be different, in different states, and might, perhaps, never have precisely the same construction, obligation or efficiency, in any two states. The public mischiefs that would attend such a state of things would be truly deplorable. ...

On the whole, the court are of opinion, that the appellate power of the United States does extend to cases pending in the state courts; and that the 25th section of the judiciary act, which authorizes the exercise of this jurisdiction in the specified cases, by a writ of error, is supported by the letter and spirit of the constitution. We find no clause in that instrument which limits this power; and we dare not interpose a limitation, where the people have not been disposed to create one. ...

It is the opinion of the whole court, that the judgment of the court of appeals of Virginia, rendered on the mandate in this cause, be reversed, and the judgment of the district court, held at Winchester, be, and the same is hereby

Affirmed.

JOHNSON, J. ... I acquiesce in their opinion, but not altogether in the reasoning or opinion of my brother who delivered it. ...

Editors' Notes

(1) **Query:** We repeat our earlier question: Article VI requires state judges to follow "the Constitution" of the United States. Does it follow that they are bound to follow what the U.S. Supreme Court has said that "Constitution" means?

(2) *Hunter's Lessee* is one of the few constitutional disputes for which John Marshall did not assign himself the task of writing the opinion of the Court. In this instance, he did not sit because he had become involved in the land speculation that revolved around the ownership of property once possessed by Loyalists during the Revolutionary War, whose title was at issue in this case. But Marshall was not quite so pure as his formal recusal indicates. He worked behind the scene to perfect Martin's appeal and to "assist" his brethren in reaching the "correct" decision. For details, see: G. Edward White, *The Marshall Court and Cultural Change, 1815–35*, vols. III–IV of The Oliver Wendell Holmes Devise, *History of the Supreme Court of the United States* (Paul A. Freund and Stanley N. Katz, eds.) (New York: Macmillan, 1988), pp. 165–173. The critical general issues of federalism might have provided the Chief Justice a rationalization for his informal participation. But Marshall's (and perhaps most judges') sense of propriety was different from that of our time. For instance: He apparently did not find it troublesome to sit in Marbury v. Madison (1803; reprinted above, p. 298), where he himself and his brother had been significant actors in precipitating the dispute.

(3) To avoid further conflict with Virginia's Court of Appeals, the Supreme Court sent its order directly to the state trial court in Winchester.

(4) Virginia's attack on § 25 was only one among many. See the two-part article by Charles Warren, "Legislative and Judicial Attacks on the

Supreme Court of the United States—A History of the Twenty–Fifth Section of the Judiciary Act," 47 *Am.L.Rev.* 1; 47 *ibid.* 161 (1913).

(5) **Query:** Story asserted that Congress was constitutionally obligated to create an entire system of federal courts. Does that conclusion follow from the plain words of Article III? Does it follow from the logic of federalism? See the discussion in Chapter 11, below. Canada and the Federal Republic of Germany, both federal systems, have depended primarily on the equivalent of state courts for the bulk of national civil and criminal jurisdiction. And it was not until after the Civil War that Congress conferred on federal courts anything approaching the full jurisdiction listed in Article III, and more recently—in the Emergency Price Control Act of 1942, for example—has specifically authorized enforcement of federal law, at least in civil cases, in state tribunals. See the discussion in Paul M. Bator, et al., eds., *Hart and Wechsler's The Federal Courts and the Federal System* (3rd ed.; Westbury, NY: Foundation Press, 1988), pp. 10–11, 479–500; Martin H. Redish, *Federal Jurisdiction* (Indianapolis: Bobbs–Merrill, 1980), pp. 21–24; and Henry J. Friendly, *Federal Jurisdiction* (New York: Columbia University Press, 1973), pp. 1–14.

"Do the courts of the States stand ... in the relation of the inferior to the Supreme Court of the United States?"

A DISCOURSE ON THE CONSTITUTION AND GOVERNMENT OF THE UNITED STATES

John C. Calhoun (1851).

Although Calhoun came to Congress in 1811 as an ardent nationalist, by 1828 he had become a sectionalist. As Vice President of the United States, U.S. Senator from South Carolina, Secretary of State, and elder statesman, he was the most elegant and systematic spokesman for nullification and then, following the iron road of his own logic, for secession as principles inherent in the American Constitution.

... Now, as there is nothing in the constitution which vests authority in the government of the United States, or any of its departments, to enforce its decision against that of the separate government of a State; and nothing in this clause [Art. III, Sec. 2, U.S. Con.] which makes the several States amenable to its process, it is manifest that there is nothing in it, which can possibly give the judicial power authority to enforce the decision of the government of the United States, against that of a separate State. ...

It is, in the last place, contended,—that the Supreme Court of the United States has the right to decide on the constitutionality of all laws; and, in virtue of this, to decide, in the last resort, all questions involving a conflict between the constitution of the United States and laws and treaties made in pursuance thereof, on the one side, and the constitutions and laws of the several States on the other.

It is admitted, that the court has the right, in all questions of a judicial character which may come before it, where the laws and treaties of the United States, and the constitution and laws of a State are in conflict or brought in question, to decide which is, or is not consistent with the constitution of the United States. But it is denied that this power is peculiar to it; or that its decision, in the last resort, is binding on any but the parties to it, and its co-departments. So far from being peculiar to it, the right appertains, not only to the Supreme Court of the United States, but to all courts of the several States, superior and inferior. ... Now, as the constitution of the United States is, within its sphere, supreme over all others appertaining to the system, it necessarily results, that where any law conflicts with it, it is the duty of the court, before which the question arises, to pronounce the constitution to be paramount. If it be the Supreme Court of the United States, its decision,—being that of the highest judicial tribunal, in the last resort, of the parties to the case or controversy,—is, of course, final as it respects them,—but only as it respects them. It results, that its decision is not binding as between the United States and the several States, as neither can make the other defendant in any controversy between them. ...

[Calhoun moved to a discussion of § 25 of the Judiciary Act of 1789.] The question is thus narrowed down to a single point;—Has Congress the authority ... to make a law providing for an appeal from the courts of the several States to the Supreme Court of the United States?

There is, on the face of the two clauses [the jurisdictional clauses of Art. III], nothing whatever to authorize the making of such a law. Neither of them names or refers, in the slightest manner to the States, or to the courts of the States; or gives the least authority, apparently, to legislate over or concerning either. The object of the former of these two clauses, is simply to extend the judicial power, so as to make it commensurate with the other powers of the government. ... While the latter simply provides, in what cases the Supreme Court of the United States shall have original, and in what, appellate jurisdiction. ...

Such being the plain meaning and intent of these clauses,—the question is;—How can Congress derive from them, authority to make a law providing for an appeal from the highest courts of the several States, in the cases specified in the 25th sect. of the Judiciary Act, to the Supreme Court of the United States?

To this question no answer can be given, without assuming that the State courts,—even the highest,—stand in the relation of inferior courts to the Supreme Court of the United States, wherever a question touching their authority comes before them. Without such an assumption, there is not, and cannot be a shadow of authority to warrant an appeal from the former to the latter. But does the fact sustain the assumption? Do the courts of the States stand, as to such questions, in the relation of the inferior to the Supreme Court of the United States? If so, it must be by some provision of the constitution of the United States. It cannot be a matter of course. How can it be reconciled with the admitted principle, that the federal government and those of the several States, are each supreme in their respective spheres? Each, it is admitted, is supreme, as it regards the other, in its proper sphere; and, of course, as has been shown, coequal and co-ordinate.

If this be true, then, the respective departments of each must be necessarily and equally so;—as the whole includes the parts. The State courts are the representatives of the reserved rights, vested in the governments of the several States, as far as it relates to the judicial power. Now, as these are reserved *against* the federal government,—as the very object and intent of the reservation, was to place them beyond the reach of its control,—how can the courts of the States be inferior to the Supreme Court of the United States; and, of course, subject to have their decisions re-examined and reversed by it, without, at the same time, subjecting the portion of the reserved rights of the governments of the several States, vested in it, to the control of the federal government?
. . .

I have now shown that the 25th section of the judiciary act is unauthorized by the constitution; and that it rests on an assumption which would give to Congress the right to enforce, through the judiciary department, whatever measures it might think proper to adopt; and to put down all resistance by force. The effect of this is to make the government of the United States the sole judge . . . as to the extent of its powers, and to place the States and their separate governments and institutions at its mercy. . . .

Editors' Notes

(1) **Query:** To what extent is Calhoun merely echoing Jefferson's argument in the Kentucky Resolutions?

(2) **Query:** What, read together, do Articles III and VI and the Tenth Amendment tell us about the relative interpretive authority of federal and state judges?

"[N]o power is more clearly conferred by the Constitution and laws of the United States, than the power of this court to decide, ultimately and finally, all cases arising under such Constitution and laws. ..."

ABLEMAN v. BOOTH

62 U.S. (21 How.) 506, 16 L.Ed. 169 (1859).

In the mid–1850s, a federal marshal arrested Sherman M. Booth, an abolitionist editor from Milwaukee, Wisconsin, and charged him with violating the Fugitive Slave Act by helping a slave to escape. Because there was no federal prison in the area, the marshal placed Booth in a local jail. The

prisoner then petitioned the Wisconsin supreme court for habeas corpus.*
That court granted the writ and declared the Fugitive Slave Act unconstitutional. The marshal obtained review in the U.S. Supreme Court. Before the
justices heard the case, a federal trial court convicted Booth, sentenced him to
a year in prison, and ordered him to pay a fine of $1,000. Again he sought
habeas corpus from the Wisconsin supreme court, and again that court
granted the writ, holding that the federal trial court's action was as unconstitutional as the statute on which the conviction was based. The local jailer freed
Booth. The marshal asked the U.S. Supreme Court to review this second
state decision as well. The justices consolidated the two appeals.

Mr. Chief Justice **TANEY** delivered the opinion of the court.   . . .

If the judicial power exercised in this instance has been reserved to
the States, no offence against the laws of the United States can be
punished by their own courts, without the permission and according to
the judgment of the courts of the State in which the party happens to be
imprisoned; for, if the Supreme Court of Wisconsin possessed the power
it has exercised . . . it necessarily follows that they must have the same
judicial authority in relation to any other law of the United States.   . . .
And, moreover, if the power is possessed by the Supreme Court of the
State of Wisconsin, it must belong equally to every other State in the
Union, when the prisoner is within its territorial limits; and it is very
certain that the State courts would not always agree in opinion; and it
would often happen, that an act which was admitted to be an offence,
and justly punished, in one State, would be regarded as innocent, and
indeed as praiseworthy, in another.   . . .

The judges of the Supreme Court of Wisconsin do not distinctly state
from what source they suppose they have derived this judicial power.
There can be no such thing as judicial authority, unless it is conferred by
a Government or sovereignty; and if the judges and courts of Wisconsin
possess the jurisdiction they claim, they must derive it either from the
United States or the State. It certainly has not been conferred on them
by the United States; and it is equally clear that it was not in the power
of the State to confer it . . . for no State can authorize one of its judges
or courts to exercise judicial power . . . within the jurisdiction of another
and independent Government. And although the State of Wisconsin is
sovereign within its territorial limits to a certain extent, yet that
sovereignty is limited and restricted by the Constitution of the United
States. And the powers of the General Government, and of the State,
although both exist and are exercised within the same territorial limits,
are yet separate and distinct sovereignties, acting separately and independently of each other, within their respective spheres. And the sphere
of action appropriate to the United States is as far beyond the reach of
the judicial process issued by a State judge or a State court, as if the line
of division was traced by landmarks and monuments visible to the eye.
. . .

---

* An order to a jailer or other person having custody of a prisoner instructing him to
bring that prisoner to court and show legal cause for holding him or her in custody.—**Eds.**

... The Constitution was not formed merely to guard the States against danger from foreign nations, but mainly to secure union and harmony at home ... and to accomplish this purpose, it was felt by the people who adopted it, that it was necessary that many of the rights of sovereignty which the States then possessed should be ceded to the General Government; and that, in the sphere of action assigned to it, should be supreme, and strong enough to execute its own laws by its own tribunals, without interruption from a State or from State authorities. ...

The language of the Constitution, by which this power is granted, is too plain to admit of doubt or to need comment. It declares that "this Constitution, and the laws of the United States which shall be passed in pursuance thereof, and all treaties made, or which shall be made, under the authority of the United States, shall be the supreme law of the land, and the judges in every State shall be bound thereby, anything in the Constitution or laws of any State to the contrary notwithstanding."

But the supremacy thus conferred on this Government could not peacefully be maintained, unless it was clothed with judicial power, equally paramount in authority to carry it into execution; for if left to the courts of justice of the several States, conflicting decisions would unavoidably take place, and the local tribunals could hardly be expected to be always free from the local influences of which we have spoken. ...

Accordingly, it was conferred on the General Government, in clear, precise, and comprehensive terms. It is declared that its judicial power shall (among other subjects enumerated) extend to all cases in law and equity arising under the Constitution and laws of the United States, and that in such cases, as well as the others there enumerated, this court shall have appellate jurisdiction both as to law and fact, with such exceptions and under such regulations as Congress shall make. The appellate power, it will be observed, is conferred on this court in all cases or suits in which such a question shall arise. It is not confined to suits in the inferior courts of the United States, but extends to all cases where such a question arises, whether it be in a judicial tribunal of a State or of the United States. And it is manifest that this ultimate appellate power in a tribunal created by the Constitution itself was deemed essential to secure the independence and supremacy of the General Government in the sphere of action assigned to it; to make the Constitution and laws of the United States uniform, and the same in every State. ...

This judicial power was justly regarded as indispensable, not merely to maintain the supremacy of the laws of the United States, but also to guard the States from any encroachment upon their reserved rights by the General Government. And as the Constitution is the fundamental and supreme law, if it appears that an act of Congress is not pursuant to it and within the limits of the power assigned to the Federal Government, it is the duty of the courts of the United States to declare it unconstitutional and void. ... And as the final appellate power in all such questions is given to this court, controversies as to the respective

—— powers of the United States and the States, instead of being determined by military and physical force are heard, investigated, and finally settled with the calmness and deliberation of judicial inquiry. ...

... No State judge or court, after they are judicially informed that the party is imprisoned under the authority of the United States, has any right to interfere with him, or to require him to be brought before them. And if the authority of a State, in the form of judicial process or otherwise, should attempt to control the marshal or other authorized officer or agent of the United States, in any respect, in the custody of his prisoner, it would be his duty to resist it. ... No judicial process ... can have any lawful authority outside of the limits of the jurisdiction of the court or judge by whom it is issued; and an attempt to enforce it beyond these boundaries is nothing less than lawless violence.

Nor is there anything in this supremacy of the General Government, or the jurisdiction of its judicial tribunals, to awaken the jealousy or offend the natural and just pride of State sovereignty. Neither this Government, nor the powers of which we are speaking, were forced upon the States. The Constitution of the United States, with all the powers conferred by it on the General Government, and surrendered by the States, was the voluntary act of the people of the several States, deliberately done, for their own protection and safety against injustice from one another. ...

... [N]o power is more clearly conferred by the Constitution and laws of the United States, than the power of this court to decide, ultimately and finally, all cases arising under such Constitution and laws; and for that purpose to bring here for revision, by writ of error, the judgment of a State court, where such questions have arisen, and the right claimed under them denied by the highest judicial tribunal in the State. ...

The judgment of the Supreme Court of Wisconsin must therefore be reversed. ...

Editors' Notes

(1) In addressing the question of WHO, to what extent did Taney rely on the words of the constitutional text? To what extent on political prudence?

(2) The Wisconsin legislature adopted a resolution branding the U.S. Supreme Court's ruling "an act of undelegated power, and therefore without authority, void and of no force"; then repeated some of the language of the Second Kentucky Resolutions of 1799 (reprinted above, p. 354):

> That the government formed by the Constitution of the United States was not made the exclusive or final judge of the extent of the powers delegated to itself; but that as in all other cases of compact among parties having no common judge, each party has an equal right to judge for itself as well of infractions as the mode and measure of redress. ...

Nevertheless, federal officers rearrested Booth in March, 1860, and he again sought habeas corpus from the state supreme court. This time, however, he did not succeed. One judge had to recuse himself because he had been the prisoner's attorney during early stages of the litigation, and the other two judges disagreed with each other about their authority to issue the writ. Booth was locked up in the federal building in Milwaukee. He was something of a popular hero who further embarrassed his jailers by refusing to pay the fine or to ask for a presidential pardon. An abolitionist mob provided the practical solution by freeing him. In 1861, the Wisconsin supreme court ruled that the U.S. district court had had jurisdiction to try Booth. Arnold v. Booth (1861). For details, see Charles Warren, *The Supreme Court in U.S. History,* II, ch. 27; Note, "Interposition vs. Judicial Power," 1 *Race Rels.L.Rep.* 465, 490–496 (1956); and Carl B. Swisher, *The Taney Period, 1836–64*, vol. V of the Holmes Devise (New York: Macmillan, 1974), ch. 26.

(3) Wisconsin's resistance to the Fugitive Slave Act was not an isolated event. At least ten other northern and western states tried to suspend the statute's operation within their borders. See, Note, "Interposition vs. Judicial Power," 1 *Race Rel.L.Rep.* 465, 496 (1956); and Anthony J. Sebok, "Judging the Fugitive Slave Acts," 100 *Yale L.J.* 1835 (1991). For a more general treatment of the moral and constitutional problems of slavery, Robert M. Cover, *Justice Accused: Antislavery and the Judicial Process* (New Haven: Yale University Press, 1975), and Christopher L. M. Eisgruber, "Justice Story, Slavery, and the Natural Law Foundations of American Constitutionalism," 55 *U. Chi. L. Rev.* 273 (1988).

"We pledge ourselves to use all lawful means to bring about a reversal of this decision. ...."—The Southern Manifesto

"[T]he interpretation of the Fourteenth Amendment enunciated by this Court in the Brown Case is the supreme law of the land, and Art. 6 of the Constitution makes it of binding effect on the States. ...."—U.S. Supreme Court

NULLIFYING AND REAFFIRMING BROWN v. BOARD OF EDUCATION

In 1954, the Supreme Court in Brown v. Board of Education declared compulsory segregation in public schools to be a violation of the equal protection clause of the Fourteenth Amendment. The initial reaction of most southern public officials—and at that time all southern public officials were whites—was one of stunned disbelief. Then southern leaders mounted a massive counterattack that included "pupil placement" plans, efforts to outlaw the National Association for the Advancement of Colored People, closing public schools, outright physical violence, and, of course, nullification.

"We reaffirm our reliance on the Constitution as the fundamental law of the land."

A. THE SOUTHERN MANIFESTO: A DECLARATION OF CONSTITUTIONAL PRINCIPLES (1956).*

The unwarranted decision of the Supreme Court in the public school cases is now bearing the fruit always produced when men substitute naked power for established law.

The Founding Fathers gave us a Constitution of checks and balances because they realized the inescapable lesson of history that no man or group of men can be safely entrusted with unlimited power. They framed this Constitution with its provisions for change by amendment in order to secure the fundamentals of government against the dangers of temporary popular passion or the personal predilections of public office-holders.

We regard the decision of the Supreme Court in the school cases as a clear abuse of judicial power. It climaxes a trend in the federal judiciary undertaking to legislate, in derogation of the authority of Congress, and to encroach upon the reserved rights of the States and the people.

The original Constitution does not mention education. Neither does the 14th amendment nor any other amendment. The debates preceding the submission of the 14th amendment clearly show that there was no intent that it should affect the system of education maintained by the States.

The very Congress which proposed the amendment subsequently provided for segregated schools in the District of Columbia.

When the amendment was adopted in 1868, there were 37 States of the Union. Every one of the 26 States that had any substantial racial differences among its people, either approved the operation of segregated schools already in existence or subsequently established such schools by action of the same law-making body which considered the 14th amendment. ...

This interpretation [the principle of "separate but equal"], restated time and again, became a part of the life of the people of many of the States and confirmed their habits, customs, traditions, and way of life. It is founded on elementary humanity and common sense, for parents should not be deprived by Government of the right to direct the lives and education of their own children.

Though there has been no constitutional amendment or act of Congress changing this established legal principle almost a century old, the Supreme Court of the United States, with no legal basis for such action, undertook to exercise their naked judicial power and substituted their personal political and social ideas for the established law of the land.

---

* 102 *Congressional Record* 4460; 1 *Race Relations Law Reporter* 435 (1956). The declaration was signed by 19 Senators and 77 Representatives.

This unwarranted exercise of power by the Court, contrary to the Constitution, is creating chaos and confusion in the States principally affected. It is destroying the amicable relations between the white and Negro races that have been created through 90 years of patient effort by the good people of both races. It has planted hatred and suspicion where there has been heretofore friendship and understanding.

Without regard to the consent of the governed, outside agitators are threatening immediate and revolutionary changes in our public-school system. If done, this is certain to destroy the system of public education in some of the States.

With the gravest concern for the explosive and dangerous condition created by this decision and inflamed by outside meddlers:

We reaffirm our reliance on the Constitution as the fundamental law of the land.

We decry the Supreme Court's encroachments on rights reserved to the States and to the people, contrary to established law, and to the Constitution.

We commend the motives of those States which have declared the intention to resist forced integration by any lawful means.

We appeal to the States and people who are not directly affected by these decisions to consider the constitutional principles involved against the time when they too, on issues vital to them, may be the victims of judicial encroachment.

Even though we constitute a minority in the present Congress, we have full faith that a majority of the American people believe in the dual system of government which has enabled us to achieve our greatness and will in time demand that the reserved rights of the States and of the people be made secure against judicial usurpation.

We pledge ourselves to use all lawful means to bring about a reversal of this decision which is contrary to the Constitution and to prevent the use of force in its implementation.

In this trying period, as we all seek to right this wrong, we appeal to our people not to be provoked by the agitators and troublemakers invading our States and to scrupulously refrain from disorder and lawless acts.

———

"[A] question of contested power has arisen. ..."

B. ALABAMA'S NULLIFICATION RESOLUTION *

Eight southern state legislatures—Alabama, Arkansas, Florida, Georgia, Louisiana, Mississippi, South Carolina, and Virginia—formally "nullified" Brown v. Board of Education.

Whereas the Constitution of the United States was formed by the sanction of the several states, given by each in its sovereign capacity; and

Whereas the states being the parties to the constitutional compact, it follows of necessity that there can be no tribunal above their authority to decide, in the last resort, whether the compact made by them be violated; and, consequently, they must decide themselves in the last resort, such questions as may be of sufficient magnitude to require their interposition; and

Whereas a question of contested power has arisen: The Supreme Court of the United States asserts, for its part, that the states did, in fact, in 1868 upon the adoption of the Fourteenth Amendment, prohibit unto themselves the power to maintain racially separate public institutions; the State of Alabama, for its part, asserts that it and its sister states have never surrendered such right; and

Whereas this assertion upon the part of the Supreme Court of the United States, accompanied by threats of coercion and compulsion against the sovereign states of this Union, constitutes a deliberate, palpable, and dangerous attempt by the court to prohibit to the states certain rights and powers never surrendered by them; and

Whereas the question of contested power asserted in this resolution is not within the province of the court to determine, but that as in other cases in which one party to a compact asserts an infraction thereof, the judgment of all other equal parties to the compact must be sought to resolve the question; be it

Resolved by the legislature of Alabama, both houses thereof concurring:

That until the issue between the State of Alabama and the General Government is decided by the submission to the states, pursuant to Article V of the Constitution, of a suitable constitutional amendment that would declare, in plain and unequivocal language, that the states do surrender their power to maintain public schools and other public facilities on a basis of separation as to race, the Legislature of Alabama declares the decisions and orders of the Supreme Court of the United States relating to separation of races in the public schools are, as a matter of right, null, void, and of no effect; and the Legislature of Alabama declares to all men as a matter of right, this State is not bound

---

* This resolution became an Act on February 2, 1956, without approval of the Governor. 1 *Race Relations Law Reporter* 437 (1956).

to abide thereby; we declare, further, our firm intention to take all appropriate measures honorably and constitutionally available to us, to avoid this illegal encroachment upon our rights, and to urge upon our sister states their prompt and deliberate efforts to check further encroachment by the General Government, through judicial legislation, upon the reserved powers of all states. ...

"No state ... officer can war against the Constitution without violating his undertaking to support it."

COOPER v. AARON

358 U.S. 1, 78 S.Ct. 1401, 3 L.Ed.2d 5 (1958).

In 1955, after the Supreme Court's decision in Brown v. Board of Education declaring compulsory segregation in public education unconstitutional, Little Rock's school board drew up a plan for gradual desegregation of the city's schools. The National Association for the Advancement of Colored People sued to compel the board to follow a more rapid program, but the federal district court and the Court of Appeals for the Eighth Circuit approved the school board's timetable. Meanwhile, the Arkansas legislature joined with other southern legislatures in "nullifying" Brown and also adopted a bevy of statutes to avoid compliance with the ruling. Little Rock's school board, however, persisted in its plan; and when the first African–American children showed up at Central High School in September 1958, the Governor ordered the National Guard to bar their entry. After much legal maneuvering, mob violence, and federal military intervention, the children were admitted to the school.

At the end of the year the school board asserted that Central High School had become so disrupted by tension and turmoil that education had become impossible. The board therefore asked the district court for permission to suspend desegregation for two and a half years, until popular feeling had calmed down. The district judge granted the request, but the court of appeals reversed his decision. The board sought and obtained certiorari from the Supreme Court.

Opinion of the Court by the Chief Justice [**WARREN**], Mr. Justice **BLACK**, Mr. Justice **FRANKFURTER**, Mr. Justice **DOUGLAS**, Mr. Justice **BURTON**, Mr. Justice **CLARK**, Mr. Justice **HARLAN**, Mr. Justice **BRENNAN**, and Mr. Justice **WHITTAKER**. ...

The constitutional rights of respondents are not to be sacrificed or yielded to the violence and disorder which have followed upon the actions of the Governor and Legislature. ... Thus law and order are not here to be preserved by depriving the Negro children of their constitutional rights. The record before us clearly establishes that the growth of the Board's difficulties to a magnitude beyond its unaided power to control is the product of state action. Those difficulties, as counsel for the Board forthrightly conceded on the oral argument in this Court, can also be brought under control by state action.

The controlling legal principles are plain. The command of the Fourteenth Amendment is that no "State" shall deny to any person within its jurisdiction the equal protection of the law. ... [T]he prohibitions of the Fourteenth Amendment extend to all action of the State denying equal protection of the laws; whatever the agency of the State taking the action, see Virginia v. Rives [1880]; Pennsylvania v. Board of Directors of City Trusts [1957]; Shelley v. Kraemer [1948], or whatever the guise in which it is taken. ... In short, the constitutional rights of children not to be discriminated against in school admission on grounds of race or color declared by this Court in the Brown case can neither be nullified openly and directly by state legislators or state executive or judicial officers, nor nullified indirectly by them through evasive schemes for segregation whether attempted "ingeniously or ingenuously." Smith v. Texas [1940].

What has been said ... is enough to dispose of the case. However, we should answer the premise of the actions of the Governor and Legislature that they are not bound by our holding in the Brown case. It is necessary only to recall some basic constitutional propositions which are settled doctrine.

Article 6 of the Constitution makes the Constitution the "supreme Law of the Land." In 1803, Chief Justice Marshall, speaking for a unanimous Court, referring to the Constitution as "the fundamental and paramount law of the nation," declared in the notable case of Marbury v. Madison that "It is emphatically the province and duty of the judicial department to say what the law is." This decision declared the basic principle that the federal judiciary is supreme in the exposition of the law of the Constitution, and that principle has ever since been respected by this Court and the Country as a permanent and indispensable feature of our constitutional system. It follows that the interpretation of the Fourteenth Amendment enunciated by this Court in the Brown Case is the supreme law of the land, and Art. 6 of the Constitution makes it of binding effect on the States "any Thing in the Constitution or Laws of any State to the Contrary notwithstanding." Every state legislator and executive and judicial officer is solemnly committed by oath taken pursuant to Art. 6, cl. 3 "to support this Constitution." Chief Justice Taney, speaking for a unanimous Court in 1859, said that this requirement reflected the framers' "anxiety to preserve it [the Constitution] in full force, in all its powers, and to guard against resistance to or evasion of its authority, on the part of a State. ..." Ableman v. Booth [1859].

No state legislator or executive or judicial officer can war against the Constitution without violating his undertaking to support it. Chief Justice Marshall spoke for a unanimous Court in saying that: "If the legislatures of the several states may, at will, annul the judgments of the courts of the United States, and destroy the rights acquired under those judgments, the constitution itself becomes a solemn mockery. ..."

United States v. Peters [1809]. A Governor who asserts a power to nullify a federal court order is similarly restrained. If he had such power, said Chief Justice Hughes, in 1932, also for a unanimous Court, "it is manifest that the fiat of a state Governor, and not the Constitution of the United States, would be the supreme law of the land; that the restrictions of the Federal Constitution upon the exercise of state power would be but impotent phrases. ..."

It is, of course, quite true that the responsibility for public education is primarily the concern of the States, but it is equally true that such responsibilities, like all other state activity, must be exercised consistently with federal constitutional requirements. ... The Constitution created a government dedicated to equal justice under law. The Fourteenth Amendment embodied and emphasized that ideal. State support of segregated schools through any arrangement, management, funds, or property cannot be squared with the Amendment's command that no State shall deny to any person within its jurisdiction the equal protection of the laws. The right of a student not to be segregated on racial grounds in schools so maintained is indeed so fundamental and pervasive that it is embraced in the concept of due process of law, Bolling v. Sharpe [1954]. The basic decision in *Brown* was unanimously reached by this Court only after the case had been briefed and twice argued and the issues had been given the most serious consideration. Since the first *Brown* opinion three new Justices have come to the Court. They are at one with the Justices still on the Court who participated in that basic decision as to its correctness, and that decision is now unanimously reaffirmed. The principles announced in that decision and the obedience of the States to them, according to the command of the Constitution, are indispensable for the protection of the freedoms guaranteed by our fundamental charter for all of us. Our constitutional ideal of equal justice under law is thus made a living truth.

Concurring opinion of Mr. Justice **FRANKFURTER**.

While unreservedly participating with my brethren in our joint opinion, I deem it appropriate also to deal individually with the great issue here at stake. ...

> ... The conception of a government by laws dominated the thoughts of those who founded this Nation and designed its Constitution, although they knew as well as the belittlers of the conception that laws have to be made, interpreted and enforced by men. To that end, they set apart a body of men, who were to be the depositories of law, who by their disciplined training and character and by withdrawal from the usual temptations of private interest may reasonably be expected to be 'as free, impartial, and independent as the lot of humanity will admit.' So strongly were the framers of the Constitution bent on securing a reign of law that they endowed the judicial office with extraordinary safeguards and prestige. No one, no matter how exalted his public office or how righteous his private motive, can be judge in his own case. That is what courts are for. United States v. United Mine Workers (concurring opinion) [1947].

The duty to abstain from resistance to "the supreme Law of the Land," U.S. Const. Art. 6, ¶ 2, as declared by the organ of our Government for ascertaining it, does not require immediate approval of it nor does it deny the right of dissent. Criticism need not be stilled. Active obstruction or defiance is barred. Our kind of society cannot endure if the controlling authority of the Law as derived from the Constitution is not to be the tribunal specially charged with the duty of ascertaining and declaring what is "the supreme Law of the Land." ... Particularly is this so where the declaration of what "the supreme Law" commands on an underlying moral issue is not the dubious pronouncement of a gravely divided Court but is the unanimous conclusion of a long-matured deliberative process. The Constitution is not the formulation of the merely personal views of the members of this Court, nor can its authority be reduced to the claim that state officials are its controlling interpreters. Local customs, however hardened by time, are not decreed in heaven. Habits and feelings they engender may be counteracted and moderated. Experience attests that such local habits and feelings will yield, gradually though this be, to law and education. And educational influences are exerted not only by explicit teaching. They vigorously flow from the fruitful exercise of the responsibility of those charged with political official power and from the almost unconsciously transforming actualities of living under law. ...

Editors' Note

Query: To what extent can it be validly argued that the justices' claim that "the interpretation of the Fourteenth Amendment enunciated by this Court in the Brown Case is the supreme law of the land, and Art. 6 of the Constitution makes it of binding effect on the States" did not constitute an amendment to "the Constitution"? Did not the justices, in effect, assert that their interpretations become part of the text? How could it be otherwise? What are the alternatives? What is the line between interpretation and amendment? What does the Court's claim tell us about WHAT "the Constitution" includes?

IV

How to Interpret the Constitution

SECTION E: MAINTAINING CONSTITUTIONAL DEMOCRACY: PROTECTING FUNDAMENTAL RIGHTS

Earlier Parts of this book discussed the context of constitutional interpretation and questions of WHAT "the Constitution" is and WHO its authoritative interpreters are. This Part focuses on the query: HOW does one interpret "the Constitution" in a coherent and intellectually defensible manner? There is, as readers are by now painfully aware, no intelligent way to answer any of the three questions around which this book is organized without becoming enmeshed in the others.

There is also no infallible way or set of ways to interpret "the Constitution." The best that commentators, judges, and other public officials have been able to develop is an array of methods, each one flawed and each one dependent on a wider view of politics, indeed on a political theory, however inchoate or unconscious. As Chapter 3 pointed out and Chapter 9 will emphasize, how an interpreter views the political theory or mixture of theories underpinning "the Constitution" affects the methodological choices that he or she will make.

This Part of the book is by far the longest. It opens with Chapter 9, a lengthy essay that offers summary sketches of eight of the more common "approaches" to constitutional interpretation. Decisions about WHAT "the Constitution" is—its content, authority, and functions—restricts choices among approaches.

Although many of the illustrations in Chapter 9 will be familiar, most readers will find this analysis difficult because of its abstraction and its demands for self-conscious choice about processes of interpretation. It is likely that we all use many of these approaches in other phases of our lives that require interpretive judgment, but few of us have thought about them—or why we choose them rather than some others. We suggest that readers peruse this chapter and then return to it, or portions of it, as they study material in ensuing chapters and again when they have completed the book. At the end, this chapter may seem simple, no more—or less—than common sense. In any event, keeping its main points in mind may help keep constitutional interpretation from degenerating into rationalization for selecting personally pleasing outcomes to controversies.

Chapters 10–18 flesh out Chapter 9 by organizing much of what is usually called constitutional law under several interpretive approaches: *structuralism, reinforcing representative democracy,* and *protecting fundamental rights.* This organization, we think, shows that there can be more coherence to constitutional interpretation than judges, commentators, or even students may believe.

A

GENERAL PROBLEMS

9

How to Interpret the Constitution: An Overview

This chapter begins analysis of the basic interrogative HOW by identifying and assessing various "approaches" to constitutional interpretation. Some of what we say will relate back to earlier parts of this book; some, however, will make full sense only after readers have addressed material in later chapters. Our objective is to provide an overview of recurring interpretive themes and methods. We suggest reading this chapter carefully now and returning (perhaps often) to its discussions of particular approaches as they become relevant in later chapters.

Throughout the remainder of this book, we use the term "approach" in a straightforward way to refer to the intellectual path an interpreter follows to seek meaning from that "thing" to be interpreted. Just as intelligent human beings would approach a kitten very differently from a full-grown tiger, thoughtful interpreters would analyze a constitution contained in a single document quite differently from one that includes more than that text. So, too, they would analyze a constitution that merely prescribed processes of governmental decision making quite differently from one that also embodied fundamental substantive values and aspired to direct its people toward a public life characterized by concepts (or conceptions) of liberty and justice. And, precisely as differences about what is to be interpreted are critical, so too are questions about WHO should use what approach. Thus we repeat our message about close relationships among the basic interrogatives of WHAT, WHO, and HOW.

Without any claim to being exhaustive, this chapter examines eight of the more frequently discussed approaches. Each of these leaves some questions unanswered and we shall sketch the costs and benefits of each. We relegate four other approaches, discussed more often by commentators than by public officials, to an Appendix.

Many of these approaches overlap and interact with each other. Indeed, all interact with *textualism*, analysis of the constitutional document itself, for they all claim to be seeking the meaning of that text. Each also involves philosophic issues, for interpreters' choices among approaches depends heavily on WHAT they believe "the Constitution" includes, how authoritative it is, and the roles it plays in the American political system. Furthermore, it probable, given the experience of constitutional interpreters, that prudential judgments will play a continuous part in the enterprise.

No approach or combination of approaches can turn constitutional interpretation into an exact science or eliminate controversy about what "the Constitution," whether as text or text plus, means. But because the interpretive enterprise will always partake of an art does not mean we cannot understand it more systematically than we now do. That understanding will not come easily. The intellectual difficulties, as readers are now well aware, are formidable. Chapter 2 and again Chapter 4 noted the obvious fact that constitutional interpretation involves more than intellectual analysis. It is a political act and, like many political acts in a constitutional democracy, involves both creativity and compromise.

Rarely can Congress adopt an important bill except after long and hard bargaining among competing forces. In that process, legislators often feel it necessary to bow to their colleagues' views on the best public policy. And issues of constitutional interpretation are not fully exempt. So, too, a President usually finds himself not only beset by opposing demands from within his own party, his cabinet, and even his personal advisers, but also by differing forces within Congress. To accomplish his objectives, he, too, must compromise, sometimes on constitutional issues. Franklin Roosevelt, for example, signed the Lend Lease Act of 1940, which he deemed critically important to national defense, despite constitutional scruples about Congress's including a "legislative veto." (Chapter 10, at p. 479, reprints his own constitutional interpretation and his reasons for giving in.)

Negotiation and compromise also frequently occur within the Supreme Court, indeed, within any tribunal or board composed of several people of equal authority. As Chapter 4 showed, the requirement that at least five justices sign an opinion for it to be labelled that of the Court means that adjustment in reasoning will be the typical means of securing agreement. The private papers of justices display frequent wistful notes about reluctant agreement. Justice Sutherland's comment: "Probably bad—but only a small baby. Let it go"; and Chief Justices Hughes's: "I choke a little at swallowing your analysis, still I do not think it would serve any useful purpose to expose my views"[1] are typical. But, even where the issues are important, as in *Hirabayashi* and *Korematsu*, discussed at length in Chapter 4, the justices are apt to try to adjust what they write in order to secure agreement.

---

1. For context, see Walter F. Murphy, *Elements of Judicial Strategy* (Chicago: University of Chicago Press, 1964), ch. 3; the quotations are from p. 53.

These processes of compromise may be a price of constitutional democracy; they may even be good for this or any other kind of political system by requiring consideration of different arguments and interests; but they can wreak havoc with intellectual neatness, complicating our ability to understand what is really going on. And they can mask officials' individual responsibility.

Because Chapters 1, 2, and 4 have confronted the problems of political context, this chapter will concentrate on intellectual issues, though, as when we discuss a *prudential approach*, we shall occasionally resurrect the specter of practical difficulties. In general, particular approaches to constitutional interpretation tend to stress either: (1) determinacy and predictability and so limit the discretion of interpreters as well as provide guidelines for public officials and private citizens about their rights and duties; or (2) flexibility to accommodate changing needs for governmental power and/or individual rights. In fact, many interpreters strive for both sets of benefits, increasing the likelihood of compromise and intellectual inconsistency—and further increasing problems of understanding.

I. TEXTUALISM

As Chapter 5 pointed out, parts of the American constitutional document sometimes lack authority. Consider the Ninth Amendment. In 1987, Judge Robert Bork provoked heated debate when he referred to it as an "ink blot." Had he made that claim three decades earlier, his remark would probably have provoked only bored yawns. The Ninth had long been called "the forgotten amendment." [2] Indeed, in 1954 Justice Robert H. Jackson admitted he could not even remember what that part of the text was all about.[3] Not until 1965, in Griswold v. Connecticut (reprinted above, p. 147), did the Court cite it in invalidating a statute; and, even since, as Prof. Randy Barnett has observed, the justices have "generally interpreted" that amendment "in a manner that denies it any role in the constitutional structure." [4]

---

2. Bennett B. Patterson, *The Forgotten Ninth Amendment* (Indianapolis: Bobbs–Merrill, 1955).

3. *The Supreme Court in the American System of Government* (Cambridge: Harvard University Press, 1955), p. 74.

4. "Reconceiving the Ninth Amendment," 74 *Corn.L.Rev.* 1, 2 (1988). Barnett argues that the amendment's functions are broader and more important than the Court has allowed. Although many commentators agree—for instance, Sotirios A. Barber, "The Ninth Amendment: Inkblot or Another Hard Nut to Crack?" 64 *Chi.-Kent L.Rev.* 67 (1988), other commentators do not. John Hart Ely argues that the Ninth authorizes judges only to enforce procedural rights. *Democracy and Distrust* (Cambridge: Harvard University Press, 1980), pp. 33–40. Andrzej Rapaczynski would dispose of the amendment through an answer to the question WHO. Its terms, he claims, do not speak to judges, only to elected officials. "The Ninth Amendment and the Unwritten Constitution: The Problems of Constitutional Interpretation," 64 *Chi.-Kent L.Rev.* 177 (1988). A reading of the amendment to exclude its application by judges strengthens the document's democratic

Other clauses, such as the Tenth Amendment, have also suffered from periodic or even chronic impotence. Speaking for the Court in United States v. Darby Lumber Co. (1941), Chief Justice Harlan Fiske Stone dismissed that amendment as no more than a "truism." [5] Moreover, no Congress ever carried out the Fourteenth Amendment's instructions to reduce the representation in the House of any state that discriminated against African–American voters. Nor has any Congress has yet taken literally the command of Article I, § 9 to publish "from time to time" a "regular Statement and Accounting" of public receipts and expenditures, unless we construe "regular Statement" as meaning incomplete and misleading accountings.

Notwithstanding these and other examples, almost all responsible constitutional interpreters and commentators treat the amended document of 1787–88 very seriously. [6] Even if it is not the entire constitution, that text forms the core of the larger constitution. Determining what those words mean marks the beginning, if not the end, of all American constitutional interpretation. Thus, to a great extent, each of the approaches discussed here is "textualist"; that is, each at very least purports to explain what that document means.

As a separable approach, *textualism* claims to find meaning in the plain words of the document, through a straightforward, uncontroversial reading of words and phrases. Most basically, textualists are readers; their principal tools are dictionaries and grammars. The process is not unlike translating from one language to another, a project that requires talent as well as knowledge.

We shall discuss three varieties of *textualism*: "*clause bound*," "*structuralist*," and "*purposive*." What we call *clause-bound textualism* takes the document as a series of more or less independent

---

basis and weakens its constitutionalist content; but such a reading also requires a strained form of *textualism*. Alternatively, that reading requires judges either to renounce judicial review—certainly not implausible from a strict *textualist* perspective—or to utilize a *philosophic approach* (discussed later in this chapter) to use democratic theory to justify excluding constitutional theory.

5. Although the Tenth Amendment has from time to time enjoyed a vigorous interpretive life, in 1789, when Congress proposed the change, states righters had voiced an assessment similar to Stone's. See William W. Crosskey, *Politics and the Constitution* (Chicago: University of Chicago Press, 1953), I, ch. 22.

6. We deliberately use the qualifiers "almost all" and "responsible." One can occasionally find, as in the debate on the Judiciary Act of 1802, reprinted above, p. 289, public officials who will throw the text aside when it gets in their way. Moreover, even a jurist as eminent as Judge Learned Hand could treat the constitutional document as not binding. See his *The Bill of Rights* (Cambridge: Harvard University Press, 1958); Gerald Gunther's monumental biography, *Learned Hand: The Man and the Judge* (New York: Knopf, 1994); and Jeffrey Rosen's trenchant review, "The Craftsman and the Nihilist," *The New Republic* (July 4, 1994), pp. 36ff. One might also reasonably argue that philosophic pragmatism, like much of deconstructionism, post-structuralism, and post-modernism, leads to a form of textual nihilism that cannot, consistently with its own premises, take the constitutional document seriously. See Sotirios A. Barber, "Stanley Fish and the Future of Pragmatism in Legal Theory," 58 *U.Chi.L.Rev.* 1033 (1991).

clauses.[7] When a problem arises, say, an attack on a statute that subsidizes textbooks in science for religious as well as public schools, a *clause-bound approach* would turn to that part of the First Amendment which reads "Congress shall make no law regarding an establishment of religion," and carefully construe it as a free standing proscription. But the meaning of these ten words may well depend on other sections of the document. Therefore it may make more sense to engage in *textual structuralism*, that is, to scrutinize any particular clause as part of larger whole—in the example of a possible establishment of religion, to expand the unit of analysis to include at very least the clause that immediately follows: "or prohibiting the free exercise thereof," perhaps the "equal protection" clause, and Article VI's ban on religious tests for federal officials. Indeed, it might be appropriate to look at the First Amendment as but one segment of the entire document. In sum, it is quite possible that, read in the context of the whole text, any single clause would take on quite a different meaning from that which it would have in isolation. As Judge Learned Hand once remarked, "a melody is more than the notes." [8]

Theologians and literary critics have long faced similar problems of fit, conflict, and reconciliation among parts of complex texts and have recognized what they call "the hermeneutic circle": Readers cannot understand the whole without understanding the parts; but neither can they understand the parts without understanding the whole. Constitutional interpretation cannot escape this dilemma. *Clause-bound textualism* focuses on the parts; *structural textualism* focuses on the entire document as forming a coherent whole. The Constitutional Court of the Federal Republic of Germany has given one of the lucid statements of what the latter sort of approach is all about:

> A constitution has an inner unity, and the meaning of any one part is linked to that of other provisions. Taken as a unit, a constitution reflects certain overarching principles and fundamental decisions to which individual provisions are subordinate.[9]

Griswold v. Connecticut (1965; reprinted above, p. 147) provides variations on *structuralist* themes. In conflict were a state's authority to forbid advising people about contraception and private citizens' putative right to privacy. For the Court, William O. Doug-

---

7. It may seem implausible that this approach has been widely used, and it may well be that no interpreter has consistently been "clause bound." Nevertheless, Prof. Charles L. Black claimed that, "in dealing with questions of constitutional law, we have preferred the method of purported explication or exegesis of the particular textual passage considered as a directive of action, as opposed to the method of inference from the structures and relationships created by the constitution in all its parts or some principal part." *Structure and Relationship in Constitutional Law* (Baton Rouge: Louisiana State University Press, 1969), p. 7.

8. Helvering v. Gregory (U.S.C.A., 2d Cir.1934).

9. The Southwest Case (1951); reprinted in Walter F. Murphy and Joseph Tanenhaus, eds., *Comparative Constitutional Law* (New York: St. Martin's, 1977), p. 208.

las began by looking at the constitutional document; but he did not restrict analysis to any one clause. Instead, he examined the interplay among the First, Third, Fourth, Fifth, and Ninth Amendments. Individually, these clauses provided textual roots for rights to privacy in specific areas, but Douglas construed them as a unit and argued that together they protected a general right to privacy, implied by but not spelled out in the document.

Purposive textualism differs from both *clause-bound* and *structural* textualism, though it may be complementary to either. *Purposive textualism* seeks the basic goal(s) that either an isolated clause or the text as a whole attempts to achieve, then interprets the clause or document in light of this objective. In *Federalist* No. 40, Madison explained this kind of approach:

> There are two rules of construction, dictated by plain reason, as well as founded on legal axioms. The one is that every part of the expression ought, if possible, be made to conspire to some common end. The other is, that where the several parts cannot be made to coincide, the less important should give way to the more important part; the means should be sacrificed to the end, rather than the end to the means.

The greatest attraction of both *structural* and *purposive analyses* is that it makes good sense to try to discover unity and coherence in a document, and, in that process, to find a central objective or objectives around which all or part of it is structured (or around which an interpreter can create a structure). The drawbacks of *textual structuralism* revolve around the fact that it is the interpreter who must articulate the skeletal structure on which the constitutional document hangs. The constitutional texts of some nations may expressly stipulate their own structure, but that of the United States does not. It implies more than it explicitly stipulates, with the result that "structure" may be something interpreters impose as much as find.

Because it is frequently the interpreters who articulate the structure, different structuralists can reasonably view a problem quite differently. (See, for example, the debates among the justices in National League of Cities v. Usery [1976; reprinted below, p. 565], Garcia v. San Antonio MTA [1985; reprinted below, p. 576], and New York v. United States [1992; reprinted below, p. 585].) It may make good sense for a textualist to use a *structural approach*, but that form of analysis does not impose a tight rein on interpretive discretion, nor does it offer a cure for indeterminacy.

Because the Preamble to the American constitutional text lays out a set of goals, a *purposive approach* seems essential to taking that document seriously. Indeed, it is almost impossible to make a rational case for an interpreters' failing to use a *purposive approach*, either at the level of individual clauses or the text as a whole. And this point may be so obvious that most interpreters,

most of the time, do not mention it.   Still, a *purposive approach*
may not always be sufficient, for the level of generality of the
Preamble's objectives is quite high.   Precisely how authority to
"provide for the general Welfare" should be divided among Congress, the President, and the courts and between the national
government and the states is something about which the document
speaks extensively, but not precisely.   Moreover, the Preamble's
goals may be difficult to reconcile with each other.   One does not,
for instance, have to be married to understand that it is not always
easy to simultaneously enjoy "domestic Tranquility" and "the Blessings of Liberty."

The purpose of particular clauses or sections may be less
abstract; but a moment's thought about such mundane delegations
to Congress as the power "to lay and collect Taxes . . . to pay the
Debts and provide for the common Defense and general Welfare of
the United States" demonstrates that even these terms are sufficiently broad to denote several competing purposes.   Do these grants
authorize Congress to regulate, by means of taxes or subsidies,
activities that would otherwise fall outside delegations of specific
powers but do pertain to the "general Welfare"?   Like structuralism
itself, a *purposive approach* depends heavily on interpreters' reading specific meanings into the text's more or less general instructions, and different interpreters can make reasonable cases for
different understandings.   No more than *structuralism*, then, does
a *purposive approach* remove the twin problems of indeterminacy
and interpretive discretion.

II. ORIGINALISM

In the United States, we said, most thoughtful, responsible
interpreters do not envision "the Constitution" as completely enveloped within the text.   Nevertheless, many interpreters stoutly argue
that it is almost entirely so contained.   These people insist that the
appropriate dictionaries, grammars, and other linguistic tools to
discover meaning are those used by the founding generation or the
generation that adopted the amendment whose message is at issue.
As Chief Justice Roger Brooke Taney said for the Court in the Dred
Scott case (1857; reprinted above, p. 195), any provision of the
constitutional text

> must be construed as it was understood at the time of its
> adoption.   It is not only the same in words, but the same in
> meaning and delegates the same powers to the Government and
> reserves and secures the same rights and privileges to the citizen;
> and as long as it continues to exist in its present form, it speaks
> not only in the same words, but with the same meaning and
> intent with which it spoke when it came from the hands of its
> framers, and was voted on and adopted by the people of the
> United States.

There are two major (and many minor) varieties of *originalism*: One, now most prominently identified with Justice Antonin Scalia,[10] focuses on the "understanding" of the founding generation, the other on the founders' "intentions." [11]   In this context, "founders" and "founding generation" are defined as the people of 1787–88 or of the time an amendment under analysis became part of the document.   For the sake of space, we shall refer to both of these sects simply as *originalists* and their approach as *originalism*.

An *originalist approach* has several attractions.   Most obviously, it links Americans to their revered founding fathers and the miracle they worked at Philadelphia.   In addition, it promises to shrink interpreters' (especially judges') discretion and so enhance determinacy and predictability in constitutional interpretation.   Third, *originalism* rests on a sort of democratic theory: The people of 1787–88 and of the periods in which amendments became part of the official text spoke their minds about the basic principles and more specific rules under which they wished to live.

But, as even Justice Scalia has conceded, originalism is also fraught with difficulties.   First, the argument from democratic theory is itself flawed.   Although the ratifying conventions of 1787–88 were probably the most democratically chosen bodies that had been assembled in modern history, no woman, no slave, and not even all white male citizens had been eligible to vote for the delegates. Furthermore, it is seems clear that, although the majority of delegates at Philadelphia wanted to ground the new system on "the consent of the governed," they did not equate that concept with full democratic rule.   In fact, one of the most frequent of the Anti-Federalists' charges against the new text was that it was anti-democratic.   Later, the Fourteenth Amendment, for all of its democratic and constitutionalist virtues was, as Chapter 6 pointed out, imposed by federal force on many of the "ratifying" states.

There are also serious problems in reading the founders' minds.   Constitutional scholars tend to agree that the framers wanted to construct a stronger, though still limited, central government, to leave considerable but still restricted authority with the states, and, by accomplishing these twin tasks, to enhance the liberty of individual citizens.   Once we go beyond those sorts of general statements, however, we glide on thin evidentiary ice.   We do not have "a record" of the debates at Philadelphia, merely notes taken by various delegates as they debated each other.   All of these

---

10.   See his "Originalism: The Lesser Evil," reprinted above, p. 231.

11.   At one time, Judge Robert H. Bork was among the most prominent of those seeking intention, but more recently he has spoken of "original understanding." *The Tempting of America: The Political Seduction of the Law* (New York: The Free Press, 1990).   Before Bork, Raoul Berger was the leading "intentionalist."   See his *Government by Judiciary* (Cambridge: Harvard University Press, 1977), and the review by Walter F. Murphy, "Constitutional Interpretation: The Art of the Historian, Magician, or Statesman?" 87 *Yale L.J.* 1752 (1978).

are fragmentary, and some are contradictory, and one set, those allegedly written by Robert Yates of New York, may well be heavily tainted by forgery.[12] Even Madison's famous "Notes," the most detailed and probably the most accurate account, provide only a partial picture. Participants in seminars today can use those notes as a script for a play and usually read out loud in less than an hour all the speeches Madison included from each day's four-to six-hour session. Furthermore, he conceded that he edited his journal some weeks after the Convention had adjourned.

In some ways, the debates on ratification paint a richer portrait. But, again, the "records" of what went on in the ratifying conventions are problematic; shorthand was not yet fully developed, and official stenographers were sometimes partisans who felt small duty to report speeches accurately. On the other hand, we have wonderful collections of the arguments on both sides in the campaign that led to the election of delegates to the conventions.[13] As the selections we reprinted earlier from "Brutus" and "Publius" show,[14] these debates displayed an intellectual splendor that Americans of the late twentieth century can only envy: not 30–second "sound bites," but serious, reasoned arguments and counterarguments conducted in newspapers, pamphlets, and public discussions. We can learn a great deal from this marvelous political drama; it is not possible, however, to discern a set of common intentions or understandings that can settle current disagreements about constitutional interpretation. No less than our own debates, those of the founding generation reveal sharp and multi-faceted differences rather than consensus or two-clear cut divisions about meaning.[15]

---

12. See espec. James H. Hutson, "The Creation of the Constitution: The Integrity of the Documentary Record," 65 *Tex.L.Rev.* 1 (1986).

13. In 1830, Jonathan Elliot published the first of several editions of a 4–volume collection of what purported to be records of the ratifying conventions. *The Debates in the Several State Conventions on the Adoption of the Federal Constitution.* ... These were incomplete and inaccurate. In 1976, Merrill Jensen began publication of efforts to restore a much more reliable record. He and his associates have managed to put together different accounts of what was said in the conventions and, equally or even more helpful, to assemble many of the contemporary documents circulated during the campaigns to choose delegates. Later John P. Kaminski and Gaspare J. Saldino took over as general editors. As of December, 1994, volumes 1–3, 8–10, and 13–16 had appeared. *The Documentary History of the Ratification of the Constitution* (Madison: University of Wisconsin Press, 1976–). Among the more useful collection of documents for the Bill of Rights are: Helen E. Veit and Kenneth E. Bowling, eds., *Creating the Bill of Rights: The Documentary Record from the First Federal Congress* (Baltimore: Johns Hopkins University Press, 1981); and Bernard Schwartz, ed., *The Bill of Rights* (New York: Chelsea House, 1971), 2 vols.

14. See Brutus, p. 281, and *The Federalist* No. 78, p. 285; see also *ibid.*, Nos. 10 and 39, reprinted below at p. 1087 and p. 526.

15. *Originalism* faces another serious difficulty, which most originalists ignore. By the time of the Revolution, American and British English had diverged in significant ways. And, although there were several early dictionaries of American English—*e.g.*, Caleb Alexander, *The Columbian Dictionary of the English Language* (1800)—the first comprehensive American work, *The American Dictionary of the English Language*, was not published until 1828, 40 years after adoption of the constitutional document and 37 years after ratification of the Bill of Rights. Moreover, the compiler of this tome was Noah

Originalists also face grave normative problems. They must provide justifications both for their choices among various founders' competing "intentions" and "understandings" and, more fundamentally, for including any or all founders' "intentions" or "understandings" within the constitutional canon. This latter task is one that *originalism* cannot perform by itself. To demonstrate that "the Constitution" includes the founders' "intentions" or "understandings"—or, to phrase the matter slightly differently, that later interpreters are bound by what the founders "intended" or "understood" their words to mean—requires justification outside of history. To argue that we are bound by what the founders intended or understood because the founders so intended or understood is to go around in a logical circle.

To make matters even more difficult for originalists, what we have of an historical record raises doubts that the founders of 1787–88 intended their intentions or understandings, rather than the document they drafted and ratified, to form authoritative interpretive guides.[16] But even if the founders, who neglected to say so, meant their intentions or understandings to bind later generations, why are those people so bound? Ratifiers voted on the terms of the initial document and later on the terms of its amendments, not on the diverse "intentions" and "understandings" of various drafters and other ratifiers. As Justice Frankfurter once noted in discussing the legislative history of the Fourteenth Amendment: In the final analysis, Congress voted on the amendment, not the speeches for and against it.[17]

Despite *originalism*'s difficulties, its claims have been part of the practice of constitutional interpretation since the time of John Marshall. Having been a member of Virginia's ratifying convention,

---

Webster, a sturdy and active Federalist, who saw his task as instructing his readers in politics as well as in linguistics. See: Noah Webster, *Collection of Essays and Fugitive Writings on Moral, Historical, Political and Literary Subjects* (1790); and, more generally, David Simpson, *The Politics of American English, 1776–1850* (New York: Oxford University Press, 1986), espec. ch. 2.

Originalists might, of course, use a more or less contemporary dictionary of British English, such as that compiled by Dr. Samuel Johnson, as a rough approximation. But rough approximations seldom yield answers precise enough to settle important disputes about constitutional meaning. Originalists might also rely on Sir William Blackstone's *Commentaries on the Laws of England, Coke on Littleton*, or one of the several other treatises widely read by American lawyers of the day. But, there is no reason to assume that the founders wished to adopt the British common law in its entirety. More serious is the fact that most originalists anchor their claims in democratic theory and so would have to root "the Constitution" in the American population at large, not merely in lawyers. And we have no evidence that Blackstone and Coke were every-day reading in the colonies. For a determined effort to reconstruct a late eighteenth-century legal dictionary for constitutional interpretation, see Crosskey, *op. cit.*, supra note 5, espec. vols. I and II. Among the reviewers who engaged Crosskey on the accuracy of his definitions was Henry M. Hart, Jr., "Professor Crosskey and Judicial Review," 67 *Harv.L.Rev.* 1456 (1954).

16. See espec. H. Jefferson Powell, "The Original Understanding of Original Intent," 98 *Harv.L.Rev.* 885 (1985); and Hutson, "The Creation of the Constitution," supra note 12.

17. Adamson v. California, concur. op. (1947).

he considered himself a founder and was perfectly prepared to treat as authoritative *his* intentions and understandings, if not those of others. As we shall see in reading McCulloch v. Maryland (1819; reprinted below, p. 530), Marshall disregarded the authors of *The Federalist* when they disagreed with him. For later generations, supposed opinions of the founders of 1787–88 have taken on an aura of dispassionate wisdom. The names of Madison, Washington, Marshall, Hamilton, and even Jefferson, though he was in France at the time, can cast a magic spell. There are, of course, good reasons beyond filial piety to heed what these people had to say. They were men of experience, judgment, prudence, and probity. Only a fool would not care what they thought about problems they shared with us—and, at bottom, many of their problems were similar to our own. But a prudential obligation to consult the founders' *wisdom* does not mean "the Constitution" includes their intentions or understandings or that we are obliged to apply to our world the specific solutions they thought best fit theirs.

III. DOCTRINALISM

Thomas Reed Powell, who taught constitutional law at Harvard Law School in the 1920s and '30s, would begin his course by warning his students never to read the constitutional text. "It will only confuse you," he claimed, for students would not find there such doctrines as "direct and indirect effects," "separate but equal," and "liberty of contract." And it was these and other ideas, which the Supreme Court had read into the text, that formed the bulk of constitutional law.

Powell was exaggerating to make a valid point: Some interpretations have, in effect, become part of the larger *constitution*. Judaism, Michael Walzer has written, "is not found in the text [of the Bible] so much as in the interpretations of the text." [18] Much the same thing could be said about the American "Constitution." Certainly few people, in or out of public office, would today question the legitimacy of judicial review,[19] claim that Lincoln was wrong when he asserted the Union was indissoluble,[20] or deny the principle of "one person, one vote." Yet, all of these interpreta-

---

18. *Exodus and Revolution* (New York: Basic Books, 1985), p. 144.

19. For a modern argument against what we call "judicial review," see W. W. Crosskey, *op. cit.* supra note 5, espec. Part IV. The sparsity of recent challenges by no means implies agreement about the scope of judicial review, as much of this book illustrates.

20. For a more general analysis that criticizes Lincoln's claim on the grounds that constitutions may decay over time and thus, whatever their textual claims to perpetuity, may dissolve, see Mark E. Brandon, "Free in the World," unpub'd Ph.D. diss. (Princeton, 1992). For more general analyses of constitutional change, see John E. Finn, *Constitutions in Crisis* (New York: Oxford University Press, 1991); William F. Harris II, *The Interpretable Constitution* (Baltimore: Johns Hopkins University Press, 1993), ch. 4; and the essays in Sanford V. Levinson, ed., *Responding to Imperfection* (Princeton: Princeton University Press, 1995).

tions were heatedly attacked when announced and may by some criteria have been wrong when given; but long acceptance and application—in short, their infusion into American political culture—have made these and other interpretations part of the broader constitution.

A *doctrinal approach* searches out past interpretations as they relate to specific problems such as "equal protection of the laws" and tries to organize them into a coherent whole and fit the solution of current problems into that whole. In the style of the common law, the object is to preserve continuity even if effecting change. As one would expect, *doctrinalism* is the typical method of teaching constitutional law. The standard casebook is organized topically, collecting decisions on such issues as federal regulation of commerce, congressional power to tax, and the meaning of "establishment of religion." [21]

Doctrinalists typically claim their approach is based on the notion of a developing rather than a static "Constitution." Thus fidelity to the text may have to make peace with fidelity to what judges have said the text means. Sometimes that peace comes easily, for the meaning of some clauses does not shift much over time. For example, Justice Chase's definition of "ex post facto law" in Calder v. Bull (1798; reprinted above, p. 121) still holds today, though the Court has broadened the scope of what constitutes punishment.[22] Sometimes, however, that peace will be uncomfortable, for interpretations of parts of the document may evolve. One can trace, for example, gradual expansions and contractions of congressional authority over "commerce among the several states" or of the limitations the two due-process clauses place on governmental regulation of labor-management relations. Of itself, each decision may make only a marginal change, but together their impact may be immense. One also sometimes sees sudden, dramatic shifts. West Coast Hotel v. Parrish (1937; reprinted below, p. 1123 marked an abrupt, dramatic transformation, wiping out decades of jurisprudence that had read laissez faire into the constitutional text. *Parrish* represented, Edward S. Corwin asserted, a "constitutional revolution," [23] setting the stage for a new doctrine that allowed deep governmental regulation of economic affairs.

The advantage of *doctrinalism* lies in permitting adaption to current problems, allowing flexibility to cope with new crises, to build on past interpretations by "reasoning by analogy," and permitting the country to move, step by step from the solution of one

---

21. For a wonderful exception, see Paul Brest and Sanford V. Levinson, *Processes of Constitutional Decisionmaking* (3d ed.; Boston: Little, Brown, 1992).

22. For example, Ex parte Garland (1867).

23. *Constitutional Revolution, Ltd.* (Claremont, CA: Claremont Press, 1941); see also Bruce Ackerman, *We the People: Foundations* (Cambridge: Harvard University Press, 1991), who characterizes the New Deal as fundamentally changing the American political system.

problem to another and so facilitate change while preserving continuity. In sum, *doctrinalism* epitomizes the method the common
law that Chapter 2 described. Still, *doctrinalism* brings its own
difficulties. First, a strict textualist would contend, *doctrinalism*
distracts attention from the constitutional document itself to what
others have said about it. Although Justice Felix Frankfurter did not
(or at least not often) limit his view of "the Constitution" to the
text, he summed up that conception when he wrote: "the ultimate
touchstone of constitutionality is the Constitution itself and not
what we have said about it." [24]

Second, although *doctrinalists* claim to limit judicial discretion,
their approach achieves that goal only partially, if at all. It inevitably allows, even encourages, a certain amount of creativity. Doctrines do not exist from the beginning of time; they have been
created, assembled, and reassembled. And the creators and/or
(re)assemblers have usually been judges. Furthermore, as we said
earlier, most doctrines expand or contract. That mixture of stability
and change is, of course, *doctrinalism's* promise; but fulfillment
comes at a cost. Interpreters seeking analogies from previous
constitutional constructions still have a range of choice among
options that allow continuity with the past. In fact, much of the
disagreement among justices of the Supreme Court centers on the
relevance and meaning of earlier decisions, for what a previous
interpretation, whether by judges, legislators, or executives, *really*
means is frequently as difficult to decipher as the text itself. Moreover, after 200 years under this political system, assiduous research-
ers can find respectable precedents for many interpretations of the
constitutional text. "Many" is not the same as "any," so it is not
fair to criticize *doctrinalism* as giving interpreters a free hand, but it
is fair to say that it does not narrowly confine their discretion and
thus does not ensure predictability.

Third, focus on doctrine allows interpreters to evade responsibility by concealing the play of more basic interpretive notions, such
as the interrogatives of WHAT, WHO, and HOW. This diversion of
attention increases discretion by allowing interpreters to avoid
providing *public* explanations of and justifications for what are, in
effect, the major premises of their arguments.

IV. ANOTHER FORM OF HISTORICAL APPROACH: CONSTITUTIONAL DEVELOPMENT

Originalism is one form of historical approach; it uses history
as a snap shot, a picture of the past as an event frozen in time.
There are, of course, other views of history—for example, one that
values it as an ongoing process, as a moving picture which contin-

---

24. Graves v. New York ex rel. O'Keefe, concur. op. (1939).

ues into and beyond the present. And there are, as Chapter 6 said, competing notions of the paths that constitutional change may legitimately follow. Some interpreters believe "the Constitution" is subject to an evolutionary process, a developing rather than a static concept.

This sort of *developmental approach* would combine elements of both *doctrinalism* and *textualism* to enlarge the interpretive arena to include broader historical events, such as informal practices, usages, and even political culture to see how meaning has evolved. For instance, in Trop v. Dulles (1958; reprinted above, p. 219), Earl Warren sought the meaning of the Eighth Amendment not merely in earlier judicial rulings but also—perhaps primarily— in "the evolving standards of decency that mark the progress of a maturing society."

The promises of *developmentalism* are very much the same as those of *doctrinalism* with the supposed advantage of drawing from a wider experience than that of formal interpretations. *Developmentalists* would also claim to make the text more meaningful to current citizens by reading it in their language rather than that of earlier periods.[25] Not unexpectedly, a *developmental approach* also shares the problems of *doctrinalism*, and some of those difficulties are writ large. In expanding the historical stage on which it performs, *developmentalism* also runs into all the obstacles of understanding the past that we earlier catalogued in discussing *originalism*. Those difficulties might ease a bit for more recent historical tracings, for interpreters are apt to be more familiar with changes in language, customs, and values that have taken place in their own lifetimes than with the mental pictures that existed in the heads of earlier generations. Nevertheless, interpretations of recent history are likely to be controversial and the road to justification arduous.

Furthermore, a *developmental approach* does little to advance the goal of stability, for by its very nature it accepts not merely the legitimacy of constitutional change from the past to the present but also the legitimacy as well as the probability of constitutional change from the present to an unknown future. And there is more at risk than preservation of the status quo. In *Trop*, Earl Warren assumed that the direction of change would be toward strengthening constitutional democracy. But, as John Randolph of Roanoke was fond of repeating, change is not the same as progress. Nations decay as well as mature and, in either process, are likely to go through cycles of greater and lesser attachment to the values of constitutional democracy.

Normative difficulties are equally formidable, though they differ in intensity depending on WHO is doing the interpreting, WHAT

---

25. If we want yet another word of art, we could call such an approach *contemporary textualism*.

interpreters believe they are interpreting, and, more particularly, whether the standards are more those of democratic or of constitutionalist theory. Speaking from a democratic perspective, Hugo Black protested in *Griswold* that

> many good and able men have eloquently spoken and written, sometimes in rhapsodical strains, about the duty of this Court to keep the Constitution in tune with the times. The idea is that the Constitution must be changed from time to time and that this Court is charged with a duty to make those changes. For myself, I must with all deference reject that philosophy. The Constitution makers knew the need for change and provided for it. Amendments suggested by the people's elected representatives can be submitted to the people or their selected agents for ratification.

Constitutionalists have been equally concerned about legislative and executive interpretations that would have altered existing principles of that system, as for instance, when in the last third of the twentieth century presidents were interpreting Article II of the text as conferring on them most of the war-making power (see below, Chapter 10) or in the 1930s when Franklin Roosevelt and a Democratic Congress laid the groundwork for a regulatory and welfare state (see below, Chapter 16).

V. A PHILOSOPHIC APPROACH

The "debate" between Chief Justice William H. Rehnquist ("The Notion of a Living Constitution," reprinted above, p. 243) [26] and Prof. Ronald Dworkin ("Taking Rights Seriously," reprinted above, p. 249) about the appropriate role of moral and political philosophy in constitutional interpretation marks the dispute about a *philosophic approach*. No one can deny that many interpreters, including judges, utilize philosophy in their search for constitutional meaning, though they are more likely to do so without openly acknowledging, or even being aware of, this use. Interpreters are as apt to make such assumptions when they deny that "the Constitution" includes moral and/or political theory as when they affirm such a proposition. Indeed, Rehnquist's own argument proceeded from a set of controversial normative notions about the relations among law and other phases of politics. Without conceding, or perhaps realizing, what he was doing, he argued from philosophic assumptions based partially on democratic theory and partially on a normative theory called "legal positivism." The hidden moves in the Chief's argument indicate how difficult it is for interpreters to avoid utilizing controversial philosophic assumptions.

---

26. Judge Robert H. Bork has repeatedly made this same argument. See his: "Neutral Principles and Some First Amendment Problems," 47 *Ind.L.J.* 2 (1971); "The Struggle Over the Role of the Court," *National Rev.* (Sept. 17, 1982), p. 1137; and *The Tempting of America*, supra note 11. For a forceful critique, see Ronald Dworkin, "Bork's Jurisprudence," 57 *U.Chi.L.Rev.* 657 (1990).

Philosophic reflection and debate are the activities through which we try to comprehend the nature of ideas like "liberty" and "property" as well as of notions like "interpretation," "tradition," and "history." Every approach to constitutional interpretation requires long and hard thought about such matters. Thus philosophic activity or passive acceptance of others' philosophic activity is essential to all forms of constitutional interpretation.

What distinguishes a *philosophic approach* in constitutional interpretation is the advice it issues to all interpreters to "theorize," to seek the meaning of words and phrases like "due process" or "commerce" and to pursue that meaning through an open and open-minded exchange of reasons that other people can respect. Proponents of a *philosophic approach* argue that philosophic decisions inevitably inhere in any proposition about constitutional meaning and, therefore, the choice is not between a *philosophic* and and a *non-philosophic approach,* but rather between philosophic methods pursued responsibly and, on the other hand, philosophic methods pursued irresponsibly. Merely citing plain words that signal complex concepts, the alleged "intent of the framers," or precedents, they say, constitutes a refusal to put the interpreter's own choices on the table so that others may evaluate and debate them.[27]

But demonstrating that all interpreters inevitably employ philosophic assumptions and methods does nothing to reduce a host of difficulties. First of all, American constitutional interpretation has seen a variety of philosophic teachings, including natural rights, various forms of relativism such as legal positivism and pragmatism, as well as the two around which much of this book is organized, democratic and constitutionalist theory. Second, Judge Bork was correct when he said that few judges are professional philosophers. Probably an even smaller proportion of other public officials and ordinary citizens are well enough educated in philosophy to make sophisticated choices among the bevy of options that present themselves. Third, as Bork has also pointed out, philosophic reflection seems endless, and forcing philosophic methods on constitutional interpretation risks destabilizing the political system.

An interpreter could concede the difficulties of a *philosophic approach* and respond by paraphrasing Justice Robert H. Jackson in the Second Flag Salute Case (1943; reprinted below, p. 1174): Interpreters use a *philosophic approach* not by reason of their

---

27. The reasons for using a *philosophic approach* become even more obvious when the constitution that is being interpreted is based on or includes one or more moral or political theories. Proponents deny that the American constitutional text is intelligible if it is not read through the lens of democratic and constitutionalist theories. What sense, they ask, can readers make of the First Amendment's protections of freedom of speech, press, and petition and the Fourteenth's guarantee of "the equal protection of the laws" if they lack sophisticated understanding of democratic theory? Is it possible to comprehend the right to privacy that some interpreters have found within the broader constitution without understanding constitutionalism?

competence but by force of their commissions. At the most elementary level, one cannot intelligently construe the words of a text without analyzing the nature of the concepts and conceptions to which those words refer.

Judge Bork's warnings, however, should encourage caution and, equally as important, introspection. If the options open to interpreters are to engage in philosophic analysis "by reflection and choice" or through assumptions hidden from the public and perhaps from themselves, then the wiser course is to make open choices among and within *philosophic approaches* and provide public justifications for those choices. The aim of a *philosophic approach*, its proponents stress, is not to turn interpreters into philosophers but to alert them to the choices they are making and equip them to make those choices consciously, carefully, and publicly. And, in that process, the framers' wisdom as well as those of previous interpreters may be of great help, allowing interpreters to build on what is worth saving from earlier analyses and to reject what does not stand the test of later and perhaps more sophisticated reasoning.

VI. MORE ABOUT STRUCTURALISM: SYSTEMIC AND TRANSCENDENT

If, for persuasive and publicly defended reasons, interpreters have concluded that the constitution to be construed is the political system, they would then have to use—and more or less simultaneously—an array of interpretive approaches. As always, a *textual approach* would be necessary, as would variations on *historical* and *philosophic* approaches as the interpreters sought out patterns of behavior then tried to discern and rank underlying values.

Another form of *structuralism* might also be useful, a version called *systemic structuralism*. It would represent an effort to do at a macro-level what *textual structuralism* does for the clauses of a document: to seek "an inner unity," a "common end," to which the various segments of the system aim. In this context, the unit of analysis would be the entire political system; the text, traditions, practices, and interpretations would be parts of the unit which interpreters examine.

We can return to Douglas' opinion in *Griswold* for an example of the use, however unreflective, of *systemic structuralism*. We saw that he began by using *textual structuralism*, linking the protections of the First, Third, Fourth, Fifth, and Ninth amendments. Then, without offering either explanation or warning, he shifted the target of his analysis from the document's plain words to the opaque areas at the edges of the shadows of the text and said that specific clauses had "penumbras formed by emanations from those guarantees that give them life and substance." As in his dissent in *Poe*, he sought reinforcement for a general right to privacy from what he saw as "the totality of the constitutional scheme under which we live"—a kind of structural approach more abstract than the *textual structuralism* with which he had begun.

We can see other, though less boldly sweeping, examples of *systemic structuralism* when problems involving federalism or separation of functions within the national government occur. Sometimes interpreters explain their decisions by explicitly referring to such controversial notions of constitutional structure—see, for example, the opinion of Chief Justice Salmon P. Chase in Texas v. White (1869; reprinted below, p. 546). Sometimes such references are only implicit; sometimes they are awkward and fumbling, with only blurred and fleeting images of structure. Sometimes the explanation reproduces, as did John Marshall's of federal-state relations in McCulloch v. Maryland (1819; reprinted below, p. 530), a comprehensive conception of the system's structure. But, as with Douglas in *Griswold*, interpreters frequently move beyond the text to governmental structures without warning and sometimes without awareness of their own moves. Indeed, it would be difficult not to make such a move when federalism is involved because the document's words about that structure are so few, so cryptic, and so important. It is only somewhat easier to stay within the document's four corners when resolving disputes between branches of the national government because the text, while more detailed in that respect, allocates powers less by precise verbal directions than by intricately woven patterns of dividing and sharing.

Suppose interpreters decide that the constitution also includes one or more political theories as well as practices, interpretations, and traditions. Interpreters would then find it necessary to employ *philosophy* to understand those political theories and their implications for constitutional meaning. But they might need yet another approach to help them bring the text, practices, traditions, and interpretations into a coherent whole with the normative demands of the relevant political theories. We call this approach *transcendent structuralism*.[28]

We may be repeating the obvious, but *systemic* and *transcendent structuralism*, while offering interpreters a clearer overview of their work, escape none of the problems of *textual structuralism*. Indeed, the larger the arena for the play of interpretive discretion, the larger these problems become.

VII. SYSTEMIC PURPOSE

Construing the constitution as the text, the political system, and one or more normative political theories is extraordinarily complex

---

28. Harris, *supra* note 20, ch. 3, calls this approach "ultra-structuralist" and uses the term "transcendental structuralism" for what we call "systemic structuralism."

work. It requires, in computerese, several gigabytes of RAM to consider each of the relevant elements separately while simultaneously analyzing the ways in which they intermesh. One method of coping with these difficulties is analogous to the *purposive* version of *textualism*, visualizing the broader constitution as having purposes and using these objectives to help discern the structure of the political system and the ordering of its values. Madison described the nub of *systemic structuralism* when he talked about construing the different elements of the constitution "to conspire to some common end." And, under this view of the constitutional universe, an interpreter could not discover that "common end" without understanding the normative theories that hold the system's parts together.

Earlier we recognized some of the problems of a *purposive approach* when we discussed its *textualist* version. Those difficulties are equally, if not more, severe when the target increases in size to become the political system and its political theories. On the other hand, either at the level of the text or of the political system, it is difficult to imagine intelligent and coherent interpretive efforts that do not take purpose(s) into account.

We shall discuss five different kinds of *purposive approaches* that have been much used in American constitutional interpretation, though, of course, interpreters have seldom carefully explained or justified their use. The first such form we examine, a *prudential approach*, sees constitutional interpretation as statecraft. Its premise is that the constitutional text as well as the polity that has developed from it have as their goal not only that the United States "endure for ages to come" but also it endure as a constitutional democracy. The words of the document, its surrounding practices, the commands of tradition, and the meaning of underlying normative theories must, therefore, be construed not as moral imperatives for saints in a heaven on earth but as means to insure the survival of flawed people in a flawed world.

Chapter 4 explained how political exigencies may constrain interpreters by excluding ideal solutions. Chapter 19 will discuss how demands for national survival affect constitutional interpretation. But, in a larger sense, a *prudential approach* is a "brooding omnipresence in the sky" of constitutional interpretation. Although threats to national or even institutional survival are relatively rare, every interpreter is a person of limited power, operating in a world of competing interests and ambitions that influence judgments about what "the Constitution" means. Even when reinforced by lucid historical and brilliant philosophic analyses, cold logic may be unable to translate "constitutional truth" into viable public policy. The objective of a *prudential approach* is to transform into political reality as much of that "truth" as possible.[29]

---

29. For a study of *prudential analysis*, see Murphy, *op. cit.* supra note 1.

One example will have to suffice. During the mid–1940s, when the Supreme Court was hearing a series of challenges to state laws segregating people by race, most of the justices came to believe that such regulations were unconstitutional. On the other hand, they doubted that a sweeping ruling to that effect would help eradicate racism from American life. Indeed, the justices feared such a ruling would do far more harm than good: The white South would resist and the rest of the country did not seem prepared to make the hard fight needed to carry out the constitutional command of "equal protection of the laws." Therefore, some of the justices made a conscious choice to avoid ringing rhetoric about how the Fourteenth Amendment forbade a caste society and instead to move slowly, to proceed case by case in classic common-law style, to undermine the old doctrine of "separate but equal." Then, even after the decision in Brown v. Board of Ed. (1954; reprinted below, p. 912) invalidated segregation in public schools, the Court moved slowly to carry out its decision, ordering merely that states act "with all deliberate speed" to dismantle dual systems of public education. The point is not that this strategy was wise or foolish, only that the justices thought that constitutional interpretation required practical wisdom as well as *textual, doctrinal, historical,* and *philosophic* analyses.

Because prudence involves anticipating an uncertain future and looks to the long run as well as the short, interpreters who utilize this approach are apt to disagree sharply with each other. Moreover, interpreters who view "the Constitution" as a set of textual commands fixed in meaning are apt to brand a *prudential approach* as irrelevant or even anathema. Justice Sutherland, dissenting in West Coast Hotel v. Parrish (1937; reprinted below, p. 1123) against the Court's abandoning, under pressure from the President, the doctrine of "substantive due process" [30] in the economic sphere, claimed that a judge who allowed prudential considerations to affect his decision stood "forsworn." A judge's duty, as Sutherland had said earlier in the Minnesota Moratorium Case (1934; reprinted above, p. 210), was to interpret the document as written, regardless of the consequences. If the people disapproved, they could amend the text.

---

30. This doctrine, discussed in detail in Chapter 16, prevailed from 1890 until 1937 and was a potent weapon against government's regulating the economy. Its gist is that the prohibitions in the Fifth and Fourteenth amendments against government's taking "life, liberty, or property, without due process of law" impose substantive as well as procedural constraints. There are some forms of liberty that government may not take away, no matter what procedures it uses. John Hart Ely has responded: " 'substantive due process' is a contradiction in terms—sort of like 'green pastel redness.' ... [A]nd 'procedural due process' is redundant." *Democracy and Distrust,* supra note 4, p. 18. Although the justices say they no longer apply the doctrine to strike down regulations of private property, they continue to use a modified version to protect other "fundamental rights." See espec. the cases in Chapter 18. Moreover, Justice Stevens charged in 1994 that the Court was resurrecting substantive due process in cases involving economic regulation. Dolan v. Tigard, dis. op.

Given that most justices have had some experience in practical politics before going to the bench, and that presidents, legislators, and state officials face electorates, prudential considerations have seldom been absent from constitutional interpretation. At its best, a *prudential approach* preserves "the Constitution" and the country by wisely construing—or by deciding not to construe—its content. At its worst, a *prudential approach* turns constitutional interpretation into mere expediency and so abandons any notion of "the Constitution" as an authoritative set of fundamental principles.

A second *purposive approach*, "the doctrine of the clear mistake," addresses the question of WHO as much as HOW. It seeks to maintain a political system that is both democratic and constitutionalist by apportioning interpretive authority in ways congruent with the duality of that objective. It was first fully articulated in 1893 by Prof. James Bradley Thayer of the Harvard Law School in a famous article "The Origin and Scope of the American Doctrine of Constitutional Law" (reprinted below, p. 602). Justice Frankfurter referred to Thayer as "our great master of constitutional law" [31] and called this article "the most important single essay" ever published in the field; [32] but Thayer's real impact came long after his death. [33] He wrote just as the Court was beginning to etch laissez faire into the larger constitution. Against this trend, Thayer argued for judicial deference to decisions of Congress. Judges should hold federal statutes invalid only "when those who have a right to make laws have not merely made a mistake, but have made a very clear one,— so clear that it is not open to question. . . ."

In part, Thayer relied on democratic theory [34] and, in part, on a notion of separation of functions. It is the duty of Congress to weigh the costs and benefits of policies as well as their permissibility under "the Constitution." The first of these determinations, Thayer contended, judges must completely accept. Judges must also accept the second, he claimed, *unless* the violation of "the Constitution" were too plain for rational doubt. "The Constitution" often admits of "different interpretations"; and, within a wide margin, courts should accord Congress "a free foot."

---

31. "A Note on Advisory Opinions," 37 *Harv.L.Rev.* 1002, 1004 (1924).

32. *Felix Frankfurter Reminisces* (Harlan B. Phillips, ed.; New York: Reynal, 1960), p. 301.

33. In 1993 Northwestern University Law School held a conference to celebrate the centennial of Thayer's article. See Symposium, "One Hundred Years of Judicial Review," 88 *Nw.U.L.Rev.* 1 (1993).

34. Thayer could not push a democratic argument very hard. Although by 1893 some state legislatures had begun to approve popular preferences among senatorial candidates, the Seventeenth Amendment, requiring that senators be elected by popular vote, was still twenty years in the future, and the Nineteenth, with its prohibition against denying women the right to vote, was even more distant. Even today one can still raise the objection that each state's having two senators, regardless of population, taints the Senate as a democratic institution.

Thayer's approach would simplify constitutional interpretation for judges but, as Justice Gibson argued in Eakin v. Raub (1825; reprinted above p. 308), it would greatly increase burdens on the electorate and the federal officials they selected. Although Thayer did not speak only as a democratic theorist, there is grave doubt that a judge could follow this doctrine without forsaking constitutionalism in the name of a particular governmental arrangement—separate institutions sharing power—one of whose chief purposes is supposedly to protect constitutionalism. In any event, Thayer's arguments have encouraged those who are more democrats than constitutionalists to construct an emended version of his approach.

The third form of *purposive analysis* we look at, "reinforcing representative democracy," follows both chronologically and logically from the democratic elements in Thayer's article. As its title indicates, this approach stresses judges' obligations to support open political processes. *Reinforcing representative democracy* had its modern origin in Justice Harlan Fiske Stone's celebrated footnote 4 in an otherwise unremarkable case, United States v. Carolene Products (1938; reprinted below, p. 609) and for a time was called the "doctrine of preferred freedoms."

The sentence to which the footnote was appended said that the usual duty of judges was to presume legislation constitutional. In indirect and guarded language, Stone then listed in separate paragraphs three exceptional sets of circumstances in which judges might relax that presumption: (1) when legislation infringed on one of the text's specific prohibitions, such as those of the Bill of Rights; (2) when "legislation which restricts those political processes which can ordinarily be expected to bring about a repeal of undesirable legislation"; or (3) when "prejudice against discrete and insular minorities" may "tend[ ] seriously to curtail the operation of those political processes ordinarily thought to be relied upon to protect minorities. ..."

Some judges and commentators—most significantly in recent years, John Hart Ely[35]—believe that only under the circumstances outlined by the last two paragraphs of Stone's footnote should judges invalidate legislative actions. Ely argues that, for the most part, the constitutional text delineates procedural rights and ways of getting policies enacted; it identifies very few substantive values. This "general theory," he says, "is one that bounds judicial review under the Constitution's open-ended provisions by insisting that it can appropriately concern itself only with questions of open participation—under which he would include protection of minorities against discriminatory legislation—and not with the substantive

---

35. *Democracy and Distrust*, supra note 4. An even more recent commentator, Cass R. Sunstein, *The Partial Constitution* (Cambridge: Harvard University Press, 1993), may be intellectually closer to Ely than either thinks. See James E. Fleming, "Constructing the Substantive Constitution," 72 *Tex.L.Rev.* 211 (1993); and Sunstein's response, "Liberal Constitutionalism and Liberal Justice," 72 *ibid.* 305 (1993).

merits of the political choice under attack." [36]   But, within the
confines of this role of guarding democratic government, Ely's
theory strongly empowers judges and all other interpreters to act
against elected officials.

Although in some respects *reinforcing representative democracy* prescribes wider scope for judicial power than does Thayer's
doctrine of the clear mistake, it also offers a much narrower scope
than do theories which stress the political system's commitment to
constitutionalism.   This interpretive approach is thus open to attack
as prescribing both too broad and too narrow a jurisprudence.
Justice Frankfurter thought it too broad.   (See the Editors' Note on
the history of footnote 4, below, pp. 618-621.)   During his early
years on the Court, he several times claimed to agree with *Carolene
Products*; later, however, he sharply criticized Stone's contention
that the degree of judicial scrutiny of challenged legislation should
vary with the kind of legislation being challenged.   "There is no
warrant in the constitutional basis of this Court's authority," Frankfurter wrote, "for attributing different roles to it depending upon
the nature of the challenge to the legislation.   ..." [37]

It is undeniable that, when subjected to *a "clause-bound
textualist approach*," rather than read as an organic whole, the
document's plain words offer small support [38] for such a special
judicial role.   To justify judges' reinforcing representation, one has
to argue that the preservation of democracy is one of "the Constitution's" controlling purposes.

Reinforcing representation may also be vulnerable to attack as
too narrow.   The authority it allocates to judges may in some
aspects serve constitutionalism, as for instance in heightening concern for minorities, but it may depreciate constitutionalism in other
respects.   The objective of Ely's version of reinforcing representation was to steer judges away from protecting substantive rights.
He thus summarily dismissed the first of Stone's three paragraphs,
which suggested a special judicial role when "legislation appears on
its face to be within a specific prohibition of the Constitution, such
as those of the first ten amendments.   ..." And "the first ten
amendments" certainly include the Ninth.   Moreover, Stone had
inserted the first paragraph at the insistence of Chief Justice Charles
Evans Hughes, who was no stranger to generous readings of the
document.   "Behind the words of the constitutional provisions,"
the Chief had earlier written for the Court, "are postulates which

---

36. Supra note 4, p. 181.

37. West Virginia v. Barnette, dis. op. (1943; reprinted below, p. 1174). Cf. Chief
Justice Rehnquist's remark in Dolan v. Tigard (1994), quoted below, Eds.' Note 6, p. 1148,
that the Fifth Amendment's "just compensation" clause was not a "poor relation."

38. Justice Hugo Black argued that the wording of the First Amendment, "Congress
shall make no law," gives courts greater authority over the validity of legislation than does
the Fourth Amendment's only forbidding "unreasonable searches and seizures."

limit and control" [39]—fancy jargon for a claim that "the Constitution" includes more than the text itself.

In 1940, when regulations requiring children to salute the flag first came before the Court, Stone did not consider it to be sufficient that the processes for political change were open and that the regulations did not discriminate. "The Constitution," he said, "expresses more than the conviction of the people that democratic processes must be preserved at all costs. It is also an expression of faith and a command that our freedom of mind and spirit must be preserved." (Minersville v. Gobitis, dis. op. [reprinted below, p. 1165.])

A fourth version of a *purposive approach*, "protecting fundamental rights," operates from the premise that, insofar as the broader constitution embraces constitutionalism, it requires interpreters, particularly judges, to be especially protective not only of rights to political participation but also of substantive rights against threats by officials who were fairly chosen through open elections.[40]

Just as democratic theory and its corollary rights to political participation reflect certain values, so do constitutionalism and its corollary substantive rights.[41] As Chapter 3 indicated, those values are almost identical for both theories: individual dignity and autonomy. During the period 1890–1937, a majority of the Supreme Court saw rights to private property and "liberty of contract" as essential to those values. In more recent decades, however, most justices, like most elected officials, have deemed complete liberty of contract to be dysfunctional to autonomy and dignity. Instead, most interpreters have seen rights to equal governmental treatment, to privacy, and to "personhood," as essential to the basic values of constitutionalism and democracy—which is not to say that judges, legislators, executives, or commentators agree with each other or among themselves about the reach of any of these rights.

In Meyer v. Nebraska (1923; reprinted below, p. 1247), James C. McReynolds, a crusty advocate of laissez faire, put the notion of *fundamental rights* in terms the Court still quotes. He tied this interpretive approach to the text through the word "liberty" in the

---

39. Monaco v. Mississippi (1934).

40. Prof. Laurence H. Tribe maintains that *reinforcing representation* is only a particular kind of *fundamental-rights approach*, with such rights restricted to those of political participation and equal treatment. "The Puzzling Persistence of Process–Based Constitutional Theories", 89 *Yale.L.J.* 1063 (1980); reprinted as ch. 2 of his *Constitutional Choices* (Cambridge: Harvard University Press, 1985).

41. Commentators and interpreters sometimes use the terms "fundamental rights" and "fundamental values" as if they were interchangeable, sowing confusion among the unwary. "Value," of course, is a broader concept than "right." Rights are likely to be a subset of values and to point to values beyond rights, as, for example, rights of every person to "due process of law" and "equal protection of the laws" point to abstract values of fair treatment and equal dignity. This section and the materials in Chapters 16–18 speak mostly of "rights," although notions of "values," to which particular rights point, lurk in the background.

Fifth and Fourteenth Amendments. That word, he argued, reflected a broad concept that

> denotes not merely freedom from bodily restraint but also the right of any individual to contract, to engage in any of the common occupations of life, to acquire useful knowledge, to marry, establish a home and bring up children, to worship God according to the dictates of his own conscience, and generally to enjoy those privileges long recognized at common law as essential to the orderly pursuit of happiness by free men.

McReynolds got much interpretive mileage from the word "liberty," but a tight textual tie, some interpreters and commentators assume, is not essential. The general theory of constitutionalism, as Chapter 3 showed, presumes the document floats in "an ocean of rights": If a textual connection is necessary, it is supplied by the Preamble's goals of justice, tranquility, and liberty; by the Bill of Rights, especially the First, Fifth, Eighth, and Ninth Amendments; and by the Thirteenth and Fourteenth amendments.

The advantages of an interpretive approach that tries to carry out the putative constitutional purpose of protecting fundamental rights are plain, at least to those who endorse constitutionalism. Justice William J. Brennan's speech on contemporary ratification of "the Constitution" (reprinted above, p. 236) explains some of these, as does Chapter 3 of this book.

The drawbacks are equally manifest. This approach gives interpreters a broad range of discretion and, by so doing, diminishes predictability. Constitutionalist as well as democratic theorists might stay awake nights worrying about what contemporaries might ratify. In addition, there is the problem of classifying rights listed in the text as more or less fundamental. No advocate of a *fundamental-rights approach* has yet produced such a calculus. In Palko v. Connecticut (1937; reprinted above, p. 128), Justice Benjamin N. Cardozo claimed that some rights mentioned in the first eight amendments are "of the very essence of a scheme of ordered liberty" and are "so rooted in the traditions and conscience of our people as to be ranked as fundamental." Even interpreters who agree that the text contains a hierarchy of rights can find little specific guidance in Cardozo's words; in effect, he offered a plausible hypothesis, but did not provide persuasive justification for it. Indeed, in recent years, property has been making a constitutional come back. Chief Justice William H. Rehnquist said for the Court in 1994 that the right to "just compensation" for private property taken for a public use, a right protected by the Fourteenth as well as the Fifth Amendment, should no longer be "relagated to the status of a poor relation." [42]

It is even more difficult to provide clear guidelines for identifying unlisted rights that deserve constitutional status. Justice John

---

42. Dolan v. City of Tigard (1994).

Marshall Harlan's efforts in Poe v. Ullman (1961; reprinted above p. 141) were heroic; but his message that American constitutional democracy was a synthesis of "the liberty of the individual" and "the demands of organized society," based on "what history teaches are the traditions from which it developed as well as the traditions from which it broke" was no less indeterminate than his call for "judgment and restraint" in discovering that synthesis.

Democratic theorists worry about appointed federal judges' using this interpretive approach. On the other hand, when elected officials show solicitude for *fundamental rights* questions of democratic legitimacy do not arise, though their concern may weaken their chances for reelection just as anxiety about reelection may sap elected officials' readiness to defend unpopular rights. And, those people who stress the system's constitutionalism are quick to argue that, in a *constitutional* democracy, it is precisely the "electoral connection" which requires appointed officials to defend fundamental rights against popular attacks. As Madison said:

> [I]nvasion of private rights is chiefly to be apprehended, not from acts of Government contrary to the sense of its constituents, but from acts in which Government is the mere instrument of the major number of its constituents.[43]

A fifth version of *purposivism* is aspirational. It operates from the premise that "the Constitution," whether the text or the text plus, is more than a set of rules for government but has, as the Preamble states, certain goals that point the nation toward an attainable good life. An *aspirational approach* requires interpreters to look for purposes in a very deep sense, to ask what kind of society "the Constitution" pushes the United States to become. In short, it takes the nation's ideals very seriously and uses them to structure constitutional interpretation.[44]

This approach is probably the most complex of all. Used intelligently it involves *textual, philosophic*, and *historical* approaches, as well as attention to *tradition* and previous interpretations. We can sometimes see it shine clearly through presidential addresses—in Lincoln's first inaugural (reprinted above, p. 314) or his Gettysburg Address, or in judicial opinions as in Black's dissent in *Barenblatt* (reprinted below, p. 803), or Earl Warren's opinion in Trop v. Dulles (1958; reprinted above, p. 219), or in his opinion for the Court in Bolling v. Sharpe, the school segregation case from the District of Columbia (1954; reprinted below, p. 917).

---

43. Letter to Jefferson, October 17, 1788. A convenient source is Marvin Meyers, ed., *The Mind of the Framer* (Indianapolis: Bobbs–Merrill, 1973), pp. 206–209.

44. For discussions of this interpretive approach, see espec.: Sotirios A. Barber, *On What the Constitution Means* (Baltimore: Johns Hopkins University Press, 1984), ch. 5; James E. Fleming, "Constructing the Substantive Constitution," 72 *Tex.L.Rev.* 211, 268–273 (1993); and Gary J. Jacobsohn, *The Supreme Court and the Decline of Constitutional Aspiration* (Totowa, NJ: Rowman & Littlefield, 1986). For a perplexed critique, see Lino A. Graglia's review of Barber: "Constitutional Mysticism: The Aspirational Defense of Judicial Review," 98 *Harv.L.Rev.* 1331 (1985).

More often than not, however, an *aspirational approach* moves "by silent foot," shaping the way interpreters read the document, understand traditions, construe previous interpretations, and apply political theories. And, the term "interpreters" includes all interpreters, not merely those like Justice Brennan who openly proclaim what they think are the system's aspirations. For example, a careful reading of the opinions and other writings of Chief Justice Rehnquist and Justice Scalia reprinted in this book [45] shows that each has a vision of what the United States should be all about, what sort of society "the Constitution" pushes the nation to become. For Rehnquist and even more for Scalia, it is the world as they believe the founding generations conceived it, their specific conceptions about that world and well as their broader concepts about political life. What makes it sometimes difficult to perceive these two justices as being guided by constitutional aspiration is that they argue for a modest judicial role. Their aspirations are more democratic than constitutionalist, more those of a distant past than a developing future, and in a peculiar sense simultaneously both Burkean and Rousseauean.

There can be little doubt that an *aspirational approach* opens a very wide field to interpretive discretion and generates vast indeterminacy, for it suffers from all the defects of the other forms of approach to which it is allied. Furthermore, under some circumstances, it may stand in very uneasy tension and perhaps even in open conflict with a *prudential approach*. If the principal danger of interpretation based solely on prudence is to degrade "the Constitution" from "the supreme law of the land" into a collection of pious admonitions to public officials to act wisely, the main threat of constitutional construction based solely on aspirationalism is to encourage interpreters to ignore the practical effects of their work, to say *"Fiat justitia, ruat coelum"*—Let justice be done though the heavens fall.

These difficulties are exacerbated by the fact that interpreters so seldom explain and justify the aspirations that guide their work and, as with Rehnquist and Scalia, may not even be aware of how their visions of the good American society shape their constitutional interpretation. On the other hand, as for *purpose* in general, it is difficult to justify interpretations that do not take into account that the political system has ideals, that the American people and their "Constitution" stand for certain substantive values. That these are difficult to enunciate and even more difficult to rank order underlines one of this book's basic themes: Interpreters need to be more aware of what it is they are doing and be more ready to offer reasoned justifications for their choices.

---

45. See espec. Rehnquist, "The Notion of a Living Constitution" (reprinted above, p. 243), and Scalia's opinion in *Michael H.* (1989; reprinted above, p. 158).

VIII. BALANCING

Yet another interpretive approach [46] goes under the name of *balancing*, a metaphor borrowed from the image of a blindfolded goddess of justice holding a set of scales in which she weighs opposing claims. During the late middle ages, English judges verbalized this symbol. Chancellors sometimes spoke of their task as "balancing the equities," and this language came to permeate the common-law system. The analogy is apt, for both parties in litigation often have some right—and some wrong—on their sides.

Modern use of *balancing* received great impetus in American law during the early years of this century when Roscoe Pound, who was to become dean of Harvard Law School, began to spread the gospel of "sociological jurisprudence." Society, he claimed, is composed of many interests, each pressing different and at times conflicting demands. "Law" consists of the rules society devises to resolve those struggles. And those rules must be sufficiently malleable to change as society's needs shift. "Law must be stable, and yet it cannot stand still" [47] was one of Pound's constant refrains. In this process, he saw judges as playing the crucial role of "social engineers": Through a study of history, economics, and sociology, they would analyze the interests vying for legal protection, "balance" those demands against each other, and create "appropriate" rules to resolve conflicts.

Constitutional interpreters have often used *balancing* as an adjunct to *textualism* when different clauses seem to state inconsistent rules, to *doctrinalism* when different doctrines clash, to *fundamental rights* when two rights collide, and to *purposivism* when goals compete. Faced with opposing claims, interpreters frequently say they must *balance* legitimate demands. Some clauses in the document invite such an approach: The Fourth Amendment, for example, forbids only "unreasonable" searches and seizures, the Eighth Amendment bars only "excessive" bail or fines, and the Fifth Amendment requires "just compensation" for private property taken for public use. What is unreasonable, excessive, or just, one might argue, can only be answered by assessing and "balancing" competing claims in the circumstances of a particular factual setting.

Balancing also attracts interpreters when simultaneous reliance on different parts of the constitutional document poses a conflict. For instance, one person's supposed right to freedom of expression,

---

46. Critics might object that *balancing*, like *prudence*, is more a strategy of organizing interpretive approaches than itself a separate approach. We concede that critics could make a good case for such a distinction, but we believe that, if we keep in mind that interpreters can and do use several approaches together, treating *balancing* (and *prudence*) as discrete approaches furthers understanding by allowing us to consider them on their own terms.

47. *Interpretations of Legal History* (New York: Macmillan, 1923), p. 1.

even of racist ideas, may clash with another's supposed right to enjoy the status of equal citizenship. (See R.A.V. v. St. Paul [1992; reprinted below, p. 686]). *Balancing* promises to resolve these competing claims and to do so without invoking controversial, abstract principles. And, by keeping the level of generality low, it provides considerable opportunity for interpretive flexibility.

Barenblatt v. United States (1959; reprinted below, p. 803) set the stage for a classic debate about *balancing* in constitutional interpretation. The clash was between, on the one hand, the authority of a congressional committee to compel a witness to testify about earlier membership in the Communist party, a supposed threat to national security, and, on the other, the witness's right, under the First Amendment, to refuse to disclose his political associations.[48] For the Court, Justice Harlan sustained the authority of Congress:

> [R]esolution of the issue always involves a balancing by the courts of the competing private and public interests at stake in the particular circumstances shown. ... We conclude that the balance between the individual and the governmental interests here at stake must be struck in favor of the latter, and that therefore the provisions of the First Amendment have not been offended.

In a passionate dissent, Hugo Black protested:

> I do not agree that laws directly abridging First Amendment freedoms can be justified by a congressional or a judicial balancing procedure. ... To apply the Court's balancing test under such circumstances is to read the First Amendment to say
>
> > Congress shall pass no law abridging freedom of speech, press, assembly and petition, unless Congress and the Supreme Court reach the joint conclusion that on balance the interest of the Government in stifling these freedoms is greater than the interest of the people in having them exercised.

Black reasoned that the plain words of the constitutional text ended the matter. The First Amendment said "Congress shall make no law" abridging these freedoms; and "no law" meant "no law at all," not "no law unless on balance."

Specific constitutional issues have changed but the debate goes on.[49] Recently, Justice Antonin Scalia has played the role Hugo

---

48. Earlier, in NAACP v. Alabama (1958; reprinted below, p. 798), the Court, speaking through Justice Harlan, had held that the First Amendment protected a right to privacy in one's political associations. It was this right, not the Fifth Amendment's protection against self-incrimination, that Barenblatt had invoked.

49. As we shall see in Chapters 14–15 and 17–18, the justices have developed a test called "strict scrutiny" to determine the constitutionality of legislation that uses certain "suspect classifications" or infringes on "fundamental rights." In essence, this test requires government to demonstrate that the particular regulation serves a "compelling interest" and is "narrowly tailored" in its coverage. Many decades ago, C. Herman Pritchett said the early forms of this test were a kind of *balancing* in which the judge acts like "the butcher who consistently weighs his thumb along with the meat" to favor claims

Black marked out. In general, Scalia has charged, *balancing* has an Alice-in-Wonderland character: "[T]he scale analogy is not really appropriate, since the interests on both sides are incommensurate. It is more like judging whether a particular line is longer than a particular rock is heavy." [50]

It is easy to ridicule particular uses of *balancing*. Even a staunch proponent concedes that Harlan's employment of it in *Barenblatt* was a "sham." [51] Dean Pound had warned that there were different levels of interests and judges should be careful to compare them on the same plane. "If we put one as an individual interest and the other as a social interest we may decide the question ... by our very way of putting it." [52] And, of course, it was precisely such a skewed balance that Harlan attempted in *Barenblatt*. As Black noted, if *balancing* were legitimate, what should have been weighed against Congress' authority to obtain information was not the right of a single person to privacy in his political associations, but, rather, the right of all citizens to make political choices, even mistakes, without fear of governmental reprisal.

A related, common misuse involves weighing of the marginal benefit of one interest against the total cost of another. In 1978, arguing against excluding illegally obtained evidence, Chief Justice Warren Burger proposed that the Court "balance the costs to society of losing perfectly competent evidence against the prospect of incrementally enhancing Fourth Amendment values." [53] What

---

of private citizens against government. *Civil Liberties and the Vinson Court* (Chicago: University of Chicago Press, 1954), p. 249. Some question remains, however, whether, in fact, "strict scrutiny" belongs to the genre of *balancing*. We raise this point in notes to several cases in these later chapters.

50. Bendix Corp. v. Midwesco, concur. op. (1988). This case centered on the validity of a state regulation that affected "commerce among the several States." A few sentences later Scalia qualified his general characterization of *balancing*: "We sometimes make similar 'balancing' judgments in determining how far the needs of the State can intrude upon liberties of the individual, but that is the essence of the courts' function as the nonpolitical branch. Weighing the governmental interest of a State against the needs of interstate commerce is, by contrast, a task squarely within the responsibility of Congress." Scalia did not offer further explanation of this distinction. On the other hand, in an article published the following year, he launched a broad attack on *balancing* as a threat to the rule of law. Near the conclusion of this piece, he wrote:

"We will have ... balancing modes of analysis with us forever—and for my sins, I will probably write some of the opinions that use them. All I urge is that these modes of analysis be avoided where possible; that the *Rule of Law*, the law of *rules*, be extended as far as the nature of the question allows. ..." ("The Rule of Law as a Law of Rules," 56 *U.Chi.L.Rev.* 1175 [1989].)

Dissenting in Morrison v. Olson (1988; discussed below, p. 513), Scalia expressed much the same view. For a perceptive analysis of the disagreements between Scalia, on the one hand, and Justices O'Connor, Souter, and Stevens, on the other, about *balancing* and "rules," see Kathleen M. Sullivan, "Foreword: The Justices of Rules and Standards," 106 *Harv.L.Rev.* 24 (1992).

51. Dean Alfange, "The Balancing of Interests in Free Speech Cases: In Defense of an Abused Doctrine," 2 *Law in Transition* Q. 1, 24 (1965).

52. "A Survey of Social Interests," 57 *Harv.L.Rev.* 1, 2 (1943).

53. United States v. Ceccolini, concur. op. (1978).

the Chief should have balanced against an incremental gain in deterring unlawful police conduct was the incremental cost to society of losing one particular piece of evidence, not the overall costs. Alternatively, he could have balanced the full advantage of the exclusionary rule in deterring police misconduct against the total social cost of losing probative evidence. But by balancing the total cost against an incremental gain, Burger rigged the scales.

Misuse, of course, may be a more persuasive argument for proper use than for abandonment. And *balancing*'s promises are attractive. It appears to provide, Prof. Louis Henkin has written, "bridges between the abstractions of principle and the life of facts. It bespeaks moderation and reasonableness, the Golden Mean." [54] But these appeals may come at a high cost to other values and, indeed, be deceptive.

First, *balancing* deeply enmeshes judges in policy choices. To be sure, this involvement was precisely the reason that Roscoe Pound advocated this approach; but judicial policy making is of profound concern to democrats. Concurring in Dennis v. United States (1951; reprinted below, p. 658), Justice Frankfurter asserted that demands of free speech and national security were "better served by candid and informed weighing of the competing interests . . . than by announcing dogmas too inflexible for the non-Euclidian problems to be solved." But, he then invoked the interrogative WHO: "[W]ho is to balance the relevant factors and ascertain which is in the circumstances to prevail? . . . Primary responsibility for adjusting the interests which compete in the situation before us of necessity belongs to the Congress."

Second, of concern to both democrats and constitutionalists, *balancing* may be no more than a black box from which interpreters extract whatever answer they want. To blandly say, as judges, legislators, and executive officials often do, that "on balance" we think the government's claims under a particular clause outweigh a citizen's claims under another clause masks from interpreters themselves as well as from observers the reasoning, if any, behind a supposed interpretation.

Balancers need to explain and justify the nature of the scale on which they profess to compare competing and possibly incommensurate interests as well as the relative weights they accord each item to be measured. Accomplishing such tasks is likely to entail *textual*, *structural*, *purposive*, and *philosophic* analyses as well as relating these approaches to a coherent and justified conception of WHAT is "the Constitution" and its aspirations that are being construed—frustrating *balancing*'s promise to limit the levels of abstraction and generality.

---

54. "Infallibility under the Law: Constitutional Balancing," 78 *Colum.L.Rev.* 1022, 1047 (1978).

Thus, critics argue, when one looks behind *balancing*'s symbolism of fairness one is usually left with an announcement of a decision, not a reasoned justification. Justice Cardozo frankly conceded the point: "If you ask how he [the judge] is to know when one interest outweighs another, I can only answer that he must get his knowledge just as the legislator gets it, from experience and study and reflection; in brief, from life itself." [55] As Henkin comments, "balancing seems to emerge as an answer instead of a process, and the metaphor of balancing as the whole message." [56]

APPENDIX

Undoubtedly, informed readers have noted that this chapter did not discuss several supposed approaches, usually expressed as distinctions, even dichotomies: Strict v. Liberal Construction; Judicial Activism v. Self–Restraint; Substance v. Procedure; and Interpretivism v. Non–Interpretivism. We think all four lead into blind analytic alleys; but, because many commentators refer to them, we shall briefly discuss each.

1. Strict v. Liberal Construction

One cannot consistently interpret the constitutional text strictly or liberally without becoming mired in massive contradictions. How, for instance, does one "strictly" interpret the Ninth Amendment? Does a strict interpretation require that more or fewer rights be protected? More generally, when one strictly interprets government's powers, one usually thereby also liberally interprets individual rights. Conversely, when one strictly interprets individual rights, one usually liberally interprets governmental power. An effort to interpret both powers and rights equally strictly is likely to leave the interpreter in a gigantic muddle. One could attempt always to interpret rights liberally and powers strictly. Constitutionalism would certainly prescribe such a general course, but there is small authority in the text for doing so. And bringing in political theory involves using a *philosophic approach* and raises the dilemma to another level of abstraction: Do we strictly or liberally construe a relevant normative theory? And how do we do strictly construe one such theory without liberally interpreting the other(s)?

A similar sort of difficulty arises in conflicts between governmental agencies. Normally, liberally construing the powers of one means strictly interpreting the powers of the other, triggering the same logical dilemma as with rights, a dilemma that can be resolved

---

55. *The Nature of the Judicial Process* (New Haven: Yale University Press, 1921), p. 113.

56. Supra note 54, p. 1048.

only on the basis of a theory not expressed in the words of the document.

Further complicating matters is the fact that sometimes governmental powers and individual rights (or two sets of governmental powers) are not in a zero-sum relationship. We all need public officials to protect us from our fellow citizens. "If men were angels," Madison said in *Federalist* No. 51. "no government would be necessary." There are frequent occasions, as when police intervene to prevent a murder or when federal officials enforce the Fourteenth Amendment, in which individual rights depend on government's exercising its powers. So, too, states' rights—even states' existence—may depend on the federal government's power to conduct foreign relations or to ameliorate an economic crisis like the Great Depression.

2. Judicial Activism v. Judicial Self-Restraint

Initially used to call attention to the need for limits on judicial discretion,[57] this alternative is now more often an ideological epithet: Any interpretation critics dislike is "activist," any they like represents an example of "self-restraint." Nevertheless, the distinction tries to illuminate a problem. A constitutional democracy cannot tolerate judges' reading their purely personal values into "the Constitution." Used in a principled fashion to limit judicial discretion, this distinction implies that judges are obliged to defer to legislative or presidential interpretations and possibly to those of state officials as well. In that sense, the distinction fits under the question of WHO shall interpret. It says nothing about HOW judges should interpret "the Constitution." And, because the constitutional document nowhere expresses a judicial duty of habitual deference to other branches of government, to argue for such a stance requires elaboration of democratic theory.[58]

And, to the extent that the American constitutional system also rests on a theory of constitutionalism, on a notion of limitations on the power even of those who represent the people, it may require that judges actively oppose the choices of elected officials. Thus, used evaluatively, the distinction poses a dilemma: From different perspectives, judges may be activist either if they strike down legislation that, in their judgment, unconstitutionally expands powers or if they accept the validity of such legislation.

---

57. The first time this phrase struck wide public notice was when, dissenting in United States v. Butler (1936), Harlan Stone referred to "our own sense of self-restraint." C. Herman Pritchett was among the first academic commentators to use the term for analytic purposes. See his path-breaking work, *The Roosevelt Court* (New York: Macmillan, 1948).

58. For a critical analysis of the claim that judges should generally defer to other officials, see Sotirios A. Barber, *The Constitution of Judicial Power* (Baltimore: Johns Hopkins University Press, 1993).

As a constitutional caution, activism/restraint is of some value. Few, if any, judges (or other interpreters) claim authority to read their personal views into "the Constitution"; but, in fact, all interpreters as well as commentators and private citizens sometimes do so. And they behave in this fashion because at many places the text extends interpreters an invitation to exercise discretion and at other places compels them to do so. It may well be that most interpreters believe "the Constitution" commands all the choices they make, but to "invite" or even "compel" choice is not the same as to "command" a particular choice. And we once more chant our chorus about the need for public justifications of these choices based on a coherent theory of the WHAT, WHO, and HOW of constitutional interpretation.

3. Substance v. Procedure

Should we read the constitutional document as primarily procedural—prescribing rules about how things are to be done—or primarily substantive—prescribing rules about what government is and is not to do? John Hart Ely presents an impressive theory of "the Constitution" as almost entirely procedural: The document is replete with commands about how officials are to be chosen and the processes they are to follow in creating public policy, but it contains very few rules about the content of public policy.[59]

This distinction is somewhat more helpful than the first two in that it makes some sense in analyzing parts of the written text. But the question quickly arises about how much help a differentiation between process and substance offers. Some, certainly; but substantive values typically underlie procedural choices, such as requirements of elections, search warrants, and public trials.[60] In the real world, the two are so interrelated that it is often difficult to distinguish them. Moreover, as Ely openly acknowledges, his use of this distinction is not simply a product of *textualism* but also of a *philosophic* approach that stresses a form of democratic theory and crowds constitutionalism almost completely out of the American political system.

4. Interpretivism v. Non–Interpretivism

This supposed distinction confounds the possibility of real insights in problems of constitutional interpretation. Thomas Grey, who was responsible for popularizing the term, defined "interpretivism" as an effort to find all constitutional meaning within the four corners of the document and "non-interpretivism" as allowing

---

59. Supra note 4.

60. Laurence H. Tribe makes this point, "The Puzzling Persistence of Process–Based Constitutional Theories," supra note 40, as does James E. Fleming, "Constructing the Substantive Constitution," supra note 35.

interpreters to move beyond the document and import values not there.[61] The first difficulty is that interpretivism is impossible except for the simplest of issues on which there is unlikely to be disagreement to begin with. Plain words, as we saw, restrain choices in constitutional interpretation, but they seldom determine them. Thus all interpretivists concede that one should look beyond the document, at least to what the founders "intended" or "understood" to have been within the four corners.[62] In effect this process would present another set of documents—records of speeches or writings of framers and ratifiers—whose words must also be collated, reconciled, interpreted, and applied. And we resurrect the difficulties of *originalism*.

Further, although some Legal Realists of an earlier generation thought the power of text to constrain was small,[63] a claim repeated by some contemporary members of the Critical Legal Studies Movement,[64] few responsible interpreters publicly assert authority to ignore or contradict the plain words,[65] except, perhaps, in the most dire national emergencies. (See, below, Chapter 19.) Mostly, interpreters insist they are only explaining what those words mean for the political system. And those whom self-labelled interpretivists brand as non-interpretivists may be displaying a greater fidelity to that text. For they take seriously words such as those of the Preamble and the Ninth Amendment that instruct interpreters to go beyond the document itself.

Thus what began as a clear distinction about the question HOW quickly turns to interpretive smog. We are all interpretivists, we are all non-interpretivists. This supposed distinction obscures the real issues in constitutional interpretation, which relate precisely to drawing—and justifications for drawing—lines between WHAT is and is not included in "the Constitution," WHO determines in an authoritative manner such issues for the polity, and HOW those authoritative interpreters make and justify their decisions. Indeed, Thomas Grey,[66] who sired the interpretive/non-interpretive distinc-

---

61. "Do We Have an Unwritten Constitution?" 27 *Stan.L.Rev.* 703 (1975). Ely, who freely acknowledged his debt to Grey, helped bring the term into common usage among commentators. *Op. cit.* supra note 4, espec. chs. 1–2.

62. Grey asserted that interpretivism would sometimes authorize "[n]ormative inferences ... from silences and omissions, from structures and relationships, as well as from explicit commands." Supra note 61, at 706 n. Given the open-ended nature of *structuralism* and the far greater variety of plausible inferences from "silences and omissions," it is difficult to imagine what one could import into "the Constitution" via non-interpretivism that one could not through interpretivism.

63. See, for example, Charles P. Curtis, "The Role of Constitutional Text," in Edmond Cahn, ed., *Supreme Court and Supreme Law* (Bloomington: Indiana University Press, 1954).

64. See, for example, Mark Tushnet, "A Note on the Revival of Textualism in Constitutional Theory," 58 *So.Cal.L.Rev.* 683 (1985).

65. See note 6 supra, for a caveat.

66. "The Constitution as Scripture," 37 *Stan.L.Rev.* 1 (1984).

tion, has since renounced his child as ill-conceived.[67]

SELECTED BIBLIOGRAPHY

Ackerman, Bruce A. *We the People: Foundations* (Cambridge: Harvard University Press, 1991).

————. "Discovering the Constitution," 93 *Yale L.J.* 1013 (1984).

————. "Constitutional Politics/Constitutional Law," 99 *Yale L.J.* 453 (1989).

Aleinikoff, T. Alexander. "Constitutional Law in the Age of Balancing," 96 *Yale L.J.* 943 (1987).

Arkes, Hadley. *Beyond the Constitution* (Princeton: Princeton University Press, 1990).

Barber, Sotirios A. *On What the Constitution Means* (Baltimore: Johns Hopkins University Press, 1984).

————. "The Ninth Amendment: Inkblot or Another Hard Nut to Crack?" 64 *Chi.-Kent L.Rev.* 67 (1988).

————. "Whither Moral Realism in Constitutional Theory?" 64 *Chi.-Kent L.Rev.* 111 (1988).

————. "Stanley Fish and the Future of Pragmatism in Legal Theory," 58 *U.Chi.L.Rev.* 1033 (1991).

————. *The Constitution of Judicial Power* (Baltimore: Johns Hopkins University Press, 1993.)

Berger, Raoul. *Government by Judiciary* (Cambridge: Harvard University Press, 1977).

Berns, Walter F. *Taking the Constitution Seriously* (New York: Simon & Schuster, 1987).

Black, Charles L. *Structure and Relationship in Constitutional Law* (Baton Rouge: Louisiana State University Press, 1969).

Black, Hugo L. *A Constitutional Faith* (New York: Knopf, 1969).

Bobbitt, Philip. *Constitutional Interpretation* (Cambridge, MA.: Basil Blackwell, 1991).

Bork, Robert H. *The Tempting of America: The Political Seduction of the Law* (New York: The Free Press, 1990).

---

67. For further analyses of the distinctions made in this Appendix, see Harris, *op. cit.*, note 20 above, pp. 124–28; and Walter F. Murphy, "The Art of Constitutional Interpretation," in M. Judd Harmon, ed., *Essays on the Constitution of the United States* (Port Washington, NY: Kennikat Press, 1978).

Brest, Paul, and Sanford V. Levinson. *Processes of Constitutional Decisionmaking: Cases and Materials* (3d ed. Boston: Little, Brown, 1992).

Brigham, John. *Constitutional Language* (Westport, CN: Greenwood Press, 1978).

Brison, Susan J., and Walter Sinnott–Armstrong, eds. *Contemporary Perspectives on Constitutional Interpretation* (Boulder, CO: Westview Press, 1993).

Chemerinsky, Erwin. *Interpreting the Constitution* (New York: Praeger, 1987).

Corwin, Edward S. "Constitution v. Constitutional Theory," 19 *Am.Pol.Sci.Rev.* 290 (1925); reprinted in Alpheus Thomas Mason and Gerald Garvey, eds., *American Constitutional History* (New York: Harper, 1964).

————. "The Constitution as Instrument and Symbol," 30 *Am. Pol.Sci.Rev.* 1071 (1936); reprinted in Richard Loss, ed., *Corwin on the Constitution* (Ithaca: Cornell University Press, 1981), vol. I.

Dworkin, Ronald. *Taking Rights Seriously* (Cambridge: Harvard University Press, 1977).

————. *A Matter of Principle* (Cambridge: Harvard University Press, 1985).

————. *Law's Empire* (Cambridge: Harvard University Press, 1986).

————. *Life's Dominion* (New York: Knopf, 1993).

Eisgruber, Christopher L. "Justice and the Text: Rethinking the Constitutional Relation Between Principle and Prudence," 43 *Duke L.J.* 1 (1993).

Ely, John Hart. *Democracy and Distrust* (Cambridge: Harvard University Press, 1980).

Fleming, James E. "Constructing the Substantive Constitution," 72 *Tex.L.Rev.* 211 (1993).

Garvey, John H. and T. Alexander Aleinikoff, eds. *Modern Constitutional Theory: A Reader* (3d ed.; St. Paul: West, 1994).

Gerhardt, Michael J., and Thomas D. Rowe, Jr., eds. *Constitutional Theory: Arguments and Perspectives* (Charlottesville, VA: Michie, 1993).

Gibson, Alan. "The Legacy and Authority of the Founders," 56 *Rev. of Pols.* 555 (1994).

Gottlieb, Stephen E. "The Paradox of Balancing Significant Interests," 45 *Hast.L.J.* 825 (1994).

Harris, William F. II. *The Interpretable Constitution* (Baltimore: Johns Hopkins University Press, 1993).

Henkin, Louis. "Infallibility under the Law: Constitutional Balancing," 78 *Colum.L.Rev.* 1022 (1978).

Hirsch, Harry N. *A Theory of Liberty: The Constitution and Minorities* (New York: Routledge, 1992).

Jacobsohn, Gary J. *The Supreme Court and the Decline of Constitutional Aspiration* (Totowa, NJ: Rowman & Littlefield, 1986).

————. *The Apple of Gold: Constitutionalism in Israel and the United States.* (Princeton: Princeton University Press, 1993).

Kahn, Ronald. *The Supreme Court & Constitutional Theory, 1953–1993* (Lawrence: University of Kansas Press, 1994).

Levinson, Sanford V. *Constitutional Faith* (Princeton: Princeton University Press, 1988).

Mason, Alpheus Thomas. *Harlan Fiske Stone: Pillar of the Law* (New York: Viking, 1956), espec. chs. 19–22.

————. *The Supreme Court from Taft to Burger* (Baton Rouge: Louisiana State University Press, 1979).

Miller, Arthur S. and Ronald F. Howell. "The Myth of Neutrality in Constitutional Adjudication," 27 *U.Chi.L.Rev.* 661 (1960).

Miller, Charles A. *The Supreme Court and the Uses of History* (Cambridge: Harvard University Press, 1969).

Monaghan, Henry P. "Foreword: Constitutional Common Law," 89 *Harv.L.Rev.* 1 (1975).

Murphy, Walter F. "The Art of Constitutional Interpretation," in M. Judd Harmon, ed., *Essays on the Constitution of the United States* (Port Washington, NY: Kennikat Press, 1978).

————. "Constitutional Interpretation: The Art of the Historian, Magician, or Statesman?" 87 *Yale L.J.* 1752 (1978).

————. "An Ordering of Constitutional Values," 53 *So.Cal.L.Rev.* 703 (1980).

————. "Constitutional Interpretation: Text, Values, and Processes," 9 *Revs. in Am. Hist.* 7 (1981).

————. "Staggering Toward the New Jerusalem of Constitutional Theory," 37 *Am.J.Juris.* 337 (1992).

Nelson, William E. "History and Neutrality in Constitutional Adjudication," 72 *Va.L.Rev.* 1237 (1986).

Nimmer, Melville B. "The Right to Speak from *Times* to *Time*," 56 *Calif.L.Rev.* 935 (1968).

Powell, H. Jefferson. "The Original Understanding of Original Intent," 98 *Harv.L.Rev.* 885 (1985).

————. *The Moral Tradition of American Constitutionalism: A Theological Interpretation* (Durham: Duke University Press, 1993).

Powell, Thomas Reed. *Vagaries and Varieties in Constitutional Interpretation* (New York: Columbia University Press, 1956).

_____. "The Logic and Rhetoric of Constitutional Law," 15 *Jo. of Phil., Psych., & Sc. Method* 654 (1918); reprinted in Robert G. McCloskey, ed., *Essays in Constitutional Law* (New York: Knopf, 1957).

Rakove, Jack N. *Interpreting the Constitution: The Debate Over Original Intent* (Boston: Northeastern University Press, 1990).

Schauer, Frederick. "An Essay on Constitutional Language," 29 *UCLA L. Rev.* 797 (1982).

Sunstein, Cass R. *The Partial Constitution* (Cambridge: Harvard University Press, 1993).

_____. "Liberal Constitutionalism and Liberal Justice: A Response," 72 *Tex.L.Rev.* 305 (1993).

Symposium on Interpretation. 58 *So.Cal.L.Rev.* 1 (1985).

Tribe, Laurence H. *Constitutional Choices* (Cambridge: Harvard University Press, 1985).

_____, and Michael H. Dorf. *On Reading the Constitution* (Cambridge: Harvard University Press, 1991).

Walker, Graham. *Moral Foundations of Constitutional Thought: Current Problems, Augustinian Prospects* (Princeton: Princeton University Press, 1990).

Wechsler, Herbert. "Toward Neutral Principles of Constitutional Law," 73 *Harv.L.Rev.* 1 (1959).

Wellington, Harry H. *Interpreting the Constitution: The Supreme Court and the Process of Adjudication* (New Haven: Yale University Press, 1990).

B

STRUCTURALISM

Chapter 9 spoke in general terms about the nature of structural analysis, of its concern with the whole of the object to be interpreted, not merely of its discrete parts. Overt use of structuralism in American constitution making began with the Philadelphia Convention, if not earlier. In the notes we have of the debates there, one can discern recurrent concern among the delegates about the wholeness of the polity they were striving to create; and, on occasion, there was real resistance to the document's spelling out details. At least some delegates wanted to construct a framework that was even more stark than the document that emerged.

Use of structural analysis in American constitutional interpretation began soon thereafter in the *Federalist Papers*. Chapter 9 quoted Madison's argument in No. 40:

> There are two rules of construction, dictated by plain reason, as well as founded on legal axioms. The one is, that every part of the expression ought, if possible, be made to conspire to some common end. The other is, that where the several parts cannot be made to coincide, the less important should give way to the more important part; the means should be sacrificed to the end, rather than the end to the means.

When in Chisholm v. Georgia (1793) the Court faced its first important case testing the nature of federalism, it was appropriate that the justices looked not merely to specific clauses of the document, but also to the more general ideas that held the document—and the larger political system—together. Perhaps the most significant of early uses of structuralism came in John Marshall's opinion for the Court in McCulloch v. Maryland (1819; reprinted below, p. 530).

The point is not that structuralism is the most ancient approach to interpretation or that somehow it is "the best," only that it has been with us from the beginning despite the fact that neither the

Founders nor early interpreters put that twentieth-century label on it. Still, we must keep in mind the difficulties that structuralism carries, most seriously the necessity for an interpreter to articulate the structure, whether of the document, the broader political system, or the theories that surround and support both the document and the system.

The chapters in this section illustrate a *structural approach* to constitutional interpretation by taking up its two most obvious uses, settling problems of allocations of power among the branches of the national government (Chapter 10) and between the national and state governments (Chapter 11). One should keep in mind, however, that *structuralism* need not have such narrow ambitions. One can make a strong case that the structure of the document, system, and/or its underlying theories is one of representative democracy. Accepting such an argument would have broad implications for constitutional interpretation, quite like those that a purposive approach of *reinforcing representative democracy*—developed in Chapters 12 and 13—explores.

One could make a similarly strong case for a constitutionalist structure to face the sorts of problems of fundamental rights that Chapters 16–18 address. Or one could, as we do throughout this book, argue that the system is one of constitutional democracy and organize most, if not all, of constitutional interpretation around a variety of *structural approaches*. We have been more modest, but we think readers should be aware that the claims for a *structuralist approach* can be exceedingly ambitious.

SELECTED BIBLIOGRAPHY

Black, Charles L., Jr. *Structure and Relationship in Constitutional Law* (Baton Rouge: Louisiana State University Press, 1969).

Bobbitt, Philip. *Constitutional Fate* (New York: Oxford University Press, 1982), ch. 6.

_____. *Constitutional Interpretation* (Cambridge, MA: Blackwell, 1991).

Brigham, John. *Constitutional Language* (Westport, CN: Greenwood Press, 1978).

Choper, Jesse H. *Judicial Review and the National Political Process* (Chicago: University of Chicago Press, 1980).

Ely, John Hart. *Democracy and Distrust* (Cambridge: Harvard University Press, 1980).

Harris, William F. II. *The Interpretable Constitution* (Baltimore: Johns Hopkins University Press, 1993).

Tribe, Laurence H., and Michael C. Dorf. *On Reading the Constitution* (Cambridge: Harvard University Press, 1991).

Tushnet, Mark V. "Legal Realism, Structural Review, and Prophecy," 8 *U. of Dayton L.Rev.* 809 (1983).

10

Structural Analysis: Sharing Power at the National Level

Early constitutional arguments by Madison, Jefferson, Marshall, and Story, later arguments by Jackson, Calhoun, Lincoln, Holmes, and more recent arguments by Rehnquist and Dworkin all support by example Justice Harlan Stone's call to read particular provisions of the constitutional text "as ... part[s] of an organic whole." [1] Indeed, it seems impossible to interpret relations among various branches of the national government or between state and national levels without either a conscious general idea or some regulative assumptions regarding the constitutional system's purposes—some idea or assumptions regarding the *structure not only* of the basic document but also of the institutions it created, the traditions that surround it, and the theories that inform its words and shape practices under it.

As Chapter 3 indicated, many of the founders were quite conscious of the general framework of government they were establishing. Part of Madison's grand strategy was to pit some economic, social, and institutional interests against other economic, social, and institutional interests, to set power against power, and thus to avoid tyranny and enhance the probability of good government. *Federalist* Nos. 10 (reprinted below, p. 1087) and 51 (reprinted below, p. 432) explain his design. Its function is not so much to separate *powers* but, as Richard E. Neustadt put it, to separate *institutions* and require them to share powers. [2]

Chapter 3 also provided detailed information about some of the ways in which these shared powers allow each of the three branches to check the other two. The President is part of the legislative process; he can propose legislation, negotiate with individual legislators to approve or disapprove particular bills, and veto those he strongly dislikes. Congress participates in the executive process by creating and funding all federal agencies. The Senate's power to advise and consent (or not consent) to the appointment of most high level executive officers involves that house even more formally

---

1. Wright v. United States, concur. op. (1938).

2. *Presidential Power* (rev. ed., New York: John Wiley, 1976), p. 101.

in administrative processes, but individual members of the House can play important roles here too. Both Congress and the President wield some judicial power in choosing judges, enacting and approving (or vetoing) laws regulating jurisdiction, and determining what litigation will be brought in the name of the United States.[3] And judges, in defining and interpreting "the Constitution" as well as the often general language of congressional enactments, frequently act as legislators, just as in making sense of the bureaucratic language of executive orders and applying laws to concrete cases judges' work may merge with that of administrators.

Questions of control over war and foreign policy provide a contested battleground of shared powers. Article I authorizes Congress "to declare war . . . to raise and support armies . . . to provide and maintain a navy . . . [and] to make rules for the government and regulation of the land and naval forces. . . ." Article II, however, makes the President commander-in-chief of the armed forces, authorizes him to conduct diplomacy, requires him to swear "to preserve, protect and defend the Constitution," and instructs him to "take care that the laws be faithfully executed."

These clauses, as Prof. Edward S. Corwin once remarked, form "an invitation to struggle for the privilege of directing American foreign policy."[4] And, of course, practical necessity seldom displays respect for constitutional texts. Presidents since George Washington have asserted authority to take military action to defend the United States without a declaration of war or other congressional approval. In response, individual legislators and Congress as an institution have periodically contested the President's claim. The War Powers Act of 1973 (reprinted below, p. 455) and the Gulf War Resolution of 1991 (reprinted below, p. 461) represent two phases of this struggle between the executive and the legislature. Although judges have sometimes become involved—see, for example, Little v. Barreme (1804; reprinted below, p. 435), and the Prize Cases (1863; reprinted below, p. 438)—the Supreme Court has usually been sufficiently prudent to keep out of this dangerous field.[5]

Economic policy has shaped a different kind of battlefield. Since the New Deal of the 1930s, Congress has assumed a positive responsibility to regulate and, in part, direct the nation's economy. It has used means that vary from prohibiting, tightly restricting, or heavily taxing certain kinds of operations, to setting minimum

---

3. Congress's power to investigate may also fulfill a judicial function. It is not unusual for congressional hearings to expose both private citizens and governmental officials to merciless publicity about alleged wrong doings.

4. *The President: Office and Powers* (4th rev. ed.; New York: New York University Press, 1957), p. 171.

5. See the Court's artful dodging of cases from the Vietnam War, especially Massachusetts v. Laird (1970) and Mora v. McNamara (1967), and later of the question of the validity of President Carter's abrogation of the defense treaty with Taiwan. Goldwater v. Carter (1979).

wages, to subsidizing selected industries. More broadly, federal legislation now tries to insure monetary stability by creating the Federal Reserve System and to cushion economic disasters by providing financial help for the aged, the disabled, and the unemployed. In considering legislation for such a complex world, Congress has seen its options as either setting broad policy goals and delegating large measures of discretionary authority to administrative officials or prescribing massive, intricately detailed, codes that require frequent and equally intricate renewals. In the belief that Congress is institutionally ill-equipped for this second approach, legislators have typically opted for the first alternative.

The constitutional course of this choice has been choppy. After more than a century of approving ever broader delegations of congressional power, the revolutionary changes the New Deal threatened to create in American life caused some justices to rethink the issue. Panama Refining Co. v. Ryan (1935) and Schechter v. Schechter Poultry Corp. (1935) ruled that two New Deal delegations had gone too far. Because these holdings threatened the efficacy of modern government as a whole, Schechter and Panama did not long survive as meaningful precedents. The Court later returned to its traditional approval of broad delegations on the theory (often the fiction) that Congress was delegating in ways that provided meaningful guidance to administrative and executive agencies.[6]

But discretion in formulating the details of a broadly phrased public policy and determining how and when it takes effect often means that administrators are really legislating. In delegating power as a way of exercising power under modern conditions, legislators could be contributing to a situation in which they lose power to administrators. To counter this result, representatives and senators have resorted to a bevy of tactics. Three have been especially important. The first has been to exercise "administrative oversight"—a euphemism for intervening in the administration of laws, supposedly the President's task—through control of the budget and the power to investigate administrative practices, supposedly to inquire into a need for new legislation. The second tactic has been to increase the number of so-called independent regulatory commissions headed by people appointed in the regular fashion but serving for set terms and not responsible to or removable by the President. The third tactic has been to delegate broad legislative authority but to tie a string to the delegation through what is called the legislative veto.

---

6. See Justice White's dis. op. in *Chadha* (1983; reprinted below, p. 485). For a more general analysis, see Sotirios A. Barber, *The Constitution and the Delegation of Congressional Power* (Chicago: University of Chicago Press, 1975). Theodore W. Lowi has argued that the pattern of congressional delegation constitutes an abdication of responsibility as well as a surrender of all hope of achieving coordinated and just public policies at the national level. *The End of Liberalism* (2nd ed.; New York: Norton, 1979).

Congressional authority to appropriate money and to enact laws—and thus to learn how effective current laws are—has meant the first tactic has encountered few constitutional difficulties, though it has often fomented bitter partisan and institutional struggles. Indeed, individual legislators have frequently used their positions of power within Congress to make it attractive for the President to choose their people rather than his own to head various federal bureaus or become federal judges. On the other hand, the constitutionality of the other two devices has been less certain.

Congress's establishment of "independent regulatory commissions" provoked interesting constitutional debate. Prior to the New Deal, Myers v. United States (1926) had decided that the President did not have to seek the Senate's approval for removing a postmaster from office. Dicta in that case suggested that Congress could place no limitations on the President's removal power, notwithstanding Congress's attempt to do so several times since Andrew Johnson's presidency. But the Court later decided that Congress could insulate some, albeit not all, administrators from presidential control. Postmasters, said the Court, were "executive" officers and therefore answerable to the President; commissioners of the independent regulatory agencies, such as the Interstate Commerce Commission, the Federal Trade Commission, and the Federal Power Commission, were somehow different. Because Congress created them to achieve the aims of particular enactments, it could validly provide that commissioners of independent agencies should serve for specific terms, rather than at the pleasure of the President.[7] This reasoning has not been convincing to all practical politicians or constitutional commentators.

The third tactic, the legislative veto, has had an even stormier course. Congress has often required that, as part of its delegation of power to an administrative agency,[8] the agency lay detailed plans before Congress; if Congress (sometimes the legislation will provide that if either house) takes no action within specified period, the regulations go into effect and have the force of law.

The benefits of allowing elected officials to regulate the work of appointed administrators is obvious; but the price of the legislative veto is to eliminate or severely constrict the presidential veto. In approving a set of regulations, Congress may be effecting substantial change in the meaning of existing laws; and its action does not go to the White House for the President's approval. One might contend that, as Chief Executive, the President may direct federal

---

7. Humphrey's Executor v. United States (1935). See also Wiener v. United States (1958). In Morrison v. Olson (1988; discussed below, p. 513, the Court rejected the suggestion that *all* executive officials (in this case, special prosecutors under the Ethics in Government Act of 1978) must be appointed and removed at the President's discretion.

8. We use the term "agency" here very broadly. Congress has even delegated lawmaking authority to the Supreme Court. See Eds.' Note 3 to INS v. Chadha (1983; reprinted below, p. 485).

administrators; but, as we hinted a few paragraphs ago, this view might be grossly oversimple. Not only has Congress by law exempted some agencies from the President's chain of command and, again by law, placed most bureaucrats under the protection of civil service regulations, but also congressional control of the budget and a strongly felt need of many Presidents to get their own social or economic policies enacted into law have put influential members of Congress in a strong position to bargain about who gets what federal jobs. Thus the heads of executive agencies are sometimes beholden to—and know they are beholden to—particular senators or representatives rather than to the President.

The constitutional problems surrounding the legislative veto have not yet been resolved. In INS v. Chadha (1983; reprinted below, p. 485), the Supreme Court declared the practice unconstitutional. But since that time Congress has continued to use it, though often in a more subtle form, and another battle—and possible clarification or modification of *Chadha*—seems likely.

Below the surface of such clashes are structural questions of the proper judicial role in settling disputes between Congress and the President. Prof. Jesse H. Choper has made a long and powerful argument that courts have no legitimate part to play as arbiter between Congress and the President or between the nation and the states. Each of these units, Choper reasons, has an array of political checks against the other. And judges, he concludes, should husband their authority in order to protect individuals against government, in what would otherwise be an unequal struggle.[9] Choper's argument has been widely persuasive, but far from universally so. However one evaluates his thesis, it is interesting that in the *Federalist*—see espec. No. 10, reprinted below, p. 1087, and No. 51, reprinted below, p. 432—Madison did not mention judicial review or even judges generally as elements in his grand design of pitting interests against interests and power against power at the national level. Only in *Federalist* No. 39 (reprinted below, p. 526) did he speak of judges as having an important role in maintaining the system's structure, and then merely insofar as relations between the nation and the states were concerned.[10]

Whatever the proper role of judges or other federal officials, the sharing of power among the branches of the national government blurs lines of responsibility and leaves no branch completely autonomous. Yet we expect each branch to retain a degree of institutional integrity sufficient to prevent domination by one or two so. The purpose is to secure a governmental system that can act in ways that

---

9. *Judicial Review and the National Political Process* (Chicago: University of Chicago Press, 1980).

10. It is worth noting that, at the Philadelphia Convention, Madison wanted judges linked to the executive in a council of revision that would pass on the constitutionality of legislative proposals. Later, in 1791, when he introduced the Bill of Rights, he also argued that judges would be important defenders of that part of the constitutional text.

insure thoughtful deliberation, democratic accountability, and respect for constitutionalism. This combination of goals is difficult to achieve, to say the very least. At the edges, making law, applying law, and interpreting law bleed into one another; it is thus sometimes almost impossible to discern the exact character of a specific action. Still, the system operates on the assumption that there is a core function that is legislative, a core that is executive, and yet a third core that is judicial. For example, the guilt or innocence of particular persons is a judicial issue,[11] what classes of acts are crimes is a legislative matter,[12] and arresting people is a task for executive officials. But, just as appropriating money for executive agencies and advising and consenting to the appointment of federal officials involves Congress and even more so the Senate in the executive process, so applying the law requires the executive department to interpret the statute, and, as with judges, interpretation often requires creative law making, thus involving both the executive and judicial departments in a kind of legislative activity.

Because distinctions among making, interpreting, and applying law are neither "natural" nor linguistically compelling, only roughly shaped by the constitutional text and long usage that predates ratification in 1787–88, what powers lie at the core of an institution's functions is a critical question for constitutional interpretation. Interpreters must decide, for example, when Congress' authority to make "exceptions" to the Supreme Court's appellate jurisdiction so trench on judicial power as to destroy the Court's integrity as a separate institution of government. (See Ex parte McCardle [1869; reprinted below, p. 467] and the editors' notes that follow it.) Interpreters must decide when the judiciary's power to remedy a constitutional violation puts judges in the legislative position of enacting tax laws[13] And judges must even decide whether considering a plaintiff's claim that the executive is violating the law would encroach on the President's power to execute the law.[14]

Cases like these are likely to turn on an interpreter's beliefs about "the Constitution's" architectural scheme, either as outlined in the document, or as indicated by the operations of the larger political system, or perhaps as both the document and the system's

---

11. After listing the general powers of Congress, Art. I, § 9 provides: "No bill of attainder or ex post facto law shall be passed." Art. I, § 10 lays the same prohibitions against the states. A bill of attainder is a legislative act that convicts a person of a crime and imposes punishment for that alleged deed. As defined in Calder v. Bull (1798; reprinted above, p. 121), an ex post facto law has retroactive effect; it makes an act, legal when committed, a crime, or increases the punishment for an act committed in the past, or lowers the standards of proof for an act committed before passage of the bill.

12. United States v. Hudson & Goodwin (1812) held that there were no "common law crimes" against the United States; that is, only Congress could establish the criminal law, though, of course, judges might interpret what Congress had enacted.

13. See, for instance, Missouri v. Jenkins (1989).

14. See Lujan v. Defenders of Wildlife (1992).

development are thought to reflect some broader political theory. The cases reprinted here show the justices drawing—usually implicitly but sometimes explicitly—the structural lines that they see as outlining the institutions of the national government. Occasionally these cases also exhibit the justices' deeper visions of the American polity.

To illustrate the complexities of shared powers among separate and quasi-autonomous yet interdependent institutions, we have divided the cases and materials in this chapter into four sections. The first is general in nature and consists of Madison's effort in *Federalist* No. 51 to sketch an overall scheme. The second section takes up one of the most troublesome of shared powers, that to wage war. The third addresses problems of preserving institutional integrity in a system of shared powers. The final section returns to problems of institutional interaction and confronts the nature of the powers to appoint, to remove, to claim executive privilege, and to exercise the veto, legislative as well as executive.

SELECTED BIBLIOGRAPHY

Abraham, Henry J. *Justices and Presidents* (3d ed.; New York: Oxford University Press, 1991).

Arnold, R. Douglas. *Congress and the Bureaucracy* (New Haven, Conn.: Yale University Press, 1979).

Ball, Howard. *"We Have a Duty": The Supreme Court and the Watergate Tapes Litigation* (New York: Greenwood Press, 1991).

Berger, Raoul. *Impeachment: The Constitutional Problems* (Cambridge: Harvard University Press, 1973).

Bessette, Joseph M., and Jeffrey Tulis, eds. *The Presidency in the Constitutional Order* (Baton Rouge: Louisiana State University Press, 1981).

Corwin, Edward S. *The President: Office and Powers* 4th rev. ed. (New York: New York University Press, 1957).

Choper, Jesse H. *Judicial Review and the National Political Process* (Chicago: University of Chicago Press, 1980).

Ely, John Hart. *War and Responsibility* (Princeton: Princeton University Press, 1993).

Fisher, Louis. *Presidential Spending Power* (Princeton: Princeton University Press, 1975).

————. *The Politics of Shared Power: Congress and the Executive* (3rd ed.; Washington, DC: Congressional Quarterly Press, 1992).

_____. *Constitutional Conflicts Between Congress and the President* (3rd ed.; Lawrence: University of Kansas Press, 1991).

_____. *Presidential War Power* (Lawrence: University of Kansas Press, 1995).

Franck, Thomas M. *Political Questions, Judicial Answers: Does the Rule of Law Apply to Foreign Affairs?* (Princeton: Princeton University Press, 1992).

Glennon, Michael J. *Constitutional Diplomacy* (Princeton: Princeton University Press, 1990).

Harris, Joseph P. *Congressional Control of Administration* (Washington, DC: The Brookings Institution, 1964).

Henkin, Louis, Michael Glennon, and William Rogers, eds. "The United States Constitution in its Third Century: Foreign Affairs," 83 *Am. J. of Intern'l L.* (1989).

Henkin, Louis. *Constitutionalism, Democracy, and Foreign Affairs* (New York: Columbia University Press, 1992).

Koh, Harold Hongju. *The National Security Constitution: Sharing Power After the Iran–Contra Affair* (New Haven: Yale University Press, 1990).

Maas, Arthur. *Muddy Waters: The Army Engineers and the Nation's Rivers* (Cambridge: Harvard University Press, 1951).

Mann, Thomas E., ed. *A Question of Balance: The President, the Congress, and Foreign Policy* (Washington, DC: The Brookings Institution, 1990).

Mansfield, Harvey C., Jr. *Taming the Prince: The Ambivalence of Modern Executive Power* (New York: The Free Press, 1989).

May, Christopher N. *In the Name of War: Judicial Review and the War Powers Since 1918* (Cambridge: Harvard University Press, 1989).

Murphy, Walter F. *Congress and the Court* (Chicago: University of Chicago Press, 1962).

Neudstadt, Richard E. *Presidential Power: The Politics of Leadership* (rev. ed.; New York: John Wiley, 1976).

Pritchett, C. Herman. *Congress versus the Supreme Court, 1957–1960* (Minneapolis: University of Minnesota Press, 1961).

Public Broadcasting System. "The War Powers: The President and Congress" (Videotape of seminar available from Media and Society Seminars, 204 Journalism, Columbia University, New York, NY 10027).

Pyle, Christopher H., and Richard M. Pious, eds. *The President, Congress, and the Constitution* (New York: The Free Press, 1984).

Schlesinger, Arthur M., Jr. *The Imperial Presidency* (New York: Popular Library, 1973).

Sofaer, Abraham D. *War, Foreign Affairs and Constitutional Power: The Origins* (Cambridge, MA; Ballinger, 1976).

Vile, M.J.C. *Constitutionalism and the Separation of Powers* (London: Oxford University Press, 1967).

I. A SYSTEM OF SHARED POWERS

"Ambition must be made to counteract ambition."

FEDERALIST NO. 51
James Madison (1788).

To what expedient, then, shall we finally resort, for maintaining in practice the necessary partition of power among the several departments as laid down in the Constitution? The only answer that can be given is that as all these exterior provisions are found to be inadequate the defect must be supplied, by so contriving the interior structure of the government as that its several constituent parts may, by their mutual relations, be the means of keeping each other in their proper places. ... I will hazard a few general observations which may perhaps place it in a clearer light, and enable us to form a more correct judgment of the principles and structure of the government planned by the convention.

In order to lay a due foundation for that separate and distinct exercise of the different powers of government, which to a certain extent is admitted on all hands to be essential to the preservation of liberty, it is evident that each department should have a will of its own; and consequently should be so constituted that the members of each should have as little agency as possible in the appointment of the members of the others. Were this principle rigorously adhered to, it would require that all the appointments ... should be drawn from the same fountain of authority, the people, through channels having no communication whatever with one another. ... Some difficulties, however, and some additional expense would attend the execution of it. Some deviations, therefore, from the principle must be admitted. In the constitution of the judiciary department in particular, it might be inexpedient to insist rigorously on the principle: first, because peculiar qualifications being essential in the members, the primary consideration ought to be to select that mode of choice which best secures these qualifications; second, because the permanent tenure by which the appointments are held in that department must soon destroy all sense of dependence on the authority conferring them.

It is equally evident that the members of each department should be as little dependent as possible on those of the others for the emoluments annexed to their offices. Were the executive magistrate, or the judges, not independent of the legislature in this particular, their independence in every other would be merely nominal.

But the great security against a gradual concentration of the several powers in the same department consists in giving to those who administer each department the necessary constitutional means and personal motives to resist encroachments of the others. The provision for defense must in this, as in all other cases, be made commensurate to the danger of attack. Ambition must be made to counteract ambition. The interest of the man must be connected with the constitutional rights of the place. It may be a reflection on human nature that such devices should be necessary to control the abuses of government. But what is government itself but the greatest of all reflections on human nature? If men were angels, no government would be necessary. If angels were to govern men, neither external nor internal controls on government would be necessary. In framing a government which is to be administered by men over men, the great difficulty lies in this: you must first enable the government to control the governed; and in the next place oblige it to control itself. A dependence on the people is, no doubt, the primary control on the government; but experience has taught mankind the necessity of auxiliary precautions.

This policy of supplying, by opposite and rival interests, the defect of better motives, might be traced through the whole system of human affairs.   ... We see it particularly displayed in all the subordinate distributions of power, where the constant aim is to divide and arrange the several offices in such a manner as that each may be a check on the other—that the private interest of every individual may be a sentinel over the public rights.   ...

But it is not possible to give to each department an equal power of self-defense. In republican government, the legislative authority necessarily predominates. The remedy for this inconvenience is to divide the legislature into different branches; and to render them, by different modes of election and different principles of action, as little connected with each other as the nature of their common functions and their common dependence on the society will admit. It may even be necessary to guard against dangerous encroachments by still further precautions. As the weight of the legislative authority requires that it should be thus divided, the weakness of the executive may require, on the other hand, that it should be fortified. An absolute negative on the legislature appears, at first view, to be the natural defense with which the executive magistrate should be armed. But perhaps it would be neither altogether safe nor alone sufficient.   ... May not this defect of an absolute negative be supplied by some qualified connection between this weaker department and the weaker branch of the stronger department, by which the latter may be led to support the constitutional rights of the former, without being too much detached from the rights of its own department? . . .

There are, moreover, two considerations particularly applicable to the federal system of America, which place that system in a very interesting point of view.

First. In a single republic, all the power surrendered by the people is submitted to the administration of a single government; and the usurpations are guarded against by a division of the government into distinct and separate departments. In the compound republic of America, the power surrendered by the people is first divided between two distinct governments, and then the portion allotted to each subdivided among distinct and separate departments. Hence a double security arises to the rights of the people. The different governments will control each other, at the same time that each will be controlled by itself.

Second. It is of great importance in a republic not only to guard the society against the oppression of its rulers, but to guard one part of the society against the injustice of the other part. Different interests necessarily exist in different classes of citizens. If a majority be united by a common interest, the rights of the minority will be insecure. There are but two methods of providing against this evil: the one by creating a will in the community independent of the majority—that is, of the society itself; the other, by comprehending in the society so many separate descriptions of citizens as will render an unjust combination of a majority of the whole very improbable, if not impracticable. The first method prevails in all governments possessing an hereditary or self-appointed authority. This, at best, is but a precarious security; because a power independent of the society may as well espouse the unjust views of the major as the rightful interests of the minor party, and may possibly be turned against both parties. The second method will be exemplified in the federal republic of the United States. Whilst all authority in it will be derived from and dependent on the society, the society itself will be broken into so many parts, interests and classes of citizens, that the rights of individuals, or of the minority, will be in little danger from interested combinations of the majority. In a free government the security for civil rights must be the same as that for religious rights. It consists in the one case in the multiplicity of interests, and in the other in the multiplicity of sects. The degree of security in both cases will depend on the number of interests and sects; and this may be presumed to depend on the extent of country and number of people comprehended under the same government. . . . Justice is the end of government. It is the end of civil society. It ever has been and ever will be pursued until it be obtained, or until liberty be lost in the pursuit. In a society under the forms of which the stronger faction can readily unite and oppress the weaker, anarchy may as truly be said to reign as in a state of nature. . . . In the extended republic of the United States, and among the great variety of interests, parties, and sects which it embraces, a coalition of a majority of the whole society could seldom take place on any other principles than those of justice and the general good; whilst there being thus less danger to a minor from the will of a major party, there must be less pretext, also, to provide for the security of the former, by introducing into the government a will not dependent on the latter, or, in other words, a will independent of the society itself. It is no less certain than it is important ... that the larger the society, provided it lie within a practicable sphere, the more duly capable it will be of self-government. And happily for the *republican cause*, the practicable sphere may be carried to a very great extent by a judicious modification and mixture of the *federal principle*.

Publius

Editors' Notes

(1) Madison's argument here parallels his more general theme in *Federalist* No. 10, reprinted below, p. 1087.

(2) For an analysis of the development of the general notion of playing off human frailties against each other as a principle of political and economic statesmanship, a notion connected to the case for capitalism, see Albert O. Hirschman, *The Passions and the Interests* (Princeton: Princeton University Press, 1977).

II. SHARING POWERS: THE POWER TO WAGE WAR

"[T]he legislature seem to have prescribed ... the manner in which this law shall be carried into execution. ..."

LITTLE v. BARREME (THE FLYING FISH)
6 U.S. (2 Cranch) 170, 2 L.Ed. 243 (1804).

During the Quasi–Naval War with France (1797–1800), Congress authorized the President to instruct U.S. naval vessels to seize any American ship bound *to* a French port. The Secretary of the Navy ordered the seizure of American ships bound *to* or *from* a French port. In pursuance of that order, the frigate *Boston,* commanded by Captain Little, captured *The Flying Fish,* bound *from* the French West Indies, took her to an American port, and filed a libel (an action in maritime law to seize a ship) against her, alleging she was an American vessel. The trial judge held that the ship was actually Danish and disallowed the seizure but refused to award damages against Little because there had been probable cause to think *The Flying Fish* was American. The circuit court reversed, ruling that, because the ship was coming *from* not *to* a French port, she would not have been liable to seizure even if American. Little appealed to the U.S. Supreme Court.

MARSHALL, Chief Justice, now delivered the opinion of the Court.
    ...

It is by no means clear that the president of the United States, whose high duty it is to "take care that the laws be faithfully executed," and who is commander in chief of the armies and navies of the United States, might not, without any special authority for that purpose, in the then existing state of things, have empowered the officers commanding armed vessels of the United States, to seize and send into port for adjudication, American vessels which were forfeited by being engaged in this illicit commerce. But when it is observed ... that the 5th section [of the statute] gives a special authority to seize on the high seas, and limits that authority to the seizure of vessels bound or sailing *to* a French port, the legislature seem to have prescribed that the manner in which this law shall be carried into execution, was to exclude a seizure of any vessel not bound *to* a French port. Of consequence, however strong the circumstances might be, which induced Captain Little to suspect *The Flying Fish* to be an American vessel, they could not excuse the detention of her, since he would not have been authorized to detain her had she been really American.

It was so obvious, that if only vessels sailing to a French port could be seized on the high seas, that the law would be very often evaded, that this act of congress appears to have received a different construction from the executive of the United States; a construction much better calculated to give it effect. ...

I confess, the first bias of my mind was very strong in favor of the opinion, that though the instructions of the executive could not give a right, they might yet excuse [Captain Little] from damages. I was much inclined to think, that a distinction ought to be taken between acts of civil and those of military officers; and between proceedings within the body of the country and those on the high seas. That implicit obedience which military men usually pay to the orders of their superiors, which indeed is indispensably necessary to every military system, appeared to me strongly to imply the principle that those orders, if not to perform a prohibited act, ought to justify the person whose general duty it is to obey them, and who is placed by the laws of his country in a situation which in general requires that he should obey them. I was strongly inclined to think that, where, in consequence of orders from the legitimate authority, a vessel is seized, with pure intention, the claim of the injured party for damages would be against that government from which the orders proceeded, and would be a proper subject for negotiation. But I have been convinced that I was mistaken, and I have receded from this first opinion. I acquiesce in that of my brethren, which is, that the instructions cannot change the nature of the transaction, or legalize an act which, without those instructions, would have been a plain trespass.

It becomes, therefore, unnecessary to inquire whether the probable cause afforded by the conduct of *The Flying Fish* to suspect her of being an American, would excuse Captain Little from damages for having seized and sent her into port, since, had she been an American, the seizure would have been unlawful?

Captain Little, then, must be answerable in damages to the owner of this neutral vessel, and as the account taken by order of the circuit court is not objectionable on its face, and has not been excepted to by counsel before the proper tribunal, this court can receive no objection to it.

There appears, then, to be no error in the judgment of the circuit court, and it must be affirmed with costs.

Editors' Notes

(1) On first reading, *The Flying Fish* seems perhaps important for international law in its holding that military and naval officers are liable for acting illegally, even when obeying direct orders of superiors. Otherwise, however, the case appears of little interest. But is there more here? What did this apparently trivial opinion of Marshall imply about the relations among Congress, the President, and the courts? Whose interpretation of a statute and more importantly of the constitutional document's (or even the broader constitution's) allocations of authority is to prevail? For a different attitude toward the weight to be accorded the President's interpretation of statutes, see Rust v. Sullivan (1991; reprinted below, p. 749) and Justice Scalia's opinion for the Court in Lujan v. Defenders of Wildlife (1992).

(2) **Query:** What did Marshall imply about the President's power to wage war, even limited war, when Congress has laid down explicit terms? In the absence of any congressional directive? See Justice Clark's use of this ruling in his concur. op. in the Steel Seizure Case (1952; reprinted below, p. 443).

(3) In Little v. Barreme, Marshall skewered Jefferson almost as neatly as he had in *Marbury*. Not only did the Chief Justice claim judicial authority to determine the constitutional boundaries between congressional and presidential power, but he had done so on a substantive issue on which Jefferson would have found it embarrassing to disagree publicly and assert a departmental theory of constitutional interpretation, for he was on record as opposing the quasi–war with France that John Adams and his Federalists had waged.

————

"**Whether the President ... has met with such armed hostile resistance, and a civil war of such alarming proportions as will compel him to accord to them the character of belligerents, is a question to be decided** *by him,* **and this Court must be governed by the decisions and** acts of the political department of the Government to which this power was entrusted."—Justice GRIER

[B]efore this insurrection against the established Government can be dealt with on the footing of a civil war, ... it must be recognized or declared by the war-making power of the Government.—Justice NELSON

THE PRIZE CASES
67 U.S. (2 Black) 635, 17 L.Ed. 459 (1863).

In 1861, after the attack on Fort Sumter, President Lincoln proclaimed a blockade of Southern ports, even though Congress had not declared war. The Union navy seized and brought to port as prizes several ships carrying goods to the Confederacy. The U.S. district court condemned the vessels, and the owners appealed.

Mr. Justice **GRIER** delivered the opinion of the court. ...

Let us enquire whether, at the time this blockade was instituted, a state of war existed which would justify a resort to these means of subduing the hostile force. ...

By the Constitution, Congress alone has the power to declare a national or foreign war. It cannot declare war against a State, or any number of States, by virtue of any clause in the Constitution. The Constitution confers on the President the whole Executive power. He is bound to take care that the laws be faithfully executed. He is Commander-in-chief of the Army and Navy of the United States, and of the militia of the several States when called into the actual service of the United States. He has no power to initiate or declare a war either against a foreign nation or a domestic State. But by the Acts of Congress of February 28th, 1795, and 3d of March, 1807, he is authorized to called out the militia and use the military and naval forces of the United States in case of invasion by foreign nations, and to suppress insurrection against the government of a State or of the United States.

If a war be made by invasion of a foreign nation, the President is not only authorized but bound to resist force by force. He does not initiate the war, but is bound to accept the challenge without waiting for any special legislative authority. And whether the hostile party be a foreign invader, or States organized in rebellion, it is none the less a war, although the declaration of it be "*unilateral*." ...

This greatest of civil wars ... sprung forth suddenly from the parent brain, a Minerva in the full panoply of *war*. The President was bound to meet it in the shape it presented itself, without waiting for Congress to baptize it with a name; and no name given to it by him or them could change the fact.

It is not the less a civil war, ... because it may be called an "insurrection" by one side, and the insurgents be considered as rebels or traitors. It is not necessary that the independence of the revolted province or State be acknowledged in order to constitute it a party belligerent in a war according to the law of nations. Foreign nations acknowledge it as war by a declaration of neutrality. The condition of neutrality cannot exist unless there be two belligerent parties. ...

As soon as the news of the attack on Fort Sumter, and the organization of a government by the seceding States, assuming to act as belligerents, could become known in Europe, ... the Queen of England issued her proclamation of neutrality. ... This was immediately followed by similar declarations or silent acquiescence by other nations. ...

Whether the President in fulfilling his duties, as Commander-in-chief, in suppressing an insurrection, has met with such armed hostile resistance, and a civil war of such alarming proportions as will compel him to accord to them the character of belligerents, is a question to be decided *by him,* and this Court must be governed by the decisions and acts of the political department of the Government to which this power was entrusted. ... The proclamation of blockade is itself official and conclusive evidence to the Court that a state of war existed which demanded and authorized a recourse to such a measure, under the circumstances peculiar to the case. ...

If it were necessary to the technical existence of a war, that it should have a legislative sanction, we find it in almost every act passed at the extraordinary session of the Legislature of 1861, which was wholly employed in enacting laws to enable the Government to prosecute the war with vigor and efficiency. And finally, in 1861, we find Congress ... in anticipation of such astute objections, passing an act "approving, legalizing, and making valid all the acts, proclamations, and orders of the President, & c., as if they had been *issued and done under the previous express authority* and direction of the Congress of the United States."

Without admitting that such an act was necessary under the circumstances, it is plain that if the President had in any manner assumed powers which it was necessary should have the authority or sanction of Congress, ... this ratification has operated to perfectly cure the defect. ...

The objection made to this act of ratification, that it is *ex post facto,* and therefore unconstitutional and void, might possibly have some weight on the trial of an indictment in a criminal Court. But precedents from that source cannot be received as authoritative in a tribunal administering public and international law.

... [T]herefore we are of the opinion that the President had a right, *jure belli,* to institute a blockade of ports in possession of the States in rebellion, which neutrals are bound to regard. ...

Mr. Justice **NELSON,** dissenting. ...

... [B]efore this insurrection against the established Government can be dealt with on the footing of a civil war, ... it must be recognized or declared by the war-making power of the Government. ... There is no difference in this respect between a civil or a public war. ...

An idea seemed to be entertained that all that was necessary to constitute a war was organized hostility in the district of country in a state of rebellion. ...

Now, in one sense, no doubt this is war, ... but it is a statement simply of its existence in a material sense, and has no relevancy or weight when the question is what constitutes war in a legal sense, in the sense of the law of nations, and of the Constitution of the United States? For it must be a war in this sense to attach to it all the consequences that belong to belligerent rights. ... [T]o constitute a civil war in the [legal] sense ... it must be recognized or declared by the sovereign power of the State, and which sovereign power by our Constitution is lodged in the Congress of the United States—civil war, therefore, under our system of government, can exist only by an act of Congress, which requires the assent of two of the great departments of the Government, the Executive and Legislative. ...

The Acts of 1795 and 1807 did not, and could not under the Constitution, confer on the President the power of declaring war against a State of this Union, or of deciding that war existed, and upon that ground authorize the capture and confiscation of the property of every citizen of the State whenever it was found on the waters. The laws of war, whether the war be civil or *inter gentes*, ... convert every citizen of the hostile State into a public enemy, and treat him accordingly, whatever may have been his previous conduct. This great power over the business and property of the citizen is reserved to the legislative department by the express words of the Constitution. It cannot be delegated or surrendered to the Executive. Congress alone can determine whether war exists or should be declared; and until they have acted, no citizen of the State can be punished in his person or property, unless he has committed some offence against a law of Congress passed before the act was committed, which made it a crime, and defined the punishment. ...

... I am compelled to the conclusion that no civil war existed between this Government and the States in insurrection till recognized by the Act of Congress 13th of July, 1861; ... and, consequently, that the President had no power to set on foot a blockade under the law of nations, and that the capture of the vessel and cargo in this case, and in all cases before us in which the capture occurred before the 18th of July, 1861, for breach of blockade, or as enemies' property, are illegal and void, and that the decrees of condemnation should be reversed and the vessel and cargo restored.

Mr. Chief Justice **TANEY,** Mr. Justice **CATRON** and Mr. Justice **CLIFFORD,** concurred in the dissenting opinion of Mr. Justice **NELSON.**

Editors' Note

The Dred Scott Case (1857; reprinted above, p. 195) ruled that a black person could not be a citizen of the United States, slaves were mere property, and therefore the Missouri Compromise of 1820, which had forbidden slavery in the territories north of latitude 36° 30′, deprived slaveowners of their property without due process of law. Because of this decision, many Republican politicians looked on the Supreme Court as pro-Southern. Two deaths and a resignation among the justices allowed Lincoln to change the orientation of the Court; but the closeness of the vote in the Prize Cases (5–4) helped persuade Congress to adopt a bill, already under consideration, to increase the number of the justices to ten and so allow Lincoln to increase what was perceived as a narrow Unionist majority.

"[T]he President alone has the power to speak or listen as a representative of the nation."

UNITED STATES v. CURTISS–WRIGHT EXPORT CORP.

299 U.S. 304, 57 S.Ct. 216, 81 L.Ed. 255 (1936).

In 1934 Congress adopted a Joint Resolution authorizing the President to prohibit the sale of arms and munitions to Bolivia and Paraguay, who were fighting over the Chaco, if he believed that such an embargo would contribute to peace. President Roosevelt immediately issued a proclamation forbidding arms shipments to either country. Shortly thereafter, the Department of Justice secured an indictment against Curtiss–Wright for selling machine guns to Bolivia. In the trial court, the corporation claimed that the President's proclamation had no legal force because Congress had unconstitutionally delegated legislative power to the executive. The district judge agreed and the government appealed directly to the Supreme Court.

Mr. Justice **SUTHERLAND** delivered the opinion of the Court. ...

Whether, if the Joint Resolution had related solely to internal affairs it would be open to the challenge that it constituted an unlawful delegation of legislative power to the Executive, we find it unnecessary to determine. The whole aim of the resolution is to affect a situation entirely external to the United States, and falling within the category of foreign affairs. ... [A]ssuming (but not deciding) that the challenged delegation, if it were confined to internal affairs, would be invalid, may it nevertheless be sustained on the ground that its exclusive aim is to afford a remedy for a hurtful condition within a foreign territory?

It will contribute to the elucidation of the question if we first consider the differences between the powers of the Federal government in respect of foreign or external affairs and those in respect of domestic or internal affairs. ...

The two classes of powers are different, both in respect of their origin and their nature. The broad statement that the Federal government can exercise no powers except those specifically enumerated in the Constitution, and such implied powers as are necessary and proper to carry into effect the enumerated powers, is categorically true only in respect of our internal affairs. In that field, the primary purpose of the Constitution was to carve from the general mass of legislative powers *then possessed by the states* such portions as it was thought desirable to vest in the Federal government, leaving those not included in the enumeration still in the states. That this doctrine applies only to powers which the states had, is self-evident. And since the states severally never possessed international powers, such powers could not have been carved from the mass of state powers but obviously were transmitted to the United States from some other source. ...

The Union existed before the Constitution, which was ordained and established among other things to form "a more perfect Union." Prior to that event, it is clear that the Union, declared by the Articles of Confederation to be "perpetual," was the sole possessor of external sovereignty, and in the Union it remained without change save in so far as the Constitution in express terms qualified its exercise. ...

It results that the investment of the Federal government with the powers of external sovereignty did not depend upon the affirmative grants of the Constitution. The powers to declare and wage war, to conclude peace, to make treaties, to maintain diplomatic relations with other sovereignties, if they had never been mentioned in the Constitution, would have vested in the Federal government as necessary concomitants of nationality. ... As a member of the family of nations, the right and power of the United States in that field are equal to the right and power of the other members of the international family. Otherwise, the United States is not completely sovereign. ... Thus the court [has] recognized, and [has] found the warrant for its conclusions not in the provisions of the Constitution, but in the law of nations. ...

Not only is the Federal power over external affairs in origin and essential character different from that over internal affairs, but participation in the exercise of the power is significantly limited. In this vast external realm, with its important, complicated, delicate and manifold problems, the President alone has the power to speak or listen as a representative of the nation. He *makes* treaties with the advice and consent of the Senate: but he alone negotiates. ...

It is important to bear in mind that we are here dealing not alone with an authority vested in the President by an exertion of legislative power, but with such an authority plus the very delicate, plenary and exclusive power of the President as the sole organ of the Federal government in the field of international relations—a power which does not require as a basis for its exercise an act of Congress, but which, of course, like every other governmental power, must be exercised in subordination to the applicable provisions of the Constitution. It is quite apparent that if, in the maintenance of our international relations, embarrassment—perhaps serious embarrassment—is to be avoided and success for our aims achieved, congressional legislation which is to be made effective through negotiation and inquiry within the international field must often accord to the President a degree of discretion and freedom from statutory restriction which would not be admissible were domestic affairs alone involved.   Moreover, he, not Congress, has the better opportunity of knowing the conditions which prevail in foreign countries, and especially is this true in time of war.   He has his confidential sources of information.   He has his agents in the form of diplomatic, consular and other officials.   Secrecy in respect of information gathered by them may be highly necessary, and the premature disclosure of it productive of harmful results.   ...

This consideration, in connection with what we have already said on the subject, discloses the unwisdom of requiring Congress in this field of governmental power to lay down narrowly definite standards by which the President is to be governed.   ...

Reversed.

Mr. Justice **McREYNOLDS** [dissented].

Mr. Justice **STONE** took no part in the consideration or decision of this case.

"The Constitution is neither silent nor equivocal about who shall make the laws which the President is to execute"—Justice BLACK

"The actual art of governing under our Constitution does not and cannot conform to judicial definitions of the power of any of its branches based on isolated clauses or even single Articles torn from context."—Justice JACKSON

"[The President] is left powerless because a power not expressly given to Congress is nevertheless found to rest exclusively with Congress."—Chief Justice VINSON

YOUNGSTOWN SHEET & TUBE CO. v. SAWYER

343 U.S. 579, 72 S.Ct. 863, 96 L.Ed. 1153 (1952).

In April, 1952, during the Korean War, after months of bargaining among the United Steel Workers, the steel industry, and the government, the union called a strike that would have shut down most of the country's steel production.   Just a few hours before the strike was to begin, President Harry S Truman issued Executive Order 10340, directing Secretary of Commerce Charles Sawyer to seize the mills and operate them.   "Seizure" consisted of sending telegrams to all the companies affected, telling them of the action taken and appointing the president of each firm as manager for the government.   All assets and liabilities were to remain with the owners, although

Sawyer's announced intention of reopening negotiations with the union might well have cost the companies future profits.

The day after the seizure, the President notified Congress of his action and said he would follow whatever course Congress prescribed. Congress took no action, but the steel companies, claiming they would suffer irreparable injury from the government's negotiating with the union, obtained an injunction against the seizure. The government won a stay of this order from the court of appeals and petitioned the Supreme Court for certiorari. The Court granted the writ, heard lengthy argument within several days, and handed down its decision a month later.

Mr. Justice **BLACK** delivered the opinion of the Court. ...

The President's power, if any, to issue the order must stem either from an act of Congress or from the Constitution itself. There is no statute that expressly authorizes the President to take possession of property as he did here. Nor is there any act of Congress to which our attention has been directed from which such a power can fairly be implied. Indeed, we do not understand the Government to rely on statutory authorization for this seizure. There are two statutes which do authorize the President to take both personal and real property under certain conditions. However, the Government admits that ... the President's order was not rooted in either. ...

Moreover, the use of the seizure technique to solve labor disputes ... was not only unauthorized by any congressional enactment; prior to this controversy, Congress had refused to adopt that method of settling labor disputes. When the Taft–Hartley Act was under consideration in 1947, Congress rejected an amendment which would have authorized such governmental seizures in cases of emergency. ...

... [T]he plan Congress adopted in that Act did not provide for seizure under any circumstances. Instead, the plan sought to bring about settlements by use of the customary devices of mediation, concilia-tion, investigation by boards of inquiry, and public reports. In some instances temporary injunctions were authorized to provide cooling-off periods. All this failing, the unions were left free to strike if the majority of the employees, by secret ballot, expressed a desire to do so.

It is clear [then] that if the President had authority to issue the order he did, it must be found in some provisions of the Constitution. And it is not claimed that express constitutional language grants this power to the President. The contention is that presidential power should be implied from the aggregate of his powers under the Constitu-tion. Particular reliance is placed on provisions in Art. II which say that "the executive Power shall be vested in a President ...."; that "he shall take Care that the Laws be faithfully executed"; and that he "shall be Commander in Chief of the Army and Navy of the United States."

The order cannot properly be sustained as an exercise of the President's military power as Commander in Chief of the Armed Forces. The Government attempts to do so by citing a number of cases upholding broad powers in military commanders engaged in day-to-day fighting in a theater of war. Such cases need not concern us here. Even though "theater of war" be an expanding concept, we cannot with faithfulness to our constitutional system hold that the Commander in Chief of the Armed Forces has the ultimate power as such to take possession of private property in order to keep labor disputes from stopping production. This is a job for the Nation's lawmakers, not for its military authorities.

Nor can the seizure order be sustained because of the several constitutional provisions that grant executive power to the President. In the framework of our Constitution, the President's power to see that the laws are faithfully executed refutes the idea that he is to be a lawmaker. The Constitution limits his functions in the law-making process to the recommending of laws he thinks wise and the vetoing of laws he thinks bad. And the Constitution is neither silent nor equivocal about who shall make laws which the President is to execute. The first section of the first article says that "All legislative Powers herein granted shall be vested in a Congress of the United States. ..."

The President's order does not direct that a congressional policy be executed in a manner prescribed by Congress—it directs that a presidential policy be executed in a manner prescribed by the President. The preamble of the order itself, like that of many statutes, sets out reasons why the President believes certain policies should be adopted, proclaims these policies as rules of conduct to be followed, and again, like a statute, authorizes a government official to promulgate additional rules and regulations consistent with the policy proclaimed and needed to carry that policy into execution. The power of Congress to adopt such public policies as those proclaimed by the order is beyond question. It can authorize the taking of private property for public use. It can make laws regulating the relationships between employers and employees, prescribing rules designed to settle labor disputes, and fixing wages and working conditions in certain fields of our economy. The Constitution did not subject this law-making power of Congress to presidential or military supervision or control.

It is said that other Presidents without congressional authority have taken possession of private business enterprises in order to settle labor disputes. But even if this be true, Congress has not thereby lost its exclusive constitutional authority to make laws necessary and proper to carry out the powers vested by the Constitution "in the Government of the United States, or any Department or Officer thereof."

The Founders of this Nation entrusted the lawmaking power to the Congress alone in both good and bad times. It would do no good to recall the historical events, the fears of power and the hopes for freedom that lay behind their choice. Such a review would but confirm our holding that this seizure order cannot stand.

The judgment of the District Court is

Affirmed.

Mr. Justice **FRANKFURTER** [concurring].

Although the considerations relevant to the legal enforcement of the principle of separation of powers seem to me more complicated and flexible than may appear from what Mr. Justice BLACK has written, I join his opinion because I thoroughly agree with the application of the principle to the circumstances of this case. ...

... The Founders of this Nation were not imbued with the modern cynicism that the only thing that history teaches is that it teaches nothing. They acted on the conviction that the experience of man sheds a good deal of light on his nature. ...

... For them the doctrine of separation of powers was not mere theory; it was a felt necessity. ... These long-headed statesmen had no illusion that our people enjoyed biological or psychological immunities from the hazards of concentrated power. It is absurd to see a dictator in a representative product of the sturdy democratic traditions of the Mississippi Valley. The accretion of dangerous power does not come in a day. It does come, however slowly, from the generative force of un-checked disregard of the restrictions that fence in even the most disin-terested assertion of authority.

The Framers, however, did not make the judiciary the overseer of our government. ... Rigorous adherence to the narrow scope of the judicial function is especially demanded in controversies that arouse appeals to the Constitution. The attitude with which this Court must approach its duty when confronted with such issues is precisely the opposite of that normally manifested by the general public. So-called constitutional questions seem to exercise a mesmeric influence over the popular mind. This eagerness to settle—preferably forever—a specific problem on the basis of the broadest possible constitutional pronounce-ments may not unfairly be called one of our minor national traits. ...

The path of duty for this Court, it bears repetition, lies in the opposite direction. ...

So here our first inquiry must be not into the powers of the President, but into the powers of a District Judge to issue a temporary injunction in the circumstances of this case. Familiar as that remedy is, it remains an extraordinary remedy. To start with a consideration of the relation between the President's powers and those of Congress ... is to start at the wrong end. A plaintiff is not entitled to an injunction if money damages would fairly compensate him for any wrong he may have suffered. ... Again, a court of equity ought not to issue an injunction, even though a plaintiff otherwise makes out a case for it, if the plaintiff's right to an injunction is overborne by a commanding public interest against it. ... To deny inquiry into the President's power in a case like this, because of the damage to the public interest to be feared from upsetting its exercise by him, would in effect always preclude inquiry into challenged power, which presumably only avowed great public interest brings into action. And so, with the utmost unwillingness, with every desire to avoid judicial inquiry into the powers and duties of the other two branches of the government, I cannot escape consideration of the legality of Executive Order No. 10340.

The pole-star for constitutional adjudications is John Marshall's greatest judicial utterance that "it is a *constitution* we are expounding." McCulloch v. Maryland [1819] That requires both a spacious view in applying an instrument of government "made for an undefined and expanding future," Hurtado v. California [1884], and as narrow a delimitation of the constitutional issues as the circumstances permit. Not the least characteristic of great statesmanship which the Framers manifested was the extent to which they did not attempt to bind the future. It is no less incumbent upon this Court to avoid putting fetters upon the future by needless pronouncements today. ...

The issue before us can be met, and therefore should be, without attempting to define the President's powers comprehensively. ... The judiciary may ... have to intervene in determining where authority lies as between the democratic forces in our scheme of government. But in doing so we should be wary and humble. Such is the teaching of this Court's role in the history of the country. ...

The question before the Court comes in this setting. Congress has frequently—at least 16 times since 1916—specifically provided for executive seizure of production, transportation, communications, or storage facilities. In every case it has qualified this grant of power with limitations and safeguards. ... The power to seize has uniformly been given only for a limited period or for a defined emergency, or has been repealed after a short period. Its exercise has been restricted to particular circumstances such as "time of war or when war is imminent," the needs of "public safety" or of "national security or defense," or "urgent and impending need."

Congress in 1947 was again called upon to consider whether governmental seizure should be used to avoid serious industrial shutdowns. Congress decided against conferring such power. ...

It cannot be contended that the President would have had power to issue this order had Congress explicitly negated such authority in formal legislation. Congress has expressed its will to withhold this power from the President as though it had said so in so many words. ...

By the Labor Management Relations Act of 1947, Congress said to the President, "You may not seize. Please report to us and ask for seizure power if you think it is needed in a specific situation." ...

No authority that has since been given to the President can by any fair process of statutory construction be deemed to withdraw the restriction or change the will of Congress as expressed by a body of enactments, culminating in the Labor Management Relations Act of 1947. ...

A scheme of government like ours no doubt at times feels the lack of power to act with complete, all-embracing, swiftly moving authority. No doubt a government with distributed authority, subject to be challenged in the courts of law, at least long enough to consider and adjudicate the challenge, labors under restrictions from which other governments are free. It has not been our tradition to envy such governments. In any event our government was designed to have such restrictions. The price was deemed not too high in view of the safeguards which these restrictions afford. . . .

Mr. Justice **DOUGLAS,** concurring. . . .

Mr. Justice **JACKSON,** concurring in the judgment and opinion of the Court. . . .

A judge, like an executive adviser, may be surprised at the poverty of really useful and unambiguous authority applicable to concrete problems of executive power as they actually present themselves. Just what our forefathers did envision, or would have envisioned had they foreseen modern conditions, must be divined from materials almost as enigmatic as the dreams Joseph was called upon to interpret for Pharaoh. A century and a half of partisan debate and scholarly speculation yields no net result but only supplies more or less apt quotations from respected sources on each side of any question. They largely cancel each other. And court decisions are indecisive because of the judicial practice of dealing with the largest questions in the most narrow way.

The actual art of governing under our Constitution does not and cannot conform to judicial definitions of the power of any of its branches based on isolated clauses or even single Articles torn from context. While the Constitution diffuses power the better to secure liberty, it also contemplates that practice will integrate the dispersed powers into a workable government. It enjoins upon its branches separateness but interdependence, autonomy but reciprocity. Presidential powers are not fixed but fluctuate, depending upon their disjunction or conjunction with those of Congress. We may well begin by a somewhat oversimplified grouping of practical situations in which a President may doubt, or others may challenge, his powers, and by distinguishing roughly the legal consequences of this factor of relativity.

1. When the President acts pursuant to an express or implied authorization of Congress, his authority is at its maximum, for it includes all that he possesses in his own right plus all that Congress can delegate. . . . A seizure executed by the President pursuant to an Act of Congress would be supported by the strongest of presumptions. . . .

2. When the President acts in absence of either a congressional grant or denial of authority, he can only rely upon his own independent powers, but there is a zone of twilight in which he and Congress may have concurrent authority, or in which its distribution is uncertain. . . . In this area, any actual test of power is likely to depend on the imperatives of events and contemporary imponderables rather than on abstract theories of law.

3. When the President takes measures incompatible with the expressed or implied will of Congress, his power is at its lowest ebb, for then he can rely only upon his own constitutional powers minus any constitutional powers of Congress over the matter. Courts can sustain exclusive Presidential control in such a case only by disabling the Congress from acting upon the subject. Presidential claim to a power at once so conclusive and preclusive must be scrutinized with caution, for what is at stake is the equilibrium established by our constitutional system.

Into which of these classifications does this executive seizure of the steel industry fit? It is eliminated from the first by admission, for it is conceded that no congressional authorization exists for this seizure. ...

Can it then be defended under flexible texts available to the second category? It seems clearly eliminated from that class because Congress has not left seizure of private property an open field but has covered it by three statutory policies inconsistent with this seizure. ...

This leaves the current seizure to be justified only by the severe tests under the third grouping, where it can be supported only by any remainder of executive power after subtraction of such powers as Congress may have over the subject. In short, we can sustain the President only by holding that seizure of such strike-bound industries is within his domain and beyond control by Congress. ...

The Solicitor General seeks the power of seizure in three clauses of the Executive Article, the first reading, "The executive Power shall be vested in a President of the United States of America." Lest I be thought to exaggerate, I quote the interpretation which his brief puts upon it: "In our view, this clause constitutes a grant of all the executive powers of which the Government is capable." If that be true, it is difficult to see why the forefathers bothered to add several specific items, including some trifling ones.

 ... I cannot accept the view that this clause is a grant in bulk of all conceivable executive power but regard it as an allocation to the presidential office of the generic powers thereafter stated.

The clause on which the Government next relies is that "The President shall be Commander in Chief of the Army and Navy of the United States. ..." ... [T]his loose appellation is sometimes advanced as support for any presidential action, internal or external, involving use of force, the idea being that it vests power to do anything, anywhere, that can be done with an army or navy.

That seems to be the logic of an argument tendered at our bar—that the President having, on his own responsibility, sent American troops abroad derives from that act "affirmative power" to seize the means of producing a supply of steel for them. ... [I]t is said he has invested himself with "war powers."

I cannot foresee all that it might entail if the Court should indorse this argument. Nothing in our Constitution is plainer than that declaration of a war is entrusted only to Congress. Of course, a state of war may in fact exist without a formal declaration. But no doctrine that the Court could promulgate would seem to me more sinister and alarming than that a President whose conduct of foreign affairs is so largely uncontrolled, and often even is unknown, can vastly enlarge his mastery over the internal affairs of the country by his own commitment of the Nation's armed forces to some foreign venture. ...

There are indications that the Constitution did not contemplate that the title Commander-in-Chief *of the Army and Navy* will constitute him also Commander-in-Chief of the country, its industries and its inhabitants. He has no monopoly of "war powers," whatever they are. While Congress cannot deprive the President of the command of the army and navy, only Congress can provide him an army or navy to command. ...

That military powers of the Commander-in-Chief were not to supersede representative government of internal affairs seems obvious from the Constitution and from elementary American history. ...

We should not use this occasion to circumscribe, much less to contract, the lawful role of the President as Commander-in-Chief. I should indulge the widest latitude of interpretation to sustain his exclusive function to command the instruments of national force, at least when turned against the outside world for the security of our society. But, when it is turned inward, not because of rebellion but because of a lawful economic struggle between industry and labor, it should have no such indulgence. His command power is not such an absolute as might be implied from that office in a militaristic system but is subject to limitations consistent with a constitutional Republic whose law and policy-making branch is a representative Congress. The purpose of lodging dual titles in one man was to insure that the civilian would control the military, not to enable the military to subordinate the presidential office. No penance would ever expiate the sin against free government of holding that a President can escape control of executive powers by law through assuming his military role. ...

The third clause in which the Solicitor General finds seizure powers is that "he shall take Care that the Laws be faithfully executed. ..." That authority must be matched against words of the Fifth Amendment that "No person shall be ... deprived of life, liberty or property, without due process of law. ..." One gives a governmental authority that reaches so far as there is law, the other gives a private right that authority shall go no farther. These signify about all there is of the principle that ours is a government of laws, not of men, and that we submit ourselves to rulers only if under rules.

The Solicitor General lastly grounds support of the seizure upon nebulous, inherent powers never expressly granted but said to have accrued to the office from the customs and claims of preceding administrations. The plea is for a resulting power to deal with a crisis or an emergency according to the necessities of the case, the unarticulated assumption being that necessity knows no law. ...

... [C]ontemporary foreign experience may be inconclusive as to the wisdom of lodging emergency powers somewhere in a modern government. But it suggests that emergency powers are consistent with free government only when their control is lodged elsewhere than in the Executive who exercises them. That is the safeguard that would be nullified by our adoption of the "inherent powers" formula. Nothing in my experience convinces me that such risks are warranted by any real necessity, although such powers would, of course, be an executive convenience.

In the practical working of our Government we already have evolved a technique within the framework of the Constitution by which normal executive powers may be considerably expanded to meet an emergency. Congress may and has granted extraordinary authorities which lie dormant in normal times but may be called into play by the Executive in war or upon proclamation of a national emergency. ...

... I have no illusion that any decision by this Court can keep power in the hands of Congress if it is not wise and timely in meeting its problems. A crisis that challenges the President equally, or perhaps primarily, challenges Congress. If not good law, there was worldly wisdom in the maxim attributed to Napoleon that "The tools belong to the man who can use them." We may say that power to legislate for emergencies belongs in the hands of Congress, but only Congress itself can prevent power from slipping through its fingers.

The essence of our free Government is "leave to live by no man's leave, underneath the law"—to be governed by those impersonal forces which we call law. Our Government is fashioned to fulfill this concept so far as humanly possible. The Executive, except for recommendation and veto, has no legislative power. The executive action we have here originates in the individual will of the President and represents an exercise of authority without law. ... With all its defects, delays and inconveniences, men have discovered no technique for long preserving free government except that the Executive be under the law, and that the law be made by parliamentary deliberations.

Such institutions may be destined to pass away. But it is the duty of the Court to be last, not first, to give them up.

Mr. Justice **BURTON,** concurring in both the opinion and judgment of the Court. ...

Mr. Justice **CLARK,** concurring in the judgment of the Court. ...

One of this Court's first pronouncements upon the powers of the President under the Constitution was made by Chief Justice John Marshall some one hundred and fifty years ago. In Little v. Barreme [1804; reprinted above, p. 435], he used this characteristically clear language in discussing the power of the President to instruct the seizure of the "Flying–Fish," a vessel bound from a French port:

> It is by no means clear that the president of the United States whose high duty it is to "take care that the laws be faithfully executed," and who is commander in chief of the armies and navies of the United States, might not, without any special authority for that purpose, in the then existing state of things, have empowered the officers commanding the armed vessels of the United States, to seize and send into port for adjudication, American vessels which were forfeited by being engaged in this illicit commerce. But when it is observed that [an Act of Congress] gives a special authority to seize on the high seas, and limits that authority to the seizure of vessels bound or sailing *to* a French port, the legislature seem to have prescribed that the manner in which this law shall be carried into execution, was to exclude a seizure of any vessel *not* bound *to* a French port.

Accordingly, a unanimous Court held that the President's instructions had been issued without authority and that they could not "legalize an act which without those instructions would have been a plain trespass." I know of no subsequent holding of this Court to the contrary. ...

I conclude that where Congress has laid down specific procedures to deal with the type of crisis confronting the President, he must follow those procedures in meeting the crisis; but that in the absence of such action by Congress, the President's independent power to act depends upon the gravity of the situation confronting the nation. I cannot sustain the seizure in question because here, as in Little v. Barreme, Congress had prescribed methods to be followed by the President in meeting the emergency at hand. ...

Mr. Chief Justice **VINSON,** with whom Mr. Justice **REED** and Mr. Justice **MINTON** join, dissenting. ...

Those who suggest that this is a case involving extraordinary powers should be mindful that these are extraordinary times. A world not yet recovered from the devastation of World War II has been forced to face the threat of another and more terrifying global conflict. ...

... As an illustration of the magnitude of the over-all program, Congress has appropriated $130 billion for our own defense and for military assistance to our allies since the June, 1950, attack in Korea.

Even before Korea, steel production at levels above theoretical 100 per cent capacity was not capable of supplying civilian needs alone. Since Korea, the tremendous military demand for steel has far exceeded the increases in productive capacity. ...

The President has the duty to execute the foregoing legislative programs. Their successful execution depends upon continued production of steel and stabilized prices for steel. ...

... The Union and the steel companies may well engage in a lengthy struggle. Plaintiff's counsel tells us that "sooner or later" the mills will operate again. That may satisfy the steel companies and, perhaps, the Union. But our soldiers and our allies will hardly be cheered with the assurance that the ammunition upon which their lives depend will be forthcoming—"sooner or later," or, in other words, "too little and too late."

Accordingly, if the President has any power under the Constitution to meet a critical situation in the absence of express statutory authorization, there is no basis whatever for criticizing the exercise of such power in this case.

The steel mills were seized for a public use. ... Plaintiffs cannot complain that any provision in the Constitution prohibits the exercise of the power of eminent domain in this case. The Fifth Amendment provides: "nor shall private property be taken for public use, without just compensation." It is no bar to this seizure for, if the taking is not otherwise unlawful, plaintiffs are assured of receiving the required just compensation. ...

Admitting that the Government could seize the mills, plaintiffs claim that the implied power of eminent domain can be exercised only under an Act of Congress. ...

Under this view, the President is left powerless at the very moment when the need for action may be most pressing and when no one, other than he, is immediately capable of action. ... [H]e is left powerless because a power not expressly given to Congress is nevertheless found to rest exclusively with Congress. ...

... [I]n this case, we need only look to history and time-honored principles of constitutional law—principles that have been applied consistently by all branches of the Government throughout our history. It is those who assert the invalidity of the Executive Order who seek to amend the Constitution in this case.

A review of executive action demonstrates that our Presidents have on many occasions exhibited the leadership contemplated by the Framers when they made the President Commander in Chief, and imposed upon him the trust to "take Care that the Laws be faithfully executed." With or without explicit statutory authorization, Presidents have at such times dealt with national emergencies by acting promptly and resolutely to enforce legislative programs, at least to save those programs until Congress could act. Congress and the courts have responded to such executive initiative with consistent approval. ...

[Vinson then cited a series of instances of seizure by Presidents Lincoln, Taft, and Franklin Roosevelt.]

Focusing now on the situation confronting the President on the night of April 8, 1952, we cannot but conclude that the President was performing his duty under the Constitution "to take Care that the Laws be faithfully executed"—a duty described by President Benjamin Harrison as "the central idea of the office."

The President reported to Congress the morning after the seizure that he acted because a work stoppage in steel production would immediately imperil the safety of the Nation by preventing execution of the legislative programs for procurement of military equipment. ...

... The President's action served the same purpose as a judicial stay entered to maintain the status quo in order to preserve the jurisdiction of a court. ...

Plaintiffs place their primary emphasis on the Labor Management Relations Act of 1947 ... but do not contend that that Act contains any provision prohibiting seizure. ...

The diversity of views expressed in the six opinions of the majority, the lack of reference to authoritative precedent, the repeated reliance upon prior dissenting opinions, the complete disregard of the uncontroverted facts showing the gravity of the emergency and the temporary nature of the taking all serve to demonstrate how far afield one must go to affirm the order of the District Court.

The broad executive power granted by Art. II to an officer on duty 365 days a year cannot, it is said, be invoked to avert disaster. Instead, the President must confine himself to sending a message to Congress recommending action. Under this messenger-boy concept of the Office, the President cannot even act to preserve legislative programs from destruction so that Congress will have something left to act upon. ...

Editors' Notes

(1) **Query:** Compare Jackson's opinion with Black's in the Steel Case. To what extent did each implicitly use structural analysis? How did the structures they visualized differ? Or did the difference lie more in Black's use of textual structuralism and Jackson's of both textual and systemic structuralism? Was Frankfurter's opinion more or less broadly structuralist than Black's or Jackson's? To what extent was Vinson's dissent also structuralist? Was it textualist, systemic, transcendent, or some other version?

(2) **Query:** Black asserted that Congress possesses "exclusive constitutional authority to make laws necessary and proper to carry out the powers vested by the Constitution 'in the Government of the United States, or any Department or Officer thereof.'" Does the constitutional text vest this power exclusively in Congress or does it require Congress to share it with the President?

(3) Compare the language of In re Neagle (1890), which grew out of a feud between Justice Stephen Field and his former law partner David Terry, who had threatened to kill Field because the Justice had, while riding circuit, held that Mrs. Terry's divorce from her first husband was not valid and therefore she was not legally married to Terry. Some time later, Terry approached Field, riding circuit in California, and began what a marshal, assigned to act as Filed's bodyguard, thought was an attack. The marshal then shot and killed Terry and was arrested by state officials. The Department of Justice asked for a writ of habeas corpus under statutes that provided that federal officers should be tried in federal courts for acts committed while on duty. The case reached the Supreme Court; and the President's authority, in

the absence of an act of Congress, to assign marshals for such protective duty was an important preliminary issue. The Court asked:

> Is this duty [of the President to "take care that the laws be faithfully executed"] limited to the enforcement of acts of Congress or of treaties of the United States, according to their *express terms,* or does it include the rights, duties and obligations growing out of the Constitution itself, our international relations, and the protection implied by the nature of the government under the Constitution?

The Court's answer was emphatically in favor of a broad scope for presidential power.

(4) On the afternoon of the Court's decision in *Youngstown,* Truman ordered the mills returned to management. That same day the United Steel Workers began a strike that lasted more than seven weeks, aggravating an existing shortage of ammunition for the troops heavily engaged in combat in Korea. On the background and effects of the seizure, see: Grant McConnell, *The President Seizes the Steel Mills* (University: University of Alabama Case Program, 1960); Richard E. Neustadt, *Presidential Power* (rev. ed.; New York: Wiley, 1976), ch. 2; Alan F. Westin, ed., *The Anatomy of a Constitutional Law Case* (New York: Macmillan, 1958). Truman claimed the ammunition shortage began after the strike—*Memoirs* (Garden City, N.Y.: Doubleday, 1955), II, ch. 29—but it had actually begun months before. For analyses of the justices' opinions, see Edward S. Corwin, "The Steel Seizure Case: A Judicial Brick Without Straw," 53 *Colum.L.Rev.* 53 (1953); Paul G. Kauper, "The Steel Seizure Case," 51 *Mich.L.Rev.* 141 (1952); and C. Herman Pritchett, *Civil Liberties and the Vinson Court* (Chicago: University of Chicago Press, 1954), pp. 206–213.

"The constitutional powers of the President ... to introduce United States Armed Forces into hostilities ... are exercised only pursuant to (1) a declaration of war, (2) specific statutory authorization, or (3) a national emergency created by an attack upon the United States. ..."

THE WAR POWERS RESOLUTION*

Joint Resolution Concerning the War Powers of Congress and the President

Resolved by the Senate and House of Representatives of the United States of America in Congress assembled, That: ...

PURPOSE AND POLICY

Sec. 2. (a) It is the purpose of this joint resolution to fulfill the intent of the framers of the Constitution of the United States and insure that the collective judgment of both the Congress and the President will

---

* H.J.Res. 542; Pub.L. 93–148 (1973); 87 Stat.555; 50 U.S.C. §§ 1541–1548. Passed over Presidential veto Nov. 7, 1973.

apply to the introduction of United States Armed Forces into hostilities, or into situations where imminent involvement in hostilities is clearly indicated by the circumstances, and to the continued use of such forces in hostilities or in such situations.

(b) Under article I, section 8, of the Constitution, it is specifically provided that the Congress shall have the power to make all laws necessary and proper for carrying into execution, not only its own powers but also all other powers vested by the Constitution in the Government of the United States, or in any department or officer thereof.

(c) The constitutional powers of the President as Commander-in-Chief to introduce United States Armed Forces into hostilities, or into situations where imminent involvement in hostilities is clearly indicated by the circumstances, are exercised only pursuant to (1) a declaration of war, (2) specific statutory authorization, or (3) a national emergency created by attack upon the United States, its territories or possessions, or its armed forces.

CONSULTATION

Sec. 3. The President in every possible instance shall consult with Congress before introducing United States Armed Forces into hostilities or into situations where imminent involvement in hostilities is clearly indicated by the circumstances, and after every such introduction shall consult regularly with the Congress until United States Armed Forces are no longer engaged in hostilities or have been removed from such situations.

Sec. 4. (a) In the absence of a declaration of war, in any case in which United States Armed Forces are introduced—

(1) into hostilities or into situations where imminent involvement in hostilities is clearly indicated by the circumstances;

(2) into the territory, airspace or waters of a foreign nation, while equipped for combat, except for deployments which relate solely to supply, replacement, repair, or training of such forces; or

(3) in numbers which substantially enlarge United States Armed Forces equipped for combat already located in a foreign nation;

the President shall submit within 48 hours to the Speaker of the House of Representatives and to the President pro tempore of the Senate a report, in writing, setting forth—

(A) the circumstances necessitating the introduction of United States Armed Forces;

(B) the constitutional and legislative authority under which such introduction took place; and

(C) the estimated scope and duration of the hostilities or involvement.

(b) The President shall provide such other information as the Congress may request in the fulfillment of its constitutional responsibilities with respect to committing the Nation to war and to the use of United States Armed Forces abroad.

(c) Whenever United States Armed Forces are introduced into hostilities or into any situation described in subsection (a) of this section, the President shall, so long as such armed forces continue to be engaged in such hostilities or situation, report to the Congress periodically on the status of such hostilities or situation as well as on the scope and duration of such hostilities or situation, but in no event shall he report to the Congress less often than once every six months.

CONGRESSIONAL ACTION

Sec. 5. (a) Each report submitted pursuant to section 4(a)(1) shall be transmitted to the Speaker of the House of Representatives and to the President pro tempore of the Senate on the same calendar day. Each report so transmitted shall be referred to the Committee on Foreign Affairs of the House of Representatives and to the Committee on Foreign Relations of the Senate for appropriate action. If, when the report is transmitted, the Congress has adjourned sine die or has adjourned for any period in excess of three calendar days, the Speaker of the House of Representatives and the President pro tempore of the Senate, if they deem it advisable (or if petitioned by at least 30 percent of the membership of their respective Houses) shall jointly request the President to convene Congress in order that it may consider the report and take appropriate action pursuant to this section.

(b) Within sixty calendar days after a report is submitted or is required to be submitted pursuant to section 4(a)(1), whichever is earlier, the President shall terminate any use of United States Armed Forces with respect to which such report was submitted (or required to be submitted), unless the Congress (1) has declared war or has enacted a specific authorization for such use of United States Armed Forces, (2) has extended by law such sixty-day period, or (3) is physically unable to meet as a result of an armed attack upon the United States. Such sixty-day period shall be extended for not more than an additional thirty days if the President determines and certifies to the Congress in writing that unavoidable military necessity respecting the safety of United States Armed Forces requires the continued use of such armed forces in the course of bringing about a prompt removal of such forces.

(c) Notwithstanding subsection (b), at any time that United States Armed Forces are engaged in hostilities outside the territory of the United States, its possessions and territories without a declaration of war or specific statutory authorization, such forces shall be removed by the President if the Congress so directs by concurrent resolution.*. . . .

---

* **Eds.' Note:** In 1983 Congress amended the act so as to replace "concurrent resolution" with "joint resolution." See Eds.' Note (4) below.

INTERPRETATION OF JOINT RESOLUTION

Sec. 8. (a) Authority to introduce United States Armed Forces into hostilities or into situations wherein involvement in hostilities is clearly indicated by the circumstances shall not be inferred—

(1) from any provision of law (whether or not in effect before the date of the enactment of this joint resolution), including any provision contained in any appropriation Act, unless such provision specifically authorizes the introduction of United States Armed Forces into hostilities or into such situations and states that it is intended to constitute specific statutory authorization within the meaning of this joint resolution; or

(2) from any treaty heretofore or hereafter ratified unless such treaty is implemented by legislation specifically authorizing the introduction of United States Armed Forces into hostilities or into such situations and stating that it is intended to constitute specific statutory authorization within the meaning of this joint resolution.

(b) Nothing in this joint resolution shall be construed to require any further specific statutory authorization to permit members of United States Armed Forces to participate jointly with members of the armed forces of one or more foreign countries in the headquarters operations of high-level military commands which were established prior to the date of enactment of this joint resolution and pursuant to the United Nations Charter or any treaty ratified by the United States prior to such date.

(c) For purposes of this joint resolution, the term "introduction of United States Armed Forces" includes the assignment of members of such armed forces to command, coordinate, participate in the movement of, or accompany the regular or irregular military forces of any foreign country or government when such military forces are engaged, or there exists an imminent threat that such forces will become engaged, in hostilities.

(d) Nothing in this joint resolution—

(1) is intended to alter the constitutional authority of the Congress or of the President, or the provisions of existing treaties; or

(2) shall be construed as granting any authority to the President with respect to the introduction of United States Armed Forces into hostilities or into situations wherein involvement in hostilities is clearly indicated by the circumstances which authority he would not have had in the absence of this joint resolution.

SEPARABILITY CLAUSE

Sec. 9. If any provision of this joint resolution or the application thereof to any person or circumstance is held invalid, the remainder of the joint resolution and the application of such provision to any other person or circumstance shall not be affected thereby. . . .

Editors' Notes

(1) A Joint Resolution has the same force as a statute. It must be passed by both houses of Congress and (i) signed by the President; or (ii) remain

unsigned for ten days when Congress is in session; or (iii) if the President vetoes it, as happened in this instance, be repassed by a two-thirds majority of each house.

(2) **Query**: To what extent can one argue that this Resolution binds the President more than an ordinary statute because it is explicitly directed at him and only at him, whereas most statutes are general in their coverage? Insofar as this Resolution is a congressional interpretation of the President's constitutional power does it bind him at all? What would Presidents Jefferson, Jackson, Lincoln, and Franklin Roosevelt have said? What should Justice Robert H. Jackson have said, had he extrapolated from his concurring opinion in *Youngstown* (1952; reprinted above, p. 443)?

(3) **Query**: More narrowly, because § 2 of the War Powers Resolution is only a general statement of purpose and policy and does not require any action by the President, does it have any binding force? Is it no more than a statement of Congress' constitutional interpretation? How does its force differ, if at all, from that of §§ 3–4?

(4) **Query**: Suppose a President were to defy the Resolution, what counteraction could Congress take? How politically feasible would it be for senators and representatives to vote to cut off money to provide supplies and ammunition for American troops engaged in combat? Is it likely that Congress would try to take its case to the Supreme Court? If that happened, is it likely the justices would hear and decide the case on its merits? If the Court did take the case, what would be the most probable outcome?

(5) Sec. 5(c) of the War Powers Resolution, authorizing Congress, by concurrent resolution, to direct the President to remove American forces from a theater of hostilities outside of the United States or its territories, contained a variant of the legislative veto. Concurrent resolutions are not submitted to the President for his approval or veto. INS v. Chadha (1983; reprinted below, p. 485) held the legislative veto unconstitutional because it removed this power of the President. To forestall challenge on that ground, Congress amended § 5(c) so as to replace "concurrent resolution" with "joint resolution," which, of course, is subject to a presidential veto. 97 Stat. 1062–63 (1983).

(6) For detailed analyses of the Resolution, see Robert Scigliano, "The War Powers Resolution and the War Powers," in Jeffrey M. Bessette and Jeffrey Tulis, eds., *The Presidency in the Constitutional Order* (Baton Rouge: Louisiana State University Press, 1981); and Christopher H. Pyle and Richard M. Pious, eds., *The President, Congress and the Constitution* (New York: The Free Press, 1984), ch. 3. See also: Graham T. Allison, "Making War," 40 *L. & Contemp. Probs.* 86 (1976); John Hart Ely, *War and Responsibility* (Princeton: Princeton University Press, 1993); J. Terry Emerson, "War Powers Resolution Tested," 51 *Notre Dame Lawyer* 187 (1975); Louis Henkin, *Constitutionalism, Democracy, and Foreign Affairs* (New York: Columbia University Press, 1990),

espec. ch. 1; and Newell L. Highsmith, "Policing Executive Adventurism," 19 *Harv.J. of Legn.* 327 (1982).

"Nothing in this resolution supersedes any requirement of the War Powers Resolution."

Six or seven times President Gerald Ford (1974–77) placed American forces in combat or in situations that were likely to have led to combat; in none of these did he comply with the terms of the War Powers Resolution. President James E. Carter (1977–81) engaged in one such operation, the abortive rescue effort of American diplomats in Iran in 1980. He did not have congressional authorization nor did he consult with Congress in advance; but he aborted the mission before it engaged in hostile action. President Ronald Reagan (1981–89) did not follow the Resolution's terms when he sent Marines into Lebanon in 1982 or when he invaded Grenada in 1983. In 1983, however, after Marines began taking heavy casualties in Lebanon, he largely complied with the provisions, though without conceding a constitutional obligation to do so. Thus, during the Resolution's first 17 years, Presidents tended to ignore it rather than to follow or openly defy it.

The so-called Gulf War of 1990–91 provided another test of presidential-legislative powers. In August 1990, Iraq invaded and occupied oil-rich Kuwait and threatened Saudi Arabia, thereby menacing a huge share of the world's supply of oil. In swift diplomatic moves, President George Bush wove an alliance of NATO, Japan, and many Arab nations, including Egypt and Syria as well as Saudi Arabia, to adopt resolutions in the United Nations condemning Iraq's action, calling for an immediate withdrawal, and imposing severe economic sanctions until the Iraqi complied. At the same time, Bush sent large numbers of American troops, ships, planes and military equipment into Saudi Arabia to defend that country and persuaded NATO and the major Arab nations to contribute armed forces and the Japanese to supply billions of dollars. In addition, he was able to secure the assistance, though not the military aid, of the new Russian Republic, the former patron of the Iraqi regime.

After several months of sanctions had not budged the Iraqi, Bush decided that military action was necessary. But such a course was not only politically controversial, it was constitutionally cloudy. Many public officials and constitutional scholars made the obvious points that (1) the massive strength of the Iraqi army would mean operations would be large and brutal, in effect a war, not a quick skirmish as in Grenada; and (2) only Congress could declare war. Furthermore, the War Power Resolution had never been repealed, even if it had been ignored. Initially, the President was inclined to use military force on his own authority, claiming to be responding to treaty obligations, including those imposed by the UN's Charter. Eventually, however, he realized that a constitutional controversy could undermine the legitimacy of his plans and agreed to ask Congress to approve use of American forces in combat. The joint resolution easily passed in the House (250–183) but did so in the Senate by a much narrower margin (52–47), with most Democrats opposed.

AUTHORIZATION FOR USE OF MILITARY FORCES AGAINST IRAQ RESOLUTION*

. . .

Section 2. Authorization for the Use of United States Armed Forces

(a) AUTHORIZATION.—The President is authorized, subject to subsection (b), to use United States Armed Forces pursuant to United Nations Security Council Resolution 678 (1990) in order to achieve implementation of Security Council Resolutions 660, 661, 662, 664, 665, 666, 667, 669, 670, 674, and 677.

(b) REQUIREMENTS FOR DETERMINATION THAT USE OF MILITARY FORCES IS NECESSARY.—Before exercising the authority granted in subsection (a), the President shall make available to the Speaker of the House of Representatives and the President pro tempore of the Senate his determination that—

(1) the United States has used all appropriate diplomatic and other peaceful means to obtain compliance by Iraq with the United Nations Security resolutions cited in subsection (a); and

(2) that those efforts have not been successful in obtaining such compliance.

(c) WAR POWERS RESOLUTIONS REQUIREMENTS.—

(1) SPECIFIC STATUTORY AUTHORIZATION.—Consistent with section 8(a)(1) of the War Powers Resolution, the Congress declares that this section is meant to constitute specific statutory authorization within the meaning of section (5)(b) of the War Powers Resolution.

(2) APPLICABILITY OF OTHER REQUIREMENTS.—Nothing in this resolution supersedes any requirement of the War Powers Resolution.

Section 4. REPORTS TO CONGRESS.

At least once every 60 days, the President shall submit to the Congress a summary of the status of efforts to obtain compliance by Iraq with the resolutions adopted by the United Nations Security Council in response to Iraq's aggression.

Editors' Note

Shortly after Congress adopted this resolution, the United States and its allies mounted a massive aerial bombardment of Iraq and Kuwait that lasted several weeks. The ground action that ensued was equally devastating. The allied forces suffered only several hundred casualties, the Iraqis perhaps 100,000. After 100 hours, the Iraqi were driven out of Kuwait and asked for an armistice.

---

* H.J.Res. 77 (1991).

III. INSTITUTIONAL INTEGRITY IN
A SYSTEM OF SHARED POWERS

"The Congress is the legislative department of the government; the President is the executive department.
Neither can be restrained in its actions by the judicial
department; though the acts of both, when performed,
are, in proper cases, subject to its cognizance."

MISSISSIPPI v. JOHNSON
71 U.S. (4 Wall.) 475, 18 L.Ed. 437 (1867).

After the Civil War, Congress passed a series of statutes called the
Reconstruction Acts. In essence, these imposed martial law on the states of
the former Confederacy, disfranchised many ex-Confederates, and established
a lengthy procedure through which these states could be readmitted to the
Union—a Union, so Lincoln had consistently claimed, they had never left.
Officials of Mississippi filed suit in the Supreme Court, invoking its original
jurisdiction to hear cases to which a state is a party, asking the justices to
enjoin President Andrew Johnson from enforcing two of these statutes.

The Chief Justice [**CHASE**] delivered the opinion of the Court. ...

The single point which requires consideration is this: Can the
President be restrained from carrying into effect an act of Congress
alleged to be unconstitutional?

It is assumed by the counsel for the State of Mississippi, that the
President, in the execution of the Reconstruction Acts, is required to
perform a mere ministerial duty. In this assumption there is, we think,
a confounding of the terms ministerial and executive, which are by no
means equivalent in import.

A ministerial duty, the performance of which may, in proper cases,
be required of the head of a department, by judicial process, is one in
respect to which nothing is left to discretion. It is a simple, definite
duty, arising under conditions admitted or proved to exist, and imposed
by law.

The case of Marbury v. Madison [1803] furnishes an illustration. A
citizen had been nominated, confirmed, and appointed a justice of the
peace for the District of Columbia, and his commission had been made
out, signed, and sealed. Nothing remained to be done except delivery,
and the duty of delivery was imposed by law on the Secretary of State.
It was held that the performance of this duty might be enforced by
mandamus issuing from a court having jurisdiction.

So, in the case of Kendall, Postmaster–General v. Stockton & Stokes
[1838] an act of Congress had directed the Postmaster–General to credit
Stockton & Stokes with such sums as the Solicitor of the Treasury

should find due to them; and that officer refused to credit them with certain sums, so found due. It was held that the crediting of this money was a mere ministerial duty, the performance of which might be judicially enforced.

In each of these cases nothing was left to discretion. There was no room for the exercise of judgment. The law required the performance of a single specific act; and that performance, it was held, might be required by mandamus.

Very different is the duty of the President in the exercise of the power to see that the laws are faithfully executed, and among these laws the acts named in the bill. By the first of these acts he is required to assign generals to command in the several military districts, and to detail sufficient military force to enable such officers to discharge their duties under the law. By the supplementary act, other duties are imposed on the several commanding generals, and these duties must necessarily be performed under the supervision of the President as commander-in-chief. The duty thus imposed on the President is in no just sense ministerial. It is purely executive and political.

An attempt on the part of the judicial department of the government to enforce the performance of such duties by the President might be justly characterized, in the language of Chief Justice Marshall, as "an absurd and excessive extravagance."

It is true that in the instance before us the interposition of the court is not sought to enforce action by the Executive under constitutional legislation, but to restrain such action under legislation alleged to be unconstitutional. But we are unable to perceive that this circumstance takes the case out of the general principles which forbid judicial interference with the exercise of Executive discretion.

It was admitted in the argument that the application now made to us is without a precedent; and this is of much weight against it.

Had it been supposed at the bar that this court would, in any case, interpose, by injunction, to prevent the execution of an unconstitutional act of Congress, it can hardly be doubted that applications with that object would have been heretofore addressed to it.

Occasions have not been wanting. ...

It will hardly be contended that Congress [the courts?] can interpose, in any case, to restrain the enactment of an unconstitutional law; and yet how can the right to judicial interposition to prevent such an enactment, when the purpose is evident and the execution of that purpose certain, be distinguished, in principle, from the right to such interposition against the execution of such a law by the President?

The Congress is the legislative department of the government; the President is the executive department. Neither can be restrained in its action by the judicial department; though the acts of both, when performed, are, in proper cases, subject to its cognizance.

The impropriety of such interference will be clearly seen upon consideration of its possible consequences.

Suppose the bill filed and the injunction prayed for allowed. If the President refuse obedience, it is needless to observe that the court is without power to enforce its process. If, on the other hand, the President complies with the order of the court and refuses to execute the acts of Congress, is it not clear that a collision may occur between the executive and legislative departments of the government? May not the House of Representatives impeach the President for such refusal? And in that case could this court interfere, in behalf of the President, thus endangered by compliance with its mandate, and restrain by injunction the Senate of the United States from sitting as a court of impeachment? Would the strange spectacle be offered to the public wonder of an attempt by this court to arrest proceedings in that court?

These questions answer themselves. . . .

It has been suggested that the bill contains a prayer that, if the relief sought cannot be had against Andrew Johnson, as President, it may be granted against Andrew Johnson as a citizen of Tennessee. But it is plain that relief as against the execution of an act of Congress by Andrew Johnson, is relief against its execution by the President. A bill praying an injunction against the execution of an act of Congress by the incumbent of the presidential office cannot be received, whether it describes him as President or as a citizen of a State.

The motion for leave to file the bill is, therefore,

Denied.

Editors' Notes

(1) Within a few days, Georgia's officials tried a different tack. They also sued under the Court's original jurisdiction asking for an injunction against the Secretary of War, forbidding him to enforce the Reconstruction Acts. The Court dismissed that suit: "[T]he rights for the protection of which our authority is invoked, are the rights of sovereignty, of political jurisdiction, of government, of corporate existence as a State, with all its constitutional powers and privileges. No case of private rights or private property . . . is presented by the bill, in a judicial form, for the judgment of the court." Georgia v. Stanton (1867).

(2) The timing in these cases—the question of WHEN to interpret—was critical. *Mississippi* was argued in April and *Georgia* in May of 1867. Ex parte McCardle (1867; reprinted below, p. 467), in which a private citizen who had been sentenced to death by a military court challenged the validity of that section of the Reconstruction Acts imposing martial law, had been argued in March. While *McCardle* was in progress and just before *Mississippi* and *Georgia* were argued, Congress, fearing the justices would invalidate the statute, removed the Court's appellate jurisdiction under which it was hearing *McCardle*. Furthermore, Congress was also warring against the President; indeed, he and the ex–Confederates were Congress' main targets, not the justices. The House had recently impeached President Johnson and his trial

was scheduled to begin soon in the Senate. Thus there was no doubt that the Radical Republicans were firmly in control of Congress, were determined to curb the presidency, and were even more determined to maintain martial law in the South. The justices, as in *McCardle,* undoubtedly thought it wiser to avoid unnecessary conflict with such a Congress.

(3) For general discussions of constitutional interpretation during Reconstruction see: Michael Les Benedict, *A Compromise of Principle* (New York: Norton, 1974); Charles Fairman, *Reconstruction and Reunion, 1864–1888* (New York: Macmillan, 1971); Harold M. Hyman, *A More Perfect Union* (New York: Knopf, 1973); and Stanley I. Kutler, *Judicial Power and Reconstruction Politics* (Chicago: University of Chicago Press, 1968).

" 'The Executive is as independent of either house of Congress as either house of Congress is independent of him. ...' "

TRUMAN REFUSES TO OBEY A SUBPOENA*

In 1953, almost a year after Harry S Truman had left the presidency, the House Committee on Un–American Activities subpoenaed him to appear and testify. The committee was planning to question him about "subversives" who had been in the federal government during his administration, in particular about Harry Dexter White, an alleged Soviet spy. Mr. Truman responded in a letter to the committee's chairman.

Dear Sir:

I have your subpoena dated Nov. 9, 1953, directing my appearance before your committee on Friday, Nov. 13, in Washington. The subpoena does not state the matters upon which you seek my testimony, but I assume from the press stories that you seek to examine me with respect to matters which occurred during my tenure of the Presidency of the United States.

In spite of my personal willingness to cooperate with your committee, I feel constrained by my duty to the people of the United States to decline to comply with the subpoena.

In doing so, I am carrying out the provisions of the Constitution of the United States; and am following a long line of precedents, commencing with George Washington himself in 1796. Since his day, Presidents Jefferson, Monroe, Jackson, Tyler, Polk, Fillmore, Buchanan, Lincoln, Grant, Hayes, Cleveland, Theodore Roosevelt, Coolidge, Hoover and Franklin D. Roosevelt have declined to respond to subpoenas or demands for information of various kinds by Congress.

---

* From the files of the House UnAmerican Activities Committee.

The underlying reason for this clearly established and universally recognized constitutional doctrine has been succinctly set forth by Charles Warren, one of our leading constitutional authorities, as follows:

> In this long series of contests by the Executive to maintain his constitutional integrity, one sees a legitimate conclusion from our theory of government. ... Under our Constitution, each branch of the Government is designed to be a coordinate representative of the will of the people. ... Defense by the Executive of his constitutional powers becomes in very truth, therefore, defense of popular rights—defense of power which the people granted to him.

> It was in that sense that President Cleveland spoke of his duty to the people not to relinquish any of the powers of his great office. It was in that sense that President Buchanan stated the people have rights and prerogatives in the execution of his office by the President which every President is under a duty to see "shall never be violated in his person" but "passed to his successors unimpaired by the adoption of a dangerous precedent." In maintaining his rights against a trespassing Congress, the President defends not himself, but popular government; he represents not himself but the people.

President Jackson repelled an attempt by the Congress to break down the separation of powers in these words:

> For myself I shall repel all such attempts as an invasion of the principles of justice as well as of the Constitution, and I shall esteem it my sacred duty to the people of the United States to resist them as I would the establishment of a Spanish Inquisition.

I might commend to your reading the opinion of one of the committees of the House of Representatives in 1879, House Report 141, March 3, 1879, Forty-fifth Congress, Third Session, in which the House Judiciary Committee said the following:

> The Executive is as independent of either house of Congress as either house of Congress is independent of him, and they cannot call for the records of his actions, or the action of his officers against his consent, any more than he can call for any of the journals or records of the House or Senate.

It must be obvious to you that if the doctrine of separation of powers and the independence of the Presidency is to have any validity at all, it must be equally applicable to a President after his term of office has expired when he is sought to be examined with respect to any acts occurring while he is President.

The doctrine would be shattered, and the President, contrary to our fundamental theory of constitutional government, would become a mere arm of the Legislative Branch of the Government if he would feel during his term of office that his every act might be subject to official inquiry and possible distortion for political purposes.

If your intention, however, is to inquire into any acts as a private individual either before or after my Presidency and unrelated to any acts as President, I shall be happy to appear.

Yours Very Truly,
Harry S Truman

_____

"I, too, shall adhere to this precedent."

NIXON REFUSES TO TESTIFY*

In February, 1977, Rep. Lester L. Wolff (Dem., N.Y.) invited former President Richard M. Nixon to testify before the Subcommittee on Asian and Pacific Affairs of the House Committee on International Relations on the question of obligations the United States might have undertaken in its cease-fire agreement with North Vietnam to provide economic aid to that country. Nixon responded on May 14, 1977.

Dear Congressman Wolff:

As I am sure you are aware, your request of February 22 presents some fundamental and serious constitutional questions.

In 1953 a Committee of the House of Representatives sought to subpoena former President Truman to inquire about matters of which he had personal knowledge while he served as President. President Truman's response states what I believe is the correct constitutional guideline which a former President must follow. ...

I, too, shall adhere to this precedent. However, because the issue of aid to the Hanoi Government is currently under consideration in the Congress, and without waiving the separation-of-powers principle, I want to be as helpful as I can in providing voluntarily my recollection of events surrounding the aid negotiation. ... [Nixon then gave a detailed account of his remembrances and concluded that there was "no commitment of any kind, moral or legal, to provide aid to the Hanoi Government."]

_____

"We are not at liberty to inquire into the motives of the legislature. We can only examine its power under the Constitution. ..."

EX PARTE McCARDLE

74 U.S. (7 Wall.) 506, 19 L.Ed. 264 (1869).

_____

* From the files of the House Subcommittee on Asian and Pacific Affairs.

As part of its plan of Reconstruction, the Radical Republicans in Congress pushed through statutes instituting martial law in the former Confederate states. In 1861, Chief Justice Roger Brooke Taney, riding circuit, had held unconstitutional Lincoln's use of military rule in Maryland during the early stages of the Civil War. Ex parte Merryman. (See below, Chapter 19.) Shortly after the war, in Ex parte Milligan (1866; reprinted below, p. 1376) the full Supreme Court declared unconstitutional that part of Lincoln's program, carried through without statutory authorization, using martial law in border states during the war. All nine justices agreed that the President, acting alone, had no such authority, and five went out of their way to say that even Congress could not have authorized trials of civilians by courts martial in areas where the dangers of war were not so severe as to make it impossible for regular civilian courts to operate.

Milligan thus threw a constitutional pall over military rule of the South, a policy the Radicals considered to be the heart of their program. The occasion for a test soon developed. The army arrested William McCardle, a bitter ex-Confederate colonel turned newspaper editor in Mississippi. He was charged with disturbing the peace and impeding Reconstruction by publishing editorials urging white people to boycott elections sponsored by the military government and threatening to publish the names of "the cowards, dogs and scoundrels" who did participate. While he was being held for trial by a court martial, he sought habeas corpus from a circuit court, and on losing appealed to the Supreme Court. Ironically, he invoked not the Judiciary Act of 1789 but a statute Congress had enacted in 1867 to protect federal officers administering Reconstruction.

The Court set the case down for argument in early March, 1868. Chief counsel for McCardle was the noted former judge and sometime Reporter of the Supreme Court, Jeremiah S. Black, who had also successfully argued *Milligan*. His strategy "was nothing less than to free the Old South from the grasp of Congress,"[1] a plan that was evident to Radical leaders. To prevent the judicial axe from falling on their program, they looked to Article III, § 2 of the Constitution:

> In all other cases before mentioned, the supreme court shall have
> appellate jurisdiction, both as to law and fact, with such exceptions,
> and under such regulations as the Congress shall make.

Argument closed on March 9. By March 27, Congress had passed, President Johnson (though under impeachment and awaiting trial by the Senate) had vetoed, and Congress had repassed over his veto a bill repealing the act of 1867 that McCardle had used to get his case before the Court. Very much aware of the Radicals' mood, the justices delayed a decision while repeal was going through the legislative process. Justices Stephen Field and Robert Grier dissented. Grier's memorandum—never published in the official reports—was angry:

> By the postponement of the case we shall subject ourselves, whether
> justly or unjustly, to the imputation that we have evaded the perfor-
> mance of a duty imposed on us by the Constitution, and have waited

---

1. Charles Fairman, *Reconstruction and Reunion 1864–1888* (New York: Macmillan, 1971), I, 456.

for legislation to interpose to supersede our action and relieve us from our responsibility. I am not willing to be a partaker of the eulogy or opprobrium that may follow. ...[2]

Jeremiah Black's comment was even more scathing: "The court stood still to be ravished and did not even hallo while the thing was getting done. ..."[3]

The justices set reargument for the following term on the question whether the Court had jurisdiction to decide the case on its merits.

The Chief Justice [**CHASE**] delivered the opinion of the court.

The first question necessarily is that of jurisdiction; for, if the act of March, 1868, takes away the jurisdiction defined by the act of February, 1867, it is useless, if not improper, to enter into any discussion of other questions. It is quite true, as was argued by the counsel for the petitioner, that the appellate jurisdiction of this court is not derived from acts of Congress. It is, strictly speaking, conferred by the Constitution. But it is conferred "with such exceptions and under such regulations as Congress shall make." ...

The source of that jurisdiction, and the limitations of it by the Constitution and by statute, have been on several occasions subjects of consideration here. In the case of Durousseau v. The United States [1810], particularly, the whole matter was carefully examined, and the court held, that while "the appellate powers of this court are not given by the judicial act, but are given by the Constitution," they are, nevertheless, "limited and regulated by that act, and by such other acts as have been passed on the subject." The court said, further, that the judicial act was an exercise of the power given by the Constitution to Congress "of making exceptions to the appellate jurisdiction of the Supreme Court." "They have described affirmatively," said the court, "its jurisdiction, and this affirmative description has been understood to imply a negation of the exercise of such appellate power as is not comprehended within it." ...

The exception to appellate jurisdiction in the case before us, however, is not an inference from the affirmation of other appellate jurisdiction. ... The provision of the act of 1867, affirming the appellate jurisdiction of this court in cases of *habeas corpus* is expressly repealed. It is hardly possible to imagine a plainer instance of positive exception.

We are not at liberty to inquire into the motives of the legislature. We can only examine into its power under the Constitution; and the power to make exceptions to the appellate jurisdiction of this court is given by express words. What, then, is the effect of the repealing act upon the case before us? We cannot doubt as to this. Without jurisdiction the court cannot proceed at all in any cause. Jurisdiction is power to declare the law, and when it ceases to exist, the only function remaining to the court is that of announcing the fact and dismissing the

---

2. Quoted in *ibid.*, 474.

3. *Ibid.*, 478.

cause. And this is not less clear upon authority than upon principle.
. . .

It is quite clear, therefore, that this court cannot proceed to pronounce judgment in this case, for it has no longer jurisdiction of the
appeal; and judicial duty is not less fitly performed by declining un-
granted jurisdiction than in exercising firmly that which the Constitution and the laws confer.

Counsel seem to have supposed, if effect be given to the repealing
act in question, that the whole appellate power of the court, in cases of
habeas corpus, is denied. But this is an error. The act of 1868 does not
except from that jurisdiction any cases but appeals from Circuit Courts
under the act of 1867. It does not affect the jurisdiction which was
previously exercised.

The appeal of the petitioner in this case must be

Dismissed for want of jurisdiction.

Editors' Notes

(1) One should read carefully the last substantive paragraph in the Chief
Justice's opinion. Ex parte Yerger (1869) came up shortly after *McCardle;*
there the Court ruled it had appellate jurisdiction because the litigant had
invoked the Act of 1789, not the repealed statute of 1867.

(2) **Query**: Does *McCardle* imply that Congress could use its power to
make exceptions to the justices' jurisdiction so as to cripple the Court? Is
there a constitutional difference between making an exception and abolishing
an entire bloc of jurisdiction? Does the term "exceptions" imply a significant
residuum? Prof. Henry M. Hart argued: "[T]he exceptions must not be such
as will destroy the essential role of the Supreme Court in the constitutional
plan." ("The Power of Congress to Limit the Jurisdiction of Federal Courts,"
66 *Harv.L.Rev.* 1362, 1365 [1953].) Invoking either a broad theory of constitutionalism or narrower structuralist view of the constitutional text as requiring
three branches of government that can effectively function, the Court might
invalidate any drastic effort at jurisdictional surgery.

And some justices have hinted at just such a possibility. In *Yerger* Chief
Justice Chase noted the circumstances in *McCardle* were "peculiar." Almost
a century later, in a diversity-of-citizenship case that splintered the Court into
three factions, Justices Harlan, Brennan, and Stewart reasoned by analogy
that, if Congress could make exceptions to the Supreme Court's jurisdiction, it
could also do so to that of the Court of Claims. But they promptly added,
"The authority is not, of course, unlimited." This disclaimer was not sufficient
for Douglas and Black. They chided Harlan et al. for even citing *McCardle*
with approval, noting, "There is a serious question whether the McCardle Case
could command a majority view today." Glidden v. Zdanok (1962).

Perhaps *McCardle* stands for only two propositions: (1) In times of
political crisis, the justices are not apt to take on the dominant branch of
government—and with the President impeached, the Radicals in command of
Congress, and the more extreme among them making threats to abolish the
Supreme Court, Congress in 1868–69 was the dominant branch and seemed

determined to exploit its dominance; and (2) Even in a crisis, or perhaps especially in a crisis, the justices are willing to take—and suffer—great pains to retain control not only over HOW but also WHEN they will interpret the constitutional text or the broader constitution.

(3) For analyses that take a narrow view of the reach of congressional authority to control the Court's appellate jurisdiction, see in addition to Hart, cited above: Lawrence G. Sager, "Congressional Limitations on Congress' Authority to Regulate the Appellate Jurisdiction of the Federal Courts," 95 *Harv.L.Rev.* 17 (1981); and Gerald Gunther, "Congressional Power to Curtail Federal Court Jurisdiction," 36 *Stan.L.Rev.* 895 (1984). For analyses that take a broad view of congressional authority, see: Michael J. Perry, *The Constitution, the Courts, and Human Rights* (New Haven: Yale University Press, 1982), pp. 129–145; and Herbert Wechsler, "The Court and the Constitution," 65 *Colum.L.Rev.* 1001 (1965). For an ingenious discussion of the problem of congressional control over the Court's appellate jurisdiction in the broader context of the structure of the national government, see Charles L. Black, "The Presidency and Congress," 32 *Wash. & Lee L.Rev.* 841 (1975).

(4) For the background of *McCardle,* see especially: Charles Fairman, *Reconstruction and Reunion 1864–1888* (New York: Macmillan, 1971), I, ch. 10; Harold M. Hyman, *A More Perfect Union* (New York: Knopf, 1973), ch. 27; and Stanley L. Kutler, *Judicial Power and Reconstruction Politics* (Chicago: University of Chicago Press, 1968).

(5) **Query:** To what extent can Congress frustrate judicial review by granting federal courts jurisdiction to enforce statutes but at the same time denying them authority to determine the constitutionality of those statutes? During World War II, the Emergency Price Control Act provided for criminal prosecutions in federal district courts but limited jurisdiction to hear attacks on the constitutionality of price control regulations to a special tribunal, the Emergency Court of Appeals, staffed by three federal judges serving during good behavior. The Supreme Court could review by certiorari. In Yakus v. United States (1944) the Court sustained this arrangement. The majority opinion, written by Chief Justice Stone, said:

> There is no constitutional requirement that that test [of constitutionality] be made in one tribunal rather than in another, so long as there is opportunity to be heard and for judicial review which satisfies the demands of due process, as is the case here.

Dissenting for himself and Justice Murphy, Rutledge protested:

> It is one thing for Congress to withhold jurisdiction. It is entirely another to confer it and direct that it be exercised in a manner inconsistent with constitutional requirements or ... without regard to them. Once it is held that Congress can require the courts criminally to enforce unconstitutional laws or statutes ... or to do so without regard to their validity, the way will have been found to circumvent the supreme law and, what is more, to make the courts parties to doing so. This Congress cannot do.

Rutledge continued:

> There are limits to the judicial power. Congress may impose others. And in some matters Congress or the President has final say under

the Constitution. But whenever the judicial power is called into play, it is responsible directly to the fundamental law and no other authority can intervene to force or authorize the judicial body to disregard it. The problem therefore is not solely one of individual right or due process of law. It is equally one of the separation of the powers of government and of the constitutional integrity of the judicial process, more especially in criminal trials.

Yakus, like *McCardle,* was decided in the midst of crisis; and Stone's opinion, like Chase's, indicated the justices were well aware of the troubled times in which they were living. "The Constitution as a continuously operative charter of government does not," Stone wrote, "demand the impossible or the impracticable."

"I believe that the Senators are entitled to know how you feel. ..."

HEARINGS ON THE NOMINATION OF WILLIAM J. BRENNAN, JR., TO BE AN ASSOCIATE JUSTICE OF THE U.S. SUPREME COURT*

In September 1956, during the middle of that year's presidential campaign, Justice Sherman Minton announced his retirement. As his successor, President Dwight D. Eisenhower chose William J. Brennan, Jr.; and because the Senate was not in session, the President, as the plain words of Article II, § 3 of the constitutional text authorize, gave Brennan a recess appointment that would expire at the close of the next session of Congress. He immediately took his place on the Court and began participating in decision making. As soon as Congress reconvened in January 1957, the President sent Brennan's nomination to the Senate for its advice and consent on his appointment during "good behavior." The Committee on the Judiciary then conducted its hearings.

SENATOR JOSEPH McCARTHY OF WISCONSIN. ... On the basis of that part of his record that I am familiar with, I believe that Justice Brennan has demonstrated an underlying hostility to congressional attempts to expose the Communist conspiracy.

I can only conclude that his decisions on the Supreme Court are likely to harm our efforts to fight communism. I shall, therefore, vote against his confirmation unless he is able to persuade me today that I am not in possession of the true facts with respect to his views.

I shall want to know if it is true that Justice Brennan, in his public speeches, has referred to congressional investigations of communism, for example, as "Salem witch hunts," and "inquisitions," and has accused

---

Hearings before the Committee on the Judiciary, U.S. Senate, on the Nomination of William J. Brennan, Jr., to be an Associate Justice of the U.S. Supreme Court, 85th Cong. 1st Sess., pp. 5, 17–22, 34.

congressional investigating committees of "barbarism." I have evidence that he has done so. ...

I would like to ask Mr. Brennan a few questions if I may. ... Do you approve of congressional investigations and exposure of the Communist conspiracy set up?

MR. BRENNAN. Not only do I approve, Senator, but personally I cannot think of a more vital function of the Congress than the investigatory function of its committees, and I can't think of a more important or vital objective of any committee investigation than that of rooting out subversives in Government.

SENATOR MCCARTHY. You, of course, I assume, will agree with me—and a number of the members of the committee—that communism is not merely a political way of life, it is a conspiracy designed to overthrow the United States Government.

MR. BRENNAN. Will you forgive me an embarrassment, Senator. You appreciate that I am a sitting Justice of the Court. There are presently pending before the Court some cases in which I believe will have to be decided the question what is communism, at least in the frame of reference in which those particular cases have come before the Court. I know, too, that you appreciate that having taken an oath of office it is my obligation not to discuss any of those pending matters. With that qualification, whether under the label communism or any other label, any conspiracy to overthrow the Government of the United States is a conspiracy that I not only would do anything appropriate to aid suppressing, but a conspiracy which, of course, like every American, I abhor.

SENATOR MCCARTHY. Mr. Brennan, I don't want to press you unnecessarily, but the question was simple. You have not been confirmed yet as a member of the Supreme Court. There will come before that Court a number of questions involving the all-important issue of whether or not communism is merely a political party or whether it represents a conspiracy to overthrow this Government.

I believe that the Senators are entitled to know how you feel about that and you won't be prejudicing then any cases by answering that question.

MR. BRENNAN. Well, let me answer it, try to answer it, this way, Senator. Of course, my nomination is now before the Senate for consideration, nevertheless since October 16 I have in fact been sitting as a member of the Court. The oath I took, I took as unreservedly as I know you took your own, and as I know every Senator took his. And I know, too, that your oath imposes upon you the obligation to ask just such questions as these. But I am in the position of having an oath of my own by which I have to guide my conduct and that oath obligates me not to discuss any matter presently pending before the Court. ...

SENATOR MCCARTHY. Mr. Brennan, we are asked to either vote to confirm or reject you. One of the things I have maintained is that you have adopted the gobbledegook that communism is merely a political party, it is not a conspiracy. The Supreme Court has held that it is a conspiracy to overthrow the Government of this country. I am merely asking you a very simple question. It doesn't relate to any lawsuit pending before the Supreme Court. Let me repeat it. Do you consider communism merely as a political party or do you consider it as a conspiracy to overthrow this country?

MR. BRENNAN. I can only answer, Senator, that believe me there are cases now pending in which the contention is made, at least in the frame of reference in which the case comes to the Court, that the definitions which have been given by the Congress to communism do not fit the particular circumstances. ...

SENATOR MCCARTHY. You know that the Congress has defined communism as a conspiracy. You are aware of that, aren't you?

MR. BRENNAN. I know the Congress has enacted a definition, yes, sir.

SENATOR MCCARTHY. And I think it is important before we vote on your confirmation that we know whether you agree with that?

MR. BRENNAN. You see, Senator, that is my difficulty, that I can't very well say more to you than that there are contending positions taken in given cases before us. ...

SENATOR MCCARTHY. ... This is all important, I would like to know whether or not the young man who is proposed for the Supreme Court feels that communism is a conspiracy or merely a political party. Now just so you won't be in the dark about my reason for asking that, the *Daily Worker*, all of the Communist-lip papers, and the Communist witnesses who have appeared before my committee, I assume the same is true of Senator Eastland's committee, have taken the position that it is merely a political party. I want to know whether you agree with that. That will affect your decision. It will affect my decision on how to vote on your confirmation. I hope it will affect the decision of other Senators.

MR. BRENNAN. Senator, believe me I appreciate that what to one man is the path of duty may to another man be the path of folly, but I simply cannot venture any comment whatever that touches upon any matter pending before the Court.

SENATOR MCCARTHY. Mr. Brennan, I am not asking you to touch upon anything pending before the Court. I am asking you the general question: Do you consider communism merely as a political party or do you consider it as a conspiracy to overthrow this country? ...

MR. BRENNAN. Senator, I cannot answer, I am sorry to say, beyond what I have. ...

SENATOR O'MAHONEY. Just let me clarify this. The Senator from Wisconsin has made it perfectly clear, as I understand it, that he is not asking the Justice to make any statement with respect to a pending case.

Therefore, the oath of office that the Justice may have taken is not involved.

SENATOR McCARTHY. Right.

SENATOR O'MAHONEY. There is now pending before the Senate a resolution, sent here by the executive branch of the Government, by the President of the United States, who appeared before us in a joint session of Congress in which he asked Congress to pass a resolution authorizing him to employ the Armed Forces of the United States in the defense of any nation in the Middle East, undescribed though the Middle East was in the resolution, at the request of any nation there, which was being attacked by international communism. Now the question I think that is in the mind of the Senator from Wisconsin is the question which I think has already been settled and on which you must have clear views. Do you believe that international communism is a conspiracy against the United States as well as against all other free nations?

MR. BRENNAN. Yes, that question I answer definitely and affirmatively. I did not understand that was the question the Senator was asking me. ...

SENATOR JENNER. May I interrupt right there? Does the Senator from Wyoming and does the Senator from Wisconsin draw a distinction between international communism and communism?

SENATOR O'MAHONEY. I don't.

SENATOR McCARTHY. I don't draw a distinction.

SENATOR JENNER. I would like to know Mr. Justice Brennan's answer to that. Do you draw a distinction between international communism and communism?

MR. BRENNAN. Let me put it this way, Senator. This is the difficulty. There are cases where, as I recall it, the particular issue is whether membership, what is membership, and whether if there is membership, does that come within the purview of the congressional statutes aimed at the conspiracy? I can't necessarily comment on those aspects because they are actual issues before the Court under the congressional legislation.

SENATOR JENNER. That is why it raises a question in my mind. In other words, if we have a Communist Party in the United States and the congressional committee has ascertained that it is hooked up with international communism, yet the domestic party might contend they are just national Communists, would that influence your thinking?

MR. BRENNAN. Nothing would influence my thinking. All I am trying to get across is that I do have an obligation not to discuss any issues that are touched upon in cases before the Court.

SENATOR JENNER. I think in the question that Senator O'Mahoney placed—read the question, will you, please, Mr. Reporter, and the answer?

(Question and answer read.)

SENATOR JENNER. Delete the word "international" and just leave in the word "communism," what would be your answer?

MR. BRENNAN. Of course, I accept the findings as they have been made by the Congress. The only thing I am trying to do, Senator, is to make certain that nothing I say touches upon the actual issues before us growing out of that legislation as applied in particular cases. ...

SENATOR JENNER. My question, Mr. Chairman, was not based on cases pending. My question was in a similar vein. In view of that would you answer the question?

MR. BRENNAN. The answer is "Yes." I'm sorry to have confused the gentlemen.

THE CHAIRMAN. Senator McCarthy, you may proceed.

SENATOR MCCARTHY. Let's see if we finally have the answer to this, Mr. Justice. You do agree that communism, striking the word "international" from it, communism does constitute a conspiracy against the United States—I am not talking about any case pending.

MR. BRENNAN. Yes.

SENATOR MCCARTHY. Thank you. ...

SENATOR O'MAHONEY. Mr. Chairman, let me address the question to the nominee, Associate Justice Brennan. I read it again from the statement filed with this committee under date of February 26, 1957, by Mr. Charles Smith.

> You are bound by your religion to follow the pronouncements of the Pope on all matters of faith and morals. There may be some controversies which involve matters of faith and morals and also matters of law and justice. But in matters of law and justice, you are bound by your oath to follow not papal decrees and doctrines, but the laws and precedents of this Nation. If you should be faced with such a mixed issue, would you be able to follow the requirements of your oath or would you be bound by your religious obligations?

MR. BRENNAN. Senator, I think the oath that I took is the same one that you and all of the Congress, every member of the executive department up and down all levels of government take to support the Constitution and laws of the United States. I took that oath just as unreservedly as I know you did, and every member and everyone else of our faith in whatever office elected or appointive he may hold. And I say not that I recognize that there is any obligation superior to that, rather that there isn't any obligation of our faith superior to that. And my answer to the question is categorically that in everything I have ever done, in every office I have held in my life or that I shall ever do in the future, what shall control me is the oath that I took to support the Constitution and laws of the United States and so act upon the cases that come before me for decision that it is that oath and that alone which governs. ...

Editors' Notes

(1) **Query:** To fulfill their constitutionally imposed duty to "advise and consent" (or not consent) to presidential nominations, senators must have authority to elicit enough information from a judicial nominee to make a judgment about his or her fitness for office. On the other hand, for a judicial nominee to explain how he or she would vote in a particular case would undermine the integrity of the judiciary. What, if any, are the *constitutional* limits on the sorts of questions that senator may ask a nominee? Are senators *constitutionally* restricted to asking questions about personal integrity and professional competence, or do judgments about "fitness" for the bench necessarily include matters of general jurisprudential orientation? How does one draw a line between "general jurisprudential orientation" and how a judge might vote in a particular case?

(2) At her hearings in 1993, Judge Ruth Bader Ginsburg began by reiterating Justice Brennan's point that she could not speak about issues before the Court or very likely soon to appear on its docket. As soon, however, as the question of the constitutional status of abortion was raised, she informed the senators of her view that women had a constitutional right to choose such an option.

(3) The hearings in 1987 on the nomination of Judge Robert H. Bork, thought by many to epitomize "Reagan jurisprudence," to be an associate justice of the Supreme Court dramatized the problems. The judge took on his senatorial interrogators in lengthy intellectual debates about constitutional interpretation. Outside the committee room, the White House staff lobbied busily, if ineffectively, to win support for the Judge, while interest groups associated with liberal causes were lobbying even more busily, and far more effectively, to ruin the Judge's chances—thereby creating a new synonym for "to destroy": To Bork. In the end, by a vote of 58–42, the Senate voted not to consent. The 6,511 pages of testimony and documents are collected in: *Hearings: Nomination of Robert H. Bork to be Associate Justice of the Supreme Court of the United States*, 100th Cong., 1st sess. (1987). For Bork's bitter comments on his fate, see his *The Tempting of America: The Political Seduction of the Law* (New York: The Free Press, 1990), espec. Part III. For sympathetic accounts of the campaign "to Bork" Bork, see Michael Pertschuk and Wendy Schaetzel, *The People Rising: The Campaign Against the Bork Nomination* (New York: Thunder Mouth's Press, 1989). For an effort to present a more even-handed assessment, see Ethan Bronner, *Battle for Justice: How the Bork Nomination Shook America* (New York: Norton, 1989).

(4) **Query:** Since Bork's defeat, the hearings on nominees for the Supreme Court have been less of a circus, though the charges of sexual harassment leveled against Clarence Thomas in 1991 added an element of salaciousness not previously present. For a general lamentation about the process, see Stephen L. Carter, *The Confirmation Mess: Cleaning Up the Federal Appointments Process* (New York: Basic Books, 1994). Whatever tinkering can be done with the process, did adoption in 1913 of the Seventeeth Amendment providing for the popular election of senators make it very

likely, perhaps inevitable, that confirmation of judges would become partisan political issues? If the answer is yes, how can one reconcile constitutionalist and democratic theory?

(5) Soon after confirmation, Brennan joined in several rulings, most notably Watkins v. United States (1957), restricting the power of Congress to investigate, and others, especially Yates v. United States (1957; reprinted below, p. 666), curtailing congressional efforts to outlaw domestic communism.

(6) Eisenhower also had given recess appointments to Earl Warren as Chief Justice and Potter Stewart. In each instance, having to sit for some months before being confirmed caused embarrassment for the justices and at least some senators. See the staff study of the House Committee on the Judiciary, *Recess Appointment of Federal Judges,* 86th Cong., 1st Sess. (1959). In 1960, the Senate passed S.Res. 334, stating that it was the sense of the Senate that the President should not make recess appointments to the Supreme Court except to prevent or end a breakdown in the administration of the Court's business. The vote, 48–37, was strictly along party lines, not surprising considering that the Senate was controlled by the Democrats and Eisenhower was a Republican.

(7) In 1984, a panel of the Court of Appeals for the Ninth Circuit (courts of appeals normally sit in panels of three judges to review decisions of district courts) vacated a federal conviction resulting from a trial conducted by a judge who had a recess appointment. The court reasoned that a judge whose confirmation was pending would "scarcely be oblivious to the effect his decision may have on the vote of those officials," and Article III requires federal judicial power be exercised only by judges who were truly independent, that is, serving during good behavior. Woodley v. United States. On rehearing, the full Court of Appeals, sitting en banc, reversed the panel and reinstated the conviction. United States v. Woodley (1985). Woodley did not seek certiorari from the Supreme Court.

(8) *Woodley* raises very important issues of constitutional interpretation. First, the panel's opinion questions the validity of decisions in which Brennan and Warren may have played significant roles before their confirmations—for Warren the School Segregation Cases (1954; reprinted below, p. 912) are the most obvious. Although he was confirmed before the decision was announced, he held a recess appointment during crucial stages of decision making. Second, although the panel's opinion in *Woodley* did not explicitly say so, it must be logically based on a conception of "the Constitution" as including a hierarchy of values. That is, the *panel*—though not the full Court of Appeals—held, in effect, that a specific clause authorizing the President to make recess appointments must give way to the higher value of an independent judiciary, even though the document does not explicitly state that value and does explicitly authorize recess appointments.

———

IV. INSTITUTIONAL INTERACTIONS IN A SYSTEM OF SHARED POWERS

"[W]e must weigh the importance of the general privilege of confidentiality of presidential communications ... against the inroads of such a privilege on the fair administration of criminal justice."

UNITED STATES v. NIXON

418 U.S. 683, 94 S.Ct. 3090, 41 L.Ed.2d 1039 (1974).

This case, dealing with a President's claim to executive privilege pitted against criminal defendants' claims to need tapes in his possession to defend themselves at a criminal trial, is reprinted above at p. 323.

" 'I deem it an imperative duty to maintain the supremacy of that sacred instrument (the Constitution) and the immunities of the Department entrusted to my care.' "

A PRESIDENTIAL LEGAL OPINION*

Robert H. Jackson.

... [It] is extraordinary for the President to render a legal opinion to the Attorney General. The occasion for this unusual procedure was a provision of the Lend–Lease Act which the President thought constitutionally objectionable but politically necessary. It reads:

> After June 30, 1943, or after the passage of a concurrent resolution of the two Houses before June 30, 1943, which declares that the powers conferred by or pursuant to subsection (a) are no longer necessary to promote the defense of the United States, neither the President nor the head of any department or agency shall exercise any of the powers conferred by or pursuant to subsection (a).

The Bill drafted by joint efforts of several executive departments and proposed by the President contained no such provision. I do not recall ... whether during the congressional consideration the President personally agreed to it. Mr. [Edward R.] Stettinius mentions it, however, as an amendment that administration forces in Congress accepted as not damaging to the essential principles of the Bill and designed to meet criticism from the opposition that the Bill gave too much power to the Executive. As thus passed, the President approved it on March 11, 1941. Two days later Senator Murdock, who had argued in debate that

---

* 66 *Harvard Law Review* 1353–1361 (1953). Reprinted with permission of the Harvard Law Review Association.

Robert H. Jackson was an Associate Justice of the United States Supreme Court (1941–54); he had served as Attorney General before going to the Court.

the provision was unconstitutional, wrote to the President recounting objections to the provision. The President discussed with me his concern about it and later sent me the following note:

> The White House
> March 17, 1941

Memorandum for the Attorney General:

> I should like to file with the Attorney General an official memorandum placing me on record in regard to that provision of the Lend–Lease Bill which seeks to repeal legislation by concurrent resolution of the two houses of Congress.

> Would you try your hand at drafting such a memorandum? I should say in it, of course, that the emergency was so great that I signed the bill in spite of a clearly unconstitutional provision contained in it.

> I enclose letter from Senator Murdock, together with marked passages relating to the debate and relating to legislative rules and precedents.

F.D.R.

This reached me the day before I was to leave Washington as a guest of the President, who, weary from the Lend–Lease battle, had arranged a fishing trip to the Bahamas. I passed the memorandum and letter to Alexander Holtzoff, Special Assistant to the Attorney General, to formulate the statement requested. While we were at sea, Congress passed the bill making appropriations to carry Lend–Lease into execution. ... This event brought about renewed discussion of the obnoxious clause of the Lend–Lease Act. It did no immediate harm. ... I really regarded the question as interesting but rather academic.

But the President feared the long-range effect of the precedent. Obviously it was a device to evade the veto which the Constitution gave to the President. It enabled a bare majority of a quorum in each of the two Houses to terminate his powers. But for the provision, they could not be cut off before the fixed date of expiration except by passing a repealing Act, which would be subject to veto. He could thus preserve his powers, unless two-thirds of each House voted to override his veto. The scheme of the Act ... took this powerful weapon away from the Executive. And the President was impressed by the question which Senator Murdock asked in the debates: "could we not attach the same clause, or a similar clause, to every piece of legislation which leaves the Congress, and by so doing destroy the veto power of the President?" It was a stratagem, as the President pointed out, never useful to the administration but only useful to increase the leverage of the opposition.

But was it unconstitutional? That was a different question. ... The question on which my doubts were not fully satisfied never bothered the President in the least. It seemed to me to depend on whether the provision was to be considered as a reservation or limitation by which the granted power would expire or terminate on the contingency of a concurrent resolution or was to be regarded as authorizing a repeal by concurrent resolution. Senator Connally, in support of the President on the Lend–Lease Bill, had argued:

> If we may terminate this bill by its terms on June 30, 1943, then we may terminate it upon any other happening or any other event which may transpire in the future.

> The reason for that is that it is in the act itself; it is a limitation upon the length of time and the length of operation of the act itself, and in no sense a repeal or modification of an existing act. The provision is written in the heart of the measure that the bill shall not last longer than June 30, 1943, and, prior to that date, it shall not last beyond any time after the Congress shall pass a concurrent resolution.

> . . . [T]he Supreme Court of the United States has held that Congress in enacting legislation has the right to hinge its operation either upon some antecedent event or upon some subsequent event, and that upon the happening of that event, such as a proclamation by the President, if that is provided in the law, the act shall either terminate or shall become operative, as the case may be, as provided in the legislation.

The President, however, invariably referred to the offending procedure as a repeal. His reasoning was that so well put on the floor by Senator Murdock:

> When you bring the measure back to the Congress and invoke the legislative will to terminate legislation, in my opinion you violate the Constitution, unless you follow the procedure set forth in the Constitution.

Then why should the President not say so, publicly and at once, by a press release, a speech, or in answer to a question planted at press conference? . . . The reason was political. His views, strangely enough, were those used by the opponents of the Lend–Lease Bill, some of whom were his consistent political enemies, to justify their opposition to the Bill. They argued that the device for recalling their grant of power was unconstitutional and therefore illusory. His loyal supporters, on the other hand, had argued that the provision was valid and therefore effective as a check on any runaway executive action. For the President to make public his views at that time would confirm and delight his opposition and let down his friends. It might seriously alienate some of his congressional support at a time when he would need to call on it frequently. It would also strengthen fear in the country that he was seeking to increase his personal power.

Why, then, not drop the matter entirely? He had to reckon on the possibility, even if remote, of an attempt to invoke the provision. If he then challenged its constitutionality, he would be confronted with his own signature to the Act he was contesting. Therefore, he wanted a record that his constitutional scruples did not arise only after the shoe began to pinch, and, so far as possible, to excuse his approval and counteract its effect. He did not want the precedent created by his yielding to ripen into a custom which would impair the powers which properly appertained to his great office. Only a statement of his own could do that. ...

Returning to Washington on April 1, I received from Mr. Holtzoff the memorandum he had prepared. He, like the President, assumed—what seemed the debatable point—that concurrent resolutions under the provision would be the same as repealing legislation. But it stated faithfully the President's position, and that was what mattered and what was requested. I forwarded it to the President on April 3. Without further discussion with me and without change, he signed it on the date it bears. It reads:

THE WHITE HOUSE

WASHINGTON
April 7, 1941

MEMORANDUM FOR THE ATTORNEY GENERAL

On March 11, 1941, I attached my approval to the bill (H.R.1776) entitled "An Act to Promote the Defense of the United States." The bill was an outstanding measure which sought to meet a momentous emergency of great magnitude in world affairs. In view of this impelling consideration, I felt constrained to sign the measure, in spite of the fact that it contained a provision which, in my opinion, is clearly unconstitutional. I have reference to the clause of Section 3(c) of the Act, providing that after the passage of a concurrent resolution by the two Houses before June 30, 1943, which declares that the powers conferred by or pursuant to subsection (a) are no longer necessary to promote the defense of the United States, neither the President nor the head of any Department or agency shall exercise any of the powers conferred by or pursuant to subsection (a), with certain specified exceptions. In effect, this provision is an attempt by Congress to authorize a repeal by means of a concurrent resolution of the two Houses, of certain provisions of an Act of Congress.

The Constitution of the United States, Article I, Section 7, prescribes the mode in which laws shall be enacted. It provides that "Every bill which shall have passed the House of Representatives and the Senate, shall, before it become a law, be presented to the President of the United States; if he approves he shall sign it, but if not he shall return it, with his objections to that House in which it shall have originated." It is thereupon provided that if after reconsideration two-thirds of each House shall agree to pass the bill, it shall become law. The Constitution contains no provision whereby the Congress may legislate by concurrent resolution without the approval of the President. The only instance in which a bill may become law without the approval of the President is when the President vetoes a bill and it is then repassed by two-thirds vote in each House.

It is too clear for argument that action repealing an existing Act itself constitutes an Act of Congress and, therefore, is subject to the foregoing requirements. A repeal of existing provisions of law, in whole or in part, therefore, may not be accomplished by a concurrent resolution of the two Houses.

In order that I may be on record as indicating my opinion that the foregoing provision of the so-called Lend–Lease Act is unconstitutional, and in order that my approval of the bill, due to the existing exigencies of the world situation, may not be construed as a tacit acquiescence in any contrary view, I am requesting you to place this memorandum in the official files of the Department of Justice. I am desirous of having this done for the further reason that I should not wish my action in approving the bill which includes this invalid clause, to be used as a precedent for any future legislation comprising provisions of a similar nature.

In conclusion, I may refer to the following pertinent remarks of President Andrew Jackson: "I deem it an imperative duty to maintain the supremacy of that sacred instrument (the Constitution) and the immunities of the Department entrusted to my care."

/s/ Franklin D. Roosevelt

The following note, however, accompanied the return of the opinion to me:

THE WHITE HOUSE
WASHINGTON

April 7, 1941.

MEMORANDUM FOR

        THE ATTORNEY GENERAL

        I enclose herewith the formal
memorandum placing me on record
in regard to the unconstitutionality
of that provision of Section 3 (c)
of the Lend-Lease Act, Public No.
11, 77th Congress, which authorizes
repeal by a concurrent resolution
of the Congress.

        I think that this formal
memorandum from me to you should
be published some day as an official document, and I leave the
method thereof to your discretion.

                    F D R

[D7644]

It evidently was dictated by the President and, after the custom of
those days, his initials were typed at its end. These he had crossed out
and had signed the same initials in longhand. Then he struck those out
and signed his full name. Also, he penned in the salutation. ...

**"Explicit and unambiguous provisions of the Constitu-
tion prescribe and define the respective functions of the
Congress and the President in the legislative process."—
Chief Justice BURGER**

**"On its face, the House's action appears clearly adjudica-
tory."—Justice POWELL**

"**[The legislative veto] is a necessary check on the unavoidably expanding power of the agencies, both executive and independent, as they engage in exercising authority delegated by Congress.**"—**Justice WHITE**

IMMIGRATION AND NATURALIZATION SERVICE v. CHADHA

462 U.S. 919, 103 S.Ct. 2764, 77 L.Ed.2d 317 (1983).

Jagdish Rai Chadha came to the United States in 1966 on a student visa, which expired in 1972. The Immigration and Naturalization Service (INS) began proceedings to deport him. After hearings, the attorney general recommended Chadha not be deported and his status changed to permanent resident alien. Under § 244(c)(2) of the Immigration and Nationality Act, either house of Congress could veto such recommendations:

[I]f [within a specified time after the attorney general's recommenda-
tion] . . . either the Senate or the House of Representatives passes a
resolution stating . . . that it does not favor the suspension of such
deportation, the Attorney General shall deport such alien. . . . If . . .
neither the Senate nor the House of Representatives shall pass such
a resolution, the Attorney General shall cancel deportation proceedings.

In 1975, within the time allowed by the Act, the House voted to reject the attorney general's recommendation and to deport Chadha and five other aliens. Chadha exhausted his administrative remedies by contesting (and losing) the order within INS and appealed to the U.S. Court of Appeals for the Ninth Circuit. That court invited the Senate and House to intervene as *amici curiae*, then ruled that the House had violated the concept of separation of powers. INS appealed to the Supreme Court.

Chief Justice **BURGER** delivered the opinion of the Court. . . .

II . . .

G. Political Question

. . . It is argued that Congress' Article I power "To establish an uniform Rule of Naturalization," combined with the Necessary and Proper Clause, grants it unreviewable authority over the regulation of aliens. The plenary authority of Congress over aliens under Art. I, § 8, cl. 4 is not open to question, but what is challenged here is whether Congress has chosen a constitutionally permissible means of implement-ing that power. As we made clear in Buckley v. Valeo (1976); "Con-gress has plenary authority in all cases in which it has substantive legislative jurisdiction, McCulloch v. Maryland (1819), so long as the exercise of that authority does not offend some other constitutional restriction."

... As identified in Baker v. Carr (1962), a political question may arise when any one of the following circumstances is present:

> a textually demonstrable constitutional commitment of the issue to a coordinate political department; or a lack of judicially discoverable and manageable standards for resolving it; or the impossibility of deciding without an initial policy determination of a kind clearly for nonjudicial discretion; or the impossibility of a court's undertaking independent resolution without expressing lack of the respect due coordinate branches of government; or an unusual need for unquestioning adherence to a political decision already made; or the potentiality of embarrassment from multifarious pronouncements by various departments on one question.

Congress apparently directs its assertion of nonjusticiability to the first of the *Baker* factors by asserting that Chadha's claim is "an assault on the legislative authority to enact Section 244(c)(2)." But if this turns the question into a political question virtually every challenge to the constitutionality of a statute would be a political question. Chadha indeed argues that one House of Congress cannot constitutionally veto the Attorney General's decision to allow him to remain in this country. No policy underlying the political question doctrine suggests that Congress or the Executive, or both acting in concert and in compliance with Art. I, can decide the constitutionality of a statute; that is a decision for the courts.[1]

Other *Baker* factors are likewise inapplicable to this case. ... Art. I provides the "judicially discoverable and manageable standards" of *Baker* for resolving the question presented by this case ... and ... there is no possibility of "multifarious pronouncements" on this question.

It is correct that this controversy may, in a sense, be termed "political." But the presence of constitutional issues with significant political overtones does not automatically invoke the political question doctrine. ... Resolution of litigation challenging the constitutional authority of one of the three branches cannot be evaded by courts because the issues have political implications in the sense urged by Congress. *Marbury* was also a "political" case, involving as it did claims under a judicial commission alleged to have been duly signed by the President but not delivered. But "courts cannot reject as 'no law suit' a bona fide controversy as to whether some action denominated 'political' exceeds constitutional authority." *Baker..* ...

---

1. The suggestion is made that § 244(c)(2) is somehow immunized from constitutional scrutiny because the Act containing § 244(c)(2) was passed by Congress and approved by the President. Marbury v. Madison (1803), resolved that question. The assent of the Executive to a bill which contains a provision contrary to the Constitution does not shield it from judicial review. See Smith v. Maryland (1979); National League of Cities v. Usery (1976); Buckley v. Valeo (1976); Myers v. United States (1926). In any event, eleven Presidents, from Mr. Wilson through Mr. Reagan, who have been presented with this issue have gone on record at some point to challenge Congressional vetoes as unconstitutional. ... Furthermore, it is not uncommon for Presidents to approve legislation containing parts which are objectionable on constitutional grounds. ... [Footnote by the Court.]

III

A. Structure of the Constitution

... We begin, of course, with the presumption that the challenged statute is valid. Its wisdom is not the concern of the courts. ... By the same token, the fact that a given law or procedure is efficient, convenient, and useful in facilitating functions of government, standing alone, will not save it if it is contrary to the Constitution. Convenience and efficiency are not the primary objectives—or the hallmarks—of democratic government and our inquiry is sharpened rather than blunted by the fact that Congressional veto provisions are appearing with increasing frequency in statutes which delegate authority to executive and independent agencies. ...

Justice White undertakes to make a case for the proposition that the one-House veto is a useful "political invention," and we need not challenge that assertion. ... But policy arguments supporting even useful "political inventions" are subject to the demands of the Constitution. ...

Explicit and unambiguous provisions of the Constitution prescribe and define the respective functions of the Congress and of the Executive in the legislative process. ... Art. I provides:

> All legislative Powers herein granted shall be vested in a Congress of the United States, which shall consist of a Senate *and* a House of Representatives.

> Every Bill which shall have passed the House of Representatives *and* the Senate, *shall*, before it become a Law, be presented to the President of the United States; ...

> *Every* Order, Resolution, or Vote to which the Concurrence of the Senate and House of Representatives may be necessary (except on a question of Adjournment) *shall be* presented to the President of the United States; and before the Same shall take Effect, *shall be* approved by him, or being disapproved by him, *shall be* repassed by two thirds of the Senate and House of Representatives, according to the Rules and Limitations prescribed in the Case of a Bill. (Emphasis added.)

These provisions of Art. I are integral parts of the constitutional design for the separation of powers. ... Just as we relied on the textual provision of Art. II, § 2, cl. 2, to vindicate the principle of separation of powers in *Buckley*, we find that the purposes underlying the Presentment Clauses and the bicameral requirement guide our resolution of the important question presented in this case. The very structure of the articles delegating and separating powers under Arts. I, II, and III exemplify the concept of separation of powers, and we now turn to Art. I.

B. The Presentment Clauses

The records [*sic*] of the Constitutional Convention reveal that the requirement that all legislation be presented to the President before becoming law was uniformly accepted by the Framers. Presentment to the President and the Presidential veto were considered so imperative that the draftsmen took special pains to assure that these requirements could not be circumvented. During the final debate on Art. I, § 7, cl. 2, James Madison expressed concern that it might easily be evaded by the simple expedient of calling a proposed law a "resolution" or "vote" rather than a "bill." As a consequence, Art. I, § 7, cl. 3, was added.

The decision to provide the President with a limited and qualified power to nullify proposed legislation by veto was based on the profound conviction of the Framers that the powers conferred on Congress were the powers to be most carefully circumscribed. It is beyond doubt that lawmaking was a power to be shared by both Houses and the President. . . .

The President's role in the lawmaking process also reflects the Framers' careful efforts to check whatever propensity a particular Congress might have to enact oppressive, improvident, or ill-considered measures. The President's veto role in the legislative process was described later during public debate on ratification:

> It establishes a salutary check upon the legislative body, calculated to guard the community against the effects of faction, precipitancy, or of any impulse unfriendly to the public good which may happen to influence a majority of that body. . . . The primary inducement to conferring the power in question upon the Executive is to enable him to defend himself; the secondary one is to increase the chances in favor of the community against the passing of bad laws through haste, inadvertence, or design. *The Federalist* No. 73.

The Court also has observed that the Presentment Clauses serve the important purpose of assuring that a "national" perspective is grafted on the legislative process:

> The President is a representative of the people just as the members of the Senate and of the House are, and it may be, at some times, on some subjects, that the President elected by all the people is rather more representative of them all than are the members of either body of the Legislature whose constituencies are local and not countrywide. . . . *Myers.*

C. Bicameralism

The bicameral requirement of Art. I, §§ 1, 7 was of scarcely less concern to the Framers than was the Presidential veto and indeed the two concepts are interdependent. By providing that no law could take effect without the concurrence of the prescribed majority of the Members of both Houses, the Framers reemphasized their belief . . . that legislation should not be enacted unless it has been carefully and fully considered by the Nation's elected officials. In the Constitutional Convention debates on the need for a bicameral legislature, James Wilson, later to become a Justice of this Court, commented:

> Despotism comes on mankind in different shapes. Sometimes in an Executive, sometimes in a military, one. Is there danger of a Legislative despotism? Theory & practice both proclaim it. If the Legislative

authority be not restrained, there can be neither liberty nor stability; and it can only be restrained by dividing it within itself, into distinct and independent branches. In a single house there is no check, but the inadequate one, of the virtue & good sense of those who compose it. ...

... The President's participation in the legislative process was to protect the Executive Branch from Congress and to protect the whole people from improvident laws. The division of the Congress into two distinctive bodies assures that the legislative power would be exercised only after opportunity for full study and debate in separate settings. The President's unilateral veto power, in turn, was limited by the power of two thirds of both Houses of Congress to overrule a veto thereby precluding final arbitrary action of one person. It emerges clearly that the prescription for legislative action in Art. I, §§ 1, 7 represents the Framers' decision that the legislative power of the Federal government be exercised in accord with a single, finely wrought and exhaustively considered, procedure.

IV ...

Although not "hermetically" sealed from one another, *Buckley,* the powers delegated to the three Branches are functionally identifiable. When any Branch acts, it is presumptively exercising the power the Constitution has delegated to it. See Hampton & Co. v. United States (1928). ... Beginning with this presumption, we must nevertheless establish that the challenged action under § 244(c)(2) is of the kind to which the procedural requirements of Art. I, § 7 apply. ...

... Whether actions taken by either House are, in law and fact, an exercise of legislative power depends not on their form but upon "whether they contain matter which is properly to be regarded as legislative in its character and effect." Examination of the action taken here by one House pursuant to § 244(c)(2) reveals that it was essentially legislative. ... The one-House veto operated in this case to overrule the Attorney General and mandate Chadha's deportation; absent the House action, Chadha would remain in the United States. Congress has *acted* and its action has altered Chadha's status.

The legislative character of the one-House veto in this case is confirmed by the character of the Congressional action it supplants. ... Without the challenged provision in § 244(c)(2), this [deportation] could have been achieved, if at all, only by legislation requiring deportation. Similarly, a veto by one House of Congress under § 244(c)(2) cannot be justified as an attempt at amending the standards set out in § 244(a)(1), or as a repeal of § 244 as applied to Chadha. Amendment and repeal of statutes, no less than enactment, must conform with Art. I.

... [W]hen the Framers intended to authorize either House of Congress to act alone and outside of its prescribed bicameral legislative role, they narrowly and precisely defined the procedure for such action. There are but four provisions in the Constitution, explicit and unambiguous, by which one House may act alone with the unreviewable force of law, not subject to the President's veto:

(a) The House of Representatives alone was given the power to initiate impeachments. Art. I, § 2, cl. 6;

(b) The Senate alone was given the power to conduct trials following impeachment on charges initiated by the House and to convict following trial. Art. I, § 3, cl. 5;

(c) The Senate alone was given final unreviewable power to approve or to disapprove presidential appointments. Art. II, § 2, cl. 2;

(d) The Senate alone was given unreviewable power to ratify treaties negotiated by the President. Art. II, § 2, cl. 2.

Clearly, when the Draftsmen sought to confer special powers on one House, independent of the other House, or of the President, they did so in explicit, unambiguous terms. ... [2] These exceptions are narrow, explicit, and separately justified; none of them authorize the action challenged here. On the contrary, they provide further support for the conclusion that Congressional authority is not to be implied and for the conclusion that the veto provided for in § 244(c)(2) is not authorized by the constitutional design of the powers of the Legislative Branch. ...

Affirmed.

Justice **POWELL** concurring in the judgment. ...

The Framers perceived that "[t]he accumulation of all powers legislative, executive and judiciary in the same hands, whether of one, a few or many, and whether hereditary, self appointed, or elective, may justly be pronounced the very definition of tyranny." The *Federalist* No. 47. Theirs was not a baseless fear. Under British rule, the colonies suffered the abuses of unchecked executive power that were attributed, at least popularly, to an hereditary monarchy. ... During the Confederation, the States reacted by removing power from the executive and placing it in the hands of elected legislators. But many legislators proved to be little better than the Crown. ...

One abuse that was prevalent during the Confederation was the exercise of judicial power by the state legislatures. The Framers were well acquainted with the danger of subjecting the determination of the rights of one person to the "tyranny of shifting majorities." ...

---

2. An exception from the Presentment Clauses was ratified in Hollingsworth v. Virginia (1798). There the Court held presidential approval was unnecessary for a proposed constitutional amendment which had passed both Houses of Congress by the requisite two-thirds majority.

One might also include another "exception" to the rule that Congressional action having the force of law be subject to the bicameral requirement and the Presentment Clauses. Each House has the power to act alone in determining specified internal matters. Art. I, § 7, cl. 2, 3, and § 5, cl. 2. However, this "exception" only empowers Congress to bind itself and is noteworthy only insofar as it further indicates the Framers' intent that Congress not act in any legally binding manner outside a closely circumscribed legislative arena, except in specific and enumerated instances. ... [Footnote by the Court.]

It was to prevent the recurrence of such abuses that the Framers vested the executive, legislative, and judicial powers in separate branches. Their concern that a legislature should not be able unilaterally to impose a substantial deprivation on one person was expressed not only in this general allocation of power, but also in more specific provisions, such as the Bill of Attainder Clause, Art. I, § 9, cl. 3. As the Court recognized in United States v. Brown (1965), "the Bill of Attainder Clause was intended not as a narrow, technical ... prohibition, but rather as an implementation of the separation of powers, a general safeguard against legislative exercise of the judicial function, or more simply—trial by legislature." This Clause, and the separation of powers doctrine generally, reflect the Framers' concern that trial by a legislature lacks the safeguards necessary to prevent the abuse of power.

The Constitution does not establish three branches with precisely defined boundaries. Rather, as Justice Jackson wrote, "[w]hile the Constitution diffuses power the better to secure liberty, it also contemplates that practice will integrate the dispersed powers into a workable government. It enjoins upon its branches separateness but interdependence, autonomy but reciprocity." Youngstown Sheet & Tube Co. v. Sawyer (1952) (concurring opinion). The Court thus has been mindful that the boundaries between each branch should be fixed "according to common sense and the inherent necessities of the governmental coordination." J.W. Hampton, Jr. & Co. v. United States (1928). But where one branch has impaired or sought to assume a power central to another branch, the Court has not hesitated to enforce the doctrine. See *Buckley*.

Functionally, the doctrine may be violated in two ways. One branch may interfere impermissibly with the other's performance of its constitutionally assigned function. See Nixon v. Administrator of General Services (1977); United States v. Nixon (1974). Alternatively, the doctrine may be violated when one branch assumes a function that more properly is entrusted to another. See *Youngstown*; Springer v. Philippine Islands (1928). This case presents the latter situation. ...

On its face, the House's action appears clearly adjudicatory. The House did not enact a general rule; rather it made its own determination that six specific persons did not comply with certain statutory criteria. It thus undertook the type of decision that traditionally has been left to other branches. ... Where, as here, Congress has exercised a power "that cannot possibly be regarded as merely in aid of the legislative function of Congress," *Buckley,* the decisions of this Court have held that Congress impermissibly assumed a function that the Constitution entrusted to another branch, see *id.*; cf. *Springer*.

The impropriety of the House's assumption of this function is confirmed by the fact that its action raises the very danger the Framers sought to avoid—the exercise of unchecked power. In deciding whether Chadha deserves to be deported, Congress is not subject to any internal constraints that prevent it from arbitrarily depriving him of the right to remain in this country.   Unlike the judiciary or an administrative agency, Congress is not bound by established substantive rules.   Nor is it subject to the procedural safeguards, such as the right to counsel and a hearing before an impartial tribunal, that are present when a court or an agency adjudicates individual rights.   The only effective constraint on Congress' power is political, but Congress is most accountable politically when it prescribes rules of general applicability.   When it decides rights of specific persons, those rights are subject to "the tyranny of a shifting majority."

Chief Justice Marshall observed: "It is the peculiar province of the legislature to prescribe general rules for the government of society; the application of those rules would seem to be the duty of other departments."   Fletcher v. Peck (1810).   In my view, when Congress undertook to apply its rules to Chadha, it exceeded the scope of its constitutionally prescribed authority.   I would not reach the broader question whether legislative vetoes are invalid under the Presentment Clauses.

Justice **WHITE,** dissenting.   ...

I   ...

The prominence of the legislative veto mechanism in our contemporary political system and its importance to Congress can hardly be overstated.   It has become a central means by which Congress secures the accountability of executive and independent agencies.   Without the legislative veto, Congress is faced with a Hobson's choice: either to refrain from delegating the necessary authority, leaving itself with a hopeless task of writing laws with the requisite specificity to cover endless special circumstances across the entire policy landscape, or in the alternative, to abdicate its lawmaking function to the executive branch and independent agencies.   ... Accordingly, over the past five decades, the legislative veto has been placed in nearly 200 statutes.   ...

... [T]he legislative veto is more than "efficient, convenient, and useful."   It is an important if not indispensable political invention that allows the President and Congress to resolve major constitutional and policy differences, assures the accountability of independent regulatory agencies, and preserves Congress' control over lawmaking.   Perhaps there are other means of accommodation and accountability, but the increasing reliance of Congress upon the legislative veto suggests that the alternatives to which Congress must now turn are not entirely satisfactory.

The history of the legislative veto also makes clear that it has not been a sword with which Congress has struck out to aggrandize itself at the expense of the other branches—the concerns of Madison and Hamilton.   Rather, the veto has been a means of defense, a reservation of ultimate authority necessary if Congress is to fulfill its designated role under Article I as the nation's lawmaker.   While the President has often objected to particular legislative vetoes, generally those left in the hands of congressional committees, the Executive has more often agreed to legislative review as the price for a broad delegation of authority. To be sure, the President may have preferred unrestricted power, but that could be precisely why Congress thought it essential to retain a check on the exercise of delegated authority.

II

For all these reasons, the apparent sweep of the Court's decision today is regrettable. The Court's Article I analysis appears to invalidate all legislative vetoes irrespective of form or subject. ... Courts should always be wary of striking statutes as unconstitutional; to strike an entire class of statutes based on consideration of a somewhat atypical and more-readily indictable exemplar of the class is irresponsible. It was for cases such as this one that Justice Brandeis wrote:

> ... The Court will not "formulate a rule of constitutional law broader than is required by the precise facts to which it is to be applied." Ashwander v. Tennessee Valley Authority (1936) (concurring opinion).
> ...

If the legislative veto were as plainly unconstitutional as the Court strives to suggest, its broad ruling today would be more comprehensible. But, the constitutionality of the legislative veto is anything but clear cut. The issue divides scholars, courts, attorneys general, and the two other branches of the National Government. If the veto devices so flagrantly disregarded the requirements of Article I as the Court today suggests, I find it incomprehensible that Congress, whose members are bound by oath to uphold the Constitution, would have placed these mechanisms in nearly 200 separate laws over a period of 50 years.

... The Constitution does not directly authorize or prohibit the legislative veto. Thus, our task should be to determine whether the legislative veto is consistent with the purposes of Art. I and the principles of Separation of Powers which are reflected in that Article and throughout the Constitution. We should not find the lack of a specific constitutional authorization for the legislative veto surprising, and I would not infer disapproval of the mechanism from its absence. From the summer of 1787 to the present the government of the United States has become an endeavor far beyond the contemplation of the Framers. ... But the wisdom of the Framers was to anticipate that the nation would grow and new problems of governance would require different solutions. ...

... In my view, neither Article I of the Constitution nor the doctrine of separation of powers is violated by this mechanism by which our elected representatives preserve their voice in the governance of the nation.

III ...

... There is no question that a bill does not become a law until it is approved by both the House and the Senate, and presented to the

President.   ... I agree with the Court that the President's qualified veto power is a critical element in the distribution of powers under the Constitution.   ... I also agree that the bicameral approval required by Art. I, §§ 1, 7 "was of scarcely less concern to the Framers than was the Presidential veto," and that the need to divide and disperse legislative power figures significantly in our scheme of Government.   ...

It does not, however, answer the constitutional question before us. The power to exercise a legislative veto is not the power to write new law without bicameral approval or presidential consideration.   The veto must be authorized by statute and may only negative what an Executive department or independent agency has proposed.   On its face, the legislative veto no more allows one House of Congress to make law than does the presidential veto confer such power upon the President.   ...

... The Court's holding today that all legislative-type action must be enacted through the lawmaking process ignores that legislative authority is routinely delegated to the Executive branch, to the independent regulatory agencies, and to private individuals and groups.   ...

This Court's decisions sanctioning such delegations make clear that Article I does not require all action with the effect of legislation to be passed as a law.

Theoretically, agencies and officials were asked only to "fill up the details," and the rule was that "Congress cannot delegate any part of its legislative power except under a limitation of a prescribed standard." United States v. Chicago, Milwaukee R. Co. (1931).   ... In practice, however, restrictions on the scope of the power that could be delegated diminished and all but disappeared.   In only two instances did the Court find an unconstitutional delegation.   Panama Refining Co. v. Ryan (1935); Schechter Poultry Corp. v. United States (1935).   In other cases, the "intelligible principle" through which agencies have attained enormous control over the economic affairs of the country was held to include such formulations as "just and reasonable," Tagg Bros. & Moorhead v. United States (1930), "public interest," New York Central Securities Corp. v. United States (1932), "public convenience, interest, or necessity," Federal Radio Comm. v. Nelson Bros. Bond & Mortgage Co. (1933), and "unfair methods of competition."   FTC v. Gratz (1920).

... [T]hese cases establish that by virtue of congressional delegation, legislative power can be exercised by independent agencies and Executive departments without the passage of new legislation.   ...

If Congress may delegate lawmaking power to independent and executive agencies, it is most difficult to understand Article I as forbidding Congress from also reserving a check on legislative power for itself. Absent the veto, the agencies receiving delegations of legislative or quasi-legislative power may issue regulations having the force of law without bicameral approval and without the President's signature.   ...

Nor are there strict limits on the agents that may receive such delegations of legislative authority so that it might be said that the legislature can delegate authority to others but not to itself. While most authority to issue rules and regulations is given to the executive branch and the independent regulatory agencies, statutory delegations to private persons have also passed this Court's scrutiny. ... Currin v. Wallace (1939) ... United States v. Rock Royal Co-operative (1939). ... Assuming *Currin* and *Rock Royal Co-operative* remain sound law, the Court's decision today suggests that Congress may place a "veto" power over suspensions of deportation in private hands or in the hands of an independent agency, but is forbidden from reserving such authority for itself. ...

More fundamentally ... the Court concedes that certain administrative agency action, such as rulemaking, "may resemble lawmaking" and recognizes that "[t]his Court has referred to agency activity as being 'quasi-legislative' in character." ... Such rules and adjudications by the agencies meet the Court's own definition of legislative action for they "alter[ ]the legal rights, duties, and relations of persons ... outside the legislative branch," and involve "determinations of policy." Under the Court's analysis, the Executive Branch and the independent agencies may make rules with the effect of law while Congress, in whom the Framers confided the legislative power, Art. I, § 1, may not exercise a veto which precludes such rules from having operative force. ...

The Court also takes no account of perhaps the most relevant consideration: However resolutions of disapproval under § 244(c)(2) are formally characterized, in reality, a departure from the status quo occurs only upon the concurrence of opinion among the House, Senate, and President. Reservations of legislative authority to be exercised by Congress should be upheld if the exercise of such reserved authority is consistent with the distribution of and limits upon legislative power that Article I provides. ...

The central concern of the presentation and bicameralism requirements of Article I is that when a departure from the legal status quo is undertaken, it is done with the approval of the President and both Houses of Congress—or, in the event of a presidential veto, a two-thirds majority in both Houses. This interest is fully satisfied by the operation of § 244(c)(2). ...

IV

... It is true that the purpose of separating the authority of government is to prevent unnecessary and dangerous concentration of power in one branch. For that reason, the Framers saw fit to divide and balance the powers of government so that each branch would be checked by the others. ... But the history of the separation of powers doctrine is also a history of accommodation and practicality. Apprehensions of an overly powerful branch have not led to undue prophylactic measures that handicap the effective working of the national government as a whole. The Constitution does not contemplate total separation of the three branches of Government. *Buckley.* ...

Our decisions reflect this judgment. ... The separation of powers doctrine has heretofore led to the invalidation of government action only when the challenged action violated some express provision in the Constitution. ...

This is the teaching of Nixon v. Administrator of Gen. Servs. (1977), which ... set forth a framework for evaluating such claims:

> [I]n determining whether the Act disrupts the proper balance between the coordinate branches, the proper inquiry focuses on the extent to which it prevents the Executive Branch from accomplishing its constitutionally assigned functions. United States v. Nixon (1974). Only where the potential for disruption is present must we then determine whether that impact is justified by an overriding need to promote objectives within the constitutional authority of Congress.

Section 244(c)(2) survives this test. The legislative veto provision does not "prevent the Executive Branch from accomplishing its constitutionally assigned functions." First, it is clear that the Executive Branch has no "constitutionally assigned" function of suspending the deportation of aliens. " 'Over no conceivable subject is the legislative power of Congress more complete than it is over' the admission of aliens." Kleindiest v. Mandel (1972). Nor can it be said that the inherent function of the Executive Branch in executing the law is involved. ... Here, § 244 grants the executive only a qualified suspension authority and it is only that authority which the President is constitutionally authorized to execute.

Moreover, the Court believes that the legislative veto we consider today is best characterized as an exercise of legislative or quasi-legislative authority. Under this characterization, the practice does not, even on the surface, constitute an infringement of executive or judicial prerogative. The Attorney General's suspension of deportation is equivalent to a proposal for legislation. ... So understood, congressional review does not undermine ... the "weight and dignity" that attends the decisions of the Executive Branch.

Nor does § 244 infringe on the judicial power, as Justice Powell would hold. Section 244 makes clear that Congress has reserved its own judgment as part of the statutory process. Congressional action does not substitute for judicial review of the Attorney General's decisions. The Act provides for judicial review of the refusal of the Attorney General to suspend a deportation and to transmit a recommendation to Congress. INS v. Wang (1981) (per curiam). But the courts have not been given the authority to review whether an alien should be given permanent status; review is limited to whether the Attorney General has properly applied the statutory standards for essentially denying the alien a recommendation that his deportable status be changed by the Congress. ...

I do not suggest that all legislative vetoes are necessarily consistent with separation of powers principles. A legislative check on an inherently executive function, for example that of initiating prosecutions, poses an entirely different question. But the legislative veto device here—and in many other settings—is far from an instance of legislative tyranny over the Executive. It is a necessary check on the unavoidably expanding power of the agencies, both executive and independent, as they engage in exercising authority delegated by Congress.

Justice **REHNQUIST**, with whom Justice **WHITE** joins, dissenting.

. . .

Editors' Notes

(1) **Query:** Compare the opinions of Burger and White across several of the approaches to constitutional interpretation discussed in Chapter 9. Which looked for constitutional meaning mainly in the text and original intent and which looked more to the operations of the larger system? In what senses did both use structural analyses?

(2) **Query:** "No policy," Burger wrote, supra p. 486, "underlying the political question doctrine suggests that Congress or the Executive, or both acting in concert and in compliance with Art. I, can decide the constitutionality of a statute; that is a decision for the courts." Was the Chief Justice inserting a claim for judicial supremacy in constitutional interpretation? A judicial monopoly? Can the President or members of Congress approve a bill if they have grave doubts of its constitutionality? See Franklin Roosevelt's response in his memo for the files of the Attorney General, above, p. 479.

(3) **Query:** Does *Chadha* undermine its own legitimacy—perhaps even the validity of all federal judicial proceedings? The case went through the federal judicial system under procedural rules that, though they had the force of law, had been insulated from a presidential veto. Congress has authorized the Supreme Court (in fact special committees of the Judicial Conference of the United States) to draft rules for bankruptcy as well as for civil, criminal, and appellate procedure for all federal courts. If not disapproved by Congress within 90 days, these rules take on the force of law and repeal all conflicting federal statutes. (The statute authorizing the Court to set the rules of civil procedure is found at 28 U.S.C. § 2072; for criminal procedure, at 18 U.S.C. §§ 3771–3772.) Justices Black and Douglas several times objected to this process not only because of the Court's role as mere conduit for the Judicial Conference but also because: "The Constitution, as we read it, provides that all laws shall be enacted by the House, the Senate, and the President, not by the mere failure of Congress to reject proposals of an outside agency. . . ." 374 U.S. 865–866 (1963). Justice Frankfurter objected because he thought that by promulgating rules the Court was prejudging issues that might come before it. 323 U.S. 821 (1944).

(4) Whatever the long-range effects of *Chadha*, its doctrine about the legislative veto may not long stand unmodified, or at least it may have only limited practical effect. As Louis Fisher, a noted authority on relations among the three branches of government, put it: "Are they [provisions for legislative vetoes] unconstitutional? By the Court's definition they are. Will this change the behavior between [congressional] committees and [executive] agencies? Probably not." "Legislative Vetoes, Phoenix Style," *Extensions* (Spring, 1984); reprinted in Walter F. Murphy and C. Herman Pritchett, eds., *Courts, Judges,*

and Politics (4th ed.; New York: Random House, 1986). In the first year after *Chadha* Congress included a legislative veto in 53 bills and the President signed them all into law, though with disclaimers similar to that of FDR about the Lend–Lease Act. More subtly, chairmen of various congressional committees and subcommittees have been working out informal legislative vetoes with agency heads, while the leadership has been carrying out involuted procedures under the formal rules of each house and also substituting joint resolutions for the one-house veto. The net effect may be to weaken rather than strengthen executive power. See Fisher: "Constitutional Interpretation by Members of Congress," 63 *N.C.L.Rev.* 707 (1985); "Judicial Misjudgments about the Lawmaking Process," 45 *Pub.Admin.Rev.* 705 (1985); and, more generally, *Constitutional Conflicts Between Congress and the President* (3rd ed.; Lawrence: University of Kansas Press, 1991).

(5) Among the authorities who had supported the constitutionality of the legislative veto was Edward S. Corwin, *The Presidency: Office and Powers* (4th rev. ed.; New York: New York University Press, 1957), pp. 129–130; for an extended defense of the legislative veto, written long before *Chadha,* see Murray Dry, "The Congressional Veto and the Constitutional Separation of Powers," in Joseph M. Bessette and Jeffrey Tulis, eds., *The Presidency in the Constitutional Order* (Baton Rouge: Louisiana State University Press, 1981).

(6) For a general study of the legislative veto, see Barbara Hinkson Craig, *The Legislative Veto* (Boulder, Colo.: Westview Press, 1983). For intensive surveys of congressional, judicial, and scholarly reactions to *Chadha,* see Louis Fisher, "One year after *INS v. Chadha,*" Library of Congress, Congressional Research Service, mimeo'ed, 1984; and his other writings cited in Eds.' Note (4). See also: U.S. House of Representatives, Committee on Rules, *Hearings: Legislative Veto after Chadha,* 98th Cong., 2d sess. (1984); (then Judge, later Justice) Stephen Breyer, "The Legislative Veto after *Chadha,*" 72 *Geo.L.J.* 785 (1984); Donald E. Elliott, "INS v. Chadha," 1983 *Sup.Ct.Rev.* 125; Elliott H. Levitas and Stanley M. Brand, "Congressional Review of Executive and Agency after *Chadha:* 'The Son of Legislative Veto' Lives On," 72 *Geo.L.J.* 801 (1984); Peter L. Strauss, "Was There a Baby in the Bathwater?" 1983 *Duke L.J.* 789; Strauss, "The Place of Agencies in Government," 84 *Colum.L.Rev.* 573 (1984); Laurence H. Tribe, "The Legislative Veto Decision," 21 *Harv.J. on Leg'n* 1 (1984); and Note, "Severability of Legislative Veto Provisions," 97 *Harv.L.Rev.* 1184 (1984).

"The Constitution does not contemplate an active role for Congress in the supervision of officers charged with the execution of the laws it enacts."—Chief Justice **BURGER**

"[W]hen Congress, or a component or an agent of Congress, seeks to make policy that will bind the Nation, it must follow the procedures mandated by Article I of the Constitution—through passage by both Houses and presentment to the President."—Justice **STEVENS**

"The wisdom of vesting 'executive' powers in an officer removable by joint resolution may indeed be debatable ... but such matters are for the most part to be worked out between the Congress and the President through the legislative process, which affords each branch ample opportunity to defend its interests."—Justice WHITE

BOWSHER v. SYNAR

478 U.S. 714, 106 S.Ct. 3181, 92 L.Ed.2d 583 (1986).

In an effort to reduce the federal deficit, Congress passed and the President signed the Balanced Budget and Emergency Deficit Control Act of 1985, popularly called the "Gramm–Rudman–Hollings Act." The statute set a maximum deficit for each of the fiscal years 1985–1991 and mandated across-the-board cuts in federal spending, with certain programs excepted, if the deficit exceeded a certain specified amount. The procedure for these supposedly "automatic" reductions was quite complex, requiring the Comptroller General to review reports from the directors of the Office of Management and Budget in the White House and the Congressional Budget Office and then submit his own conclusions on cuts to the President, who was obliged to carry them out. Twelve Representatives and the National Treasury Workers Union sued the Comptroller General in a special three-judge district court, asking for a declaratory judgment that the Act was unconstitutional. The court so held, and the Comptroller General appealed directly to the Supreme Court.

Chief Justice **BURGER** delivered the opinion of the Court.

The question presented ... is whether the assignment by Congress to the Comptroller General of the United States of certain functions under the Balanced Budget and Emergency Deficit Control Act of 1985 violates the doctrine of separation of powers. ...

II

A threshold issue is whether the Members of Congress, members of the National Treasury Employees Union, or the Union itself have standing to challenge the constitutionality of the Act in question. It is clear that members of the Union ... will sustain injury by not receiving a scheduled increase in benefits. This is sufficient to confer standing. ... We therefore need not consider the standing issue as to the Union or Members of Congress. ...

III

... The declared purpose of separating and dividing the powers of government, of course, was to "[diffuse] power the better to secure liberty." Youngstown Sheet & Tube Co. v. Sawyer (1952) (Jackson, J., concurring). Justice Jackson's words echo the famous warning of Montesquieu, quoted by James Madison in *The Federalist* No. 47, that " 'there can be no liberty where the legislative and executive powers are united in the same person, or body of magistrates'. ..."

That this system of division and separation of powers produces conflicts, confusion, and discordance at times is inherent, but it was deliberately so structured to assure full, vigorous, and open debate on the great issues affecting the people and to provide avenues for the operation of checks on the exercise of governmental power.

The Constitution does not contemplate an active role for Congress in the supervision of officers charged with the execution of the laws it enacts. The President appoints "Officers of the United States" with the "Advice and Consent of the Senate. ..." Art. II, § 2. Once the appointment has been made and confirmed, however, the Constitution explicitly provides for removal of Officers of the United States by Congress only upon impeachment by the House of Representatives and conviction by the Senate ... Art. II, § 4. A direct congressional role in the removal of officers charged with the execution of the laws beyond this limited one is inconsistent with separation of powers.

This was made clear in debate in the First Congress in 1789. When Congress considered an amendment to a bill establishing the Department of Foreign Affairs, the debate centered around whether the Congress "should recognize and declare the power of the President under the Constitution to remove the Secretary of Foreign Affairs without the advice and consent of the Senate." Myers v. United States (1925). James Madison urged rejection of a congressional role in the removal of Executive Branch officers, other than by impeachment. ... Madison's position ultimately prevailed, and a congressional role in the removal process was rejected. This "Decision of 1789" provides "contemporaneous and weighty evidence" of the Constitution's meaning since many of the Members of the First Congress "had taken part in framing that instrument." Marsh v. Chambers (1983).

This Court first directly addressed this issue in Myers v. United States (1926). ... At issue ... was a statute providing that certain postmasters could be removed only "by and with the advice and consent of the Senate." The President removed one such Postmaster without Senate approval, and a lawsuit ensued. Chief Justice Taft, writing for the Court, declared the statute unconstitutional on the ground that for Congress to "draw to itself, or to either branch of it, the power to remove or the right to participate in the exercise of that power ... would ... infringe the constitutional principle of the separation of governmental powers." ...

A decade later, in Humphrey's Executor v. United States (1935) ... a Federal Trade Commissioner who had been removed by the President sought back pay. Humphrey's Executor involved an issue not presented either in the Myers case or in this case—i.e., the power of Congress to limit the President's powers of removal of a Federal Trade Commissioner. ... The relevant statute permitted removal "by the President," but only "for inefficiency, neglect of duty, or malfeasance in office." Justice Sutherland, speaking for the Court, upheld the statute, holding that "illimitable power of removal is not possessed by the President [with respect to Federal Trade Commissioners]." . . . The Court distinguished *Myers*, reaffirming its holding that congressional participation in the removal of executive officers is unconstitutional. . . . The Court reached a similar result in Wiener v. United States (1958), concluding that, under *Humphrey's Executor*, the President did not have unrestrained removal authority over a member of the War Claims Commission.

. . . The statutes establishing independent agencies typically specify either that the agency members are removable by the President for specified causes . . . [such as] "inefficiency, neglect of duty, or malfeasance in office" . . . or else do not specify a removal procedure. . . . This case involves nothing like these statutes, but rather a statute that provides for direct congressional involvement over the decision to remove the Comptroller General. Appellants have referred us to no independent agency whose members are removable by the Congress for certain causes short of impeachable offenses, as is the Comptroller General.

In light of these precedents, we conclude that Congress cannot reserve for itself the power of removal of an officer charged with the execution of the laws except by impeachment. To permit the execution of the laws to be vested in an officer answerable only to Congress would, in practical terms, reserve in Congress control over the execution of the laws. . . . The structure of the Constitution does not permit Congress to execute the laws; it follows that Congress cannot grant to an officer under its control what it does not possess.

. . . To permit an officer controlled by Congress to execute the laws would be, in essence, to permit a congressional veto. Congress could simply remove, or threaten to remove, an officer for executing the laws in any fashion found to be unsatisfactory to Congress. This kind of congressional control over the execution of the laws, *Chadha* makes clear, is constitutionally impermissible.

. . . With these principles in mind, we turn to consideration of whether the Comptroller General is controlled by Congress.

IV . . .

The critical factor lies in the provisions of the statute defining the Comptroller General's office relating to removability. Although the Comptroller General is nominated by the President from a list of three individuals recommended by the Speaker of the House of Representatives and the President pro tempore of the Senate . . . and confirmed by the Senate, he is removable only at the initiative of Congress. He may be removed not only by impeachment but also by joint resolution of Congress "at any time" resting on any one of the following bases: "(i) permanent disability; (ii) inefficiency; (iii) neglect of duty; (iv) malfeasance; or (v) a felony or conduct involving moral turpitude." . . . This provision was included, as one Congressman explained in urging passage of the Act, because Congress "felt that . . . at any moment when it found [the Comptroller] was inefficient and was not carrying on the duties of his office as he should and as the Congress expected, [Congress] could remove him without the long, tedious process of a trial by impeachment." . . .

Justice White [dissenting] contends: "The statute does not permit anyone to remove the Comptroller at will; removal is permitted only for specified cause, with the existence of cause to be determined by Congress following a hearing. Any removal under the statute would presumably be subject to post-termination judicial review to ensure that a hearing had in fact been held and that the finding of cause for removal was not arbitrary." . . .

[But] . . . the dissent's assessment of the statute fails to recognize the breadth of the grounds for removal. The statute permits removal for "inefficiency," "neglect of duty," or "malfeasance." These terms are very broad and, as interpreted by Congress, could sustain removal of a Comptroller General for any number of actual or perceived transgressions of the legislative will. The Constitutional Convention chose to permit impeachment of executive officers only for "Treason, Bribery, or other high Crimes and Misdemeanors." It rejected language that would have permitted impeachment for "maladministration," with Madison arguing that "[so] vague a term will be equivalent to a tenure during pleasure of the Senate." . . .

We need not decide whether "inefficiency" or "malfeasance" are terms as broad as "maladministration" in order to reject the dissent's position that removing the Comptroller General requires "a feat of bipartisanship more difficult than that required to impeach and convict." . . . (White, J., dissenting.) Surely no one would seriously suggest that judicial independence would be strengthened by allowing removal of federal judges only by a joint resolution finding "inefficiency," "neglect of duty," or "malfeasance."

Justice White, however, assures us that "[realistic] consideration" of the "practical result of the removal provision" . . . reveals that the Comptroller General is unlikely to be removed by Congress. The separated powers of our Government cannot be permitted to turn on judicial assessment of whether an officer exercising executive power is on good terms with Congress. The Framers recognized that, in the long term, structural protections against abuse of power were critical to preserving liberty. In constitutional terms, the removal powers over the Comptroller General's office dictate that he will be subservient to Congress.

This much said, we must also add that the dissent is simply in error to suggest that the political realities reveal that the Comptroller General is free from influence by Congress. . . . It is clear that Congress has consistently viewed the Comptroller General as an officer of the Legislative Branch. The Reorganization Acts of 1945 and 1949, for example, both stated that the Comptroller General and the G[eneral] A[ccounting] O[ffice] are "a part of the legislative branch of the Government." . . .

... The remaining question is whether the Comptroller General has been assigned such [executive] powers in the Balanced Budget and Emergency Deficit Control Act of 1985.

V ...

Appellants suggest that the duties assigned to the Comptroller General in the Act are essentially ministerial and mechanical so that their performance does not constitute "execution of the law" in a meaningful sense. On the contrary, we view these functions as plainly entailing execution of the law in constitutional terms. Interpreting a law enacted by Congress to implement the legislative mandate is the very essence of "execution" of the law. ... [T]he Comptroller General must exercise judgment concerning facts that affect the application of the Act. He must also interpret the provisions of the Act to determine precisely what budgetary calculations are required. Decisions of that kind are typically made by officers charged with executing a statute.

The executive nature of the Comptroller General's functions under the Act is revealed in § 252(a)(3) which gives the Comptroller General the ultimate authority to determine the budget cuts to be made. Indeed, the Comptroller General commands the President himself to carry out, without the slightest variation (with exceptions not relevant to the constitutional issues presented), the directive of the Comptroller General as to the budget reductions. ...

... [A]s *Chadha* makes clear, once Congress makes its choice in enacting legislation, its participation ends. Congress can thereafter control the execution of its enactment only indirectly—by passing new legislation. ... By placing the responsibility for execution of the Balanced Budget and Emergency Deficit Control Act in the hands of an officer who is subject to removal only by itself, Congress in effect has retained control over the execution of the Act and has intruded into the executive function. The Constitution does not permit such intrusion.

Justice **STEVENS**, with whom Justice **MARSHALL** joins, concurring in the judgment.

When this Court is asked to invalidate a statutory provision that has been approved by both Houses of the Congress and signed by the President ... it should only do so for the most compelling constitutional reasons. I agree with the Court that the "Gramm–Rudman–Hollings" Act contains a constitutional infirmity so severe that the flawed provision may not stand. I disagree with the Court, however, on the reasons why. ... It is not the dormant, carefully circumscribed congressional removal power that represents the primary constitutional evil. Nor do I agree with the conclusion of both the majority and the dissent that the analysis depends on a labeling of the functions assigned to the Comptroller General as "executive powers." ... Rather, I am convinced that the Comptroller General must be characterized as an agent of Congress because of his longstanding statutory responsibilities; that the powers assigned to him under the Gramm–Rudman–Hollings Act require him to make policy that will bind the Nation; and that, when Congress ... seeks to make policy that will bind the Nation, it must follow the procedures mandated by Article I of the Constitution—through passage by both Houses and presentment to the President. In short, Congress may not exercise its fundamental power to formulate national policy by delegating that power to one of its two Houses, to a legislative committee, or to an individual agent of the Congress. ...

I

The fact that Congress retained for itself the power to remove the Comptroller General is important evidence supporting the conclusion that he is a member of the Legislative Branch of the Government. Unlike the Court, however, I am not persuaded that the congressional removal power is either a necessary, or a sufficient, basis for concluding that his statutory assignment is invalid.

As Justice White explains ... Congress does not have the power to remove the Comptroller General at will, or because of disagreement with any policy determination that he may be required to make in the administration of this, or any other, Act. The statute provides a term of 15 years for the Comptroller General; it further provides that he must retire upon becoming 70 years of age, and that he may be removed at any time by impeachment or by "joint resolution of Congress, after notice and an opportunity for a hearing, only for—(i) permanent disability; (ii) inefficiency; (iii) neglect of duty; (iv) malfeasance; or (v) a felony or conduct involving moral turpitude." ... Far from assuming that this provision creates a " 'here-and-now subservience' " ... we should presume that Congress will adhere to the law. ... The notion that the removal power at issue here automatically creates some kind of "here-and-now subservience" of the Comptroller General to Congress is belied by history. There is no evidence that Congress has ever removed, or threatened to remove, the Comptroller General for reasons of policy. ...

II

In assessing the role of the Comptroller General, it is appropriate to consider his already existing statutory responsibilities. Those responsibilities leave little doubt that one of the identifying characteristics of the Comptroller General is his statutorily required relationship to the Legislative Branch.

... The statute that created the Comptroller General's office—the Budget and Accounting Act of 1921—provided that four of the five statutory responsibilities given to the Comptroller General be exercised on behalf of Congress, three of them exclusively so. On at least three occasions since 1921, moreover, in considering the structure of Government, Congress has defined the Comptroller General as being a part of the Legislative Branch. In the Reorganization Act of 1945, Congress specified that the Comptroller General and the General Accounting Office "are a part of the legislative branch of the Government." ... In the Reorganization Act of 1949, Congress again confirmed that the Comptroller General and the General Accounting Office "are a part of the legislative branch of the Government." ... Finally, in the Budget and Accounting Procedures Act of 1950, Congress referred to the "auditing for the Government, conducted by the Comptroller General of the United States as an agent of the Congress." ...

III

Everyone agrees that the powers assigned to the Comptroller General by ... the Gramm–Rudman–Hollings Act are extremely important. They require him to exercise sophisticated economic judgment concerning anticipated trends in the Nation's economy, projected levels of unemployment, interest rates, and the special problems that may be confronted by the many components of a vast federal bureaucracy. His duties are anything but ministerial—he is not merely a clerk wearing a "green eyeshade" as he undertakes these tasks. ... Unless we make the naive assumption that the economic destiny of the Nation could be safely entrusted to a mindless bank of computers, the powers that this Act vests in the Comptroller General must be recognized as having transcendent importance. ...

The Court concludes that the Gramm–Rudman–Hollings Act impermissibly assigns the Comptroller General "executive powers." ... Justice White's dissent agrees. ... This conclusion is not only far from obvious but also rests on the unstated and unsound premise that there is a definite line that distinguishes executive power from legislative power.

"The great ordinances of the Constitution do not establish and divide fields of black and white." Springer v. Philippine Islands (1928) (Holmes, J., dissenting). "The men who met in Philadelphia in the summer of 1787 were practical statesmen, experienced in politics, who viewed the principle of separation of powers as a vital check against tyranny. But they likewise saw that a hermetic sealing off of the three branches of Government from one another would preclude the establishment of a Nation capable of governing itself effectively." Buckley v. Valeo (1976). As Justice Brandeis explained in his dissent in Myers v. United States: "The separation of the powers of government did not make each branch completely autonomous. It left each, in some measure, dependent upon the others, as it left to each power to exercise, in some respects, functions in their nature executive, legislative and judicial."

One reason that the exercise of legislative, executive, and judicial powers cannot be categorically distributed among three mutually exclusive branches of Government is that governmental power cannot always be readily characterized with only one of those three labels. On the contrary, as our cases demonstrate, a particular function, like a chameleon, will often take on the aspect of the office to which it is assigned.

For this reason, "[when] any Branch acts, it is presumptively exercising the power the Constitution has delegated to it." INS v. Chadha.

The Chadha case itself illustrates this basic point. The governmental decision that was being made was whether a resident alien who had overstayed his student visa should be deported. From the point of view of the Administrative Law Judge who conducted a hearing on the issue ... the decision took on a judicial coloring. From the point of view of the Attorney General of the United States to whom Congress had delegated the authority to suspend deportation of certain aliens, the decision appeared to have an executive character. But, as the Court held, when the House of Representatives finally decided that *Chadha* must be deported, its action "was essentially legislative in purpose and effect."

The powers delegated to the Comptroller General by ... the Act before us today have a similar chameleon-like quality. Thus, I do not agree that the Comptroller General's responsibilities under the Gramm–Rudman–Hollings Act must be termed "executive powers," or even that our inquiry is much advanced by using that term. ... If the delegation to a stranger is permissible, why may not Congress delegate the same responsibilities to one of its own agents? That is the central question before us today.

IV

Congress regularly delegates responsibility to a number of agents who provide important support for its legislative activities. Many perform functions that could be characterized as "executive" in most contexts—the Capitol Police can arrest and press charges against lawbreakers, the Sergeant at Arms manages the congressional payroll, the Capitol Architect maintains the buildings and grounds, and its Librarian has custody of a vast number of books and records. Moreover, the Members themselves necessarily engage in many activities that are merely ancillary to their primary lawmaking responsibilities—they manage their separate offices, they communicate with their constituents, they conduct hearings, they inform themselves about the problems confronting the Nation, and they make rules for the governance of their own business. ...

The Gramm–Rudman–Hollings Act assigns to the Comptroller General the duty to make policy decisions that have the force of law. ... It is the Comptroller General's report that the President must follow and that will have conclusive effect. It is, in short, the Comptroller General's report that will have a profound, dramatic, and immediate impact on the Government and on the Nation at large. Article I of the Constitution specifies the procedures that Congress must follow when it makes policy that binds the Nation: its legislation must be approved by both of its Houses and presented to the President. ...

If Congress were free to delegate its policymaking authority to one of its components, or to one of its agents, it would be able to evade "the carefully crafted restraints spelled out in the Constitution." ... That danger—congressional action that evades constitutional restraints—is not present when Congress delegates lawmaking power to the executive or to an independent agency.

The distinction between the kinds of action that Congress may delegate to its own components and agents and those that require either compliance with Article I procedures or delegation to another branch pursuant to defined standards is reflected in the practices that have developed over the years regarding congressional resolutions. The joint resolution, which is used for "special purposes and ... incidental matters," ... makes binding policy and "requires an affirmative vote by both Houses and submission to the President for approval" ...—the full Article I requirements. A concurrent resolution, in contrast, makes no binding policy; it is "a means of expressing fact, principles, opinions, and purposes of the two Houses" ... and thus does not need to be presented to the President. It is settled, however, that if a resolution is intended to make policy that will bind the Nation and thus is "legislative in its character and effect," ...—then the full Article I requirements must be observed. ...

In my opinion, Congress itself could not exercise the Gramm–Rudman–Hollings functions through a concurrent resolution. ... I think it equally clear that Congress may not simply delegate those functions to an agent such as the Congressional Budget Office. Since I am persuaded that the Comptroller General is also fairly deemed to be an agent of Congress, he too cannot exercise such functions. ...

In short, even though it is well settled that Congress may delegate legislative power to independent agencies or to the Executive, and thereby divest itself of a portion of its lawmaking power, when it elects to exercise such power itself, it may not authorize a lesser representative of the Legislative Branch to act on its behalf. ...

Justice **WHITE**, dissenting.

The Court, acting in the name of separation of powers, takes upon itself to strike down the Gramm–Rudman–Hollings Act, one of the most novel and far-reaching legislative responses to a national crisis since the New Deal. ... I cannot concur in the Court's action. ... In attaching dispositive significance to what should be regarded as a triviality, the Court neglects what has in the past been recognized as a fundamental principle governing consideration of disputes over separation of powers:

> "The actual art of governing under our Constitution does not and cannot conform to judicial definitions of the power of any of its branches based on isolated clauses or even single Articles torn from context. While the Constitution diffuses power the better to secure liberty, it also contemplates that practice will integrate the dispersed powers into a workable government." *Youngstown* (1952) (Jackson, J. concurring).

I

... I wish to emphasize what it is that the Court quite pointedly and correctly does not hold: namely, that "executive" powers of the sort granted the Comptroller by the Act may only be exercised by officers removable at will by the President. The Court's apparent unwillingness to accept this argument ... is fully consistent with the Court's long-standing recognition that it is within the power of Congress under the "Necessary and Proper" Clause, Art. I, § 8, to vest authority that falls within the Court's definition of executive power in officers who are not subject to removal at will by the President and are therefore not under the President's direct control. See, e.g., Humphrey's Executor v. United States (1935); Wiener v. United States (1958). ... [W]ith the advent and triumph of the administrative state and the accompanying multiplication of the tasks undertaken by the Federal Government, the Court has been virtually compelled to recognize that Congress may reasonably deem it "necessary and proper" to vest some among the broad new array of governmental functions in officers who are free from the partisanship that may be expected of agents wholly dependent upon the President.

The Court's recognition of the legitimacy of legislation vesting "executive" authority in officers independent of the President does not imply derogation of the President's own constitutional authority—indeed, duty—to "take Care that the Laws be faithfully executed," Art. II, § 3, for any such duty is necessarily limited to a great extent by the content of the laws enacted by the Congress. ... In determining whether a limitation on the President's power to remove an officer performing executive functions constitutes a violation of the constitutional scheme of separation of powers, a court must "[focus] on the extent to which [such a limitation] prevents the Executive Branch from accomplishing its constitutionally assigned functions." Nixon v. Administrator of General Services (1977). ... This inquiry is, to be sure, not one that will beget easy answers; it provides nothing approaching a bright-line rule or set of rules. Such an inquiry, however, is necessitated by the recognition that "formalistic and unbending rules" in the area of separation of powers may "unduly constrict Congress' ability to take needed and innovative action pursuant to its Article I powers." Commodity Futures Trading Comm'n v. Schor (1986).

It is evident ... that the powers exercised by the Comptroller General under the Gramm–Rudman–Hollings Act are not such that vesting them in an officer not subject to removal at will by the President would in itself improperly interfere with Presidential powers. Determining the level of spending by the Federal Government is not by nature a function central either to the exercise of the President's enumerated powers or to his general duty to ensure execution of the laws; rather, appropriating funds is a peculiarly legislative function, and one expressly committed to Congress by Art. I, § 9. ... In enacting Gramm–Rudman–Hollings, Congress has chosen to exercise this legislative power to establish the level of federal spending by providing a detailed set of criteria for reducing expenditures below the level of appropriations in the event that certain conditions are met. Delegating the execution of this legislation ... to an officer independent of the President's will does not deprive the President of any power that he would otherwise have or that is essential to the performance of the duties of his office. ... To be sure, if the budget-cutting mechanism required the responsible officer to exercise a great deal of policymaking discretion, one might argue that having created such broad discretion Congress had some obligation based upon Art. II to vest it in the Chief Executive or his agents. In Gramm–Rudman–Hollings, however, Congress has done no such thing. ... Such a delegation deprives the President of no authority that is rightfully his.

II

If, as the Court seems to agree, the assignment of "executive" powers under Gramm–Rudman–Hollings to an officer not removable at will by the President would not in itself represent a violation of the constitutional scheme of separated powers, the question remains whether ... the fact that the officer to whom Congress has delegated the authority to implement the Act is removable by a joint resolution of Congress should require invalidation of the Act. The Court's decision ... is based on a syllogism: the Act vests the Comptroller with "executive power"; such power may not be exercised by Congress or its agents; the Comptroller is an agent of Congress because he is removable by Congress; therefore the Act is invalid. I have no quarrel with the proposition that the powers exercised by the Comptroller under the Act may be characterized as "executive" in that they involve the interpretation and carrying out of the Act's mandate. I can also accept the general proposition that although Congress has considerable authority in designating the officers who are to execute legislation ... the constitutional scheme of separated powers does prevent Congress from reserving an executive role for itself or for its "agents." Buckley v. Valeo (White, J., concurring in part and dissenting in part). I cannot accept, however, that the exercise of authority by an officer removable for cause by a joint resolution of Congress is analogous to the impermissible execution of the law by Congress itself, nor would I hold that the congressional role in the removal process renders the Comptroller an "agent" of the Congress, incapable of receiving "executive" power. ...

... As interpreted in Chadha, the Constitution prevents Congress from interfering with the actions of officers of the United States through means short of legislation satisfying the demands of bicameral passage and presentment to the President for approval or disapproval. ... Today's majority concludes that the same concerns that underlay Chadha indicate the invalidity of a statutory provision allowing the removal by joint resolution for specified cause of any officer performing executive functions. Such removal power, the Court contends, constitutes a "congressional veto" analogous to that struck down in Chadha, for it permits Congress to "remove, or threaten to remove, an officer for executing the laws in any fashion found to be unsatisfactory." The

Court concludes that it is "[this] kind of congressional control over the execution of the laws" that *Chadha* condemns.

The deficiencies in the Court's reasoning are apparent. First, the Court baldly mischaracterizes the removal provision when it suggests that it allows Congress to remove the Comptroller for "executing the laws in any fashion found to be unsatisfactory"; in fact, Congress may remove the Comptroller only for one or more of five specified reasons, which "although not so narrow as to deny Congress any leeway, circumscribe Congress' power to some extent by providing a basis for judicial review of congressional removal." ... Second, and more to the point, the Court overlooks or deliberately ignores the decisive difference between the congressional removal provision and the legislative veto struck down in *Chadha*: under the Budget and Accounting Act, Congress may remove the Comptroller only through a joint resolution, which by definition must be passed by both Houses and signed by the President. ... In other words, a removal of the Comptroller under the statute *satisfies the requirements of bicameralism and presentment laid down in* Chadha. ...

To the extent that it has any bearing on the problem now before us, *Chadha* would seem to suggest the legitimacy of the statutory provision making the Comptroller removable through joint resolution, for the Court's opinion in *Chadha* reflects the view that the bicameralism and presentment requirements of Art. I represent the principal assurances that Congress will remain within its legislative role in the constitutionally prescribed scheme of separated powers. Action taken in accordance with the "single, finely wrought, and exhaustively considered, procedure" established by Art. I, *Chadha,* ... should be presumptively viewed as a legitimate exercise of legislative power. That such action may represent a more or less successful attempt by Congress to "control" the actions of an officer of the United States surely does not in itself indicate that it is unconstitutional, for no one would dispute that Congress has the power to "control" administration through legislation imposing duties or substantive restraints on executive officers, through legislation increasing or decreasing the funds made available to such officers, or through legislation actually abolishing a particular office. Indeed, *Chadha* expressly recognizes that while congressional meddling with administration of the laws outside of the legislative process is impermissible, congressional control over executive officers exercised through the legislative process is valid. ...

... The [remaining] question ... is whether the threat of removal of the Comptroller General for cause through joint resolution ... renders the Comptroller sufficiently subservient to Congress that investing him with "executive" power can be realistically equated with the unlawful retention of such power by Congress itself; more generally, the question is whether there is a genuine threat of "encroachment or aggrandizement of one branch at the expense of the other." ...

Common sense indicates that the existence of the removal provision poses no such threat. ...

The statute does not permit anyone to remove the Comptroller at will; removal is permitted only for specified cause, with the existence of cause to be determined by Congress following a hearing. Any removal under the statute would presumably be subject to post-termination judicial review to ensure that a hearing had in fact been held and that the finding of cause for removal was not arbitrary. ... These procedural and substantive limitations on the removal power militate strongly against the characterization of the Comptroller as a mere agent of Congress. ... Removal authority limited in such a manner is more properly viewed as motivating adherence to a substantive standard established by law than as inducing subservience. ...

More importantly, the substantial role played by the President in the process of removal through joint resolution reduces to utter insignificance the possibility that the threat of removal will induce subservience to the Congress. ... The requirement of Presidential approval obviates the possibility that the Comptroller will perceive himself as so completely at the mercy of Congress that he will function as its tool. If the Comptroller's conduct in office is not so unsatisfactory to the President as to convince the latter that removal is required under the statutory standard, Congress will have no independent power to coerce the Comptroller unless it can muster a two-thirds majority in both Houses—a feat of bipartisanship more difficult than that required to impeach and convict. ...

The practical result of the removal provision is not to render the Comptroller unduly dependent upon or subservient to Congress, but to render him one of the most independent officers in the entire federal establishment. Those who have studied the office agree that the procedural and substantive limits on the power of Congress and the President to remove the Comptroller make dislodging him against his will practically impossible. ...

Realistic consideration of the nature of the Comptroller General's relation to Congress thus reveals that the threat to separation of powers conjured up by the majority is wholly chimerical. ...

The majority's contrary conclusion rests on the rigid dogma that, outside of the impeachment process, any "direct congressional role in the removal of officers charged with the execution of the laws ... is inconsistent with separation of powers." ... Reliance on such an unyielding principle to strike down a statute posing no real danger of aggrandizement of congressional power is extremely misguided and insensitive to our constitutional role. The wisdom of vesting "executive" powers in an officer removable by joint resolution may indeed be debatable ... but such matters are for the most part to be worked out between the Congress and the President through the legislative process, which affords each branch ample opportunity to defend its interests. The Act vesting budget-cutting authority in the Comptroller General represents Congress' judgment that the delegation of such authority to counteract ever-mounting deficits is "necessary and proper" to the exercise of the powers granted the Federal Government by the Constitution; and the President's approval of the statute signifies his unwillingness to reject the choice made by Congress. ... Under such circumstances, the role of this Court should be limited to determining whether the Act so alters the balance of authority among the branches of government as to pose a genuine threat to they basic division between the lawmaking power and the power to execute the law. ... I see no such threat. ...

Justice **BLACKMUN**, dissenting. ...

Editors' Notes

(1) **Query:** The Papers of Justice Thurgood Marshall (Library of Congress, Manuscripts Division, File No. 396) reveal that five members of the majority thought that the Chief Justice's first circulating draft of the Court's opinion, in Justice O'Connor's words, "cast doubt on the constitutionality of the independent [regulatory] agencies." Marshall, O'Connor, Stevens, Brennan, and Powell believed that Burger was suggesting Congress could delegate the power it wanted to give to the Comptroller only to an official removable by the President. As Marshall described it, Burger's draft focused on the President's need to be "master in his own house"—master, that is, over all officials performing any "executive functions," including commissioners of the FCC, SEC, ICC, and other independent agencies. Disclaiming any intention to undermine the independent regulatory commissions, Burger rewrote the opinion. Stevens, however, remained unsatisfied, insisting that the Court avoid labeling the Comptroller's functions under the Act as "executive" and that the rationale for invalidating the Act rest on *Chadha*. But is there any way other than Justice White's approach to avoid reviving old doubts about the independent regulatory agencies? If, as per *Chadha* and Stevens' opinion in *Bowsher*, Congress may not delegate legislative powers to one of its own agencies, how may it delegate those same powers to any other body? And if the independent regulatory agencies are not part of the executive branch, are they not in some sense "agents" of Congress?

(2) **Query:** Burger cited "the Decision of 1789" as important for determining constitutional meaning. To what extent was he implicitly endorsing a version of departmentalism? Was he treating this decision of the First Congress as contemporaneous evidence of the founders' intent and thus as evidence of constitutional meaning that would bind Congress and the Court? If, indeed, Burger was implying that "the Decision of 1789" bound later Congresses, was he holding the legislative branch to a stricter version of stare decisis than judges hold courts?

(3) **Query:** Burger said that "The Constitution does not contemplate an active role for Congress in the supervision of officers charged with the execution of the laws it enacts." Assuming that the Chief Justice was correct insofar as the plain words of the text are concerned, to what extent was he accurately describing the institutional practices of the American political system? To what extent are these practices constitutional? What do answers to

these questions—indeed, the questions themselves—tell us about the broader constitution?   Does any justice confront these problems?   Why or why not?

(4) Two terms later Chief Justice Rehnquist wrote the opinion in Morrison v. Olson (1988), upholding the Ethics in Government Act of 1978.   That Act allowed panels of federal judges to appoint special prosecutors to investigate and prosecute high governmental officials.   These special prosecutors were removable only "for good cause," and then by the Attorney General.   The Act thus allowed a group of executive officials a significant measure of independence from the President.   For the Court, Rehnquist noted that, although Article II gives the President exclusive power to nominate the principal officers of government, it enables Congress to vest appointment of "inferior officers" in officials other than the President, including federal judges.   The Chief Justice reasoned that, although the Act to some extent restricted the President's control of federal prosecutors, it did not impermissibly interfere with the President's duty to ensure prosecutorial fidelity to the law.

In a long, bitter, and lonely dissent, Justice Scalia denied that independent prosecutors were inferior officials, since their independence meant they did not have to take orders from others.   He accused the majority of ignoring the plain words of the constitutional text—words that vested *all* executive power, not merely some, in the President.   Echoing Justice Black in *Griswold* (1965; reprinted above, p. 147), Scalia protested that the Court had substituted its own discretion for those plain words.

11

Sharing Powers: The Nature of the Union

The concept of federalism shares at least one trait with that of separation of powers: Its popularity far exceeds its precision. At very least, however, a federal system requires that political power be shared between a central government and local governments. It differs from a unitary system in that local governments possess authority independent of the will of the central government. It differs from a confederation in that, first, the central government does not need the consent of local units to act within its orbit of authority and, second, the central government can operate directly on citizens rather than only indirectly through local governments.

But these distinctions are quite modern. There were no exact models of what we now call federalism for the founders to follow. Indeed, as the peculiar phrasing of Madison's essay in *Federalist* No. 39 (reprinted below, p. 526) shows, the very term "federalism" did not then exist in its current meaning. It is a creation not only of the Philadelphia Convention but also of decades of constitutional development.

Much of the debate at Philadelphia focused on the structure that the new government would take. Madison initially joined Edmund Randolph in sponsoring the Virginia Plan, which would have come close to reducing the states to administrative subdivisions of the nation. But even the unhappy experiences under the Articles of Confederation had not convinced a majority of the delegates that such a centralization of power was justified—or could be justified to the American people. Here, as in their broader political perspective, many of the founders distrusted great concentrations of power.

The principal reasons for opposing ratification were fear of the potential strength of the new national government and the allegedly unrepresentative and undemocratic character of the proposed Congress. The opponents, the Anti–Federalists, lost because people like Madison and Hamilton convinced the electorate that the new "compound republic" [1] was not a threat to their liberties and would

---

1. Madison, *Federalist*, No. 51; reprinted above, p. 432.

better secure national defense and nourish commercial interests than would a weaker political system. Nevertheless, the Anti–Federalists did not roll over and die. They continued—and their successors still continue—to struggle to maximize local autonomy within the constitutional framework.

I. STRUCTURALISM

The plain words of the constitutional document provide only limited guidance about distributions of power between state and nation. Article VI contains the clearest clause:

> This Constitution, and the laws of the United States which shall be made in pursuance thereof; and all treaties made, or which shall be made, under the authority of the United States, shall be the supreme law of the land; and the judges in every state shall be bound thereby, any thing in the Constitution or laws of any state to the contrary notwithstanding.

But to say "the Constitution" is supreme tells nothing about how it distributes power. The critical questions here are: WHAT is "the Constitution"? Is it a contract among sovereign states, as Thomas Jefferson contended? Or is it a charter for securing the will of the people of the nation as a whole, as Alexander Hamilton and John Marshall argued? HOW should we interpret the document? Narrowly so as to restrict national power, as Jefferson contended, or, as Marshall in fact did, with an eye to historical designs and current social needs? And WHO is to interpret "the Constitution"? The Supreme Court, Congress, each department of the national government for itself, or perhaps even the states, as Jefferson, Calhoun, and white supremists of the 1950s insisted?

Several sections of the document offer somewhat different clues about distributions of power. The Tenth Amendment provides the strongest textual support for a deep residuum of state authority:

> The powers not delegated to the United States by the Constitution, nor prohibited by it to the States, are reserved to the States respectively, or to the people.

That amendment, however, was at best only a partial victory for opponents of a muscular national government. Several times they had tried to repeat the words of the Articles of Confederation by inserting "expressly" before "delegated." Each time they were voted down and so failed to repudiate the notion of implied national powers contained in the "sweeping clause" of Article I, which delegates to Congress authority "to make all laws which shall be necessary and proper for carrying into execution the foregoing [specifically listed] powers, and all other powers vested by this Constitution in the Government of the United States, or in any Department or officer thereof."

In another sense, the Tenth Amendment represented both a victory for popular sovereignty and a defeat for state sovereignty. The amendment's last four words, "or to the people," do not recognize a dual division of power between state and nation, but rather, paralleling the Ninth Amendment, a tripartite division: powers delegated to the national government, powers reserved to the states, and yet other powers denied to both levels of government and reserved to the people.

The words of the Tenth Amendment are not particularly helpful in resolving concrete cases except as read in a larger context—a context that must be determined by some background political theory or by interpretations of constitutional history. And it is in insisting on a larger context that structuralists make their contributions to constitutional interpretation. Put another way, structuralists proceed from theories of the constitutional text or the broader constitution, "taken as a whole." Alas, neither the document nor constitutional history provides a clear definition of the phrase "taken as a whole." Some structuralists have sought to start with all of the document's principal clauses, from the Preamble to each provision of the Bill of Rights, the Civil War Amendments, and beyond. Yet moving blindly from the bottom up encounters a high hurdle: American constitutional history has largely been a chronicle of disagreement over what these specific provisions mean.

Although particular textual provisions do lay down principles that prevent many kinds of disputes from arising, even taken together they leave important problems unresolved. What does congressional authority to "regulate commerce among the several states" include? How far does it reach into matters that, on their face, seem local? Does regulation include prohibition? Does the phrase "necessary and proper" in Article I, § 8 restrict Congress to means that are *absolutely essential* to carry out an explicitly delegated power or does it authorize whatever laws Congress thinks convenient? In either instance, what are the "powers not delegated to the United States" of which the Tenth Amendment speaks? When can federal judges substitute their judgments about "the Constitution's" nature, scope, and content for those of senators and representatives in Washington or of officials in the states?

To solve these sorts of difficulties every constitutional interpreter has brought to his or her reading of the document a larger concept of the structure of the federal system. As John Marshall explained in McCulloch v. Maryland (1819; reprinted below, p. 530), when the Court sustained congressional authority to charter a national bank:

> There is no express provision for the case, but the claim has been sustained on a principle which so entirely pervades the constitution, is so intermixed with the materials which compose it, so interwoven with its web, so blended with its texture, as to be

incapable of being separated from it, without rending it into shreds.

To the justices, that "principle" may have been one that "entirely pervades the constitution," but Thomas Jefferson could not find it there. The constitutional text, he complained, had become "a mere thing of wax in the hands of the judiciary, which they may twist and shape into any form they please." [2]   And even Marshall's most admiring biographer thought that in *McCulloch* the Chief Justice had proceeded with "sublime audacity." [3]   During the following summer, Marshall spent much of his time writing a series of newspaper articles under the pen name "A Friend of the Constitution," [4] replying to articles by Virginia judges (also published under pen names), who had not only castigated *McCulloch* for having "rendered the Constitution the sport of legal ingenuity," [5] but had also furiously attacked its conception of federalism.

The long lived acidity of this debate underlines both the necessity and the illusiveness of structural arguments, for, no less than Marshall—and no less than modern justices in National League of Cities v. Usery (1976; reprinted below, p. 565) and Garcia v. San Antonio MTA (1985; reprinted below, p. 576)—the jurists from Virginia envisioned an architectural scheme of American federalism whose outlines the constitutional document sketches only in rough and ambiguous terms, if at all—terms that accommodate opposing visions. Although the other Virginians' vision differed from Marshall's, perhaps one was as faithful to the document as the other; and certainly the document excluded neither.

II.   THEORIES OF AMERICAN FEDERALISM

A.   National Supremacy

As early as 1793, Chisholm v. Georgia held that a citizen of one state could sue another state in a federal court without the other state's permission, thus suggesting a wide reach for the nation's supremacy over the states. The Eleventh Amendment reversed *Chisholm's* specific holding about federal jurisdiction, but not its broader claims for federal supremacy. And through most of John

---

2. To Spencer Roane, September 6, 1819, in Andrew A. Lipscomb, ed., *The Writings of Thomas Jefferson* (Washington, DC: The Thomas Jefferson Memorial Association, 1903), XV, 213. It is worth noting, in light of the discussion of Who shall interpret in Chapters 7 and 8, that Jefferson was criticizing Marshall for *not* declaring an act of Congress unconstitutional. Was Jefferson being inconsistent with his departmental theory of interpretation?

3. Albert J. Beveridge, *The Life of John Marshall* (Boston: Houghton Mifflin Co., 1919), IV, 302.

4. See Gerald Gunther, ed., *John Marshall's Defense of McCulloch v. Maryland* (Stanford: Stanford University Press, 1969).

5. Quoted in Charles Warren, *The Supreme Court in United States History* (Rev. ed.; Boston: Little, Brown, 1926), I, 557.

Marshall's tenure as Chief Justice (1801–1835), the Court did not retreat from that basic doctrine. Fletcher v. Peck (1810; reprinted below, p. 1091) was the first instance[6] in which the justices declared a state statute unconstitutional, and Martin v. Hunter's Lessee (1816; reprinted above, p. 359) reaffirmed earlier pronouncements that federal judges were superior to state jurists in constitutional interpretation.

McCulloch offered the classic structuralist justification for national supremacy. First, Marshall argued that the federal government is not the creature of the state governments. Rather, like the constitutional document itself, the national government "proceeds directly from the people; is 'ordained and established' in the name of the people. ... The government of the Union, then ... is, emphatically and truly, a government of the people."[7] Second, Marshall joined this "fact" of the people as the source of national authority to his reading of the supremacy clause to conclude that:

> If any one proposition could command the universal consent of mankind, we might expect it would be this—that the government of the Union, though limited in its powers, is supreme within its sphere of action. This would seem to result necessarily from its nature. It is the government of all; its powers are delegated by all; it represents all, and acts for all.

Third, the Chief Justice went on to construe the "sweeping clause" broadly and to interpret "necessary and proper" to mean "appropriate." Thus he concluded that Congress not only had authority to incorporate a bank but also that "the states have no power, by taxation or otherwise, to retard, impede, burden, or in any manner control the operation of constitutional laws enacted by Congress. ..."

B. "Dual Federalism"

Even when reasoned as cleverly as John Marshall's, judicial opinions seldom fully and finally resolve the problems of federalism they confront. Among the difficulties that *McCulloch* did not have to face was that of state regulation of matters that apparently fell within the ambit of federal control but over which Congress had not acted. And for ensuing generations, state regulation of commerce has provided a frequent battleground.

Marshall dodged this issue in Gibbons v. Ogden (1824), involving the authority of New York to regulate commerce between itself and New Jersey; he found an obscure federal licensing statute that

---

6. In effect, Ware v. Hylton (1796) invalidated a Virginia statute as conflicting with Jay's Treaty, though the justices did not specifically hold the state statute unconstitutional.

7. Madison in *Federalist* No. 39 (reprinted below, p. 526) had offered a somewhat less nationalistic explanation of "the Constitution's" source; but he was trying to persuade people to accept a greater degree of centralized power than in their existing system.

enabled him to point to a congressional exercise of its power. In his final years, as he was losing control of his Court to new justices more concerned to protect state interests, he ignored that same licensing act when, for the Court, he sustained state control over navigable waters [8]—in effect, giving up a little to preserve as much national supremacy as he could.

Marshall's successor as Chief Justice, Roger Brooke Taney, had a much less nationalistic view of federalism. Whereas Marshall saw the nation as supreme, within its sphere, over the states and the Court as an agent of national supremacy, Taney and a majority of his colleagues tended to see state and nation as almost co-equal sovereigns. As Edward S. Corwin said, "the Court under Taney sometimes talked as if it regarded all the reserved powers of the States as limiting national power. ..." [9] Taney's approach, later called "dual federalism," made the Court more powerful politically, because it forced the justices to act as umpires between two relative equals. When, however, states challenged federal *judicial* authority, and in a manner contrary to Taney's vision of "the Constitution's" substantive objectives, he and his brethren could speak as nationalistically as Marshall, as the Court's opinion in Ableman v. Booth (1859; reprinted above, p. 367) illustrates.

Near the end of the nineteenth century, when the justices became persuaded that "the Constitution" required, perhaps included, an economic theory of laissez-faire, they turned to dual federalism as a weapon against federal regulation of the economy. There was a great deal of irony here, for Taney had largely developed his doctrine to allow state governments to regulate commercial affairs in the absence of congressional action. From 1890 until 1937, however, the justices often used dual federalism to strike down congressional regulation on grounds that it somehow interfered with powers reserved to the states. When, for example, the U.S. government tried to break up a monopoly that controlled 97 per cent of sugar refining, [10] the Court held it irrelevant that the business was involved in commerce on a national scale. Manufacturing was local and therefore under state authority; that authority limited the power of Congress to "regulate commerce ... among the several States."

Reading laissez-faire into "the Constitution" required the justices to play games with stare decisis by either ignoring or misstating Marshall's jurisprudence; it was also useful, if not essential, to sin against textualism. To justify striking down a congressional effort to ban goods made by child labor from being shipped in interstate

---

8. Willson v. Blackbird Creek Marsh Co. (1829).

9. "Introduction to the 1953 Edition," reprinted in Lester S. Jayson et al., eds., *The Constitution of the United States of America: Analysis and Interpretation* (Washington, DC: Government Printing Office, 1973), p. xix.

10. United States v. E.C. Knight (1895).

commerce, the Court not only took a narrow view of the "sweeping clause," it also read the Tenth Amendment so expansively as to include the word expressly, which the states righters of the First Congress had been unable to put in. Justice Day thus wrote for the Court:

> In interpreting the Constitution it must never be forgotten that the Nation is made up of States to which are entrusted the powers of local government. And to them and to the people the powers not *expressly* delegated to the National Government are reserved.[11] [Italics added.]

Using such reasoning, the justices could strike down federal efforts to regulate economic affairs as invading state authority under the Tenth Amendment and state efforts to regulate the same matters as violating the due process clause of the Fourteenth Amendment.

C. A Return to National Supremacy

As we have seen, Roosevelt's landslide victory in the election of 1936 helped move the justices to end their constitutional liaison with laissez-faire. In the spring of 1937, the old justices began expanding their views about the reach of the commerce clause.[12] In 1941, Justice Stone quoted Marshall in Gibbons v. Ogden to hold for the Court that the "power of Congress over interstate commerce 'is complete in itself, may be exercised to its utmost extent, and acknowledges no limitations other than are prescribed in the Constitution.' " The Tenth Amendment, Stone continued,

> states but a truism that all is retained which has not been surrendered. There is nothing in the history of its adoption to suggest that it was more than declaratory of the relationship between the national and state government as it had been established by the Constitution before the amendment or that its purpose was other than to allay fears that the new national government might seek to exercise powers not granted, and that the states might not be able to exercise fully their reserved powers.[13]

Wickard v. Filburn (1942) showed just how far the President, Congress, and the Court were willing to go. There the justices upheld a fine against a farmer for planting 11 more acres of wheat than the quota set by the Secretary of Agriculture. That Farmer Filburn intended to consume the wheat on his own farm was of no import, because, the Court reasoned, if he could do it so could other farmers, and a large number of farmers consuming wheat produced in excess of their quotas could depress the national market for wheat.

---

11. Hammer v. Dagenhart (1918).

12. See espec. NLRB v. Jones & Laughlin (1937); NLRB v. Fruehauf Trailer Co. (1937); NLRB v. Friedman–Harry Marks Clothing Co. (1937).

13. United States v. Darby Lumber Co. (1941).

During the decades that followed the justices treated as settled Congress' constitutional authority to regulate almost any commercial activity. It was under this broad view of the commerce power that the Court sustained provisions of the Civil Rights Act of 1964 outlawing segregation in most hotels, restaurants, and similar facilities.[14]

Federal regulations and taxes touching on state governments, as contrasted with private or nongovernmental entities, have generated more lasting problems. In dual federalist fashion, the Court, beginning with Collector v. Day (1871), extrapolated from *M'Culloch* 's insistence on the immunity of federal instrumentalities from state taxation, to the immunity of state instrumentalities from federal taxation. This state shield did not cover ordinary commercial activities not normally conducted by government, such as selling liquor or operating a railroad, but that shield did protect salaries of governmental employees. The Court even went so far as to exempt a private manufacturer from federal taxes on the sale of motorcycles to a municipal police department.[15]

Shortly after the constitutional revolution of 1937, Helvering v. Gerhart (1939) abandoned one aspect of dual federalism by agreeing that a group of state employees had to pay federal income taxes on their salaries. But something of the doctrine of state immunity from federal taxation remains and with it such problems as what separates an essential governmental function from ordinary commercial activities and when a tax is a so-called user fee to which the immunity doctrine has been held inapplicable.[16]

The most important of these remaining questions is, of course, what background constitutional theory and interpretation might justify reading the document to include *any* state immunity from federal taxation. Textualism does not help. For the Sixteenth Amendment authorized Congress "to lay and collect taxes on, from whatever source derived. . . ." Resort to the founders raises other kinds of questions. Were Madison and Marshall off the mark when they argued, respectively, in *The Federalist* (espec. No. 10; reprinted below, p. 1087) and *McCulloch* that the national government would be a better repository for liberty than the states (Madison) and that (Marshall) national goals were paramount to those of the states? Did Marshall miss something about the requirements of democratic legitimacy in *McCulloch* when he reasoned that state burdens on federal policy were undemocratic because Congress represented all Americans, including the people of a given state, while the several states represented only fractions of the whole

---

14. See espec. Heart of Atlanta Motel v. United States (1964). But see United States v. Lopez (1995; discussed below, p. 596).

15. Indian Motorcycle Co. v. United States (1931).

16. See, e.g., New York v. United States (1947; upholding a federal tax applied to sales of mineral water bottled by a state); and Massachusetts v. United States (1978; upholding an annual federal registration tax applied to a state helicopter as a method of recovering the costs of federal services used by the nation's civil aircraft).

people? Would better theories of liberty and democracy find an essential place for small, local governments with real rights to pursue their own policies, even when opposed by the rest of the nation? Can states as large and as culturally diverse as California, New York, and Florida satisfy the criteria of some better theory of democracy?

The Court revisited some of these problems in 1976 when it returned to dual federalism by inferring a doctrine of state *regulatory* immunity from the surviving doctrine of state *tax* immunity. Even general regulations not related to taxation, such as those setting minimum wage and hours, when applied to state employees, can have a significant impact on a state's expenditures and, therewith, its policies. The Court invalidated one such federal regulation in National League of Cities v. Usery (1976; reprinted below, p. 565). But the times did not favor a strong doctrine of state regulatory immunity. After almost a decade in which the Court resisted extending *League of Cities*, the justices overruled that case and returned to the spirit of *McCulloch* in Garcia v. San Antonio MTA (1985; reprinted below, p. 576). The dissenters in *Garcia* angrily vowed they would continue the fight for states rights, however, and in the most recent round, New York v. United States (1992; reprinted below, p. 585), the states' righters prevailed, perhaps not unexpectedly in an area—disposal of radioactive waste—whose practical consequences and underlying philosophic assumptions remain controversial.

III. PROTECTING FEDERALISM: A TASK FOR JUDGES OR LEGISLATORS?

"Federalism," a noted English scholar claimed, "means legalism—the predominance of the judiciary in the Constitution." [17] This aspect of limited powers returns us directly to the question Chapters 7 and 8 addressed: WHO shall interpret "the Constitution"? Certainly American judges have usually played a prominent part in safeguarding the federal nature of the system.

Still, the efficacy of that role is open to dispute. Political scientists like Morton Grodzins [18] and Daniel J. Elazar [19] have claimed that the strongest protection for the states comes not from judges but from the way federalism permeates all American political structures, formal and informal. Political parties, like most interest groups, are federal in their organization. Senators and representatives are elected from individual states, not from the nation as a whole. And while they take oaths as national officials, they cannot

---

17. A.V. Dicey, *Introduction to the Study of the Law of the Constitution* (6th ed.; London: Macmillan, 1902), pp. 170–171.

18. *The American System*, ed. Daniel J. Elazar, (Chicago: Rand, McNally, 1966).

19. *American Federalism* (3d ed.; New York: Harper & Row, 1984).

afford to run roughshod over the wishes—and bases of power—of those on whom they depend for reelection.[20]

The President's constituency is national, but to get anything done he has to win Congress' consent; and, even within the executive branch, he must operate through sets of bureaucracies that often display deeper loyalty to senators and representatives on budgetary subcommittees (and those legislators' concerns for local interests) than to a temporary tenant of the White House. Furthermore, to save money, create jobs for constituents, and ease the appearance of a threat to state authority, Congress often provides that state and local officials will share in administering federal laws.

Some legal scholars not only agree that judges are not very helpful federal umpires but also assert, as does Jesse H. Choper, for instance, that such a role is an imprudent if not improper one for judges. They should, he argues, conserve their time, energy, and power to protect individual rights, for private citizens seldom have the political strength to stand up against governmental officials, state or national.[21]

It is worthwhile to note that reservations about the judiciary's role in this area do not inevitably signal a bias in favor of state over national interests. John Marshall, after all, suggested a substantial, though not exclusive, reliance on the states' representation in Congress as way to protect states' interests. And Hugo Black did not want the Court to decide when state regulation of commerce trespassed on congressional power because, he reasoned, it was to Congress that the constitutional text delegated the power to regulate commerce. And Congress was quite capable of exercising that authority: "A century and a half of constitutional history and government admonishes this Court to leave that choice to the elected representatives of the people themselves, where it properly belongs both on democratic principles and the requirements of efficient government." [22]

League of Cities, Garcia, and New York v. United States (not to mention *Lopez*) have continued this debate. Blackmun's view for

---

20. For a study linking congressional behavior with a felt necessity for reelection, see David R. Mayhew, *Congress: The Electoral Connection* (New Haven: Yale University Press, 1974).

21. *Judicial Review and the National Political Process* (Chicago: University of Chicago Press, 1980). As Chapter 10 indicated, Choper also makes a similar argument against judges' marking boundaries of power between Congress and the President. For an earlier similar argument on federalism, see also Herbert Wechsler, "The Political Safeguards of Federalism: The Role of the States in the Composition and Selection of the National Government," 54 *Col.L.Rev.* 543 (1954).

22. Dissenting in Southern Pacific Co. v. Arizona (1945); see also his dissent in Hood v. Du Mond (1949). In both these cases Justice Jackson joined the majority, but he apparently also accepted the primacy of political processes as protectors as federalism. As he wrote for the Court in Wickard v. Filburn (1942): Marshall in Gibbons v. Ogden (1824) had "made emphatic the embracing and penetrating nature of [the commerce power] by warning that effective restraints on its exercise must proceed from political rather than from judicial processes."

the majority in *Garcia* was that "the principal means chosen by the Framers to ensure the role of the States in the federal system lies in the structure of the Federal Government itself." After echoing the reasoning of Grodzins and Elazar, Blackmun concluded:

> [T]he Framers chose to rely on a federal system in which special restraints on federal power over the States inhered principally in the workings of the National Government itself, rather than in discrete limitations on the objects of federal authority. State sovereign interests, then, are more properly protected by procedural safeguards inherent in the structure of the federal system than by judicially created limitations on federal power.

But, like *Garcia*, these arguments go against the grain of judicial history. As Justice William O. Douglas once noted: "We sit as a court of law functioning primarily as a referee in the federal system." [23] And Justice O'Connor redeemed the promise she had made with Justices Rehnquist and Powell in *Garcia* that the dissenters would rise again. In 1992, she spoke for the Court in New York v. United States, holding that: The Tenth Amendment does reserve a "core of sovereignty" to the states; this core limits Congress's power just as does the First Amendment; *and* the Court has a solemn responsibility to determine Congress if "oversteps the boundary between federal and state authority."

IV. THE CONTINUING STRUGGLE

Until after the Civil War, differences about the nature of the Union posed the most serious threat to the survival of the American Republic. Although the nature of the union persists as a problem for constitutional interpretation, after the Civil War it was replaced at center stage by a question that accompanied the rise of American capitalism: How can the polity accommodate economic liberty in an age of increasing interdependence? This problem, though also still with us to some extent, has in turn been replaced by the problem of what such "fundamental rights" like privacy and equality should mean to a people whose religious, racial, ethnic, and other differences stand as stubborn barriers to achieving a consensus on fundamental values.

And this problem of deep cultural differences within a broader American community has always attracted a states' rights response. Instead of one uniform national solution to such issues as abortion, school prayer, and racial justice, it is wiser to have a number of local solutions and a right of each American to move to the community that reflects his or her values. So, at any rate, goes the "small republic" theme of the Anti–Federalists opponents of the constitutional text of 1787–88, a theme that resonates with the conservative

---

23. Walker v. Birmingham, dis. op. (1967).

mainstream of the 1990s [24] and has in the past and continues today to resonate among more liberal groups. Little wonder, then, that a Supreme Court dominated by judges chosen by Ronald Reagan and George Bush should have lost little time in rejecting the theoretical underpinnings of *Garcia*, as New York v. United States did.[25] And it is not at all clear that President William Jefferson Clinton would want to change this particular aspect of the Court's constitutional jurisprudence. In his first years in the White House, the former Governor of Arkansas showed tender regard for claims of dispersed federalism. For example, his plans for universal medical care and for higher standards in education had been national programs that state officials would apply on a state-by-state basis.

SELECTED BIBLIOGRAPHY

Amar, Akhil Reed. "Of Sovereignty and Federalism," 96 *Yale L.J.* 1425 (1987).

Barber, Sotirios A. *On What the Constitution Means* (Baltimore: The Johns Hopkins University Press, 1984), ch. 4.

Berns, Walter. "The Meaning of the 10th Amendment," in Robert A. Goldwin, ed., *A Nation of States* (Chicago: Rand, McNally, 1974).

Black, Charles L. *Structure and Relationship in American Constitutional Law* (Baton Rouge: Louisiana State University Press, 1969).

Choper, Jesse H. *Judicial Review and the National Political Process* (Chicago: University of Chicago Press, 1980).

Corwin, Edward S. "The Passing of Dual Federalism," 36 *Va.L.Rev.* 1 (1950).

Diamond, Martin. "What the Framers Meant by Federalism," in Robert A. Goldwin, ed., *A Nation of States* (Chicago: Rand, McNally, 1974).

Duchachek, Ivo D. *Comparative Federalism* (New York: Holt, Rinehart & Winston, 1970).

Elazar, Daniel J. *American Federalism* (3rd ed.; New York: Harper & Row, 1984).

Freund, Paul. "A Supreme Court in a Federation," 53 *Colum.L.Rev.* 597 (1953).

---

24. See William A. Schambra, "Progressive Liberalism and American Community," 80 *The Public Interest* 31 (1985).

25. See also Gregory v. Ashcroft (1991).

————. "Umpiring the Federal System," in Arthur W. MacMahon, ed. *Federalism Mature and Emergent* (New York: Doubleday, 1955).

Grodzins, Morton. *The American System*, ed. Daniel J. Elazar. (Chicago: Rand, McNally, 1966).

Harris, William F. II. *The Interpretable Constitution* (Baltimore: Johns Hopkins University Press, 1993), ch. 2.

Lofgren, Charles A. "The Origins of the Tenth Amendment," in Ronald K.L. Collins, ed., *Constitutional Government in America* (Durham, NC: Carolina Academic Press, 1980).

McConnell, Michael W. "Federalism: Evaluating the Framers' Design," 54 *U.Chi.L.Rev.* 1484 (1987).

McWhinney, Edward. *Comparative Federalism* (Toronto: University of Toronto Press, 1962).

Mason, Alpheus Thomas, ed. *The States Rights Debate: Anti–Federalism and the Constitution* (2d ed.; Englewood Cliffs, NJ: Prentice–Hall, 1972).

Pritchett, C. Herman. *The Constitutional Law of the Federal System* (Englewood Cliffs, NJ: Prentice–Hall, 1984), chs. 4–5, 11–13.

Riker, William H. *Federalism: Origin, Operation, Significance* (Boston: Little, Brown, 1964).

Storing, Herbert J. *What the Anti–Federalists Were For* (Chicago: University of Chicago Press, 1981).

"The proposed Constitution ... is, in strictness, neither a national nor a federal Constitution, but a composition of both."

FEDERALIST NO. 39

James Madison (1788).

... The first question that offers itself is whether the general form and aspect of the government be strictly republican. It is evident that no other form would be reconcilable with the genius of the people of America; with the fundamental principles of the Revolution; or with that honorable determination which animates every votary of freedom to rest all our political experiments on the capacity of mankind for self-government. ...

If we resort for a criterion to the different principles on which different forms of government are established, we may define a republic to be ... a government which derives all its powers directly or indirectly from the great body of the people, and is administered by persons holding their offices during pleasure for a limited period, or during good behavior. It is *essential* to such a government that it be derived from the great body of the society, not from an inconsiderable proportion or a favored class of it. ... It is *sufficient* for such a government that the persons administering it be appointed, either directly or indirectly, by the people; and that they hold their appointments by either of the tenures just specified. ...

On comparing the Constitution planned by the convention with the standard here fixed, we perceived at once that it is, in the most rigid sense, conformable to it. The House of Representatives ... is elected immediately by the great body of the people. The Senate ... derives its appointment indirectly from the people. The President is indirectly derived from the choice of the people, according to the example in most of the States. Even the judges, with all other officers of the Union, will, as in the several States, be the choice, though a remote choice, of the people themselves. The duration of the appointments is equally conformable to the republican standard and to the model of State constitutions. ...

Could any further proof be required of the republican complexion of this system, the most decisive one might be found in its absolute prohibition of titles of nobility, both under the federal and the State governments; and in its express guaranty of the republican form to each of the latter.

"But it was not sufficient," say the adversaries of the proposed Constitution, "for the convention to adhere to the republican form. They ought with equal care to have preserved the *federal** form, which regards the Union as a *Confederacy* of sovereign states; instead of which they have framed a *national* government, which regards the Union as a *consolidation* of the States." And it is asked by what authority this bold and radical innovation was undertaken? ...

... [I]t will be necessary ... first, to ascertain the real character of the government in question; secondly, to inquire how far the convention were authorized to propose such a government; and thirdly, how far the duty they owed to their country could supply any defect of regular authority.

First.—In order to ascertain the real character of the government, it may be considered in relation to the foundation on which it is to be

---

* Madison uses the term "federal" to refer to an arrangement closer to what modern analysts would call a confederation, that is, a union of sovereign states with a weak central government that operates only vis-à-vis the states and not directly on citizens of those states. Today we refer to the mixed system Madison describes here as "federal" and make a three-fold distinction among a confederation, a federal system, and a unitary system in which the central government is supreme in all spheres and local governments are merely its creatures. Each individual American state has a unitary system: Local governments exist at the sufferance of the state government, at least in formal terms, though the actual power of some local officials may be such as to make them more influential than many state officials.—**Eds.' Note.**

established; to the sources from which its ordinary powers are to be drawn; to the operation of those powers; to the extent of them; and to the authority by which future changes in the government are to be introduced.

On examining the first relation, it appears, on one hand, that the Constitution is to be founded on the assent and ratification of the people of America, given by deputies elected for the special purpose; but, on the other, that this assent and ratification is to be given by the people, not as individuals composing one entire nation, but as composing the distinct and independent States to which they respectively belong. It is to be the assent and ratification of the several States, derived from the supreme authority in each State—the authority of the people themselves. The act, therefore, establishing the Constitution will not be a *national* but a *federal* act.

That it will be a federal and not a national act ... is obvious from this single consideration: that it is to result neither from the decision of a *majority* of the people of the Union, nor from that of a *majority* of the States. It must result from the *unanimous* assent of the several States that are parties to it, differing no otherwise from their ordinary assent than in its being expressed, not by the legislative authority, but by that of the people themselves. Were the people regarded in this transaction as forming one nation, the will of the majority of the whole people of the United States would bind the minority. ... Each State, in ratifying the Constitution, is considered as a sovereign body independent of all others, and only to be bound by its own voluntary act. In this relation, then, the new Constitution will, if established, be a *federal* and not a *national* constitution.

The next relation is to the sources from which the ordinary powers of government are to be derived. The House of Representatives will derive its powers from the people of America; and the people will be represented in the same proportion and on the same principle as they are in the legislature of a particular State. So far the government is *national,* not *federal.* The Senate, on the other hand, will derive its powers from the States as political and coequal societies; and these will be represented on the principle of equality in the Senate, as they now are in the existing Congress. So far the government is *federal,* not *national.* The executive power will be derived from a very compound source. The immediate election of the President is to be made by the States in their political characters. The votes allotted to them are in a compound ratio, which considers them partly as distinct and coequal societies, partly as unequal members of the same society. The eventual election again, is to be made by that branch of the legislature* which consists of the national representatives; but in this particular act they are to be thrown into the form of individual delegations from so many distinct and co-equal bodies

---

*This comment is one of several hints that many of the founders expected that the Electoral College would usually nominate candidates for the presidency and the House would make the final choice.—**Eds.**

politic. From this aspect of the government it appears to be of a mixed character, presenting at least as many *federal* as *national* features.

... [As to] the *operation of the government* ... the Constitution ... falls under the *national* not the *federal* character; though perhaps not so completely as has been understood. In several cases, and particularly in the trial of controversies to which States may be parties, they must be viewed and proceeded against in their collective and political capacities only. But the operation of the government on the people in their individual capacities, in its ordinary and most essential proceedings, will, in the sense of its opponents, on the whole, designate it, in this relation, a *national* government.

But if the government be national with regard to the *operation* of its powers, it changes its aspect again when we contemplate it in relation to the extent of its powers. The idea of a national government involves in it not only an authority over the individual citizens, but an indefinite supremacy over all persons and things, so far as they are objects of lawful government. Among a people consolidated into one nation, this supremacy is completely vested in the national legislature. Among communities united for particular purposes, it is vested partly in the general and partly in the municipal legislatures. In the former case, all local authorities are subordinate to the supreme; and may be controlled, directed, or abolished by it at pleasure. In the latter, the local or municipal authorities form distinct and independent portions of the supremacy, no more subject, within their respective spheres, to the general authority than the general authority is subject to them, within its own sphere. In this relation, then, the proposed government cannot be deemed a *national* one; since its jurisdiction extends to certain enumerated objects only, and leaves to the several States a residuary and inviolable sovereignty over all other objects. It is true that in controversies relating to the boundary between the two jurisdictions, the tribunal which is ultimately to decide is to be established under the general government. But this does not change the principle of the case. The decision is to be impartially made, according to the rules of the Constitution; and all the usual and most effectual precautions are taken to secure this impartiality. Some such tribunal is clearly essential to prevent an appeal to the sword and a dissolution of the compact; and that it ought to be established under the general rather than under the local governments, or, to speak more properly, that it could be safely established under the first alone, is a position not likely to be combated.

If we try the Constitution by its last relation to the authority by which amendments are to be made, we find it neither wholly *national* nor wholly *federal*. ... In requiring more than a majority, and particularly in computing the proportion by *States*, not by *citizens*, it departs from the national and advances towards the *federal* character; in rendering the concurrence of less than the whole number of States sufficient, it loses again the *federal* and partakes of the *national* character.

The proposed Constitution, therefore ... is, in strictness, neither a national nor a federal Constitution, but a composition of both. In its foundation it is federal, not national; in the sources from which the ordinary powers of the government are drawn, it is partly federal and partly national; in the operation of these powers, it is national, not federal; in the extent of them, again, it is federal, not national; and, finally in the authoritative mode of introducing amendments, it is neither wholly federal nor wholly national.

Publius.

"It is a mistake, that the constitution was not designed to operate upon the states, in their corporate capacities."

MARTIN v. HUNTER'S LESSEE

14 U.S. (1 Wheat.) 304, 4 L.Ed. 97 (1816).

This case, upholding the supremacy of a national treaty over a state law and of constitutional interpretations by federal over those of state judges, is reprinted above at p. 359.

"[T]he government of the Union, though limited in its powers, is supreme within its sphere of action."

McCULLOCH v. MARYLAND

17 U.S. (4 Wheat.) 316, 4 L.Ed. 579 (1819).

In 1811, during James Madison's first administration, the Jeffersonians allowed the Bank of the United States, originally chartered in 1791 at the urging of the arch-Federalist, Alexander Hamilton, to die. But, in 1816, national fiscal difficulties following the War of 1812 persuaded the Jeffersonians to recharter the Bank, which quickly became an aggressive financial institution successful in attracting much of the business of competing state banks. Local banks sought relief from their own legislatures, and many states, including Maryland, began to tax the national bank. Maryland required banks not chartered by its legislature to issue notes only on special, stamped, paper which the state would supply at an annual fee of $15,000 plus an additional charge for each note. James McCulloch, cashier of the Baltimore branch of the Bank of the United States, took time out from his systematic looting of the bank's resources to refuse to pay the tax. Maryland then obtained a judgment for the taxes from the Baltimore County court, and the state's Court of Appeals sustained the ruling. McCulloch sought a writ of error from the U.S. Supreme Court.

MARSHALL, Ch. J., delivered the opinion of the court:

In the case now to be determined, the defendant, a sovereign state, denies the obligation of a law enacted by the legislature of the Union, and the plaintiff, on his part, contests the validity of an act which has been passed by the legislature of that state. The constitution of our country, in its most interesting and vital parts, is to be considered; the conflicting powers of the government of the Union and of its members, as marked in that constitution, are to be discussed; and an opinion given, which may essentially influence the great operations of the government. No tribunal can approach such a question without a deep sense of its importance, and of the awful responsibility involved in its decision. But it must be decided peacefully, or remain a source of hostile legislation, perhaps of hostility of a still more serious nature; and if it is to be so decided, by this tribunal alone can the decision be made. On the Supreme Court of the United States has the constitution of our country devolved this important duty.

The first question made in the cause is, has Congress power to incorporate a bank?

It ... can scarcely be considered as an open question, entirely unprejudiced by the former proceedings of the nation respecting it. The principle now contested was introduced at a very early period of our history, has been recognized by many successive legislatures, and has been acted upon by the judicial department, in cases of peculiar delicacy, as a law of undoubted obligation.

It will not be denied that a bold and daring usurpation might be resisted, after an acquiescence still longer and more complete than this. But it is conceived that a doubtful question, one on which human reason may pause, and the human judgment be suspended, in the decision of which the great principles of liberty are not concerned, but the respective powers of those who are equally the representatives of the people, are to be adjusted; if not put at rest by the practice of the government, ought to receive a considerable impression from that practice. An exposition of the constitution, deliberately established by legislative acts, on the faith of which an immense property has been advanced, ought not to be lightly disregarded.

The power now contested was exercised by the first Congress elected under the present constitution.

The bill for incorporating the bank of the United States did not steal upon an unsuspecting legislature, and pass unobserved. Its principle was completely understood, and was opposed with equal zeal and ability. ... The original act was permitted to expire; but a short experience of the embarrassments to which the refusal to revive it exposed the government, convinced those who were most prejudiced against the measure of its necessity and induced the passage of the present law. It would require no ordinary share of intrepidity to assert that a measure adopted under these circumstances was a bold and plain usurpation, to which the constitution gave no countenance.

These observations belong to the cause; but they are not made under the impression that, were the question entirely new, the law would be found irreconcilable with the constitution.

In discussing this question, the counsel for the state of Maryland have deemed it of some importance in the construction of the constitution, to consider that instrument not as emanating from the people, but as the act of sovereign and independent states. The powers of the general government, it has been said, are delegated by the states, who alone are truly sovereign; and must be exercised in subordination to the states, who alone possess supreme dominion.

It would be difficult to sustain this proposition. The convention which framed the constitution was indeed elected by the state legislatures. But the instrument, when it came from their hands, was a mere proposal, without obligation, or pretensions to it. It was reported to the then existing Congress of the United States, with a request that it might "be submitted to a convention of delegates, chosen in each state by the people thereof, under the recommendation of its legislature, for their assent and ratification." This mode of proceeding was adopted; and by the convention, by Congress, and by the state legislatures, the instrument was submitted to the people. They acted upon it in the only manner in which they can act safely, effectively, and wisely, on such a subject, by assembling in convention. It is true, they assembled in their several states—and where else should they have assembled? No political dreamer was ever wild enough to think of breaking down the lines which separate the states, and of compounding the American people into one common mass. Of consequence, when they act, they act in their states. But the measures they adopt do not, on that account, cease to be the measures of the people themselves, or become the measures of the state governments.

From these conventions the constitution derives its whole authority. The government proceeds directly from the people; is "ordained and established" in the name of the people. ... The assent of the states, in their sovereign capacity, is implied in calling a convention, and thus submitting that instrument to the people. But the people were at perfect liberty to accept or reject it; and their act was final. It required not the affirmance, and could not be negatived, by the state governments. The constitution, when thus adopted, was of complete obligation, and bound the state sovereignties.

It has been said that the people had already surrendered all their powers to the state sovereignties, and had nothing more to give. But, surely, the question whether they may resume and modify the powers granted to government does not remain to be settled in this country. ... To the formation of a league, such as was the confederation, the state sovereignties were certainly competent. But when, "in order to form a more perfect union," it was deemed necessary to change this alliance into an effective government, possessing great and sovereign powers, and acting directly on the people, the necessity of referring it to the people, and of deriving its powers directly from them, was felt and acknowledged by all.

The government of the Union, then (whatever may be the influence of this fact on the case), is, emphatically, and truly, a government of the people. In form and in substance it emanates from them. Its powers are granted by them, and are to be exercised directly on them, and for their benefit.

This government is acknowledged by all to be one of enumerated powers. . . . But the question respecting the extent of the powers actually granted, is perpetually arising, and will probably continue to arise, as long as our system shall exist.

In discussing these questions, the conflicting powers of the general and state governments must be brought into view, and the supremacy of their respective laws, when they are in opposition, must be settled.

If any one proposition could command the universal assent of mankind, we might expect it would be this—that the government of the Union, though limited in its powers, is supreme within its sphere of action. This would seem to result necessarily from its nature. It is the government of all; its powers are delegated by all; it represents all, and acts for all. Though any one state may be willing to control its operations, no state is willing to allow others to control them. The nation, on those subjects on which it can act, must necessarily bind its component parts. But this question is not left to mere reason; the people have, in express terms, decided it by saying, "this constitution, and the laws of the United States, which shall be made in pursuance thereof," "shall be the supreme law of the land," and by requiring that the members of the state legislatures, and the officers of the executive and judicial departments of the states shall take the oath of fidelity to it.

The government of the United States, then, though limited in its powers, is supreme; and its laws, when made in pursuance of the constitution, form the supreme law of the land, "anything in the constitution or laws of any state to the contrary notwithstanding."

Among the enumerated powers, we do not find that of establishing a bank or creating a corporation. But there is no phrase in the instrument which, like the articles of confederation, excludes incidental or implied powers; and which requires that everything granted shall be expressly and minutely described. Even the 10th amendment, which was framed for the purpose of quieting the excessive jealousies which had been excited, omits the word "expressly," and declares only that the powers "not delegated to the United States, nor prohibited to the states, are reserved to the states or to the people;" thus leaving the question, whether the particular power which may become the subject of contest has been delegated to the one government, or prohibited to the other, to depend on a fair construction of the whole instrument. The men who drew and adopted this amendment had experienced the embarrassments resulting from the insertion of this word in the articles of confederation, and probably omitted it to avoid those embarrassments. A constitution, to contain an accurate detail of all the subdivisions of which its great powers will admit, and of all the means by which they may be carried into execution, would partake of a prolixity of a legal code, and could scarcely be embraced by the human mind. It would probably never be understood by the public. Its nature, therefore, requires, that only its great outlines should be marked, its important objects designated, and the minor ingredients which compose those objects be deduced from the nature of the objects themselves. That this idea was entertained by the framers of the American constitution, is not only to be inferred from the nature of the instrument, but from the language. Why else were some of the limitations, found in the ninth section of the 1st article, introduced? It is also, in some degree, warranted by their having omitted to use any restrictive term which might prevent its receiving a fair and just interpretation. In considering this question, then, we must never forget that it is *a constitution* we are expounding.

Although, among the enumerated powers of government, we do not find the word "bank" or "incorporation," we find the great powers to lay and collect taxes; to borrow money; to regulate commerce; to declare and conduct a war; and to raise and support armies and navies. The sword and the purse, all the external relations, and no inconsiderable portion of the industry of the nation, are entrusted to its government. It can never be pretended that these vast powers draw after them others of inferior importance, merely because they are inferior. ... But it may with great reason be contended, that a government, entrusted with such ample powers, on the due execution of which the happiness and prosperity of the nation so vitally depends, must also be entrusted with ample means for their execution. The power being given, it is the interest of the nation to facilitate its execution. It can never be their interest, and cannot be presumed to have been their intention, to clog and embarrass its execution by withholding the most appropriate means. Throughout this vast republic, from the St. Croix to the Gulf of Mexico, from the Atlantic to the Pacific, revenue is to be collected and expended, armies are to be marched and supported. ... Is that construction of the constitution to be preferred which would render these operations difficult, hazardous, and expensive? Can we adopt that construction (unless the words imperiously require it) which would impute to the framers of that instrument, when granting these powers for the public good, the intention of impeding their exercise by withholding a choice of means? If, indeed, such be the mandate of the constitution, we have only to obey; but that instrument does not profess to enumerate the means by which the powers it confers may be executed; nor does it prohibit the creation of a corporation, if the existence of such a being be essential to the beneficial exercise of those powers. It is, then, the subject of fair inquiry, how far such means may be employed. It is not denied that the powers given to the government imply the ordinary means of execution.

... But it is denied that the government has its choice of means; or, that it may employ the most convenient means, if, to employ them, it be necessary to erect a corporation.

On what foundation does this argument rest? On this alone: The power of creating a corporation, is one appertaining to sovereignty, and is not expressly conferred on Congress. This is true. But all legislative powers appertain to sovereignty. ...

The government which has a right to do an act, and has imposed on it the duty of performing that act, must, according to the dictates of reason, be allowed to select the means; and those who contend that it may not select any appropriate means, that one particular mode of effecting the object is excepted, take upon themselves the burden of establishing that exception. ...

... The power of creating a corporation, though appertaining to sovereignty, is not, like the power of making war, or levying taxes, or of regulating commerce, a great substantive and independent power, which cannot be implied as incidental to other powers, or used as a means of executing them. It is never the end for which other powers are exercised, but a means by which other objects are accomplished. ... No sufficient reason is, therefore, perceived, why it may not pass as incidental to those powers which are expressly given, if it be a direct mode of executing them.

But the constitution of the United States has not left the right of Congress to employ the necessary means for the execution of the powers conferred on the government to general reasoning. To its enumeration of powers is added that of making "all laws which shall be necessary and proper, for carrying into execution the foregoing powers, and all other powers vested by this constitution, in the government of the United States, or in any department thereof."

The counsel for the State of Maryland have urged ... that this clause, though in terms a grant of power, is not so in effect; but is really restrictive of the general right, which might otherwise be implied, of selecting means for executing the enumerated powers.

In support of this proposition, they have found it necessary to contend, that this clause was inserted for the purpose of conferring on Congress the power of making laws. ...

... [W]ould it have entered into the mind of a single member of the convention that an express power to make laws was necessary to enable the legislature to make them? That a legislature, endowed with legislative powers, can legislate, is a proposition too self-evident to have been questioned.

But the argument on which most reliance is placed, is drawn from the peculiar language of this clause. Congress is not empowered by it to make all laws, which may have relation to the powers conferred on the government, but such only as may be *"necessary and proper"* for carrying them into execution. The word *"necessary"* is considered as controlling the whole sentence, and as limiting the right to pass laws for the execution of the granted powers, to such as are indispensable, and without which the power would be nugatory. That it excludes the choice of means, and leaves to Congress, in each case, that only which is most direct and simple.

Is it true that this is the sense in which the word "necessary" is always used? Does it always import an absolute physical necessity, so strong that one thing, to which another may be termed necessary, cannot exist without that other? We think it does not. If reference be had to its use, in the common affairs of the world, or in approved authors, we find that it frequently imports no more than that one thing is convenient, or useful, or essential to another. To employ the means necessary to an end, is generally understood as employing any means calculated to produce the end, and not as being confined to those single means, without which the end would be entirely unattainable. Such is the character of human language, that no word conveys to the mind, in all situations, one single definite idea; and nothing is more common than to use words in a figurative sense. Almost all compositions contain words, which, taken in their rigorous sense, would convey a meaning different from that which is obviously intended. It is essential to just construction, that many words which import something excessive should be understood in a more mitigated sense—in that sense which common usage justifies. The word "necessary" is of this description. It has not a fixed character peculiar to itself. It admits of all degrees of comparison. ... A thing may be necessary, very necessary, absolutely or indispensably necessary. To no mind would the same idea be conveyed by these several phrases. ... It is, we think, impossible to compare the sentence which prohibits a state from laying "imposts or duties on imports or exports, except what may be *absolutely* necessary for executing its inspection laws," [Art. I, § 10] with that which authorizes Congress "to make all laws which shall be necessary and proper for carrying into execution" the powers of the general government, without feeling a conviction that the convention understood itself to change materially the meaning of the word "necessary," by prefixing the word "absolutely." This word, then, like others, is used in various senses; and, in its construction, the subject, the context, the intention of the person using them, are all to be taken into view.

Let this be done in the case under consideration. The subject is the execution of those great powers on which the welfare of a nation essentially depends. It must have been the intention of those who gave these powers, to insure, as far as human prudence could insure, their beneficial execution. This could not be done by confining the choice of means to such narrow limits as not to leave it in the power of Congress to adopt any which might be appropriate, and which were conducive to the end. This provision is made in a constitution intended to endure for ages to come, and, consequently, to be adapted to the various *crises* of human affairs. To have prescribed the means by which government should, in all future time, execute its powers, would have been to change, entirely, the character of the instrument, and give it the properties of a legal code. It would have been an unwise attempt to provide, by immutable rules, for exigencies which, if foreseen at all, must have been seen dimly, and which can be best provided for as they occur. To have declared that the best means shall not be used, but those alone without which the power given would be nugatory, would have been to deprive the legislature of the capacity to avail itself of experience, to exercise its reason, and to accommodate its legislation to circumstances. If we apply this principle of construction to any of the powers of the government, we shall find it so pernicious in its operation that we shall be compelled to discard it. ...

In ascertaining the sense in which the word "necessary" is used in this clause of the constitution, we may derive some aid from that with which it is associated. Congress shall have power "to make all laws which shall be necessary and proper to carry into execution" the powers of the government. If the word "necessary" was used in that strict and rigorous sense for which the counsel for the state of Maryland contend, it would be an extraordinary departure from the usual course of the human mind, as exhibited in composition, to add a word, the only possible effect of which is to qualify that strict and rigorous meaning; to present to the mind the idea of some choice of means of legislation not straightened and compressed within the narrow limits for which gentlemen contend.

But the argument which most conclusively demonstrates the error of the construction contended for by the counsel for the state of Maryland, is founded on the intention of the convention, as manifested in the whole clause. To waste time and argument in proving that without it Congress might carry its powers into execution, would be not much less idle than to hold a lighted taper to the sun. As little can it be required to prove, that in the absence of this clause, Congress would have some choice of means. That it might employ those which, in its judgment, would most advantageously effect the object to be accomplished. That any means adapted to the end, any means which tended directly to the execution of the constitutional powers of the government, were in themselves constitutional. This clause, as construed by the state of Maryland, would abridge, and almost annihilate this useful and necessary right of the legislature to select its means. That this could not be intended, is, we should think, had it not been already controverted, too apparent for controversy. We think so for the following reasons:

1st. The clause is placed among the powers of Congress, not among the limitations on those powers.

2d. Its terms purport to enlarge, not to diminish the powers vested in the government. It purports to be an additional power, not a restriction on those already granted. No reason has been, or can be assigned for thus concealing an intention to narrow the discretion of the national legislature under words which purport to enlarge it. ... If, then, their intention had been, by this clause, to restrain the free use of means which might otherwise have been implied, that intention would have been inserted in another place, and would have been expressed in terms resembling these. "In carrying into execution the foregoing powers, and all others," & c., "no laws shall be passed but such as are necessary and proper." ...

We admit, as all must admit, that the powers of the government are limited, and that its limits are not to be transcended. But we think the sound construction of the constitution must allow to the national legislature that discretion, with respect to the means by which the powers it confers are to be carried into execution, which will enable that body to perform the high duties assigned to it, in the manner most beneficial to the people. Let the end be legitimate, let it be within the scope of the constitution, and all means which are appropriate, which are plainly adapted to that end, which are not prohibited, but consist with the letter and spirit of the constitution, are constitutional.

That a corporation must be considered as a means not less usual, not of higher dignity, not more requiring a particular specification than other means, has been sufficiently proved. ...

... Should Congress, in the execution of its powers, adopt measures which are prohibited by the constitution; or should Congress, under the pretext of executing its powers pass laws for the accomplishment of objects not intrusted to the government, it would become the painful duty of this tribunal, should a case requiring such a decision come before it, to say that such an act was not the law of the land. But where the law is not prohibited, and is really calculated to effect any of the objects entrusted to the government, to undertake here to inquire into the degree of its necessity, would be to pass the line which circumscribes the judicial department, and to tread on legislative ground. This court disclaims all pretensions to such a power. ...

It being the opinion of the court that the act incorporating the bank is constitutional, and that the power of establishing a branch in the state of Maryland might be properly exercised by the bank itself, we proceed to inquire:

2. Whether the state of Maryland may, without violating the constitution, tax that branch?

That the power of taxation is one of vital importance; that it is retained by the states; that it is not abridged by the grant of a similar power to the government of the Union; that it is to be concurrently exercised by the two governments: are truths which have never been denied. But, such is the paramount character of the constitution that its capacity to withdraw any subject from the action of even this power, is admitted. The states are expressly forbidden to lay any duties on imports or exports, except what may be absolutely necessary for executing their inspection laws. If the obligation of this prohibition must be conceded ... the same paramount character would seem to restrain ... a state from such other exercise of this power, as is in its nature incompatible with, and repugnant to, the constitutional laws of the Union. A law, absolutely repugnant to another, as entirely repeals that other as if express terms of repeal were used.

On this ground the counsel for the bank place its claim to be exempted from the power of a state to tax its operations. There is no express provision for the case, but the claim has been sustained on a principle which so entirely pervades the constitution, is so intermixed with the materials which compose it, so interwoven with its web, so blended with its texture, as to be incapable of being separated from it without rending it into shreds.

This great principle is, that the constitution and the laws made in pursuance thereof are supreme; that they control the constitution and laws of the respective states, and cannot be controlled by them. From this, which may be almost termed an axiom, other propositions are deduced as corollaries. ... These are, 1st. That a power to create implies a power to preserve. 2d. That a power to destroy if wielded by a different hand, is hostile to, and incompatible with these powers to create and to preserve. 3d. That where this repugnancy exists, that authority which is supreme must control, not yield to that over which it is supreme. ...

That the power of taxing it by the states may be exercised so as to destroy it, is too obvious to be denied. But taxation is said to be an absolute power, which acknowledges no other limits than those expressly prescribed in the constitution, and like sovereign power of every other description, is trusted to the discretion of those who use it. But the very terms of this argument admit that the sovereignty of the state, in the article of taxation itself, is subordinate to, and may be controlled by the constitution of the United States. How far it has been controlled by that instrument must be a question of construction. In making this construction, no principle not declared can be admissible, which would defeat the legitimate operations of a supreme government. It is of the very essence of supremacy to remove all obstacles to its action within its own sphere, and so to modify every power vested in subordinate governments as to exempt its own operations from their own influence. This effect need not be stated in terms. It is so involved in the declaration of supremacy, so necessarily implied in it, that the expression of it could not make it more certain. We must, therefore, keep it in view while construing the constitution. ...

... It is admitted that the power of taxing the people and their property is essential to the very existence of government, and may be legitimately exercised on the objects to which it is applicable, to the utmost extent to which the government may chose to carry it. The only security against the abuse of this power is found in the structure of the government itself. In imposing a tax the legislature acts upon its constituents. This is in general a sufficient security against erroneous and oppressive taxation.

The people of a state, therefore, give to their government a right of taxing themselves and their property, and as the exigencies of government cannot be limited, they prescribe no limits to the exercise of this right, resting confidently on the interest of the legislator, and on the influence of the constituents over their representative, to guard them against its abuse. But the means employed by the government of the Union have no such security, nor is the right of a state to tax them sustained by the same theory. Those means are not given by the people of a particular state, not given by the constituents of the legislature, which claim the right to tax them, but by the people of all the states. They are given by all, for the benefit of all—and upon theory, should be subjected to that government only which belongs to all. ...

If we measure the power of taxation residing in a state, by the extent of sovereignty which the people of a single state possess, and can confer on its government, we have an intelligible standard, applicable to every case to which the power may be applied. We have a principle which leaves the power of taxing the people and property of a state unimpaired; which leaves to a state the command of all its resources, and which places beyond its reach, all those powers which are conferred by the people of the United States on the government of the Union, and all those means which are given for the purpose of carrying those powers into execution. ... The attempt to use it [the state's power to tax] on the means employed by the government of the Union, in pursuance of the constitution, is itself an abuse, because it is the usurpation of a power which the people of a single state cannot give. ...

... Would the people of any one state trust those of another with a power to control the most insignificant operations of their state government? We know they would not. Why, then, should we suppose that the people of any one state should be willing to trust those of another with a power to control the operations of a government to which they have confided the most important and most valuable interests? In the legislature of the Union alone, are all represented. The legislature of the Union alone, therefore, can be trusted by the people with the power of controlling measures which concern all, in the confidence that it will not be abused. ...

If the states may tax one instrument, employed by the [national] government in the execution of its powers, they may tax any and every other instrument. They may tax the mail; they may tax the mint; they may tax patent-rights; they may tax the papers of the custom-house; they may tax judicial process; they may tax all the means employed by the government, to an excess which would defeat all the ends of government. This was not intended by the American people. They did not design to make their government dependent on the states.

In the course of the argument, *The Federalist* has been quoted; and the opinions expressed by the authors of that work have been justly supposed to be entitled to great respect in expounding the constitution. No tribute can be paid to them which exceeds their merit; but in applying their opinions to the cases which may arise in the progress of our government, a right to judge of their correctness must be retained; and, to understand the argument, we must examine the proposition it maintains, and the objections against which it is directed. ...

The objections to the constitution which are noticed in these numbers [of *The Federalist*], were to the undefined power of the government to tax, not to the incidental privilege of exempting its own measures from state taxation. ...

It has also been insisted, that, as the power of taxation in the general and state governments is acknowledged to be concurrent, every argument which would sustain the right of the general government to tax banks chartered by the states, will equally sustain the right of the states to tax banks chartered by the general government.

But the two cases are not on the same reason. The people of all the states have created the general government, and have conferred upon it the general power of taxation. The people of all the states, and the states themselves, are represented in Congress, and, by their representatives, exercise this power. When they tax the chartered institutions of the states, they tax their constituents; and these taxes must be uniform. But, when a state taxes the operations of the government of the United States, it acts upon institutions created, not by their own constituents, but by people over whom they claim no control. It acts upon the measures of a government created by others as well as themselves, for the benefit of others in common with themselves. The difference is that which always exists, and always must exist, between the action of the whole on a part, and the action of a part on the whole—between the laws of a government declared to be supreme, and those of a government which, when in opposition to those laws, is not supreme.

But if the full application of this argument could be admitted, it might bring into question the right of Congress to tax the state banks, and could not prove the right of the states to tax the Bank of the United States. ...

We are unanimously of opinion that the law passed by the legislature of Maryland, imposing a tax on the Bank of the United States, is unconstitutional and void.

This opinion does not deprive the states of any resources which they originally possessed. It does not extend to a tax paid by the real property of the bank, in common with the other real property within the state, nor to a tax imposed on the interest which the citizens of Maryland may hold in this institution, in common with other property of the same description throughout the state. But this is a tax on the operations of the bank, and is, consequently, a tax on the operation of an instrument employed by the government of the Union to carry its powers into execution. Such a tax must be unconstitutional.

Editors' Notes

(1) **Query:** What sort of structural approach to constitutional interpretation did Marshall employ? Merely textual? Systemic? Transcendent? To what extent did he combine a purposive approach with structuralism?

(2) Compare Marshall's view of the structure of American federalism with that of Madison in *Federalist* No. 39, reprinted above, p. 526. To what extent did Madison agree with Marshall's claim that the national government (and so "the Constitution") "proceeds directly from the people; is 'ordained and established' in the name of the people"?

(3) "[W]e must never forget that it is a *constitution* we are expounding" is probably the most often quoted passage in American constitutional law. As Justice Frankfurter remarked: "It bears repeating because it is, I believe, the single most important utterance in the literature of constitutional law—most important because most comprehensive and comprehending." What is "most comprehensive and comprehending" about it? Presumably proponents of alternative concepts of "the Constitution" discussed in Chapters 5 and 6 would contend that they never forget that it is a *constitution* they are expounding, but they would disagree about the nature of "the Constitution" to be expounded. What was Marshall's conception of "the Constitution"? How did it fit with the various views discussed in Chapters 5 and 6? Would his meaning have been expressed more aptly had he written: "[W]e must never forget WHAT the Constitution is that we are expounding"?

(4) **Query:** To what extent did Marshall base his reasoning on the assumption that the most important restraint on the taxing power is that of the ballot box? Put differently, to what extent was Marshall's argument based on democratic theory?

(5) **Query:** Note how Marshall spoke of "the intent" of the constitutional instrument and also brushed aside counterarguments from *The Federalist*. To what extent was he an originalist?

(6) As the headnote to this case indicated, the Bank was an explosive issue in the politics of the time. In that context, the justices feared Maryland's court of appeals would not obey their ruling. Thus, rather than merely reversing the state court, the justices entered an unusual decree:

> . . . It is, therefore, Adjudged and Ordered, that the said judgment of the said Court of Appeals of the State of Maryland in this case be, and the same hereby is, reversed and annulled. And this Court, proceeding to render such judgment as the said Court of Appeals should have rendered; it is further Adjudged and Ordered, that the judgment of the said Baltimore County Court be reversed and annulled, and that judgment be entered in the said Baltimore County Court for the said James W. McCulloch.

That judgment ended this particular piece of litigation, but the basic issue returned to the Court. See especially Osborn v. Bank of the U.S. (1824), when Ohio used physical force to extract a similar tax. The Court held such action unconstitutional. The battle against the Bank continued until Andrew Jackson's veto of the Bank bill in 1832 spelled the death of the BUS as an important national institution. His references in the veto message (reprinted above, p. 313) to a decision of the Supreme Court were, of course, to

McCulloch. Bray Hammond, *Banks and Politics in America from the Revolution to the Civil War* (Princeton: Princeton University Press, 1957) still ranks among the best accounts of the war against the bank.

(7) As the introductory essay to this chapter pointed out, after the Civil War, Marshall's dictum regarding federal authority to tax state instrumentalities experienced a rollercoaster history. Beginning with Collector v. Day (1871), the Court handed down a long series of rulings setting up walls of reciprocal tax immunity. As part of its doctrine of "dual federalism," the Court held that states were entitled to the same protection against federal taxation as the United States was against states. How does dual federalism conflict with Marshall's view of the structure of the Union? For an excellent account of the rise and fall of reciprocal tax immunity through the end of World War II, see Samuel J. Konefsky, *Chief Justice Stone and the Supreme Court* (New York: Macmillan, 1946). Although the conflicting 5–4 decisions in National League of Cities v. Usery (1976; reprinted below, p. 565), Garcia v. San Antonio MTA (1985; reprinted below, p. 576), and New York v. United States (1992; reprinted below, p. 585) demonstrate that problems of state-federal relations are hardly fully resolved, it is likely that the Court would sustain a federal tax that reached any state activity except one that is uniquely capable of being performed by a state, for example, collecting taxes or operating a legislature. Conversely, the Court would probably sustain any clear congressional decision to exempt federal activity from state taxation.

"The people of these United States constitute one nation."

CRANDALL v. NEVADA
73 U.S. (6 Wall.) 35, 18 L.Ed. 744 (1868).

In 1865, three years before adoption of the Fourteenth Amendment, Nevada levied a tax of one dollar on every person leaving the state by public conveyance and required the transporting company to collect the tax and turn it over to the state treasury. Later, Nevada officials arrested Crandall, an agent for the Pioneer Stage Co. at Carson City, for refusing to collect the tax. In his defense, he asserted that the levy was unconstitutional. After losing in state courts, he obtained a writ of error from the U.S. Supreme Court.

Mr. Justice **MILLER** delivered the opinion of the court. . . .

The people of these United States constitute one nation. They have a government in which all of them are deeply interested. This government has necessarily a capital established by law, where its principal operations are conducted. Here sits its legislature, composed of Senators and Representatives, from the states and from the people of the states. Here resides the President, directing through thousands of agents, the execution of the laws over all this vast country. Here is the seat of the supreme judicial power of the nation, to which all its citizens have a right to resort to claim justice at its hands. Here are the great

Executive Departments, administering the offices of the mails, of the public lands, of the collection and distribution of the public revenues, and of our foreign relations. These are all established and conducted under the admitted powers of the Federal government. That government has a right to call to this point any or all of its citizens to aid in its service, as members of the Congress, of the courts, of the Executive Departments, and to fill all its other offices; and this right cannot be made to depend upon the pleasure of a state over whose territory they must pass to reach the point where these services must be rendered. The government also, has its offices of secondary importance in all other parts of the country. On the seacoasts and on the rivers it has its ports of entry. In the interior it has its land offices, its revenue offices, and its sub-treasuries. In all these it demands the services of its citizens, and is entitled to bring them to those points from all quarters of the nation, and no power can exist in a state to obstruct this right that would not enable it to defeat the purposes for which the government was established.

The Federal power has a right to declare and prosecute wars and, as a necessary incident, to raise and transport troops through and over the territory of any state of the Union.

If this right is dependent in any sense, however limited, upon the pleasure of a state, the government itself may be overthrown by an obstruction to its exercise. Much the largest part of the transportation of troops during the late Rebellion was by railroads, and largely through states whose people were hostile to the Union. If the tax levied by Nevada on railroad passengers had been the law of Tennessee, enlarged to meet the wishes of her people, the Treasury of the United States could not have paid the tax necessary to enable its armies to pass through her territory.

But if the government has these rights on her own account, the citizen also has correlative rights. He has the right to come to the seat of government to assert any claim he may have upon that government, or to transact any business he may have with it. To seek its protection, to share its offices, to engage in administering its functions, he has a right to free access to its sea-ports, through which all the operations of foreign trade and commerce are conducted, to the sub-treasuries, the land offices, the revenue offices, and the court of justice in the several states, and this right is in its nature independent of the will of any state over whose soil he must pass in the exercise of it.

The views here advanced are neither novel nor unsupported by authority. The question of the taxing power of the states, as its exercise has affected the functions of the Federal government, has been repeatedly considered by this court, and the right of the states in this mode to impede or embarrass the constitutional operations of that government, or the rights which its citizens hold under it, has been uniformly denied.

The leading case of this class is that of McCulloch v. Maryland [1819]. . . .

It is not possible to condense the conclusive argument of Chief Justice Marshall in that case, and it is too familiar to justify its reproduction here; but an extract or two, in which the results of his reasoning are stated, will serve to show its applicability to the case before us. "That the power of taxing the bank by the states," he says, "may be exercised so as to destroy it, is too obvious to be denied. But taxation is said to be an absolute power which acknowledges no other limits than those prescribed by the Constitution; and, like sovereign power of any description, is trusted to the discretion of those who use it. But the very terms of this argument admit that the sovereignty of the state in the article of taxation is subordinate to, and may be controlled by, the Constitution of the United States." . . .

It will be observed that it was not the extent of the tax in that case which was complained of, but the right to levy any tax of that character. So in the case before us, it may be said that a tax of one dollar for passing through the state of Nevada, by stage coach, or by railroad, cannot sensibly affect any function of the government, or deprive a citizen of any valuable right. But if the state can tax a railroad passenger one dollar, it can tax him $1,000. If one state can do this, so can every other state. And thus one or more states covering the only practicable routes of travel from the east to the west, or from the north to the south, may totally prevent or seriously burden all transportation of passengers from one part of the country to the other. . . .

Those principles, as we have already stated them in this opinion, must govern the present case.

The judgment of the Supreme Court of the State of Nevada is, therefore, reversed, and the case remanded to that court, with directions to discharge the plaintiff in error from custody.

Mr. Justice **CLIFFORD**. . . .

. . . I hold that the act of the state legislature is inconsistent with the power conferred upon Congress to regulate commerce among the several states, and I think the judgment of the court should have been placed exclusively upon that ground. . . .

The Chief Justice [**CHASE**] also dissents, and concurs in the views I have expressed.

————

"The Constitution, in all its provisions, looks to an indestructible Union, composed of indestructible States."— Chief Justice CHASE

"If I regard the truth of history for the last eight years, I cannot discover the State of Texas as one of these United States."—Justice GRIER

TEXAS v. WHITE

74 U.S. (7 Wall.) 700, 19 L.Ed. 227 (1869).

As an indemnification for adjustments in Texas's boundary, Congress in 1851 gave that state 5,000 U.S. bonds, with a face value of $1,000 each, redeemable in gold in 1865. During the last months of the Civil War, the Texas Military Board turned over some of these bonds to George W. White and John Chiles in exchange for a promise to deliver supplies needed for the war. The arrangement smacked of fraud: The Confederacy was crumbling and the agreement called for White and Chiles, if they could not deliver the supplies, to return not the gold U.S. bonds but an equivalent amount in almost worthless state bonds.

Not surprisingly, White and Chiles did not deliver the supplies; instead, shortly after the war, they produced the now totally worthless Confederate paper to fulfill their obligation. The provisional governor refused to accept the "paper" and branded the agreement a swindle. In February, 1867, Texas filed an original suit in the U.S. Supreme Court—Article III of the constitutional document allows a state to invoke the Court's original jurisdiction—asking for an order that White and Chiles return the U.S. bonds.

During the leisurely course of litigation—the Court would not decide the case until almost two years after it was filed—Congress enacted much more stringent policies of Reconstruction than Presidents Lincoln and Johnson had followed. The new legislation denied the former Confederate states representation in Congress and removed their elected civil state governments. In their place, Congress established military officers as rulers. Thus the Court confronted a series of questions: What was Texas's constitutional status during the Civil War? What was its status immediately after the war when the suits were filed? And, assuming that the Court would rule that secession was unconstitutional and so Texas had always remained a member of the Union, what was its status now, when it had no senators or representatives and was under military rule? Was it still a state in the sense the constitutional text used that term? If so, was it not entitled to representation in Congress and were its people not entitled, as Article IV of the constitutional document ordered the federal government to guarantee them, to a "republican" not a military form of government? In sum, if Texas were still a state in the constitutional sense, then were not the policies of Radical Reconstruction invalid?

The answers to these questions were all the more difficult and delicate because of the belligerent mood of Congress. Not only were the Radicals determined to exact retribution from the South for the bloody Civil War, but they were also determined to control all three branches of the federal government. They had impeached and tried Andrew Johnson during the time the case had been on the Court's docket; and, in an effort to prevent the justices from declaring part of Reconstruction unconstitutional, Congress had also removed part of the Court's appellate jurisdiction. (See the discussion of Ex parte McCardle [1869], in Chapter 10 at pp. 467-72.)

We reprint here only those parts of the opinions dealing with questions relating to Texas's statehood—and so to the structure of the American constitutional system.

The Chief Justice [**CHASE**] delivered the opinion of the Court. ...

If ... it is true that the State of Texas was not at the time of filing this bill, or is not now, one of the United States, we have no jurisdiction of this suit. ...

In the Constitution the term "state" most frequently expresses the combined idea ... of people, territory, and government. A state, in the ordinary sense of the Constitution, is a political community of free citizens, occupying a territory of defined boundaries, and organized under a government sanctioned and limited by a written constitution, and established by the consent of the governed. It is the union of such states, under a common constitution, which forms the distinct and greater political unit, which that Constitution designates as the United States, and makes of the people and states which compose it one people and one country. ...

Did Texas, in consequence of these acts [of seceding, joining the Confederacy, and warring against the United States], cease to be a State? Or, if not, did the State cease to be a member of the Union? ...

The Union of the States never was a purely artificial and arbitrary relation. It began among the colonies and grew out of common origin, mutual sympathies, kindred principles, similar interests, and geographical relations. It was confirmed and strengthened by the necessities of war, and received definite form, and character, and sanction from the Articles of Confederation. By these the Union was solemnly declared to "be perpetual." And when these Articles were found to be inadequate to the exigencies of the country, the Constitution was ordained "to form a more perfect Union." It is difficult to convey the idea of indissoluble unity more clearly than by these words. What can be indissoluble if a perpetual Union, made more perfect, is not?

But the perpetuity and indissolubility of the Union, by no means implies the loss of distinct and individual existence, or of the right of self-government by the States. Under the Articles of Confederation each State retained its sovereignty, freedom, and independence, and every power, jurisdiction, and right not expressly delegated to the United States. Under the Constitution, though the powers of the States were much restricted, still, all powers not delegated to the United States, nor prohibited to the States, are reserved to the States respectively, or to the people. ... Not only, therefore, can there be no loss of separate and independent autonomy to the States, through their union under the Constitution, but it may be not unreasonably said that the preservation of the States, and the maintenance of their governments, are as much within the design and care of the Constitution as the preservation of the Union and the maintenance of the National government. The Constitution, in all its provisions, looks to an indestructible Union, composed of indestructible States.

When, therefore, Texas became one of the United States, she entered into an indissoluble relation. All the obligations of perpetual union, and all the guaranties of republican government in the Union, attached at once to the State. The act which consummated her admission into the Union was something more than a compact; it was the incorporation of a new member into the political body. And it was final. The union between Texas and the other States was as complete, as perpetual, and as indissoluble as the union between the original States. There was no place for reconsideration, or revocation, except through revolution, or through consent of the States.

Considered therefore as transactions under the Constitution, the ordinance of secession, adopted by the convention and ratified by a majority of the citizens of Texas, and all the acts of her legislature intended to give effect to that ordinance, were absolutely null. ...

Our conclusion therefore is, that Texas continued to be a State, and a State of the Union, notwithstanding the transactions to which we have referred. And this conclusion, in our judgment, is not in conflict with any act or declaration of any department of the National government, but entirely in accordance with the whole series of such acts and declarations since the first outbreak of the rebellion.

But in order to the exercise, by a State, of the right to sue in this court, there needs to be a State government, competent to represent the State in its relations with the National government, so far at least as the institution and prosecution of a suit is concerned.

And it is by no means a logical conclusion, from the premises which we have endeavored to establish, that the governmental relations of Texas to the Union remained unaltered. Obligations often remain unimpaired, while relations are greatly changed. ...

... No one has been bold enough to contend that, while Texas was controlled by a government hostile to the United States, and in affiliation with a hostile confederation, waging war upon the United States, senators chosen by her legislature, or representatives elected by her citizens, were entitled to seats in Congress; or that any suit, instituted in her name, could be entertained in this court. All admit that, during this condition of civil war, the rights of the State as a member, and of her people as citizens of the Union, were suspended. The government and the citizens of the State, refusing to recognize their constitutional obligations, assumed the character of enemies, and incurred the consequences of rebellion.

These new relations imposed new duties upon the United States. The first was that of suppressing the rebellion. The next was that of re-establishing the broken relations of the State with the Union. ...

The authority for the performance of the first had been found in the power to suppress insurrection and carry on war; for the performance of the second, authority was derived from the obligation of the United States to guarantee to every State in the Union a republican form of government. ...

There being no government in Texas in constitutional relations with the Union, it became the duty of the United States to provide for the restoration of such a government. ...

In the exercise of the power conferred [on the United States] by the guaranty clause [Art. IV, § 4], as in the exercise of every other constitutional power, a discretion in the choice of means is necessarily allowed. It is essential only that the means must be necessary and proper for carrying into execution the power conferred, through the restoration of the State to its constitutional relations ... and that no acts be done, and no authority exerted, which is [sic] either prohibited or unsanctioned by the Constitution.

It is not important to review, at length, the measures which have been taken ... by the executive and legislative departments of the National government. ...

... [Congress] proceeded, after long deliberation, to adopt various measures for reorganization and restoration. These measures were embodied in proposed amendments to the Constitution, and in the acts known as the Reconstruction Acts, which have been so far carried into effect, that a majority of the States which were engaged in the rebellion have been restored to their constitutional relations, under forms of government, adjudged to be republican by Congress, through the admission of their "Senators and Representatives into the councils of the Union." ...

... We do not inquire here into the constitutionality of this legislation so far as it relates to military authority, or to the paramount authority of Congress. It suffices to say, that the terms of the acts necessarily imply recognition of actually existing governments; and that in point of fact, the governments thus recognized, in some important respects, still exist. ...

In the case before us each [governor of Texas] has given his sanction to the prosecution of the suit, and we find no difficulty ... in holding that the sanction thus given sufficiently warranted the action of the solicitor and counsel in behalf of the State. The necessary conclusion is that the suit was instituted and is prosecuted by competent authority.

The question of jurisdiction being thus disposed of, we proceed to the consideration of the merits. ... [The Court held that Texas was entitled to recover the bonds.]

Mr. Justice **GRIER**, dissenting. ...

The original jurisdiction of this court can be invoked only by one of the United States. ... Is Texas one of these United States? ... This is to be decided as *a political fact*, not as a *legal fiction*. This court is bound to know and notice the public history of the nation. If I regard the truth of history for the last eight years, I cannot discover the State of Texas as one of these United States. ...

Is Texas a State, now represented by members chosen by the people of that State and received on the floor of Congress? Has she two senators to represent her as a State in the Senate of the United States? Has her voice been heard in the late election of President? Is she not now held and governed as a conquered province by military force? The act of Congress of March 2d, 1867, declares Texas to be a "rebel State," and provides for its government until a legal and republican State government could be legally established. It constituted Louisiana and Texas the fifth military district, and made it subject, not to the civil authority, but to the "military authorities of the United States."

It is true that no organized rebellion now exists there, and the courts of the United States now exercise jurisdiction over the people of that province. But this is no test of the State's being in the Union; Dacotah [sic] is no State, and yet the courts of the United States administer justice there as they do in Texas. The Indian tribes, who are governed by military force, cannot claim to be States of the Union. Wherein does the condition of Texas differ from theirs? ...

... I am not disposed to join in any essay to prove Texas to be a State of the Union, when Congress have decided that she is not. It is a question of fact, I repeat, and of fact only. *Politically,* Texas is not *a State in this Union.* Whether rightfully out of it or not is a question not before the court. ...

[Mr. Justice **SWAYNE** and Mr. Justice **MILLER** concurred with Mr. Justice **GRIER**]

"[W]e do not see in those amendments any purpose to destroy the main features of the general system."—Justice MILLER

"[G]rants of exclusive privilege, such as is made by the act in question, are opposed to the whole theory of free government, and it requires no aid from any bill of rights to render them void."—Justice FIELD

"But even if the Constitution were silent, the fundamental privileges and immunities of citizens, as such, would be no less real and no less inviolable than they now are."—Justice BRADLEY

"Fairly construed these amendments may be said to rise to the dignity of a new Magna Charta."—Justice SWAYNE

SLAUGHTER-HOUSE CASES

83 U.S. (16 Wall.) 36, 21 L.Ed. 394 (1873).

Congress proposed the Fourteenth Amendment in 1866, and slightly more than two years later the Secretary of State certified that the necessary twenty-eight of the then thirty-seven states had ratified it. That process, however, had been very difficult and controversial. Many states had refused to assent because their officials believed the amendment would radically change the federal structure of the political system. Indeed, the final five state legislatures agreed only under coercion. They were members of the former Confederacy, and the Reconstruction Congress had made ratification a condition for their "readmission" into the Union. Even then ratification was immediately possible only because the Secretary of State refused to accept notices from the legislatures of New Jersey, Ohio, and Oregon revoking their earlier ratifications. (The Supreme Court heard no challenge to the validity of the Fourteenth Amendment, but decades later ruled in Coleman v. Miller [1939] that when an amendment became part of the constitutional document was a political not a justiciable question.)

Very quickly, however, the Court was presented with questions about the new amendment's scope. In 1869, the Crescent City Live–Stock Landing and Slaughter–House Co. bribed officials of New Orleans and the carpetbag legislature of Louisiana to grant the company a twenty-five year monopoly to operate meat-slaughtering facilities for New Orleans. Several hundred butchers joined together in the Butchers Benevolent Association and hired John A. Campbell, who at the outbreak of the Civil War had resigned his seat on the U.S. Supreme Court and returned to Alabama, to direct their attack on the monopoly. The "foreign" character of the state legislature and its ties to "Radical Reconstruction" stirred up glowing embers of hatred both among ex-Confederates and staunch Unionists.

In an ironic twist, Campbell invoked the Fourteenth Amendment to attack state authority in the name of nationally protected rights of the individual. He lost in state courts but obtained a writ of error from his former colleagues.

Mr. Justice **MILLER** ... delivered the opinion of the court. ...

The plaintiffs in error ... allege that the statute is a violation of the Constitution of the United States in ...:

That it creates involuntary servitude ...

That it abridges the privileges and immunities of citizens of the United States;

That it denies to the plaintiffs the equal protection of the laws; and,

That it deprives them of their property without due process of law.
...

This court is thus called upon for the first time to give construction to these articles. We do not conceal from ourselves the great responsibility which this duty devolves upon us. No questions so far-reaching and pervading in their consequences, so profoundly interesting to the people of this country, and so important in their bearing upon the relations of the United States, and of the several States to each other and to the citizens of the States and the United States, have been before this court during the official life of any of its present members. We have given every opportunity for a full hearing at the bar; we have discussed it freely and compared views among ourselves; we have taken ample time for careful deliberation. ...

The most cursory glance at these articles [Thirteenth, Fourteenth, and Fifteenth Amendments] discloses a unity of purpose, when taken in connection with the history of the times, which cannot fail to have an important bearing on any question of doubt concerning their true meaning. Nor can such doubts, when any reasonably exist, be safely and rationally solved without a reference to that history; for in it is found the occasion and the necessity for recurring again to the great source of power in this country, the people of the States, for additional guarantees of human rights; additional powers to the Federal government; additional restraints upon those of the States. Fortunately that history is fresh within the memory of us all, and its leading features ... free from doubt. ...

... [I]n the light of this recapitulation of events [the Civil War and Reconstruction], almost too recent to be called history ... and on the most casual examination of the language of these amendments, no one can fail to be impressed with the one pervading purpose found in them all ... the freedom of the slave race, the security and firm establishment of that freedom, and the protection of the newly-made freeman and citizen from the oppression of those who had formerly exercised unlimited dominion over him. It is true that only the fifteenth amendment, in terms, mentions the negro by speaking of his color and his slavery. But it is just as true that each of the other articles was addressed to the grievances of that race. ...

We do not say that no one else but the negro can share in this protection. Both the language and the spirit of these articles are to have their fair and just weight in any question of construction. ... But what we do say ... is, that in any fair and just construction of any section or phrase of these amendments, it is necessary to look to the purpose which we have said was the pervading spirit of them all, the evil they were intended to remedy, and the process of continued addition to the Constitution, until that purpose was supposed to be accomplished, as far as constitutional law can accomplish it.

The first section of the fourteenth article ... opens with a definition of citizenship—not only citizenship of the United States, but citizenship of the States. No such definition was previously found in the Constitution. ... But it had been held by this court, in the celebrated Dred Scott case, only a few years before the outbreak of the civil war, that a man of African descent, whether a slave or not, was not and could not be a citizen of a State or of the United States. This decision, while it met the condemnation of some of the ablest statesmen and constitutional lawyers of the country, had never been overruled. ...

To remove this difficulty primarily, and to establish a clear and comprehensive definition of citizenship ... the first clause of the first section was framed. "All persons born or naturalized in the United

States, and subject to the jurisdiction thereof, are citizens of the United States and of the State wherein they reside." ... It declares that persons may be citizens of the United States without regard to their citizenship of a particular State, and it overturns the Dred Scott decision by making all persons born within the United States and subject to its jurisdiction citizens of the United States. That its main purpose was to establish the citizenship of the negro can admit of no doubt. ...

It is quite clear, then, that there is a citizenship of the United States, and a citizenship of a State, which are distinct from each other, and which depend upon different characteristics or circumstances in the individual. ... The argument, however, in favor of the plaintiffs [in error] rests wholly on the assumption that the citizenship is the same, and the privileges and immunities guaranteed by the clause are the same.

The language is, "No State shall make or enforce any law which shall abridge the privileges or immunities of citizens of *the United States.*" It is a little remarkable, if this clause was intended as a protection to the citizen of a State against the legislative power of his own State, that the word citizen of the State should be left out when it is so carefully used, and used in contradistinction to citizens of the United States, in the very sentence which precedes it. It is too clear for argument that the change in phraseology was adopted understandingly and with a purpose.

Of the privileges and immunities of the citizen of the United States, and of the privileges and immunities of the citizen of the State ... it is only the former which are placed by this clause under the protection of the Federal Constitution. ... [The] provision is found in section two of the fourth article, in the following words: "The citizens of each State shall be entitled to all the privileges and immunities of citizens of the several States." There can be but little question that the purpose of both these provisions is the same, and that the privileges and immunities intended are the same in each. ...

Fortunately we are not without judicial construction of this clause of the Constitution. The first and the leading case on the subject is that of Corfield v. Coryell [1823], decided by Mr. Justice Washington in the Circuit Court. ... "The inquiry," he says, "is, what are the privileges and immunities of citizens of the several States? We feel no hesitation in confining these expressions to those privileges and immunities which are fundamental; which belong of right to the citizens of all free governments, and which have at all times been enjoyed by citizens of the several States which compose this Union. ... What these fundamental principles are, it would be more tedious than difficult to enumerate. They may all, however, be comprehended under the following general heads: protection by the government, with the right to acquire and possess property of every kind, and to pursue and obtain happiness and safety, subject, nevertheless, to such restraints as the government may prescribe for the general good of the whole." This definition ... is adopted in the main by this court in Ward v. Maryland [1871]. ...

In ... Paul v. Virginia [1869], the [U.S. Supreme] court, in expounding this clause of the Constitution, says that "the privileges and immunities secured to citizens of each State in the several States ... are those privileges and immunities which are common to the citizens in the latter States under their constitution and laws by virtue of their being citizens."

The constitutional provision there alluded to did not create those rights, which it called privileges and immunities of citizens of the States. ... Nor did it profess to control the power of the State governments over the rights of its own citizens. Its sole purpose was to declare to the several States, that whatever those rights, as you grant or establish them to your own citizens, or as you limit or qualify, or impose restrictions on their exercise, the same, neither more nor less, shall be the measure of the rights of citizens of other States within your jurisdiction.

... [U]p to the adoption of the recent amendments, no claim or pretense was set up that those rights depended on the Federal government for their existence or protection, beyond the very few express limitations which the Federal Constitution imposed upon the States—such, for instance, as the prohibition against *ex post facto* laws, bills of attainder, and laws impairing the obligation of contracts. But with the exception of these and a few other restrictions, the entire domain of the privileges and immunities of citizens of the States ... lay within the constitutional and legislative power of the States. ... Was it the purpose of the fourteenth amendment, by the simple declaration that no State should make or enforce any law which shall abridge the privileges and immunities of citizens of the United States, to transfer the security and protection of all the civil rights which we have mentioned, from the States to the Federal government? And where it is declared that Congress shall have the power to enforce that article, was it intended to bring within the power of Congress the entire domain of civil rights heretofore belonging exclusively to the States?

All this and more must follow, if the proposition of the plaintiffs be sound. For not only are these rights subject to the control of Congress whenever in its discretion any of them are supposed to be abridged by State legislation, but that body may also pass laws in advance, limiting and restricting the exercise of legislative power by the States, in their most ordinary and usual function, as in its judgment it may think proper on all such subjects. And still further, such a construction ... would constitute this court a perpetual censor upon all legislation of the States, on the civil rights of their own citizens. ... The argument, we admit, is not always the most conclusive which is drawn from the consequences urged against the adoption of a particular construction of an instrument. But when, as in the case before us, these consequences are so serious, so far-reaching and pervading, so great a departure from the structure and spirit of our institutions when the effect is to fetter and degrade the State governments by subjecting them to the control of Congress, in the exercise of powers heretofore universally conceded to them of the most ordinary and fundamental character; when in fact it radically changes the whole theory of the relations of the State and Federal governments to each other and of both these governments to the people; the argument has a force that is irresistible, in the absence of language which expresses such a purpose too clearly to admit of doubt.

We are convinced that no such results were intended by the Congress which proposed these amendments, nor by the legislatures of the States which ratified them.

Having shown that the privileges and immunities relied on in the argument are those which belong to citizens of the States as such, and that they are left to the State governments for security and protection ... we may hold ourselves excused from defining the privileges and immunities of citizens of the United States which no State can abridge, until some case involving those privileges may make it necessary to do so. But lest it should be said that no such privileges and immunities are to be found if those we have been considering are excluded, we venture to suggest some which owe their existence to the Federal government, its National character, its Constitution, or its laws.

One of these is well described in the case of Crandall v. Nevada [1868] ... [,] the right of the citizens of this great country, protected by implied guarantees of its Constitution, "to come to the seat of government to assert any claim he may have upon that government, to transact any business he may have with it, to seek its protection, to share its offices, to engage in administering its functions. He has the right of free access to its seaports ... to the sub-treasuries, land offices, and courts of justice in the several States." And " ... for all the great purposes for which the Federal government was established, we are one people, with one common country, we are all citizens of the United States;" . ...

Another privilege of a citizen of the United States is to demand the care and protection of the Federal government over his life, liberty, and property when on the high seas or within the jurisdiction of a foreign government. ... The right to peaceably assemble and petition for redress of grievances, the privilege of the writ of *habeas corpus,* are rights of the citizen guaranteed by the Federal Constitution. The right to use the navigable waters of the United States, however they may penetrate the territory of the several States, all rights secured to our citizens by treaties with foreign nations, are dependent upon citizenship of the United States, and not citizenship of a State. One of these privileges is conferred by the very article under consideration. It is that a citizen of the United States can, of his own volition, become a citizen of any State of the Union by a *bona fide* residence therein, with the same rights as other citizens of that State. To these may be added the rights secured by the thirteenth and fifteenth articles of amendment, and by the other clause of the fourteenth, next to be considered.

But it is useless to pursue this branch of the inquiry, since we are of opinion that the rights claimed by these plaintiffs in error, if they have any existence, are not privileges and immunities of citizens of the United States. ...

The argument has not been much pressed in these cases that the defendant's charter deprives the plaintiffs [in error] of their property without due process of law, or that it denies them the equal protection of the law. The first of these paragraphs has been in the Constitution since the adoption of the fifth amendment, as a restraint upon the Federal power. ... We are not without judicial interpretation ... of the meaning of this clause. And it is sufficient to say that under no construction of that provision that we have ever seen, or that we deem admissible, can the restraint imposed by ... Louisiana ... be held to be a deprivation of property within the meaning of that provision.

"Nor shall any State deny to any person within its jurisdiction the equal protection of the laws."

In the light of the history of these amendments, and the pervading purpose of them ... it is not difficult to give a meaning to this clause. The existence of laws in the States where the newly emancipated negroes resided, which discriminated with gross injustice and hardship against them as a class, was the evil to be remedied. ...

If, however, the States did not conform their laws to its requirements, then by the fifth section of the article of amendment Congress was authorized to enforce it by suitable legislation. We doubt very much whether any action of a State not directed by way of discrimination against the negroes as a class, or on account of their race, will ever be held to come within the purview of this provision. It is so clearly a provision for that race and that emergency, that a strong case would be necessary for its application to any other. But as it is a State that is to be dealt with, and not alone the validity of its laws, we may safely leave that matter until Congress shall have exercised its power, or some case of State oppression, by denial of equal justice in its courts, shall have claimed a decision at our hands. ...

The adoption of the first eleven amendments to the Constitution so soon after the original instrument was accepted, shows a prevailing sense of danger at that time from the Federal power. And it cannot be denied that such jealousy continued to exist with many patriotic men until the breaking out of the late civil war. It was then discovered that the true danger of the perpetuity of the Union was in the capacity of the State organizations to combine and concentrate all the powers of the State, and of contiguous States, for a determined resistance to the General Government. Unquestionably this has given great force to the argument, and added largely to the number, of those who believe in the necessity of a strong National government.

But, however pervading this sentiment, and however it may have contributed to the adoption of the amendments we have been considering, we do not see in those amendments any purpose to destroy the main features of the general system. Under the pressure of all the excited feeling growing out of the war, our statesmen have still believed that the existence of the States with powers for domestic and local government, including the regulation of civil rights—the rights of person and of property—was essential to the perfect working of our complex form of government, though they may have thought proper to impose additional limitations on the States, and to confer additional power on that of the Nation.

But whatever fluctuations may be seen in the history of public opinion on this subject during the period of our national existence, we think it will be found that this court, so far as its functions require, has always held with a steady and even hand the balance between State and Federal power, and we trust that such may continue to be the history of its relation to that subject so long as it shall have duties to perform which demand of it a construction of the Constitution, or any of its parts. ...

Affirmed.

Mr. Justice **FIELD**, dissenting. ...

The first clause of the fourteenth amendment ... recognizes in express terms, if it does not create, citizens of the United States, and it makes their citizenship dependent upon the place of their birth, or the fact of their adoption, and not upon the constitution or laws of any State or the condition of their ancestry. A citizen of a State is now only a citizen of the United States residing in that State. The fundamental rights, privileges, and immunities now belong to him as a citizen of the United States, and are not dependent upon his citizenship of any State. ...

The amendment does not attempt to confer any new privileges or immunities upon citizens, or to enumerate or define those already existing. It assumes that there are such privileges and immunities which belong of right to citizens as such, and ordains that they shall not be abridged by State legislation. If this inhibition has no reference to privileges and immunities of this character but only refers ... to such privileges and immunities as were before its adoption specially designated in the Constitution or necessarily implied as belonging to citizens of the United States, it was a vain and idle enactment, which accomplished nothing, and most unnecessarily excited Congress and the people on its passage. The supremacy of the Constitution and the laws of the United States always controlled any State legislation of that character. But if the amendment refers to the natural and inalienable rights which belong to all citizens, the inhibition has a profound significance and consequence.

What then are the privileges and immunities which are secured against abridgment by State legislation?

In the first section of the Civil Rights Act [of 1866] Congress has given its interpretation to these terms, or at least has stated some of the rights which, in its judgment, these terms include ... the right "to make and enforce contracts, to sue, be parties and give evidence, to inherit, purchase, lease, sell, hold, and convey real and personal property, and to full and equal benefit of all laws and proceedings for the security of person and property." That act, it is true, was passed before the fourteenth amendment, but the amendment was adopted ... to obviate objections to legislation of similar character, extending the protection of the National government over the common rights of all citizens of the United States. Accordingly, after its ratification, Congress re-enacted the act under the belief that whatever doubts may have previously existed of its validity, they were removed by the amendment. ...

[Field then recited the same history of the term "privileges and immunities" as had Miller and also quoted the same passage from Corfield v. Coryell (1823).] ... The privileges and immunities designated are those *which of right belong to the citizens of all free governments.* Clearly among these must be placed the right to pursue a lawful employment in a lawful manner without other restraint than such as equally affects all persons. In the discussions in Congress upon the passage of the Civil Rights Act repeated reference was made to this language of Mr. Justice Washington. ...

What the clause in question [in Art. IV] did for the protection of citizens of one State against hostile and discriminating legislation of other States, the fourteenth amendment does for the protection of every citizen of the United States against hostile and discriminating legislation against him in favor of others, whether they reside in the same or different States. If under the fourth article of the Constitution equality of privileges and immunities is secured between citizens of different States, under the fourteenth amendment the same equality is secured between citizens of the United States.

It will not be pretended that under the fourth article of the Constitution any State could create a monopoly in any known trade or manufacture in favor of her own citizens, or any portion of them, which would exclude an equal participation in the trade or manufacture monopolized by citizens of other States. ...

Now, what the clause in question does for the protection of citizens of one State against the creation of monopolies in favor of citizens of other States, the fourteenth amendment does for the protection of every citizen of the United States against the creation of any monopoly whatsoever. The privileges and immunities of citizens of the United States, of every one of them, is secured against abridgment in any form by any State. The fourteenth amendment places them under the guardianship of the National authority. All monopolies in any known trade or manufacture are an invasion of these privileges, for they encroach upon the liberty of citizens to acquire property and pursue happiness, and were held void at common law. ...

In all these cases there is a recognition of the equality of right among citizens in the pursuit of the ordinary avocations of life, and a declaration that all grants of exclusive privilege ... are against common right, and void. ... And when the Colonies separated from the mother country no privilege was more fundamentally recognized or more completely incorporated into the fundamental law of the country than that every free subject ... was entitled to pursue his happiness by following any of the known established trades and occupations ... subject only to such restraints as equally affected all others. The immortal document which proclaimed the independence of the country declared as self-evident truths that the Creator had endowed all men "with certain inalienable rights, and that among these are life, liberty, and the pursuit of happiness; and that to secure these rights governments are instituted among men." ...

This equality of right ... is the distinguishing privilege of citizens of the United States. ... The State may prescribe such regulations as will promote the public health, secure the good order and advance the general prosperity of society, but when once prescribed, the pursuit or calling must be free to be followed by every citizen who is within the conditions designated, and will conform to the regulations. This is the fundamental idea upon which our institutions rest, and unless adhered to in the legislation of the country our government will be a republic only in name. The fourteenth amendment ... makes it essential to the validity of the legislation of every State that this equality of right should be respected. ... [G]rants of exclusive privilege, such as is made by the act in question, are opposed to the whole theory of free government, and it requires no aid from any bill of rights to render them void. That only is a free government, in the American sense of the term, under which the inalienable right of every citizen to pursue his happiness is unrestrained, except by just, equal, and impartial laws.

I am authorized by the Chief Justice [**CHASE**], Mr. Justice **SWAYNE**, and Mr. Justice **BRADLEY** to state that they concur with me in this dissenting opinion.

Mr. Justice **BRADLEY**, also dissenting. ...

... A citizen of the United States has a perfect constitutional right to go to and reside in any State he chooses, and to claim citizenship therein, and an equality of rights with every other citizen; and the whole power of the nation is pledged to sustain him in that right. ... Citizenship of the United States ought to be, and, according to the Constitution, is, a sure and undoubted title to equal rights in any and every State in this Union, subject to such regulations as the legislature may rightfully prescribe. If a man be denied full equality before the law, he is denied one of the essential rights of citizenship as a citizen of the United States.

Every citizen, then, being primarily a citizen of the United States, and, secondarily, a citizen of the State where he resides, what, in general, are the privileges and immunities of a citizen of the United States? Is the right, liberty, or privilege of choosing any lawful employment one of them? ... This seems to me to be the essential question before us. ... And, in my judgment, the right of any citizen to follow whatever lawful employment he chooses to adopt (submitting himself to all lawful regulations) is one of his most valuable rights, and one which the legislature of a State cannot invade, whether restrained by its own constitution or not.

The right of a State to regulate the conduct of its citizens is undoubtedly a very broad and extensive one. ... But there are certain fundamental rights which this right of regulation cannot infringe. It may prescribe the manner of their exercise, but it cannot subvert the rights themselves. I speak now of the rights of citizens of any free government. ... In this free country, the people of which inherited certain traditional rights and privileges from their ancestors, citizenship means something. It has certain privileges and immunities attached to it which the government, whether restricted by express or implied limitations, cannot take away or impair. ... And these privileges and immunities attach as well to citizenship of the United States as to citizenship of the States.

The people of this country brought with them to its shores the rights of Englishmen; the rights which had been wrested from English sovereigns at various periods of the nation's history. ...

... [P]ersonal rights ... were claimed by the very first Congress of the Colonies, assembled in 1774, as the undoubted inheritance of the people of this country; and the Declaration of Independence, which was the first political act of the American people in their independent sovereign capacity, lays the foundation of our National existence upon this broad proposition: "That all men are created equal; that they are endowed by their Creator with certain inalienable rights; that among these are life, liberty, and the pursuit of happiness." Here again we have the great threefold division of the rights of free-men, asserted as the rights of man. Rights to life, liberty, and the pursuit of happiness are equivalent to the rights of life, liberty, and property. These are the fundamental rights which can only be taken away by due process of law, and which can only be interfered with, or the enjoyment of which can only be modified, by lawful regulations necessary or proper for the mutual good of all; and these rights, I contend, belong to the citizens of every free government.

For the preservation, exercise, and enjoyment of these rights the individual citizen, as a necessity, must be left free to adopt such calling, profession, or trade as may seem to him most conducive to that end. Without this right he cannot be a freeman. This right to choose one's calling is an essential part of that liberty which it is the object of government to protect; and a calling, when chosen, is a man's property and right. Liberty and property are not protected where these rights are arbitrarily assailed.

... [C]itizenship is not an empty name, but ... in this country at least, it has connected with it certain incidental rights, privileges, and immunities of the greatest importance. And to say that these rights and immunities attach only to State citizenship, and not to citizenship of the United States, appears to me to evince a very narrow and insufficient estimate of constitutional history and the rights of men, not to say the rights of the American people. ...

[Justice Bradley here also quoted *Corfield*.]

But we are not bound to resort to implication, or to the constitutional history of England, to find an authoritative declaration of some of the most important privileges and immunities of citizens of the United States. It is in the Constitution itself. The Constitution, it is true, as it stood prior to the recent amendments, specifies, in terms, only a few of the personal privileges and immunities of citizens, but they are very comprehensive in their character. The States were merely prohibited from passing bills of attainder, *ex post facto* laws, laws impairing the obligation of contracts, and perhaps one or two more. But others of the greatest consequence were enumerated, although they were only secured, in express terms, from invasion by the Federal government; such as the right of *habeas corpus*, the right of trial by jury, of free exercise of religious worship, the right of free speech and a free press, the right peaceably to assemble for the discussion of public measures, the right to be secure against unreasonable searches and seizures, and above all, and including almost all the rest, the right of *not being deprived of life, liberty, or property, without due process of law*. These, and still others are specified in the original Constitution, or in the early amendments of it, as among the privileges and immunities of citizens of the United States, or, what is still stronger for the force of the argument, the rights of all persons, whether citizens or not.

But even if the Constitution were silent, the fundamental privileges and immunities of citizens, as such, would be no less real and no less inviolable than they now are. It was not necessary to say in words that the citizens of the United States should have and exercise all the privileges of citizens; the privilege of buying, selling, and enjoying property; the privilege of engaging in any lawful employment for a livelihood; the privilege of resorting to the laws for redress of injuries, and the like. Their very citizenship conferred these privileges, if they did not possess them before. And these privileges they would enjoy whether they were citizens of any State or not. ...

The granting of monopolies, or exclusive privileges to individuals or corporations, is an invasion of the right of others to choose a lawful calling, and an infringement of personal liberty. ...

It is futile to argue that none but persons of the African race are intended to be benefited by this amendment. They may have been the primary cause of the amendment, but its language is general, embracing all citizens, and I think it was purposely so expressed.

The mischief to be remedied was not merely slavery and its incidents and consequences; but that spirit of insubordination and disloyalty to the National government which had troubled the country for so many years in some of the States, and that intolerance of free speech and free discussion which often rendered life and property insecure, and led to much unequal legislation. The amendment was an attempt to give voice to the strong National yearning for that time and that condition of things, in which American citizenship should be a sure guaranty of safety, and in which every citizen of the United States might stand erect on every portion of its soil, in the full enjoyment of every right and privilege belonging to a freeman, without fear of violence or molestation.

But great fears are expressed that this construction of the amendment will lead to enactments by Congress interfering with the internal affairs of the States, and establishing therein civil and criminal codes of law for the government of the citizens, and thus abolishing the State governments in everything but name; or else, that it will lead the Federal courts to draw to their cognizance the supervision of State tribunals on every subject of judicial inquiry, on the plea of ascertaining whether the privileges and immunities of citizens have not been abridged.

In my judgment no such practical inconveniences would arise. Very little, if any, legislation on the part of Congress would be required to carry the amendment into effect. Like the prohibition against passing a law impairing the obligation of a contract, it would execute itself. The point would be regularly raised, in a suit at law, and settled by final reference to the Federal court. As the privileges and immunities protected are only those fundamental ones which belong to every citizen, they would soon become so far defined as to cause but a slight accumulation of business in the Federal courts. Besides, the recognized existence of the law would prevent its frequent violation. But even if the business of the National courts should be increased, Congress could easily supply the remedy by increasing their number and efficiency. The great question is, What is the true construction of the amendment? When once we find that, we shall find the means of giving it effect. ...

Mr. Justice **SWAYNE**, dissenting. ...

The first eleven amendments to the Constitution were intended to be checks and limitations upon the government which that instrument called into existence. They had their origin in a spirit of jealousy on the part of the States, which existed when the Constitution was adopted. ...

... [The Thirteenth, Fourteenth, and Fifteenth] amendments are a new departure, and mark an important epoch in the constitutional history of the country. They trench directly upon the power of the States, and deeply affect those bodies. They are, in this respect, at the opposite pole from the first eleven. Fairly construed these amendments may be said to rise to the dignity of a new Magna Charta. ...

The first section of the fourteenth amendment is alone involved in the consideration of these cases. No searching analysis is necessary to eliminate its meaning. Its language is intelligible and direct. Nothing can be more transparent. Every word employed has an established signification. There is no room for construction. There is nothing to construe. Elaboration may obscure, but cannot make clearer, the intent and purpose sought to be carried out. ...

These amendments are all consequences of the late civil war. The prejudices and apprehension as to the central government which prevailed when the Constitution was adopted were dispelled by the light of experience. The public mind became satisfied that there was less danger of tyranny in the head than of anarchy and tyranny in the members. The provisions of this section are all eminently conservative in their character. They are a bulwark of defence, and can never be made an engine of oppression. The language employed is unqualified in its scope. There is no exception in its terms, and there can be properly none in their application. By the language "citizens of the United States" was meant *all* such citizens; and by "any person" was meant *all* persons within the jurisdiction of the State. No distinction is intimated on account of race or color. This court has no authority to interpolate a limitation that is neither expressed nor implied. Our duty is to execute the law, not to make it. The protection provided was not intended to be confined to those of any particular race or class, but to embrace equally all races, classes, and conditions of men. It is objected that the power conferred is novel and large. The answer is that the novelty was known and the measure deliberately adopted. The power is beneficent in its nature, and cannot be abused. It is such as should exist in every well-ordered system of polity. Where could it be more appropriately lodged than in the hands to which it is confided? It is necessary to enable the government of the nation to secure to every one within its jurisdiction the rights and privileges enumerated, which, according to the plainest considerations of reason and justice and the fundamental principles of the social compact, all are entitled to enjoy. Without such authority any government claiming to be national is glaringly defective. The construction adopted by the majority of my brethren is, in my judgment, much too narrow. It defeats, by a limitation not anticipated, the intent of those by whom the instrument was framed and of those by whom it was adopted. To the extent of that limitation it turns, as it were, what was meant for bread into a stone. By the Constitution, as it stood before the war, ample protection was given against oppression by the Union, but little was given against wrong and oppression by the States. That want was intended to be supplied by this amendment. ...

Editors' Notes

(1) **Query**: To what extent did Miller's opinion rest on a structural approach? A purposive approach? To what extent did he resort to a form of (intuitive?) originalism? What about Field? Bradley? Swayne?

(2) **Query**: According to Justice Miller, what was the effect of the Fourteenth Amendment on the structure of American federalism? Bradley? Swayne? Did Field need the Fourteenth Amendment to justify his conclusions?

(3) **Query**: To what extent did each of the dissents rest on a political theory much like constitutionalism?

(4) **Query**: To varying degrees, all the opinions here accept the notion that before the Fourteenth Amendment the constitutional text imposed few federal restraints on the states. Marshall certainly so held in Barron v. Baltimore (1833), when he ruled that the Bill of Rights does not apply to the states; but what about his opinion in Fletcher v. Peck (1810; reprinted below p. 1091) and Chase's in Calder v. Bull (1798; reprinted above, p. 121).

(5) **Query**: Was Miller hinting that there are limits to valid constitutional change? For an argument that such was the thrust of his opinion, see Walter F. Murphy, "*Slaughter-House, Civil Rights*, and Limits on Constitutional Change," 32 *Am.J.Jurisp.* 1 (1987).

(6) As far as "privileges or immunities" are concerned, *Slaughter-House* still stands, though it would have been more logical for the Court to have read the Bill of Rights into the Fourteenth Amendment through that clause than through due process. One objection to "privileges or immunities" as such a vehicle is that it only prohibits states from abridging the "privileges or immunities of citizens of the United States," apparently leaving open the possibility of denying such rights to aliens and to corporations who, while legal persons, are not citizens. But, as John Hart Ely has pointed out, the ban is not against denying citizens their privileges or immunities but against denying such rights; thus grammatically the clause could protect aliens as well as corporations. *Democracy and Distrust* (Cambridge: Harvard University Press, 1980), p. 25.

(7) The Court has expanded the scope of the Thirteenth Amendment to combat some forms of discrimination; see, e.g., Runyon v. McCrary (1976). It has, however, completely gutted *Slaughter-House* 's interpretation of the equal protection and due process clauses. Indeed, Swayne's description of the Fourteenth Amendment as "a new Magna Charta" has almost become a reality.

––––––––

> **"[W]hen we are dealing with words that also are a constituent act, like the Constitution of the United States, we must realize that they have called into life a being the development of which could not have been foreseen completely by the most gifted of its begetters."**

MISSOURI v. HOLLAND

252 U.S. 416, 40 S.Ct. 382, 64 L.Ed. 641 (1920).

This case, sustaining the constitutionality of a treaty against a challenge from a state that it was invalid because of "some invisible radiation from the general terms of the Tenth Amendment," is reprinted above at p. 206.

"Congress may not exercise that power [over commerce] so as to force directly upon the States its choices as to how essential decisions regarding the conduct of integral governmental functions are to be made."—Justice REHNQUIST

"This Court is simply not at liberty to erect a mirror of its own conception of a desirable governmental structure."—Justice BRENNAN

NATIONAL LEAGUE OF CITIES v. USERY
426 U.S. 833, 96 S.Ct. 2465, 49 L.Ed.2d 245 (1976).

In 1974 Congress amended the Fair Labor Standards Act so as to bring within its minimum wage and maximum hours coverage almost all public employees in the states and cities. Individual cities, states, the National League of Cities, and the National Governors' Conference brought suit in a special three-judge federal district court to enjoin the secretary of labor from enforcing these amendments, claiming they violated the Tenth Amendment. The district court dismissed the suit, and plaintiffs appealed directly to the U.S. Supreme Court.

Mr. Justice **REHNQUIST** delivered the opinion of the Court. ...

II

It is established beyond peradventure that the Commerce Clause of Article I of the Constitution is a grant of plenary authority to Congress. That authority is, in the words of Mr. Chief Justice Marshall in Gibbons v. Ogden (1824), "the power to regulate; that is, to prescribe the rule by which commerce is to be governed." When considering the validity of asserted applications of this power to wholly private activity, the Court has made it clear that

> [e]ven activity that is purely intrastate in character may be regulated by Congress, where the activity, combined with like conduct by others similarly situated, affects commerce among the States or with foreign nations. Fry v. United States (1975).

Congressional power over areas of private endeavor, even when its exercise may pre-empt express state law determinations contrary to the result which has commended itself to the collective wisdom of Congress, has been held to be limited only by the requirement that "the means chosen by [Congress] must be reasonably adapted to the end permitted by the Constitution." Heart of Atlanta Motel v. United States (1964).

Appellants in no way challenge these decisions establishing the breadth of authority granted Congress under the commerce power. Their contention ... is that when Congress seeks to regulate directly the activities of States as public employers, it transgresses an affirmative limitation on the exercise of its power akin to other commerce power affirmative limitations contained in the Constitution. ... Appellants' essential contention is that the 1974 amendments to the Act, while undoubtedly within the scope of the Commerce Clause, encounter a ... constitutional barrier because they are to be applied directly to the States and subdivisions of States as employers.

This Court has never doubted that there are limits upon the power of Congress to override state sovereignty, even when exercising its otherwise plenary powers to tax or to regulate commerce. ... In [Maryland v.] Wirtz [1968], for example, the Court took care to assure the appellants that it had "ample power to prevent ... 'the utter destruction of the State as a sovereign political entity.'" In *Fry*, the Court recognized that an express declaration of this limitation is found in the Tenth Amendment:

> While the Tenth Amendment has been characterized as a "truism," stating merely that "all is retained which has not been surrendered," United States v. Darby (1941), it is not without significance. The Amendment expressly declares the constitutional policy that Congress may not exercise power in a fashion that impairs the States' integrity or their ability to function effectively in a federal system.

In New York v. United States (1946), Mr. Chief Justice Stone, speaking for four Members of an eight-Member Court in rejecting the proposition that Congress could impose taxes on the States so long as it did so in a non-discriminatory manner, observed:

> A State may, like a private individual, own real property and receive income. But in view of our former decisions we could hardly say that a general nondiscriminatory real estate tax (apportioned), or an income tax laid upon citizens and States alike could be constitutionally applied to the State's capitol, its State-house, its public school houses, public parks, or its revenues from taxes or school lands, even though all real property and all income of the citizen is taxed. ...

The expressions in these more recent cases trace back to earlier decisions of this Court recognizing the essential role of the States in our federal system of government. Mr. Chief Justice Chase,. ... [i]n Texas v. White (1869), declared that "[t]he Constitution, in all its provisions, looks to an indestructible Union, composed of indestructible States." In Lane County v. Oregon (1869), his opinion for the Court said:

> Both the States and the United States existed before the Constitution. ... [I]n many articles of the Constitution the necessary existence of the States, and, within their proper spheres, the independent authority of the States, is distinctly recognized. ...

Appellee Secretary argues that the cases in which this Court has upheld sweeping exercises of authority by Congress, even though those exercises pre-empted state regulation of the private sector, have already curtailed the sovereignty of the States quite as much as the 1974 amendments to the Fair Labor Standards Act. We do not agree. It is one thing to recognize the authority of Congress to enact laws regulating individual businesses necessarily subject to the dual sovereignty of the government of the Nation and of the State in which they reside. It is quite another to uphold a similar exercise of congressional authority directed, not to private citizens, but to the States as States. We have repeatedly recognized that there are attributes of sovereignty attaching to every state government which may not be impaired by Congress, not because Congress may lack an affirmative grant of legislative authority to reach the matter, but because the Constitution prohibits it from exercising the authority in that manner. . . .

One undoubted attribute of state sovereignty is the States' power to determine the wages which shall be paid to those whom they employ in order to carry out their governmental functions, what hours those persons will work, and what compensation will be provided where these employees may be called upon to work overtime. The question we must resolve here, then, is whether these determinations are " 'functions essential to separate and independent existence.' " Coyle v. Oklahoma (1911), quoting from Lane County, so that Congress may not abrogate the States' otherwise plenary authority to make them. . . .

Judged solely in terms of increased costs in dollars, these allegations show a significant impact on the functioning of the governmental bodies involved. The Metropolitan Government of Nashville and Davidson County, Tenn., for example, asserted that the Act will increase its costs of providing essential police and fire protection, without any increase in service or in current salary levels, by $938,000 per year. . . . The State of California . . . estimated that application of the Act to its employment practices will necessitate an increase in its budget of between $8 million and $16 million.

Increased costs are not, of course, the only adverse effects which compliance with the Act will visit upon state and local governments. . . . [F]or example, California asserted that it could not comply with the overtime costs (approximately $750,000 per year) which the Act required to be paid to California Highway Patrol cadets during their academy training program. California reported that it had thus been forced to reduce its academy training program from 2,080 hours to only 960 hours, a compromise undoubtedly of substantial importance to those whose safety and welfare may depend upon the preparedness of the California Highway Patrol.

This type of forced relinquishment of important governmental activities is further reflected in the complaint's allegation that the city of Inglewood, Cal. has been forced to curtail its affirmative action program for providing employment opportunities for men and women interested in a career in law enforcement. . . .

Quite apart from the substantial costs imposed upon the States and their political subdivisions, the Act displaces state policies regarding the manner in which they will structure delivery of those governmental services which their citizens require. The Act, speaking directly to the States qua States, requires that they shall pay all but an extremely limited minority of their employees the minimum wage rates currently chosen by Congress. It may well be that as a matter of economic policy it would be desirable that States, just as private employers, comply with these minimum wage requirements. But it cannot be gainsaid that the federal requirement directly supplants the considered policy choices of the States' elected officials and administrators as to how they wish to structure pay scales in state employment. ... The only "discretion" left to them under the Act is either to attempt to increase their revenue to meet the additional financial burden imposed upon them by paying congressionally prescribed wages to their existing complement of employees, or to reduce that complement to a number which can be paid the federal minimum wage without increasing revenue.

This dilemma presented by the minimum wage restrictions may seem not immediately different from that faced by private employers, who have long been covered by the Act. ... The difference, however, is that a State is not merely a factor in the "shifting economic arrangements" of the private sector of the economy, Kovacs v. Cooper (1949) (Frankfurter, J., concurring), but is itself a coordinate element in the system established by the Framers for governing our Federal Union. ...

Our examination of the effect of the 1974 amendments ... satisfies us that both the minimum wage and the maximum hour provisions will impermissibly interfere with the integral governmental functions of these bodies. ... [T]heir application will ... significantly alter or displace the States' abilities to structure employer-employee relationships in such areas as fire prevention, police protection, sanitation, public health, and parks and recreation. These activities are typical of those performed by state and local governments in discharging their dual functions of administering the public law and furnishing public services. Indeed, it is functions such as these which governments are created to provide, services such as these which the States have traditionally afforded their citizens. If Congress may withdraw from the States the authority to make those fundamental employment decisions upon which their systems for performance of these functions must rest, we think there would be little left of the States' " 'separate and independent existence.' " Coyle. Thus, even if appellants may have overestimated the effect which the Act will have upon their current levels and patterns of governmental activity, the dispositive factor is that Congress has attempted to exercise its Commerce Clause authority to prescribe minimum wages and maximum hours to be paid by the States in their capacities as sovereign governments. In so doing, Congress has sought to wield its power in a fashion that would impair the States' "ability to function effectively in a federal system." Fry. This exercise of congressional authority does not comport with the federal system of government embodied in the Constitution. We hold that insofar as the challenged amendments operate to directly displace the States' freedom to structure integral operations in areas of traditional governmental functions, they are not within the authority granted Congress by Art I, § 8, cl. 3.

III

One final matter requires our attention.   Appellee has vigorously urged that we cannot, consistently with the Court's decisions in *Wirtz* and *Fry* rule against him here.   ...

We think our holding today quite consistent with *Fry*.   The enactment at issue there was occasioned by an extremely serious problem which endangered the well-being of all the component parts of our federal system and which only collective action by the National Government might forestall.   The means selected were carefully drafted so as not to interfere with the States' freedom beyond a very limited, specific period of time.   The effect of the across-the-board freeze authorized by that Act, moreover, displaced no state choices as to how governmental operations should be structured, nor did it force the States to remake such choices themselves.   Instead, it merely required that the wage scales and employment relationships which the States themselves had chosen be maintained during the period of the emergency.   Finally, the Economic Stabilization Act operated to reduce the pressures upon state budgets rather than increase them.   These factors distinguish the statute in *Fry* from the provisions at issue here.   The limits imposed upon the commerce power when Congress seeks to apply it to the States are not so inflexible as to preclude temporary enactments tailored to combat a national emergency.   ...

With respect to the Court's decision in *Wirtz*, we reach a different conclusion.   ... There are undoubtedly factual distinctions between the two situations, but in view of the conclusions expressed earlier in this opinion we do not believe the reasoning in *Wirtz* may any longer be regarded as authoritative.

Wirtz relied heavily on the Court's decision in United States v. California (1936).   The opinion quotes the following language from that case:

> "[We] look to the activities in which the states have traditionally engaged as marking the boundary of the restriction upon the federal taxing power.   But there is no such limitation upon the plenary power to regulate commerce.   The state can no more deny the power if its exercise has been authorized by Congress than can an individual."

But we have reaffirmed today that the States as States stand on a quite different footing from an individual or a corporation when challenging the exercise of Congress' power to regulate commerce.   We think the dicta from United States v. California, simply wrong.   Congress may not exercise that power so as to force directly upon the States its choices as to how essential decisions regarding the conduct of integral governmental functions are to be made.   We agree that such assertions of power, if unchecked, would indeed, as Mr. Justice Douglas cautioned in his dissent in *Wirtz,* allow "the National Government [to] devour the essentials of state sovereignty" ... and would therefore transgress the bounds of the authority granted Congress under the Commerce Clause. While there are obvious differences between the schools and hospitals involved in *Wirtz,* and the fire and police departments affected here, each provides an integral portion of those governmental services which the States and their political subdivisions have traditionally afforded their citizens. We are therefore persuaded that *Wirtz* must be overruled.

Reversed.

Mr. Justice **BLACKMUN,** concurring.

... Although I am not untroubled by certain possible implications of the Court's opinion ... I do not read the opinion so despairingly as does my Brother Brennan. In my view, the result with respect to the statute under challenge here is necessarily correct. I may misinterpret the Court's opinion, but it seems to me that it adopts a balancing approach, and does not outlaw federal power in areas such as environmental protection, where the federal interest is demonstrably greater and where state facility compliance with federal standards would be essential. With this understanding on my part of the Court's opinion, I join it.

Mr. Justice **BRENNAN,** with whom Mr. Justice **WHITE** and Mr. Justice **MARSHALL** join, dissenting.

The Court concedes that Congress enacted the 1974 amendments pursuant to its exclusive power under Art I, § 8, cl. 3, of the Constitution "[t]o regulate Commerce ... among the several States." It must therefore be surprising that my Brethren should choose this bicentennial year of our independence to repudiate principles governing judicial interpretation of our Constitution settled since the time of Mr. Chief Justice John Marshall, discarding his postulate that the Constitution contemplates that restraints upon exercise by Congress of its plenary commerce power lie in the political process and not in the judicial process. For 152 years ago Mr. Chief Justice Marshall enunciated that principle to which, until today, his successors on this Court have been faithful.

> [T]he power over commerce ... is vested in Congress as absolutely as it would be in a single government. ... *The wisdom and the discretion of Congress, their identity with the people, and the influence which their constituents possess at elections, are ... the sole restraints on which they have relied, to secure them from its abuse. They are the restraints on which the people must often rely solely, in all representative governments.* Gibbons v. Ogden (1824) [emphasis added].

Only 34 years ago, Wickard v. Filburn (1942) reaffirmed that "[a]t the beginning Chief Justice Marshall ... made emphatic the embracing and penetrating nature of [Congress' commerce] power by warning that effective restraints on its exercise must proceed from political rather than from judicial processes."

My Brethren do not successfully obscure today's patent usurpation of the role reserved for the political process by their purported discovery in the Constitution of a restraint derived from sovereignty of the States on Congress' exercise of the commerce power. Mr. Chief Justice Marshall recognized that limitations "prescribed in the constitution," Gibbons v. Ogden, restrain Congress' exercise of the power. ... Thus laws within the commerce power may not infringe individual liberties protected by the First Amendment, ... the Fifth Amendment, ... or the Sixth Amendment. ... But there is no restraint based on state sovereignty requiring or permitting judicial enforcement anywhere expressed in the Constitution; our decisions over the last century and a half have explicitly rejected the existence of any such restraint on the commerce power. ...

My Brethren thus have today manufactured an abstraction without substance, founded neither in the words of the Constitution nor on precedent. An abstraction having such profoundly pernicious consequences is not made less so by characterizing the 1974 amendments as legislation directed against the "States qua States." ... [M]y Brethren make no claim that the 1974 amendments are not regulations of "commerce"; rather they overrule *Wirtz* in disagreement with historic principles that United States v. California reaffirmed. ... [M]y Brethren are also repudiating the long line of our precedents holding that a judicial finding that Congress has not unreasonably regulated a subject matter of "commerce" brings to an end the judicial role. "Let the end be legitimate, let it be within the scope of the constitution, and all means which are appropriate, which are plainly adapted to that end, which are not prohibited, but consist with the letter and spirit of the constitution, are constitutional." McCulloch v. Maryland [1819].

The reliance of my Brethren upon the Tenth Amendment as "an express declaration of [a state sovereignty] limitation," ... not only suggests that they overrule governing decisions of this Court that address this question but must astound scholars of the Constitution. For not only early decisions, *Gibbons*, *McCulloch*, and Martin v. Hunter's Lessee (1816), hold that nothing in the Tenth Amendment constitutes a limitation on congressional exercise of powers delegated by the Constitution to Congress. Rather, as the Tenth Amendment's significance was more recently summarized:

> The amendment states but a truism that all is retained which has not been surrendered. There is *nothing in the history of its adoption to suggest that it was more than declaratory of the relationship between the national and state governments as it had been established by the Constitution before the amendment.* ... United States v. Darby [emphasis added].

My Brethren purport to find support for their novel state-sovereignty doctrine in the concurring opinion of Mr. Chief Justice Stone in New York v. United States (1946). That reliance is plainly misplaced, ... [for] the Chief Justice was addressing not the question of a state sovereignty restraint upon the exercise of the commerce power, but rather the principle of implied immunity of the States and Federal Government from taxation by the other. ...

In contrast, the apposite decision that Term to the question whether the Constitution implies a state sovereignty restraint upon congressional exercise of the commerce power is Case v. Bowles (1946). ... The Court ... in an opinion joined by Mr. Chief Justice Stone, reason[ed]:

> [T]he [State's] argument is that the extent of that power as applied to state functions depends on whether these are "essential" to the state government. The use of the same criterion in measuring the constitutional power of Congress to tax has proved to be unworkable, and we reject it as a guide in the field here involved. Cf. United States v. California. ...

... Even more significant for our purposes is ... United States v. California. ...[which] directly presented the question whether any state sovereignty restraint precluded application of the Federal Safety Appliance Act to a state-owned and -operated railroad. ... Mr. Justice Stone rejected the contention in an opinion for a unanimous Court. His rationale is a complete refutation of today's holding:

> ... The sovereign power of the states is necessarily diminished to the extent of the grants of power to the federal government in the Constitution. ...

Today's repudiation of this unbroken line of precedents that firmly reject my Brethren's ill-conceived abstraction can only be regarded as a transparent cover for invalidating a congressional judgment with which they disagree. The only analysis even remotely resembling that adopted today is found in a line of opinions dealing with the Commerce Clause and the Tenth Amendment that ultimately provoked a constitutional crisis for the Court in the 1930's. E.g. Carter v. Carter Coal Co. (1936); United States v. Butler (1936); Hammer v. Dagenhart (1918). We tend to forget that the Court invalidated legislation during the Great Depression, not solely under the Due Process Clause, but also and primarily under the Commerce Clause and the Tenth Amendment. It may have been the eventual abandonment of that overly restrictive construction of the commerce power that spelled defeat for the Court-packing plan, and preserved the integrity of this institution, ... see, e.g. United States v. Darby (1941); NLRB v. Jones & Laughlin Steel Corp. (1937), but my Brethren today are transparently trying to cut back on that recognition of the scope of the commerce power. My Brethren's approach to this case is not far different from the dissenting opinions in the cases that averted the crisis.

That no precedent justifies today's result is particularly clear from the awkward extension of the doctrine of state immunity from federal taxation—an immunity conclusively distinguished by Mr. Justice Stone in *California*, and an immunity that is "narrowly limited" because "the people of all the states have created the national government and are represented in Congress," Helvering v. Gerhardt (1938) (Stone, J.)—to fashion a judicially enforceable restraint on Congress' exercise of the commerce power that the Court has time and again rejected as having no place in our constitutional jurisprudence. "[W]here [Congress] keeps within its sphere and violates no express constitutional limitation it has been the rule of this Court, going back almost to the founding days of the Republic, not to interfere." Katzenbach v. McClung (1964). . . . The 1974 amendments are . . . an entirely legitimate exercise of the commerce power, not in the slightest restrained by any doctrine of state sovereignty cognizable in this Court. . . . [S]ince *Wirtz* is overruled, the Fair Labor Standards Act is invalidated in its application to all state employees "in [any areas] that the States have regarded as integral parts of their governmental activities." This standard is a meaningless limitation on the Court's state-sovereignty doctrine, and thus today's holding goes beyond even what the States of Washington and California urged in *Case* and *California*, and by its logic would overrule those cases. . . . I cannot recall another instance in the Court's history when the reasoning of so many decisions covering so long a span of time has been discarded in such a roughshod manner. That this is done without any justification not already often advanced and consistently rejected, clearly renders today's decision an ipse dixit reflecting nothing but displeasure with a congressional judgment. . . .

Certainly the paradigm of sovereign action—action qua State—is in the enactment and enforcement of state laws. Is it possible that my Brethren are signaling abandonment of the heretofore unchallenged principle that Congress "can, if it chooses, entirely displace the States to the full extent of the far-reaching Commerce Clause"? Bethlehem Steel Co. v. New York State Board (1947) (opinion of Frankfurter, J.) [T]he ouster of state laws obviously curtails or prohibits the States' prerogatives to make policy choices respecting subjects clearly of greater significance to the "State qua State" than the minimum wage paid to state employees. . . .

My Brethren do more than turn aside longstanding constitutional jurisprudence that emphatically rejects today's conclusion. More alarming is the startling restructuring of our federal system, and the role they create therein for the federal judiciary. This Court is simply not at liberty to erect a mirror of its own conception of a desirable governmental structure. If the 1974 amendments have any "vice," . . . my Brother Stevens is surely right that it represents "merely . . . a policy issue which has been firmly resolved by the branches of government having power to decide such questions." It bears repeating "that effective restraints on . . . exercise [of the commerce power] must proceed from political rather than from judicial processes." *Wickard.*

It is unacceptable that the judicial process should be thought superior to the political process in this area. Under the Constitution the Judiciary has no role to play beyond finding that Congress has not made an unreasonable legislative judgment respecting what is "commerce." . . .

Judicial restraint in this area merely recognizes that the political branches of our Government are structured to protect the interests of the States, as well as the Nation as a whole, and that the States are fully able to protect their own interests in the premises. Congress is constituted of representatives in both the Senate and House elected from the States. *The Federalist* No. 45. ... Decisions upon the extent of federal intervention under the Commerce Clause into the affairs of the States are in that sense decisions of the States themselves. Judicial redistribution of powers granted the National Government by the terms of the Constitution violates the fundamental tenet of our federalism that the extent of federal intervention into the States' affairs in the exercise of delegated powers shall be determined by the States' exercise of political power through their representatives in Congress. There is no reason whatever to suppose that in enacting the 1974 amendments Congress, even if it might extensively obliterate state sovereignty by fully exercising its plenary power respecting commerce, had any purpose to do so. Surely the presumption must be to the contrary. Any realistic assessment of our federal political system, dominated as it is by representatives of the people *elected from the States*, yields the conclusion that it is highly unlikely that those representatives will ever be motivated to disregard totally the concerns of these States. *The Federalist* No. 46. ...

My Brethren's disregard for precedents recognizing these long-settled constitutional principles is painfully obvious in their cavalier treatment of *Wirtz*. Without even a passing reference to the doctrine of stare decisis, *Wirtz*—regarded as controlling only last Term, *Fry* ...—is by exercise of raw judicial power overruled.

No effort is made to distinguish the FLSA amendments sustained in *Wirtz* from the 1974 amendments. We are told at the outset that "the 'far-reaching implications' of *Wirtz* should be overruled," ... later it is said that the "reasoning in *Wirtz* " is no longer "authoritative." My Brethren then merely restate their essential-function test and say that *Wirtz* must "therefore" be overruled. There is no analysis whether *Wirtz* reached the correct result, apart from any flaws in reasoning, even though we are told that "there are obvious differences" between this case and *Wirtz*. Are state and federal interests being silently balanced, as in the discussion of *Fry*? The best I can make of it is that the 1966 FLSA amendments are struck down and *Wirtz* is overruled on the basis of the conceptually unworkable essential-function test; and that the test is unworkable is demonstrated by my Brethren's inability to articulate any meaningful distinctions among state-operated railroads, ... state-operated schools and hospitals, and state-operated police and fire departments.

We are left then with a catastrophic judicial body blow at Congress' power under the Commerce Clause. Even if Congress may nevertheless accomplish its objectives—for example, by conditioning grants of federal funds upon compliance with federal minimum wage and overtime standards, cf. Oklahoma v. CSC (1947)—there is an ominous portent of disruption of our constitutional structure implicit in today's mischievous decision. I dissent.

Mr. Justice **STEVENS**, dissenting.

The Court holds that the Federal Government may not interfere with a sovereign State's inherent right to pay a substandard wage to the janitor at the state capitol. The principle on which the holding rests is difficult to perceive.

The Federal Government may, I believe, require the State to act impartially when it hires or fires the janitor, to withhold taxes from his paycheck, to observe safety regulations when he is performing his job, to forbid him from burning too much soft coal in the capitol furnace, from dumping untreated refuse in an adjacent waterway, from overloading a state-owned garbage truck, or from driving either the truck or the governor's limousine over 55 miles an hour. Even though these and many other activities of the capitol janitor are activities of the State qua State, I have no doubt that they are subject to federal regulation.

I agree that it is unwise for the Federal Government to exercise its power in the ways described in the Court's opinion. ...

My disagreement with the wisdom of this legislation may not, of course, affect my judgment with respect to its validity. On this issue there is no dissent from the proposition that the Federal Government's power over the labor market is adequate to embrace these employees. Since I am unable to identify a limitation on that federal power that would not also invalidate federal regulation of state activities that I consider unquestionably permissible, I am persuaded that this statute is valid. ...

Editors' Notes

(1) **Query:** How did Rehnquist's and Brennan's structuralist approaches and their visions of the broader constitution differ? To what extent did each (or either) seek and find support in the constitutional text? To what extent did each reinforce his structuralism with a doctrinal approach?

(2) **Query:** Rehnquist is usually identified as the democratic theorist, who wants judges to defer to the judgments of the people's elected representatives (see his "The Notion of a Living Constitution," reprinted above, p. 243), and Brennan as the constitutionalist, who advocates a strong role for judges vis-à-vis elected officials (see his "The Constitution of the United States: Contemporary Ratification," reprinted above, p. 236). To what extent did the two switch sides in *National League of Cities*?

(3) **Query:** With the vote 5–4, Blackmun's joining Rehnquist's opinion was essential to its becoming the opinion of the Court rather than merely expressing the views of four justices. To what extent was Blackmun's interpretation of Rehnquist's opinion justified? In effect, was Blackmun publicly serving notice that he would not endorse a return to dual federalism?

Compare his opinion for the Court in Garcia v. San Antonio MTA (1985), the very next case we reprint.

(4) Brennan's assertion that *National League of Cities* would "astound scholars of the Constitution" turned out to be accurate. See espec.: Sotirios A. Barber, "National League of Cities v. Usery: New Meaning for the Tenth Amendment," 1976 *Sup.Ct.Rev.* 161; Karen Flax, "In the Wake of National League of Cities v. Usery: A Derelict Makes Waves," 34 *So.Car.L.Rev.* 649 (1983); Charles A. Lofgren, "National League of Cities v. Usery: Dual Federalism Reborn," 4 *Claremont Jo. of Pub. Affrs.* 19 (1977); Frank I. Michelman, "States' Rights and States' Roles: The Permutations of 'Sovereignty' in *National League of Cities v. Usery*," 86 *Yale L.J.* 1165 (1977); C. Herman Pritchett, *Constitutional Law of the Federal System* (Englewood Cliffs, N.J.: Prentice–Hall, 1983), pp. 234–235; Laurence H. Tribe, "Unravelling *National League of Cities*," 90 *Harv.L Rev.* 1065 (1977).

"Apart from the limitation on federal authority inherent in the delegated nature of Congress' Article I powers, the principal means ... to ensure the role of States in the federal system is the structure of the Federal Government itself."—Justice BLACKMUN

"[I]t does not seem to have occurred to the Court that *it*—an unelected majority of five Justices—today rejects almost 200 years of the understanding of the constitutional status of federalism."—Justice POWELL

GARCIA v. SAN ANTONIO METROPOLITAN TRANSIT AUTHORITY

469 U.S. 528, 105 S.Ct. 1005, 83 L.Ed.2d 1016 (1985).

It became clear from Blackmun's vote in Equal Employment Opportunity Commission v. Wyoming (1983), in which he joined the four dissenters in *National League of Cities* to erode that ruling, that the ambivalence he had expressed in 1976 had not abated in the intervening seven years. Thus the stage was set for a new constitutional battle when the U.S. Department of Labor claimed that the San Antonio Metropolitan Transit Authority (SAMTA), a county-owned agency operating a system of mass transit, had to abide by the Fair Labor Standards Act as amended in 1974. SAMTA filed suit against the Department of Labor, claiming, on the basis of *National League of Cities*, constitutional immunity from the Act. It won in the lower courts. The Department of Labor appealed to the Supreme Court.

Justice **BLACKMUN** delivered the opinion of the Court. ...

We revisit ... an issue raised in National League of Cities v. Usery (1976). In that litigation, this Court, by a sharply divided vote, ruled that the Commerce Clause does not empower Congress to enforce the minimum-wage and overtime provisions of the Fair Labor Standards Act

(FLSA) against the States "in areas of traditional governmental functions." Although *National League of Cities* supplied some examples of "traditional governmental functions," it did not offer a general explanation of how a "traditional" function is to be distinguished from a "nontraditional" one. Since then, federal and state courts have struggled with the task, thus imposed, of identifying a traditional function for purposes of state immunity under the Commerce Clause. ...

Our examination of this "function" standard applied in these and other cases over the last eight years now persuades us that the attempt to draw the boundaries of state regulatory immunity in terms of "traditional governmental function" is not only unworkable but is inconsistent with established principles of federalism and, indeed, with those very federalism principles on which *National League of Cities* purported to rest. That case, accordingly, is overruled. ...

II

Appellees have not argued that SAMTA is immune from regulation under the FLSA on the ground that it is a local transit system engaged in intrastate commercial activity. In a practical sense, SAMTA's operations might well be characterized as "local." Nonetheless, it long has been settled that Congress' authority under the Commerce Clause extends to intrastate economic activities that affect interstate commerce. See, e.g., Hodel v. Virginia Surface Mining & Recl. Assn. (1981); Heart of Atlanta Motel, Inc. v. United States, (1964); Wickard v. Filburn (1942); United States v. Darby (1941). Were SAMTA a privately owned and operated enterprise, it could not credibly argue that Congress exceeded the bounds of its Commerce Clause powers in prescribing minimum wages and overtime rates for SAMTA's employees. Any constitutional exemption from the requirements of the FLSA therefore must rest on SAMTA's status as a governmental entity rather than on the "local" nature of its operations.

The prerequisites for governmental immunity under *National League of Cities* were summarized by this Court in *Hodel.* Under that summary, four conditions must be satisfied before a state activity may be deemed immune from a particular federal regulation under the Commerce Clause. First, it is said that the federal statute at issue must regulate "the 'States as States.'" Second, the statute must "address matters that are indisputably 'attribute[s] of state sovereignty.'" Third, state compliance with the federal obligation must "directly impair [the States'] ability 'to structure integral operations in areas of traditional governmental functions.'" Finally, the relation of state and federal interests must not be such that "the nature of the federal interest ... justifies state submission."

The controversy in the present cases has focused on the third *Hodel* requirement—that the challenged federal statute trench on "traditional governmental functions." ... Just how troublesome the task has been is revealed by the results reached in other federal cases. Thus, courts have held that regulating ambulance services, licensing automobile drivers, operating a municipal airport, performing solid waste disposal, and operating a highway authority are functions *protected* under *National League of Cities*. At the same time, courts have held that issuance of industrial development bonds, regulation of intrastate natural gas sales, regulation of traffic on public roads, regulation of air transportation, operation of a telephone system, leasing and sale of natural gas, operation of a mental health facility, and provision of in-house domestic serves for the handicapped are *not* entitled to immunity. We find it difficult, if not impossible, to identify an organizing principle that places each of the cases in the first group on one side of a line and each of the cases in the second group on the other side. The constitutional distinction between licensing drivers and regulating traffic, for example, or between operating a highway authority and operating a mental health facility, is elusive at best.

... The only other case in which the Court has had occasion to address the problem is [Transportation Union v.] Long Island [1982]. We there observed: "The determination of whether a federal law impairs a state's authority with respect to 'areas of traditional [state] functions' may at times be a difficult one." The accuracy of that statement is demonstrated by this Court's own difficulties in *Long Island* in developing a workable standard for "traditional governmental functions." ...

... Neither do any of the alternative standards that might be employed to distinguish between protected and unprotected governmental functions appear manageable. We rejected the possibility of making immunity turn on a purely historical standard of "tradition" in *Long Island,* and properly so. The most obvious defect of a historical approach to state immunity is that it prevents a court from accommodating changes in the historical functions of States, changes that have resulted in a number of once-private functions like education being assumed by the States and their subdivisions. ...

A nonhistorical standard for selecting immune governmental functions is likely to be just as unworkable. ... The goal of identifying "uniquely" governmental functions, for example, has been rejected by the Court in the field of government tort liability in part because the notion of a "uniquely" governmental function is unmanageable. See Indian Towing Co. v. United States (1955); see also Lafayette v. Louisiana Power & Light Co. (1978) (dissenting opinion). ...

We believe, however, that there is a more fundamental problem at work here. ... The problem is that neither the governmental/proprietary distinction nor any other that purports to separate out important governmental functions can be faithful to the role of federalism in a democratic society. The essence of our federal system is that within the realm of authority left open to them under the Constitution, the States must be equally free to engage in any activity that their citizens choose for the common weal, no matter how unorthodox or unnecessary anyone else—including the judiciary—deems state involvement to be. Any rule of state immunity that looks to the "traditional," "integral," or "necessary" nature of governmental functions inevitably invites an unelected federal judiciary to make decisions about which state policies it favors and which ones it dislikes. ...

We therefore now reject, as unsound in principle and unworkable in practice, a rule of state immunity from federal regulation that turns on a judicial appraisal of whether a particular governmental function is "integral" or "traditional." Any such rule leads to inconsistent results at the same time that it disserves principles of democratic self-governance, and it breeds inconsistency precisely because it is divorced from those principles. ...

III

The central theme of *National League of Cities* was that the States occupy a special position in our constitutional system and that the scope of Congress' authority under the Commerce Clause must reflect that position. Of course, the Commerce Clause by its specific language does not provide any special limitation on Congress' actions with respect to the States. It is equally true, however, that the text of the Constitution provides the beginning rather than the final answer to every inquiry into questions of federalism, for "[b]ehind the words of the constitutional provisions are postulates which limit and control." Monaco v. Mississippi (1934). *National League of Cities* reflected the general conviction that the Constitution precludes "the National Government [from] devour[ing] the essentials of state sovereignty." Maryland v. Wirtz [1968] (dissenting opinion). In order to be faithful to the underlying federal premises of the Constitution, courts must look for the "postulates which limit and control."

What has proved problematic is not the perception that the Constitution's federal structure imposes limitations on the Commerce Clause, but rather the nature and content of those limitations. ...

We doubt that courts ultimately can identify principled constitutional limitations on the scope of Congress' Commerce Clause powers over the States merely by relying on *a priori* definitions of state sovereignty. In part, this is because of the elusiveness of objective criteria for "fundamental" elements of state sovereignty, a problem we have witnessed in the search for "traditional governmental functions." There is, however, a more fundamental reason: the sovereignty of the States is limited by the Constitution itself. A variety of sovereign powers, for example, are withdrawn from the States by Article I, § 10. Section 8 of the same Article works an equally sharp contraction of state sovereignty by authorizing Congress to exercise a wide range of legislative powers and (in conjunction with the Supremacy Clause of Article VI) to displace contrary state legislation. By providing for final review of questions of federal law in this Court, Article III curtails the sovereign power of the States' judiciaries to make authoritative determinations of law. Finally, the developed application, through the Fourteenth Amendment, of the greater part of the Bill of Rights to the States limits the sovereign authority that States otherwise would possess to legislate with respect to their citizens and to conduct their own affairs.

The States unquestionably do "retai[n] a significant measure of sovereign authority." EEOC v. Wyoming (Powell, J., dissenting). They do so, however, only to the extent that the Constitution has not divested them of their original powers and transferred those powers to the Federal Government. In the words of James Madison to the Members of the First Congress: "Interference with the power of the States was no constitutional criterion of the power of Congress. If the power was not given, Congress could not exercise it; if given, they might exercise it, although it should interfere with the laws, or even the Constitution of the States." ...

As a result, to say that the Constitution assumes the continued role of the States is to say little about the nature of that role. ...

When we look for the States' "residuary and inviolable sovereignty," the *Federalist* No. 39 (J. Madison), in the shape of the constitutional scheme rather than in predetermined notions of sovereign power, a different measure of state sovereignty emerges. Apart from the limitation on federal authority inherent in the delegated nature of Congress' Article I powers, the principal means chosen by the Framers to ensure the role of the States in the federal system lies in the structure of the Federal Government itself. It is no novelty to observe that the composition of the Federal Government was designed in large part to protect the States from overreaching by Congress. The Framers thus gave the States a role in the selection both of the Executive and the Legislative Branches of the Federal Government. The States were vested with indirect influence over the House of Representatives and the Presidency by their control of electoral qualifications and their role in presidential elections. U.S. Const., Art. I, § 2, and Art. II, § 1. They were given more direct influence in the Senate, where each State received equal representation and each Senator was to be selected by the legislature of his State. Art. I, § 3. The significance attached to the States' equal representation in the Senate is underscored by the prohibition of any constitutional amendment divesting a State of equal representation without the State's consent. Art. V. ...

... In short, the Framers chose to rely on a federal system in which special restraints on federal power over the States inhered principally in the workings of the National Government itself, rather than in discrete limitations on the objects of federal authority. State sovereign interests, then, are more properly protected by procedural safeguards inherent in the structure of the federal system than by judicially created limitations on federal power.

The effectiveness of the federal political process in preserving the States' interests is apparent even today in the course of federal legislation. On the one hand, the States have been able to direct a substantial proportion of federal revenues into their own treasuries in the form of general and program-specific grants in aid. The federal role in assisting state and local governments is a longstanding one; Congress provided federal land grants to finance state governments from the beginning of the Republic, and direct cash grants were awarded as early as 1887 under the Hatch Act. In the past quarter-century alone, federal grants to States and localities have grown from $7 billion to $96 billion. As a result, federal grants now account for about one-fifth of state and local government expenditures. ... [A]t the same time that the States have exercised their influence to obtain federal support, they have been able to exempt themselves from a wide variety of obligations imposed by Congress under the Commerce Clause. For example, the Federal Power Act, the National Labor Relations Act, the Labor–Management Reporting and Disclosure Act, the Occupational Safety and Health Act, the Employee Retirement Insurance Security Act, and the Sherman Act all contain express or implied exemptions for States and their subdivisions. The fact that some federal statutes such as the FLSA extend general obligations to the States cannot obscure the extent to which the political position of the States in the federal system has served to minimize the burdens that the States bear under the Commerce Clause.

We realize that changes in the structure of the Federal Government have taken place since 1789, not the least of which has been the substitution of popular election of Senators by the adoption of the Seventeenth Amendment in 1913, and that these changes may work to alter the influence of the States in the federal political process. Nonetheless ... we are convinced that the fundamental limitation that the constitutional scheme imposes on the Commerce Clause to protect the "States as States" is one of process rather than one of result. Any substantive restraint on the exercise of Commerce Clause powers must find its justification in the procedural nature of this basic limitation, and it must be tailored to compensate for possible failings in the national political process rather than to dictate a "sacred province of state autonomy." EEOC v. Wyoming.

Insofar as the present cases are concerned, then, we need go no further than to state that we perceive nothing in the overtime and minimum-wage requirements of the FLSA, as applied to SAMTA, that is destructive of state sovereignty or violative of any constitutional provision. ...

IV ...

We do not lightly overrule recent precedent. We have not hesitated, however, when it has become apparent that a prior decision has departed from a proper understanding of congressional power under the Commerce Clause. See United States v. Darby (1941). Due respect for the reach of congressional power within the federal system mandates that we do so now.

National League of Cities v. Usery is overruled. The judgment of the District Court is reversed, and these cases are remanded to that court for further proceedings consistent with this opinion.

It is so ordered.

Justice **POWELL**, with whom the Chief Justice [**BURGER**], Justice **REHNQUIST**, and Justice **O'CONNOR** join, dissenting. ...

There are, of course, numerous examples over the history of this Court in which prior decisions have been reconsidered and overruled. There have been few cases, however, in which the principle of *stare decisis* and the rationale of recent decisions were ignored as abruptly as we now witness. The reasoning of the Court in *National League of Cities,* and the principle applied there, have been reiterated consistently over the past eight years. Since its decision in 1976, *National League of Cities* has been cited and quoted in opinions joined by every member of the present Court. Hodel v. Virginia Surface Mining & Recl. Assn. (1981); United Transportation Union v. Long Island R. Co. (1982); FERC v. Mississippi (1982). Less than three years ago, in *Long Island R. Co.,* a unanimous Court reaffirmed the principles of *National League of Cities* but found them inapplicable to the regulation of a railroad heavily engaged in interstate commerce. ...

The Court in that case recognized that the test "may at times be a difficult one," but it was considered in that unanimous decision as settled constitutional doctrine. ...

Although the doctrine is not rigidly applied to constitutional questions, "any departure from the doctrine of *stare decisis* demands special justification." Arizona v. Rumsey (1984). See also Oregon v. Kennedy (1982) (Stevens, J., concurring). In the present case, the five Justices who compose the majority today participated in *National League of Cities* and the cases reaffirming it. The stability of judicial decision, and with it respect for the authority of this Court, are not served by the precipitous overruling of multiple precedents that we witness in this case.

Whatever effect the Court's decision may have in weakening the application of *stare decisis,* it is likely to be less important than what the Court has done to the Constitution itself. A unique feature of the United States is the *federal* system of government guaranteed by the Constitution and implicit in the very name of our country. Despite some genuflecting in [the] Court's opinion to the concept of federalism, today's decision effectively reduces the Tenth Amendment to meaningless rhetoric when Congress acts pursuant to the Commerce Clause. ...

To leave no doubt about its intention, the Court renounces its decision in *National League of Cities* because it "inevitably invites an unelected federal judiciary to make decisions about which state policies its favors and which ones it dislikes." In other words, the extent to which the States may exercise their authority, when Congress purports to act under the Commerce Clause, henceforth is to be determined from time to time by political decisions made by members of the federal government, decisions the Court says will not be subject to judicial review. I note that it does not seem to have occurred to the Court that *it*—an unelected majority of five Justices—today rejects almost 200 years of the understanding of the constitutional status of federalism. In doing so, there is only a single passing reference to the Tenth Amendment. Nor is so much as a dictum of any court cited in support of the view that the role of the States in the federal system may depend upon the grace of elected federal officials, rather than on the Constitution as interpreted by this Court. ...

The Court apparently thinks that the States' success at obtaining federal funds for various projects and exemptions from the obligations of some federal statutes is indicative of the "effectiveness of the federal political process in preserving the States' interests. ..." But such political success is not relevant to the question whether the political *processes* are the proper means of enforcing constitutional limitations. The fact that Congress generally does not transgress constitutional limits on its power to reach State activities does not make judicial review any less necessary to rectify the cases in which it does do so. The States' role in our system of government is a matter of constitutional law, not of legislative grace. "The powers not delegated to the United States by the Constitution, nor prohibited by it to the States, are reserved to the States, respectively, or to the people." U.S. Const., Amend. 10.

More troubling than the logical infirmities in the Court's reasoning is the result of its holding, i.e., that federal political officials, invoking the Commerce Clause, are the sole judges of the limits of their own power. This result is inconsistent with the fundamental principles of our constitutional system. See, e.g., The *Federalist* No. 78 (Hamilton). At least since Marbury v. Madison [1803] it has been the settled province of the federal judiciary "to say what the law is" with respect to the constitutionality of acts of Congress. In rejecting the role of the judiciary in protecting the States from federal overreaching, the Court's opinion offers no explanation for ignoring the teaching of the most famous case in our history. ...

... [T]he Court today propounds a view of federalism that pays only lip service to the role of the States. ... [I]t fails to recognize the broad, yet specific areas of sovereignty that the Framers intended the States to retain. Indeed, the Court barely acknowledges that the Tenth Amendment exists. ... The Court recasts this language to say that the States retain their sovereign powers "only to the extent that the Constitution has not divested them of their original powers and transferred those powers to the Federal Government." This rephrasing is not a distinction without a difference; rather, it reflects the Court's unprecedented view that Congress is free under the Commerce Clause to assume a State's traditional sovereign power, and to do so without judicial review of its action. Indeed, the Court's view of federalism appears to relegate the States to precisely the trivial role that opponents of the Constitution feared they would occupy. ...

Justice **REHNQUIST**, dissenting. ...

I join both Justice Powell's and Justice O'Connor's thoughtful dissents. ... I do not think it incumbent on those of us in dissent to spell out further the fine points of a principle that will, I am confident, in time again command the support of a majority of this Court.

Justice **O'CONNOR**, with whom Justice **POWELL** and Justice **REHN-QUIST** join, dissenting.

The Court today surveys the battle scene of federalism and sounds a retreat. Like Justice Powell, I would prefer to hold the field and, at the very least, render a little aid to the wounded. I join Justice Powell's opinion. I also write separately to note my fundamental disagreement with the majority's views of federalism and the duty of this Court. ...

It has been difficult for this Court to craft the bright lines defining the scope of state autonomy protected by *National League of Cities.* Such difficulty is to be expected whenever constitutional concerns as important as federalism and the effectiveness of the commerce power come into conflict. Regardless of the difficulty, it is and will remain the duty of this Court to reconcile these concerns in the final instance. That the Court shuns this task today by appealing to the "essence of federalism" can provide scant comfort to those who believe our federal system requires something more than a unitary, centralized government. I would not shirk the duty acknowledged by *National League of Cities* and its progeny, and I share Justice Rehnquist's belief that this Court will in time again assume its constitutional responsibility. ...

Editors' Notes

(1) **Query**: To what extent did Blackmun and Powell rely on structural approaches? What sorts of structural analyses? Textual? Systemic? Transcendent? How did the justices differ?

(2) **Query**: In his concurrence in *National League of Cities,* Justice Blackmun had said that the majority opinion had used a balancing test and that he joined with that understanding. To what extent had the majority in *National League of Cities* in fact used a balancing test? To what extent did Blackmun in *Garcia*?

(3) **Query**: Powell protested that five *unelected* justices were overturning 200 years of constitutional interpretation of the nature of federalism. Would John Marshall have agreed?

(4) **Query**: To what extent was the debate in *National League of Cities* and *Garcia* a debate over WHO shall interpret? Which justices offered the more democratic responses?

"**The Tenth Amendment ... directs us to determine [whether] an incident of state sovereignty is protected by a limitation on an Article I power.**"—**Justice O'CONNOR**

NEW YORK v. UNITED STATES
505 U.S. 144, 112 S.Ct. 2408, 120 L.Ed.2d 120 (1992).

In response to proposals of the National Governors Association and other state leaders, Congress enacted the Low–Level Radioactive Waste Policy Amendments Act of 1985. The statute encouraged states either to dispose of the wastes generated within their borders or form interstate compacts for regional disposal of atomic wastes. Because most states had been unwilling to do either, by 1985 the wastes of 31 "unsited" states were being shipped to only three disposal facilities. It was then that Congress acted, giving the unsited states until January, 1993, to arrange for disposing of their own wastes. To foster compliance, the Act authorized the three existing disposal facilities to charge a graduated surcharge of from $10 per cubic foot of wastes in 1986 to more than $40 in 1990. The Act gave the states other incentives, including monetary rewards for meeting the deadlines and, ultimately, an option: compliance by 1996 or taking title to, and thereby assuming legal liability for, all low-level radioactive wastes generated within their several borders.

New York challenged in a federal district court all of the Act's incentives as inconsistent with the Tenth Amendment. That tribunal dismissed the complaint; the Court of Appeals affirmed; and New York obtained certiorari.

Justice **O'CONNOR** delivered the opinion of the Court. ...

This case implicates one of our Nation's newest problems of public policy and perhaps our oldest question of constitutional law. ... The constitutional question is as old as the Constitution: It consists of discerning the proper division of authority between the Federal Government and the States. We conclude that while Congress has substantial power under the Constitution to encourage the States to provide for the disposal of the radioactive waste generated within their borders, the Constitution does not confer upon Congress the ability simply to compel the States to do so. We therefore find that only two of the Act's three provisions at issue are consistent with the Constitution's allocation of power to the Federal Government. ...

II

A

At least as far back as Martin v. Hunter's Lessee (1816), the Court has resolved questions "of great importance and delicacy" in determining whether particular sovereign powers have been granted by the Constitution to the Federal Government or have been retained by the States.

These questions can be viewed in either of two ways. In some cases the Court has inquired whether an Act of Congress is authorized by one of the powers delegated to Congress in Article I of the Constitution. See, e.g., Perez v. United States (1971); *McCulloch*. In other cases the Court has sought to determine whether an Act of Congress invades the province of state sovereignty reserved by the Tenth Amendment. See, e.g., *Garcia*; Lane County v. Oregon (1869). In a case like this one, involving the division of authority between federal and state governments, the two inquiries are mirror images of each other. If a power is delegated to Congress in the Constitution, the Tenth Amendment expressly disclaims any reservation of that power to the States; if a power is an attribute of state sovereignty reserved by the Tenth Amendment, it is necessarily a power the Constitution has not conferred on Congress. . . .

It is in this sense that the Tenth Amendment "states but a truism that all is retained which has not been surrendered." United States v. Darby (1941). . . . This has been the Court's consistent understanding: "The States unquestionably do retain a significant measure of sovereign authority . . . to the extent that the Constitution has not divested them of their original powers and transferred those powers to the Federal Government." *Garcia*.

Congress exercises its conferred powers subject to the limitations contained in the Constitution. Thus, for example, under the Commerce Clause Congress may regulate publishers engaged in interstate commerce, but Congress is constrained in the exercise of that power by the First Amendment. The Tenth Amendment likewise restrains the power of Congress, but this limit is not derived from the text of the Tenth Amendment itself, which . . . is essentially a tautology. Instead, the Tenth Amendment confirms that the power of the Federal Government is subject to limits that may, in a given instance, reserve power to the States. The Tenth Amendment thus directs us to determine, as in this case, whether an incident of state sovereignty is protected by a limitation on an Article I power.

. . . Our task would be the same even if one could prove that federalism secured no advantages to anyone. It consists not of devising our preferred system of government, but of understanding and applying the framework set forth in the Constitution. . . .

This framework [of federalism] has been sufficiently flexible over the past two centuries to allow for enormous changes in the nature of government. The Federal Government undertakes activities today that would have been unimaginable to the Framers. . . . Yet the powers conferred upon the Federal Government by the Constitution were phrased in language broad enough to allow for the expansion of the Federal Government's role. Among the provisions of the Constitution that have been particularly important in this regard, three concern us here.

First, the Constitution allocates to Congress the power "to regulate Commerce ... among the several States." Art. I, § 8, cl. 3. ... Second, the [power] ... "to pay the Debts and provide for the ... general Welfare of the United States." Art. I, § 8, cl. 1. ... Finally, the Constitution provides that "the Laws of the United States ... shall be the supreme Law of the Land ... any Thing in the Constitution or Laws of any State to the Contrary notwithstanding." Art. VI, cl. 2. As the Federal Government's willingness to exercise power within the confines of the Constitution has grown, the authority of the States has correspondingly diminished to the extent that federal and state policies have conflicted. We have observed that the Supremacy Clause gives the Federal Government "a decided advantage in the delicate balance" the Constitution strikes between State and Federal power. Gregory v. Ashcroft.

The actual scope of the Federal Government's authority with respect to the States has changed over the years, therefore, but the constitutional structure underlying and limiting that authority has not. ...

B

Petitioners do not contend that Congress lacks the power to regulate the disposal of low level radioactive waste. Space in radioactive waste disposal sites is frequently sold by residents of one State to residents of another. Regulation of the resulting interstate market in waste disposal is therefore well within Congress' authority under the Commerce Clause. Petitioners likewise do not dispute that under the Supremacy Clause Congress could, if it wished, pre-empt state radioactive waste regulation. Petitioners contend only that the Tenth Amendment limits the power of Congress to regulate in the way it has chosen. Rather than addressing the problem of waste disposal by directly regulating the generators and disposers of waste, petitioners argue, Congress has impermissibly directed the States to regulate in this field.

Most of our recent cases interpreting the Tenth Amendment have concerned the authority of Congress to subject state governments to generally applicable laws. The Court's jurisprudence in this area has traveled an unsteady path. See Maryland v. Wirtz (1968) (state schools and hospitals are subject to Fair Labor Standards Act); National League of Cities v. Usery (1976) (overruling *Wirtz*) (state employers are not subject to Fair Labor Standards Act); Garcia v. San Antonio Metropolitan Transit Authority (1985) (overruling *National League of Cities*) (state employers are once again subject to Fair Labor Standards Act). This case presents no occasion to apply or revisit the holdings of any of these cases, as this is not a case in which Congress has subjected a State to the same legislation applicable to private parties.

This case instead concerns the circumstances under which Congress may use the States as implements of regulation; that is, whether Congress may direct or otherwise motivate the States to regulate in a particular field or a particular way. Our cases have established a few principles that guide our resolution of the issue.

1 ...

... While Congress has substantial powers to govern the Nation directly, including in areas of intimate concern to the States, the Constitution has never been understood to confer upon Congress the ability to require the States to govern according to Congress' instructions. See Coyle v. Oklahoma (1911). The Court has been explicit about this distinction. "Both the States and the United States existed before the Constitution. The people, through that instrument, established a more perfect union by substituting a national government, acting, with ample power, directly upon the citizens, instead of the Confederate government, which acted with powers, greatly restricted, only upon the States." The Court has made the same point with more rhetorical flourish, although perhaps with less precision, on a number of occasions. ...

Indeed, the question whether the Constitution should permit Congress to employ state governments as regulatory agencies was a topic of lively debate among the Framers. ...

In the end, the Convention opted for a Constitution in which Congress would exercise its legislative authority directly over individuals rather than over States. ... Oliver Ellsworth, a member of the Connecticut delegation in Philadelphia, explained the distinction to his State's convention: "This Constitution does not attempt to coerce sovereign bodies, states, in their political capacity. ... But this legal coercion singles out the ... individual." Charles Pinckney, another delegate at the Constitutional Convention, emphasized to the South Carolina House of Representatives that in Philadelphia "the necessity of having a government which should at once operate upon the people, and not upon the states, was conceived to be indispensable by every delegation present." Rufus King, one of Massachusetts' delegates, returned home to support ratification by recalling the Commonwealth's unhappy experience under the Articles of Confederation and arguing: "Laws, to be effective, therefore, must not be laid on states, but upon individuals." [Alexander] Hamilton ... exclaimed: "But can we believe that one state will ever suffer itself to be used as an instrument of coercion? The thing is a dream; it is impossible. Then we are brought to this dilemma— either a federal standing army is to enforce the requisitions, or the federal treasury is left without supplies, and the government without support. What, sir, is the cure for this great evil? Nothing, but to enable the national laws to operate on individuals, in the same manner as those of the states do." At North Carolina's convention, Samuel Spencer recognized that "all the laws of the Confederation were binding on the states in their political capacities ... but now the thing is entirely different. The laws of Congress will be binding on individuals." *

---

* All of Justice O'Connor's citations were to Jonathan Elliot, ed., *Debates on the Federal Constitution* (2d ed., 1863). She gave no hint that she was aware of the fragile (at best)

In providing for a stronger central government, therefore, the Framers explicitly chose a Constitution that confers upon Congress the power to regulate individuals, not States. As we have seen, the Court has consistently respected this choice. We have always understood that even where Congress has the authority under the Constitution to pass laws requiring or prohibiting certain acts, it lacks the power directly to compel the States to require or prohibit those acts. ...

2

This is not to say that Congress lacks the ability to encourage a State to regulate in a particular way, or that Congress may not hold out incentives to the States as a method of influencing a State's policy choices. Our cases have identified a variety of methods, short of outright coercion, by which Congress may urge a State to adopt a legislative program consistent with federal interests. Two of these methods are of particular relevance here.

First, under Congress' spending power, "Congress may attach conditions on the receipt of federal funds." ... Where the recipient of federal funds is a State, as is not unusual today, the conditions attached to the funds by Congress may influence a State's legislative choices. ... Second, where Congress has the authority to regulate private activity under the Commerce Clause, we have recognized Congress' power to offer States the choice of regulating that activity according to federal standards or having state law pre-empted by federal regulation. ...

By either of these two methods ... the residents of the State retain the ultimate decision as to whether or not the State will comply. If a State's citizens view federal policy as sufficiently contrary to local interests, they may elect to decline a federal grant. If state residents would prefer their government to devote its attention and resources to problems other than those deemed important by Congress, they may choose to have the Federal Government rather than the State bear the expense of a federally mandated regulatory program, and they may continue to supplement that program to the extent state law is not preempted. Where Congress encourages state regulation rather than compelling it, state governments remain responsive to the local electorate's preferences; state officials remain accountable to the people.

By contrast, where the Federal Government compels States to regulate, the accountability of both state and federal officials is diminished. If the citizens of New York, for example, do not consider that making provision for the disposal of radioactive waste is in their best interest, they may elect state officials who share their view. That view can always be pre-empted under the Supremacy Clause if is contrary to

---

condition of this collection as a "record" of what was actually said in the various ratifying conventions. The very most one can say for these "speeches" is that they were the notes written down by people, often partisan, who did not know modern shorthand and that the participants, when they read them in newspapers, often bitterly complained of their inaccuracy. For a general discussion, see James H. Hutson, "The Creation of the Constitution: The Integrity of the Documentary Record," 65 *Tex.L Rev.* 1 (1986).—**Eds.**

the national view, but in such a case it is the Federal Government that makes the decision in full view of the public, and it will be federal officials who suffer the consequences if the decision turns out to be detrimental or unpopular. But where the Federal Government directs the States to regulate, it may be state officials who will bear the brunt of public disapproval, while the federal officials who devised the regulatory program may remain insulated from the electoral ramifications of their decision. ...

With these principles in mind, we turn to the three challenged provisions of the Low–Level Radioactive Waste Policy Amendments Act of 1985.

III

Construed as a whole, the Act comprises three sets of "incentives" for the States to provide for the disposal of low level radioactive waste generated within their borders. We consider each in turn.

A

The first set ... works in three steps. First, Congress has authorized States with disposal sites to impose a surcharge on radioactive waste received from other States. Second, the Secretary of Energy collects a portion of this surcharge and places the money in an escrow account. Third, States achieving a series of milestones receive portions of this fund. ...

Petitioners contend ... that the form of these expenditures removes them from the scope of Congress' spending power. Petitioners emphasize the Act's instruction to the Secretary of Energy to "deposit all funds received in a special escrow account. The funds so deposited shall not be the property of the United States." Petitioners argue that because the money collected and redisbursed to the States is kept in an account separate from the general treasury, because the Secretary holds the funds only as a trustee, and because the States themselves are largely able to control whether they will pay into the escrow account or receive a share, the Act "in no manner calls for the spending of federal funds."

The Constitution's grant to Congress of the authority to "pay the Debts and provide for the ... general Welfare" has never, however, been thought to mandate a particular form of accounting. A great deal of federal spending comes from segregated trust funds collected and spent for a particular purpose. See, e.g., Highway Trust Fund, Federal Old–Age and Survivors Insurance Trust Fund, Federal Disability Insurance Trust Fund, [and] Federal Supplementary Medical Insurance Trust Fund. The Spending Clause has never been construed to deprive Congress of the power to structure federal spending in this manner. ...

The Act's first set of incentives, in which Congress has conditioned grants to the States upon the States' attainment of a series of milestones, is thus well within the authority of Congress under the Commerce and Spending Clauses. Because the first set of incentives is supported by affirmative constitutional grants of power to Congress, it is not inconsistent with the Tenth Amendment.

B

In the second set of incentives, Congress has authorized States and regional compacts with disposal sites gradually to increase the cost of access to the sites, and then to deny access altogether, to radioactive waste generated in States that do not meet federal deadlines. As a simple regulation, this provision would be within the power of Congress to authorize the States to discriminate against interstate commerce. Where federal regulation of private activity is within the scope of the Commerce Clause, we have recognized the ability of Congress to offer states the choice of regulating that activity according to federal standards or having state law pre-empted by federal regulation.

This is the choice presented to nonsited States by the Act's second set of incentives: States may either regulate the disposal of radioactive waste according to federal standards by attaining local or regional self-sufficiency, or their residents who produce radioactive waste will be subject to federal regulation authorizing sited States and regions to deny access to their disposal sites. The affected States are not compelled by Congress to regulate, because any burden caused by a State's refusal to regulate will fall on those who generate waste and find no outlet for its disposal, rather than on the State as a sovereign. A State whose citizens do not wish it to attain the Act's milestones may devote its attention and its resources to issues its citizens deem more worthy; the choice remains at all times with the residents of the State, not with Congress. The State need not expend any funds, or participate in any federal program, if local residents do not view such expenditures or participation as worthwhile. Nor must the State abandon the field if it does not accede to federal direction; the State may continue to regulate the generation and disposal of radioactive waste in any manner its citizens see fit.

The Act's second set of incentives thus represents a conditional exercise of Congress' commerce power, along the lines of those we have held to be within Congress' authority. As a result, the second set of incentives does not intrude on the sovereignty reserved to the States by the Tenth Amendment.

C

The take title provision is of a different character. This third so-called "incentive" offers States, as an alternative to regulating pursuant to Congress' direction, the option of taking title to and possession of the low level radioactive waste generated within their borders and becoming liable for all damages waste generators suffer as a result of the States' failure to do so promptly. In this provision, Congress has crossed the line distinguishing encouragement from coercion. ...

The take title provision offers state governments a "choice" of either accepting ownership of waste or regulating according to the instructions of Congress. Respondents do not claim that the Constitution would authorize Congress to impose either option as a freestanding requirement. On one hand, the Constitution would not permit Congress simply to transfer radioactive waste from generators to state governments. Such a forced transfer, standing alone, would in principle be no different than [sic] a congressionally compelled subsidy from state governments to radioactive waste producers. The same is true of the provision requiring the States to become liable for the generators' damages. ... [This] type of federal action would "commandeer" state governments into the service of federal regulatory purposes, and would for this reason be inconsistent with the Constitution's division of authority between federal and state governments. On the other hand, the second alternative held out to state governments—regulating pursuant to Congress' direction—would, standing alone, present a simple command to state governments to implement legislation enacted by Congress. As we have seen, the Constitution does not empower Congress to subject state governments to this type of instruction.

Because an instruction to state governments to take title to waste, standing alone, would be beyond the authority of Congress, and because a direct order to regulate, standing alone, would also be beyond the authority of Congress, it follows that Congress lacks the power to offer the States a choice between the two. Unlike the first two sets of incentives, the take title incentive does not represent the conditional exercise of any congressional power enumerated in the Constitution. In this provision, Congress has not held out the threat of exercising its spending power or its commerce power; it has instead held out the threat, should the States not regulate according to one federal instruction, of simply forcing the States to submit to another federal instruction. A choice between two unconstitutionally coercive regulatory techniques is no choice at all. ...

The take title provision appears to be unique. No other federal statute has been cited which offers a state government no option other than that of implementing legislation enacted by Congress. Whether one views the take title provision as lying outside Congress' enumerated powers, or as infringing upon the core of state sovereignty reserved by the Tenth Amendment, the provision is inconsistent with the federal structure of our Government established by the Constitution. ...

Justice **WHITE**, with whom Justice **BLACKMUN** and Justice **STEVENS** join, concurring in part and dissenting in part.

The Court today affirms the constitutionality of two facets of the Low–Level Radioactive Waste Policy Amendments Act of 1985. ... The Court strikes down and severs a third component of the 1985 Act, the "take title" provision ... [as] unconstitutional under principles of federalism. Because I believe the Court has mischaracterized the essential inquiry, misanalyzed the inquiry it has chosen to undertake, and undervalued the effect the seriousness of this public policy problem should have on the constitutionality of the take title provision, I can only join

Parts **III-A** and **III-B**, and I respectfully dissent from the rest of its opinion. ...

IV

The Court announces that it has no occasion to revisit such decisions as *Garcia* and *National League of Cities* because "this is not a case in which Congress has subjected a State to the same legislation applicable to private parties." Although this statement sends the welcome signal that the Court does not intend to cut a wide swath through our recent Tenth Amendment precedents, it nevertheless is unpersuasive. I have several difficulties with the Court's analysis in this respect: it builds its rule around an insupportable and illogical distinction in the types of alleged incursions on state sovereignty ... and it omits any discussion of the most recent and pertinent test for determining the take title provision's constitutionality.

The Court's distinction between a federal statute's regulation of States and private parties for general purposes, as opposed to a regulation solely on the activities of States, is unsupported by our recent Tenth Amendment cases. In no case has the Court rested its holding on such a distinction. Moreover, the Court makes no effort to explain why this purported distinction should affect the analysis of Congress' power under general principles of federalism and the Tenth Amendment. The distinction, facilely thrown out, is not based on any defensible theory. Certainly one would be hard-pressed to read the spirited exchanges between the Court and dissenting Justices in *National League of Cities* and in *Garcia*, as having been based on the distinction now drawn by the Court. An incursion on state sovereignty hardly seems more constitutionally acceptable if the federal statute that "commands" specific action also applies to private parties. The alleged diminution in state authority over its own affairs is not any less because the federal mandate restricts the activities of private parties.

... I would also submit ... that the Court's attempt to carve out a doctrinal distinction for statutes that purport solely to regulate State activities is especially unpersuasive after *Garcia*. ... Just last Term ... Justice O'CONNOR wrote for the Court [in Gregory v. Ashcroft (1991)] that "this Court in *Garcia* has left primarily to the political process the protection of the States against intrusive exercises of Congress' Commerce Clause powers." ...

... In *Garcia*, we stated the proper inquiry: "We are convinced that the fundamental limitation that the constitutional scheme imposes on the Commerce Clause to protect the States as States' is one of process rather than one of result. Any substantive restraint on the exercise of Commerce Clause powers must find its justification in the procedural nature of this basic limitation, and it must be tailored to compensate for possible failings in the national political process rather than to dictate a sacred province of state autonomy.' " Where it addresses this aspect of respondents' argument, the Court tacitly concedes that a failing of the political process cannot be shown in this case because it refuses to rebut the unassailable arguments that the States were well able to look after themselves in the legislative process that culminated in the 1985 Act's passage. Indeed, New York acknowledges that its "congressional delegation participated in the drafting and enactment of both the 1980 and the 1985 Acts." The Court rejects this process-based argument by resorting to generalities and platitudes about the purpose of federalism being to protect individual rights.

Ultimately, I suppose, the entire structure of our federal constitutional government can be traced to an interest in establishing checks and balances to prevent the exercise of tyranny against individuals. But these fears seem extremely far distant to me in a situation such as this. We face a crisis of national proportions in the disposal of low-level radioactive waste, and Congress has acceded to the wishes of the States by permitting local decision making rather than imposing a solution from Washington. New York itself participated and supported passage of this legislation at both the gubernatorial and federal representative levels, and then enacted state laws specifically to comply with the deadlines and timetables agreed upon by the States in the 1985 Act. For me, the Court's civics lecture has a decidedly hollow ring at a time when action, rather than rhetoric, is needed to solve a national problem. ...

V

The ultimate irony of the decision today is that in its formalistically rigid obeisance to "federalism," the Court gives Congress fewer incentives to defer to the wishes of state officials in achieving local solutions to local problems. This legislation was a classic example of Congress acting as arbiter among the States in their attempts to accept responsibility for managing a problem of grave import. The States urged the National Legislature not to impose from Washington a solution to the country's low-level radioactive waste management problems. Instead, they sought a reasonable level of local and regional autonomy consistent with Art. I, § 10 cl. 3, of the Constitution. By invalidating the measure designed to ensure compliance for recalcitrant States, such as New York, the Court upsets the delicate compromise achieved among the States and forces Congress to erect several additional formalistic hurdles to clear before achieving exactly the same objective. ...

Justice **STEVENS**, concurring in part and dissenting in part.

Under the Articles of Confederation, the Federal Government had the power to issue commands to the States. See Arts. VIII, IX. Because that indirect exercise of federal power proved ineffective, the Framers of the Constitution empowered the Federal Government to exercise legislative authority directly over individuals within the States, even though that direct authority constituted a greater intrusion on State sovereignty. Nothing in that history suggests that the Federal Government may not also impose its will upon the several States as it did under the

Articles. The Constitution enhanced, rather than diminished, the power of the Federal Government.

The notion that Congress does not have the power to issue "a simple command to state governments to implement legislation enacted by Congress" is incorrect and unsound. There is no such limitation in the Constitution. The Tenth Amendment surely does not impose any limit on Congress' exercise of the powers delegated to it by Article I. Nor does the structure of the constitutional order or the values of federalism mandate such a formal rule. To the contrary, the Federal Government directs state governments in many realms. The Government regulates state-operated railroads, state school systems, state prisons, state elections, and a host of other state functions. Similarly, there can be no doubt that, in time of war, Congress could either draft soldiers itself or command the States to supply their quotas of troops. I see no reason why Congress may not also command the States to enforce federal water and air quality standards or federal standards for the disposition of low-level radioactive wastes. ...

Editors' Notes

(1) **Query:** To what extent did Justice O'Connor rely on a structuralist approach? A doctrinal approach? Originalism? To what extent was her reasoning textualist? Did she, implicitly at least, rely on a version of democratic theory? Where, exactly, did she get her vision of federalism?

(2) **Query:** What about Justice White? What answers would one give to the questions in Note (1)? What about Justice Stevens?

(3) **Query:** Our note on pp. 588–89 pointed out that O'Connor's citations to Elliot's *Debates* on ratification gave no hint of doubts about the validity of these alleged records. But how probable is it that even biased and inaccurate reporters at five different state conventions could have thought that five people from the Philadelphia Convention had said essentially the same thing? But is it clear that these quotations, even assuming the delegates actually used the words attributed to them, were addressing the point that O'Connor was trying to make? That is, were they *both* asserting that the new constitutional text would authorize the national government to operate directly on individual citizens and denying it could operate directly on the states?

(4) **Query:** Stevens claimed that the constitutional text does implicitly authorize, under some circumstances, federal action against the states. How strong a case do the plain words (including passages Stevens did not cite) make for such a claim?

(5) **Query:** Does the question of WHO shall interpret lurk in the background of any of the opinions in this case?

(6) **Query:** Justices from Marshall in *McCulloch* to Rehnquist in *League of Cities* have proceeded as if *two* questions are typically involved in challenges to congressional power: (1) whether the act in question falls within a power of Congress; and (2) whether, even if within Congress's power, the act is prohibited by some part of the Bill of Rights or other textual exemption from Congress's power. Thus, Rehnquist could agree in *League of Cities* that "congressional enactments which [in answer to question (1)] may be fully

within the grant of legislative authority contained in the Commerce Clause may nevertheless be invalid because found [in answer to question (2)] to offend against the right to trial by jury" or other individual right. Putting states' rights in the same logical place as individual rights vis-à-vis national power, the theory of dual federalism contends that states' reserved powers are exemptions from the powers of Congress akin to those in the Bill of Rights.

Both dual federalists and their opponents have traditionally agreed that the first question is appropriate in states'-rights challenges to national power. A state can legitimately ask, in other words, whether the constitutional text authorizes some congressional act. But only dual federalists ask the second question in cases involving states' rights. Only dual federalists ask whether a congressional act, though authorized by a specific textual grant of power, nevertheless encroaches on some area reserved to the states. Opponents of dual federalism do not ask the second question when states challenge national power because, they say, the constitutional document contains no states'-rights exemptions akin to protected individual and minority rights.

In New York v. United States, Justice O'Connor collapsed these two questions—those of (1) congressional power and (2) states' rights. She contended, in effect, that the question of states' rights is one element of the question of congressional power: that the finding of an appropriate states' right answers (in the negative) the question of Congress's authorization. If the traditional two-question understanding was good enough for Rehnquist in *League of Cities*, why might O'Connor have abandoned it in New York v. United States? What does her merger of the two questions tell us about her vision of federalism and the structure of the American political system?

(7) **Query**: To what extent did New York v. United States overrule *Garcia*?

(8) United States v. Lopez (1995), voided the Gun–Free School Zones Act of 1990, which had forbidden private possession of firearms near schools. In declaring the Act exceeded Congress's power under the Commerce Clause, a 5–4 Court interrupted a modern judicial tradition of two strands. One dates from the 1890s and involves congressional reliance on the Commerce Clause to reach problems beyond those directly implicated by the Constitution's enumeration of specific national powers. This tradition includes laws against: racial segregation, racketeering, interstate travel to incite riots, and interstate kidnapping. A related strand dates from the late 1930s and defers to Congress's judgment about whether a noncommercial problem is sufficiently connected with commerce to warrant action under the Commerce Clause. An ambiguous opinion by Chief Justice Rehnquist causes doubt about the further growth of these traditions, but leaves little doubt about the current status of Justice Blackmun's approach in *Garcia*.

C

REINFORCING REPRESENTA-TIVE DEMOCRACY: KEEPING POLITICAL PROCESSES OPEN

Chapter 3 discussed the competing political theories of constitutionalism and democracy that underpin the American political system. Chapter 9 elaborated a bevy of "approaches" to constitutional interpretation. Chapters 10 and 11 tried to focus on various forms of one of these, *structuralism*, though, as Chapter 9 had warned, other approaches, such as *textualism, originalism, doctrinalism, philosophy,* and *prudence,* kept intruding on our analysis. The pair of chapters that follow try, subject to the same sorts of incursions, to concentrate on one *purposive* approach to constitutional interpretation, "reinforcing representative democracy." But, as so often happens, one has to move backward before going forward, and we begin by discussing its intellectual antecedent, deference to representative democracy through "the doctrine of the clear mistake." Although the two differ in significant ways, each seeks to constrain judges' interpretive power.

The "doctrine of the clear mistake" was most clearly stated by Prof. James Bradley Thayer of the Harvard Law School in 1893, just as the Supreme Court was beginning to etch the economics of laissez faire in the margins of the constitutional text. Earlier that year, Justice David Brewer had told the New York State Bar Association that the country faced grave dangers from "the black flag of anarchism, flaunting destruction to property," and "the red flag of socialism, inviting a redistribution of property." Identifying the labor movement and governmental regulation as immediate perils, he saw "the multitudes—the majority" as ready to ransack rights to own property and engage in business. Brewer's solution was straightforward: "strengthen the judiciary."

> I am firmly persuaded that the salvation of the Nation, the
> permanence of government of and by the people, rests upon the
> independence and vigor of the judiciary, to stay the waves of
> popular feeling, to restrain the greedy hand of the many from
> filching from the few that which they have honestly acquired.
> . . . [1]

In contrast, Thayer argued that judges should leave policy making to
the officials whom the people had elected to Congress and uphold
the validity of *federal* statutes except when their constitutional
infirmity was clear beyond a reasonable doubt. (We reprint his
article at p. 602.)

"Reinforcing representative democracy" builds on Thayer's article but entails a broader, though still limited, set of roles for courts.
In general, as with "the doctrine of the clear mistake," judges
should presume that statutes are valid and place the burden of
proving otherwise on the challenger. (Because their concern is
with democracy at all levels, proponents of "reinforcing" typically
presume the validity of state as well as federal law.) Justice Harlan
Fiske Stone initially put the elements of this approach to constitutional interpretation into a coherent, if not yet complete, form in
footnote 4 to his opinion for the Court in United States v. Carolene
Products (1938; reprinted below, p. 609). There he suggested
three exceptions to the general presumption of constitutionality
(and thus to Thayer's doctrine). Later judges and commentators,[2]
including Louis Lusky, who as Stone's law clerk drafted the earliest
version of the footnote,[3] have expanded and reinterpreted the
model that Stone sketched.

The timing of the footnote is important. During much of the
previous fifty years, a majority of the justices had been following
Brewer rather than Thayer and had read their own economic views
into and out of the constitutional text so as to thwart both state and
federal efforts to cope with the problems of industrial and finance
capitalism. The Great Depression that enveloped the country in
1929 and the judiciary's war against Roosevelt's New Deal left
laissez faire—and the Supreme Court's reputation for wisdom—in
shambles. By 1938 the justices had retreated, returning to an older
doctrine of presuming economic regulation constitutional. This
withdrawal caused much heart-wrenching among some of the breth-

---

1. "The Movement of Coercion," 16 *Procs. of the N.Y.St.Bar Ass'n* 37 (1893).

2. See, for example: Alpheus Thomas Mason, *The Supreme Court from Taft to Burger*
(Baton Rouge: Louisiana State University Press, 1979); John Hart Ely, *Democracy and
Distrust* (Cambridge: Harvard University Press, 1980); and Cass R. Sunstein, *The Partial
Constitution* (Cambridge: Harvard University Press, 1993). Although a political philoso-
pher rather than a "constitutional commentator," Michael Walzer has expounded a theory
quite similar to Ely's: "Philosophy and Democracy," 9 *Pol. Theory* 379 (1981). But see
Walzer's later essay, "Flight From Philosophy," *N.Y. Rev. Books*, Feb. 2, 1989, at 42.

3. See Lusky's own discussions, several decades later: *By What Right?* (Charlottesville, VA: Michie, 1975), and "Footnote Redux: A *Carolene Products* Reminiscence," 82
Colum.L.Rev. 1093 (1982).

ren (see George Sutherland's dissent in West Coast Hotel v. Parrish [1937; reprinted below, p. 1123]) and raised fundamental questions about future judicial involvement in constitutional interpretation. If judges were to presume economic regulation constitutional, why not all regulation? On what principles could they draw lines?

Other problems, practical, moral, and intellectual, were also looming. In Europe, totalitarianism had become a widespread and established fact. With varying amounts of murderous violence, Mussolini, Stalin, and Hitler each suppressed political dissent. In addition, the atrocity of Nazism's racism was becoming increasingly plain. These developments helped sharpen some Americans' awareness of their own country's intolerance toward dissent and an ugly racism that belied ideals of equality. Well before the end of the 1930s, the justices had begun acting more boldly in upholding First–Amendment freedoms and had taken a few tentative steps toward questioning the validity of governmentally imposed segregation. A year before *Carolene Products*, Palko v. Connecticut (1937; reprinted above, p. 128) had stated that "the Constitution" contained a hierarchy of values and that the First Amendment was near the apex of that scale.

In this context, Stone (and his clerk Lusky) [4] outlined what people at the time called "the preferred position," what more recent commentators have subtly changed and rechristened "reinforcing representative democracy." The gist of the argument is that the American political system is basically a representative democracy in which the various conditions listed in Chapter 3 obtain. The people are entitled to rule themselves by being able to choose their government after full and open debate and through an electoral process in which each citizen can participate. "The Constitution" (usually construed to include only the document plus a version of democratic theory) does prescribe some specific limitations on governmental choice; but, as with "the clear mistake," judges should allow the people's elected representatives—and therefore the people themselves—latitude in interpreting that "Constitution." It is the fact that laws are made by the people's duly elected representatives and do not clearly violate the text or democratic theory that gives such laws legitimacy, not their conformity to other values judges deem fundamental.

But if the text and adherence to democratic theory convey legitimacy, it follows that judges should change [5] the presumption

---

4. The footnote's genesis is described by Alpheus Thomas Mason: *Security Through Freedom* (Ithaca: Cornell University Press, 1955), and *Harlan Fiske Stone* (New York: Viking, 1956), espec. ch. 31. Stone always denied his ideas were novel; he got them, he said, from Holmes and Brandeis. Lusky, too, modestly minimized his own very important role.

5. Some commentators and interpreters would relax the presumption, others would drop it, and still others would reverse it.

of constitutionality in several kinds of situations. The presumption does not hold: first, when legislation restricts rights to free political communication and open political processes; and, second, when legislation singles out for disadvantage minorities who lack political power. At the urging of Chief Justice Hughes, Stone added a third exception (placed first in his footnote) which some commentators, including Lusky, would like to discount heavily: when legislation impinges on a right of an individual citizen listed in the constitutional document.

Carolene Products has become the centerpiece of latter-day constitutional interpretation. More than a half century later, judges and commentators are still wrangling over the validity, utility, and implications of the jurisprudence that Stone so tantalizingly suggested. Indeed, we organize much of the rest of the book around its contents. By focusing on *reinforcing representative democracy* as an approach to constitutional interpretation, Chapters 12 and 13 examine a few of the more obvious problems of what became Stone's second exception: freedom of speech and press and the rights to associate with others to influence political decisions and, of course, to vote, to have one's vote counted, and to have it counted equally.

Section D, Chapters 14 and 15, discusses what became Stone's third exception and some of the complexities of "equal protection of the laws." There the approaches of *doctrinalism, developmentalism, originalism, prudence,* and *philosophy* mix with *purposive* approaches. Section E, Chapters 16–18 illustrates the *purposive* approach of *protecting fundamental rights*.

It should be clear that, although the approach the following two chapters put at center stage, *reinforcing representative democracy*, directly concerns constitutional interpretation as influenced by democratic theory, constitutionalism is not indifferent or irrelevant to preserving a democratic system. The right of a citizen to participate in his or her government is as much a part of constitutionalism's concept of human dignity as self-expression is vital to constitutionalism's concept of the individual's right to full development.

SELECTED BIBLIOGRAPHY

Anastaplo, George. *The Constitutionalist* (Dallas: Southern Methodist University Press, 1971).

Barber, Sotirios A. *On What the Constitution Means* (Baltimore: Johns Hopkins University Press, 1984).

_____. *The Constitution of Judicial Power* (Baltimore: Johns Hopkins University Press, 1993).

Choper, Jesse H. *Judicial Review and the National Political Process* (Chicago: University of Chicago Press, 1980).

Douglas, William O. *We, the Judges* (New York: Doubleday, 1955), espec. ch. 9.

Dworkin, Ronald. "The Forum of Principle," 56 *N.Y.U.L.Rev.* 469 (1981); reprinted as ch. 2 in his *A Matter of Principle* (Cambridge: Harvard University Press, 1985).

Elliott, Ward. E.Y. *The Rise of Guardian Democracy* (Cambridge: Harvard University Press, 1974).

Ely, John Hart. *Democracy and Distrust* (Cambridge: Harvard University Press, 1980).

_____. "Another Such Victory: Constitutional Theory and Practice in a World Where Courts Are No Different From Legislatures," 77 *Va.L.Rev.* 833 (1991).

Emerson, Thomas I. *Toward a General Theory of the First Amendment* (New York: Random House, 1963).

Fleming, James E. "Constructing the Substantive Constitution," 72 *Tex.L.Rev.* 211 (1993).

Gabin, Sanford B. *Judicial Review and the Reasonable Doubt Test* (Port Washington, NY: Kennikat Press, 1980)

Lusky, Louis. *By What Right?* (Charlottesville, VA: Michie, 1975).

Mason, Alpheus Thomas. *Security Through Freedom* (Ithaca: Cornell University Press, 1955).

_____. *Harlan Fiske Stone* (New York: Viking, 1956), espec. ch. 31.

_____. *The Supreme Court from Taft to Burger* (Baton Rouge: Louisiana State University Press, 1979).

Meiklejohn, Alexander. *Free Speech and Its Relation to Self–Government* (New York: Harpers, 1948).

Schwartz, Bernard. *Super Chief: Earl Warren and his Supreme Court* (New York: New York University Press, 1983).

Sunstein, Cass R. *The Partial Constitution* (Cambridge: Harvard University Press, 1993).

Symposium. "Judicial Review versus Democracy," 42 *Ohio St.L.J.* (1981).

Symposium. "Constitutional Adjudication and Democratic Theory," 56 *N.Y.U.L.Rev.* 259 (1981).

Symposium. "*Democracy and Distrust*: Ten Years Later," 77 *Va. L.Rev.* 631 (1991).

Tribe, Laurence H. "The Puzzling Persistence of Process–Based Constitutional Theories," 89 *Yale L.J.* 1063 (1980); reprinted as ch. 2 in his *Constitutional Choices* (Cambridge: Harvard University Press, 1985).

"[W]hatever choice is rational is constitutional."

THE ORIGIN AND SCOPE OF THE AMERICAN DOCTRINE OF CONSTITUTIONAL LAW*

James Bradley Thayer (1893).

I

How did our American doctrine, which allows to the judiciary the power to declare legislative Acts unconstitutional, and to treat them as null, come about, and what is the true scope of it? It is a singular fact that [before 1792] the State constitutions did not give this power to the judges in express terms; it was inferential. ... So far as the grounds for this remarkable power are found in the mere fact of a constitution being in writing, or in judges being sworn to support it, they are quite inadequate. Neither the written form nor the oath of the judges necessarily involves the right of reversing, displacing, or disregarding any action of the legislature or the executive which these departments are constitutionally authorized to take, or the determination of those departments that they are so authorized. ...

How came we then to adopt this remarkable practice? Mainly as a natural result of our political experience before the War of Independence,—as being colonists, governed under written charters of government proceeding from the English Crown. The terms and limitations of these charters, so many written constitutions, were enforced by various means,—by forfeiture of the charters, by Act of Parliament, by the direct annulling of legislation by the Crown, by judicial proceedings and an ultimate appeal to the Privy Council. Our practice was a natural result of this; but it was by no means a necessary one. ...

The Revolution came, and ... we cut the cord that tied us to Great Britain, and there was no longer an external sovereign. Our conception now was that "the people" took his place; that is to say, our own home population in the several States were now their own sovereign. So far as existing institutions were left untouched, they were construed by translating the name and style of the English sovereign into that of our new ruler,—ourselves, the People. After this the charters, and still more obviously the new constitutions, were not so many orders from without,

---

* 7 *Harvard Law Review* 129 (1893).

Thayer was Professor at the Harvard Law School.

backed by an organized outside government, which simply performed an ordinary function in enforcing them; they were precepts from the people themselves who were to be governed, addressed to each of their own number, and especially to those who were charged with the duty of conducting the government. No higher power existed to support these orders by compulsion of the ordinary sort. The sovereign himself, having written these expressions of his will, had retired into the clouds; in any regular course of events he had no organ to enforce his will, except those to whom his orders were addressed in these documents. How then should his written constitution be enforced if these agencies did not obey him, if they failed, or worked amiss?

Here was really a different problem from that which had been presented under the old state of things. And yet it happened that no new provisions were made to meet it. The old methods and the old conceptions were followed. ... But it is instructive to see that this new application of judicial power [to declare legislative Acts void as being contrary to the Constitution] was not universally assented to. It was denied by several members of the Federal convention, and was referred to as unsettled by various judges in the last two decades of the last century. ... As late as 1807 and 1808, judges were impeached by the legislature of Ohio for holding Acts of that body to be void.

II

When at last this power of the judiciary was everywhere established, and added to the other bulwarks of our written constitutions, how was the power to be conceived of? Strictly as a judicial one. ... Therefore, ... in the first place, there were many cases where [this purely judicial power] had no operation. In the case of purely political acts and of the exercise of mere discretion, it mattered not that other departments were violating the constitution, the judiciary could not interfere; on the contrary, they must accept and enforce their acts. ...

Again, where the power of the judiciary did have place, its whole scope was this; namely, to determine, for the mere purpose of deciding a litigated question properly submitted to the court, whether a particular disputed exercise of power was forbidden by the constitution. In doing this the court was so to discharge its office as not to deprive another department of any of its proper power, or to limit it in the proper range of its discretion. Not merely, then, do these questions, when presenting themselves in the courts for judicial action, call for a peculiarly large method in the treatment of them, but especially they require an allowance to be made by the judges for the vast and not definable range of legislative power and choice, for that wide margin of considerations which address themselves only to the practical judgment of a legislative body. Within that margin, as among all these legislative considerations, the constitutional law-makers must be allowed a free foot. In so far as legislative choice, ranging here unfettered, may select one form of action or another, the judges must not interfere, since *their* question is a naked judicial one.

Moreover, such is the nature of this particular judicial question that the preliminary determination by the legislature is a fact of very great importance, since the constitutions expressly intrust to the legislature this determination; they cannot act without making it. Furthermore, the constitutions not merely intrust to the legislatures a preliminary determination of the question, but they contemplate that this determination may be the final one; for they secure no revision of it. It is only as litigation may spring up, and as the course of it may happen to raise the point of constitutionality, that any question for the courts can regularly emerge. It may be, then, that the mere legislative decision will accomplish results throughout the country of the profoundest importance before any judicial question can arise or be decided. ...

It is plain that where a power so momentous as this primary authority to interpret is given, the actual determinations of the body to whom it is intrusted are entitled to a corresponding respect; and this not on mere grounds of courtesy or conventional respect, but on very solid and significant grounds of policy and law. The judiciary may well reflect that if they had been regarded by the people as the chief protection against legislative violation of the constitution, they would not have been allowed merely this incidental and postponed control. They would have been let in, as it was sometimes endeavored in the conventions to let them in, to a revision of the laws before they began to operate. As the opportunity of the judges to check and correct unconstitutional Acts is so limited, it may help us to understand why the extent of their control, when they do have the opportunity, should also be narrow. ...

The rigor of this limitation upon judicial action is sometimes freely recognized, yet in a perverted way which really operates to extend the judicial function beyond its just bounds. The court's duty, we are told, is the mere and simple office of construing two writings and comparing one with another, as two contracts or two statutes are construed and compared when they are said to conflict; of declaring the true meaning of each, and, if they are opposed to each other, of carrying into effect the constitution as being of superior obligation,—an ordinary and humble judicial duty, as the courts sometimes describe it. This way of putting it easily results in the wrong kind of disregard of legislative considerations; not merely in refusing to let them directly operate as grounds of judgment, but in refusing to consider them at all. Instead of taking them into account and allowing for them as furnishing possible grounds of legislative action, there takes place a pedantic and academic treatment of the texts of the constitution and the laws. And so we miss that combination of a lawyer's rigor with a statesman's breadth of view which should be found in dealing with this class of questions in constitutional law. Of this petty method we have many specimens. ...

In order, however, to avoid falling into these narrow and literal methods, in order to prevent the courts from forgetting, as Marshall said, that "it is a constitution we are expounding," these literal precepts about the nature of the judicial task have been accompanied by a rule of administration which has tended, in competent hands, to give matters a very different complexion.

III

Let us observe the course which the courts, in point of fact, have taken, in administering this interesting jurisdiction. They began by resting it upon the very simple ground that the legislature had only a delegated and limited authority under the constitutions; that these restraints, in order to be operative, must be regarded as so much law; and, as being law, that they must be interpreted and applied by the court. This was put as a mere matter of course. The reasoning was simple and narrow. Such was Hamilton's method in the *Federalist* [No. 78] in 1788. ... [I]n 1803 came Marbury v. Madison, with the same severe line of argument. ...

But these simple precepts were supplemented by a very significant rule of administration,—one which corrected their operation, and brought into play large considerations not adverted to in the reasoning so far mentioned. In 1811, Chief Justice Tilghman, of Pennsylvania, while asserting the power of the court to hold laws unconstitutional, but declining to exercise it in a particular case, stated this rule as follows:—

> For weighty reasons, it has been assumed as a principle in constitutional construction by the Supreme Court of the United States, by this court, and every other court of reputation in the United States, that an Act of the legislature is not to be declared void unless the violation of the constitution is so manifest as to leave no room for reasonable doubt.

. . .

IV

... [T]he rule in question is something more than a mere form of language, a mere expression of courtesy and deference. It means far more than that. The courts have perceived with more or less distinctness that this exercise of the judicial function does in truth go far beyond the simple business which judges sometimes describe. If their duty were in truth merely and nakedly to ascertain the meaning of the text of the constitution and of the impeached Act of the legislature, and to determine, as an academic question, whether in the court's judgment the two were in conflict, it would, to be sure, be an elevated and important office, one dealing with great matters, involving large public considerations, but yet a function far simpler than it really is. Having ascertained all this, yet there remains a question—the really momentous question—whether, after all, the court can disregard the Act. It cannot do this as a mere matter of course,—merely because it is concluded that upon a just and true construction the law is unconstitutional. That is precisely the significance of the rule of administration that the courts lay down. It can only disregard the Act when those who have the right to make laws have not merely made a mistake, but have made a very clear one,—so clear that it is not open to rational question. That is the standard of

duty to which the courts bring legislative Acts; that is the test which
they apply,—not merely their own judgment as to constitutionality, but
their conclusion as to what judgment is permissible to another department which the constitution has charged with the duty of making it.
This rule recognizes that, having regard to the great, complex, ever-
unfolding exigencies of government, much which will seem unconstitutional to one man, or body of men, may reasonably not seem so to
another; that the constitution often admits of different interpretations;
that there is often a range of choice and judgment; that in such cases
the constitution does not impose upon the legislature any one specific
opinion, but leaves open this range of choice; and that whatever choice
is rational is constitutional. This is the principle which the rule that I
have been illustrating affirms and supports. The meaning and effect of
it are shortly and very strikingly intimated by a remark of Judge
[Thomas] Cooley, to the effect that one who is a member of a legislature
may vote against a measure as being, in his judgment, unconstitutional;
and, being subsequently placed on the bench, when this measure, having
been passed by the legislature in spite of his opposition, comes before
him judicially, may there find it his duty, although he has in no degree
changed his opinion, to declare it constitutional. ...

It must indeed be studiously remembered, in judicially applying such
a test as this of what a legislature may reasonably think, that virtue,
sense, and competent knowledge are always to be attributed to that
body. The conduct of public affairs must always go forward upon
conventions and assumptions of that sort. "It is a *postulate*," said Mr.
Justice Gibson, "in the theory of our government ... that the people are
wise, virtuous, and competent to manage their own affairs." "It would
be indecent in the extreme," said Marshall, C.J., "upon a private
contract between two individuals to enter into an inquiry respecting the
corruption of the sovereign power of a State." And so in a court's
revision of legislative acts, as in its revision of a jury's acts, it will always
assume a duly instructed body; and the question is not merely what
persons may rationally do who are such as we often see ... but what
those other persons, competent, well-instructed, sagacious, attentive,
intent only on public ends, fit to represent a self-governing people, such
as our theory of government assumes to be carrying on our public
affairs,—what such persons may reasonably think or do, what is the
permissible view for them. ... The reasonable doubt, then, of which
our judges speak is that reasonable doubt which lingers in the mind of a
competent and duly instructed person who has carefully applied his
faculties to the question. ... *[T]he ultimate question is not what is the
true meaning of the constitution, but whether legislation is sustainable or
not.*

It may be suggested that this is not the way in which the judges in
fact put the matter; e.g., that Marshall, in McCulloch v. Maryland, seeks
to establish the court's own opinion of the constitutionality of the
legislation establishing the United States Bank. But in recognizing that
this is very often true, we must remember that where the court is

sustaining an Act, and finds it to be constitutional in its own opinion, it is fit that this should be said, and that such a declaration is all that the case calls for; it disposes of the matter. But it is not always true; there are many cases where the judges sustain an Act because they are in doubt about it; where they are not giving their own opinion that it is constitutional, but are merely leaving untouched a determination of the legislature; as in the case where a Massachusetts judge concurred in the opinion of his brethren that a legislative Act was "competent for the legislature to pass, and was not unconstitutional," "upon the single ground that the Act is not so clearly unconstitutional, its invalidity so free from reasonable doubt, as to make it the duty of the judicial department, in view of the vast interests involved in the result, to declare it void." . . .

. . . What really took place in adopting our theory of constitutional law was this: we introduced for the first time into the conduct of government through its great departments a judicial sanction, as among these departments,—not full and complete, but partial. The judges were allowed, indirectly and in a degree, the power to revise the action of other departments and to pronounce it null. In simple truth, while this is a mere judicial function, it involves . . . taking a part, a secondary part, in the political conduct of government. If that be so, then the judges must apply methods and principles that befit their task. In such a work there can be no permanent or fitting *modus vivendi* between the different departments unless each is sure of the full co-operation of the others, so long as its own action conforms to any reasonable and fairly permissible view of its constitutional power. The ultimate arbiter of what is rational and permissible is indeed always the courts, so far as litigated cases bring the question before them. This leaves to our courts a great and stately jurisdiction. It will only imperil the whole of it if it is sought to give them more. They must not step into the shoes of the law-maker, or be unmindful of the hint that is found in the sagacious remark of an English bishop nearly two centuries ago, quoted lately from Mr. Justice Holmes:—

> Whoever hath an absolute authority to interpret any written or spoken laws, it is he who is truly the lawgiver, to all intents and purposes, and not the person who first wrote or spoke them.

V . . .

. . . [There are also] questions arising out of the existence of our double system, with two written constitutions, and two governments, one of which, within its sphere, is of higher authority than the other. The relation to the States of the paramount government as a whole . . . seem[s] to fix also the duty of each of its departments; namely, that of maintaining this paramount authority in its true and just proportions, to be determined by itself. If a State legislature passes a law which is impeached in the due course of litigation before the national courts, as being in conflict with the supreme law of the land, those courts may have to ask themselves a question different from that which would be

applicable if the enactments were those of a co-ordinate department.
. . . Fundamentally, it involves the allotment of power between the two
governments,—where the line is to be drawn. True, the judiciary is still
debating whether a legislature has transgressed its limit; but the
departments are not co-ordinate, and the limit is at a different point.
The judiciary now speaks as representing a paramount constitution and
government, whose duty it is, in all its departments, to allow to that
constitution nothing less than its just and true interpretation; and
having fixed this, to guard it against any inroads from without. . . .

[VI]

. . . No doubt our doctrine of constitutional law has had a tendency
to drive out questions of justice and right, and to fill the mind of
legislators with thoughts of mere legality, of what the constitution
allows. And moreover, even in the matter of legality, they have felt little
responsibility; if we are wrong, they say, the courts will correct it. If
what I have been saying is true, the safe and permanent road towards
reform is that of impressing upon our people a far stronger sense than
they have of the great range of possible harm and evil that our system
leaves open, and must leave open, to the legislatures, and of the clear
limits of judicial power; so that responsibility may be brought sharply
home where it belongs. The checking and cutting down of legislative
power, by numerous detailed prohibitions in the constitution, cannot be
accomplished without making the government petty and incompetent.
. . . Under no system can the power of courts go far to save a people from
ruin; our chief protection lies elsewhere. If this should be true, it is of
the greatest public importance to put the matter in its true light.

Editors' Notes

(1) **Query:** Felix Frankfurter regarded Thayer's essay as "the most important single essay" in the history of American constitutional law. *Felix Frankfurter Reminisces* (Harlan B. Phillips, ed.; New York: Reynal, 1960), p. 301. How
can one justify such a high opinion of this article?

(2) **Query:** Much of Thayer's essay raises the question of WHO. He said
that the federal and state constitutions not merely make legislatures the
"preliminary" constitutional interpreters "but they [also] contemplate that this
determination may be the final one; for they secure no revision of it." Does
the federal constitutional text support such a claim? What about the broader
constitution? What was his conception of what "the Constitution" includes?

(3) **Query:** To what extent was Thayer's approach to constitutional
interpretation *textualist*? *Structuralist*? *Originalist*? *Purposive*?

(4) **Query:** Thayer asserted that Marshall's justification for judicial review
in *Marbury* (reprinted above, p. 298) was the same as Hamilton's in *Federalist*
No. 78 (reprinted above, p. 285). Was he correct?

(5) **Query:** Felix Cohen, a famous Legal Realist, argued that a test of
minimum rationality like Thayer's turns courts into "lunacy commissions sitting
in judgment upon the mental capacity of legislators" and that no legislature is
so mad that it would enact or retain an utterly unreasonable (and therefore,

under this test, unconstitutional) law. "Transcendental Nonsense and the Functional Approach," in *The Legal Conscience* (Lucy Kramer Cohen, ed.; New Haven: Yale University Press, 1960), p. 44. Is Cohen's charge fair? Or, as Thayer argued, would his test "leave to our courts a great and stately jurisdiction"?

(6) In 1993, Northwestern University School of Law held a symposium to mark the centennial of the publication of Thayer's essay. See 88 *Nw.U.L.Rev.* 1 (1993).

"It is unnecessary to consider now whether legislation which restricts those political processes which can ordinarily be expected to bring about repeal of undesirable legislation, is to be subjected to more exacting judicial scrutiny. ..."

UNITED STATES v. CAROLENE PRODUCTS CO.
304 U.S. 144, 58 S.Ct. 778, 82 L.Ed. 1234 (1938).

The Filled Milk Act of 1923 forbade shipment in interstate commerce of skimmed milk compounded with fat or oils obtained from products other than milk and made to look like milk. A federal grand jury indicted the Carolene Products Co. for shipping such a product, Milnut. The company demurred to the indictment, in effect said that even if the facts alleged by the government were true, they did not constitute a violation of a valid statute. The trial judge held the act unconstitutional and sustained the demurrer; the United States appealed.

This case was argued on April 6, 1938, almost exactly a year after the famous "switch in time that saved nine"—the Supreme Court's acceptance of the legitimacy of a greater governmental role in economic life and a concomitantly broader view of the reach of congressional power under the commerce clause. Thus, it was reasonably clear what would be the response of a majority of the justices to the basic substantive question in the case regarding congressional authority to regulate commerce. Two justices, Cardozo and Reed, did not participate, and only one, McReynolds, had strong enough objections to the statute's constitutionality to dissent—though Justice Butler probably had serious reservations.

As it turned out, the only thorny issue revolved around what at first seems like a niggling, technical point: Could the defendant introduce evidence that the legislative findings supporting the statute were erroneous or at least did not fit the company's practices and so make the law, even if generally valid, unconstitutional as applied specifically to this case? (See, below, the section of the opinion of the Court marked *Third.*)

After the conference on April 9, Chief Justice Hughes assigned the task of writing the opinion of the Court to Harlan Fiske Stone, who after being selected by Calvin Coolidge in 1925, had quickly become a judicial ally of Holmes and Brandeis and later of Cardozo. During the Court's war with the

New Deal, Stone had often voted and written to sustain governmental power and had urged his brethren to distinguish between the commands of "the Constitution" and their personal values.

As the general introduction to this set of chapters indicated, at the time of *Carolene Products,* constitutional jurisprudence was in a state of flux if not chaos. The justices had just repudiated their former role of protectors of the individual's formal—as opposed, sometimes, to real—economic autonomy and in doing so had returned to an even older doctrine, that of presuming acts of Congress and the states to be constitutional. In retrospect, the Court's casting off form for reality does not appear as so momentous a change in a general policy of protecting constitutionalism's value of individual autonomy. At the time, however, the future was not so clearly charted. Until this period, the Court had on some occasions protected aspects of individual liberty besides private property and "freedom of contract" against government, but overall its record had been spotty if not spotted.

On the one hand, Stone thought the country was well rid of judges as makers of economic policy. On the other hand, he was deeply troubled by other aspects of civil liberty. He spent his summers traveling, often in Europe, and there he had witnessed the evils of Nazism. Worse, he had seen much evidence of religious and racial hatred in the United States. These experiences moved him to take the opportunity to craft a new jurisprudence, one that would leave economic policy making to democratically elected officials while not placing other civil liberties, especially those of small minorities, at the mercy of representatives of majorities.

Stone's solution was to plant the seeds of a new jurisprudence in a footnote to this otherwise unremarkable case. It was a tactic he liked to employ, one that took advantage of his more conservative colleagues' reverence for stare decisis. He often operated, a law clerk remarked, "like a squirrel storing nuts to be pulled out at some later time. And there was mischief as well as godliness in his delight when his ruse was undetected and the chestnuts safely stored away."

We reprint excerpts from the text of the opinion, indicate where Stone placed his famous footnote and then discuss separately the genesis and history of that appendage.

Mr. Justice **STONE** delivered the opinion of the Court. ...

First. The power to regulate commerce is the power "to prescribe the rule by which commerce is to be governed," Gibbons v. Ogden [1824], and extends to the prohibition of shipments in such commerce, Reid v. Colorado [1902]; Lottery Case (Champion v. Ames) [1903]. The power "is complete in itself, may be exercised to its utmost extent and acknowledges no limitations other than are prescribed by the Constitution." *Gibbons.* Hence Congress is free to exclude from interstate commerce articles whose use in the states for which they are destined it may reasonably conceive to be injurious to the public health, morals or welfare, *Reid*; Lottery Case; Hipolite Egg Co. v. United States [1911]; Hoke v. United States [1913], or which contravene the policy of the state of their destination. Kentucky Whip & Collar Co. v. Illinois C.R. Co.

[1937]. Such a regulation is not a forbidden invasion of state power either because its motive or its consequence is to restrict the use of articles of commerce within the states of destination, and is not prohibited unless by the Due Process Clause of the Fifth Amendment. ...

Second. The prohibition of shipment of appellee's product in interstate commerce does not infringe the Fifth Amendment. Twenty years ago this Court, in Hebe Co. v. Shaw [1919], held that a state law which forbids the manufacture and sale of a product assumed to be wholesome and nutritive, made of condensed skimmed milk, compounded with coconut oil, is not forbidden by the Fourteenth Amendment. The power of the legislature to secure a minimum of particular nutritive elements in a widely used article of food and to protect the public from fraudulent substitutions, was not doubted; and the Court thought that there was ample scope for the legislative judgment that prohibition of the offending article was an appropriate means of preventing injury to the public.

We see no persuasive reason for departing from that ruling here, where the Fifth Amendment is concerned; and since none is suggested, we might rest decision wholly on the presumption of constitutionality. But affirmative evidence also sustains the statute. In twenty years evidence has steadily accumulated of the danger to the public health from the general consumption of foods which have been stripped of elements essential to the maintenance of health. The Filled Milk Act was adopted by Congress after committee hearings, in the course of which eminent scientists and health experts testified. An extensive investigation was made of the commerce in milk compounds in which vegetable oils have been substituted for natural milk fat, and of the effect upon the public health of the use of such compounds as a food substitute for milk. The conclusions drawn from evidence presented at the hearings were embodied in reports of the House Committee on Agriculture and the Senate Committee on Agriculture and Forestry. Both committees concluded, as the statute itself declares, that the use of filled milk as a substitute for pure milk is generally injurious to health and facilitates fraud on the public. ...

There is nothing in the Constitution which compels a legislature, either national or state, to ignore such evidence, nor need it disregard the other evidence which amply supports the conclusions of the Congressional committees that the danger is greatly enhanced where an inferior product, like appellee's, is indistinguishable from a valuable food of almost universal use, thus making fraudulent distribution easy and protection of the consumer difficult. ...

Appellee raises no valid objection to the present statute by arguing that its prohibition has not been extended to oleomargarine or other butter substitutes in which vegetable fats or oils are substituted for butter fat. The Fifth Amendment has no equal protection clause, and even that of the Fourteenth, applicable only to the states, does not compel their legislatures to prohibit all like evils, or none. A legislature may hit at an abuse which it has found, even though it has failed to strike at another. Central Lumber Co. v. South Dakota [1912].

Third. We may assume for present purposes that no pronounce-ment of a legislature can forestall attack upon the constitutionality of the prohibition which it enacts by applying opprobrious epithets to the prohibited act, and that a statute would deny due process which preclud-ed the disproof in judicial proceedings of all facts which would show or tend to show that a statute depriving the suitor of life, liberty or property had a rational basis.

But such we think is not the purpose or construction of the statuto-ry characterization of filled milk as injurious to health and as a fraud upon the public. There is no need to consider it here as more than a declaration of the legislative findings deemed to support and justify the action taken as a constitutional exertion of the legislative power, aiding informed judicial review, as to the reports of legislative committees, by revealing the rationale of the legislation. Even in the absence of such aids the existence of facts supporting the legislative judgment is to be presumed, for regulatory legislation affecting ordinary commercial trans-actions is not to be pronounced unconstitutional unless in the light of the facts made known or generally assumed it is of such a character as to preclude the assumption that it rests upon some rational basis within the knowledge and experience of the legislators.[4] The present statutory findings affect appellee no more than the reports of the Congressional committees; and since in the absence of the statutory findings they would be presumed, their incorporation in the statute is no more prejudicial than surplusage.

Where the existence of a rational basis for legislation whose consti-tutionality is attacked depends upon facts beyond the sphere of judicial notice, such facts may properly be made the subject of judicial inquiry, Borden's Farm Products Co. v. Baldwin [1934], and the constitutionality of a statute predicated upon the existence of a particular state of facts may be challenged by showing to the court that those facts have ceased to exist. Chastleton Corp. v. Sinclair [1924]. Similarly we recognize that the constitutionality of a statute, valid on its face, may be assailed by proof of facts tending to show that the statute as applied to a particular article is without support in reason because the article, although within the prohibited class, is so different from others of the class as to be without the reason for the prohibition, Railroad Retire-ment Bd. v. Alton R. Co. [1935]; see Whitney v. California [1927]. ... But by their very nature such inquiries, where the legislative judgment is drawn in question, must be restricted to the issue whether any state of facts either known or which could reasonably be assumed affords sup-port for it. Here the demurrer challenges the validity of the statute on its face and it is evident from all the considerations presented to

---

4. It was at this point that Stone inserted the historic footnote 4. We reprint it in its original and final draft, together with correspondence between Stone and Chief Justice Hughes, after the concurrence of Justice Butler.—**Eds.**

Congress, and those of which we may take judicial notice, that the question is at least debatable whether commerce in filled milk should be left unregulated, or in some measure restricted, or wholly prohibited. As that decision was for Congress, neither the finding of a court arrived at by weighing the evidence, nor the verdict of a jury can be substituted for it. Price v. Illinois [1915]; South Carolina State Highway Dept. v. Barnwell Bros. [1938]. ...

The prohibition of shipment in interstate commerce of appellee's product, as described in the indictment, is a constitutional exercise of the power to regulate interstate commerce. ...

Reversed.

Mr. Justice **BLACK** concurs in the result and in all of the opinion except the part marked "Third."

Mr. Justice **McREYNOLDS** thinks that the judgment should be affirmed.

Mr. Justice **CARDOZO** and Mr. Justice **REED** took no part in the consideration or decision of this case.

Mr. Justice **BUTLER**

I concur in the result. ...

Stone turned to his clerk, Louis Lusky, who was later to become a distinguished professor of law at Columbia University, to draft the footnote and accepted, almost without change, what Lusky wrote. (Lusky later explained some of the philosophy behind the footnote in "Minority Rights and the Public Interest," 52 *Yale L.J.* 1 [1942], in *By What Right?* [Charlottesville, VA: Michie, 1975], and in "Footnote Redux: A *Carolene Products* Reminiscence," 82 *Colum. L. Rev.* 1093 [1982].)

As circulated, that note was appended to the following sentence: "Even in the absence of such aids [extensive legislative findings of facts] the existence of facts supporting the legislative judgment is to be presumed, for regulatory legislation affecting ordinary commercial transactions is not to be pronounced unconstitutional unless in the light of the facts made known or generally assumed it is of such a character as to preclude the assumption that it rests upon some rational basis within the knowledge and experience of the legislators."

As Stone initially circulated the opinion among the justices for their comments, the footnote read:

[4] Different considerations may apply, and one attacking the constitutionality of a statute may be thought to bear a lighter burden, when the legislation aims at restricting the corrective political processes which

can ordinarily be expected to bring about repeal of undesirable legislation. So, statutory interferences with political organizations, Stromberg v. California [1931]; Fiske v. Kansas [1927]; Whitney v. California [1927]; Herndon v. Lowry [1937]; and see Holmes, J., in Gitlow v. New York [1925], and with the dissemination of information, Near v. Minnesota [1931]; Grosjean v. American Press Co. [1936]; Lovell v. Griffin [1938], have been subjected to a more exacting judicial test than have been other types of statutes. Like considerations may be relevant in comparable situations, as when the right to vote, cf. Nixon v. Condon [1932], or peaceably to assemble is involved, or when a statute is directed at particular religions, Pierce v. Society of Sisters [1925], at a national, Meyer v. Nebraska [1923]; Bartels v. Iowa [1923]; Farrington v. Tokushige [1927], or at racial minorities. Nixon v. Herndon [1927]; Nixon v. Condon. Prejudice against discrete and insular minorities may be a special condition in such situations, which tends seriously to curtail the operation of those political processes normally to be relied on to protect minorities, and which may call for a correspondingly more searching judicial scrutiny. Compare McCulloch v. Maryland [1819]; South Carolina v. Barnwell Bros. [1938], n. 2, and cases cited.*

Chief Justice Hughes, who had a keener eye than most of the brethren, read footnote 4 with care. Some of its implications displeased him. As he wrote Stone:

Supreme Court of the United States
Washington, D.C.
April 18, 1938.

No. 640.—*United States v. Carolene Products Co.*

Dear Justice Stone:

I am somewhat disturbed by your Note 4 on page 6. Is it true that "different considerations" apply in the instances you mention? Are the "considerations" different or does the difference lie not in the *test* but in the nature of the right invoked? When we say that a statute is invalid on its face, do we not mean that, in relation to the right invoked against it, the legislative action raises no presumption in its favor and has no rational support? Thus, in dealing with freedom of speech and of the

---

* Note 2 in *Barnwell* was another of Stone's doctrinal plants, that one specifically related to the reach of state authority over commerce. Similar to *Carolene Products,* it put forth as one reason for close judicial oversight the absence of political control by the voters of one state over what the legislature of another state might do. In this respect, Stone's argument paralleled that of Chief Justice Marshall in McCulloch v. Maryland (1819; reprinted above, p. 530) and what Justice Blackmun would later write in Garcia v. SAMTA (1985; reprinted above, p. 575.—**Eds.**

press, as in the recent Lovell case, the legislative action putting the press broadly under license and censorship is directly opposed to the constitutional guaranty and for that reason has no presumption to support it. Of course, the test, whether there is a rational basis, must always have regard to the particular matter to which the test is applied and in that sense there may be different considerations in different cases. In that view the distinction between the two forms of statement may be only a verbal one, but may not the phrasing of your note lead to some misunderstanding and bring us in the future into an unnecessary controversy over forms of expression?

Faithfully,

Mr. Justice Stone.

The vote at conference had been 6–1 to reverse the district court and to sustain the statute, but Justice Black expressed concern that the third section of Stone's opinion allowed dangerous judicial intrusions into the legislative domain, while Justice Butler thought that section dangerously curtailed judicial power. Stone was trying to keep the two justices in his camp, though their conflicting views made it impossible to satisfy both. Knowing he had little chance with Butler, who was still smarting under the Court's withdrawal in 1937, Stone concentrated on persuading Black. They differed, but on the margins of doctrine rather than at the core—or at least so they both then thought. Black, though, was a very stubborn man, as Stone knew. Furthermore, Stone had little intellectual respect for his new colleague, whom he thought to be unlearned and precipitate rather than scholarly and judicious in striving for goals they both desired. In the end, despite Stone's efforts at reconciliation, Black refused to join in the third part of the opinion.

When he received Hughes's note, Stone could not yet be sure that he would lose both Butler and Black. But he did know that if neither joined his opinion, he would not have a majority of the full Court, though he would have a majority of the seven sitting justices, and so technically could speak for "the Court." If, however, Hughes also went his own way, Stone would speak for only three justices (himself, Brandeis and Roberts), not for the Court as an institution. And what he hoped would be the seeds of a new constitutional jurisprudence would be denied the soil in which they could best grow. Thus keeping the Chief Justice in the fold was a practical necessity. It was also a practical possibility, despite ideological differences between the Chief and Stone, for Hughes, like his predecessor William Howard Taft, always tried to avoid writing dissenting or concurring opinions. He thought it was his role as chief justice to lead the Court, not to criticize it.

Within a day of receiving the Chief's letter, Stone had reworked footnote 4. He replied to Hughes:

April 19, 1938

Dear Chief Justice:

I am recirculating my opinion in No. 640, United States v. Carolene Products Company, with some changes in the body of the opinion at pages 6 and 7. In view of your letter I have also revised the note on page 6.

You are quite right in saying that the specific prohibitions of the first ten amendments and the same prohibitions when adopted by the Fourteenth Amendment leave no opportunity for presumption of constitutionality where statutes on their face violate the prohibition. There are, however, possible restraints on liberty and political rights which do not fall within those specific prohibitions and are forbidden only by the general words of the due process clause of the Fourteenth Amendment. I wish to avoid the possibility of having what I have written in the body of the opinion about the presumption of constitutionality in the ordinary run of due process cases applied as a matter of course to these other more exceptional cases. For that reason it seemed to me desirable to file a caveat in the note, without, however, committing the Court to any proposition contained in it. The notion that the Court should be more alert to protect constitutional rights in those cases where there is danger that the ordinary political processes for the correction of undesirable legislation may not operate has been announced for the Court by many judges, notably Chief Justice Marshall in McCulloch v. Maryland, with reference to taxation of governmental instrumentalities, and Justices Bradley, Field and Miller in state taxation or regulation affecting interstate commerce—cases collected in Note 2 in South Carolina v. Barnwell Bros., Inc., No. 161 this term.

I hope you will find the note acceptable in its present form, but if not I shall be glad if you will let me know.

Yours faithfully,

The Chief Justice.

Stone

To further placate the Chief Justice, Stone inserted a reference to Hughes's opinion in DeJonge v. Oregon (1937) and, more importantly, added a fresh opening paragraph to the footnote. Stone also divided the original footnote into two paragraphs so that he now addressed three separate exceptions to the general presumption of constitutionality—and in his usual indirect manner. The Chief found the new version acceptable and joined Stone's opinion, which thus became the opinion of the Court, though representing the views of only four of the seven justices who heard *Carolene*

Products. As it appears in the U.S. Reports, the three paragraphs of footnote 4 read:

[4] There may be narrower scope for operation of the presumption of constitutionality when legislation appears on its face to be within a specific prohibition of the Constitution, such as those of the first ten amendments, which are deemed equally specific when held to be embraced within the Fourteenth. See Stromberg v. California [1931]; Lovell v. Griffin [1938].

It is unnecessary to consider now whether legislation which restricts those political processes which can ordinarily be expected to bring about repeal of undesirable legislation, is to be subjected to more exacting judicial scrutiny under the general prohibitions of the Fourteenth Amendment than are most other types of legislation. On restrictions upon the right to vote, see Nixon v. Herndon [1927]; Nixon v. Condon [1932]; on restraints upon the dissemination of information, see Near v. Minnesota [1931]; Grosjean v. American Press Co. [1936]; Lovell v. Griffin [1938]; on interferences with political organizations, see Stromberg v. California [1931]; Fiske v. Kansas [1927]; Whitney v. California [1927]; Herndon v. Lowry [1937]; and see Holmes, J., in Gitlow v. New York [1925]; as to peaceable assembly, see DeJonge v. Oregon [1937].

Nor need we inquire whether similar considerations enter into the review of statutes directed at particular religious, Pierce v. Society of Sisters [1925], or national, Meyer v. Nebraska [1923]; Bartels v. Iowa [1923]; Farrington v. Tokushige [1927], or racial minorities, Nixon v. Herndon [1927]; Nixon v. Condon [1932]; whether prejudice against discrete and insular minorities may be a special condition, which tends seriously to curtail the operation of those political processes ordinarily thought to be relied upon to protect minorities, and which may call for a correspondingly more searching judicial inquiry. Compare McCulloch v. Maryland [1819]; South Carolina State Highway Department v. Barnwell [1938], note 2, and cases cited.

Editors' Notes

(1) **Query:** How did Stone's approach to constitutional interpretation differ from Thayer's?

(2) **Query:** To what extent did Stone simultaneously address the questions of WHO and HOW? Can we completely separate the two?

(3) **Query:** To what extent is *reinforcing representative democracy*, even in this early form, a *structuralist* approach? A *philosophic* approach? To what extent did Stone rely on a *doctrinal* approach?

(4) **Query:** Was footnote 4, in its final form, based solely in democratic theory or was it also grounded in constitutionalism?

(5) In light of later developments in the way Congress, the Court, and the President have interpreted the meaning of equality in the American political system, it is interesting to see Stone writing: "The Fifth Amendment has no

equal protection clause, and even that of the Fourteenth, applicable only to the states, does not compel their legislatures to prohibit all like evils, or none."

THE HISTORY OF FOOTNOTE FOUR

As the Introductory Essay to this section said, much of American constitutional interpretation from 1938 until the present unfolds in the history of this footnote. The approach to constitutional interpretation usually labelled "reinforcing representative democracy," which accords a special place to the rights to vote and to communicate political ideas, owes much of its intellectual power to the democratic rationale behind paragraph 2. The roots of what is termed the "modern" (and extraordinarily complex) doctrine of equal protection and its levels (or "tiers") of judicial scrutiny of challenged legislation run back to paragraph 3 of that footnote. And, the approach to constitutional interpretation labelled *protecting fundamental rights* finds support in paragraph 1, as does the Court's insistence on strict governmental observance of the procedural guarantees of the Bill of Rights in criminal prosecutions.

That importance, however, does not imply that the principles behind the footnote may not conflict with each other—nor that the approaches it spurred may not collide. Neither does that significance mean that the justices have uniformly carried out the logic of Stone's jurisprudence. Even he nodded at times. In Colegrove v. Green (1946), one of the last cases he heard, he argued in conference that Illinois's gerrymandering congressional districts so grossly as to make some in downstate contain one-eighth the population of others in Chicago did not present an issue that the justices should decide. "It isn't court business," Justice Murphy recorded Stone as saying. Somehow he had forgotten the justification for the Court's protecting fair and open political processes—what paragraph 2 was all about.

Still, Stone made ready disciples among some of the new men who came to the Court. Black (despite his exception to the third part of Stone's opinion in *Carolene Products*), Douglas, Murphy, Rutledge, and, for a time, Frankfurter and Jackson found the footnote to foreshadow a new and welcome jurisprudence. Indeed, Black, Douglas, Murphy, and Rutledge wanted to extend paragraph 2 to the point of presuming unconstitutional any legislation that restricted rights to speak, write, or vote.[1] It was not, however, until the period of the Warren Court (1953–69) that Stone's seeds would come to full flower.[2]

Initially, the opposition to Stone's approach came principally from four justices, Sutherland, Van Devanter, McReynolds, and Butler, who objected to judicial deference in general rather than to his rubrics for relaxing deference. (See West Coast Hotel v. Parrish [1937; reprinted below, p. 1123].) After those so-called "Four Horsemen" left the bench, Justice Felix Frankfurter would become the leader of the opposition. In 1938, however, Frankfurter's

---

1. See the debates in Thomas v. Collins (1945) and Kovacs v. Cooper (1949); many of the cases are analyzed in C. Herman Pritchett: *The Roosevelt Court* (New York: Macmillan, 1948), chs. 5, 7, 9, & 10; and *Civil Liberties and the Vinson Court* (Chicago: University of Chicago Press, 1954), pp. 32–36.

2. See Alpheus Thomas Mason, *The Supreme Court from Taft to Burger* (Baton Rouge: Louisiana State University Press, 1979), chs. 4–7; John Hart Ely, *Democracy and Distrust* (Cambridge: Harvard University Press, 1980), chs. 4–6; Walter F. Murphy, "Deeds under a Doctrine," 59 *Am.Pol.Sci.Rev.* 64 (1965).

opposition still lay in the future. Indeed, while still a professor at the Harvard Law School, he congratulated Stone on footnote 4:

> You, yourself, wrote an admirable opinion in the milk case, and I was especially excited by your note 4. I have just finished a series of lectures to the laity on The Court and Mr. Justice Holmes, in which I've tried to reconcile his latitudinarian attitude toward constitutionality in cases other than civil liberties, to use a loose phrase, with his attitude in civil liberties cases. That bit in these lectures, when they are published, may interest you. Your note is extremely suggestive and opens up new territory.[3]

Frankfurter's letter must have comforted Stone, for he thought he was articulating what was latent in earlier opinions of Holmes and Brandeis. As far as paragraph 2 was concerned, this modesty was probably accurate. The two older justices had, after some hesitation, come to see freedom of speech and press as a central value in the political system, one that the Court should be alert to protect.[4] Indeed, Frankfurter had written that Holmes believed the Court should be wary of deferring to legislative judgment when a statute restricted freedom of speech or press.

On the other hand, it is difficult to find much of either Holmes or Brandeis in paragraph 3. Holmes in particular tended to denigrate arguments based on equal protection. For example, in Buck v. Bell [1927; reprinted below, p. 1254], he dismissed appeals to equal protection as "the usual last resort of constitutional arguments." And Brandeis's views on deference to legislative judgment often led to similar results.[5]

But it was easy for Frankfurter to accept paragraph 2 and stay loyal to his trinity of Holmes, Brandeis, and even Thayer. And during his early years on the Court, Frankfurter claimed to be a true believer. During debate on the First Flag Salute Case (1940; reprinted below, p. 1165), he tried to persuade Stone to join his opinion:

> I am aware of the important distinction which you skillfully adumbrated in your footnote 4 (particularly the second paragraph of it). ... I agree with that distinction; I regard it as basic. [The complete text of this letter is reprinted below, pp. 1166–68.]

And, eight months later, Frankfurter wrote for the Court in AFL v. Swing (1941) that judges should protect freedom of discussion "with a jealous eye." He cited footnote 4 as one of three authorities for that role.

Soon, however, Frankfurter began to withdraw his endorsement of footnote 4, whether for personal or jurisprudential reasons.[6] More and more often, he dissociated himself from Stone as well as Black, Douglas, Murphy,

---

3. Frankfurter to Stone, April 27, 1938; the Stone Papers, the Library of Congress. We are indebted to Claire Laporte of the Princeton Class of 1982 for providing this letter.

4. Compare their views in Schenck v. United States (1919) and its companion cases with those in Abrams v. United States (1919), Gitlow v. New York (1925), and, most especially, Whitney v. California (1927; reprinted below, p. 651).

5. See his dissent for himself and Holmes in Royster Guano v. Virginia (1920).

6. For a fascinating inquiry into Frankfurter's personality and its possible effects on his change of mind, see Harry N. Hirsch, *The Enigma of Felix Frankfurter* (New York: Basic Books, 1981).

and later Rutledge when they gave preference to claims to freedom of political expression. In 1943, dissenting in the Second Flag Salute Case (reprinted below, p. 1174), Frankfurter repudiated his earlier view of a hierarchy among constitutional values:

> The Constitution does not give us greater veto power when dealing with one phase of "liberty" than with another. . . . Judicial restraint is equally necessary whenever an exercise of political or legislative power is challenged. There is no warrant in the constitutional basis of this Court's authority for attributing different roles to it depending upon the nature of the challenge to the legislation. Our power does not vary according to the particular provision of the Bill of Rights which is invoked. The right not to have one's property taken without just compensation has, so far as the scope of judicial power is concerned, the same constitutional dignity as the right to be protected against unreasonable searches and seizures, and the latter has no less claim than freedom of the press or freedom of speech or religious freedom.

In 1949, concurring in Kovacs v. Cooper, he directly attacked *Carolene Products* for having produced "mischievous" results. "A footnote," he added, "hardly seems to be an appropriate way of announcing a new constitutional doctrine." He then went to considerable lengths to show that Stone's note had neither contained anything original nor implied that legislation touching the First Amendment was presumptively invalid. In 1951 Frankfurter returned to the offensive: "It has been suggested, with the casualness of a footnote, that such legislation is not presumptively valid." [7] *All* legislation, he reasserted, carried presumptive validity. (Recall his reverence for Thayer's "doctrine of the clear mistake," discussed in the Editors' Notes to Thayer's article, reprinted above, at 602.)

Carrying the fight to a more personal level, Frankfurter was determined to undermine Stone's reputation as a jurist. Thus he was gleeful when in 1955 he read in Alpheus Thomas Mason's *Security Through Freedom* not only that Louis Lusky had drafted footnote 4 but also that Stone often allowed his clerks such authority during the last months of their tenure. "I have good grounds," Frankfurter wrote to a friend at Harvard, "for believing that Lusky wrote the heart of that footnote, but it never occurred to me that it was 'a striking example of Justice Stone's custom.' . . . In light of this disclosure by Mason, I should think my phrase 'the casualness of a footnote' . . . is a model of moderation." [8]

Neither Stone's death nor those of Frankfurter, Murphy, Rutledge, Black, Douglas, and the other members of the Roosevelt Court ended disputes over the meaning of footnote 4 and its centrality for constitutional interpretation. In 1973, for instance, Justice Rehnquist repeated several of Frankfurter's objections and added some of his own.[9] But Rehnquist spoke in dissent; and the majority, though citing footnote 4, ignored critiques of *Carolene Products*.

---

7. Dennis v. United States, concur. op. (1951).

8. Frankfurter to Paul Freund, October 24, 1955; the Frankfurter Papers, the Library of Congress.

9. Sugarman v. Dougall, dis. op.

That treatment has been typical of the Court's behavior. Not since Kovacs v. Cooper in 1949 have the justices engaged in a full scale debate of *Carolene Products*. Nevertheless, footnote 4 continues to be the hinge on which much of modern constitutional argument turns. Justice Lewis F. Powell has called it "the most celebrated footnote in constitutional law." [10] A great deal of recent academic controversy revolves around that note; [11] and, among the justices, one can hear its creak in such opinions as Harris v. McRae (1980; reprinted below, p. 1271), where Justice Stewart wrote for the majority that "[i]t is well settled that ... if a law 'impinges upon a fundamental right explicitly or implicitly secured by the Constitution [it] is presumptively unconstitutional,' " [12] or Justice Antonin Scalia's more recent dissents in which he argues for the presumptive validity of legislation that results from democratic processes.[13]

---

10. Lewis F. Powell, *"Carolene Products* Revisited," 82 *Colum.L.Rev.* 1087, 1087 (1982).

11. For example: Bruce A. Ackerman, "Beyond *Carolene Products*," 98 *Harv.L.Rev.* 713 (1985); Geoffrey P. Miller, "The True Story of *Carolene Products*," 1987 *Sup. Ct. Rev.* 397; Louis Lusky, *By What Right?* (Charlottesville, VA: Michie, 1975); Walter F. Murphy, "The Art of Constitutional Interpretation," in M. Judd Harmon, ed., *Essays on the Constitution of the United States* (Port Washington, NY: Kennikat Press, 1978); and Mason, *supra* note 2. Ely's *Democracy and Distrust* drew the most attention. For analyses, see: Paul Brest, "The Fundamental Rights Controversy," 90 *Yale L.J.* 1063 (1981); Ronald Dworkin, "The Forum of Principle," 56 *N.Y.U.L.Rev.* 469 (1981) (reprinted as ch. 2 in his *A Matter of Principle* [Cambridge: Harvard University Press, 1985]); James E. Fleming, "A Critique of John Hart Ely's Quest for the Ultimate Constitutional Interpretivism of Representative Democracy," 80 *Mich.L.Rev.* 634 (1982); Sanford V. Levinson, "Judicial Review and the Problem of the Comprehensible Constitution," 59 *Tex.L.Rev.* 395 (1981); Walter F. Murphy, "Constitutional Interpretation," 9 *Revs. in Am.Hist.* 7 (1981); Symposium, "Judicial Review versus Democracy," 42 *Ohio State L.J.* 1 (1981); Symposium, "Constitutional Adjudication and Democratic Theory," 56 *N.Y.U.L.Rev.* 259 (1981); and Laurence H. Tribe, "The Puzzling Persistence of Process–Based Constitutional Theories," 89 *Yale L.J.* 1063 (1980) (reprinted as ch. 2 in his *Constitutional Choices* [Cambridge: Harvard University Press, 1985]). For more recent reassessments of Ely's theory, see Symposium, *"Democracy and Distrust:* Ten Years Later," 77 *Va.L.Rev.* 631 (1991). That symposium includes an essay by Ely, "Another Such Victory: Constitutional Theory and Practice in a World Where Courts Are No Different From Legislatures," 77 *Va.L.Rev.* 833 (1991). For a recent theory that is similar to Ely's, see Cass R. Sunstein, *The Partial Constitution* (Cambridge: Harvard University Press, 1993), criticized in James E. Fleming, "Constructing the Substantive Constitution," 72 *Tex.L.Rev.* 211 (1993).

12. See also Richmond v. J. A. Croson Co. (1989; reprinted below, p. 954), where Justice O'Connor wrote for the plurality that "[i]f one aspect of the judiciary's role under the Equal Protection Clause is to protect 'discrete and insular minorities' from majoritarian prejudice or indifference, see *Carolene Products* n. 4, some maintain that these concerns are not implicated when the 'white majority' places burdens upon itself. See Ely, *Democracy and Distrust* 170 (1980)." But see Marshall's dissenting opinion in *Croson*.

13. See, in particular, his opinion in Planned Parenthood v. Casey (1992; reprinted below, p. 1281).

12

Freedom of Political Communication

The U.S. Reports are studded with eloquent panegyrics to freedom of political communication. As Hugo Black said in 1941:

> ... I view the guaranties of the First Amendment as the foundation upon which our governmental structure rests. ... Freedom to speak and write about public questions is as important to the life of our government as the heart is to the human body. In fact, this privilege is the heart of our government. If that heart be weakened, the result is debilitation; if it be stilled, the result is death.[1]

But inspiring rhetoric does not solve fundamental political problems. This chapter will examine, as part of the larger question of HOW to interpret, the ways in which American public officials have addressed troublesome constitutional issues involving freedom of political communication.

We would like to focus on one relevant approach to constitutional interpretation, that of *reinforcing representative democracy*. As in other chapters, however, we shall find interpreters using mixes of approaches as they quest after constitutional meaning. Indeed, *reinforcing representative democracy* is itself a species of *purposive* approach and also partially utilizes both a *structuralist* and a *philosophic* approach—the former insofar as it proposes to consider the text and political system as a single whole, and the latter insofar as it makes arguments based on democratic theory.

Furthermore, although *reinforcing representative democracy* has its proximate origins in footnote 4 of *Carolene Products* (1938; reprinted above, p. 609), it owes its development as a coherent theory of, or approach to, constitutional interpretation more to academic commentators like John Hart Ely [2] than to judges or other public officials. Thus, readers will have to be alert to catch glimpses of this constitutional snark—indeed, to treat only as a hypothesis that it is worthwhile to think of *reinforcing representative democracy* as a useful approach.

---

1. Milkwagon Drivers Union v. Meadowmoor Dairies, dis. op. (1941).

2. *Democracy and Distrust* (Cambridge: Harvard University Press, 1980).

I. COMMUNICATION AND CONSTITUTIONAL INTERPRETATION

A. From Democratic Theory to Literal Interpretation

The core of democratic theory is formed around free political communication. It is, as Justice Holmes said, "more than self-expression, it is the essence of self-government." [3] If the people are to choose their leaders and influence those leaders' selections of policies, citizens must have an opportunity to learn about candidates and their proposals for public policy. Only then can the people's choices be intelligent and free. Two distinct, equally important, and functionally interlocking rights are involved: that of every citizen to participate in self-government by trying to win support for his or her politically relevant ideas; and that of potential listeners to hear and be informed so that they may decide how best—in *their* judgments—to allocate political resources.

Like democratic theory, constitutionalism also highly values freedom of communication. Insofar as government censors a person's ideas, a constitutionalist would argue, it denies him or her both full participation in self-government and free development of personality. By trying to determine what thoughts its people may lawfully express, such a government degrades its people. Indeed, constitutionalism would move a step further than democratic theory and accord protection, though not necessarily the same protection, to the expression of ideas that have no apparent political relevance.

Interpreters who, without consciously endorsing *reinforcing representative democracy*, take a *structuralist* or *philosophic* approach might make similar arguments. (See Brennan's concur. op. in Richmond Newspapers v. Virginia [1980; reprinted below, p. 642] and his majority opinion in New York Times v. Sullivan [1964; reprinted below, p. 634].) The plain words of the constitutional text, the way the system operates, and the architectural scheme prescribed by the underlying political theories of democracy and constitutionalism, all point toward a critical role for free political communication.

In contending that constitutional interpretation should be limited to ascertaining the meaning of the words of the document, a *textual* approach should also push its adherents to argue for the

---

3. Abrams v. United States, dis. op. (1919). Closely related to the "self-government" rationale for protecting freedom of political communication is a rationale stemming from the idea of the search for truth in the "marketplace of ideas," which Holmes also expressed in his dissent in *Abrams*:

[W]hen men have realized that time has upset many fighting faiths, they may come to believe even more than they believe the very foundations of their own conduct that the ultimate good desired is better reached by free trade in ideas—that the best test of truth is the power of the thought to get itself accepted in the competition of the market. ... That at any rate is the theory of our Constitution.

centrality of the First Amendment's guarantees of freedom of speech, press, assembly, and petition. For, unlike many other parts of the Bill of Rights, the First Amendment is cast in absolute terms. The Fourth Amendment, for example, forbids only "unreasonable" searches and seizures, and the Fifth does not forbid all takings of "life, liberty, or property," but only such takings "without due process of law" or without "just compensation." In contrast, the First Amendment reads: "Congress shall make no law ... abridging the freedom of speech, or of the press; or the right of the people peaceably to assemble to petition the Government for a redress of grievances." "My view is," the Supreme Court's great literalist wrote,

> without exception, without any ifs, buts, or whereases, that free-
> dom of speech means the government shall not do anything to
> people, or, in the words of Magna Carta, move against people
> either for the views they have or the views they express or the
> words they speak or write. ... I simply believe that "Congress
> shall make no law" means Congress shall make no law.[4]

B. The Interplay of Other Values

If democratic theorists, constitutionalists, structuralists, and textualists are unanimous that free communication of political ideas is an imperative for the American polity, it would seem that any constitutional problems would be easily resolved. In fact, however, freedom of communication is among the most troubled and hotly disputed areas of constitutional interpretation. In part the cause lies in the failure of judges as well as legislators and executives to articulate clearly and apply consistently a coherent theory of why they are protecting communication. But, in part, the difficulty also arises from the complicated interplay of different sets of values in political life and therefore in constitutional interpretation.

In the abstract, there is agreement that government lacks authority either to deny the people the information they need to formulate political judgments or to express those judgments so as to influence their fellow citizens and the course of public policy. In particular situations, however, most people are willing to grant exceptions, for there are other values at work than those of open political processes or free self expression. First, the line between what is politically relevant and what is not—a line that would not be as significant for a constitutionalist as for a democratic theorist—is fuzzy. In Chaplinsky v. New Hampshire (1942; reprinted below, p. 677), the Court stated that "[t]here are certain well-defined and narrowly limited classes of speech, the prevention and punishment of which have never been thought to raise any Constitutional

---

4. Hugo L. Black, *A Constitutional Faith* (New York: Knopf, 1969), p. 45. See also his numerous opinions in cases involving the First Amendment, for example, his dissent in Barenblatt v. United States (1959; reprinted below, p. 803).

problem" because "such utterances are no essential part of any exposition of ideas." The categories of unprotected speech have historically included "the lewd and obscene, the profane, the libelous, and the insulting or 'fighting' words." Yet these are inexact categories and many subsequent cases have broken down or eroded these supposedly "well-defined and narrowly limited classes."

In some situations the political element may be apparent, but it may occur alongside other values. Cohen v. California (1971; reprinted below, p. 705) addresses a situation in which a young man phrased his indisputably political message in vulgar terms that offended many people. In other situations, patently political expression may be harmful to other persons or classes of persons. Beauharnais v. Illinois (1952; reprinted below, p. 680) and R.A.V. v. St. Paul (1992; reprinted below, p. 686), involved expressions of hate-filled ideas that not only libeled members of a racial group but seemed designed to undermine their status as equal citizens. American Booksellers Association v. Hudnut (7th Cir.1985; reprinted below, p. 710) involved pornography, which may be related to freedom of expression but which also may contribute to violence against women and more generally may tend to subordinate and silence them.

Furthermore, there may be limits to how far a democratic theorist would push the concept of politically relevant communication or a constitutionalist the concept of free communication as necessary to the expression of one's individuality. Few, for example, would claim that a group of Mafiosi who were conspiring to bribe a senator were protected in their plotting because their speech was related to public policy or because it was necessary to develop their personalities by voicing the evil within their souls.

Even speech or writing filled with obvious political content that does not involve what people ordinarily think of as crime might cause difficulties. How far may one go in the rough and tumble of political debate to assail the character of an opponent? Or to mock public figures so as to inflict emotional distress on them? Do the rights of some citizens to decent reputations and to lives free of emotional distress automatically yield to the rights of other citizens to voice their political views as forcefully (or, in some instances, as outrageously) as they can? On the other hand, if those arguing for or against particular candidates and policies have to stop to analyze complex laws of defamation, can debate truly be free and open? Here some versions of constitutionalist and democratic theories might offer quite different responses. New York Times v. Sullivan (1964; reprinted below, p. 634) and Hustler Magazine, Inc. v. Falwell (1988; reprinted below, p. 717) take up those sorts of problems.

Perhaps the most intractable constitutional difficulties concern national security. Not many people claim that the public's right to information includes access to the codes used to program the Air Force's nuclear tipped missiles or the Drug Enforcement Agency's lists of informants within Columbian cartels. Yet without some detailed and accurate information it is impossible for voters to make informed judgments about the adequacy of defense policy or various wars against crime—certainly primary political concerns. And who, without actually knowing some details, can distinguish between protecting vital military secrets and hiding information that might embarrass officials? During the Vietnam War, for instance, the American voters were the last to learn about American bombings of Cambodia. The Pentagon Papers Case (1971; reprinted below, p. 739) presented some of these issues. That case and Near v. Minnesota (1931; reprinted below, p. 733) raise the more general problem of prior restraints on expression.

Constitutional interpretation is further complicated by the fact that absolutely free political communication raises difficulties even for democratic theory. The nub of democracy is that, after full debate and free elections, the people's chosen representatives shall govern, subject only to such restraints as the people have put on themselves and their representatives. But what about threats to harm or even kill a public official?[5] Or speech that urges people to resort to violence to stop minorities from exercising their rights as full citizens? (See Brandenburg v. Ohio [1969; reprinted below at p. 672].) Or speech and writing that try to identify U.S. intelligence agents in foreign countries and so expose them to assassination?[6] All these means threaten to negate democratic processes.

Even more basic are questions about the legitimacy of efforts to organize a group to use violence to destroy a democratic political system. Such efforts present the age-old problem of sedition; and protecting democracy against internal subversion raises difficulties similar to those of protecting military secrets. On an even wider scale than assassination or illegal action against minorities, sedition emphatically tries to overturn democratic procedures.[7]

On the other hand, it is always tempting for those in office to label opponents as seditionists. In this century, that charge has been levelled not only against communists, but also against socialists, pacifists, union organizers, career diplomats who thought in the late 1940s that the United States should recognize Red China, opponents of racial segregation, critics of the FBI, foes of the war in Vietnam, enemies of Richard Nixon, and advocates of nuclear disarmament. In the eighteenth century, the charge of sedition was also made against Thomas Jefferson, whose vision of democracy was too

---

5. See Gooding v. Wilson (1972) and Watts v. United States (1969).

6. See Haig v. Agee (1981).

7. See the discussion in Walter F. Murphy, "Excluding Political Parties: Problems for Democratic and Constitutional Theory," in Paul Kirchhof and Donald P. Kommers, eds., *Germany and Its Basic Law* (Baden–Baden: Nomos, 1993).

radical for many Federalists. Although he himself escaped prosecution, many of his followers did not and were jailed under the Sedition Act of 1798. It was out of these experiences that Jefferson urged in his first inaugural address:

> [L]et us reflect that, having banished from our land that religious intolerance under which mankind has so long bled and suffered, we have gained little if we countenance a political intolerance as despotic, as wicked, and capable of as bitter and bloody persecutions. ... If there be any among us who would wish to dissolve this Union or to change its republican form, let them stand undisturbed as monuments of the safety with which error of opinion may be tolerated where reason is free to combat it.[8]

In 1937, speaking for the Court in De Jonge v. Oregon, Chief Justice Charles Evans Hughes echoed Jefferson's message:

> The greater the importance of safeguarding the community from incitements to overthrow of our institutions by force and violence, the more imperative is the need to preserve inviolate the constitutional rights of free speech, free press and free assembly in order to maintain the opportunity for free political discussion, to the end that government may be responsive to the will of the people and that changes, if desired, may be obtained by peaceful means. Therein lies the security of the Republic, the very foundation of constitutional government.

Where charges of sedition or subversion have been made, the Supreme Court has only intermittently given close attention either to Jefferson's specific words or to the democratic theory on which they were based.[9] As a result, it has awkwardly grappled with such conundra, as shown by Dennis v. United States (1951), Yates v. United States (1957), and Barenblatt v. United States (1959) (all reprinted below). In these as in other cases, the justices have left themselves vulnerable to attack for their failure to state coherent theories of constitutional interpretation. One should keep in mind, however, that if legislators or executives had more clearly thought through the theoretical and practical difficulties of punishing communication of political ideas, judges would probably not have had to face such constitutional dilemmas. At the same time, one should bear in mind that judges, despite their relative institutional independence, are subject to many of the same fears as are legislators and executives. "The great tides and currents which engulf the rest of men," Justice Cardozo wrote, "do not turn aside in their course and pass the judges by." [10]

---

8. Andrew A. Lipscomb, ed., *The Writings of Thomas Jefferson* (Washington, DC: The Thomas Jefferson Memorial Association, 1903), III, 318–319.

9. Note also the Court's ducking the issue of whether illegal federal surveillance of radical groups exerted such a "chilling effect" on freedom of political communication as to violate the First Amendment: Laird v. Tatum (1972).

10. *The Nature of the Judicial Process* (New Haven: Yale University Press, 1921), p. 168.

II. PRINCIPLES OF INTERPRETATION

Although Stone's exceptions to the general rule of judicial deference in United States v. Carolene Products (1938; reprinted above, p. 609) have formed a pivot around which modern constitutional interpretation squeaks, there has been wide disagreement about the legitimacy as well as the meaning of those exceptions. Some justices have ignored them; others, like Felix Frankfurter, came to think them fundamentally wrong (see above, pp. 618–20); others, like Black and Douglas and later Potter Stewart,[11] extended Stone's suggestions; yet others, like Chief Justice Warren Burger[12] and Chief Justice Rehnquist,[13] would have restricted them; and even Stone himself at times seemed unsure about where his new approach led.[14]

Carolene Products did not enter a doctrinal vacuum, but neither was constitutional jurisprudence regarding political participation well developed in 1938. In fact, before World War I there had been almost no judicial interpretations of the First Amendment. Even the Sedition Act of 1798, a federal statute, did not generate a challenge that reached the Supreme Court. And it was not until 1925 in Gitlow v. New York that the Court held that the Fourteenth Amendment protected free speech against state encroachment.

Between World War I and *Carolene Products*, the Court usually applied one of two standards to test legislation challenged under the First Amendment's free speech or press clauses. Neither fit smoothly with what would become an approach of *reinforcing representative democracy*, a *structural* approach, or, for that matter, a *textual* approach. The first standard was the so-called "clear and present danger" test. As enunciated by Holmes in cases growing out of opposition to World War I, this test would sustain restrictions upon communication if what was spoken or written posed a "clear and present danger" of a substantive evil that

---

11. See, for example, Stewart's opinion for the Court in Harris v. McRae (1980; reprinted below, p. 1271), quoting his plurality opinion in Mobile v. Bolden (1980): "It is well settled that ... if a law 'impinges upon a fundamental right explicitly or implicitly secured by the Constitution [it] is presumptively unconstitutional.'"

12. See Burger's plurality opinion in Fullilove v. Klutznick (1980) quoting his opinion for the Court in Columbia Broadcasting Sys. v. Democratic National Committee (1973) that the Court accords "'great weight to the decisions of Congress' even though the legislation implicate[s] constitutional rights guaranteed by the First Amendment." See also Burger's opinion for the Court in Landmark Communications v. Virginia (1978).

13. Sugarman v. Dougall, dis. op. (1973).

14. Stone voted in Colegrove v. Green (1946) that legislative malapportionment did not present a justiciable issue. See the discussion above in Note "History of Footnote Four," p. 618, along with the discussion below in the headnote to Baker v. Carr (1962; reprinted below, p. 769).

government might legitimately prevent.[15] In this test's initial applications, the Court used it to justify sending people to jail for
arguing that the draft was unconstitutional and that the United
States should not intervene in the Russian civil war.[16] Later,
Holmes and Brandeis tried to refine "clear and present danger" to
protect rather than restrict free speech. As Brandeis explained in
his concurring opinion in Whitney v. California (1927; reprinted
below, p. 651):

> [N]o danger flowing from speech can be deemed clear and
> present, unless the incidence of evil apprehended is so imminent
> that it may befall before there is opportunity for full discussion.
> If there be time to expose through discussion the falsehood and
> fallacies ... the remedy to be applied is more speech, not
> enforced silence. Only an emergency can justify repression. ...
>
> Moreover, even imminent danger cannot justify resort to
> prohibition of these functions essential to effective democracy,
> unless the evil apprehended is relatively serious. ... The fact
> that speech is likely to result in some violence or in destruction of
> property is not enough to justify its suppression. There must be
> the probability of serious injury to the State.

For a time, "clear and present danger" managed to coexist with
the budding jurisprudence of Carolene Products. But, by the early
1950s, both those who were terrified by the specter of domestic
communism and those who, like Justice Douglas, dismissed communist agitators as "miserable merchants of unwanted ideas," agreed
that "clear and present danger" test was not a useful instrument to
interpret the First Amendment. The former thought it was too
restrictive of governmental power, the latter found it too restrictive
of freedom of speech and the democratic theory on which the
political system was based. The Court subsequently reformulated
the test in Brandenburg v. Ohio (1969; reprinted below, p. 672),
toughening it up to require "incitement to imminent lawless action."

The second test, much less compatible with *textualism, structuralism,* or *reinforcing representative democracy*, bore the label
"bad tendency." It was never so lucidly expressed as was "clear
and present danger," but Justice Sanford ponderously summarized
it for the Court in *Whitney*:

> a State in the exercise of it police power may punish those who
> abuse this freedom [of expression] by utterances inimical to the
> public welfare, tending to incite to crime, disturb the public
> peace, or endanger the foundations of organized government and
> threaten its overthrow by unlawful means. ...

By the early 1930s, the Court dropped the "bad tendency" test, but
something like it reappeared in Beauharnais v. Illinois (1952; re-

---

15. Schenck v. United States (1919).

16. Abrams v. United States (1919) and Debs v. United States (1919).

printed below, p. 680) and in the plurality's watered-down formulation of the "clear and present danger" test in Dennis v. United States (1951; reprinted below, p. 658).

Since *Carolene Products*, the Court has also occasionally used various forms of a *balancing* approach when confronted with a challenge under the First Amendment. And all the difficulties of *balancing* that Chapter 9 mentioned became quickly evident. Barenblatt v. United States (1959; reprinted below, p. 803) offered the starkest example, and we refer readers to the critique at pp. 410–14.

As Felix Frankfurter distanced himself from *Carolene Products*, he also became less enamored with "clear and present danger," a rejection that must have come hard because of his deep personal and as well as professional attachment to both Holmes and Brandeis. Casting about for a new approach, Frankfurter joined the majority's *balancing* in *Barenblatt*. Eight years earlier, however, he had argued that in a democracy the legislature must strike the balance, not the judiciary:

> Courts are not representative bodies. They are not designed to be a good reflex of a democratic society. . . . Primary responsibility for adjusting the interests that compete . . . of necessity belongs to the Congress. [Dennis v. United States, concur. op. (1951; reprinted below, p. 658).]

Judges, Frankfurter maintained, should only ensure that the "balance" that the legislature set falls within reasonable limits, not whether it is "correct" or the "best" of possible alternatives. This reasoning, of course, owes much to that of James Bradley Thayer,[17] another of his heroes. Frankfurter's intellectual voyage from *Carolene Products*, "clear and present danger," and "legislative balancing" to "judicial balancing" marks more than personal waffling. With the possible exception of Hugo Black, most other justices and commentators were not noticeably more consistent.

It might seem, then, that the simplest approach to these constitutional problems is *textualism*, *à la* Black. But, as Chapters 1 and 9 pointed out, often *textualism* alone does not move us very far, and Black's own record reflects some of the difficulties of using that approach by itself as well as shifts over time. In fact, one might reasonably argue that, on various occasions, Black mixed his *textualism* with a bit of *structuralism*,[18] some *philosophic* analysis insofar as he included democratic theory with his "Constitution," and even with an *aspirational* approach. "Our First Amendment," he

---

17. "The Origin and Scope of the American Doctrine of Constitutional Law" (1893; reprinted above, p. 602).

18. See his dis. op. in Milkwagon Drivers Union v. Meadowmoor Dairies (1941), quoted at the beginning of this chapter.

said in 1960, "was a bold effort ... to establish a country with no legal restrictions of any kind upon the subjects people could investigate, discuss and deny." [19]

In any event, Black excluded from constitutional protection "symbolic" acts of communication as picketing,[20] wearing armbands in a public school,[21] or burning a draft card [22] or an American flag.[23] He also wanted to sustain convictions of demonstrators for parading in an orderly fashion outside a courtroom. "Justice cannot be rightly administered," he explained, "nor are the lives and safety of prisoners secure, when throngs of people clamor against the processes of justice outside the courthouse or jailhouse door." [24]

These distinctions may make practical sense but they are not solely the products of *textualism.* In addition to evidence of *structural, philosophic,* and *aspirational* approaches, some *prudential* analysis is also manifest. Furthermore, even in textual terms, any distinction between political words and action is thin. Not only is the usual purpose of words to cause deeds—words are "the triggers of action," Judge Learned Hand once wrote,[25] and "[e]very idea is an incitement" to action, as Justice Holmes put it [26]—but verbal persuasion is typically interlaced with symbols. The flag, the log cabin, the burning cross, the swastika, "Watergate," "Wall Street," "star wars," and "Whitewater," all express politically laden values. United States v. O'Brien (1968; reprinted below, p. 721), United States v. Eichman (1990; reprinted below, p. 727), and R.A.V. v. St. Paul (1992: reprinted below, p. 686) show the justices awkwardly grappling with legislative attempts to restrict symbolic expression, such as burning draft cards, American flags, and crosses. The words of the text, "Congress shall make no law," set general guidelines, they do not inexorably yield self-evident truth. As is often the case, a *textual* approach provides a starting point rather than an ending point for constitutional interpretation.

Among the central questions in the readings that follow are: First, how far does *reinforcing representative democracy* move us beyond *textualism*? And, second, what costs does such an approach impose on constitutionalist theory? Are there "better" approaches? Better for what purposes?

---

19. "The Bill of Rights," 35 *N.Y.U.L.Rev.* 865 (1960).

20. Milkwagon Drivers Union v. Meadowmoor Dairies, dis. op. (1941); Giboney v. Empire Storage (1949).

21. Tinker v. Des Moines, dis. op. (1969).

22. United States v. O'Brien (1968).

23. Street v. New York, dis. op. (1969).

24. Cox v. Louisiana, dis. op. (1965).

25. Masses Publishing Co. v. Patten (S.D.N.Y.1917).

26. Gitlow v. New York, dis. op. (1925).

SELECTED BIBLIOGRAPHY

Baker, C. Edwin. *Human Liberty and Freedom of Speech* (New York: Oxford University Press, 1989).

Barber, Sotirios A. *On What the Constitution Means* (Baltimore: John Hopkins University Press, 1984).

Black, Hugo L. *A Constitutional Faith* (New York: Knopf, 1969).

Bollinger, Lee C. *The Tolerant Society: Freedom of Speech and Extremist Speech in America* (New York: Oxford University Press, 1986).

Bork, Robert H. "Neutral Principles and Some First Amendment Problems," 47 *Ind.L.J.* 1 (1971).

Chafee, Zechariah. *Free Speech in the United States* (Cambridge: Harvard University Press, 1941).

Choper, Jesse H. *Judicial Review and the National Political Process* (Chicago: University of Chicago Press, 1980).

Dworkin, Ronald. "The Coming Battles over Free Speech," *New York Review of Books* (June 11, 1992), pp. 55ff.

Ely, John Hart. *Democracy and Distrust* (Cambridge: Harvard University Press, 1980).

Emerson, Thomas I. *Toward a General Theory of the First Amendment* (New York: Random House, 1963).

————. *The System of Freedom of Expression* (New York: Random House, 1970).

Graber, Mark A. *Transforming Free Speech: The Ambiguous Legacy of Civil Libertarianism* (Berkeley: University of California Press, 1991).

Greenawalt, Kent. *Speech, Crime, and the Uses of Language* (New York: Oxford University Press, 1989).

Kalven, Harry. *A Worthy Tradition: Freedom of Speech in America* (Jamie Kalven, ed.; New York: Harper & Row, 1988).

Levy, Leonard W. *The Emergence of a Free Press* (New York: Oxford University Press, 1985).

Lusky, Louis. *By What Right?* (Charlottesville, VA: Michie, 1975).

Mason, Alpheus T. *The Supreme Court from Taft to Burger* (Baton Rouge: Louisiana State University Press, 1979).

Meiklejohn, Alexander. *Free Speech and Its Relation to Self–Government* (New York: Harpers, 1948).

Miller, J.C. *Crisis in Freedom: The Alien and Sedition Acts* (Boston: Little, Brown, 1951).

Murphy, Walter F. "Excluding Political Parties: Problems for Democratic and Constitutional Theory," in Paul Kirchhof and Donald

P. Kommers, eds., *Germany and Its Basic Law* (Baden–Baden: Nomos, 1993).

Powe, Lucas A. *The Fourth Estate and the Constitution: Freedom of the Press in America* (Berkeley: University of California Press, 1991).

Rabban, David M. "The First Amendment in its Forgotten Years," 90 *Yale L.J.* 514 (1981).

_____. "The Emergence of Modern First Amendment Doctrine," 50 *U.Chi.L.Rev.* 1207 (1983).

Randall, Richard S. *Freedom and Taboo: Pornography and the Politics of a Self Divided* (Berkeley: University of California Press, 1989).

Scanlon, T.M. "A Theory of Freedom of Expression," 1 *Phil. & Pub. Affairs* 204 (1972).

_____. "Freedom of Expression and Categories of Expression," 40 *U.Pitt.L.Rev.* 519 (1979).

Schauer, Frederick. *Free Speech: A Philosophical Enquiry* (New York: Cambridge University Press, 1982).

Shiffrin, Steven H. *The First Amendment, Democracy, and Romance* (Cambridge: Harvard University Press, 1990).

Smith, James Morton. *Freedom's Fetters: The Alien and Sedition Laws and American Civil Liberties* (Ithaca: Cornell University Press, 1956).

Sunstein, Cass R. *The Partial Constitution* (Cambridge: Harvard University Press, 1993).

_____. *Democracy and the Problem of Free Speech* (New York: Basic Books, 1993).

Tribe, Laurence H. *American Constitutional Law* (2d ed.; Mineola, NY: The Foundation Press, 1988), ch. 12.

I. THE STRUCTURAL ROLE OF FREEDOM OF POLITICAL COMMUNICATION

"[W]e consider this case against the background of a profound national commitment to the principle that debate on public issues should be uninhibited, robust, and wide-open, and that it may well include vehement, caustic, and sometimes unpleasantly sharp attacks on government and public officials."—Justice BRENNAN

"**[T]he First and Fourteenth Amendments not merely 'delimit' a State's power to award damages to 'public officials against critics of their official conduct' but completely prohibit a State from exercising such a power.**"—Justice **BLACK**

"**Purely private defamation has little to do with the political ends of a self-governing society.**"—Justice **GOLDBERG**

NEW YORK TIMES v. SULLIVAN

376 U.S. 254, 84 S.Ct. 710, 11 L.Ed.2d 686 (1964).

In 1960, when the Civil Rights Movement in the South was gaining momentum, the *New York Times* printed an advertisement, "Heed Their Rising Voices," which described the brutal reaction of police in Montgomery, Ala., and Orangeburg, S.C., to peaceful protests by black students seeking to affirm their constitutional rights to "human dignity." Peaceful efforts at reform, the advertisement claimed, were "being met by an unprecedented wave of terror by those who would deny and negate that document . . ." L.B. Sullivan, a city commissioner of Montgomery, whose work included supervision of police, sued the *Times* and four persons whose names had appeared (without their permission) as sponsoring the advertisement. The *Times* conceded that the ad was inaccurate in some of its details, but noted that it had not named any individual as responsible for the violence. The jury awarded damages of $500,000. The Alabama supreme court affirmed, holding the advertisement was libelous *per se* and not privileged under the First and Fourteenth amendments. By the time the *Times* had sought and obtained certiorari and presented oral argument, eleven other suits by local officials in the South, asking for $5.6 million, were pending against it.

Mr. Justice **BRENNAN** delivered the opinion of the Court.

We are required in this case to determine for the first time the extent to which the constitutional protections for speech and press limit a State's power to award damages in a libel action brought by a public official against critics of his official conduct. . . .

I

We may dispose at the outset of two grounds asserted to insulate the judgment of the Alabama courts from constitutional scrutiny. The first is the proposition relied on by the State Supreme Court—that "The Fourteenth Amendment is directed against State action and not private action." That proposition has no application to this case. Although this is a civil lawsuit between private parties, the Alabama courts have applied a state rule of law which petitioners claim to impose invalid restrictions on their constitutional freedoms of speech and press. . . .

The second contention is that the constitutional guarantees of freedom of speech and of the press are inapplicable here . . . because the allegedly libelous statements were published as part of a paid, "commercial" advertisement. ... The publication here ... communicated information, expressed opinion, recited grievances, protested claimed abuses, and sought financial support on behalf of a movement whose existence and objectives are matters of the highest public interest and concern. ... That the *Times* was paid for publishing the advertisement is as immaterial ... as is the fact that newspapers and books are sold. ... Any other conclusion would discourage newspapers from carrying "editorial advertisements" of this type, and so might shut off an important outlet for the promulgation of information and ideas by persons who do not themselves have access to publishing facilities—who wish to exercise their freedom of speech even though they are not members of the press. ...

II ...

Respondent relies heavily, as did the Alabama courts, on statements of this Court to the effect that the Constitution does not protect libelous publications. Those statements do not foreclose our inquiry here. None of the cases sustained the use of libel laws to impose sanctions upon expression critical of the official conduct of public officials. ... Like insurrection, contempt, advocacy of unlawful acts, breach of the peace, obscenity, solicitation of legal business, and the various other formulae for the repression of expression that have been challenged in this Court, libel can claim no talismanic immunity from constitutional limitations. It must be measured by standards that satisfy the First Amendment.

The general proposition that freedom of expression upon public questions is secured by the First Amendment has long been settled by our decisions. ... Thus we consider this case against the background of a profound national commitment to the principle that debate on public issues should be uninhibited, robust, and wide-open, and that it may well include vehement, caustic, and sometimes unpleasantly sharp attacks on government and public officials. The present advertisement, as an expression of grievance and protest on one of the major public issues of our time, would seem clearly to qualify for the constitutional protection. The question is whether it forfeits that protection by the falsity of some of its factual statements and by its alleged defamation of respondent.

Authoritative interpretations of the First Amendment guarantees have consistently refused to recognize an exception for any test of truth—whether administered by judges, juries, or administrative officials—and especially one that puts the burden of proving truth on the speaker. Cf. Speiser v. Randall [1958]. The constitutional protection does not turn upon "the truth, popularity, or social utility of the ideas and beliefs which are offered." NAACP v. Button [1963]. ... As Madison said, "Some degree of abuse is inseparable from the proper use of every thing; and in no instance is this more true than in that of the press." ...

Injury to official reputation affords no more warrant for repressing speech that would otherwise be free than does factual error. Where judicial officers are involved, this Court has held that concern for the dignity and reputation of the courts does not justify the punishment as criminal contempt of criticism of the judge or his decision. Bridges v. California [1941]. ... This is true even though the utterance contains "half-truths" and "misinformation." Pennekamp v. Florida [1946]. Such repression can be justified, if at all, only by a clear and present danger of the obstruction of justice. ... If judges are to be treated as "men of fortitude, able to thrive in a hardy climate," Craig v. Harney [1947], surely the same must be true of other government officials. ... Criticism of their official conduct does not lose its constitutional protection merely because it ... diminishes their official reputations.

If neither factual error nor defamatory content suffices to remove the constitutional shield from criticism of official conduct, the combination of the two elements is no less inadequate. This is the lesson to be drawn from the great controversy over the Sedition Act of 1798, ... which first crystallized a national awareness of the central meaning of the First Amendment. ...

Madison prepared the Report [Of the Virginia legislature against the Alien and Sedition laws, discussed above, Chapter 8, at pp. 353–59— **Eds.**] in support of the protest. His premise was that the Constitution created a form of government under which "The people, not the government, possess the absolute sovereignty." The structure of the government dispersed power in reflection of the people's distrust of concentrated power, and of power itself at all levels. ... Earlier, in a debate in the House of Representatives, Madison had said: "If we advert to the nature of Republican Government, we shall find that the censorial power is in the people over the Government, and not in the Government over the people." ... The right of free public discussion of the stewardship of public officials was thus, in Madison's view, a fundamental principle of the American form of government. ...

The state rule of law is not saved by its allowance of the defense of truth. ... Allowance of the defense of truth, with the burden of proving it on the defendant, does not mean that only false speech will be deterred. ... Under such a rule, would-be critics of official conduct may be deterred from voicing their criticism, even though it is believed to be true and even though it is in fact true, because of doubt whether it can be proved in court or fear of the expense of having to do so. ... The rule thus dampens the vigor and limits the variety of public debate. It is inconsistent with the First and Fourteenth Amendments.

The constitutional guarantees require, we think, a federal rule that prohibits a public official from recovering damages for a defamatory falsehood relating to his official conduct unless he proves that the statement was made with "actual malice"—that is, with knowledge that it was false or with reckless disregard of whether it was false or not. ...

Such a privilege for criticism of official conduct is appropriately analogous to the protection accorded a public official when *he* is sued for libel by a private citizen. ... The reason for the official privilege is said to be that the threat of damage suits would otherwise "inhibit the fearless, vigorous, and effective administration of policies of government" and "dampen the ardor of all but the most resolute, or the most irresponsible, in the unflinching discharge of their duties." Barr v. Matteo [1959]. Analogous considerations support the privilege for the citizen-critic of government. It is as much his duty to criticize as it is the official's duty to administer. ... It would give public servants an unjustified preference over the public they serve, if critics of official conduct did not have a fair equivalent of the immunity granted to the officials themselves. ...

III ...

Since respondent may seek a new trial, ... considerations of effective judicial administration require us to review the evidence in the present record to determine whether it could constitutionally support a judgment for respondent. This Court's duty is not limited to the elaboration of constitutional principles; we must also in proper cases review the evidence to make certain that those principles have been constitutionally applied. This is such a case, particularly since the question is one of alleged trespass across "the line between speech unconditionally guaranteed and speech which may legitimately be regulated." *Speiser.* ... In cases where that line must be drawn, the rule is that we "examine for ourselves the statements in issue and the circumstances under which they were made to see ... whether they are of a character which the principles of the First Amendment, as adopted by the Due Process Clause of the Fourteenth Amendment, protect." *Pennekamp.* ...

Applying these standards, we consider that the proof presented to show actual malice lacks the convincing clarity which the constitutional standard demands, and hence that it would not constitutionally sustain the judgment for respondent under the proper rule of law. ... We also think the evidence was constitutionally defective in another respect: it was incapable of supporting the jury's finding that the allegedly libelous statements were made "of and concerning" respondent. ... There was no reference to respondent in the advertisement, either by name or official position. ...

Reversed and remanded.

Mr. Justice **BLACK,** with whom Mr. Justice **DOUGLAS** joins, concurring.

... I base my vote to reverse on the belief that the First and Fourteenth Amendments not merely "delimit" a State's power to award damages to "public officials against critics of their official conduct" but completely prohibit a State from exercising such a power. The Court goes on to hold that a State can subject such critics to damages if "actual malice" can be proved against them. "Malice," even as defined by the Court, is an elusive, abstract concept, hard to prove and hard to disprove. The requirement that malice be proved provides at best an evanescent protection for the right critically to discuss public affairs and certainly does not measure up to the sturdy safeguard embodied in the First Amendment. . . .

In my opinion the Federal Constitution has dealt with this deadly danger to the press in the only way possible without leaving the free press open to destruction—by granting the press an absolute immunity for criticism of the way public officials do their public duty. . . .

This Nation, I suspect, can live in peace without libel suits based on public discussions of public affairs and public officials. But I doubt that a country can live in freedom where its people can be made to suffer physically or financially for criticizing their government, its actions, or its officials. "For a representative democracy ceases to exist the moment that the public functionaries are by any means absolved from their responsibility to their constituents; and this happens whenever the constituent can be restrained in any manner from speaking, writing, or publishing his opinions upon any public measure, or upon the conduct of those who may advise or execute it." [1] An unconditional right to say what one pleases about public affairs is what I consider to be the minimum guarantee of the First Amendment. . . .

Mr. Justice **GOLDBERG** with whom Mr. Justice **DOUGLAS** joins, concurring in the result. . . .

In my view, the First and Fourteenth Amendments to the Constitution afford to the citizen and to the press an absolute, unconditional privilege to criticize official conduct despite the harm which may flow from excesses and abuses. . . . The right should not depend upon a probing by the jury of the motivation of the citizen or press. The theory of our Constitution is that every citizen may speak his mind and every newspaper express its view on matters of public concern and may not be barred from speaking or publishing because those in control of government think that what is said or written is unwise, unfair, false, or malicious. . . .

This is not to say that the Constitution protects defamatory statements directed against the private conduct of a public official or private citizen. Freedom of press and of speech insures that government will respond to the will of the people and that changes may be obtained by peaceful means. Purely private defamation has little to do with the political ends of a self-governing society. . . .

The conclusion that the Constitution affords the citizen and the press an absolute privilege for criticism of official conduct does not leave the public official without defenses against unsubstantiated opinions or deliberate misstatements. "Under our system of government, counterargument and education are the weapons available to expose these matters, not abridgment . . . of free speech. . . ." Wood v. Georgia

---

1. 1 Tucker, *Blackstone's Commentaries* (1803), 297. [Footnote by Justice Black.]

[1962]. The public official certainly has equal if not greater access than most private citizens to media of communication. ...

Editors' Notes

(1) The U.S. Supreme Court's reexamination of the trial record of a state court, especially where the state supreme court had affirmed the trial court's findings, was unusual but not unprecedented. See, for example, Fiske v. Kansas (1927). Rule 52(a) of the Federal Rules of Civil Procedure establishes a similar policy for review of cases from federal courts. Furthermore, Bose Corp. v. Consumers Union (1984) held that both Rule 52(a) and *New York Times* stated

> a rule of federal constitutional law. It emerged from the exigency of deciding concrete cases; it is law in its purest form under our common law heritage. It reflects a deeply held conviction that judges—and particularly members of this Court—must exercise such review in order to preserve the precious liberties established and ordained by the Constitution.

(2) **Query:** In *New York Times*, Brennan's approach to constitutional interpretation differed from Black's and also Goldberg's. Which had the firmest basis in the text? In the structure of "the Constitution"? (What "Constitution"?) In democratic theory? In constitutionalism? How much emphasis did each place on a *doctrinal approach*?

(3) **Query:** Would constitutionalism be more protective of a public official's reputation than would democratic theory? But how far would a democratic theorist want to push Black's or Goldberg's reasoning, or even Brennan's? Might some of those opinions work to keep decent people out of politics? Justice Fortas, for example, vainly protested in St. Amant v. Thompson (1968) against the Court's reversing a judgment for damages secured by a public official against a man who, on a television program, falsely accused him of being a criminal:

> The First Amendment does not require that we license shotgun attacks on public officials in virtually unlimited open-season. The occupation of public officeholder does not forfeit one's membership in the human race.

It has been possible, however, for at least a few public officials to win judgments for libel under *New York Times.* Senator Barry Goldwater did so against *Fact Magazine,* which during the presidential campaign of 1964 pictured him as having a dangerously paranoid personality. The Supreme Court denied certiorari, over dissents from Black and Douglas. Ginzburg v. Goldwater (1970).

(4) *New York Times* concerned public officials, and Brennan was silent about whether the press's special protection when writing about public officials applied to stories about private citizens. In a public interview, two years before *New York Times,* Black had said he thought the First Amendment banned all libel actions.

> I have no doubt that the provision ... intended that there should be no libel or defamation law in the United States ... just absolutely none so far as I am concerned. ... ["Justice Black and First

Amendment 'Absolutes': A Public Interview," 37 *NYU.L.Rev.* 549,
557–558 (1962), reprinted in Irving Dilliard, ed., *One Man's Stand for
Freedom* (New York: Knopf, 1971), pp. 467ff.]

When the Court faced such questions, it constructed a middle category of
people, whom it labeled "public figures," a term that included those who attain
prominent positions or play influential roles in society—such as a retired
general who had vocally supported many political causes (Associated Press v.
Walker [1967]) or a nationally famous football coach at a large university
(Curtis Publishing Co. v. Butts [1967]).

Later in Rosenbloom v. Metromedia (1971), Black (joined by Douglas)
would have written into law the view he had expressed in the interview.
Brennan would have extended the requirement of "actual malice" to suits by
private citizens if the allegedly libelous statements concerned matters of public
interest; but the eight justices split five different ways, with no majority
opinion.

Three years after *Rosenbloom,* the Court held, 5–4, that *New York Times's*
requirement of "actual malice" did not apply when the plaintiff was a private
citizen. Gertz v. Robert Welch, Inc. (1974). That case also held, however,
that (1) while states had wide latitude to set their own standards in defamation
suits between private citizens and news media, they could not make the media
liable for damages without a showing of fault; and (2) even private citizens
could not recover "punitive"—as contrasted with "actual"—damages in the
absence of a finding of "actual malice." In addition, *Gertz* offered a somewhat
more precise, and narrower, definition of a "public figure":

> For the most part those who attain this status have assumed roles of
> especial prominence in the affairs of society. Some occupy positions
> of such persuasive power and influence that they are deemed public
> figures for all purposes. More commonly, those classed as public
> figures have thrust themselves to the forefront of particular public
> controversies in order to influence the resolution of the issues in-
> volved.

(5) Time, Inc. v. Firestone (1976) further considered the question of who
is a public figure. It involved a libel suit by a member of one of the nation's
wealthiest families, against *Time Magazine* for erroneously reporting that her
divorce was granted on grounds of extreme cruelty and adultery. She won a
judgment of $100,000, which the state supreme court sustained. The U.S.
Supreme Court, 5–3, rejected *Time*'s argument that Mrs. Firestone was a
public figure: She "did not assume any role of especial prominence in the
affairs of society, other than perhaps Palm Beach society, and she did not
thrust herself to the forefront of any particular public controversy in order to
influence the resolution of the issues involved in it." The Court also rejected
Time's argument for extension of *New York Times's* standard of actual malice
to all reports of judicial proceedings.

(6) **Query:** The Court's apparent emphasis on Mrs. Firestone's right to
reputation made its ruling three weeks later in Paul v. Davis (1976) all the more
puzzling. In an opinion also written by Rehnquist, the Court held, by the same
5–3 division as in *Time,* that there was no constitutionally protected right to a
good name. In dissent, Brennan remarked:

It is strange that the Court should hold that the interest in one's good name and reputation is not embraced within the concept of "liberty" or "property" under the Fourteenth Amendment, and yet hold that the same interest, when recognized under state law, is sufficient to overcome the specific protections of the First Amendment.

Is it possible to construct a coherent approach to or theory of constitutional interpretation that would simultaneously produce *Time* and *Paul*?

(7) The Court has only begun to settle problems of what evidence is sufficient to show "actual malice." Herbert v. Lando (1979) allowed a public figure to question the defendant, a TV producer, about such matters as his decisions to include and exclude evidence and his opinions about the veracity of some of his own witnesses. After the Supreme Court's ruling, the Court of Appeals for the Second Circuit dismissed Herbert's suit, holding that nine specific statements lacked any evidence of actual malice. In 1985 General William Westmoreland's suit against the Columbia Broadcasting System for allegedly damaging his reputation was settled out of court in CBS's favor before the end of a long trial. The General claimed that CBS so selected evidence, edited the film, and coached hostile witnesses as to have shown reckless disregard for the truth of its claim that he had misled the President about the strength of North Vietnamese forces in South Vietnam.

(8) Dun & Bradstreet v. Greenmoss Builders (1985) involved a suit stemming from a false report by a credit reporting agency that a contractor had filed a voluntary petition for bankruptcy. In affirming that the jury could award punitive damages without a showing of actual malice, the U.S. Supreme Court further limited *New York Times.* In so doing, the majority compounded *Gertz* 's distinction between public and private figures with a distinction between speech that is and speech that is not about matters of public concern.

(9) In *Gertz,* the Court stated that "[u]nder the First Amendment there is no such thing as a false idea," but also said that "there is no constitutional value in false statements of fact." In Milkovich v. Lorain Journal Co. (1990), the Court concluded that *Gertz* did not require a separate inquiry into whether the statements were "opinion" or "fact." The justices explained that such a "dichotomy" was unnecessary because Philadelphia Newspapers, Inc. v. Hepps (1986) already "stands for the proposition that a statement on matters of public concern must be provable as false" before liability can be imposed upon a media defendant.

(10) Justice Brennan later provided his own analysis of *New York Times:* "The Supreme Court and the Meiklejohn Interpretation of the First Amendment," 79 *Harv.L.Rev.* 1 (1965). For discussions of the cases since, see: David A. Anderson, "Libel and Press Self–Censorship," 53 *Tex.L.Rev.* 422 (1975); Richard A. Epstein, "Was *New York Times v. Sullivan* Wrong?" 53 *U.Chi.L.Rev.* 782 (1986); Harry Kalven, Jr., "The *New York Times* Case: A Note on 'The Central Meaning of the First Amendment,' " 1964 *Sup.Ct.Rev.* 191; Pierre N. Leval, "The No–Money, No–Fault Libel Suit: Keeping *Sullivan* in Its Proper Place," 101 *Harv.L.Rev.* 1287 (1988); Anthony Lewis, *Make No Law: The Sullivan Case and the First Amendment* (New York: Random House, 1991); Melville B. Nimmer, "The Right to Speak from *Times* to *Time,*" 56 *Calif.L.Rev.* 935 (1968); C. Herman Pritchett, *Constitutional Civil Liberties* (Englewood Cliffs, NJ: Prentice–Hall, 1984), pp. 101–108; Rodney A. Smolla,

"Let the Author Beware: The Rejuvenation of the American Law of Libel," 132 *U.Pa.L.Rev.* 1 (1984); Symposium, "Defamation and the First Amendment: New Perspectives," 25 *Wm. & Mary L.Rev.* 745 (1984); and Laurence H. Tribe, *American Constitutional Law* (2d ed.; Mineola, NY: The Foundation Press, 1988), ch. 12.

———

> **"We hold that the right to attend criminal trials is implicit in the guarantees of the First Amendment. . . ."—Chief Justice BURGER**
>
> **"[T]he First Amendment . . . has a *structural* role to play in . . . our Republican system of self-government."—Justice BRENNAN**
>
> **"Being unable to find any prohibition [against excluding spectators at a trial when neither side objects] in the First, Sixth, Ninth, or any other Amendments . . . or in the Constitution itself, I dissent."—Justice REHNQUIST**

RICHMOND NEWSPAPERS, INC. v. VIRGINIA
448 U.S. 555, 100 S.Ct. 2814, 65 L.Ed.2d 973 (1980).

In 1976 a state court in Richmond convicted a man named Stevenson of second-degree murder. The Virginia supreme court reversed, and the second and third trials ended in mistrials. In 1978, just before the fourth trial began, defense counsel asked the judge to close the courtroom to spectators and journalists so that jurors would not read inaccurate news summaries of testimony or speculation about evidence the judge had excluded. The prosecution did not object, and the judge so ordered, citing his statutory authority to exclude persons in order to ensure a fair trial, "provided that the right of the accused to a public trial shall not be violated." Richmond Newspapers, Inc., objected to being barred from the courtroom; and, after a hearing, from which reporters were also barred, the judge reaffirmed his order. The state supreme court dismissed an appeal of the ruling, and Richmond Newspapers, Inc., obtained certiorari from the U.S. Supreme Court.

Mr. Chief Justice **BURGER** announced the judgment of the Court and
    delivered an opinion in which Mr. Justice **WHITE** and Mr. Justice
    STEVENS joined. . . .

II . . .

A

The origins of the proceeding which has become the modern criminal trial in Anglo–American justice can be traced back beyond reliable historical records. . . . What is significant for present purposes is that throughout its evolution, the trial has been open to all who cared to observe.

In the days before the Norman Conquest, cases in England were generally brought before moots, such as the local court of the hundred or the county court, which were attended by the freemen of the community. Somewhat like modern jury duty, attendance at these early meetings was compulsory on the part of the freemen, who were called upon to render judgment. ... From these early times, although great changes in courts and procedure took place, one thing remained constant: the public character of the trial at which guilt or innocence was decided. ...

We have found nothing to suggest that the presumptive openness of the trial, which English courts were later to call "one of the essential qualities of a court of justice," Daubney v. Cooper (1829), was not also an attribute of the judicial systems of colonial America. In Virginia, for example, such records as there are of early criminal trials indicate that they were open. ... In some instances, the openness of trials was explicitly recognized as part of the fundamental law of the colony. ...

B

... [T]he historical evidence demonstrates conclusively that at the time when our organic laws were adopted, criminal trials both here and in England had long been presumptively open. This is no quirk of history; rather, it has long been recognized as an indispensable attribute of an Anglo–American trial. ... The early history of open trials in part reflects the widespread acknowledgement, long before there were behavioral scientists, that public trials had significant community therapeutic value. Even without such experts to frame the concept in words, people sensed from experience and observation that, especially in the administration of criminal justice, the means used to achieve justice must have the support derived from public acceptance of both the process and its results.

When a shocking crime occurs, a community reaction of outrage and public protest often follows. ... Thereafter the open processes of justice serve an important prophylactic purpose, providing an outlet for community concern, hostility, and emotion. Without an awareness that society's responses to criminal conduct are underway, natural human reactions of outrage and protest are frustrated and may manifest themselves in some form of vengeful "self-help," as indeed they did regularly in the activities of vigilante "committees" on our frontiers. ...

Civilized societies withdraw both from the victim and the vigilante the enforcement of criminal laws, but they cannot erase from people's consciousness the fundamental, natural yearning to see justice done—or even the urge for retribution. The crucial prophylactic aspects of the administration of justice cannot function in the dark; no community catharsis can occur if justice is "done in a corner [or] in any covert manner." It is not enough to say that results alone will satiate the natural community desire for "satisfaction." ... To work effectively, it is important that society's criminal process "satisfy the appearance of justice," Offutt v. United States (1954), and the appearance of justice can best be provided by allowing people to observe it. ...

C

From this unbroken, uncontradicted history, supported by reasons as valid today as in centuries past, we are bound to conclude that a presumption of openness inheres in the very nature of a criminal trial under our system of justice. ...

Despite the history of criminal trials being presumptively open since long before the Constitution, the State presses its contention that neither the Constitution nor the Bill of Rights contains any provision which by its terms guarantees to the public the right to attend criminal trials. Standing alone, this is correct, but there remains the question whether, absent an explicit provision, the Constitution affords protection against exclusion of the public from criminal trials.

III

A

The First Amendment, in conjunction with the Fourteenth, prohibits governments from "abridging the freedom of speech, or of the press; or the right of the people peaceably to assemble, and to petition the Government for a redress of grievances." These expressly guaranteed freedoms share a common core purpose of assuring freedom of communication on matters relating to the functioning of government. Plainly it would be difficult to single out any aspect of government of higher concern and importance to the people than the manner in which criminal trials are conducted; as we have shown, recognition of this pervades the centuries-old history of open trials and the opinions of this Court.

The Bill of Rights was enacted against the backdrop of the long history of trials being presumptively open. ... [T]he First Amendment can be read as protecting the right of everyone to attend trials so as to give meaning to those explicit guarantees. ... Free speech carries with it some freedom to listen. "In a variety of contexts this Court has referred to a First Amendment right to 'receive information and ideas.' " Kleindienst v. Mandel (1972). What this means in the context of trials is that the First Amendment guarantees of speech and press, standing alone, prohibit government from summarily closing courtroom doors which had long been open to the public at the time that amendment was adopted. "For the First Amendment does not speak equivocally. ... It must be taken as a command of the broadest scope that explicit language, read in the context of a liberty-loving society, will allow." Bridges v. California (1941). ... The explicit, guaranteed rights to speak and to publish concerning what takes place at a trial would lose much meaning if access to observe the trial could, as it was here, be foreclosed arbitrarily.

B

The right of access to places traditionally open to the public, as criminal trials have long been, may be seen as assured by the amalgam of the First Amendment guarantees of speech and press; and their affinity to the right of assembly is not without relevance. ... [1]

"The right of peaceable assembly is a right cognate to those of free speech and free press and is equally fundamental." DeJonge v. Oregon (1937). People assemble in public places not only to speak or to take action, but also to listen, observe, and learn; indeed, they may "assembl[e] for any lawful purpose," Hague v. C.I.O. (1939) (opinion of Stone, J.). Subject to the traditional time, place, and manner restrictions, see, e.g. Cox v. New Hampshire (1941); see also Cox v. Louisiana (1965), streets, sidewalks, and parks are places traditionally open, where First Amendment rights may be exercised. ... [A] trial courtroom also is a public place where the people generally—and representatives of the media—have a right to be present, and where their presence historically has been thought to enhance the integrity and quality of what takes place. ...

C

The State argues that the Constitution nowhere spells out a guarantee for the right of the public to attend trials, and that accordingly no such right is protected. The possibility that such a contention could be made did not escape the notice of the Constitution's draftsmen; they were concerned that some important rights might be thought disparaged because not specifically guaranteed. It was even argued that because of this danger no Bill of Rights should be adopted. See, e.g., A. Hamilton,

---

1. When the First Congress was debating the Bill of Rights, it was contended that there was no need separately to assert the right of assembly because it was subsumed in freedom of speech. Mr. Sedgwick of Massachusetts argued that inclusion of "assembly" among the enumerated rights would tend to make the Congress "appear trifling in the eyes of their constituents. ... If people freely converse together, they must assemble for that purpose; it is a self-evident, unalienable right which the people possess; it is certainly a thing that never would be called in question. ..."

... Since the right existed independent of any written guarantee, Sedgwick went on to argue that if it were the drafting committee's purpose to protect all inherent rights of the people by listing them, "they might have gone into a very lengthy enumeration of rights," but this was unnecessary, he said, "in a Government where none of them were intended to be infringed." ...

Mr. Page of Virginia responded, however, that at times "such rights have been opposed," and that "people have ... been prevented from assembling together on their lawful occasions":

[T]herefore it is well to guard against such stretches of authority, by inserting the privilege in the declaration of rights. If the people could be deprived of the power of assembly under any pretext whatsoever, they might be deprived of every other privilege contained in the clause. *Ibid.* The motion to strike "assembly" was defeated. ...

[Footnote by the Chief Justice.]

The Federalist no. 84. In a letter to Thomas Jefferson in October of 1788, James Madison explained why he, although "in favor of a bill of rights," had "not viewed it in an important light" up to that time: "I conceive that in a certain degree ... the rights in question are reserved by the manner in which the federal powers are granted." He went on to state "there is great reason to fear that a positive declaration of some of the most essential rights could not be obtained in the requisite latitude." [2]

But arguments such as the State makes have not precluded recognition of important rights not enumerated. Notwithstanding the appropriate caution against reading into the Constitution rights not explicitly defined, the Court has acknowledged that certain unarticulated rights are implicit in enumerated guarantees. For example, the rights of association and of privacy, the right to be presumed innocent and the right to be judged by a standard of proof beyond a reasonable doubt in a criminal trial, as well as the right to travel, appear nowhere in the Constitution or Bill of Rights. Yet these important but unarticulated rights have nonetheless been found to share constitutional protection in common with explicit guarantees. [3] The concerns expressed by Madison and others have thus been resolved; fundamental rights, even though not expressly guaranteed, have been recognized by the Court as indispensable to the enjoyment of rights explicitly defined.

We hold that the right to attend criminal trials is implicit in the guarantees of the First Amendment; without the freedom to attend such trials, which people have exercised for centuries, important aspects of freedom of speech and "of the press could be eviscerated." Branzburg [v. Hayes (1972)]. ...

D

... Absent an overriding interest articulated in findings [of a particular set of circumstances], the trial of a criminal case must be open to the public. [4]

                                                                Reversed.

---

2. Madison's comments in Congress also reveal the perceived need for some sort of constitutional "saving clause," which, among other things, would serve to foreclose application to the Bill of Rights of the maxim that the affirmation of particular rights implies a negation of those not expressly defined. Madison's efforts, culminating in the Ninth Amendment, served to allay the fears of those who were concerned that expressing certain guarantees could be read as excluding others. [Footnote by the Chief Justice.]

3. See, e.g., NAACP v. Alabama (1958); Griswold v. Connecticut (1965) and Stanley v. Georgia (1969); Estelle v. Williams (1976) and Taylor v. Kentucky (1978); In re Winship (1970); United States v. Guest (1966) and Shapiro v. Thompson (1969). [Footnote by the Chief Justice.]

4. We have no occasion here to define the circumstances in which all or parts of a criminal trial may be closed to the public ..., but our holding today does not mean that the First Amendment rights of the public and representatives of the press are absolute. ... [A] trial judge, in the interest of the fair administration of justice, [may] impose reasonable limitations on access to a trial. ... [Footnote by the Chief Justice.]

Mr. Justice **POWELL** took no part in the consideration or decision in this case.

Mr. Justice **WHITE,** concurring. ...

Mr. Justice **STEVENS,** concurring. ...

Mr. Justice **BRENNAN,** with whom Mr. Justice **MARSHALL** joins, concurring in the judgment. ...

I ...

The Court's approach in right of access cases simply reflects the special nature of a claim of First Amendment right to gather information. Customarily, First Amendment guarantees are interposed to protect communication between speaker and listener. When so employed against prior restraints, free speech protections are almost insurmountable. See Nebraska Press Assn. v. Stuart (1976); New York Times Co. v. United States (1971). See generally Brennan, Address, 32 *Rutgers L.Rev.* 173, 176 (1979). But the First Amendment embodies more than a commitment to free expression and communicative interchange for their own sakes; it has a *structural* role to play in securing and fostering our republican system of self-government. See United States v. Carolene Prods. Co. n.4 (1938); Grosjean v. American Press Co. (1936); Stromberg v. California (1931); Ely, *Democracy and Distrust* 93–94 (1980); Emerson, *The System of Freedom of Expression* 7 (1970); Meiklejohn, *Free Speech and Its Relation to Self-Government* (1948). Implicit in this structural role is not only "the principle that debate on public issues should be uninhibited, robust, and wide-open," New York Times [v. Sullivan (1964)], but the antecedent assumption that valuable public debate—as well as other civic behavior—must be informed. The structural model links the First Amendment to that process of communication necessary for a democracy to survive, and thus entails solicitude not only for communication itself, but for the indispensable conditions of meaningful communication.[1]

... [S]o far as the participating citizen's need for information is concerned, "[t]here are few restrictions on action which could not be clothed by ingenious argument in the garb of decreased data flow." Zemel v. Rusk (1965). An assertion of the prerogative to gather information must accordingly be assayed by considering the information sought and the opposing interests invaded. This judicial task is as much a matter of sensitivity to practical necessities as it is of abstract reasoning. But at least two helpful principles may be sketched. First, the case for a right of access has special force when drawn from an enduring and vital tradition of public entree to particular proceedings or information.

---

1. The technique of deriving specific rights from the structure of our constitutional government, or from other explicit rights, is not novel. The right of suffrage has been inferred from the nature of "a free and democratic society" and from its importance as a "preservative of other basic civil and political rights. ..." Reynolds v. Sims (1964). [Footnote by Justice Brennan.]

Such a tradition commands respect in part because the Constitution carries the gloss of history. More importantly, a tradition of accessibility implies the favorable judgment of experience. Second, the value of access must be measured in specifics. Analysis is not advanced by rhetorical statements that all information bears upon public issues; what is crucial in individual cases is whether access to a particular government process is important in terms of that very process. ...

II ...

This Court too has persistently defended the public character of the trial process. In re Oliver [1948] established that the Due Process Clause of the Fourteenth Amendment forbids closed criminal trials. ... Even more significantly for our present purpose, *Oliver* recognized that open trials are bulwarks of our free and democratic government: public access to court proceedings is one of the numerous "checks and balances" of our system, because "contemporaneous review in the forum of public opinion is an effective restraint on possible abuse of judicial power." Tradition, contemporaneous state practice, and this Court's own decisions manifest a common understanding that "[a] trial is a public event. What transpires in the court room is public property." Craig v. Harney (1947).

III

Publicity serves to advance several of the particular purposes of the trial (and, indeed, the judicial) process. Open trials play a fundamental role in furthering the efforts of our judicial system to assure the criminal defendant a fair and accurate adjudication of guilt or innocence. But, as a feature of our governing system of justice, the trial process serves other, broadly political, interests, and public access advances these objectives as well. To that extent, trial access possesses specific structural significance.

The trial is a means of meeting "the notion, deeply rooted in the common law, that 'justice must satisfy the appearance of justice.' " Levine v. United States (1960). For a civilization founded upon principles of ordered liberty to survive and flourish, its members must share the conviction that they are governed equitably. It also mandates a system of justice that demonstrates the fairness of the law to our citizens. One major function of the trial, hedged with procedural protections and conducted with conspicuous respect for the rule of law, is to make that demonstration. Secrecy is profoundly inimical to this demonstrative purpose of the trial process. ...

But the trial is more than a demonstrably just method of adjudicating disputes and protecting rights. It plays a pivotal role in the entire judicial process, and, by extension, in our form of government. Under our system, judges are not mere umpires, but, in their own sphere, lawmakers—a coordinate branch of *government*. While individual cases turn upon the controversies between parties, or involve particular prosecutions, court rulings impose official and practical consequences upon members of society at large. Moreover, judges bear responsibility for the vitally important task of construing and securing constitutional rights. Thus, so far as the trial is the mechanism for judicial factfinding, as well as the initial forum for legal decisionmaking, it is a genuine governmental proceeding.

It follows that the conduct of the trial is preeminently a matter of public interest. ...

IV

... What countervailing interests might be sufficiently compelling to reverse this presumption of openness need not concern us now, for the statute at stake here authorizes trial closures at the unfettered discretion of the judge and parties. ...

Mr. Justice **STEWART,** concurring in the judgment. ...

Mr. Justice **BLACKMUN,** concurring in the judgment. ...

... I remain convinced that the right to a public trial is to be found where the Constitution explicitly placed it—in the Sixth Amendment.

The Court, however, has eschewed the Sixth Amendment route. The plurality turns to other possible constitutional sources and invokes a veritable potpourri of them—the speech clause of the First Amendment, the press clause, the assembly clause, the Ninth Amendment, and a cluster of penumbral guarantees recognized in past decisions. This course is troublesome. ...

Having said all this, and with the Sixth Amendment set to one side in this case, I am driven to conclude, as a secondary position, that the First Amendment must provide some measure of protection for public access to the trial. ...

Mr. Justice **REHNQUIST,** dissenting.

In the Gilbert & Sullivan operetta *Iolanthe,* the Lord Chancellor recites:

The Law is the true embodiment
of everything that's excellent,
It has no kind of fault or flaw,
And I, my lords, embody the law.

It is difficult not to derive more than a little of this flavor from the various opinions supporting the judgment in this case. ...

... I do not believe that either the First or Sixth Amendments, as made applicable to the States by the Fourteenth, require that a State's reasons for denying public access to a trial, where both the prosecuting attorney and the defendant have consented to an order of closure approved by the judge, are subject to any additional constitutional review at our hands. And I most certainly do not believe that the Ninth

Amendment confers upon us any such power to review orders of state trial judges closing trials in such situations.

We have at present 50 state judicial systems and one federal judicial system in the United States, and our authority to reverse a decision by the highest court of the State is limited to only those occasions when the state decision violates some provision of the United States Constitution. And that authority should be exercised with a full sense that the judges whose decisions we review are making the same effort as we to uphold the Constitution. As said by Mr. Justice Jackson, concurring in the result in Brown v. Allen [1953], "we are not final because we are infallible, but we are infallible only because we are final."

The proper administration of justice in any nation is bound to be a matter of the highest concern to all thinking citizens. But to gradually rein in, as this Court has done over the past generation, all of the ultimate decisionmaking power over how justice shall be administered, not merely in the federal system but in each of the 50 States, is a task that no Court consisting of nine persons, however gifted, is equal to. Nor is it desirable that such authority be exercised by such a tiny numerical fragment of the 220 million people who compose the population of this country. In the same concurrence just quoted, Mr. Justice Jackson accurately observed that "[t]he generalities of the Fourteenth Amendment are so indeterminate as to what state actions are forbidden that this Court has found it a ready instrument, in one field or another, to magnify federal, and incidentally its own, authority over the states."
. . .

The issue here is not whether the "right" to freedom of the press conferred by the First Amendment to the Constitution overrides the defendant's "right" to a fair trial conferred by other amendments to the Constitution; it is instead whether any provision in the Constitution may fairly be read to prohibit what the trial judge in the Virginia state court system did in this case. Being unable to find any such prohibition in the First, Sixth, Ninth, or any other Amendments to the United States Constitution, or in the Constitution itself, I dissent.

Editors' Notes

(1) **Query:** Burger, Brennan, and Rehnquist all claimed to follow a *structuralist* approach. How is it that they reason so differently? (In fact, how far apart were Burger and Brennan?) In this case, at least, how much of a *textualist approach* did each of the four justices follow? A *doctrinal approach*? What was the implicit answer of each to the question, "What does 'the Constitution' include?"

(2) **Query:** "Under our system," Brennan wrote, "judges are not mere umpires, but, in their own sphere, lawmakers—a coordinate branch of *government.*" What does such a claim imply for the structure of the national government and the so-called doctrine of separation of powers? (See Chapter 10, above.)

(3) **Query:** What was Burger's conception of the "core purpose" of the First Amendment? Brennan's conception? To what extent did either or both rest his argument on democratic theory?

(4) **Query:** Sometimes rights under the First Amendment to free speech and press may conflict with the Sixth Amendment's guarantee of a fair trial. How helpful are any of the opinions here in resolving such a conflict?

(5) **Query:** Burger's opinion for the plurality in *Richmond Newspapers,* together with Goldberg's concur. op. in Griswold v. Connecticut (1965; reprinted above, p. 147), are the most important judicial invocations of the Ninth Amendment in justifying the recognition of "unenumerated" constitutional rights. Was Burger's conception of the Ninth Amendment different from Goldberg's? What should be the role of the Ninth Amendment in interpreting the Constitution? For collections of essays on the Ninth Amendment, see *The Rights Retained by the People* (Randy Barnett ed.; Fairfax, VA: George Mason University Press, 1989 & 1993); "Symposium on Interpreting the Ninth Amendment," 64 *Chi.-Kent L.Rev.* 1 (1988); and "Symposium: The Bill of Rights and the Unwritten Constitution," 16 *S. Ill.U.L.J.* 267 (1992).

II. ADVOCACY OR INCITEMENT OF UNLAWFUL ACTION

"[A] State in the exercise of its police power may punish those who abuse this freedom by utterances inimical to the public welfare, tending to incite to crime, disturb the public peace, or endanger the foundations of organized government and threaten its overthrow by unlawful means. ..."—Justice SANFORD

"If there be time to expose through discussion the falsehood and fallacies, to avert the evil by the process of education, the remedy to be applied is more speech, not enforced silence."—Justice BRANDEIS

WHITNEY v. CALIFORNIA
274 U.S. 357, 47 S.Ct. 641, 71 L.Ed. 1095 (1927).

In 1919 Anita Whitney attended a convention in Oakland, held to organize a state branch of the Communist Labor party, which had links to the Communist International in Moscow. The national party's program called for "a unified revolutionary working class movement in America" to reorganize society and bring about a communist commonwealth. During the convention she signed a proposal urging the value of political action and electoral activity.

The resolution did not pass; instead, the convention adopted the national party's program. Whitney stayed at the convention and remained an active member of the party. She was later convicted under California's Criminal Syndicalism Act, which made it a felony to organize or join a group advocating, aiding, or abetting acts of violence to achieve political or industrial change. She obtained a writ of error from the U.S. Supreme Court after state appellate courts affirmed her conviction.

Mr. Justice **SANFORD** delivered the opinion of the Court. ...

1. While it is not denied that the evidence warranted the jury in finding that the defendant became a member of and assisted in organizing the Communist Labor Party of California, and that this was organized to advocate, teach, aid or abet criminal syndicalism as defined by the Act, it is urged that the Act, as here construed and applied, deprived the defendant of her liberty without due process of law in that it has made her action in attending the Oakland convention unlawful by reason of "a subsequent event brought about against her will, by the agency of others," with no showing of a specific intent on her part to join in the forbidden purpose of the association, and merely because, by reason of a lack of "prophetic" understanding she failed to foresee the quality that others would give to the convention. ...

This contention, while advanced in the form of a constitutional objection to the Act, is in effect nothing more than an effort to review the weight of the evidence for the purpose of showing that the defendant did not join and assist in organizing the Communist Labor Party of California with a knowledge of its unlawful character and purpose. This question, which is foreclosed by the verdict of the jury—sustained by the Court of Appeal over the specific objection that it was not supported by the evidence—is one of fact merely which is not open to review in this Court, involving as it does no constitutional question whatever. And we may add that the argument entirely disregards the facts. ... [S]he not only remained in the convention, without protest, until its close, but subsequently manifested her acquiescence by attending as an alternate member of the State Executive Committee and continuing as a member of the Communist Labor Party.

2. It is clear that the Syndicalism Act is not repugnant to the due process clause by reason of vagueness and uncertainty of definition. ... The Act, plainly, meets the essential requirement of due process that a penal statute be "sufficiently explicit to inform those who are subject to it, what conduct on their part will render them liable to its penalties," and be couched in terms that are not "so vague that men of common intelligence must necessarily guess at its meaning and differ as to its application." ... So, as applied here, the Syndicalism Act required of the defendant no "prophetic" understanding of its meaning. ...

4. Nor is the Syndicalism Act as applied in this case repugnant to the due process clause as a restraint of the rights of free speech, assembly, and association. That the freedom of speech which is secured by the Constitution does not confer an absolute right to speak, without

responsibility, whatever one may choose, or an unrestricted and unbridled license giving immunity for every possible use of language and preventing the punishment of those who abuse this freedom; and that a State in the exercise of its police power may punish those who abuse this freedom by utterances inimical to the public welfare, tending to incite to crime, disturb the public peace, or endanger the foundations of organized government and threaten its overthrow by unlawful means, is not open to question. Gitlow v. New York [1925].

By enacting the provisions of the Syndicalism Act the State has declared, through its legislative body, that to knowingly be or become a member of or assist in organizing an association to advocate, teach or aid and abet the commission of crimes or unlawful acts of force, violence or terrorism as a means of accomplishing industrial or political changes, involves such danger to the public peace and the security of the State, that these acts should be penalized in the exercise of its police power. That determination must be given great weight. Every presumption is to be indulged in favor of the validity of the statute ... and it may not be declared unconstitutional unless it is an arbitrary or unreasonable attempt to exercise the authority vested in the State in the public interest. ...

The essence of the offense denounced by the Act is the combining with others in an association for the accomplishment of the desired ends through the advocacy and use of criminal and unlawful methods. It partakes of the nature of a criminal conspiracy. That such united and joint action involves even greater danger to the public peace and security than the isolated utterances and acts of individuals, is clear. We cannot hold that, as here applied, the Act is an unreasonable or arbitrary exercise of the police power of the State, unwarrantably infringing any right of free speech, assembly or association. ...

Affirmed.

Mr. Justice **BRANDEIS** [joined by Justice **HOLMES**], concurring. ...

[Under this statute,] [t]he mere act of assisting in forming a society for teaching syndicalism, of becoming a member of it, or of assembling with others for that purpose is given the dynamic quality of crime. There is guilt although the society may not contemplate immediate promulgation of the doctrine. Thus the accused is to be punished, not for contempt, incitement or conspiracy, but for a step in preparation, which, if it threatens the public order at all, does so only remotely. The novelty in the prohibition introduced is that the statute aims, not at the practice of criminal syndicalism, nor even directly at the preaching of it, but at association with those who propose to preach it.

Despite arguments to the contrary which had seemed to me persuasive, it is settled that the due process clause of the Fourteenth Amendment applies to matters of substantive law as well as to matters of procedure. Thus all fundamental rights comprised within the term liberty are protected by the Federal Constitution from invasion by the

States. The right of free speech, the right to teach and the right of
assembly are, of course, fundamental rights. See Meyer v. Nebraska
[1923]; Pierce v. Society of Sisters [1925]; Gitlow v. New York [1925];
Farrington v. Tokushige [1927]. These may not be denied or abridged.
But, although the rights of free speech and assembly are fundamental,
they are not in their nature absolute. Their exercise is subject to
restriction, if the particular restriction proposed is required in order to
protect the State from destruction or from serious injury, political,
economic or moral. That the necessity which is essential to a valid
restriction does not exist unless speech would produce, or is intended to
produce, a clear and imminent danger of some substantive evil which the
State constitutionally may seek to prevent has been settled. See
Schenck v. United States [1919].

   ... The legislature must obviously decide, in the first instance,
whether a danger exists which calls for a particular protective measure.
But where a statute is valid only in case certain conditions exist, the
enactment of the statute cannot alone establish the facts which are
essential to its validity. Prohibitory legislation has repeatedly been held
invalid, because unnecessary, where the denial of liberty involved was
that of engaging in a particular business. The power of the courts to
strike down an offending law is no less when the interests involved are
not property rights, but the fundamental personal rights of free speech
and assembly.

   This Court has not yet fixed the standard by which to determine
when a danger shall be deemed clear; how remote the danger may be
and yet be deemed present; and what degree of evil shall be deemed
sufficiently substantial to justify resort to abridgement of free speech
and assembly as the means of protection. To reach sound conclusions
on these matters, we must bear in mind why a State is, ordinarily,
denied the power to prohibit dissemination of social, economic and
political doctrine which a vast majority of its citizens believes to be false
and fraught with evil consequence.

   Those who won our independence believed that the final end of the
State was to make men free to develop their faculties; and that in its
government the deliberative forces should prevail over the arbitrary.
They valued liberty both as an end and as a means. They believed
liberty to be the secret of happiness and courage to be the secret of
liberty. They believed that freedom to think as you will and to speak as
you think are means indispensable to the discovery and spread of
political truth; that without free speech and assembly discussion would
be futile; that with them, discussion affords ordinarily adequate protection against the dissemination of noxious doctrine; that the greatest
menace to freedom is an inert people; that public discussion is a political
duty; and that this should be a fundamental principle of the American
government.[1] They recognized the risks to which all human institutions

   1. Compare Thomas Jefferson ...: "If there be any among us who would wish to
dissolve this union or change its republican form, let them stand undisturbed as monu-

are subject. But they knew that order cannot be secured merely through fear of punishment for its infraction; that it is hazardous to discourage thought, hope and imagination; that fear breeds repression; that repression breeds hate; that hate menaces stable government; that the path of safety lies in the opportunity to discuss freely supposed grievances and proposed remedies; and that the fitting remedy for evil counsels is good ones. Believing in the power of reason as applied through public discussion, they eschewed silence coerced by law—the argument of force in its worst form. Recognizing the occasional tyrannies of governing majorities, they amended the Constitution so that free speech and assembly should be guaranteed.

Fear of serious injury cannot alone justify suppression of free speech and assembly. Men feared witches and burnt women. It is the function of speech to free men from the bondage of irrational fears. To justify suppression of free speech there must be reasonable ground to fear that serious evil will result if free speech is practiced. There must be reasonable ground to believe that the danger apprehended is imminent. There must be reasonable ground to believe that the evil to be prevented is a serious one. Every denunciation of existing law tends in some measure to increase the probability that there will be violation of it. ... But even advocacy of violation, however reprehensible morally, is not a justification for denying free speech where the advocacy falls short of incitement and there is nothing to indicate that the advocacy would be immediately acted on. The wide difference between advocacy and incitement, between preparation and attempt, between assembling and conspiracy, must be borne in mind. In order to support a finding of clear and present danger it must be shown either that immediate serious violence was to be expected or was advocated, or that the past conduct furnished reason to believe that such advocacy was then contemplated.

Those who won our independence by revolution were not cowards. They did not fear political change. They did not exalt order at the cost of liberty. To courageous, self-reliant men, with confidence in the power of free and fearless reasoning applied through the processes of popular government, no danger flowing from speech can be deemed clear and present, unless the incidence of the evil apprehended is so imminent that it may befall before there is opportunity for full discussion. If there be time to expose through discussion the falsehood and fallacies, to avert the evil by the processes of education, the remedy to be applied is more speech, not enforced silence. Only an emergency can justify repression. Such must be the rule if authority is to be reconciled with freedom. Such, in my opinion, is the command of the Constitution. ...

Moreover, even imminent danger cannot justify resort to prohibition of these functions essential to effective democracy, unless the evil apprehended is relatively serious. Prohibition of free speech and assembly is a measure so stringent that it would be inappropriate as the means

---

ments of the safety with which error of opinion may be tolerated where reason is left free to combat it." [Footnote by Justice Brandeis.]

for averting a relatively trivial harm to society. A police measure may be unconstitutional merely because the remedy, although effective as means of protection, is unduly harsh or oppressive. . . . The fact that speech is likely to result in some violence or in destruction of property is not enough to justify its suppression. There must be the probability of serious injury to the State. Among free men, the deterrents ordinarily to be applied to prevent crime are education and punishment for violations of the law, not abridgment of the rights of free speech and assembly. . . .

. . . I am unable to assent to the suggestion in the opinion of the Court that assembling with a political party, formed to advocate the desirability of a proletarian revolution by mass action at some date necessarily far in the future, is not a right within the protection of the Fourteenth Amendment. In the present case, however, there was other testimony which tended to establish the existence of a conspiracy, on the part of members of the International Workers of the World, to commit present serious crimes; and likewise to show that such a conspiracy would be furthered by the activity of the society of which Miss Whitney was a member. Under these circumstances the judgment of the state court cannot be disturbed. . . .

Editors' Notes

(1) The plurality opinion in Dennis v. United States (1951; reprinted below, p. 658) said: "Although no case subsequent to *Whitney* and Gitlow [v. New York (1925)] has expressly overruled the majority opinions in those cases, there can be no doubt that subsequent opinions have inclined toward the Holmes–Brandeis rationale." *Gitlow* had applied the "bad tendency" test, but it had also held for the first time that the Fourteenth Amendment protected against state infringement on freedom of speech. On the latter point it remains good law. See Eds.' Notes to Palko v. Connecticut (1937), above, at p. 133. In 1969, Brandenburg v. Ohio (reprinted below, p. 672), explicitly overruled *Whitney.*

(2) **Query:** To what extent did Sanford's opinion in *Whitney* merely extend Thayer's doctrine of the clear mistake ("The Origin and Scope of the American Doctrine of Constitutional Law," reprinted above, p. 602) to judicial scrutiny of state legislative judgments?

(3) **Query:** To what extent did Brandeis take an *originalist* approach? To what extent was his approach *philosophic* in the sense of arguing from democratic theory? Does his dissent support Stone's claim that paragraph 2 of *Carolene Products'* footnote 4 owed much to Brandeis?

(4) **Query:** How accurate was Brandeis' claim that the founders were avid advocates of free speech? Not only did the Sedition Act of 1798 (1 Stat. 596) punish attempting violent overthrow of the government, it also made it a felony for any person to:

> write, print, utter, or publish or . . . cause or procure to be written, printed, uttered, or published, or . . . knowingly and willingly assist or aid in writing, printing, uttering or publishing any false, scandalous and malicious writing or writings against the government of the

United States, or either house of the Congress of the United States, or the President of the United States, with intent to defame ... or to bring them, or either of them, into contempt or disrepute. ...

Prosecutors and judges took a capacious view of the Act. David Brown's offense was not atypical. He called the Federalists who controlled Congress and the presidency "a tyrannic association of five hundred out of five millions" who reaped "all the benefits of public property and live upon the ruins of the rest of the community." For this crime, Justice Chase—Supreme Court justices in those days "rode circuit" and presided at trials—carried out his belief that "[t]here is nothing we should dread more than the licentiousness of the press," and sentenced Brown to pay a fine of $450 and to serve 18 months in prison. See John C. Miller, *Crisis in Freedom: The Alien and Sedition Acts* (Boston: Little, Brown, 1951), pp. 114–119. (Chase, incidentally, had signed the Declaration of Independence but had opposed ratification of the constitutional text of 1787–88. His zealous prosecution of the Sedition Act was one of the causes for his impeachment.)

According to Leonard Levy, initially Madison's and Jefferson's principal constitutional reason for opposing the Sedition Act was that it interfered with state authority, not that it violated the First Amendment. Only in the course of the debate did Jeffersonians begin to formulate a theory of free speech and press as we would recognize them. See Levy, *Emergence of a Free Press* (New York: Oxford University Press, 1985).

(5) **Query:** Even conceding that Brandeis's history might be more rhetoric than fact, to what extent did he articulate the theory or theories the First Amendment necessarily implies? What is his explication of the underlying rationale(s) of the First Amendment? *Search for truth in the marketplace of ideas?* (See Abrams v. United States [1919] (Holmes, J., dissenting); John Stuart Mill, *On Liberty* [1859]; Stanley Ingber, "The Marketplace of Ideas: A Legitimizing Myth," 1984 *Duke L.J.* 1.) *Self-government?* (See Alexander Meiklejohn, *Free Speech and Its Relation to Self-Government* [New York: Harpers, 1948]; John Hart Ely, *Democracy and Distrust* [Cambridge: Harvard University Press, 1980]; and Cass R. Sunstein, *Democracy and the Problem of Free Speech* [New York: Basic Books, 1993].) *Self-fulfillment or autonomy?* (See T.M. Scanlon, "A Theory of Freedom of Expression," 1 *Phil. & Pub. Aff.* 204 [1972].) *A synthesis of some or all of these rationales?*

(6) **Query:** Is "more speech" rather than "enforced silence" always a sufficient remedy? Consider this question in connection with pornography (see American Booksellers Ass'n, Inc. v. Hudnut [1985; reprinted below, p. 710]) and racism (see Beauharnais v. Illinois [1952; reprinted below, p. 680] and R.A.V. v. St. Paul [1992; reprinted below, p. 686]). Can such expression silence women and minorities? See Kenneth Karst, "Boundaries and Reasons: Freedom of Expression and the Subordination of Groups," 1990 *Ill. L.Rev.* 95.

"Speech is not an absolute, above and beyond control by the legislature when its judgment ... is that certain

kinds of speech are so undesirable as to warrant criminal sanction."—Chief Justice VINSON

"It is not for us to decide how we would adjust the clash
of interests which this case presents. ..."—Justice
FRANKFURTER

"I cannot agree that the First Amendment permits us to
sustain laws suppressing freedom of speech and press on
the basis of Congress' or our own notions of mere 'reasonableness.' "—Justice BLACK

"The First Amendment makes confidence in the common
sense of our people and in their maturity of judgment
the great postulate of our democracy."—Justice DOUG-
LAS

DENNIS v. UNITED STATES
341 U.S. 494, 71 S.Ct. 857, 95 L.Ed. 1137 (1951).

In 1949 a federal district court convicted eleven leaders of the Communist
party for violating §§ 2 and 3 of the Smith Act. Sec. 2 makes it a crime "to
knowingly and willfully advocate, abet, advise, or teach the duty, necessity,
desirability, or propriety of overthrowing or destroying any government in the
United States by force or violence, or by assassination of any officer of such
government"; or, with intent to cause such overthrow, to publish or display
written material advocating violent overthrow of government; or to organize or
help organize a group to carry out such aims. Sec. 3 makes it a crime to
attempt any of the actions specified in § 2. The Court of Appeals for the
Second Circuit sustained the convictions, and Dennis et al. sought certiorari
from the Supreme Court. The justices granted the writ, limited to whether the
Smith Act abridged freedom of speech or association or was "void for
vagueness."

Mr. Chief Justice **VINSON** announced the judgment of the Court and an
    opinion in which Mr. Justice **REED**, Mr. Justice **BURTON** and Mr.
    Justice **MINTON** join. ...

II

The obvious purpose of the statute is to protect existing Government, not from change by peaceable, lawful and constitutional means,
but from change by violence, revolution and terrorism. That it is within
the *power* of the Congress to protect the Government of the United
States from armed rebellion is a proposition which requires little discussion. Whatever theoretical merit there may be to the argument that
there is a "right" to rebellion against dictatorial governments is without
force where the existing structure of the government provides for peaceful and orderly change. We reject any principle of governmental help-
lessness in the face of preparation for revolution, which principle ...
carried to its logical conclusion must lead to anarchy. ... The question
with which we are concerned here is not whether Congress has such

power, but whether the *means* which it has employed conflict with the First and Fifth Amendments to the Constitution.

One of the bases for the contention that the means which Congress has employed are invalid takes the form of an attack on the face of the statute on the grounds that by its terms, it prohibits academic discussion of the merits of Marxism–Leninism, that it stifles ideas and is contrary to all concepts of a free speech and a free press. ...

The very language of the Smith Act negates th[at] interpretation. ... It is directed at advocacy, not discussion. Thus, the trial judge properly charged the jury that they could not convict if they found that petitioners did "no more than pursue peaceful studies and discussions or teaching and advocacy in the realm of ideas." ...

III ...

No important case involving free speech was decided by this Court prior to Schenck v. United States (1919). The question the Court faced was whether the evidence was sufficient to sustain the conviction. Writing for a unanimous Court, Justice Holmes stated that the "question in every case is whether the words used are used in such circumstances and are of such a nature as to create a clear and present danger that they will bring about the substantive evils that Congress has a right to prevent." ...

In several later cases involving convictions under the Criminal Espionage Act, the nub of the evidence the Court held sufficient to meet the "clear and present danger" test ... was ...: Frohwerk v. United States (1919)—publication of twelve newspaper articles attacking the war; Debs v. United States (1919)—one speech attacking United States' participation in the war; Abrams v. United States (1920)—circulation of copies of two different socialist circulars attacking the war; Schaefer v. United States (1920)—publication of a German-language newspaper with allegedly false articles, critical of capitalism and the war; Pierce v. United States (1920)—circulation of copies of a four-page pamphlet written by a clergyman, attacking the purposes of the war and United States' participation therein. ...

The rule we deduce from these cases is that where an offense is specified by a statute in nonspeech or nonpress terms, a conviction relying upon speech or press as evidence of violation may be sustained only when the speech or publication created a "clear and present danger" of attempting or accomplishing the prohibited crime, e.g., interference with enlistment. ...

The next important case before the Court in which free speech was the crux of the conflict was Gitlow v. New York (1925). There New York had made it a crime to "advocate ... the necessity or propriety of overthrowing ... the government by force. ..." The evidence of violation of the statute was that the defendant had published a Manifesto attacking the Government and capitalism. The convictions were sustained, Justices Holmes and Brandeis dissenting. The majority refused to apply the "clear and present danger" test to the specific utterance. ... Justices Holmes and Brandeis refused to accept this approach. [I]n Whitney v. California (1927) ... the Court was confronted with a conviction under the California Criminal Syndicalist statute. The Court sustained the conviction, Justices Brandeis and Holmes concurring in the result. In their concurrence they repeated that even though the legislature had designated certain speech as criminal, this could not prevent the defendant from showing that there was no danger that the substantive evil would be brought about.

Although no case subsequent to *Whitney* and *Gitlow* has expressly overruled the majority opinions in those cases, there is little doubt that subsequent opinions have inclined toward the Holmes–Brandeis rationale. ... American Communications Asso. v. Douds [1950] suggested that neither Justice Holmes nor Justice Brandeis ever envisioned that a shorthand phrase should be crystallized into a rigid rule to be applied inflexibly without regard to the circumstances of each case. Speech is not an absolute, above and beyond control by the legislature when its judgment, subject to review here, is that certain kinds of speech are so undesirable as to warrant criminal sanction. Nothing is more certain in modern society than the principle that there are no absolutes, that a name, a phrase, a standard has meaning only when associated with the considerations which gave birth to the nomenclature. ... To those who would paralyze our Government in the face of impending threat by encasing it in a semantic strait jacket we must reply that all concepts are relative.

In this case we are squarely presented with the application of the "clear and present danger" test, and must decide what that phrase imports. We first note that many of the cases in which this Court has reversed convictions by use of this or similar tests have been based on the fact that the interest which the States was attempting to protect was itself too insubstantial to warrant restriction of speech. ... Overthrow of the Government by force and violence is certainly a substantial enough interest for the Government to limit speech. Indeed this is the ultimate value of any society, for if a society cannot protect its very structure from armed internal attack, it must follow that no subordinate value can be protected. ...

Obviously, the words cannot mean that before the Government may act, it must wait until the *putsch* is about to be executed, the plans have been laid and the signal is awaited. ... Certainly an attempt to overthrow the Government by force, even though doomed from the outset because of inadequate numbers or power of the revolutionists, is a sufficient evil for Congress to prevent. The damage which such attempts create both physically and politically to a nation makes it impossible to measure the validity in terms of the probability of success, or the immediacy of a successful attempt. In the instant case the trial judge charged the jury that they could not convict unless they found that petitioners intended to overthrow the Government "as speedily as circumstances would permit." This does not mean, and could not properly mean, that they would not strike until there was certainty of success. What was meant was that the revolutionists would strike when they thought the time was ripe. We must therefore reject the contention that success or probability of success is the criterion.

The situation with which Justices Holmes and Brandeis were concerned in *Gitlow* was a comparatively isolated event, bearing little relation in their minds to any substantial threat to the safety of the community. ... They were not confronted with any situation comparable to the instant one—the development of an apparatus designed and dedicated to the overthrow of the Government in the context of world crisis after crisis.

Chief Judge Learned Hand, writing for the majority below, interpreted the phrase as follows: "In each case [courts] must ask whether the gravity of the 'evil,' discounted by its improbability, justifies such invasion of free speech as is necessary to avoid the danger." We adopt this statement of the rule. ...

The formation by petitioners of such a highly organized conspiracy, with rigidly disciplined members subject to call when the leaders, these petitioners, felt that the time had come for action, coupled with the inflammable nature of world conditions, similar uprisings in other countries, and the touch-and-go nature of our relations with countries with whom petitioners were in the very least ideologically attuned, convince us that their convictions were justified on this score. And this analysis disposes of the contention that a conspiracy to advocate, as distinguished from the advocacy itself, cannot be constitutionally restrained, because it comprises only the preparation. It is the existence of the conspiracy which creates the danger. ... If the ingredients of the reaction are present, we cannot bind the Government to wait until the catalyst is added. ...

Affirmed.

Mr. Justice **CLARK** took no part in the consideration or decision of this case.

Mr. Justice **FRANKFURTER** concurring in affirmance of the judgment.
. . .

The demands of free speech in a democratic society as well as the interest in national security are better served by candid and informed weighing of the competing interests, within the confines of the judicial process, than by announcing dogmas too inflexible for the non-Euclidian problems to be solved.

But how are competing interests to be assessed? Since they are not subject to quantitative ascertainment, the issue necessarily resolves itself into asking who is to make the adjustment?—who is to balance the relevant factors and ascertain which interest is in the circumstances to prevail? Full responsibility for the choice cannot be given to the courts.

Courts are not representative bodies. They are not designed to be a good reflex of a democratic society. Their judgment is best informed, and therefore most dependable, within narrow limits. Their essential quality is detachment, founded on independence. History teaches that the independence of the judiciary is jeopardized when courts become embroiled in the passions of the day and assume primary responsibility in choosing between competing political, economic and social pressures.

Primary responsibility for adjusting the interests which compete in the situation before us of necessity belongs to the Congress. ... We are to set aside the judgment of those whose duty it is to legislate only if there is no reasonable basis for it. Sinking Fund Cases [1879]; Mugler v. Kansas [1887]; United States v. Carolene Products [1938]. We are to determine whether a statute is sufficiently definite to meet the constitutional requirements of due process, and whether it respects the safeguards against undue concentration of authority secured by separation of power. United States v. Cohen Grocery [1921]. We must assure fairness of procedure. And, of course, the proceedings in a particular case before us must have the warrant of substantial proof. Beyond these powers we must not go. ... Above all we must remember that this Court's power of judicial review is not "an exercise of the powers of a super-legislature." ...

Some members of the Court—and at times a majority—have done more. They have suggested that our function in reviewing statutes restricting freedom of expression differs sharply from our normal duty in sitting in judgment on legislation. ... It has been suggested, with the casualness of a footnote, that such legislation is not presumptively valid, see Carolene Products, and it has been weightily reiterated that freedom of speech has a "preferred position" among constitutional safeguards. Kovacs v. Cooper [1949].

Free speech cases are not an exception to the principle that we are not legislators, that direct policy-making is not our province. How best to reconcile competing interests is the business of legislatures, and the balance they strike is a judgment not to be displaced by ours, but to be respected unless outside the pale of fair judgment. ...

On the one hand is the interest in security. The Communist Party was not designed by these defendants as an ordinary political party. ...

On the other hand is the interest in free speech. The right to exert all governmental powers in aid of maintaining our institutions and resisting their physical overthrow does not include intolerance of opinions and speech that cannot do harm although opposed and perhaps alien to dominant, traditional opinion. The treatment of its minorities, especially their legal position, is among the most searching tests of the level of civilization attained by a society. It is better for those who have almost unlimited power of government in their hands to err on the side of freedom. We have enjoyed so much freedom for so long that we are perhaps in danger of forgetting how much blood it cost to establish the Bill of Rights. ...

... Suppressing advocates of overthrow inevitably will also silence critics who do not advocate overthrow but fear that their criticism may be so construed. ... It is a sobering fact that in sustaining the conviction before us we can hardly escape restriction on the interchange of ideas. ... Freedom of expression is the well-spring of our civilization—the civilization we seek to maintain and further by recognizing the right of Congress to put some limitation upon expression. Such are the paradoxes of life. ...

It is not for us to decide how we would adjust the clash of interests which this case presents were the primary responsibility for reconciling it ours. Congress has determined that the danger created by advocacy of overthrow justifies the ensuing restriction on freedom of speech. The determination was made after due deliberation, and the seriousness of the congressional purpose is attested by the volume of legislation passed to effectuate the same ends.

Can we then say that the judgment Congress exercised was denied it by the Constitution? Can we establish a constitutional doctrine which forbids the elected representatives of the people to make this choice? Can we hold that the First Amendment deprives Congress of what it deemed necessary for the Government's protection? To make validity of legislation depend on judicial reading of events still in the womb of time—a forecast, that is, of the outcome of forces at best appreciated only with knowledge of the topmost secrets of nations—is to charge the judiciary with duties beyond its equipment. ...

Civil liberties draw at best only limited strength from legal guaranties. Preoccupation by our people with the constitutionality, instead of with the wisdom, of legislation or of executive action is preoccupation with a false value. ... Focusing attention on constitutionality tends to make constitutionality synonymous with wisdom. When legislation touches freedom of thought and freedom of speech, such a tendency is a formidable enemy of the free spirit. Much that should be rejected as illiberal, because repressive and envenoming, may well be not unconstitutional. The ultimate reliance for the deepest needs of civilization must be found outside their vindication in courts of law; apart from all else, judges, howsoever they may conscientiously seek to discipline themselves against it, unconsciously are too apt to be moved by the deep undercurrents of public feeling. ... The mark of a truly civilized man is confidence in the strength and security derived from the inquiring mind. ... Without open minds there can be no open society. And if society be not open the spirit of man is mutilated and becomes enslaved. ...

Mr. Justice **JACKSON**, concurring. ...

This prosecution is the latest of never-ending, because never successful, quests for some legal formula that will secure an existing order against revolutionary radicalism. It requires us to reappraise, in the light of our own times and conditions, constitutional doctrines devised under other circumstances to strike a balance between authority and liberty. ...

The highest degree of constitutional protection is due to the individual acting without conspiracy. But even an individual cannot claim that the Constitution protects him in advocating or teaching overthrow of government by force or violence. I should suppose no one would doubt that Congress has power to make such attempted overthrow a crime. But the contention is that one has the constitutional right to work up a public desire and a will to do what it is a crime to attempt. I think direct incitement by speech or writing can be made a crime, and I think there can be a conviction without also proving that the odds favored its success by 99 to 1, or some other extremely high ratio. ...

Mr. Justice **BLACK,** dissenting. ...

... These petitioners were not charged with an attempt to overthrow the Government. They were not charged with overt acts of any kind designed to overthrow the Government. They were not even charged with saying anything or writing anything designed to overthrow the Government. The charge was that they agreed to assemble and to talk and publish certain ideas at a later date: The indictment is that they conspired to organize the Communist Party and to use speech or newspapers and other publications in the future to teach and advocate the forcible overthrow of the Government. No matter how it is worded, this is a virulent form of prior censorship of speech and press, which I believe the First Amendment forbids. ...

So long as this Court exercises the power of judicial review ... I cannot agree that the First Amendment permits us to sustain laws suppressing freedom of speech and press on the basis of Congress' or our own notions of mere "reasonableness." Such a doctrine waters down the First Amendment so that it amounts to little more than an admonition to Congress. The Amendment as so construed is not likely to protect any but those "safe" or orthodox views which rarely need its protection. ...

Public opinion being what it now is, few will protest the conviction of these Communist petitioners. There is hope, however, that in calmer times, when present pressures, passions and fears subside, this or some later Court will restore the First Amendment liberties to the high preferred place where they belong in a free society.

Mr. Justice **DOUGLAS,** dissenting.

If this were a case where those who claimed protection under the First Amendment were teaching the techniques of sabotage, the assassination of the President, the filching of documents from public files, the planting of bombs, the art of street warfare, and the like, I would have no doubts. The freedom to speak is not absolute; the teaching of methods of terror and other seditious conduct should be beyond the pale along with obscenity and immorality. This case was argued as if those were the facts. ...

So far as the present record is concerned, what petitioners did was to organize people to teach and themselves teach the Marxist–Leninist doctrine contained chiefly in four books: *Foundations of Leninism* by Stalin (1924), *The Communist Manifesto* by Marx and Engels (1848), *State and Revolution* by Lenin (1917), *History of the Communist Party of the Soviet Union* (B) (1939). ...

How it can be said that there is a clear and present danger that this advocacy will succeed is, therefore, a mystery. Some nations less resilient than the United States, where illiteracy is high and where democratic traditions are only budding, might have to take drastic steps and jail these men for merely speaking their creed. But in America they are miserable merchants of unwanted ideas. ... The fact that their ideas are abhorrent does not make them powerful. ...

The First Amendment provides that "Congress shall make no law ... abridging the freedom of speech." The Constitution provides no exception. This does not mean, however, that the Nation need hold its hand until it is in such weakened condition that there is no time to protect itself from incitement to revolution. Seditious conduct can always be punished. But the command of the First Amendment is so clear that we should not allow Congress to call a halt to free speech except in the extreme case of peril from the speech itself. The First Amendment makes confidence in the common sense of our people and in their maturity of judgment the great postulate of our democracy. ... The First Amendment reflects the philosophy of Jefferson "that it is time enough for the rightful purposes of civil government for its officers to interfere when principles break out into overt acts against peace and good order." The political censor has no place in our public debates. ...

Editors' Notes

(1) **Query:** Was Vinson's formulation for the plurality of the clear and present danger test (adopting the "gravity of the evil" test developed by Chief Judge Learned Hand of the Court of Appeals for the Second Circuit) as protective of freedom of speech as Brandeis's formulation in his concurring opinion in *Whitney*? For a further development of Hand's test, which was a variation on his theory of negligence law, see Richard A. Posner, "Free Speech in an Economic Perspective," 20 *Suffolk U.L.Rev.* 1 (1986).

(2) **Query:** The clear and present danger test would seem to require that a court analyze two factors: (a) how clear and present, or imminent, or probable, is the danger and (b) how serious is the evil that the government is seeking to avert. Did Vinson analyze both of these factors? In what way(s) was Vinson's version of clear and present danger distinguishable from the "bad tendency" test of *Whitney*? Which of the approaches used by the various opinion writers would most and least restrict free speech?

(3) **Query:** Exactly what, according to the justices in the majority in *Dennis*, was the serious evil in question here?

(4) **Query:** Did the opinions on the opposing sides in *Dennis* presuppose competing theories of democracy? If so, how did these theories differ? Frankfurter's concurring opinion pointed to an alleged "paradox of life" (or of democracy) as justifying these convictions for advocacy of overthrow: To preserve democracy and freedom of expression, we must limit freedom of expression. To what extent was he correct? For a comparative analysis, see Walter F. Murphy, "Excluding Political Parties: Problems for Democratic and Constitutional Theory," in Paul Kirchhof and Donald P. Kommers, eds., *Germany and Its Basic Law* (Baden–Baden: Nomos, 1993).

(5) **Query:** John Hart Ely has argued that Frankfurter's approach to the First Amendment—which he characterizes as "ad hoc balancing tempered with substantial deference to the legislative judgment"—"mocks our commitment to an open political process." *Democracy and Distrust* (Cambridge: Harvard University Press, 1980), pp. 108–109. Is this charge accurate?

(6) Vinson cited American Communications Ass'n v. Douds (1950), which, by a 4–4 vote, had sustained the Taft–Hartley Act's requirement that labor union officials swear not only that they were not members of the Communist party but also that they did not *believe* in its doctrines. Congress repealed this section in 1959; and in 1965, reviewing a conviction for perjury under the old section, the Court in effect reversed *Douds,* holding that the requirement of the oath constituted a bill of attainder. United States v. Brown (1965).

(7) For a perceptive analysis of *Dennis,* see: C. Herman Pritchett, *Civil Liberties and the Vinson Court* (Chicago: University of Chicago Press, 1954), pp. 71–79.

————

"**The distinction between advocacy of abstract doctrine and advocacy directed at promoting unlawful action is one that has been consistently recognized in the opinions of this Court. ...**"—Justice HARLAN

"**[T]he First Amendment forbids Congress to punish people for talking about public affairs, whether or not such discussion incites to action, legal or illegal.**"—Justice BLACK

"**I have studied the section of the opinion concerning the instructions and frankly its 'artillery of words' leaves me confused as to why the majority concludes that the charge as given was insufficient.**"—Justice CLARK

YATES v. UNITED STATES
354 U.S. 298, 77 S.Ct. 1064, 1 L.Ed.2d 1356 (1957).

Shortly after *Dennis,* the Department of Justice obtained convictions under the Smith Act against fourteen lower echelon leaders of the Communist party.

The specific charges and evidence were quite similar to those lodged in *Dennis*. The court of appeals affirmed and the Supreme Court granted certiorari.

Mr. Justice **HARLAN** delivered the opinion of the Court. ...

[The first part of the opinion dealt with the meaning of the word "organize" in the Smith Act. Harlan concluded that it meant only the initial founding of a group. Thus, because the Smith Act was subject to a three-year statute of limitations, the Communist party had been "organized" in 1945 (it was disbanded during World War II), and the indictments had not been obtained until 1951, petitioners could not be tried for violating that section of the Act.]

II. Instructions to the Jury

Petitioners contend that the instructions to the jury were fatally defective in that the trial court refused to charge that, in order to convict, the jury must find that the advocacy which the defendants conspired to promote was a kind calculated to "incite" persons to action for the forcible overthrow of the Government. It is argued that advocacy of forcible overthrow as mere *abstract doctrine* is within the free speech protection of the First Amendment; that the Smith Act, consistently with that constitutional provision, must be taken as proscribing only the sort of advocacy which incites to illegal *action*. ...

There can be no doubt from the record that in so instructing the jury the court regarded as immaterial, and intended to withdraw from the jury's consideration, any issue as to the character of the advocacy in terms of its capacity to stir listeners to forcible action. ... We are thus faced with the question whether the Smith Act prohibits advocacy and teaching of forcible overthrow as an abstract principle, divorced from any effort to instigate action to that end, so long as such advocacy or teaching is engaged in with evil intent. We hold that it does not.

The distinction between advocacy of abstract doctrine and advocacy directed at promoting unlawful action is one that has been consistently recognized in the opinions of this Court, beginning with Fox v. Washington [1915] and Schenck v. United States [1919]. This distinction was heavily underscored in Gitlow v. New York [1925]. ...

We need not, however, decide the issue before us in terms of constitutional compulsion, for our first duty is to construe this statute. In doing so we should not assume that Congress chose to disregard a constitutional danger zone so clearly marked, or that it used the words "advocate" and "teach" in their ordinary dictionary meanings when they had already been construed as terms of art carrying a special and limited connotation. ... Cf. United States v. Carolene Products [1938]. The legislative history of the Smith Act and related bills shows beyond all question that Congress was aware of the distinction between the advocacy or teaching of abstract doctrine and the advocacy or teaching of action, and that it did not intend to disregard it. The statute was aimed at the advocacy and teaching of concrete action for the forcible overthrow of the Government, and not of principles divorced from action.

The Government's reliance on this Court's decision in Dennis v. United States (1951) is misplaced. The jury instructions which were refused here were given there, and were referred to by this Court as requiring "the jury to find the facts *essential* to establish the substantive crime." ... It is true that at one point in the late Chief Justice's opinion it is stated that the Smith Act "is directed at advocacy, not discussion," ... but it is clear that the reference was to advocacy of action, not ideas, for in the very next sentence the opinion emphasizes that the jury was properly instructed that there could be no conviction for "advocacy in the realm of ideas." The two concurring opinions in that case likewise emphasize the distinction with which we are concerned. ...

In light of the foregoing we are unable to regard the District Court's charge upon this aspect of the case as adequate. The jury was never told that the Smith Act does not denounce advocacy in the sense of preaching abstractly the forcible overthrow of the Government. ... The essential distinction is that those to whom the advocacy is addressed must be urged to *do* something, now or in the future, rather than merely to *believe* in something. ...

III.   The Evidence

The determinations already made require a reversal of these convictions. Nevertheless, in the exercise of our power ... to "direct the entry of such appropriate judgment ... as may be just under the circumstances," we have conceived it to be our duty to scrutinize this lengthy record with care, in order to determine whether the way should be left open for a new trial of all or some of these petitioners. ...

... [W]hen it comes to Party advocacy or teaching in the sense of a call to forcible action at some future time we cannot but regard this record as strikingly deficient. At best this voluminous record shows but a half dozen or so scattered incidents which even under the loosest standards could be deemed to show such advocacy. Most of these were not connected with any of the petitioners, or occurred many years before the period covered by the indictment. We are unable to regard this sporadic showing as sufficient to justify viewing the Communist Party as the nexus between these petitioners and the conspiracy charged. We need scarcely say that however much one may abhor even the abstract preaching of forcible overthrow of government, or believe that forcible overthrow is the ultimate purpose to which the Communist Party is dedicated, it is upon the evidence in the record that the petitioners must be judged in this case. ...

[The Court then found the evidence too insubstantial to permit the retrial of five of the defendants and so directed an acquittal. The Court found the evidence against the other nine to be sufficiently weighty to allow the government to seek a retrial if it wished.]

Mr. Justice **BURTON,** concurring in the result. ...

Mr. Justice **BRENNAN** and Mr. Justice **WHITTAKER** took no part in the consideration or decision of this case.

Mr. Justice **BLACK,** with whom Mr. Justice **DOUGLAS** joins, concurring in part and dissenting in part.

... In my judgment the statutory provisions on which these prosecutions are based abridge freedom of speech, press and assembly. ...

Since the Court proceeds on the assumption that the statutory provisions involved are valid, however, I feel free to express my views about the issues it considers. *First.*—I agree with Part I of the Court's opinion that deals with the statutory term, "organize". ... *Second.*—I also agree with the Court insofar as it holds that the trial judge erred in instructing that persons could be punished under the Smith Act for teaching and advocating forceful overthrow as an abstract principle. But ... I cannot agree that the instruction which the Court indicates it might approve is constitutionally permissible. ... I believe that the First Amendment forbids Congress to punish people for talking about public affairs, whether or not such discussion incites to action, legal or illegal. ... *Third.*—I also agree with the Court that [five of the] petitioners ... should be ordered acquitted. ... I think the same action should also be taken as to the remaining nine. ...

In essence, petitioners were tried upon the charge that they believe in and want to foist upon this country ... a despicable form of authoritarian government in which voices criticizing the existing order are summarily silenced. I fear that the present type of prosecutions are more in line with the philosophy of authoritarian government than with that expressed by our First Amendment.

Doubtlessly, dictators have to stamp out causes and beliefs which they deem subversive to their evil regimes. But governmental suppression of causes and beliefs seems to me to be the very antithesis of what our Constitution stands for. ... The First Amendment provides the only kind of security system that can preserve a free government—one that leaves the way wide open for people to favor, discuss, advocate or incite causes and doctrines however obnoxious and antagonistic such views may be to the rest of us.

Mr. Justice **CLARK** dissenting. ...

The petitioners ... were engaged in this conspiracy with the defendants in *Dennis.* ... The conspiracy includes the same group of defendants as in the Dennis case though petitioners here occupied a lower echelon in the party hierarchy. They, nevertheless, served in the same

army and were engaged in the same mission. The convictions here were
based upon evidence closely paralleling that adduced in *Dennis*. ...

... [This] Court has freed five of the convicted petitioners and
ordered new trials for the remaining nine. As to the five, it says that
the evidence is "clearly insufficient." I agree with the Court of Appeals,
the District Court, and the jury that the evidence showed guilt beyond a
reasonable doubt. ... In any event, this Court should not acquit anyone
here. In its long history I find no case in which an acquittal has been
ordered by this Court solely on the *facts*. It is somewhat late to start in
now usurping the function of the jury. ...

... I have studied the section of the opinion concerning the instructions and frankly its "artillery of words" leaves me confused as to why
the majority concludes that the charge as given was insufficient. I
thought that *Dennis* merely held that a charge was sufficient where it
requires a finding that "the Party advocates the theory that there is a
duty and necessity to overthrow the Government by force and violence
... not as a prophetic insight or as a bit of ... speculation, but as a
program for winning adherents and as a policy to be translated into
action" as soon as the circumstances permit. ... I notice, however, that
to the majority

> The essence of the *Dennis* holding was that indoctrination of a
> group in preparation for future violent action, as well as exhortation to
> immediate action, by advocacy found to be directed to "action for the
> accomplishment" of forcible overthrow, to violence "as a rule or princi-
> ple of action," and employing "language of incitement," ... is not
> constitutionally protected when the group is of sufficient size and
> cohesiveness, is sufficiently oriented toward action, and other circum-
> stances are such as reasonably to justify apprehension that action will
> occur.

I have read this statement over and over but do not seem to grasp
its meaning for I see no resemblances between it and what the respected
Chief Justice wrote in *Dennis*, nor do I find any such theory in the
concurring opinions. As I see it, the trial judge charged in essence all
that was required under the *Dennis* opinions. ...

Editors' Notes

(1) **Query:** To what extent does Harlan's distinction between "advocacy
of abstract doctrine" and "advocacy directed at promoting unlawful action"
conform to the plain words or even general sense of the Smith Act? To the
plain words of the First Amendment? To what extent does that distinction
make sense in the real world? Would an interpreter who took seriously a
theory of "reinforcing representative democracy" find that reading Harlan's
distinction into the Smith Act preserved the statute's constitutionality?

(2) Note the narrowness of Harlan's opinion. He managed to encapsu-
late, perhaps even disguise, critical constitutional questions about protection
of democratic processes within statutory interpretation. What sort of approach
to constitutional interpretation does this style manifest?

(3) Why the shift between *Dennis* and *Yates?* Changes among the justices had some effect. John Marshall Harlan, II, had replaced Robert H. Jackson; and Earl Warren, whose chief justiceship was to become synonymous with civil liberty, had succeeded Fred Vinson. Two other members of the majority in *Dennis,* Sherman Minton and Stanley Reed, had retired, though their replacements, William J. Brennan, Jr., and Charles E. Whittaker, did not sit in *Yates.* Thus only two of the six members of the majority in *Dennis,* Harold Burton and Felix Frankfurter, were still on the Court when *Yates* was decided. Both of the dissenters in *Dennis,* Black and Douglas, were still sitting. Frankfurter switched sides, at least to the extent of joining Harlan's "constitutional interpretation as statutory interpretation." Burton also switched, though he had reservations. Tom Clark, who had been attorney general when *Dennis* began, had taken no part in that ruling, though his dissent in *Yates* indicates how he would have voted. Brennan, of course, became closely allied with the views of Warren, Douglas, and Black on the First Amendment.

There may have been other reasons for change. In 1951, the anti-Communist hysteria fanned by Richard Nixon and Joseph McCarthy was near its peak. Six years later, the mood of the country had sobered. It is unlikely that judges were unaffected by either set of sentiments. See Justice Cardozo's comments on this point, above, p. 627.

(4) When the justices met in conference after *Yates* had been argued, the vote was four (Reed, Burton, Minton, and Clark) to affirm the convictions, three (Warren, Black, and Douglas) to reverse, and two justices (Frankfurter and Harlan) "passed." Warren suggested postponing a final vote for a few weeks. During that interval Minton retired and Frankfurter and Harlan joined Warren et al. to make the vote 5–3 to reverse. Warren assigned the task of writing the opinion of the Court to Harlan, hoping that because of his middle position he might persuade some of the dissenters to join him. By the time the decision was announced, Reed had also retired, leaving the final vote 5–2. We recite this history because it helps explain some other rulings, notably Barenblatt v. United States (1959; reprinted below, p. 803), in which Harlan and Frankfurter apparently flipflopped. The point is that they were never firm members of the liberal bloc of the Warren Court (at that time Warren, Black, and Douglas, and when Minton retired Brennan, and some years later Goldberg then Fortas and Marshall). See the analysis in Bernard Schwartz, *Super Chief* (New York: New York University Press, 1983), pp. 232–234.

(5) After *Yates,* the Department of Justice dropped all prosecutions under the Smith Act that involved charges of advocacy, did not retry any of the nine defendants whose retrial the Supreme Court had allowed, and through 1995 had not again used these clauses. The reactions to *Yates* varied. Communists were delighted. "We rejoice. Victory is, indeed, sweet," *The People's World* crowed. Conservatives wept. "The boys in the Kremlin," the *Chicago Tribune* lamented, "may wonder why they need a 5th column in the United States so long as the Supreme Court is determined to be so helpful." Reaction in Congress took the form of a massive attack on the Court. For details, see C. Herman Pritchett, *Congress versus the Supreme Court* (Minneapolis: University of Minnesota Press, 1961), and Walter F. Murphy, *Congress and the Court* (Chicago: University of Chicago Press, 1962). After several

legislative battles, Congress amended the Smith Act to define "organize" to include the day-to-day operations of maintaining a group.

"Where First Amendment rights are asserted to bar governmental interrogation resolution of the issue always involves a balancing by the courts of the competing private and public interests at stake."—Justice HARLAN

"This is closely akin to the notion that neither the First Amendment nor any other provision of the Bill of Rights should be enforced unless the Court believes it is *reasonable* to do so."—Justice BLACK

BARENBLATT v. UNITED STATES
360 U.S. 109, 79 S.Ct. 1081, 3 L.Ed.2d 1115 (1959).

This case, involving a clash between Barenblatt's right under the First Amendment to be silent about his political associations and a claim by a congressional committee to be able to obtain answers from him about his participation in the Communist party, is reprinted below, p. 803.

"[T]he constitutional guarantees of free speech and free press do not permit a State to forbid or proscribe advocacy of the use of force or of law violation except where such advocacy is directed to inciting or producing imminent lawless action and is likely to incite or produce such action."—The COURT

"I see no place in the regime of the First Amendment for any 'clear and present danger' test, whether strict and tight as some would make it, or free-wheeling as the Court in *Dennis* rephrased it."—Justice DOUGLAS

BRANDENBURG v. OHIO
395 U.S. 444, 89 S.Ct. 1827, 23 L.Ed.2d 430 (1969).

Ohio's Criminal Syndicalism Act made it a crime to "advocate ... the duty, necessity, or propriety of crime, sabotage, violence, or unlawful methods of terrorism as a means of accomplishing industrial or political reform" or to "voluntarily assemble with any society, group, or assemblage of persons to teach or advocate the doctrines of political syndicalism." Clarence Brandenburg, a leader of the Ku Klux Klan, was convicted under this statute for organizing Klan meetings and arranging for their filming and broadcasting. All of the participants were hooded, but only some were armed. Included in the speeches were such remarks as, "Personally, I believe the nigger should be returned to Africa, the Jew to Israel," and: "We're not a revengent organization, but if our President, our Congress, our Supreme Court continues to suppress the white, Caucasian race, it's possible that there might have to be some revengeance taken."

The Ohio appellate courts sustained the conviction and Brandenburg appealed to the U.S. Supreme Court.

PER CURIAM. ...

... In 1927, this Court sustained the constitutionality of California's Criminal Syndicalism Act, the text of which is quite similar to that of the laws of Ohio. Whitney v. California. ... But *Whitney* has been thoroughly discredited by later decisions. See Dennis v. United States [1951]. These later decisions have fashioned the principle that the constitutional guarantees of free speech and free press do not permit a State to forbid or proscribe advocacy of the use of force or of law violation except where such advocacy is directed to inciting or producing imminent lawless action and is likely to incite or produce such action. As we said in Noto v. United States (1961), "the mere abstract teaching ... of the moral propriety or even moral necessity for a resort to force and violence, is not the same as preparing a group for violent action and steeling it to such action." See also Herndon v. Lowry (1937); Bond v. Floyd (1966). A statute which fails to draw this distinction impermissibly intrudes upon the freedoms guaranteed by the First and Fourteenth Amendments. It sweeps within its condemnation speech which our Constitution has immunized from governmental control. Cf. Yates v. United States (1957); DeJonge v. Oregon (1937); Stromberg v. California (1931).

Measured by this test, Ohio's Criminal Syndicalism Act cannot be sustained. ... Neither the indictment nor the trial judge's instructions to the jury in any way refined the statute's bald definition of the crime in terms of mere advocacy not distinguished from incitement to imminent lawless action. ... Such a statute falls within the condemnation of the First and Fourteenth Amendments. The contrary teaching of *Whitney* cannot be supported, and that decision is therefore overruled.

Reversed.

Mr. Justice **BLACK,** concurring. ...

Mr. Justice **DOUGLAS,** concurring. ...

The "clear and present danger" test was adumbrated by Mr. Justice Holmes in a case arising during World War I—a war "declared" by the Congress, not by the Chief Executive. The case was Schenck v. United States [1919], where the defendant was charged with attempts to cause insubordination in the military and obstruction of enlistment. The pamphlets that were distributed urged resistance to the draft, denounced conscription, and impugned the motives of those backing the war effort. The First Amendment was tendered as a defense. Mr. Justice Holmes in rejecting that defense said:

The question in every case is whether the words used are used in such circumstances and are of such a nature as to create a clear and present danger that they will bring about the substantive evils that Congress has a right to prevent. It is a question of proximity and degree.

Frohwerk v. United States [1919], also authored by Mr. Justice Holmes, involved prosecution and punishment for publication of articles very critical of the war effort in World War I. *Schenck* was referred to as a conviction for obstructing security "by words of persuasion." And the conviction in *Frohwerk* was sustained because "the circulation of the paper was in quarters where a little breath would be enough to kindle a flame." Debs v. United States [1919], was the third of the trilogy of the 1918 Term. Debs was convicted of speaking in opposition to the war where his "opposition was so expressed that its natural and intended effect would be to obstruct recruiting."

If that was intended and if, in all the circumstances, that would be its probable effect, it would not be protected by reason of its being part of a general program and expressions of a general and conscientious belief.

In the 1919 Term, the Court applied the *Schenck* doctrine to affirm the convictions of other dissidents in World War I. Abrams v. United States [1919] was one instance. Mr. Justice Holmes, with whom Mr. Justice Brandeis concurred, dissented. While adhering to *Schenck*, he did not think that on the facts a case for overriding the First Amendment had been made out:

It is only the present danger of immediate evil or an intent to bring it about that warrants Congress in setting a limit to the expression of opinion where private rights are not concerned. Congress certainly cannot forbid all effort to change the mind of the country.

... Mr. Justice Holmes, though never formally abandoning the "clear and present danger" test, moved closer to the First Amendment ideal when he said in dissent in Gitlow v. New York [1925]:

Every idea is an indictment. It offers itself for belief and if believed it is acted on unless some other belief outweighs it or some failure of energy stifles the movement at its birth. The only difference between the expression of an opinion and an incitement in the narrower sense is the speaker's enthusiasm for the result. Eloquence may set fire to reason. But whatever may be thought of the redundant discourse before us it had no chance of starting a present conflagration. If in the long run the beliefs expressed in proletarian dictatorship are destined to be accepted by the dominant forces of the community, the only meaning of free speech is that they should be given their chance and have their way.

We have never been faithful to the philosophy of that dissent. ...

My own view is quite different. I see no place in the regime of the First Amendment for any "clear and present danger" test, whether strict and tight as some would make it, or free-wheeling as the Court in *Dennis* rephrased it.

When one reads the opinions closely and sees when and how the "clear and present danger" test has been applied, great misgivings are aroused. First, the threats were often loud but always puny and made serious only by judges so wedded to the status quo that critical analysis made them nervous. Second, the test was so twisted and perverted in *Dennis* as to make the trial of those teachers of Marxism an all-out political trial which was part and parcel of the cold war that has eroded substantial parts of the First Amendment.

Action is often a method of expression and within the protection of the First Amendment. Suppose one tears up his own copy of the Constitution in eloquent protest to a decision of this Court. May he be indicted? ... Last Term the Court held in United States v. O'Brien [1968] that a registrant under Selective Service who burned his draft card in protest of the war in Vietnam could be prosecuted. The First Amendment was tendered as a defense and rejected, the Court saying:

> The issuance of certificates indicating the registration and eligibility classification of individuals is a legitimate and substantial administrative aid in the functioning of this system. And legislation to insure the continuing availability of issued certificates serves a legitimate and substantial purpose in the system's administration.

But O'Brien was not prosecuted for not having his draft card available when asked for by a federal agent. He was indicted, tried, and convicted for burning the card. And this Court's affirmance of that conviction was not, with all respect, consistent with the First Amendment.

The act of praying often involves body posture and movement as well as utterances. It is nonetheless protected by the Free Exercise Clause. Picketing, as we have said on numerous occasions, is "free speech plus." ... That means it can be regulated when it comes to the "plus" or "action" side of the protest. It can be regulated as to the number of pickets and the place and hours, because traffic and other community problems would otherwise suffer.

But none of these considerations are implicated in the symbolic protest of the Vietnam war in the burning of a draft card.

One's beliefs have long been thought to be sanctuaries which government could not invade. *Barenblatt* is one example of the ease with which that sanctuary can be violated. The lines drawn by the Court between the criminal act of being an "active" Communist and the innocent act of being a nominal or inactive Communist mark the difference only between deep and abiding belief and casual or uncertain belief. But I think that all matters of belief are beyond the reach of subpoenas or the probings of investigators. That is why the invasions of privacy made by investigating committees were notoriously unconstitutional. That is the deep-seated fault in the infamous loyalty-security hearings which, since 1947 when President Truman launched them, have processed 20,000,000 men and women. Those hearings were primarily concerned with one's thoughts, ideas, beliefs, and convictions. They were the most blatant violations of the First Amendment we have ever known.

The line between what is permissible and not subject to control and what may be made impermissible and subject to regulation is the line between ideas and overt acts. The example usually given by those who would punish speech is the case of one who falsely shouts fire in a crowded theatre. This is, however, a classic case where speech is brigaded with action. They are indeed inseparable and a prosecution can be launched for the overt acts actually caused. Apart from rare instances of that kind, speech is, I think, immune from prosecution. Certainly there is no constitutional line between advocacy of abstract ideas as in *Yates* and advocacy of political action as in *Scales*. The quality of advocacy turns on the depth of the conviction; and government has no power to invade that sanctuary of belief and conscience.

Editors' Notes

(1) **Query:** To what extent did the Court in this case rely on a *doctrinal approach* to constitutional interpretation? Justice Douglas? To the extent the majority did so rely, how strong is its claim that previous decisions, such as *Dennis*, "have fashioned the principle" adopted in *Brandenburg*? See Hans Linde, " 'Clear and Present Danger' Reexamined: Dissonance in the *Brandenburg* Concerto," 22 *Stan.L.Rev.* 1163 (1970).

(2) What is the argument that *Brandenburg* provides an example of the Court's using *reinforcing representative democracy* as an approach to constitutional interpretation? For Douglas' so doing?

(3) Much of Douglas' opinion did not directly pertain to *Brandenburg*. The case arose during the war in Vietnam, a conflict he thought unconstitutionally waged by the President, and was accompanied by what he considered to be echoes of the repression of free speech and even thought that had occurred during the late 1940s and early 1950s, at the outset of the Cold War. See also his dissent in United States v. O'Brien (1968; reprinted below, p. 721).

(4) **Query:** How would a constitutionalist respond to Holmes's dissenting statement in *Gitlow*, quoted by Douglas: "If in the long run the beliefs expressed in proletarian dictatorship are destined to be accepted by the dominant forces of the community, the only meaning of free speech is that they should be given their chance and have their way." Is constitutionalism neutral as to results? Is democratic theory quite so neutral as Holmes? Would constitutionalism set limits to political communication different from those of democratic theory?

(5) **Query:** Is a hyperbolic threat against the President constitutionally protected speech? See Watts v. United States (1969), where, at a political rally near the Washington Monument during the Vietnam War, Robert Watts allegedly stated: "If they ever make me carry a rifle the first man I want to get my sights on is L[yndon]. B. J[ohnson]. ..."

Watts was convicted of violating a 1917 federal statute forbidding any person "knowingly and willfully" to make "any threat to take the life of or to inflict bodily harm upon the President of the United States." The Court conceded that the statute "is constitutional on its face," but it reversed the conviction on the ground that "the kind of political hyperbole" indulged in by

Watts did not fit within the statutory term "threat." The justices explained: "[W]e must interpret the language Congress chose 'against the background of a profound national commitment to the principle that debate on public issues should be uninhibited, robust, and wide-open, and that it may well include vehement, caustic, and sometimes unpleasantly sharp attacks on government and public officials'" (quoting *New York Times v. Sullivan* [1964; reprinted above, p. 634]). The Court concluded that Watts's "only offense here was 'a kind of very crude offensive method of stating a political opposition. ...'"

(6) In NAACP v. Claiborne Hardware (1982), the Court unanimously reversed a damage award against alleged participants in an economic boycott by African Americans against white merchants in Mississippi. "If we catch any of you going in any of them racist stores," Charles Evers, the leader of the boycott, had publicly stated, "we're gonna break your damn neck." The Court held that "mere *advocacy* of the use of force or violence does not remove speech from the protection of the First Amendment." And the fact that no acts of violence occurred until weeks after the speech indicated Mr. Evers's "emotionally charged rhetoric ... did not transcend the bounds of protected speech set forth in *Brandenburg*."

III. CATEGORIES OF UNPROTECTED EXPRESSION

A. Fighting Words

"[T]he right of free speech is not absolute at all times and under all circumstances. There are certain well-defined and narrowly limited classes of speech, the prevention and punishment of which have never been thought to raise any Constitutional problem."

CHAPLINSKY v. NEW HAMPSHIRE
315 U.S. 568, 62 S.Ct. 766, 86 L.Ed. 1031 (1942).

Walter Chaplinsky, a Jehovah's Witness, was distributing literature and talking to people on the streets of a small town in New Hampshire on a Saturday afternoon. When local citizens complained to the town marshal about Chaplinsky's calling all religion "a racket," the marshal replied that Chaplinsky had a lawful right to do speak, but also warned Chaplinsky that the crowd was getting restless. Later, after an incident near a busy intersection, a traffic policeman took Chaplinsky into custody. The marshal, having heard a riot had started, came on the scene and repeated his warning to Chaplinsky. The marshal claimed that Chaplinsky then replied, "You are a God damned racketeer" and "a damned Fascist." Chaplinsky admitted using such terms, except for the name of God, but he also insisted that the marshal had cursed him when he asked for protection against hecklers.

Chaplinsky was convicted under a statute which made it a crime to "address any offensive, derisive or annoying word to any other person who is lawfully in any street or public place," or to "call him by any offensive or derisive name," or to "make any noise or exclamation in his presence and hearing with intent to deride, offend or annoy him, or to prevent him from pursuing his lawful business or occupation." State courts sustained the conviction, and Chaplinsky appealed to the U.S. Supreme Court.

Mr. Justice **MURPHY** delivered the opinion of the Court. . . .

It is now clear that "Freedom of speech and freedom of the press, which are protected by the First Amendment from infringement by Congress, are among the fundamental personal rights and liberties which are protected by the Fourteenth Amendment from invasion by state action." Lovell v. Griffin [1938]. Freedom of worship is similarly sheltered. Cantwell v. Connecticut [1940].

Appellant assails the statute as a violation of all three freedoms, speech, press, and worship, but only an attack on the basis of free speech is warranted. The spoken, not the written, word is involved. And we cannot conceive that cursing a public officer is the exercise of religion in any sense of the term. But even if the activities of the appellant which preceded the incident could be viewed as religious in character, and therefore entitled to the protection of the Fourteenth Amendment, they would not cloak him with immunity from the legal consequences for concomitant acts committed in violation of a valid criminal statute. . . .

Allowing the broadest scope to the language and purpose of the Fourteenth Amendment, it is well understood that the right of free speech is not absolute at all times and under all circumstances. There are certain well-defined and narrowly limited classes of speech, the prevention and punishment of which have never been thought to raise any Constitutional problem. These include the lewd and obscene, the profane, the libelous, and the insulting or "fighting" words—those which by their very utterance inflict injury or tend to incite an immediate breach of the peace. It has been well observed that such utterances are no essential part of any exposition of ideas, and are of such slight social value as a step to truth that any benefit that may be derived from them is clearly outweighed by the social interest in order and morality. "Resort to epithets or personal abuse is not in any proper sense communication of information or opinion safeguarded by the Constitution, and its punishment as a criminal act would raise no question under that instrument." Cantwell. . . .

. . . [T]he state [supreme] court declared that the statute's purpose was to preserve the public peace, no words being "forbidden except such as have a direct tendency to cause acts of violence by the persons to whom, individually, the remark is addressed." It was further said:

The word "offensive" is not to be defined in terms of what a particular addressee thinks. . . . The test is what men of common intelligence would understand would be words likely to cause an average addressee to fight. . . . The English language has a number of words and expressions which by general consent are "fighting words" when said without a disarming smile. . . . Such words, as ordinary men know, are likely to cause a fight. So are threatening, profane or obscene revilings. . . . The statute, as construed, does no more than prohibit the face-to-face words plainly likely to cause a breach of the peace by the addressee, words whose speaking constitute a breach of the peace by the speaker—including . . . profanity, obscenity and threats.

We are unable to say that the limited scope of the statute as thus construed contravenes the Constitutional right of free expression. It is a statute narrowly drawn and limited to define and punish specific conduct lying within the domain of state power, the use in a public place of words likely to cause a breach of the peace. Cf. *Cantwell*; Thornhill v. Alabama [1940]. . . . A statute punishing verbal acts, carefully drawn so as not unduly to impair liberty of expression, is not too vague for a criminal law. Cf. Fox v. Washington [1915]. Nor can we say that the application of the statute to the facts disclosed by the record substantially or unreasonably impinges upon the privilege of free speech. Argument is unnecessary to demonstrate that the applications "damned racketeer" and "damned Fascist" are epithets likely to provoke the average person to retaliation, and thereby cause a breach of the peace. . . .

Affirmed.

Editors' Notes

(1) In *Chaplinsky,* the Court articulated a "two-level" theory of the First Amendment, under which certain categories of expression are of "slight social value" and therefore do not receive the full protection that is accorded to higher value expression that does not fall within those categories. Traditional categories of unprotected speech included those mentioned in *Chaplinsky*—the "lewd and obscene," the "profane," the "libelous," and the "insulting or 'fighting' words"—as well as incitement to imminent lawless action. To what extent have subsequent cases, beginning with New York Times v. Sullivan (1964; reprinted above, p. 634) broken down or at least eroded these categories?

(2) **Query:** The Court suggested that "fighting words" are constitutionally unprotected because they "are no essential part of any exposition of ideas." Does the First Amendment, by its own terms, protect the "emotive force" as well as the "cognitive content" of expression? Does the approach of *reinforcing representative democracy*? See Cohen v. California (1971; reprinted below, p. 705).

(3) **Query:** The Court also suggested that "fighting words" are unprotected because they "tend to incite an immediate breach of the peace." Is this formulation more akin to a stringent "clear and present danger test" as in Brandenburg v. Ohio (1969; reprinted above, p. 672), or to a "bad tendency test," like that applied in Whitney v. California (1927; reprinted above, p. 651)?

Do such words, when addressed to a police officer, constitute criticism of government policy and personnel that the First Amendment, according to *New York Times* (1964; reprinted above, p. 634), protects? See Stephen W. Gard, "Fighting Words As Free Speech," 58 *Wash.U.L.Q.* 531 (1980).

(4) In Gooding v. Wilson (1972), the Court reaffirmed *Chaplinsky* but diluted the fighting words doctrine. While involved in a protest against the war in Vietnam, Johnny Wilson had made such remarks to a police officer as: "White son of a bitch, I'll kill you," and "You son of a bitch, I'll choke you to death." He was convicted under a Georgia law which made it a crime "without provocation, [to] use to or of another, and in his presence ... opprobrious words or abusive language, tending to cause a breach of the peace. ..." The U.S. Supreme Court reversed, holding the Georgia statute unconstitutionally overbroad, for state courts had construed it to sweep beyond the class of "fighting" words *Chaplinsky* defined.

(5) **Query:** As in *Gooding*, the Court often cites *Chaplinsky*, but, as of January, 1995, it had not upheld another conviction for "fighting words." Does *Chaplinsky* today "strike[ ] a quaint, almost nostalgic note" and "bespeak[ ] the gentility of a bygone era"? Does that fate represent a changing and, many would say, more vulgar culture, changing the meaning of the constitutional text? See Harry Kalven, Jr., *A Worthy Tradition: Freedom of Speech in America* (Jamie Kalven, ed.; New York: Harper & Row, 1988), pp. 17, 78.

B. Defamation of Groups

"[I]t would be out of bounds for the judiciary to deny the legislature a choice of policy, provided it is not unrelated to the problem and not forbidden by some explicit limitation on the State's power."—Justice FRANKFURTER

"I think the First Amendment, with the Fourteenth, 'absolutely' forbids such laws without any 'ifs' or 'buts' or 'whereases.'"—Justice BLACK

"The Framers of the Constitution ... chose liberty. That should be our choice today no matter how distasteful to us the pamphlet of Beauharnais may be."—Justice DOUGLAS

BEAUHARNAIS v. ILLINOIS
343 U.S. 250, 72 S.Ct. 725, 96 L.Ed. 919 (1952).

Joseph Beauharnais, president of the White Circle League, distributed a leaflet calling on the Mayor and City Council of Chicago "to halt the further encroachment, harassment and invasion of white people, their property, neighborhoods and persons, by the Negro." The leaflet urged "One million self respecting white people in Chicago to unite," adding: "If persuasion and the need to prevent the white race from becoming mongrelized by the negro will not unite us, then the aggressions ... rapes, robberies, knives, guns and marijuana of the negro, surely will." The leaflet also attached an application for membership in the White Circle League.

Beauharnais was convicted of violating an Illinois statute that made it unlawful to "manufacture, sell, or offer for sale, advertise or publish, present or exhibit in any public place in this state any lithograph, moving picture, play, drama or sketch which ... portrays depravity, criminality, unchastity, or lack of virtue of a class of citizens, of any race, color, creed or religion which ... exposes the citizens of any race, color, creed or religion to contempt, derision, or obloquy or which is productive of breach of the peace or riots." The trial judge instructed the jury that, to convict, they did not need to find the pamphlet "was likely to produce a clear and present danger of a serious substantive evil that rises far above public inconvenience, annoyance or unrest." Beauharnais claimed the statute, as so interpreted, violated the First and Fourteenth Amendments. The state supreme court sustained his conviction, and he obtained certiorari from the U.S. Supreme Court.

Mr. Justice **FRANKFURTER** delivered the opinion of the Court.

... Today, every American jurisdiction ... punish[es] libels directed at individuals.

> There are certain well-defined and narrowly limited classes of speech, the prevention and punishment of which have never been thought to raise any Constitutional problem. These include the lewd and obscene, the profane, the libelous, and the insulting or 'fighting' words—those which by their very utterance inflict injury or tend to incite an immediate breach of the peace. It has been well observed that such utterances are no essential part of any exposition of ideas, and are of such slight social value as a step to truth that any benefit that may be derived from them is clearly outweighed by the social interest in order and morality.
> ... Chaplinsky v. New Hampshire [1942].

No one will gainsay that it is libelous falsely to charge another with being a rapist, robber, carrier of knives and guns, and user of marijuana. The precise question before us, then, is whether the protection of "liberty" in the Due Process Clause of the Fourteenth Amendment prevents a State from punishing such libels—as criminal libel has been defined, limited and constitutionally recognized time out of mind— directed at designated collectivities and flagrantly disseminated. ... [I]f an utterance directed at an individual may be the object of criminal sanctions, we cannot deny to a State power to punish the same utterance directed at a defined group, unless we can say that this is a wilful and purposeless restriction unrelated to the peace and well-being of the State.

Illinois did not have to look beyond her own borders ... to conclude that wilful purveyors of falsehood concerning racial and religious groups promote strife and tend powerfully to obstruct the manifold adjustments required for free, ordered life in a metropolitan, polyglot community. From the murder of the abolitionist Lovejoy in 1837 to the Cicero riots of 1951, Illinois has been the scene of exacerbated tension between races, often flaring into violence. ... In many of these outbreaks, utterances of the character here in question, so the Illinois legislature could conclude, played a significant part. ...

In the face of this history and its frequent obligato of extreme racial and religious propaganda, we would deny experience to say that the Illinois legislature was without reason in seeking ways to curb false or malicious defamation of racial and religious groups, made in public places and by means calculated to have a powerful emotional impact on those to whom it was presented. ...

It may be argued, and weightily, that this legislation will not help matters. ... [But] it would be out of bounds for the judiciary to deny the legislature a choice of policy, provided it is not unrelated to the problem and not forbidden by some explicit limitation on the State's power. ... It would ... be arrant dogmatism ... for us to deny that the Illinois legislature may warrantably believe that a man's job and his educational opportunities and the dignity accorded him may depend as much on the reputation of the racial and religious group to which he willy-nilly belongs, as on his own merits. This being so, we are precluded from saying that speech concededly punishable when immediately directed at individuals cannot be outlawed if directed at groups with whose position and esteem in society the affiliated individual may be inextricably involved.

We are warned that the choice open to the Illinois legislature here may be abused, that the law may be discriminatorily enforced; prohibiting libel of a creed or of a racial group, we are told, is but a step from prohibiting libel of a political party.[1] Every power may be abused, but the possibility of abuse is a poor reason for denying Illinois the power to adopt measures against criminal libels sanctioned by centuries of Anglo–American law. "While this Court sits" it retains and exercises authority to nullify action which encroaches on freedom of utterance under the guise of punishing libel. ...

Libelous utterances not being within the area of constitutionally protected speech, it is unnecessary ... to consider the issues behind the phrase "clear and present danger." Certainly no one would contend that obscene speech, for example, may be punished only upon a showing of such circumstances. Libel, as we have seen, is in the same class.

Affirmed.

Mr. Justice **BLACK**, with whom Mr. Justice **DOUGLAS** concurs, dissenting. ...

The Court condones this expansive state censorship by painstakingly analogizing it to the law of criminal libel. As a result of this refined

---

1. ... The rubric "race, color, creed or religion" which describes the type of group libel of which is punishable, has attained too fixed a meaning to permit political groups to be brought within it. If a statute sought to outlaw libels of political parties, quite different problems not now before us would be raised. For one thing, the whole doctrine of fair comment as indispensable to the democratic political process would come into play. Political parties, like public men, are, as it were, public property. [Footnote by the Court.]

analysis, the Illinois statute emerges labeled a "group libel law." This label may make the Court's holding more palatable for those who sustain it, but the sugar-coating does not make the censorship less deadly. . . . Every expansion of the law of criminal libel so as to punish discussions of matters of public concern means a corresponding invasion of the area dedicated to free expression by the First Amendment. . . .

The Court's reliance on *Chaplinsky* is also misplaced. New Hampshire had a state law making it an offense to direct insulting words at an *individual* on a public street. . . . Whether the words used in their context here are "fighting" words in the same sense is doubtful, but . . . they are not addressed to or about *individuals*. Moreover, the leaflet used here was also the means adopted by an assembled group to enlist interest in their efforts to have legislation enacted. . . . Freedom of petition, assembly, speech and press could be greatly abridged by a practice of meticulously scrutinizing every editorial, speech, sermon or other printed matter to extract two or three naughty words on which to hang charges of "group libel." The *Chaplinsky* case makes no such broad inroads on First Amendment freedoms. . . .

This Act sets up a system of state censorship which is at war with the kind of free government envisioned by those who forced adoption of our Bill of Rights. The motives behind the state law may have been to do good. But the same can be said about most laws making opinions punishable as crimes. . . .

We are told that freedom of petition and discussion are in no danger "while this Court sits." . . . I do not agree that the Constitution leaves freedom of petition, assembly, speech, press or worship at the mercy of a case-by-case, day-by-day majority of this Court. . . . I think the First Amendment, with the Fourteenth, "absolutely" forbids such laws without any "ifs" or "buts" or "whereases." Whatever the danger, if any, in such public discussions, it is a danger the Founders deemed outweighed by the danger incident to the stifling of thought and speech. . . .

Mr. Justice **REED**, with whom Mr. Justice **DOUGLAS** joins, dissenting.
    . . .

Mr. Justice **DOUGLAS**, dissenting.

Hitler and his Nazis showed how evil a conspiracy could be which was aimed at destroying a race by exposing it to contempt, derision, and obloquy. I would be willing to concede that such conduct directed at a race or group in this country could be made an indictable offense. For such a project would be more than the exercise of free speech. Like picketing, it would be free speech plus. I would also be willing to concede that even without the element of conspiracy there might be times and occasions when the legislative or executive branch might call a halt to inflammatory talk, such as the shouting of "fire" in a school or a theatre.

My view is that if in any case other public interests are to override the plain command of the First Amendment, the peril of speech must be clear and present, leaving no room for argument, raising no doubts as to the necessity of curbing speech in order to prevent disaster.

The First Amendment is couched in absolute terms. ... Speech has therefore a preferred position as contrasted to some other civil rights. ... Yet recently the Court in this and in other cases [e.g., Dennis v. United States (1951)] has engrafted the right of regulation onto the First Amendment by placing in the hands of the legislative branch the right to regulate "within reasonable limits" the right of free speech. This to me is an ominous and alarming trend. The free trade in ideas which the Framers of the Constitution visualized disappears. In its place there is substituted a new orthodoxy—an orthodoxy that changes with the whims of the age or the day, an orthodoxy which the majority by solemn judgment proclaims to be essential to the safety, welfare, security, morality, or health of society. ...

... Intemperate speech is a distinctive characteristic of man. Hotheads blow off and release destructive energy in the process. They shout and rave. ... The Framers of the Constitution knew human nature as well as we do. They too had lived in dangerous days; they too knew the suffocating influence of orthodoxy and standardized thought. They weighed the compulsions for restrained speech and thought against the abuses of liberty. They chose liberty. That should be our choice today no matter how distasteful to us the pamphlet of Beauharnais may be. ...

Mr. Justice **JACKSON**, dissenting. ...

Editors' Notes

(1) **Query:** What was Frankfurter's standard for reviewing regulatory legislation under the First Amendment? Was it merely an extension of Thayer's argument to state legislation? Or did Frankfurter's opinion have a firmer grounding in democratic theory? What was the basis of the distinction he drew in footnote 1? What medley of approaches to constitutional interpretation did Frankfurter use?

(2) **Query:** Who had the best *textualist* argument here, Frankfurter, Black, or Douglas? To what extent were any (or all) of their opinions *originalist*? How close did either Black or Douglas come to articulating a theory of *reinforcing representative democracy*? What about Frankfurter, taking into account his footnote 1? To what extent were any of these opinions *structuralist*? Why did no justice rely heavily on a *doctrinal approach*?

(3) In 1977, the American Nazis planned to march in Skokie, Illinois, a predominantly Jewish suburb of Chicago whose residents included approximately 5,000 survivors of Nazi concentration camps. Among other measures, Skokie enacted three ordinances to prohibit the march: (1) requiring applicants for parade permits to obtain $300,000 in public liability insurance and $50,000 in property damage insurance; (2) prohibiting the "dissemination of any material which promotes and incites hatred against persons by reason of their race, national origin, or religion, and is intended to do so"; and (3) prohibiting public demonstrations "on behalf of any political party while

wearing a military-style uniform." The district court held that all three ordinances violated the First Amendment, and the Court of Appeals for the Seventh Circuit affirmed. Collin v. Smith (1978). The Supreme Court denied Skokie's request for a stay of the order of the Court of Appeals. Having won their right to march, the Nazis cancelled their plans for Skokie, instead holding a rally in Chicago. There were numerous arrests but no serious violence.

(4) **Query:** See the query in Editors' Note 5 to Whitney v. California (1927) at p. 651.

(5) In recent years, a number of colleges and universities, both state and private, have adopted codes to prohibit or punish hate-filled racist speech. For example, the University of Michigan prohibited any person from stigmatizing an individual "on the basis of race, ethnicity, religion, sex, sexual orientation, creed, national origin, ancestry, age, marital status, handicap or Viet–Nam era veteran status" with the "purpose or reasonably foreseeable effect of interfering with an individual's academic efforts, employment, participation in University sponsored extra-curricular activities or personal safety." In Doe v. University of Michigan (1989), a federal district court held that code unconstitutional under the First Amendment. In UWM Post, Inc. v. Board of Regents (1991), a federal district court struck down a similar code from the University of Wisconsin.

Stanford University adopted a code focused on "discriminatory harassment" and modeled on the "fighting words" category of unprotected expression. At the University of Texas, the President's Ad Hoc Committee on Racial Harassment rejected the "fighting words" approach, instead proposing a ban on "racial harassment" based on the common-law tort of intentional infliction of emotional distress. This alternative approach is similar to that recommended by Richard Delgado in "Words That Wound: A Tort Action for Racial Insults, Epithets, and Name–Calling," 17 *Harv.Civ.Rts.—Civ.Lib.L.Rev.* 133 (1982). Mari Matsuda offers a still different approach: recognition of a category of unprotected expression consisting of racist hate speech. "Public Response to Racist Speech: Considering the Victim's Story," 87 *Mich.L.Rev.* 2320 (1989). On Matsuda's view, the constitutionally unprotected characteristics of racist hate speech include the message's being "directed against a historically oppressed group." What about hate speech directed against a historically dominant group? Should the First Amendment countenance asymmetry in this respect?

(6) The literature on regulating racist speech on campus includes: Richard Delgado, "Campus Antiracism Rules," 85 *Nw.U.L.Rev.* 343 (1991); Kent Greenawalt, "Insults and Epithets: Are They Protected Speech?," 42 *Rutgers L.Rev.* 287 (1990); Charles Lawrence, "If He Hollers Let Him Go: On Regulating Racist Speech on Campus," 1990 *Duke L.J.* 431; Nadine Strossen, "Regulating Racist Speech on Campus: A Modest Proposal?" 1990 *ibid.* 484.

————

"[St. Paul] has proscribed fighting words ... that communicate messages of racial, gender, or religious intolerance. Selectivity of this sort creates the possibility that

the city is seeking to handicap the expression of particular ideas."—Justice SCALIA

" 'Such a simplistic, all-or-nothing-at-all approach to the First Amendment is at odds with common sense and with our jurisprudence as well.' "—Justice WHITE

"The Court today turns First Amendment law on its head."—Justice STEVENS

R.A.V. v. ST. PAUL
505 U.S. 377, 112 S.Ct. 2538, 120 L.Ed.2d 305 (1992).

Police in St. Paul, MN, arrested R.A.V. and several of his friends for burning a cross on the lawn of an African American family. The city could have tried him under such laws as those prohibiting terroristic threats, arson, and criminal damage to property, but chose to charge these juveniles only under the city's Bias–Motivated Crime Ordinance:

> Whoever places on public or private property a symbol, object, appellation, characterization or graffiti, including, but not limited to, a burning cross or Nazi swastika, which one knows or has reasonable grounds to know arouses anger, alarm or resentment in others on the basis of race, color, creed, religion or gender commits disorderly conduct and shall be guilty of a misdemeanor.

R.A.V.'s attorney claimed the ordinance violated the First Amendment. The trial court agreed, but the state supreme court reversed because, as construed in prior cases, the phrase "arouses anger, alarm or resentment in others" limited the reach of the ordinance to conduct that amounts to "fighting words," i.e., "conduct that itself inflicts injury or tends to incite immediate violence." Thus the ordinance only punished expression "that the First Amendment does not protect." The court also concluded that the ordinance was not impermissibly content-based because it "is a narrowly tailored means toward accomplishing the compelling governmental interest in protecting the community against bias-motivated threats to public safety and order." The U.S. Supreme Court granted certiorari.

Justice **SCALIA** delivered the opinion of the Court. . . .

I

In construing the St. Paul ordinance, we are bound by the construction given to it by the Minnesota court. Accordingly, we accept the Minnesota Supreme Court's authoritative statement that the ordinance reaches only those expressions that constitute "fighting words" within the meaning of Chaplinsky v. New Hampshire (1942). . . . [W]e nonetheless conclude that the ordinance is facially unconstitutional in that it prohibits otherwise permitted speech solely on the basis of the subjects the speech addresses.

The First Amendment generally prevents government from proscribing speech, see, e.g., Cantwell v. Connecticut (1940), or even expressive conduct, see, e.g., Texas v. Johnson (1989), because of disapproval of the

ideas expressed.   Content-based regulations are presumptively invalid.
Simon & Schuster v. NY State Crime Victims Bd. (1991);   Police Dept. v.
Mosley (1972).   From 1791 to the present, however, our society, like
other free but civilized societies, has permitted restrictions upon the
content of speech in a few limited areas, which are "of such slight social
value as a step to truth that any benefit that may be derived from them
is clearly outweighed by the social interest in order and morality."
Chaplinsky. We have recognized that "the freedom of speech" referred
to by the First Amendment does not include a freedom to disregard these
traditional limitations.   See, e.g., Roth v. United States (1957) (obscenity); Beauharnais v. Illinois (1952) (defamation); *Chaplinsky* ("fighting
words").   Our decisions since the 1960's have narrowed the scope of the
traditional categorical exceptions for defamation, see New York Times
Co. v. Sullivan (1964);   Gertz v. Robert Welch (1974);   see generally
Milkovich v. Lorain Journal (1990), and for obscenity, see Miller v.
California (1973), but a limited categorical approach has remained an
important part of our First Amendment jurisprudence.

We have sometimes said that these categories of expression are "not
within the area of constitutionally protected speech," *Roth, Beauharnais,
Chaplinsky*, or that the "protection of the First Amendment does not
extend" to them, Bose Corp. v. Consumers Union (1984); Sable Communications v. FCC (1989).   Such statements must be taken in context,
however, and are no more literally true than is the occasionally repeated
shorthand characterizing obscenity "as not being speech at all."   What
they mean is that these areas of speech can, consistently with the First
Amendment, be regulated *because of their constitutionally proscribable
content* (obscenity, defamation, etc.)—not that they are categories of
speech entirely invisible to the Constitution, so that they may be made
the vehicles for content discrimination unrelated to their distinctively
proscribable content.   Thus, the government may proscribe libel; but it
may not make the further content discrimination of proscribing *only*
libel critical of the government.   . . .

Our cases surely do not establish the proposition that the First
Amendment imposes no obstacle whatsoever to regulation of particular
instances of such proscribable expression.   . . . Such a simplistic, all-or-
nothing-at-all approach to First Amendment protection is at odds with
common sense and with our jurisprudence as well.[1]   It is not true that

---

1. Justice White concedes that a city council cannot prohibit only those legally obscene
works that contain criticism of the city government, but asserts that to be the consequence,
not of the First Amendment, but of the Equal Protection Clause.   Such content-based
discrimination would not, he asserts, "be rationally related to a legitimate government
interest."   But of course the only *reason* that government interest is not a "legitimate"
one is that it violates the First Amendment.   This Court itself has occasionally fused the
First Amendment into the Equal Protection Clause in this fashion, but at least with the
acknowledgment (which Justice White cannot afford to make) that the First Amendment
underlies its analysis.   See *Mosley*. . . .

Justice Stevens seeks to avoid the point by dismissing the notion of obscene antigovernment speech as "fantastical," apparently believing that any reference to politics
prevents a finding of obscenity.   Unfortunately for the purveyors of obscenity, that is
obviously false.   A shockingly hard core pornographic movie that contains a model sporting

"fighting words" have at most a "de minimis" expressive content, or that their content is *in all respects* "worthless and undeserving of constitutional protection"; sometimes they are quite expressive indeed. We have not said that they constitute "*no* part of the expression of ideas," but only that they constitute "no *essential* part of any exposition of ideas." *Chaplinsky* (emphasis added).

The proposition that a particular instance of speech can be proscribable on the basis of one feature (e.g., obscenity) but not on the basis of another (e.g., opposition to the city government) is commonplace. ... We have long held, for example, that nonverbal expressive activity can be banned because of the action it entails, but not because of the ideas it expresses—so that burning a flag in violation of an ordinance against outdoor fires could be punishable, whereas burning a flag in violation of an ordinance against dishonoring the flag is not. ...

In other words, the exclusion of "fighting words" from the scope of the First Amendment simply means that ... the unprotected features of the words are, despite their verbal character, essentially a "nonspeech" element of communication. Fighting words are thus analogous to a noisy sound truck: Each is, as Justice Frankfurter recognized, a "mode of speech," Niemotko v. Maryland (1951) (concurring in result); both can be used to convey an idea; but neither has, in and of itself, a claim upon the First Amendment. As with the sound truck, however, so also with fighting words: The government may not regulate use based on hostility—or favoritism—towards the underlying message expressed.[2]

The concurrences describe us as setting forth a new First Amendment principle that prohibition of constitutionally proscribable speech cannot be "underinclusive" (White, J.)—a First Amendment "absolutism" whereby "within a particular 'proscribable' category of expression, ... a government must either proscribe *all* speech or no speech at all" (Stevens, J.). That easy target is of the concurrences' own invention. In our view, the First Amendment imposes not an "underinclusiveness" limitation but a "content discrimination" limitation upon a State's prohibition of proscribable speech. There is no problem whatever, for example, with a State's prohibiting obscenity (and other forms of proscribable expression) only in certain media or markets, for although that prohibition would be "underinclusive," it would not discriminate on the basis of content. See, e.g., *Sable Communications* (upholding 47 U.S.C. § 223(b)(1), which prohibits obscene *telephone* communications). ...

---

a political tattoo can be found, "*taken as a whole* [to] lack serious literary, artistic, political, or scientific value," *Miller* (emphasis added). ... [Footnote by the Court.]

2. Although Justice White asserts that our analysis disregards "established principles of First Amendment law," he cites not a single case (and we are aware of none) that even involved, much less considered and resolved, the issue of content discrimination through regulation of "unprotected" speech—though we plainly *recognized* that as an issue in Ferber [v. New York (1982)]. It is of course contrary to all traditions of our jurisprudence to consider the law on this point conclusively resolved by broad language in cases where the issue was not presented or even envisioned. [Footnote by the Court.]

When the basis for the content discrimination consists entirely of the very reason the entire class of speech at issue is proscribable, no significant danger of idea or viewpoint discrimination exists. Such a reason, having been adjudged neutral enough to support exclusion of the entire class of speech from First Amendment protection, is also neutral enough to form the basis of distinction within the class. To illustrate: ... the Federal Government can criminalize only those threats of violence that are directed against the President—since the reasons why threats of violence are outside the First Amendment (protecting individuals from the fear of violence, from the disruption that fear engenders, and from the possibility that the threatened violence will occur) have special force when applied to the person of the President. See Watts v. United States (1969). ... But the Federal Government may not criminalize only those threats against the President that mention his policy on aid to inner cities. ...

Another valid basis for according differential treatment to even a content-defined subclass of proscribable speech is that the subclass happens to be associated with particular "secondary effects" of the speech, so that the regulation is *"justified* without reference to the content of the ... speech," Renton v. Playtime Theatres (1986). ... A State could, for example, permit all obscene live performances except those involving minors. Moreover, since words can in some circumstances violate laws directed not against speech but against conduct (a law against treason, for example, is violated by telling the enemy the nation's defense secrets), a particular content-based subcategory of a proscribable class of speech can be swept up incidentally within the reach of a statute directed at conduct rather than speech. Thus, for example, sexually derogatory "fighting words" ... may produce a violation of Title VII's general prohibition against sexual discrimination in employment practices, 42 U.S.C. §§ 2000e–2. Where the government does not target conduct on the basis of its expressive content, acts are not shielded from regulation merely because they express a discriminatory idea or philosophy.

... There may be other such bases as well. Indeed, to validate such selectivity (where totally proscribable speech is at issue) it may not even be necessary to identify any particular "neutral" basis, so long as the nature of the content discrimination is such that there is no realistic possibility that official suppression of ideas is afoot. ... Save for that limitation, the regulation of "fighting words," like the regulation of noisy speech, may address some offensive instances and leave other, equally offensive, instances alone.[3]

---

3. Justice Stevens cites a string of opinions as supporting his assertion that "selective regulation of speech based on content" is not presumptively invalid. Analysis reveals, however, that they do not support it. To begin with, three of them did not command a majority of the Court, Young v. American Mini Theatres (1976) (plurality); FCC v. Pacifica Foundation (1978) (plurality); Lehman v. Shaker Heights (1974) (plurality); and two others did not even discuss the First Amendment, Morales [v. TWA (1992)]; Jacob Siegel Co. v. FTC (1946). In any event, all that their contents establish is what we readily concede: that presumptive invalidity does not mean invariable invalidity, leaving room for

II

... [E]ven as narrowly construed by the Minnesota Supreme Court, the ordinance is facially unconstitutional. Although the phrase in the ordinance, "arouses anger, alarm or resentment in others," has been limited by ... construction to reach only those symbols or displays that amount to "fighting words," the remaining, unmodified terms make clear that the ordinance applies only to "fighting words" that insult, or provoke violence, "on the basis of race, color, creed, religion or gender." Displays containing abusive invective, no matter how vicious or severe, are permissible unless they are addressed to one of the specified disfavored topics. Those who wish to use "fighting words" in connection with other ideas—to express hostility, for example, on the basis of political affiliation, union membership, or homosexuality—are not covered. The First Amendment does not permit St. Paul to impose special prohibitions on those speakers who express views on disfavored subjects. See *Simon & Schuster.*

In its practical operation, moreover, the ordinance goes even beyond mere content discrimination, to actual viewpoint discrimination. Displays containing some words—odious racial epithets, for example—would be prohibited to proponents of all views. But "fighting words" that do not themselves invoke race, color, creed, religion, or gender—aspersions upon a person's mother, for example—would seemingly be usable ad libitum in the placards of those arguing *in favor* of racial ... tolerance and equality, but could not be used by that speaker's opponents. One could hold up a sign saying, for example, that all "anti-Catholic bigots" are misbegotten; but not that all "papists" are, for that would insult and provoke violence "on the basis of religion." St. Paul has no such authority to license one side of a debate to fight freestyle, while requiring the other to follow Marquis of Queensbury Rules.

What we have here ... is not a prohibition of fighting words that are directed at certain persons or groups (which would be *facially* valid if it met the requirements of the Equal Protection Clause); but rather, a prohibition of fighting words that contain ... messages of "bias-motivated" hatred and in particular, as applied to this case, messages "based on virulent notions of racial supremacy." One must wholeheartedly agree with the Minnesota Supreme Court that "it is the responsibility, even the obligation, of diverse communities to confront such notions in whatever form they appear," but the manner of that confrontation cannot consist of selective limitations upon speech. ... The point of the First Amendment is that majority preferences must be expressed in some fashion other than silencing speech on the basis of its content.

Despite the fact that the Minnesota Supreme Court and St. Paul acknowledge that the ordinance is directed at expression of group hatred, Justice Stevens suggests that this "fundamentally misreads" the ordinance. It is directed, he claims, not to speech of a particular

---

such exceptions as reasonable and viewpoint-neutral content-based discrimination in nonpublic forums. [Footnote by the Court.]

content, but to particular "injur[ies]" that are "qualitatively different" from other injuries. This is wordplay. What makes the anger, fear, sense of dishonor, etc. produced by violation of this ordinance distinct from the anger, fear, sense of dishonor, etc. produced by other fighting words is nothing other than the fact that it is caused by a distinctive idea, conveyed by a distinctive message. The First Amendment cannot be evaded that easily. It is obvious that the symbols which will arouse "anger, alarm or resentment in others on the basis of race, color, creed, religion or gender" are those symbols that communicate a message of hostility based on one of these characteristics. St. Paul concedes in its brief that the ordinance applies only to "racial, religious, or gender-specific symbols" such as "a burning cross, Nazi swastika or other instrumentality of like import." ...

Th[is] content-based discrimination ... comes within neither any of the specific exceptions to the First Amendment prohibition we discussed earlier, nor within a more general exception for content discrimination that does not threaten censorship of ideas. It assuredly does not fall within the exception for content discrimination based on the very reasons why the particular class of speech at issue (here, fighting words) is proscribable. ... [T]he reason why fighting words are categorically excluded from the protection of the First Amendment is not that their content communicates any particular idea, but that their content embodies a particularly intolerable (and socially unnecessary) *mode* of expressing *whatever* idea the speaker wishes to convey. St. Paul has not singled out an especially offensive mode of expression. ... Rather, it has proscribed fighting words of whatever manner that communicate messages of racial, gender, or religious intolerance. Selectivity of this sort creates the possibility that the city is seeking to handicap the expression of particular ideas. That possibility would alone be enough to render the ordinance presumptively invalid, but St. Paul's comments and concessions in this case elevate the possibility to a certainty.

St. Paul argues that the ordinance comes within ... the specific exception ... that allows content discrimination aimed only at the "secondary effects" of the speech. According to St. Paul, the ordinance is intended, "not to impact on [sic] the right of free expression of the accused," but rather to "protect against the victimization of a person or persons who are particularly vulnerable because of their membership in a group that historically has been discriminated against." ... [I]t is clear that the St. Paul ordinance is not directed to secondary effects within the meaning of *Renton*. As we said in Boos v. Barry (1988), "[l]isteners' reactions to speech are not the type of 'secondary effects' we referred to in *Renton*." ...

Finally, St. Paul ... assert[s] that the ordinance helps to ensure the basic human rights of members of groups that have historically been subjected to discrimination, including the right of such group members to live in peace where they wish. We do not doubt that these interests are compelling, and that the ordinance can be said to promote them.

But the "danger of censorship" presented by a facially content-based statute requires that that weapon be employed only where it is "*necessary* to serve the asserted [compelling] interest," Burson v. Freeman (1992) (plurality) (emphasis added). The existence of adequate content-neutral alternatives thus "undercuts significantly" any defense of such a statute. *Boos.* ...

... The dispositive question in this case, therefore, is whether content discrimination is reasonably necessary to achieve St. Paul's compelling interests; it plainly is not. An ordinance not limited to the favored topics, for example, would have precisely the same beneficial effect. In fact the only interest distinctively served by the content limitation is that of displaying the city council's special hostility towards the particular biases thus singled out.[4] That is precisely what the First Amendment forbids. ...

Let there be no mistake about our belief that burning a cross in someone's front yard is reprehensible. But St. Paul has sufficient means at its disposal to prevent such behavior without adding the First Amendment to the fire.

The judgment of the Minnesota Supreme Court is reversed. ...

Justice **WHITE**, with whom Justice **BLACKMUN** and Justice **O'CONNOR** join, and with whom Justice **STEVENS** joins except as to Part I(A), concurring in the judgment.

I agree with the majority that the judgment ... should be reversed. However, our agreement ends there.

This case could easily be decided within the contours of established First Amendment law by holding, as petitioner argues, that the St. Paul ordinance is fatally overbroad because it criminalizes not only unprotected expression but expression protected by the First Amendment. Instead, "finding it unnecessary" to consider the questions upon which we granted review, the Court holds the ordinance facially unconstitutional on a ground that was never presented to the Minnesota Supreme Court, a ground that has not been briefed by the parties before this Court, a ground that requires serious departures from the teaching of prior cases and is inconsistent with the plurality opinion in Burson v. Freeman (1992), which was joined by two of the five Justices in the majority in the present case.

---

4. A plurality of the Court reached a different conclusion with regard to the Tennessee anti-electioneering statute considered earlier this Term in *Burson*. In light of the "logical connection" between electioneering and the State's compelling interest in preventing voter intimidation and election fraud—an inherent connection borne out by a "long history" and a "wide-spread and time-tested consensus"—the plurality concluded that it was faced with one of those "rare cases" in which the use of a facially content-based restriction was justified by interests unrelated to the suppression of ideas. Justice White and Justice Stevens are therefore quite mistaken when they seek to convert the *Burson* plurality's passing comment that "the First Amendment does not require States to regulate for problems that do not exist" into endorsement of the revolutionary proposition that the suppression of particular ideas can be justified when only those ideas have been a source of trouble in the past. [Footnote by the Court.]

This Court ordinarily is not so eager to abandon its precedents. ...

But in the present case, the majority casts aside long-established First Amendment doctrine without the benefit of briefing and adopts an untried theory. This is hardly a judicious way of proceeding, and the Court's reasoning in reaching its result is transparently wrong.

I

A

This Court's decisions have plainly stated that expression falling within certain limited categories so lacks the values the First Amendment was designed to protect that the Constitution affords no protection to that expression. *Chaplinsky.* ... Thus, as the majority concedes, this Court has long held certain discrete categories of expression to be proscribable on the basis of their content. All of these categories are content based. But the Court has held that First Amendment does not apply to them because their expressive content is worthless or of de minimis value to society. *Chaplinsky.* ... This categorical approach has provided a principled and narrowly focused means for distinguishing between expression that the government may regulate freely and that which it may regulate on the basis of content only upon a showing of compelling need.

Today, however, the Court announces that earlier Courts did not mean their repeated statements that certain categories of expression are "not within the area of constitutionally protected speech." *Roth.* The present Court submits that such clear statements "must be taken in context" and are not "literally true."

To the contrary, those statements meant precisely what they said: The categorical approach is a firmly entrenched part of our First Amendment jurisprudence. ... Nevertheless, the majority holds that the First Amendment protects those narrow categories of expression long held to be undeserving of First Amendment protection—at least to the extent that lawmakers may not regulate some fighting words more strictly than others because of their content. ... Should the government want to criminalize certain fighting words, the Court now requires it to criminalize all fighting words.

To borrow a phrase, "Such a simplistic, all-or-nothing-at-all approach to First Amendment protection is at odds with common sense and with our jurisprudence as well." It is inconsistent to hold that the government may proscribe an entire category of speech because the content of that speech is evil, *Ferber;* but that the government may not treat a subset of that category differently without violating the First Amendment; the content of the subset is by definition worthless and undeserving of constitutional protection.

The majority's observation that fighting words are "quite expressive indeed" is no answer. Fighting words are not a means of exchanging views, rallying supporters, or registering a protest; they are directed against individuals to provoke violence or to inflict injury. Therefore, a ban on all fighting words or on a subset of the fighting words category would restrict only the social evil of hate speech, without creating the danger of driving viewpoints from the marketplace. ...

Any contribution of this holding to First Amendment jurisprudence is surely a negative one, since it necessarily signals that expressions of violence, such as the message of intimidation and racial hatred conveyed by burning a cross on someone's lawn, are of sufficient value to outweigh the social interest in order and morality that has traditionally placed such fighting words outside the First Amendment.[1] Indeed, by characterizing fighting words as a form of "debate," the majority legitimates hate speech as a form of public discussion. ...

B

In a second break with precedent, the Court refuses to sustain the ordinance even though it would survive under the strict scrutiny applicable to other protected expression. ... St. Paul has urged that its ordinance ... "helps to ensure the basic human rights of members of groups that have historically been subjected to discrimination. ..." The Court expressly concedes that this interest is compelling and is promoted by the ordinance. Nevertheless, ... [u]nder the majority's view, a narrowly drawn, content-based ordinance could never pass constitutional muster if the object of that legislation could be accomplished by banning a wider category of speech. This appears to be a general renunciation of strict scrutiny review, a fundamental tool of First Amendment analysis. ... *

Although the First Amendment does not apply to categories of unprotected speech, such as fighting words, the Equal Protection Clause requires that the regulation of unprotected speech be rationally related to a legitimate government interest. ...

Turning to the St. Paul ordinance and assuming arguendo, as the majority does, that the ordinance is not constitutionally overbroad, there is no question that it would pass equal protection review. The ordinance proscribes a subset of "fighting words," those that injure "on the basis of race, color, creed, religion or gender." This selective regulation

---

1. This does not suggest, of course, that cross burning is always unprotected. Burning a cross at a political rally would almost certainly be protected expression. Cf. Brandenburg v. Ohio (1969). But in such a context, the cross burning could not be characterized as a "direct personal insult or an invitation to exchange fisticuffs," Texas v. Johnson (1989), to which the fighting words doctrine applies. [Footnote by Justice White.]

* "Strict scrutiny" is a term derived from footnote 4 of *Carolene Products*. Developed in cases involving equal protection and later transplanted to other constitutional fields, it essentially means that, where legislation involves a "suspect classification" (an open-ended concept) or a "fundamental right" (equally capacious), courts should not only relax the usual presumption of constitutionality but also place the burden on government to show (1) a regulation meets a "compelling" public need and (2) more narrowly tailored regulation could not meet this need. For its use in interpreting the First Amendment, see United States v. O'Brien (1968; reprinted below, p. 721), the equal protection clause, see Chapters 14–15, below, and rights to religious exercise and privacy, see Chapters 17–18, below.—**Eds.**

reflects the City's judgment that harms based on race, color, creed, religion, or gender are more pressing public concerns than the harms caused by other fighting words. In light of our Nation's long and painful experience with discrimination, this determination is plainly reasonable. Indeed, as the majority concedes, the interest is compelling.

C

The Court has patched up its argument with an apparently nonexhaustive list of ad hoc exceptions. ... For instance, if the majority were to give general application to the rule on which it decides this case, today's decision would call into question the constitutionality of the statute making it illegal to threaten the life of the President. Surely, this statute, by singling out certain threats, incorporates a content-based distinction; it indicates that the Government especially disfavors threats against the President as opposed to threats against all others. But because the Government could prohibit all threats and not just those directed against the President, under the Court's theory, the compelling reasons justifying the enactment of special legislation to safeguard the President would be irrelevant, and the statute would fail First Amendment review.

To save the statute, the majority has engrafted the following exception onto its newly announced First Amendment rule: Content-based distinctions may be drawn within an unprotected category of speech if the basis for the distinctions is "the very reason the entire class of speech at issue is proscribable." ...

The exception swallows the majority's rule. Certainly, it should apply to the St. Paul ordinance, since "the reasons why [fighting words] are outside the First Amendment ... have special force when applied to [groups that have historically been subjected to discrimination]."

To avoid the result of its own analysis, the Court suggests that fighting words are simply a mode of communication, rather than a content-based category, and that the St. Paul ordinance has not singled out a particularly objectionable mode of communication. Again, the majority confuses the issue. A prohibition on fighting words is not a time, place, or manner restriction; it is a ban on a class of speech that conveys an overriding message of personal injury and imminent violence, a message that is at its ugliest when directed against groups that have long been the targets of discrimination. Accordingly, the ordinance falls within the first exception to the majority's theory.

As its second exception, the Court posits that certain content-based regulations will survive under the new regime if the regulated subclass "happens to be associated with particular 'secondary effects' of the speech." ... Again, there is a simple explanation for the Court's eagerness to craft an exception to its new First Amendment rule: Under the general rule the Court applies in this case, Title VII hostile work environment claims would suddenly be unconstitutional.

Title VII makes it unlawful to discriminate "because of [an] individual's race, color, religion, sex, or national origin," and the regulations covering hostile workplace claims forbid "sexual harassment," which includes "unwelcome sexual advances, requests for sexual favors, and other verbal or physical conduct of a sexual nature" which creates "an intimidating, hostile, or offensive working environment." The regulation does not prohibit workplace harassment generally; it focuses on what the majority would characterize as the "disfavored topic" of sexual harassment. In this way, Title VII is similar to the St. Paul ordinance ... because it "imposes special prohibitions on those speakers who express views on disfavored subjects." ...

Hence, the majority's second exception, which the Court indicates would insulate a Title VII hostile work environment claim from an underinclusiveness challenge because "sexually derogatory 'fighting words' ... may produce a violation of Title VII's general prohibition against sexual discrimination in employment practices." But application of this exception to a hostile work environment claim does not hold up under close examination.

First, the hostile work environment regulation ... would no more fall within a secondary effects exception than does the St. Paul ordinance. Second, the majority's focus on the statute's general prohibition on discrimination glosses over the language of the specific regulation governing hostile working environment, which reaches beyond any "incidental" effect on speech. If the relationship between the broader statute and specific regulation is sufficient ... then all St. Paul need do to bring its ordinance within this exception is to add some prefatory language concerning discrimination generally.

As the third exception to the Court's theory for deciding this case, the majority concocts a catchall exclusion to protect against unforeseen problems. ... This final exception would apply in cases in which "there is no realistic possibility that official suppression of ideas is afoot." ... [T]his case does not concern the official suppression of ideas. The majority discards this notion out-of-hand. ...

II

... I would decide the case on overbreadth grounds. ...

In attempting to narrow the scope of the St. Paul antibias ordinance, the Minnesota Supreme Court relied upon two of the categories of speech and expressive conduct that fall outside the First Amendment's protective sphere: words that incite "imminent lawless action," Brandenburg v. Ohio (1969), and "fighting" words, Chaplinsky. ... [It] drew upon the definition of fighting words that appears in Chaplinsky—words "which by their very utterance inflict injury or tend to incite an immediate breach of the peace." However, [it] was far from clear in identifying the "injuries" inflicted by the expression that St. Paul sought to regulate. Indeed, the Minnesota court emphasized ... that "the ordinance censors only those displays that one knows or should know will create anger, alarm or resentment based on racial, ethnic, gender or religious bias." I therefore understand the court to have ruled that St. Paul may constitutionally prohibit expression that "by its very utterance" causes "anger, alarm or resentment."

Our fighting words cases have made clear, however, that such generalized reactions are not sufficient to strip expression of its constitutional protection. The mere fact that expressive activity causes hurt feelings, offense, or resentment does not render the expression unprotected. See United States v. Eichman (1990); Texas v. Johnson (1989); Hustler Magazine, Inc. v. Falwell (1988); Cohen v. California (1971).

In the First Amendment context, "[c]riminal statutes must be scrutinized with particular care; those that make unlawful a substantial amount of constitutionally protected conduct may be held facially invalid even if they also have legitimate application." Houston v. Hill (1987). The St. Paul antibias ordinance is such a law. Although the ordinance reaches conduct that is unprotected, it also makes criminal expressive conduct that causes only hurt feelings, offense, or resentment, and is protected by the First Amendment. The ordinance is therefore fatally overbroad and invalid on its face. ...

Justice **BLACKMUN**, concurring in the judgment. ...

... [T]he Court seems to abandon the categorical approach, and inevitably to relax the level of scrutiny applicable to content-based laws. As Justice White points out, this weakens the traditional protections of speech. If all expressive activity must be accorded the same protection, that protection will be scant. ... It is sad that in its effort to reach a satisfying result in this case, the Court is willing to weaken First Amendment protections. ... I fear that the Court has been distracted from its proper mission by the temptation to decide the issue over "politically correct speech" and "cultural diversity," neither of which is presented here. ... I concur in the judgment ... because I agree with Justice White that this particular ordinance reaches beyond fighting words to speech protected by the First Amendment.

Justice **STEVENS**, with whom Justice **WHITE** and Justice **BLACK-MUN** join as to Part I, concurring in the judgment.

Conduct that creates special risks or causes special harms may be prohibited by special rules. Lighting a fire near an ammunition dump or a gasoline storage tank is especially dangerous; such behavior may be punished more severely than burning trash in a vacant lot. Threatening someone because of her race or religious beliefs may cause particularly severe trauma or touch off a riot, and threatening a high public official may cause substantial social disruption; such threats may be punished more severely than threats against someone based on, say, his support of a particular athletic team. There are legitimate, reasonable, and neutral justifications for such special rules.

This case involves the constitutionality of one such ordinance. Because the regulated conduct has some communicative content—a message of racial, religious or gender hostility—the ordinance raises two quite different First Amendment questions. Is the ordinance "overbroad" because it prohibits too much speech? If not, is it "underbroad" because it does not prohibit enough speech?

In answering these questions, my colleagues today wrestle with two broad principles: first, that certain "categories of expression [including fighting words] are 'not within the area of constitutionally protected speech,' " (White, J., concurring); and second, that "content-based regulations [of expression] are presumptively invalid." (Opinion of the Court.) Although in past opinions the Court has repeated both of these maxims, it has—quite rightly—adhered to neither with the absolutism suggested by my colleagues. Thus, while I agree that the St. Paul ordinance is unconstitutionally overbroad for the reasons stated in Part II of Justice White's opinion, I write separately to suggest how the allure of absolute principles has skewed the analysis of both the majority and concurring opinions.

I

Fifty years ago, the Court articulated a categorical approach to First Amendment jurisprudence. *Chaplinsky*. ... The Court today revises this categorical approach. It is not, the Court rules, that certain "categories" of expression are "unprotected," but rather that certain "elements" of expression are wholly "proscribable." To the Court, an expressive act, like a chemical compound, consists of more than one element. Although the act may be regulated because it contains a proscribable element, it may not be regulated on the basis of another (nonproscribable) element it also contains. Thus, obscene antigovernment speech may be regulated because it is obscene, but not because it is antigovernment. It is this revision of the categorical approach that allows the Court to assume that the St. Paul ordinance proscribes only fighting words, while at the same time concluding that the ordinance is invalid because it imposes a content-based regulation on expressive activity.

As an initial matter, the Court's revision of the categorical approach seems to me something of an adventure in a doctrinal wonderland, for the concept of "obscene antigovernment" speech is fantastical. ...

I am, however, even more troubled by the second step of the Court's analysis—namely, its conclusion that the St. Paul ordinance is an unconstitutional content-based regulation of speech. Drawing on broadly worded dicta, the Court establishes a near-absolute ban on content-based regulations of expression and holds that the First Amendment prohibits the regulation of fighting words by subject matter. Thus, while the Court rejects the "all-or-nothing-at-all" nature of the categorical approach, it promptly embraces an absolutism of its own: within a particular "proscribable" category of expression, the Court holds, a government must either proscribe all speech or no speech at all. This aspect of the Court's ruling fundamentally misunderstands the role and constitutional status of content-based regulations on speech, conflicts with the very nature of First Amendment jurisprudence, and disrupts well settled principles of First Amendment law.

Although the Court has, on occasion, declared that content-based regulations of speech are "never permitted," Police Dept. v. Mosley (1972), such claims are overstated. . . . Contrary to the broad dicta in *Mosley* and elsewhere, our decisions demonstrate that content-based distinctions, far from being presumptively invalid, are an inevitable and indispensable aspect of a coherent understanding of the First Amendment.

This is true at every level of First Amendment law. In broadest terms, our entire First Amendment jurisprudence creates a regime based on the content of speech. The scope of the First Amendment is determined by the content of expressive activity: Although the First Amendment broadly protects "speech," it does not protect the right to "fix prices, breach contracts, make false warranties, place bets with bookies, threaten, [or] extort." . . . Similarly, "the line between permissible advocacy and impermissible incitation to crime or violence depends, not merely on the setting in which the speech occurs, but also on exactly what the speaker had to say." *American Mini Theatres* (plurality opinion).

Likewise, whether speech falls within one of the categories of "unprotected" or "proscribable" expression is determined, in part, by its content. Whether a magazine is obscene, a gesture a fighting word, or a photograph child pornography is determined, in part, by its content. Even within categories of protected expression, the First Amendment status of speech is fixed by its content. *New York Times* and *Dun & Bradstreet* establish that the level of protection given to speech depends upon its subject matter: speech about public officials or matters of public concern receives greater protection than speech about other topics. . . .

Consistent with this general premise, we have frequently upheld content-based regulations of speech. For example, in *American Mini Theatres,* the Court upheld zoning ordinances that regulated movie theaters based on the content of the films shown. In *Pacifica Foundation* (plurality opinion), we upheld a restriction on the broadcast of specific indecent words. In *Lehman* (plurality opinion), we upheld a city law that permitted commercial advertising, but prohibited political advertising, on city buses. In Broadrick v. Oklahoma (1973), we upheld a state law that restricted the speech of state employees, but only as concerned partisan political matters. We have long recognized the power of the Federal Trade Commission to regulate misleading advertising and labeling, see, e.g., Siegel Co. v. FTC (1946), and the National Labor Relations Board's power to regulate an employer's election-related speech on the basis of its content. See, e.g., NLRB v. Gissel Packing

(1969). It is also beyond question that the Government may choose to limit advertisements for cigarettes, but not for cigars; choose to regulate airline advertising, see *Morales,* but not bus advertising; or choose to monitor solicitation by lawyers, see *Ohralik,* but not by doctors.

All of these cases involved the selective regulation of speech based on content—precisely the sort of regulation the Court invalidates today. ... Disregarding this vast body of case law, the Court today goes beyond even the overstatement in *Mosley* and applies the prohibition on content-based regulation to speech that the Court had until today considered wholly "unprotected" by the First Amendment—namely, fighting words. This new absolutism in the prohibition of content-based regulations severely contorts the fabric of settled First Amendment law.

Our First Amendment decisions have created a rough hierarchy in the constitutional protection of speech. Core political speech occupies the highest, most protected position; commercial speech and nonobscene, sexually explicit speech are regarded as a sort of second-class expression; obscenity and fighting words receive the least protection of all. Assuming that the Court is correct that this last class of speech is not wholly "unprotected," it certainly does not follow that fighting words and obscenity receive the same sort of protection afforded core political speech. Yet in ruling that proscribable speech cannot be regulated based on subject matter, the Court does just that. ... The Court today turns First Amendment law on its head: Communication that was once entirely unprotected (and that still can be wholly proscribed) is now entitled to greater protection than commercial speech— and possibly greater protection than core political speech. See Burson v. Freeman (1992).

Perhaps because the Court recognizes these perversities, it quickly offers some ad hoc limitations on its newly extended prohibition on content-based regulations. ... [But] [j]ust as Congress may determine that threats against the President entail more severe consequences than other threats, so St. Paul's City Council may determine that threats based on the target's race, religion, or gender cause more severe harm to both the target and to society than other threats. This latter judgment—that harms caused by racial, religious, and gender-based invective are qualitatively different from that caused by other fighting words— seems to me eminently reasonable and realistic. ...

Similarly, it is impossible to reconcile the Court's analysis of the St. Paul ordinance with its recognition that "a prohibition of fighting words that are directed at certain persons or groups ... would be facially valid." ... Whether the selective proscription of proscribable speech is defined by the protected target ("certain persons or groups") or the basis of the harm (injuries "based on race, color, creed, religion or gender") makes no constitutional difference: what matters is whether the legislature's selection is based on a legitimate, neutral, and reasonable distinction.

In sum, the central premise of the Court's ruling—that "content-based regulations are presumptively invalid"—has simplistic appeal, but lacks support in our First Amendment jurisprudence. To make matters worse, the Court today extends this overstated claim to reach categories of hitherto unprotected speech and, in doing so, wreaks havoc in an area of settled law. Finally, although the Court recognizes exceptions to its new principle, those exceptions undermine its very conclusion that the St. Paul ordinance is unconstitutional. Stated directly, the majority's position cannot withstand scrutiny.

II

Although I agree with much of Justice White's analysis, I do not join Part I–A of his opinion because I have reservations about the "categorical approach" to the First Amendment. ... Admittedly, the categorical approach to the First Amendment has some appeal: either expression is protected or it is not—the categories create safe harbors for governments and speakers alike. But this approach sacrifices subtlety for clarity and is ... ultimately unsound. ...

Perhaps sensing the limits of such an all-or-nothing approach, the Court has applied its analysis less categorically than its doctrinal statements suggest. The Court has recognized intermediate categories of speech (for example, for indecent nonobscene speech and commercial speech) and geographic categories of speech (public fora, limited public fora, nonpublic fora) entitled to varying levels of protection. ... [T]he history of the categorical approach is largely the history of narrowing the categories of unprotected speech.

III

... Unlike the Court, I do not believe that all content-based regulations are equally infirm and presumptively invalid; unlike Justice White, I do not believe that fighting words are wholly unprotected by the First Amendment. To the contrary, I believe our decisions establish a more complex and subtle analysis, one that considers the content and context of the regulated speech, and the nature and scope of the restriction on speech. ...

In applying this analysis to the St. Paul ordinance, I assume arguendo—as the Court does—that the ordinance regulates only fighting words and therefore is not overbroad. Looking to the content and character of the regulated activity, two things are clear. First, by hypothesis the ordinance bars only low-value speech, namely, fighting words. ... Second, the ordinance regulates "expressive conduct [rather] than ... the written or spoken word." Texas v. Johnson.

Looking to the context of the regulated activity, it is again significant that the statute (by hypothesis) regulates only fighting words. Whether words are fighting words is determined in part by their context. Fighting words are not words that merely cause offense; fighting words must be directed at individuals so as to "by their very utterance inflict injury." By hypothesis, then, the St. Paul ordinance restricts speech in confrontational and potentially violent situations. The case at hand is illustrative. The cross-burning ...—directed as it was to a single African–American family trapped in their home—was nothing more than a crude form of physical intimidation. That this cross-burning sends a message of racial hostility does not automatically endow it with complete constitutional protection.

Significantly, the St. Paul ordinance regulates speech not on the basis of its subject matter or the viewpoint expressed, but rather on the basis of the *harm* the speech causes. In this regard, the Court fundamentally misreads the St. Paul ordinance. The Court describes the St. Paul ordinance as regulating expression "addressed to one of [several] specified disfavored *topics*," as "policing disfavored *subjects*," and as "prohibit[ing] ... speech solely on the basis of the *subjects* the speech addresses." (Emphases supplied [by Justice Stevens].) Contrary to the Court's suggestion, the ordinance regulates only a subcategory of expression that causes *injuries* based on "race, color, creed, religion or gender," not a subcategory that involves *discussions* that concern those characteristics.[1] ...

Moreover, even if the St. Paul ordinance did regulate fighting words based on its subject matter, such a regulation would, in my opinion, be constitutional. ... [S]ubject-matter regulations generally do not raise the same concerns of government censorship and the distortion of public discourse presented by viewpoint regulations. ... Contrary to the suggestion of the majority, the St. Paul ordinance does *not* regulate expression based on viewpoint. The Court contends that the ordinance requires proponents of racial intolerance to "follow the Marquis of Queensbury Rules" while allowing advocates of racial tolerance to "fight freestyle." The law does no such thing. ...

The St. Paul ordinance is evenhanded. In a battle between advocates of tolerance and advocates of intolerance, the ordinance does not prevent either side from hurling fighting words at the other on the basis of their conflicting ideas, but it does bar *both* sides from hurling such words on the basis of the target's "race, color, creed, religion or gender."

---

1. The Court contends that this distinction is "wordplay," reasoning that "what makes [the harms caused by race-based threats] distinct from [the harms] produced by other fighting words is ... the fact that [the former are] caused by a *distinctive idea*." (Emphasis added [by Justice Stevens].) In this way, the Court concludes that regulating speech based on the injury it causes is no different from regulating speech based on its subject matter. This analysis fundamentally miscomprehends the role of "race, color, creed, religion [and] gender" in contemporary American society. One need look no further than the recent social unrest in the Nation's cities to see that race-based threats may cause more harm to society and to individuals than other threats. [Stevens was referring to the riots that swept Los Angeles in April and May 1992 after a state jury acquitted four policemen of brutally beating Rodney King, a black man they had arrested—Eds.] Just as the statute prohibiting threats against the President is justifiable because of the place of the President in our social and political order, so a statute prohibiting race-based threats is justifiable because of the place of race in our social and political order. Although it is regrettable that race occupies such a place and is so incendiary an issue, until the Nation matures beyond that condition, laws such as St. Paul's ordinance will remain reasonable and justifiable. [Footnote by Justice Stevens.]

To extend the Court's pugilistic metaphor, the St. Paul ordinance simply bans punches "below the belt"—*by either party*. It does not, therefore, favor one side of any debate.

Finally, it is noteworthy that the St. Paul ordinance is, as construed by the Court today, quite narrow. The St. Paul ordinance does not ban all "hate speech," nor does it ban, say, all cross-burnings or all swastika displays. Rather it only bans a subcategory of the already narrow category of fighting words. Such a limited ordinance leaves open and protected a vast range of expression on the subjects of racial, religious, and gender equality. As construed by the Court today, the ordinance certainly does not " 'raise the specter that the Government may effectively drive certain ideas or viewpoints from the marketplace.' " Petitioner is free to burn a cross to announce a rally or to express his views about racial supremacy, he may do so on private property or public land, at day or at night, so long as the burning is not so threatening and so directed at an individual as to "by its very [execution] inflict injury." Such a limited proscription scarcely offends the First Amendment.

. . . . Thus, were the ordinance not overbroad, I would vote to uphold it.

Editors' Notes

(1) **Query:** The opinions in this case are passionate as well as prolix and require careful reading and rereading. What were the chief issues of disagreement among the justices? To what extent did each depend on a *doctrinal approach* to constitutional interpretation? What role did the text itself play in the debate? Did any of the justices use a *purposive approach*? A *structuralist approach*?

(2) **Query:** To what extent is it accurate to label Scalia's opinion as an example of "clause-bound interpretivism"? Did he focus single-mindedly on the First Amendment, to the exclusion of other textual provisions (and the values they serve) such as the Equal Protection Clause of the Fourteenth Amendment, to say nothing of the Thirteenth Amendment? For a critique along these lines, see Akhil Reed Amar, "The Case of the Missing Amendments: *R.A.V. v. City of St. Paul*," 106 *Harv.L.Rev.* 124 (1992); for a response, see Alex Kozinski & Eugene Volokh, "A Penumbra Too Far," 106 *ibid.* 1639 (1993).

(3) **Query:** To what extent is it fair to say that Scalia accepted the notion that the First Amendment (and by implication the entire constitution) requires governmental neutrality between those who advocate the goals and ideals of the constitutional text and those who would destroy those goals and ideals? (Cf. Holmes's claim in *Abrams*, quoted above at p. 623.) To the extent this criticism is correct, did Scalia reject not only for judges but for all other public officials as well an *aspirational approach* to constitutional interpretation? A *purposive approach*?

(4) Compare the Canadian Supreme Court's decision in Queen v. Keestra (1990), which sustained an anti-hate speech law very much like St. Paul's. Amendments to that country's constitutional text adopted in 1981 included § 2:

Everyone has the following fundamental freedoms . . .

> (b) freedom of thought, belief, opinion, and expression, including freedom of the press and other media of communication.   . . .

Still, a close 4–3 majority reasoned that the law was constitutional because it furthered democratic principles and because racial, ethnic, or religious slurs were not essential to the purposes of free expression. In stark contrast to Scalia's opinion, Chief Justice Dickson stated for the majority:

> While we must guard carefully against judging expression according to its popularity, it is equally destructive of free expression values, as well as those other values which underlie a free and democratic society, to treat all expression as equally crucial to those principles at the core of s. 2(b).

Which premise, Scalia's that government must be largely neutral about the content of speech or Dickson's that a free society need not be completely neutral, better fits with democratic theory? Constitutionalist theory?

(5) Despite *R.A.V.*, Wisconsin v. Mitchell (1993) unanimously upheld a statute imposing harsher sentences on criminals who intentionally select their victims on the basis of race, religion, color, disability, sexual orientation, national origin or ancestry. But in Rosenberger v. University of Virginia (1995), a 5–4 ruling held that a state university could not discriminate against "selected viewpoints" by denying a student-run religious magazine a share of student-activities fees that the university made available to non-religious student publications. And in Capitol Square Review Bd. v. Pinette (1995), a 7–2 ruling held, under the First Amendment, that a municipality could not bar the Ku Klux Klan from erecting a cross on a public square open to other forms of private expression.

C. Defamation of Public Officials and Public Figures

"[W]e consider this case against the background of a profound national commitment to the principle that debate on public issues should be uninhibited, robust, and wide-open, and that it may well include vehement, caustic, and sometimes unpleasantly sharp attacks on government and public officials."

NEW YORK TIMES v. SULLIVAN
376 U.S. 254, 84 S.Ct. 710, 11 L.Ed.2d 686 (1964).

This case, involving a state's power to award damages in a libel action brought by public officials against critics of their official conduct, is reprinted above, at p. 634.

D. Offensive Expression

"We cannot sanction the view that the Constitution ... has little or no regard for that emotive function which ... may often be the more important element in the overall message. ..."—Justice HARLAN

"Cohen's absurd and immature behavior was mainly conduct and little speech."—Justice BLACKMUN

COHEN v. CALIFORNIA

403 U.S. 15, 91 S.Ct. 1780, 29 L.Ed.2d 284 (1971).

Paul Robert Cohen was sentenced to 30 days imprisonment for violating a state law against disturbing "the peace or quiet of any neighborhood or person." To protest the draft and the war in Vietnam, he had gone to a state courthouse, wearing a jacket bearing the slogan, "Fuck the draft." There was no evidence that he had spoken any words in the courthouse prior to his arrest. An appellate court sustained the conviction, the California supreme court refused review, and Cohen appealed to the U.S. Supreme Court.

Mr. Justice **HARLAN** delivered the opinion of the Court. ...

I ...

The conviction quite clearly rests upon the asserted offensiveness of the *words* Cohen used to convey his message to the public. The only "conduct" which the State sought to punish is the fact of communication. Thus, we deal here with a conviction resting solely upon "speech," not upon any separately identifiable conduct. ... Cf. United States v. O'Brien (1968). Further, the State certainly lacks power to punish Cohen for the underlying content of the message the inscription conveyed. At least so long as there is no showing of an intent to incite disobedience to or disruption of the draft, Cohen could not, consistently with the First and Fourteenth Amendments, be punished for asserting the evident position on the inutility or immorality of the draft his jacket reflected. Yates v. United States (1957).

Appellant's conviction, then, rests squarely upon his exercise of the "freedom of speech" protected from arbitrary governmental interference by the Constitution and can be justified, if at all, only as a valid regulation of the manner in which he exercised that freedom, not as a permissible prohibition on the substantive message it conveys. This does not end the inquiry, of course, for the First and Fourteenth Amendments have never been thought to give absolute protection to every individual to speak whenever or wherever he pleases, or to use any form of address in any circumstances that he chooses. In this vein, too, however, we think it important to note that several issues typically associated with such problems are not presented here.

In the first place, Cohen was tried under a statute applicable throughout the entire State. Any attempt to support this conviction on the ground that the statute seeks to preserve an appropriately decorous atmosphere in the courthouse where Cohen was arrested must fail. ... In the second place ... this case cannot be said to fall within those relatively few categories of instances where prior decisions have established the power of government to deal more comprehensively with certain forms of individual expression simply upon a showing that such a form was employed. This is not, for example, an obscenity case. ... It cannot plausibly be maintained that this vulgar allusion to the Selective Service System would conjure up such psychic stimulation in anyone likely to be confronted with Cohen's crudely defaced jacket.

This Court has also held that the States are free to ban the simple use, without a demonstration of additional justifying circumstances, of so-called "fighting words." ... *Chaplinsky* (1942). While the four-letter word displayed by Cohen in relation to the draft is not uncommonly employed in a personally provocative fashion, in this instance it was clearly not "directed to the person of the hearer." Cantwell v. Connecticut (1940). No individual actually or likely to be present could reasonably have regarded the words on appellant's jacket as a direct personal insult. Nor do we have here an instance of the exercise of the State's police power to prevent a speaker from intentionally provoking a given group to hostile reaction. Cf. Feiner v. New York (1951). There is ... no showing that anyone who saw Cohen was in fact violently aroused or that appellant intended such a result.

Finally ... much has been made of the claim that Cohen's distasteful mode of expression was thrust upon unwilling or unsuspecting viewers, and that the State might therefore legitimately act as it did in order to protect the sensitive. ... Of course, the mere presumed presence of unwitting listeners or viewers does not serve automatically to justify curtailing all speech capable of giving offense. While this Court has recognized that government may properly act in many situations to prohibit intrusion into the privacy of the home of unwelcome views and ideas which cannot be totally banned from the public dialogue, e.g., Rowan v. Post Office Dept. (1970), we have at the same time consistently stressed that "we are often 'captives' outside the sanctuary of the home and subject to objectionable speech." *Ibid.* The ability of government, consonant with the Constitution, to shut off discourse solely to protect others from hearing it is, in other words, dependent upon a showing that substantial privacy interests are being invaded in an essentially intolerable manner. Any broader view of this authority would effectively empower a majority to silence dissidents simply as a matter of personal predilections. ...

II

... [T]he issue flushed by this case stands out in bold relief. It is whether California can excise, as "offensive conduct," one particular scurrilous epithet from the public discourse, either upon the theory of the court below that its use is inherently likely to cause violent reaction or upon a more general assertion that the States, acting as guardians of public morality, may properly remove this offensive word from the public vocabulary.

The rationale of the California court is plainly untenable. At most it reflects an "undifferentiated fear or apprehension of disturbance [which] is not enough to overcome the right to freedom of expression." Tinker v. Des Moines (1969). We have been shown no evidence that substantial numbers of citizens are standing ready to strike out physically at whoever may assault their sensibilities with execrations like that uttered by Cohen. There may be some persons about with such lawless and violent proclivities, but that is an insufficient base upon which to erect, consistently with constitutional values, a governmental power to force persons who wish to ventilate their dissident views into avoiding particular forms of expression. . . .

Admittedly, it is not so obvious that the First and Fourteenth Amendments must be taken to disable the States from punishing public utterance of this unseemly expletive in order to maintain what they regard as a suitable level of discourse within the body politic. We think, however, that examination and reflection will reveal the shortcomings of a contrary viewpoint.

. . . [W]e cannot overemphasize that, in our judgment, most situations where the State has a justifiable interest in regulating speech will fall within one or more of the various established exceptions . . . to the usual rule that governmental bodies may not prescribe the form or content of individual expression. Equally important to our conclusion is the constitutional backdrop against which our decision must be made. The constitutional right of free expression is powerful medicine in a society as diverse and populous as ours. It is designed and intended to remove governmental restraints from the arena of public discussion, putting the decision as to what views shall be voiced largely into the hands of each of us, in the hope that use of such freedom will ultimately produce a more capable citizenry and more perfect polity and in the belief that no other approach would comport with the premise of individual dignity and choice upon which our political system rests. See Whitney v. California (1927) (Brandeis, J., concurring).

To many, the immediate consequence of this freedom may often appear to be only verbal tumult, discord, and even offensive utterance. These are, however, within established limits, in truth necessary side effects of the broader enduring values which the process of open debate permits us to achieve. That the air may at times seem filled with verbal cacophony is, in this sense not a sign of weakness but of strength. . . .

Against this perception of the constitutional policies involved, we discern certain more particularized considerations that peculiarly call for reversal of this conviction. First, the principle contended for by the State seems inherently boundless. How is one to distinguish this from any other offensive word? Surely the State has no right to cleanse public debate to the point where it is grammatically palatable to the most squeamish among us.   Yet no readily ascertainable general principle exists for stopping short of that result were we to affirm the judgment below.   For, while the particular four-letter word being litigated here is perhaps more distasteful than most others of its genre, it is nevertheless often true that one man's vulgarity is another's lyric. Indeed, we think it is largely because governmental officials cannot make principled distinctions in this area that the Constitution leaves matters of taste and style so largely to the individual.

Additionally, we cannot overlook ... that much linguistic expression serves a dual communicative function: it conveys not only ideas capable of relatively precise, detached explication, but otherwise inexpressible emotions as well.   In fact, words are often chosen as much for their emotive as their cognitive force.   We cannot sanction the view that the Constitution, while solicitous of the cognitive content of individual speech, has little or no regard for that emotive function which, practically speaking, may often be the more important element of the overall message sought to be communicated.   ...

Finally ... we cannot indulge the facile assumption that one can forbid particular words without also running a substantial risk of suppressing ideas in the process.   Indeed, governments might soon seize upon the censorship of particular words as a convenient guise for banning the expression of unpopular views.   ...

Reversed.

Mr. Justice **BLACKMUN,** with whom the Chief Justice [**BURGER**] and Mr. Justice **BLACK** join.

I dissent.   ... 1. Cohen's absurd and immature behavior was mainly conduct and little speech.   ... Further, the case appears to me to be well within the sphere of *Chaplinsky* (1942).   ... As a consequence, this Court's agonizing First Amendment values seems misplaced and unnecessary.   2. I am not at all certain that the California Court of Appeal's construction of [the state statute] is now the authoritative California construction.   ...

Mr. Justice **WHITE** concurs in para. 2 of Mr. Justice **BLACKMUN's** dissenting opinion.

Editors' Notes

(1) **Query:** To what extent did *Cohen* depend on a *textual approach* to constitutional interpretation? A *doctrinal approach*? A *structuralist approach*? A general *purposive approach* or *reinforcing representative democracy* in particular?

(2) **Query:** Recall that in *Chaplinsky* (1942; reprinted above, p. 677), the Court had listed "profane" and "insulting or 'fighting' words" as categories of unprotected expression. To what extent did *Cohen* undermine these categories and accord full protection under the First Amendment to such expression?

To what extent did *Cohen* support Justice Scalia's reasoning in *R.A.V.*? Justices Stevens's?

(3) **Query:** Did *Chaplinsky* presuppose that the First Amendment protects only the cognitive content of a message, to the exclusion of its emotive force? Did *Cohen* reject this rationalistic model of freedom of expression? Which is more congruent with democratic theory? Constitutionalism?

(4) For discussions of *Cohen,* see David L. Paletz and William F. Harris II, "Four–Letter Threats to Authority," 37 *Jo. of Pols.* 955 (1975); and Daniel Farber, "Civilizing Public Discourse: An Essay on Professor Bickel, Justice Harlan, and the Enduring Significance of Cohen v. California," 1980 *Duke L.J.* 283.

(5) The strongest dissent against the principles enunciated in *Cohen* came a year later, after Lewis F. Powell had replaced Hugo Black and William Rehnquist had taken John Marshall Harlan II's place. The Court remanded three cases—Rosenfeld v. New Jersey (1972), Lewis v. New Orleans (1972), and Brown v. Oklahoma (1972)—to lower courts for reconsideration in light of *Cohen* and Gooding v. Wilson (1972; discussed above, p. 680). Powell, joined by Burger and Blackmun, dissented, noting that Rosenfeld had spoken before an audience of about 150 people, including about 40 children and 25 women, and had used "the adjective 'M_____ F_____' on four occasions, to describe the teachers, the school board, the town and his own country." He had been convicted under a state statute making it disorderly conduct to utter indecent language in a public place. Powell added:

> The preservation of the right to free and robust speech is accorded high priority in our society and under the Constitution. Yet, there are other significant values. One of the hallmarks of a civilized society is the level and quality of discourse. We have witnessed in recent years a disquieting deterioration in the standards of taste and civility in speech. For the increasing number of persons who derive satisfaction from vocabularies dependent upon filth and obscenities, there are abundant opportunities to gratify their debased tastes. ... The shock and sense of affront, and sometimes the injury to mind and spirit, can be as great from words as from some physical attacks.
>
> . . .

Chief Justice Burger—joined by Blackmun and Rehnquist—was more foreboding:

> It is barely a century since men in parts of this country carried guns constantly because the law did not afford protection. In that setting, the words used in these cases, if directed toward such an armed civilian, could well have led to death or serious bodily injury. When we undermine the general belief that the law will give protection against fighting words and profane and abusive language such as the utterances involved in these cases, we take steps to return to the law of the jungle. ...

We repeat our question from Editors' Note 5 to *Chaplinsky,* above, p. 680: Do cases like *Cohen, Gooding,* and *Rosenfeld* demonstrate how American culture has changed constitutional meaning?

E. Harmful Expression

"The Constitution forbids the state to declare one perspective right and silence opponents."

AMERICAN BOOKSELLERS ASSOCIATION, INC. v. HUDNUT
771 F.2d 323 (U.S. Court of Appeals, 7th Cir., 1985).

The Supreme Court has held that "obscenity" is an unprotected category of expression. To be "obscene," a publication "must, taken as a whole, appeal to the prurient interest, must contain patently offensive depictions or descriptions of specified sexual conduct, and on the whole have no serious literary, artistic, political, or scientific value." Brockett v. Spokane Arcades, Inc. (1985) (interpreting Miller v. California [1973]). Both offensiveness assessed by the standards of the community and an appeal to something other than "normal, healthy sexual desires" are essential elements of "obscenity." Id. Pornography as distinguished from obscenity, however, has traditionally received First Amendment protection.

Conceiving pornography as denigrating women, Catharine A. MacKinnon and Andrea Dworkin drafted an anti-pornography ordinance that the Minneapolis City Council adopted in 1983. The Mayor, however, vetoed it as infringing on freedom of speech and press. Subsequently, Indianapolis adopted a similar ordinance, which prohibited people to "traffic" in pornography, "coerce" others into performing in pornographic works, or "force" pornography on anyone. It also provided that anyone injured by someone who has seen or read pornography could sue the maker or seller. A number of distributors and readers of books, magazines, and films challenged the constitutionality of the ordinance, arguing that it violated the First Amendment. The district court held it unconstitutional. The City appealed to the Court of Appeals for the Seventh Circuit.

EASTERBROOK, Circuit Judge. ...

"Pornography" under the ordinance is "the graphic sexually explicit subordination of women, whether in pictures or in words, that also includes [presenting women]":

(1) ... as sexual objects who enjoy pain or humiliation; or

(2) ... as sexual objects who experience sexual pleasure in being raped; or

(3) ... as sexual objects tied up or cut up or mutilated or bruised or physically hurt, or as dismembered or truncated or fragmented or severed into body parts; or

(4) ... as being penetrated by objects or animals; or

(5) ... in scenarios of degradation, injury, abasement, torture, shown as filthy or inferior, bleeding, bruised, or hurt in a context that makes these conditions sexual; or

(6) . . . as sexual objects for domination, conquest, violation, exploitation, possession, or use, or through postures or positions of servility or submission or display.

The statute provides that the "use of men, children, or transsexuals in the place of women in paragraphs (1) through (6) above shall also constitute pornography under this section." The ordinance as passed in April 1984 defined "sexually explicit" to mean actual or simulated intercourse or the uncovered exhibition of the genitals, buttocks or anus. An amendment in June 1984 deleted this provision, leaving the term undefined.

The Indianapolis ordinance does not refer to the prurient interest, to offensiveness, or to the standards of the community. It demands attention to particular depictions, not to the work judged as a whole. It is irrelevant under the ordinance whether the work has literary, artistic, political, or scientific value. The City and many *amici* point to these omissions as virtues. They maintain that pornography influences attitudes, and the statute is a way to alter the socialization of men and women rather than to vindicate community standards of offensiveness. And as one of the principal drafters of the ordinance has asserted, "if a woman is subjected, why should it matter that the work has other value?" Catharine A. MacKinnon, "Pornography, Civil Rights, and Speech," 20 *Harv.Civ.Rts.—Civ.Lib.L.Rev.* 1, 21 (1985). . . .

We do not try to balance the arguments for and against an ordinance such as this. The ordinance discriminates on the ground of the content of the speech. Speech treating women in the approved way—in sexual encounters "premised on equality" (MacKinnon, supra, at 22)—is lawful no matter how sexually explicit. Speech treating women in the disapproved way—as submissive in matters sexual or as enjoying humiliation—is unlawful no matter how significant the literary, artistic, or political qualities of the work taken as a whole. The state may not ordain preferred viewpoints in this way. The Constitution forbids the state to declare one perspective right and silence opponents. . . .

III

"If there is any fixed star in our constitutional constellation, it is that no official, high or petty, can prescribe what shall be orthodox in politics, nationalism, religion, or other matters of opinion or force citizens to confess by word or act their faith therein." W.Va. St. Bd. of Ed'n v. Barnette (1943). Under the First Amendment the government must leave to the people the evaluation of ideas. Bald or subtle, an idea is as powerful as the audience allows it to be. . . . A pernicious belief may prevail. Totalitarian governments today rule much of the planet, practicing suppression of billions and spreading dogma that may enslave others. One of the things that separates our society from theirs is our absolute right to propagate opinions that the government finds wrong or even hateful.

The ideas of the Klan may be propagated. Brandenburg v. Ohio (1969). Communists may speak freely and run for office. DeJonge v. Oregon (1937). The Nazi Party may march through a city with a large Jewish population. Collin v. Smith (7th Cir.), *cert. denied* (1978). ... People may teach religions that other despise. People may seek to repeal laws guaranteeing equal opportunity in employment or to revoke the constitutional amendments granting the vote to blacks and women. They may do this because "above all else, the First Amendment means that government has no power to restrict expression because of its message [or] its ideas. ..." Police Department v. Mosley (1972).

Under the ordinance graphic sexually explicit speech is "pornography" or not depending on the perspective the author adopts. Speech that "subordinates" women ... is forbidden, no matter how great the literary or political value of the work taken as a whole. Speech that portrays women in positions of equality is lawful, no matter how graphic the sexual content. This is thought control. It establishes an "approved" view of women, of how they may react to sexual encounters, of how the sexes may relate to each other. Those who espouse the approved view may use sexual images; those who do not, may not.

Indianapolis justifies the ordinance on the ground that pornography affects thoughts. Men who see women depicted as subordinate are more likely to treat them so. Pornography is an aspect of dominance. It does not persuade people so much as change them. It works by socializing, by establishing the expected and the permissible. In this view pornography is not an idea; pornography is the injury.

There is much to this perspective. Beliefs are also facts. People often act in accordance with the images and patterns they find around them. People raised in a religion tend to accept the tenets of that religion, often without independent examination. People taught from birth that black people are fit only for slavery rarely rebelled against that creed; beliefs coupled with the self-interest of the masters established a social structure that inflicted great harm while enduring for centuries. Words and images act at the level of the subconscious before they persuade at the level of the conscious. Even the truth has little chance unless a statement fits within the framework of beliefs that may never have been subjected to rational study.

Therefore we accept the premises of this legislation. Depictions of subordination tend to perpetuate subordination. The subordinate status of women in turn leads to affront and lower pay at work, insult and injury at home, battery and rape on the streets.[1] ...

---

1. MacKinnon's article collects empirical work that supports this proposition. The social science studies are very difficult to interpret, however, and they conflict. ... In saying that we accept the finding that pornography as the ordinance defines it leads to unhappy consequences, we mean only that there is evidence to this effect, that this evidence is consistent with much human experience, and that as judges we must accept the legislative resolution of such disputed empirical questions. See Gregg v. Georgia (1976) (opinion of Stewart, Powell, and Stevens, J.J.). [Footnote by the Court.]

Yet this simply demonstrates the power of pornography as speech. All of these unhappy effects depend on mental intermediation. Pornography affects how people see the world, their fellows, and social relations. If pornography is what pornography does, so is other speech. Hitler's orations affected how some Germans saw Jews. Communism is a world view, not simply a *Manifesto* by Marx and Engels or a set of speeches. Efforts to suppress communist speech in the United States were based on the belief that the public acceptability of such ideas would increase the likelihood of totalitarian government. Religions affect socialization in the most pervasive way. ... Many people believe that the existence of television, apart from the content of specific programs, leads to intellectual laziness, to a penchant for violence, to many other ills. The Alien and Sedition Acts passed during the administration of John Adams rested on a sincerely held belief that disrespect for the government leads to social collapse and revolution—a belief with support in the history of many nations. Most governments of the world act on this empirical regularity, suppressing critical speech. In the United States, however, the strength of the support for this belief is irrelevant. Seditious libel is protected speech unless the danger is not only grave but also imminent. See New York Times Co. v. Sullivan (1964); cf. *Brandenburg;* New York Times Co. v. United States (1971).

Racial bigotry, anti-semitism, violence on television, reporters' biases—these and many more influence the culture and shape our socialization. None is directly answerable by more speech, unless that speech too finds its place in the popular culture. Yet all is protected as speech, however insidious. Any other answer leaves the government in control of all of the institutions of culture, the great censor and director of which thoughts are goods for us.

Sexual responses often are unthinking responses, and the association of sexual arousal with the subordination of women therefore may have a substantial effect. But almost all cultural stimuli provoke unconscious responses. Religious ceremonies condition their participants. Teachers convey messages by selecting what not to cover. ... Television scripts contain unarticulated assumptions. People may be conditioned in subtle ways. If the fact that speech plays a role in a process of conditioning were enough to permit governmental regulation, that would be the end of freedom of speech.

It is possible to interpret the claim that pornography is the harm in a different way. Indianapolis emphasizes the injury that models in pornographic films and pictures may suffer. The record contains materials depicting sexual torture, penetration of women by red-hot irons and the like. These concerns have nothing to do with written materials subject to the statute, and physical injury can occur with or without the "subordination" of women. [A] state may make injury in the course of producing a film unlawful independent of the viewpoint expressed in the film.

The more immediate point, however, is that the image of pain is not necessarily pain. In *Body Double,* a suspense film directed by Brian DePalma, a woman who has disrobed and presented a sexually explicit display is murdered . . .—yet no one believes that the actress suffered pain or died. In *Barbarella* a character played by Jane Fonda is at times displayed in sexually explicit ways and at times shown "bleeding, bruised, [and] hurt in a context that makes these conditions sexual"— and again no one believes that Fonda was actually tortured to make the film. In *Carnal Knowledge* a women grovels to please the sexual whims of a character played by Jack Nicholson; no one believes that there was a real sexual submission, and the Supreme Court held the film protected by the First Amendment. Jenkins v. Georgia (1974). And this works both ways. The description of women's sexual domination of men in *Lysistrata* was not real dominance. Depictions may affect slavery, war, or sexual roles, but a book about slavery is not itself slavery, or a book about death by poison a murder.

Much of Indianapolis's argument rests on the belief that when speech is "unanswerable," and the metaphor that there is a "market-place of ideas" does not apply, the First Amendment does not apply either. The metaphor is honored; Milton's *Aeropagitica* and John Stewart [sic] Mill's *On Liberty* defend freedom of speech on the ground that the truth will prevail, and many of the most important cases under the First Amendment recite this position. The Framers undoubtedly believed it. As a general matter it is true. But the Constitution does not make the dominance of truth a necessary condition of freedom of speech. To say that it does would be to confuse an outcome of free speech with a necessary condition for the application of the amendment.

A power to limit speech on the ground that truth has not yet prevailed and is not likely to prevail implies the power to declare truth. . . . Under the First Amendment, however, there is no such thing as a false idea, Gertz v. Robert Welch, Inc. (1974), so the government may not restrict speech on the ground that in a free exchange truth is not yet dominant. . . .

We come, finally, to the argument that pornography is "low value" speech, that it is enough like obscenity that Indianapolis may prohibit it. Some cases hold that speech far removed from politics and other subjects at the core of the Framers' concerns may be subjected to special regulation. E.g., FCC v. Pacifica Foundation (1978); Young v. American Mini Theatres (1976) (plurality opinion); *Chaplinsky* (1942). [But t]hese cases do not sustain statutes that select among viewpoints. . . .

At all events, "pornography" is not low value speech within the meaning of these cases. . . . But Indianapolis left out of its definition any reference to literary, artistic, political, or scientific value. The ordinance applies to graphic sexually explicit subordination in works great and small.[2] The Court sometimes balances the value of speech

---

2. Indianapolis briefly argues that *Beauharnais* (1952) . . . supports the ordinance. In *Collin,* we concluded that cases such as *New York Times* had so washed away the

against the costs of its restriction, but it does this by category of speech and not by the content of particular works. Indianapolis has created an approved point of view and so loses the support of these cases.

Any rationale we could imagine in support of this ordinance could not be limited to sex discrimination. Free speech has been on balance an ally of those seeking change. Governments that want stasis start by restricting speech. Culture is a powerful force of continuity; Indianapolis paints pornography as part of the culture of power. Change in any complex system ultimately depends on the ability of outsiders to challenge accepted views and the reigning institutions. Without a strong guarantee of freedom of speech, there is no effective right to challenge what is. ...

Affirmed.

SWYGERT, Senior Circuit Judge, concurring. ...

Editors' Notes

(1) In 1986 the Supreme Court summarily affirmed the decision of the Seventh Circuit. Chief Justice Burger and Justices Rehnquist and O'Connor dissented, urging that the case be set for oral argument.

(2) **Query:** Granted that efforts to control pornography raise problems for freedom of communication, what are the relevant issues for democratic theory? Assuming that anti-pornography legislation is enacted by freely chosen officials, what problems arise for democratic theory? Does *reinforcing representative democracy* have anything relevant to say here? What about constitutionalism?

(3) **Query:** Is the remedy of more speech or writing, which Brandeis suggested for discourse that is directly political (*Whitney* [1927; reprinted above, p. 651]), likely to be effective in protecting women against pornography? Some feminists argue that pornography (1) so denigrates women that their voices will not be heard; and (2) operates on the subconscious, and thus is not directly answerable by more speech. (Such feminists point to parallels with racist speech.) Did Judge Easterbrook adequately respond to these arguments?

(4) In *Hudnut* Easterbrook and, to some extent, Scalia in *R.A.V.* adopt Holmes's position in Gitlow v. New York (1925) that the First Amendment requires government to be indifferent to the outcomes of political debates. Does democratic theory require such a neutral attitude? Does constitutionalism? Does the American constitutional text, read as a whole? The larger constitutional system? What does Holmes's interpretation of the First Amend-

---

foundations of *Beauharnais* that it could not be considered authoritative. If we are wrong in this, however, the case still does not support the ordinance. It is not clear that depicting women as subordinate in sexually explicit ways, even combined with a depiction of pleasure in rape, would fit within the definition of a group libel. The well received film *Swept Away* used explicit sex, plus taking pleasure in rape, to make a political statement, not to defame. Work must be an insult or slur for its own sake to come within the ambit of *Beauharnais,* and a work need not be scurrilous at all to be "pornography" under the ordinance. [Footnote by the Court.]

ment say to the question WHO? To the question WHAT does "the Constitution" include?

(5) Enactment of MacKinnon and Dworkin's anti-pornography ordinance was the result of a remarkable coalition of strange bedfellows, radical feminists and the Moral Majority. See Donald A. Downs, *The New Politics of Pornography* (Chicago: University of Chicago Press, 1989). MacKinnon's writings on pornography include *Only Words* (Cambridge: Harvard University Press, 1993); "Pornography as Defamation and Discrimination," 71 *B.U.L.Rev.* 793 (1991); "Pornography, Civil Rights, and Speech," 20 *Harv.Civ.Rts.—Civ.Lib. L.Rev.* 1 (1985), cited in the opinion above; and "Not a Moral Issue," 2 *Yale L. & Pol. Rev.* 321 (1984). The latter two articles are reprinted in her *Feminism Unmodified* (Cambridge: Harvard University Press, 1987). Andrea Dworkin's publications on the subject include *Pornography: Men Possessing Women* (New York: Perigee, 1981); and "Pornography Is a Civil Rights Issue for Women," 21 *U.Mich.J.L.Ref.* 55 (1987).

(6) In Butler v. The Queen (1992), the Supreme Court of Canada, while acknowledging that the country's criminal obscenity law restricted freedom of expression, upheld the law on the ground that it was justifiable to ban pornography that harms women. The decision redefined "obscenity" as "sexually explicit material that involves violence or degradation." In explicitly accepting the argument that pornography harms women, the Court stated: "If true equality between male and female persons is to be achieved, we cannot ignore the threat to equality resulting from exposure to audiences of certain types of violent and degrading material." Which argument, that of Easterbrook or the Canadian Supreme Court, is more congruent with democratic theory? With constitutionalism?

(7) The enormous literature dealing with the regulation of pornography includes, in addition to the works cited above: David Copp & Susan Wendells, eds., *Pornography and Censorship* (Buffalo: Prometheus Books, 1983); Nan D. Hunter and Sylvia A. Law, "Brief Amici Curiae of Feminist Anti–Censorship Taskforce et al. in *American Booksellers Association v. Hudnut*," reprinted in 21 *U.Mich.J.L.Ref.* 69 (1987); Kenneth Karst, "Boundaries and Reasons: Freedom of Expression and the Subordination of Groups," 1990 *U.Ill.L.Rev.* 95; Laura Lederer ed., *Take Back the Night: Women on Pornography* (New York: William Morrow, 1980); Carlin Meyer, "Sex, Sin, and Women's Liberation: Against Porn–Suppression," 72 *Tex.L.Rev.* 1097 (1994); Frank Michelman, "Conceptions of Democracy in American Constitutional Argument: The Case of Pornography Regulation," 56 *Tenn.L.Rev.* 291 (1989); Nadine Strossen, *Defending Pornography: Free Speech, Sex, and the Fight for Women's Rights* (New York: Scribner's, 1994); Cass R. Sunstein, "Pornography and the First Amendment," 1986 *Duke L.J.* 589; Sunstein, *Democracy and the Problem of Free Speech* (New York: The Free Press, 1993), ch. 7; Laurence H. Tribe, *American Constitutional Law* (2d ed.; Mineola, NY: Foundation Press, 1988), pp. 920–28; and Robin West, "The Feminist–Conservative Anti–Pornography Alliance and the 1986 Attorney General's Commission on Pornography Report," 1987 *Am.B.Found.Res.J.* 681.

F. Outrageous Expression

" 'Outrageousness' in the area of political and social discourse has an inherent subjectiveness about it which would allow a jury to impose liability on the basis of the jurors' tastes or views. ..."

HUSTLER MAGAZINE, INC. v. FALWELL

485 U.S. 46, 108 S.Ct. 876, 99 L.Ed.2d 41 (1988).

Hustler Magazine published a "parody" of an advertisement for Campari Liqueur that contained the name and picture of nationally known television evangelist and political activist Jerry Falwell and was entitled "Jerry Falwell talks about his first time." The parody included an alleged "interview" in which Falwell stated that his "first time" was during a drunken incestuous rendezvous with his mother in an outhouse. The parody also suggested that he was a hypocrite who preached only when drunk. In small print at the bottom of the page, the ad contained the disclaimer, "ad parody—not to be taken seriously." The magazine's table of contents also listed the ad as "Fiction; Ad and Personality Parody."

Rev. Falwell sued *Hustler* and its publisher, Larry Flynt, for invasion of privacy, libel, and intentional infliction of emotional distress. Falwell did not dispute that he was a "public figure" under New York Times v. Sullivan (1964; reprinted above, p. 634) and later cases. The district judge directed a verdict against Falwell on the privacy claim but submitted the other two claims to a jury. The jury found for *Hustler* and Flynt on the libel claim but for Falwell on his claim for intentional infliction of emotional distress and awarded compensatory damages of $100,000 and punitive damages of $50,000 each against *Hustler* and Flynt. The court of appeals affirmed, and the Supreme Court granted certiorari.

Chief Justice **REHNQUIST** delivered the opinion of the Court. ...

... Respondent would have us find that a State's interest in protecting public figures from emotional distress is sufficient to deny First Amendment protection to speech that is patently offensive and is intended to inflict emotional injury, even when that speech could not reasonably have been interpreted as stating actual facts about the public figure involved. This we decline to do.

At the heart of the First Amendment is the recognition of the fundamental importance of the free flow of ideas and opinions on matters of public interest and concern. ... The sort of robust political debate encouraged by the First Amendment is bound to produce speech that is critical of those who hold public office or those public figures who are "intimately involved in the resolution of important public questions or, by reason of their fame, shape events in areas of concern to society at large." AP v. Walker, decided with Curtis Publishing Co. v. Butts (1967) (Warren, C. J., concurring in result). ... Such criticism, inevitably, will not always be reasoned or moderate; public figures as well as public officials will be subject to "vehement, caustic, and sometimes unpleasantly sharp attacks," *New York Times* [1964]. ...

Of course, this does not mean that *any* speech about a public figure is immune from sanction in the form of damages. Since *New York Times,* we have consistently ruled that a public figure may hold a speaker liable for the damage to reputation caused by publication of a defamatory falsehood, but only if the statement was made "with knowledge that it was false or with reckless disregard of whether it was false or not." False statements of fact are particularly valueless; they interfere with the truth-seeking function of the marketplace of ideas, and they cause damage to an individual's reputation that cannot easily be repaired by counterspeech, however persuasive or effective. See Gertz [v. Robert Welch, Inc. (1974)]. But even though falsehoods have little value in and of themselves, they are "nevertheless inevitable in free debate," *id.,* and a rule that would impose strict liability on a publisher for false factual assertions would have an undoubted "chilling" effect on speech relating to public figures that does have constitutional value. ...

Respondent argues, however, that a different standard should apply in this case because here the State seeks to prevent not reputational damage, but the severe emotional distress suffered by the person who is the subject of an offensive publication. ... It is the intent to cause injury that is the gravamen of the tort, and the State's interest in preventing emotional harm simply outweighs whatever interest a speaker may have in speech of this type.

Generally speaking the law does not regard the intent to inflict emotional distress as one which should receive much solicitude, and it is quite understandable that most if not all jurisdictions have chosen to make it civilly culpable where the conduct in question is sufficiently "outrageous." But in the world of debate about public affairs, many things done with motives that are less than admirable are protected by the First Amendment. In Garrison v. Louisiana (1964), we held that even when a speaker or writer is motivated by hatred or ill will his expression was protected by the First Amendment. ... Thus while such a bad motive may be deemed controlling for purposes of tort liability in other areas of the law, we think the First Amendment prohibits such a result in the area of public debate about public figures.

Were we to hold otherwise, there can be little doubt that political cartoonists and satirists would be subjected to damages awards without any showing that their work falsely defamed its subject. ... The appeal of the political cartoon or caricature is often based on exploitation of unfortunate physical traits or politically embarrassing events—an exploitation often calculated to injure the feelings of the subject of the portrayal. The art of the cartoonist is often not reasoned or evenhanded, but slashing and one-sided. ...

Despite their sometimes caustic nature, from the early cartoon portraying George Washington as an ass down to the present day, graphic depictions and satirical cartoons have played a prominent role in public and political debate. ... From the viewpoint of history it is clear that our political discourse would have been considerably poorer without them.

Respondent contends, however, that the caricature in question here was so "outrageous" as to distinguish it from more traditional political cartoons. There is no doubt that the caricature of respondent and his mother published in Hustler is at best a distant cousin of the political cartoons described above, and a rather poor relation at that. If it were possible by laying down a principled standard to separate the one from the other, public discourse would probably suffer little or no harm. But we doubt that there is any such standard, and we are quite sure that the pejorative description "outrageous" does not supply one. "Outrageousness" in the area of political and social discourse has an inherent subjectiveness about it which would allow a jury to impose liability on the basis of the jurors' tastes or views, or perhaps on the basis of their dislike of a particular expression. An "outrageousness" standard thus runs afoul of our longstanding refusal to allow damages to be awarded because the speech in question may have an adverse emotional impact on the audience. See NAACP v. Claiborne Hardware Co. (1982) ("Speech does not lose its protected character ... simply because it may embarrass others or coerce them into action.") And, as we stated in FCC v. Pacifica Foundation (1978):

> [T]he fact that society may find speech offensive is not a sufficient reason for suppressing it. Indeed, if it is the speaker's opinion that gives offense, that consequence is a reason for according it constitutional protection. For it is a central tenet of the First Amendment that the government must remain neutral in the marketplace of ideas.

Admittedly, these oft-repeated First Amendment principles, like other principles, are subject to limitations. We recognized in *Pacifica Foundation* that speech that is " 'vulgar,' 'offensive,' and 'shocking' " is "not entitled to absolute constitutional protection under all circumstances." In *Chaplinsky* (1942), we held that a State could lawfully punish an individual for the use of insulting "fighting" words. ... These limitations are but recognition of the observation in Dun & Bradstreet, Inc. v. Greenmoss Builders, Inc. (1985) that this Court has "long recognized that not all speech is of equal First Amendment importance." But the sort of expression involved in this case does not seem to us to be governed by any exception to the general First Amendment principles stated above.

We conclude that public figures and public officials may not recover for the tort of intentional infliction of emotional distress by reason of publications such as the one here at issue without showing in addition that the publication contains a false statement of fact which was made with "actual malice," i.e., with knowledge that the statement was false or with reckless disregard as to whether or not it was true. This is not merely a "blind application" of the *New York Times* standard, it reflects our considered judgment that such a standard is necessary to give adequate "breathing space" to the freedoms protected by the First Amendment.

Reversed.

Justice **KENNEDY** took no part in the consideration or decision of this case.

Justice **WHITE**, concurring in the judgment. . . .

Editors' Notes

(1) **Query:** Recall that Rehnquist had urged an approach to constitutional interpretation blending *textualism* and *originalism*. ("The Notion of a Living Constitution," reprinted above, p. 243.) Did he use either approach in this opinion? What approach(es) did he use? To what extent did he rely on a *doctrinal approach*?

(2) **Query:** Would the opposite result in *Hustler* have given public figures an opportunity to outflank *New York Times*'s standard of "actual malice" to sue critics for libel? Does the actual result in *Hustler* give critics an easy way around *New York Times*'s standard of "actual malice" in that all they need do to lodge false charges is to label them a spoof, knowing that some tar will stick?

(3) **Query:** An approach including democratic theory in "the Constitution" or requiring interpreters to construe the First Amendment as being based on such a theory might seem to justify the results in *New York Times* and *Hustler* as well as in R.A.V. v. St. Paul (1992; reprinted above, p. 686). But do these results mean that democratic theory is ultimately self-destructive in requiring society to stand idly by if political discussion disintegrates into vulgar name calling? Is the version of democratic theory that would justify these sorts of decisions the only version available under the American constitutional system? What would another version look like? (Most European countries who think themselves constitutional democracies make it much easier than does the United States for public officials to obtain libel judgments.)

(4) For an account of this case, see Rodney A. Smolla, *Jerry Falwell v. Larry Flynt: The First Amendment on Trial* (New York: St. Martin's Press, 1988). See also Robert Post, "The Constitutional Concept of Public Discourse: Outrageous Opinion, Democratic Deliberation, and *Hustler Magazine v. Falwell*," 103 *Harv.L.Rev.* 601 (1990).

———

IV. SYMBOLIC EXPRESSION

"We cannot accept the view that an apparently limitless variety of conduct can be labeled 'speech' whenever the person engaging in the conduct intends thereby to express an idea."—Chief Justice WARREN

"The underlying and basic problem in this case, however, is whether conscription is permissible in the absence of a declaration of war."—Justice DOUGLAS

UNITED STATES v. O'BRIEN

391 U.S. 367, 88 S.Ct. 1673, 20 L.Ed.2d 672 (1968).

David O'Brien and three other protesters against the war in Vietnam, burned their draft cards on the steps of the South Boston Courthouse before a large crowd, some of whose members began attacking the protestors. FBI agents arrested the protestors for violating the 1965 amendment to the Universal Military Training and Service Act of 1948, which provides criminal punishment for anyone who "knowingly destroys, [or] knowingly mutilates" a draft card. O'Brien was convicted, but the court of appeals reversed, holding the 1965 amendment violated the First Amendment. The Department of Justice obtained certiorari.

Mr. Chief Justice **WARREN** delivered the opinion of the Court. . . .

II

O'Brien first argues that the 1965 Amendment is unconstitutional as applied to him because his act of burning his registration certificate was protected "symbolic speech" within the First Amendment. His argument is that the freedom of expression which the First Amendment guarantees includes all modes of "communication of ideas by conduct," and that his conduct is within this definition because he did it in "demonstration against the war and against the draft."

We cannot accept the view that an apparently limitless variety of conduct can be labeled "speech" whenever the person engaging in the conduct intends thereby to express an idea. However, even on . . . [O'Brien's view], it does not necessarily follow that the destruction of a registration certificate is constitutionally protected activity. This Court has held that when "speech" and "nonspeech" elements are combined in the same course of conduct, a sufficiently important governmental interest in regulating the nonspeech element can justify incidental limitations on First Amendment freedoms. To characterize the quality of the governmental interest which must appear, the Court has employed a variety of descriptive terms: compelling; substantial; subordinating; paramount; cogent; strong. Whatever imprecision inheres in these terms, we think it clear that a government regulation is sufficiently justified if it is within the constitutional power of the Government; if it furthers an important or substantial governmental interest; if the governmental interest is unrelated to the suppression of free expression; and if the incidental restriction on alleged First Amendment freedoms is no greater than is essential to the furtherance of that interest. We find that the 1965 Amendment to § 12(b)(3) of the Universal Military Training and Service Act meets all of these requirements. ...

The constitutional power of Congress to raise and support armies and to make all laws necessary and proper to that end is broad and sweeping. Lichter v. United States (1948); Selective Draft Law Cases [1918]. The power of Congress to classify and conscript manpower for military service is "beyond question." *Lichter;* Selective Draft Law Cases. Pursuant to this power, Congress may establish a system of registration for individuals liable for training and service, and may require such individuals within reason to cooperate in the registration system. The issuance of certificates indicating the registration and eligibility classification of individuals is a legitimate and substantial administrative aid in the functioning of this system. ...

O'Brien ... essentially adopts the position that such certificates are so many pieces of paper ... to be retained or tossed in the wastebasket according to the convenience or taste of the registrant. ... We agree that the registration certificate contains much information of which the registrant needs no notification. This circumstance, however, does not lead to the conclusion that the certificate serves no purposes but that, like the classification certificate, it serves purposes in addition to initial notification. Many of these purposes would be defeated by the certificates' destruction or mutilation. Among these are:

1. The registration certificate serves as proof that the individual described thereon has registered for the draft. .... [A]vailability of the certificates for such display relieves the Selective Service System of the administrative burden it would otherwise have in verifying the registration and classification of all suspected delinquents. ... Additionally, in a time of national crisis, reasonable availability to each registrant of the two small cards assures a rapid and uncomplicated means for determining his fitness for immediate induction. ...

2. The information supplied on the certificates facilitates communication between registrants and local boards, simplifying the system and benefiting all concerned. ...

3. Both certificates carry continual reminders that the registrant must notify his local board of any change of address, and other specified changes in his status. ...

4. The regulatory scheme involving Selective Service certificates includes clearly valid prohibitions against the alteration, forgery, or similar deceptive misuse of certificates. The destruction or mutilation of certificates obviously increases the difficulty of detecting and tracing

abuses such as these. Further, a mutilated certificate might itself be used for deceptive purposes. ...

We think it apparent that the continuing availability to each registrant of his Selective Service certificates substantially furthers the smooth and proper functioning of the system that Congress has established to raise armies. We think it also apparent that the Nation has a vital interest in having a system for raising armies that functions with maximum efficiency and is capable of easily and quickly responding to continually changing circumstances. For these reasons, the Government has a substantial interest in assuring the continuing availability of issued Selective Service certificates.

It is equally clear that the 1965 Amendment specifically protects this substantial governmental interest. We perceive no alternative means that would more precisely and narrowly assure the continuing availability of issued Selective Service certificates than a law which prohibits their wilful mutilation or destruction. Compare Sherbert v. Verner (1963), and the cases cited therein. The 1965 Amendment prohibits such conduct and does nothing more. ... When O'Brien deliberately rendered unavailable his registration certificate, he wilfully frustrated this governmental interest. For this noncommunicative impact of his conduct, and for nothing else, he was convicted. ...

III

O'Brien finally argues that the 1965 Amendment is unconstitutional as enacted because what he calls the "purpose" of Congress was "to suppress freedom of speech." We reject this argument because under settled principles the purpose of Congress, as O'Brien uses that term, is not a basis for declaring this legislation unconstitutional. It is a familiar principle of constitutional law that this Court will not strike down an otherwise constitutional statute on the basis of an alleged illicit legislative motive. ...

Inquiries into congressional motives or purposes are a hazardous matter. When the issue is simply the interpretation of legislation, the Court will look to statements by legislators for guidance as to the purpose of the legislature,[1] because the benefit to sound decision-making in this circumstance is thought sufficient to risk the possibility of misreading Congress' purpose. It is entirely a different matter when we are asked to void a statute that is, under well-settled criteria, constitutional on its face, on the basis of what fewer than a handful of Congressmen said about it. What motivates one legislator to make a speech about a statute is not necessarily what motivates scores of others to enact it, and the stakes are sufficiently high for us to eschew guesswork. We decline to void essentially on the ground that it is unwise legislation which Congress had the undoubted power to enact

---

1. The Court may make the same assumption in a very limited and well-defined class of cases where the very nature of the constitutional question requires an inquiry into legislative purpose. ... [Footnote by the Court.]

and which could be reenacted in its exact form if the same or another legislator made a "wiser" speech about it.

Mr. Justice **MARSHALL** took no part in the consideration or decision of these cases.

Mr. Justice **HARLAN,** concurring.

The crux of the Court's opinion, which I join, is of course its general statement that "a government regulation is sufficiently justified if it is within the constitutional power of the Government; if it furthers an important or substantial governmental interest; if the governmental interest is unrelated to the suppression of free expression; and if the incidental restriction on alleged First Amendment freedoms is no greater than is essential to the furtherance of that interest."

I wish to make explicit my understanding that this passage does not foreclose consideration of First Amendment claims in those rare instances when an "incidental" restriction upon expression, imposed by a regulation which furthers an "important or substantial" governmental interest and satisfies the Court's other criteria, in practice has the effect of entirely preventing a "speaker" from reaching a significant audience with whom he could not otherwise lawfully communicate. ...

Mr. Justice **DOUGLAS,** dissenting.

The Court states that the constitutional power of Congress to raise and support armies is "broad and sweeping" and that Congress' power "to classify and conscript manpower for military service is 'beyond question.' " This is undoubtedly true in times when, by declaration of Congress, the Nation is in a state of war. The underlying and basic problem in this case, however, is whether conscription is permissible in the absence of a declaration of war. That question has not been briefed nor was it presented in oral argument; but it is, I submit, a question upon which the litigants and the country are entitled to a ruling. I have discussed in Holmes v. United States [1968] the nature of the legal issue and it will be seen from my dissenting opinion in that case that this Court has never ruled on the question. It is time that we made a ruling. This case should be put down for reargument and heard with Holmes v. United States and with Hart v. United States, in which the Court today denies certiorari. ...

Editors' Notes

(1) When *O'Brien* was first discussed at conference, the justices unanimously agreed to reverse the court of appeals. Warren's first circulated draft placed much nonverbal communication outside the Constitution's protection: "[A]n act unrelated to the employment of language or other inherently expressive symbols is not speech within the First Amendment if as a matter of fact the act has an immediate and harmful impact not completely apart from any impact arising by virtue of the claimed communication itself." (Quoted in Bernard Schwartz, *Super Chief* [New York: New York University Press, 1983],

p. 684.)   This rationale pleased Hugo Black, but it disturbed some of the other justices, particularly Harlan and Brennan.   The former circulated a concurrence critical of the Chief's draft;   the latter tried to persuade the Chief that O'Brien had raised valid First Amendment issues, but the government's interest in regulating such conduct was compelling, reasoning like that which Brennan had used in NAACP v. Button (1963;   reprinted below, p. 811) to strike down a state statute.

(2) **Query:** Given Earl Warren's avid defense of democratic theory (for instance, his opinion for the Court in Reynolds v. Sims [1964;   reprinted below, p. 777]), how can we account for the approach to the First Amendment that he took in his draft opinion in *O'Brien*?   In his published opinion?

(3) **Query:** How *textualist* was Warren's approach?   How could Hugo Black, the great literalist, have agreed with Warren?   To what extent does the test of strict scrutiny—the Court's turning presumption of constitutionality on its head and demanding that government justify a statute as meeting a compelling need and being "narrowly tailored" to achieve that purpose— comport with the constitutional text?   With democratic theory?   With *structuralism*?

(4) In later rulings involving equal protection, the Court has often said administrative convenience is not a compelling governmental interest.   See, e.g., Frontiero v. Richardson (1973;   reprinted below, p. 986)   and Shapiro v. Thompson (1969;   reprinted below, p. 1019).

(5) The Court has not been nearly so consistent in closing its eyes to legislative motivation as Warren's opinion would lead one to believe.   See, e.g., Washington v. Davis (1976;   discussed below, p. 931), espec. the concur. op. of Stevens, criticizing the Court's use of this sort of search and his similar critique dissenting in Rogers v. Lodge (1982;   reprinted below, p. 933);   and Paul Brest, "Palmer v. Thompson: An Approach to the Problem of Unconstitutional Legislative Motivation," 1971 *Sup.Ct.Rev.* 95.   Some commentators, most notably John Hart Ely, believe that the Court should look for legislative motivation in constitutional interpretation: "Legislative and Administrative Motivation in Constitutional Law," 79 *Yale L.J.* 1205 (1970), critiquing *O'Brien;* and *Democracy and Distrust* (Cambridge: Harvard University Press, 1980), pp. 136–148.   Ely, however, argues that "the inquiry's most important ingredient by far must be the actual terms of the law or provision in issue, read in light of its foreseeable effects and a healthy dose of common sense, and not, though it can help occasionally, its legislative history."   (*Democracy and Distrust,* p. 130.)

Perhaps the root of the difficulty here lies in a failure to distinguish among *motivation,* the factors working on and within a person to cause him or her to act in a particular way, *intent,* what one immediately has in mind to accomplish, and *purpose,* the larger objective one tries to attain by a certain action. The first, *motivation,* probably lies beyond the competence of judges or even psychiatrists to discover in a group the size of a legislature.   The second and third are difficult to distinguish because in some respects *intent* may be a shorter range form of *purpose.* But if it is correct to assume that legislators are rational people who mean to accomplish the results that logically follow from their actions, *purpose* can often be seen in what a legislature does.

(6) **Query:** To what extent do the problems Warren saw in discerning legislative intent or motivation apply to quests for original intentions or understandings of those who proposed and ratified the constitutional text of 1787–88 and its various amendments?

(7) A year after *O'Brien*, Tinker v. Des Moines (1969) presented another issue of symbolic speech. A small group of teen-aged students had planned to wear black armbands to classes to protest the war in Vietnam, but school principals forbade the demonstration and threatened to suspend students who disobeyed the order. Several students defied the principals' edict and were suspended. Their families unsuccessfully sought an injunction from a U.S. district court forbidding the principals and the school district to discipline the children for their symbolic protest. The Court, reversing, held that the symbolic act of wearing an armband was "closely akin to 'pure speech' ... entitled to comprehensive protection under the First Amendment" and that the school authorities' "undifferentiated fear or apprehension of disturbance is not enough to overcome the right to freedom of expression." The Court also proclaimed: "It can hardly be argued that either students or teachers shed their constitutional rights to freedom of speech or expression at the school-house gate." Justices Black and Harlan dissented.

(8) Street v. New York (1969) involved yet another form of symbolic protest, burning the American flag. On hearing of the murder of James Meredith, the African American civil rights leader, Sidney Street burned an American flag and told a crowd, "If they did that to Meredith, we don't need an American flag." He was convicted under a state statute making it a misde-meanor "publicly [to] mutilate, deface, defile, or defy, trample upon or cast contempt upon, either by words or act," an American flag. Justice Harlan, who had dissented in *Tinker,* wrote the opinion of the Court reversing the conviction: Either Street's speech or his burning the flag or both might have provided the basis for his conviction, and his speech was constitutionally protected. Warren, Black, White, and Fortas dissented. Fortas, author of the Court's opinion in *Tinker,* had initially joined the majority, but later changed his mind. See Schwartz, *Super Chief,* pp. 732–734.

Smith v. Goguen (1974) reversed the conviction of a man who wore a small cloth version of the American flag on the seat of his jeans and held that a Massachusetts statute that punished anyone who "treats contemptuously" the American flag was "void for vagueness," that is, the statute's terms were so unclear as to give no warning about the kind of conduct outlawed.

(9) **Query:** Is the wearing of masks or hoods in public a form of symbolic expression that is protected by the First Amendment? Is there a constitutional right to make public statements anonymously? Or is a ban on wearing masks or hoods in public a permissible regulation of conduct that only incidentally burdens expression? Is forbidding members of the Ku Klux Klan to wear hoods tantamount to compelling them to disclose their membership in that organization, and to subject them to harassment and reprisals? In Knights of the Ku Klux Klan v. Martin Luther King Jr. Worshippers (M.D.Tenn.1990), a federal district judge struck down a statute that forbade marchers in a parade (in this instance members of the KKK) to wear "frightening masks." See NAACP v. Alabama (1958; reprinted below, p. 798).

"Punishing desecration of the flag dilutes the very freedom that makes this emblem so revered, and worth revering."—Justice BRENNAN

"[T]he flag uniquely symbolizes the ideas of liberty, equality, and tolerance. ..."—Justice STEVENS

UNITED STATES v. EICHMAN
496 U.S. 310, 110 S.Ct. 2404, 110 L.Ed.2d 287 (1990).

In Texas v. Johnson (1989), the Supreme Court invalidated as an infringement on the First and Fourteenth Amendments a state statute that made it a crime knowingly to desecrate a state or national flag, defining "desecrate" as to "deface, damage, or otherwise physically mistreat in a way that the actor knows will seriously offend one or more persons likely to observe or discover his action." Immediately thereafter, the U.S. Senate by a vote of 97–3 passed a resolution expressing "profound disappointment" with Johnson. The House approved a similar resolution by a vote of 411–5. President George Bush called for a constitutional amendment to overrule Johnson by authorizing the states or the federal government to punish desecration of the flag. Others contended that the Supreme Court might uphold a carefully drawn federal statute designed to protect the physical integrity of the flag under all circumstances. The Flag Protection Act of 1989 was the compromise. Exempting burning of worn or soiled flags, the Act amended 18 USC § 700 and imposed criminal penalties on anyone who "knowingly mutilates, defaces, physically defiles, burns, maintains on the floor or ground, or tramples upon" an American flag. Shortly after passage, the government arrested several people who had, as part of political protests, burned American flags. The district judges held the Flag Protection Act unconstitutional, and the United States appealed directly to the Supreme Court.

Justice **BRENNAN** delivered the opinion of the Court. ...

The Government concedes in this case, as it must, that appellees' flag-burning constituted expressive conduct, but invites us to reconsider our rejection in [Texas v. Johnson (1989)] of the claim that flag-burning as a mode of expression, like obscenity or "fighting words," does not enjoy the full protection of the First Amendment. Cf. *Chaplinsky* (1942). This we decline to do. The only remaining question is whether the Flag Protection Act is sufficiently distinct from the Texas statute that it may constitutionally be applied to proscribe appellees' expressive conduct.

The Government contends that[,] unlike the statute addressed in *Johnson,* the Act does not target expressive conduct on the basis of the content of its message. The Government asserts an interest in "protect[ing] the physical integrity of the flag under all circumstances" in order to safeguard the flag's identity " 'as the unique and unalloyed symbol of the Nation.' " The Act proscribes conduct (other than disposal) that damages or mistreats a flag, without regard to the actor's motive, his intended message, or the likely effects of his conduct on onlookers.   By contrast, the Texas statute expressly prohibited only those acts of physical flag desecration "that the actor knows will seriously offend" onlookers, and the former federal statute prohibited only those acts of desecration that "cas[t] contempt upon" the flag.

Although the Act contains no explicit content-based limitation on the scope of prohibited conduct, it is nevertheless clear that the Government's asserted *interest* is "related 'to the suppression of free expression,'" and concerned with the content of such expression. The Government's interest in protecting the "physical integrity" of a privately owned flag rests upon a perceived need to preserve the flag's status as a symbol of our Nation and certain national ideals. But the mere destruction or disfigurement of a particular physical manifestation of the symbol, without more, does not diminish or otherwise affect the symbol itself in any way. For example, the secret destruction of a flag in one's own basement would not threaten the flag's recognized meaning. Rather, the Government's desire to preserve the flag as a symbol for certain national ideals is implicated "only when a person's treatment of the flag communicates [a] message" to others that is inconsistent with those ideals.[1]

Moreover, the precise language of the Act's prohibitions confirms Congress' interest in the communicative impact of flag destruction. The Act criminalizes the conduct of anyone who "knowingly mutilates, defaces, physically defiles, burns, maintains on the floor or ground, or tramples upon any flag." Each of the specified terms—with the possible exception of "burns"—unmistakably connotes disrespectful treatment of the flag and suggests a focus on those acts likely to damage the flag's symbolic value. And the explicit exemption for disposal of "worn or soiled" flags protects certain acts traditionally associated with patriotic respect for the flag.

As we explained in *Johnson:* "[I]f we were to hold that a State may forbid flag-burning wherever it is likely to endanger the flag's symbolic role, but allow it wherever burning a flag promotes that role—as where, for example, a person ceremoniously burns a dirty flag—we would be ... permitting a State to 'prescribe what shall be orthodox' by saying that one may burn the flag to convey one's attitude toward it and its referents only if one does not endanger the flag's representation of nationhood and national unity" [quoting West Virginia v. Barnette (1943)]. Although Congress cast the Act in somewhat broader terms than the Texas statute at issue in *Johnson,* the Act still suffers from the

---

1.   ... We concede that the Government has a legitimate interest in preserving the flag's function as an "incident of sovereignty," though we need not address today the extent to which this interest may justify any laws regulating conduct that would thwart this core function, as might a commercial or like appropriation of the image of the United States flag. *Amici* do not, and cannot, explain how a statute that penalizes anyone who knowingly burns, mutilates, or defiles any American flag is designed to advance this asserted interest in maintaining the association between the flag and the Nation. Burning a flag does not threaten to interfere with this association in any way; indeed, the flag-burner's message depends in part on the viewer's ability to make this very association. [Footnote by the Court.]

same fundamental flaw: it suppresses expression out of concern for its likely communicative impact. Despite the Act's wider scope, its restriction on expression cannot be " 'justified without reference to the content of the regulated speech.' " Boos [v. Barry (1988)]. ... The Act therefore must be subjected to "the most exacting scrutiny," Boos, and for the reasons stated in Johnson, the Government's interest cannot justify its infringement on First Amendment rights. We decline the Government's invitation to reassess this conclusion in light of Congress' recent recognition of a purported "national consensus" favoring a prohibition on flag-burning. Even assuming such a consensus exists, any suggestion that the Government's interest in suppressing speech becomes more weighty as popular opposition to that speech grows is foreign to the First Amendment.

III ...

We are aware that desecration of the flag is deeply offensive to many. But the same might be said, for example, of virulent ethnic and religious epithets, see Terminiello v. Chicago (1949), vulgar repudiations of the draft, see Cohen v. California (1971), and scurrilous caricatures, see Hustler Magazine, Inc. v. Falwell (1988). "If there is a bedrock principle underlying the First Amendment, it is that the Government may not prohibit the expression of an idea simply because society finds the idea itself offensive or disagreeable." Johnson. Punishing desecration of the flag dilutes the very freedom that makes this emblem so revered, and worth revering. The judgments of the District Courts are affirmed.

Justice **STEVENS**, with whom The Chief Justice [**REHNQUIST**], Justice **WHITE** and Justice **O'CONNOR** join, dissenting.

The Court's opinion ends where proper analysis of the issue should begin. Of course "the Government may not prohibit the expression of an idea simply because society finds the idea itself offensive or disagreeable." ... But it is equally well settled that certain methods of expression may be prohibited if (a) the prohibition is supported by a legitimate societal interest that is unrelated to suppression of the ideas the speaker desires to express; (b) the prohibition does not entail any interference with the speaker's freedom to express those ideas by other means; and (c) the interest in allowing the speaker complete freedom of choice among alternative methods of expression is less important than the societal interest supporting the prohibition.

... [I]t is now conceded that the Federal Government has a legitimate interest in protecting the symbolic value of the American flag. ... [That value] has at least these two components: In times of national crisis, it inspires and motivates the average citizen to make personal sacrifices in order to achieve societal goals of overriding importance; at all times, it serves as a reminder of the paramount importance of pursuing the ideals that characterize our society.

The first question the Court should consider is whether the interest in preserving the value of that symbol is unrelated to suppression of the ideas that the flag burners are trying to express. In my judgment the answer depends, at least in part, on what those ideas are. A flag burner might intend various messages. The flag burner may wish simply to convey hatred, contempt, or sheer opposition directed at the United States. ... A flag burner may also, or instead, seek to convey the depth of his personal conviction about some issue, by willingly provoking the use of force against himself. In so doing, he says that "my disagreement with certain policies is so strong that I am prepared to risk physical harm (and perhaps imprisonment) in order to call attention to my views." This second possibility apparently describes the expressive conduct of the flag burners in these cases. Like the protesters who dramatized their opposition to our engagement in Vietnam by publicly burning their draft cards—and who were punished for doing so—their expressive conduct is consistent with affection for this country and respect for the ideals that the flag symbolizes. There is at least one further possibility: A flag burner may intend to make an accusation against the integrity of the American people who disagree with him. By burning the embodiment of America's collective commitment to freedom and equality, the flag burner charges that the majority has forsaken that commitment. ... Such a charge may be made even if the flag burner loves the country and zealously pursues the ideals that the country claims to honor.

The idea expressed by a particular act of flag burning is necessarily dependent on the temporal and political context in which it occurs. ... In *Johnson,* it apparently expressed opposition to the platform of the Republican Party. In these cases, the respondents have explained that it expressed their opposition to racial discrimination, to the failure to care for the homeless, and of course to statutory prohibitions of flag burning. In any of these examples, the protestors may wish both to say that their own position is the only one faithful to liberty and equality, and to accuse their fellow citizens of hypocritical indifference to—or even of a selfish departure from—the ideals which the flag is supposed to symbolize. ...

The Government's legitimate interest in preserving the symbolic value of the flag is, however, essentially the same regardless of which of many different ideas may have motivated a particular act of flag burning. ... [T]he flag uniquely symbolizes the ideas of liberty, equality, and tolerance—ideas that Americans have passionately defended and debated throughout our history. The flag embodies the spirit of our national commitment to those ideals. The message thereby transmitted does not take a stand upon our disagreements, except to say that those disagreements are best regarded as competing interpretations of shared ideals. It does not judge particular policies, except to say that they command respect when they are enlightened by the spirit of liberty and equality. To the world, the flag is our promise that we will continue to strive for these ideals. To us, the flag is a reminder both that the struggle for liberty and equality is unceasing. . . .

Thus, the Government may—indeed, it should—protect the symbolic value of the flag without regard to the specific content of the flag burners' speech. The prosecution in this case does not depend upon the object of the defendants' protest. It is, moreover, equally clear that the prohibition does not entail any interference with the speaker's freedom to express his or her ideas by other means. . . .

This case therefore comes down to a question of judgment. Does the admittedly important interest in allowing every speaker to choose the method of expressing his or her ideas . . . outweigh the societal interest in preserving the symbolic value of the flag? This question, in turn, involves three different judgments: (1) The importance of the individual interest in selecting the preferred means of communication; (2) the importance of the national symbol; and (3) the question whether tolerance of flag burning will enhance or tarnish that value. . . . [R]easonable judges may differ with respect to each of these judgments.

The individual interest is unquestionably a matter of great importance. Indeed, it is one of the critical components of the idea of liberty that the flag itself is intended to symbolize. Moreover, it is buttressed by the societal interest in being alerted to the need for thoughtful response to voices that might otherwise go unheard. The freedom of expression protected by the First Amendment embraces not only the freedom to communicate particular ideas, but also the right to communicate them effectively. That right, however, is not absolute—the communicative value of a well-placed bomb in the Capitol does not entitle it to the protection of the First Amendment.

Burning a flag is not, of course, equivalent to burning a public building. Assuming that the protestor is burning his own flag, it causes no physical harm to other persons or to their property. The impact is purely symbolic, and . . . some thoughtful persons believe that impact, far from depreciating the value of the symbol, will actually enhance its meaning. I most respectfully disagree. Indeed, what makes this case particularly difficult for me is what I regard as the damage to the symbol that has already occurred as a result of this Court's decision to place its stamp of approval on the act of flag burning. A formerly dramatic expression of protest is now rather commonplace. In today's marketplace of ideas, the public burning of a Vietnam draft card is probably less provocative than lighting a cigarette. Tomorrow flag burning may produce a similar reaction. . . .

The symbolic value of the American flag is not the same today as it was yesterday. . . . [Some citizens] now have difficulty understanding the message that the flag conveyed to their parents and grandparents— whether born abroad and naturalized or native born. Moreover, the integrity of the symbol has been compromised by those leaders who seem to advocate compulsory worship of the flag even by individuals whom it offends, or who seem to manipulate the symbol of national purpose into a pretext for partisan disputes about meaner ends.[1] And, as I have suggested, the residual value of the symbol after this Court's decision in *Johnson* is surely not the same as it was a year ago. . . .

Editors' Notes

(1) **Query:** Compare Brennan's approach to constitutional interpretation with Stevens'. Which relied more heavily on democratic theory? On *textualism*? To what extent did either follow the approach called *reinforcing representative democracy*? Did Stevens utilize a *balancing approach*?

(2) **Query:** Here as in *R.A.V.* and similar cases, the Court required government to be neutral about the content of speech, including symbolic speech. How convincing is Stevens's argument that the statute is neutral? On the other hand, would a legislative decision *not* to punish publicly burning a flag itself convey a message and thus not be "content neutral"?

(3) **Query:** Apparently in the early days of the Republic neither the federal government nor any state specifically criminalized publicly burning a flag. Would such an absence—in effect, a silent interpretation—lend *originalist* support to *Eichman*?

(4) **Query:** In Texas v. Johnson (1989), the earlier flag-burning case discussed in the headnote to *Eichman*, Brennan said for the Court: "The First Amendment does not guarantee that other concepts virtually sacred to our Nation as a whole—such as the principle that discrimination on the basis of race is odious and destructive—will go unquestioned in the marketplace of ideas. *Brandenburg.*" In dissent, Rehnquist claimed: "[s]urely one of the high purposes of a democratic society is to legislate against conduct that is regarded as evil and profoundly offensive to the majority of people." Which assertion is more congruent with democratic theory? Constitutionalism?

(5) **Query:** If Brennan were correct in *Johnson* and *Eichman* when he said, "if there is a bedrock principle underlying the First Amendment, it is that the government may not prohibit the expression of an idea simply because society finds the idea itself offensive or disagreeable," can society legitimately criminalize preaching other principles, such as assassination of public officials or rape of women? How strong is the distinction the Court stressed in Yates v. United States (1957; reprinted above, p. 666) between advocacy and incitement? How accurate was Holmes when he wrote in *Gitlow* (1925) that "Every idea is an incitement"? What good does it do to be able to advocate a principle if one will go to jail for acting on it? Does a democratic system necessarily lack authority to preserve the values that it supposedly fosters?

(6) *Eichman* prompted renewed efforts to amend the constitutional text: "The Congress and the States shall have power to prohibit the physical desecration of the flag of the United States." In 1990, this proposal failed to secure the necessary two-thirds vote in the House of Representatives (254–177, 34 votes short) as well as in the Senate (58–42, nine votes short). But in

---

1. The allusion was to George Bush's attack during the presidential campaign of 1988 on his opponent for vetoing a state bill that would have forced public school teachers to lead students in saluting the flag.—**Eds.**

1995, as this edition went to press, the House had just endorsed the proposal by a vote of 312–120; the Senate had not yet voted on it.

(7) The literature on the recent flag burning cases is voluminous. Among the more interesting are: Kent Greenawalt, "O'er the Land of the Free: Flag Burning as Speech," *UCLA L.Rev.* 925 (1990); Arnold Loewy, "The Flag–Burning Case: Freedom of Speech When We Need It Most," 68 *N.C.L.Rev.* 165 (1989); Frank I. Michelman, "Saving Old Glory: On Constitutional Iconography," 42 *Stan.L.Rev.* 1337 (1990); Jeff Rosen, "Note: Was the Flag Burning Amendment Unconstitutional?" 100 *Yale L.J.* 1073 (1991); Geoffrey R. Stone, "Flag Burning and the Constitution," 75 *Ia.L.Rev.* 111 (1989).

––––––––

V. PRIOR RESTRAINT OF EXPRESSION

"[L]iberty of the press, historically considered and taken up by the Federal Constitution, has meant, principally, although not exclusively, immunity from previous restraints or censorship."—Chief Justice HUGHES

"The decision of the court … gives to freedom of the press a meaning and a scope not heretofore recognized and construes 'liberty' in the due process clause of the 14th Amendment to put upon the states a Federal restriction that is without precedent."—Justice BUTLER

NEAR v. MINNESOTA
283 U.S. 697, 51 S.Ct. 625, 75 L.Ed. 1357 (1931).

In a series of articles published during Prohibition for the alleged purpose of pushing reform in Minneapolis' government, *The Saturday Press* vilified, among others, the mayor, the police chief, and the city's two largest newspapers for taking orders from "Jew Gangsters." One article asserted that "Practically every vendor of vile hooch, every owner of a moonshine still, every snake-faced gangster and embryonic yegg in the Twin Cities is a JEW," and urged Jews to "rid themselves of the odium and stigma the RODENTS OF THEIR OWN RACE HAVE BROUGHT UPON THEM."

The local prosecutor invoked a state statute that allowed a court to enjoin, as a public nuisance, a "malicious, scandalous and defamatory newspaper, magazine or other periodical." The trial court issued an order against the publisher, J.M. Near, barring future issues of the paper. The state supreme court affirmed. Near appealed to the U.S. Supreme Court.

Mr. Chief Justice **HUGHES** delivered the opinion of the Court. …

This statute … is unusual, if not unique, and raises questions of grave importance transcending the local interests involved in the partic-

ular action. It is no longer open to doubt that the liberty of the press
and of speech is within the liberty safeguarded by the due process clause
of the 14th Amendment from invasion by state action. ... Gitlow v.
New York [1925]; Whitney v. California [1927]; Stromberg v. California
[1931]. In maintaining this guaranty, the authority of the State to enact
laws to promote the health, safety, morals and general welfare of its
people is necessarily admitted. The limits of this sovereign power must
always be determined with appropriate regard to the particular subject
of its exercise. ... [T]his court has held that the power of the state
stops short of interference with what are deemed to be certain indispensable requirements of the liberty assured. ... [Like liberty of contract,]
[l]iberty of speech and of the press is also not an absolute right, and the
state may punish its abuse. ... Liberty, in each of its phases, has its
history and connotation and, in the present instance, the inquiry is as to
the historic conception of the liberty of the press and whether the
statute under review violates the essential attributes of that liberty. ...

   ... [I]n passing upon constitutional questions the court has regard
to substance and not to mere matters of form, and ... in accordance
with familiar principles, the statute must be tested by its operation and
effect. ... If we cut through mere details of procedure, the operation
and effect of the statute ... is that public authorities may bring the
owner or publisher of a newspaper or periodical before a judge upon a
charge of conducting a business of publishing scandalous and defamatory
matter ... and unless the owner or publisher is able and disposed to
bring competent evidence to satisfy the judge that the charges are true
and are published with good motives and for justifiable ends, his newspaper or periodical is suppressed and further publication is made punishable as a contempt. This is of the essence of censorship.

   The question is whether a statute authorizing such proceedings in
restraint of publication is consistent with the conception of the liberty of
the press as historically conceived and guaranteed. In determining the
extent of the constitutional protection, it has been generally, if not
universally, considered that it is the chief purpose of the guaranty to
prevent previous restraints upon publication. The struggle in England,
directed against the legislative power of the licenser, resulted in renunciation of the censorship of the press. ... The distinction was early
pointed out between the extent of the freedom with respect to censorship
under our constitutional system and that enjoyed in England. Here, as
Madison said, "The great and essential rights of the people are secured
against legislative as well as against executive ambition. They are
secured, not by laws paramount to prerogative, but by constitutions
paramount to laws. This security of the freedom of the press requires
that it should be exempt not only from previous restraint by the
executive, as in Great Britain, but from legislative restraint also."

   ... The preliminary freedom extends as well to the false as to the
true; the subsequent punishment may extend as well to the true as to

the false. This was the law of criminal libel apart from statute in most cases, if not in all. ...

... [I]t is recognized that punishment for the abuse of the liberty accorded to the press is essential to the protection of the public, and that the common law rules that subject the libeler to responsibility for the public offense, as well as for the private injury, are not abolished by the protection extended in our constitutions. ... In the present case, we have no occasion to inquire as to the permissible scope of subsequent punishment. For whatever wrong the appellant has committed or may commit, by his publications, the state appropriately affords both public and private redress by its libel laws. ... [T]he statute in question does not deal with punishments; it provides for no punishment, except in case of contempt for violation of the court's order, but for suppression and injunction, that is, for restraint upon publication.

The objection has also been made that the principle as to immunity from previous restraint is stated too broadly, if every such restraint is deemed to be prohibited. That is undoubtedly true; the protection even as to previous restraint is not absolutely unlimited. But the limitation has been recognized only in exceptional cases. "When a nation is at war many things that might be said in time of peace are such a hindrance to its effort that their utterance will not be endured so long as men fight and that no court could regard them as protected by any constitutional right." Schenck v. United States [1919]. No one would question but that a government might prevent actual obstruction to its recruiting service or the publication of the sailing dates of transports or the number and location of troops. On similar grounds, the primary requirements of decency may be enforced against obscene publications. The security of the community life may be protected against incitements to acts of violence and the overthrow by force of orderly government. The constitutional guaranty of free speech does not "protect a man from an injunction against uttering words that may have all the effect of force." Gompers v. Bucks Stove & Range Co. [1911]; Schenck. These limitations are not applicable here. ...

The exceptional nature of its limitations places in a strong light the general conception that liberty of the press, historically considered and taken up by the Federal Constitution, has meant, principally, although not exclusively, immunity from previous restraints or censorship. The conception of the liberty of the press in this country had broadened with the exigencies of the colonial period and with the efforts to secure freedom from oppressive administration. That liberty was especially cherished for the immunity it afforded from previous restraint of the publication of censure of public officers and charges of official misconduct. ...

... Madison, who was the leading spirit in the preparation of the 1st Amendment of the Federal Constitution, thus described the practice and sentiment which led to the guaranties of liberty of the press in state constitutions:

In every state, probably, in the Union, the press has exerted a freedom in canvassing the merits and measures of public men of every description which has not been confined to the strict limits of the common law. On this footing the freedom of the press has stood; on this footing it yet stands. ... Some degree of abuse is inseparable from the proper use of everything, and in no instance is this more true than in that of the press. It has accordingly been decided by the practice of the states, that it is better to leave a few of its noxious branches to their luxuriant growth, than, by pruning them away, to injure the vigour of those yielding the proper fruits. And can the wisdom of this policy be doubted by any who reflect that to the press alone, chequered as it is with abuses, the world is indebted for all the triumphs which have been gained by reason and humanity over error and oppression; who reflect that to the same beneficent source the United States owe much of the lights which conducted them to the ranks of a free and independent nation, and which have improved their political system into a shape so auspicious to their happiness? Had "Sedition Acts," forbidding every publication that might bring the constituted agents into contempt or disrepute, or that might excite the hatred of the people against the authors of unjust or pernicious measures, been uniformly enforced against the press, might not the United States have been languishing at this day under the infirmities of a sickly Confederation? Might they not, possibly, be miserable colonies, groaning under a foreign yoke?

The fact that for approximately one hundred and fifty years there has been almost an entire absence of attempts to impose previous restraints upon publications relating to the malfeasance of public officers is significant of the deep-seated conviction that such restraints would violate constitutional right. ...

The importance of this immunity has not lessened. ... [T]he administration of government has become more complex, the opportunities for malfeasance and corruption have multiplied, crime has grown to most serious proportions, and the danger of its protection by unfaithful officials and of the impairment of the fundamental security of life and property by criminal alliances and official neglect, emphasizes the primary need of a vigilant and courageous press, especially in great cities. The fact that the liberty of the press may be abused by miscreant purveyors of scandal does not make any the less necessary the immunity of the press from previous restraint in dealing with official misconduct. Subsequent punishment for such abuses as may exist is the appropriate remedy, consistent with constitutional privilege. ...

For these reasons we hold the statute, so far as it authorized the proceedings in this action under clause (b) of section one, to be an infringement of the liberty of the press guaranteed by the 14th Amendment. We should add that this decision rests upon the operation and effect of the statute, without regard to the question of the truth of the charges contained in the particular periodical. ...

Mr. Justice **BUTLER**, dissenting:

The decision of the court in this case declares Minnesota and every other state powerless to restrain by injunction the business of publishing and circulating among the people malicious, scandalous and defamatory periodicals that in due course of judicial procedure has been adjudged to be a public nuisance. It gives to freedom of the press a meaning and a scope not heretofore recognized and construes "liberty" in the due process clause of the 14th Amendment to put upon the states a Federal restriction that is without precedent. ...

In his work on the Constitution, ... Justice [Joseph] Story [, John Marshall's colleague, said] ...:

> That this amendment was intended to secure to every citizen an absolute right to speak, or write, or print whatever he might please, without any responsibility, public or private, therefor, is a supposition too wild to be indulged by any rational man. This would be to allow to every citizen a right to destroy at his pleasure the reputation, the peace, the property, and even the personal safety of every other citizen. ... Civil society could not go on under such circumstances. Men would then be obliged to resort to private vengeance to make up for the deficiencies of the law. ... It is plain, then, that the language of this amendment imports no more than that every man shall have a right to speak, write, and print his opinions upon any subject whatsoever, without any prior restraint, so always that he does not injure any other person in his rights, person, property, or reputation; and so always that he does not thereby disturb the public peace, or attempt to subvert the government. ...

The Minnesota statute does not operate as a *previous* restraint on publication within the proper meaning of that phrase. It does not authorize administrative control in advance such as was formerly exercised by the licensers and censors but prescribes a remedy to be enforced by a suit in equity. In this case there was previous publication made in the course of the business of regularly producing malicious, scandalous and defamatory periodicals. ... The restraint authorized is only in respect of continuing to do what has been duly adjudged to constitute a nuisance. ... As that resulting from lewd publications constitutionally may be enjoined it is hard to understand why the one resulting from a regular business of malicious defamation may not. ...

Mr. Justice **VAN DEVANTER**, Mr. Justice **McREYNOLDS**, and Mr. Justice **SUTHERLAND**, concur in this opinion.

Editors' Notes

(1) **Query**: How useful for this case was a *textualist* approach? What other sort(s) of approach(es) did Hughes use? Butler? Did either consider "the Constitution" as including *only* the text? If not, what more?

(2) *Near* was the first case in which the Court held that the Fourteenth Amendment "incorporated" the First Amendment's protection of freedom of the press. Perhaps it is the fact that this was an initial voyage that made Hughes's opinion so cautious, so careful to point out limitations on freedom of the press rather than to explain its breadth. The Court has since reduced many of the limitations that Hughes mentioned, especially libel laws where public officials have allegedly suffered injury. See *New York Times* (1964;

reprinted above, p. 634) and *Hudnut* (1985; reprinted above, p. 710). Moreover, even judges now have very limited power to punish criticism as contempt.   C. Herman Pritchett has analyzed the cases: *Constitutional Civil
Liberties* (Englewood Cliffs, NJ: Prentice–Hall, 1984), pp. 73–75.

(3) **Query:** Is there a theory, internally coherent and consistent with both
the First Amendment and democratic theory, that would accord standards of
"civility" the weight that Butler assigned them?   Would it be more constitutionalist or democratic in nature—or would it be neither?

(4) Hughes said that Minnesota's statute was unusual if not unique,
implying widespread legal support for freedom of communication.   Such
nostalgia may have been misplaced.   See David M. Rabban, "The First
Amendment in its Forgotten Years," 90 *Yale L.J.* 514 (1981), who argues that
there was much litigation involving claims to freedom of speech and press
during the early twentieth century and that the "overwhelming majority of pre
[World War I] decisions in all jurisdictions rejected free speech claims.   ... No
court was more unsympathetic to freedom of expression than the Supreme
Court.   ..."

" 'Any system of prior restraints of expression comes to
this Court bearing a heavy presumption against its constitutional validity.' "—The COURT

"In seeking injunctions against these newspapers ... the
Executive Branch seems to have forgotten the essential
purpose and history of the First Amendment ..."—Justice BLACK

"The dominant purpose of the First Amendment was to
prohibit the widespread practice of governmental suppression of embarrassing information."—Justice DOUG-
LAS

"[T]he First Amendment tolerates absolutely no prior
judicial restraints of the press predicated upon surmise
or conjecture.   ..."—Justice BRENNAN

"The responsibility must be where the power is."—Justice STEWART

"I do not say that in no circumstances would the First
Amendment permit an injunction against publishing information about government plans or operations."—Justice WHITE

"The issue is whether this Court or the Congress has the
power to make law."—Justice MARSHALL

"An issue of this importance should be tried and heard
in a judicial atmosphere conducive to thoughtful, reflective deliberation.   ..."—Chief Justice BURGER

"I consider that the Court has been almost irresponsibly feverish in dealing with these cases."—Justice HARLAN

"The First Amendment, after all, is only one part of an entire Constitution."—Justice BLACKMUN

THE PENTAGON PAPERS CASE (NEW YORK TIMES v. UNITED STATES)

403 U.S. 713, 91 S.Ct. 2140, 29 L.Ed.2d 822 (1971).

In 1971, the *New York Times* and the *Washington Post* obtained copies of a classified study stolen from the Department of Defense, *History of U.S. Decision–Making Process on Viet Nam Policy,* popularly called *The Pentagon Papers.* After some delay, the newspapers began publishing the documents. The Department of Justice sought injunctions from federal district courts in New York and the District of Columbia against further publication. Both courts refused the requests, but the Court of Appeals for the Second Circuit sent the case back to the district court in New York for further hearings and granted a temporary injunction. In Washington, the Court of Appeals for the District of Columbia sustained the refusal. Both sides petitioned for expedited review. The Supreme Court agreed but issued an order restraining publication until after its decision on the merits. Four days after oral argument, the Court announced its judgment.

PER CURIAM. . . .

"Any system of prior restraints of expression comes to this Court bearing a heavy presumption against its constitutional validity." Bantam Books, Inc. v. Sullivan (1963); see also Near v. Minnesota (1931). The Government "thus carries a heavy burden of showing justification for the imposition of such a restraint." Organization for a Better Austin v. Keefe (1971). The District Court for the Southern District of New York in the *New York Times* case and the District Court for the District of Columbia and the Court of Appeals for the District of Columbia Circuit in the *Washington Post* case held that the Government had not met that burden. We agree. . . .

Mr. Justice **BLACK**, with whom Mr. Justice **DOUGLAS** joins, concurring. . . .

. . . [F]or the first time in the 182 years since the founding of the Republic, the federal courts are asked to hold that the First Amendment does not mean what it says, but rather means that the Government can halt the publication of current news of vital importance to the people of this country.

In seeking injunctions against these newspapers and in its presentation to the Court, the Executive Branch seems to have forgotten the essential purpose and history of the First Amendment. . . . The Bill of Rights changed the original Constitution into a new charter under which no branch of government could abridge the people's freedoms of press, speech, religion, and assembly. Yet the Solicitor General argues and

some members of the Court appear to agree that the general powers of
the Government adopted in the original Constitution should be interpreted to limit and restrict the specific and emphatic guarantees of the
Bill of Rights adopted later. I can imagine no greater perversion of
history. Madison and the other Framers of the First Amendment ...
wrote in language they earnestly believed could never be misunderstood:
"Congress shall make no law ... abridging the freedom ... of the press.
..." Both the history and language of the First Amendment support the
view that the press must be left free to publish news, whatever the
source, without censorship, injunctions, or prior restraints.

In the First Amendment the Founding Fathers gave the free press
the protection it must have to fulfill its essential role in our democracy.
The press was to serve the governed, not the governors. The Government's power to censor the press was abolished so that the press would
remain forever free to censure the Government. The press was protected so that it could bare the secrets of government and inform the people.
Only a free and unrestrained press can effectively expose deception in
government. And paramount among the responsibilities of a free press
is the duty to prevent any part of the government from deceiving the
people and sending them off to distant lands to die of foreign fevers and
foreign shot and shell. ...

The Government's case here is based on premises entirely different
from those that guided the Framers of the First Amendment. The
Solicitor General has carefully and emphatically stated:

> Now, Mr. Justice [Black], your construction of ... [the First
> Amendment] is well known, and I certainly respect it. You say that no
> law means no law, and that should be obvious. I can only say, Mr.
> Justice, that to me it is equally obvious that "no law" does not mean
> "no law," and I would seek to persuade the Court that that is true. ...
> [T]here are other parts of the Constitution that grant powers and
> responsibilities to the Executive, and ... the First Amendment was not
> intended to make it impossible for the Executive to function or to
> protect the security of the United States.

And the Government argues in its brief that in spite of the First
Amendment, "[t]he authority of the Executive Department to protect
the nation against publication of information whose disclosure would
endanger the national security stems from two interrelated sources: the
constitutional power of the President over the conduct of foreign affairs
and his authority as Commander-in-Chief." ...

... To find that the President has "inherent power" to halt the
publication of news by resort to the courts would wipe out the First
Amendment and destroy the fundamental liberty and security of the
very people the Government hopes to make "secure." ...

The word "security" is a broad, vague generality whose contours
should not be invoked to abrogate the fundamental law embodied in the
First Amendment. ... The guarding of military and diplomatic secrets
at the expense of informed representative government provides no real

security for our Republic. The Framers of the First Amendment ...
sought to give this new society strength and security by providing that
freedom of speech, press, religion, and assembly should not be abridged.
...

Mr. Justice **DOUGLAS**, with whom Mr. Justice **BLACK** joins, concurring. ...

It should be noted at the outset that the First Amendment provides
that "Congress shall make no law ... abridging the freedom of speech,
or of the press." That leaves, in my view, no room for governmental
restraint on the press. There is, moreover, no statute barring the
publication by the press of the material which the *Times* and the *Post*
seek to use. ... So any power that the Government possesses must
come from its "inherent power."

The power to wage war is "the power to wage war successfully."
See Hirabayashi v. United States [1943]. But the war power stems from
a declaration of war. The Constitution by Art. I, § 8, gives Congress,
not the President, power "[t]o declare War." Nowhere are presidential
wars authorized. We need not decide therefore what leveling effect the
war power of Congress might have. These disclosures may have a
serious impact. But that is no basis for sanctioning a previous restraint
on the press. ...

The Government says that it has inherent powers to go into court
and obtain an injunction to protect the national interest, which in this
case is alleged to be national security. Near v. Minnesota [1931]
repudiated that expansive doctrine in no uncertain terms.

The dominant purpose of the First Amendment was to prohibit the
widespread practice of governmental suppression of embarrassing information. ... A debate of large proportions goes on in the Nation over
our posture in Vietnam. That debate antedated the disclosure of the
contents of the present documents. The latter are highly relevant to the
debate in progress. Secrecy in government is fundamentally anti-democratic, perpetuating bureaucratic errors. Open debate and discussion of
public issues are vital to our national health. On public questions there
should be "uninhibited, robust, and wide-open" debate. New York
Times Co. v. Sullivan [1964]. ...

Mr. Justice **BRENNAN,** concurring. ...

... The entire thrust of the Government's claim throughout these
cases has been that publication of the material sought to be enjoined
"could," or "might," or "may" prejudice the national interest in various
ways. But the First Amendment tolerates absolutely no prior judicial
restraints of the press predicated upon surmise or conjecture that
untoward consequences may result. Our cases, it is true, have indicated
that there is a single, extremely narrow class of cases in which the First
Amendment's ban on prior judicial restraint may be overridden. Our
cases have thus far indicated that such cases may arise only when the

Nation "is at war," Schenck v. United States (1919), during which times "[n]o one would question but that a government might prevent actual obstruction to its recruiting service or the publication of the sailing dates of transports or the number and location of troops." Near v. Minnesota (1931). Even if the present world situation were assumed to be tantamount to a time of war, or if the power of presently available armaments would justify even in peacetime the suppression of information that would set in motion a nuclear holocaust, in neither of these actions has the Government presented or even alleged that publication of items from or based upon the material at issue would cause the happening of an event of that nature. ...

Mr. Justice **STEWART**, with whom Mr. Justice **WHITE** joins, concurring.

In the governmental structure created by our Constitution, the Executive is endowed with enormous power in the two related areas of national defense and international relations. This power, largely unchecked by the Legislative and Judicial branches, has been pressed to the very hilt since the advent of the nuclear missile age. For better or for worse, the simple fact is that a President of the United States possesses vastly greater constitutional independence in these two vital areas of power than does, say, a prime minister of a country with a parliamentary form of government.

In the absence of the governmental checks and balances present in other areas of our national life, the only effective restraint upon executive policy and power in the areas of national defense and international affairs may lie in an enlightened citizenry—in an informed and critical public opinion which alone can here protect the values of democratic government. For this reason, it is perhaps here that a press that is alert, aware, and free most vitally serves the basic purpose of the First Amendment. For without an informed and free press there cannot be an enlightened people.

Yet it is elementary that the successful conduct of international diplomacy and the maintenance of an effective national defense require both confidentiality and secrecy. Other nations can hardly deal with this Nation in an atmosphere of mutual trust unless they can be assured that their confidences will be kept. And within our own executive departments, the development of considered and intelligent international policies would be impossible if those charged with their formulation could not communicate with each other freely, frankly, and in confidence. In the area of basic national defense the frequent need for absolute secrecy is, of course, self-evident.

I think there can be but one answer to this dilemma, if dilemma it be. The responsibility must be where the power is. If the Constitution gives the Executive a large degree of unshared power in the conduct of foreign affairs and the maintenance of our national defense, then under the Constitution the Executive must have the largely unshared duty to determine and preserve the degree of internal security necessary to exercise that power successfully. It is an awesome responsibility, requiring judgment and wisdom of a high order. ...

This is not to say that Congress and the courts have no role to play. Undoubtedly Congress has the power to enact specific and appropriate criminal laws to protect government property and preserve government secrets. ... And if a criminal prosecution is instituted, it will be the responsibility of the courts to decide the applicability of the criminal law under which the charge is brought. Moreover, if Congress should pass a specific law authorizing civil proceedings in this field, the courts would likewise have the duty to decide the constitutionality of such a law as well as its applicability to the facts proved.

But in the cases before us we are asked neither to construe specific regulations nor to apply specific laws. We are asked, instead, to perform a function that the Constitution gave to the Executive, not the Judiciary. We are asked, quite simply, to prevent the publication by two newspapers of material that the Executive Branch insists should not, in the national interest, be published. I am convinced that the Executive is correct with respect to some of the documents involved. But I cannot say that disclosure of any of them will surely result in direct, immediate, and irreparable damage to our Nation or its people. That being so, there can under the First Amendment be but one judicial resolution of the issues before us. ...

Mr. Justice **WHITE**, with whom Mr. Justice **STEWART** joins, concurring.

I concur in today's judgments, but only because of the concededly extraordinary protection against prior restraints enjoyed by the press under our constitutional system. I do not say that in no circumstances would the First Amendment permit an injunction against publishing information about government plans or operations. Nor, after examining the materials the Government characterizes as the most sensitive and destructive, can I deny that revelation of these documents will do substantial damage to public interests. Indeed, I am confident that their disclosure will have that result. But I nevertheless agree that the United States has not satisfied the very heavy burden that it must meet to warrant an injunction against publication in these cases. ...

... That the Government mistakenly chose to proceed by injunction does not mean that it could not successfully proceed in another way. ... I am not, of course, saying that either of these newspapers has yet committed a crime or that either would commit a crime if it published all the material now in its possession. ...

Mr. Justice **MARSHALL**, concurring.

... The issue is whether this Court or the Congress has the power to make law. ... The problem here is whether in these particular cases the Executive Branch has authority to invoke the equity jurisdiction of the courts to protect what it believes to be the national interest.   ...

In these cases we are not faced with a situation where Congress has failed to provide the Executive with broad power to protect the Nation from disclosure of damaging state secrets.   Congress has on several occasions given extensive consideration to the problem of protecting the military and strategic secrets of the United States.   This consideration has resulted in the enactment of statutes making it a crime to receive, disclose, communicate, withhold, and publish certain documents, photographs, instruments, appliances, and information.   ...

...   Congress has specifically rejected passing legislation that would have clearly given the President the power he seeks here and made the current activity of the newspapers unlawful.   When Congress specifically declines to make conduct unlawful it is not for this Court to redecide those issues—to overrule Congress.   See *Youngstown Sheet & Tube Co.* ...

Mr. Chief Justice **BURGER**, dissenting.

...   In these cases, the imperative of a free and unfettered press comes into collision with another imperative, the effective functioning of a complex modern government and specifically the effective exercise of certain constitutional powers of the Executive.   Only those who view the First Amendment as an absolute in all circumstances—a view I respect, but reject—can find such cases as these to be simple or easy.   ...

Why are we in this posture, in which only those judges to whom the First Amendment is absolute and permits of no restraint in any circumstances or for any reason, are really in a position to act?   I suggest we are in this posture because these cases have been conducted in unseemly haste.   ...   The prompt setting of these cases reflects our universal abhorrence of prior restraint.   But prompt judicial action does not mean unjudicial haste.

Here, moreover, the frenetic haste is due in large part to the manner in which the *Times* proceeded from the date it obtained the purloined documents.   It seems reasonably clear now that the haste precluded reasonable and deliberate judicial treatment of these cases and was not warranted.   The precipitate action of this Court aborting trials not yet completed is not the kind of judicial conduct that ought to attend the disposition of a great issue.

The newspapers make a derivative claim under the First Amendment; they denominate this right as the public "right to know"; by implication, the *Times* asserts a sole trusteeship of that right by virtue of its journalistic "scoop."   The right is asserted as an absolute.   Of course, the First Amendment right itself is not an absolute.   ...[1] An

---

1.   ...   [T]he *Times* has copyrighted its material and there were strong intimations in the oral argument that the *Times* contemplated enjoining its use by any other publisher in violation of its copyright.   Paradoxically this would afford it a protection, analogous to

issue of this importance should be tried and heard in a judicial atmosphere conducive to thoughtful, reflective deliberation, especially when haste, in terms of hours, is unwarranted in light of the long period the *Times,* by its own choice, deferred publication.

It is not disputed that the *Times* has had unauthorized possession of the documents for three to four months, during which it has had its expert analysts studying them, presumably digesting them and preparing the material for publication. During all of this time, the *Times,* presumably in its capacity as trustee of the public's "right to know," has held up publication for purposes it considered proper and thus public knowledge was delayed. No doubt this was for a good reason; the analysis of 7,000 pages of complex material drawn from a vastly greater volume of material would inevitably take time and the writing of good news stories takes time. But why should the United States Government, from whom this information was illegally acquired by someone, along with all the counsel, trial judges, and appellate judges be placed under needless pressure? After these months of deferral, the alleged "right to know" has somehow and suddenly become a right that must be vindicated *instanter.* . . .

The consequences of all this melancholy series of events is that we literally do not know what we are acting on. . . .

Mr. Justice **HARLAN**, with whom The Chief Justice [**BURGER**] and
    Mr. Justice **BLACKMUN** join, dissenting. . . .

. . . With all respect, I consider that the Court has been almost irresponsibly feverish in dealing with these cases. . . .

. . . It is plain to me that the scope of the judicial function in passing upon the activities of the Executive Branch of the Government in the field of foreign affairs is very narrowly restricted. This view is, I think, dictated by the concept of separation of powers upon which our constitutional system rests. In a speech on the floor of the House of Representatives, Chief Justice John Marshall, then a member of that body, stated: "The President is the sole organ of the nation in its external relations, and its sole representative with foreign nations." . . . From this constitutional primacy in the field of foreign affairs, it seems to me that certain conclusions necessarily follow. . . .

The power to evaluate the "pernicious influence" of premature disclosure is not, however, lodged in the Executive alone. I agree that, in performance of its duty to protect the values of the First Amendment against political pressures, the judiciary must review the initial Executive determination to the point of satisfying itself that the subject matter of the dispute does lie within the proper compass of the President's foreign relations power. Constitutional considerations forbid "a complete abandonment of judicial control." . . . Moreover, the judiciary may properly insist that the determination that disclosure of the subject

---

prior restraint, against all others—a protection the *Times* denies the Government of the United States. [Footnote by Chief Justice Burger.]

matter would irreparably impair the national security be made by the head of the Executive Department concerned—here the Secretary of State or the Secretary of Defense—after actual personal consideration by that officer. This safeguard is required in the analogous area of executive claims of privilege for secrets of state. ...

But in my judgment the judiciary may not properly go beyond these two inquiries and redetermine for itself the probable impact of disclosure on the national security. ...

Even if there is some room for the judiciary to override the executive determination, it is plain that the scope of review must be exceedingly narrow. ... Pending further hearings in each case conducted under the appropriate ground rules, I would continue the restraints on publication. ...

Mr. Justice **BLACKMUN**, dissenting.

The country would be none the worse off were the cases tried quickly, to be sure, but in the customary and properly deliberative manner. The most recent of the material, it is said, dates no later than 1968, already about three years ago, and the *Times* itself took three months to formulate its plan of procedure and, thus, deprived its public for that period.

The First Amendment, after all, is only one part of an entire Constitution. Article II of the great document vests in the Executive Branch primary power over the conduct of foreign affairs and places in that branch the responsibility for the Nation's safety. Each provision of the Constitution is important, and I cannot subscribe to a doctrine of unlimited absolutism for the First Amendment at the cost of downgrading other provisions. First Amendment absolutism has never commanded a majority of this Court. What is needed here is a weighing, upon properly developed standards, of the broad right of the press to print and of the very narrow right of the Government to prevent. Such standards are not yet developed. The parties here are in disagreement as to what those standards should be. But even the newspapers concede that there are situations where restraint is in order and is constitutional. ...

Editors' Notes

(1) **Query**: Did Black's *textual approach* force him to contradict himself? In other cases, he would have limited constitutional rights to those explicitly listed in the constitutional document; see espec. his dis. op. in Griswold v. Connecticut (1965; reprinted above p. 147). But what right does the First Amendment explicitly establish against either judicial or executive interference with freedom of the press? That amendment says "Congress shall make no law," not "Government shall not interfere with. ..." Did Black extract himself from this contradiction by employing (an)other approach(es) to constitutional interpretation in conjunction with *textualism*? If so, how well did he succeed?

(2) **Query**: Recall Dworkin's distinction between "concepts" and "conceptions" in constitutional interpretation. ("Taking Rights Seriously," reprint-

ed above, p. 249.) Reread the text of the First Amendment. To the extent Dworkin's distinction is valid, can Black legitimately claim to be a literalist?

(3) **Query:** Unlike in *Griswold*, Douglas also used a *textual approach* in *Pentagon Papers*; but, as a constitutionalist, he demanded that government put its finger on a clause in the document authorizing interference with freedom of the press. Obviously, he took several other approaches to constitutional interpretation in this case. Did he use any version of *structuralism* that he employed in *Griswold*? If we assume *arguendo* that Douglas's mixture of approaches was more congruent with constitutionalism than Black's, was it more congruent with democratic theory than Black's?

(4) **Query:** Which justice(s) followed a *structural approach* in *Pentagon Papers*? What sort(s) of *structuralism* did he or they follow? Is there evidence in the opinions themselves that any of the justices used a *prudential approach*? How heavily did any justice rely on a *doctrinal approach*?

(5) **Query:** As always, the question of WHO interprets was bubbling beneath the surface of this case. How did each of the justices explicitly or implicitly resolve that issue?

(6) **Query:** Compare the various opinions here as they relate to divisions of power within the national government with those in the Steel Seizure Case (1952; reprinted above, p. 443) and INS v. Chadha (1983; reprinted above, p. 485). Did any opinion have the sophistication of Jackson's concurring opinion in *Steel Seizure*?

(7) Unlike most nations, the United States has no "Official Secrets Act." Thus, when the Department of Justice indicted Daniel Ellsberg for passing the *Pentagon Papers* to the press, it had to charge him in very general terms. The prosecution foundered when it became known that, under orders from Nixon's White House, the government had engaged in assorted crimes, including breaking into the office of Ellsberg's psychiatrist to try to obtain information that might embarrass him. No criminal action was ever brought against the newspapers.

(8) Less than a month after the Court's decision in *Pentagon Papers*, the version printed in the *Times* was published as a paperback book, *The Pentagon Papers* (New York: Bantam Books, 1971), under the supervision of James L. Greenfield, based on investigative reporting by Neil Sheehan. It contained much embarrassing information about the way in which presidents from Eisenhower to Johnson had bungled American relations with and in IndoChina, but no great military secrets escaped.

(9) For analyses of the Court's ruling and its various opinions, see: Louis Henkin, "The Right to Know and the Duty to Withhold," 120 *U.Pa.L.Rev.* 271 (1971); C. Herman Pritchett, *Constitutional Civil Liberties* (Englewood Cliffs, NJ: Prentice–Hall, 1984), ch. 4; David M. O'Brien, *The Public's Right to Know* (New York: Praeger, 1981), pp. 155–165; Martin Shapiro, *The Pentagon Papers and the Courts* (San Francisco: Chandler, 1972); Sanford J. Ungar, *The Papers and the Papers* (New York: Dutton, 1972). For a consideration of the constitutionality of the Vietnam War, see John Hart Ely, *War and Responsibility: Constitutional Lessons of Vietnam and Its Aftermath* (Princeton: Princeton University Press, 1993).

(10) In Haig v. Agee (1981), the Court, speaking through Chief Justice Burger, upheld revocation of the passport of James Agee, a former CIA agent who had announced that he was launching a "campaign" to "fight the United States CIA wherever it is operating" and "to expose CIA officers and agents and take the measures necessary to drive them out of the countries where they are operating." Burger acknowledged that the revocation "rests in part on the content of his speech: specifically, his repeated disclosures of intelligence operations and names of intelligence personnel." But the Chief Justice observed, quoting *Near,* that "[l]ong ago ... this Court recognized that '[n]o one would question but that a government might prevent actual obstruction to its recruiting service or the publication of the sailing dates of transports or the number and location of troops.'" He concluded: "The mere fact that Agee is also engaged in criticism of the Government does not render his conduct beyond the reach of the law."

(11) In 1978 Frank W. Snepp, III, a former CIA agent, published *Decent Interval* (New York: Random House), a critical analysis of earlier American policy in Vietnam. He had not submitted the manuscript to the Agency for review as his contract of employment had required. On the other hand, the government conceded that the book contained no classified information that had not already been published elsewhere. Six justices, without hearing oral argument or having briefs on the merits, treated the case solely as a matter of breach of contract and ordered Snepp to give the government all royalties the book earned. Snepp v. United States (1980). Stevens, joined by Brennan and Marshall, dissented. (Perhaps one reason that the Court ignored the basic issue of free criticism of public policy was that *Snepp* came up just after publication of Bob Woodward and Scott Armstrong, *The Brethren* (New York: Simon & Schuster, 1979), which purported to be an inside history of the Burger Court and was heavily based on gossip (some of it true) provided by young law clerks who had, without doubt, betrayed their justices' trust.)

(12) CIA v. Sims (1985) held that Congress had given the CIA very broad exemption from the obligation to disclose information under the Freedom of Information Act.

VI.   UNCONSTITUTIONAL CONDITIONS

"The condition that federal funds will be used only to further the purposes of a grant does not violate constitutional rights."—Chief Justice REHNQUIST

"Whatever may be the Government's power to condition the receipt of its largesse upon the relinquishment of constitutional rights, it surely does not extend to a con-

dition that suppresses the recipient's cherished freedom
of speech based solely upon the content or viewpoint of
that speech."—Justice BLACKMUN

RUST v. SULLIVAN

500 U.S. 173, 111 S.Ct. 1759, 114 L.Ed.2d 233 (1991).

As amended, Title X of the Public Health Service Act of 1970 authorized the Secretary of the Department of Health and Human Services to assist in family planning by making grants to public and non-profit private organizations. Section 1008 provides, however: "None of the funds appropriated under this subchapter shall be used in programs where abortion is a method of family planning." In 1988 the Secretary changed the department's long standing regulations to explicitly prohibit grantees from using federal funds to engage in activities that "encourage, promote or advise abortion as a method of family planning." The Secretary also set down specific rules requiring an organization that did engage in such abortion-related activities to separate those activities—and personnel—from its federally financed operations. A group of doctors and organizations receiving grants sued in a federal district court, challenging the regulations on the grounds that they were not authorized by Title X and that they violated the First and Fifth Amendments. The challengers lost in the district court and in the court of appeals, but obtained certiorari from the Supreme Court.

Chief Justice **REHNQUIST** delivered the opinion of the Court.   ...

[The Chief Justice concluded that the Secretary's administrative regulations did not exceed his authority under the statute.]

III

Petitioners contend that the regulations violate the First Amendment by impermissibly discriminating based on viewpoint because they prohibit "all discussion about abortion as a lawful option—including counseling, referral, and the provision of neutral and accurate information about ending a pregnancy—while compelling the clinic or counselor to provide information that promotes continuing a pregnancy to term."
...   Relying on Regan v. Taxation With Representation [1983], and Arkansas Writers v. Ragland (1987), petitioners also assert that while the Government may place certain conditions on the receipt of federal subsidies, it may not "discriminate invidiously in its subsidies in such a way as to 'a[im] at the suppression of dangerous ideas.' "

There is no question but that the statutory prohibition contained in § 1008 is constitutional. In Maher v. Roe [1977] we upheld a state welfare regulation under which Medicaid recipients received payments for services related to childbirth, but not for nontherapeutic abortions. ... The Government can, without violating the Constitution, selectively fund a program to encourage certain activities it believes to be in the public interest, without at the same time funding an alternate program which seeks to deal with the problem in another way. In so doing, the Government has not discriminated on the basis of viewpoint; it has merely chosen to fund one activity to the exclusion of the other. . . . "[A] legislature's decision not to subsidize the exercise of a fundamental right does not infringe the right." *Regan.* . . .

The challenged regulations implement the statutory prohibition by prohibiting counseling, referral, and the provision of information regarding abortion as a method of family planning. They are designed to ensure that the limits of the federal program are observed. The Title X program is designed not for prenatal care, but to encourage family planning. A doctor who wished to offer prenatal care to a project patient who became pregnant could properly be prohibited from doing so because such service is outside the scope of the federally funded program. . . . This is not a case of the Government "suppressing a dangerous idea," but of a prohibition on a project grantee or its employees from engaging in activities outside of the project's scope.

. . . Petitioners' assertions ultimately boil down to the position that if the government chooses to subsidize one protected right, it must subsidize analogous counterpart rights. But the Court has soundly rejected that proposition. *Regan; Maher.* Within far broader limits than petitioners are willing to concede, when the government appropriates public funds to establish a program it is entitled to define the limits of that program. . . .

Petitioners also contend that the restrictions on the subsidization of abortion-related speech contained in the regulations are impermissible because they condition the receipt of a benefit . . . on the relinquishment of a constitutional right, the right to engage in abortion advocacy and counseling. Relying on Perry v. Sindermann (1972) and FCC v. League of Women Voters of Cal. (1984), petitioners argue that "even though the government may deny [a] . . . benefit for any number of reasons, there are some reasons upon which the government may not rely. It may not deny a benefit to a person on a basis that infringes his constitutionally protected interests—especially, his interest in freedom of speech."

Petitioners' reliance on these cases is unavailing, however, because here the government is not denying a benefit to anyone, but is instead simply insisting that public funds be spent for the purposes for which they were authorized. The Secretary's regulations do not force the Title X grantee to give up abortion-related speech; they merely require that the grantee keep such activities separate and distinct from Title X activities. . . .

In contrast, our "unconstitutional conditions" cases involve situations in which the government has placed a condition on the *recipient* of the subsidy rather than on a particular program or service, thus effectively prohibiting the recipient from engaging in the protected conduct outside the scope of the federally funded program. In *League of Women Voters,* we invalidated a federal law providing that noncommercial television and radio stations that receive federal grants may not "engage in editorializing." Under that law, a recipient of federal funds was "barred absolutely from all editorializing" because it "is not able to segregate its activities according to the source of its funding" and thus "has no way of

limiting the use of its federal funds to all noneditorializing activities."
. . .

Similarly, in *Regan* we held that Congress could . . . reasonably refuse to subsidize the lobbying activities of tax-exempt charitable organizations by prohibiting such organizations from using tax-deductible contributions to support their lobbying efforts. In so holding, we explained that such organizations remained free "to receive deductible contributions to support . . . nonlobbying activit[ies]." . . . The condition that federal funds will be used only to further the purposes of a grant does not violate constitutional rights. . . .

The same principles apply to petitioners' claim that the regulations abridge the free speech rights of the grantee's staff. . . . The regulations, which govern solely the scope of the Title X project's activities, do not in any way restrict the activities of those persons acting as private individuals. The employees' freedom of expression is limited during the time that they actually work for the project; but this limitation is a consequence of their decision to accept employment in a project, the scope of which is permissibly restricted by the funding authority.

This is not to suggest that funding by the Government, even when coupled with the freedom of the fund recipients to speak outside the scope of the Government-funded project, is invariably sufficient to justify government control over the content of expression. For example, this Court has recognized that the existence of a Government "subsidy," in the form of Government-owned property, does not justify the restriction of speech in areas that have "been traditionally open to the public for expressive activity," United States v. Kokinda (1990); Hague v. CIO (1939)(opinion of Roberts, J.), or have been "expressly dedicated to speech activity." *Kokinda;* Perry Education Assn. v. Perry Local Educators' Assn. (1983). Similarly, we have recognized that the university is a traditional sphere of free expression so fundamental to the functioning of our society that the Government's ability to control speech within that sphere by means of conditions attached to the expenditure of Government funds is restricted by the vagueness and overbreadth doctrines of the First Amendment, Keyishian v. Board of Regents (1967).
. . .

IV . . .

[The Chief Justice addressed and rejected claims that the Secretary's regulations violated the Fifth Amendment's due process clause by interfering with women's rights to obtain abortions.]

Affirmed.

Justice **BLACKMUN**, with whom Justice **MARSHALL** joins, with whom Justice **STEVENS** joins as to Parts II and III, and with whom Justice **O'CONNOR** joins as to Part I, dissenting. . . .

I . . .

Because I conclude that a plainly constitutional construction of § 1008 "is not only 'fairly possible' but entirely reasonable," Machinists [v. Street (1961)], I would reverse the judgment of the Court of Appeals on this ground without deciding the constitutionality of the Secretary's Regulations.

II

I also strongly disagree with the majority's disposition of petitioners' constitutional claims, and because I feel that a response thereto is indicated, I move on to that issue.

A

Until today, the Court never has upheld viewpoint-based suppression of speech simply because that suppression was a condition upon the acceptance of public funds. Whatever may be the Government's power to condition the receipt of its largess upon the relinquishment of constitutional rights, it surely does not extend to a condition that suppresses the recipient's cherished freedom of speech based solely upon the content or viewpoint of that speech. ...

Nothing in the Court's opinion in *Regan* can be said to challenge this long-settled understanding. In *Regan,* the Court upheld a content-neutral provision of the Internal Revenue Code that disallowed a particular tax-exempt status to organizations that "attempt[ed] to influence legislation," while affording such status to veterans' organizations irrespective of their lobbying activities. ... [T]he Court explained: "The case would be different if Congress were to discriminate invidiously in its subsidies in such a way as to 'a[im] at the suppression of dangerous ideas.' " ...

It cannot seriously be disputed that the counseling and referral provisions at issue in the present cases constitute content-based regulation of speech. Title X grantees may provide counseling and referral regarding any of a wide range of family planning and other topics, save abortion.

The Regulations are also clearly viewpoint-based. While suppressing speech favorable to abortion with one hand, the Secretary compels anti-abortion speech with the other. For example, the Department of Health and Human Services' own description of the Regulations makes plain that "Title X projects are *required* to facilitate access to prenatal care and social services, including adoption services, that might be needed by the pregnant client to promote her well-being and that of her child, while making it abundantly clear that the project is not permitted to promote abortion by facilitating access to abortion through the referral process." (Emphasis added [by Judge Blackmun].)

Moreover, the Regulations command that a project refer for prenatal care each woman diagnosed as pregnant, irrespective of the woman's expressed desire to continue or terminate her pregnancy. If a client asks directly about abortion, a Title X physician or counselor is required to say, in essence, that the project does not consider abortion to be an appropriate method of family planning. Both requirements are anti-thetical to the First Amendment.

The Regulations pertaining to "advocacy" are even more explicitly viewpoint-based. These provide: "A Title X project may not *encourage, promote* or *advocate* abortion as a method of family planning." (Empha-sis added [by Justice Blackmun].) . . . The Regulations do not, however, proscribe or even regulate anti-abortion advocacy. These are clearly restrictions aimed at the suppression of "dangerous ideas."

Remarkably, the majority concludes that "the Government has not discriminated on the basis of viewpoint; it has merely chosen to fund one activity to the exclusion of another." But the majority's claim that the Regulations merely limit a Title X project's speech to preventive or preconceptual services rings hollow in light of the broad range of non-preventive services that the Regulations authorize Title X projects to provide.[1] By refusing to fund those family-planning projects that advo-cate abortion *because* they advocate abortion, the Government plainly has targeted a particular viewpoint. The majority's reliance on the fact that the Regulations pertain solely to funding decisions simply begs the question. Clearly, there are some bases upon which government may not rest its decision to fund or not to fund. For example, the Members of the majority surely would agree that government may not base its decision to support an activity upon considerations of race. See, e.g., Yick Wo v. Hopkins (1886). . . . [O]ur cases make clear that ideological viewpoint is a similarly repugnant ground upon which to base funding decisions.

. . . [I]n addition to their impermissible focus upon the viewpoint of regulated speech, the provisions intrude upon a wide range of communi-cative conduct, including the very words spoken to a woman by her physician. By manipulating the content of the doctor/patient dialogue, the Regulations upheld today force each of the petitioners "to be an instrument for fostering public adherence to an ideological point of view [he or she] finds unacceptable." Wooley v. Maynard [1977]. . . .

B

The Court concludes that the challenged Regulations do not violate the First Amendment rights of Title X staff members because any limitation of the employees' freedom of expression is simply a conse-quence of their decision to accept employment at a federally funded project. But it has never been sufficient to justify an otherwise uncon-stitutional condition upon public employment that the employee may escape the condition by relinquishing his or her job. It is beyond question "that a government may not require an individual to relinquish rights guaranteed him by the First Amendment as a condition of public

---

1. In addition to requiring referral for prenatal care and adoption services, the Regulations permit general health services such as physical examinations, screening for breast cancer, treatment of gynecological problems, and treatment for sexually transmitted diseases. None of the latter are strictly preventive, preconceptual services. [Footnote by Justice Blackmun.]

employment." Abood v. Detroit Board of Education (1977), citing Elrod
v. Burns (1976) and cases cited therein; Perry v. Sindermann (1972);
Keyishian v. Board of Regents (1967). Nearly two decades ago, it was
said:

> "For at least a quarter-century, this Court has made clear that even
> though a person has no 'right' to a valuable governmental benefit and
> even though the government may deny him the benefit for any number
> of reasons, there are some reasons upon which the government may not
> rely. It may not deny a benefit to a person on a basis that infringes his
> constitutionally protected interests—especially, his interest in freedom
> of speech. For if the government could deny a benefit to a person
> because of his constitutionally protected speech or associations, his
> exercise of those freedoms would in effect be penalized and inhibited.
> This would allow the government to 'produce a result which [it] could
> not command directly.' " Perry v. Sindermann, quoting Speiser v.
> Randall (1958).

The majority attempts to circumvent this principle by emphasizing
that Title X physicians and counselors "remain free ... to pursue
abortion-related activities when they are not acting under the auspices of
the Title X project." ... Under the majority's reasoning, the First
Amendment could be read to tolerate *any* governmental restriction upon
an employee's speech so long as that restriction is limited to the funded
workplace. This is a dangerous proposition, and one the Court has
rightly rejected in the past. ...

C

Finally, it is of no small significance that the speech the Secretary
would suppress is truthful information regarding constitutionally protected conduct of vital importance to the listener. One can imagine no
legitimate governmental interest that might be served by suppressing
such information. Concededly, the abortion debate is among the most
divisive and contentious issues that our Nation has faced in recent years.
"But freedom to differ is not limited to things that do not matter much.
That would be a mere shadow of freedom. The test of its substance is
the right to differ as to things that touch the heart of the existing
order." W.Va. v. Barnette (1943). ...

Justice **STEVENS**, dissenting. ...

Justice **O'CONNOR**, dissenting. ...

Editors' Notes

(1) **Query:** What general problems for democratic theory does selective
governmental funding raise? For constitutionalism?

(2) **Query:** To what extent did either Rehnquist or Blackmun rely on a
textual approach to constitutional interpretation? A *structuralist approach*? A
purposive approach? A *doctrinal approach*? How consistent was Rehnquist
with his argument in "The Notion of a Living Constitution," reprinted above, p.
243.

(3) **Query:** Scalia joined the majority in this case. How could he square Rehnquist's reasoning with his own in *R.A.V.* (1992; reprinted above, p. 686) that government could not prefer symbolic speech that fostered racial equality over hate speech? Did *originalism* play any role in Rehnquist's opinion?

(4) **Query:** Suppose *Rust* was wrongly decided, as many commentators do. Suppose also that the year is 1857, a few months after *Dred Scott* (reprinted above, p. 195), and new breeds of insects are ruining farms all across the United States. Would it then be constitutional for Congress to fund a program of agricultural assistance which forbids recipients, during the hours they are actually working under the federal grants, to teach the desirability, utility, or necessity of slavery?

(5) The reaction to *Rust* was heavily negative, and Congress passed a bill to remove the grounds for the Secretary's ban on counselling abortion under Title X. The *Washington Post* reported that "a recent Harris poll found that 78 percent of Americans interviewed opposed the Supreme Court ruling ... with most of them favoring a veto override if Bush opposes the legislation." (June 21, 1991, p. A4.) Nevertheless, George Bush did veto the bill. The Senate voted 72–25 to override, but the House vote fell several votes short of the necessary two-thirds majority. One of William J. Clinton's first official acts as President was to sign an administrative order lifting the so-called "gag rule" *Rust* had upheld. He did so on January 22, 1993, the twentieth anniversary of the Supreme Court's decision in Roe v. Wade (1973; reprinted below, p. 1258).

(6) Under *Rust*, may the government stipulate that no federal funds be distributed to artists whose work is "offensive," "indecent," or "obscene"? The so-called Helms Amendment of 1989 to the statute funding the National Endowment for the Arts was prompted by controversy over NEA's underwriting an exhibition of Robert Mapplethorpe's works. The Helms Amendment provided: "None of the funds ... may be used to promote, disseminate, or produce materials which in the judgment of the National Endowment for the Arts ... may be considered obscene. ..." The next year, Congress enacted the Arts, Humanities, and Museum Amendments of 1990, which decreed that "obscenity ... shall not be funded," but left the judgment of obscenity to the courts, and further provided that, if NEA funds did support a work that a court subsequently determined to be obscene, the recipient would have to repay the funds and would not be eligible for additional financial assistance until those funds were fully repaid.

(7) **Query:** May the government require an individual to relinquish constitutional rights as a condition of holding public employment? Pickering v. Bd. of Ed. (1968) invalidated the firing of a public school teacher for openly criticizing a board of education's allocation of money. For the Court, Justice Marshall held that Pickering's comments were about "a matter of legitimate public concern" and so were protected by the First and Fourteenth Amendments. The majority's reasoning, however, was not clear. At one point Marshall identified *balancing* as the proper approach:

> The problem in any case is to find a balance between the interests of the [employee], as a citizen, in commenting upon matters of public concern and the interest of the State, as employer, in promoting the efficiency of the public services it performs through its employees.

But, toward the end of his opinion, Marshall said: "absent proof of false statements knowingly or recklessly made by him, a teacher's exercise of his right to speak on issues of public importance may not furnish the basis for his dismissal from public employment."

(8) A constitutional democracy should not want civil servants who are partisans of one political party or interest group. On the other hand, constitutional democracy strongly values rights to political expression and participation. Sec. 9(a) of the Hatch Act opted for civil servants who were, overtly at least, non-partisan over those who were openly expressing their political choices:

> An employee in an Executive Agency or an individual employed by the government of the District of Columbia may not (1) use his official authority or influence for the purpose of interfering with or affecting the result of an election; or (2) take an active part in political management or in political campaigns.

In 1947 United Public Workers v. Mitchell sustained the validity of this provision. During the next twenty-five years, however, the Supreme Court became more sensitive of and concerned to protect rights of political association and participation. And several groups as well as individual federal employees filed suit in a federal district court re-challenging the constitutionality of § 9a. A special three-judge district court agreed that constitutional doctrine had changed since *Mitchell* and invalidated § 9a.

In United States Civil Service Comm'n v. Nat'l Ass'n of Letter Carriers (1973), the Supreme Court per Justice White reversed, reaffirming *Mitchell*. In doing so, White quoted *Pickering*'s endorsement of a *balancing approach and* observed that "the government has an interest in regulating the conduct and 'the speech of its employees that differ[s] significantly from those it possesses in connection with regulation of the speech of the citizenry in general.'" Emphasizing that "[n]either the right to associate nor the right to participate in political activities is absolute," White concluded: "We agree with the basic holding of *Mitchell* that plainly identifiable acts of political management and political campaigning may constitutionally be prohibited on the part of federal employees." Justice Douglas vigorously dissented, and was joined by Justices Brennan and Marshall.

(9) Connick v. Myers (1983) sustained a district attorney's firing of one of his assistants for what he alleged was insubordination in circulating a questionnaire to fellow staff members regarding some of the office's internal policies. The assistant alleged that her discharge violated her rights under the First and Fourteenth amendments. White wrote for the Court again: "For at least 15 years, it has been settled that a state cannot condition public employment on a basis that infringes the employee's constitutionally protected interest in freedom of expression." But White explicitly refused to lay down a general standard; instead, he again quoted *Pickering*'s endorsement of a *balancing approach* and concluded that "the balance" was against the employee.

(10) Over the years, there have been several attempts to amend the Hatch Act substantially, none of which has succeeded.

(11) For discussions of the issue of unconstitutional conditions, see Richard A. Epstein: *Bargaining With the State* (Princeton: Princeton University Press, 1994), and "Foreword: Unconstitutional Conditions, State Power, and the Limits of Consent," 102 *Harv.L.Rev.* 4 (1988); Michael McConnell, "The Selective Funding Problem: Abortions and Religious Schools," 104 *Harv. L.Rev.* 989 (1991); Kathleen Sullivan, "Unconstitutional Conditions," 102 *Harv. L.Rev.* 1413 (1989); and Cass R. Sunstein, "Why the Unconstitutional Conditions Doctrine Is an Anachronism," 70 *B.U.L.Rev.* 593 (1990).

13

Political Participation

Problems of freedom of political communication are intricate and fascinating in their own right, so much so that they may distract attention from the fundamental problem: HOW should "the Constitution," whatever that term encompasses, be interpreted? This pair of chapters is focusing on one answer to that question: Judges' proper approach to constitutional interpretation is to keep the political processes open, to *reinforce representative democracy*, so that popularly chosen officials can decide most of the substantive issues of public policy, even those issues involving constitutional interpretation.

Chapter 3 discussed six minimal institutional conditions necessary for representative democracy: (1) Popular election for limited terms of the most important policy makers to governmental offices that allow a majority to govern; (2) Universal adult suffrage; (3) Electoral districts of approximately equal population that are not skewed to give disproportionate advantages to particular political parties or interests; (4) Free entry of citizens as candidates for electoral office; (5) Freedom of political communication so that citizens can be as informed as they wish to be about issues and candidates competing for public office; and, closely related to several of these, (6) Freedom to associate with other people to try to convince them of the rightness of one's views and/or to join with others of similar views to influence campaigns (to electioneer) and officeholders (to lobby). This sixth category includes a right to privacy so that people who espouse unpopular causes may associate with each other without fear of governmental or societal reprisal.

The problems of freedom of political communication Chapter 12 considered are inseparable from the difficulties involved in achieving the other freedoms essential to representative democracy. One cannot effectively campaign, join with others, lobby, or even vote intelligently if government controls what may and may not be communicated. Most basically, if government controls all or even a large share of politically relevant information, elections become charades.

And, as with political communication, no regulation at all of the rights of political participation might well produce anarchy. A

758

chaos of bribery, fraudulent voting, frivolous candidacies, and criminal conspiracies might flourish in the name of free political participation. At very least, government must protect the rights to participate from interference by other private citizens, lest violence determine electoral results. In the United States, federalism and racial hatred have complicated matters;[1] but, after some initial hesitation, the Supreme Court sustained efforts of Reconstruction Congresses to protect black voters from violence. As the justices unanimously held in Ex parte Yarbrough (1884), affirming the conviction of a group of whites for beating up a black man who was trying to vote:

> If [the federal] government is anything more than a mere aggregation of delegated agents of other States and governments ... it must have the power to protect the elections on which its existence depends from open violence and insidious corruption.

The history of state, mostly but not exclusively southern, efforts to keep African Americans from voting is long and sordid. Southern influence in the Senate forced proponents of civil rights to wage their countercampaign in the federal courts. Although African Americans suffered significant defeats,[2] they finally succeeded in persuading the Supreme Court to invalidate the white primary,[3] which had once been the principal "legal" means of racial disfranchisement. It was not, however, until the School Segregation Cases (1954; reprinted below, p. 912) helped trigger the Civil Rights Movement that Congress finally enacted a comprehensive statute, the Voting Rights Act of 1965 (amended in 1970, 1975, and 1982), to protect against both subtle and not-so-subtle forms of fraud that for much of a century had kept blacks (and often poor whites) from voting.[4] South Carolina v. Katzenbach (1966) and its progeny[5] sustained the main provisions of the law.

Protecting citizens against violence and fraud in the electoral processes are, as Ex parte Yarborough held, obvious governmental duties. But what else must or even may government do to protect or even enhance rights to political participation?

---

1. See, e.g., United States v. Reese (1876), and United States v. Cruikshank (1876).

2. For example: Williams v. Mississippi (1898), Giles v. Harris (1903), and Grovey v. Townsend (1935).

3. Smith v. Allwright (1944) and Terry v. Adams (1953).

4. See C. Herman Pritchett, *Constitutional Civil Liberties* (Englewood Cliffs, NJ: Prentice–Hall, 1984), pp. 342–346 for summaries of the Act of 1965 and its amendments. See also Howard Ball, Dale Crane, and Thomas P. Lasuth, *Compromised Compliance: Implementation of the 1965 Voting Rights Act* (Westport, CN: Greenwood Press, 1982).

5. See the discussion in Editors' Notes to *Katzenbach*, above pp. 333–335; United States v. Mississippi (1965); Mobile v. Bolden (1980), and Rome v. United States (1980); and Alexander Bickel, "The Voting Rights Cases," 1966 *Sup.Ct.Rev.* 79.

I. TO WHAT EXTENT DOES THE CONSTITUTION INCLUDE DEMOCRATIC THEORY?

The reach of participatory rights and the degree to which they are protected by the constitutional text or the broader constitution are problematic. It takes a broad leap over text, logic, history, and practice to claim that "the Constitution" fully incorporates democratic theory. Even assuming the validity of that claim, there would remain disagreement concerning what conception of democratic theory one has in mind. For example, is it a theory of interest-group pluralism (in which individuals and groups pursuing their own interests clash and form coalitions in a veritable marketplace of ideas) or a theory of civic republicanism (in which public-spirited citizens deliberate about the common good)?[6] Or indeed under the text does there lurk a political hybrid in which elements of both these conceptions of democracy coexist in tension with each other as well as with constitutionalism?

Originalism does not help much. The Federalists were wary of democracy, as evidenced by such patently non-majoritarian institutions as a Senate equally representing each state regardless of population, an electoral college skewed to overrepresent less populous states, and an appointed judiciary.

Even the constitutional status of the simple act of voting poses interpretive problems, for the text speaks tersely about a right to cast a ballot. Article I provides that those eligible to vote for the most numerous house of their state legislature are eligible to vote for candidates for the House of Representatives; and the Seventeenth Amendment, ratified in 1913, set the same standards for senatorial elections. All the document's other provisions, however, are negative: The Fifteenth Amendment forbids discrimination against potential voters on account of race, the Nineteenth on account of sex, the Twenty-sixth on account of age for those over eighteen, and the Twenty-fourth, which applies only to senatorial, congressional, and presidential elections, on account of failure to pay a tax.[7] Thus a narrow, literal interpretation of the Constitution would produce the same result today as the Court's ruling in 1875 that "the Constitution of the United States does not confer the right

---

6. For theories of interest-group pluralism, see, e.g., David B. Truman, *The Governmental Process* (2d ed.; New York: Knopf, 1971) and Robert A. Dahl, *A Preface to Democratic Theory* (Chicago: University of Chicago Press, 1956). For theories of civic republicanism, see, e.g., Gordon S. Wood, *The Creation of the American Republic, 1776–1787* (Chapel Hill: University of North Carolina Press, 1969); Benjamin Barber, *Strong Democracy: Participatory Politics for a New Age* (Berkeley: University of California Press, 1984); Cass R. Sunstein, "Beyond the Republican Revival," 97 *Yale L.J.* 1539 (1988); Sunstein, *The Partial Constitution* (Cambridge: Harvard University Press, 1993); Frank Michelman, "Foreword: Traces of Self–Government," 100 *Harv.L.Rev.* 4 (1986); and Michelman, "Law's Republic," 97 *Yale L.J.* 1493 (1988).

7. Harper v. Virginia (1966; reprinted above, p. 225) went further, holding that the equal protection clause forbids making the right to vote depend on the payment of any tax, and so applies to elections of state as well as federal officers.

of suffrage on any one. ..." [8]

A theory of representative democracy may also demand electoral districts of equal population, but the constitutional text itself says
nothing directly about such a requirement. Both the Founders and
those who proposed and ratified the Fourteenth and Fifteenth
Amendments were intimately familiar with gerrymandering. Indeed, Elbridge Gerry, for whom the American practice of deliberately drawing unfair electoral lines was named, was himself a member
of the Philadelphia Convention. Moreover, the framers of the
Fourteenth Amendment apparently did not think that the equal
protection clause applied to suffrage, for they quickly proposed the
Fifteenth Amendment, which forbids discrimination among prospective voters, but only on the basis of race or previous condition of
servitude; it does not mention other factors, such as maldistricting.[9]

An interpreter who primarily relies on a *structuralist approach*
might argue, as would many democratic theorists, that the architectural scheme of the document as well as the historical development
of the political system require "one person, one vote." [10] But the
advent of that rule in American constitutional law is quite recent.
(See Baker v. Carr [1962; reprinted below, p. 769] and Reynolds v.
Sims [1964: reprinted below, p. 777].) And Warren's opinion for
the Court in *Reynolds*, like Douglas's in Gray v. Sanders (1963)—
which first set out the principle of "one person, one vote"—had
much deeper roots in contemporary forms of democratic theory
than in the constitutional document or the history of the political
system.

Thus, to a considerable extent, the Supreme Court in this
century has taken the leap across text, logic, history, and practice to
read much, though not all, of democratic theory into "the Constitution." Stone's footnote four in *Carolene Products* (1938; reprinted
above, p. 609) was by no means the first decision to stress the
importance of the political process in protecting all constitutional
rights, but it marked out as the judiciary's special responsibility to

8. Minor v. Happersett (1875), sustaining a state constitutional provision limiting the
suffrage to males. The Nineteenth Amendment, adopted in 1920, formally changed the
constitutional rule, although by that time most states allowed women to vote.

9. For an argument that "suffrage was intentionally excluded from the rights that the
Fourteenth Amendment and Civil Rights Act of 1866 were to guarantee," in order to
reduce political opposition to Reconstruction measures, see Robert Kaczorowski, "Revolutionary Constitutionalism in the Era of the Civil War and Reconstruction," 61
N.Y.U.L.Rev. 863, 881–82 (1986).

10. Like structuralists, democratic theorists have to confront the harsh fact that
weighting votes equally may exclude minorities from having effective representation in
governmental institutions chosen by popular election. United Jewish Organizations v.
Carey (1977) and Doe v. Bolton (1973) presented this problem, but the Court brushed it
aside in both instances. See also Rogers v. Lodge (1982; reprinted below, p. 933) and
Mobile v. Bolden (1980; cited in *Rogers* and discussed in the Editors' Notes to that case).
Interpreters who endorse majoritarian theories of democracy rely on either "virtual"
representation to protect such minorities or cross-cutting cleavages with the community
that can make the political power of even small groups significant. See the discussion in
Chapter 3, above, at pp. 43–44.

keep the political processes open. And Warren's opinion in *Reynolds* highlighted the linkage between constitutional interpretation and democratic theory: "The right to vote freely for the candidate of one's choice is of the essence of a democratic society, and any restrictions on that right strike at the heart of representative government." In dissent, Harlan eloquently protested that the Court was applying a particular version of democratic theory, not a doctrine found in the explicit terms of the constitutional document or in the system's accepted practices. And he challenged imposition of that form of democratic theory by unelected judges as itself anti-democratic.

In sum, Warren and Harlan disagreed fundamentally about the Court's function, about whether it should interpret the constitutional text so as to include democratic theory, and about whether it could articulate specific standards to "reinforce representative democracy." Warren and Harlan also differed profoundly on the interpretation of democratic theory, illustrating that even agreement about the text's democratic character does not automatically eliminate interpretive uncertainty. Ironically, Hugo Black, the great literalist, was on Warren's side, not Harlan's; but, as we have suggested, Black laced his literalism with political theory.[11]

II. PRACTICAL PROBLEMS

A. Voting: Problems of Districting, Literacy, and Residence

Interpreters who accept the principle of "one person, one vote" face many practical problems. First, the mobility of the American people makes it impossible to draw electoral lines that encompass equal populations or, given the diversity of the country, that do not somehow give an advantage to particular interests or parties. How much deviation from the norm is permissible? The Warren Court seemed to be moving to near mathematical uniformity,[12] but later the justices have been less strict, allowing variations in districts that reached as high as sixteen per cent,[13] but not those that reached twenty per cent.[14] Even assuming exactly equal population among districts, gerrymandering presents judges with even thornier problems, and so far the Court has warily entered this particular corner of the "political thicket" of apportionment. See Davis v. Bandemer (1986; reprinted below, p. 788).[15]

---

11. Black even wrote the opinion of the Court in Wesberry v. Sanders (1964), which applied the principle of "one person, one vote" to congressional districting.

12. Swann v. Adams (1967) and Kirkpatrick v. Preisler (1967).

13. Mahan v. Howell (1973).

14. Chapman v. Meier (1975).

15. See also: Wright v. Rockefeller (1964), United Jewish Organizations v. Carey (1977), and Karcher v. Daggett (1983). In Gaffney v. Cummings (1973), the Court upheld,

Second, does "the Constitution," even if liberally suffused with democratic theory, allow government to condition voting on literacy in English? The document is utterly silent on the point, except insofar as the equal protection clause may be involved. The argument in favor of the limitation is that it may increase the likelihood that voting (which has an impact on all citizens' lives, not merely that of the voter) will be an informed act. There are two arguments against it: (1) Literacy is not a legitimate basis on which to distinguish among citizens; and (2) literacy tests lend themselves to discriminatory administration. Recent constitutional debate has centered more on the second than the first point.

Around the turn of the twentieth century, the Court upheld such tests, even though it was obvious that southern states were unfairly administering them to exclude blacks.[16] In 1959, the Court unanimously reiterated this view, holding that it was not unreasonable for North Carolina to conclude that only those who could read English were likely to be politically informed.[17] Congress later concluded that state officials were often using literacy tests so as to deny some citizens equal protection and, interpreting the Constitution for itself, forbade states to refuse the ballot to anyone who had completed six years of education in the United States *or* Puerto Rico. This provision provoked a furious debate within the Court about WHO was the authoritative interpreter of the Constitution, but Katzenbach v. Morgan (1966; reprinted above, p. 327) upheld the validity of the clause. In 1970 Congress suspended for five years all literacy tests as prerequisites to voting—sustained by Oregon v. Mitchell (1970)—and five years later made the suspension permanent.[18]

A third difficulty involves residency and registration requirements for voting. If government had no such requirements, nothing would prevent people from voting two or more times in the same election, a rather common occurrence in large cities before enactment of laws requiring registration of voters. But demanding long periods of residence may deprive citizens of equal protection. How long is too long? Dunn v. Blumstein (1972) held that Tennes-

---

against a charge of political gerrymandering, a state redistricting scheme formulated in a bipartisan effort to provide political representation approximately proportional to the strength of political parties in the state. Shaw v. Reno (1993) and Miller v. Johnson (1995) involved racial gerrymandering to create "safe" electoral districts where a majority of the voters are black. These three cases are discussed in Davis v. Bandemer (1986; reprinted below, p. 788) and the Notes to that case.

16. Giles v. Harris (1903) and Guinn v. United States (1915). See also Williams v. Mississippi (1890).

17. Lassiter v. Northampton (1959). The Court, however, became much more cynical about requirements that prospective voters show registrars that they "understood" or could "interpret" the state or national constitutions. *Giles* and *Williams* sustained such tests, but Louisiana v. United States (1965) struck them down.

18. 42 U.S.C. §§ 1973b(e)(2).

see's requirement of one year's residence to vote in state elections infringed the rights to vote and to travel freely. Thirty days residence, the Court noted, was the period Congress set in the Voting Rights Act of 1970 for eligibility to vote in presidential elections, and that "appears to be an ample period of time for the State to complete whatever administrative tasks are necessary to prevent fraud—and a year, or three months, too much." But then Marston v. Lewis (1973) and Burns v. Fortson (1973) sustained state claims that fifty days were necessary to complete accurate voting lists.

While these cases differ in detail, they do agree on two points: (1) To protect against fraud, states may require a minimum period of residency; and (2) "minimum" is measured in weeks, not months, lest it interfere with the rights to vote and to move one's residence freely within the country.

B.   The Right to Associate

At first glance, the right to associate seems free of such difficulties. It is fundamental to representative democracy, and the First Amendment specifically recognizes "the right of the people peaceably to assemble, and to petition the government for a redress of grievances." But rights to assemble and petition may be more limited than a general right to associate. Do these rights encompass association for all political purposes? Do they include a right of communists to form a political party that would preach the propriety and necessity of forcefully overthrowing the constitutional system? (See Barenblatt v. United States [1959; reprinted below, p. 803].) Do these rights allow small, unpopular groups who advocate peaceful change to keep their membership secret lest supporters be subject to community pressures? (See NAACP v. Alabama [1958; reprinted below, p. 798].) May the Ku Klux Klan assert such a right to secrecy? (See New York v. Zimmerman [1928; reprinted below, p. 795].) Does "the Constitution" protect freedom of intimate association as well as freedom of expressive association? (See Roberts v. United States Jaycees [1984; reprinted below, p. 818].)

C.   Money and Politics: Contributing and Spending

Money poses special dangers for democratic politics. The costs of political campaigning are astronomical. Do rights of political participation allow wealthy individuals or groups to *contribute* as much money as they wish to particular candidates? Do those rights allow wealthy candidates, individuals, or groups to *spend* however much money it takes to blanket the mass media of communications to try to influence voters? For government to limit the amount of money one may contribute or spend certainly limits the capacity of candidates and their partisans to communicate freely. On the other hand, does representative democracy have a "compelling interest" in making certain that elections are held rather than bought, or more generally protecting the political processes against both corruption and the appearance of corruption? The Court wrestled with these issues in Buckley v. Valeo (1976; reprinted below, p. 828), First National Bank v. Bellotti (1978; reprinted below, p. 834, and Austin v. Michigan State Chamber of Commerce (1990; reprinted below, p. 842).

D. Regulation of the Mass Media to Improve the Political Process

Closely related to questions about campaign finances is the issue of access to mass media of communications, an aspect of the larger question whether the government may regulate the mass media to improve the political process. To operate a radio or television station and perhaps even more so a newspaper of any size requires huge amounts of capital. Because of such costs and the finite number of radio frequencies and TV channels available, control over these media is typically highly concentrated and so gives the owners immense advantages in reaching the public with their opinions. May government constitutionally require the owners of such mass media to accord equal space and time to allow those whom they criticize to respond? (See Miami Herald v. Tornillo [1974; reprinted below, p. 866], involving a newspaper, and Red Lion Broadcasting Co. v. FCC [1969; discussed below, p. 869], involving radio and television stations.) May government condition a broadcaster's receipt of federal funds upon its agreement not to engage in editorializing? (See FCC v. League of Women Voters (1984; discussed below, pp. 869–70)).

E. Lobbying

Lobbying raises similar issues. It is a right closely connected to rights of free political communication—who better to communicate ideas to than one who holds power? And, human nature being what it is, lobbying is much more likely to be effective when the lobbyist has something besides sweet reason to offer. His or her votes and those of associates are, of course, at stake; but what about money, perhaps contributions to campaign chests? The line between lobbying—essential we would *now*[19] all agree to representative democracy—and bribery can be fine indeed. Where can one legitimately draw it? To what extent may government regulate such activities? (The Court tried hard to avoid this cluster of issues in

---

19. See, however, Trist v. Child (1874), which, in effect, held lobbying to be against public morals and voided a contract by which a client agreed to pay a lobbyist. The case is discussed in a note to NAACP v. Button (1963; reprinted below, at p. 811).

United States v. Harriss [1954; discussed in the Editors' Notes to NAACP v. Button (1963; reprinted below, p. 811)].)

If there is a right to lobby legislators and executives, is there also a right to "lobby" judges in the sense of instituting lawsuits to bring the power of the courts to bear to protect particular rights and interests? After all, constitutional interpretation makes a substantial difference not only in the general ways the polity operates but also in the specific policies it pursues. One need only watch the flurry of political activity that precedes and accompanies the selection of judges to realize how well leaders of interest groups understand the importance of judicial decisions on public policy. And organizational support is often available—in fact, sometimes to seek out and recruit—litigants to use the courts to achieve public policy goals. Groups like the NAACP, the National Association of Manufacturers, and the AFL–CIO stand ready to support litigants who share their interests, just as the American Civil Liberties Union often assists in cases begun by others that raise constitutional issues.

For people who have no hope of achieving influence in the legislative process, courts may stand as the only havens against oppression. (See the third paragraph of *Carolene Products'* footnote 4; reprinted above, p. 609.) For individuals acting on their own to go to court to protect their rights seems unproblematic. But does the situation change when people, who have used their right to associate to form organizations, bring their collective resources, financial and otherwise, to bear in the judicial process? The Court first fully confronted the issues of judicial lobbying in NAACP v. Button (1963; reprinted below, p. 811).

F. Term Limitations

Term limitations on members of Congress raise complex issues for the approach of *reinforcing representative democracy*: Through such measures, the people would *limit* their own power to reelect representatives or senators in order to *enhance* democracy. The Twenty-second Amendment, ratified in 1951 (after Franklin D. Roosevelt was four times elected to the presidency), imposes a limit of two four-year terms upon the President. It is commonplace to observe that people attack Congress, yet love their own representatives and Senators and repeatedly reelect them. Until November, 1994, it had been the usual result that more than 90 per cent of incumbents who choose to run were reelected. Term limitations, which many states have adopted in recent years for both state and national legislators, are a response to this situation. Like Ulysses, who bound himself to the mast of his ship so he could hear the sirens singing but could not steer into the rocks, the people bind themselves so they will not succumb to their incumbents' pleas to be reelected repeatedly. The Supreme Court invalidated term limitations that a state imposed upon members of Congress elected from that state and clearly indicated that a constitutional amendment would be necessary to institute such measures.[20]

III. REINFORCING REPRESENTATIVE DEMOCRACY AND REDUCING JUDICIAL DISCRETION

No less than for freedom of communication, defining the existence and extent of other rights essential to representative democracy poses difficult problems for constitutional interpretation. Because of the document's silence, one must first read a version or versions of democratic theory into "the Constitution" to derive from that instrument many basic participatory principles such as "one person, one vote." As compared with constitutionalism's defense of an active role for judges in protecting such fundamental substantive rights as those to property and privacy (see Chapters 16–18), *reinforcing representative democracy* may seek to limit judicial discretion and judicial policy making. But this approach by no means eliminates either.

Indeed, this answer to the question of HOW to interpret is grounded on the legitimacy of judges' making three great and related interpretive decisions that are not commanded by the document's plain words: (1) That "the Constitution" includes or is based on a theory of representative democracy; (2) that judges therefore have a special obligation to insure the political processes are open, so the electorate in fact has the opportunity to choose public officials to represent their views on public policy; and (3) that judges must thereafter defer on most other issues, including many of substantive constitutional interpretation, to the judgment of such elected officials.

The first decision responds to the WHAT interrogative, the second and third to WHO. Constitutionalists might accept the first and second decisions as correct, though incomplete, but consider the third an abdication of responsibility.

SELECTED BIBLIOGRAPHY

Abernathy, Glenn. *The Right of Assembly and Association* (Columbia: University of South Carolina Press, 1961).

---

20. U.S. Term Limits, Inc. v. Thornton (1995). For a spirited defense of term limits, specifically on the ground that they will help to restore deliberation in democracy, see George F. Will, *Restoration: Congress, Term Limits, and the Recovery of Deliberative Democracy* (New York: Free Press, 1992).

Barber, Benjamin. *Strong Democracy: Participatory Politics for a New Age* (Berkeley: University of California Press, 1984).

Dworkin, Ronald. "What Is Equality? Part 4: Political Equality," 22 *U.San Fran.L.Rev.* 1 (1987).

————. "Equality, Democracy, and Constitution: We the People in Court," 28 *Alberta L.Rev.* 324 (1990).

Elliott, Ward E.Y. *The Rise of Guardian Democracy: The Supreme Court's Role in Voting Rights Disputes, 1845–1969* (Cambridge: Harvard University Press, 1974).

Fellman, David. "Constitutional Rights of Association," 1961 *Sup. Ct.Rev.* 74.

Horn, Robert A. *Groups and the Constitution* (Stanford: Stanford University Press, 1956.)

Michelman, Frank. "Law's Republic," 97 *Yale L.J.* 1493 (1988).

Murphy, Walter F., C. Herman Pritchett, and Sotirios A. Barber, eds., *Courts, Judges, and Politics* (5th ed.; Boston: McGraw–Hill, 1995), ch. 5.

Pateman, Carole. *Participation and Democratic Theory* (Cambridge: Cambridge University Press, 1970).

Pennock, J. Roland and Chapman, John W. *Participation in Politics* NOMOS XVI (New York: Lieber–Atherton, 1975).

Pritchett, C. Herman. *Constitutional Civil Liberties* (Englewood Cliffs, NJ: Prentice–Hall, 1984), ch. 6.

Still, Jonathan W. "Political Equality and Election Systems," 91 *Ethics* 375 (1981).

Sunstein, Cass R. "Beyond the Republican Revival," 97 *Yale L.J.* 1539 (1988).

Tribe, Laurence H. *American Constitutional Law* (2d ed.; Mineola, NY: The Foundation Press, 1988), chs. 12–13.

I. THE RIGHT TO VOTE AND HAVE ONE'S VOTE COUNTED EQUALLY

"[T]he mere fact that the suit seeks protection of a political right does not mean it presents a political question."—Justice BRENNAN

"In a democratic society like ours, relief must come through an aroused popular conscience that sears the

> conscience of the people's representatives."—Justice
> **FRANKFURTER**

BAKER v. CARR

369 U.S. 186, 82 S.Ct. 691, 7 L.Ed.2d 663 (1962).

The Supreme Court squarely confronted the issue of malapportionment of legislative districts in Colegrove v. Green (1946). For many decades the rural, Republican legislature of Illinois had declined to reapportion the state, thus maintaining district lines that did not reflect the great shift in population from farms to cities. Three professors from the Chicago area sued in a federal district court, claiming that this gerrymandering-by-default of congressional districts deprived them of an equal right to vote: Some districts in and around Chicago had nine times the population of those in rural regions.

The district court dismissed the suit and the professors appealed. One would have expected that, when the case reached the Supreme Court, Chief Justice Stone as author of footnote four of *Carolene Products* would have invoked the second paragraph of that footnote and asserted a special judicial role to protect a right of citizens to have their votes counted equally. He, however, wanted no part of this controversy and told the conference "This isn't court business." According to Frank Murphy's notes of that discussion Justice Black was equally wary: "I don't want to get involved in control of elections in state and nation. I don't think [the] courts had power to make them [states] act." Apparently, only William O. Douglas spoke out for reversing the district court. (Murphy's notes indicate that he voted with Douglas, but Justice Burton's notes record Murphy as passing when his turn came.)

Stone died before the decision in *Colegrove* was announced and Justice Jackson did not participate—he was at Nuremberg serving as chief Allied prosecutor at the trials of Nazi leaders. In the meantime, Douglas had persuaded Black; and Murphy, if he had wavered at the conference, also joined Black and Douglas. The switches, Stone's death, and Jackson's nonparticipation left a peculiar situation. There were three votes to affirm (Frankfurter, Reed, and Burton), three to reverse (Black, Douglas, and Murphy). The seventh justice, Wiley Rutledge, pretty much agreed with Douglas et al. that the issue was justiciable, but thought that it was so close to the election of 1946 that the courts would do more harm than good if they intervened. So he voted to affirm.

As the senior justice in the majority, Frankfurter announced the *judgment* of the Court; but, because Rutledge had his own reasons, Frankfurter's *opinion* was not that of the Court. Still, because of the power and eloquence of that opinion, most commentators assumed that the Court had treated districting as a political question. And, indeed, the Court later dismissed several other challenges to malapportioned systems. Then in 1960 Gomillion v. Lightfoot struck down, as a violation of the Fifteenth Amendment, Alabama's efforts to redraw the electoral districts in Tuskegee so as to exclude most African American residents. Many observers construed *Gomillion,* especially since Frankfurter had written the opinion of the Court, as signalling a reversal of *Colegrove*; quickly new attacks on maldistricting began. The first to reach the Supreme Court came from Tennessee, which had not redrawn the lines for state legislative districts since 1901.

When the justices met in conference after oral argument, they were again equally divided, with one justice, Potter Stewart, badly torn between the two sides. Black and Douglas had remained adamant over the years. They were now joined by Brennan and even Warren, who as governor of California had presided over what he later admitted was the most malapportioned state in the country and had opposed reapportionment for, he frankly conceded, reasons of political expediency. Frankfurter had also not changed his mind. For him *Gomillion* differed from *Colegrove* because *Gomillion* involved racial discrimination, a violation of the Fifteenth Amendment's plain words. Harlan agreed, as to some extent did Tom Clark. Charles Whittaker was not sure that *Colegrove* had been correctly decided but did not want to see it overturned by a closely divided Court. Stewart saw much reason in both positions and did not vote. The Court ordered reargument for the fall of 1961.

Reargument left eight of the justices unchanged, but Stewart tentatively voted with Douglas et al. Thus the initial, if not very firm, decision was 5–4; but, Stewart would agree only that legislative districting presented a justiciable rather than a political question. He was not yet sure what sort of remedy judges could provide, so there could be no opinion on the merits, only directions to the district court, which had dismissed the suit, to hear it.

Black and Douglas talked to Warren and suggested that he not assign the opinion to himself or to either of them. All three had taken public stands on the issue and none was especially diplomatic. Assigning the opinion to Stewart might keep him in the fold, but his differences with the other four on reapportionment were real, and he and Douglas had sharp disagreements about judicial style. On the other hand, Brennan, as both a master at negotiation and a good friend of Stewart, was ideal. Warren agreed. The opinion went through almost twenty drafts, as Brennan patiently wrote and rewrote to meet the fresh objections that occurred to Stewart as he listened to the strong counterarguments of Frankfurter and Harlan.

Shortly before the decision was to be announced, Whittaker retired because of ill health, leaving the vote 5–3. Then, after having initially been pleased with Frankfurter's dissent, Clark began to have doubts. Eventually, he switched sides, putting the vote at 6–2. He, like Warren, Black, Douglas, and Brennan himself, wanted to decide the case on the merits and hold that Tennessee's apportionment denied urban citizens equal protection of the laws. Five votes for that sort of decision were there; but at such a late stage Stewart might well have asked that the case be argued once again, and it would be difficult to oppose him. The new majority contented themselves with the thought that once the Court held that maldistricting presented a justiciable issue, there would be ample opportunity to speak to the merits.

Mr. Justice **BRENNAN** delivered the opinion of the Court. ...

IV

Justiciability

In holding that the subject matter of this suit was not justiciable, the District Court relied on Colegrove v. Green [1946] and subsequent *per curiam* cases. We understand the District Court to have read the cited cases as compelling the conclusion that since the appellants sought to have a legislative apportionment held unconstitutional, their suit presented a "political question" and was therefore nonjusticiable. ...

Of course the mere fact that the suit seeks protection of a political right does not mean it presents a political question. Such an objection "is little more than a play upon words." Nixon v. Herndon [1927]. Rather, it is argued that apportionment cases ... can involve no federal constitutional right except one resting on the guaranty of a republican form of government, and that complaints based on that clause have been held to present political questions which are nonjusticiable. We hold that the claim pleaded here neither rests upon nor implicates the Guaranty Clause and that its justiciability is therefore not foreclosed by our decisions of cases involving that clause. ...

Our discussion ... requires review of a number of political question cases, in order to expose the attributes of the doctrine—attributes which, in various settings, diverge, combine, appear, and disappear in seeming disorderliness. ... That review reveals that in the Guaranty Clause cases and in the other "political question" cases, it is the relationship between the judiciary and the coordinate branches of the Federal Government, and not the federal judiciary's relationship to the States, which gives rise to the "political question."

We have said that "in determining whether a question falls within [the political question] category, appropriateness under our system of government of attributing finality to the action of the political departments and also the lack of satisfactory criteria for a judicial determination are dominant considerations." Coleman v. Miller [1939]. The nonjusticiability of a political question is primarily a function of the separation of powers. Much confusion results from the capacity of the "political question" label to obscure the need for case-by-case inquiry. Deciding whether a matter has in any measure been committed by the Constitution to another branch of government, or whether the action of that branch exceeds whatever authority has been committed, is itself a delicate exercise in constitutional interpretation, and is a responsibility of this Court as ultimate interpreter of the Constitution. To demonstrate this requires no less than to analyze representative cases and to infer from them the analytical threads that make up the political question doctrine. We shall then show that none of those threads catches this case.

Foreign relations. There are sweeping statements to the effect that all questions touching foreign relations are political questions. Not only does resolution of such issues frequently turn on standards that defy judicial application, or involve the exercise of a discretion demonstrably committed to the executive or legislature; but many such questions uniquely demand single-voiced statement of the Government's views. Yet it is error to suppose that every case or controversy which touches foreign relations lies beyond judicial cognizance. Our cases in this field

seem invariably to show a discriminating analysis of the particular
question posed, in terms of the history of its management by the political
branches, of its susceptibility to judicial handling in the light of its
nature and posture in the specific case, and of the possible consequences
of judicial action. . . .

Dates of duration of hostilities. Though it has been stated broadly
that "the power which declared the necessity is the power to declare its
cessation, and what the cessation requires," Commercial Trust Co. v.
Miller [1923], here too analysis reveals isolable reasons for the presence
of political questions, underlying this Court's refusal to review the
political departments' determination of when or whether a war has
ended. Dominant is the need for finality in the political determination.
. . .

Validity of enactments. In *Coleman* this Court held that the questions of how long a proposed amendment to the Federal Constitution
remained open to ratification, and what effect a prior rejection had on a
subsequent ratification, were committed to congressional resolution and
involved criteria of decision that necessarily escaped the judicial grasp.
. . .

The status of Indian tribes. This Court's deference to the political
departments in determining whether Indians are recognized as a tribe,
while it reflects familiar attributes of political questions . . . also has a
unique element in that "the relation of the Indians to the United States
is marked by peculiar and cardinal distinctions which exist no where
else. . . ." Cherokee Nation v. Georgia [1831]. . . .

It is apparent that several formulations which vary slightly according to the settings in which the questions arise may describe a political
question, although each has one or more elements which identifies it as
essentially a function of the separation of powers. Prominent on the
surface of any case held to involve a political question is found a
textually demonstrable constitutional commitment of the issue to a
coordinate political department; or a lack of judicially discoverable and
manageable standards for resolving it; or the impossibility of deciding
without an initial policy determination of a kind clearly for nonjudicial
discretion; or the impossibility of a court's undertaking independent
resolution without expressing lack of the respect due coordinate branches of government; or an unusual need for unquestioning adherence to a
political decision already made; or the potentiality of embarrassment
from multifarious pronouncements by various departments on one question.

Unless one of these formulations is inextricable from the case at bar,
there should be no dismissal for nonjusticiability on the ground of a
political question's presence. The doctrine of which we treat is one of
"political questions," not one of "political cases." The courts cannot
reject as "no law suit" a bona fide controversy as to whether some action
denominated "political" exceeds constitutional authority. . . .

We come, finally to the ultimate inquiry whether our precedents as to what constitutes a nonjusticiable "political question" bring the case before us under the umbrella of that doctrine. A natural beginning is to note whether any of the common characteristics which we have been able to identify and label descriptively are present. We find none: The question here is the consistency of state action with the Federal Constitution. We have no question decided, or to be decided, by a political branch of government coequal with this Court. Nor do we risk embarrassment of our government abroad, or grave disturbance at home if we take issue with Tennessee as to the constitutionality of her action here challenged. Nor need the appellants, in order to succeed in this action, ask the Court to enter upon policy determinations for which judicially manageable standards are lacking. Judicial standards under the Equal Protection Clause are well developed and familiar, and it has been open to courts since the enactment of the Fourteenth Amendment to determine, if on the particular facts they must, that a discrimination reflects *no* policy, but simply arbitrary and capricious action. ...

Reversed and remanded.

Mr. Justice **WHITTAKER** did not participate in the decision of this case.

Mr. Justice **DOUGLAS,** concurring. ...

Mr. Justice **CLARK,** concurring. ...

Mr. Justice **STEWART,** concurring. ...

Mr. Justice **FRANKFURTER,** with whom Mr. Justice **HARLAN** joins, dissenting. ...

We were soothingly told at the bar of this Court that we need not worry about the kind of remedy a court could effectively fashion once the abstract constitutional right to have courts pass on a state-wide system of electoral districting is recognized as a matter of judicial rhetoric, because legislatures would heed the Court's admonition. This is not only a euphoric hope. It implies a sorry confession of judicial impotence in place of a frank acknowledgement that there is not under our Constitution a judicial remedy for every political mischief. ... In this situation as in others of like nature, appeal for relief does not belong here. Appeal must be to an informed, civically militant electorate. In a democratic society like ours, relief must come through an aroused popular conscience that sears the conscience of the people's representatives. ...

In sustaining appellants' claim ... this Court's uniform course of decision over the years is overruled or disregarded. ... The *Colegrove* doctrine ... represents long judicial thought and experience. From its earliest opinions this Court has consistently recognized a class of controversies which do not lend themselves to judicial standards and judicial remedies. ...

1.   The cases concerning war or foreign affairs, for example, are usually explained by the necessity of the country's speaking with one voice in such matters. While this concern alone undoubtedly accounts for many of the decisions, others do not fit the pattern. ... A controlling factor in such cases is that, decision respecting these kinds of complex matters of policy being traditionally committed not to courts but to the political agencies of government for determination by criteria of political expediency, there exists no standard ascertainable by settled judicial experience or process by reference to which a political decision affecting the question at issue between the parties can be judged. ...

2.   The Court has been particularly unwilling to intervene in matters concerning the structure and organization of the political institutions of the States. The abstention from judicial entry into such areas has been greater even than that which marks the Court's ordinary approach to issues of state power challenged under broad federal guarantees. ...

3.   The cases involving Negro disfranchisement are no exception to the principle. ... For here the controlling command of Supreme Law is plain and unequivocal. An end of discrimination against the Negro was the compelling motive of the Civil War Amendments. ...

4.   The Court has refused to exercise its jurisdiction to pass on "abstract questions of political power, of sovereignty, of government." Massachusetts v. Mellon [1923]. ... The crux of the matter is that courts are not fit instruments of decision where what is essentially at stake is the composition of those large contests of policy traditionally fought out in non-judicial forums, by which governments and the actions of governments are made and unmade. ...

5.   The influence of these converging considerations—the caution not to undertake decision where standards meet for judicial judgment are lacking, the reluctance to interfere with matters of state government in the absence of an unquestionable and effectively enforceable mandate, the unwillingness to make courts arbiters of the broad issues of political organization historically committed to other institutions and for whose adjustment the judicial process is ill-adapted—has been decisive of the settled line of cases, reaching back more than a century, which holds that Art. IV, § 4, of the Constitution, guaranteeing to the States "a Republican Form of Government," is not enforceable through the courts. ...

The present case involves all of the elements that have made the Guarantee Clause cases non-justiciable. It is, in effect a Guarantee Clause claim masquerading under a different label. But it cannot make the case more fit for judicial action that appellants invoke the Fourteenth Amendment rather than Art. IV, § 4, where, in fact, the gist of their complaint is the same. ...

Here appellants attack "the State as a State. ..." Their complaint is that the basis of representation of the Tennessee Legislature hurts them. They assert that "a minority now rules in Tennessee," that the apportionment statute results in a "distortion of the constitutional system," that the General Assembly is no longer "a body representative of the people of the State of Tennessee," all "contrary to the basic principle of representative government. ..." Accepting appellants' own formulation of the issue, one can know this handsaw from a hawk. Such a claim would be non-justiciable not merely under Art. IV, § 4, but under any clause of the Constitution, by virtue of the very fact that a federal court is not a forum for political debate. ...

But appellants, of course, do not rest on this claim *simpliciter*. In invoking the Equal Protection Clause, they assert that the distortion of representative government complained of is produced by systematic discrimination against them, by way of "a debasement of their votes. ..."

... Appellants invoke the right to vote and to have their votes counted. But they are permitted to vote and their votes are counted. They go to the polls, they cast their ballots, they send their representatives to the state councils. Their complaint is simply that the representatives are not sufficiently numerous or powerful. ... What is actually asked of the Court in this case is to choose among competing bases of representation—ultimately, really, among competing theories of political philosophy—in order to establish an appropriate frame of government for the State of Tennessee and thereby for all the States of the Union.

... This is not a case in which a State has, through a device however oblique and sophisticated, denied Negroes or Jews or redheaded persons a vote, or given them only a third or a sixth of a vote. That was Gomillion v. Lightfoot [1961]. ... What Tennessee illustrates is an old and still widespread method of representation—representation by local geographical division, only in part respective of population—in preference to others, others, forsooth, more appealing. Appellants contest this choice and seek to make this Court the arbiter of the disagreement. They would make the Equal Protection Clause the charter of adjudication, asserting that the equality which it guarantees comports, if not the assurance of equal weight to every voter's vote, at least the basic conception that representation ought to be proportionate to population, a standard by reference to which the reasonableness of apportionment plans may be judged.

To find such a political conception legally enforceable in the broad and unspecific guarantee of equal protection is to rewrite the Constitution. ...

Dissenting opinion of Mr. Justice **HARLAN,** whom Mr. Justice **FRANKFURTER** joins. ...

Editors' Notes

(1) **Query:** In his *Memoirs* (New York: Doubleday, 1977), p. 306, Earl Warren said that not the School Segregation Cases (1954; reprinted below, p.

912) but Baker v. Carr "was the most important case of my tenure on the Court." How justified was that claim?

(2) **Query:** Arguments about "political questions" are a subspecies of arguments about the interrogative WHO, which, in turn, raises basic questions about democratic and constitutionalist theories. Who was more faithful to democratic theory, Brennan or Frankfurter? Why? To what extent did their disagreement stem from different conceptions of democracy, and to what extent from different conceptions of the proper roles of courts? Who was more faithful to the text of the constitutional document?

(3) That Frankfurter used a *doctrinal approach* is obvious. But what other approach(es) to constitutional interpretation did he employ? How much did he argue from considerations of *prudence*? Brennan's approach, Frankfurter claimed, required the justice to choose "among competing theories of political philosophy." To what extent was he correct? To what extant did Frankfurter's own approach(es) require him to make the same sort of choice?

(4) **Query:** It is in *Baker* that the Court first referred to itself "as the ultimate interpreter of the Constitution." Does that claim appear as uncontestable now as it did when we first encountered it in Chapter 7?

(5) The expectation that the Court would receive more cases involving reapportionment was quickly fulfilled. See Reynolds v. Sims (1964; reprinted next) and accompanying notes.

(6) Art. IV, § 4 of the constitutional text reads: "The United States shall guarantee to every State in this Union a Republican Form of Government." Luther v. Borden (1849) held that the question of which of two rival groups was the lawful state government was a nonjusticiable, political question for Congress to decide. *Baker* explicitly rejected *Colgrove* 's view that legislative apportionment raised a political question but explicitly adhered to *Luther* 's holding that claims under the Guarantee Clause are nonjusticiable. Although the Guarantee Clause itself thus has been virtually a dead letter for constitutional adjudication since *Luther,* the Court sometimes seems to draw inferences from political theories of a republican form of government. For analyses of the Guarantee Clause, see William M. Wiecek, *The Guarantee Clause of the U.S. Constitution* (Ithaca, NY: Cornell University Press, 1972); Note, "A Niche for the Guarantee Clause," 94 *Harv.L.Rev.* 681 (1981).

"[R]epresentative government is in essence self-government ... and each and every citizen has an inalienable right to full and effective participation in the political processes of his State's legislative bodies."—Chief Justice WARREN

"The Constitution is not a panacea for every blot upon the public welfare, nor should this Court ... be thought of as a general haven for reform movements."—Justice HARLAN

REYNOLDS v. SIMS

377 U.S. 533, 84 S.Ct. 1362, 12 L.Ed.2d 506 (1964).

Soon after Baker v. Carr, the Court was presented with opportunities to decide the substantive constitutional issues presented by maldistricting. Announcing for the first time the principle of "one person, one vote," Gray v. Sanders (1963) invalidated Georgia's "county unit" system, under which votes of residents of rural counties counted for more than those in urban areas. Wesberry v. Sanders (1964) applied that principle to congressional districting. Quickly the Court faced fourteen cases challenging other aspects of legislative districting. In *Reynolds,* a group of citizens challenged Alabama's apportionment of seats in the state legislature. That apportionment had not changed since the census of 1900. According to the 1960 census, population in districts for the lower house ranged from 6,700 to 104,000, and for the senate from 15,000 to 634,000. The U.S. district court rejected several state proposals for redistricting because they still included wide disparities in population and ordered state officials to carry out the court's own plan for reapportionment. For different reasons, both the private citizens and the state appealed to the U.S. Supreme Court.

Mr. Chief Justice **WARREN** delivered the opinion of the Court. . . .

II

Undeniably the Constitution of the United States protects the right of all qualified citizens to vote, in state as well as in federal elections. A consistent line of decisions by this Court in cases involving attempts to deny or restrict the right of suffrage has made this indelibly clear. . . . And history has seen a continuing expansion of the scope of the right of suffrage in this country. The right to vote freely for the candidate of one's choice is of the essence of a democratic society, and any restrictions on that right strike at the heart of representative government. And the right of suffrage can be denied by a debasement or dilution of the weight of a citizen's vote just as effectively as by wholly prohibiting the free exercise of the franchise. . . .

III

A predominant consideration in determining whether a State's legislative apportionment scheme constitutes an invidious discrimination violative of rights asserted under the Equal Protection Clause is that the rights allegedly impaired are individual and personal in nature. . . . Undoubtedly, the right of suffrage is a fundamental matter in a free and democratic society. Especially since the right to exercise the franchise in a free and unimpaired manner is preservative of other basic civil and political rights, any alleged infringement of the right of citizens to vote must be carefully and meticulously scrutinized. . . . [I]n Yick Wo v. Hopkins [1886] the Court referred to "the political franchise of voting" as "a fundamental political right, because preservative of all rights."

Legislators represent people, not trees or acres. Legislators are elected by voters, not farms or cities or economic interests. As long as ours is a representative form of government, and our legislatures are those instruments of government elected directly by and directly representative of the people, the right to elect legislators in a free and unimpaired fashion is a bedrock of our political system. ... Weighting the votes of citizens differently, by any method or means, merely because of where they happen to reside, hardly seems justifiable. One must be ever aware that the Constitution forbids "sophisticated as well as simple-minded modes of discrimination." Lane v. Wilson [1939]. ...

State legislatures are, historically, the fountainhead of representative government in this country. ... But representative government is in essence self-government through the medium of elected representatives of the people, and each and every citizen has an inalienable right to full and effective participation in the political processes of his State's legislative bodies. Most citizens can achieve this participation only as qualified voters through the election of legislators to represent them. Full and effective participation by all citizens in state government requires, therefore, that each citizen have an equally effective voice in the election of members of his state legislature. Modern and viable state government needs, and the Constitution demands, no less.

... [I]n a society ostensibly grounded on representative government, it would seem reasonable that a majority of the people of a State could elect a majority of that State's legislators. To conclude differently ... would appear to deny majority rights in a way that far surpasses any possible denial of minority rights that might otherwise be thought to result. Since legislatures are responsible for enacting laws by which all citizens are to be governed, they should be bodies which are collectively responsive to the popular will. And the concept of equal protection has been traditionally viewed as requiring the uniform treatment of persons standing in the same relation to the governmental action questioned or challenged. With respect to the allocation of legislative representation, all voters, as citizens of a State, stand in the same relation regardless of where they live. ... [T]he Equal Protection Clause guarantees the opportunity for equal participation by all voters in the election of state legislators. Diluting the weight of votes because of place of residence impairs basic constitutional rights under the Fourteenth Amendment just as much as invidious discriminations based upon factors such as race. Brown v. Board [1954], or economic status, Griffin v. Illinois [1956], Douglas v. California [1963]. Our constitutional system amply provides for the protection of minorities by means other than giving them majority control of state legislatures. ...

We are told that the matter of apportioning representation in a state legislature is a complex and many faceted one. We are advised that States can rationally consider factors other than population in apportioning legislative representation. We are admonished not to restrict the power of the States to impose differing views as to political philosophy on their citizens. We are cautioned about the dangers of entering into political thickets and mathematical quagmires. Our answer is this: a denial of constitutionally protected rights demands judicial protection; our oath and our office require no less of us. ...

To the extent that a citizen's right to vote is debased, he is that much less a citizen. The fact that an individual lives here or there is not a legitimate reason for overweighting or diluting the efficacy of his vote. ... Representation schemes once fair and equitable become archaic and outdated. But the basic principle of representative government remains, and must remain, unchanged—the weight of a citizen's vote cannot be made to depend on where he lives. ... This is at the heart of Lincoln's vision of "government of the people, by the people, [and] for the people." The Equal Protection Clause demands no less ... for all citizens, of all places as well as of all races. ...

V

... [We] find the federal analogy inapposite and irrelevant to state legislative districting schemes. ... The system of representation in the two Houses of the Federal Congress is one ingrained in our Constitution, as part of the law of the land. It is one conceived out of compromise and concession indispensable to the establishment of our federal republic. Arising from unique historical circumstances, it is based on the consideration that in establishing our type of federalism a group of formerly independent States bound themselves together under one national government. ...

Political subdivisions of States—counties, cities, or whatever—never were and never have been considered as sovereign entities. Rather, they have been traditionally regarded as subordinate governmental instrumentalities created by the State to assist in the carrying out of state governmental functions. ... The right of a citizen to equal representation and to have his vote weighted equally with those of all other citizens in the election of members of one house of a bicameral state legislature would amount to little if States could effectively submerge the equal-population principle in the apportionment of seats in the other house. ...

We do not believe that the concept of bicameralism is rendered anachronistic and meaningless when the predominant basis of representation in the two state legislative bodies is required to be the same—population. A prime reason for bicameralism, modernly considered, is to insure mature and deliberate consideration of, and to prevent precipitate action on, proposed legislative measures. Simply because the controlling criterion for apportioning representation is required to be the same in both houses does not mean that there will be no differences in the composition and complexion of the two bodies. Different constituencies can be represented in the two houses. One body could be composed of single-member districts while the other could have at least some multi-member districts. The length of terms of the legislators in the separate bodies could differ. The numerical size of the two bodies could be made to differ, even significantly, and the geographical size of districts ... could also be made to differ. And apportionment in one house could be arranged so as to balance off minor inequities in the representation of certain areas in the other. ...

VI

... [T]he Equal Protection Clause requires that a State make an honest and good faith effort to construct districts, in both houses of its legislature, as nearly of equal population as is practicable. We realize that it is a practical impossibility to arrange legislative districts so that each one has an identical number of residents, or citizens, or voters. Mathematical exactness or precision is hardly a workable constitutional requirement. ...

A State may legitimately desire to maintain the integrity of various political subdivisions, insofar as possible, and provide for compact districts of contiguous territory in designing a legislative apportionment scheme. Valid considerations may underlie such aims. Indiscriminate districting, without any regard for political subdivision or natural or historical boundary lines, may be little more than an open invitation to partisan gerrymandering. ...

... So long as the divergences from a strict population standard are based on legitimate considerations incident to the effectuation of a rational state policy, some deviations from the equal-population principle are constitutionally permissible. ... But neither history alone, nor economic or other sorts of group interests, are permissible factors in attempting to justify disparities from population-based representation. Citizens, not history or economic interests, cast votes. Considerations of area alone provide an insufficient justification for deviations from the equal-population principle. Again, people, not land or trees or pastures, vote. Modern developments and improvements in transportation and communications make rather hollow, in the mid–1960's, most claims that deviations from population-based representation can validly be based solely on geographical considerations. ...

A consideration that appears to be of more substance in justifying some deviations from population-based representation in state legislatures is that of insuring some voice to political subdivisions, as political subdivisions. ... In many States much of the legislature's activity involves the enactment of so-called local legislation, directed only to the concerns of particular political subdivisions. And a State may legitimately desire to construct districts along political subdivision lines to deter the possibilities of gerrymandering. However, ... if even as a result of a clearly rational state policy of according some legislative representation to political subdivisions, population is submerged as the controlling consideration in the apportionment of seats in the particular legislative body, then the right of all of the State's citizens to cast an effective and adequately weighted vote would be unconstitutionally impaired.

VII

One of the arguments frequently offered as a basis for upholding a State's legislative apportionment arrangement, despite substantial disparities from a population basis in either or both houses, is grounded on congressional approval, incident to admitting States into the Union, of state apportionment plans containing deviations from the equal-population principle. Proponents of this argument contend that congressional approval of such schemes ... indicates that such arrangements are plainly sufficient as establishing a "republican form of government." As we stated in Baker [v. Carr (1962)], some questions raised under the Guaranty Clause are nonjusticiable, where "political" in nature and where there is a clear absence of judicially manageable standards. Nevertheless, it is not inconsistent with this view to hold that, despite congressional approval of state legislative apportionment plans at the time of admission into the Union ... the Equal Protection Clause can and does require more. And an apportionment scheme in which both houses are based on population can hardly be considered as failing to satisfy the Guaranty Clause requirement. Congress presumably does not assume, in admitting States into the Union, to pass on all constitutional questions relating to the character of state governmental organization. In any event, congressional approval, however well-considered, could hardly validate an unconstitutional state legislative apportionment. Congress simply lacks the constitutional power to insulate States from attack with respect to alleged deprivations of individual constitutional rights. ...

[*Affirmed.*]

Mr. Justice **HARLAN**, dissenting. ...

... Whatever may be thought of this holding as a piece of political ideology—and even on that score the political history and practices of this country from its earliest beginnings leave wide room for debate (see the dissenting opinion of Frankfurter, J., in *Baker*)—I think it demonstrable that the Fourteenth Amendment does not impose this political tenet on the States or authorize this Court to do so.

... Stripped of aphorisms, the Court's argument boils down to the assertion that appellees' right to vote has been invidiously "debased" or "diluted" by systems of apportionment which entitle them to vote for fewer legislators than other voters, an assertion which is tied to the Equal Protection Clause only by the constitutionally frail tautology that "equal" means "equal."

Had the Court paused to probe more deeply into the matter, it would have found that the Equal Protection Clause was never intended to inhibit the States in choosing any democratic method they pleased for the apportionment of their legislatures. This is shown by the language of the Fourteenth Amendment taken as a whole, by the understanding of those who proposed and ratified it, and by the political practices of the States at the time the Amendment was adopted. It is confirmed by numerous state and congressional actions since the adoption of the Fourteenth Amendment, and by the common understanding of the Amendment as evidenced by subsequent constitutional amendments and decisions of this Court before *Baker* made an abrupt break with the past in 1962. ...

... Since it can ... be shown beyond doubt that state legislative apportionments ... are wholly free of constitutional limitations, save such as may be imposed by the Republican Form of Government Clause (Art. IV, § 4), the Court's action now bringing them within the purview of the Fourteenth Amendment amounts to nothing less than an exercise of the amending power by this Court. ...

I

[Harlan then examined in great detail the history of the adoption of the Fourteenth Amendment and concluded:]

The facts recited above show beyond any possible doubt:

(1) that Congress, with full awareness of and attention to the possibility that the States would not afford full equality in voting rights to all their citizens, nevertheless deliberately chose not to interfere with the States' plenary power in this regard when it proposed the Fourteenth Amendment;

(2) that Congress did not include in the Fourteenth Amendment restrictions on the States' power to control voting rights because it believed that if such restrictions were included, the Amendment would not be adopted; and

(3) that at least a substantial majority, if not all, of the States which ratified the Fourteenth Amendment did not consider that in so doing, they were accepting limitations on their freedom, never before questioned, to regulate voting rights as they chose. ...

II

The Court's elaboration of its new "constitutional" doctrine indicates how far—and how unwisely—it has strayed from the appropriate bounds of its authority. The consequence of today's decision is that in all but the handful of States ... [courts] are given blanket authority and the constitutional duty to supervise apportionment of the State Legislatures. It is difficult to imagine a more intolerable and inappropriate interference by the judiciary with the independent legislatures of the States. ...

Although the Court—necessarily, as I believe—provides only generalities in elaboration of its main thesis, its opinion nevertheless fully demonstrates how far removed these problems are from fields of judicial competence. Recognizing that "indiscriminate districting" is an invitation to "partisan gerrymandering," the Court nevertheless excludes virtually every basis for the formation of electoral districts other than "indiscriminate districting." ... (1) history; (2) "economic or other sorts of group interests"; (3) area; (4) geographical considerations; (5) a desire "to insure effective representation for sparsely settled areas"; (6) "availability of access of citizens to their representatives"; (7) theories of bicameralism (except those approved by the Court); (8) occupation; (9) "an attempt to balance urban and rural power"; (10) the preference of a majority of voters in the State.

So far as presently appears, the *only* factor which a State may consider, apart from numbers, is political subdivisions. But even "a clearly rational state policy" recognizing this factor is unconstitutional if "population is submerged as the controlling consideration. ..."

I know of no principle of logic or practical or theoretical politics, still less any constitutional principle, which establishes all or any of these exclusions. ... So far as the Court says anything at all on this score, it says only that "legislators represent people, not trees or acres"; that "citizens, not history or economic interests, cast votes"; that "people, not land or trees or pastures, vote." All this may be conceded. But it is surely equally obvious, and, in the context of elections, more meaningful to note that people are not ciphers and that legislators can represent their electors only by speaking for their interests—economic, social, political—many of which do reflect the place where the electors live. The Court does not establish, or indeed even attempt to make a case for the proposition that conflicting interests within a State can only be adjusted by disregarding them when voters are grouped for purposes of representation.

CONCLUSION

... What is done today deepens my conviction that judicial entry into this realm is profoundly ill-advised and constitutionally impermissible. ... I believe that the vitality of our political system, on which in the last analysis all else depends, is weakened by reliance on the judiciary for political reform; in time a complacent body politic may result.

These decisions also cut deeply into the fabric of our federalism. What must follow from them may eventually appear to be the product of state legislatures. Nevertheless, no thinking person can fail to recognize that the aftermath of these cases, however desirable it may be thought in itself, will have been achieved at the cost of a radical alteration in the relationship between the States and the Federal Government, more particularly the Federal Judiciary. Only one who has an overbearing impatience with the federal system and its political processes will believe that that cost was not too high or was inevitable.

Finally, these decisions give support to a current mistaken view of the Constitution and the constitutional function of this Court. This view, in a nutshell, is that every major social ill in this country can find its cure in some constitutional "principle," and that this Court should "take the lead" in promoting reform when other branches of government fail to act. The Constitution is not a panacea for every blot upon the public welfare, nor should this Court, ordained as a judicial body, be thought of as a general haven for reform movements. The Constitution is an instrument of government, fundamental to which is the premise that in a diffusion of governmental authority lies the greatest promise that this Nation will realize liberty for all its citizens. This Court, limited in function in accordance with that premise, does not serve its high purpose when it exceeds its authority, even to satisfy justified impatience with the slow workings of the political process. For when, in the name of constitutional interpretation, the Court *adds* something to the Constitution that was deliberately excluded from it, the Court in reality substitutes its view of what should be so for the amending process. ...

Mr. Justice **STEWART**, whom Mr. Justice **CLARK** joins, dissenting.*
...

What the Court has done is to convert a particular political philosophy into a constitutional rule, binding upon each of the 50 States. ... My own understanding of the various theories of representative government is that no one theory has ever commanded unanimous assent among political scientists, historians, or others who have considered the problem. But even if it were thought that the rule announced today by the Court is, as a matter of political theory, the most desirable general rule which can be devised as a basis for the make-up of the representative assembly of a typical State, I could not join in the fabrication of a constitutional mandate which imports and forever freezes one theory of political thought into our Constitution, and forever denies to every State any opportunity for enlightened and progressive innovation in the design of its democratic institutions. ...

Representative government is a process of accommodating group interests through democratic institutional arrangements. ... Appropriate legislative apportionment, therefore, should ideally be designed to insure effective representation in the State's legislature, in cooperation with other organs of political power, of the various groups and interests making up the electorate.

... [L]egislators do not represent faceless numbers. They represent ... people with identifiable needs and interests ... which can often be related to the geographical areas in which these people live. The very fact of geographic districting, the constitutional validity of which the Court does not question, carries with it an acceptance of the idea of legislative representation of regional needs and interests. Yet if geographical residence is irrelevant, as the Court suggests, and the goal is solely that of equally "weighted" votes, I do not understand why the

---

* Justices Stewart and Clark concurred in the result in *Reynolds,* but dissented in companion cases, WMCA v. Lomenzo and Lucas v. Colorado (1964).—**Eds.**

Court's constitutional rule does not require the abolition of districts and the holding of all elections at large.

The fact is, of course, that population factors must often to some degree be subordinated in devising a legislative apportionment plan which is to achieve the important goal of ensuring a fair, effective, and balanced representation of the regional, social, and economic interests within a State. And the further fact is that throughout our history the apportionments of State Legislatures have reflected the strongly felt American tradition that the public interest is composed of many diverse interests, and that in the long run it can better be expressed by a medley of component voices than by the majority's monolithic command. What constitutes a rational plan reasonably designed to achieve this objective will vary from State to State, since each State is unique, in terms of topography, geography, demography, history, heterogeneity and concentration of population, variety of social and economic interests, and in the operation and interrelation of its political institutions. But so long as a State's apportionment plan reasonably achieves, in the light of the State's own characteristics, effective and balanced representation of all substantial interests, without sacrificing the principle of effective majority rule, that plan cannot be considered irrational. ...

... I think that the Equal Protection Clause demands but two basic attributes of any plan of state legislative apportionment. First, ... in the light of the State's own characteristics and needs, the plan must be a rational one. Secondly, ... the plan must be such as not to permit the systematic frustration of the will of a majority of the electorate of the State. I think it is apparent that any plan of legislative apportionment which could be shown to reflect no policy, but simply arbitrary and capricious action or inaction, and that any plan which could be shown systematically to prevent ultimate effective majority rule, would be invalid under accepted Equal Protection Clause standards. But, beyond this, I think there is nothing in the Federal Constitution to prevent a State from choosing any electoral legislative structure it thinks best suited to the interests, temper, and customs of its people. ...

Editors' Notes

(1) **Query:** What are the fundamental differences between Warren and Harlan? Where do Stewart and Clark fit into this debate? To what extent was the debate ultimately about competing political theories? To what extent was the debate here about WHO shall interpret?

(2) **Query:** Minor v. Happersett (1875) ruled that "the Constitution of the United States does not confer the right of suffrage on any one. ..." Yet in *Reynolds,* Warren stated: "Undeniably the Constitution of the United States protects the right of all qualified citizens to vote. ..." It would seem that the plain words of the document are on *Minor*'s side. What "Constitution" was Warren speaking about? How can it be that Hugo Black joined Warren's opinion? Rereading Chapter 9's discussion of different *textual approaches* might help here.

(3) **Query:** As did Frankfurter in *Baker*, Harlan accused the majority of making choices among competing political theories. To what extent did Harlan make similar choices? Are such choices inevitable?

(4) In *Reynolds* Warren denied the Court was requiring mathematical exactness, but during the next few years several rulings came close to demanding such equality. More recent decisions have taken a somewhat looser attitude, though the Court did invalidate a districting scheme that contained variations in population of 20 per cent.

(5) Sophisticated computer programs can carve out districts of approximately equal populations to give particular office holders, parties, or interests great advantages. In Gomillion v. Lightfoot (1960; discussed above at pp. 769–70) the justices boldly faced up to racial gerrymandering. (See Bernard Taper, *Gomillion versus Lightfoot* [New York: McGraw–Hill, 1962]; and Jo Desha Lucas, "Dragon in the Thicket," 1961 *Sup.Ct.Rev.* 194.) For cases involving political gerrymandering, see Karcher v. Daggett (1983), discussed in the Introduction to this Chapter, above, pp. 762–63, and Davis v. Bandemer (1986; reprinted below, p. 788). For cases involving racial gerrymandering under the Voting Rights Act of 1965 to create "safe" districts for African Americans, see Shaw v. Reno (1993) and Miller v. Johnson (1995).

(6) **Query:** Does "one person, one vote" apply to all kinds of elections? Kramer v. Union Free School District (1969) struck down a New York statute limiting the right to vote in school district elections to certain kinds of taxpayers or parents of children attending public schools. Cipriano v. Houma (1969) and Phoenix v. Kolodziejski (1970) yielded much the same reasoning and results.

In 1973, however, Salyer Land Co. v. Tulare Lake Basin Water Storage District sustained a state law limiting to landowners the right to vote for directors of a water district. Ball v. James (1981) extended *Salyer* to uphold an Arizona law limiting eligibility to vote for directors of a large water reclamation district to those who own land and apportioning voting power among landowners according to how much land they owned: not "one person, one vote," but "one acre, one vote." Laurence H. Tribe argues that *"Salyer* and *Ball* rest on the most problematic of foundations and should be treated as a limited exception to the powerful general principle that interest based restrictions [on the right to vote] are constitutionally disfavored." *American Constitutional Law* (2d ed.; Mineola, NY: The Foundation Press, 1988), p. 1088.

Then Quinn v. Millsap (1989) unanimously held that a requirement that only owners of real property could be members of a board of freeholders (a body empowered to recommend reorganizations of the local governments) did not pass "rational basis scrutiny" under the Equal Protection Clause. In doing so, the Court rejected the claim that *Salyer* and *Ball* had meant the Equal Protection Clause was inapplicable "when the local unit of government does not exercise general governmental powers." The Court also narrowly construed *Salyer* and *Ball*, indicating that it had been rational for the states in the water district cases to limit voting rights to land owners because the purpose of those bodies was "so directly linked with land ownership."

(7) United States Dep't of Commerce v. Montana (1992) unanimously sustained the constitutionality of a federal law determining the allocation of

congressional districts among the states. The law, a district court had concluded, ignored the Court's principle of "equal representation for equal numbers of people." The Supreme Court held that the lower court had mistakenly transplanted the principle of one person, one vote from the context of districting *within* states to the context of districting *between* states.

"[W]ealth or fee paying has ... no relation to voting qualifications; the right to vote is too precious, too fundamental to be so burdened or conditioned."

HARPER v. VIRGINIA STATE BOARD OF ELECTIONS
383 U.S. 663, 86 S.Ct. 1079, 16 L.Ed.2d 169 (1966).

This case, invalidating as a denial of equal protection Virginia's requirement that voters in state elections pay a tax of $1.50, is reprinted above, p. 225.

Editors' Notes

(1) **Query:** Paraphrasing Warren in *Reynolds*, Douglas said in *Harper* that "the right to vote in federal elections is conferred by Art. I, § 2 of the Constitution." Douglas was thus more textualist than Warren, but does that provision explicitly confer a right to vote? Hugo Black dissented in *Harper*. Was that vote more or less consistent with his general approach to constitutional interpretation than his vote in *Reynolds*?

(2) **Query:** To what extent did Douglas's reasoning in *Harper* and Warren's in *Reynolds* (1964; reprinted above, p. 777) depend on a *structural approach*? To the degree either justice used a form of structural analyses, was it mainly of the document? Or did it extend to the political system? Beyond to the logic of the political theory(ies) on which the broader constitution supposedly rests? (See the discussion of structuralism in constitutional interpretation in Chapter 9.)

(3) **Query:** In his famous dissent in Lochner v. New York (1905; reprinted below, p. 1110), Justice Holmes argues that "a constitution is not intended to embody a particular economic theory." Does the American "Constitution" embody a political theory or combination of political theories? Both Douglas for the majority and Black and Harlan in dissent invoke Holmes's dissent. Who has the better argument?

"At-large voting schemes and multimember districts tend to minimize the voting strength of minority groups. ... [But] this Court has repeatedly held that they are not unconstitutional per se."

ROGERS v. LODGE

458 U.S. 613, 102 S.Ct. 3272, 73 L.Ed.2d 1012 (1982).

This case affirmed lower court decisions that the political system of a Georgia county that elected its governing board from the county as a whole, without division into subunits, violated the equal protection clause. The justices debated the proper standards to apply when faced with a policy that produced an adverse impact on a racial minority. The opinions are reprinted below, p. 933.

————

"[U]nconstitutional vote dilution ... occurs only when the electoral system is arranged in a manner that will consistently degrade a voter's or a group of voters' influence on the political process as a whole."—Justice WHITE

"The rights asserted in this case are group rights to an equal share of political power and representation."—Justice O'CONNOR

"Computer technology now enables gerrymanderers to achieve their purpose while adhering perfectly to the requirement that districts be of equal population."—Justice POWELL

DAVIS v. BANDEMER

478 U.S. 109, 106 S.Ct. 2797, 92 L.Ed.2d 85 (1986).

In 1981, when the state legislature of Indiana began reapportioning the state's legislative districts pursuant to the 1980 census, Republicans had a majority in both the 100 member House and the 50 member Senate, and the Governor was Republican. The legislative conference committee that developed the reapportionment plan that ultimately became law consisted entirely of Republicans, and the districting map it used was produced through a computerized study (by an outside firm) funded by the Republican State Committee. The plan "stacked" Democrats into districts with large Democratic majorities and "split" them in other districts so as to give Republicans safe but not excessive majorities in those districts. As the Speaker of the House said: "We wanted to save as many incumbent Republicans as possible."

The November 1982 election was held under the new districting plan. Democratic candidates for the House received 51.9% of the votes cast statewide and Republican candidates 48.1%; yet, out of the 100 seats to be filled, Democratic candidates won only 43 and Republicans 57. In the Senate, 53.1% of the votes cast statewide were for Democratic candidates, who won 52% (13 out of 25) of the seats to be filled. But in Marion and Allen Counties, both of which were divided into multimember House districts, Democrats drew 46.6% of the vote, but won only 3 of 21, or 14%, of the seats.

In early 1982, several Indiana Democrats filed suit, alleging that the 1981 reapportionment plan constituted a political gerrymander that violated their right, as Democrats, to equal protection of the laws. A divided three-judge district court invalidated the reapportionment.   The Republicans appealed.

Justice **WHITE** announced the judgment of the Court and delivered the opinion of the Court as to Part **II** and an opinion as to Parts **I, III,** and **IV,** in which Justice **BRENNAN**, Justice **MARSHALL**, and Justice **BLACKMUN** join.   . . .

III . . .

A

. . . [T]he appellees' claim . . . is that Democratic voters over the State as a whole, not Democratic voters in particular districts, have been subjected to unconstitutional discrimination.   . . . We . . . agree with the District Court that in order to succeed the plaintiffs were required to prove both intentional discrimination against an identifiable political group and an actual discriminatory effect on that group.   See, e.g., Mobile v. Bolden [1980].   Further, we are confident that if the law challenged here had discriminatory effects on Democrats, this record would support a finding that the discrimination was intentional.   . . . As long as redistricting is done by a legislature, it should not be very difficult to prove that the likely political consequences of the reapportionment were intended.

B

. . . The District Court held that because any apportionment scheme that purposely prevents proportional representation is unconstitutional, Democratic voters need only show that their proportionate voting influence has been adversely affected.   Our cases, however, clearly foreclose any claim that the Constitution requires proportional representation or that legislatures in reapportioning must draw district lines to come as near as possible to allocating seats to the contending parties in proportion to what their anticipated statewide vote will be.   Whitcomb v. Chavis [1971]; White v. Regester [1973].

The typical election for legislative seats in the United States is conducted in described geographical districts, with the candidate receiving the most votes in each district winning the seat allocated to that district. If all or most of the districts are competitive . . . even a narrow statewide preference for either party would produce an overwhelming majority for the winning party in the state legislature.   This consequence, however, is inherent in winner-take-all, district-based elections, and we cannot hold that such a reapportionment law would violate the Equal Protection Clause because the voters in the losing party do not have representation in the legislature in proportion to the statewide vote received by their party candidates.   . . .

To draw district lines to maximize the representation of each major party would require creating as many safe seats for each party as the demographic and predicted political characteristics of the State would permit. This in turn would leave the minority in each safe district without a representative of its choice. We upheld this "political fairness" approach in Gaffney v. Cummings [1973], despite its tendency to deny safe district minorities any realistic chance to elect their own representatives. But *Gaffney* in no way suggested that the Constitution requires the approach that Connecticut had adopted in that case.

In cases involving individual multimember districts, we have required a substantially greater showing of adverse effects than a mere lack of proportional representation to support a finding of unconstitutional vote dilution. Only where there is evidence that excluded groups have "less opportunity to participate in the political processes and to elect candidates of their choice" have we refused to approve the use of multimember districts. Rogers v. Lodge [1982]. See also *White; Whitcomb.* In these cases, we have also noted the lack of responsiveness by those elected to the concerns of the relevant groups. ...

These holdings rest on a conviction that the mere fact that a particular apportionment scheme makes it more difficult for a particular group in a particular district to elect the representatives of its choice does not render that scheme constitutionally infirm. This conviction, in turn, stems from a perception that the power to influence the political process is not limited to winning elections. An individual or a group of individuals who votes for a losing candidate is usually deemed to be adequately represented by the winning candidate and to have as much opportunity to influence that candidate as other voters in the district. We cannot presume in such a situation, without actual proof to the contrary, that the candidate elected will entirely ignore the interests of those voters. This is true even in a safe district where the losing group loses election after election. ...

As with individual districts, where unconstitutional vote dilution is alleged in the form of statewide political gerrymandering, the mere lack of proportional representation will not be sufficient to prove unconstitutional discrimination. Again, without specific supporting evidence, a court cannot presume in such a case that those who are elected will disregard the disproportionately underrepresented group. Rather, unconstitutional discrimination occurs only when the electoral system is arranged in a manner that will consistently degrade a voter's or a group of voters' influence on the political process as a whole. ...

C

... In reaching its conclusion, the District Court relied primarily on the results of the 1982 elections. ... Relying on a single election to prove unconstitutional discrimination is unsatisfactory. The District Court observed ... that Indiana is a swing State. Voters sometimes prefer Democratic candidates, and sometimes Republican. The District

Court did not find that ... the 1981 reapportionment would consign the Democrats to a minority status in the Assembly throughout the 1980's or that the Democrats would have no hope of doing any better in the reapportionment that would occur after the 1990 census. ...

Furthermore, in determining the constitutionality of multimember districts challenged as racial gerrymanders, we have rejected the view that "any group with distinctive interests must be represented in legislative halls if it is numerous enough to command at least one seat and represents a minority living in an area sufficiently compact to constitute a single-member district." *Whitcomb.* Rather, we have required that there be proof that the complaining minority "had less opportunity ... to participate in the political processes and to elect legislators of their choice." *Id.* In *Whitcomb,* ... we concluded that the failure of the minority "to have legislative seats in proportion to its population emerges more as a function of losing elections than of built-in bias against poor Negroes. The voting power of ghetto residents may have been 'cancelled out' as the District Court held, but this seems a mere euphemism for political defeat at the polls." *Id.* ...

... For constitutional purposes, the Democratic claim in this case, insofar as it challenges vel non the legality of the multimember districts in certain counties, is like that of the Negroes in *Whitcomb* who failed to prove a racial gerrymander, for it boils down to a complaint that they failed to attract a majority of the voters in the challenged multimember districts.

D

... Justice Powell suggests an alternative method for evaluating equal protection claims of political gerrymandering. In his view, courts should look at a number of factors in considering these claims. ... [T]he crux of Justice Powell's analysis seems to be that—at least in some cases—the intentional drawing of district boundaries for partisan ends and for no other reason violates the Equal Protection Clause in and of itself. We disagree ... with this conception of a constitutional violation. Specifically, even if a state legislature redistricts with the specific intention of disadvantaging one political party's election prospects, we do not believe that there has been an unconstitutional discrimination against members of that party unless the redistricting does in fact disadvantage it at the polls. ... Justice Powell's view would allow a constitutional violation to be found where the only proven effect on a political party's electoral power was disproportionate results in one (or possibly two) elections. ...

Reversed.

Chief Justice **BURGER**, concurring in the judgment. ...

Justice **O'CONNOR**, with whom The Chief Justice [**BURGER**] and Justice **REHNQUIST** join, concurring in the judgment.

Today the Court holds that claims of political gerrymandering lodged by members of one of the political parties that make up our two-

party system are justiciable under the Equal Protection Clause. ...
Nothing in our precedents compels us to take this step, and there is
every reason not to do so. ...

The step taken today is a momentous one, which if followed in the
future can only lead to political instability and judicial malaise. If
members of the major political parties are protected by the Equal
Protection Clause from dilution of their voting strength, then members
of every identifiable group that possesses distinctive interests and tends
to vote on the basis of those interests should be able to bring similar
claims. ... There is simply no clear stopping point to prevent the
gradual evolution of a requirement of roughly proportional representation for every cohesive political group. ...

... The right asserted in Baker [v. Carr (1962)] was an individual
right to a vote whose weight was not arbitrarily subjected to "debasement." The rights asserted in this case are group rights to an equal
share of political power and representation. ... [T]his Court's racial
gerrymandering cases [do not] require the recognition of any such group
right outside the context of racial discrimination. ...

I would avoid the difficulties generated by the plurality's efforts to
confine the effects of a generalized group right to equal representation
by not recognizing such a right in the first instance. ... Racial
gerrymandering should remain justiciable, for the harms it engenders
run counter to the central thrust of the Fourteenth Amendment. But
no such justification can be given for judicial intervention on behalf of
mainstream political parties, and the risks such intervention poses to our
political institutions are unacceptable. ...

Justice **POWELL**, with whom Justice **STEVENS** joins, concurring in
part and dissenting in part. ...

... Since the essence of a gerrymandering claim is that the members of a political party as a group have been denied their right to "fair
and effective representation," Reynolds v. Sims (1964), I believe that the
claim cannot be tested solely by reference to "one person, one vote."
Rather, a number of other relevant neutral factors must be considered.
...

The Equal Protection Clause guarantees citizens that their State
will govern them impartially. See Karcher v. Daggett [1983] (Stevens,
J., concurring). In the context of redistricting, that guarantee is of
critical importance because the franchise provides most citizens their
only voice in the legislative process. ... The Court's decision in Reynolds illustrates two concepts that are vitally important in evaluating an
equal protection challenge to redistricting. First, the Court recognized
that equal protection encompasses a guarantee of equal representation,
requiring a State to seek to achieve through redistricting "fair and
effective representation for all citizens." The concept of "representation" necessarily applies to groups: groups of voters elect representatives, individual voters do not. ...

Second, at the same time that it announced the principle of "one person, one vote" ... , the Court plainly recognized that redistricting should be based on a number of neutral criteria, of which districts of equal population was only one. *Reynolds.* ... For example, the Court observed that districts should be compact and cover contiguous territory, precisely because the alternative, "[indiscriminate] districting," would be "an open invitation to partisan gerrymandering." Similarly, a State properly could choose to give "independent representation" to established political subdivisions. Adherence to community boundaries, the Court reasoned, would both "deter the possibilities of gerrymandering," and allow communities to have a voice in the legislature that directly controls their local interests. ...

In *Karcher,* Justice Stevens, echoing the decision in *Reynolds,* described factors that I believe properly should guide both legislators who redistrict and judges who test redistricting plans against constitutional challenges. The most important of these factors are the shapes of voting districts and adherence to established political subdivision boundaries. Other relevant considerations include the nature of the legislative procedures by which the apportionment law was adopted and legislative history reflecting contemporaneous legislative goals. To make out a case of unconstitutional partisan gerrymandering, the plaintiff should be required to offer proof concerning these factors, which bear directly on the fairness of a redistricting plan, as well as evidence concerning population disparities and statistics tending to show vote dilution. No one factor should be dispositive.

In this case, appellees offered convincing proof of the ease with which mapmakers, consistent with the "one person, one vote" standard, may design a districting plan that purposefully discriminates against political opponents as well as racial minorities. Computer technology now enables gerrymanderers to achieve their purpose while adhering perfectly to the requirement that districts be of equal population. Relying on the factors correctly described by Justice Stevens in *Karcher,* the District Court carefully reviewed appellees' evidence and found that the redistricting law was intended to and did unconstitutionally discriminate against Democrats as a group. We have held that a district court's ultimate determination that a redistricting plan was "being maintained for discriminatory purposes," as well as its "subsidiary findings of fact," may not be set aside by a reviewing court unless they are clearly erroneous. *Rogers;* see, e.g., White v. Regester. The plurality ignores these precedents. The plurality also disregards the various factors discussed by the District Court as adequate indicia of unconstitutional gerrymandering. ...

... I would affirm the judgment of the District Court.

Editors' Notes

(1) **Query:** To what extent did White, Powell, and O'Connor each use a *philosophic approach* to constitutional interpretation in this case? Which was

truest to democratic theory? Can one answer that question without asking "Which democratic theory?" How does one find an answer to that question?

(2) **Query:** Questions of justiciability are inevitably questions about WHO. White thought the Democrats' claims did not raise a "political question," O'Connor thought they did because Democrats were presenting "group rights." Were not voters hurt by the districting systems in Baker v. Carr (1962; reprinted above, p. 769) and Reynolds v. Sims (1964; reprinted above, p. 777) also presenting "group rights" as well as individual rights? African American children in the School Segregation Cases (1954; reprinted below, p. 912)? How did O'Connor's reasoning differ from Frankfurter's in *Baker*?

(3) **Query:** If O'Connor had commanded a majority of the Court, what remedy would be open to members of minority parties if a legislature gerrymandered a state so as, for all practical purposes, to exclude them from political power? What was Frankfurter's remedy in *Baker*?

(4) **Query:** Was White's standard really that which Stewart had unsuccessfully urged in his dissent in *Reynolds* (pp. 784–85)?

(5) For analyses see: "Symposium: Gerrymandering and the Courts," 33 *UCLA L.Rev.* 1 (1985), espec. the articles by Sanford V. Levinson and Martin Shapiro; and Peter H. Schuck, "The Thickest Thicket: Partisan Gerrymandering and Judicial Regulation of Politics," 87 *Colum.L.Rev.* 1325 (1987).

(6) Gomillion v. Lightfoot (1960) invalidated an effort by officials of Tuskegee, Alabama to minimize black voting power. What about efforts, designed to *benefit* members of historically disadvantaged racial minority groups, to draw district boundary lines of "bizarre" or "dramatically irregular shape" to create federal congressional districts that have a majority of African American voters? Shaw v. Reno (1993) grew out of such efforts. Pursuant to the Voting Rights Act of 1965, as amended, 42 U.S.C. § 1973c, and following the 1990 census, the North Carolina legislature passed legislation creating two "majority-black districts," one of which was approximately 160 miles long and, for much of its length, no wider than the corridor of I-85, an interstate highway. Five white voters brought suit in federal district court, alleging that the plan constituted an unconstitutional racial gerrymander. The district court dismissed their suit, but the Supreme Court reversed, holding that the white voters had stated a claim under the Equal Protection Clause by "alleging that the [legislature] adopted a reapportionment scheme so irrational on its face that it can be understood only as an effort to segregate voters into separate voting districts because of their race, and that the separation lacks sufficient justification." The Court remanded the case to the district court for a trial of the voters' claims. The Court was careful to state: "we express no view as to whether 'the intentional creation of majority-minority districts, without more' always gives rise to an equal protection claim." See also Johnson v. De Grandy (1994), which interpreted the Voting Rights Act of 1965 not to require a state to create the maximum number of legislative districts in which members of minorities make up a majority of the voters, and Miller v. Johnson (1995), which held that the use of race as a "predominant factor" in drawing district lines is presumably unconstitutional and invalidated the creation of a majority-black congressional district in Georgia.

(7) There is much controversy concerning whether the interests of historically disadvantaged racial minority groups are better served through creating "majority-minority districts" or through creating districts in which they do not

constitute a majority but nonetheless make up a substantial enough bloc that representatives must take their interests into account if they wish to be reelected. For analyses of such issues, see Carol M. Swain, *Black Faces, Black Interests: The Representation of African Americans in Congress* (Cambridge: Harvard University Press, 1993) and Justice Thomas's dissent in Johnson v. De Grandy (1994), which argued that the Court has consistently misinterpreted the Voting Rights Act of 1965.

II. THE RIGHT TO ASSOCIATE

"The right of membership in the association ..., like most other personal rights, must yield to the rightful exertion of the police power."

NEW YORK ex rel. BRYANT v. ZIMMERMAN
278 U.S. 63, 49 S.Ct. 61, 73 L.Ed. 184 (1928).

With certain exceptions for labor unions and benevolent associations, New York required every incorporated and unincorporated society of more than twenty members that imposed an oath as a condition of membership to file with the secretary of state a copy of its constitution, by-laws, and oath, as well as an annual list of officers and members. Any person who became or remained a member of an association that failed to comply with the registration provisions committed a misdemeanor. The Ku Klux Klan did not register, and George W. Bryant, a Klansman from Buffalo, was convicted and sent to jail. Later he sought habeas corpus from a state judge, alleging that he had been prosecuted under an unconstitutional statute. He lost at all three levels of state courts and obtained a writ of error from the U.S. Supreme Court.

Mr. Justice **VAN DEVANTER** delivered the opinion of the Court. ...

The relator's contention under the due process clause is that the statute deprives him of liberty in that it prevents him from exercising his right of membership in the association. But his liberty in this regard, like most other personal rights, must yield to the rightful exertion of the police power. There can be no doubt that under that power the State may prescribe and apply to associations having an oath-bound membership any reasonable regulation calculated to confine their purposes and activities within limits which are consistent with the rights of others and the public welfare. The requirement ... that each association shall file with the secretary of state a sworn copy of its constitution, oath of membership, etc., with a list of members and officers is such a regulation. It proceeds on the two-fold theory that the State within whose territory and under whose protection the association exists is entitled to be informed of its nature and purpose, of whom it is composed and by whom its activities are conducted, and that requiring this information to be supplied for the public files will operate as an effective or substantial deterrent from violations of public and private right to which the association might be tempted if such a disclosure were not required. The requirement is not arbitrary or oppressive, but reasonable and likely to be of real effect. Of course, power to require the disclosure includes authority to prevent individual members of an association which has failed to comply from attending meetings or retaining membership with knowledge of its default. We conclude that the due process clause is not violated.

The main contention made under the equal protection clause is that the statute discriminates against the Knights of the Ku Klux Klan and other associations in that it excepts from its requirements several associations having oath-bound membership, such as labor unions, the Masonic fraternity, the Independent Order of Odd Fellows, the Grand Army of the Republic and the Knights of Columbus. ...

The courts below ... reached the conclusion that the classification was justified by a difference between the two classes of associations shown by experience, and that the difference consisted (a) in a manifest tendency on the part of one class to make the secrecy surrounding its purposes and membership a cloak for acts and conduct inimical to personal rights and public welfare, and (b) in the absence of such a tendency on the part of the other class. In pointing out this difference one of the courts said of the Ku Klux Klan, the principal association in the included class: "It is a matter of common knowledge that this organization functions largely at night, its members disguised by hoods and gowns and doing things calculated to strike terror into the minds of the people"; and later said of the other class: "These organizations and their purposes are well known, many of them having been in existence for many years. Many of them are oath-bound and secret. But we hear no complaints against them regarding violation of the peace or interfering with the rights of others." ...

We assume that the legislature had before it such information as was readily available, including the published report of a hearing before a committee of the House of Representatives of the 57th Congress relating to the formation, purposes and activities of the Ku Klux Klan. If so, it was advised—putting aside controverted evidence—that the order was a revival of the Ku Klux Klan of an earlier time with additional features borrowed from the Know Nothing and the A.P.A. orders of other periods; that its membership was limited to native born, gentile, protestant whites; that in part of its constitution and printed creed it proclaimed the widest freedom for all and full adherence to the Constitution of the United States, in another exacted of its members an oath to shield and preserve "white supremacy," and in still another declared any person actively opposing its principles to be "a dangerous ingredient in the body politic of our country and an enemy to the weal of our national commonwealth"; that it was conducting a crusade against Catholics, Jews and Negroes and stimulating hurtful religious and race prejudices; that it was striving for political power and assuming a sort of guardianship over the administration of local, state and national affairs; and that at times it was taking into its own hands the punishment of what some of its members conceived to be crimes.

We think it plain that the action of the courts below in holding that there was a real and substantial basis for the distinction made between the two sets of associations or orders was right and should not be disturbed. . . .

Judgment affirmed.

Separate opinion of Mr. Justice **McREYNOLDS.**

. . . I think we have no jurisdiction of this writ of error and that it should be dismissed. . . .

Editors' Notes

(1) The date of this case is 1928. Only three years earlier, Gitlow v. New York had for the first time held that the Fourteenth Amendment applied the First Amendment to the states. One year earlier, Whitney v. California (reprinted above, p. 651) had assumed without discussion that the Due Process Clause incorporated not only rights of free speech and assembly but also association. Like the opinion in *Whitney,* Van Devanter's opinion here took a general liberty of association for granted, though it is difficult to know how broad he thought that right. The meaning and scope of a constitutional right to associate later became more central—and controversial—in constitutional interpretation. See espec. NAACP v. Alabama (1958), the next case.

(2) **Query:** Given the Court's greater solicitude for freedom of association as well as the hate speech case, R.A.V. v. St. Paul (1992; reprinted above, p. 686), and lower courts' refusals to enjoin Nazis from marching in Skokie to intimidate Jewish survivors of the Holocaust, would the Court now sustain a regulation like the one in *Zimmerman*? What response can one give to the claim that, if the state must be neutral among contending political views, it must allow the same freedom to those who preach hate as to those who preach the message of the Preamble and the Fourteenth Amendment?

"[S]tate action which may have the effect of curtailing the freedom to associate is subject to the closest scrutiny."

NAACP v. ALABAMA
357 U.S. 449, 78 S.Ct. 1163, 2 L.Ed.2d 1488 (1958).

Following the National Association for the Advancement of Colored People's great victory in the School Segregation Cases (1954), ten southern states began a concerted counter-attack against the organization, branding it, among other things, a communist-inspired group. (See, for example, the two-volume pamphlet issued by the Georgia Education Commission, *Communism and the NAACP.*) These states convened legislative investigations, began lawsuits to produce membership lists and prosecutions for allegedly "fomenting" litigation and failing to register under Anti–Ku Klux Klan laws, similar to that upheld in *New York ex rel. Bryant* (1928; reprinted above, p. 795). A Louisiana statute threatened with dismissal any public school teacher who was found "advocating or in any manner performing any act toward bringing about integration of the races within the public school system," and Georgia would have punished such advocacy or action by revoking the teacher's license "forever."

Alabama's attack was the first to reach the U.S. Supreme Court. The attorney general asked a state court to enjoin the NAACP from carrying on activities in the state because it had failed to provide its records and membership lists. The trial judge issued a temporary injunction and also ordered the Association to produce its records and membership lists. The NAACP gave all the records requested except the names of rank-and-file members, who, it said, would be subjected to hurtful harassment in communities hostile to desegregation. (During the proceedings, the judge won re-election on a platform promising to drive the NAACP out of the state; after the election he refused to disqualify himself from presiding at the rest of the trial.)

When the Association did not comply with the order regarding membership lists, the judge held it in contempt and fined it $100,000. The Alabama supreme court twice refused to review the ruling, and the NAACP obtained certiorari from the U.S. Supreme Court.

Mr. Justice **HARLAN** delivered the opinion of the Court. ...

II

The Association both urges that it is constitutionally entitled to resist official inquiry into its membership lists, and that it may assert, on behalf of its members, a right personal to them to be protected from compelled disclosure by the State of their affiliation with the Association as revealed by the membership lists. We think that petitioner argues more appropriately the rights of its members, and that its nexus with them is sufficient to permit that it act as their representative before this Court. In so concluding, we reject respondent's argument that the Association lacks standing to assert here constitutional rights pertaining to the members, who are not of course parties to the litigation.

To limit the breadth of issues which must be dealt with in particular litigation, this Court has generally insisted that parties rely only on constitutional rights which are personal to themselves. Tileston v. Ullman [1943]. This rule is related to the broader doctrine that constitutional adjudication should where possible be avoided. See Ashwander v. Tennessee Valley Authority (concurring opinion) [1938]. The principle is not disrespected where constitutional rights of persons who are not immediately before the Court could not be effectively vindicated except through an appropriate representative before the Court. See Barrows v. Jackson [1953]; Joint Anti–Fascist Refugee Committee v. McGrath (concurring opinion) [1951].

If petitioner's rank-and-file members are constitutionally entitled to withhold their connection with the Association despite the production order, it is manifest that this right is properly assertable by the Association. To require that it be claimed by the members themselves would result in nullification of the right at the very moment of its assertion. Petitioner is the appropriate party to assert these rights, because it and its members are in every practical sense identical. ... Cf. Pierce v. Society of Sisters [1925].

III

We thus reach petitioner's claim that the production order in the state litigation trespasses upon fundamental freedoms protected by the Due Process Clause of the Fourteenth Amendment. ...

Effective advocacy of both public and private points of view, particularly controversial ones, is undeniably enhanced by group association, as this Court has more than once recognized by remarking upon the close nexus between the freedoms of speech and assembly. De Jonge v. Oregon [1937]; Thomas v. Collins [1945]. It is beyond debate that freedom to engage in association for the advancement of beliefs and ideas is an inseparable aspect of the "liberty" assured by the Due Process Clause of the Fourteenth Amendment, which embraces freedom of speech. See Gitlow v. New York [1925]; Palko v. Connecticut [1937]; Cantwell v. Connecticut [1940]; Staub v. Baxley [1958]. Of course, it is immaterial whether the beliefs sought to be advanced by association pertain to political, economic, religious or cultural matters, and state action which may have the effect of curtailing the freedom to associate is subject to the closest scrutiny.

The fact that Alabama ... has taken no direct action, to restrict the right of petitioner's members to associate freely, does not end inquiry into the effect of the production order. In the domain of these indispensable liberties, whether of speech, press, or association, the decisions of this Court recognize that abridgement of such rights, even though unintended, may inevitably follow from varied forms of governmental action. ... Similar recognition of possible unconstitutional intimidation of the free exercise of the right to advocate underlay this Court's narrow construction of the authority of a congressional committee investigating lobbying and of an Act regulating lobbying, although in neither case was there an effort to suppress speech. United States v. Rumely [1953]; United States v. Harriss [1954]. The governmental action challenged may appear to be totally unrelated to protected liberties. Statutes imposing taxes upon rather than prohibiting particular activity have been struck down when perceived to have the consequence of unduly curtailing the liberty of freedom of press assured under the Fourteenth

Amendment. Grosjean v. American Press Co. [1936]; Murdock v. Pennsylvania [1943].

It is hardly a novel perception that compelled disclosure of affiliation with groups engaged in advocacy may constitute as effective a restraint on freedom of association as the forms of governmental action in the cases above were thought likely to produce upon the particular constitutional rights there involved. This Court has recognized the vital relationship between freedom to associate and privacy in one's associations. ... Inviolability of privacy in group association may in many circumstances be indispensable to preservation of freedom of association, particularly where a group espouses dissident beliefs.

... Petitioner has made an uncontroverted showing that on past occasions revelation of the identity of its rank-and-file members has exposed these members to economic reprisal, loss of employment, threat of physical coercion, and other manifestations of public hostility. Under these circumstances, we think it apparent that compelled disclosure of petitioner's Alabama membership is likely to affect adversely the ability of petitioner and its members to pursue their collective effort to foster beliefs which they admittedly have the right to advocate, in that it may induce members to withdraw from the Association and dissuade others from joining it because of fear of exposure of their beliefs shown through their associations and of the consequences of this exposure.

It is not sufficient to answer, as the State does here, that whatever repressive effect compulsory disclosure of names of petitioner's members may have upon participation by Alabama citizens in petitioner's activities follows not from *state* action but from *private* community pressures. The crucial factor is the interplay of governmental and private action, for it is only after the initial exertion of state power represented by the production order that private action takes hold.

We turn to the final question whether Alabama has demonstrated an interest in obtaining the disclosures ... which is sufficient to justify the deterrent effect which we have concluded these disclosures may well have on the free exercise by petitioner's members of their constitutionally protected right of association. Such a "... subordinating interest of the State must be compelling," Sweezy v. N.H. (concur. op.) [1957]. It is not of moment that the State has here acted solely through its judicial branch, for whether legislative or judicial, it is still the application of state power which we are asked to scrutinize.

It is important to bear in mind that petitioner asserts no right to absolute immunity from state investigation, and no right to disregard Alabama's laws. ... Petitioner has not objected to divulging the identity of its members who are employed by or hold official positions with it. It has urged the rights solely of its ordinary rank-and-file members. ...

Whether there was "justification" in this instance turns solely on the substantiality of Alabama's interest in obtaining the membership lists. ... The issues in the litigation commenced by Alabama ... were whether the character of petitioner and its activities in Alabama had been such as to make petitioner subject to the registration statute, and whether the extent of petitioner's activities without qualifying suggested its permanent ouster from the State. Without intimating the slightest view upon the merits of these issues, we are unable to perceive that the disclosure of the names of petitioner's rank-and-file members has a substantial bearing on either of them. As matters stand in the state court, petitioner (1) has admitted its presence and conduct of activities in Alabama since 1918; (2) has offered to comply in all respects with the state qualification statute, although preserving its contention that the statute does not apply to it; and (3) has apparently complied satisfactorily with the production order, except for the membership lists, by furnishing the Attorney General with varied business records, its charter and statement of purposes, the names of all of its directors and officers, and with the total number of its Alabama members and the amount of their dues. ... [W]hatever interest the State may have in obtaining names of ordinary members has not been shown to be sufficient to overcome petitioner's constitutional objections to the production order.

From what has already been said, we think it apparent that N.Y. ex rel. Bryant v. Zimmerman [1928] cannot be relied on in support of the State's position, for that case involved markedly different considerations in terms of the interest of the State in obtaining disclosure. ... The decision was based on the particular character of the Klan's activities, involving acts of unlawful intimidation and violence, which the Court assumed was before the state legislature when it enacted the statute, and of which the Court itself took judicial notice. Furthermore, the situation before us is significantly different from that in *Bryant*, because the organization there had made no effort to comply with any of the requirements of New York's statute but rather had refused to furnish the State with *any* information as to its local activities.

We hold that the immunity from state scrutiny of membership lists which the Association claims on behalf of its members is here so related to the right of the members to pursue their lawful private interests privately and to associate freely with others in so doing as to come within the protection of the Fourteenth Amendment. And we conclude that Alabama has fallen short of showing a controlling justification for the deterrent effect on the free enjoyment of the right to associate which disclosure of membership lists is likely to have. Accordingly, the judgment of civil contempt and the $100,000 fine which resulted from petitioner's refusal to comply with the production order in this respect must fall. ...

Reversed.

Editors' Notes

(1) For the background to this and similar cases, see Walter F. Murphy, "The South Counterattacks: The Anti–NAACP Laws," 12 *West.Pol.Q.* 371 (1959).

(2) The Supreme Court "remanded" the case "for proceedings not inconsistent with this opinion." The case then went back to Alabama's supreme court. Twice the NAACP moved that that court direct the trial judge to proceed in accordance with the U.S. Supreme Court's ruling. In 1959, however, the Alabama supreme court held that the U.S. Supreme Court had acted on a "mistaken premise" and therefore reaffirmed the trial judge's adjudication of contempt. The NAACP returned to the U.S. Supreme Court and won a second, but limited victory. It had sought a writ of mandamus—a direct order to the court below in place of the usual diplomatic formula regarding "proceedings not inconsistent with" the Court's opinion—but the justices contented themselves with reversing the Alabama supreme court and noting: "[T]he Alabama Supreme Court is foreclosed from reexamining the grounds of our disposition. ... We assume that the State Supreme Court, thus advised, will not fail to proceed promptly with the disposition of the matters left open under our mandate. ..." NAACP v. Alabama (1959).

The assumption was unwarranted. The NAACP was unable to obtain a hearing in the Alabama supreme court for more than a year, during which time the injunction against it remained in force. The Association then began an action in a U.S. district court to obtain a federal injunction against the operation of the state injunction. The district court dismissed, and the Court of Appeals for the Fifth Circuit affirmed, holding that the doctrine of "equitable abstention" required that the issues be settled in state courts. The NAACP again obtained review in the U.S. Supreme Court. In October, 1961, the justices directed the court of appeals to instruct the district judge to hold hearings unless "within a reasonable time, no later than January 2, 1962," the state courts had proceeded. NAACP v. Gallion (1961).

In December, 1961, five years after the state trial court had issued its "temporary" injunction, that court held its first hearings on the merits of the case. Shortly after, the trial court made its injunction permanent. Alabama's supreme court affirmed, and in 1964 the case came to the U.S. Supreme Court for the fourth time.

The justices still spoke softly, but this time they brandished their big stick:

> The judgment below must be reversed. ... [W]e are asked to formulate a decree for entry in the state courts which will insure the Association's right to conduct activities in Alabama without further delay. While such a course undoubtedly lies within this Court's power, Martin v. Hunter's Lessee [1816], we prefer to follow our usual practice and remand the case to the Supreme Court of Alabama for further proceedings not inconsistent with this opinion. Such proceedings should include the prompt entry of a decree ... vacating in all respects the permanent injunction ... and permitting the Association to take all steps necessary to qualify it to do business in Alabama. Should we unhappily be mistaken in our belief that the Supreme Court of Alabama will promptly implement this decision, leave is given the Association to apply to this Court for further appropriate relief. NAACP v. Alabama (1964).

Six weeks later, President Lyndon Johnson signed into law the Civil Rights Act of 1964, which for the first time put federal executive and legislative power unmistakably behind the concept of racial justice that the U.S. Supreme Court had been vindicating since Brown v. Board of Education (1954). Shortly thereafter, the Alabama judges dissolved the injunction.

(3) **Query:** In *NAACP*, the Court protected "privacy in one's associations" because it is "indispensable to preservation of freedom of association." To what extent was Harlan's approach *textual*? *Doctrinal*? What other approach(es) did he use? To what extent did Harlan foreshadow the assorted lines of reasoning that Douglas used in *Griswold* (1965; reprinted above, p. 147)? There Douglas said *NAACP* had held that "the First Amendment has a penumbra where privacy is protected from governmental intrusion." Is Harlan's or Douglas's reasoning less bound to or constrained by the constitutional text? How could Black have joined Harlan in *NAACP* and dissented—vehemently—in *Griswold*?

(4) **Query:** Did Harlan persuasively distinguish this case from the KKK Case (reprinted above, p. 795)?

———

"We conclude that the balance between the individual and the governmental interests here at stake must be struck in favor of the latter. . . ."—Justice HARLAN

"I do not agree that laws directly abridging First Amendment freedoms can be justified by a congressional or judicial balancing process."—Justice BLACK

BARENBLATT v. UNITED STATES
360 U.S. 109, 79 S.Ct. 1081, 3 L.Ed.2d 1115 (1959).

Rule XI of the House of Representatives authorized the Committee on Un-American Activities to investigate propaganda that was "un-American" or attacked the "principle of the form of government guaranteed by our Constitution." Investigating supposed communist influence in education, the committee called as a witness Lloyd Barenblatt, who had been a graduate student and teaching assistant at the University of Michigan and later an instructor at Vassar and had been identified by another witness as having been a communist while at Michigan. He refused to answer questions, claiming that the committee was abridging his rights under the First, Ninth, and Tenth Amendments, conducting a legislative trial, and subjecting him to a bill of attainder. He was cited for contempt of Congress and convicted in a district court; the court of appeals affirmed.

Meanwhile, Watkins v. United States (1957) reversed another conviction for contempt of Congress on narrow grounds: The committee had not clearly informed Watkins of the relevance of its questions to a valid legislative purpose. Warren's opinion for the Court, however, had gone out of its way to castigate congressional investigations that tried to expose and punish people for their political views. In and outside of Congress, *Watkins* was read as a warning that the Court was going to protect the First Amendment against congressional campaigns for political orthodoxy. And, when Barenblatt petitioned for certiorari, the Court granted the writ and remanded the case to the court of appeals for reconsideration in light of *Watkins.*

The court of appeals reaffirmed its decision and Barenblatt again sought and obtained certiorari. In the interim between *Watkins* and *Barenblatt,* another set of events occurred. Southern Democrats and conservative Republicans had joined together in a multi-pronged attack on the Supreme Court for its decisions in *Watkins,* the School Segregation Cases, *Yates,* and several other rulings that had protected alleged subversives in government as well as the rights of the criminally accused. Due to the work of a coalition of liberal Democrats and Republicans and to Lyndon Johnson's adroitness as majority leader of the Senate and his ambition to become President, all but one of the attacks failed, although several came very close to passage—close enough to constitute a warning to the justices of congressional power.

Mr. Justice **HARLAN** delivered the opinion of the Court.

Once more the Court is required to resolve the conflicting constitutional claims of congressional power and of an individual's right to resist its exercise. ...

... In the present case congressional efforts to learn the extent of a nationwide, indeed world wide, problem have brought one of its investigating committees into the field of education. Of course, broadly viewed, inquiries cannot be made into the teaching that is pursued in any of our educational institutions. When academic teaching-freedom and its corollary learning-freedom, so essential to the well-being of the Nation, are claimed, this Court will always be on the alert against intrusion by Congress into this constitutionally protected domain. But this does not mean that the Congress is precluded from interrogating a witness merely because he is a teacher. An educational institution is not a constitutional sanctuary from inquiry into matters that may otherwise be within the constitutional legislative domain merely for the reason that inquiry is made of someone within its walls. ...

Our function, at this point, is purely one of constitutional adjudication in the particular case and upon the particular record before us, not to pass judgment upon the general wisdom or efficacy of the activities of this Committee in a vexing and complicated field. The precise constitutional issue confronting us is whether the Subcommittee's inquiry into petitioner's past or present membership in the Communist Party transgressed the provisions of the First Amendment, which of course reach and limit congressional investigations. *Watkins* [1957].

The Court's past cases establish sure guides to decision. Undeniably, the First Amendment in some circumstances protects an individual from being compelled to disclose his associational relationships. However, the protections of the First Amendment, unlike a proper claim of the privilege against self-incrimination under the Fifth Amendment, do not afford a witness the right to resist inquiry in all circumstances. Where First Amendment rights are asserted to bar governmental interrogation resolution of the issue always involves a balancing by the courts of the competing private and public interests at stake in the particular circumstances shown. These principles were recognized in the Watkins Case, where, in speaking of the First Amendment in relation to congressional inquiries, we said: "It is manifest that despite the adverse effects which follow upon compelled disclosure of private matters, not all such inquiries are barred. ... The critical element is the existence of, and the weight to be ascribed to, the interest of the Congress in demanding disclosures from an unwilling witness." More recently in NAACP v. Alabama [1958] we applied the same principles in judging state action claimed to infringe rights of association assured by the Due Process Clause of the Fourteenth Amendment, and stated that the " 'subordinating interest of the State must be compelling' " in order to overcome the individual constitutional rights at stake. See Sweezy v. N.H. concur. op. [1957]. In light of these principles we now consider petitioner's First Amendment claims.

The first question is whether this investigation was related to a valid legislative purpose, for Congress may not constitutionally require an individual to disclose his political relationships or other private affairs except in relation to such a purpose. See *Watkins*.

That Congress has wide power to legislate in the field of Communist activity in this Country, and to conduct appropriate investigations in aid thereof, is hardly debatable. The existence of such power has never been questioned by this Court, and it is sufficient to say, without particularization, that Congress has enacted or considered in this field a wide range of legislative measures, not a few of which have stemmed from recommendations of the very Committee whose actions have been drawn in question here. In the last analysis this power rests on the right of self-preservation, "the ultimate value of any society." Dennis v. United States [1951]. Justification for its exercise in turn rests on the long and widely accepted view that the tenets of the Communist Party include the ultimate overthrow of the Government of the United States by force and violence, a view which has been given formal expression by the Congress.

On these premises, this Court in its constitutional adjudications has consistently refused to view the Communist Party as an ordinary political party, and has upheld federal legislation aimed at the Communist problem which in a different context would certainly have raised constitutional issues of the gravest character. On the same premises this Court has upheld under the Fourteenth Amendment state legislation requiring those occupying or seeking public office to disclaim knowing membership in any organization advocating overthrow of the Government by force and violence, which legislation none can avoid seeing was aimed at membership in the Communist Party. Similarly, in other areas, this Court has recognized the close nexus between the Communist Party and violent overthrow of government. ... To suggest that because the Communist Party may also sponsor peaceable political reforms the constitutional issues before us should now be judged as if that Party were just an ordinary political party from the standpoint of national security, is to ask this Court to blind itself to world affairs which have determined the whole course of our national policy since the close of World War II ... and to the vast burdens which these conditions have entailed for the entire Nation.

We think that investigatory power in this domain is not to be denied Congress solely because the field of education is involved. ...

Nor can we accept the further contention that this investigation should not be deemed to have been in furtherance of a legislative purpose because the true objective of the Committee and of the Congress was purely "exposure." So long as Congress acts in pursuance of its constitutional power, the Judiciary lacks authority to intervene on the basis of the motives which spurred the exercise of that power. Arizona v. California [1931].

"It is, of course, true," as was said in McCray v. United States [1904], "that if there be no authority in the judiciary to restrain a lawful exercise of power by another department of the government, where a wrong motive or purpose has impelled to the exertion of the power, that abuses of a power conferred may be temporarily effectual. The remedy for this, however, lies, not in the abuse by the judicial authority of its functions, but in the people, upon whom, after all, under our institutions, reliance must be placed for the correction of abuses committed in the exercise of a lawful power."

Finally, the record is barren of other factors which in themselves might sometimes lead to the conclusion that the individual interests at stake were not subordinate to those of the state. There is no indication in this record that the Subcommittee was attempting to pillory witnesses. Nor did petitioner's appearance as a witness follow from indiscriminate dragnet procedures. ... And the relevancy of the questions put to him by the Subcommittee is not open to doubt.

We conclude that the balance between the individual and the governmental interests here at stake must be struck in favor of the latter, and that therefore the provisions of the First Amendment have not been offended.

Mr. Justice **BLACK,** with whom The Chief Justice **[WARREN]** and Mr. Justice **DOUGLAS** concur, dissenting. ...

II

The First Amendment says in no equivocal language that Congress shall pass no law abridging freedom of speech, press, assembly or petition. The activities of this Committee, authorized by Congress, do precisely that, through exposure, obloquy and public scorn. See *Watkins.* ... The Court does not really deny this fact but relies on a combination of three reasons for permitting the infringement: **(A)** The notion that despite the First Amendment's command Congress can abridge speech and association if this Court decides that the governmental interest in abridging speech is greater than an individual's interest in exercising that freedom, **(B)** the Government's right to "preserve itself," **(C)** the fact that the Committee is only after Communists or suspected Communists in this investigation.

A

I do not agree that laws directly abridging First Amendment freedoms can be justified by a congressional or judicial balancing process. There are, of course, cases suggesting that a law which primarily regulates conduct but which might also indirectly affect speech can be upheld if the effect on speech is minor in relation to the need for control of the conduct. With these cases I agree. Typical of them are Cantwell v. Connecticut [1940] and Schneider v. Irvington [1939]. Both of these involved the right of a city to control its streets. In *Cantwell*, a man had been convicted of breach of the peace for playing a phonograph on the street. He defended on the ground that he was disseminating religious views and could not, therefore, be stopped. We upheld his defense, but in so doing we pointed out that the city did have substantial power over conduct on the streets even where this power might to some extent affect speech. A State, we said, might "by general and non-discriminatory legislation regulate the times, the places, and the manner of soliciting upon its streets, and holding meetings thereon." ... But even such laws governing conduct, we emphasized, must be tested, though only by a balancing process, if they indirectly affect ideas. On one side of the balance, we pointed out, is the interest of the United States in seeing that its fundamental law protecting freedom of communication is not abridged; on the other the obvious interest of the State to regulate conduct within its boundaries. In *Cantwell* we held that the need to control the streets could not justify the restriction made on speech. We stressed the fact that where a man had a right to be on a street, "he had a right peacefully to impart his views to others." ... Similar views were expressed in *Schneider,* which concerned ordinances prohibiting the distribution of handbills to prevent littering. ... But we did not in *Schneider,* any more than in *Cantwell,* even remotely suggest that a law directly aimed at curtailing speech and political persuasion could be saved through a balancing process. Neither these cases, nor any others, can be read as allowing legislative bodies to pass laws abridging freedom of speech, press and association merely because of hostility to views peacefully expressed in a place where the speaker had a right to be. Rule XI, on its face and as here applied, since it attempts inquiry into beliefs, not action—ideas and associations, not conduct—does just that.

To apply the Court's balancing test under such circumstances is to read the First Amendment to say

> Congress shall pass no law abridging freedom of speech, press, assembly and petition, unless Congress and the Supreme Court reach the joint conclusion that on balance the interest of the Government in stifling these freedoms is greater than the interest of the people in having them exercised.

This is closely akin to the notion that neither the First Amendment nor any other provision of the Bill of Rights should be enforced unless the Court believes it is *reasonable* to do so. ... [T]his violate[s] the genius of our *written* Constitution. ...

But even assuming what I cannot assume, that some balancing is proper in this case, I feel that the Court after stating the test ignores it completely. At most it balances the right of the Government to preserve itself, against Barenblatt's right to refrain from revealing Communist affiliations. Such a balance, however, mistakes the factors to be weighed. In the first place, it completely leaves out the real interest in Barenblatt's silence, the interest of the people as a whole in being able to join organizations, advocate causes and make political "mistakes" without later being subjected to governmental penalties for having dared to think for themselves. It is this right, the right to err politically, which keeps us strong as a Nation. For no number of laws against communism can have as much effect as the personal conviction which comes from having heard its arguments and rejected them, or from having once accepted its tenets and later recognized their worthlessness. Instead, the obloquy which results from investigations such as this not only stifles "mistakes" but prevents all but the most courageous from hazarding any views which might at some later time become disfavored. This result, whose importance cannot be overestimated, is doubly crucial when it affects the universities, on which we must largely rely for the experimentation and development of new ideas essential to our country's welfare. It is these interests of society, rather that Barenblatt's own right to silence, which I think the Court should put on the balance against the demands of the Government, if any balancing process is to be tolerated. Instead they are not mentioned. ... Such a result reduces "balancing" to a mere play on words and is completely inconsistent with the rules this Court has previously given for applying a "balancing test," where it is proper: "[T]he courts should be *astute* to examine the *effect* of the challenged legislation. Mere *legislative preferences or beliefs* ... may well support regulation directed at other personal activities, but be insufficient to justify such as diminishes the exercise of rights so vital to the maintenance of democratic institutions." *Schneider*. (Italics supplied.)

B

Moreover, I cannot agree with the Court's notion that First Amendment freedoms must be abridged in order to "preserve" our country. That notion rests on the unarticulated premise that this Nation's security hangs upon its power to punish people because of what they think, speak or write about, or because of those with whom they associate for political purposes. ... I challenge this premise, and deny that ideas can be proscribed under our Constitution. I agree that despotic governments cannot exist without stifling the voice of opposition to their oppressive practices. The First Amendment means to me, however, that the only constitutional way our Government can preserve itself is to leave its people the fullest possible freedom to praise, criticize or discuss, as they see fit, all governmental policies and to suggest, if they desire, that even its most fundamental postulates are bad and should be changed; "Therein lies the security of the Republic, the very foundation of constitutional government." [De Jonge v. Oregon (1937).] ...

C

The Court implies, however, that the ordinary rules and requirements of the Constitution do not apply because the Committee is merely after Communists and they do not constitute a political party but only a criminal gang. ... Of course it has always been recognized that members of the Party who, either individually or in combination, commit acts in violation of valid laws can be prosecuted. But the Party as a whole and innocent members of it could not be attainted merely because it had some illegal aims and because some of its members were lawbreakers. ...

... [N]o matter how often or how quickly we repeat the claim that the Communist Party is not a political party, we cannot outlaw it, as a group, without endangering the liberty of all of us. The reason is not hard to find, for mixed among those aims of communism which are illegal are perfectly normal political and social goals. ...

... History should teach us then, that in times of high emotional excitement minority parties and groups which advocate extremely unpopular social or governmental innovations will always be typed as criminal gangs and attempts will always be made to drive them out. It was knowledge of this fact, and of its great dangers, that caused the Founders of our land to enact the First Amendment as a guarantee that neither Congress nor the people would do anything to hinder or destroy the capacity of individuals and groups to seek converts and votes for any cause, however radical or unpalatable their principles might seem under the accepted notions of the time. ...

III

Finally, I think Barenblatt's conviction violates the Constitution because the chief aim, purpose and practice of the House Un–American Activities Committee, as disclosed by its many reports, is to try witnesses and punish them because they are or have been Communists or because they refuse to admit or deny Communist affiliations. The punishment imposed is generally punishment by humiliation and public shame. There is nothing strange or novel about this kind of punishment. It is in fact one of the oldest forms of governmental punishment known to mankind; branding, the pillory, ostracism and subjection to public hatred being but a few examples of it. ...

... [T]he Constitution proscribes *all* bills of attainder by State or Nation. ... It does this because the Founders believed that punishment was too serious a matter to be entrusted to any group other than an independent judiciary and a jury of twelve men acting on previously passed, unambiguous laws, with all the procedural safeguards they put in the Constitution as essential to a fair trial. . . .

Mr. Justice **BRENNAN,** dissenting. . . .

Editors' Notes

(1) **Query:** *Barenblatt* raises a host of questions concerning proper approaches to constitutional interpretation. It is the classic debate over *balancing*. See pp. 410–14 in Chapter 9 for a general discussion of that approach. But what other approaches did Harlan employ? Black?

(2) **Query:** To what extent was Harlan using a form of a *prudential approach*? That is, to what extent was he trimming the Court's sails to avoid Congress's wrath? See Walter F. Murphy, *Congress and the Court* (Chicago: University of Chicago Press, 1962), espec. Pt. III.

(3) **Query:** Black spoke of "the genius of our *written* Constitution." What is that "genius"? Did Black limit himself to using a *textualist*'s understanding of that "genius"?

(4) *Barenblatt* was one of a number of cases decided at the height of the Cold War era involving legislative investigation (both federal and state) into political association, especially membership in the Communist party, and convictions for contempt for refusing to answer questions concerning such membership.

(5) **Query:** In Scales v. United States (1961), the Court per Justice Harlan upheld, 5–4, the conviction of Junius Irving Scales, former chairman of the Communist party in North and South Carolina, under the clause of the Smith Act making it a crime to be a member of an organization that advocated violent overthrow of a government in the United States. How can one distinguish between, on the one hand, *Barenblatt* and *Scales*, and, on the other hand, NAACP v. Alabama (1958; reprinted above, p. 798), in which Harlan also wrote the opinion of the Court? Are the former cases more akin to the KKK Case (1928; reprinted above, p. 795)?

By the time the Court decided *Scales* in 1961, he had broken with the party. Thus a reformed communist was the only person in prison in the United States for being a communist. President Kennedy pardoned Scales at Christmas, 1962.

(6) Noto v. United States (1961), decided the same day as *Scales* and by the same majority, again speaking through Harlan, reversed the conviction of another communist under the Smith Act's membership clause. The Court did so on grounds that the evidence had been insufficient to prove that the Communist party had advocated direct action to overthrow the government by force. Also on the same day, Communist Party v. Subversive Activities Control Board (SACB) (1961) upheld, again 5–4, the constitutionality of a requirement of the Internal Security Act of 1950 that groups held by the SACB to be "communist controlled" register with the attorney general and give, among other items, the names and addresses of all members.

When the Communist party refused to register, the attorney general tried to enforce another section of the 1950 act that required, under such circumstances, all individual members to register. Albertson v. SACB (1965) unanimously held that section of the law unconstitutional. The effects of the Smith Act as upheld by *Scales*, the Court reasoned, made compulsory registration equivalent to compulsory self-incrimination. *Aptheker v. Secretary of State* (1964) invalidated the section of the Internal Security Act of 1950 that refused passports to American citizens who belonged to a communist organization, and *United States v. Robel* (1967) struck down the section that made it a crime for a member of such an organization to hold a job in a defense industry once the SACB had ordered the organization to register. In 1973 the Nixon administration allowed the SACB to die by declining to ask Congress to appropriate funds to keep it in existence.

(7) *Gibson v. Florida Legislative Committee* (1963) involved a state legislative investigation into alleged subversive influences in the NAACP. The Committee announced that "the inquiry would be directed at Communists and Communist activities, including infiltration of Communists into organizations operating [in] described fields" such as race relations. Gibson, the President of the Miami branch of the NAACP, refused to produce the records relating to the identity of members of and contributors to the Miami and state NAACP organizations. The state court found him in contempt; the U.S. Supreme Court reversed, distinguishing *Barenblatt* on the basis of differences between the NAACP (a "concededly legitimate" group that "was and is against communism") and the Communist Party ("not an ordinary or legitimate political party") and emphasizing that the "evidence discloses the utter failure to demonstrate the existence of any substantial relationship between the NAACP and subversive or Communist activities."

(8) With the treatment of the Communist party during the height of the Cold War era, contrast *Brown v. Socialist Workers Party* (1982), which held that the defendant party, "a minor political party which historically has been the object of harassment by government officials and private parties," could not be constitutionally required to disclose information concerning contributions to its campaigns. This case is also discussed in the Editors' Notes to *Buckley v. Valeo* (1976; reprinted below, p. 828).

———

"[O]nly a compelling state interest in the regulation of a subject within the State's constitutional power to regulate can justify limiting First Amendment freedoms."— Justice BRENNAN

"The problem in each such case is to weigh the legitimate interest of the State against the effect of the regulation on individual rights."—Justice HARLAN

NAACP v. BUTTON
371 U.S. 415, 83 S.Ct. 328, 9 L.Ed.2d 405 (1963).

As part of its program of "massive resistance" to thwart implementation of the School Segregation Cases (1954), Virginia joined the southern attack on the NAACP (see the headnote to NAACP v. Alabama, above, p. 798), enacting a bevy of laws to curb the organization's capacity "to litigate by day and to think about litigation by night." Given the NAACP's frequent tactic of urging its members to file law suits—under the rules of standing an individual litigant is almost always necessary—and even asking people at meetings to sign blank forms authorizing the Association to file suits in their names, southern states' readily available weapons were statutes regulating the practice of law and redefining the old crimes of barratry ("habitual stirring up of quarrels"), champerty (assisting another to start or continue a law suit), and maintenance ("officious intermeddling" in a law suit by encouraging another to sue, usually by paying money to the potential litigant).

The NAACP attacked the constitutionality of five of these statutes in a federal district court, which struck down three but under the doctrine of equitable abstention refused to rule on the others until they had been interpreted by state courts. Virginia appealed to the U.S. Supreme Court, which held that the district court should have applied equitable abstention to all five. Harrison v. NAACP (1959).

The NAACP went into state courts to repeat its challenge to four of the five acts. State judges declared two of the statutes inapplicable to the Association's activities and another unconstitutional. The NAACP then obtained certiorari to contest the other statute, chapter 33 of the Acts of the Assembly, 1956 Extra Session. That chapter banned in very general terms "improper solicitation of any legal or professional business."

Mr. Justice **BRENNAN** delivered the opinion of the Court. ...

II

Petitioner challenges the decision of the Supreme Court of Appeals on many grounds. But we reach only one: that Chapter 33 as construed and applied abridges the freedoms of the First Amendment, protected against state action by the Fourteenth. More specifically, petitioner claims that the chapter infringes the right of the NAACP and its members and lawyers to associate for the purpose of assisting persons who seek legal redress for infringements of their constitutionally guaranteed and other rights. We think petitioner may assert this right on its own behalf, because, though a corporation, it is directly engaged in those activities, claimed to be constitutionally protected, which the statute would curtail. Cf. Grosjean v. American Press [1936]. We also think petitioner has standing to assert the corresponding rights of its members. See NAACP v. Alabama [1958]; Bates v. Little Rock [1960]; Louisiana ex rel. Gremillion v. NAACP [1961]. ...

A

We meet at the outset the contention that "solicitation" is wholly outside the area of freedoms protected by the First Amendment. To this contention there are two answers. The first is that a state cannot foreclose the exercise of constitutional rights by mere labels. The second is that abstract discussion is not the only species of communication which the Constitution protects; the First Amendment also protects vigorous advocacy, certainly of lawful ends, against governmental intrusion. Thomas v. Collins [1945]; Herndon v. Lowry [1937]. In the context of NAACP objectives, litigation is not a technique of resolving private differences; it is a means for achieving the lawful objectives of equality of treatment by all government, federal, state and local, for the members of the Negro community in this country. It is thus a form of political expression. Groups which find themselves unable to achieve their objectives through the ballot frequently turn to the courts. Just as it was true of the opponents of New Deal legislation during the 1930's, for example, no less is it true of the Negro minority today. And under the conditions of modern government, litigation may well be the sole practicable avenue open to a minority to petition for redress of grievances.

We need not, in order to find constitutional protection for the kind of cooperative, organizational activity disclosed by this record ... subsume such activity under a narrow, literal conception of freedom of speech, petition or assembly. For there is no longer any doubt that the First and Fourteenth Amendments protect certain forms of orderly group activity. Thus we have affirmed the right "to engage in association for the advancement of beliefs and ideas." NAACP v. Alabama. We have deemed privileged, under certain circumstances, the efforts of a union official to organize workers. *Thomas*. ... And we have refused to countenance compelled disclosure of a person's political associations. ...

The NAACP is not a conventional political party; but the litigation it assists, while serving to vindicate the legal rights of members of the American Negro community, at the same time and perhaps more importantly, makes possible the distinctive contribution of a minority group to the ideas and beliefs of our society. For such a group, association for litigation may be the most effective form of political association.

B

Our concern is with the impact of enforcement of Ch. 33 upon First Amendment freedoms. ... For us, the words of Virginia's highest court are the words of the statute. Hebert v. Louisiana [1926]. ... We read the decree of the Virginia Supreme Court of Appeals ... as proscribing any arrangement by which prospective litigants are advised to seek the assistance of particular attorneys. No narrower reading is plausible. ...

... It is enough that a vague and broad statute lends itself to selective enforcement against unpopular causes. We cannot close our eyes to the fact that the militant Negro civil rights movement has engendered the intense resentment and opposition of the politically dominant white community of Virginia; litigation assisted by the NAACP has been bitterly fought. In such circumstances, a statute broadly curtailing group activity leading to litigation may easily become a weapon of oppression, however evenhanded its terms appear. Its mere existence could well freeze out of existence all such activity on behalf of the civil rights of Negro citizens. ...

... If there is an internal tension between proscription and protection in the statute, we cannot assume that, in its subsequent enforcement, ambiguities will be resolved in favor of adequate protection of First Amendment rights. Broad prophylactic rules in the area of free expression are suspect. See e.g., Near v. Minnesota [1931]. Precision of regulation must be the touchstone in an area so closely touching our most precious freedoms.

C

The second contention is that Virginia has a subordinating interest in the regulation of the legal profession. ... However, the State's attempt to equate the activities of the NAACP and its lawyers with common-law barratry, maintenance and champerty, and to outlaw them accordingly, cannot obscure the serious encroachment worked by Ch. 33 upon protected freedoms of expression. The decisions of this Court have consistently held that only a compelling state interest in the regulation of a subject within the State's constitutional power to regulate can justify limiting First Amendment freedoms. ... For a State may not, under the guise of prohibiting professional misconduct, ignore constitutional rights. ... [I]n *Bates*, we said, "[w]here there is a significant encroachment upon personal liberty, the State may prevail only upon showing a subordinating interest which is compelling." ...

However valid may be Virginia's interest in regulating the traditionally illegal practices of barratry, maintenance and champerty, that interest does not justify the prohibition of the NAACP activities disclosed by this record. Malicious intent was of the essence of the common-law offenses of fomenting or stirring up litigation. And whatever may be or may have been true of suits against government in other countries, the exercise in our own, as in this case, of First Amendment rights to enforce constitutional rights through litigation, as a matter of law, cannot be deemed malicious. ...

Mr. Justice **WHITE**, concurring in part and dissenting in part. ...

Mr. Justice **HARLAN**, whom Mr. Justice **CLARK** and Mr. Justice **STEWART** join, dissenting. ...

II

Freedom of expression embraces more than the right of an individual to speak his mind. It includes also his right to advocate and his right to join with his fellows in an effort to make that advocacy effective. Thomas v. Collins [1945]; NAACP v. Alabama [1958]; Bates v. Little Rock [1960]. And just as it includes the right jointly to petition the legislature for redress of grievances, so it must include the right to join together for purposes of obtaining judicial redress. ... Litigation is often the desirable and orderly way of resolving disputes of broad public significance, and of obtaining vindication of fundamental rights. This is particularly so in the sensitive area of racial relationships.

But to declare that litigation is a form of conduct that may be associated with political expression does not resolve this case. Neither the First Amendment nor the Fourteenth constitutes an absolute bar to government regulation in the fields of free expression and association. This Court has repeatedly held that certain forms of speech are outside the scope of the protection of those Amendments, and that, in addition, "general regulatory statutes, not intended to control the content of speech but incidentally limiting its unfettered exercise," are permissible "when they have been found justified by subordinating valid governmental interests." The problem in each such case is to weigh the legitimate interest of the State against the effect of the regulation on individual rights. . . .

. . . [T]he basic rights in issue are those of the petitioner's members to associate, to discuss, and to advocate. Absent the gravest danger to the community, these rights must remain free from frontal attack or suppression, and the state court has recognized this. . . . But litigation, whether or not associated with the attempt to vindicate constitutional rights, is *conduct:* it is speech *plus.* Although the State surely may not broadly prohibit individuals with a common interest from joining together to petition a court for redress of their grievances, it is equally certain that the State may impose reasonable regulations limiting the permissible form of litigation. . . .

So here, the question is whether the particular regulation of conduct concerning litigation has a reasonable relation to the furtherance of a proper state interest, and whether that interest outweighs any foreseeable harm to the furtherance of protected freedoms.

III

The interest which Virginia has here asserted is that of maintaining high professional standards among those who practice law within its borders. This Court has consistently recognized the broad range of judgments that a State may properly make in regulating any profession. But the regulation of professional standards for members of the bar comes to us with even deeper roots in history and policy, since courts for centuries have possessed disciplinary powers incident to the administration of justice. See Cohen v. Hurley [1961]; Konigsberg v. California [1957]; Martin v. Walton [1961].

The regulation before us has its origins in the long-standing common-law prohibitions of champerty, barratry, and maintenance, the closely related prohibitions in the Canons of Ethics against solicitation and intervention by a law intermediary, and statutory provisions forbidding the unauthorized practice of law. . . .

First, with regard to the claimed absence of the pecuniary element, . . . the attorneys here . . . are in fact compensated for their work. Nor can it tenably be argued that petitioner's litigating activities fall into the accepted category of aid to indigent litigants. . . . [A]voidance of improper pecuniary gain is not the only relevant factor in determining standards of professional conduct. Running perhaps even deeper is the desire of the profession, of courts, and of legislatures to prevent any interference with the uniquely personal relationship between lawyer and client and to maintain untrammeled by outside influences the responsibility which the lawyer owes to the courts he serves.

When an attorney is employed by an association or corporation to represent individual litigants, two problems arise ... no matter how unimpeachable its motives. The lawyer becomes subject to the control of a body that is not itself a litigant and that, unlike the lawyers it employs, is not subject to strict professional discipline as an officer of the court. In addition, the lawyer necessarily finds himself with a divided allegiance—to his employer and to his client—which may prevent full compliance with his basic professional obligations. ...

Second, it is claimed that the interests of petitioner and its members are sufficiently identical to eliminate any "serious danger" of "professionally reprehensible conflicts of interest." ...

... [I]t may be in the interests of the Association in every case to make a frontal attack on segregation ... to sacrifice minor points that may win a given case for the major points that may win other cases too. But in a particular litigation ... a Negro parent, concerned that a continued frontal attack could result in schools closed for years, might prefer to wait with his fellows a longer time for good-faith efforts by the local school board than is permitted by the centrally determined policy of the NAACP. Or he might see a greater prospect of success through discussions with local school authorities than through the litigation deemed necessary by the Association. The parent, of course, is free to withdraw his authorization, but is his lawyer, retained and paid by petitioner and subject to its directions on matters of policy, able to advise the parent with that undivided allegiance that is the hallmark of the attorney-client relation? I am afraid not. ...

Third, it is said that the practices involved here must stand on a different footing because the litigation that petitioner supports concerns the vindication of constitutionally guaranteed rights. ... The true question is whether the State has taken action which unreasonably obstructs the assertion of federal rights. Here, it cannot be said that the underlying state policy is inevitably inconsistent with federal interests. The State has sought to prohibit the solicitation and sponsoring of litigation by those who have no standing to initiate that litigation themselves and who are not simply coming to the assistance of indigent litigants. ...

The impact of such a prohibition on the rights of petitioner and its members to free expression and association cannot well be deemed so great as to require that it be struck down in the face of this substantial state interest. The important function of organizations like petitioner in vindicating constitutional rights is not of course to be minimized, but that function is not, in my opinion, substantially impaired by this statute. Of cardinal importance, this regulatory enactment as construed does not in any way suppress assembly, or advocacy of litigation in general or in particular. ...

Editors' Notes

(1) **Query:** To what extent did Brennan's approach to constitutional interpretation exemplify *reinforcing representative democracy*? Was Harlan again using a *balancing approach* as in Barenblatt v. United States (1959; reprinted above, p. 803)? To what extent did the two justices directly engage each other on the issue of the proper *approach*?

(2) **Query:** To what extent did either Brennan or Harlan use a *doctrinal approach*? A *purposive approach*? Is it possible to reconcile Harlan's dissent here with his opinion for the Court in NAACP v. Alabama (1958; reprinted above, p. 798)?

(3) **Query:** Brennan's opinion alluded to southern states' resistance to the School Segregation Cases (1954; reprinted below, p. 912), and the defiance publicly voiced by southern officials, including those of Virginia, must have moved the justices to read with suspicion supposedly neutral statutes. But he did not mention that, in most of the South it was extraordinarily difficult if not impossible for African Americans to vote. (The Voting Rights Act of 1965 was still two years in the future.) Thus, if Ch. 33 was, as its legislative authors boasted, an effort to keep the NAACP from litigating and if Virginia continued to be successful in barring blacks from the polls, what other avenues for social change were open to African Americans in the state? Against that background, was Harlan's dissenting opinion naive? Is the implication of his argument that African Americans could only "appeal to heaven," that is, resort to revolution? Cf. John Locke, *The Second Treatise of Civil Government* (1690), § 242. On the other hand, can one make a reasoned argument that Harlan was defending democratic theory, even utilizing *reinforcing representative democracy*?

(4) In *Button* and United States v. Harriss (1954), the Court was solicitous of a right to lobby public officials, though conscious of the possibility of its misuse. *Harriss* upheld, against a First Amendment challenge, provisions of the Federal Regulation of Lobbying Act requiring "every person receiving any contributions or expending any money" to influence passage or defeat of congressional legislation to file the name and address of each person who makes a contribution of $500 or more, or to whom $10 or more is paid, as well as the total of all contributions and expenditures.

Indeed, in both of these cases the justices practically assumed without discussion that a right to lobby is protected by the First Amendment. It had not always been so. Trist v. Child (1874) invalidated a contract under which Nicholas Trist agreed to give L.M. Child a share of what Child could persuade Congress to pay Trist for his negotiating the Treaty of Guadelupe Hidalgo with Mexico (1848). The Court treated lobbying, even as here where there was no evidence of any effort at bribery, with great moral disdain:

> If the instances were numerous, open, and tolerated, they would be regarded as measuring the decay of public morals and the degeneracy of the times. ... If the agent is truthful, and conceals nothing, all is well. If he uses nefarious means with success, the spring-head and the stream of legislation are polluted. To legalize

the traffic of such service, would open a door at which fraud and falsehood would not fail to enter and make themselves felt at every accessible point.

(5) For an analysis of *Button,* see: Walter F. Murphy and Robert F. Birkby, "Interest Group Conflict in the Judicial Arena: The First Amendment and Group Access to the Court," 42 *Tex.L.Rev* 1018 (1964). For a general approach to interest groups in the courts, see: Clement E. Vose, "Litigation as a Form of Pressure Group Activity," 319 *The Annals* 20 (1958); and Walter F. Murphy, C. Herman Pritchett, and Sotirios A. Barber, *Courts, Judges, and Politics* (5h ed,; Boston: McGraw Hill, 1995), ch. 7. For detailed studies of the NAACP's tactics, see: Vose, *Caucasians Only* (Berkeley: University of California Press, 1959); and Mark V. Tushnet, *The NAACP's Legal Strategy Against Segregated Education* (Chapel Hill: University of North Carolina Press, 1987). For an analysis of the problems of attorney-client relationships in litigation designed to change public policy, see Derrick Bell, "Serving Two Masters: Integration Ideals and Client Interests in School Desegregation Litigation," 85 *Yale L.J.* 470 (1976).

(6) Brotherhood of Railroad Trainmen v. Virginia (1964), United Mine Workers v. Illinois State Bar (1967), and United Transportation Union v. State Bar of Michigan (1971) applied, to economic organizations, *Button* 's inclusion of a right under the First Amendment of groups to utilize the courts. Harlan did not change his stance, though he dissented only in part in the Michigan case.

———

"The right to associate for expressive purposes is not . . . absolute. Infringements on that right may be justified by regulations adopted to serve compelling state interests, unrelated to the expression of ideas, that cannot be achieved through means significantly less restrictive of associational freedoms."

ROBERTS v. UNITED STATES JAYCEES
468 U.S. 609, 104 S.Ct. 3244, 82 L.Ed.2d 462 (1984).

The United States Jaycees, or Junior Chamber of Commerce, is a national organization whose objectives are "to inculcate . . . a spirit of genuine Americanism and civic interest . . . and to provide [members] with opportunity for personal development and achievement and an avenue for intelligent participation . . . in the affairs of their community, state and nation. . . ." Before this case, membership was limited to males between the ages of 18 and 35.

In 1974 and 1975, two local chapters in Minnesota began admitting women and were sanctioned by the national association and threatened with expulsion. Several of the women members then filed charges of discrimination with the state Department of Human Rights. While those proceedings were in progress, the national organization sued in a federal district court alleging the Minnesota Human Rights Act was unconstitutional. The district judge certified to the state supreme court the question whether the Act covered the Jaycees, and that tribunal ruled it did. After full trial, the district court sustained the statute, but the Court of Appeals for the Eighth Circuit reversed. The state then appealed to the U.S. Supreme Court.

Justice **BRENNAN** delivered the opinion of the Court. ...

II

Our decisions have referred to constitutionally protected "freedom of association" in two distinct senses. In one line of decisions, the Court has concluded that choices to enter into and maintain certain intimate human relationships must be secured against undue intrusion by the State because of the role of such relationships in safeguarding the individual freedom that is central to our constitutional scheme. In this respect, freedom of association receives protection as a fundamental element of personal liberty. In another set of decisions, the Court has recognized a right to associate for the purpose of engaging in those activities protected by the First Amendment—speech, assembly, petition for the redress of grievances, and the exercise of religion. The Constitution guarantees freedom of association of this kind as an indispensable means of preserving other individual liberties.

The intrinsic and instrumental features of constitutionally protected association may, of course, coincide. In particular, when the State interferes with individuals' selection of those with whom they wish to join in a common endeavor, freedom of association in both of its forms may be implicated. The Jaycees contend that this is such a case. Still, the nature and degree of constitutional protection afforded freedom of association may vary depending on the extent to which one or the other aspect of the constitutionally protected liberty is at stake in a given case. We therefore find it useful to consider separately the effect of applying the Minnesota statute to the Jaycees on what could be called its members' freedom of intimate association and their freedom of expressive association.

A

The Court has long recognized that, because the Bill of Rights is designed to secure individual liberty, it must afford the formation and preservation of certain kinds of highly personal relationships a substantial measure of sanctuary from unjustified interference by the State. E.g., Pierce v. Society of Sisters (1925); Meyer v. Nebraska (1923). ... [W]e have noted that certain kinds of personal bonds have played a critical role in the culture and traditions of the Nation by cultivating and transmitting shared ideals and beliefs; they thereby foster diversity and act as critical buffers between the individual and the power of the State. See, e.g., Zablocki v. Redhail (1978); Moore v. East Cleveland (1977) (plurality opinion); Wisconsin v. Yoder (1973); Griswold v. Connecticut (1965); *Pierce*. See also Gilmore v. Montgomery (1974); NAACP v. Alabama (1958); Poe v. Ullman (1961) (Harlan, J., dissenting). More-

over, the constitutional shelter afforded such relationships reflects the
realization that individuals draw much of their emotional enrichment
from close ties with others. Protecting these relationships from unwarranted state interference therefore safeguards the ability independently
to define one's identity that is central to any concept of liberty.

The personal affiliations that exemplify these considerations, and
that therefore suggest some relevant limitations on the relationships
that might be entitled to this sort of constitutional protection, are those
that attend the creation and sustenance of a family—marriage, e.g.,
Zablocki; childbirth, e.g., Carey [v. Population Services (1977)]; the
raising and education of children, e.g., Smith v. Organization of Foster
Families; and cohabitation with one's relatives, e.g., Moore. Family
relationships, by their nature, involve deep attachments and commitments to the necessarily few other individuals with whom one shares not
only a special community of thoughts, experiences, and beliefs but also
distinctively personal aspects of one's life. ... As a general matter, only
relationships with these sorts of qualities are likely to reflect the
considerations that have led to an understanding of freedom of association as an intrinsic element of personal liberty. Conversely, an association lacking these qualities—such as a large business enterprise—seems
remote from the concerns giving rise to this constitutional protection.
Accordingly, the Constitution undoubtedly imposes constraints on the
State's power to control the selection of one's spouse that would not
apply to regulations affecting the choice of one's fellow employees.

Between these poles, of course, lies a broad range of human relationships that may make greater or lesser claims to constitutional protection.
... Determining the limits of state authority over an individual's freedom to enter into a particular association therefore unavoidably entails a
careful assessment of where that relationship's objective characteristics
locate it on a spectrum from the most intimate to the most attenuated of
personal attachments. See generally Runyon v. McCrary (1976) (Powell,
J., concurring). ... We note only that factors that may be relevant
include size, purpose, policies, selectivity, congeniality, and other characteristics that in a particular case may be pertinent. In this case,
however, several features of the Jaycees clearly place the organization
outside of the category of relationships worthy of this kind of constitutional protection.

The undisputed facts reveal that the local chapters of the Jaycees
are large and basically unselective groups. ... Apart from age and sex,
neither the national organization nor the local chapters employs any
criteria for judging applicants for membership, and new members are
routinely recruited and admitted with no inquiry into their backgrounds.
In fact, a local officer testified that he could recall no instance in which
an applicant had been denied membership on any basis other than age or
sex. ... Furthermore, despite their inability to vote, hold office, or
receive certain awards, women affiliated with the Jaycees attend various
meetings, participate in selected projects, and engage in many of the

organization's social functions. ... Accordingly, we conclude that the Jaycees chapters lack the distinctive characteristics that might afford constitutional protection to the decision of its members to exclude women. ...

B

An individual's freedom to speak, to worship, and to petition the Government for the redress of grievances could not be vigorously protected from interference by the State unless a correlative freedom to engage in group effort toward those ends were not also guaranteed. See, e.g., Rent Control Coalition for Fair Housing v. Berkeley (1981). According protection to collective effort on behalf of shared goals is especially important in preserving political and cultural diversity and in shielding dissident expression from suppression by the majority. See, e.g. Gilmore; Griswold; NAACP v. Button (1963); NAACP v. Alabama. Consequently, we have long understood as implicit in the right to engage in activities protected by the First Amendment a corresponding right to associate with others in pursuit of a wide variety of political, social, economic, educational, religious, and cultural ends. See, e.g., NAACP v. Claiborne Hardware Co. (1982); Larson v. Valente (1982); In re Primus (1978); Abood v. Detroit Board of Education (1977). ... [T]hat right is plainly implicated in this case.

... There can be no clearer example of an intrusion into the internal structure or affairs of an association than a regulation that forces the group to accept members it does not desire. Such a regulation may impair the ability of the original members to express only those views that brought them together. Freedom of association therefore plainly presupposes a freedom not to associate.

The right to associate for expressive purposes is not, however, absolute. Infringements on that right may be justified by regulations adopted to serve compelling state interests, unrelated to the suppression of ideas, that cannot be achieved through means significantly less restrictive of associational freedoms. E.g., Brown v. Socialist Workers (1982); Democratic Party v. Wisconsin (1981); Buckley v. Valeo (1976); Cousins v. Wigoda (1975); American Party v. White (1974); NAACP v. Button; Shelton v. Tucker (1960). We are persuaded that Minnesota's compelling interest in eradicating discrimination against its female citizens justifies the impact that application of the statute to the Jaycees may have on the male members' associational freedoms.

On its face, the Minnesota Act does not aim at the suppression of speech, does not distinguish between prohibited and permitted activity on the basis of viewpoint, and does not license enforcement authorities to administer the statute on the basis of such constitutionally impermissible criteria. ... Instead, as the Minnesota Supreme Court explained, the Act reflects the State's strong historical commitment to eliminating discrimination. ... That goal, which is unrelated to the suppression of expression, plainly serves compelling state interests of the highest order.

The Minnesota Human Rights Act ... here is an example of public accommodations laws that were adopted by some States beginning a decade before enactment of their federal counterpart, the Civil Rights Act of 1875. ... In 1973, the Minnesota legislature added discrimination on the basis of sex to the types of conduct prohibited by the statute.

By prohibiting gender discrimination in places of public accommodation, the Minnesota Act protects the State's citizenry from a number of serious social and personal harms. In the context of reviewing state actions under the Equal Protection Clause, this Court has frequently noted that discrimination based on archaic and overbroad assumptions about the relative needs and capacities of the sexes forces individuals to labor under stereotypical notions that often bear no relationship to their actual abilities. It thereby both deprives persons of their individual dignity and denies society the benefits of wide participation in political, economic, and cultural life. See, e.g., Heckler v. Mathews (1984); Mississippi University for Women v. Hogan (1982); Frontiero v. Richardson (1973) (plurality opinion). ... Thus, in upholding Title II of the Civil Rights Act of 1964, which forbids race discrimination in public accommodations, we emphasized that its "fundamental object ... was to vindicate 'the deprivation of personal dignity that surely accompanies denials of equal access to public establishments.' " Heart of Atlanta Motel v. United States (1964). ...

In applying the Act to the Jaycees, the State has advanced those interests through the least restrictive means of achieving its ends. Indeed, the Jaycees have failed to demonstrate that the Act imposes any serious burdens on the male members' freedom of expressive association. ... To be sure, as the Court of Appeals noted, a "not insubstantial part" of the Jaycees' activities constitutes protected expression on political, economic, cultural, and social affairs. ... There is, however, no basis in the record for concluding that admission of women as full voting members will impede the organization's ability to engage in these protected activities or to disseminate its preferred views. The Act requires no change in the Jaycees' creed of promoting the interests of young men, and it imposes no restrictions on the organization's ability to exclude individuals with ideologies or philosophies different from those of its existing members. Cf. Democratic Party v. Wisconsin (recognizing the right of political parties to "protect themselves 'from intrusion by those with adverse political principles' "). Moreover, the Jaycees already invite women to share the group's views and philosophy and to participate in much of its training and community activities. Accordingly, any claim that admission of women as full voting members will impair a symbolic message conveyed by the very fact that women are not permitted to vote is attenuated at best.

... [T]he Court of Appeals nonetheless entertained the hypothesis that women members might have a different view or agenda with respect to these matters so that, if they are allowed to vote, "some change in the Jaycees' philosophical cast can reasonably be expected." It is similarly arguable that, insofar as the Jaycees is organized to promote the views of young men . . . admission of women as voting members will change the message communicated by the group's speech. . . . Neither supposition, however, is supported by the record. In claiming that women might have a different attitude about such issues as the federal budget, school prayer, voting rights, and foreign relations, or that the organization's public positions would have a different effect if the group were not "a purely young men's association," the Jaycees rely solely on unsupported generalizations. . . . [W]e have repeatedly condemned legal decision-making that relies uncritically on such assumptions. See, e.g., Palmore v. Sidoti (1984); Heckler v. Mathews. . . . [W]e decline to indulge in the sexual stereotyping that underlies appellee's contention. . . .

. . . [E]ven if enforcement of the Act causes some incidental abridgement of the Jaycees' protected speech, that effect is no greater than is necessary to accomplish the State's legitimate purposes. . . . [A]cts of invidious discrimination in the distribution of publicly available goods, services, and other advantages cause unique evils that government has a compelling interest to prevent—wholly apart from the point of view such conduct may transmit. Accordingly, like violence or other types of potentially expressive activities that produce special harms distinct from their communicative impact, such practices are entitled to no constitutional protection. Runyon v. McCrary (1976). In prohibiting such practices, the Minnesota Act therefore "responds precisely to the substantive problem which legitimately concerns" the State and abridges no more speech or associational freedom than is necessary to accomplish that purpose. See City Council v. Taxpayers for Vincent (1984). . . .

Reversed.

Justice **REHNQUIST** concurs in the judgment.

The Chief Justice [**BURGER**] and Justice **BLACKMUN** took no part in the decision of this case.

Justice **O'CONNOR**, concurring in part and concurring in the judgment.

I join Parts **I** and **III** of the Court's opinion. . . . With respect to Part **II-A** . . . I agree. . . . I part company with the Court over its First Amendment analysis in Part **II-B** of its opinion. I agree with the Court that application of the Minnesota law to the Jaycees does not contravene the First Amendment, but I reach that conclusion for reasons distinct from those offered by the Court. . . .

I

The Court analyzes Minnesota's attempt to regulate the Jaycees' membership using a test that I find both over-protective of activities undeserving of constitutional shelter and under-protective of important First Amendment concerns. The Court declares that the Jaycees' right of association depends on the organization's making a "substantial" showing that the admission of unwelcome members "will change the message communicated by the group's speech." I am not sure what showing the Court thinks would satisfy its requirement of proof of a membership-message connection, but whatever it means, the focus on such a connection is objectionable.

Imposing such a requirement, especially in the context of the balancing-of-interests test articulated by the Court, raises the possibility that certain commercial associations, by engaging occasionally in certain kinds of expressive activities, might improperly gain protection for discrimination. The Court's focus raises other problems as well. How are we to analyze the First Amendment associational claims of an organization that invokes its right, settled by the Court in NAACP v. Alabama (1958), to protect the privacy of its membership? And would the Court's analysis of this case be different if, for example, the Jaycees membership had a steady history of opposing public issues thought (by the Court) to be favored by women? ... Whether an association is or is not constitutionally protected in the selection of its membership should not depend on what the association says or why its members say it.

The Court's readiness to inquire into the connection between membership and message reveals a more fundamental flaw in its analysis. The Court pursues this inquiry as part of its mechanical application of a "compelling interest" test. ... The Court entirely neglects to establish at the threshold that the Jaycees is an association whose activities or purposes should engage the strong protections that the First Amendment extends to expressive associations.

On the one hand, an association engaged exclusively in protected expression enjoys First Amendment protection of both the content of its message and the choice of its members. Protection of the message itself is judged by the same standards as protection of speech by an individual. Protection of the association's right to define its membership derives from the recognition that the formation of an expressive association is the creation of a voice, and the selection of members is the definition of that voice. ... A ban on specific group voices on public affairs violates the most basic guarantee of the First Amendment—that citizens, not the government, control the content of public discussion.

On the other hand, there is only minimal constitutional protection of the freedom of *commercial* association. There are, of course, some constitutional protections of commercial speech—speech intended and used to promote a commercial transaction with the speaker. But the State is free to impose any rational regulation on the commercial transaction itself. The Constitution does not guarantee a right to choose employees, customers, suppliers, or those with whom one engages in simple commercial transactions, without restraint from the State. A shopkeeper has no constitutional right to deal only with persons of one sex.

The dichotomy between rights of commercial association and rights of expressive association is also found in the more limited constitutional protections accorded an association's recruitment and solicitation activities and other dealings with its members and the public. ... Thus, after careful scrutiny, we have upheld regulations on matters such as the financial dealings between an association and its members, see *Buckley*, disclosure of membership lists to the State, see NAACP v. Alabama; *Shelton*, access to the ballot, time limits on registering before elections, and similar matters, see, e.g., Rosario v. Rockefeller (1973); Dunn v. Blumstein (1972); Williams v. Rhodes (1968). See also Heffron v. International Society for Krishna Consciousness, Inc. (1981). By contrast, an organization engaged in commercial activity enjoys only minimal constitutional protection of its recruitment, training, and solicitation activities. ...

Many associations cannot readily be described as purely expressive or purely commercial. No association is likely ever to be exclusively engaged in expressive activities. ... The standard must nevertheless give substance to the ideal of complete protection for purely expressive association, even while it readily permits state regulation of commercial affairs.

In my view, an association should be characterized as commercial, and therefore subject to rationally related state regulation of its membership and other associational activities, when, and only when, the association's activities are not predominantly of the type protected by the First Amendment. It is only when the association is predominantly engaged in protected expression that state regulation of its membership will necessarily affect, change, dilute, or silence one collective voice that would otherwise be heard. An association must choose its market. Once it enters the marketplace of commerce in any substantial degree it loses the complete control over its membership that it would otherwise enjoy if it confined its affairs to the marketplace of ideas.

Determining whether an association's activity is predominantly protected expression will often be difficult. ... The purposes of an association, and the purposes of its members in adhering to it, are doubtless relevant in determining whether the association is primarily engaged in protected expression. ... A group boycott or refusal to deal for political purposes may be speech, NAACP v. Claiborne Hardware Co., though a similar boycott for purposes of maintaining a cartel is not.

The considerations that may enter into the determination of when a particular association of persons is predominantly engaged in expression are therefore fluid and somewhat uncertain. But the Court has recognized the need to draw similar lines in the past. Two examples, both addressed in cases decided this Term, stand out.

The first concerns claims of First Amendment protection made by lawyers. On the one hand, some lawyering activity is undoubtedly protected by the First Amendment. ... *Primus*; see NAACP v. Button. On the other hand, ordinary law practice for commercial ends has never been given special First Amendment protection. ... *Hishon* ... rejected a large commercial law firm's claim to First Amendment protection for

alleged gender-based discriminatory partnership decisions for associates
of the firm.   ... As a commercial enterprise, the law firm could claim no
First Amendment immunity from employment discrimination laws, and
that result would not have been altered by a showing that the firm
engaged even in a substantial amount of activity entitled to First
Amendment protection.

We have adopted a similar analysis in our cases concerning association with a labor union. A State is free to impose rational regulation of
the membership of a labor union representing "the general *business*
needs of employees." Railway Mail Assn. v. Corsi (1945) (emphasis
added). The State may not, on the other hand, compel association with
a union engaged in ideological activities. *Abood.* ... We applied this
distinction in Ellis v. Railway Clerks (1984), decided this Term. Again,
the constitutional inquiry is not qualified by any analysis of governmental interests and does not turn on an individual's ability to establish
disagreement with the particular views promulgated by the union. It is
enough if the individual simply expresses unwillingness to be associated
with the union's ideological activities.

In summary, this Court's case law recognizes radically different
constitutional protections for expressive and non-expressive associations.
... The proper approach to analysis of First Amendment claims of
associational freedom is, therefore, to distinguish non-expressive from
expressive associations and to recognize that the former lack the full
constitutional protections possessed by the latter.

II

Minnesota's attempt to regulate the membership of the Jaycees
chapters operating in that State presents a relatively easy case for
application of the expressive-commercial dichotomy. ... Notwithstanding its protected expressive activities, the Jaycees ... is, first and
foremost, an organization that, at both the national and local levels,
promotes and practices the art of solicitation and management. The
organization claims that the training it offers its members gives them an
advantage in business, and business firms do indeed sometimes pay the
dues of individual memberships for their employees. ...

Recruitment and selling are commercial activities ... Minnesota has
a legitimate interest in ensuring nondiscriminatory access to the commercial opportunity presented by membership in the Jaycees.   ...

Editors' Notes

(1) **Query:** How, if at all, did Brennan's and O'Connor's vision of "the
Constitution" differ?

(2) **Query:** Do constitutionalist and democratic theories make different
demands in this case? Would constitutionalist theory protect both freedom of
intimate association and freedom of expressive association? Would democratic theory protect only freedom of expressive association? Does the First
Amendment encompass only freedom of association aimed at political expres-

sion? Why does it not protect other kinds of expression or, to the extent it does protect them, do so to a lesser degree? Does the text offer an answer here? Would a *purposive approach* help find an answer? Did either justice use such an approach? Or does the text also embrace (at least some aspects of) freedom of intimate association? For an analysis of freedom of intimate association, see Kenneth L. Karst, "The Freedom of Intimate Association," 89 *Yale L.J.* 624 (1980). See also Douglas O. Linder, "Freedom of Association after *Roberts v. United States Jaycees,*" 82 *Mich.L.Rev.* 1878 (1984).

(3) **Query:** O'Connor said that Brennan followed a *balancing approach.* Was she correct? Is "strict scrutiny," with its requirement that the state show a compelling interest, a form of *balancing*? Does "strict scrutiny" meet the criticisms that Chapter 9 (pp. 410–14) directed at balancing in constitutional interpretation?

(4) **Query:** For other cases dealing with classification by sex, see Chapter 15. Is *Roberts* a victory or a defeat for women's rights? Should it make a difference, for purposes of constitutional interpretation, if the Jaycees could prove that women indeed do have "a different view or agenda," or that there is a different "women's point of view"? Consider Carol Gilligan, *In a Different Voice* (Cambridge: Harvard University Press, 1982); and Deborah L. Rhode, *Justice and Gender* (Cambridge: Harvard University Press, 1989), ch. 11.

(5) Bd. of Directors of Rotary Intern'l v. Rotary Club of Duarte (1987) unanimously followed *Roberts,* holding that a California antidiscrimination law barring exclusion of women from membership in local Rotary clubs did not "interfere unduly with the [male] members' freedom of private association" or violate their "right of expressive association." Similarly, N.Y. State Club Ass'n v. City of N.Y. (1988) unanimously upheld New York City's Human Rights Law, rejecting a challenge that the law infringed freedom of association by prohibiting racial, religious, or sex discrimination in any institution, club, or place of accommodation that has more than 400 members, provides regular meal service, and regularly receives payment from nonmembers for trade or business. Dallas v. Stanglin (1989) upheld a city ordinance restricting admission to certain dance halls to persons between the ages of 14 and 18. Although the Court acknowledged that the opportunity of minors to dance with adults, and of adults to dance with minors, "might be described as 'associational' in common parlance," the Court concluded:

We think the activity of these dance-hall patrons—coming together to engage in recreational dancing—is not protected by the First Amendment. Thus this activity qualifies neither as a form of "intimate association" nor as a form of "expressive association" as those terms were described in *Roberts.*

The Court also stated: "[W]e do not think the Constitution recognizes a generalized right of 'social association' that includes chance encounters in dance halls."

———

III.   REGULATION OF THE POLITICAL PROCESS TO PRESERVE ITS INTEGRITY

A.   Money and Politics: Regulation of Contributions and Expenditures

"The First Amendment denies government the power to determine that spending to promote one's political views is wasteful, excessive or unwise."—The COURT

"Congress has not merely treated the two major parties differently from minor parties and independents, but has discriminated in favor of the former in such a way as to run afoul of the Fifth and First Amendments. . . ."— Justice REHNQUIST

BUCKLEY v. VALEO
424 U.S. 1, 96 S.Ct. 612, 46 L.Ed.2d 659 (1976).

As a result of the scandals inherent in the high cost of running for public office and the frequent necessity for candidates to rely on financial contributions from a few large donors, and more particularly as a result of the scandals during Richard Nixon's presidency when he and his aides pressured many businessmen for gifts of money (and in turn were pressured by those donors for special treatment), Congress in 1974 extensively amended the Federal Election Campaign Act:

1.   Limiting to $1,000 contributions by individuals to any candidate for federal office and to $25,000 contributions by any committee;

2.   Forbidding individuals or groups acting independently of a candidate for federal office to spend more than $1,000 to aid that candidate;

3.   Requiring candidates for federal office to report for the public record contributions beyond a certain amount;

4.   Providing for public funding of presidential campaigns;

5.   Establishing a Federal Election Commission to oversee administration of the act's provisions.

A wide array of political figures, including former Senator Eugene McCarthy, a noted liberal, and James Buckley, then a conservative senator from New York, quickly filed suit in a federal district court, attacking the constitutionality of various provisions. In an unusual procedure, the district judge "certified" the questions to the Court of Appeals for the Second Circuit. That tribunal upheld the statute, and the challengers appealed to the Supreme Court.

PER CURIAM. . . .

A.   General Principles

The Act's contribution and expenditure limitations operate in an area of the most fundamental First Amendment activities. Discussion of public issues and debate on the qualifications of candidates are integral to the operation of the system of government established by our Constitution. The First Amendment affords the broadest protection to such political expression. ...

The First Amendment protects political association as well as political expression. The constitutional right of association explicated in NAACP v. Alabama (1958) stemmed from the Court's recognition that "[e]ffective advocacy of both public and private points of view, particularly controversial ones, is undeniably enhanced by group association." Subsequent decisions have made clear that the First and Fourteenth Amendments guarantee " 'freedom to associate with others for the common advancement of political beliefs and ideas,' " a freedom that encompasses " '[t]he right to associate with the political party of one's choice.' " Kusper v. Pontikes (1973). ...

Appellees contend that what the Act regulates is conduct, and that its effect on speech and association is incidental at most. Appellants respond that contributions and expenditures are at the very core of political speech, and that the Act's limitations thus constitute restraints on First Amendment liberty that are both gross and direct. ...

The expenditure of money simply cannot be equated with such conduct as destruction of a draft card. Some forms of communication made possible by the giving and spending of money involve speech alone, some involve conduct primarily, and some involve a combination of the two. Yet this Court has never suggested that the dependence of a communication on the expenditure of money operates itself to introduce a nonspeech element or to reduce the exacting scrutiny required by the First Amendment. ...

... [T]he governmental interests advanced in support of the Act involve "suppressing communication." The interests served by the Act include restricting the voices of people and interest groups who have money to spend and reducing the overall scope of federal election campaigns. Although the Act does not focus on the ideas ... it is aimed in part at equalizing the relative ability of all voters to affect electoral outcomes by placing a ceiling on expenditures for political expression by citizens and groups. ... [I]t is beyond dispute that the interest in regulating the alleged "conduct" of giving or spending money "arises in some measure because the communication allegedly integral to the conduct is itself thought to be harmful." O'Brien.

Nor can the Act's contribution and expenditure limitations be sustained, as some of the parties suggest, by reference to the constitutional principles reflected [by cases that permit governmental limitations that are reasonable regulations of time, place, and manner of expression]. ... The critical difference between this case and those time, place, and manner cases is that the present Act's contribution and expenditure limitations impose direct quantity restrictions on political communication and association by persons, groups, candidates, and political parties in addition to any reasonable time, place, and manner regulations otherwise imposed.

A restriction on the amount of money a person or group can spend on political communication during a campaign necessarily reduces the quantity of expression by restricting the number of issues discussed, the depth of their exploration, and the size of the audience reached. This is because virtually every means of communicating ideas in today's mass society requires the expenditure of money. ... The expenditure limitations ... represent substantial ... restraints on the quantity and diversity of political speech. The $1,000 ceiling on spending "relative to a clearly identified candidate," ... would appear to exclude all citizens and groups except candidates, political parties, and the institutional press from any significant use of the most effective modes of communication. ...

By contrast ... a limitation upon the amount that any one person or group may contribute to a candidate or political committee entails only a marginal restriction upon the contributor's ability to engage in free communication. A contribution serves as a general expression of support for the candidate and his views, but does not communicate the underlying basis for the support. The quantity of communication by the contributor does not increase perceptibly with the size of the contribution, since the expression rests solely on the undifferentiated symbolic act of contributing. At most, the size of the contribution provides a very rough index of the intensity of the contributor's support for the candidate. A limitation on the amount of money a person may give to a candidate or campaign organization thus involves little direct restraint on his political communication. ... While contributions may result in political expression if spent by a candidate or an association to present views to the voters, the transformation of contributions into political debate involves speech by someone other than the contributor. ...

The Act's contribution and expenditure limitations also impinge on protected associational freedoms. Making a contribution, like joining a political party, serves to affiliate a person with a candidate. In addition, it enables like-minded persons to pool their resources. ... The Act's contribution ceilings thus limit one important means of associating ... but leave the contributor free to become a member of any political association and to assist personally in the association's efforts on behalf of candidates. And the Act's contribution limitations permit associations and candidates to aggregate large sums of money to promote effective advocacy. By contrast, the Act's $1,000 limitation on independent expenditures "relative to a clearly identified candidate" precludes most associations from effectively amplifying the voice of their adherents, the original basis for the recognition of First Amendment protection of the freedom of association. ...

In sum, although the Act's contribution and expenditure limitations both implicate fundamental First Amendment interests, its expenditure ceilings impose significantly more severe restrictions on protected freedoms of political expression and association than do its limitations on financial contributions. ...

[In the next 123 pages of its opinion, the Court took up the Act's provisions one by one and applied the "exacting scrutiny test" (sometimes called "strict scrutiny") to each that touched on the First Amendment, that is, dropped the usual presumption of constitutionality and placed the burden of proof on the government to show that the regulation was aimed at securing a "compelling" governmental interest and was narrowly tailored to attain that goal. The Court held:

[1. The limit of $1,000 on individual contributions met the compelling governmental interest of avoiding the reality and appearance of corruption and focused precisely (was "narrowly tailored") on a means necessary to achieve that objective.

[2. The governmental interest of avoiding the reality and appearance of corruption was insufficient to justify the restriction on individual expression imposed by the limitation on what independent citizens could spend in a campaign.

[3. Limitations on what candidates for federal office could spend from their own and their families' private funds also failed the test. The real justification for these limits, "equalizing the relative financial resources of candidates" was "wholly foreign" to the First Amendment.

[4. The limits on the total amounts that candidates for federal office could spend was similarly flawed.

[5. Requiring candidates to keep records of contributors, contributions, and expenditures "directly serve[s] substantial governmental interests" and was a specific means of preventing corruption. Some appellant claimed that revealing contributors names might expose them to the sort of pressures against which NAACP v. Alabama (1958; reprinted above, p. 798) had protected. The Court found none of the appellants were so threatened but expressed a willingness to examine any such claim that might arise: "The evidence proffered need only show a reasonable probability that the compelled disclosure of a party's contributors' names will subject them to threats, harassment, or reprisals from either Government officials or private parties."

[6. The plan for financing of presidential campaigns, even though it used different procedures to subsidize the two established parties and minor or new parties, did not discriminate against the latter. (The Democrats and the Republicans would each receive a multi-million dollar subsidy at the close of their national conventions, whereas new and minor parties would be reimbursed after the election according to the percentage of the vote they polled.)

[Chief Justice Burger and Justices White, Marshall, Blackmun, and Rehnquist concurred in part and dissented in part, with enough joining different sections of the Per Curiam opinion that it became the opinion of the Court. Rehnquist was disturbed by difference between how the Act would fund the established parties and new or minor parties:

I would hold that, as to general election financing, Congress has not merely treated the two major parties differently from minor parties and independents, but has discriminated in favor of the former in such a way as to run afoul of the Fifth and First Amendments to the Constitution.]

Editors' Notes

(1) *Buckley* also held unconstitutional the way in which members of Federal Election Commission were appointed. See the discussion in Bowsher v. Synar (1986; reprinted above, p. 499).

(2) **Query:** As it did in several other opinions we have read, the Court applied the so-called "exacting scrutiny" (or "strict scrutiny") test here. What does that test, in any of its incarnations, say about WHAT is "the Constitution" to be interpreted? About its purposes? Structure? About WHO shall interpret? In general is this test more congruent with democratic theory or constitutionalism?

(3) **Query:** The Court stated that it is "wholly foreign" to the First Amendment for the government to "equaliz[e] the relative ability of individuals and groups to influence the outcome of elections." Is this claim persuasive? Is doing so "wholly foreign" to the constitutional text as a whole? Is it wholly foreign to the First Amendment and the Equal Protection Clause to limit the spending of wealthy citizens in an effort to secure equal participation or an equally effective voice in the political process for all citizens? Reynolds v. Sims (1964; reprinted above, p. 777) stated that the Equal Protection Clause guarantees "equal participation by all voters in the election of state legislators" and that "each and every citizen has an inalienable right to full and effective participation in the political processes of his State's legislative bodies," adding that the right requires that "each citizen have an equally effective voice in the election of members of his state legislature." Assuming that the equal protection component of the Fifth Amendment applies the same principles against the federal government, is it possible to reconcile *Buckley* with *Reynolds*?

(4) **Query:** Would government's equalizing the relative capacities of individual citizens to influence public policy offend democratic theory? Constitutionalism? If the answer to either is no, how then did the Court find the First Amendment outlawed such efforts? If the answer is yes, was the Court not utilizing (without warning and perhaps without being aware) a *philosophic approach*? To what extent did *Buckley* present a clash between two different views of democracy, namely between interest group pluralism in which the political arena functions much as an economic market does for competing buyers and sellers and, on the other hand, a civic republican vision in which there is a public interest that all participants should be seeking?

(5) John Rawls has argued (*Political Liberalism* [New York: Columbia University Press, 1993], p. 362):

If the Court means what it says in *Wesberry* and *Reynolds*, *Buckley* must sooner or later give way. The First Amendment no more enjoins a system of representation according to influence effectively exerted in free political rivalry between unequals than the Fourteenth Amendment enjoins a system of liberty of contract and free competition between unequals in the economy, as the Court thought in the *Lochner* era.

For a similar argument that *Buckley* is an "heir" to *Lochner*, see Cass R. Sunstein, *"Lochner's* Legacy," 87 *Colum.L.Rev.* 873, 874–75 (1987); and his *The Partial Constitution* (Cambridge: Harvard University Press, 1993). See also Mark V. Tushnet, "An Essay on Rights," 62 *Tex.L.Rev.* 1363, 1387 (1984) ("The first amendment has replaced the due process clause as the primary guarantor of the privileged.").

(6) *Buckley* denied minor parties a blanket exemption from disclosing names of contributors but hinted at a sympathetic hearing if there arose a claim of harassment because of such disclosure. Brown v. Socialist Workers Party (1982) fulfilled that promise by holding unconstitutional Ohio's requirement of disclosure of contributors, as applied to the Socialist Workers Party (a small group devoted to "the abolition of capitalism," and the target of dozens of burglaries by the FBI during the 1960s). For a five-judge majority, Marshall wrote: "In Buckley v. Valeo (1976), this Court held that the First Amendment prohibits the government from compelling disclosures by a minor party that can show a 'reasonable probability' that the compelled disclosures will subject those identified to 'threats, harassment, or reprisals.' "

(7) FEC v. Nat'l Conservative PAC (1985) invalidated § 9012(f) of the 1974 Act as a violation of the First Amendment. That section forbade political action committees to spend more than $1,000 to assist a presidential candidate who had accepted federal campaign subsidies. Speaking for five members of the Court, Rehnquist relied heavily on *Buckley:* "[A]llowing the presentation of views while forbidding the expenditure of more than $1,000 to present them [in a presidential campaign] is much like allowing a speaker in a public hall to express his views while denying him use of an amplifying system." Stevens concurred in part and dissented in part. White commented: "The First Amendment protects the right to speak, not the right to spend"; and he, along with Brennan and Marshall, thought governmental interests in preventing corruption justified whatever intrusion the section made on freedom of communication.

(8) For commentaries on *Buckley,* see: Marlene A. Nicholson, "Buckley v. Valeo," 1977 *Wis.L.Rev.* 323 (1976); Daniel D. Polsby, "Buckley v. Valeo: The Special Nature of Political Speech," 1976 *Sup.Ct.Rev.* 1; Laurence H. Tribe, *American Constitutional Law* (2d ed.; Mineola, NY: Foundation Press, 1988), pp. 1132–53; J. Skelly Wright, "Politics and the Constitution: Is Money Speech?" 85 *Yale L.J.* 1001 (1976), and Wright, "Money and the Pollution of Politics: Is the First Amendment an Obstacle to Political Equality?" 82 *Colum.L.Rev.* 609 (1982). See also Frank J. Sorauf, *Inside Campaign Finance: Myths and Realities* (New Haven: Yale University Press, 1992); J. L. Balkin, "Some Realism About Pluralism: Legal Realist Approaches to the First Amendment," 1990 *Duke L.J.* 375; and Lillian R. BeVier, "Money and Politics: A Perspective on the First Amendment and Campaign Finance Reform," 73 *Calif.L.Rev.* 1045 (1985).

"[T]he First Amendment goes beyond protection of the press and the self-expression of individuals to prohibit government from limiting the stock of information from which members of the public may draw."—Justice POWELL

"This is not only a policy which a State may adopt consistent with the First Amendment but one which protects the very freedoms that this Court has held to be guaranteed by the First Amendment."—Justice WHITE

FIRST NATIONAL BANK OF BOSTON v. BELLOTTI
435 U.S. 765, 98 S.Ct. 1407, 55 L.Ed.2d 707 (1978).

Chapter 55, § 8 of the Massachusetts General Laws forbade certain kinds of corporations, including banks, trusts, insurance companies, and public power firms, to contribute to candidates for public office or to campaigns for or against public referenda. In 1976, two banks and three other corporations covered by § 8 announced they were going to spend money to publicize their opposition to a proposal for a graduated income tax, scheduled for a referendum that year. The state attorney general warned he would proceed against the corporations under § 8 if they carried out their plan. They then sued in a state court to have the statute declared unconstitutional as a violation of the First Amendment. Eventually, the Supreme Judicial Court of Massachusetts sustained § 8, and the corporations appealed to the U.S. Supreme Court.

Mr. Justice **POWELL** delivered the opinion of the Court. . . .

III . . .

A

The speech proposed by appellants is at the heart of the First Amendment's protection. . . . In appellants' view, the enactment of a graduated personal income tax, as proposed to be authorized by constitutional amendment, would have a seriously adverse effect on the economy of the State. The importance of the referendum issue to the people and government of Massachusetts is not disputed. Its merits, however, are the subject of sharp disagreement.

As the Court said in Mills v. Alabama (1966), "there is practically universal agreement that a major purpose of [the First] Amendment was to protect the free discussion of governmental affairs." If the speakers here were not corporations, no one would suggest that the State could silence their proposed speech. It is the type of speech indispensable to decisionmaking in a democracy, and this is no less true because the speech comes from a corporation rather than an individual. The inherent worth of the speech in terms of its capacity for informing the public does not depend upon the identity of its source, whether corporation, association, union, or individual. . . .

... The question in this case, simply put, is whether the corporate identity of the speaker deprives this proposed speech of what otherwise would be its clear entitlement to protection. We turn now to that question.

B

The court below ... concluded that a corporation's First Amendment rights must derive from its property rights under the Fourteenth. This is an artificial mode of analysis, untenable under decisions of this Court. ... Freedom of speech and the other freedoms encompassed by the First Amendment always have been viewed as fundamental components of the liberty safeguarded by the Due Process Clause, see Gitlow v. New York (1925); NAACP v. Alabama (1958); Stromberg v. California (1931); DeJonge v. Oregon (1937); [Charles] Warren, The New "Liberty" Under the Fourteenth Amendment, 39 *Harv.L.Rev.* 431 (1926), and the Court has not identified a separate source for the right when it has been asserted by corporations. ...

The press cases emphasize the special and constitutionally recognized role of that institution in informing and educating the public, offering criticism, and providing a forum for discussion and debate. *Mills.* But the press does not have a monopoly on either the First Amendment or the ability to enlighten. Cf. Buckley v. Valeo [1976]; Red Lion Broadcasting Co. v. FCC (1969); New York Times v. Sullivan (1964); AP v. United States (1945). Similarly, the Court's decisions involving corporations in the business of communication or entertainment are based not only on the role of the First Amendment in fostering individual self-expression but also on its role in affording the public access to discussion, debate, and the dissemination of information and ideas.[1] See *Red Lion;* Stanley v. Georgia (1969); Time v. Hill (1967). Even decisions seemingly based exclusively on the individual's right to express himself acknowledge that the expression may contribute to society's edification. Winters v. New York (1948).

Nor do our recent commercial speech cases lend support to appellee's business interest theory. They illustrate that the First Amendment goes beyond protection of the press and the self-expression of individuals to prohibit government from limiting the stock of information from which members of the public may draw. A commercial advertisement is constitutionally protected not so much because it pertains to the seller's business as because it furthers the societal interest in the "free flow of commercial information." Va. State Bd. of Pharmacy v. Va. Citizens Consumer Council (1976); see Linmark Asso's v. Willingboro [1977]. ...

---

1. The suggestion in Mr. Justice White's dissent that the First Amendment affords less protection to ideas that are not the product of "individual choice" would seem to apply to newspaper editorials and every other form of speech created under the auspices of a corporate body. No decision of this Court lends support to such a restrictive notion. [Footnote by the Court.]

In the realm of protected speech, the legislature is constitutionally disqualified from dictating the subjects about which persons may speak and the speakers who may address a public issue. Police Dept. of Chicago v. Mosley (1972). If a legislature may direct business corporations to "stick to business," it also may limit other corporations— religious, charitable, or civic—to their respective "business" when addressing the public. Such power in government to channel the expression of views is unacceptable under the First Amendment. ...

IV

The constitutionality of § 8's prohibition of the "exposition of ideas" by corporations turns on whether it can survive the exacting scrutiny necessitated by a state-imposed restriction of freedom of speech. Especially where, as here, a prohibition is directed at speech itself, and the speech is intimately related to the process of governing, "the State may prevail only upon showing a subordinating interest which is compelling," Bates v. Little Rock (1960), "and the burden is on the government to show the existence of such an interest." Elrod v. Burns (1976). Even then, the State must employ means "closely drawn to avoid unnecessary abridgment. ..." *Buckley*. ...

A

Preserving the integrity of the electoral process, preventing corruption, and "sustain[ing] the active, alert responsibility of the individual citizen in a democracy for the wise conduct of government" are interests of the highest importance. *Buckley*; United States v. Automobile Workers (1957); Burroughs v. United States (1934). Preservation of the individual citizen's confidence in government is equally important. *Buckley;* CSC v. Letter Carriers (1973).

Appellee advances a number of arguments in support of his view that these interests are endangered by corporate participation in discussion of a referendum issue. They hinge upon the assumption that such participation would exert an undue influence on the outcome of a referendum vote, and—in the end—destroy the confidence of the people in the democratic process and the integrity of government. According to appellee, corporations are wealthy and powerful and their views may drown out other points of view. If appellee's arguments were supported by record or legislative findings that corporate advocacy threatened imminently to undermine democratic processes ... these arguments would merit our consideration. Cf. *Red Lion*. But there has been no showing that the relative voice of corporations has been overwhelming or even significant in influencing referenda in Massachusetts, or that there has been any threat to the confidence of the citizenry in government. ...

... To be sure, corporate advertising may influence the outcome of the vote; this would be its purpose. But the fact that advocacy may persuade the electorate is hardly a reason to suppress it: The Constitution "protects expression which is eloquent no less than that which is unconvincing." Kingsley Int'l Pictures Corp. v. Regents [1959]. ... Moreover, the people in our democracy are entrusted with the responsibility for judging and evaluating the relative merits of conflicting arguments. They may consider, in making their judgment, the source and credibility of the advocate. But if there be any danger that the people cannot evaluate the information and arguments advanced by appellants, it is a danger contemplated by the Framers of the First Amendment. ...

B

Finally, appellee argues that § 8 protects corporate shareholders, an interest that is both legitimate and traditionally within the province of state law. The statute is said to serve this interest by preventing the use of corporate resources in furtherance of views with which some shareholders may disagree. This purpose is belied, however, by the provisions of the statute, which are both underinclusive and overinclusive.

The underinclusiveness of the statute is self-evident. Corporate expenditures with respect to a referendum are prohibited, while corporate activity with respect to the passage or defeat of legislation is permitted. ... Nor does § 8 prohibit a corporation from expressing its views, by the expenditure of corporate funds, on any public issue until it becomes the subject of a referendum, though the displeasure of disapproving shareholders is unlikely to be any less. ... Nor is the fact that § 8 is limited to banks and business corporations without relevance. Excluded from its provisions and criminal sanctions are entities or organized groups in which numbers of persons may hold an interest or membership, and which often have resources comparable to those of large corporations. Minorities in such groups or entities may have interests with respect to institutional speech quite comparable to those of minority shareholders in a corporation. ...

The overinclusiveness of the statute is demonstrated by the fact that § 8 would prohibit a corporation from supporting or opposing a referendum proposal even if its shareholders unanimously authorized the contribution or expenditure. ...

[*Reversed.*]

Mr. Chief Justice **BURGER** concurring. ...

Mr. Justice **WHITE,** with whom Mr. Justice **BRENNAN** and Mr. Justice **MARSHALL** join, dissenting. ...

... The Court's fundamental error is its failure to realize that the state regulatory interests in terms of which the alleged curtailment of First Amendment rights accomplished by the statute must be evaluated are themselves derived from the First Amendment. ...

I

There is now little doubt that corporate communications come within the scope of the First Amendment. This, however, is merely the starting point of analysis, because an examination of the First Amendment values that corporate expression furthers and the threat to the functioning of a free society it is capable of posing reveals that it is not fungible with communications emanating from individuals and is subject to restrictions which individual expression is not. Indeed, what some have considered to be the principal function of the First Amendment, the use of communication as a means of self-expression, self-realization, and self-fulfillment, is not at all furthered by corporate speech. It is clear that the communications of profitmaking corporations are not "an integral part of the development of ideas, of mental exploration and of the affirmation of self." They do not represent a manifestation of individual freedom or choice. Undoubtedly, as this Court has recognized, see NAACP v. Button (1963), there are some corporations formed for the express purpose of advancing certain ideological causes shared by all their members or, as in the case of the press, of disseminating information and ideas. Under such circumstances, association in a corporate form may be viewed as merely a means of achieving effective self-expression. But this is hardly the case generally with corporations operated for the purpose of making profits. Shareholders in such entities do not share a common set of political or social views, and they certainly have not invested their money for the purpose of advancing political or social causes or in an enterprise engaged in the business of disseminating news and opinion. In fact ... the government has a strong interest in assuring that investment decisions are not predicated upon agreement or disagreement with the activities of corporations in the political arena.

... [T]here is no basis whatsoever for concluding that these views are expressive of the heterogeneous beliefs of their shareholders whose convictions on many political issues are undoubtedly shaped by considerations other than a desire to endorse any electoral or ideological cause which would tend to increase the value of a particular corporate investment. This is particularly true where, as in this case ... [the managers] have not been able to demonstrate that the issue involved has any material connection with the corporate business. ...

The self-expression of the communicator is not the only value encompassed by the First Amendment. One of its functions ... is to protect the interchange of ideas. Any communication of ideas, and consequently any expenditure of funds which makes the communication of ideas possible, it can be argued, furthers the purposes of the First Amendment. This proposition does not establish, however, that the right of the general public to receive communications financed by means of corporate expenditures is of the same dimension as that to hear other forms of expression. In the first place ... corporate expenditures designed to further political causes lack the connection with individual self-expression. ... Ideas which are not a product of individual choice are entitled to less First Amendment protection. Secondly, the restriction of corporate speech concerned with political matters impinges much less severely upon the availability of ideas to the general public than do restrictions upon individual speech. Even the complete curtailment of corporate communications concerning political or ideological questions not integral to day-to-day business functions would leave individuals, including corporate shareholders, employees, and customers, free to communicate their thoughts. ...

I recognize that there may be certain communications undertaken by corporations which could not be restricted without impinging seriously upon the right to receive information. ... None of these considerations, however, are implicated by a prohibition upon corporate expenditures relating to referenda concerning questions of general public concern having no connection with corporate business affairs.

It bears emphasis here that the Massachusetts statute forbids the expenditure of corporate funds in connection with referenda but in no way forbids the board of directors of a corporation from formulating and making public what it represents as the views of the corporation even though the subject addressed has no material effect whatsoever on the business of the corporation. These views could be publicized at the individual expense of the officers, directors, stockholders, or anyone else interested in circulating the corporate view on matters irrelevant to its business.

The governmental interest in regulating corporate political communications ... also raises considerations which differ significantly from those governing the regulation of individual speech. Corporations are artificial entities created by law for the purpose of furthering certain economic goals. In order to facilitate the achievement of such ends, special rules relating to such matters as limited liability, perpetual life, and the accumulation, distribution, and taxation of assets are normally applied to them. States have provided corporations with such attributes in order to increase their economic viability and thus strengthen the economy generally. It has long been recognized, however, that the special status of corporations has placed them in a position to control vast amounts of economic power which may, if not regulated, dominate not only the economy but also the very heart of our democracy, the electoral process. ... [T]he interest of Massachusetts and the many other States which have restricted corporate political activity is ... preventing institutions which have been permitted to amass wealth as a result of special advantages extended by the State for certain economic purposes from using that wealth to acquire an unfair advantage in the political process. ... The State need not permit its own creation to consume it. ...

This Nation has for many years recognized the need for measures designed to prevent corporate domination of the political process. The Corrupt Practices Act, first enacted in 1907, has consistently barred

corporate contributions in connection with federal elections. This Court
has repeatedly recognized that one of the principal purposes of this
prohibition is "to avoid the deleterious influences on federal elections
resulting from the use of money by those who exercise control over large
aggregations of capital." *Automobile Workers.* See Pipefitters v. United
States (1972); United States v. CIO [1948]. Although this Court has
never adjudicated the constitutionality of the Act, there is no suggestion
in its cases construing it, that this purpose is in any sense illegitimate or
deserving of other than the utmost respect. ...

II

There is an additional overriding interest related to the prevention
of corporate domination ...: assuring that shareholders are not compelled to support and financially further beliefs with which they disagree
where, as is the case here, the issue involved does not materially affect
the business, property, or other affairs of the corporation. The State has
not interfered with the prerogatives of corporate management to communicate about matters that have material impact on the business
affairs entrusted to them. ... In short, corporate management may not
use corporate monies to promote what does not further corporate affairs
but what in the last analysis are the purely personal views of the
management, individually or as a group.

This is not only a policy which a State may adopt consistent with the
First Amendment but one which protects the very freedoms that this
Court has held to be guaranteed by the First Amendment. In Bd. of Ed.
v. Barnette (1943), the Court struck down a West Virginia statute which
compelled children enrolled in public school to salute the flag and pledge
allegiance to it on the ground that the First Amendment prohibits public
authorities from requiring an individual to express support for or agreement with a cause with which he disagrees or concerning which he
prefers to remain silent. ... Last Term, in Abood v. Detroit Bd. of Ed.
(1977), we confronted these constitutional questions and held that a
State may not, even indirectly, require an individual to contribute to the
support of an ideological cause he may oppose as a condition of employment. ...

... The interest which the State wishes to protect here is identical
to that which the Court has previously held to be protected by the First
Amendment: the right to adhere to one's own beliefs and to refuse to
support the dissemination of the personal and political views of others,
regardless of how large a majority they may compose. ...

Mr. Justice **REHNQUIST**, dissenting.

This Court decided at an early date, with neither argument nor
discussion, that a business corporation is a "person" entitled to the
protection of the Equal Protection Clause of the Fourteenth Amendment. Santa Clara County v. So. Pac. R. Co. (1886). Likewise, it soon
became accepted that the property of a corporation was protected under

the Due Process Clause of that same Amendment. See, e.g., Smyth v. Ames (1898). Nevertheless, we concluded soon thereafter that the liberty protected by that Amendment "is the liberty of natural, not artificial persons." Northwestern Nat. Life Ins. Co. v. Riggs (1906). Before today, our only considered and explicit departures from that holding have been that a corporation engaged in the business of publishing or broadcasting enjoys the same liberty of the press as is enjoyed by natural persons, Grosjean v. American Press Co. (1936), and that a nonprofit membership corporation organized for the purpose of "achieving . . . equality of treatment by all government, federal, state and local, for the members of the Negro community" enjoys certain liberties of political expression. NAACP v. Button (1963). . . .

. . . The appellants herein either were created by the Commonwealth or were admitted into the Commonwealth only for the limited purposes described in their charters and regulated by state law. Since it cannot be disputed that the mere creation of a corporation does not invest it with all the liberties enjoyed by natural persons, United States v. White (1944) (corporations do not enjoy the privilege against self-incrimination), our inquiry must seek to determine which constitutional protections are "incidental to its very existence." . . .

. . . A State grants to a business corporation the blessings of potentially perpetual life and limited liability to enhance its efficiency as an economic entity. It might reasonably be concluded that those properties, so beneficial in the economic sphere, pose special dangers in the political sphere. . . . I can see no basis for concluding that the liberty of a corporation to engage in political activity with regard to matters having no material effect on its business is necessarily incidental to the purposes for which the Commonwealth permitted these corporations to be organized or admitted within its boundaries. . . .

. . . The free flow of information is in no way diminished by the Commonwealth's decision to permit the operation of business corporations with limited rights of political expression. All natural persons, who owe their existence to a higher sovereign than the Commonwealth, remain as free as before to engage in political activity. Cf. Maher v. Roe (1977). . . .

Editors' Notes

(1) **Query**: How much help does a *textualist approach* to constitutional interpretation offer here? A *purposive approach*? A *structural approach*? To what extent did any of the opinions follow these and/or other approaches?

(2) **Query**: The opinions here claim the First Amendment's protection of freedom of communication has three objectives: (i) The public's right to hear or receive information so it can make wise political choices (Powell, White, and Rehnquist); (ii) individual "self-expression, self-realization, and self-fulfillment" (White); and, (iii) implicit in all three opinions, the personal right to influence the political processes (perhaps "self-government" rather than "self-realiza-

tion" or self-fulfillment).   Which of these pertain to democratic theory, which to constitutionalism?

(3) **Query**: To what extent can it be said that each of these opinions used the approach called *reinforcing representative democracy*?

(4) **Query:** Was Justice White correct that the majority's "fundamental error is its failure to realize that the state regulatory interests ... are themselves derived from the First Amendment," in particular, from the value of promoting free political discussion by preventing corporate domination? What sort of showing would have been necessary to persuade Justice Powell and the majority that corporations through expressing their views were indeed "drown[ing] out other points of view"? Does *Bellotti* signal a return to the era of Lochner v. New York (1905; reprinted below, p. 1110)? Consider again the Editors' Notes to *Buckley* asking whether that decision is also part of *"Lochner's* Legacy."

(5) For analyses of *Bellotti* and corporate speech, *see:* Charles R. O'Kelley, "The Constitutional Rights of Corporations Revisited," 67 *Geo.L.J.* 1347 (1979); Thomas R. Kiley, "PACing the Burger Court: The Corporate Right to Speak and the Public Right to Hear after First National Bank of Boston v. Bellotti," 22 *Ariz.L.Rev.* 427 (1980); Comment, "The Corporation and the Constitution," 90 *Yale L.J.* 1883 (1981); Victor Brudney, "Business Corporations and Stockholders' Rights Under the First Amendment," 91 *Yale L.J.* 235 (1981); Daniel H. Lowenstein, "Campaign Spending and Ballot Propositions: Recent Experience, Public Choice Theory and the First Amendment," 29 *UCLA L.Rev.* 505 (1982); Mark V. Tushnet, "Corporations and Free Speech," in *The Politics of Law* (David Kairys ed.; New York: Pantheon Books, 1982).

"[W]e must ascertain whether [Michigan's restriction on corporate political expenditures] burdens the exercise of political speech and, if it does, whether it is narrowly tailored to serve a compelling state interest."—Justice MARSHALL.

"I doubt that those who framed and adopted the First Amendment would agree.   ..."—Justice SCALIA.

"The State cannot demonstrate that a compelling interest supports its speech restriction, nor can it show that its law is narrowly tailored to the purported statutory end."—Justice KENNEDY

AUSTIN v. MICHIGAN STATE CHAMBER OF COMMERCE
494 U.S. 652, 110 S.Ct. 1391, 108 L.Ed.2d 652 (1990).

Section 54(1) of the Michigan Campaign Finance Act prohibits corporations from using corporate treasury funds for independent expenditures in support of, or in opposition to, any candidate in elections for state office. Corporations are permitted, however, to make such expenditures from segregated funds used solely for political purposes. Section 54(1) was modeled on a provision of the Federal Election Campaign Act of 1971, as amended, that requires corporations and labor unions to use segregated funds to finance independent expenditures made in federal elections.

The Michigan State Chamber of Commerce (the Chamber), a non-profit state corporation, comprises more than 8,000 members, three-quarters of whom are for-profit corporations. The Chamber's general treasury is funded through annual dues required of all members. In June 1985, when Michigan scheduled a special election to fill a vacancy in the state House of Representatives, the Chamber tried to use not its separate political fund but its general funds to buy an advertisement supporting a specific candidate. The Chamber also brought suit in federal district court for injunctive relief against enforcement of the Act, arguing that the restriction on expenditures violated the First and the Fourteenth Amendments. The trial court upheld the statute, but the court of appeals reversed. The state appealed to the U.S. Supreme Court. We reprint only those portions of the opinions dealing with interpretation of the First Amendment.

Justice **MARSHALL** delivered the opinion of the Court.

. . . Although we agree that expressive rights are implicated in this case, we hold that application of § 54(1) to the Chamber is constitutional because the provision is narrowly tailored to serve a compelling state interest. Accordingly, we reverse the judgment of the Court of Appeals. . . .

II

. . . [W]e must ascertain whether [Michigan's restriction on corporate political expenditures] burdens the exercise of political speech and, if it does, whether it is narrowly tailored to serve a compelling state interest. Buckley v. Valeo (1976). Certainly, the use of funds to support a political candidate is "speech"; independent campaign expenditures constitute "political expression 'at the core of our electoral process and of the First Amendment freedoms.'" Id. The mere fact that the Chamber is a corporation does not remove its speech from the ambit of the First Amendment. See, e.g., First Nat'l Bank of Boston v. Bellotti (1978).

A

This Court concluded in FEC v. Mass. Citizens for Life, Inc. (1986) (MCFL), that a federal statute requiring corporations to make independent political expenditures only through special segregated funds burdens corporate freedom of expression. The Court reasoned that the small nonprofit corporation in that case would face certain organizational and financial hurdles in establishing and administering a segregated political fund. . . . These hurdles "impose[d] administrative costs that many small entities [might] be unable to bear" and "create[d] a disincentive for such organizations to engage in political speech."

Despite the Chamber's success in administering its separate political fund, Michigan's segregated fund requirement still burdens the Chamber's exercise of expression because "the corporation is not free to use its general funds for campaign advocacy purposes." *MCFL.* The Act imposes requirements similar to those in the federal statute involved in *MCFL:* a segregated fund must have a treasurer; and its administrators must keep detailed accounts of contributions, and file with state officials a statement of organization. In addition, a nonprofit corporation like the Chamber may solicit contributions to its political fund only from members, stockholders of members, officers or directors of members, and the spouses of any of these persons. Although these requirements do not stifle corporate speech entirely, they do burden expressive activity. Thus they must be justified by a compelling state interest.

B

The State contends that the unique legal and economic characteristics of corporations necessitate some regulation of their political expenditures to avoid corruption or the appearance of corruption. See FEC v. Nat'l Conservative PAC (1985) (*NCPAC*). State law grants corporations special advantages—such as limited liability, perpetual life, and favorable treatment of the accumulation and distribution of assets—that enhance their ability to attract capital and to deploy their resources in ways that maximize the return on their shareholders' investments. These state-created advantages not only allow corporations to play a dominant role in the Nation's economy, but also permit them to use "resources amassed in the economic marketplace" to obtain "an unfair advantage in the political marketplace." *MCFL.* As the Court explained in *MCFL,* the political advantage of corporations is unfair because

> [t]he resources in the treasury of a business corporation . . . are not an indication of popular support for the corporation's political ideas. They reflect instead the economically motivated decisions of investors and customers. The availability of these resources may make a corporation a formidable political presence, even though the power of the corporation may be no reflection of the power of its ideas.

We therefore have recognized that "the compelling governmental interest in preventing corruption support[s] the restriction of the influence of political war chests funneled through the corporate form." *NCPAC;* see also *MCFL.*

. . . [T]his Court has . . . recognized that a legislature might demonstrate a danger of real or apparent corruption posed by such expenditures when made by corporations to influence candidate elections, *Bellotti.* . . . Michigan's regulation aims at a different type of corruption in the political arena: the corrosive and distorting effects of immense aggregations of wealth that are accumulated with the help of the corporate form and that have little or no correlation to the public's support for the corporation's political ideas. The Act does not attempt "to equalize the relative influence of speakers on elections"; rather, it ensures that expenditures reflect actual public support for the political ideas espoused by corporations. . . . Corporate wealth can unfairly influence elections when it is deployed in the form of independent expenditures, just as it can when it assumes the guise of political contributions. We therefore hold that the State has articulated a sufficiently compelling rationale to support its restriction on independent expenditures by corporations.

C

We next turn to the question whether the Act is sufficiently narrowly tailored. ... We find that the Act is precisely targeted to eliminate the distortion caused by corporate spending while also allowing corporations to express their political views. Contrary to the dissents' critical assumptions, the Act does not impose an absolute ban on all forms of corporate political spending but permits corporations to make independent political expenditures through separate segregated funds. Because persons contributing to such funds understand that their money will be used solely for political purposes, the speech generated accurately reflects contributors' support for the corporation's political views. See *MCFL.*

III

The Chamber contends that even if the Act is constitutional with respect to for-profit corporations, it nonetheless cannot be applied to a nonprofit ideological corporation like a chamber of commerce. In *MCFL,* we held that the nonprofit organization there had "features more akin to voluntary political associations than business firms, and therefore should not have to bear burdens on independent spending solely because of [its] incorporated status." In reaching that conclusion, we enumerated three characteristics of the corporation that were "essential" to our holding. Because the Chamber does not share these crucial features, the Constitution does not require that it be exempted from the generally applicable provisions of § 54(1).

The first characteristic of Mass. Citizens for Life, Inc., that distinguished it from ordinary business corporations was that the organization "was formed for the express purpose of promoting political ideas, and cannot engage in business activities." MCFL's narrow political focus thus "ensure[d] that [its] political resources reflect[ed] political support." In contrast, the Chamber's bylaws set forth more varied purposes, several of which are not inherently political. ... Unlike MCFL's, the Chamber's educational activities are not expressly tied to political goals; many of its seminars, conventions, and publications are politically neutral and focus on business and economic issues. ...

We described the second feature of MCFL as the absence of "shareholders or other persons affiliated so as to have a claim on its assets or earnings. This ensures that persons connected with the organization will have no economic disincentive for disassociating with it if they disagree with its political activity." Although the Chamber also lacks shareholders, many of its members may be similarly reluctant to withdraw as members even if they disagree with the Chamber's political expression, because they wish to benefit from the Chamber's nonpolitical programs and to establish contacts with other members of the business community. The Chamber's political agenda is sufficiently distinct from its educational and outreach programs that members who disagree with the former may continue to pay dues to participate in the latter. ... Thus, we are persuaded that the Chamber's members are more similar to shareholders of a business corporation than to the members of MCFL in this respect.[1]

The final characteristic upon which we relied in *MCFL* was the organization's independence from the influence of business corporations. On this score, the Chamber differs most greatly. ... MCFL was not established by, and had a policy of not accepting contributions from, business corporations. Thus it could not "serv[e] as [a] condui[t] for the type of direct spending that creates a threat to the political market-place." *MCFL*. In striking contrast, more than three-quarters of the Chamber's members are business corporations, whose political contributions and expenditures can constitutionally be regulated by the State. As we read the Act, a corporation's payments into the Chamber's general treasury would not be considered payments to influence an election, so they would not be "contributions" or "expenditures," and would not be subject to the Act's limitations. Business corporations therefore could circumvent the Act's restriction by funneling money through the Chamber's general treasury. Because the Chamber accepts money from for-profit corporations, it could, absent application of § 54(1), serve as a conduit for corporate political spending. ...

IV

The Chamber also attacks § 54(1) as underinclusive because it does not regulate the independent expenditures of unincorporated labor unions. Whereas unincorporated unions, and indeed individuals, may be able to amass large treasuries, they do so without the significant state-conferred advantages of the corporate structure. ... Moreover, labor unions differ from corporations in that union members who disagree with a union's political activities need not give up full membership in the organization to avoid supporting its political activities. ... As a result, the funds available for a union's political activities more accurately reflect members' support for the organization's political views than does a corporation's general treasury. Michigan's decision to exclude unincorporated labor unions from the scope of § 54(1) is therefore justified by the crucial differences between unions and corporations. ...

[Reversed.]

---

1. A requirement that the Chamber disclose the nature and extent of its political activities (Kennedy, J., dissenting) would not eliminate the possible distortion of the political process inherent in independent expenditures from general corporate funds. Given the significant incentive for members to continue their financial support for the Chamber in spite of their disagreement with its political agenda, disclosure will not ensure that the funds in the Chamber's treasury correspond to members' support for its ideas. [Footnote by the Court.]

Justice **BRENNAN**, concurring.

... As one of the "Orwellian" "censor[s]" derided by the dissents, and as the author of our recent decision in *MCFL*, I write separately to explain my views in this case.

The Michigan law ... is not an across-the-board prohibition on political participation by corporations or even a complete ban on corporate political expenditures. Rather, the statute merely requires those corporations wishing to make independent expenditures in support of candidates to do so through segregated funds or political action committees (PAC's) rather than directly from their corporate treasuries. ... [T]he dissents significantly overstate their case in several important respects and ... the Court's decision today is faithful to our prior opinions ... particularly *MCFL*. ...

The PAC requirement may be unconstitutional as applied to some corporations because they do not present the dangers at which expenditure limitations are aimed. Indeed, we determined that Massachusetts Citizens for Life ... fell into this category.[1] ...

... Justice Kennedy, by repeatedly using the qualifier "nonprofit" ... appears to concede that the Michigan law legitimately may be applied to for-profit business corporations, or at least that the Court's rationale might "suffice to justify restricting political speech by for-profit corporations." If that is so, Justice Kennedy's failure to sustain the statute as applied in this case is perplexing, because the Chamber, unlike other nonprofits such as MCFL, is clearly a conduit for corporations barred from making independent expenditures directly.[2] ...

Justice **STEVENS**, concurring. ...

Justice **SCALIA**, dissenting.

"Attention all citizens. To assure the fairness of elections by preventing disproportionate expression of the views of any single powerful group, your Government has decided that the following associations

---

1. Justice Kennedy is mistaken when he suggests that by upholding the as-applied challenge in *MCFL* and rejecting it here, we are embarking on "value-laden, content-based speech suppression that permits some non-profit corporate groups but not others to engage in political speech." ... Whether an organization presents the threat at which the campaign finance laws are aimed has to do with the particular characteristics of the organization at issue and not with the content of its speech. Of course, if a correlation between the two factors could be shown to exist, a group would be free to mount a First Amendment challenge on that basis. Cf. *Buckley*. Neither respondent nor Justice Kennedy's dissent has provided any reason to believe that such a relationship exists here. [Footnote by Justice Brennan.]

2. According to Justice Kennedy's dissent, the majority holds that "it is now a felony in Michigan for the Sierra Club, or the American Civil Liberties Union" to make independent expenditures. This characterization is inaccurate. Not only are those groups not part of the proceeding before us, but the dissent has overlooked the central lesson of *MCFL* that the First Amendment may require exemptions, on an as-applied basis, from expenditure restrictions. If a nonprofit corporation is formed with the express purpose of promoting political ideas, is not composed of members who face an economic incentive for disassociating with it, and does not accept contributions from business corporations or labor unions, then it would be governed by our *MCFL* holding. [Footnote by Justice Brennan.]

of persons shall be prohibited from speaking or writing in support of any candidate: _____." In permitting Michigan to make private corporations the first object of this Orwellian announcement, the Court today endorses the principle that too much speech is an evil that the democratic majority can proscribe. I dissent because that principle is contrary to our case law and incompatible with the absolutely central truth of the First Amendment: that government cannot be trusted to assure, through censorship, the "fairness" of political debate.

The Court's opinion says that political speech of corporations can be regulated because "[s]tate law grants [them] special advantages," and because this "unique state-conferred corporate structure ... facilitates the amassing of large treasuries." This analysis seeks to create one good argument by combining two bad ones. Those individuals who form that type of voluntary association known as a corporation are, to be sure, given special advantages. ... But so are other associations and private individuals ... , ranging from tax breaks to contract awards to public employment to outright cash subsidies. It is rudimentary that the State cannot exact as the price of those special advantages the forfeiture of First Amendment rights. See Pickering v. Bd. of Ed. (1968). The categorical suspension of the right of any person, or of any association of persons, to speak out on political matters must be justified by a compelling state need. See *Buckley*. That is why the Court puts forward its second bad argument, the fact that corporations "amas[s] large treasuries." But that alone is also not sufficient justification for the suppression of political speech, unless one thinks it would be lawful to prohibit men and women whose net worth is above a certain figure from endorsing political candidates. Neither of these two flawed arguments is improved by combining them. ...

... We held in *Buckley* ... that independent expenditures to express the political views of individuals and associations do not raise a sufficient threat of corruption to justify prohibition. Neither the Court's opinion nor either of the concurrences makes any effort to distinguish that case—except, perhaps, by misdescribing the case as involving "federal laws regulating individual donors" [rather than corporations]. ... *Buckley* should not be overruled, because it is entirely correct. The contention that prohibiting overt advocacy for or against a political candidate satisfies a "compelling need" to avoid "corruption" is easily dismissed. [*Buckley*.]

The Court does not try to defend the proposition that independent advocacy poses a substantial risk of political "corruption". ... Rather, it asserts that that concept (which it defines as " 'financial quid pro quo' corruption") is really just a narrow subspecies of a hitherto unrecognized genus of political corruption. "Michigan's regulation," we are told, "aims at a different type of corruption in the political arena: the corrosive and distorting effects of immense aggregations of wealth that are accumulated with the help of the corporate form and that have little or no correlation to the public's support for the corporations's political ideas." Under this mode of analysis, virtually anything the Court deems politically undesirable can be turned into political corruption—by simply describing its effects as politically "corrosive," which is close enough to "corruptive" to qualify. It is sad to think that the First Amendment will ultimately be brought down not by brute force but by poetic metaphor.

The Court's opinion ultimately rests upon that proposition whose violation constitutes the "New Corruption": expenditures must "reflect actual public support for the political ideas espoused." This illiberal free-speech principle of "one man, one minute" was proposed and soundly rejected in *Buckley:* "... the concept that government may restrict the speech of some elements of our society in order to enhance the relative voice of others is wholly foreign to the First Amendment. ..." ...

I would not do justice to the significance of today's decision to discuss only its lapses from case precedent and logic. Infinitely more important ... is its departure from long-accepted premises of our political system regarding the benevolence that can be expected of government in managing the arena of public debate, and the danger that is to be anticipated from powerful private institutions that compete with government, and with one another, within that arena.

Perhaps the Michigan law before us here has an unqualifiedly noble objective—to "equalize" the political debate by preventing disproportionate expression of corporations' points of view. But governmental abridgement of liberty is always undertaken with the very best of announced objectives (dictators promise to bring order, not tyranny), and often with the very best of genuinely intended objectives (zealous policemen conduct unlawful searches in order to put dangerous felons behind bars). The premise of our Bill of Rights, however, is that there are some things—even some seemingly desirable things—that government cannot be trusted to do. The very first of these is establishing the restrictions upon speech that will assure "fair" political debate. The incumbent politician who says he welcomes full and fair debate is no more to be believed than the entrenched monopolist who says he welcomes full and fair competition. ... The fundamental approach of the First Amendment, I had always thought, was to assume the worst, and to rule the regulation of political speech "for fairness' sake" simply out of bounds.

I doubt that those who framed and adopted the First Amendment would agree that avoiding the New Corruption, that is, calibrating political speech to the degree of public opinion that supports it, is even a *desirable* objective, much less one that is important enough to qualify as a compelling state interest. Those Founders designed, of course, a system in which popular ideas would ultimately prevail; but also, through the First Amendment, a system in which true ideas could readily become popular. For the latter purpose, the calibration that the Court today endorses is precisely backwards: To the extent a valid proposition has scant public support, it should have wider rather than narrower circulation. I am confident, in other words, that Jefferson and Madison would not have sat at these controls; but if they did they would have turned them in the opposite direction.

Ah, but then there is the special element of corporate wealth: What would the Founders have thought of that? They would have endorsed, I think what Tocqueville wrote in 1835:

> "When the members of an aristocratic community adopt a new opinion ... they give it a station ... upon the lofty platform where they stand; and opinions and sentiments so conspicuous to the eyes of the multitude are easily introduced into the hearts and minds of all around. In the democratic countries the governing power alone is naturally in a condition to act in this manner; but it is easy to see that its action is always inadequate, and often dangerous. ... No sooner does a government attempt to go beyond its political sphere and to enter upon this new track than it exercises, even unintentionally, an insupportable tyranny. ... Worse still will be the case if the government really believes itself interested in preventing all circulation of ideas. ... Governments, therefore, should not be the only active powers; associations ought, in democratic nations, to stand in lieu of those powerful private individuals whom the equality of condition has swept away." 2 A. de Tocqueville. *Democracy in America* 109 (P. Bradley ed. 1948). ...

Despite all the talk about "corruption and the appearance of corruption" ... it is entirely obvious that the object of the law we have approved today is not to prevent wrongdoing but to prevent speech. Since those private associations known as corporations have so much money, they will speak so much more, and their views will be given inordinate prominence in election campaigns. This is not an argument that our democratic traditions allow. ... The premise of our system is that there is no such thing as too much speech—that the people are not foolish but intelligent, and will separate the wheat from the chaff. ...

Justice **KENNEDY**, with whom Justice **O'CONNOR** and Justice **SCALIA** join, dissenting.

The majority opinion validates not one censorship of speech but two. One is Michigan's content-based law which decrees it a crime for a nonprofit corporate speaker to endorse or oppose candidates for Michigan public office. ... The other censorship scheme ... is of our own creation. It is value-laden, content-based speech suppression that permits some nonprofit corporate groups, but not others, to engage in political speech. After failing to disguise its animosity and distrust for the particular kind of political speech here at issue ... the Court adopts a rule that allows Michigan to stifle the voices of some of the most respected groups in public life on subjects central to the integrity of our democratic system. Each of these schemes is repugnant to the First Amendment and contradicts its central guarantee, the freedom to speak in the electoral process. ...

The State has conceded that among those communications prohibited by its statute are the publication by a nonprofit corporation of its own assessment of a candidate's voting record. With the imprimatur of this Court, it is now a felony in Michigan for the Sierra Club, or the American Civil Liberties Union, or the Michigan Chamber of Commerce, to advise the public how a candidate voted on issues of urgent concern to its members. In both practice and theory, the prohibition aims at the heart of political debate. ...

First, the Act prohibits corporations from speaking on ... the subject of candidate elections. It is a basic precept that the State may not confine speech to certain subjects. Content-based restrictions are the essence of censorial power. *Bellotti.* ... Second, the Act discriminates on the basis of the speaker's identity. Under the Michigan law, any person or group other than a corporation may engage in political debate over candidate elections; but corporations, even nonprofit corporations that have unique views of vital importance to the electorate, must remain mute. Our precedents condemn this censorship. See *Bellotti;* Police Dept. of Chicago v. Mosley (1972); Carey v. Brown (1980). ...

By using distinctions based upon both the speech and the speaker, the Act engages in the rawest form of censorship: the State censors what a particular segment of the political community might say with regard to candidates who stand for election. ... The Act does not meet our standards for laws that burden fundamental rights. The State cannot demonstrate that a compelling interest supports its speech restriction, nor can it show that its law is narrowly tailored to the purported statutory end. See *Bellotti.* ...

Our cases acknowledge the danger that corruption poses for the electoral process, but draw a line in permissible regulation between payments to candidates ("contributions") and payments or expenditures to express one's own views ("independent expenditures"). Today's decision abandons this distinction and threatens once-protected political speech. The Michigan statute prohibits independent expenditures by a nonprofit corporate speaker to express its own views about candidate qualifications. Independent expenditures are entitled to greater protection than campaign contributions. *MCFL.* See also *Buckley.* ...

The majority almost admits that ... the danger of a political quid pro quo is insufficient to justify a restriction of this kind. Since the specter of corruption ... is missing ... the majority invents a new interest: combating the "corrosive and distorting effects of immense aggregations of wealth" accumulated in corporate form. ... The majority styles this novel interest as simply a different kind of corruption, but has no support for its assertion. While it is questionable whether such imprecision would suffice to justify restricting political speech by for-profit corporations, it is certain that it does not apply to nonprofit entities. ...

In *Buckley* and *Bellotti,* ... we rejected the argument that the expenditure of money to increase the quantity of political speech somehow fosters corruption. The key to the majority's reasoning appears to be that because some corporate speakers are well supported and can buy press space or broadcast time to express their ideas, government may ban all corporate speech to ensure that it will not dominate political debate. The argument is flawed in at least two respects. First, the statute is overinclusive because it covers all groups which use the corporate form, including all nonprofit corporations. Second, it assumes that the government has a legitimate interest in equalizing the relative influence of speakers. ... An argument similar to that made by the majority was rejected in *Bellotti.* ...

The Court purports to distinguish *MCFL* on the ground that the nonprofit corporation permitted to speak in that case received no funds from profit-making corporations. It is undisputed that the Chamber is itself a nonprofit corporation. The crucial difference, it is said, is that the Chamber receives corporate contributions. But this distinction rests on the fallacy that the source of the speaker's funds is somehow relevant to the speaker's right of expression or society's interest in hearing what the speaker has to say. ... The more narrow alternative of recordkeeping and funding disclosure is available. See *MCFL.* A wooden rule prohibiting independent expenditures by nonprofit corporations that receive funds from business corporations invites discriminatory distinctions. The principled approach is to acknowledge that where political speech is concerned, freedom to speak extends to all nonprofit corporations, not the special favorites of a majority of this Court.

... To create second-class speakers that can be stifled on the subject of candidate qualifications is to silence some of the most significant participants in the American public dialogue, as evidenced by the amici briefs filed on behalf of the Chamber of Commerce by the American Civil Liberties Union, the Center for Public Interest Law, the American Medical Association, the National Association of Realtors, the American Insurance Association, the National Organization for Women, Greenpeace Action, the National Abortion Rights Action League, the National Right to Work Committee, the Planned Parenthood Federation of America, the Fund for the Feminist Majority, the Washington Legal Foundation, and the Allied Educational Foundation. ...

Editors' Notes

(1) **Query:** "[T]he use of funds to support a political candidate," Marshall said for the Court, "is 'speech'". ... None of the justices challenged this equation, but can a *textualist approach* equate "speech" with using money? A *philosophic approach*? Any other approach?

(2) **Query:** To what extent did Marshall's opinion argue—or assume—the Court has a special obligation to assure the integrity of the political process? In short, was Marshall following an approach of *reinforcing representative democracy*? What about the opinions of Scalia and Kennedy? To what extent did the controversy here center on a question of WHO? Which

institution, if any, can constitutionally diagnose and correct distortions in the political process? And WHO makes that determination of "which institution"?

(3) **Query:** To what extent did all of the opinions use a *doctrinal approach*? Were Scalia and Kennedy correct in suggesting that *Austin* undermined *Buckley* and *Bellotti*?

(4) **Query:** Scalia and Kennedy joined the majority in Rust v. Sullivan (1991; reprinted above, p. 749) to sustain the so-called "gag-rule." How could they reconcile their opposition here and in *R.A.V.* (1992; reprinted above, p. 686) to "content-based" bans on speech?

(5) **Query:** Scalia wrote: "I doubt that those who framed and adopted the First Amendment would agree that avoiding the New Corruption ... is even a desirable objective, much less one that is important enough to qualify as a compelling state interest." He cited no historical evidence to support his doubts, beyond offering a long quotation from Alexis de Tocqueville, *Democracy in America*, II, 109 (P. Bradley ed. 1948), and saying that he thought the Founders would have agreed, though again without citing any evidence to support his belief about endorsement. Why would anyone *assume* that the Founders would have agreed with what a very perceptive French aristocrat wrote a half century after ratification? Why would anyone *assume* that he or she knew how the Founders would have responded to phenomena, such as large, rich corporations, about which they knew very little? What sort of evidence would Scalia need to support his "originalism"? Indeed, to what extent was Scalia using an *originalist approach* and to what extent was he using a *purposive approach*?

(6) **Query:** Kennedy emphasized the importance of group identity and association in American character and democracy. Yet in Adarand Constructors v. Pena (1995; discussed below, p. 970), involving affirmative action, he joined O'Connor's opinion of the court, in which she stressed that "the Constitution" protects persons not groups. How can Kennedy's two positions be reconciled?

B. Regulation of Campaign Promises and Access to the Ballot

"It remains to determine the standards by which we might distinguish between those 'private arrangements' that are inconsistent with democratic government, and those candidate assurances that promote the representative foundation of our political system."

BROWN v. HARTLAGE
456 U.S. 45, 102 S.Ct. 1523, 71 L.Ed.2d 732 (1982).

Sec. 121.055 of the Revised Statutes of Kentucky reads:

No candidate for nomination or election to any state, county, city or district office shall expend, pay, promise, loan or become pecuniarily

liable in any way for money or other thing of value, either directly or
indirectly, to any person in consideration of the vote or financial or
moral support of that person.

In Sparks v. Boggs (1960) the Kentucky Court of Appeals interpreted
§ 121.055 to outlaw a pledge made by a candidate to serve in office at a
reduced salary. In 1979, Carl Brown, a candidate for county commissioner,
attacked the "outrageous salaries" paid to commissioners and promised that
if elected he would reduce the commissioners' compensation. Upon learning
of Sparks, Brown withdrew his pledge to reduce salaries. He won the election
anyway, but his opponent, Earl Hartlage, filed suit in a state court, asking the
judge to void the election because Brown had engaged in a corrupt practice in
violation of § 121.055.

Hartlage lost in the trial court; but the court of appeals reversed on the
basis of Sparks, and Kentucky's supreme court refused to hear the case.
Brown then sought and obtained certiorari from the U.S. Supreme Court.

Justice **BRENNAN** delivered the opinion of the Court. ...

II

... Just as a State may take steps to ensure that its governing
political institutions and officials properly discharge public responsibilities and maintain public trust and confidence, a State has a legitimate
interest in upholding the integrity of the electoral process itself. But
when a State seeks to uphold that interest by restricting speech, the
limitations on state authority imposed by the First Amendment are
manifestly implicated.

At the core of the First Amendment are certain basic conceptions
about the manner in which political discussion in a representative
democracy should proceed. As we noted in Mills v. Alabama (1966):

> Whatever differences may exist about interpretations of the First
> Amendment, there is practically universal agreement that a major
> purpose of that Amendment was to protect the free discussion of
> governmental affairs. This of course includes discussions of candidates,
> structures and forms of government, the manner in which government
> is operated or should be operated, and all such matters relating to
> political processes.

The free exchange of ideas provides special vitality to the process
traditionally at the heart of American constitutional democracy—the
political campaign. "[I]f it be conceded that the First Amendment was
'fashioned to assure the unfettered interchange of ideas for the bringing
about of political and social changes desired by the people,' then it can
hardly be doubted that the constitutional guarantee has its fullest and
most urgent application precisely to the conduct of campaigns for political office." Monitor Patriot Co. v. Roy (1971). The political candidate
does not lose the protection of the First Amendment when he declares
himself for public office. Quite to the contrary. ...

When a State seeks to restrict directly the offer of ideas by a
candidate to the voters, the First Amendment surely requires that the

restriction be demonstrably supported not only by a legitimate state interest, but a compelling one, and that the restriction operate without unnecessarily circumscribing protected expression.

III

On its face, § 121.055 prohibits a candidate from offering material benefits to voters in consideration for their votes, and, conversely, prohibits candidates from accepting payments in consideration for the manner in which they serve their public function. Sparks v. Boggs (1960) placed a not entirely obvious gloss on that provision with respect to candidate utterances concerning the salaries of the office for which they were running, by barring the candidate from promising to reduce his salary when that salary was already "fixed by law." We thus consider the constitutionality of § 121.055 with respect to the proscription evident on the face of the statute, and in light of the more particularized concerns suggested by the *Sparks* gloss. We discern three bases upon which the application of the statute to Brown's promise might conceivably be justified: first, as a prohibition on buying votes; second, as facilitating the candidacy of persons lacking independent wealth; and third, as an application of the State's interests and prerogatives with respect to factual misstatements.

A

The first sentence of § 121.055 prohibits a political candidate from giving, or promising to give, anything of value to a voter in exchange for his vote or support. In many of its possible applications, this provision would appear to present little constitutional difficulty. ... No body politic worthy of being called a democracy entrusts the selection of leaders to a process of auction or barter. ... The fact that such an agreement necessarily takes the form of words does not confer upon it, or upon the underlying conduct, the constitutional immunities that the First Amendment extends to speech. ... See Hoffman Estates v. Flipside (1982); Central Hudson Gas & Elec. v. Pub. Service Comm'n (1980); Pittsburgh Press Co. v. Human Relations Comm'n (1973).

... [I]t is equally plain that there are constitutional limits on the State's power to prohibit candidates from making promises in the course of an election campaign. Some promises are universally acknowledged as legitimate, indeed "indispensable to decision-making in a democracy," First National Bank of Boston v. Bellotti (1978); and the "maintenance of the opportunity for free political discussion to the end that government may be responsive to the will of the people and that changes may be obtained by lawful means ... is a fundamental principle of our constitutional system." Stromberg v. California (1931). Candidate commitments enhance the accountability of government officials to the people whom they represent, and assist the voters in predicting the effect of their vote. The fact that some voters may find their self-interest reflected in a candidate's commitment does not place that commitment beyond the reach of the First Amendment. We have never insisted that the franchise be exercised without taint of individual benefit; indeed, our tradition of political pluralism is partly predicated on the expectation that voters will pursue their individual good through the political process, and that the summation of these individual pursuits will further the collective welfare. So long as the hoped-for personal benefit is to be achieved through the normal processes of government, and not through some private arrangement, it has always been, and remains, a reputable basis upon which to cast one's ballot.

It remains to determine the standards by which we might distinguish between those "private arrangements" that are inconsistent with democratic government, and those candidate assurances that promote the representative foundation of our political system. ...

It is clear that the statements of petitioner Brown in the course of the August 15 press conference were very different in character from the corrupting agreements and solicitations historically recognized as unprotected by the First Amendment. Notably, Brown's commitment to serve at a reduced salary was made openly, subject to the comment and criticism of his political opponent and to the scrutiny of the voters. We think the fact that the statement was made in full view of the electorate offers a strong indication that the statement contained nothing fundamentally at odds with our shared political ethic.

... [T]here is no *constitutional* basis upon which Brown's pledge to reduce his salary might be equated with a candidate's promise to pay voters for their support from his own pocketbook. ... Brown did not offer the voters a payment from his personal funds. ... At least to outward appearances, the commitment was fully in accord with our basic understanding of legitimate activity by a government body. Before any implicit monetary benefit to the individual taxpayer might have been realized, public officials—among them, of course, Brown himself—would have had to approve that benefit in accordance with the good faith exercise of their public duties. ...

In addition ... it is impossible to discern in Brown's generalized commitment any invitation to enter into an agreement that might place the statement outside the realm of unequivocal protection that the Constitution affords to political speech. Not only was the source of the promised benefit the public fisc, but that benefit was to extend beyond those voters who cast their ballots for Brown, to all taxpayers and citizens. ...

In sum, Brown did not offer some private payment or donation in exchange for voter support. ... Like a promise to lower taxes, to increase efficiency in government, or indeed to increase taxes in order to provide some group with a desired public benefit or public service, Brown's promise to reduce his salary cannot be deemed beyond the reach of the First Amendment, or considered as inviting the kind of corrupt arrangement the appearance of which a State may have a compelling interest in avoiding. See Buckley v. Valeo [1976]. ... [A] candidate's promise to confer some ultimate benefit on the voter, qua taxpayer, citizen, or member of the general public, does not lie beyond the pale of First Amendment protection.

B

Sparks relied in part on the interest a State may have in ensuring that the willingness of some persons to serve in public office without remuneration does not make gratuitous service the sine qua non of plausible candidacy. The State might legitimately fear that such emphasis on free public service might result in persons of independent wealth but less ability being chosen over those who, though better qualified, could not afford to serve at a reduced salary. But if § 121.055 was designed to further this interest, it chooses a means unacceptable under the First Amendment. In barring certain public statements with respect to this issue, the State ban runs directly contrary to the fundamental premises underlying the First Amendment as the guardian of our democracy. That Amendment embodies our trust in the free exchange of ideas as the means by which the people are to choose between good ideas and bad, and between candidates for political office. The State's fear that voters might make an ill-advised choice does not provide the State with a compelling justification for limiting speech. It is simply not the function of government to "select which issues are worth discussing or debating," Police Department of Chicago v. Mosley (1972), in the course of a political campaign. ...

[*Reversed.*]

The Chief Justice [**BURGER**] concurs in the judgment.

Justice **REHNQUIST**, concurring in the result. ...

Editors' Notes

(1) **Query:** Brennan began to discuss "the standards by which we might distinguish between those 'private arrangements' that are inconsistent with democratic government, and those candidate assurances that promote the representative foundation of our political system." What are those standards? Cf. Madison in *Federalist* No. 10, reprinted below, p. 1087.

(2) **Query:** Why would inconsistency with principles of democratic government raise a constitutional question? Brennan observed that "the States have a legitimate interest in preserving the integrity of their electoral processes." Do courts have a special constitutional obligation to assure the integrity of the political processes?

(3) **Query:** If voting is a constitutional right of the individual citizen, why can he or she not sell his or her vote or exchange it for something else of value? In what *constitutionally* significant way does selling one's vote differ from voting for a candidate whom a voter knows will reward him or her with public office or some other benefit, such as a tax reduction for people in a particular income bracket or welfare payments for others?

(4) Notice that the U.S. Supreme Court takes § 121.055 as it has been interpreted by the courts of Kentucky. The Supreme Court could not, as it did

for a federal statute in *Yates* (1957; reprinted above, p. 666), interpret a state statute so as to avoid constitutional questions.

"Only after weighing all these factors is the reviewing court in a position to decide whether the challenged provision is unconstitutional."—Justice STEVENS

"[I]n cases like this ... we have never required that States meet some kind of "narrowly tailored" standard in order to pass constitutional muster. "—Justice REHNQUIST

ANDERSON v. CELEBREZZE

460 U.S. 780, 103 S.Ct. 1564, 75 L.Ed.2d 547 (1983).

Ohio required independent candidates for the presidency to file a statement and nominating petition signed by 5,000 qualified voters 75 days before the primary election (229 days before the general election). In 1980, John Anderson did not file the necessary papers until May, two months after the deadline but some weeks before the state primary elections and well before the national nominating conventions were to meet. Ohio officials denied him a place on the ballot, and he filed suit in federal district court. The judge ordered the state to place Anderson's name on the ballot, but the Court of Appeals for the Sixth Circuit reversed. Noting that the courts of appeals for the First and Fourth Circuits had sustained orders against enforcement of similar laws in Maine and Maryland, the Supreme Court granted certiorari.

Justice **STEVENS** delivered the opinion of the Court. ...

I

... "[T]he rights of voters and the rights of candidates do not lend themselves to neat separation; laws that affect candidates always have at least some theoretical, correlative effect on voters." Bullock v. Carter (1972). Our primary concern is with the tendency of ballot access restrictions "to limit the field of candidates from which voters might choose." Therefore, "[i]n approaching candidate restrictions, it is essential to examine in a realistic light the extent and nature of their impact on voters."

The impact of candidate eligibility requirements on voters implicates basic constitutional rights. Writing for a unanimous Court in NAACP v. Alabama (1958), Justice Harlan stated that it "is beyond debate that freedom to engage in association for the advancement of beliefs and ideas is an inseparable aspect of the 'liberty' assured by the Due Process Clause of the Fourteenth Amendment, which embraces freedom of speech." In our first review of Ohio's electoral scheme, Williams v. Rhodes (1968), this Court explained the interwoven strands of "liberty" affected by ballot access restrictions:

[T]he state laws place burdens on two different, although overlapping, kinds of rights—the right of individuals to associate for the advancement of political beliefs, and the right of qualified voters, regardless of their political persuasion, to cast their votes effectively. Both of these rights, of course, rank among our most precious freedoms.

As we have repeatedly recognized, voters can assert their preferences only through candidates or parties or both. ... The right to vote is "heavily burdened" if that vote may be cast only for major-party candidates at a time when other parties or other candidates are "clamoring for a place on the ballot." *Williams.* The exclusion of candidates also burdens voters' freedom of association, because an election campaign is an effective platform for the expression of views on the issues of the day, and a candidate serves as a rallying-point for like-minded citizens.

Although these rights of voters are fundamental, not all restrictions imposed by the States on candidates' eligibility for the ballot impose constitutionally-suspect burdens on voters' rights to associate or to choose among candidates. We have recognized that, "as a practical matter, there must be a substantial regulation of elections if they are to be fair and honest and if some sort of order, rather than chaos, is to accompany the democratic processes." Storer v. Brown (1974). To achieve these necessary objectives, States have enacted comprehensive and sometimes complex election codes. ... [T]he state's important regulatory interests are generally sufficient to justify reasonable, nondiscriminatory restrictions.

Constitutional challenges to specific provisions of a State's election laws therefore cannot be resolved by any "litmus-paper test" that will separate valid from invalid restrictions. *Storer.* Instead, a court must resolve such a challenge by an analytical process that parallels its work in ordinary litigation. It must first consider the character and magnitude of the asserted injury to the rights protected by the First and Fourteenth Amendments. ... It then must identify and evaluate the precise interests put forward by the State as justifications for the burden imposed by its rule. In passing judgment, the Court must not only determine the legitimacy and strength of each of those interests; it also must consider the extent to which those interests make it necessary to burden the plaintiff's rights. Only after weighing all these factors is the reviewing court in a position to decide whether the challenged provision is unconstitutional. ...

II

An early filing deadline may have a substantial impact on independent-minded voters. In election campaigns, particularly those which are national in scope, the candidates and the issues simply do not remain static over time. ... Such developments will certainly affect the strategies of candidates who have already entered the race; they may also create opportunities for new candidacies. Yet Ohio's filing deadline prevents persons who wish to be independent candidates from entering the significant political arena established in the State by a Presidential election campaign—and creating new political coalitions of Ohio voters—at any time after mid-to-late March. At this point developments in campaigns for the major-party nominations have only begun, and the major parties will not adopt their nominees and platforms for another five months. ...

[The statute] also burdens the signature-gathering efforts of independents who decide to run in time to meet the deadline. When the primary campaigns are far in the future and the election itself is even more remote, the obstacles facing an independent candidate's organizing efforts are compounded. ...

... [I]t is especially difficult for the State to justify a restriction that limits political participation by an identifiable political group whose members share a particular viewpoint, associational preference, or economic status. "Our ballot access cases ... focus on the degree to which the challenged restrictions operate as a mechanism to exclude certain classes of candidates from the electoral process. The inquiry is whether the challenged restriction unfairly or unnecessarily burdens 'the availability of political opportunity.'" Clements v. Fashing (1982) (plurality opinion), quoting Lubin v. Panish (1974).[1]

A burden that falls unequally on new or small political parties or on independent candidates impinges, by its very nature, on associational choices protected by the First Amendment. It discriminates against those candidates and—of particular importance—against those voters whose political preferences lie outside the existing political parties. By limiting the opportunities of independent-minded voters to associate in the electoral arena to enhance their political effectiveness as a group, such restrictions threaten to reduce diversity and competition in the marketplace of ideas. In short, the primary values protected by the First Amendment—"a profound national commitment to the principle that debate on public issues should be uninhibited, robust, and wide-open," New York Times v. Sullivan (1964)—are served when election campaigns are not monopolized by the existing political parties.

Furthermore, in the context of a Presidential election, state-imposed restrictions implicate a uniquely important national interest. For the President and the Vice President of the United States are the only elected officials who represent all the voters in the Nation. Moreover, the impact of the votes cast in each State is affected by the votes cast for the various candidates in other States. Thus in a Presidential election a State's enforcement of more stringent ballot access requirements, including filing deadlines, has an impact beyond its own borders. Similarly, the State has a less important interest in regulating Presidential elec-

---

1. In addition, because the interests of minor parties and independent candidates are not well represented in state legislatures, the risk that the First Amendment rights of those groups will be ignored in legislative decisionmaking may warrant more careful judicial scrutiny. [S]ee generally United States v. Carolene Products (1938); J. Ely, *Democracy and Distrust: A Theory of Judicial Review* 73–88 (1980). [Footnote by the Court.]

tions than statewide or local elections, because the outcome of the former will be largely determined by voters beyond the State's boundaries. ...

III

The State identifies three separate interests that it seeks to further by its early filing deadline for independent Presidential candidates. ...

Voter Education

There can be no question about the legitimacy of the State's interest in fostering informed and educated expressions of the popular will in a general election. Moreover, the Court of Appeals correctly identified that interest as one of the concerns that motivated the Framers' decision not to provide for direct popular election of the President. We are persuaded, however, that the State's important and legitimate interest in voter education does not justify the specific restriction on participation in a Presidential election that is at issue in this case.

The passage of time since the Constitutional Convention in 1787 has brought about two changes that are relevant to the reasonableness of Ohio's statutory requirement that independents formally declare their candidacy at least seven months in advance of a general election. First ... today even trivial details about national candidates are instantaneously communicated nationwide in both verbal and visual form. Second ... today the vast majority of the electorate not only is literate but is informed on a day-to-day basis about events and issues that affect election choices. ... [I]t is somewhat unrealistic to suggest that it takes more than seven months to inform the electorate about the qualifications of a particular candidate simply because he lacks a partisan label.
...

It is also by no means self-evident that the interest in voter education is served at all by a requirement that independent candidates must declare their candidacy before the end of March. ... As we observed in another First Amendment context, it is often true "that the best means to that end is to open the channels of communication rather than to close them." Virginia Pharmacy Board v. Virginia Consumer Council (1976).

Equal Treatment

We also find no merit in the State's claim that the early filing deadline serves the interest of treating all candidates alike. ... The consequences of failing to meet the statutory deadline are entirely different for party primary participants and independents. The name of the nominees of the Democratic and Republican parties will appear on the Ohio ballot in November even if they did not decide to run until after Ohio's March deadline had passed, but the independent is simply denied a position on the ballot if he waits too long.[2] Thus, under Ohio's scheme, the major parties may include all events preceding their national conventions in the calculus that produces their respective nominees and campaign platforms, but the independent's judgment must be based on a history that ends in March. ...

Political Stability

... The State's brief explains that the State has a substantial interest in protecting the two major political parties from "damaging intraparty feuding." ... Ohio's asserted interest in political stability amounts to a desire to protect existing political parties from competition. ... In *Williams* we squarely held that protecting the Republican and Democratic parties from external competition cannot justify the virtual exclusion of other political aspirants from the political arena. Addressing Ohio's claim that it "may validly promote a two-party system in order to encourage compromise and political stability," we wrote:

> ... There is, of course, no reason why two parties should retain a permanent monopoly on the right to have people vote for or against them. Competition in ideas and governmental policies is at the core of our electoral process and of the First Amendment freedoms. ...

... [*Storer*] recognized the legitimacy of the State's interest in preventing "splintered parties and unrestrained factionalism." But we did not suggest that a political party could invoke the powers of the State to assure monolithic control over its own members and supporters. Political competition that draws resources away from the major parties cannot, for that reason alone, be condemned as "unrestrained factionalism." ... Moreover, we pointed out that the policy "involves no discrimination against independents."

Ohio's challenged restriction is substantially different from the California provisions upheld in *Storer*. ... [T]he early filing deadline does discriminate against independents. And the deadline is neither a "sore loser" provision nor a disaffiliation statute. Furthermore, it is important to recognize that *Storer* upheld the State's interest in avoiding political fragmentation in the context of elections wholly within the boundaries of California. The State's interest in regulating a nation-wide Presidential election is not nearly as strong. ... The Ohio deadline does not serve any state interest in "maintaining the integrity of the various routes to the ballot" for the Presidency, because Ohio's Presidential preference primary does not serve to narrow the field for the general election. ... In addition, the national scope of the competition for delegates at the Presidential nominating conventions assures that "intraparty feuding" will continue until August. ...

Reversed.

---

2. It is true, of course, that Ohio permits "write-in" votes for independents. We have previously noted that this opportunity is not an adequate substitute for having the candidate's name appear on the printed ballot. ... [Citing Lubin v. Panish (1974).] [Footnote by the Court.]

Justice **REHNQUIST**, with whom Justice **WHITE**, Justice **POWELL**, and Justice **O'CONNOR** join, dissenting.

Article II of the Constitution provides that "[e]ach State shall appoint, in such Manner as the Legislature thereof may direct, a Number of Electors" who shall select the President of the United States. This provision, one of few in the Constitution that grants an express plenary power to the States, conveys "the broadest power of determination" and "[i]t recognizes that [in the election of a President] the people act through their representatives in the legislature, and *leaves it to the legislature exclusively to define the method of effecting the object.*" McPherson v. Blacker (1892) (emphasis added). ...

... [T]he Constitution does not require that a State allow any particular Presidential candidate to be on its ballot, and so long as the Ohio ballot access laws are rational and allow nonparty candidates reasonable access to the general election ballot,[1] this Court should not interfere with Ohio's exercise of its Article II, § 1, cl. 2 power. ...

Anderson makes no claim, and thus has offered no evidence to show, that the early filing deadline impeded his "signature-gathering efforts." That alone should be enough to prevent the Court from finding that the deadline has such an impact. A statute "is not to be upset upon hypothetical and unreal possibilities, if it would be good upon the facts as they are." Pullman Co. v. Knott (1914). What information the record does contain on this point leads to a contrary conclusion. The record shows that in 1980 five independent candidates submitted nominating petitions with the necessary 5,000 signatures by the March 20 deadline and thus qualified for the general election ballot in Ohio. ...

... [T]he effect of the Ohio filing deadline is quite easily summarized: it requires that a candidate, who has already decided to run for President, decide by March 20 which route his candidacy will take. ... Anderson ... submitted in a timely fashion his nominating petition for Ohio's Republican Primary. Then, realizing that he had no chance for the Republican nomination, Anderson sought to change the form of this candidacy. The Ohio filing deadline prevented him from making this change. Quite clearly, rather than prohibiting him from seeking the Presidency, the filing deadline only prevented Anderson from having two shots at it in the same election year.

Thus, Ohio's filing deadline does not create a restriction "denying the franchise to citizens." Likewise, Ohio's filing deadline does not create a restriction that makes it "virtually impossible" for new-party candidates or nonparty candidates to qualify for the ballot, such as those

---

1. Anderson would not have been totally excluded from participating in the general election since Ohio allows for "write-in" candidacies. The Court suggests, however, that ... a write-in procedure "is not an adequate substitute for having the candidate's appear on the printed ballot." [Footnote 2, above.] Until today the Court had not squarely so held and in fact in earlier decisions the Court had treated the availability of write-in candidacies as quite relevant. See *Storer*. [Footnote by Justice Rehnquist.]

addressed in *Williams, Bullock,* and *Lubin.* ... [W]e are not without guidance from prior decisions by this Court.

In *Storer,* the Court was faced with a California statute prohibiting an independent candidate from affiliating with a political party for 12 months preceding the primary election. This required a prospective candidate to decide on the form of his candidacy at a date some eight months earlier than Ohio requires. In upholding, in the face of a First Amendment challenge, this disaffiliation statute and a statute preventing candidates who had lost a primary from running as independents, the Court determined that the laws were "expressive of a general state policy aimed at maintaining the integrity of various routes to the ballot," and that the statutes furthered "the State's interest," described by the Court as "compelling," "in the stability of its political system." ... The similarities between the effect of the Ohio filing deadline and the California disaffiliation statute are obvious.

Refusing to own up to the conflict its opinion creates with *Storer,* the Court tries to distinguish it, saying that it "did not suggest that a political party could invoke the powers of the State to assure monolithic control over its own members and supporters." The Court asserts that the Ohio filing deadline is more like the statutory scheme in *Williams,* which were designed to protect " 'two particular parties—the Republicans and the Democrats—and in effect tends to give them a complete monopoly.' " ... But this simply is not the case. The Ohio filing deadline in no way makes it "virtually impossible" ... for new parties or nonparty candidates to secure a position on the general election ballot. ... What the Ohio filing deadline prevents is a candidate such as Anderson from seeking a party nomination and then, finding that he is rejected by the party, bolting from the party to form an independent candidacy. This is precisely the same behavior that California sought to prevent by the disaffiliation statute this Court upheld in *Storer.* ...

The Court further notes that "*Storer* upheld the State's interest in avoiding political fragmentation in the context of elections wholly within the boundaries of California. The State's interest in regulating a nationwide Presidential election is not nearly as strong." ... The Court's characterization of the election simply is incorrect. The Ohio general election in 1980, among other things, was for the appointment of Ohio's representatives to the Electoral College. The Court ... fails to come to grips with this fact. While Ohio may have a lesser interest in who is ultimately selected by the Electoral College, its interest in who is supported by its own Presidential electors must be at least as strong as its interest in electing other representatives. ...

The point the Court misses is that in cases like this and *Storer,* we have never required that States meet some kind of "narrowly tailored" standard in order to pass constitutional muster. In reviewing election laws like Ohio's filing deadline, we have said before that a court's job is to ensure that the State "in no way freezes the status quo, but implicitly recognizes the potential fluidity of American political life." *Jenness v.*

Fortson (1971). If it does not freeze the status quo, then the State's laws will be upheld if they are "tied to a particularized legitimate purpose, and [are] in no sense invidious or arbitrary." Rosario v. Rockefeller (1973). The Court tries to avoid the rules set forth in some of these cases, saying that such rules were "applicable only to party primaries" and that "this case involves restrictions on access to the general election ballot." The fallacy in this reasoning is quite apparent: one cannot restrict access to the primary ballot without also restricting access to the general election ballot. ...

The Ohio filing deadline easily meets the test described above. [T]he interest of the "stability of its political system," *Storer*, ... alone is sufficient to support Ohio ballot access laws. ... But this is not the only interest furthered by Ohio's laws. Ohio maintains that requiring an early declaration of candidacy gives its voters a better opportunity to take a careful look at the candidates and see how they withstand the close scrutiny of a political campaign. ... But the Court finds that "the State's important and legitimate interest in voter education does not justify the specific restriction on participation in a Presidential election that is at issue in this case." ...

I cannot agree with the suggestion that the early deadline reflects a lack of "faith" in the voters. That Ohio wants to give its voters as much time as possible to gather information on the potential candidates would seem to lead to the contrary conclusion. ... Besides, the Court's assertion that it does not take seven months to inform the electorate is difficult to explain in light of the fact that Anderson allowed himself some 19 months to complete this task; and we are all well aware that Anderson's decision to make an early go of it is not atypical. ...

Editors' Notes

(1) As the debate between Stevens and Rehnquist indicates, in earlier cases involving restrictions on access to the ballot neither the Court's doctrinal reasoning nor its general approach to constitutional interpretation had been consistent. See espec. Clements v. Fashing (1982), which sustained a Texas law forbidding state judges and certain other officials to run for the state legislature.

(2) **Query:** In *Anderson,* Stevens prescribed the proper decisional strategy as that of "weighing" the various interests and factors at stake: The Court

> must first consider the character and magnitude of the asserted injury to the rights protected by the First and Fourteenth Amendments. ...
> It must then identify and evaluate the precise interests put forward by the State. ... [T]he Court must not only determine the legitimacy and strength of each of those interests; it must also consider the extent to which those interests make it necessary to burden the plaintiff's rights.

How does this sort of test differ from "strict (or exacting) scrutiny" used in Buckley v. Valeo (1976; reprinted above, p. 828) and other cases in this Chapter? To what degree is Stevens prescribing a *balancing approach*?

Recall O'Connor's claim in Roberts v. Jaycees (1984; reprinted above, p. 818) that "strict scrutiny" is really a form of *balancing*. Did Stevens give more weight to O'Connor's claim? Is *balancing* compatible with *reinforcing representative democracy*?

IV. REGULATION OF THE MASS MEDIA TO IMPROVE THE POLITICAL PROCESS

"A responsible press is an undoubtedly desirable goal, but press responsibility is not mandated by the Constitution. ..."

MIAMI HERALD PUBLISHING CO. v. TORNILLO
418 U.S. 241, 94 S.Ct. 2831, 41 L.Ed.2d 730 (1974).

A Florida statute required a newspaper to print, at no cost, with equal space and in as prominent a position and typeface as the original story or editorial, any response that political candidates may make to the paper's charges concerning his or her official conduct or personal character. In 1972, the *Miami Herald* published two editorials critical of the candidacy of Pat Tornillo, Jr., for the state house of representatives. The *Herald* refused Tornillo's request to print his rebuttal. He then sued in a state court, but the trial judge held the statute violated the First Amendment. Florida's supreme court reversed, reasoning that the right-of-reply statute enhanced rather than abridged the rights to freedom of communication protected by the First Amendment. The *Herald* appealed to the U.S. Supreme Court.

Mr. Chief Justice **BURGER** delivered the opinion of the Court. ...

III ...

B

The appellee and supporting advocates of an enforceable right of access to the press vigorously argue that government has an obligation to ensure that a wide variety of views reach the public. ... It is urged that at the time the First Amendment to the Constitution was enacted in 1791 as part of our Bill of Rights the press was broadly representative of the people it was serving. While many of the newspapers were intensely partisan and narrow in their views, the press collectively presented a broad range of opinions to readers. Entry into publishing was inexpensive; pamphlets and books provided meaningful alternatives to the organized press for the expression of unpopular ideas and often treated events and expressed views not covered by conventional newspapers. A true marketplace of ideas existed in which there was relatively easy access to the channels of communication.

Access advocates submit that although newspapers of the present are superficially similar to those of 1791 the press of today is in reality very different from that known in the early years of our national existence. In the past half century a communications revolution has seen the introduction of radio and television into our lives, the promise of a global community through the use of communications satellites, and the spectre of a "wired" nation by means of an expanding cable television network with two-way capabilities. The printed press, it is said, has not escaped the effects of this revolution. Newspapers have become big business and there are far fewer of them to serve a larger literate population. Chains of newspapers, national newspapers, national wire and news services, and one-newspaper towns, are the dominant features of a press that has become noncompetitive and enormously powerful and influential in its capacity to manipulate popular opinion and change the course of events. Major metropolitan newspapers have collaborated to establish news services national in scope. Such national news organizations provide syndicated "interpretive reporting" as well as syndicated features and commentary, all of which can serve as part of the new school of "advocacy journalism."

The elimination of competing newspapers in most of our large cities, and the concentration of control of media that results from the only newspaper's being owned by the same interests which own a television station and a radio station, are important components of this trend toward concentration of control of outlets to inform the public.

The result of these vast changes has been to place in a few hands the power to inform the American people and shape public opinion. . . . In effect, it is claimed, the public has lost any ability to respond or to contribute in a meaningful way to the debate on issues. The monopoly of the means of communication allows for little or no critical analysis of the media except in professional journals of very limited readership. . . .

Access advocates note that Mr. Justice Douglas a decade ago expressed his deep concern regarding the effects of newspaper monopolies:

> "Where one paper has a monopoly in an area, it seldom presents two sides of an issue. It too often hammers away on one ideological or political line using its monopoly position not to educate people, not to promote debate, but to inculcate in its readers one philosophy, one attitude—and to make money." "The newspapers that give a variety of views and news that is not slanted or contrived are few indeed. And the problem promises to get worse." . . .

IV . . .

. . . A responsible press is an undoubtedly desirable goal, but press responsibility is not mandated by the Constitution and like many other virtues it cannot be legislated.

Appellee's argument that the Florida statute does not amount to a restriction of appellant's right to speak because "the statute in question here has not prevented the *Miami Herald* from saying anything it wished" begs the core question. ... The Florida statute operates as a command in the same sense as a statute or regulation forbidding appellant to publish specified matter. Governmental restraint on publishing need not fall into familiar or traditional patterns to be subject to constitutional limitations on governmental powers. Grosjean v. American Press Co. (1936). The Florida statute exacts a penalty on the basis of the content of a newspaper. The first phase of the penalty resulting from the compelled printing of a reply is exacted in terms of the cost in printing and composing time and materials and in taking up space that could be devoted to other material the newspaper may have preferred to print. ...

Faced with the penalties that would accrue to any newspaper that published news or commentary arguably within the reach of the right-of-access statute, editors might well conclude that the safe course is to avoid controversy. Therefore, under the operation of the Florida statute, political and electoral coverage would be blunted or reduced. Government-enforced right of access inescapably "dampens the vigor and limits the variety of public debate," New York Times v. Sullivan (1964). ...

... [T]he Florida statute [also] fails to clear the barriers of the First Amendment because of its intrusion into the function of editors. A newspaper is more than a passive receptacle or conduit for news, comment, and advertising. The choice of material to go into a newspaper, and the decisions made as to limitations on the size and content of the paper, and treatment of public issues and public officials—whether fair or unfair—constitute the exercise of editorial control and judgment. It has yet to be demonstrated how governmental regulation of this crucial process can be exercised consistent with First Amendment guarantees of a free press as they have evolved to this time. ...

Reversed.

Mr. Justice **BRENNAN,** with whom Mr. Justice **REHNQUIST** joins, concurring. ...

Mr. Justice **WHITE,** concurring.

... According to our accepted jurisprudence, the First Amendment erects a virtually insurmountable barrier between government and the print media so far as government tampering, in advance of publication, with news and editorial content is concerned. New York Times v. United States (1971). A newspaper or magazine is not a public utility subject to "reasonable" governmental regulation in matters affecting the exercise of journalistic judgment as to what shall be printed. Cf. Mills v. Alabama (1966). We have learned, and continue to learn, from what we view as the unhappy experiences of other nations where government has been allowed to meddle in the internal editorial affairs of newspapers. Regardless of how beneficent-sounding the purposes of controlling the press might be, we prefer "the power of reason as applied through public discussion" and remain intensely skeptical about those measures that would allow government to insinuate itself into the editorial rooms of this Nation's press. ...

Editors' Notes

(1) **Query:** How helpful is a *textualist approach* in settling the problems raised here? How much assistance does a *structural approach* offer? A *balancing approach*? What interests could an interpreter intelligently "balance" here? What would be their relative weights in such a process? To what extent was *Miami Herald* congruent with the demands of democratic theory? To what extent did this case provide an example of *reinforcing representative democracy*? How does it foster robust debate to allow the sole newspaper in a community to print only one side of an issue? Does constitutionalism have anything important to add?

(2) **Query:** Red Lion Broadcasting Co. v. Federal Communications Commission (1969) sustained the FCC's "fairness doctrine," which required radio and television stations to allow time for response by people personally attacked in broadcasts or by political candidates whose opponents a station may have endorsed. Conceding the First Amendment was relevant to broadcasting but noting far more people were seeking licenses to broadcast than there were frequencies available, the Court held: "It does not violate the First Amendment to treat licensees given the privilege of using scarce radio frequencies as proxies for the entire community, obligated to give suitable time and attention to matters of great public concern." Thus, the Court upheld a limited right of access to the broadcasting media, finding that such access would "enhance rather than abridge the freedoms of speech and press." Is it possible to reconcile *Red Lion* and *Miami Herald*? Which would be financially more difficult to start, a new radio station or a daily newspaper? Is the answer to that question relevant to constitutional interpretation? Constitutional interpretation by whom?

(3) Although the Court upheld the fairness doctrine in *Red Lion,* the FCC dropped the requirement in 1987, stating that it unconstitutionally "chilled" the First Amendment rights of broadcasters.

(4) Three years earlier, FCC v. League of Women Voters (1984) had thrown additional doubt on *Red Lion.* A group of litigants, including the League of Women Voters and the Pacifica Foundation, which operated several stations and received federal grants, challenged § 339 of the Public Broadcasting Act of 1967. That section forbade educational broadcasting stations receiving grants from the federal government to "engage in editorializing" about political campaigns or candidates. For the majority, Brennan applied "most exacting scrutiny." He acknowledged that the federal government had authority to regulate the "scarce and valuable national resource" of limited frequencies and that that authority was more extensive than over newspapers. Nevertheless, "broadcasters are engaged in a vital and independent form of communicative activity" that fell under the First Amendment's shield, and he

found § 339's ban was much too sweeping, restricting "precisely that form of speech which the Framers of the Bill of Rights were most anxious to protect."

Burger, White, Rehnquist, and White dissented. In an opinion that adumbrated Rust v. Sullivan (1991; reprinted above, p. 749) concerning "unconstitutional conditions," Rehnquist wrote:

Congress in enacting § 399 of the Public Broadcasting Act has simply determined that public funds shall not be used to subsidize noncommercial, educational broadcasting stations which engage in "editorializing" or which support or oppose any political candidate. I do not believe that anything in the First Amendment prevents Congress from choosing to spend public moneys in that manner.   ...

   ... Congress has rationally determined that the bulk of the taxpayers whose moneys provide the funds for grants ... would prefer not to see the management of local educational stations promulgate its own private views on the air at taxpayer expense. Accordingly Congress simply has decided not to subsidize stations which engage in that activity.   ...

This is not to say that the Government may attach any condition to its largess; it is only to say that when the Government is simply exercising its power to allocate its own public funds, we need only find that the condition imposed has a rational relationship to Congress' purpose in providing the subsidy and that it is not primarily "aimed at the suppression of dangerous ideas." In this case Congress' prohibition is directly related to its purpose in providing subsidies for public broadcasting, and it is plainly rational for Congress to have determined that taxpayer moneys should not be used to subsidize management's views or to pay for management's exercise of partisan politics. Indeed, it is entirely rational for Congress to have wished to avoid the appearance of Government sponsorship of a particular view or a particular political candidate. Furthermore, Congress' prohibition is strictly neutral.

D

MAINTAINING CONSTITU-TIONAL DEMOCRACY: TREATING EQUALS EQUALLY

The Declaration of Independence's ringing proclamation that "all men are created equal" stated one of the foundational beliefs of both constitutionalism and democracy. Yet neither the constitutional text of 1787–88 nor the Bill of Rights said much explicitly about equality, even equality before the law. Article I denied federal and state authority to "grant any title of nobility," and Article IV said that "citizens of each State shall be entitled to all privileges and immunities of citizens of the several States," though without listing those "privileges and immunities" or specifying who was to define and protect them.[1]

The authors of the *Federalist Papers* took up the problem of equality but mostly, as far as domestic politics was concerned, in the context of fair representation in Congress between large and small states. The only extensive discussion of equality among citizens came in *Federalist* No. 10 (reprinted below, p. 1087), in which Madison spoke of men's "unequal faculties of acquiring property," the protection of which, he asserted, "is the first object of Government."

During the next few generations, slavery left the constitutional issue of equality festering. In the 1830s, as abolitionism grew stronger in the North and Midwest,[2] southern spokesmen fought back.[3] John C. Calhoun even had the temerity to attack the quasi-sacred Declaration of Independence. There was not a word of truth in it, he said in a speech in the Senate in June, 1848. Men were not born at all, babies were; and what was "self-evident" was that these babies were not born equal. On the other hand, Lincoln eloquently echoed the Declaration's proclamation, abolitionists rallied around those words, which became a battle cry during the war, and later moved many of the supporters of the Thirteenth and Fourteenth amendments.[4]

After the Civil War, the Thirteenth Amendment ended slavery's legitimacy:

---

1. One might also point to states' equal representation in the Senate and the prohibition in Article I, § 9 against Congress's giving preference to the ports of one state over another as well as § 8's requirement that all federal "Duties, Imposts, and Excises shall be uniform throughout the United States." But these provisions relate to a different kind of equality from that which the Fourteenth Amendment addresses.

2. One should not think that in the period between 1787 and 1861 the South was completely solid on slavery. During the first few decades of the nineteenth century, emancipation societies flourished in the South. While Chief Justice, John Marshall was the president of such a society in Virginia and vice-president of a national group. These organizations typically wanted gradual, peaceful emancipation, with the masters compensated and the ex-slaves relocated in what is now Liberia. Marshall's successor, Roger Brooke Taney, also thought slavery was immoral (though constitutionally protected), and even Robert E. Lee believed slavery was wrong.

3. For a collection of such essays, see Eric L. McKitrick, ed., *Slavery Defended: The Views of the Old South* (Englewood Cliffs, NJ: Prentice-Hall, 1963).

4. See espec. Jacobus tenBroek, *Equal Under Law* (New York: Macmillian, 1965). Originally published in 1951 under the title, *The Antislavery Origins of the Fourteenth Amendment.*

> Neither slavery nor involuntary servitude, except as a punishment
> for crime whereof the party shall have been duly convicted, shall
> exist within the United States.

But, as massive a blow for both liberty and equality as that amendment was, by itself it did not automatically create equality of people
of all races before the law.   Unreconstructed white legislators in
southern states quickly enacted "black codes" to keep the newly
freed slaves from full citizenship.   The effective movement for
equality before the law came from the Radical Republicans' program
of Reconstruction and, more specifically, the federal Civil Rights Act
of 1866, which recognized a right, regardless of race,

> to make and enforce contracts, to sue, be parties, and give
> evidence, to inherit, purchase, lease, sell, hold and convey real
> and personal property, and to full and equal benefit of all laws
> and proceedings for the security of persons and property.

Equality before the law came close to reality—but only for a few
fleeting moments.

The origins of the Fourteenth Amendment are complex, but in
part it was a reaction to the complaint that the Thirteenth Amendment could not support such statutes as the Civil Rights Act of
1866.[5]   The amendment's "equal protection clause" is deceptively
simple: "No State shall ... deny to any person within its jurisdiction the equal protection of the laws."   These words do not
command equal treatment in all respects, only "equal protection of
the laws"—and what that phrase means is complex and controversial.

No more than had the Continental Congress meant the Declaration of Independence to free slaves would many politically active
members of the generation of 1868 have read the equal protection
clause as recognizing that every American, or even every adult
citizen, had a right, enforceable against government, much less
against fellow residents, to equal dignity and respect.   By standards
of the late (or even mid) twentieth century, Lincoln had been a
racist, as had been most of the Radical Republicans who controlled
Congress after the war.   Indeed, it is difficult to know how much of
the Radicals' campaign on behalf of the newly freed slaves was
driven by hatred of southern whites and how much by zeal for
constitutionalist and democratic principles.   Furthermore, most
men of that generation were, by current standards, sexist, anxious
to protect women but loath to acknowledge their full legal equality
with males.

---

5. In part, of course, the Fourteenth Amendment was an effort to expunge *Dred Scott*'s
narrow definition of citizenship and in part it was an effort both to punish white
southerners and keep them from becoming politically powerful again.   Three of the
amendment's five sections, each one lengthier than § 1, dealt exclusively with such
punitive matters, and § 5 authorized Congress to enforce the entire amendment.

I. INTERPRETING EQUALITY: TEXTUALISM

The Fourteenth Amendment's terms are Delphic. Let us begin, as have most interpreters, with a *textualist approach*. The immediate problems are to define "state," "person," "equal," and "protection."

A. State Action

The Supreme Court has construed the phrase "nor shall any state" to exclude constitutional protection against unequal treatment by fellow citizens. The Civil Rights Cases (1883) struck down a federal statute that forbade private citizens who operated businesses such as inns, theaters, and restaurants, to discriminate on account of race in their accommodations. The government argued that § 1 of the amendment defined who was an American citizen and § 5 empowered Congress to protect those citizens against individual as well as state action. The Court, however, refused to look at the sentence defining citizenship and insisted on a myopic form of a *textualist approach*, not even clause-bound but sentence-bound: "Individual invasion of individual rights is not the subject-matter of the amendment."

It is painfully obvious that the heavy hand of the state can be felt even where public officials are not physically present. In recent decades judges have been more sensitive to this fact, and the Civil Rights Cases have been obliquely overruled. Invoking congressional power to regulate "Commerce . . . among the several states," the Court has sustained federal legislation directed against individual discrimination.[6] Nevertheless, Congress, the presidency, and the Court continue to hold the view that, for § 1 of the Fourteenth Amendment to come directly into play, there must be a palpable connection between the state and the private individual or group doing the discriminating.

Operating within this peculiar framework, judges have tended more to address specific problems presented by particular cases

---

6. See espec. Heart of Atlanta Motel v. United States (1964) and Katzenbach v. McClung (1964), sustaining the Civil Rights Act of 1964, which was even broader in its protection of civil rights than the act of 1875 that *Civil Rights* invalidated. The justices distinguished *Civil Rights* because there the Court had not considered the reach of the commerce clause. Concurring, Justice Douglas bluntly said that he would base the ruling on § 5 of the Fourteenth Amendment and so would expressly overrule *Civil Rights*. In any event, the Court's finding in *Katzenbach* that the commerce clause allowed Congress to regulate the affairs of a small barbecue restaurant, when coupled with the Court's equally imperial view of the commerce clause in other cases—see espec. Wickard v. Filburn (1942; discussed above, p. 520)—leaves little that Congress may not regulate. (But see United States v. Lopez [1995; discussed above, p. 596].) Nevertheless, it is important to realize that these cases validate *congressional* protection of civil rights; they do not require either the states or Congress to protect individual rights against discrimination by other private citizens or, in the absence of explicit congressional authorization, federal courts to do so either.

than to offer general guidelines to determine when state action is present. One point, however, seems clear: A state may not escape the Fourteenth (or the Fifteenth) Amendment by allowing private citizens or corporations to perform such public functions as elections [7] and possibly education. [8] Beyond that point, we confront what Tennyson would have called "a wilderness of single instances."

The specific limitation of "state action" has been punctured in another way. In many early cases, the justices had noted that the equal protection clause did not bind the federal government, only the states. But in Hirabayashi v. United States (1943), upholding the curfew against Japanese–Americans, Chief Justice Stone's opinion for the majority acknowledged some federal obligation to govern even-handedly and vaguely hinted that, had the equal protection clause applied to the federal government, the Court might have decided in favor of the Nisei.

The justices continued to think about the problem, and eleven years later the school segregation case from the District of Columbia, Bolling v. Sharpe (1954; reprinted below, p. 917), ruled the due process clause of the Fifth Amendment also imposes a requirement of equal protection. But Chief Justice Warren was careful to say that, although both equal protection and due process stem from "our American ideal of fairness," "we do not imply that the two are always interchangeable phrases."

Gradually, however, the justices began to blend the two clauses and concepts. In 1975 Weinberger v. Wiesenfeld asserted that the "Court's approach to Fifth Amendment equal protection claims has always been precisely the same as to equal protection claims under the Fourteenth Amendment." Although later decisions have backed away from a complete merger, [9] we witness not only an erasure of decades of decisions but also a reverse twist on the incorporation

---

7. This is the teaching of the later white primary cases, espec. Terry v. Adams (1953).

8. See, for example, Griffin v. Prince Edward County (1964); Walter F. Murphy, "Public Education with Private Funds?" 20 *J. of Pols.* 635 (1958). For more recent studies of the concept of "state action," see, e.g.: Robert J. Glennon, Jr., and John E. Nowak, "A Functional Analysis of the Fourteenth Amendment 'State Action' Requirement," 1976 *Sup.Ct.Rev.* 221; L.F. Goldstein, "The Death and Transfiguration of the State Action Doctrine," 4 *Hast.Con.L.Q.* 1 (1977); Jesse Choper, "Thoughts on State Action," 1979 *Wash.U.L.Q.* 775; Paul Brest, "State Action and Liberal Theory," 130 *U.Pa.L.Rev.* 1296 (1982); and Cass R. Sunstein, *The Partial Constitution* (Cambridge: Harvard University Press, 1993), espec. chs. 3, 5, and pp. 203ff.

9. Hampton v. Mow Sun Wong (1976) noted that "the two protections are not always coextensive. Not only does the language of the two Amendments differ, but more importantly, there may be overriding national interests which justify selective federal legislation that would be unacceptable for an individual State." Brennan, the author of the Court's opinion in *Weinberger*, was apparently troubled by these sentences and filed a brief concurring opinion. The justices have vigorously debated the question whether Congress may adopt affirmative action programs which, if adopted by state or local governments, would be unconstitutional: see Richmond v. J. A. Croson Co. (1989; reprinted below, p. 954) and Metro Broadcasting v. FCC (1990) and Adarand Constuctors v. Pena (1995), discussed below, pp. 969–70).

doctrine (see above, p. 133): Instead of deciding that the Fourteenth Amendment incorporated part of the Bill of Rights, the Court
ruled that the Bill of Rights incorporated part of the Fourteenth
Amendment. As *clause-bound textualism*, this reasoning is
strange—John Hart Ely called it "gibberish both syntactically and
historically"[10]—but it could make good sense as the product of
textual structuralism, especially when combined with a *philosophic
approach*. For his part, Ely argues that a *textualist approach*
would be better: To seek the principle of equal protection that
applies to the federal government in the Ninth Amendment.[11]

B. Who Is a "Person"?

"Person" also presents difficult issues of definition. Does the
word refer only to humans or does it include corporations? Without hearing argument on the point, the Court in Santa Clara County
v. Southern Pacific (1886) held that a corporation was a "person"
for purposes of the Fourteenth Amendment. And so, despite an
occasional protest, the matter stands today.

A more emotionally charged issue is whether a human fetus is a
"person" entitled not merely to due process and equal protection
but to any constitutionally cognizable claim of protection and
respect by government. Roe v. Wade (1973; reprinted below, p.
1258) held that a fetus was not a person under the Fourteenth
Amendment; but, as the ferocious debate over various proposals to
protect fetal life shows, the issue is still very much alive. Nonetheless, Planned Parenthood v. Casey (1992; reprinted below, p. 1281)
reaffirmed *Roe* in this respect. Indeed, in his separate opinion,
Stevens claimed that "no member of the Court has ever questioned
this fundamental proposition."[12]

Also of great importance is the question whether the term
"person" basically pertains to an individual as an individual or as a
member of a group. A *textual approach* to the equal protection
clause may seem to yield an individualized meaning; but, one might
argue, a *purposive approach* would look behind those words to a
broader conception. And, so the argument goes, the amendment's
goal was to protect disadvantaged groups—some, like newly freed
slaves, rather easily identifiable; others, like the poor, quite amorphous and, from an *originalist* perspective, beyond the pale of the

---

10. *Democracy and Distrust* (Cambridge: Harvard University Press, 1980), p. 32.

11. As we shall see below, p. 919, this argument might be *structuralist*, which, Chapter
9 pointed out, can be *textualist, systemic,* or *transcendent*.

12. Actually, William O. Douglas, a member of the majority in *Roe*, had earlier argued
that bears and river basins had "standing to sue" in federal courts and thus were
"persons" of a sort. Sierra Club v. Morton (1972). It would have been fascinating to
know how a river basin was a person but a fetus was not. Furthermore, Thurgood
Marshall, also a member of the majority in *Roe,* claimed in Burns v. Alcala (1975) that a
fetus qualified as a "dependent child" for purposes of welfare. It would be difficult to
imagine that a being who qualified as a "child" was not a person.

constitutional text as well as the understandings of the amendment's framers and ratifiers.

The distinction between an individual and a group basis for equal protection is hardly sharp, for, although we suffer injury as individuals, we identify ourselves—and are identified by others—as members of groups, in most cases of several groups.[13] Still, there are politically significant differences. For example, an "affirmative action" plan that tries to repair past damage by giving preference to members of groups who had previously suffered from official discrimination needs a constitutional base that recognizes a wider degree of group disadvantage as well as of group liability than a purely individualized conception of "person"—and of disadvantage and liability—would allow. The latter would not necessarily oppose affirmative action, but it would tend to limit the benefits of such programs to individuals who could show that discrimination had injured them personally, not simply their group generally.

Part of the difficulty the justices have had in resolving problems of affirmative action (see espec. Regents v. Bakke [1978; reprinted below, p. 942], Richmond v. J.A. Croson Co. [1989; reprinted below, p. 954], and Metro Broadcasting v. FCC [1990] and Adarand Constructors v. Pena [1995], discussed below, pp. 969–70]) is due to their failure to face up to these two views of the reach of the amendment—and of the nature of the rights it protects—and to offer a carefully reasoned choice between them.[14]

C. What Does "Equal" Mean?

If, as a practical matter, the equal protection clause forbade states to make distinctions, it would be self-destructive. "Sometimes," as the Court observed in Jenness v. Fortson (1971), "the grossest discrimination can lie in treating things that are different as though they were exactly alike. . . ." A law that exacted the same amount of taxes from a poor as from a rich person or required universal military service without exempting the physically disabled would magnify existing inequality. Statutes that allowed the blind as well as the sighted to drive automobiles, pilot aircraft, or perform surgery or the mentally handicapped to dispense medical prescriptions, teach in public schools, or serve as law enforcement officials would be absurdly destructive of life and property.

---

13. For a debate on this issue, which indicates how much the two views have in common as well as how much they differ, see: Owen M. Fiss, "Groups and the Equal Protection Clause," 5 Phil. & Pub. Aff. 107 (1976); and Paul Brest, "In Defense of the Anti–Discrimination Principle," 90 Harv.L.Rev. 1 (1976). See also Vernon Van Dyke, "Justice as Fairness: For Groups?" 69 Am.Pol.Sci.Rev. 607 (1975).

14. See Charles Fried, "Metro Broadcasting, Inc. v. FCC: Two Concepts of Equality," 104 Harv.L.Rev. 107 (1990) (criticizing Metro and arguing for a individual-rights conception rather than a group-rights conception of equality); Patricia J. Williams, "Metro Broadcasting, Inc. v. FCC: Regrouping in Singular Times," 104 Harv.L.Rev. 525 (1990) (defending Metro on the ground that it marks an important step toward a recognition of multiculturalism and of the need to take active steps to nurture such diversity).

"The Equal Protection Clause is itself a classic paradox," William H. Rehnquist once said:

> It creates a requirement of equal treatment to be applied to the process of legislation—legislation whose very purpose is to draw lines in such a way that different people are treated differently. The problem presented is one of sorting the legislative distinctions which are acceptable from those which involve invidiously unequal treatment. ... [E]qual protection does not mean that all persons must be treated alike. Rather, its general principle is that persons similarly situated should be treated similarly.[15]

But even that statement of high principle, Rehnquist conceded, does little to settle specific cases. "For the crux of the problem is *whether persons are similarly situated* for purposes of the state action at issue." Complicating analysis is the severe temptation of human beings to see themselves as differently situated, to place their own interests ahead of others', and, consequently, for those who have or can influence political power to use government for self-advancement. In effect, though seldom in name, we are all tempted to make self-serving distinctions and to rationalize them as being objectively valid and socially necessary.

Thus constitutional interpretation is left with a knotty problem: On the one hand, classification is essential in a complex world. On the other, we all tend to see distinctions that benefit us as "necessary." Moreover, treatment that is in fact based on "objective" criteria may sometimes confer advantages closely correlated with wealth, status, and ethnic background. For example, performance on the standardized tests often used for admission to universities is highly correlated with the quality of secondary education, thus giving an advantage to those young people whose families live in affluent neighborhoods or can afford private schools and/or tutors. By what criteria can constitutional interpreters distinguish between useful, perhaps necessary, distinctions and those that deny equal protection of the laws?

D. What Is "Protection"?

The word "protection" has a negative connotation in the sense of "defending" a person or thing *from* danger posed by some other person or thing. Usually it does not signify a positive act of furthering, only of guarding against. Thus, in the context of the Fourteenth Amendment, "protection" might reasonably be interpreted to command the state's equally defending from harm all persons within its jurisdiction, but to say nothing, or very little, about how a state should advance various persons' interests or dispense public benefits. Ironically, judges have turned this *textualist* analysis on its head. From the earliest days, courts have seen

---

15. Trimble v. Gordon, dis. op. (1977).

governmental distributions of benefits to fall under the term "protection" and have required that such be more or less equal—though without necessarily settling what "equal" entails. Education provides the most dramatic though by no means the sole example.

On the other hand, judges have disagreed sharply whether a state's failure or refusal to protect people within its jurisdiction falls within the purview of the amendment. The sticking point seems to be a concern that "state inaction" is not the same as "state action." Here *doctrinalism* has sometimes overridden the plain words of the text, for the amendment does not use the term "action," only "state." Rather, those words speak directly against a failure to protect, which by any common sense understanding must refer to inaction or feeble action. Nevertheless, DeShaney v. Winnebago County Department of Social Services (1989; reprinted below, p. 1350) [16] held that a state was not liable for civil damages for severe brain damage done to a child after its officers, though repeatedly warned that the child was being badly beaten by his father, refused to protect the boy. The case was decided on grounds of due process rather than equal protection, but the problem of "protection" requiring "action" is the same.

II. BEYOND TEXTUALISM

Readers of earlier chapters will have guessed at a glance the subtext of this introductory essay: Interpreters have typically begun by following a *textual approach*; but, when confronted with problems about the meaning of the amendment's critical terms and the relations among those terms and other constitutional provisions, interpreters have also been quick to follow other approaches as well. The most prominent has been *doctrinalism*. Judges and other public officials have moved, like good products of a common-law system, from case to case, building up a body of rules.

The next two chapters reveal angry and learned disputes among interpreters about the meaning and implications of earlier interpretations of equal protection. These disagreements are not unimportant, for, as common-law lawyers, judges often think in *doctrinal* terms. But we would make two points here about these quarrels. First, they illustrate one of the principal defects of a *doctrinal approach*: It frequently yields not one but several conflicting answers. *Stare decisis*, as we saw in Chapter 2, is more than a mechanism to preserve the status quo; it also provides a means for gradual change. Not all interpreters want change, and those who do often want different kinds of changes. *Doctrinalism* and its instrument, *stare decisis*, can easily accommodate most of the contending parties. One side may be able to muster more convinc-

---

16. See the discussion in David A. Strauss, "Due Process, Government Inaction, and Private Wrongs," 1989 *Sup.Ct.Rev.* 53.

ing analyses of previous decisions than the other, but often a *doctrinal approach* is congenial to all contestants.

Second, disputes about doctrine may conceal, both from the creators and consumers of constitutional interpretation, deeper disagreements. Interpreters themselves may not always be aware that they are using other approaches besides *textualism* and *doctrinalism.* Frequently, for example, they will innocently, perhaps naively or even unconsciously, follow a *philosophic approach.* In the section on a *textual approach*, the discussion of "state," "person," "equal," and "protection" may have seemed peculiarly truncated, for analysis of each of those concepts poses important—and difficult—questions for political theory and even more basic philosophy. Legislators and judges offer "legal" definitions of these terms, all of which rest on moral, philosophic, and sometimes even theological assumptions. To return to the explosive issue of abortion: Does a decision that a fetus is neither a "human" nor a "person" rest any less on moral/philosophic/theological arguments (or assumptions) than does a decision that the fetus is a "human" and a "person"? That interpreters fail to examine their assumptions or beg important moral and philosophical questions does not mean these issues are not playing a significant, perhaps even a crucial, role in determining constitutional meaning.

Interpreters often use a *structuralist approach*, looking at the text as a whole or the text plus the political system, or even using as the unit of analysis both of these plus underlying political theories. One could argue, as Justice Arthur Goldberg did in defending the Court's holding the federal government was also bound to accord equal protection, that "the idea of equality pervades the [constitutional] document." [17] Article I forbids both the state and federal governments to bestow titles of nobility, eliminating the possibility of a hereditary aristocracy.[18] Article IV constrains both levels of government by guaranteeing to each state a "Republican Form of Government" and so rejects the ancient distinction between king and vassal. The privileges and immunities clause of Article IV requires states to treat all American citizens more or less equally.[19]

---

17. "Equality and Governmental Action," 39 *N.Y.U.L.Rev.* 205, 206 (1964).

18. Justice John Paul Stevens made this point dissenting in Fullilove v. Klutznick (1980), but it fits Goldberg's argument.

19. Goldberg also used an *originalist approach*: The document was framed against a background of written agreements, running back from the Mayflower Compact, with its promise of "the framing of 'just & equall lawes,'" to the newer state constitutional texts, many of which guaranteed equal protection. In this context, equality before the law, he argued, was an accepted assumption that did not have to be explicitly stated. But Goldberg's picture of American history may not have been altogether accurate. Some states did write professions of equality in their constitutional texts, but others did not. See, generally, Stanley N. Katz, "The Strange Birth and Unlikely History of Constitutional Equality," 75 *J. of Am. Hist.* 747 (1988); and Willi Paul Adams, *The First American Constitutions: Republican Ideology and the Making of State Constitutions in the Revolutionary Era* (Rita and Robert Kimber, trans.) (Chapel Hill: University of North Carolina Press, 1980), espec. ch. 8.

And, as we noted at the beginning of this introduction, both democratic and constitutionalist theory postulate the equal dignity and respect due to all citizens.

Furthermore, since *Slaughter-House* (1873; reprinted above, p. 550) and Strauder v. West Virginia (1880; reprinted below, p. 896), a *purposive approach*, looking to "the general objects" the amendment sought, has been critically important. Sometimes interpreters have sought *purpose* at a very specific level. As Justice Miller said in *Slaughter-House*:

> [N]o one can fail to be impressed with the one pervading purpose found in all the [three post-Civil War amendments:] ... the freedom of the slave race, the security and firm establishment of that freedom, and the protection of the newly made freeman and citizen from the oppression of those who had formerly exercised unlimited dominion over him.

At other times, the purpose has been much broader, to require equal governmental benefits as well as protection not merely for African Americans but also for people of other ethnic groups,[20] aliens,[21] and women.[22] An interpreter combining a *developmentalist* with a *purposive approach* could contend that American constitutional history records a march, sometimes broken, even doglegged, toward fulfillment of this objective.

III. EQUAL PROTECTION AND THE HOW, WHAT, AND WHO OF CONSTITUTIONAL INTERPRETATION

The introductory essays and the cases reprinted in the next two chapters try to illustrate the ways in which the Supreme Court and indirectly Congress have tried, however stumblingly, to cope with problems of equality before the law. We once again caution users of this book, in reading these chapters, not to become mesmerized by the twists and turns of developing legal doctrines. These are interesting as well as important in their own right, but they are more important as instruments to help us better understand the HOW of constitutional interpretation, an interrogative whose answer(s) inevitably depend on WHAT interpreters believe "the Constitution" is.

---

20. Hernandez v. Texas (1954; reprinted below, p. 923).

21. Yick Wo v. Hopkins (1886; reprinted below, p. 900).

22. For example, Craig v. Boren (1976; reprinted below, p. 992).

To an interpreter who views "the Constitution" as no more than the document, "equal protection of the laws" may mean only that a legislature must offer a reason for its classification that does not offend the document's specific terms. To an interpreter with a broader view of "the Constitution," the equal protection and due process clauses may serve two much broader functions. First, they may operate as the document's references to a political theory that demands not only that government accord to all persons within its jurisdiction equal concern and respect, but also that the policies it formulates to control relations among private citizens reflect a similar imperative. Second and related, those clauses may manifest a vision of a society in which citizens enjoy freedom from governmental and societal prejudice based on such irrelevant factors as race, ethnicity, sex, sexual orientation, or wealth.

The differences between these interpreters may lie not only in their conceptions of WHAT "the Constitution" includes and the visions of the society to which it points, but also in differing answers to the question of WHO interprets which aspects of the constitutional text and the broader constitution. We are studying mainly judicial action, and, as we have frequently seen, a judge may well conclude that his or her role is peripheral to that of elected public officials in some facets of constitutional interpretation. Thus we continue to need to keep the larger process of constitutional interpretation in focus as we work within the convoluted doctrines that judges have created to cope with discrete problems. In every important piece of constitutional interpretation, the cords of WHAT, WHO, and HOW braid together.

SELECTED BIBLIOGRAPHY

Ball, Milner S. *The Promise of American Law* (Athens: University of Georgia Press, 1981).

Dworkin, Ronald. "What is Equality? Part 3: The Place of Liberty," 73 *Iowa L.Rev.* 1 (1987).

Ely, John Hart. *Democracy and Distrust* (Cambridge: Harvard University Press, 1980).

Gunther, Gerald. "In Search of Evolving Doctrine on a Changing Court," 86 *Harv.L.Rev.* 1 (1972).

Hartz, Louis. *The Liberal Tradition in America* (New York: Harcourt, Brace, 1955).

Karst, Kenneth L. *Belonging to America: Equal Citizenship and the Constitution* (New Haven: Yale University Press, 1989).

Katz, Stanley N. "The Strange Birth and Unlikely History of Constitutional Equality," 75 *Jo. of Am.Hist.* 747 (1988).

Pennock, J. Roland, and John W. Chapman, eds. *Equality* (New York: Lieber–Atherton, 1967).

Perry, Michael J. "Modern Equal Protection: A Conceptualization and an Appraisal," 79 *Colum.L.Rev.* 1023 (1979).

Pole, J.R. *The Pursuit of Equality in American History* (Berkeley: University of California Press, 1978).

Pritchett, C. Herman. *Constitutional Civil Liberties* (Englewood Cliffs, NJ: Prentice–Hall, 1984), chs. 10, 12.

Rodgers, Daniel T. *Contested Truths: Keywords in American Politics Since Independence* (New York: Basic Books, 1987).

Sandalow, Terrence. "Judicial Protection of Minorities," 75 *Mich. L.Rev.* 1162 (1977).

Sartori, Giovanni. *Democratic Theory* (New York: Praeger, 1965), chs. 13–15.

Sunstein, Cass R. "Public Values, Private Interests, and the Equal Protection Clause," 1982 *Sup.Ct.Rev.* 127.

————. *The Partial Constitution* (Cambridge: Harvard University Press, 1993).

tenBroek, Jacobus. *Equal Under Law* (New York: Macmillan, 1965). (Originally published in 1951 under the title, *The Antislavery Origins of the Fourteenth Amendment.*)

Tribe, Laurence H. *American Constitutional Law* (2d ed.; Mineola, NY: Foundation Press, 1988), ch. 16.

Tussman, Joseph, and Jacobus tenBroek. "The Equal Protection of the Laws," 37 *Calif.L.Rev.* 341 (1949).

Westen, Peter. *Speaking of Equality: An Analysis of the Rhetorical Force of Equality in Moral and Legal Discourse* (Princeton: Princeton University Press, 1993).

Williams, Bernard A.O. "The Idea of Equality," in H.A. Bedau, ed., *Justice and Equality* (Englewood Cliffs, NJ: Prentice–Hall, 1971).

14

The Problems of Equal Protection, I

The Slaughter–House Cases (1873; reprinted above, p. 550) provided the first important opportunity for judicial interpretation of the Fourteenth Amendment, but the justices gave the equal protection clause short shrift. For the majority, Samuel Miller found it inapplicable to the butchers' plight, and the dissenters were much more concerned with due process and privileges or immunities. But if *Slaughter-House* augured for a limited scope for equal protection generally, it suggested great promise for African Americans. It "is not difficult," Miller wrote,

> to give a meaning to this clause. The existence of laws in the States where the newly emancipated negroes resided, which discriminated with gross injustice and hardship against them as a class, was the evil to be remedied.

I. FROM *SLAUGHTER-HOUSE* TO *CAROLENE PRODUCTS*

A. Race Relations

In this respect, *Slaughter-House* echoed Railroad Co. v. Brown (1873), which interpreted a congressional act granting a franchise to the Washington and Alexandria Railroad to operate in the District of Columbia. One of the conditions of the franchise was that no person should be excluded because of race. The railroad allowed anyone who could pay to travel, but it ran separate cars for whites and blacks. In this initial test of "separate but equal," the Court was curt: "This is an ingenious attempt to evade a compliance with the obvious meaning of the requirement." Segregation was "discrimination," the justices unanimously held.

A few other early cases picked up on *Slaughter-House* 's promise. Strauder v. Virginia (1880; reprinted below, p. 896) said that the Fourteenth Amendment secured for blacks "exemption from legal discriminations, implying inferiority in civil society. ..." And Yick Wo v. Hopkins (1886; reprinted below, p. 900) indicated a judicial willingness to look beyond legal rules to the reality of their administration. There the justices struck down a San Francisco ordinance that supposedly regulated all laundries but had in fact been administered to harass those operated by Chinese. "Though the law itself be fair on its face and impartial in its appearance," the Court said,

> yet, if it is applied and administered with an evil eye and an unequal hand, so as practically to make unjust and illegal discriminations between persons in similar circumstances, material to their rights, the denial of equal justice is still within the prohibition of the Constitution.

But these decisions were islands in a sea of judicial indifference to the rights of persons who were not white males.[1] To resolve the disputed Hayes–Tilden election, the Compromise of 1877 allowed the Republicans to retain the White House in exchange for ending Reconstruction in the South, a promise of new capital to develop the area, and the transfer of responsibility for protecting civil rights of African Americans from federal to southern state officials, who, of course, would be white. The eminent historian C. Vann Woodward[2] sees the Civil Rights Cases (1883) as a judicial ratification of that compromise in its denial of federal authority to protect blacks against private discrimination in public accommodations. And it is worth noting that Justice Joseph P. Bradley, who wrote the majority opinion in the Civil Rights Cases, had been the "neutral" member of the special commission that resolved the Hayes–Tilden deadlock. He had cast his vote for Hayes in each contested election.

More indicative of the Court's attitude than *Railroad Co.* and *Yick Wo* were cases like Hall v. DeCuir (1876), which invalidated as burdening interstate commerce a state statute that forbade transportation companies to segregate passengers by race, and Louisville, New Orleans & Texas Rr. v. Mississippi (1890), which, despite the commerce clause and despite *Hall*, sustained a state statute requiring segregation in transportation.[3]

Plessy v. Ferguson (1896; reprinted below, p. 902) was the landmark ruling that repudiated *Slaughter-House*'s promise by fully validating "separate but equal." By a 7–1 vote the justices upheld a Louisiana statute mandating segregation in transportation. The Fourteenth Amendment, the majority wrote, "could not have been intended to abolish distinctions based upon color, or to enforce social, as distinguished from political equality, or a commingling of the two races upon terms unsatisfactory to either." The principal

---

1. See, for instance, the Court's sustaining in Bradwell v. Illinois (1873) a state law that did not allow women to practice law, and in Minor v. Happersett (1875) a state law denying women the right to vote.

2. *The Strange Career of Jim Crow* (2d ed.; New York: Oxford University Press, 1966); *Reunion and Reaction* (Garden City, NY.: Doubleday, 1951); *Origins of the New South* (Baton Rouge: Louisiana State University Press, 1951).

3. For analyses of these cases, see Derrick A. Bell, Jr., *Race, Racism and American Law* (3d ed.; Boston: Little, Brown, 1992), ch. 4.

criterion the Court applied to test segregation's validity was its "reasonableness," and that test was easily met:

> In determining the question of reasonableness [the State] is at liberty to act with reference to the established usages, customs and traditions of the people, and with a view to the promotion of their comfort, and the preservation of the public peace and good order.

Just as in the Civil Rights Cases, so in *Plessy*, Justice John Marshall Harlan, I, dissented. Although he had owned slaves and opposed adoption of both the Thirteenth and Fourteenth amendments—he said he had fought to save the Union, not to lose his slaves—he asserted: "Our Constitution is color-blind, and neither knows nor tolerates classes among citizens."

Harlan's prediction in *Plessy* that "the judgment this day rendered will, in time, prove to be quite as pernicious as the decision made by this tribunal in the *Dred Scott* case" was prophetic. *Plessy*'s rationale, soon applied to other areas of social life,[4] legitimized Jim Crow and ensured that vestiges of slavery would continue to plague Americans through the next century. Only several decades after *Plessy* did the Court begin to show interest in protecting African Americans' civil rights, and even then the judicial record hardly demonstrated sensitivity toward people suffering "legal discriminations, implying inferiority in civil society."[5] Notwithstanding the Civil War and the Civil War amendments to the Constitution, blacks for all practical purposes remained second-class citizens. They had some but only some "rights which a white man was bound to respect."

In the late 1920s and early 1930s, the justices looked skeptically at the white primary,[6] but in 1935 Grovey v. Townsend held that it was constitutional for a political party, even in a one-party southern state, to restrict voting in primaries to whites, as long as state law did not require such a restriction. (Smith v. Allwright reversed this decision in 1944.)

B. Economic Regulation

Without a doubt, racism colored the way the justices, like most white Americans, viewed the separate and unequal world of African

---

4. For education, see: Cumming v. Board (1899); Berea College v. Kentucky (1908); and Gong Lum v. Rice (1927).

5. McCabe v. Atchison, Topeka & Santa Fe (1914) conceded the right of blacks travelling interstate to accommodations that were in fact equal even though separate, but held that the plaintiffs had no standing to sue. Buchanan v. Warley (1917) and its companion cases struck a blow for equality by invalidating state statutes requiring segregated housing. At issue was not only equal protection, but also the right to own and dispose of private property, a right to which the Court from 1890 to 1937 usually gave special solicitude. Guinn v. United States (1915) held unconstitutional a state statute that imposed strict restrictions on the right to vote but granted exceptions to all those whose ancestors had been eligible to vote in 1866, i.e., whites.

6. Nixon v. Herndon (1927); Nixon v. Condon (1932).

Americans. But there was also a general judicial indifference to equal protection. During an age when judges were crusading for "substantive due process" to guard property rights against governmental regulation, equality was simply not a value that the legal system was championing. Justice Holmes was not far from the judicial norm when he sneered in Buck v. Bell (1927; reprinted below, p. 1254) that an appeal to equal protection was "the usual last resort of constitutional arguments."

The Court was quite content to allow government broad leeway, in economic regulations as well as race relations, to establish classifications. (*Slaughter-House* itself had involved an economic regulation.) As in *Plessy*, the rule was that of reasonableness. "If the selection or classification is neither capricious nor arbitrary, and rests upon some reasonable consideration of difference or policy, there is no denial of equal protection of the laws." [7] Lindsley v. Natural Carbonic Gas Co. (1911) spelled out these components in some detail:

1.   The equal protection clause ... does not take from the State the power to classify in the adoption of police laws, but admits of the exercise of a wide scope of discretion ... and avoids what is done only when it is without any reasonable basis and therefore is purely arbitrary.

2.   A classification having some reasonable basis does not offend against that clause merely because it is not made with mathematical nicety or because in practice it results in some inequality.

3.   When the classification in such a law is called into question, if any state of facts reasonably can be conceived that would sustain it, the existence of that state of facts at the time the law was enacted must be assumed.

4.   One who assails the classification in such a law must carry the burden of showing that it does not rest upon any reasonable basis, but is essentially arbitrary.

C. Caste in America and the Shadow of Nazism

The 1930s brought not only the New Deal but also the beginnings of a change in judicial and popular attitudes toward race relations. As the evils of Nazism and its persecution of Jews became more apparent, it grew increasingly difficult to justify America's own caste society, harshly silhouetted by frequent lynchings (at least 75 between 1930 and 1936) and kangaroo courts. In Scottsboro, Alabama, for instance, seven young black men had been accused of raping two white women. The evidence that the crimes had actually occurred was flimsy, but the police did not feel it necessary to conduct any sort of investigation beyond taking the "victims'" complaint. The defendants were divided into three groups, and

---

7.   Brown–Forman Co. v. Kentucky (1910).

each trial was completed in less than a day, a pace made easier by the court's dispensing with such niceties as right to counsel. The jury, from which African Americans had been excluded, did its part, almost instantly finding all defendants guilty and imposing the death penalty.

Twice, in 1932 and 1935, the cases reached the U.S. Supreme Court; twice the justices reversed the convictions, establishing for the first time indigents' right to court-appointed counsel in state cases, though only under limited circumstances,[8] and reaffirming the right to be tried by a jury from which members of one's race had not been systematically excluded.[9] Nevertheless, as in NAACP v. Alabama (1958; reprinted above, p. 798), the state drove ahead and reconvicted four of the seven.

In 1936, a case from Mississippi presented the justices with a shocking example of brutality against African Americans.[10] There a deputy sheriff, accompanied by friends, arrested three black men for murder. They hanged one from a tree, lowering him periodically to ask if he would confess. When this tactic failed, they tied him to the tree and whipped him. When this tactic also failed, they released this suspect but later rearrested him. After additional hours of torture, the man confessed when promised that if he did so the beatings would stop. The other two accused were also tortured, though somewhat less cruelly, until they, too, agreed to confess.

At the trial, the rope scars were still plainly visible on the throat of the first defendant, but all three were convicted and sentenced to death after a proceeding that rivaled Scottsboro's in swiftness and was also unencumbered by defense counsel. Mississippi's supreme court found the case to be disgraceful but said the Fifth Amendment's protection against self-incrimination did not bind the states, as, indeed, Twining v. New Jersey (1908) had held. The U.S. Supreme Court reversed without overruling *Twining*, holding, *inter alia*, that use of torture violated due process and hence voided any confession so obtained.

These sorts of cases must have brought home to the justices what at some level of consciousness they had already known, that the caste system was unspeakably cruel to African Americans. Moreover, there was no hope for change through the political processes. Blacks in the South, where more than three-quarters of them then lived, were disenfranchised, and southern senators were able to filibuster to death every serious proposal for new civil rights laws. That same legislative influence and the ability to deliver the electoral votes of "the solid South" to the Democratic party's presidential candidate meant that the Department of Justice was not about to

---

8. Powell v. Alabama (1932).

9. Norris v. Alabama (1935).

10. Brown v. Mississippi (1936).

enforce existing federal statutes protecting civil rights.[11] Thus there were only two avenues of political change: the courts or violence.[12]

African Americans were not alone in their plight. On the West Coast, Asians were subjected to legal and social discrimination, in the Southwest Mexican–Americans, and Native American Indians wherever they found themselves. In no part of the country were women the equals of men where law and economics were concerned. Anti–Semitism and anti-Catholicism suffused much of American social life, though there were no legal barriers against these minorities. It was, rather, the Jehovah's Witnesses who dramatized the prevalence of religious bigotry. Not only were the Witnesses subjected to legal harassment by being arrested for distributing religious pamphlets without a license to sell—something no policeman would have dared ask of white Protestants—but they were also often subjected to physical beatings plus tarrings and featherings. As a tiny group, the Witnesses had no hope of wielding influence in the electoral processes, but the courts were open to them. And in the 1930s a trickle of their cases began to reach the Supreme Court.[13]

II. *CAROLENE PRODUCTS*

After 1937 and the death of "substantive due process" to protect economic rights (see West Coast Hotel v. Parrish [1937]; reprinted below, p. 1123), the justices were searching for a new jurisprudence in a context that boded ill for the ideals of constitutionalism and democracy. In Europe, totalitarianism had conquered Russia and Germany, and authoritarian regimes controlled Spain, Portugal, Italy, Poland, and much of the Balkans. In the United States, religious and racial intolerance seemed triumphant, and the Court's gross political and economic error in trying to write laissez-faire into the constitutional text had injured its capacity to educate the American people. The justices' crushing defeat at the hands of Franklin Roosevelt made it tempting for them to abandon constitutionalism, presume all legislation constitutional, and let the people rely on the political checks of democratic processes. On the other hand, the plight of minorities in Europe and the United States

---

11. At least not until Frank Murphy became Attorney General in 1939. See Robert K. Carr, *Federal Protection of Civil Rights* (Ithaca: Cornell University Press, 1947), and J. Woodford Howard, *Mr. Justice Murphy* (Princeton: Princeton University Press, 1968), ch. 9. But even those efforts were cut short; Murphy went to the Supreme Court a year later and World War II focused the attention of Roosevelt's administration on foreign affairs.

12. The Communist party made concerted but unsuccessful efforts to persuade blacks that revolution was the only solution. See Wilson Record, *The Negro and the Communist Party* (Chapel Hill: University of North Carolina Press, 1951). For a reversal of a conviction of a Communist organizer in Georgia, see Herndon v. Lowry (1937), decided a year before *Carolene Products*.

13. For an account of the Witnesses' use of the courts, see David R. Manwaring, *Render unto Caesar* (Chicago: University of Chicago Press, 1962).

pointed to the dangers of such a course. The political processes were often choked and even where open offered little chance for unpopular groups.

It was to cope with these difficulties that Justice Harlan Fiske Stone formulated footnote 4 in *Carolene Products* (1938; reprinted above, p. 609). Its third paragraph contemplated the problem of equal protection:

> Nor need we inquire whether similar considerations [regarding the Court's presuming a statute constitutional] enter into the review of statutes directed at particular religious, or national, or racial minorities: whether prejudice against discrete and insular minorities may be a special condition, which tends seriously to curtail the operation of those political processes ordinarily to be relied upon to protect minorities, and which may call for a correspondingly more searching judicial inquiry.

To some extent, Stone was prescribing a new jurisprudence; to some extent he was also providing a general justification of what the justices were beginning to do, even though they themselves—and even Stone—may have only been dimly aware of the theories they were weaving. Very rapidly, some of his prescription became part of a description. Eight months after *Carolene Products*, the Court launched the first of what would be many attacks against Jim Crow, holding unconstitutional Missouri's plan to provide legal education for blacks by paying their tuition to law schools out of state.[14]

As we have seen (above, pp. 619–20), several of the justices whom Roosevelt nominated—Black, Douglas, Murphy, and Rutledge in particular, to a lesser extent Jackson, and, for a time, even Frankfurter—were or soon became adherents of Stone's message in *Carolene Products*. As we saw in Chapters 12 and 13, much of their work centered around paragraph two and its emphasis on the necessity of open political processes; thus they gave a "preferred position" to the First Amendment. But no less doggedly and with far greater harmony they worked first to undermine and then to end the legal life of segregation. Brown v. Board of Education (1954; reprinted below, p. 912) came as the climax to a long campaign that played out the common law's usage of stare decisis, gradually expanding exceptions to the doctrine of "separate but equal" until there was nothing left of it but a shell.[15]

---

14. Missouri ex rel. Gaines v. Canada (1938).

15. See, for example: *Transportation*: Mitchell v. United States (1941); Morgan v. Virginia (1946); Bob–Lo Excursion Co. v. Michigan (1948); Henderson v. United States (1950); *Education*: Sipuel v. Bd. of Regents (1948); Fisher v. Hurst (1948); Sweatt v. Painter (1950); McLaurin v. Oklahoma State Regents (1950). See Mark V. Tushnet, *The NAACP's Legal Strategy Against Segregated Education, 1925–1950* (Chapel Hill: University of North Carolina Press, 1987).

A. The Limited Scope of "Deferential Scrutiny"

In cases challenging economic regulation, the Court contin-ued—and still continues—basically to follow the rules laid down in *Lindsley* (1911), what has been called "deferential scrutiny." As the Court stated this test in McGowan v. Maryland (1961): "[a] statuto-ry discrimination will not be set aside if any state of facts reasonably may be conceived to justify it." The justices presume that the legislation is constitutional; the burden of proof to the contrary falls on the challenger. The government does not even have to demonstrate a "rational basis" for its classifications. The Court's use of passive voice indicates that judges as well as legislators may "conceive" the necessary facts; the justices may also hypothesize legitimate purposes to uphold the legislation even without any evidence that the legislature actually intended to pursue such purposes.

It is almost impossible for the challenger to win when a court applies this minimal test of deferential scrutiny. Since the late 1930s, the justices have insisted on using it where the challenge is to economic regulation. (See Williamson v. Lee Optical [1955; reprinted below, p. 908].) Those justices who would insist upon a showing of actual legitimate governmental purpose have been dis-senters. (See Editors' Notes accompanying *Williamson*, below, p. 911.)

B. The Development of "Strict Scrutiny"

During the period after 1938, however, the Court began to develop a different standard for other kinds of problems involving equal protection. The volatility of American race relations made the justices reluctant to spell out clearly their new jurisprudence, but where classification by race was concerned, they relaxed the pre-sumption of constitutionality. In *Carolene Products* Stone had suggested a "more searching judicial inquiry" for the review of statutes directed at "discrete and insular minorities." In Skinner v. Oklahoma (1942; reprinted below, p. 1014), Justice Douglas penned what would eventually become the Court's term of art, "strict scrutiny," in striking down on equal protection grounds a statute requiring sterilization of habitual criminals that exempted persons who committed certain "white collar" crimes.

Skinner, however, had no overt racial content (although it invoked the specter of use of the power to sterilize against groups or types of individuals who are inimical to the dominant group). Ironically, it was Hirabayashi v. United States (1943) and Korematsu v. United States (1944), sustaining first a curfew on and then the internment of Japanese–Americans, that prefigured much of the new egalitarian doctrine. In *Hirabayashi* Stone said:

> Distinctions between citizens solely because of their ancestry are
> by their very nature odious to a free people whose institutions are

founded upon the doctrine of equality. For that reason, legislative classification or discrimination based on race alone has often been held to be a denial of equal protection.

Stone cited three cases to support his last sentence, none of which had quite held that classification by race was, alone, enough to deny equal protection, but all of which pointed in that direction. Thus the Chief Justice was, as in *Carolene Products*, reshaping constitutional doctrine even as he was pretending to describe it.

Hugo Black, speaking for the Court in *Korematsu*, penned two other seminal phrases. First, he said "most rigid scrutiny"—a variation on "strict scrutiny"—was the standard to be applied to classifications involving racial minorities. Second, he explicitly used a concept to which Stone had alluded in both *Carolene Products* and *Hirabayashi*, "suspect classification":

[A]ll legal restrictions which curtail the civil rights of a single racial group are immediately suspect. That it not to say that all such restrictions are unconstitutional. It is to say that courts must subject them to more rigid scrutiny.

Brown v. Board of Education (1954) removed much of the necessity for diplomatic veiling of the new jurisprudence of equal protection; perhaps it also made clearer to the justices themselves precisely what they were doing. In any event, over the next few decades the Court developed the notions of strict scrutiny and suspect classification and then melded them with a concept of "fundamental rights"—which we saw in Chapters 12 and 13 and will see again in Chapters 16–18—to create a nest of tests to assess the constitutionality of statutes challenged as denying equal protection.

The essence of these tests is that where neither a "suspect classification" nor a "fundamental right" is involved, the Court applies "deferential scrutiny," or "rational basis review." It asks only for a reasonable or rational relationship between the legislation and a legitimate governmental goal, and presumes the existence of facts to support the legislature's judgment. Where, however, either a "suspect classification" or a "fundamental right" is involved, the Court invokes "strict scrutiny."

From time to time the justices have used slightly different phrases to describe the test of this "upper tier," but essentially it means that the burden of proof shifts from the challenger to the government to show that: (1) a "compelling" governmental interest is at stake; (2) the connection (or fit) between the challenged governmental action and that compelling governmental interest is very close or "narrowly tailored" (on occasion the Court has said that the connection must be "necessary" [16]) and (3) government could not secure that compelling interest by a different classification

---

16. Shapiro v. Thompson (1969; reprinted below, p. 1019); Adarand Constructors v. Pena (1995; discussed below, p. 970).

or by a lesser infringement on a fundamental right—by "less drastic means," was the way Shelton v. Tucker (1960) put it.

The Court's use of these very different sets of standards has been called a "two-tiered" approach. But, as we shall see in Chapter 15 (espec. San Antonio v. Rodriguez [1973; reprinted below, p. 1002]), there is serious question whether the Court has not in fact used a sliding scale rather than two tiers. Further complicating analysis, the justices in 1976 [17] articulated a middle tier of "intermediate scrutiny" for reviewing classifications such as those based on gender, which the justices concluded were neither so suspicious as to trigger strict scrutiny nor so harmless as to allow deferential scrutiny.

We have passed over the questions of what makes a classification "suspect," what makes a right "fundamental," and what makes a governmental interest "compelling." Chapter 15 takes up those issues, though with no claim to resolving them any more satisfactorily than the justices have. Here we note only that race has been *the* paradigmatic suspect classification. Its use usually carries not a halo of reasonableness but a mark of invidiousness. As Justice Stewart wrote for the Court in 1979:

> Certain classifications ... in themselves supply a reason to infer antipathy. Race is the paradigm. A racial classification, regardless of the purported motivation, is presumptively invalid and can be upheld only upon extraordinary justification.[18]

Beyond the category of race, fog swirls. The Court has said that national origin or ethnicity as well as alienage are also suspect, but the cases are not consistent. (See Hernandez v. Texas (1954; reprinted below, p. 923) and accompanying notes.)

Since *Brown*, the Court has sometimes strained mightily for doctrinal coherence here, as the cases involving affirmative action show. (See Regents v. Bakke [1978; reprinted below, p. 942]; City of Richmond v. J.A. Croson Co. [1989; reprinted below, p. 954]; and Metro Broadcasting v. FCC [1990] and Adarand Constructors v. Pena [1995], discussed in the Editors' Notes following *Croson*.]) The core of the Supreme Court's difficulty in deciding cases involving affirmative action—efforts to eliminate the effects of *past* racial discrimination by taking race into account *now*—lies in deciding the extent to which the Fourteenth Amendment applies to groups and the extent to which it applies only to individuals.

---

17. Craig v. Boren (1976; reprinted below, p. 992).

18. Personnel Administrator v. Feeney (1979). The matter, however, is not always so simple, as the next paragraph indicates. See also the concur. op. of Black, Harlan, and Stewart in Lee v. Washington (1968), where the Court unanimously struck down segregation in Alabama's prisons: "[P]rison authorities have the right, acting in good faith and in particularized circumstances, to take into account racial tensions in maintaining security, discipline, and good order in prisons and jails."

Without an answer to that question, the justices can only awkwardly grope for standards by which to test constitutionality: strict, intermediate, or some other kind of scrutiny. Racial classifications historically have discriminated against African Americans and other racial and ethnic minorities; therefore courts have, during the last decades, subjected them to strict scrutiny. But what test should judges apply to legislation that "benignly" rather than "invidiously" uses racial classifications to try to remedy evils that racial discrimination caused? What test should judges apply to legislation that is not narrowly remedial but nonetheless serves important governmental interests that benefit African Americans and other racial and ethnic minorities? In *Croson*, the majority held that a "set-aside" program for minority business enterprises adopted by a local government is subject to strict scrutiny. In *Metro Broadcasting,* the majority applied intermediate scrutiny to a "benign" measure adopted by Congress. But in *Adarand Constructors,* a different majority held that all racial classifications, whether "benign" or "invidious," and whether adopted by federal, state, or local governments, are subject to strict scrutiny.

Dissenting in *Bakke*, Justice Blackmun put the problem as a dilemma: "In order to get beyond racism, we must first take account of race. ... And in order to treat some people equally, we must treat them differently." On the other hand, before going to the Court, Antonin Scalia argued that to treat people differently is to mistake "the disease as cure." [19] On the bench, he has quoted the first Justice Harlan's dissenting opinion in *Plessy*: "Our Constitution is color-blind." Much in this difficult and controversial area remains unsettled; the only thing that is certain is that "We the People" and judges will continue to debate the meaning of equal protection and equal citizenship in the third century under "the Constitution."

III. THE ORGANIZATION OF THE CASES

Section I of this chapter focuses on the background of equal protection, the early promise and then the bitter reality. Section II examines several modern applications of deferential scrutiny to economic regulation, showing how part of the early jurisprudence is still operating. Then Section III deals with the development of the notion of suspect classifications, restricted here to race and ethnicity, and leaving for Chapter 15 the expansion of that concept and the development of the fundamental rights strand of equal protection. Section IV takes up the problem of distinguishing governmental action that stems from a racially discriminatory purpose from that which merely results in a racially disproportionate impact. Finally, Section V addresses another problem of how to end racial inequality, the constitutionality of affirmative action measures.

---

19. "The Disease as Cure," 1979 *Wash.U.L.Q.* 147.

We repeat our caution that readers should not allow the inherent complexity and fascination of the substantive problems to distract from the purpose of this bloc of chapters: To explore the question, HOW to interpret. We shall see the justices relying heavily on a *doctrinal approach* to augment the usual *textualism*. But we should be alert to see what other *approaches* they are following.

SELECTED BIBLIOGRAPHY

Bell, Derrick A., Jr. *Race, Racism and American Law* (3d ed.; Boston: Little, Brown, 1992).

_____. *And We Are Not Saved* (New York: Basic Books, 1987).

_____. *Faces at the Bottom of the Well* (New York: Basic Books, 1992).

Bickel, Alexander M. "The Original Understanding and the Segregation Decision," 69 *Harv.L.Rev.* 1 (1955).

Brest, Paul. "In Defense of the Antidiscrimination Principle," 90 *Harv.L.Rev.* 1 (1976).

Cohen, Marshall, Thomas Nagel and Thomas Scanlon, eds. *Equality and Preferential Treatment* (Princeton: Princeton University Press, 1977).

Dworkin, Ronald. *A Matter of Principle* (Cambridge: Harvard University Press, 1985), chs. 14–16.

Ely, John Hart. *Democracy and Distrust* (Cambridge: Harvard University Press, 1980), espec. chs. 4, 6.

Fiss, Owen M. "Groups and the Equal Protection Clause," 5 *Phil. & Pub.Aff.* 107 (1976).

Goldman, Alan H. *Justice and Reverse Discrimination* (Princeton: Princeton University Press, 1979).

Gunther, Gerald, "In Search of Evolving Doctrine on a Changing Court," 86 *Harv.L.Rev.* 1 (1972).

Kaczorowski, Robert J. "Revolutionary Constitutionalism in the Era of the Civil War and Reconstruction," 61 *N.Y.U.L.Rev.* 863 (1986).

Kirp, David L., *Just Schools: The Idea of Racial Equality in American Education* (Berkeley: University of California Press, 1982).

Kluger, Richard. *Simple Justice: The History of Brown v. Board of Education and Black America's Struggle for Equality* (New York: Knopf, 1976).

Mason, Alpheus Thomas. *Harlan Fiske Stone* (New York: Viking, 1956), espec. chs. 19–22.

Pritchett, C. Herman. *Constitutional Civil Liberties* (Englewood Cliffs, NJ: Prentice–Hall, 1984), chs. 10, 12.

Sowell, Thomas. *Civil Rights: Rhetoric or Reality?* (New York: Thomas Morrow, 1984).

Tribe, Laurence H. *American Constitutional Law* (2d ed.; Mineola, NY: Foundation Press, 1988), ch. 16.

————. *Constitutional Choices* (Cambridge: Harvard University Press, 1985), chs. 14–16.

Wilkinson, J. Harvie, III. *From Brown to Bakke* (New York: Oxford University Press, 1979).

I. HISTORICAL BACKGROUND: THE PROMISE AND THE REALITY

"The true spirit and meaning of the amendments ... cannot be understood without keeping in view the history of the times when they were adopted, and the general objects they plainly sought to accomplish."

STRAUDER v. WEST VIRGINIA
100 U.S. (10 Otto) 303, 25 L.Ed. 664 (1880).

A West Virginia grand jury indicted Strauder, a black man, for murder; and a petit (trial) jury convicted him of that crime. State law forbade blacks to serve on either kind of jury, and Strauder's counsel unsuccessfully contended at the trial and on appeal within the state judicial system that this exclusion denied his client equal protection of the laws. The U.S. Supreme Court granted a writ of error.

Mr. Justice **STRONG** delivered the opinion of the Court. ...

... [The controlling question] is not whether a colored man ... has a right to a grand or a petit jury composed in whole or in part of persons of his own race or color; but it is whether ... all persons of his race or color may be excluded by law, solely because of their race or color, so that by no possibility can any colored man sit upon the jury.

The questions are important, for they demand a construction of the recent amendments of the Constitution. ... The Fourteenth Amendment ... is one of a series of constitutional provisions having a common purpose; namely, securing to a race recently emancipated ... all the civil rights that the superior race enjoy. The true spirit and meaning of the amendments, as we said in the Slaughter–House Cases [1873], cannot be understood without keeping in view the history of the times when they were adopted, and the general objects they plainly sought to accomplish. ... [I]t required little knowledge of human nature to anticipate that those who had long been regarded as an inferior and subject race would, when suddenly raised to the rank of citizenship, be looked upon with jealousy and positive dislike, and that State Laws might be enacted or enforced to perpetuate the distinctions that had before existed. Discriminations against them had been habitual. It was well known that in some States laws making such discriminations then existed, and others might well be expected. The colored race, as a race, was abject and ignorant, and in that condition was unfitted to command the respect of those who had superior intelligence. Their training had left them mere children, and as such they needed the protection which a wise government extends to those who are unable to protect themselves. They especially needed protection against unfriendly action in the States where they were resident. It was in view of these considerations the Fourteenth Amendment was framed and adopted. It was designed to assure to the colored race the enjoyment of all the civil rights that under the law are enjoyed by white persons, and to give to that race the protection of the general government, in that enjoyment, whenever it should be denied by the States. It not only gave citizenship and the privileges of citizenship to persons of color, but it denied to any State the power to withhold from them the equal protection of the laws, and authorized Congress to enforce its provisions by appropriate legislation. To quote ... *Slaughter-House:* "No one can fail to be impressed with the one pervading purpose found in all the amendments, lying at the foundation of each, and without which none of them would have been suggested— ... the freedom of the slave race, the security and firm establishment of that freedom, and the protection of the newly made freeman and citizen from the oppressions of those who had formerly exercised unlimited dominion over them." ... "We doubt very much whether any action of a State, not directed by way of discrimination against the negroes, as a class, will ever be held to come within the purview of this provision."

If this is the spirit and meaning of the amendment, whether it means more or not, it is to be construed liberally, to carry out the purposes of its framers. ... [It declares] that the law in the States shall be the same for the black as for the white; that all persons, whether colored or white, shall stand equal before the laws of the States, and, in regard to the colored race, for whose protection the amendment was primarily designed, that no discrimination shall be made against them by law because of their color[.] The words of the amendment, it is true, are prohibitory, but they contain a necessary implication of a positive immunity, or right, most valuable to the colored race— ... exemption from legal discriminations, implying inferiority in civil society, lessening the security of their enjoyment of the rights which others enjoy, and discriminations which are steps towards reducing them to the condition of a subject race.

That the West Virginia statute respecting juries ... is such a discrimination ought not to be doubted. Nor would it be if the persons excluded by it were white men. If in those States where the colored people constitute a majority of the entire population a law should be enacted excluding all white men from jury service ... no one would be heard to claim that it would not be a denial to white men of the equal protection of the laws. Nor if a law should be passed excluding all naturalized Celtic Irishmen, would there be any doubt of its inconsistency with the spirit of the amendment. The very fact that colored people are singled out and expressly denied by a statute all right to participate in the administration of the law, as jurors, because of their color, though they are citizens, and may be in other respects fully qualified, is practically a brand upon them, affixed by the law; an assertion of their inferiority, and a stimulant to that race prejudice which is an impediment to securing to individuals of the race that equal justice which the law aims to secure to all others.

The right to a trial by jury is guaranteed to every citizen of West Virginia by the Constitution of that State. ... The very idea of a jury is a body of men composed of the peers or equals of the person whose rights it is selected or summoned to determine; that is, of his neighbors, fellows, associates, persons having the same legal status in society as that which he holds. ... [P]rejudices often exist against particular classes in the community, which ... operate in some cases to deny to persons of those classes the full enjoyment of that protection which others enjoy. ... The framers of the constitutional amendment must have known full well the existence of such prejudice and its likelihood to continue against the manumitted slaves and their race, and that knowledge was doubtless a motive that led to the amendment. By their manumission and citizenship the colored race became entitled to the equal protection of the laws of the States in which they resided; and the apprehension that ... there might be discrimination against them, was the inducement to bestow upon the national government the power to enforce the provision that no State shall deny to them the equal protection of the laws. ... It is not easy to comprehend how it can be said that while every white man is entitled to a trial by a jury ... selected without discrimination against his color, and a negro is not, the latter is equally protected by the law with the former. ...

We do not say that, within the limits from which it is not excluded by the amendment, a State may not prescribe the qualifications of its jurors, and in so doing make discriminations. It may confine the selection to males, to freeholders, to citizens, to persons within certain ages, or to persons having educational qualifications. We do not believe the Fourteenth Amendment was ever intended to prohibit this. Looking at its history, it is clear it had no such purpose. Its aim was against discrimination because of race or color. ... [I]ts design was to protect an emancipated race, and to strike down all possible legal discriminations against those who belong to it. "In giving construction to any of these [amendments], it is necessary to keep the main purpose steadily in view." "It is so clearly a provision for that race and that emergency, that a strong case would be necessary for its application to any other." [*Slaughter-House.*] We are not now called upon to affirm or deny that it had other purposes.

The Fourteenth Amendment makes no attempt to enumerate the rights it designed to protect. It speaks in general terms, and those are as comprehensive as possible. Its language is prohibitory; but every prohibition implies the existence of rights and immunities, prominent among which is an immunity from inequality of legal protection, either for life, liberty, or property. Any State action that denies this immunity to a colored man is in conflict with the Constitution. ...

[*Reversed.*]

Mr. Justice **FIELD** and Mr. Justice **CLIFFORD** dissented.

Editors' Notes

(1) **Query:** What approach or approaches to constitutional interpretation did Justice Strong follow? What did his conception of "the Constitution" include?

(2) **Query:** The Court in *Strauder* regarded the statute's explicit exclusion of blacks from jury service as "practically a brand upon them" and "a stimulant to that race prejudice" that impedes attainment of equal justice. Does this concern with stigma and prejudice fit more comfortably within a *Carolene Products* theory of *reinforcing representative democracy* or a constitutionalist theory of human dignity? Compare John Hart Ely, *Democracy and Distrust* (Cambridge: Harvard University Press, 1980), ch. 6, with Bruce A. Ackerman, "Beyond *Carolene Products*," 98 *Harv.L.Rev.* 713 (1985), and Charles R. Lawrence, III, "The Id, the Ego, and Equal Protection: Reckoning with Unconscious Racism," 39 *Stan.L.Rev.* 317 (1987). One might keep this concern with stigma in mind when reading Plessy v. Ferguson (1896; reprinted below, p. 902).

(3) **Query:** Did *Strauder* interpret the Fourteenth Amendment as embodying a principle of opposition to castes or a principle of racial neutrality? *See* Cass R. Sunstein, *The Partial Constitution* (Cambridge: Harvard University Press, 1993), chs. 5 & 11.

(4) **Query:** In *Strauder*, the West Virginia statute expressly discriminated against African Americans. It also discriminated against women, but the Court said that was constitutionally permissible. What if the statute's words had not been discriminatory, but the state had applied it with the purpose or effect of excluding blacks from jury service? For a general response, see Yick Wo v. Hopkins (1886: reprinted immediately below). For the specific issue of discrimination in selection of juries, see Batson v. Kentucky (1986), which held that "the Equal Protection Clause forbids the prosecutor to challenge potential jurors solely on account of their race." In J.E.B. v. Alabama ex rel. T.B. (1994),

the Court reached a similar conclusion regarding use of peremptory challenges to exclude potential jurors on the basis of their sex.

"[T]he nature and the theory of our institutions of government, the principles upon which they are supposed to rest, and ... the history of their development ... do not mean to leave room for the play and action of purely personal and arbitrary power."

YICK WO v. HOPKINS

118 U.S. 356, 6 S.Ct. 1064, 30 L.Ed. 220 (1886).

An ordinance of San Francisco County required special permission to operate a laundry in a building constructed of materials other than brick or stone. More than 300 of the approximately 320 laundries in the city were made of wood. With only one exception, the county granted all applications for special permission filed by Caucasians, but denied all 200 submitted by Chinese. Yick Wo and 150 other Chinese aliens continued to operate their laundries and were convicted under the ordinance. The state supreme court affirmed the convictions, and Yick Wo and another Chinese alien obtained a writ of error from the U.S. Supreme Court.

Mr. Justice **MATTHEWS** delivered the opinion of the Court. ...

The rights of the petitioners ... are not less because they are aliens. ... The Fourteenth Amendment to the Constitution is not confined to the protection of citizens. It says: "Nor shall any State deprive any person of life, liberty, or property without due process of law; nor deny to any person within its jurisdiction the equal protection of the laws." These provisions are universal in their application, to all persons within the territorial jurisdiction, without regard to any differences of race, of color, or of nationality; and the equal protection of the laws is a pledge of the protection of equal laws. ... [Petitioners contend that the ordinances] are void on their face, as being within the prohibitions of the Fourteenth Amendment; and, in the alternative, if not so, that they are void by reason of their administration, operating unequally, so as to punish in the present petitioners what is permitted to others as lawful, without any distinction of circumstances—an unjust and illegal discrimination, it is claimed, which, though not made expressly by the ordinances is made possible by them.

When we consider the nature and the theory of our institutions of government, the principles upon which they are supposed to rest, and review the history of their development, we are constrained to conclude that they do not mean to leave room for the play and action of purely personal and arbitrary power. Sovereignty itself is, of course, not subject to law, for it is the author and source of law; but in our system, while sovereign powers are delegated to the agencies of government, sovereignty itself remains with the people, by whom and for whom all government exists and acts. And the law is the definition and limitation of power. It is, indeed, quite true, that there must always be lodged somewhere, and in some person or body, the authority of final decision; and in many cases of mere administration the responsibility is purely political, no appeal lying except to the ultimate tribunal of the public judgment, exercised either in the pressure of opinion or by means of the suffrage. But the fundamental rights to life, liberty, and the pursuit of happiness ... are secured by those maxims of constitutional law which are the monuments showing the victorious progress of the race in securing to men the blessings of civilization under the reign of just and equal laws, so that, in the famous language of the Massachusetts Bill of Rights, the government of the commonwealth "may be a government of laws and not of men." For, the very idea that one man may be compelled to hold his life, or the means of living, or any material right essential to the enjoyment of life, at the mere will of another, seems to be intolerable in any country where freedom prevails, as being the essence of slavery itself.

There are many illustrations that might be given of this truth, which would make manifest that it was self-evident in the light of our system of jurisprudence. The case of the political franchise of voting is one. Though not regarded strictly as a natural right, but as a privilege merely conceded by society according to its will, under certain conditions, nevertheless it is regarded as a fundamental political right, because preservative of all rights. ...

... In the present cases we are not obliged to reason from the probable to the actual. ... For the cases present the ordinances in actual operation. ... Though the law itself be fair on its face and impartial in appearance, yet, if it is applied and administered by public authority with an evil eye and an unequal hand, so as practically to make unjust and illegal discriminations between persons in similar circumstances, material to their rights, the denial of equal justice is still within the prohibition of the Constitution. ...

The present cases ... are within this class. It appears that both petitioners have complied with every requisite, deemed by the law or by the public officers charged with its administration, necessary for the protection of neighboring property from fire, or as a precaution against injury to the public health. No reason whatever, except the will of the supervisors, is assigned why they should not be permitted to carry on, in the accustomed manner, their harmless and useful occupation, on which they depend for a livelihood. And while this consent of the supervisors is withheld from them and from two hundred others who have also petitioned, all of whom happen to be Chinese subjects, eighty others, not Chinese subjects, are permitted to carry on the same business under similar conditions. The fact of this discrimination is admitted. No reason for it is shown, and the conclusion cannot be resisted, that no reason for it exists except hostility to the race and nationality to which the petitioners belong, and which in the eye of the law is not justified. The discrimination is, therefore, illegal, and the public administration which enforces it is a denial of the equal protection of the laws and a violation of the Fourteenth Amendment of the Constitution. The imprisonment of the petitioners is, therefore, illegal, and they must be discharged.

[*Reversed.*]

Editors' Notes

(1) **Query:** How did Justice Matthews's approach(es) to constitutional interpretation differ from Strong's in *Strauder*?

(2) **Query:** The "fundamental rights to life, liberty, and the pursuit of happiness," Matthews wrote, "are secured by those maxims of constitutional law which are the monuments showing the victorious progress of the race in securing to men the blessings of civilization under the reign of just and equal laws, so that [we may have]' ... a government of laws and not of men.' " Where did Matthews find "those maxims of constitutional law"? What did *his* "Constitution" include?

(3) Unlike *Strauder*, which involved racial discrimination on the face of a statute, *Yick Wo* involved discrimination in the administration of an ordinance that was "fair on its face and impartial in appearance." The Court readily inferred purposeful discrimination from the racially disproportionate impact of its administration. But see the Editors' Notes on The Requirement of a Racially Discriminatory Purpose, below at p. 931, and Rogers v. Lodge (1982; reprinted below, p. 933.

(4) Compare the Court's conception of "slavery" here and in *Strauder* with that expressed in Plessy v. Ferguson (1896; reprinted immediately below).

"The object of the [Fourteenth] Amendment was undoubtedly to enforce the absolute equality of the two races before the law, but ... it could not have been intended to abolish distinctions based upon color, or to enforce social, as distinguished from political equality, or a commingling of the two races upon terms unsatisfactory to either."—Justice BROWN

"Our Constitution is color-blind, and neither knows nor tolerates classes among citizens."—Justice HARLAN

PLESSY v. FERGUSON

163 U.S. 537, 16 S.Ct. 1138, 41 L.Ed. 256 (1896).

In 1890 the Louisiana legislature enacted a law requiring railroads to provide "equal but separate" accommodations for "white" and "colored" passengers. Homer Plessy, seven-eighths white and one-eighth "colored," was convicted for refusing to comply with a conductor's order to sit in a coach assigned to "colored" passengers. The state supreme court rejected Plessy's claims that the law violated the Thirteenth and Fourteenth amendments, but he obtained a writ of error from the U.S. Supreme Court.

Mr. Justice **BROWN** delivered the opinion of the Court. ...

1. That [the act] does not conflict with the Thirteenth Amendment, which abolished slavery and involuntary servitude, except as a punishment for crime, is too clear for argument. Slavery implies involuntary servitude—a state of bondage; the ownership of mankind as a chattel, or at least the control of the labor and services of one man for the benefit of another, and the absence of a legal right to the disposal of his own person, property and services. ...

A statute which implies merely a legal distinction between the white and colored races—a distinction which is founded in the color of the two races, and which must always exist so long as white men are distinguished from the other race by color—has no tendency to destroy the legal equality of the two races, or reestablish a state of involuntary servitude. Indeed, we do not understand that the Thirteenth Amendment is strenuously relied upon by the plaintiff in error in this connection.

2. ... The object of the [Fourteenth] Amendment was undoubtedly to enforce the absolute equality of the two races before the law, but in the nature of things it could not have been intended to abolish distinctions based upon color, or to enforce social, as distinguished from political equality, or a commingling of the two races upon terms unsatisfactory to either. Laws permitting, and even requiring, their separation in places where they are liable to be brought into contact do not necessarily imply the inferiority of either race to the other and have been generally, if not universally, recognized as within the competency of the state legislatures in the exercise of their police power. The most common instance of this is connected with the establishment of separate schools for white and colored children, which has been held to be a valid exercise of the legislative power even by courts of States where the political rights of the colored race have been longest and most earnestly enforced.

One of the earliest of these cases is that of Roberts v. Boston [1849], in which the Supreme Judicial Court of Massachusetts held that the general school committee of Boston had power to make provision for the instruction of colored children in separate schools established exclusively for them, and to prohibit their attendance upon the other schools. "The great principle," said Chief Justice Shaw. ...

is that by the constitution and laws of Massachusetts, all persons without distinction of age, sex, birth or color, origin or condition, are equal before the law. ... But, when this great principle comes to be applied to the actual and various conditions of persons in society, it will not warrant the assertion, that men and women are legally clothed with the same civil and political powers, and that children and adults are

legally to have the same functions and be subject to the same treatment;
but only that the rights of all, as they are settled and regulated by law,
are equally entitled to the paternal consideration and protections of the
law for their maintenance and security.

It was held that the powers of the committee extended to the establishment of separate schools for children of different ages, sexes, and colors.
... Similar laws have been enacted by Congress under its general power
of legislation over the District of Columbia. ...

Laws forbidding the intermarriage of the two races may be said in a
technical sense to interfere with the freedom of contract, and yet have
been universally recognized as within the police power of the State. The
distinction between laws interfering with the political equality of the
negro and those requiring the separation of the two races in schools,
theatres and railway carriages has been frequently drawn by this court.
Strauder v. West Virginia [1880]. ... [W]e think the enforced separation of the races, as applied to the internal commerce of the State,
neither abridges the privileges or immunities of the colored man, deprives him of his property without due process of law, nor denies him the
equal protection of the laws, within the meaning of the Fourteenth
Amendment. ...

It is claimed by the plaintiff in error that, in any mixed community,
the reputation of belonging to the dominant race, in this instance the
white race, is *property,* in the same sense that a right of action, or of
inheritance, is property. Conceding this to be so, for the purposes of
this case, we are unable to see how this statute deprives him of, or in any
way affects his right to, such property. If he be a white man and
assigned to a colored coach, he may have his action for damages against
the company for being deprived of his so called property. Upon the
other hand, if he be a colored man and be so assigned, he has been
deprived of no property, since he is not lawfully entitled to the reputation of being a white man.

... [I]t is also suggested ... that the same argument that will
justify the state legislature in requiring railways to provide separate
accommodations for the two races will also authorize them to require
separate cars to be provided for people whose hair is of a certain color, or
who are aliens, or who belong to certain nationalities, or to enact laws
requiring colored people to walk upon one side of the street, and white
people upon the other, or requiring white men's houses to be painted
white, and colored men's black, or their vehicles or business signs to be
of different colors, upon the theory that one side of the street is as good
as the other, or that a house or vehicle of one color is as good as one of
another color. The reply to all this is that every exercise of the police
power must be reasonable, and extend only to such laws as are enacted
in good faith for the promotion for the public good, and not for the
annoyance or oppression of a particular class. Yick Wo v. Hopkins
[1886]. ...

So far, then, as a conflict with the Fourteenth Amendment is concerned, the case reduces itself to the question whether the statute of Louisiana is a reasonable regulation, and with respect to this there must necessarily be a large discretion on the part of the legislature. In determining the question of reasonableness it is at liberty to act with reference to the established usages, customs and traditions of the people, and with a view to the promotion of their comfort, and the preservation of the public peace and good order. Gauged by this standard, we cannot say that a law which authorizes or even requires the separation of the two races in public conveyances is unreasonable, or more obnoxious to the Fourteenth Amendment than the acts of Congress requiring separate schools for colored children in the District of Columbia, the constitutionality of which does not seem to have been questioned, or the corresponding acts of state legislatures.

We consider the underlying fallacy of the plaintiff's argument to consist in the assumption that the enforced separation of the two races stamps the colored race with a badge of inferiority. If this be so, it is not by reason of anything found in the act, but solely because the colored race chooses to put that construction upon it. The argument necessarily assumes that if, as has been more than once the case, and is not unlikely to be so again, the colored race should become the dominant power in the state legislature, and should enact a law in precisely similar terms, it would thereby relegate the white race to an inferior position. We imagine that the white race, at least, would not acquiesce in this assumption. The argument also assumes that social prejudices may be overcome by legislation, and that equal rights cannot be secured to the negro except by an enforced commingling of the two races. We cannot accept this proposition. If the two races are to meet upon terms of social equality, it must be the result of natural affinities, a mutual appreciation of each other's merits and a voluntary consent of individuals. ... Legislation is powerless to eradicate racial instincts or to abolish distinctions based upon physical differences, and the attempt to do so can only result in accentuating the difficulties of the present situation. If the civil and political rights of both races be equal one cannot be inferior to the other civilly or politically. If one race be inferior to the other socially, the Constitution of the United States cannot put them upon the same plane. ...

Affirmed.

Mr. Justice **HARLAN** dissenting. ...

The white race deems itself to be the dominant race in this country. And so it is, in prestige, in achievements, in education, in wealth and in power. So, I doubt not, it will continue to be for all time, if it remains true to its great heritage and holds fast to the principles of constitutional liberty. But in view of the Constitution, in the eye of the law, there is in this country no superior, dominant, ruling class of citizens. There is no caste here. Our Constitution is color-blind, and neither knows nor tolerates classes among citizens. In respect of civil rights, all citizens are equal before the law. The humblest is the peer of the most powerful. The law regards man as man, and takes no account of his surroundings or of his color when his civil rights as guaranteed by the supreme law of the land are involved. It is, therefore, to be regretted that this high tribunal, the final expositor of the fundamental law of the land, has reached the conclusion that it is competent for a State to regulate the enjoyment by citizens of their civil rights solely upon the basis of race.

In my opinion, the judgment this day rendered will, in time, prove to be quite as pernicious as the decision made by this tribunal in the *Dred Scott* case [1857]. ... [It] will not only stimulate aggressions, more or less brutal and irritating, upon the admitted rights of colored citizens, but will encourage the belief that it is possible, by means of state enactments, to defeat the beneficent purposes which the people of the United States had in view when they adopted the recent amendments of the Constitution. ... The destinies of the two races, in this country, are indissolubly linked together, and the interests of both require that the common government of all shall not permit the seeds of race hate to be planted under the sanction of law. What can more certainly arouse race hate, what more certainly create and perpetuate a feeling of distrust between these races, than state enactments, which, in fact, proceed on the ground that colored citizens are so inferior and degraded that they cannot be allowed to sit in public coaches occupied by white citizens? That, as all will admit, is the real meaning of such legislation as was enacted in Louisiana.

The sure guarantee of the peace and security of each race is the clear, distinct, unconditional recognition by our governments, National and State, of every right that inheres in civil freedom, and of the equality before the law of all citizens of the United States without regard to race. State enactments regulating the enjoyment of civil rights, upon the basis of race, and cunningly devised to defeat legitimate results of the war, under the pretence of recognizing equality of rights, can have no other result than to render permanent peace impossible, and to keep alive a conflict of races, the continuance of which must do harm to all concerned. This question is not met by the suggestion that social equality cannot exist between the white and black races in this country ...; for social equality no more exists between two races when travelling in a passenger coach or a public highway than when members of the same races sit by each other in a street car or in the jury box, or stand or sit with each other in a political assembly, or when they use in common the streets of a city or town. ...

The arbitrary separation of citizens, on the basis of race, while they are on a public highway, is a badge of servitude wholly inconsistent with the civil freedom and the equality before the law established by the Constitution. It cannot be justified upon any legal grounds. ... We boast of the freedom enjoyed by our people above all other peoples. But it is difficult to reconcile that boast with a state of the law which, practically, puts the brand of servitude and degradation upon a large class of our fellow-citizens, our equals before the law. The thin disguise of "equal" accommodations for passengers in railroad coaches will not mislead any one, nor atone for the wrong this day done. ...

I am of opinion that the statute of Louisiana is inconsistent with the personal liberty of citizens, white and black, in that State, and hostile to both the spirit and letter of the Constitution of the United States. If laws of like character should be enacted in the several States of the Union, the effect would be in the highest degree mischievous. Slavery, as an institution tolerated by law would, it is true, have disappeared from our country, but there would remain a power in the States, by sinister legislation, to interfere with the full enjoyment of the blessings of freedom; to regulate civil rights, common to all citizens, upon the basis of race; and to place in a condition of legal inferiority a large body of American citizens, now constituting a part of the political community called the People of the United States, for whom, and by whom through representatives, our government is administered. Such a system is inconsistent with the guarantee given by the Constitution to each State of a republican form of government, and may be stricken down by Congressional action, or by the courts in the discharge of their solemn duty to maintain the supreme law of the land, anything in the constitution or laws of any State to the contrary notwithstanding. ...

Mr. Justice **BREWER** did not hear the argument or participate in the decision of this case.

Editors' Notes

(1) **Query:** What approach to constitutional interpretation did Justice Brown follow? What sort of test of constitutionality did he apply? What was Justice Harlan's approach? His test? How did their "Constitutions" differ?

(2) **Query:** To what extent did Harlan make, in effect, a *structuralist* argument that the Republican Form of Government Clause (Article IV, Section 4), the Thirteenth Amendment, and the equal protection clause must be read together as a unit, and that, so read, the constitutional text invalidates denials of equal citizenship? For the interplay between the Equal Protection Clause and the Republican Form of Government Clause, see Reynolds v. Sims (1964; reprinted above, p. 777, and accompanying Editors' Notes).

(3) **Query:** Harlan's claim that "[o]ur Constitution is color-blind, and neither knows nor tolerates classes among citizens" is one of the most often quoted passages in the history of American constitutional law. Did his assertion reflect a principle of opposition to castes or a principle of racial neutrality? In recent years Harlan's dissent has served as a rallying cry for critics of affirmative action programs benefitting blacks. See, e.g., Justice Scalia's and Justice Kennedy's concurring opinions in Richmond v. J. A. Croson (1989; reprinted below, p. 954) and Kennedy's dissenting opinion, joined by Scalia, in Metro Broadcasting v. FCC (1990), discussed in the Editors' Notes following *Croson*. But the conception of equal protection as a

principle absolutely requiring racial neutrality has never commanded the assent of a majority of the Supreme Court.

(4) **Query:** Was the majority in *Plessy* right in assuming that the Fourteenth Amendment is inherently limited to protecting against deprivations of "political equality" as distinguished from "social equality"? What is the basis for such a distinction? A principled interpretation of the text of the Fourteenth Amendment or a prudential and sociological judgment that there are limits on the extent to which a state can legally enforce social and moral principles?

(5) Harlan's prediction that *Plessy* would "prove to be quite as pernicious" as *Dred Scott* proved correct. But its doctrine of "separate but equal" was not even partially overruled until more than a half-century later by Brown v. Board of Education and Bolling v. Sharpe (1954; reprinted below, p. 912 & p. 917), and then only insofar as public education was concerned. No one doubted that *Brown* killed *Plessy*, but the funeral came in terse and fragmentary ceremonies over the next few years, as the Court invalidated segregation in public parks and transportation.

II. DEFERENTIAL SCRUTINY

"The prohibition of the Equal Protection Clause goes no further than the invidious discrimination."

WILLIAMSON v. LEE OPTICAL CO.
348 U.S. 483, 75 S.Ct. 461, 99 L.Ed. 563 (1955).

Oklahoma's legislature enacted a complex statute regulating visual care. Its effect was to reduce drastically the scope of opticians' lawful activities and correspondingly to increase those phases of visual care that could be performed only by ophthalmologists or optometrists. Lee Optical Co., opticians, sued in a federal district court, claiming that, by taking away their business, the statute deprived them of their property without due process and denied them equal protection. The district court declared the statute unconstitutional, and Oklahoma appealed to the Supreme Court.

Mr. Justice **DOUGLAS** delivered the opinion of the Court. . . .

. . . First, [the District Court] held invalid under the Due Process Clause of the Fourteenth Amendment the portions of § 2 which make it unlawful for any person not a licensed optometrist or ophthalmologist to fit lenses to a face or to duplicate or replace into frames lenses or other optical appliances, except upon written prescriptive authority of an Oklahoma licensed ophthalmologist or optometrist. An ophthalmologist is a duly licensed physician who specializes in the care of the eyes. An optometrist examines eyes for refractive error, recognizes (but does not treat) diseases of the eye, and fills prescriptions for eyeglasses. The optician is an artisan qualified to grind lenses, fill prescriptions, and fit frames.

The effect of § 2 is ... that no optician can fit old glasses into new frames or supply a lens, whether it be a new lens or one to duplicate a lost or broken lens, without a prescription. The District Court conceded that it was in the competence of the police power of a State to regulate the examination of the eyes. But it rebelled at the notion that a State could require a prescription from an optometrist or ophthalmologist "to take old lenses and place them in new frames and then fit the completed spectacles to the *face* of the eyeglass wearer." ... The Court held that "Although on [the] precise issue of duplication, the legislature in the instant regulation was dealing with a matter of public interest, the particular means chosen are neither reasonably necessary nor reasonably related to the end sought to be achieved." It was, accordingly, the opinion of the court that this provision of the law violated the Due Process Clause by arbitrarily interfering with the optician's right to do business. ...

The Oklahoma law may exact a needless, wasteful requirement in many cases. But it is for the legislature, not the courts, to balance the advantages and disadvantages of the new requirement. It appears that in many cases the optician can easily supply the new frames or new lenses without reference to the old written prescription. It also appears that many written prescriptions contain no directive data in regard to fitting spectacles to the face. But ... [t]he legislature might have concluded that the frequency of occasions when a prescription is necessary was sufficient to justify this regulation of the fitting of eyeglasses. Likewise, when it is necessary to duplicate a lens, a written prescription may or may not be necessary. But the legislature might have concluded that one was needed often enough to require one in every case. Or the legislature may have concluded that eye examinations were so critical, not only for correction of vision but also for detection of latent ailments or diseases, that every change in frames and every duplication of a lens should be accompanied by a prescription from a medical expert. To be sure, the present law does not require a new examination of the eyes every time the frames are changed or the lenses duplicated. For if the old prescription is on file with the optician, he can go ahead and make the new fitting or duplicate the lenses. But the law need not be in every respect logically consistent with its aims to be constitutional. It is enough that there is an evil at hand for correction, and that it might be thought that the particular legislative measure was a rational way to correct it.

The day is gone when this Court uses the Due Process Clause of the Fourteenth Amendment to strike down state laws, regulatory of business and industrial conditions, because they may be unwise, improvident, or out of harmony with a particular school of thought. See West Coast Hotel Co. v. Parrish [1937].

Secondly, the District Court held that it violated the Equal Protection Clause of the Fourteenth Amendment to subject opticians to this regulatory system and to exempt, as § 3 of the Act does, all sellers of ready-to-wear glasses. The problem of legislative classification is a perennial one, admitting of no doctrinaire definition. Evils in the same field may be of different dimensions and proportions, requiring different remedies. Or so the legislature may think. Or the reform may take one step at a time, addressing itself to the phase of the problem which seems most acute to the legislative mind. The legislature may select one phase of one field and apply a remedy there, neglecting the others. The prohibition of the Equal Protection Clause goes no further than the invidious discrimination. We cannot say that that point has been reached here. For all this record shows, the ready-to-wear branch of this business may not loom large in Oklahoma or may present problems of regulation distinct from the other branch. ...

[*Reversed.*]

Mr. Justice **HARLAN** took no part in the consideration or decision of these cases.

Editors' Notes

(1) One of the most annoying difficulties with the Court's use of terms such as "rationality" or "rational basis test" is that the justices often use "rational" in a loose way, not in the more technical sense of instrumental rationality between ends and means that social scientists would employ that word. See, for example, Sidney Verba, "Assumptions of Rationality and Non-Rationality in Models of the International System," 14 *World Pols.* 93 (1961). In the social sciences, a "rational choice" is the alternative among many which most efficiently moves an actor toward a desired goal. Thus, one cannot begin to speak intelligently of a choice as rational without knowing what the goal is. What judges mean by rationality is often unclear.

(2) **Query:** What approach to constitutional interpretation did Justice Douglas follow? *Textualism? Purposivism? Structuralism? Balancing?* Some other?

(3) **Query:** Is there any way the state can lose if the Court applies the sort of deferential scrutiny that it did in *Williamson*? (See the discussion of Lindsley v. Natural Carbonic Gas Co. [1911] in the Introductory Essay to this Chapter.) What happens then to the promise of equal protection of the laws? Does it vanish or does deferential judicial scrutiny merely turn from the question of HOW to interpret to WHO interprets, with the Court's offering the answer that this aspect of constitutional interpretation falls almost completely within the province of legislators and administrators? In New Orleans v. Dukes (1976), the Court, in applying such deferential scrutiny to uphold an ordinance forbidding "pushcart vendors" within the old French Quarter of the New Orleans—but allowing any pushcart peddler who had been in business for eight or more years to continue to operate there—overruled the only case

in the last half century to invalidate "a wholly economic regulation solely on equal protection grounds." Morey v. Doud (1957).

(4) **Query:** Since 1937, in cases involving economic regulations, the Court has essentially speculated about the conceivable ends that the legislature might have been pursuing, and has further speculated about how the statute conceivably might further those ends. Should the Court, instead, insist upon hard evidence about actual legitimate governmental purposes, and a demonstration that the statute actually furthers those purposes? In U.S. Railroad Retirement Board v. Fritz (1980), the Court, through Justice Rehnquist, stated: "Where . . . there are plausible reasons for Congress' action, our inquiry is at an end . . . because this Court has never insisted that a legislative body articulate its reasons for enacting a statute." In dissent, Justice Brennan argued that, in recent years, "this Court has frequently recognized that the actual purposes of Congress, rather than the post hoc justifications offered by Government attorneys, must be the primary basis for analysis under the rational basis test."

Justice Lewis F. Powell would have gone further than Brennan. Dissenting in Schweiker v. Wilson (1981), Powell wrote:

> In my view, the Court should receive with some skepticism post hoc hypotheses about legislative purpose, unsupported by the legislative history. When no indication of legislative purpose appears other than the current position of [an executive officer] the Court should require that the classification bear a "fair and substantial relation" to the asserted purpose. . . . This marginally more demanding scrutiny indirectly would test the plausibility of the tendered purpose and preserve equal protection review as something more than "a mere tautological recognition of the fact that Congress did what it intended to do." (Quoting *Fritz* [Stevens, J., concurring in the judgment]).

How would a court go about ascertaining "actual purposes"?

Prof. Sanford V. Levinson has recently argued that state attorneys general should play a different role. Rather than being the legislature's "hired gun," they should look on themselves as agents of the public and not invent ends-means analysis for the legislature. "Identifying the Compelling State Interest: On 'Due Process of Lawmaking' and the Professional Responsibility of the Public Lawyer," 45 *Hastings L.J.* 1035 (1994).

(5) Railway Express Agency v. New York (1949) upheld, against both due process and equal protection challenges, a New York traffic regulation forbidding all advertising on vehicles except that related to the business of the vehicle's owner. Concurring, Justice Jackson urged that the Court should use the equal protection clause to invalidate legislation more readily than the due process clause because the former intrudes less on the choices of governmental bodies:

> Invalidation of a statute or an ordinance on due process grounds leaves ungoverned and ungovernable conduct which many people find objectionable. Invocation of the equal protection clause, on the other hand, does not disable any governmental body from dealing

with the subject at hand.   It merely means that the prohibition or regulation must have a broader impact.

Query: Is Justice Jackson's distinction between due process and equal protection persuasive?

III. THE BEGINNING OF SUSPECT CLASSIFICATIONS: RACE AND ETHNICITY

"[L]egal restrictions which curtail the civil rights of a single racial group are immediately suspect. ... [C]ourts must subject them to the most rigid scrutiny.

KOREMATSU v. UNITED STATES
323 U.S. 214, 65 S.Ct. 193, 89 L.Ed. 194 (1944).

This case, sustaining the imprisonment of American citizens of Japanese ancestry during World War II, is reprinted below, p. 1383.

"In approaching this problem, we cannot turn the clock back to 1868 when the Amendment was adopted, or even to 1896 when *Plessy* was written. We must consider public education in the light of its full development and its present place in American life throughout the Nation."

BROWN v. BOARD OF EDUCATION OF TOPEKA, I
347 U.S. 483, 74 S.Ct. 686, 98 L.Ed. 873 (1954).

From its founding in 1909, the National Association for the Advancement of Colored People fought to bring a measure of racial justice to the United States and, more specifically, to overturn Plessy v. Ferguson (1896; reprinted above, p. 902).   The group had only mixed success, but in 1938 its operations became more effective when a young black lawyer named Thurgood Marshall became director of the NAACP's Legal Defense and Educational Fund.   He converted what had been a series of scattered skirmishes into a centrally directed campaign that carefully selected plaintiffs and targets for lawsuits and coordinated legal arguments and tactics with sympathetic organizations like the American Civil Liberties Union.

Over the next dozen years, Marshall won every case he got before the U.S. Supreme Court as he pursued a strategy of gradually undermining the constitutional bases of racial segregation. In 1950 Sweatt v. Painter signalled that the climax of the judicial phase of the campaign was near. There the Court held that Texas's creation of a separate law school for African Americans did not accord equal protection. The state could provide equality in separate tangible, physical facilities, but it could not provide equality in such intangibles as prestige and alumni. If the justices were serious about the importance of intangibles, then all public school segregation was doomed, for no one pretended that black schools were equal to white on that score, and few pretended that they were often physically equal either. Many southern states began crash programs, allocating dozens of millions of dollars to improve the quality of black schools, but the move came too late. In 1951, the NAACP, in the name of African–American children, began litigation in Kansas, Delaware, South Carolina, Virginia, and the District of Columbia directly challenging the concept of "separate but equal."

The supreme court of Delaware ordered black children admitted to all-white schools but intimated that they might be re-segregated when the state completed its program to equalize physical facilities. In the other cases, federal courts reaffirmed Plessy, and the NAACP appealed to the Supreme Court.

When the cases were first heard during the 1952 term, the justices divided 5–4 and concluded that it would invite disaster to decide such a crucial and volatile issue when the Court was so closely divided. They set the cases down for reargument during the 1953 term. Shortly before that term began, Chief Justice Fred M. Vinson died and Eisenhower gave a recess appointment to Earl Warren as the new chief. Under his leadership, the Court eventually reached a unanimous decision. The last potential dissenter, Stanley Reed, gave in at the end, saying that if the decision were to be effective it would have to be unanimous, and that he loved the Court more than he treasured his personal views.

Mr. Chief Justice **WARREN** delivered the opinion of the Court. . . .

Reargument was largely devoted to the circumstances surrounding the adoption of the Fourteenth Amendment in 1868. It covered exhaustively consideration of the Amendment in Congress, ratification by the states, then existing practices in racial segregation, and the views of proponents and opponents of the Amendment. This discussion and our own investigation convince us that, although these sources cast some light, it is not enough to resolve the problem with which we are faced. At best, they are inconclusive. The most avid proponents of the post-War Amendments undoubtedly intended them to remove all legal distinctions among "all persons born or naturalized in the United States." Their opponents, just as certainly, were antagonistic to both the letter and the spirit of the Amendments and wished them to have the most limited effect. What others in Congress and the state legislatures had in mind cannot be determined with any degree of certainty.

An additional reason for the inconclusive nature of the Amendment's history, with respect to segregated schools, is the status of public education at that time. In the South, the movement toward free common schools, supported by general taxation, had not yet taken hold. Education of white children was largely in the hands of private groups. Education of Negroes was almost nonexistent, and practically all of the race were illiterate. In fact, any education of Negroes was forbidden by law in some states. Today, in contrast, many Negroes have achieved outstanding success in the arts and sciences as well as in the business and professional world. It is true that public school education at the time of the Amendment had advanced further in the North, but the effect of the Amendment on Northern States was generally ignored in the congressional debates. Even in the North, the conditions of public education did not approximate those existing today. The curriculum was usually rudimentary; ungraded schools were common in rural areas; the school term was but three months a year in many states; and compulsory school attendance was virtually unknown. As a consequence, it is not surprising that there should be so little in the history of the Fourteenth Amendment relating to its intended effect on public education.

In the first cases in this Court construing the Fourteenth Amendment, decided shortly after its adoption, the Court interpreted it as proscribing all state-imposed discriminations against the Negro race. The doctrine of "separate but equal" did not make its appearance in this Court until 1896 in the case of Plessy v. Ferguson, involving not education but transportation. American courts have since labored with the doctrine for over half a century. In this Court, there have been six cases involving the "separate but equal" doctrine in the field of public education. In Cumming v. County Bd. of Ed. [1899] and Gong Lum v. Rice [1927], the validity of the doctrine itself was not challenged. In more recent cases, all on the graduate school level, inequality was found in that specific benefits enjoyed by white students were denied to Negro students of the same educational qualifications. Missouri ex rel. Gaines v. Canada [1938]; Sipuel v. University of Oklahoma [1948]; Sweatt v. Painter [1950]; McLaurin v. Oklahoma State Regents [1950]. In none of these cases was it necessary to reexamine the doctrine to grant relief to the Negro plaintiff. And in *Sweatt,* the Court expressly reserved decision on the question whether *Plessy* should be held inapplicable to public education.

In the instant cases, that question is directly presented. Here, unlike *Sweatt,* there are findings below that the Negro and white schools involved have been equalized, or are being equalized, with respect to buildings, curricula, qualifications and salaries of teachers, and other "tangible" factors. Our decision, therefore, cannot turn on merely a comparison of these tangible factors in the Negro and white schools involved in each of the cases. We must look instead to the effect of segregation itself on public education.

In approaching this problem, we cannot turn the clock back to 1868 when the Amendment was adopted, or even to 1896 when *Plessy* was written. We must consider public education in the light of its full development and its present place in American life throughout the Nation. Only in this way can it be determined if segregation in public schools deprives these plaintiffs of the equal protection of the laws.

Today, education is perhaps the most important function of state and local governments. Compulsory school attendance laws and the great expenditures for education both demonstrate our recognition of the importance of education to our democratic society. It is required in the performance of our most basic public responsibilities, even service in the armed forces. It is the very foundation of good citizenship. Today it is a principal instrument in awakening the child to cultural values, in preparing him for later professional training, and in helping him to adjust normally to his environment. In these days, it is doubtful that any child may reasonably be expected to succeed in life if he is denied the opportunity of an education. Such an opportunity, where the state has undertaken to provide it, is a right which must be made available to all on equal terms.

We come then to the question presented: Does segregation of children in public schools solely on the basis of race, even though the physical facilities and other "tangible" factors may be equal, deprive the children of the minority group of equal educational opportunities? We believe that it does.

In *Sweatt,* in finding that a segregated law school for Negroes could not provide them equal educational opportunities, this Court relied in large part on "those qualities which are incapable of objective measurement but which make for greatness in a law school." In *McLaurin,* the Court, in requiring that a Negro admitted to a white graduate school be treated like all other students, again resorted to intangible considerations: " . . . his ability to study, to engage in discussions and exchange views with other students, and, in general, to learn his profession." Such considerations apply with added force to children in grade and high schools. To separate them from others of similar age and qualifications solely because of their race generates a feeling of inferiority as to their status in the community that may affect their hearts and minds in a way unlikely ever to be undone. The effect of this separation on their educational opportunities was well stated by a finding in the Kansas case by a court which nevertheless felt compelled to rule against the Negro plaintiffs:

> Segregation of white and colored children in public schools has a detrimental effect upon the colored children. The impact is greater when it has the sanction of the law; for the policy of separating the races is usually interpreted as denoting the inferiority of the negro group. A sense of inferiority affects the motivation of a child to learn. Segregation with the sanction of law, therefore, has a tendency to [retard] the educational and mental development of Negro children and to deprive them of some of the benefits they would receive in a racial[ly] integrated school system.

Whatever may have been the extent of psychological knowledge at the time of *Plessy*, this finding is amply supported by modern authority.[11] Any language in *Plessy* contrary to this finding is rejected.

We conclude that in the field of public education the doctrine of "separate but equal" has no place. Separate educational facilities are inherently unequal. Therefore, we hold that the plaintiffs and others similarly situated for whom the actions have been brought are, by reason of the segregation complained of, deprived of the equal protection of the laws guaranteed by the Fourteenth Amendment. This disposition makes unnecessary any discussion whether such segregation also violates the Due Process Clause of the Fourteenth Amendment.

Because these are class actions, because of the wide applicability of this decision, and because of the great variety of local conditions, the formulation of decrees in these cases presents problems of considerable complexity. On reargument, the consideration of appropriate relief was necessarily subordinated to the primary question—the constitutionality of segregation in public education. We have now announced that such segregation is a denial of the equal protection of the laws. In order that we may have the full assistance of the parties in formulating decrees, the cases will be restored to the docket, and the parties are requested to present further argument on Questions 4 and 5 previously propounded by the Court for the reargument this Term. ...

It is so ordered.

Editors' Notes

(1) The questions set for reargument dealing with the form the decree implementing the decision should take are reprinted in footnote 1 to *Brown*, II, below at p. 920.

(2) **Query:** What approach(es) to constitutional interpretation did Chief Justice Warren follow? What was his conception of WHAT "the Constitution" includes?

(3) **Query:** Warren explained why the Court did not follow an *originalist approach*. To what extent does that explanation generally undercut the validity of this approach?

(4) **Query:** What weight did the Court's references to empirical studies by social scientists carry in justifying its constitutional interpretation? Compare the Court's use of sociological evidence and reasoning in *Brown*, I, and *Plessy*. Which is more convincing? If the studies cited in *Brown*, I, were proved to be methodologically unsound, would the validity of the decision be

---

11. K.B. Clark, *Effect of Prejudice and Discrimination on Personality Development* (Midcentury White House Conference on Children and Youth, 1950); Witmer and Kotinsky, *Personality in the Making* (1952), ch VI; Deutscher and Chein, "The Psychological Effects of Enforced Segregation: A Survey of Social Science Opinion," 26 *J.Psychol.* 259 (1948); Chein, "What are the Psychological Effects of Segregation Under Conditions of Equal Facilities?" 3 *Int.J.Opinion and Attitude Res.* 229 (1949); Brameld, "Educational Costs," in *Discrimination and National Welfare* (MacIver, ed, 1949), 44–48; Frazier, *The Negro in the United States* (1949), 674–681. And see generally Myrdal, *An American Dilemma* (1944). [We have retained the Court's number for this footnote because of its fame as a target for white supremists.—**Eds.**]

damaged? See, e.g., *Symposium, The Courts, Social Science and School Desegregation,* 39 *Law & Contemp.Probs.* (Winter/Spring 1975).

(5) **Query:** Is the opinion in *Brown,* I, vulnerable to the criticism that it improperly made "sensitivity" or "the feeling of inferiority" rather than text, tradition, or even justice the paramount issue in race relations and constitutional interpretation? See Clarence Thomas, "Toward a 'Plain Reading' of the Constitution—The Declaration of Independence in Constitutional Interpretation," 30 *How.L.J.* 983, 990–91 (1987).

(6) **Query:** Does the opinion in *Brown,* I, rest upon the special importance of equal educational opportunities in our society to such an extent that its rationale cannot be generalized to other contexts? Or does it presuppose a principle of equal citizenship that would apply to all contexts?

(7) For a superb study of the origin and development of these cases in local communities, lower courts, and within the U.S. Supreme Court, see Richard Kluger, *Simple Justice* (New York: Knopf, 1976). See also Bernard Schwartz, *Super Chief* (New York: New York University Press, 1983), ch. 3; and William O. Douglas, *The Court Years, 1939–1975* (New York: Random House, 1980), ch. 5.

———

"[T]he concepts of equal protection and due process, both stemming from the American ideal of fairness, are not mutually exclusive. ... [D]iscrimination may be so unjustifiable as to be violative of due process."

BOLLING v. SHARPE

347 U.S. 497, 74 S.Ct. 693, 98 L.Ed. 884 (1954).

This is a companion case from the District of Columbia to the four suits from the states decided under *Brown,* I.

Mr. Chief Justice **WARREN** delivered the opinion of the Court. ...

We have this day held that the Equal Protection Clause of the Fourteenth Amendment prohibits the states from maintaining racially segregated public schools. The legal problem in the District of Columbia is somewhat different, however. The Fifth Amendment, which is applicable in the District of Columbia, does not contain an equal protection clause as does the Fourteenth Amendment which applies only to the states. But the concepts of equal protection and due process, both stemming from our American ideal of fairness, are not mutually exclusive. The "equal protection of the laws" is a more explicit safeguard of prohibited unfairness than "due process of law," and, therefore, we do not imply that the two are always interchangeable phrases. But, as this Court has recognized, discrimination may be so unjustifiable as to be violative of due process.

Classifications based solely upon race must be scrutinized with particular care, since they are contrary to our traditions and hence constitutionally suspect. [Korematsu v. United States (1944); Hirabayashi v. United States (1943).] As long ago as 1896, this Court declared the principle "that the Constitution of the United States, in its present form, forbids, so far as civil and political rights are concerned, discrimination by the General Government, or by the States, against any citizen because of his race." [Gibson v. Mississippi (1896).] And in Buchanan v. Warley [1917], the Court held that a statute which limited the right of a property owner to convey his property to a person of another race was, as an unreasonable discrimination, a denial of due process of law.

Although the Court has not assumed to define "liberty" with any great precision, that term is not confined to mere freedom from bodily restraint. Liberty under law extends to the full range of conduct which the individual is free to pursue, and it cannot be restricted except for a proper governmental objective. Segregation in public education is not reasonably related to any proper governmental objective, and thus it imposes on Negro children of the District of Columbia a burden that constitutes an arbitrary deprivation of their liberty in violation of the Due Process Clause.

In view of our decision that the Constitution prohibits the states from maintaining racially segregated public schools, it would be unthinkable that the same Constitution would impose a lesser duty on the Federal Government. We hold that racial segregation in the public schools of the District of Columbia is a denial of the due process of law guaranteed by the Fifth Amendment to the Constitution. ...

It is so ordered.

Editors' Notes

(1) **Query:** Warren said:

> Segregation in public education is not reasonably related to any proper governmental objective, and thus it imposes on Negro children of the District of Columbia a burden that constitutes an arbitrary deprivation of their liberty in violation of the Due Process Clause.

These words sound very much like the "rationality text" used in *Plessy*:

> So far, then, as a conflict with the Fourteenth Amendment is concerned, the case reduces itself to the question whether the statute of Louisiana is a reasonable regulation, and with respect to this there must necessarily be a large discretion on the part of the legislature.

(The introductory essay to this chapter and cases that follow, such as Williamson v. Lee Optical [1955; reprinted above, p. 908], discuss this test in detail). Did *Bolling* and *Brown*, I, really apply the same test as did *Plessy* to laws compelling racial segregation? If not, what test did *Brown*, I, and *Bolling* apply?

(2) As the introduction to this Part of the book indicated, *Bolling* marked a significant development in equal protection: The Court began to read the due process clause of the Fifth Amendment as including the command of the equal protection clause of the Fourteenth Amendment. See Weinberger v.

Wiesenfeld (1975): "[T]he Court's approach to Fifth Amendment equal protection has always been precisely the same as to equal protection claims under the Fourteenth Amendment." A year later, however, a majority in Hampton v. Mow Sun Wong (1976) admitted there were some differences: "[T]he two protections are not always coextensive. Not only does the language of the two Amendments differ, but more importantly, there may be overriding national interests which justify selective federal legislation that would be unacceptable for an individual State." What sort of approach(es) to constitutional interpretation can lead to this partial merger? *Textualism? Originalism? Structuralism? Philosophy? Developmentalism? Purposivism?* Some other(s)? Which did Warren use in *Bolling?*

(3) **Query:** Is it indeed "unthinkable," as Warren said in *Bolling,* that "the Constitution" would impose a "lesser duty" on the federal government than on the state governments? To what conclusion would a *structural approach* lead? A *purposive approach?*

(4) **Query:** Even if the concepts of equal protection and due process both stem from "our American ideal of fairness," and are "not mutually exclusive," should they nonetheless play different roles in our constitutional scheme? If so, what should those roles be? Ira Lupu, "Untangling the Strands of the Fourteenth Amendment," 77 *Mich.L.Rev.* 981, 982–85 (1979), argues that judicial protection of "unenumerated" fundamental rights should be grounded on the due process clause, while the equal protection clause should reflect a constitutional principle against discrimination (the so-called antidiscrimination principle). Cass R. Sunstein, "Sexual Orientation and the Constitution: A Note on the Relationship Between Due Process and Equal Protection," 55 *U.Chi.L.Rev.* 1161, 1168, 1174 (1988), argues that the due process clause is "backward-looking" and its scope "should be defined largely by reference to tradition," whereas the equal protection clause is "forward-looking" and "a self-conscious repudiation of history and tradition as defining constitutional principles," for "it was self-consciously designed to eliminate practices that existed at the time of ratification and that were expected to endure." Chapter 15 explores further the relationship between due process and equal protection as bases for protecting fundamental rights.

(5) The irony of the Court's citing *Hirabayashi* and *Korematsu* to strike down racial discrimination is remarkable but frequently repeated, as the discussion of *Korematsu* in Chapter 4 pointed out. See also the Court's similar use of these cases in Loving v. Virginia (1966; reprinted below, p. 926).

" ... **with all deliberate speed.** ..."

BROWN v. BOARD OF EDUCATION OF TOPEKA, II
349 U.S. 294, 75 S.Ct. 753, 99 L.Ed. 1083 (1955).

Mr. Chief Justice **WARREN** delivered the opinion of the Court. ...

These cases were decided on May 17, 1954. The opinions of that date, declaring the fundamental principle that racial discrimination in public education is unconstitutional, are incorporated herein by reference. All provisions of federal, state, or local law requiring or permitting such discrimination must yield to this principle. There remains for consideration the manner in which relief is to be accorded.

Because these cases arose under different local conditions and their disposition will involve a variety of local problems, we requested further argument on the question of relief.[1] In view of the nationwide importance of the decision, we invited the Attorney General of the United States and the Attorneys General of all states requiring or permitting racial discrimination in public education to present their views on that question. The parties, the United States, and the States of Florida, North Carolina, Arkansas, Oklahoma, Maryland, and Texas filed briefs and participated in the oral argument.

These presentations were informative and helpful to the Court in its consideration of the complexities arising from the transition to a system of public education freed of racial discrimination. The presentations also demonstrated that substantial steps to eliminate racial discrimination in public schools have already been taken, not only in some of the communities in which these cases arose, but in some of the states appearing as amici curiae, and in other states as well. ...

Full implementation of these constitutional principles may require solution of varied local school problems. School authorities have the primary responsibility for elucidating, assessing, and solving these problems; courts will have to consider whether the action of school authorities constitutes good faith implementation of the governing constitutional principles. Because of their proximity to local conditions and the possible need for further hearings, the courts which originally heard these cases can best perform this judicial appraisal. Accordingly, we believe it appropriate to remand the cases to those courts.

---

1. Further argument was requested on the following questions previously propounded by the Court:

4. Assuming it is decided that segregation in public schools violates the Fourteenth Amendment

(a) would a decree necessarily follow providing that, within the limits set by normal geographic school districting, Negro children should forthwith be admitted to schools of their choice, or

(b) may this Court, in the exercise of its equity powers, permit an effective gradual adjustment to be brought about from existing segregated systems to a system not based on color distinctions?

5. On the assumption on which questions 4(a) and (b) are based, and assuming further that this Court will exercise its equity powers to the end described in question 4 (b),

(a) should this Court formulate detailed decrees in these cases;

(b) if so, what specific issues should the decrees reach;

(c) should this Court appoint a special master to hear evidence with a view to recommending specific terms for such decrees;

(d) should this Court remand to the courts of first instance with directions to frame decrees in these cases, and if so what general directions should the decrees of this Court include and what procedures should the courts of first instance follow in arriving at the specific terms of more detailed decrees? [Footnote by the Court.]

In fashioning and effectuating the decrees, the courts will be guided by equitable principles. Traditionally, equity has been characterized by a practical flexibility in shaping its remedies and by a facility for adjusting and reconciling public and private needs. These cases call for the exercise of these traditional attributes of equity power. At stake is the personal interest of the plaintiffs in admission to public schools as soon as practicable on a nondiscriminatory basis. To effectuate this interest may call for elimination of a variety of obstacles in making the transition to school systems operated in accordance with the constitutional principles set forth in our May 17, 1954, decision. Courts of equity may properly take into account the public interest in the elimination of such obstacles in a systematic and effective manner. But it should go without saying that the vitality of these constitutional principles cannot be allowed to yield simply because of disagreement with them.

While giving weight to these public and private considerations, the courts will require that the defendants make a prompt and reasonable start toward full compliance with our May 17, 1954, ruling. Once such a start has been made, the courts may find that additional time is necessary to carry out the ruling in an effective manner. The burden rests upon the defendants to establish that such time is necessary in the public interest and is consistent with good faith compliance at the earliest practicable date. To that end, the courts may consider problems related to administration, arising from the physical condition of the school plant, the school transportation system, personnel, revision of school districts and attendance areas into compact units to achieve a system of determining admission to the public schools on a nonracial basis, and revision of local laws and regulations which may be necessary in solving the foregoing problems. They will also consider the adequacy of any plans the defendants may propose to meet these problems and to effectuate a transition to a racially nondiscriminatory school system. During this period of transition, the courts will retain jurisdiction of these cases.

The judgments below, except that in the Delaware case, are accordingly reversed and the cases are remanded to the District Courts to take such proceedings and enter such orders and decrees consistent with this opinion as are necessary and proper to admit to public schools on a racially nondiscriminatory basis with all deliberate speed the parties to these cases. The judgment in the Delaware case—ordering the immediate admission of the plaintiffs to schools previously attended only by white children—is affirmed on the basis of the principles stated in our May 17, 1954, opinion, but the case is remanded to the Supreme Court of Delaware for such further proceedings as that Court may deem necessary in light of this opinion.

It is so ordered.

Editors' Notes

THE IMPLEMENTATION OF *BROWN*

(1) Southern reactions to the School Segregation Cases were defiantly hostile. "Massive Resistance" was one response—avoiding the impact of the decisions by simple foot-dragging; using "pupil placement plans" that somehow kept blacks in segregated schools and "freedom of choice" schemes that, in effect, allowed whites to choose not to go to integrated schools; invoking the police power to justify maintaining segregation to preserve public peace; claiming immunity from suit under the Eleventh Amendment; threatening to close (and in Prince Edward County, Va., where one of the original suits had begun, actually closing) public schools; and counterattacking against the NAACP (see NAACP v. Alabama [1958; reprinted above, p. 798]; and NAACP v. Button [1963; reprinted above, p. 811]). Some state legislatures tried to reopen the question of WHO interprets for the federal system by "nullifying" *Brown* (see Alabama's resolution, reprinted above, p. 374). Most dangerous, of course, were frequent outbreaks of violence that threatened the safety of young African Americans (as well as white civil rights workers) who dared to assert what the Court had said were their constitutional rights.

During much of the next decade, the justices avoided as much as they could further discussion of the issue of segregation. Their strategy was to affirm in terse *per curiam* orders lower court decisions striking down segregation and similarly to reverse those sustaining segregation. The most notable exception was Cooper v. Aaron (1958; reprinted above, p. 375), when the Governor of Arkansas called out troops to prevent enforcement of a federal district court's order to desegregate. In several other cases raising the issue of state laws outlawing racially mixed marriages, the justices evaded the issue. See the discussion in the headnote to Loving v. Virginia (1967; reprinted below, p. 926).

In the ten years after *Brown,* II, there was some desegregation in the border states but almost none whatsoever in the South. Then Congress enacted the Civil Rights Act of 1964 (78 Stat. 241), which, in addition to making it a crime to refuse to serve all customers on an equal basis in accommodations affecting "commerce among the several states," cut off federal grants to states that did not desegregate public schools. Segregated public schools remain a reality; but, once southern state officials realized that the 1964 act meant what it said, defiance changed to compliance, though initially begrudging. Armed with presidential and congressional support, the justices in 1968 discarded their diplomacy and spoke imperatively. In Green v. New Kent County, they unanimously said: "This deliberate perpetuation of the unconstitutional dual system can only have compounded the harm of such a system. ... The burden on the school board today is to come forward with a plan that promises realistically to work, and promises realistically to work *now.*" During most of the last two and a half decades, the difficulties of desegregating public schools have differed little from region to region—which is to say that there are as many problems outside as within the South, not that the problems have vanished.

(2) In its *per curiam* orders the Court invalidated state-mandated segregation in recreational facilities—Muir v. Louisville (1954); Baltimore v. Dawson (1955); Holmes v. Atlanta (1955); and New Orleans v. Detiege (1958)—and in

local transportation—Gayle v. Browder (1956), a case growing out of the sit-in that helped turn Dr. Martin Luther King, Jr.s' Southern Christian Leadership Conference into a national civil rights movement. These orders established clearly that the rationale of *Brown* was not limited to the special status of education in a constitutional democracy but reflected a principle of equal citizenship that applies to all contexts.

(3) For analyses of the aftermath of *Brown,* see Stephen L. Wasby, A.A. D'Amato, and R. Metrailer, *Desegregation from Brown to Alexander* (Carbondale, Ill.: Southern Illinois University Press, 1977); Richard Kluger, *Simple Justice* (New York: Knopf, 1975), ch. 27; Jack W. Peltason, *58 Lonely Men: Southern Federal Judges and School Desegregation* (New York: Harcourt, Brace & World, 1961); and Jack Bass, *Unlikely Heroes* (New York: Simon & Schuster, 1981).

For analyses of school desegregation and busing, see, e.g., Gary Orfield, *Must We Bus?* (Washington, DC: The Brookings Institution, 1978); David Chang, "The Bus Stops Here: Defining the Constitutional Right of Equal Educational Opportunity and an Appropriate Remedial Process," 63 *B. U. L.Rev.* 1 (1983); Paul D. Gewirtz, "Remedies and Resistance," 92 *Yale L.J.* 585 (1983); and Paul D. Gewirtz, "Choice in the Transition: School Desegregation and the Corrective Ideal," 86 *Colum.L.Rev.* 728 (1986). For a highly critical assessment, see Lino A. Graglia, *Disaster by Decree: The Supreme Court's Decisions on Race and the Schools* (Ithaca: Cornell University Press, 1976).

"The Fourteenth Amendment is not directed solely against discrimination due to a 'two-class theory'—that is, based upon differences between 'white' and Negro."

HERNANDEZ v. TEXAS

347 U.S. 475, 74 S.Ct. 667, 98 L.Ed. 866 (1954).

Pete Hernandez, an American citizen of Mexican descent, was indicted for murder by a grand jury in Jackson County, Texas, convicted by a petit jury, and sentenced to life imprisonment. Prior to and at the trial, his counsel objected to both juries because Mexican–Americans had been systematically excluded from service on them. The judge denied these motions, the state supreme court affirmed, and the U.S. Supreme Court granted certiorari.

Mr. Chief Justice **WARREN** delivered the opinion of the Court. . . .

In numerous decisions, this Court has held that it is a denial of the equal protection of the laws to try a defendant of a particular race or color under an indictment issued by a grand jury, or before a petit jury, from which all persons of his race or color have, solely because of that race or color, been excluded by the State, whether acting through its legislature, its courts, or its executive or administrative officers. Although the Court has had little occasion to rule on the question directly, it has been recognized since Strauder v. West Virginia [1880] that the exclusion of a class of persons from jury service on grounds other than race or color may also deprive a defendant who is a member of that class of the constitutional guarantee of equal protection of the laws. The State of Texas would have us hold that there are only two classes—white and Negro—within the contemplation of the Fourteenth Amendment. The decisions of this Court do not support that view. ...

Throughout our history differences in race and color have defined easily identifiable groups which have at times required the aid of the courts in securing equal treatment under the laws. But community prejudices are not static, and from time to time other differences from the community norm may define other groups which need the same protection. Whether such a group exists within a community is a question of fact. When the existence of a distinct class is demonstrated, and it is further shown that the laws, as written or as applied, single out that class for different treatment not based on some reasonable classification, the guarantees of the Constitution have been violated. The Fourteenth Amendment is not directed solely against discrimination due to a "two-class theory"—that is, based upon differences between "white" and Negro.

... The exclusion of otherwise eligible persons from jury service solely because of their ancestry or national origin is discrimination prohibited by the Fourteenth Amendment. The Texas statute makes no such discrimination, but the petitioner alleges that those administering the law do.

The petitioner's initial burden in substantiating his charge of group discrimination was to prove that persons of Mexican descent constitute a separate class in Jackson County, distinct from "whites." One method by which this may be demonstrated is by showing the attitude of the community. Here the testimony of responsible officials and citizens contained the admission that residents of the community distinguished between "white" and "Mexican." The participation of persons of Mexican descent in business and community groups was shown to be slight. Until very recent times, children of Mexican descent were required to attend a segregated school for the first four grades. At least one restaurant in town prominently displayed a sign announcing "No Mexicans Served." On the courthouse grounds at the time of the hearing, there were two men's toilets, one unmarked, and the other marked "Colored Men" and "Hombres Aqui" ("Men Here"). No substantial evidence was offered to rebut the logical inference to be drawn from these facts, and it must be concluded that petitioner succeeded in his proof.

Having established the existence of a class, petitioner was then charged with the burden of proving discrimination. To do so, he relied on the pattern of proof established by Norris v. Alabama [1935]. In that case, proof that Negroes constituted a substantial segment of the population of the jurisdiction, that some Negroes were qualified to serve as jurors, and that none had been called for jury service over an extended period of time, was held to constitute prima facie proof of the systematic exclusion of Negroes from jury service. This holding, sometimes called the "rule of exclusion," has been applied in other cases, and it is available in supplying proof of discrimination against any delineated class.

The petitioner established that 14% of the population of Jackson County were persons with Mexican or Latin American surnames, and that 11% of the males over 21 bore such names. The County Tax Assessor testified that 6 or 7 percent of the freeholders on the tax rolls of the County were persons of Mexican descent. The State of Texas stipulated that "for the last twenty-five years there is no record of any person with a Mexican or Latin American name having served on a jury commission, grand jury or petit jury in Jackson County." The parties also stipulated that "there are some male persons of Mexican or Latin American descent in Jackson County who, by virtue of being citizens, householders, or freeholders, and having all other legal prerequisites to jury service, are eligible to serve as members of a jury commission, grand jury and/or petit jury."

The petitioner met the burden of proof imposed in Norris v. Alabama [1935]. To rebut [this] strong prima facie case ... the State offered the testimony of five jury commissioners that they had not discriminated against persons of Mexican or Latin American descent in selecting jurors. They stated that their only objective had been to select those whom they thought were best qualified. This testimony is not enough to overcome the petitioner's case. ...

Circumstances or chance may well dictate that no persons in a certain class will serve on a particular jury or during some particular period. But it taxes our credulity to say that mere chance resulted in there being no members of this class among the over six thousand jurors called in the past 25 years. The result bespeaks discrimination, whether or not it was a conscious decision on the part of any individual jury commissioner. The judgment of conviction must be reversed.

To say that this decision revives the rejected contention that the Fourteenth Amendment requires proportional representation of all the component ethnic groups of the community on every jury ignores the facts. The petitioner did not seek proportional representation, nor did he claim a right to have persons of Mexican descent sit on the particular juries which he faced. His only claim is the right to be indicted and tried by juries from which all members of his class are not systematically excluded—juries selected from among all qualified persons regardless of national origin or descent. To this much, he is entitled by the Constitution.

Reversed.

Editors' Notes

(1) **Query:** This case was decided the same day as *Brown*, I and *Bolling v. Sharpe*. Did Warren follow the same approach to constitutional interpretation in all three opinions?

(2) **Query:** What test for constitutionality did Warren use in *Hernandez*? He said that the state violates constitutional guarantees when it singles out a class for "different treatment not based on some reasonable classification." Was he using the same test as the Court used in *Plessy*? See above, p. 918, Editors' Note (1) to *Bolling*.

(3) Castaneda v. Partida (1977) added an interesting twist to *Hernandez*. Partida, a convicted rapist, sought habeas corpus from a federal district court, claiming Mexican–Americans had been excluded from his grand jury. He offered statistics to show that, although 79 per cent of the county's population was Mexican–American, during the past eleven years only 39 per cent of the grand jurors had had Spanish surnames. The district court denied habeas corpus, in part because the judge thought it unlikely that a governing majority would discriminate against itself. Partida appealed and won in the court of appeals, and Texas obtained review on cert. The Supreme Court held for Partida. For the majority, Justice Blackmun said: "Because of the many facets of human motivation, it would be unwise to presume as a matter of law that human beings of one definable group will not discriminate against members of their group." Contrast the debate between Justice O'Connor for the majority and Justice Marshall for the dissenters in Richmond v. J.A. Croson Co. (1989; reprinted below, p. 954).

(4) The Supreme Court has consistently treated classifications based on ethnicity, or national origin, as suspect. Its handling of classifications based on alienage, however, has meandered. (See discussion below, Chapter 15, pp. 975–76).

"At the very least, the Equal Protection Clause demands that racial classifications, especially suspect in criminal classifications, be subjected to 'the most rigid scrutiny' ". ...

LOVING v. VIRGINIA

388 U.S. 1, 87 S.Ct. 1817, 18 L.Ed.2d 1010 (1967).

In 1883 Pace v. Alabama sustained a statute punishing fornication between a white person and a Negro and imposing a greater penalty than for the same act committed by persons of the same race. This statute was typical of laws in most southern states which, to protect the "purity of the white race," forbade interracial marriage and sexual intercourse. As southern officials were quick to point out, the logic of the School Segregation Cases threatened the validity of these statutes. "Racial mongrelization" turned into a white southern bugaboo in the fight against desegregation. "Let them in the schools today and tomorrow they'll be marrying your daughters" became a rallying cry.

Recognizing the power of this white fear, the justices were loath to let logic dominate prudence. Shortly after *Brown, I,* they denied certiorari to a black woman whom Alabama had sentenced to prison for marrying a white man. (Jackson v. Alabama [1954].)

A case from Virginia provided a second opportunity, which the justices also cautiously declined. Using the state's anti-miscegenation statute as the basis of decision, Virginia had annulled a marriage between a white woman and a man of Chinese ancestry; the husband claimed he had been denied equal protection and appealed—that is, took his case to the U.S. Supreme Court as a matter of right. Justice Frankfurter urged his colleagues not to decide such a volatile issue so soon after the School Segregation Cases. He stressed "the Court's responsibility in not thwarting or seriously handicapping the enforcement of its decision in the segregation cases." (Quoted in Bernard Schwartz, *Super Chief* [New York: New York University Press, 1983], p. 159.) The justices temporized by remanding the case to the state courts asking for clarifications of the record. Naim v. Naim (1955).

The Virginia Supreme Court of Appeals curtly responded that the record was adequate for decision; there was no procedure for the sort of clarification the Supreme Court had asked for; and the original decision was correct anyway. Faced with this public rebuke, the justices backed away and dismissed the appeal on grounds that the lack of a clarified record "leaves the case devoid of a properly presented federal question." (Naim v. Naim [1956].) One angry law clerk who demanded an explanation from his justice was told, "One bombshell at a time is enough." Earl Warren, who along with Black had opposed the remand in *Naim,* was more pungent: "That's what happens when you turn your ass to the grandstand!" (Quoted in Schwartz, p. 162.)

But issues of interracial sex and marriage would return to the Court, as the justices knew. In McLaughlin v. Florida (1964), the justices took a small step toward invalidating anti-miscegenation laws, but once more they proceeded cautiously. They reversed a conviction for interracial cohabitation and the statute on which it was based, but only because the state had not shown "some overriding statutory purpose requiring the proscription of the specified conduct when engaged in between a white person and a Negro, but not otherwise." Stewart and Douglas preferred a flat statement that all such statutes were unconstitutional.

Three years after *McLaughlin* and passage of the Civil Rights Act of 1964, Virginia provided yet another opportunity. Richard Loving, a white man, and Mildred Jeter, a black woman, both residents of Virginia, were married in the District of Columbia. When they returned to Virginia, they were convicted for violating the state statute making interracial marriage a crime. Virginia's Supreme Court of Appeals upheld the conviction and the constitutionality of the statute. The Lovings then appealed to the U.S. Supreme Court.

Mr. Chief Justice **WARREN** delivered the opinion of the Court. ...

This case presents a constitutional question never addressed by this Court: whether a statutory scheme adopted by the State of Virginia to prevent marriages between persons solely on the basis of racial classifica-

tions violates the Equal Protection and Due Process Clauses of the
Fourteenth Amendment. ...

I

In upholding the constitutionality of these provisions, the Supreme
Court of Appeals of Virginia referred to its 1955 decision in Naim v.
Naim ... [and] court concluded that the State's legitimate purposes
were "to preserve the racial integrity of its citizens," and to prevent
"the corruption of blood," "a mongrel breed of citizens," and "the
obliteration of racial pride," obviously an endorsement of the doctrine of
White Supremacy. The court also reasoned that marriage has traditionally been subject to state regulation without federal intervention, and,
consequently, the regulation of marriage should be left to exclusive state
control by the Tenth Amendment.

While the state court is no doubt correct in asserting that marriage
is a social relation subject to the State's police power, the State does not
contend ... that its powers to regulate marriage are unlimited notwithstanding the commands of the Fourteenth Amendment. Nor could it do
so in light of Meyer v. Nebraska (1923) and Skinner v. Oklahoma (1942).
Instead, the State argues that the meaning of the Equal Protection
Clause, as illuminated by the statements of the Framers, is only that
state penal laws containing an interracial element as part of the definition of the offense must apply equally to whites and Negroes in the sense
that members of each race are punished to the same degree. Thus, the
State contends that, because its miscegenation statutes punish equally
both the white and the Negro participants in an interracial marriage,
these statutes, despite their reliance on racial classifications, do not
constitute an invidious discrimination based upon race. ...

Because ... we do not accept the State's contention that these
statutes should be upheld if there is any possible basis for concluding
that they serve a rational purpose. ... [T]he fact of equal application
does not immunize the statute from the very heavy burden of justification which the Fourteenth Amendment has traditionally required of
state statutes drawn according to race.

The State argues that statements in the Thirty-ninth Congress
about the time of the passage of the Fourteenth Amendment indicate
that the Framers did not intend the Amendment to make unconstitutional state miscegenation laws. Many of the statements alluded to by
the State concern the debates over the Freedmen's Bureau Bill ... and
the Civil Rights Act of 1866. ... While these statements have some
relevance to the intention of Congress in submitting the Fourteenth
Amendment, ... they pertained to the passage of specific statutes and
not to the broader, organic purpose of a constitutional amendment. As
for the various statements directly concerning the Fourteenth Amendment, we have said in connection with a related problem, that although
these historical sources "cast some light" they are not sufficient to
resolve the problem; "[a]t best, they are inconclusive. ..." Brown v.

Board of Education (1954). See also Strauder v. West Virginia (1880). We have rejected the proposition that the debates in the Thirty-ninth Congress or in the state legislatures which ratified the Fourteenth Amendment supported the theory advanced by the State, that the requirement of equal protection of the laws is satisfied by penal laws defining offenses based on racial classifications so long as white and Negro participants in the offense were similarly punished. McLaughlin v. Florida (1964).

The State finds support for its "equal application" theory in the decision of the Court in Pace v. Alabama (1883). In that case, the Court upheld a conviction under an Alabama statute forbidding adultery or fornication between a white person and a Negro which imposed a greater penalty than that of a statute proscribing similar conduct by members of the same race. The Court reasoned that the statute could not be said to discriminate against Negroes because the punishment for each partici-pant in the offense was the same. However, ... in rejecting the reasoning of that case, we stated "*Pace* represents a limited view of the Equal Protection Clause which has not withstood analysis in the subse-quent decisions of this Court." *McLaughlin.* ... As we there demon-strated, the Equal Protection Clause requires the consideration of whether the classifications drawn by any statute constitute an arbitrary and invidious discrimination. The clear and central purpose of the Fourteenth Amendment was to eliminate all official state sources of invidious racial discrimination in the States. Slaughter–House Cases (1873); *Strauder*; Shelley v. Kraemer (1948).

There can be no question but that Virginia's miscegenation statutes rest solely upon distinctions drawn according to race. ... Over the years, this Court has consistently repudiated "[d]istinctions between citizens solely because of their ancestry" as being "odious to a free people whose institutions are founded upon the doctrine of equality." Hirabayashi v. United States (1943). At the very least, the Equal Protection Clause demands that racial classifications, especially suspect in criminal statutes, be subjected to the "most rigid scrutiny," Koremat-su v. United States (1944), and, if they are ever to be upheld, they must be shown to be necessary to the accomplishment of some permissible state objective, independent of the racial discrimination which it was the object of the Fourteenth Amendment to eliminate. Indeed, two mem-bers of this Court have already stated that they "cannot conceive of a valid legislative purpose ... which makes the color of a person's skin the test of whether his conduct is a criminal offense." *McLaughlin* (Stew-art, J., joined by Douglas, J., concurring).

There is patently no legitimate overriding purpose independent of invidious racial discrimination which justifies this classification. The fact that Virginia prohibits only interracial marriages involving white persons demonstrates that the racial classifications must stand on their own justification, as measures designed to maintain White Supremacy. We have consistently denied the constitutionality of measures which restrict the rights of citizens on account of race. There can be no doubt that restricting the freedom to marry solely because of racial classifications violates the central meaning of the Equal Protection Clause.

II

These statutes also deprive the Lovings of liberty without due process of law in violation of the Due Process Clause of the Fourteenth Amendment. The freedom to marry has long been recognized as one of the vital personal rights essential to the orderly pursuit of happiness by free men.

Marriage is one of the "basic civil rights of man," fundamental to our very existence and survival. *Skinner*. To deny this fundamental freedom on so unsupportable a basis as the racial classifications embodied in these statutes, classifications so directly subversive of the principle of equality at the heart of the Fourteenth Amendment, is surely to deprive all the State's citizens of liberty without due process of law. The Fourteenth Amendment requires that the freedom of choice to marry not be restricted by invidious racial discriminations. Under our Constitution, the freedom to marry, or not marry, a person of another race resides with the individual and cannot be infringed by the State. ...

[Reversed.]

Mr. Justice **STEWART**, concurring. ...

Editors' Notes

(1) **Query:** Does *Loving*'s *purposive approach* (the "central purpose of the Fourteenth Amendment was to eliminate all official state sources of invidious racial discrimination in the States") provide a better justification for strict scrutiny of racial classifications than did *Brown, I*?

(2) **Query:** As in *Brown, I*, Warren rejected an *originalist approach*. Are the reasons for doing so in *Loving* stronger or weaker than in *Brown, I*? Why?

(3) **Query:** Warren offered two bases for the Court's decision, namely, that the statute: (i) used a suspect classification that could not withstand strict scrutiny and (ii) impinged on a fundamental right. Why this violation of Occam's razor? Would Occam's razor cut in favor of an equal protection rationale or a substantive due process rationale? Does the distinction between these two bases for protecting fundamental rights collapse here? See Zablocki v. Redhail (1978; reprinted below, p. 1034, and accompanying Editors' Notes).

(4) **Query:** Warren spoke of the personal rights "essential to the orderly pursuit of happiness by free men." Is this phrase analogous to "essential to the concept of ordered liberty" in Palko v. Connecticut (1937; reprinted above, p. 128)? What is the textual basis for Warren's claiming constitutional protection for the "pursuit of happiness"? It does not appear in the constitutional text; it is in the Declaration of Independence. Was Warren implying (or assuming) that "the Constitution" includes the principles proclaimed in the

Declaration of Independence? Is there some other basis for including it in the constitutional canon?

IV. RACIALLY DISCRIMINATORY PURPOSE VERSUS RACIALLY DISPROPORTIONATE IMPACT

THE REQUIREMENT OF A RACIALLY DISCRIMINATORY PURPOSE

In 1971 Griggs v. Duke Power Co. interpreted Title VII of the Civil Rights Act of 1964, aimed at banning racial discrimination in employment in businesses involved in "commerce among the several states." The Duke Power Co., which had previously limited its most desirable jobs to whites, set up educational achievements and high scores on intelligence tests as prerequisites for those jobs. Few African Americans qualified, and a group of them claimed the "prerequisites" were discriminatory. The Supreme Court agreed, holding that the "prerequisites" were not related to the actual jobs. The Court also held that Title VII does not require a showing of discriminatory purpose. A plaintiff need only prove discriminatory impact to establish a prima facie statutory claim; the burden then shifts to the employer to show that the challenged practices are justified by "business necessity."

If proof of a racially discriminatory impact is enough to establish, as a matter of statutory interpretation, a violation of Title VII, is it sufficient to establish, as a matter of constitutional interpretation, a denial of equal protection? Washington v. Davis (1976) held that it was not. In that case, several African Americans alleged the hiring practices for police in the District of Columbia violated the Fifth Amendment. To be accepted for the police training program, an applicant had to receive a grade of at least 40 out of 80 on "Test 21," an examination used throughout the federal civil service to gauge verbal ability, reading, and comprehension. Plaintiffs claimed that Test 21 excluded a far larger proportion of blacks than whites and bore no relationship to job performance. The district court found the test was a valid instrument, but the court of appeals reversed. The court of appeals followed Griggs, believing that the Title VII standard of discriminatory impact governed the constitutional question. The Supreme Court reversed: "our cases have not embraced the proposition that a law or other official act, without regard to whether it reflects a racially discriminatory purpose, is unconstitutional solely because it has a racially disproportionate impact." The Court held that Test 21 served the racially neutral purpose of requiring all applicants to meet a uniform minimal standard of literacy and communicative abilities.

What factors should be taken into account to determine whether a racially discriminatory purpose exists? Village of Arlington Heights v. Metropolitan Housing Development Corp. (1977) held that a real estate developer who had been denied a zoning permit to build racially integrated low and moderate cost housing in a suburb of Chicago had failed to show the denial was caused by a racially discriminatory purpose. " 'Disproportionate impact is not irrelevant, but it is not the sole touchstone of an invidious racial discrimination,' " Justice Powell said for the majority, quoting from Davis. "Proof of racially discriminatory intent or purpose is required to show a violation of the Equal Protection Clause." But, he added, "*Davis* does not require a plaintiff to prove that the challenged action rested solely on racially discriminatory purposes. Rarely can it be said that a legislature or administrative body operating under a broad mandate made a decision motivated solely by a single concern, or even that a particular purpose was the 'dominant' or 'primary' one." Powell then offered a summary sketch of some of the factors at which a court should look to determine whether "racially discriminatory intent existed":

> Determining whether invidious discriminatory purpose was a motivating factor demands a sensitive inquiry into such circumstantial and direct evidence of intent as may be available. The impact of the official action—whether it "bears more heavily on one race than another," *Davis*—may provide an important starting point. Sometimes a clear pattern, unexplainable on grounds other than race, emerges from the effect of the state action even when the governing legislation appears neutral on its face. Yick Wo v. Hopkins (1886); Guinn v. United States (1915); Lane v. Wilson (1939); Gomillion v. Lightfoot (1960). The evidentiary inquiry is then relatively easy. But such cases are rare. Absent a pattern as stark as that in *Gomillion* or *Yick Wo,* impact alone is not determinative, and the Court must look to other evidence.
>
> The historical background of the decision is one evidentiary source, particularly if it reveals a series of official actions taken for invidious purposes. See Lane v. Wilson [1939]; Griffin v. Sch. Bd. [1964]; Schnell v. Davis (1949); cf. Keyes v. School Dist. No. 1 [1973]. The specific sequence of events leading up to the challenged decision also may shed some light on the decisionmaker's purposes. Reitman v. Mulkey (1967); Grosjean v. American Press Co. (1936). For example, if the property involved here always had been zoned R–5 but suddenly was changed to R–3 when the town learned of MHDC's plans to erect integrated housing, we would have a far different case. Departures from the normal procedural sequence also might afford evidence that improper purposes are playing a role. Substantive departures too may be relevant, particularly if the factors usually considered important by the decisionmaker strongly favor a decision contrary to the one reached.
>
> The legislative or administrative history may be highly relevant, especially where there are contemporary statements by members of the decisionmaking body, minutes of its meetings, or reports. In some extraordinary instances the members might be called to the stand at trial to testify concerning the purpose of the official action, although even then such testimony frequently will be barred by privilege. See Tenney v. Brandhove (1951); United States v. Nixon (1974); 8 J. Wigmore, *Evidence* § 2371 (McNaughton rev. ed. 1961).

Justice White in *Davis* and Powell in *Arlington Heights* seemed to have equated "purpose" and "intent" and at times even "motive" with the other two. Would it improve doctrinal analysis were interpreters to distinguish among these three concepts?

"[F]or the Equal Protection Clause to be violated, 'the invidious quality of a law claimed to be racially discriminatory must ultimately be traced to a racially discriminatory purpose.' "—Justice WHITE

" 'The central purpose of the Equal Protection Clause of the Fourteenth Amendment is the prevention of official conduct discriminating on the basis of race.' "—Justice POWELL

"A constitutional standard that gave special protection to political groups identified by racial characteristics would be inconsistent with the basic tenet of the Equal Protection Clause."—Justice STEVENS

ROGERS v. LODGE
458 U.S. 613, 102 S.Ct. 3272, 73 L.Ed.2d 1012 (1982).

Eight African Americans living in Burke County, Georgia, filed a class action in a federal district court, claiming that the county's electoral system denied their constitutional rights under the First, Thirteenth, Fourteenth, and Fifteenth amendments, as well as their statutory rights under federal civil rights laws. The county chose the five members of its governing board by at-large elections, that is, each candidate had to win a county-wide election. No African American had ever been selected. The district judge found for the plaintiffs and ordered the county divided into five geographic areas, each of which would become the electoral district for a commissioner. The court of appeals affirmed, and the county appealed.

Mr. Justice **WHITE** delivered the opinion of the Court. ...

II

At-large voting schemes and multimember districts tend to minimize the voting strength of minority groups by permitting the political majority to elect *all* representatives of the district. A distinct minority, whether it be a racial, ethnic, economic, or political group, may be unable to elect any representatives in an at-large election, yet may be able to elect several representatives if the political unit is divided into single-member districts. The minority's voting power in a multimember district is particularly diluted when bloc voting occurs and ballots are cast along strict majority-minority lines. While multimember districts have been challenged for "their winner-take-all aspects, their tendency to submerge minorities and to over-represent the winning party," Whitcomb v. Chavis (1971), this Court has repeatedly held that they are not unconstitutional per se. Mobile v. Bolden [1980]; White v. Regester

(1973); *Whitcomb*. The Court has recognized, however, that multimember districts violate the Fourteenth Amendment if "conceived or operated as purposeful devices to further racial ... discrimination" by minimizing, cancelling out or diluting the voting strength of racial elements in the voting population. *Whitcomb*. Cases charging that multimember districts unconstitutionally dilute the voting strength of racial minorities are thus subject to the standard of proof generally applicable to Equal Protection Clause cases. Washington v. Davis (1976) and Village of Arlington Heights v. Metropolitan Housing Development Corp. (1977) made it clear that in order for the Equal Protection Clause to be violated, "the invidious quality of a law claimed to be racially discriminatory must ultimately be traced to a racially discriminatory purpose." ...[1]

Arlington Heights and *Davis* both rejected the notion that a law is invalid under the Equal Protection Clause simply because it may affect a greater proportion of one race than another. However, both cases recognized that discriminatory intent need not be proven by direct evidence. ... Thus determining the existence of a discriminatory purpose "demands a sensitive inquiry into such circumstantial and direct evidence of intent as may be available." *Arlington Heights*.

... First, and fundamentally, we are unconvinced that the District Court in this case applied the wrong legal standard. ... [It] demonstrated its understanding of the controlling standard ... and concluded that the at-large scheme of electing commissioners, "although racially neutral when adopted, is being *maintained* for invidious purposes." ...

III

We are also unconvinced that we should disturb the District Court's finding that the at-large system in Burke County was being maintained for the invidious purpose of diluting the voting strength of the black population. ...

The District Court found that blacks have always made up a substantial majority of the population in Burke County, but that they are a distinct minority of the registered voters. There was also overwhelming evidence of bloc voting along racial lines. Hence, although there had been black candidates, no black had ever been elected to the Burke County commission. These facts bear heavily on the issue of purposeful discrimination. Voting along racial lines allows those elected to ignore black interests without fear of political consequences, and without bloc voting the minority candidates would not lose elections solely because of their race. ...

Under our cases, however, such facts are insufficient in themselves to prove purposeful discrimination absent other evidence such as proof that blacks have less opportunity to participate in the political processes

---

1. Purposeful racial discrimination invokes the strictest scrutiny of adverse differential treatment. Absent such purpose, differential impact is subject only to the test of rationality. *Davis*. [Footnote by the Court.]

and to elect candidates of their choice. United Jewish Organizations v. Carey (1977); *White; Whitcomb.* See also *Mobile.* Both the District Court and the Court of Appeals thought the supporting proof in this case was sufficient to support an inference of intentional discrimination. ...

The District Court began by determining the impact of past discrimination on the ability of blacks to participate effectively in the political process. Past discrimination was found to contribute to low black voter registration because prior to the Voting Rights Act of 1965, blacks had been denied access to the political process by means such as literacy tests, poll taxes, and white primaries. The result was that "Black suffrage in Burke County was virtually non-existent." Black voter registration in Burke County has increased following the Voting Rights Act to the point that some 38 per cent of blacks eligible to vote are registered to do so. On that basis the District Court inferred that "past discrimination has had an adverse effect on black voter registration which lingers to this date." Past discrimination against blacks in education also had the same effect. Not only did Burke County schools discriminate against blacks as recently as 1969, but some schools still remain essentially segregated and blacks as a group have completed less formal education than whites.

The District Court found further evidence of exclusion from the political process. Past discrimination had prevented blacks from effectively participating in Democratic Party affairs and in primary elections. ... There were also property ownership requirements that made it difficult for blacks to serve as chief registrar in the county. There had been discrimination in the selection of grand jurors, the hiring of county employees, and in the appointments to boards and committees which oversee the county government. The District Court thus concluded that historical discrimination had restricted the present opportunity of blacks effectively to participate in the political process. Evidence of historical discrimination is relevant to drawing an inference of purposeful discrimination. ...

Extensive evidence was cited by the District Court to support its finding that elected officials of Burke County have been unresponsive and insensitive to the needs of the black community, which increases the likelihood that the political process was not equally open to blacks. This evidence ranged from the effects of past discrimination which still haunt the county courthouse to the infrequent appointment of blacks to county boards and committees; the overtly discriminatory pattern of paving county roads; the reluctance of the county to remedy black complaints, which forced blacks to take legal action to obtain school and grand jury desegregation; and the role played by the County Commissioners in the incorporation of an all-white private school to which they donated public funds for the purchase of band uniforms.

The District Court also considered the depressed socio-economic status of Burke County blacks ..., [concluding] that [it] results in part from "the lingering effects of past discrimination." Although finding that the state policy behind the at-large electoral system in Burke County was "neutral in origin," the District Court concluded that the policy "has been subverted to invidious purposes." ...

The trial court considered, in addition, several factors which this Court has indicated enhance the tendency of multimember districts to minimize the voting strength of racial minorities. See *Whitcomb*. It found that the sheer geographic size of the county, which is nearly two-thirds the size of Rhode Island, "has made it more difficult for Blacks to get to polling places or to campaign for office." ... The majority vote requirement was found "to submerge the will of the minority" and thus "deny the minority's access to the system." The court also found the requirement that candidates run for specific seats enhances [appellee's] lack of access because it prevents a cohesive political group from concentrating on a single candidate. Because Burke County has no residency requirement, "[a]ll candidates could reside in Waynesboro, or in 'lilly-white' neighborhoods. To that extent, the denial of access becomes enhanced."

... As in *White*, the District Court's findings were "sufficient to sustain [its] judgment ... and, on this record, we have no reason to disturb them."

[*Affirmed.*]

Justice **POWELL,** with whom Justice **REHNQUIST** joins, dissenting. ...

The Court's decision today relies heavily on the capacity of the federal district courts—essentially free from any standards propounded by this Court—to determine whether at-large voting systems are "being maintained for the invidious purpose of diluting the voting strength of the black population." Federal courts thus are invited to engage in deeply subjective inquiries into the motivations of local officials in structuring local governments. Inquiries of this kind not only can be "unseemly," see [Kenneth] Karst, The Costs of Motive–Centered Inquiry, 15 *San Diego Law Rev.* 1163, 1164 (1978); they intrude the federal courts—with only the vaguest constitutional direction—into an area of intensely local and political concern. ...

... In the absence of compelling reasons of both law and fact, the federal judiciary is unwarranted in undertaking to restructure state political systems. This is inherently a political area, where the identification of a seeming violation does not necessarily suggest an enforceable judicial remedy—or at least none short of a system of quotas or group representation. Any such system, of course, would be antithetical to the principles of our democracy.

... "The central purpose of the Equal Protection Clause of the Fourteenth Amendment is the prevention of official conduct discriminating on the basis of race." *Davis*. Because I am unwilling to abandon this central principle in cases of this kind, I cannot join Justice Stevens's opinion. Nonetheless, I do agree with him that what he calls "objective" factors should be the focus of inquiry in vote-dilution cases. ... In the absence of proof of discrimination by reliance on [such factors], I would hold that the factors cited by the Court of Appeals are too attenuated as a matter of law to support an inference of discriminatory intent. ...

Justice **STEVENS,** dissenting.

... The record in this case amply supports the conclusion that the governing officials of Burke County have repeatedly denied black citizens rights guaranteed by the Fourteenth and Fifteenth Amendments to the Federal Constitution. No one could legitimately question the validity of remedial measures, whether legislative or judicial, designed to prohibit discriminatory conduct by public officials and to guarantee that black citizens are effectively afforded the rights to register and to vote. ... Nor, in my opinion, could there be any doubt about the constitutionality of an amendment to the Voting Rights Act that would require Burke County and other covered jurisdictions to abandon specific kinds of at-large voting schemes that perpetuate the effects of past discrimination. ...

The Court's decision today, however, is not based on either its own conception of sound policy or any statutory command. The decision rests entirely on the Court's interpretation of the requirements of the Federal Constitution. Despite my sympathetic appraisal of the Court's laudable goals, I am unable to agree with its approach to the constitutional issue that is presented. In my opinion, this case raises questions that encompass more than the immediate plight of disadvantaged black citizens. I believe the Court errs by holding the structure of the local governmental unit unconstitutional without identifying an acceptable, judicially-manageable standard for adjudicating cases of this kind. ...

III

Ever since I joined the Court, I have been concerned about the Court's emphasis on subjective intent as a criterion for constitutional adjudication. Although that criterion is often regarded as a restraint on the exercise of judicial power, it may in fact provide judges with a tool for exercising power that otherwise would be confined to the legislature. My principal concern with the subjective intent standard, however, is unrelated to the quantum of power it confers upon the judiciary. It is based on the quality of that power. For in the long run constitutional adjudication that is premised on a case-by-case appraisal of the subjective intent of local decisionmakers cannot possibly satisfy the requirement of impartial administration of the law that is embodied in the Equal Protection Clause of the Fourteenth Amendment. ...

In the future, it is not inconceivable that the white officials who are likely to remain in power under the District Court's plan will desire to perpetuate that system and to continue to control a majority of seats on the county commission. Under this Court's standard, if some of those officials harbor such an intent for an "invidious" reason, the District

Court's plan will itself become unconstitutional. It is not clear whether the invidious intent would have to be shared by all three white commissioners, by merely a majority of two, or by simply one if he were influential. It is not clear whether the issue would be affected by the intent of the two black commissioners, who might fear that a return to an at-large system would undermine the certainty of two black seats. ... In sum, as long as racial consciousness exists in Burke County, its governmental structure is subject to attack. ...

... [T]he question becomes whether the system was *maintained* for a discriminatory purpose. Whose intentions control? Obviously not the voters, although they may be most responsible for the attitudes and actions of local government. Assuming that it is the intentions of the "state actors" that is critical, how will their mental processes be discovered? Must a specific proposal for change be defeated? What if different motives are held by different legislators or, indeed, by a single official? Is a selfish desire to stay in office sufficient to justify a failure to change a governmental system?

The Court avoids these problems by failing to answer the very question that its standard asks. Presumably, according to the Court's analysis, the Burke County governmental structure is unconstitutional because it was maintained at some point for an invidious purpose. Yet the Court scarcely identifies the manner in which changes to a county governmental structure are made. There is no reference to any unsuccessful attempt to replace the at-large system with single-member districts. It is incongruous that subjective intent is identified as the constitutional standard and yet the persons who allegedly harbored an improper intent are never identified or mentioned. ...

... I am not convinced ... that the Constitution affords a right—and this is the *only* right the Court finds applicable in this case—to have every official decision made without the influence of considerations that are in some way "discriminatory." Is the failure of a state legislature to ratify the Equal Rights Amendment invalid if a federal judge concludes that a majority of the legislators harbored stereotypical views of the proper role of women in society? Is the establishment of a memorial for Jews slaughtered in World War II unconstitutional if civic leaders believe that their cause is more meritorious than that of victimized Palestinian refugees? Is the failure to adopt a state holiday for Martin Luther King, Jr. invalid if it is proved that state legislators believed that he does not deserve to be commemorated? Is the refusal to provide medicaid funding for abortions unconstitutional if officials intend to discriminate against women who would abort a fetus?

A rule that would invalidate all governmental action motivated by racial, ethnic or political considerations is too broad. Moreover, in my opinion the Court is incorrect in assuming that the intent of elected officials is invidious when they are motivated by a desire to retain control of the local political machinery. For such an intent is surely characteristic of politicians throughout the country. ...

[A] device that serves no purpose other than to exclude minority groups from effective political participation is unlawful under objective standards. But if a political majority's intent to maintain control of a legitimate local government is sufficient to invalidate any electoral device that makes it more difficult for a minority group to elect candidates—regardless of the nature of the interest that gives the minority group cohesion—the Court is not just entering a "political thicket"; it is entering a vast wonderland of judicial review of political activity.

The obvious response to this suggestion is that this case involves a racial group and that governmental decisions that disadvantage such a group must be subject to special scrutiny under the Fourteenth Amendment. I therefore must consider whether the Court's holding can legitimately be confined to political groups that are identified by racial characteristics.

IV ...

Groups of every character may associate together to achieve legitimate common goals. If they voluntarily identify themselves by a common interest in a specific issue, by a common ethnic heritage, by a common religious belief, or by their race, that characteristic assumes significance as the bond that gives the group cohesion and political strength. When referring to different kinds of political groups, this Court has consistently indicated that ... the Equal Protection Clause does not make some groups of citizens more equal than others. See Zobel v. Williams [1982] (Brennan, J., concurring). ... Indeed, in its opinion today the Court recognizes that the practical impact of the electoral system at issue applies equally to any "distinct minority, whether it be a racial, ethnic, economic, or political group."

A constitutional standard that gave special protection to political groups identified by racial characteristics would be inconsistent with the basic tenet of the Equal Protection Clause. Those groups are no more or less able to pursue their interests in the political arena than are groups defined by other characteristics. Nor can it be said that racial alliances are so unrelated to political action that any electoral decision that is influenced by racial consciousness—as opposed to other forms of political consciousness—is inherently irrational. For it is the very political power of a racial or ethnic group that creates a danger that an entrenched majority will take action contrary to the group's political interests. ... It would be unrealistic to distinguish racial groups from other political groups on the ground that race is an irrelevant factor in the political process.

Racial consciousness and racial association are not desirable features of our political system. We all look forward to the day when race is an irrelevant factor in the political process. In my opinion, however, that goal will best be achieved by eliminating the vestiges of discrimination that motivate disadvantaged racial and ethnic groups to vote as identifiable units. Whenever identifiable groups in our society are disadvantaged, they will share common political interests and tend to vote as a "bloc." In this respect, racial groups are like other political groups. A permanent constitutional rule that treated them differently would, in my opinion, itself tend to perpetuate race as a feature distinct from all others; a trait that makes persons different in the eyes of the law. ...

My conviction that all minority groups are equally entitled to constitutional protection against the misuse of the majority's political power does not mean that I would abandon judicial review of such action. ... [A] gerrymander as grotesque as the boundaries condemned in Gomillion v. Lightfoot [1960] is intolerable whether it fences out black voters, Republican voters, or Irish–Catholic voters. But if the standard the Court applies today extends to all types of minority groups, it is either so broad that virtually every political device is vulnerable or it is so undefined that federal judges can pick and choose almost at will among those that will be upheld and those that will be condemned.

There are valid reasons for concluding that certain minority groups—such as the black voters in Burke County, Georgia—should be given special protection from political oppression by the dominant majority. But those are reasons that justify the application of a legislative policy choice rather than a constitutional principle that cannot be confined to special circumstances or to a temporary period in our history. Any suggestion that political groups in which black leadership predominates are in need of a permanent constitutional shield against the tactics of their political opponents underestimates the resourcefulness, the wisdom, and the demonstrated capacity of such leaders. ...

Editors' Notes

(1) **Query:** We repeat our usual chorus of questions: What approaches to constitutional interpretation did Justices White, Powell, and Stevens follow? Did differences among the justices stem merely from different interpretations of the Equal Protection Clause or more deeply from different conceptions of our political system?

(2) **Query:** None of the justices utilized an *originalist approach*. Why not? The Reconstruction Congresses created and funded a massive program of welfare and affirmative action for the newly freed slaves administered by the Freedmen's Bureau. Of what interpretive relevance is that fact?

(3) **Query:** White wrote the opinions of the Court in both *Davis* and *Rogers*. Did *Rogers* blur *Davis*'s distinction between purpose and impact? In *Rogers*, did White offer any proof of purposeful discrimination above and beyond proof of impact of past discrimination?

(4) **Query:** Were the African Americans in *Rogers* asserting a constitutional right to group or proportional representation, as Powell implies in dissent? In Mobile v. Bolden (1980), discussed in *Rogers*, Justice Stewart

wrote for the plurality that the "Equal Protection Clause [does] not require proportional representation as an imperative of political organization." For a critique, see Note, "The Constitutional Imperative of Proportional Representation," 94 *Yale L.J.* 163 (1984). See also Cass R. Sunstein, "Beyond the Republican Revival," 97 *ibid.* 1539 (1988).

(5) **Query:** Dissenting in *Bolden*, Justice Marshall protested that the plurality had failed "to distinguish two distinct lines of equal protection decisions: those involving suspect classifications and those involving fundamental rights." Where the former were involved, "a showing of discriminatory purpose is necessary to impose strict scrutiny of facially neutral classifications having a racially discriminatory impact." On the other hand, "if a classification 'impinges upon a fundamental right explicitly or implicitly protected by the Constitution ... strict judicial scrutiny' is required, regardless of whether the infringement was intentional." And, Marshall closed his logical noose, the Court had often held that the right to a vote, an undiluted vote, equal to that of every other citizen, was a fundamental right. Thus search for discriminatory purpose in voting cases was irrelevant. In *Rogers,* however, Marshall joined the majority in its quest for discriminatory purpose. Why?

(6) **Query:** Is the logic of *Rogers* limited to political groups defined by racial characteristics or does it extend to any political group? In Davis v. Bandemer (1986; reprinted above, p. 788), the Court reversed a judgment sustaining an equal protection challenge to Indiana's 1982 state apportionment on the ground that the law unconstitutionally diluted the votes of Indiana Democrats. For a plurality, White wrote that the plaintiffs (Democrats) were required to prove "both intentional discrimination against an identifiable political group and an actual discriminatory effect on that group." The plurality concluded that the plaintiffs had easily satisfied the requirement of intent, but had failed to show the requisite effects. (Plaintiffs usually have more difficulty proving intent than effects.) Powell and Stevens dissented, as they had in *Rogers.*

(7) In addition to the article by Karst, which Powell cited above, p. 936, see also John Hart Ely, "The Centrality and Limits of Motivation Analysis," 15 *San Diego L.Rev.* 1155 (1978); these articles were part of a symposium on legislative motivation published in that volume. See also earlier works: Paul Brest, "Palmer v. Thompson: An Approach to the Problem of Unconstitutional Motive," 1971 *Sup.Ct.Rev.* 95; John Hart Ely, "Legislative and Administrative Motivation in Constitutional Law," 79 *Yale L.J.* 1205 (1970), as well as ch. 6 of his later work, *Democracy and Distrust* (Cambridge: Harvard University Press, 1980); Michael J. Perry, "The Disproportionate Impact Theory of Racial Discrimination," 125 *U.Pa.L.Rev.* 540 (1977); and Laurence H. Tribe, *American Constitutional Law* (2d ed.; Mineola, NY: Foundation Press, 1988), pp. 1076–1080.

V. HOW TO END RACIAL INEQUALITY: AFFIRMATIVE ACTION

"The guarantees of equal protection cannot mean one thing when applied to one individual and something else when applied to a person of another color."—Justice POWELL

"Our cases have always implied that an 'overriding statutory purpose' could be found that would justify racial classifications."—Justices BRENNAN, WHITE, MARSHALL, and BLACKMUN

"In order to get beyond racism, we must first take account of race."—Justice BLACKMUN

REGENTS OF THE UNIVERSITY OF CALIFORNIA v. BAKKE
438 U.S. 265, 98 S.Ct. 2733, 57 L.Ed.2d 750 (1978).

As part of its plan for "affirmative action," the Medical School of the University of California at Davis established a special admissions program for members of minority groups, allotting to them 16 of the 100 places in each entering class. In 1973 and 1974, the school denied admission to Allan Bakke, a white male, even though, according to the supposed standards for acceptance, he scored well above most candidates admitted under the special program. (The mean College Grade Point Average of those admitted in 1974 under the special program was 2.62; Bakke's was 3.51 on a scale in which A = 4, B = 3, C = 2, D = 1, and F = 0. On the national Medical College Admission Test, Bakke scored in the ninety-sixth percentile on verbal aptitude and in the ninety-seventh on scientific aptitude; the average scores of those admitted under the special program were at the thirty-fourth and thirty-seventh percentiles. Moreover, at least one person so admitted had had a C- average in college and scored in the lower third of the country on both verbal and scientific aptitude.)

After his second rejection, Bakke filed suit in a state court, which held Davis's affirmative action plan unconstitutional because it was based on race. The court, however, refused to order Bakke's admission on grounds that he had not proved that he would have been admitted in the absence of the special program. Both Bakke and Davis appealed parts of the judgment. California's Supreme Court ruled that the affirmative action plan violated both the Fourteenth Amendment and Title VI of the Civil Rights Act of 1964. (The most relevant section, 601, reads: "No person in the United States shall, on the ground of race, color, or national origin, be excluded from participation in, be denied the benefits of, or be subjected to discrimination under any program or activity receiving Federal financial assistance." The Medical School at Davis was receiving federal financial aid.) The court ordered Bakke admitted. Davis then sought and obtained certiorari from the U.S. Supreme Court.

The Justices could not agree on an opinion for the Court. Four (Brennan, White, Marshall, and Blackmun) thought the affirmative action plan constitutional and legal under Title VI and voted to deny Bakke admission. Four (Burger, Stewart, Rehnquist, and Stevens) believed that Title VI outlawed Davis's plan and voted for Bakke's admission. This even division made the role of the ninth Justice, Lewis F. Powell, decisive.

Mr. Justice **POWELL** announced the judgment of the Court. ...

... I believe that so much of the judgment of the California court as holds petitioner's special admissions program unlawful and directs that respondent be admitted to the Medical School must be affirmed. For the reasons expressed in a separate opinion, my Brothers The Chief Justice [Burger], Mr. Justice Stewart, Mr. Justice Rehnquist, and Mr. Justice Stevens concur in this judgment. ...

I also conclude ... that the portion of the court's judgment enjoining petitioner from according any consideration to race in its admissions process must be reversed. For reasons expressed in separate opinions, my Brothers Mr. Justice Brennan, Mr. Justice White, Mr. Justice Marshall, and Mr. Justice Blackmun concur in this judgment. ...

II

[Justice Powell analyzed the wording and legislative history of Title VI of the Civil Rights Act of 1964 and concluded that it proscribed "only those racial classifications that would violate the Equal Protection Clause or the Fifth Amendment." Thus he moved to the basic constitutional question: Did California's plan of affirmative action deny Bakke equal protection?]

III

A ...

... [T]he parties fight a sharp preliminary action over the proper characterization of the special admissions program. Petitioner prefers to view it as establishing a "goal" of minority representation. ... Respondent ... labels it a racial quota. This semantic distinction is beside the point: the special admissions program is undeniably a classification based on race and ethnic background. To the extent that there existed a pool of at least minimally qualified minority applicants to fill the 16 special admissions seats, white applicants could compete only for 84 seats in the entering class, rather than the 100 open to minority applicants. Whether this limitation is described as a quota or a goal, it is a line drawn on the basis of race and ethnic status.

The guarantees of the Fourteenth Amendment extend to persons. Its language is explicit: "No state shall ... deny to any person within its jurisdiction the equal protection of the laws." It is settled beyond question that the "rights created by the first section of the Fourteenth Amendment are, by its terms, guaranteed to the individual. ..." The guarantee of equal protection cannot mean one thing when applied to one individual and something else when applied to a person of another color. If both are not accorded the same protection, then it is not equal.

Nevertheless, petitioner argues that the court below erred in applying strict scrutiny to the special admissions programs because white
males ... are not a "discrete and insular minority" requiring extraordinary protection from the majoritarian political process. [United States
v.] Carolene Products Co. (1938). This rationale, however, has never
been invoked in our decisions as a prerequisite to subjecting racial or
ethnic distinctions to strict scrutiny. Nor has this Court held that
discreteness and insularity constitute necessary preconditions to a holding that a particular classification is invidious. ... These characteristics
may be relevant in deciding whether or not to add new types of
classifications to the list of "suspect" categories or whether a particular
classification survives close examination. Racial and ethnic classifications, however, are subject to stringent examination without regard to
these additional characteristics. [Korematsu v. United States (1944).]

B ...

Although many of the Framers of the Fourteenth Amendment
conceived of its primary function as bridging the vast distance between
members of the Negro race and the white "majority," the Amendment
itself was framed in universal terms, without reference to color, ethnic
origin, or condition of prior servitude. ...

Over the past 30 years, this Court has embarked upon the crucial
mission of interpreting the Equal Protection Clause with the view of
assuring to all persons "the protection of equal laws," Yick Wo [v.
Hopkins (1886)]. ... Because the landmark decisions in this area arose
in response to the continued exclusion of Negroes from the mainstream
of American society, they could be characterized as involving discrimination by the "majority" white race against the Negro minority. But they
need not be read as depending upon that characterization for their
results. It suffices to say that "[o]ver the years, this Court consistently
repudiated '[d]istinctions between citizens solely because of their ancestry' as being 'odious to a free people whose institutions are founded upon
the doctrine of equality.' " Loving v. Virginia (1967), quoting Hirabayashi v. United States (1943).

Petitioner urges us to adopt for the first time a more restrictive view
of the Equal Protection Clause and hold that discrimination against
members of the white "majority" cannot be suspect if its purpose can be
characterized as "benign." The clock of our liberties, however, cannot
be turned back to 1868. [Brown v. Board of Education (1954).] It is far
too late to argue that the guarantee of equal protection to *all* persons
permits the recognition of special wards entitled to a degree of protection
greater than that accorded others. ...

Once the artificial line of a "two-class theory" of the Fourteenth
Amendment is put aside, the difficulties entailed in varying the level of
judicial review according to a perceived "preferred" status of a particular
racial or ethnic minority are intractable. The concepts of "majority"
and "minority" necessarily reflect temporary arrangements and political

judgments. ... [T]he white "majority" itself is composed of various minority groups, most of which can lay claim to a history of prior discrimination. ... There is no principled basis for deciding which groups would merit "heightened judicial solicitude" and which would not. ...

Moreover, there are serious problems of justice connected with the idea of preference itself. First, it may not always be clear that a so-called preference is in fact benign. Courts may be asked to validate burdens imposed upon individual members of particular groups in order to advance the group's general interest. ... Nothing in the Constitution supports the notion that individuals may be asked to suffer otherwise impermissible burdens in order to enhance the societal standing of their ethnic groups. Second, preferential programs may only reinforce common stereotypes holding that certain groups are unable to achieve success without special protection. ... Third, there is a measure of inequity in forcing innocent persons ... to bear the burdens of redressing grievances not of their making.

By hitching the meaning of the Equal Protection Clause to these transitory considerations, we would be holding, as a constitutional principle, that judicial scrutiny of classifications touching on racial and ethnic background may vary with the ebb and flow of political forces. Disparate constitutional tolerance of such classifications well may serve to exacerbate racial and ethnic antagonisms rather than alleviate them. ... Also, the mutability of a constitutional principle, based upon shifting political and social judgments, undermines the chances for consistent application of the Constitution from one generation to the next, a critical feature of its coherent interpretation. ... In expounding the Constitution, the Court's role is to discern "principles sufficiently absolute to give them roots throughout the community and continuity over significant periods of time, and to lift them above the level of the pragmatic political judgments. ..." A[rchibald] Cox, *The Role of the Supreme Court in American Government* 114 (1976).

If it is the individual who is entitled to judicial protection ... rather than the individual only because of his membership in a particular group, then constitutional standards may be applied consistently. Political judgments regarding the necessity for the particular classification may be weighed in the constitutional balance ... but the standard of justification will remain constant. This is as it should be, since those political judgments are the product of rough compromise struck by contending groups within the democratic process. When they touch upon an individual's race or ethnic background, he is entitled to a judicial determination that the burden he is asked to bear on that basis is precisely tailored to serve a compelling governmental interest. ...

IV

We have held that in "order to justify the use of a suspect classification, a State must show that its purpose or interest is both constitutionally permissible and substantial, and that its use of the classification is 'necessary ... to the accomplishment' of its purpose or the safeguarding of its interest." In re Griffiths (1973); *Loving*. ...

A

If petitioner's purpose is to assure within its student body some specified percentage of a particular group merely because of its race or ethnic origin, such a preferential purpose must be rejected ... as facially invalid. Preferring members of any one group for no reason other than race or ethnic origin is discrimination for its own sake. This the Constitution forbids. E.g., *Loving, Brown.*

B

The State certainly has a legitimate and substantial interest in ameliorating, or eliminating ... the disabling effects of identified discrimination. ... We have [, however,] never approved a classification that aids persons perceived as members of relatively victimized groups at the expense of other innocent individuals in the absence of judicial, legislative, or administrative findings of constitutional or statutory violations. ... After such findings ... the governmental interest in preferring members of the injured groups at the expense of others is substantial, since the legal rights of the victims must be vindicated. ... Petitioner does not purport to have made, and is in no position to make, such findings. ... Lacking this capability, petitioner has not carried its burden of justification on this issue.

Hence, the purpose of helping certain groups whom the faculty of the Davis Medical School perceived as victims of "societal discrimination" does not justify a classification that imposes disadvantages upon persons ... who bear no responsibility for whatever harm the beneficiaries of the special admissions program are thought to have suffered. ...

C

Petitioner identifies, as another purpose of its program, improving the delivery of health care services to communities currently underserved. It may be assumed that in some situations a State's interest in facilitating the health care of its citizens is sufficiently compelling to support the use of a suspect classification. But there is virtually no evidence in the record indicating that petitioner's special admissions program is either needed or geared to promote that goal. ...

D

The fourth goal asserted by petitioner is the attainment of a diverse student body. This clearly is a constitutionally permissible goal for an institution of higher education. Academic freedom, though not a specifically enumerated constitutional right, long has been viewed as a special concern of the First Amendment. The freedom of a university to make its own judgments as to education includes the selection of its student body. ... Thus, in arguing that its universities must be accorded the right to select those students who will contribute the most to the "robust exchange of ideas," petitioner invokes a countervailing constitutional interest, that of the First Amendment. In this light, petitioner must be viewed as seeking to achieve a goal that is of paramount importance in the fulfillment of its mission.

... [E]ven at the graduate level, our tradition and experience lend support to the view that the contribution of diversity is substantial. ... Physicians serve a heterogeneous population. An otherwise qualified medical student with a particular background—whether it be ethnic, geographic, culturally advantaged or disadvantaged—may bring to a professional school of medicine experiences, outlooks and ideas that enrich the training of its student body and better equip its graduates to render with understanding their vital service to humanity.

Ethnic diversity, however, is only one element in a range of factors a university properly may consider in attaining the goal of a heterogeneous student body. Although a university must have wide discretion in making the sensitive judgments as to who should be admitted, constitutional limitations protecting individual rights may not be disregarded. ... [T]he question remains whether the program's racial classification is necessary to promote this interest. ...

V

A

... The diversity that furthers a compelling state interest encompasses a far broader array of qualifications and characteristics of which racial or ethnic origin is but a single though important element. Petitioner's special admissions program, focused solely on ethnic diversity, would hinder rather than further attainment of genuine diversity. The experience of other university admissions programs which take race into account in achieving the educational diversity valued by the First Amendment, demonstrates that the assignment of a fixed number of places to a minority group is not a necessary means toward that end. An illuminating example is found in the Harvard College program:

> In recent years Harvard College has expanded the concept of diversity to include students from disadvantaged economic, racial and ethnic groups.
> ...
>
> In practice, this new definition of diversity has meant that race has been a factor in some admission decisions. When the Committee on Admissions reviews the large middle group of applicants who are "admissible" ... the race of an applicant may tip the balance in his favor just as [may] geographic origin. ... A farm boy from Idaho can bring something ... that a Bostonian cannot offer. Similarly, a black student can usually bring something that a white person cannot offer. ...
>
> ... [T]he Committee has not set target-quotas for the number of blacks, or of musicians, football players, physicists or Californians. ... [Rather] in choosing among thousands of applicants who are not only

"admissible" academically but have other strong qualities, the Committee, with a number of criteria in mind, pays some attention to distribution among many types and categories of students. ...

In such an admissions program, race or ethnic background may be deemed a "plus" in a particular applicant's file, yet it does not insulate the individual from comparison with all other candidates for the available seats. The file of a particular black applicant may be examined for his potential contribution to diversity without the factor of race being decisive when compared, for example, with that of an applicant identified as an Italian–American if the latter is thought to exhibit qualities more likely to promote beneficial educational pluralism. Such qualities could include exceptional personal talents, unique work or service experience, leadership potential, maturity, demonstrated compassion, a history of overcoming disadvantage, ability to communicate with the poor, or other qualifications deemed important. ...

This kind of program treats each applicant as an individual in the admissions process. The applicant who loses out on the last available seat to another candidate receiving a "plus" on the basis of ethnic background will not have been foreclosed from all consideration for that seat simply because he was not the right color or had the wrong surname. It would mean only that his combined qualifications, which may have included similar nonobjective factors, did not outweigh those of the other applicant. His qualifications would have been weighed fairly and competitively, and he would have no basis to complain of unequal treatment. ...

It has been suggested that an admissions program which considers race only as one factor is simply a subtle and more sophisticated—but no less effective—means of according racial preference than the Davis program. A facial intent to discriminate, however, is evident in petitioner's preference program and not denied in this case. No such facial infirmity exists in an admissions program where race or ethnic background is simply one element—to be weighed fairly against other elements—in the selection process. ...

B ...

... [W]hen a State's distribution of benefits or imposition of burdens hinges on the color of a person's skin or ancestry, that individual is entitled to a demonstration that the challenged classification is necessary to promote a substantial state interest. Petitioner [California] has failed to carry this burden. ...

[*Affirmed in part and reversed in part.*]

Opinion of Mr. Justice **BRENNAN,** Mr. Justice **WHITE,** Mr. Justice **MARSHALL,** and Mr. Justice **BLACKMUN,** concurring in the judgment in part and dissenting. ...

I ...

The Fourteenth Amendment, the embodiment in the Constitution of our abiding belief in human equality, has been the law of our land for only slightly more than half its 200 years. And for half of that half, the Equal Protection Clause of the Amendment was largely moribund. ... Worse than desuetude, the Clause was early turned against those whom it was intended to set free, condemning them to a "separate but equal" status before the law, a status always separate but seldom equal. Not until 1954 was this odious doctrine interred by our decision in Brown v. Board of Education and its progeny. ... Even then inequality was not eliminated with "all deliberate speed." ... [O]fficially sanctioned discrimination is not a thing of the past.

Against this background, claims that law must be "colorblind" or that the datum of race is no longer relevant to public policy must be seen as aspiration rather than as description of reality. ... [W]e cannot— and ... need not under our Constitution or Title VI ...—let color blindness become myopia which masks the reality that many "created equal" have been treated within our lifetimes as inferior both by the law and by their fellow citizens.

II

[The four Justices then examined the text and legislative history of the Civil Rights Act of 1964 and concluded that the statute did not outlaw affirmative action plans such as that of Davis.]

III

A

The assertion of human equality is closely associated with the proposition that differences in color or creed, birth or status, are neither significant nor relevant to the way in which persons should be treated. Nonetheless, the position ... summed up by the shorthand phrase "[o]ur Constitution is color-blind," Plessy v. Ferguson (1896) (Harlan, J., dissenting), has never been adopted by this Court as the proper meaning of the Equal Protection Clause. Indeed, we have expressly rejected this proposition on a number of occasions.

Our cases have always implied that an "overriding statutory purpose" could be found that would justify racial classifications. ... We conclude, therefore, that racial classifications are not *per se* invalid under the Fourteenth Amendment. Accordingly, we turn to the problem of articulating what our role should be in reviewing state action that expressly classifies by race, e.g. *Loving, Korematsu.*

B ...

Unquestionably we have held that a government practice or statute which restricts "fundamental rights" or which contains "suspect classifications" is to be subjected to "strict scrutiny" and can be justified only if it furthers a compelling government purpose and, even then, only if no less restrictive alternative is available. ... But no fundamental right is involved here. ... Nor do whites as a class have any of the "traditional indicia of suspectness: the class is not saddled with such disabilities, or subjected to such a history of purposeful unequal treatment, or relegated to such a position of political powerlessness as to command extraordinary protection from the majoritarian political process." [San Antonio v. Rodriguez (1973).] See *Carolene Products* n. 4. ...

... Nor ... [do] the University's purposes contravene the cardinal principle that racial classifications that stigmatize—because they are drawn on the presumption that one race is inferior to another or because they put the weight of government behind racial hatred and separatism—are invalid without more. ...

On the other hand ... this case ... should [not] be analyzed by applying the very loose rational-basis standard of review that is the very least that is always applied in equal protection cases. ... [A] number of considerations ... lead us to conclude that racial classifications designed to further remedial purposes " 'must serve important governmental objectives and must be substantially related to achievement of those objectives.' " Craig v. Boren (1976). First, race, like "gender-based classifications too often [has] been inexcusably utilized to stereotype and stigmatize politically powerless segments of society." ... Second, race, like gender and illegitimacy, ... is an immutable characteristic which its possessors are powerless to escape or set aside. While a classification is not *per se* invalid because it divides classes on the basis of an immutable characteristic ... it is nevertheless true that such divisions are contrary to our deep belief that "legal burdens should bear some relationship to individual responsibility or wrongdoing" ... and that advancement sanctioned, sponsored, or approved by the State should ideally be based on individual merit or achievement. ...

In sum, because of the significant risk that racial classifications established for ostensibly benign purposes can be misused, ... to justify such a classification an important and articulated purpose for its use must be shown. In addition, any statute must be stricken that stigmatizes any group or that singles out those least well represented in the political process to bear the brunt of a benign program. ...

IV

Davis's articulated purpose of remedying the effects of past societal discrimination is, under our cases, sufficiently important to justify the use of race-conscious admissions programs where there is a sound basis for concluding that minority underrepresentation is substantial and chronic, and that the handicap of past discrimination is impeding access of minorities to the medical school. ...

B

Properly construed, ... our prior cases unequivocally show that a state government may adopt race-conscious programs if the purpose of such programs is to remove the disparate racial impact its actions might otherwise have and if there is reason to believe that the disparate impact is itself the product of past discrimination, whether its own or that of society at large.   There is no question that Davis's program is valid under this test.   ...

Davis clearly could conclude that the serious and persistent under-representation of minorities in medicine ... is the result of handicaps under which minority applicants labor as a consequence of a background of deliberate, purposeful discrimination against minorities in education and in society generally, as well as in the medical profession.   From the inception of our national life, Negroes have been subjected to unique legal disabilities impairing access to equal educational opportunity.   ... The generation of minority students applying to Davis Medical School since it opened in 1968 ... clearly have been victims of this discrimina-tion.   ... [T]he conclusion is inescapable that applicants to medical school must be few indeed who endured the effects of *de jure* segrega-tion, the resistance to *Brown*, or the equally debilitating pervasive discrimination fostered by our long history of official discrimination ... and yet come to the starting line with an education equal to whites.   ...

C

The second prong of our test—whether the Davis program stigma-tizes any discrete group or individual and whether race is reasonably used in light of the program's objectives—is clearly satisfied by the Davis program.

It is not even claimed that Davis's program in any way operates to stigmatize or single out any discrete and insular, or even any identifi-able, nonminority group.   Nor will harm comparable to that imposed upon racial minorities by exclusion or separation on grounds of race be the likely result of the program.   ...

Nor was Bakke in any sense stamped as inferior by the Medical School's rejection of him.   ...   Unlike discrimination against racial minorities, the use of racial preferences for remedial purposes does not inflict a pervasive injury upon individual whites in the sense that wherever they go or whatever they do there is a significant likelihood that they will be treated as second-class citizens because of their color.
...

D

We disagree with the lower courts' conclusion that the Davis pro-gram's use of race was unreasonable in light of its objectives.   ... [T]here are no practical means by which it could achieve its ends in the foreseeable future without the use of race-conscious measures.   ...

E

Finally, Davis's special admissions program cannot be said to violate the Constitution simply because it has set aside a predetermined number of places for qualified minority applicants rather than using minority status as a positive factor to be considered in evaluating applications of disadvantaged minority applicants. For purposes of constitutional adjudication, there is no difference between the two approaches. In any admissions program which accords special consideration to disadvantaged racial minorities, a determination of the degree of preference to be given is unavoidable, and any given preference that results in the exclusion of a white candidate is no more or no less constitutionally acceptable than a program such as that at Davis. ...

Separate opinion of Mr. Justice **WHITE**. ...

[Justice White contended that Title VI of the Civil Rights Act of 1964 did not provide for enforcement by private action, and that consequently the courts had no jurisdiction in Bakke's case.]

Mr. Justice **MARSHALL**. ...

Mr. Justice **BLACKMUN**. ...

I suspect that it would be impossible to arrange an affirmative action program in a racially neutral way and have it successful. To ask that this be so is to demand the impossible. In order to get beyond racism, we must first take account of race. There is no other way. And in order to treat some persons equally, we must treat them differently. We cannot—we dare not—let the Equal Protection Clause perpetuate racial supremacy. ...

Mr. Justice **STEVENS,** with whom The Chief Justice [**BURGER**], Mr. Justice **STEWART,** and Mr. Justice **REHNQUIST** join, concurring in part and dissenting in part. ...

... Our settled practice ... is to avoid the decision of a constitutional issue if a case can be fairly decided on a statutory ground. ... The more important the issue, the more force there is to this doctrine. In this case, we are presented with a constitutional question of undoubted and unusual importance. Since, however, a dispositive statutory claim was raised at the very inception of this case, and squarely decided in the portion of the trial court judgment affirmed by the California Supreme Court, it is our plain duty to confront it. Only if petitioner should prevail on the statutory issue would it be necessary to decide whether the University's admissions program violated the Equal Protection Clause of the Fourteenth Amendment.

Section 601 of the Civil Rights Act of 1964 provides:

> No person in the United States shall, on the ground of race, color, or national origin, be excluded from participation in, be denied the benefits of, or be subjected to discrimination under any program or activity receiving Federal financial assistance.

The University, through its special admissions policy, excluded Bakke from participation in its program of medical education because of his race. The University also acknowledges that it was, and still is, receiving federal financial assistance. The plain language of the statute therefore requires affirmance of the judgment below. A different result cannot be justified unless that language misstates the actual intent of the Congress that enacted the statute or the statute is not enforceable in a private action. Neither conclusion is warranted. ...

Editors' Notes

(1) **Query:** To what (varying?) extents did each of the opinion writers follow a *textualist approach*? A *structuralist approach*? A *purposive approach*?

(2) **Query:** According to Justice Powell, "Political judgments regarding the necessity for the particular classification may be weighed in the constitutional balance ... but the standard of justification will remain constant." Does this sentence, in the context of the rest of the opinion, indicate that Powell's approach is that of *balancing*? If so, how did he meet the objections to *balancing* that Chapter 9 listed? What does this sentence reveal about Powell's theory of legitimate constitutional change? To what extent did he agree with Justice Sutherland in the Minnesota Moratorium Case (1934; reprinted above, p. 210) and to what extent with Justice Cardozo in that same case?

(3) **Query:** At p. 948, Justices Brennan et al. said that the Fourteenth Amendment was "the embodiment in the Constitution of our abiding belief in human equality." Do the amendment's words "embody" an "abiding belief in human equality"? How could the four justices have so interpreted it? See Brennan's speech, "The Constitution of the United States: Contemporary Ratification" (reprinted above, p. 236).

(4) **Query:** To what degree was the division of Justice Powell from Justices Brennan, White, Marshall, and Blackmun the result of a difference on the question whether the equal protection clause protects individual rights or group rights? See the discussion of this general point in the Introductory Essay to this Section, at pp. 876–77. To what extent did it stem from a difference concerning the implications of *Carolene Products*?

(5) **Query:** The opinion of Brennan et al. made much of the claim that affirmative action does not "stigmatize" whites. To what extent is "stigma" relevant to the plain words of the equal protection clause? The structure of the Fourteenth Amendment? To the structure of the entire constitutional document? To the structure of the larger political system? To the political theories that underlie the document and the political system?

(6) The opinion of Brennan et al. also alluded to a different level of scrutiny and so to a different, lower level, test called "intermediate scrutiny," which the Court created to consider challenges to classifications based on sex; Brennan explained and applied that test for the Court in Craig v. Boren (1976; reprinted below, p. 992). That test requires that the classification "serve important [not compelling] governmental objectives and must be substantially related [not closely related or necessary] to achievement of those objectives." Brennan would have applied "intermediate scrutiny," not "strict scrutiny," to plans for affirmative action. The debate concerning whether strict scrutiny or intermediate scrutiny properly applies to such plans continues in the next case, Richmond v. J. A. Croson Co. (1989), and Metro Broadcasting

v. FCC (1990), discussed in the Editors' Notes following *Croson*. But in Adarand Constructors v. Pena (1995), also discussed there, the Court held that strict scrutiny applies.

This debate has also spilled over to the question of the proper constitutional test for governmental regulations of abortion. See Planned Parenthood v. Casey (1992; reprinted below, p. 1281).

————

"Racial classifications are suspect, and that means that simple legislative assurances of good intention cannot suffice."—Justice O'CONNOR

"A central purpose of the Fourteenth Amendment is to further the national goal of equal opportunity for all our citizens. ... [But] the Constitution requires us to evaluate our policy decisions ... primarily by studying their probable impact on the future."—Justice STEVENS

"Only such a [race neutral] program, and not one that operates on the basis of race, is in accord with the letter and the spirit of our Constitution."—Justice SCALIA

"A profound difference separates governmental actions that themselves are racist, and governmental actions that seek to remedy the effects of prior racism or to prevent neutral governmental activity from perpetuating the effects of such racism."—Justice MARSHALL

CITY OF RICHMOND v. J. A. CROSON CO.
488 U.S. 469, 109 S.Ct. 706, 102 L.Ed.2d 854 (1989).

In 1983, the Richmond City Council held public hearings that showed that, although half the city's population was African American, less than 1 percent of the construction contracts awarded by the city went to companies owned by members of racial minorities. The hearings, however, did not reveal overt discrimination by city officials or prime contractors. By a 5–2 vote, the council then adopted the Minority Business Utilization Plan, which required prime contractors to whom the city awarded construction contracts to subcontract at least 30 per cent of the dollar amount of the contract to one or more Minority Business Enterprises (MBEs), that is, firms in which blacks, Hispanics, Orientals, Native Americans, Eskimos, or Aleuts owned at least 51 per cent of the business.

Later that year J. A. Croson Co., a firm owned by whites, submitted a bid on a city project and won the contract. Before bidding, Croson had asked five or six MBEs to bid to sell it the materials it would need. The only such company to respond delayed its estimate for 30 days after the deadline and then submitted a bill that was more than 7 per cent above the market price. Citing these circumstances, Croson twice asked the city either to waive the subcontracting requirement or increase the price of the construction. The city denied the requests and reopened the project for bidding. Croson then filed suit in a federal district court, claiming the ordinance was unconstitutional on its face and as applied in this instance.

Croson lost in the district court and in the court of appeals. Both tribunals relied heavily on the Supreme Court's decision in Fullilove v. Klutznick (1980), which had upheld a similar congressional plan, one based on no specific finding of discrimination, for federal contracts. In that case, however, the justices had written four different opinions, with none commanding more than three votes. No one could tell what test, if any, a majority of the justices would use. Croson obtained certiorari from the Supreme Court, which remanded the case for further consideration in light of a later case, Wygant v. Jackson (1986). There, a similarly splintered Court had invalidated a local effort to cope with racial tension by providing that, when public schools teachers were to be "laid off," the existing proportion of white and minority teachers would be maintained, regardless of the seniority of individual educators.

On remand, the Court of Appeals applied the test of strict scrutiny and invalidated Richmond's ordinance. The city appealed to the Supreme Court.

Justice **O'CONNOR** announced the judgment of the Court and delivered the opinion of the Court with respect to Parts **I**, **III-B**, and **IV**, an opinion with respect to Part **II**, in which **THE CHIEF JUSTICE [REHNQUIST]** and Justice **WHITE** join, and an opinion with respect to Parts **III-A** and **V**, in which **THE CHIEF JUSTICE**, Justice **WHITE** and Justice **KENNEDY** join. . . .

II

The parties . . . fight an initial battle over the scope of the city's power to adopt legislation designed to address the effects of past discrimination. Relying on our decision in Wygant [v. Jackson Board of Education (1986)], appellee argues that the city must limit any race-based remedial efforts to eradicating the effects of its own prior discrimination. . . . Appellant argues that our decision in Fullilove [v. Klutznick (1980)] is controlling, and that as a result the city of Richmond enjoys sweeping legislative power to define and attack the effects of prior discrimination in its local construction industry. We find that neither of these two rather stark alternatives can withstand analysis. . . .

The principal opinion in *Fullilove*, written by Chief Justice Burger, did not employ "strict scrutiny" or any other traditional standard of equal protection review. The Chief Justice noted at the outset that although racial classifications call for close examination, the Court was at the same time, "bound to approach [its] task with appropriate deference to the Congress, a co-equal branch charged by the Constitution with the power to 'provide for the . . . general Welfare of the United States' and 'to enforce by appropriate legislation,' the equal protection guarantees of the Fourteenth Amendment." . . .

On the issue of congressional power, the Chief Justice found that Congress' commerce power was sufficiently broad to allow it to reach the practices of prime contractors on federally funded local construction projects. Congress could mandate state and local government compliance with the set-aside program under its § 5 power to enforce the Fourteenth Amendment. ...

Appellant ... rel[ies] heavily on *Fullilove* for the proposition that a city council, like Congress, need not make specific findings of discrimination to engage in race-conscious relief. ... What appellant ignores is that Congress, unlike any State or political subdivision, has a specific constitutional mandate to enforce the dictates of the Fourteenth Amendment. The power to "enforce" may at times also include the power to define situations which Congress determines threaten principles of equality and to adopt prophylactic rules to deal with those situations. See Katzenbach v. Morgan (1966). The Civil War Amendments themselves worked a dramatic change in the balance between congressional and state power over matters of race. ...

That Congress may identify and redress the effects of society-wide discrimination does not mean that, *a fortiori,* the State and their political subdivisions are free to decide that such remedies are appropriate. Section 1 of the Fourteenth Amendment is an explicit *constraint* on state power, and the States must undertake any remedial efforts in accordance with that provision. To hold otherwise would be to cede control over the content of the Equal Protection Clause to the 50 state legislatures and their myriad political subdivisions. The mere recitation of a benign or compensatory purpose for the use of a racial classification would essentially entitle the States to exercise the full power of Congress under § 5 of the Fourteenth Amendment and insulate any racial classification from judicial scrutiny under § 1. We believe that such a result would be contrary to the intentions of the Framers of the Fourteenth Amendment. ...

It would seem equally clear, however, that a state or local subdivision ... has the authority to eradicate the effects of private discrimination within its own legislative jurisdiction. ... Thus, if the city could show that it had essentially become a "passive participant" in a system of racial exclusion practiced by elements of the local construction industry, we think it clear that the city could take affirmative steps to dismantle such a system. It is beyond dispute that any public entity, state or federal, has a compelling interest in assuring that public dollars, drawn from the tax contributions of all citizens, do not serve to finance the evil of private prejudice.

III

The Equal Protection Clause of the Fourteenth Amendment provides that "[N]o State shall ... deny to *any* person within its jurisdiction the equal protection of the laws" (emphasis added). [T]he "rights created by the first section of the Fourteenth Amendment are, by its terms, guaranteed to the individual. The rights established are personal rights." Shelley v. Kraemer (1948). The Richmond Plan denies certain citizens the opportunity to compete for a fixed percentage of public contracts based solely upon their race. To whatever racial group these citizens belong, their "personal rights" to be treated with equal dignity and respect are implicated by a rigid rule erecting race as the sole criterion in an aspect of public decisionmaking.

Absent searching judicial inquiry into the justification for such race-based measures, there is simply no way of determining what classifications are "benign" or "remedial" and what classifications are in fact motivated by illegitimate notions of racial inferiority or simple racial politics. Indeed, the purpose of strict scrutiny is to "smoke out" illegitimate uses of race by assuring that the legislative body is pursuing a goal important enough to warrant use of a highly suspect tool. The test also ensures that the means chosen "fit" this compelling goal so closely that there is little or no possibility that the motive for the classification was illegitimate racial prejudice or stereotype.

Classifications based on race carry a danger of stigmatic harm. Unless they are strictly reserved for remedial settings, they may in fact promote notions of racial inferiority and lead to a politics of racial hostility. See University of California Regents v. Bakke (1978) (opinion of Powell, J.). We thus reaffirm the view expressed by the plurality in *Wygant* that the standard of review under the Equal Protection Clause is not dependent on the race of those burdened or benefitted by a particular classification. ... See also San Antonio v. Rodriguez (1973) (Marshall, J., dissenting).

Even were we to accept a reading of the guarantee of equal protection under which the level of scrutiny varies according to the ability of different groups to defend their interests in the representative process, heightened scrutiny would still be appropriate in the circumstances of this case. One of the central arguments for applying a less exacting standard to "benign" racial classifications is that such measures essentially involve a choice made by dominant racial groups to disadvantage themselves. If one aspect of the judiciary's role under the Equal Protection Clause is to protect "discrete and insular minorities" from majoritarian prejudice or indifference, see United States v. Carolene Products (1938), some maintain that these concerns are not implicated when the "white majority" places burdens upon itself. See J. Ely, *Democracy and Distrust* 170 (1980).

In this case, blacks comprise approximately 50% of the population of the city of Richmond. Five of the nine seats on the City Counsel are held by blacks. The concern that a political majority will more easily act to the disadvantage of a minority based on unwarranted assumptions or incomplete facts would seem to militate for, not against, the application of heightened judicial scrutiny in this case.

In *Bakke*, ... [Justice Powell] contrasted the "focused" goal of remedying "wrongs worked by specific instances of racial discrimination" with "the remedying of the effects of 'societal discrimination,' an amorphous concept of injury that may be ageless in its reach into the past." He indicated that for the governmental interest in remedying past discrimination to be triggered "judicial, legislative, or administrative findings of constitutional or statutory violations" must be made. Only then does the Government have a compelling interest in favoring one race over another.

In *Wygant,* four Members of the Court applied heightened scrutiny to a race-based system of employee layoffs. Justice Powell, writing for the plurality, again drew the distinction between "societal discrimination" ... and the type of identified discrimination that can support and define the scope of race-based relief. ... The lower courts had upheld the scheme, based on the theory that minority students were in need of "role models" to alleviate the effects of prior discrimination in society. This Court reversed. ...

B

We think it clear that the factual predicate offered in support of the Richmond Plan suffers from the same two defects identified as fatal in *Wygant.* The District Court found the city council's "findings sufficient to ensure that, in adopting the Plan, it was remedying the present effects of past discrimination in the *construction industry.*" (Emphasis added.) Like the "role model" theory ... a generalized assertion that there has been past discrimination in an entire industry provides no guidance for a legislative body to determine the precise scope of the injury it seeks to remedy. It "has no logical stopping point." *Wygant* (plurality opinion). "Relief" for such an ill-defined wrong could extend until the percentage of public contracts awarded to MBEs in Richmond mirrored the percentage of minorities in the population as a whole.

Appellant argues that it is attempting to remedy various forms of past discrimination that are alleged to be responsible for the small number of minority businesses in the local contracting industry. Among these the city cites the exclusion of blacks from skilled construction trade unions and training programs. ... While there is no doubt that the sorry history of both private and public discrimination in this country has contributed to a lack of opportunities for black entrepreneurs, this observation, standing alone, cannot justify a rigid racial quota in the awarding of public contracts in Richmond, Virginia. ... The 30% quota cannot in any realistic sense be tied to any injury suffered by anyone. ...

The District Court accorded great weight to the fact that the city council designated the Plan as "remedial." But the mere recitation of a "benign" or legitimate purpose for a racial classification is entitled to little or no weight. See Weinberger v. Wiesenfeld [1975]. Racial classifications are suspect, and that means that simple legislative assurances of good intention cannot suffice.

The District Court also relied on the highly conclusionary statement of a proponent of the Plan that there was racial discrimination in the construction industry "in this area, and the State, and around the nation." . . . The factfinding process of legislative bodies is generally entitled to a presumption of regulatory and deferential review by the judiciary. But when a legislative body chooses to employ a suspect classification, it cannot rest upon a generalized assertion as to the classification's relevance to its goals. See McLaughlin v. Florida (1964). A governmental actor cannot render race a legitimate proxy for a particular condition merely by declaring that the condition exists. The history of racial classifications in this country suggested that blind judicial deference to legislative or executive pronouncements of necessity has no place in equal protection analysis. See Korematsu v. United States (1944) (Murphy, J., dissenting).

Reliance on the disparity between the number of prime contracts awarded to minority firms and the minority population of the city of Richmond is similarly misplaced. . . . In this case, the city does not even know how many MBEs in the relevant market are qualified to undertake prime or subcontracting work in public construction projects. Nor does the city know what percentage of total city construction dollars minority firms now receive as subcontractors on prime contracts let by the city. . . .

The city and the District Court also relied on evidence that MBE membership in local contractors' associations was extremely low. Again, standing alone this evidence is not probative of any discrimination in the local construction industry. There are numerous explanations for this dearth of minority participation, including past societal discrimination in education and economic opportunities as well as both black and white career and entrepreneurial choices. Blacks may be disproportionately attracted to industries other than construction. . . .

Finally, the city and the District Court relied on Congress' finding in connection with the set-aside approved in *Fullilove* that there had been nationwide discrimination in the construction industry. The probative value of these findings for demonstrating the existence of discrimination in Richmond is extremely limited. . . . If all a state or local government need do is find a congressional report on the subject to enact a set-aside program, the constraints of the Equal Protection Clause will, in effect, have been rendered a nullity.

. . . The "evidence" relied upon by the dissent, the history of school desegregation in Richmond and numerous congressional reports, does little to define the scope of any injury to minority contractors in Richmond or the necessary remedy. The facts relied upon by the dissent could justify a preference of any size or duration. . . .

In sum, none of the evidence presented by the city points to any identified discrimination in the Richmond construction industry. We, therefore, hold that the city has failed to demonstrate a compelling interest in apportioning public contracting opportunities on the basis of race. To accept Richmond's claim that past societal discrimination alone can serve as the basis for rigid racial preferences would be to open the door to competing claims for "remedial relief" for every disadvantaged

group. The dream of a Nation of equal citizens in a society where race
is irrelevant to personal opportunity and achievement would be lost in a
mosaic of shifting preferences based on inherently unmeasurable claims
of past wrongs. ... We think such a result would be contrary to both
the letter and spirit of a constitutional provision whose central command
is equality. ...

IV

... [I]t is almost impossible to assess whether the Richmond Plan is
narrowly tailored to remedy prior discrimination since it is not linked to
identified discrimination in any way. ... First, there does not appear to
have been any consideration of the use of race-neutral means to increase
minority business participation in city contracting. ... The principal
opinion in *Fullilove* found that Congress had carefully examined and
rejected race-neutral alternatives before enacting the MBE set-aside.
... Second, the 30% quota cannot be said to be narrowly tailored to any
goal, except perhaps outright racial balancing. ...

V

Nothing we say today precludes a state or local entity from taking
action to rectify the effects of identified discrimination within its jurisdiction. If the city of Richmond had evidence before it that nonminority
contractors were systematically excluding minority businesses from subcontracting opportunities it could take action to end the discriminatory
exclusion. Where there is a significant statistical disparity between the
number of qualified minority contractors willing and able to perform a
particular service and the number of such contractors actually engaged
by the locality or the locality's prime contractors, an inference of
discriminatory exclusion could arise. Under such circumstances, the city
could act to dismantle the closed business system by taking appropriate
measures against those who discriminate on the basis of race or other
illegitimate criteria. In the extreme case, some form of narrowly tailored racial preference might be necessary to break down patterns of
deliberate exclusion.

Nor is local government powerless to deal with individual instances
of racially motivated refusals to employ minority contractors. Where
such discrimination occurs, a city would be justified in penalizing the
discriminator and providing appropriate relief to the victim of such
discrimination. ...

Even in the absence of evidence of discrimination, the city has at its
disposal a whole array of race-neutral devices to increase the accessibility
of city contracting opportunities to small entrepreneurs of all races.
Simplification of bidding procedures, relaxation of bonding requirements,
and training and financial aid for disadvantaged entrepreneurs of all
races would open the public contracting market to all those who have
suffered the effects of past societal discrimination or neglect. ...

... Because the city of Richmond has failed to identify the need for remedial action in the awarding of its public construction contracts, its treatment of its citizens on a racial basis violates the dictates of the Equal Protection Clause. ...

Affirmed.

Justice **STEVENS**, concurring in part and concurring in the judgment.

A central purpose of the Fourteenth Amendment is to further the national goal of equal opportunity for all our citizens. In order to achieve that goal we must learn from our past mistakes, but I believe the Constitution requires us to evaluate our policy decisions—including those that govern the relationships among different racial and ethnic groups—primarily by studying their probable impact on the future. I therefore do not agree with the premise that seems to underlie today's decision, as well as the decision in *Wygant*, that a governmental decision that rests on a racial classification is never permissible except as a remedy for a past wrong. I do, however, agree with the Court's explanation of why the Richmond ordinance cannot be justified as a remedy for past discrimination, and therefore join Parts **I**, **III-B**, and **IV** of its opinion. ...

Justice **KENNEDY**, concurring in part and concurring in the judgment.

...

The moral imperative of racial neutrality is the driving force of the Equal Protection Clause. Justice Scalia's opinion underscores that proposition. ... The rule suggested in his opinion, which would strike down all preferences which are not necessary remedies to victims of unlawful discrimination, ... would make crystal clear to the political branches, at least those of the States, that legislation must be based on criteria other than race.

Nevertheless, given that a rule of automatic invalidity for racial preferences ... would be a significant break with our precedents that require a case-by-case test, I am not convinced we need adopt it at this point. ... I accept the less absolute rule contained in Justice O'Connor's opinion. ...

Justice **SCALIA**, concurring in the judgment.

I agree with much of the Court's opinion, and, in particular, with Justice O'Connor's conclusion that strict scrutiny must be applied to all governmental classification by race, whether or not its asserted purpose is "remedial" or "benign." I do not agree, however, with [her] dictum suggesting that ... state and local governments may in some circumstances discriminate on the basis of race in order (in a broad sense) "to ameliorate the effects of past discrimination." ... At least where state or local action is at issue, only a social emergency rising to the level of imminent danger to life and limb—for example, a prison race riot, requiring temporary segregation of inmates, cf. Lee v. Washington

[1968]—can justify an exception to the principle embodied in the Four-teenth Amendment that "[o]ur Constitution is color-blind, and neither knows nor tolerates classes among citizens," Plessy v. Ferguson (1896) (Harlan, J., dissenting).

We have in some contexts approved the use of racial classifications by the Federal Government to remedy the effects of past discrimination. I do not believe that we must or should extend those holdings to the States.   ... A sound distinction between federal and state (or local) action based on race rests not only upon the substance of the Civil War Amendments, but upon social reality and governmental theory.   ... The struggle for racial justice has historically been a struggle by the national society against oppression in the individual States.   ... [R]acial discrimi-nation against any group finds a more ready expression at the state and local than at the federal level.   To the children of the Founding Fathers, this should come as no surprise.   An acute awareness of the heightened danger of oppression from political factions in small, rather than large, political units dates to the very beginning of our national history.   ... *The Federalist* No. 10.   ... [Reprinted below, p. 1087—**Eds.**]

In my view there is only one circumstance in which the States may act by race to "undo the effects of past discrimination": where that is necessary to eliminate their own maintenance of a system of unlawful racial classification.   ... This distinction explains our school desegrega-tion cases, in which we have made plain that States and localities sometimes have an obligation to adopt race-conscious remedies.   ...

I agree with the Court's dictum that a fundamental distinction must be drawn between the effects of "societal" discrimination and the effects of "identified" discrimination, and that the situation would be different if Richmond's plan were "tailored" to identify those particular bidders who "suffered from the effects of past discrimination by the city or prime contractors."   In my view, however, the reason that would make a difference is not, as the Court states, that it would justify race-conscious action but rather that it would enable race-neutral remediation.   Noth-ing prevents Richmond from according a contracting preference to identified victims of discrimination.   While most of the beneficiaries might be black, neither the beneficiaries nor those disadvantaged by the preference would be identified *on the basis of their race*.   ...

It is plainly true that in our society blacks have suffered discrimina-tion immeasurably greater than any directed at other racial groups.   But those who believe that racial preferences can help to "even the score" display, and reinforce, a manner of thinking by race that was the source of the injustice.   ... The relevant proposition is not that it was blacks, or Jews, or Irish who were discriminated against, but that it was individual men and women, "created equal," who were discriminated against.   And the relevant resolve is that that should never happen again.   ... Since blacks have been disproportionately disadvantaged by racial discrimination, any race-neutral remedial program aimed at the disadvantaged as such will have a disproportionately beneficial impact on blacks. Only such a program, and not one that operates on the basis of race, is in accord with the letter and the spirit of our Constitution. ...

Justice **MARSHALL**, with whom Justice **BRENNAN** and Justice **BLACKMUN** join, dissenting.

It is a welcome symbol of racial progress when the former capital of the Confederacy acts forthrightly to confront the effects of racial discrimination in its midst. ... Richmond's set-aside program is indistinguishable in all meaningful respects from—and in fact was patterned upon—the federal set-aside plan which this Court upheld in *Fullilove*.

... The essence of the majority's position is that Richmond has failed to catalogue adequate findings to prove that past discrimination has impeded minorities from joining or participating fully in Richmond's construction contracting industry. I find deep irony in second-guessing Richmond's judgment on this point. As much as any municipality in the United States, Richmond knows what racial discrimination is; a century of decisions by this and other federal courts has richly documented the city's disgraceful history of public and private racial discrimination. In any event, the Richmond City Council has supported its determination that minorities have been wrongly excluded from local construction contracting. ...

More fundamentally, today's decision marks a deliberate and giant step backward in this Court's affirmative action jurisprudence. Cynical of one municipality's attempt to redress the effects of past racial discrimination in a particular industry, the majority launches a grapeshot attack on race-conscious remedies in general. The majority's unnecessary pronouncements will inevitably discourage or prevent governmental entities ... from acting to rectify the scourge of past discrimination. This is the harsh reality of the majority's decision, but it is not the Constitution's command. ...

II

... My view has long been that race-conscious classifications designed to further remedial goals "must serve important governmental objectives and must be substantially related to achievement of those objectives" in order to withstand constitutional scrutiny. *Bakke* (joint separate opinion of Brennan, White, Marshall, and Blackmun, JJ.). Analyzed in terms of this two-prong standard, Richmond's set-aside, like the federal program on which it was modeled, is "plainly constitutional."

A

1. Turning first to the governmental interest inquiry, Richmond has two powerful interests in setting aside a portion of public contracting funds for minority-owned enterprises. The first is ... interest in eradicating the effects of past racial discrimination. It is far too late in the day to doubt that remedying such discrimination is a compelling, let alone an important, interest. ... Richmond has a second compelling interest in ... preventing the city's own spending decisions from reinforcing and perpetuating the exclusionary effects of past discrimination. See *Fullilove.* ...

The majority is wrong to trivialize the continuing impact of government acceptance or use of private institutions or structures once wrought by discrimination. When government channels all its contracting funds to a white-dominated community of established contractors whose racial homogeneity is the product of private discrimination, it does more than place its imprimatur on the practices which forged and which continue to define that community. It also provides a measurable boost to those economic entities that have thrived within it, while denying important economic benefits to those entities which, but for prior discrimination, might well be better qualified to receive valuable government contracts. ... Cities like Richmond may not be constitutionally required to adopt set-aside plans. But there can be no doubt that when Richmond acted affirmatively to stem the perpetuation of patterns of discrimination through its own decisionmaking, it served an interest of the highest order.

2. The remaining question ... is whether Richmond has proffered satisfactory proof of past racial discrimination to support its twin interests in remediation and in governmental nonperpetuation. ... Richmond's reliance on localized, industry-specific findings is a far cry from the reliance on generalized "societal discrimination" which the majority decries as a basis for remedial action. ... The majority also takes the disingenuous approach of disaggregating Richmond's local evidence, attacking it piecemeal, and thereby concluding that no single piece of evidence adduced by the city, "standing alone," suffices to prove past discrimination. But items of evidence do not, of course, "stan[d] alone" or exist in alien juxtaposition; they necessarily work together, reinforcing or contradicting each other.

In any event, the majority's criticisms of individual items of Richmond's evidence rest on flimsy foundations. ... First, considering how minuscule the share of Richmond public construction contracting dollars received by minority-owned businesses is, it is hardly unreasonable to conclude that this case involves a "gross statistical disparit[y]." Hazelwood School Dist. [v. United States (1977)]. There are roughly equal numbers of minorities and nonminorities in Richmond—yet minority-owned businesses receive one-seventy-fifth the public contracting funds that other businesses receive.

Second, and more fundamentally, where the issue is not present discrimination but rather whether past discrimination has resulted in the continuing exclusion of minorities from an historically tight-knit industry, a contrast between population and work force is entirely appropriate to help gauge the degree of the exclusion. [Johnson v. Transportation Agency (1987)]. ...

The majority's perfunctory dismissal of the testimony of Richmond's appointed and elected leaders is also deeply disturbing. ... When the legislatures and leaders of cities with histories of pervasive discrimination testify that past discrimination has infected one of their industries, armchair cynicism like that exercised by the majority has no place. ...

Finally, I vehemently disagree with the majority's dismissal of the congressional and Executive Branch findings noted in *Fullilove* as having "extremely limited" probative value in this case. The majority concedes that Congress established nothing less than a "presumption" that minority contracting firms have been disadvantaged by prior discrimination. The majority, inexplicably, would forbid Richmond to "share" in this information. ...

No principle of federalism or of federal power ... forbids a state or local government from drawing upon a nationally relevant historical record prepared by the Federal Government. Of course, Richmond could have built an even more compendious record of past discrimination, one including additional stark statistics and additional individual accounts of past discrimination. But nothing in the Fourteenth Amendment imposes such onerous documentary obligations upon States and localities once the reality of past discrimination is apparent.

B

... Richmond's set-aside plan also comports with the second prong of the equal protection inquiry, for it is substantially related to the interests it seeks to serve in remedying past discrimination and in ensuring that municipal contract procurement does not perpetuate that discrimination. The most striking aspect of the city's ordinance is the similarity it bears to the "appropriately limited" federal set-aside provision upheld in *Fullilove*. Like the federal provision, Richmond's is limited to five years in duration, and was not renewed when it came up for reconsideration in 1988. Like the federal provision, Richmond's contains a waiver provision freeing from its subcontracting requirements those nonminority firms that demonstrate that they cannot comply with its provisions. Like the federal provision, Richmond's has a minimal impact on innocent third parties. While the measure affects 30% of public contracting dollars, that translates to only 3% of overall Richmond area contracting.

Finally, like the federal provision, Richmond's does not interfere with any vested right of a contractor to a particular contract; instead it operates entirely prospectively. ...

These factors, far from "justify[ing] a preference of any size or duration," are precisely the factors to which this Court looked in *Fullilove*. The majority takes issue, however, with two aspects of Richmond's tailoring: the city's refusal to explore the use of race-neutral measures to increase minority business participation in contracting, and the selection of a 30% set-aside figure. ... [T]he majority's suggestion that Richmond should have first undertaken such race-neutral measures as a program of city financing for small firms, ignores the fact that such measures ... have been discredited by Congress as ineffectual ... in this very industry. For this reason, this Court in *Fullilove* refused to fault Congress for not undertaking race-neutral measures as precursors to its race-conscious set-aside. The Equal Protection Clause does not require Richmond to retrace Congress' steps when Congress has found that those steps lead nowhere. ...

As for Richmond's 30% target, the majority states that this figure "cannot be said to be narrowly tailored to any goal, except perhaps outright racial balancing." The majority ignores ... the fact that Richmond's 30% figure was patterned directly on the *Fullilove* precedent. Congress' 10% figure fell "roughly halfway between the present percentage of minority contractors and the percentage of minority group members in the Nation." The Richmond City Council's 30% figure similarly falls roughly halfway between the present percentage of Richmond-based minority contractors (almost zero) and the percentage of minorities in Richmond (50%). ...

III

I would ordinarily end my analysis at this point. ... However, I am compelled to add more, for the majority has gone beyond the facts of this case to announce a set of principles which unnecessarily restrict the power of governmental entities to take race-conscious measures to redress the effects of prior discrimination.

A

Today, for the first time, a majority of this Court has adopted strict scrutiny as its standard of Equal Protection Clause review of race-conscious remedial measures. ... A profound difference separates governmental actions that themselves are racist, and governmental actions that seek to remedy the effects of prior racism or to prevent neutral governmental activity from perpetuating the effects of such racism.

Racial classifications "drawn on the presumption that one race is inferior to another or because they put the weight of government behind racial hatred and separatism" warrant the strictest judicial scrutiny. ... By contrast, racial classifications drawn for the purpose of remedying the effects of discrimination that itself was race-based have a highly pertinent basis: the tragic and indelible fact that discrimination against blacks and other racial minorities in this Nation has pervaded our Nation's history and continues to scar our society. ...

In concluding that remedial classifications warrant no different standard of review under the Constitution than the most brutal and repugnant forms of state-sponsored racism, a majority of this Court signals that it regards racial discrimination as largely a phenomenon of the past. ... I, however, do not believe this Nation is anywhere close to eradicating racial discrimination or its vestiges. In constitutionalizing its wishful thinking, the majority today does a grave disservice not only to those victims of past and present racial discrimination ... but also to this Court's long tradition of approaching issues of race with the utmost sensitivity.

B

I am also troubled by the majority's assertion that, even if it did not believe generally in strict scrutiny of race-based remedial measures, "the circumstances of this case" require this Court to look upon the Richmond City Council's measure with the strictest scrutiny. The sole such circumstance which the majority cites, however, is the fact that blacks in Richmond are a "dominant racial grou[p]" in the city. ... [T]he majority observes that "blacks comprise approximately 50% of the population of the city of Richmond" and that "[f]ive of the nine seats on the City Council are held by blacks."

While I agree that the numerical and political supremacy of a given racial group is a factor bearing upon the level of scrutiny to be applied, this Court has never held that numerical inferiority, standing alone, makes a racial group "suspect". ... Rather, we have identified other "traditional indicia of suspectness": whether a group has been "saddled with such disabilities, or subjected to such a history of purposeful unequal treatment, or relegated to such a position of political powerlessness as to command extraordinary protection from the majoritarian political process." *San Antonio.*

It cannot seriously be suggested that nonminorities in Richmond have any "history of purposeful unequal treatment." Nor is there any indication that they have any of the disabilities that have characteristically afflicted those groups this Court has deemed suspect. ... If the majority really believes that groups like Richmond's nonminorities, which comprise approximately half the population but which are outnumbered even marginally in political fora, are deserving of suspect class status for these reasons alone, this Court's decisions denying suspect status to women, see Craig v. Boren (1976), and to persons with below-average incomes, see *San Antonio,* stand on extremely shaky ground. See Castaneda v. Partida (1977) (Marshall, J., concurring). ...

C ...

Nothing in the Constitution or in the prior decisions of this Court supports limiting state authority to confront the effects of past discrimination to those situations in which a prima facie case of a constitutional or statutory violation can be made out. ... To the degree that this parsimonious standard is grounded on a view that either § 1 or § 5 of the Fourteenth Amendment substantially disempowered States and localities from remedying past racial discrimination, the majority is seriously mistaken. With respect, first, to § 5, our precedents have never suggested that this provision ... was meant to pre-empt or limit state police power to undertake race-conscious remedial measures. ...

As for § 1, it is too late in the day to assert seriously that the Equal Protection Clause prohibits States—or for that matter, the Federal

Government, to whom the equal protection guarantee has largely been applied—from enacting race-conscious remedies. Our cases in the areas of school desegregation, voting rights, and affirmative action have demonstrated time and again that race is constitutionally germane, precisely because race remains dismayingly relevant in American life.

In adopting its prima facie standard for States and localities, the majority closes its eyes to this constitutional history and social reality. So, too, does Justice Scalia. ... [H]is approach "would freeze the status quo that is the very target" of the remedial actions of States and localities. McDaniel v. Barresi [1971]. The fact is that Congress' concern in passing the Reconstruction Amendments, and particularly their congressional authorization provisions, was that States would not adequately respond to racial violence or discrimination against newly freed slaves. To interpret any aspect of these Amendments as proscribing state remedial responses to these very problems turns the Amendments on their heads. ...

Justice **BLACKMUN**, with whom Justice **BRENNAN** joins, dissenting. ...

Editors' Notes

(1) **Query:** Justices O'Connor and Marshall debated the application of a *Carolene Products* jurisprudence to this case. Was their disagreement merely about who made up the majority and the minorities in Richmond? Was it also (or alternatively) a disagreement about whether there is a constitutionally relevant difference between "benign" and "invidious" discrimination? Or, even more deeply, was it a disagreement about the proper approach to constitutional interpretation? Whose reasoning was more coherent? More convincing?

(2) **Query:** What sort of approach to constitutional interpretation did Justice Stevens follow?

(3) **Query:** Justice Scalia, the apostle of *originalism* (see his "Originalism: The Lesser Evil," reprinted above, p. 231), did not invoke original understanding in this case. Why not? There is much history that might be very relevant to an *originalist*. After the Civil War, as an integral part of Reconstruction that included adoption of the Fourteenth Amendment, Congress created the Freedmen's Bureau to administer a cluster of programs designed to repair the wrongs African Americans had suffered. Moreover, some "carpetbag" state governments adopted similar policies. There is a huge professional literature on these efforts at affirmative action; see, *e.g.*, George R. Bentley, *A History of the Freedmen's Bureau* (Philadelphia: University of Pennsylvania Press, 1955); Barry A. Crouch, *The Freedmen's Bureau and Black Texans* (Austin: University of Texas Press, 1992); Eric Foner, *Reconstruction: America's Unfinished Revolution, 1863–1877* (New York: Harper & Row, 1988); and Willie Lee Rose, *Rehearsal for Reconstruction: The Port Royal Experiment* (Indianapolis: Bobbs–Merrill, 1964). See also Note 7, below, for Justice Brennan's reminder, in Metro Broadcasting v. FCC (1990), of these policies.

(4) **Query:** Is Scalia's distinction between "race-conscious action" whose purpose is to benefit African Americans, on the one hand, and "race-neutral remediation" whose racially disproportionate impact is to benefit African Americans, on the other, as fundamental and clear as he claimed? What in the constitutional text justifies this distinction? In the original understanding of the Fourteenth Amendment? In some political theory on which he may have silently relied? What in those same sources would support his contention that Congress, but not state and local governments, could have adopted the minority set-aside at issue here?

(5) **Query:** Scalia wrote: "The relevant proposition is not that it was blacks, or Jews, or Irish who were discriminated against, but that it was individual men and women, 'created equal,' who were discriminated against." The constitutional text, of course, does not speak of people's being "created equal"; that phrase appears in the Declaration of Independence. Was Scalia implying that his "Constitution" includes the Declaration? What plausible argument can one make for such an inclusion?

(6) **Query:** Was Justice Kennedy right that "the moral imperative of racial neutrality is the driving force of the Equal Protection Clause"? Compare Scalia's view that " '[o]ur Constitution is color-blind' " (quoting *Plessy,* Harlan, J., dissenting). Does "equal protection" mean "neutral protection"? Do the language and structure of the constitutional text support Kennedy's and Scalia's interpretations? The theories that underpin the document? The original understanding of the creators of the Fourteenth Amendment? Harlan's phrase is famous and many contemporary critics of affirmative action programs quote it, but it has never gained the assent of a majority of the Supreme Court. For arguments that "the Constitution" is color-blind, see, *e.g.*, Richard A. Posner, "The DeFunis Case and the Constitutionality of Preferential Treatment of Racial Minorities," 1974 *Sup.Ct.Rev.* 1; and Antonin Scalia, "The Disease as Cure," 1979 *Wash.U.L.Q.* 147. For critiques, see, *e.g.*, David A. Strauss, "The Myth of Colorblindness," 1986 *Sup.Ct.Rev.* 99; and Laurence H. Tribe, "In What Vision of the Constitution Must the Law be Color-Blind?," 20 *John Marshall L.Rev.* 201 (1986).

(7) The ink had barely dried on *Croson*'s apparent application of "strict scrutiny" to a local government's minority set-aside, when Metro Broadcasting v. FCC (1990) raised the question of what level of scrutiny should apply to congressional schemes for minority preference. The case involved a policy of the Federal Communications Commission, approved by Congress, to promote racial diversity in the ownership of radio and television stations by setting aside some licenses for minorities and giving them an advantage in purchasing others. In a 5–4 decision, with Justice Brennan writing for the majority, the Court held that "benign race-conscious measures mandated by Congress— even if those measures are not 'remedial' in the sense of being designed to compensate victims of past governmental or societal discrimination—are constitutionally permissible to the extent that they serve important governmental objectives within the power of Congress and are substantially related to achievement of those objectives." This test, of course, was that of "intermediate scrutiny," and the Court found the FCC's policies were substantially related to the important governmental goal of enhancing diversity of ownership within the mass media so that the American people might be presented with varying perspectives.

O'Connor protested that the phrase " 'benign' racial classification" was "a contradiction in terms." Kennedy agreed and suggested as examples of " 'benign' race-conscious measures" South Africa's apartheid, the "separate but equal" doctrine of Plessy v. Ferguson (1896), and the internment of American citizens of Japanese ancestry upheld in Korematsu v. United States (1944; discussed above, p. 87, and reprinted below, p. 1383). "I regret," he wrote, "that after a century of judicial opinions we interpret the Constitution to do no more than move us from 'separate but equal' to 'unequal but benign.' " Brennan responded: "We are confident that an 'examination of the legislative scheme and its history' will separate benign measures from other types of racial classifications." Although usually not a proponent of *originalism,* Brennan also observed: "The concept of benign race-conscious measures—even those with at least some non-remedial purposes—is as old as the Fourteenth Amendment. For example, the Freedmen's Bureau Acts authorized the provision of land, education, medical care and other assistance to Afro–Americans."

(8) In Adarand Constructors v. Pena (1995), the Court overruled *Metro Broadcasting.* In a 5–4 decision, with Justice O'Connor writing for the majority, the Court held that all racial classifications, whether "benign" or "invidious," and whether adopted by federal, state, or local governments, are subject to strict scrutiny. But O'Connor was at pains to "dispel the notion that strict scrutiny is 'strict in theory, but fatal in fact,' " (quoting *Fullilove* [Marshall, J., concurring in judgment]), stating: "The unhappy persistence of both the practice and the lingering effects of racial discrimination against minority groups in this country is an unfortunate reality, and government is not disqualified from acting in response to it." Justices Scalia and Thomas, in separate concurrences, made clear that they would have gone further and ruled that affirmative action programs are never justified.

(9) Among the better analyses of affirmative action are: Marshall Cohen, Thomas Nagel, and Thomas Scanlon, eds., *Equality and Preferential Treatment* (Princeton: Princeton University Press, 1977); Joel Dreyfuss and Charles Lawrence, III, *The Bakke Case* (New York: Harcourt, Brace, Jovanovitch, 1979); Terry Eastland and William J. Bennett, *Counting by Race* (New York: Basic Books, 1979); Ronald Dworkin, *A Matter of Principle* (Cambridge: Harvard University Press, 1985), chs. 14–16; John Hart Ely, "The Constitutionality of Reverse Discrimination," 41 *U.Chi.L.Rev.* 723 (1974); Nathan Glazier, *Affirmative Discrimination* (New York: Basic Books, 1975); Alan H. Goldman, *Justice and Reverse Discrimination* (Princeton: Princeton University Press, 1979); R. Kent Greenawalt, *Discrimination and Reverse Discrimination* (New York: Knopf, 1983); Randall Kennedy, "Persuasion and Distrust: A Comment on the Affirmative Action Debate," 99 *Harv.L.Rev.* 1327 (1986); Russell Nieli, ed., *Racial Preference and Racial Justice* (Washington, DC: Ethics and Public Policy Center, 1991); Laurence H. Tribe, *American Constitutional Law* (2d ed.; Mineola, NY: Foundation Press, 1988), pp. 1521–44; and J. Harvie Wilkinson, III, *From Brown to Bakke* (New York: Oxford University Press, 1979). See also Stephen L. Carter, *Reflections of an Affirmative Action Baby* (New York: Basic Books, 1991); Charles Fried, "*Metro Broadcasting, Inc. v. FCC:* Two Concepts of Equality," 104 *Harv.L.Rev.* 107 (1990); Patricia J. Williams, "*Metro Broadcasting, Inc. v. FCC:* Regrouping in Singular Times," 104 *ibid.* 525 (1990).

15

The Problems of Equal Protection, II

As part of a broader analysis of the question of HOW to interpret the constitutional text and the broader constitution, Chapter 14 focused on substantive problems of equal protection that classifications based on race and ethnicity raise. Left open was a host of other problems. First, in discussing the "two-tiered" model of strict and deferential scrutiny, we did not explore the reach of the concept of "suspect classification" nor that of "fundamental rights." Second, Chapter 14 alluded to but did not address a possible expansion of "tiers" of analysis from two to three or even to a finely graded scale. Also untouched was what are perhaps the two most basic questions: Are the doctrines about two-, three-, or multi-tiered models of scrutiny justifiable as incrustations on the constitutional text and are they especially useful to constitutional interpretation?

The introductory essay and the cases that follow take up those issues. We repeat our already frequently repeated caution against allowing pursuit of a necessary understanding of the Court's byzantine doctrines to distract from the basic interrogatives of WHAT, WHO, and HOW.

I. THE TWO–TIERED MODEL

At the outset, one should keep in mind a distinction that many interpreters overlook. There is an important conceptual difference between "suspect classifications" and "suspect classes." Members of the Supreme Court tend to use the terms interchangeably and so confuse their own as well as others' analyses. To discover a suspect class—in Stone's terms, a "discrete and insular" minority—an interpreter must look to the social history surrounding particular groups in this country. A "suspect classification" is one, like race or religion, whose very nature presumptively offends constitutional standards—though that definition tells us little about what classifications are suspect or where to find a full statement of those standards.[1] Because the purpose of this essay is to introduce readers to

---

1. "Suspect classification" and "suspect class" may require different kinds of analyses, or at least analyses at different levels of abstraction. For instance, to say that Arabs form

the Court's work, we shall only occasionally allude to this distinction, but we think it is an important component of any serious effort
to cope with the HOW of constitutional interpretation.

A.   What Classes/Classifications Are Suspect?

There is neither an historical nor a logical reason why Stone's
reference in *Carolene Products* to "discrete and insular minorities"
should include only racial or ethnic groups.   This open-endedness
is both a strength and a weakness of the jurisprudence that he
planted.   Its strength lies in its generality, its potential application
to a whole genre of minorities legally disadvantaged by hostile or
insensitive majorities.   The price of that generality is indefiniteness.
"It would hardly take extraordinary ingenuity," William H. Rehnquist once protested, "for a lawyer to find 'insular and discrete'
minorities at every turn in the road." [2]   But of course few such
minorities have been subject to prejudice of a sort calling for what
Stone termed "more searching judicial inquiry."

Who qualifies as a "discrete and insular" minority?   Who other
than African Americans and perhaps Native Americans can demand
the special judicial protection of "strict scrutiny"?   Justice Powell,
speaking for the Court in San Antonio v. Rodriguez (1973; reprinted below, p. 1002), tried to answer that question.   A suspect class,
he said, is one that has been

> saddled with such disabilities, or subjected to such a history of
> purposeful unequal treatment, or relegated to such a position of
> political powerlessness as to command extraordinary protection
> from the majoritarian political processes.

Powell's effort was characteristically honest; but, like Brennan's
in Plyler v. Doe (1982; reprinted below, p. 1040), it suffers from
indeterminacy.   How much "purposeful unequal treatment" must a
group have experienced "to command" special judicial protection?
How ancient (or recent) does the history of unequal treatment have
to be?   More broadly, is any group, in fact, now in a condition of
"political powerlessness"?   Before the Thirteenth, Fourteenth, and
Fifteenth amendments, slaves obviously were; blacks in the South
before the Voting Rights Act of 1965 still were; women before they
got the vote through the Nineteenth Amendment were.

The real issue, however, is seldom one of having power or
being powerless.   Power is rarely a dichotomous variable.   It is
never evenly distributed among the population, but most adult

---

a "suspect class" is much more specific than to say that ethnicity is a "suspect classification."   Furthermore, labelling Arabs as a suspect class does not tell us much about
whether Irish or Norwegians or Hispanics each also form a suspect class.   Good English
might solve the difficulty.   It is *legislative use* of certain categories that should raise
judicial suspicions.   Surely it is not the groups who are "suspect," though the justices'
syntax usually suggests otherwise.

   2.   Sugarman v. Dougall, dis. op. (1973).

citizens have *some* of that commodity. They can speak out, vote, lobby, and, as important, use the courts to affect and perhaps even effect public policy, as NAACP v. Button (1963; reprinted above, p. 811) noted. Even aliens, including illegal aliens, often have this last option, and through the judicial process they, too, can influence public policy as *Plyler* (at p. 1040) shows.

Focusing on "suspect classes" frames the central question as: How little power does it take for a group to require special protection? To that query, the Court has made no more generalized response than Powell's in *San Antonio* or Brennan's in *Plyler*[3] though individual justices have offered more detailed answers. (See the separate opinions of Stevens and Marshall in Cleburne v. Cleburne Living Center [1985; reprinted below, p. 1048].) Focusing on "suspect classifications" poses as a basic question of HOW to interpret: What types of classification does "the Constitution" outlaw or at least require government to bear a heavy burden to justify?

Specifically, the Court has had to face claims from a wide range of groups. Children born outside of marriage, the aged, the poor, aliens, and women have all sought recognition as suspect classes, as have homosexuals, individuals with disabilities, the mentally ill, and the mentally retarded, not to mention prisoners.[4] The Court has often ignored such claims by deciding cases on other grounds or by denying certiorari.[5] *Cleburne*, however, squarely addressed not

---

3. Compare Stevens's opinion of the Court in Lyng v. Castillo (1986). Litigants had challenged regulations in a food stamp program that distinguished (for purposes of definition of a "household") between, on the one hand, parents, children, and siblings, and, on the other, more distant relatives and unrelated persons. In addressing this claim, Stevens summarized the requirements for heightened scrutiny:

> The disadvantaged class [here] is that comprised by parents, children, and siblings. Close relatives are not a "suspect" or "quasi-suspect" class. As a historical matter, they have not been subjected to discrimination; they do not exhibit obvious, immutable, or distinguishing characteristics that define them as a discrete group; and they are not a minority or politically powerless.

Therefore, the Court applied deferential scrutiny, upholding the classification.

4. See, *e.g.*, Judith A. Baer, *Equality under the Fourteenth Amendment* (Ithaca: Cornell University Press, 1983), espec. chs. 7–9; Note, "The Constitutional Status of Sexual Orientation: Homosexuality as a Suspect Classification," 98 *Harv.L.Rev.* 1285 (1985); Sylvia A. Law, "Homosexuality and the Social Meaning of Gender," 1988 *Wis.L.Rev.* 187; M.P. and R. Borgdorf, "A History of Unequal Treatment: The Qualifications of Handicapped Persons as a 'Suspect Class' Under the Equal Protection Clause," 15 *Santa Clara Lawyer* 855 (1975); Comment, "Mental Illness: A Suspect Classification?" 83 *Yale L.J.* 1237 (1974). The Americans with Disabilities Act, 42 U.S.C. §§ 12101 to 12213, passed in 1990, prohibits discrimination on the basis of disability in both employment and public accommodations. (In 1988, the Fair Housing Act of 1968, 42 U.S.C. §§ 3601 to 3619, 3631, had been amended to prohibit discrimination on the basis of disability in the sale or rental of dwellings.) In Hudson v. Palmer (1984), Stevens, joined by Brennan, Marshall, and Blackmun, argued that prisoners, "the outcasts of society," form a suspect class because they "are surely a 'discrete and insular minority.'" The Court, however, rejected this view and, with Brennan, Marshall, and Blackmun now in retirement, has shown no sign of changing its collective mind.

5. In Schweiker v. Wilson (1981), the Court did not reach the question whether mental illness is a suspect classification, or the mentally ill are a discrete and insular minority. Moreover, for a time the Court declined to grant certiorari to consider any questions

only particular problems of the mentally retarded but also some of the fundamental difficulties about "suspect classes" and tiers of analysis.

"Illegitimate" children seem to fit perfectly into Powell's definition of a "suspect class." First, they are now and have historically been "saddled with" legal "disabilities" on their rights to inherit property from their fathers and to sue if their fathers have been wrongfully or accidentally killed. Second, that unequal treatment is purposeful: Statutes and judicial decisions make no effort to disguise an effort to discriminate against illegitimate in favor of legitimate children. Third, as children and therefore ineligible to vote, they are about as close to being politically powerless as any group in our society. Fourth, to add one of Stone's criteria, their treatment is the result of prejudice, to whose existence there is no more eloquent testimony than the connotation of the word "bastard." Fifth, as the Court observed in *Plyler* (at p. 1040): "Legislation imposing special disabilities upon groups disfavored by virtue of circumstances beyond their control suggests the kind of 'class or caste' treatment that the Fourteenth Amendment was designed to abolish." Yet the Court has consistently refused to recognize illegitimacy as a suspect classification; and it was Powell who wrote many of these opinions.[6]

The elderly have suffered even sharper defeats in the courts, though they have fared quite well in Congress.[7] Massachusetts v. Murgia (1976), for example, refused to regard the aged as a suspect class. At issue was a law requiring uniformed state police to retire at 50. Repeating Powell's definition, the majority, blithely mixing "class" and "classification," added:

> The class subject to the compulsory retirement ... consists of uniformed state police officers over the age of 50. [The statute]

---

concerning homosexuals. The Court did, however, hear Bowers v. Hardwick (1986; reprinted below, p. 1322) and held, 5–4, that a law prohibiting sodomy, even between consenting adults in their own home, did not violate due process. The Court expressed no opinion on the question whether such a law might violate equal protection, though Stevens's dissent raised that issue. See Cass R. Sunstein, "Sexual Orientation and the Constitution: A Note on the Relationship Between Due Process and Equal Protection," 55 *U.Chi.L.Rev.* 1161 (1988).

6. In Pickett v. Brown (1983), the Court held that legislative classifications based on illegitimacy were subject to a "heightened level of scrutiny," stating that "[a]lthough we have held that classifications based on illegitimacy are not 'suspect,' or subject to 'our most exacting scrutiny,' the scrutiny applied to them 'is not a toothless one.' " And in Clark v. Jeter (1988), the Court unanimously agreed that "intermediate" scrutiny was appropriate. See also the discussion below in Parts II and III of this introductory essay.

7. See the Age Discrimination in Employment Act of 1967, as amended in 1978 and 1986; 29 U.S.C. § 621ff. Originally, the statute forbade employers covered by the Act to discriminate against employees between the ages of 40 and 65 because of age. In 1978, Congress raised the mandatory retirement age to 70, and in 1986, eliminated mandatory retirement at any age. Moreover, Congress has extended the coverage of the Act to state and local governments as well as to private employers employing at least 20 persons. The Act makes certain exceptions for managerial personnel. The Age Discrimination Act of 1975, 42 U.S.C. § 6101ff, forbids discrimination on the basis of age in programs receiving federal funds.

cannot be said to discriminate only against the elderly. Rather, it draws the line at a certain age in middle life. But even old age does not define a "discrete and insular" group, United States v. Carolene Products (1938), in need of "extraordinary protection from the majoritarian political process." Instead, it marks a stage that each of us will reach if we live out our normal span. Even if the statute could be said to impose a penalty upon a class defined as the aged, it would not impose a distinction sufficiently akin to those classifications that have been found suspect to call for strict scrutiny.

Three years later, using much the same reasoning, Vance v. Bradley sustained compulsory retirement for foreign service officers at age 60. More recently, Gregory v. Ashcroft (1991) reaffirmed *Murgia*, upholding Missouri's requirement that state judges retire at 70.

With other claims, the Court has not always been consistent in its responses. For a time it seemed that the poor had succeeded in establishing wealth as a suspect "classification." [8] Certainly Justice Harlan thought so, and he opposed that course of decisions. See his dissent in Shapiro v. Thompson (1969; reprinted below, p. 1019). That same year, Chief Justice Warren remarked in his opinion for the Court in McDonald v. Board of Election Commissioners that "a careful examination on our part is especially warranted where lines are drawn on the basis of wealth or race, Harper v. Virginia [1966; reprinted above, p. 225], two factors which would independently render a classification suspect and thereby demand a more exacting judicial scrutiny." But in 1973 *San Antonio* swept away that apparent victory, or at least limited it to scrutiny of wealth-based classifications involving the fundamental right to vote and the fundamental interest in access to the legal system to vindicate rights.[9] In Harris v. McRae (1980; reprinted below, p. 1271), the Court reaffirmed *San Antonio*, stating that "poverty, standing alone, is not a suspect classification." [10]

Aliens also seemingly had won recognition as a suspect class, but judicial protection of that group has narrowed somewhat. "Aliens as a class," the Court said in Graham v. Richardson (1971), "are a prime example of a 'discrete and insular' minority (see United States v. Carolene Products Co. [1938]) for whom such heightened judicial solicitude is appropriate." The Court later

---

8. As, for example, eight justices said in Roberts v. LaVallee (1967): "Our decisions for more than a decade now have made it clear that differences in access to the instruments needed to vindicate legal rights, when based upon the financial situation of the defendant, are repugnant to the Constitution." See also Griffin v. Illinois (1956); Douglas v. California (1963); and Boddie v. Connecticut (1971). But see United States v. Kras (1973); Ortwein v. Schwab (1973); and Ross v. Moffitt (1974).

9. On voting and access to the ballot, see *Harper* (at p. 225); Cipriano v. City of Houma (1969); Bullock v. Carter (1972); and Lubin v. Panish (1974). On access to the legal system, see cases cited below in note 23.

10. Kadrmas v. Dickinson Public Schools (1988) reaffirmed *San Antonio,* upholding a public school system's charging a fee for school bus service.

reaffirmed this holding,[11] but then hedged, sustaining exclusions of aliens from police forces and public school teaching.[12] Speaking through Thurgood Marshall in Bernal v. Fainter (1984), a majority of eight justices found a rationale to explain its meanderings:

> As a general matter, a State law that discriminates on the basis of alienage can be sustained only if it can withstand strict judicial scrutiny. ... [T]o withstand strict scrutiny the law must advance a compelling State interest by the least restrictive means available. ... We have, however, developed a narrow exception to the rule that discrimination based on alienage triggers strict scrutiny. This exception has been labelled the "political function" exception and applies to laws that exclude aliens from positions [like police and public school teaching] intimately related to the process of democratic self-government.

In *Bernal* the Court held that the office of notary public did not qualify for the "political function" exception, joining professions such as law and engineering. Excluding aliens from these professions would trigger strict scrutiny. Not surprisingly, the Court has also held, in *Plyler* (at p. 1040), that "illegal aliens" do not constitute a suspect class.[13]

In sum, there is no short answer to the question of what other "classifications" than those based on race or ethnicity are suspect or "classes" other than racial and ethnic minorities and aliens are entitled to special judicial protection. Chief Justice Rehnquist, who is fundamentally opposed to the jurisprudence behind the *Carolene Products* footnote, has waged a long battle against including any category other than race, with a begrudging acceptance of national origin.[14]

Several times the justices have said that excluding from certain benefits people who recently arrived in a state is an "invidious"

---

11. Sugarman v. Dougall (1973); In re Griffiths (1973); Examining Bd. v. Flores (1976); Nyquist v. Mauclet (1977).

12. See Foley v. Connelie (1978) and Cabell v. Chavez–Salido (1982), sustaining state regulations requiring police officers and probation officers to be citizens, and Ambach v. Norwick (1979), upholding a state law limiting teaching in public schools to citizens. In *Cabell*, Blackmun, the author of *Graham* and several other opinions holding alienage a suspect classification, dissented: "[T]oday's decision rewrites the Court's precedents, ignores history, defies common sense, and reinstates the deadening mantle of state parochialism in public employment." For a general discussion, see David Carlinger, *The Rights of Aliens* (2d ed.; Carbondale: Southern Illinois University Press, 1990).

13. In re Griffiths (1973) (law); Examining Bd. v. Flores (1976) (civil engineering). Some cases involving states' classifications on the basis of alienage raise not only questions of equal protection but also issues of federal preemption in dealing with problems of immigration and naturalization. The Court has held that "there may be overriding national interests which justify selective federal legislation that would be unacceptable for an individual State." Hampton v. Mow Sun Wong (1976) (nonetheless striking down a policy of the Civil Service Commission to exclude aliens from most civil service jobs). See also Mathews v. Diaz (1976) (upholding a federal Medicaid program limiting participation to citizens and aliens who had continuously resided for at least five years in the United States).

14. See espec. his dissents in *Sugarman* and Trimble v. Gordon (1977).

classification.[15]   But it is not evident, in light of the Court's insistence in these and other rulings that the right to travel interstate, or
at least to "migrate" to establish a new residence, is "fundamental,"
how much those decisions to invoke strict scrutiny turned on the
existence of a suspect "class" or "classification" and how much on
a fundamental right whose exercise the state sought to penalize.
And alienage, as we have seen, is suspect only under some circumstances, pointing toward degrees of suspicion with which a majority
of the justices view different classifications, as Marshall claimed in
his dissent in *San Antonio*. We take up that point under Part II of
this introductory essay and in several of the cases reprinted below—
especially *San Antonio* (at p. 1002), Craig v. Boren (1976; at p.
992), *Plyler* (at p. 1040), and *Cleburne* (at p. 1048).

B. What Is a "Fundamental" Right?

The whole issue of what rights are "fundamental," how that
status should be determined, and who should make the decisions is
the subject of the cases and materials in Section E of this Part of the
book. As one would expect, the questions are difficult and the
debate bitter, if not always intellectually acute. (See espec. the
opinions reprinted below in *San Antonio* [p. 1002], *Shapiro* [p.
1019], Bowers v. Hardwick [p. 1322], and Planned Parenthood v.
Casey [p. 1281], as well as Michael H. v. Gerald D. [1989; reprinted
above, p. 158]). These sorts of inquiries may be logically distinct
from considerations of equality; but, because of the Court's development of the doctrine of strict scrutiny, they have become entan-
gled with problems of equal protection. At least since Skinner v.
Oklahoma (1942; reprinted below, p. 1014), the concepts of equality and liberty, along with textual provisions regarding equal protection and due process, have been competing though not mutually
exclusive bases for deriving fundamental rights. Hence Potter Stewart charged in his concurrence in Zablocki v. Redhail (1978; reprinted below, p. 1034) that, in some cases, the fundamental rights
strand of equal protection "is no more than substantive due process
by another name." To the same effect are Harlan's dissents in
Harper (at p. 225) and *Shapiro* (at p. 1019).

Here we would note only that, influenced either by democratic
theory or constitutionalism (and sometimes by both), the Court has
decided that certain rights, including some not listed in the document, are fundamental. As Chapter Three pointed out, democratic
theory stresses the primacy of rights of political expression and
participation (see espec. New York Times v. Sullivan [1964; reprinted above, p. 634] and Reynolds v. Sims [1964; reprinted above, p.
777]). Constitutionalism emphasizes others relating to individual
autonomy and dignity. The Court has applied the label "fundamen-

---

15. Shapiro v. Thompson (1969; reprinted below, p. 1019); Dunn v. Blumstein (1972);
and Memorial Hospital v. Maricopa County (1974).

tal" not only to privacy (see Griswold v. Connecticut [1965; reprint-ed above, p. 147]), but also to such rights as those to procreate,[16] to marry,[17] to vote,[18] and to travel.[19] But the justices have declined to recognize welfare,[20] the need for decent shelter,[21] and edu-cation[22] as fundamental rights. Besides fundamental rights, the Court has also recognized "fundamental interests" in access to the legal system to vindicate legal rights—interests which are not inde-pendently protected fundamental rights but which, if the govern-ment undertakes to provide them to some, it must do so equally (or at least minimally) to all.[23]

San Antonio basically said "this far and no further" would the Court go in recognizing fundamental rights and interests whose infringement triggered strict scrutiny, thereby stemming the expan-sion of these concepts as a strand of equal-protection analysis. Since 1973, the Court has essentially followed that policy of holding the line. (But see the discussion in Part III, below.)

C. What Constitutes a "Compelling" Governmental Interest?

The Court has offered no general criteria for deciding what constitutes a compelling governmental interest, or what means are necessary to or closely related to furtherance of such an interest. Instead, the justices have provided a long list of claims that do not so qualify and a short list of those that do. Neither list, however, pretends to be exhaustive. Among those claims rejected have been administrative convenience,[24] having the names of the rank-and-file members of an organization to facilitate an investigation of the

---

16. Skinner v. Oklahoma (1942; reprinted below, p. 1014).

17. Loving v. Virginia (1967; reprinted above, p. 926); Zablocki v. Redhail (1978; reprinted below, p. 1034).

18. Reynolds (at p. 777); Harper (at p. 225).

19. United States v. Guest (1966); Shapiro (1969; reprinted below, at 1019); Memorial Hospital v. Maricopa County (1974). For an attack on the notion of a fundamental right to travel, see Rehnquist's dissent in Memorial Hospital.

20. Dandridge v. Williams (1970; reprinted below, p. 1027).

21. Lindsey v. Normet (1972).

22. San Antonio v. Rodriguez (1973; reprinted below, p. 1002).

23. See Griffin v. Illinois (1956) ("[i]t is true that a State is not required by the Federal Constitution to provide appellate courts or a right to appellate review at all. ... But that is not to say that a State that does grant appellate review can do so in a way that discriminates against some convicted defendants on account of their poverty"); and Douglas v. California (1963) (extending Griffin in holding that where a state grants a statutory right to appeal a criminal conviction, it must appoint counsel for indigent defendants). But see cases cited above in note 8. See also Harper (at p. 225), where Douglas said that "the right to vote in state elections is nowhere expressly mentioned. ... [I]t is enough to say that once the franchise is granted to the electorate, lines may not be drawn which are inconsistent with the Equal Protection Clause. ..."

24. Frontiero v. Richardson (1973; reprinted below, p. 986).

association,[25] keeping the races "pure,"[26] high professional standards for lawyers,[27] filling lower civil service positions with people knowledgeable of and loyal to American traditions,[28] maintenance of state ownership of fish in offshore waters,[29] and distributing limited state funds available for welfare only to long-term residents[30] and citizens.[31]

Among those sustained as "compelling" have been a federal interest in national security,[32] a federal interest in maintaining the integrity and the appearance of integrity of the electoral processes,[33] and a strong suggestion from three concurring justices of such a state interest in preserving discipline in its prisons.[34] This second list is brief because, when the Court has found that government has used a suspect classification or infringed a fundamental right, the decision to hold the regulation unconstitutional has been almost automatic.

II. IS THE COURT ACTUALLY USING A TWO–TIERED MODEL?

A. Continua versus Two Tiers

Dissenting in *San Antonio*, Thurgood Marshall spelled out his oft-stated argument that the Court had not used and should not use a simple two-tiered model. Rather, he claimed, the test had been— and rightfully so—much less rigid and much more sophisticated, involving several continua or sliding scales along which the justices measure the amount of suspicion that they throw on the classification, the degree of fundamentality of the individual's right, and the nature of the government's interest.

Although in recent years a majority has rejected Marshall's reasoning, in Dunn v. Blumstein (1972) he wrote an opinion for the Court that pretty much used the sorts of spectra that he advocated in *San Antonio*. *Dunn* involved a challenge to a Tennessee law requiring a year's residency within the state as a prerequisite to voting for state officials. After noting that the right to travel interstate was fundamental, Marshall said for the Court:

---

25. NAACP v. Alabama (1958; reprinted above, p. 798).

26. *Loving* (1967; reprinted above, p. 926).

27. Examining Bd. v. Flores (1976).

28. Sugarman v. Dougall (1973).

29. Takahashi v. Fish & Game Commn. (1948).

30. *Shapiro* (at p. 1019; Memorial Hospital v. Maricopa County (1974).

31. Graham v. Richardson (1971).

32. Korematsu v. United States (1944; reprinted below, p. 1383).

33. Buckley v. Valeo (1976; reprinted above, p. 828).

34. Lee v. Washington (1968).

[D]urational residency laws must be measured by a strict equal protection test: they are unconstitutional unless a State can demonstrate that such laws are "*necessary* to promote a *compelling* governmental interest." Shapiro v. Thompson [1969] (first emphasis added); Kramer v. Union Free Sch. Dist. [1969].

So far his opinion was unexceptional. But he continued:

Thus phrased, the constitutional question may sound like a mathematical formula. But legal "tests" do not have the precision of mathematical formulas. The key words emphasize a *matter of degree*: that a heavy burden of justification is on the State, and that the statute will be closely scrutinized in light of its asserted purposes. [Italics supplied.]

Marshall's analysis moved Justice White in Vlandis v. Kline (1973) to remark that "it is clear that we employ not just one, or two, but as my Brother Marshall has so ably demonstrated, a 'spectrum of standards.' " Stevens' concurrence in *Cleburne* (at p. 1048) bears some affinities to Marshall's approach. The Court's treatment of illegitimate children supports Marshall's argument, as do more recent cases concerning aliens. In both areas, the Court has applied something stronger than deferential scrutiny, but weaker than strict scrutiny. Yet White in *Vlandis* and Stevens in *Cleburne* spoke only for themselves, and the Court refuses to acknowledge that it uses a continuum instead of tiers.

B. Construction of a Middle Ground: A Three-Tiered Test

Classifications by gender have been commonplace in American legal history, but the citizenry and courts have come to recognize them as reflecting outmoded stereotypes that are both invidiously discriminatory in purpose and not well founded in fact. In Frontiero v. Richardson (1973; reprinted below, p. 986), four members of the Court—Brennan, Douglas, White, and Marshall—would have held such classifications suspect, but were unable to win the fifth vote necessary to speak for the Court. A few years later, however, Craig v. Boren (1976; reprinted below, p. 992) presented an occasion for compromise. Six justices—Brennan, White, Marshall, Blackmun, Powell, and Stevens—agreed that classifications by sex were too suspect for judges to subject them only to a test of "rational basis," but not so suspect as to trigger "strict scrutiny."

In effect, *Craig* made gender a "somewhat suspicious" category, and the Court created a new test called "intermediate scrutiny," somewhere between strict and deferential scrutiny:

To withstand constitutional challenge, . . . classifications by gender must serve *important* [not compelling or merely legitimate] governmental objectives and must be *substantially* related [not closely related or necessary to nor merely rationally related] to achievement of those objectives. [Italics added.]

In Rostker v. Goldberg (1981), however, the Court gave only lip service to an intermediate tier and apparently reverted to the old rational basis test in sustaining registration of males but not females for a military draft.   It may be that the difference here was due to the case's involving military/foreign policy, problems that the justices typically avoid when they can by according great deference to executive and legislative actions.

In several later cases, Mississippi University for Women v. Hogan (1982; reprinted below, p. 997) and Heckler v. Mathews (1984), the Court reverted to the three-tier test where sex was the basis of challenged classifications.   In both cases, however, the majority used a formulation slightly different from that in *Craig*:

> [The government must show] a legitimate and "exceedingly persuasive justification" for gender based classification ... [and demonstrate] "the requisite direct, substantial relationship" between the classification and the important governmental objectives it purports to serve.

What other somewhat suspicious classifications or important but not compelling interests will also find a niche in this middle tier remains to be seen.   After getting itself into a "quagmire" in struggling with illegitimacy,[35] the Court unanimously agreed that intermediate scrutiny "generally has been applied to discriminatory classifications based on sex or illegitimacy."[36]   The Court for a time applied intermediate scrutiny to benign race-conscious measures approved by Congress, while applying strict scrutiny to such measures prescribed by state and local governments.[37]   It is possible that the Court will some day announce that all along it has been using the sorts of continua that Marshall described.   It is also possible that the Court will retreat from the middle tier with respect to certain issues, as in *Rostker*.   It is further possible that the justices, as they continue to cope with the problem of HOW to interpret, will shed their tiers and adopt a test (or set of tests) that differs in kind from strict, intermediate, and deferential scrutiny.

III.   A MODEL WITHOUT TIERS?

Readers exposed to essays on equal protection are typically confused and frustrated.   Closely analyzing the cases will decrease

---

35. See the discussion of the cases in C. Herman Pritchett, *Constitutional Civil Liberties* (Englewood Cliffs, NJ: Prentice–Hall, 1984), pp. 329–30.

36. Clark v. Jeter (1988).   One can also make a case that, taken together, these decisions involving illegitimacy evidence a new and stronger kind of test that insists on a "rational basis" for classifications.   As the Court put it in United States v. Clark (1980), classifications based on illegitimacy are "unconstitutional unless [they] bear 'an evident and substantial relation to the particular [objectives that the] statute is designed to serve'" (quoting *Lalli*).   See below, Part III of this introductory essay and *Plyler* as well as *Cleburne*.

37. Metro Broadcasting v. FCC (1990; discussed above, p. 969) and Richmond v. Croson Co. (1989; reprinted above, p. 954).   But Adarand Contractors v. Pena (1995; discussed above, p. 970) held that strict scrutiny applied in both contexts.

confusion but at the cost of increasing frustration. It may be of some comfort to know that many judges and commentators [38] share that frustration. One of the more fundamental criticisms is based on a concern that in using a two-, three- or multi-tiered model, the justices are, in effect, following a *balancing approach* generating all the problems discussed in Chapter 9, masking them even from the judges.[39]

The justices have become restive under their own doctrine, subjecting it to three levels of criticism. First is an unhappiness with the way the Court applies the tests in particular cases, exemplified by Potter Stewart's protest in one instance that he found the majority's talk of "discriminatory classifications" with respect to "fundamental rights" as "little short of fantasy." [40] Second, and at a deeper level, Thurgood Marshall claimed that the two-tiered model (and his objections hold almost as well for a three-tiered model) misstates what the Court has actually been doing and is also much too rigid. He, as we have seen, advocated modifying the model to fit along a more finely graded scale.

Third, and much more radical in his critique as well as his solution, is Chief Justice William H. Rehnquist. He has recognized that in its current doctrine the Court is simultaneously dealing with the interrogatives WHO and HOW. These tiered tests, he has said, are mere smoke screens to hide judicial policy making: Whenever the Court believes that a societal group is "discrete and insular," it has the constitutional mandate to prohibit legislation that somehow treats the group differently from some other group. Rehnquist would leave this sort of policy making to elected officials and replace all tiered models with a simpler one that would look only for a "rational" connection between a legitimate governmental end and a particular statutory classification. Race, he would add, is inherently irrational because of the overriding purpose of the Fourteenth Amendment.

John Paul Stevens has frequently disagreed with Rehnquist on the meaning of equal protection, but he, too, has expressed serious reservations about the dominant models. "There is," he wrote concurring in *Craig*, "only one Equal Protection Clause," arguing

---

38. See, for example: Richard H. Seeburger, "The Muddle of the Middle Tier," 48 *Mo.L.Rev.* 587 (1983); Steven G. Calabresi, "A Madisonian Interpretation of the Equal Protection Doctrine," 91 *Yale L.J.* 1403 (1982); Cass R. Sunstein, "Public Values, Private Interests, and the Equal Protection Clause," 1982 *Sup.Ct.Rev.* 127; Jeffrey H. Blattner, "The Supreme Court's 'Intermediate' Equal Protection Decisions," 8 *Hastings Con.L.J.* 777 (1981); Michael J. Perry, "Modern Equal Protection: A Conceptualization and Appraisal," 79 *Colum.L.Rev.* 1023 (1979). J. Harvie Wilkinson, III, "The Supreme Court, the Equal Protection Clause, and the Three Faces of Constitutional Equality," 61 *Va. L.Rev.* 945 (1975); John E. Nowak, "Realigning the Standards of Review under the Equal Protection Guarantee," 62 *Geo.L.J.* 1071 (1974).

39. Justice O'Connor, for one, has candidly labelled strict scrutiny as a form of *balancing*. See, for example, her comments in Roberts v. Jaycees (1984; reprinted above, p. 818).

40. Zablocki v. Redhail, concur. op. (1978; reprinted below, p. 1034).

that the Court's decisions "actually apply a single standard in a reasonably consistent fashion." As suggested above, his concurrence in *Cleburne* (at p. 1048) expresses ideas similar to Marshall's.[41]

Along similar lines—and some years before Stevens came to the Court—Professor Gerald Gunther suggested [42] a "newer" model of equal protection that he called an "expanded reasonable means inquiry" or "rationality review 'with bite' ":

> Stated most simply, it would have the Court take seriously a constitutional requirement that has never been formally abandoned: that legislative means must substantially further legislative ends. ... Putting consistent new bite into the old equal protection would mean that the Court would be less willing to supply justifying rationales by exercising its imagination. ... Moreover, it would have the Justices gauge the question of reasonableness of questionable means on the basis of materials that are offered to the Court, rather than resorting to rationalizations created by perfunctory judicial hypothesizing.

Gunther's model has great attraction, though it would complicate judges' work by requiring them to examine evidence and arguments to a far greater extent than they need do under the existing tests, which, at least on the strict and deferential tiers, tend to yield near-automatic answers. His model "does not take issue with the heightened scrutiny tiers of 'strict' and 'intermediate' review." "Instead," he has explained, "it is solely addressed to the appropriate intensity of review to be exercised when the lowest tier, that of rationality review, is deemed appropriate." [43] Gunther proposes putting some teeth into that lowest level of scrutiny.

We may be on the cusp of judicial change toward Gunther's model. *Plyler* and *Cleburne* show a majority of the justices applying a test of rationality that, as Harry Blackmun put it in an earlier illegitimacy case, "is not a toothless one." [44] It bears little resem-

---

41. See also U.S. Railroad Retirement Bd. v. Fritz (1980), where speaking through Rehnquist, the Court applied traditional "deferential scrutiny" to uphold classificatory changes in the statute regarding retirement benefits of railroad employees. Concurring, Stevens conceded that what was at issue was socio-economic regulation; but, he added: "When Congress deprives a small class of persons of vested rights that are protected—and, indeed, even enhanced—for others who are in a similar though not identical position, I believe the Constitution requires something more than merely a 'conceivable' or a 'plausible' explanation for the unequal treatment."

42. "In Search of Evolving Doctrine on a Changing Court," 86 *Harv.L.Rev.* 1 (1972). Gunther is apparently still willing to defend his model, see the 12th ed. of his *Constitutional Law* (Westbury, NY: Foundation Press, 1991), pp. 620–22. For skeptical appraisals of Gunther's model, see Hans Linde, "Due Process of Lawmaking," 55 *Neb.L.Rev.* 197 (1976), and Note, "Legislative Purpose, Rationality, and Equal Protection," 82 *Yale L.J.* 123 (1972).

43. Gunther, *Constitutional Law*, pp. 620–21 n.7.

44. Mathews v. Lucas (1979). Compare Powell's comment, speaking for the Court in Weber v. Aetna Casualty (1972), a challenge to a Louisiana statute that allowed illegitimate children to share in workmen's compensation benefits only to the extent that the maximum amount allowable had not been claimed by the parent's legitimate children: "The

blance to the Court's use of rationality in Williamson v. Lee Optical (1955; reprinted above, p. 908). *Plyler* used a standard of rationality, but it threw the burden on the state to prove the rational connection between its goals and the exclusion of the children of illegal aliens from public schools. Likewise, *Cleburne*, in invalidating a zoning ordinance applied to require a special permit for construction of a home for the mentally retarded, employed a standard that Marshall in concurrence termed " 'second order' rational basis review." [45]

Whether *Plyler* and *Cleburne* are turning points or merely more twists in an old road remains to be seen, as does whether the model that they may represent would supplement or rather supplant a two- or three-tiered model. In assessing the desirability of a model without tiers, one must ask to what extent the sort of jurisprudence that Stone was fostering in *Carolene Products* is viable without some variation of strict scrutiny. Indeed does constitutionalism itself demand some version of this test? Could these demands be met by a "rational basis" model that proceeded along the kind of spectrum that Marshall suggested, requiring more and more convincing arguments by government to justify classifications or restrictions of the sort previously covered by strict scrutiny? How would such a test differ from strict scrutiny?

IV. THE SCOPE AND PERMANENCE OF CONSTITUTIONAL MEANING

Through the dust raised by the Court's backing and filling across tangled masses of models and counter-models of equal protection, two obvious facts stand out. First, the doctrinal webs the justices have woven extend far from the constitutional text. Neither the older models, the now dominant model, or any of the more seriously proposed changes sinks its roots very deeply into the words of the Fourteenth or Fifth amendments. On occasion, a justice makes a weak pass at the intent of the framers and ratifiers of the Fourteenth Amendment, while others use, not always systematically or even consciously, a *philosophic approach*, alluding to but seldom analyzing political theory. Most seek and elaborate the doctrines present in previous decisions. None, however, makes the black letter of the text more than the starting point of interpretation. Thus the question HOW to interpret finds itself enmeshed in undefended, indeed usually unspoken, assumptions about WHAT "the Constitution" is.

Louisiana Supreme Court emphasized strongly the State's interest in protecting 'legitimate family relationships'. ... We do not question the importance of that interest; what we do question is how the challenged statute will promote it."

45. This change, if it is a change, has not arrived unheralded. See, for instance, *Mathews* and *Weber*, discussed above in note 44, and U.S. Railroad Retirement Bd. v. Fritz (1980), espec. Stevens' concur. op., discussed above in note 41.

Second, in trying to cope with the interrogative HOW where equal protection is involved, the Court—no doubt unintentionally—has thrown considerable light on the discussions in Chapter 6 of constitutional change. Whether "the Constitution's" meaning should or should not be permanent, over the last century the meaning of "equal protection of the laws" has several times changed and done so in politically as well as jurisprudentially consequential ways. As Justice Douglas expressed it for the Court in Harper v. Virginia State Board of Elections (1966; reprinted above, p. 225): "[T]he Equal Protection Clause is not shackled to the political theory of a particular era. . . . Notions of what constitutes equal treatment for purposes of the Equal Protection Clause *do* change." Moreover, that process of change is continuing.

SELECTED BIBLIOGRAPHY

Baer, Judith A. *Equality Under the Fourteenth Amendment* (Ithaca: Cornell University Press, 1983).

Black, Charles L., Jr. "Further Reflections on the Constitutional Justice of Livelihood," 86 *Colum.L.Rev.* 1103 (1986).

Ely, John Hart. *Democracy and Distrust* (Cambridge: Harvard University Press, 1980), ch. 6.

Gunther, Gerald. "In Search of Evolving Doctrine on a Changing Court," 86 *Harv.L.Rev.* 1 (1972).

Karst, Kenneth L. *Belonging to America: Equal Citizenship and the Constitution* (New Haven: Yale University Press, 1989).

Karst, Kenneth L. "Equal Citizenship under the Fourteenth Amendment," 91 *Harv.L.Rev.* 1 (1977).

Kirp, David L., Mark G. Yudof, & Marlene Strong Franks. *Gender Justice* (Chicago: University of Chicago Press, 1986).

Law, Sylvia A. "Rethinking Sex and the Constitution," 132 *U.Pa. L.Rev.* 955 (1984).

Lupu, Ira. "Untangling the Strands of the Fourteenth Amendment," 77 *Mich.L.Rev.* 981 (1979).

MacKinnon, Catharine A. "Reflections on Sex Equality Under Law," 100 *Yale L.J.* 1281 (1991).

Michelman, Frank I. "On Protecting the Poor Through the Fourteenth Amendment," 83 *Harv.L.Rev.* 7 (1969).

————. "The Supreme Court and Litigation Access Fees: The Right to Protect One's Rights," Parts I and II, 1973 *Duke L.J.* 1153 and 1974 *ibid.* 527.

————. "Welfare Rights in a Constitutional Democracy," 1979 *Wash.U.L.Q.* 659.

Minow, Martha. *Making All the Difference* (Ithaca: Cornell University Press, 1990).

Pritchett, C. Herman. *Constitutional Civil Liberties* (Englewood Cliffs, NJ: Prentice–Hall, 1984), chs. 10, 12.

Rhode, Deborah L. *Justice and Gender* (Cambridge: Harvard University Press, 1989).

Richards, David A. J. *Conscience and the Constitution* (Princeton: Princeton University Press, 1993).

Sunstein, Cass R. "Public Values, Private Interests, and the Equal Protection Clause," 1982 *Sup.Ct.Rev.* 127.

————. "Sexual Orientation and the Constitution: A Note on the Relationship Between Due Process and Equal Protection," 55 *U.Chi.L.Rev.* 1161 (1988).

————. *The Partial Constitution* (Cambridge: Harvard University Press, 1993).

Tribe, Laurence H. *American Constitutional Law* (2d ed.; Mineola, NY: Foundation Press, 1988), ch. 16.

I. SUSPECT CLASSIFICATIONS
A. Gender

"[C]lassifications based upon sex, like classifications based upon race, alienage, or national origin, are inherently suspect, and must therefore be subjected to strict judicial scrutiny."—Justice BRENNAN

"[T]his reaching out to pre-empt by judicial action a major political decision which is currently in process of resolution does not reflect appropriate respect for duly prescribed legislative processes."—Justice POWELL

FRONTIERO v. RICHARDSON
411 U.S. 677, 93 S.Ct. 1764, 36 L.Ed.2d 583 (1973).

Under military regulations a serviceman's wife automatically counted as his dependent for the purposes of increased housing allowances and medical benefits. On the other hand, a servicewoman's husband counted as a dependent only if the servicewoman proved that he was in fact dependent on her for half his support. Lt. Sharon Frontiero brought suit in a federal district court, contending that these regulations unconstitutionally discriminated against her and other servicewomen. The district court sustained the regulations, and she appealed to the Supreme Court.

Mr. Justice **BRENNAN** announced the judgment of the Court and delivered an opinion in which Mr. Justice **DOUGLAS**, Mr. Justice **WHITE**, and Mr. Justice **MARSHALL** join. ...

... [T]he question for decision is whether this difference in treatment constitutes an unconstitutional discrimination against servicewomen in violation of the Due Process Clause of the Fifth Amendment.[1] ...

II

At the outset, appellants contend that classifications based upon sex, like classifications based upon race, alienage, and national origin, are inherently suspect and must therefore be subjected to close judicial scrutiny. We agree and, indeed, find at least implicit support for such an approach in our unanimous decision only last Term in Reed v. Reed (1971). ... [There we] held that, even though the State's interest in achieving administrative efficiency "is not without some legitimacy," "[t]o give a mandatory preference to members of either sex over members of the other, merely to accomplish the elimination of hearings on the merits, is to make the very kind of arbitrary legislative choice forbidden by the [Constitution]. ..." This departure from "traditional" rational-basis analysis with respect to sex-based classifications is clearly justified.

There can be no doubt that our Nation has had a long and unfortunate history of sex discrimination. Traditionally, such discrimination was rationalized by an attitude of "romantic paternalism" which, in practical effect, put women, not on a pedestal, but in a cage. Indeed, this paternalistic attitude became so firmly rooted in our national consciousness that, 100 years ago, a distinguished Member of this Court was able to proclaim:

> Man is, or should be, woman's protector and defender. The natural and proper timidity and delicacy which belongs to the female sex evidently unfits it for many of the occupations of civil life. The constitution of the family organization, which is founded in the divine ordinance, as well as in the nature of things, indicates the domestic sphere as that which properly belongs to the domain and functions of womanhood. The harmony, not to say identity, of interests and views which belong, or should belong, to the family institution is repugnant to the idea of a woman adopting a distinct and independent career from that of her husband. ...

---

1. "[W]hile the Fifth Amendment contains no equal protection clause, it does forbid discrimination that is 'so unjustifiable as to be violative of due process.' " Schneider v. Rusk (1964); see Shapiro v. Thompson (1969); Bolling v. Sharpe (1954). [Footnote by Justice Brennan.]

... The paramount destiny and mission of woman are to fulfil the noble and benign offices of wife and mother. This is the law of the Creator. Bradwell v. Illinois (1873) (Bradley, J., concurring).

As a result of notions such as these, our statute books gradually became laden with gross, stereotyped distinctions between the sexes and, indeed, throughout much of the 19th century the position of women in our society was, in many respects, comparable to that of blacks under the pre-Civil War slave codes. Neither slaves nor women could hold office, serve on juries, or bring suit in their own names, and married women traditionally were denied the legal capacity to hold or convey property or to serve as legal guardians of their own children. And although blacks were guaranteed the right to vote in 1870, women were denied even that right—which is itself "preservative of other basic civil and political rights" [Reynolds v. Sims (1964)]—until adoption of the Nineteenth Amendment half a century later.

It is true, of course, that the position of women in America has improved markedly in recent decades. Nevertheless, it can hardly be doubted that, in part because of the high visibility of the sex characteristic, women still face pervasive, although at times more subtle, discrimination in our educational institutions, in the job market and, perhaps most conspicuously, in the political arena.

Moreover, since sex, like race and national origin, is an immutable characteristic determined solely by the accident of birth, the imposition of special disabilities upon the members of a particular sex because of their sex would seem to violate "the basic concept of our system that legal burdens should bear some relationship to individual responsibility. ..." Weber v. Aetna Casualty & Surety Co. (1972). And what differentiates sex from such nonsuspect statutes as intelligence or physical disability, and aligns it with the recognized suspect criteria, is that the sex characteristic frequently bears no relation to ability to perform or contribute to society. As a result statutory distinctions between the sexes often have the effect of invidiously relegating the entire class of females to inferior legal status without regard to the actual capabilities of its individual members.

We might also note that, over the past decade, Congress has itself manifested an increasing sensitivity to sex-based classifications. In Title VII of the Civil Rights Act of 1964, for example, Congress expressly declared that no employer, labor union, or other organization subject to the provisions of the Act shall discriminate against any individual on the basis of "race, color, religion, sex, or national origin." Similarly, the Equal Pay Act of 1963 provides that no employer covered by the Act "shall discriminate ... between employees on the basis of sex." And § 1 of the Equal Rights Amendment, passed by Congress on March 22, 1972, and submitted to the legislatures of the States for ratification, declares that "[e]quality of rights under the law shall not be denied or

abridged by the United States or by any State on account of sex." *
Thus, Congress itself has concluded that classifications based upon sex
are inherently invidious, and this conclusion of a coequal branch of
Government is not without significance to the question presently under
consideration.   Cf. Oregon v. Mitchell (1970) (opinion of Brennan,
White, and Marshall, JJ.); Katzenbach v. Morgan (1966).

With these considerations in mind, we can only conclude that
classifications based upon sex, like classifications based upon race, alienage, or national origin, are inherently suspect, and must therefore be
subjected to strict judicial scrutiny. Applying the analysis mandated by
that stricter standard of review, it is clear that the statutory scheme now
before us is constitutionally invalid.

III

The sole basis of the classification established in the challenged
statutes is the sex of the individuals involved. ... Moreover, the
Government concedes that the differential treatment accorded men and
women under these statutes serves no purpose other than mere "administrative convenience." In essence, the Government maintains that, as
an empirical matter, wives in our society frequently are dependent upon
their husbands, while husbands rarely are dependent upon their wives.
. . .

The Government offers no concrete evidence, however, tending to
support its view that such differential treatment in fact saves the
Government any money. In order to satisfy the demands of strict
judicial scrutiny, the Government must demonstrate, for example, that it
is actually cheaper to grant increased benefits with respect to *all* male
members, than it is to determine which male members are in fact
entitled to such benefits and to grant increased benefits only to those
members whose wives actually meet the dependency requirement. Here,
however, there is substantial evidence that, if put to the test, many of
the wives of male members would fail to qualify for benefits. ...

In any case, our prior decisions make clear that, although efficacious
administration of governmental programs is not without some importance, "the Constitution recognizes higher values than speed and efficiency." Stanley v. Illinois (1972). And when we enter the realm of
"strict judicial scrutiny," there can be no doubt that "administrative
convenience" is not a shibboleth, the mere recitation of which dictates
constitutionality. See Shapiro v. Thompson (1969). On the contrary,
any statutory scheme which draws a sharp line between the sexes, *solely*
for the purpose of achieving administrative convenience, necessarily
commands "dissimilar treatment for men and women who are ...
similarly situated," and therefore involves the "very kind of arbitrary
legislative choice forbidden by the [Constitution]. ..." *Reed.* We there-

---

* The proposed amendment was ratified by 35 states, three short of the three-quarters of
the states (38) necessary for adoption. Five of the 35 states, however, attempted to rescind
their ratifications.—**Eds.**

fore conclude that, by according differential treatment to male and female members of the uniformed services for the sole purpose of achieving administrative convenience, the challenged statutes violate the Due Process Clause of the Fifth Amendment insofar as they require a female member to prove the dependency of her husband.

Reversed.

Mr. Justice **STEWART** concurs in the judgment. ...

Mr. Justice **REHNQUIST** dissents. ...

Mr. Justice **POWELL,** with whom The Chief Justice [**BURGER**] and Mr. Justice **BLACKMUN** join, concurring in the judgment.

I agree that the challenged statutes constitute an unconstitutional discrimination against service-women ... but I cannot join the opinion of Mr. Justice Brennan. ... It is unnecessary for the Court in this case to characterize sex as a suspect classification, with all of the far-reaching implications of such a holding. *Reed,* which abundantly supports our decision today, did not add sex to the narrowly limited group of classifications which are inherently suspect. In my view, we can and should decide this case on the authority of *Reed* and reserve for the future any expansion of its rationale.

There is another, and I find compelling, reason for deferring a general categorizing of sex classifications as invoking the strictest test of judicial scrutiny. The Equal Rights Amendment, which if adopted will resolve the substance of this precise question, has been approved by the Congress and submitted for ratification by the States. If this Amendment is duly adopted, it will represent the will of the people accomplished in the manner prescribed by the Constitution. By acting prematurely and unnecessarily, as I view it, the Court has assumed a decisional responsibility at the very time when state legislatures, functioning within the traditional democratic process, are debating the proposed Amendment. It seems to me that this reaching out to pre-empt by judicial action a major political decision which is currently in process of resolution does not reflect appropriate respect for duly prescribed legislative processes.

There are times when this Court, under our system, cannot avoid a constitutional decision on issues which normally should be resolved by the elected representatives of the people. But democratic institutions are weakened, and confidence in the restraint of the Court is impaired, when we appear unnecessarily to decide sensitive issues of broad social and political importance at the very time they are under consideration within the prescribed constitutional processes.

Editors' Notes

(1) Justice Brennan's opinion in *Frontiero* is not an opinion of the Court, merely an opinion of four justices. The Court has never held that classifications based upon sex are inherently suspect and therefore subject to strict scrutiny.

(2) **Query:** What is the constitutional basis for Brennan's analogy between discrimination based on sex and that based on race? Would a *textual approach* lead to such an analogy? A *structuralist approach*? A *philosophic approach*? An *originalist approach*? A *doctrinal approach*? Any other? Whatever the analogy's constitutional basis, is it apt? Are there more situations in which sexual differences are justifiably relevant to the pursuit of important, even compelling, governmental objectives than are racial differences? Is the constitutional text or the broader constitution "sex-blind"? See Richard A. Wasserstrom, "Racism and Sexism," in *Philosophy and Social Issues* (Notre Dame: University of Notre Dame Press, 1980).

(3) **Query:** If a majority of the Court had held in *Frontiero* that sex-based classifications were suspect, would its doing so have "pre-empted" the ERA, as Justice Powell charges? Compare his argument here with James Bradley Thayer's argument that judicial review debilitates the political process, reprinted above, at p. 602. What implications, if any, does the failure of the ERA to secure adoption have for the level of scrutiny to which judges should subject sex-based classifications? How would a democratic theorist respond? A constitutionalist?

(4) **Query:** Would the type of *reinforcing representative democracy approach* that *Carolene Products* mapped subject gender-based classifications to "more searching judicial inquiry"? In his version of such an approach, John Hart Ely contends that women not only are not discrete and insular, they are not even a minority. He proposes "remanding" older statutes embodying sex-based classifications to legislatures for a "second look." *Democracy and Distrust* (Cambridge: Harvard University Press, 1980), pp. 167–70. What constitutional justification could judges offer for such a course?

(5) **Query:** To what extent would a constitutionalist agree with Ely? Does democratic theory support his conclusion? Kenneth L. Karst has argued that equal citizenship requires not only removal of obstacles to voting, but also "eradication of any discrimination which, without compelling justification, reinforces the substance or symbolism of female dependency." "Foreword: Equal Citizenship Under the Fourteenth Amendment," 91 *Harv.L.Rev.* 1, 26 (1977). See also Sylvia A. Law, "Rethinking Sex and the Constitution," 132 *U.Pa.L.Rev.* 955 (1984).

"[C]lassifications by gender must serve important governmental objectives and must be substantially related to achievement of those objectives."—Justice BRENNAN

"There are valid reasons for dissatisfaction with the 'two-tier' approach. ..."—Justice POWELL

"There is only one Equal Protection Clause."—Justice STEVENS

"The only redeeming feature of the Court's opinion ... is that it apparently signals a retreat by those who joined the plurality opinion in *Frontiero* from their view that sex is a 'suspect' classification.   ...."—Justice REHNQUIST

CRAIG v. BOREN

429 U.S. 190, 97 S.Ct. 451, 50 L.Ed.2d 397 (1976).

Title 37, §§ 241 and 245 of the Oklahoma code forbade the sale of 3.2 per cent beer to males under 21 and to females under 18. Craig, a male between 18 and 21, sued in a federal district court, alleging that §§ 241 and 245 invidiously discriminated against males 18–20 years of age. The district court sustained the constitutionality of the provisions, and Craig appealed to the Supreme Court.

Mr. Justice **BRENNAN** delivered the opinion of the Court. ...

... Reed [v. Reed (1971)] emphasized that statutory classifications that distinguish between males and females are "subject to scrutiny under the Equal Protection Clause." To withstand constitutional challenge, previous cases establish that classifications by gender must serve important governmental objectives and must be substantially related to achievement of those objectives. ... [*Reed* and subsequent cases] have rejected administrative ease and convenience as sufficiently important objectives to justify gender-based classifications. See, *e.g.*, Stanley v. Illinois (1972); Frontiero v. Richardson (1973). ...

Reed has also provided the underpinning for decisions that have invalidated statutes employing gender as an inaccurate proxy for other more germane bases of classification. Hence, "archaic and overbroad" generalizations concerning the financial position of servicewomen and working women could not justify use of a gender line in determining eligibility for certain governmental entitlements. Similarly, increasingly outdated misconceptions concerning the role of females in the home rather than in the "marketplace and world of ideas" were rejected as loose-fitting characterizations incapable of supporting state statutory schemes that were premised upon their accuracy. In light of the weak congruence between gender and the characteristic or trait that gender purported to represent, it was necessary that the legislatures choose either to realign their substantive laws in a gender-neutral fashion, or to adopt procedures for identifying those instances where the sex-centered generalization actually comported with fact.

... We turn then to the question whether, under *Reed,* the difference between males and females with respect to the purchase of 3.2% beer warrants the differential in age drawn by the Oklahoma statute. We conclude that it does not. We accept ... the District Court's identification of the objective underlying §§ 241 and 245 as the enhancement of traffic safety. Clearly, the protection of public health and safety represents an important function of state and local governments. However, appellees' statistics in our view cannot support the conclusion that the gender-based distinction closely serves to achieve that objective and therefore the distinction cannot under *Reed* withstand equal protection challenge.

The appellees introduced a variety of statistical surveys. ... Even were this statistical evidence accepted as accurate, it nevertheless offers only a weak answer to the equal protection question presented here. The most focused and relevant of the statistical surveys, arrests of 18–20–years-olds for alcohol-related driving offenses, exemplifies the ultimate unpersuasiveness of this evidentiary record. Viewed in terms of the correlation between sex and the actual activity that Oklahoma seeks to regulate—driving while under the influence of alcohol—the statistics broadly establish that .18% of females and 2% of males in that age group were arrested for that offense. While such a disparity is not trivial in a statistical sense, it hardly can form the basis for employment of a gender line as a classifying device. Certainly if maleness is to serve as a proxy for drinking and driving, a correlation of 2% * must be considered an unduly tenuous "fit." Indeed, prior cases have consistently rejected the use of sex as a decision-making factor even though the statutes in question certainly rested on far more predictive empirical relationships than this.

Moreover, the statistics exhibit a variety of other shortcomings that seriously impugn their value to equal protection analysis. Setting aside the obvious methodological problems, the surveys do not adequately justify the salient features of Oklahoma's gender-based traffic-safety law. ...

There is no reason to belabor this line of analysis. It is unrealistic to expect either members of the judiciary or state officials to be well versed in the rigors of experimental or statistical technique. But this merely illustrates that proving broad sociological propositions by statistics is a dubious business, and one that inevitably is in tension with the normative philosophy that underlies the Equal Protection Clause. Suffice to say that the showing offered by the appellees does not satisfy us that sex represents a legitimate, accurate proxy for the regulation of drinking and driving. In fact, when it is further recognized that Oklahoma's statute prohibits only the selling of 3.2% beer to young males and not their drinking the beverage once acquired (even after purchase by their 18–20–year-old female companions), the relationship between gender and traffic safety becomes far too tenuous to satisfy *Reed*'s requirement that the gender-based difference be substantially related to achievement of the statutory objective. ...

We conclude that the gender-based differential ... constitutes a denial of the equal protection of the laws to males aged 18–20. ...

[*Reversed.*]

---

* Justice Brennan badly misconceived the concept of correlation.—**Eds.**

Mr. Justice **POWELL**, concurring.

I join the opinion of the Court ... [a]lthough I do have reservations as to some of the discussion concerning the appropriate standard for equal protection analysis. ... I find it unnecessary, in deciding this case, to read [*Reed*] as broadly as some of the Court's language may imply. *Reed* and subsequent cases involving gender-based classifications make clear that the Court subjects such classifications to a more critical examination than is normally applied when "fundamental" constitutional rights and "suspect classes" are not present.[1]

Mr. Justice **STEVENS**, concurring.

There is only one Equal Protection Clause. It requires every State to govern impartially. It does not direct the courts to apply one standard of review in some cases and a different standard in other cases. Whatever criticism may be leveled at a judicial opinion implying that there are at least three such standards applies with the same force to a double standard.

I am inclined to believe that what has become known as the two-tiered analysis of equal protection claims does not describe a completely logical method of deciding cases, but rather is a method the Court has employed to explain decisions that actually apply a single standard in a reasonably consistent fashion. I also suspect that a careful explanation of the reasons motivating particular decisions may contribute more to an identification of that standard than an attempt to articulate it in all-encompassing terms. It may therefore be appropriate for me to state the principal reasons which persuaded me to join the Court's opinion.

In this case, the classification is objectionable because it is based on an accident of birth, because it is a mere remnant of the now almost universally rejected tradition of discriminating against males in this age bracket, and because, to the extent it reflects any physical difference between males and females, it is actually perverse. The question then is whether the traffic safety justification put forward by the State is sufficient to make an otherwise offensive classification acceptable.

The classification is not totally irrational. For the evidence does indicate that there are more males than females in this age bracket who drive and also more who drink. Nevertheless, ... I regard the justifica-

---

1. As is evident from our opinions, the Court has had difficulty in agreeing upon a standard of equal protection analysis that can be applied consistently to the wide variety of legislative classifications. There are valid reasons for dissatisfaction with the "two-tier" approach. ... Although viewed by many as a result-oriented substitute for more critical analysis, that approach—with its narrowly limited "upper-tier"—now has substantial precedential support. As has been true of *Reed* and its progeny, our decision today will be viewed by some as a "middle-tier" approach. While I would not endorse that characterization and would not welcome a further subdividing of equal protection analysis, candor compels the recognition that the relatively deferential "rational basis" standard of review normally applied takes on a sharper focus when we address a gender-based classification. So much is clear from our recent cases. ... [Footnote by Justice Powell.]

tion as unacceptable. ... The legislation imposes a restraint on 100% of the males in the class allegedly because about 2% of them have probably violated one or more laws relating to the consumption of alcoholic beverages. It is unlikely that this law will have a significant deterrent effect either on that 2% or on the law-abiding 98%. But even assuming some such slight benefit, it does not seem to me that an insult to all of the young men of the State can be justified by visiting the sins of the 2% on the 98%.

Mr. Justice **BLACKMUN,** concurring in part. ...

Mr. Justice **STEWART,** concurring in the judgment. ...

Mr. Chief Justice **BURGER,** dissenting. ...

Mr. Justice **REHNQUIST,** dissenting. ...

The only redeeming feature of the Court's opinion, to my mind, is that it apparently signals a retreat by those who joined the plurality opinion in *Frontiero* from their view that sex is a "suspect" classification for purposes of equal protection analysis. I think the Oklahoma statute challenged here need pass only the "rational basis" equal protection analysis expounded in cases such as *McGowan* and Williamson v. Lee Optical Co. (1955), and I believe that it is constitutional under that analysis.

... [T]he Court's application here of an elevated or "intermediate" level scrutiny, like that invoked in cases dealing with discrimination against females, raises the question of why the statute here should be treated any differently from countless legislative classifications unrelated to sex which have been upheld under a minimum rationality standard. Most obviously unavailable to support any kind of special scrutiny in this case, is a history or pattern of past discrimination, such as was relied on by the plurality in *Frontiero*. ... There is no suggestion in the Court's opinion that males in this age group are in any way peculiarly disadvantaged, subject to systematic discriminatory treatment, or otherwise in need of special solicitude from the courts. ...

The Court's conclusion that a law which treats males less favorably than females "must serve important governmental objectives and must be substantially related to achievement of those objectives" apparently comes out of thin air. The Equal Protection Clause contains no such language, and none of our previous cases adopt that standard. I would think we have had enough difficulty with the two standards of review which our cases have recognized—the norm of "rational basis," and the "compelling state interest" required where a "suspect classification" is involved—so as to counsel weightily against the insertion of still another "standard" between those two. How is this Court to divine what objectives are important? How is it to determine whether a particular law is "substantially" related to the achievement of such objective, rather than related in some other way to its achievement? Both of the phrases used are so diaphanous and elastic as to invite subjective judicial preferences or prejudices relating to particular types of legislation. ...

Our decisions indicate that application of the Equal Protection Clause in a context not justifying an elevated level of scrutiny does not demand "mathematical nicety" or the elimination of all inequality. ... The Court's criticism of the statistics relied on by the District Court conveys the impression that a legislature in enacting a new law is to be subjected to the judicial equivalent of a doctoral examination in statistics. ...

Quite apart from [the] alleged methodological deficiencies in the statistical evidence, the Court appears to hold that that evidence, on its face, fails to support the distinction drawn in the statute. The Court notes that only 2% of males (as against .18% of females) in the age group were arrested for drunk driving, and that this very low figure establishes "an unduly tenuous 'fit' "between maleness and drunk driving in the 18–20–year-old group. On this point the Court misconceives the nature of the equal protection inquiry.

The rationality of a statutory classification for equal protection purposes does not depend upon the statistical "fit" between the class and the trait sought to be singled out. It turns on whether there may be a sufficiently higher incidence of the trait within the included class than in the excluded class to justify different treatment. Therefore the present equal protection challenge to this gender-based discrimination poses only the question whether the incidence of drunk driving among young men is sufficiently greater than among young women to justify differential treatment. Notwithstanding the Court's critique of the statistical evidence, that evidence suggests clear differences between the drinking and driving habits of young men and women. Those differences are grounds enough for the State reasonably to conclude that young males pose by far the greater drunk-driving hazard. ... The gender-based difference in treatment in this case is therefore not irrational. ...

Editors' Notes

(1) **Query:** To some extent all of the opinions in *Craig* followed a *doctrinal approach.* To what extent did any of the justices also utilize a *textualist approach*? A *structuralist approach*? Any other(s)?

(2) **Query:** What is the difference between the *doctrinal* standard that the majority adopted for considering gender-based classifications ("intermediate scrutiny" or a "middle-tier" approach) and the standard that Justice Powell proposed in concurrence (deferential scrutiny but with a "sharper focus")?

(3) **Query:** Was Justice Brennan correct that "proving broad sociological propositions by statistics inevitably is in tension with the normative philosophy that underlies the Equal Protection Clause"? Recall that footnote 11 in Brown v. Board of Education (1954; reprinted above, p. 912) cited empirical social

science studies to support its conclusion that "[s]eparate educational facilities are inherently unequal." Is *Craig* consistent with this aspect of *Brown*?

(4) **Query:** A *textualist approach* might have supported Justice Stevens's claim that "There is only one Equal Protection Clause." He also claimed, in effect, that a *doctrinal approach* would lead to the same conclusion. To what extent was that latter claim correct? Was he correct in saying that the decisions of the Court "actually apply a single standard in a reasonably consistent fashion"? If so, what is that single standard? What is its basis in the constitutional text? In the political theories that underlie that text? Indeed, what does that "text" include? The Declaration of Independence as well as the amended document of 1787–88? Reconsider these questions after reading Cleburne v. Cleburne Living Center (1985; reprinted below, p. 1048).

(5) **Query:** Should judges subject statutes discriminating against men to a lower level of scrutiny than statutes discriminating against women? Or should judges use the same standard of review for both?

(6) **Query:** Using a *textualist approach*, Rehnquist objected that the "Equal Protection Clause contains no such language" as that of the majority's standard of intermediate scrutiny. Is his own proposed standard of "rational basis" any less vulnerable to such a *textualist* objection? An *originalist* objection? (Recall his essay, "The Notion of a Living Constitution," reprinted above, p. 243.)

"The purpose of requiring [intermediate scrutiny] is to assure that the validity of a [gender-based] classification is determined through reasoned analysis rather than through the mechanical application of traditional, often inaccurate, assumptions about the proper roles of men and women."—Justice O'CONNOR

"I have come to suspect that it is easy to go too far with rigid rules in this area of claimed sex discrimination. ..."—Justice BLACKMUN

"By applying heightened equal protection analysis to this case, the Court frustrates the liberating spirit of the Equal Protection Clause."—Justice POWELL

MISSISSIPPI UNIVERSITY FOR WOMEN v. HOGAN
458 U.S. 718, 102 S.Ct. 3331, 73 L.Ed.2d 1090 (1982).

In Craig v. Boren, the justices seemed to have reached a compromise—heightened but not strict scrutiny for classifications by sex, in other words, intermediate scrutiny. In 1981, however, two opinions written by Justice Rehnquist raised serious questions about how long that compromise would hold. The first, Michael M. v. Superior Court, found no sexual discrimination in a conviction of a 17½ year-old male for statutory rape of a 16½ year-old female. For four of the five justices in the majority, Rehnquist wrote:

> [W]e do not apply so-called "strict scrutiny" to [gender-based] classi-
> fications. Our cases have held, however, that the traditional minimal
> rationality test takes on a somewhat "sharper focus" when gender-
> based classifications are challenged. See Craig v. Boren (1976)
> (Powell, J., concurring).

Conceding that the purpose of punishing males for intercourse with females
under 18 but not females for intercourse with males under 18 was "somewhat
less than clear," Rehnquist accepted the state's argument that it was to
prevent pregnancies among teen-agers and that this was a "strong interest."

In the second case, Rostker v. Goldberg, Rehnquist wrote for the Court,
upholding 6–3 the Military Selective Service Act, which required only males to
register for the draft. The majority found Congress' limitation reasonable.
The opinion, redolent with deference toward congressional power to raise
armies and wage war, finessed the question of requiring any standard stricter
than a rational basis. Some observers, however, discounted the possibility
that Rostker signalled change because it involved congressional powers that
the Court had traditionally been reluctant to question. Michael M. was more
difficult to discount, though Rehnquist had made a slight bow toward a form of
heightened scrutiny.

Mississippi University for Women, a state institution in Columbus, Miss.,
provided a new test of the compromise's vitality. From its founding, MUW had
limited enrollment to women. Joe Hogan, a male nurse resident in Columbus,
applied for admission to MUW's School of Nursing to obtain a bachelor's
degree in his field. Solely on the basis of his sex, MUW denied him admission
to a degree-granting program, though he was allowed to audit classes. He
sued for an injunction in a federal district court, lost, and won on appeal.
Mississippi then sought and obtained certiorari.

Justice **O'CONNOR** delivered the opinion of the Court. . . .

II

We begin our analysis aided by several firmly-established principles.
. . . That this statute discriminates against males rather than against
females does not exempt it from scrutiny or reduce the standard of
review. Our decisions also establish that the party seeking to uphold a
statute that classifies individuals on the basis of their gender must carry
the burden of showing an "exceedingly persuasive justification" for the
classification. The burden is met only by showing at least that the
classification serves "important governmental objectives and that the
discriminatory means employed" are "substantially related to the
achievement of those objectives."

Although the test for determining the validity of a gender-based
classification is straightforward, it must be applied free of fixed notions
concerning the roles and abilities of males and females. Care must be
taken in ascertaining whether the statutory objective itself reflects
archaic and stereotypic notions. Thus, if the statutory objective is to
exclude or "protect" members of one gender because they are presumed
to suffer from an inherent handicap or to be innately inferior, the

objective itself is illegitimate. See Frontiero v. Richardson (1973) (plurality opinion).

If the State's objective is legitimate and important, we next determine whether the requisite direct, substantial relationship between objective and means is present. The purpose of requiring that close relationship is to assure that the validity of a classification is determined through reasoned analysis rather than through the mechanical application of traditional, often inaccurate, assumptions about the proper roles of men and women. ...

III

The State's primary justification for maintaining the single-sex admissions policy of MUW's School of Nursing is that it compensates for discrimination against women and, therefore, constitutes educational affirmative action. As applied to the School of Nursing, we find the State's argument unpersuasive.

In limited circumstances, a gender-based classification favoring one sex can be justified if it intentionally and directly assists members of the sex that is disproportionately burdened. However, we consistently have emphasized that "the mere recitation of a benign, compensatory purpose is not an automatic shield which protects against any inquiry into the actual purposes underlying a statutory scheme." Weinberger v. Wiesenfeld (1975). The same searching analysis must be made, regardless of whether the State's objective is to eliminate family controversy, Reed, to achieve administrative efficiency, Frontiero, or to balance the burdens borne by males and females.

It is readily apparent that a State can evoke a compensatory purpose to justify an otherwise discriminatory classification only if members of the gender benefited by the classification actually suffer a disadvantage related to the classification. ... [But] Mississippi has made no showing that women lacked opportunities to obtain training in the field of nursing or to attain positions of leadership in that field when the MUW School of Nursing opened its door or that women currently are deprived of such opportunities. In fact, in 1970, the year before the School of Nursing's first class enrolled, women earned 94 percent of the nursing baccalaureate degrees conferred in Mississippi and 98.6 percent of the degrees earned nationwide. ...

Rather than compensate for discriminatory barriers faced by women, MUW's policy of excluding males from admission to the School of Nursing tends to perpetuate the stereotyped view of nursing as an exclusively woman's job. ... Thus, we conclude that, although the State recited a "benign, compensatory purpose," it failed to establish that the alleged objective is the actual purpose underlying the discriminatory classification.

The policy is invalid also because it fails the second part of the equal protection test, for the State has made no showing that the gender-based classification is substantially and directly related to its proposed compensatory objective. To the contrary, MUW's policy of permitting men to attend classes as auditors fatally undermines its claim that women, at least those in the School of Nursing, are adversely affected by the presence of men. ...

[*Affirmed.*]

Chief Justice **BURGER**, dissenting. ...

Justice **BLACKMUN**, dissenting. ...

I have come to suspect that it is easy to go too far with rigid rules in this area of claimed sex discrimination, and to lose—indeed destroy— values that mean much to some people by forbidding the State from offering them a choice while not depriving others of an alternate choice. Justice Powell in his separate opinion advances this theme well.

While the Court purports to write narrowly ... there is inevitable spillover from the Court's ruling today. That ruling, it seems to me, places in constitutional jeopardy any state-supported educational institution that confines its student body in any area to members of one sex, even though the State elsewhere provides an equivalent program to the complaining applicant. The Court's reasoning does not stop with the School of Nursing of the Mississippi University for Women.

I hope that we do not lose all values that some think are worthwhile (and are not based on differences of race or religion) and relegate ourselves to needless conformity. The ringing words of the Equal Protection Clause of the Fourteenth Amendment—what Justice Powell aptly describes as its "liberating spirit,"—do not demand that price.

Justice **POWELL**, with whom Justice **REHNQUIST** joins, dissenting.

The Court's opinion bows deeply to conformity. Left without honor—indeed, held unconstitutional—is an element of diversity that has characterized much of American education and enriched much of American life. The Court in effect holds today that no State now may provide even a single institution of higher learning open only to women students. It gives no heed to the efforts of the State of Mississippi to provide abundant opportunities for young men and young women to attend coeducational institutions, and none to the preferences of the more than 40,000 young women who over the years have evidenced their approval of an all-women's college by choosing Mississippi University for Women (MUW) over seven coeducational universities within the State. ...

... In my view, the Court errs seriously by assuming—without argument or discussion—that the equal protection standard generally applicable to sex discrimination is appropriate here. That standard was designed to free women from "archaic and overbroad generalizations. ..." *Schlesinger*. In no previous case have we applied it to invalidate state efforts to *expand* women's choices. Nor are there prior sex discrimination decisions by this Court in which a male plaintiff, as in this case, had the choice of an equal benefit.

By applying heightened equal protection analysis to this case, the Court frustrates the liberating spirit of the Equal Protection Clause. It forbids the States from providing women with an opportunity to choose the type of university they prefer. And yet it is these women whom the Court regards as the *victims* of an illegal, stereotyped perception of the role of women in our society. The Court reasons this way in a case in which no woman has complained, and the only complainant is a man who advances no claims on behalf of anyone else. His claim ... is not that he is being denied a substantive educational opportunity, or even the right to attend an all-male or a coeducational college. It is *only* that the colleges open to him are located at inconvenient distances. ...

A distinctive feature of America's tradition has been respect for diversity. This has been characteristic of the peoples from numerous lands who have built our country. It is the essence of our democratic system. At stake in this case as I see it is the preservation of a small aspect of this diversity. But that aspect is by no means insignificant, given our heritage of available choice between single-sex and coeducational institutions of higher learning. ... The Equal Protection Clause was never intended to be applied to this kind of case.

Editors' Notes

(1) **Query:** Again, we see the justices following different *doctrinal approaches* or at least reading the landmarks on those routes differently. Did *doctrinalism* conceal deeper disagreements both about HOW to interpret and WHAT is "the Constitution" to be interpreted?

(2) **Query:** Justice Powell spoke of the "liberating spirit" of the equal protection clause. Where did he find that spirit? What sort of approach would justify such a search?

(3) **Query:** If "separate but equal" is not permissible with respect to sexually segregated public nursing schools, should it be permissible for any public undergraduate institution?

––––––––

B. Wealth?

"Wealth, like race, creed, or color, is not germane to one's ability to participate intelligently in the electoral process. Lines drawn on the basis of wealth or property, like those of race, are traditionally disfavored."

HARPER v. VIRGINIA STATE BOARD OF ELECTIONS
383 U.S. 663, 86 S.Ct. 1079, 16 L.Ed.2d 169 (1966).

This case, invalidating as a denial of equal protection Virginia's law requiring that voters pay a poll tax of $1.50 as a qualification for voting in state elections, is reprinted above, p. 225.

––––––––

"The system of alleged discrimination and the class it defines have none of the traditional indicia of suspectness. ..."—Justice POWELL

"A principled reading of what this Court has done reveals that it has applied a spectrum of standards in reviewing discrimination allegedly violative of the Equal Protection Clause."—Justice MARSHALL

SAN ANTONIO SCHOOL DISTRICT v. RODRIGUEZ

411 U.S. 1, 93 S.Ct. 1278, 36 L.Ed.2d 16 (1973).

In a program similar to that of most states at the time, Texas' Minimum Foundation School Program provided basic financial support for public schools; each district supplemented those funds through local property taxes. Because the value of taxable property varied from district to district, the amount of money available to finance public schools also widely varied. For example, in 1967–68 the expenditure in Edgewood Independent School District, a poor and heavily Mexican–American area in urban San Antonio, was $356 per pupil; it was $594 in Alamo Heights, a residential "Anglo" district. Parents of students in Edgewood brought a class action in a federal district court, claiming that Texas was denying them equal protection. Relying on cases like Harper v. Virginia (1966; reprinted above, p. 225), the district court held that wealth was a suspect classification, education was a fundamental right, the rules of strict scrutiny applied, and the unequal financing plan was unconstitutional. Texas appealed to the Supreme Court.

Mr. Justice **POWELL** delivered the opinion of the Court.　...

I ...

... We must decide, first, whether the Texas system of financing public education operates to the disadvantage of some suspect class or impinges upon a fundamental right explicitly or implicitly protected by the Constitution, thereby requiring strict judicial scrutiny. ... If not, the Texas scheme must still be examined to determine whether it rationally furthers some legitimate, articulated state purpose and therefore does not constitute an invidious discrimination in violation of the Equal Protection Clause of the Fourteenth Amendment.

II ...

... [W]e find neither the suspect-classification nor the fundamental-interest analysis persuasive.

A

The wealth discrimination discovered by the District Court in this case and by several other courts that have recently struck down school financing laws in other States is quite unlike any of the forms of wealth discrimination heretofore reviewed by this Court. ... [T]he courts in these cases have virtually assumed their findings of a suspect classification through a simplistic process of analysis: since, under the traditional systems of financing public schools, some poorer people receive less expensive educations than other more affluent people, these systems discriminate on the basis of wealth. This approach largely ignores the hard threshold questions, including whether it makes a difference for purposes of consideration under the Constitution that the class of disadvantaged "poor" cannot be identified or defined in customary equal protection terms, and whether the relative—rather than absolute—nature of the asserted deprivation is of significant consequence. ...

... The individuals, or groups of individuals, who constituted the class discriminated against in our prior cases shared two distinguishing characteristics: ... they were completely unable to pay for some desired benefit, and as a consequence, they sustained an absolute deprivation of a meaningful opportunity to enjoy that benefit. ...

Only appellees' first possible basis for describing the class disadvantaged by the Texas school-financing system—discrimination against a class of definably "poor" persons—might arguably meet the criteria established in these prior cases. Even a cursory examination, however, demonstrates that neither of the two distinguishing characteristics of wealth classifications can be found here. First, ... appellees have made no effort to demonstrate that it operates to the peculiar disadvantage of any class fairly definable as indigent, or as composed of persons whose incomes are beneath any designated poverty level. Indeed ... there is no basis on the record in this case for assuming that the poorest people ... are concentrated in the poorest districts.

Second, ... lack of personal resources has not occasioned an absolute deprivation of the desired benefit. The argument here is not that the children in districts having relatively low assessable property values are receiving no public education; rather, it is that they are receiving a poorer quality education than that available to children in districts having more assessable wealth. ... [A] sufficient answer ... is that, at least where wealth is involved, the Equal Protection Clause does not require absolute equality or precisely equal advantages. Nor, indeed, in view of the infinite variables affecting the educational process, can any system assure equal quality of education except in the most relative sense. Texas asserts that ... [b]y providing 12 years of free public school education, and by assuring teachers, books, transportation and operating funds, [it] has endeavored to "guarantee, for the welfare of the state as a whole, that all people shall have at least an adequate program of education. ..." No proof was offered at trial persuasively discrediting or refuting the State's assertion. ...

... [A]ppellees and the District Court may have embraced a second [approach,] which might be characterized as a theory of relative or comparative discrimination based on family income. Appellees sought to prove that a direct correlation exists between the wealth of families within each district and the expenditures therein for education. ...

The principal evidence adduced in support of this comparative discrimination claim is an affidavit submitted by Professor Joel S. Berke of Syracuse University's Educational Finance Policy Institute. ... Professor Berke's affidavit is based on a survey of approximately 10% of the school districts in Texas. His findings ... show only that the wealthiest few districts in the sample have the highest median family incomes and spend the most on education, and that the several poorest districts have the lowest family incomes and devote the least amount of money to education. For the remainder of the districts—96 districts comprising almost 90% of the sample—the correlation is inverted, *i.e.*, the districts that spend next to the most money on education are populated by families having next to the lowest median family incomes while the districts spending the least have the highest median family incomes. It is evident that ... no factual basis exists upon which to found a claim of comparative wealth discrimination.

This brings us, then, to the third way in which the classification scheme might be defined—*district* wealth discrimination. ... [T]he disadvantaged class might be viewed as encompassing every child in every district except the district that has the most assessable wealth and spends the most on education. Alternatively, the class might be defined more restrictively to include children in districts with assessable property which falls below the statewide average, or median, or below some other artificially defined level.

However described, it is clear that appellees' suit asks this Court to extend its most exacting scrutiny to review a system that allegedly discriminates against a large, diverse, and amorphous class, unified only by the common factor of residence in districts that happen to have less taxable wealth than other districts. The system of alleged discrimination and the class it defines have none of the traditional indicia of suspectness: the class is not saddled with such disabilities, or subjected to such a history of purposeful unequal treatment, or relegated to such a position of political powerlessness as to command extraordinary protection from the majoritarian political process.

We thus conclude that the Texas system does not operate to the peculiar disadvantage of any suspect class. But [recognizing] that this Court has never heretofore held that wealth discrimination alone provides an adequate basis for invoking strict scrutiny, appellees ... also assert that the State's system impermissibly interferes with the exercise of a "fundamental" right [to education] and that accordingly the prior decisions of this Court require the application of the strict standard of judicial review. ...

B

In Brown v. Board of Education (1954) a unanimous Court recognized that "education is perhaps the most important function of state and local governments." ... Nothing this Court holds today in any way detracts from our historic dedication to public education. ... But the importance of a service performed by the State does not determine whether it must be regarded as fundamental for purposes of examination under the Equal Protection Clause. ...

The lesson of [prior] cases ... is plain. It is not the province of this Court to create substantive constitutional rights in the name of guaranteeing equal protection of the laws. Thus the key to discovering whether education is "fundamental" is not to be found in comparisons of the relative societal significance of education as opposed to subsistence [Dandridge v. Williams (1970)] or housing [Lindsey v. Normet (1972)]. Nor is it to be found by weighing whether education is as important as the right to travel [Shapiro v. Thompson (1969)]. Rather, the answer lies in assessing whether there is a right to education explicitly or implicitly guaranteed by the Constitution. Skinner v. Oklahoma (1942).

Education, of course, is not among the rights afforded explicit protection under our Federal Constitution. Nor do we find any basis for saying it is implicitly so protected. ... It is appellees' contention, however, that education is distinguishable from other services and benefits provided by the State because it bears a peculiarly close relationship to other rights and liberties accorded protection under the Constitution. Specifically, they insist that education is itself a fundamental personal right because it is essential to the effective exercise of First Amendment freedoms and to intelligent utilization of the right to vote. In asserting a nexus between speech and education, appellees urge that the right to speak is meaningless unless the speaker is capable of articulating his thoughts intelligently and persuasively. ... A similar line of reasoning is pursued with respect to the right to vote. ...

We need not dispute any of these propositions. The Court has long afforded zealous protection against unjustifiable governmental interference with the individual's rights to speak and to vote. Yet we have never presumed to possess either the ability or the authority to guarantee to the citizenry the most *effective* speech or the most *informed* electoral choice. That these may be desirable goals of a system of freedom of expression and of a representative form of government is not to be doubted. ... But they are not values to be implemented by judicial intrusion into otherwise legitimate state activities.

Even if it were conceded that some identifiable quantum of education is a constitutionally protected prerequisite to the meaningful exercise of either right, we have no indication that the present levels of educational expenditure in Texas provide an education that ... fails to provide each child with an opportunity to acquire the basic minimal skills necessary. ...

Furthermore, the logical limitations on appellees' nexus theory are difficult to perceive. How, for instance, is education to be distinguished from the significant personal interests in the basics of decent food and shelter? Empirical examination might well buttress an assumption that the ill-fed, ill-clothed, and ill-housed are among the most ineffective participants in the political process, and that they derive the least enjoyment from the benefits of the First Amendment. If so, appellees' thesis would cast serious doubt on the authority of *Dandridge* and *Lindsey*. ...

C ...

... [We] lack both the expertise and the familiarity with local problems so necessary to the making of wise decisions with respect to the raising and disposition of public revenues. ... [T]his case also involves the most persistent and difficult questions of educational policy, another area in which this Court's lack of specialized knowledge and experience counsels against premature interference with the informed judgments made at the state and local levels. ...

It must be remembered, also, that every claim arising under the Equal Protection Clause has implications for the relationship between national and state power under our federal system. Questions of federalism are always inherent in the process of determining whether a State's laws are to be accorded the traditional presumption of constitutionality, or are to be subjected instead to rigorous judicial scrutiny. ... [I]t would be difficult to imagine a case having a greater potential impact on our federal system than the one now before us, in which we are urged to abrogate systems of financing public education presently in existence in virtually every State.

The foregoing considerations buttress our conclusion that Texas' system of public school finance is an inappropriate candidate for strict judicial scrutiny. These same considerations are relevant to the determination whether that system, with its conceded imperfections, nevertheless bears some rational relationship to a legitimate state purpose. ...

III ...

Appellees do not question the propriety of Texas' dedication to local control of education. To the contrary, they attack the school-financing system precisely because, in their view, it does not provide the same level of local control and fiscal flexibility in all districts. ... While it is no doubt true that reliance on local property taxation for school revenues provides less freedom of choice with respect to expenditures for some districts than for others, the existence of "some inequality" in the manner in which the State's rationale is achieved is not alone a sufficient basis for striking down the entire system. McGowan v. Maryland (1961). It may not be condemned simply because it imperfectly effectuates the State's goals. *Dandridge*. Nor must the financing system fail because ... other methods of satisfying the State's interest, which occasion "less drastic" disparities in expenditures, might be conceived. Only where state action impinges on the exercise of fundamental constitutional rights or liberties must it be found to have chosen the least restrictive alternative. ...

Appellees further urge that the Texas system is unconstitutionally arbitrary because it allows the availability of local taxable resources to turn on "happenstance." ... But any scheme of local taxation ... requires the establishment of jurisdictional boundaries that are inevitably arbitrary. It is equally inevitable that some localities are going to be blessed with more taxable assets than others. ...

Moreover, if local taxation for local expenditure is an unconstitutional method of providing for education then it may be an equally impermissible means of providing other necessary services customarily financed largely from local property taxes, including local police and fire protection, public health and hospitals, and public utility facilities of various kinds. We perceive no justification for such a severe denigration of local property taxation and control as would follow from appellees' contentions. ...

In sum, ... we cannot say that such disparities [among districts] are the product of a system that is so irrational as to be invidiously discriminatory. ... The Texas plan is not the result of hurried, ill-conceived legislation [or] of purposeful discrimination against any group or class. On the contrary, it is rooted in decades of experience in Texas and elsewhere, and in major part is the product of responsible studies by qualified people. ... We are unwilling to assume for ourselves a level of wisdom superior to that of legislators, scholars, and educational authorities in 49 States, especially where the alternatives proposed are only recently conceived and nowhere yet tested. The constitutional standard under the Equal Protection Clause is whether the challenged state action rationally furthers a legitimate state purpose or interest. We hold that the Texas plan abundantly satisfies this standard. ...

Reversed.

Mr. Justice **STEWART**, concurring. ...

Mr. Justice **BRENNAN**, dissenting. ...

Mr. Justice **WHITE**, with whom Mr. Justice **DOUGLAS** and Mr. Justice **BRENNAN** join, dissenting. ...

Mr. Justice **MARSHALL**, with whom Mr. Justice **DOUGLAS** concurs, dissenting. ...

... [T]he majority may believe that the Equal Protection Clause cannot be offended by substantially unequal state treatment of persons who are similarly situated so long as the State provides everyone with some unspecified amount of education which evidently is "enough." The basis for such a novel view is far from clear. It is, of course, true that the Constitution does not require precise equality in the treatment of all persons. ... But this Court has never suggested that because some "adequate" level of benefits is provided to all, discrimination in the provision of services is therefore constitutionally excusable. The Equal Protection Clause is not addressed to the minimal sufficiency but rather to the unjustifiable inequalities of state action. It mandates nothing less than that "all persons similarly circumstanced shall be treated alike." F.S. Royster Guano Co. v. Virginia (1920). ... I cannot accept [the majority's] emasculation of the Equal Protection Clause. ...

... The Court apparently seeks to establish today that equal protection cases fall into one of two neat categories which dictate the appropriate standard of review—strict scrutiny or mere rationality. But this Court's decisions ... defy such easy categorization. A principled reading of what this Court has done reveals that it has applied a spectrum of standards in reviewing discrimination allegedly violative of the Equal Protection Clause. This spectrum clearly comprehends variations in the degree of care with which the Court will scrutinize particular classifications, depending, I believe, on the constitutional and societal importance of the interest adversely affected and the recognized invidiousness of the basis upon which the particular classification is drawn. I find in fact that many of the Court's recent decisions embody the very sort of reasoned approach to equal protection analysis for which I previously argued. ... *Dandridge* (dissenting opinion).

I therefore cannot accept the majority's labored efforts to demonstrate that fundamental interests, which call for strict scrutiny of the challenged classification, encompass only established rights which we are somehow bound to recognize from the text of the Constitution itself. To be sure, some interests which the Court has deemed to be fundamental for purposes of equal protection analysis are themselves constitutionally protected rights. ... *Shapiro.* But it will not do to suggest that the "answer" to whether an interest is fundamental for purposes of equal protection analysis is *always* determined by whether that interest "is a right ... explicitly or implicitly guaranteed by the Constitution."

I would like to know where the Constitution guarantees the right to procreate, *Skinner,* or the right to vote in state elections, *e.g.,* Reynolds v. Sims (1964), or the right to an appeal from a criminal conviction, *e.g.,* Griffin v. Illinois (1956). These are instances in which, due to the importance of the interests at stake, the Court has displayed a strong concern with the existence of discriminatory state treatment. But the Court has never said or indicated that these are interests which independently enjoy full-blown constitutional protection. ...

The majority is, of course, correct when it suggests that the process of determining which interests are fundamental is a difficult one. But I do not ... accept the view that the process need necessarily degenerate into an unprincipled, subjective "picking-and-choosing" between various interests or that it must involve this Court in creating "substantive constitutional rights in the name of guaranteeing equal protection of the laws." Although not all fundamental interests are constitutionally guaranteed, the determination of which interests are fundamental should be firmly rooted in the text of the Constitution. The task in every case should be to determine the extent to which constitutionally guaranteed rights are dependent on interests not mentioned in the

Constitution. As the nexus between the specific constitutional guarantee and the nonconstitutional interest draws closer, the nonconstitutional interest becomes more fundamental and the degree of judicial scrutiny applied when the interest is infringed on a discriminatory basis must be adjusted accordingly. Thus, it cannot be denied that interests such as procreation, the exercise of the state franchise, and access to criminal appellate processes are not fully guaranteed to the citizen by our Constitution. But these interests have nonetheless been afforded special judicial consideration in the face of discrimination because they are, to some extent, interrelated with constitutional guarantees. ... Only if we closely protect the related interests from state discrimination do we ultimately ensure the integrity of the constitutional guarantee itself. ... [See, *e.g.*, Eisenstadt v. Baird (1972); Reed v. Reed (1971); and Weber v. Aetna Casualty & Surety Co. (1972)].

... In the context of economic interests, we find that discriminatory state action is almost always sustained, for such interests are generally far removed from constitutional guarantees. ... But the situation differs markedly when discrimination against important individual interests with constitutional implications and against particularly disadvantaged or powerless classes is involved. ...

... It is true that this Court has never deemed the provision of free public education to be required by the Constitution. ... Nevertheless, the fundamental importance of education is amply indicated by the prior decisions of this Court, by the unique status accorded public education by our society, and by the close relationship between education and some of our most basic constitutional values. ... Education directly affects the ability of a child to exercise his First Amendment interests, both as a source and as a receiver of information and ideas. ...

Of particular importance is the relationship between education and the political process. ... Education may instill the interest and provide the tools necessary for political discourse and debate. Indeed, it has frequently been suggested that education is the dominant factor affecting political consciousness and participation. ... [O]f most immediate and direct concern must be the demonstrated effect of education on the exercise of the franchise by the electorate. ... Data from the Presidential Election of 1968 clearly demonstrates a direct relationship between participation in the electoral process and level of educational attainment. ...

While ultimately disputing little of this, the majority seeks refuge in the fact that the Court has "never presumed to possess either the ability or the authority to guarantee to the citizenry the most *effective* speech or the most *informed* electoral choice." ... This serves only to blur what is in fact at stake. ... Appellees do not now seek the best education Texas might provide. They do seek, however, an end to state discrimination resulting from the unequal distribution of taxable district property wealth. ... As this Court held in *Brown*, the opportunity of education, "where the state has undertaken to provide it, is a right which must be made available to all on equal terms." The factors just considered ... compel us to recognize the fundamentality of education and to scrutinize with appropriate care the bases for state discrimination affecting equality of educational opportunity in Texas' school districts—a conclusion which is only strengthened when we consider the character of the classification in this case. ...

As the Court points out, ... no previous decision has deemed the presence of just a wealth classification to be sufficient basis to call forth rigorous judicial scrutiny of allegedly discriminatory state action. [This] may be explainable on a number of grounds. The "poor" may not be seen as politically powerless as certain discrete and insular minority groups. Personal poverty may entail much the same social stigma as historically attached to certain racial or ethnic groups. But personal poverty is not a permanent disability; its shackles may be escaped. Perhaps most importantly, though, personal wealth may not necessarily share the general irrelevance as a basis for legislative action that race or nationality is recognized to have. While the "poor" have frequently been a legally disadvantaged group, it cannot be ignored that social legislation must frequently take cognizance of the economic status of our citizens. Thus, we have generally gauged the invidiousness of wealth classifications with an awareness of the importance of the interests being affected and the relevance of personal wealth to those interests. See Harper v. Virginia Bd. of Elections [1966].

When evaluated with these considerations in mind, it seems to me that discrimination on the basis of group wealth in this case likewise calls for careful judicial scrutiny. First, ... while local district wealth may serve other interests, it bears no relationship whatsoever to the [important] interest of Texas school children in the educational opportunity afforded them by the State of Texas. ... Discrimination on the basis of group wealth may not, to be sure, reflect the social stigma frequently attached to personal poverty. Nevertheless, insofar as group wealth discrimination involves wealth over which the disadvantaged individual has no significant control, it represents in fact a more serious basis of discrimination than does personal wealth. ... Cf. *Weber*.

The disability of the disadvantaged class in this case extends as well into the political processes upon which we ordinarily rely as adequate for the protection and promotion of all interests. Here legislative realloca-tion of the State's property wealth must be sought in the face of inevitable opposition from significantly advantaged districts that have a strong vested interest in the preservation of the status quo, a problem not completely dissimilar to that faced by underrepresented districts prior to the Court's intervention in the process of reapportionment, see Baker v. Carr (1962).

Nor can we ignore the extent to which, in contrast to our prior decisions, the State is responsible for the wealth discrimination in this instance. ... The means for financing public education in Texas are selected and specified by the State. ...

... [Therefore,] both the nature of the interest and the classification dictate close judicial scrutiny of the purposes which Texas seeks to serve ... and of the means it has selected to serve that purpose. The only justification offered by appellants ... is local educational control. ... In Texas, [however,] statewide laws regulate in fact the most minute details of local public education. ... Moreover, even if we accept Texas' general dedication to local control in educational matters, it is difficult to find any evidence of such dedication with respect to fiscal matters. ... In fact [fiscal policy] is largely determined by the amount of taxable property located in the district—a factor over which local voters can exercise no control. ...

In my judgment, ... the State has selected means wholly inappropriate to secure its purported interest in assuring its school districts local fiscal control. ...

Editors' Notes

(1) **Query:** This dispute is basically about the state's distribution of public assets (tax monies). What, a *textualist* might ask, does the equal protection clause have to do with such a situation? What answer(s) would interpreters who follow other approaches offer?

(2) To some extent both Justices Powell and Marshall followed a *doctrinal approach* in *San Antonio*. Which offered the more accurate description of the doctrine(s) the Court *had* used in confronting various classifications? Which offered the more convincing prescription for how the Court *should* treat different classifications? One should reconsider these questions after reading the other cases on "semi-suspect" classifications, espec. Craig v. Boren (1976; reprinted above, p. 992), and Mississippi University for Women v. Hogan (1982; reprinted above, p. 997), as well as Cleburne v. Cleburne Living Center (1985; reprinted below, p. 1048). Although *Craig* appears earlier in this book, it was decided after *San Antonio*. To what extent did Powell change his mind in *Craig*?

(3) Marshall's formulation for the protection due listed and "unlisted interests" is famous though not altogether clear:

> Although not all fundamental interests are constitutionally guaranteed, the determination of which interests are fundamental should be firmly rooted in the text of the Constitution. The task in every case should be to determine the extent to which constitutionally guaranteed rights are dependent on interests not mentioned in the Constitution. As the nexus between the specific constitutional guarantee and the nonconstitutional interest draws closer, the nonconstitutional interest becomes more fundamental and the degree of judicial scrutiny applied when the interest is infringed on a discriminatory basis must be adjusted accordingly.

How can the "determination" of an interest not mentioned in the constitutional document be "firmly rooted in the text of the Constitution"? Marshall tried to answer these questions in his next two sentences. What sort of approach to constitutional interpretation did he follow? How convincing was his argument?

(4) Prior to *San Antonio,* the status of wealth as a nonsuspect classification was not nearly as clear as Powell claimed. See the discussion in the Introductory Essay, above, at p. 975. In addition, California's supreme court had invalidated, as a denial of equal protection, a financing plan similar to Texas's, Serrano v. Priest (1971); as had Michigan's Supreme Court, Milliken v. Green (1972); and, on state grounds, New Jersey's, Robinson v. Cahill (1973). Later, the Michigan Supreme Court granted a rehearing and vacated its earlier judgment, Milliken v. Green (1973), because of *San Antonio.* In Harris v. McRae (1980; reprinted below, p. 1271), the U.S. Supreme Court reaffirmed that wealth is not a suspect classification.

(5) **Query:** Are the problems the poor typically face problems of invidious discrimination against them or problems of a state's failing (or refusing) to provide certain basic goods or services for them? See John Hart Ely, *Democracy and Distrust* (Cambridge: Harvard University Press, 1980), p. 162. Does the constitutional text impose affirmative obligations upon government to provide basic goods or services? Where? Does the broader constitution? How? See Harris v. McRae (1980; reprinted below, p. 1271) and DeShaney v. Winnebago County Dep't of Social Services (1989; reprinted below, p. 1350).

(6) **Query:** How useful is Powell's test for deciding whether a claimed right, such as education, is fundamental for purposes of equal protection analysis? In Brown v. Board of Education (1954; reprinted above, p. 912), the Court said that "education is perhaps the most important function of state and local governments" and that the opportunity of an education, "where the state has undertaken to provide it, is a right which must be made available to all on equal terms." Powell quoted the former statement, but not the latter. Marshall emphasized the latter statement. Was *San Antonio* consistent with *Brown* 's view of education? Would it help here to distinguish between "fundamental rights," which the constitutional text or the broader constitution protects independently of the Equal Protection Clause, and "fundamental interests," which are not independently protected constitutional rights but which the government, if it undertakes to provide for them, must do so for all on equal terms? Did Powell acknowledge "fundamental rights" while ignoring or obliterating "fundamental interests"?

(7) **Query:** Did Powell's distinction between relative and absolute deprivation of education imply that the Equal Protection Clause is a "minimum" protection clause? What if a state abolished its system of public education altogether? Would its doing so deny equal protection? Would it deny due process?

(8) In 1989, the Texas Supreme Court invalidated the system of financing public education at issue in *San Antonio,* unanimously holding that the disparities in spending between rich and poor school districts violated the state constitution. Texas, which has no corporate or personal income taxes, adopted a new plan that shifted local property tax revenue from richer districts to poorer districts to make funding more equal statewide. The Texas Supreme Court invalidated three versions of such a plan, but upheld a tax-sharing school finance law in 1995.

(9) Among the more interesting analyses of the problems of wealth and equal protection are: Judith Areen and Leonard Ross, "The Rodriguez Case,"

1976 *Sup.Ct.Rev.* 33; Frank I. Michelman, "On Protecting the Poor through the Fourteenth Amendment," 83 *Harv.L.Rev.* 7 (1969); Frank I. Michelman, "Welfare Rights in a Constitutional Democracy," 1979 *Wash.U.L.Q.* 659; C. Herman Pritchett, *Constitutional Civil Liberties* (Englewood Cliffs, NJ: Prentice–Hall, 1984), pp. 322–324; David A. J. Richards, *Conscience and the Constitution* (Princeton: Princeton University Press, 1993), ch. 7; Laurence H. Tribe, *American Constitutional Law* (2d ed.; Mineola, NY: Foundation Press, 1988), ch. 16; and Ralph K. Winter, Jr., "Poverty, Economic Equality, and the Equal Protection Clause," 1972 *Sup.Ct.Rev.* 51.

"[T]he principal impact of the Hyde Amendment falls on the indigent. But that fact does not itself render the funding restriction constitutionally invalid, for this Court has held repeatedly that poverty, standing alone, is not a suspect classification."

HARRIS v. McRAE

448 U.S. 297, 100 S.Ct. 2671, 65 L.Ed.2d 784 (1980).

This decision, upholding a provision in an appropriation bill forbidding use of federal funds to finance abortions unless the pregnancy was caused by rape or was endangering the life of the pregnant woman, is reprinted below, p. 1271.

II. FUNDAMENTAL RIGHTS

A. Procreation

"We are dealing here with legislation which involves one of the basic civil rights of man. [S]trict scrutiny of the classification which a state makes in a sterilization law is essential, lest ... invidious discriminations are made against groups or types of individuals in violation of the constitutional guaranty of just and equal laws."—Justice DOUGLAS

"[T]he real question we have to consider is not one of equal protection, but whether the wholesale condemnation of a class to such an invasion of personal liberty, without opportunity to any individual to show that his is not the type of case which would justify resort to it, satisfies the demands of due process."—Chief Justice STONE

"There are limits to the extent to which a legislatively represented majority may conduct biological experi-

ments at the expense of the dignity and personality and natural powers of a minority—even those who have been guilty of what the majority define as crimes."—Justice JACKSON

SKINNER v. OKLAHOMA

316 U.S. 535, 62 S.Ct. 1110, 86 L.Ed. 1655 (1942).

In 1935 Oklahoma adopted a statute requiring sterilization of "habitual criminals"—persons convicted two or more times for some felonies involving moral turpitude. The act allowed a defendant an opportunity to be heard and a right to trial by jury; but the only issue triable was whether the defendant "may be rendered sexually sterile without detriment to his or her general health," not whether his or her criminal tendencies were inheritable. The statute excepted certain "white collar" crimes: "offenses arising out of the violation of the prohibitory laws [Oklahoma was a "dry" state then], revenue acts, embezzlement, or political offenses, shall not be considered to come or be considered within the terms of this Act." Buck v. Bell (1927; reprinted below, p. 1254) provided some constitutional support for the statute. There the Supreme Court had rejected challenges based on due process and equal protection and upheld compulsory sterilization of "mental defectives."

In 1926, Jack Skinner was convicted in Oklahoma of stealing chickens and in 1929 and 1934 of robbery with firearms. Because each of these felonies involved moral turpitude, the state began proceedings to order his sterilization. He challenged the substance and process of the statute as unconstitutional. After losing in state courts, he sought and obtained certiorari from the U.S. Supreme Court.

Mr. Justice **DOUGLAS** delivered the opinion of the Court. ...

This case touches a sensitive and important area of human rights. Oklahoma deprives certain individuals of a right which is basic to the perpetuation of a race—the right to have offspring. ...

... It is urged that the Act cannot be sustained as an exercise of the police power in view of the state of scientific authorities respecting inheritability of criminal traits. It is argued that due process is lacking because under this Act, unlike the act upheld in Buck v. Bell [1927], the defendant is given no opportunity to be heard on the issue as to whether he is the probable potential parent of socially undesirable offspring. ... We pass those points without intimating an opinion on them, for there is a feature of the Act which clearly condemns it. That is its failure to meet the requirements of the equal protection clause of the Fourteenth Amendment.

We do not stop to point out all of the inequalities in this Act. A few examples will suffice. ... [A clerk who embezzles money] is not subject to the pains and penalties of the Act no matter how large his embezzle-ments nor how frequent his convictions. A person who enters a chicken coop and steals chickens commits a felony; and he may be sterilized if he is thrice convicted. If, however, he is a bailee of the property and fraudulently appropriates it, he is an embezzler. Hence no matter how habitual his proclivities for embezzlement are and no matter how often his conviction, he may not be sterilized. ...

It was stated in *Buck* that the claim that state legislation violates the equal protection clause ... is "the usual last resort of constitutional arguments." Under our constitutional system the States in determining the reach and scope of particular legislation need not provide "abstract symmetry." They may mark and set apart the classes and types of problems according to the needs and as dictated or suggested by experience. ... Mr. Justice Holmes, speaking for the Court in Bain Peanut Co. v. Pinson [1931], stated, "We must remember that the machinery of government would not work if it were not allowed a little play in its joints." ... Thus, if we had here only a question as to a State's classification of crimes, such as embezzlement or larceny, no substantial federal question would be raised. ...

But the instant legislation runs afoul of the equal protection clause, though we give Oklahoma that large deference which the rule of the foregoing cases requires. We are dealing here with legislation which involves one of the basic civil rights of man. Marriage and procreation are fundamental to the very existence and survival of the race. The power to sterilize, if exercised, may have subtle, far-reaching and devastating effects. In evil or reckless hands it can cause races or types which are inimical to the dominant group to wither and disappear. There is no redemption for the individual whom the law touches. Any experiment which the State conducts is to his irreparable injury. He is forever deprived of a basic liberty. ... [S]trict scrutiny of the classification which a state makes in a sterilization law is essential, lest unwittingly or otherwise, invidious discriminations are made against groups or types of individuals in violation of the constitutional guaranty of just and equal laws. The guaranty of "equal protection of the laws is a pledge of the protection of equal laws." Yick Wo v. Hopkins [1886]. When the law lays an unequal hand on those who have committed intrinsically the same quality of offense and sterilizes one and not the other, it has made as invidious a discrimination as if it had selected a particular race or nationality for oppressive treatment. Sterilization of those who have thrice committed grand larceny with immunity for those who are embezzlers is a clear, pointed, unmistakable discrimination. Oklahoma makes no attempt to say that he who commits larceny by trespass or trick or fraud has biologically inheritable traits which he who commits embezzlement lacks. ... Only when it comes to sterilization are the pains and penalties of the law different. The equal protection clause would indeed be a formula of empty words if such conspicuous artificial lines could be drawn. In *Buck,* the Virginia [sterilization] statute was upheld though it applied only to feeble-minded persons in institutions of the State. But it was pointed out that "so far as the operations enable those who otherwise must be kept confined to be returned to the world, and thus open the asylum to others, the equality aimed at will be more nearly reached." Here there is no such saving feature. Embezzlers are forever free. Those who steal or take in other ways are not. ...

Reversed.

Mr. Chief Justice **STONE** concurring:

I concur in the result, but I am not persuaded that we are aided in reaching it by recourse to the equal protection clause. If Oklahoma may resort generally to the sterilization of criminals on the assumption that their propensities are transmissible to future generations by inheritance, I seriously doubt that the equal protection clause requires it to apply the measure to all criminals in the first instance, or to none.

Moreover, if we must presume that the legislature knows—what science has been unable to ascertain—that the criminal tendencies of any class of habitual offenders are transmissible regardless of the varying mental characteristics of its individuals, I should suppose that we must likewise presume that the legislature, in its wisdom, knows that the criminal tendencies of some classes of offenders are more likely to be transmitted than those of others. And so I think the real question we have to consider is not one of equal protection, but whether the wholesale condemnation of a class to such an invasion of personal liberty, without opportunity to any individual to show that his is not the type of case which would justify resort to it, satisfies the demands of due process.

There are limits to the extent to which the presumption of constitutionality can be pressed, especially where the liberty of the person is concerned (see United States v. Carolene Products Co., note 4 [1938]) and where the presumption is resorted to only to dispense with a procedure which the ordinary dictates of prudence would seem to demand for the protection of the individual from arbitrary action. Although petitioner here was given a hearing to ascertain whether sterilization would be detrimental to his health, he was given none to discover whether his criminal tendencies are of an inheritable type. Undoubtedly a state may, after appropriate inquiry, constitutionally interfere with the personal liberty of the individual to prevent the transmission by inheritance of his socially injurious tendencies. *Buck.* But until now we have not been called upon to say that it may do so without giving him a hearing and opportunity to challenge the existence as to him of the only facts which could justify so drastic a measure.

Science has found and the law has recognized that there are certain types of mental deficiency associated with delinquency which are inheritable. But the State does not contend—nor can there be any pretense—that either common knowledge or experience, or scientific investigation, has given assurance that the criminal tendencies of any class of habitual offenders are universally or even generally inheritable. In such circumstances, inquiry whether such is the fact in the case of any particular individual cannot rightly be dispensed with. ... A law which condemns, without hearing, all the individuals of a class to so harsh a measure as the present because some or even many merit condemnation, is lacking in the first principles of due process. And so, while the state may protect itself from the demonstrably inheritable tendencies of the individual which are injurious to society, the most elementary notions of due process would seem to require it to take appropriate steps to safeguard the liberty of the individual by affording him, before he is condemned to an irreparable injury in his person, some opportunity to show that he is without such inheritable tendencies. The state is called on to sacrifice no permissible end when it is required to reach its objective by a reasonable and just procedure adequate to safeguard rights of the individual which concededly the Constitution protects.

Mr. Justice **JACKSON** concurring:

I join the Chief Justice in holding that the hearings provided are too limited in the context of the present Act to afford due process of law. I also agree with the opinion of Mr. Justice Douglas that the scheme of classification set forth in the Act denies equal protection of the law. I disagree with the opinion of each in so far as it rejects or minimizes the grounds taken by the other. ...

There are limits to the extent to which a legislatively represented majority may conduct biological experiments at the expense of the dignity and personality and natural powers of a minority—even those who have been guilty of what the majority define as crimes. But this Act falls down before reaching this problem, which I mention only to avoid the implication that such a question may not exist because not discussed. On it I would also reserve judgment.

Editors' Notes

(1) *Skinner* represents the first time that the Court used the term "strict scrutiny" in a case involving equal protection. In *Carolene Products* Stone had spoken of "more exacting judicial scrutiny." *Skinner* is also the first case to intimate that the equal protection clause guarded against violations of fundamental rights as well as certain kinds of classifications.

(2) **Query:** Can paragraphs 2 and 3 of *Carolene Products* justify the outcome in *Skinner?* Can paragraph 1? Although Douglas intimates a concern regarding the potential danger of invidious discrimination by a dominant group against particular races or nationalities, Stone himself argued on grounds of procedural due process. Did the Court need a broader constitutionalist theory to justify *Skinner?* To what extent did Jackson's concurrence point toward such a theory?

(3) **Query:** Contrast the approaches to constitutional interpretation that Douglas, Stone, and Jackson followed. What did each assume "the Constitution" included? All three spoke of or hinted at the existence of a "fundamental right" to procreate. Where did each find that constitutional right? How did each justify its constitutionally protected status? It is interesting that the Court chose to use equal protection as the ground for decision rather than carrying through on Douglas's forthright statement that marriage and procreation were fundamental rights and holding that the state law unconstitutionally denied

those rights as a matter of substantive due process. Why might the Court have so chosen?

(4) Perhaps so soon after the Old Court's repudiation of substantive due process in West Coast Hotel v. Parrish (1937; reprinted below, p. 1123)—1937 was only five years past when *Skinner* came down—it would have been imprudent for the young justices to reinvoke that concept. Discussing *Skinner* twenty years later, Douglas said that he had thought from the beginning that it should be decided on equal-protection grounds. Stone and Roberts, the only two people from 1937 among the sitting justices, were both unhappy with the use of equal protection, but Roberts agreed not to go public with his doubts. "Murphy and Black and Frankfurter, Reed and I," Douglas recalled, "were very clear on the equal-protection point from the beginning." "Transcriptions of Conversations between Justice William O. Douglas and Prof. Walter F. Murphy," (Recorded 1961–63; Mudd Library, Princeton University), pp. 158–160.

(5) Douglas also reported that he did not want *Skinner* to disturb Buck v. Bell (1927). Might a feminist have a point in suggesting that the crucial difference between *Buck* and *Skinner* was that the first involved a woman, the second a man?

(6) Retrospectively, the Court has often construed *Skinner* as if it were a substantive due process case involving the fundamental right to procreate rather than an equal protection case. See, *e.g.*, Loving v. Virginia (1967; reprinted above, p. 926); Roe v. Wade (1973; reprinted below, p. 1258); Moore v. East Cleveland (1977; reprinted below, p. 1314), notwithstanding Douglas's eschewal of that straightforward option (see note (4) above).

B. Voting

"Especially since the right to exercise the franchise in a free and unimpaired manner is preservative of other basic civil and political rights, any alleged infringement of the right of citizens to vote must be carefully and meticulously scrutinized."

REYNOLDS v. SIMS
377 U.S. 533, 84 S.Ct. 1362, 12 L.Ed.2d 506 (1964).

This decision, which applied the equal protection principle of "one person, one vote" to invalidate Alabama's legislative apportionment scheme for its state legislature, is reprinted above, p. 777.

"While the right to vote in federal elections is conferred by Art I, § 2, of the Constitution, the right to vote in state elections is nowhere expressly mentioned. ... [But] once the franchise is granted to the electorate,

lines may not be drawn which are inconsistent with the Equal Protection Clause."

HARPER v. VIRGINIA STATE BOARD OF ELECTIONS
383 U.S. 663, 86 S.Ct. 1079, 16 L.Ed.2d 169 (1966).

This case, invalidating as a denial of equal protection Virginia's law requiring that voters pay a poll tax of $1.50 as a qualification for voting in state elections, is reprinted above, p. 225.

C. Travel

"Since the classification here touches on the fundamental right of interstate movement, its constitutionality must be judged by the stricter standard of whether it promotes a *compelling* state interest."—Justice BRENNAN

"The Court today does *not* 'pick out particular human activities, characterize them as "fundamental," and give them added protection. ...' [T]he Court simply recognizes ... an established constitutional right, and gives to that right no less protection than the Constitution itself demands."—Justice STEWART

"Since the congressional decision is rational and the restriction on travel insubstantial, I conclude that residence requirements can be imposed by Congress. ..."—Chief Justice WARREN

"[I] know of nothing which entitles this Court to pick out particular human activities, characterize them as 'fundamental,' and give them added protection under an unusually stringent equal protection test."—Justice HARLAN

SHAPIRO v. THOMPSON
394 U.S. 618, 89 S.Ct. 1322, 22 L.Ed.2d 600 (1969).

Connecticut, Pennsylvania, and the District of Columbia denied welfare benefits to people who had not resided in the jurisdiction for at least one year. Poor people filed suits in federal district courts, and each court held the denial to violate equal protection. The states and the District appealed to the Supreme Court.

Mr. Justice **BRENNAN** delivered the opinion of the Court. ...

II

... [T]he effect of the waiting-period ... is to create two classes of needy resident families indistinguishable from each other except that one is composed of residents who have resided a year or more, and the second of residents who have resided less than a year, in the jurisdiction. On the basis of this sole difference the first class is granted and the second class is denied welfare aid upon which may depend the ability of the families to obtain the very means to subsist—food, shelter, and other necessities of life. ... [A]ppellees' central contention is that the statutory prohibition of benefits to residents of less than a year creates a classification which constitutes an invidious discrimination denying them equal protection of the laws. We agree. ...

III

Primarily, appellants justify the waiting-period requirement as a protective device to preserve the fiscal integrity of state public assistance programs. It is asserted that people who require welfare assistance during their first year of residence in a State are likely to become continuing burdens on state welfare programs. Therefore, the argument runs, if such people can be deterred from entering the jurisdiction by denying them welfare benefits during the first year, state programs to assist long-time residents will not be impaired by a substantial influx of indigent newcomers. ... We do not doubt that the one-year waiting-period device is well suited to discourage the influx of poor families in need of assistance. ...

This Court long ago recognized that the nature of our Federal Union and our constitutional concepts of personal liberty unite to require that all citizens be free to travel throughout the length and breadth of our land uninhibited by statutes, rules, or regulations which unreasonably burden or restrict this movement. That proposition was early stated by Chief Justice Taney in the Passenger Cases (1849):

> For all the great purposes for which the Federal government was formed, we are one people, with one common country. We are all citizens of the United States; and, as members of the same community, must have the right to pass and repass through every part of it without interruption, as freely as in our own States.

We have no occasion to ascribe the source of this right to travel interstate to a particular constitutional provision.[1] It suffices that, as Mr. Justice Stewart said for the Court in United States v. Guest (1966):

> The constitutional right to travel from one State to another ... occupies a position fundamental to the concept of our Federal Union. It is a right that has been firmly established and repeatedly recognized. ...

---

1. In Corfield v. Coryell (1825) [Washington, J., on circuit], Paul v. Virginia (1869), and Ward v. Maryland (1871), the right to travel interstate was grounded upon the Privileges and Immunities Clause of Art. IV, § 2. See also Slaughter–House Cases (1873); Twining v. New Jersey (1908). In Edwards v. California (1941) (Douglas and Jackson, JJ., concurring), and Twining v. New Jersey reliance was placed on the Privileges and Immunities Clause of the Fourteenth Amendment. See also Crandall v. Nevada (1868). In Edwards and the Passenger Cases a commerce clause approach was employed. See also Kent v. Dulles (1958); Aptheker v. Secretary of State (1964); Zemel v. Rusk (1965), where the freedom of Americans to travel outside the country was grounded upon the Due Process Clause of the Fifth Amendment. [Footnote by the Court.]

Thus, the purpose of deterring the in-migration of indigents cannot serve as justification for the classification created by the one-year waiting period, since that purpose is constitutionally impermissible. If a law has "no other purpose ... than to chill the assertion of constitutional rights by penalizing those who choose to exercise them, then it [is] patently unconstitutional." United States v. Jackson (1968).

Alternatively, appellants argue that ... the challenged classification may be justified as a permissible state attempt to discourage those indigents who would enter the State solely to obtain larger benefits. We observe first that none of the statutes before us is tailored to serve that objective. ... In actual operation ... the three statutes enact what in effect are nonrebuttable presumptions that every applicant for assistance in his first year of residence came to the jurisdiction solely to obtain higher benefits. Nothing whatever in any of these records supplies any basis in fact for such a presumption. More fundamentally, a State may no more try to fence out those indigents who seek higher welfare benefits than it may try to fence out indigents generally. ...

Appellants argue further that the challenged classification may be sustained as an attempt to distinguish between new and old residents on the basis of the contribution they have made to the community through the payment of taxes. ... Appellants' reasoning would logically permit the State to bar new residents from schools, parks, and libraries or deprive them of police and fire protection. Indeed it would permit the State to apportion all benefits and services according to the past tax contributions of its citizens. The Equal Protection Clause prohibits such an apportionment of state services.

We recognize that a State has a valid interest in preserving the fiscal integrity of its programs. It may legitimately attempt to limit its expenditures, whether for public assistance, public education, or any other program. But a State may not accomplish such a purpose by invidious distinctions between classes of its citizens. It could not, for example, reduce expenditures for education by barring indigent children from its schools. ...

IV

Appellants next advance as justification certain administrative and related governmental objectives ... They argue that the requirement (1) facilitates the planning of the welfare budget; (2) provides an objective test of residency; (3) minimizes the opportunity for recipients fraudulently to receive payments from more than one jurisdiction; and (4) encourages early entry of new residents into the labor force.

At the outset, we reject appellants' argument that a mere showing of a rational relationship between the waiting period and these four admittedly permissible state objectives will suffice to justify the classification. See Lindsley v. Natural Carbonic Gas Co. (1911); McGowan v. Maryland (1961). ... [I]n moving from State to State or to the District of Columbia appellees were exercising a constitutional right, and any classification which serves to penalize the exercise of that right, unless shown to be necessary to promote a *compelling* governmental interest, is unconstitutional. Cf. Skinner v. Oklahoma (1942); Korematsu v. United States (1944).

The argument that the waiting-period requirement facilitates budget predictability is wholly unfounded. The records in all [these] cases are utterly devoid of evidence that either State or the District of Columbia in fact uses the one-year requirement as a means to predict the number of people who will require assistance in the budget year. ... [T]he claim ... is plainly belied by the fact that the requirement is not also imposed on applicants who are long-term residents, the group that receives the bulk of welfare payments. ...

The argument that the waiting period serves as an administratively efficient rule of thumb for determining residency similarly will not withstand scrutiny. The residence requirement and the one-year waiting-period requirement are distinct and independent prerequisites for assistance under these three statutes, and the facts relevant to the determination of each are directly examined by the welfare authorities. ... Similarly, there is no need for a State to use the one-year waiting period as a safeguard against fraudulent receipt of benefits; for less drastic means are available, and are employed, to minimize that hazard. ... [T]he investigations now conducted entail inquiries into facts relevant to that subject. ... Pennsylvania suggests that the one-year waiting period is justified as a means of encouraging new residents to join the labor force promptly. But this logic would also require a similar waiting period for long-term residents of the State. ...

We conclude therefore that appellants in these cases do not use and have no need to use the one-year requirement for the governmental purposes suggested. Thus, even under traditional equal protection tests a classification of welfare applicants according to whether they have lived in the State for one year would seem irrational and unconstitutional. But, of course, the traditional criteria do not apply in these cases. Since the classification here touches on the fundamental right of interstate movement, its constitutionality must be judged by the stricter standard of whether it promotes a *compelling* state interest. Under this standard, the waiting-period requirement clearly violates the Equal Protection Clause.[2]

V

Connecticut and Pennsylvania argue, however, that ... Congress expressly approved the imposition of the requirement by the States as part of the jointly funded AFDC program. ... But even if we were to assume, arguendo, that Congress did approve the imposition of a one-

---

2. We imply no view of the validity of waiting-period *or* residence requirements determining eligibility to vote, eligibility for tuition-free education, to obtain a license to practice a profession, to hunt or fish, and so forth. Such requirements may promote compelling state interests on the one hand, or, on the other, may not be penalties upon the exercise of the constitutional right of interstate travel. [Footnote by the Court.]

year waiting period, ... [t]he provision ... would be unconstitutional. Congress may not authorize the States to violate the Equal Protection Clause. ...

Affirmed.

Mr. Justice **STEWART,** concurring.

In joining the opinion of the Court, I add a word in response to the dissent of my Brother Harlan. ...

The Court today does *not* "pick out particular human activities, characterize them as 'fundamental,' and give them added protection. ..." To the contrary, the Court simply recognizes, as it must, an established constitutional right, and gives to that right no less protection than the Constitution itself demands.

Mr. Chief Justice **WARREN,** with whom Mr. Justice **BLACK** joins, dissenting. ...

II

Congress has imposed a residence requirement in the District of Columbia and authorized the States to impose similar requirements. The issue before us must therefore be framed in terms of whether Congress may create minimal residence requirements, not whether the States, acting alone, may do so. ... Appellees insist that ... Congress, even under its "plenary" power to control interstate commerce, is constitutionally prohibited from imposing residence requirements. ...

... The core inquiry is "the extent of the governmental restriction imposed" and the "extent of the necessity for the restriction". ... [T]ravel itself is not prohibited. Any burden inheres solely in the fact that a potential welfare recipient might take into consideration the loss of welfare benefits for a limited period of time if he changes his residence. ... [A]ppellees themselves assert there is evidence that few welfare recipients have in fact been deterred by residence requirements. ...

The insubstantiality of the restriction imposed by residence requirements must then be evaluated in light of the possible congressional reasons for such requirements. See, *e.g., McGowan.* Our cases require only that Congress have a rational basis for finding that a chosen regulatory scheme is necessary to the furtherance of interstate commerce. See, *e.g.,* Katzenbach v. McClung (1964); Wickard v. Filburn (1942). Certainly, a congressional finding that residence requirements allowed each State to concentrate its resources upon new and increased programs of rehabilitation ultimately resulting in an enhanced flow of commerce as the economic condition of welfare recipients progressively improved is rational and would justify imposition of residence requirements under the Commerce Clause. ...

... Since the congressional decision is rational and the restriction on travel insubstantial, I conclude that residence requirements can be imposed by Congress as an exercise of its power to control interstate commerce consistent with the constitutionally guaranteed right to travel. . . .

The Court's decision reveals only the top of the iceberg. Lurking beneath are the multitude of situations in which States have imposed residence requirements including eligibility to vote, to engage in certain professions or occupations or to attend a state-supported university. Although the Court takes pains to avoid acknowledging the ramifications of its decision, its implications cannot be ignored. I dissent.

Mr. Justice **HARLAN,** dissenting. . . .

II . . .

The "compelling interest" doctrine, which today is articulated more explicitly than ever before, constitutes an increasingly significant exception to the long-established rule that a statute does not deny equal protection if it is rationally related to a legitimate governmental objective. The "compelling interest" doctrine has two branches. The branch which requires that classifications based upon "suspect" criteria be supported by a compelling interest apparently had its genesis in case[s] involving racial classifications, which have, at least since *Korematsu,* been regarded as inherently "suspect." . . . The criterion of "wealth" apparently was added to the list of "suspects" as an alternative justification for the rationale in Harper v. Virginia Bd. of Elections (1966). . . . Today the list apparently has been further enlarged to include classifications based upon recent interstate movement, and perhaps those based upon the exercise of *any* constitutional right. . . .

I think that this branch of the "compelling interest" doctrine is sound when applied to racial classifications, for historically the Equal Protection Clause was largely a product of the desire to eradicate legal distinctions founded upon race. However, I believe that the more recent extensions have been unwise. For the reasons stated in my dissenting opinion in *Harper,* I do not consider wealth a "suspect" statutory criterion. And when, as in the present case, a classification is based upon the exercise of rights guaranteed against state infringement by the Federal Constitution, then there is no need for any resort to the Equal Protection Clause; in such instances, this Court may properly and straightforwardly invalidate any undue burden upon those rights under the Fourteenth Amendment's Due Process Clause.

The second branch of the "compelling interest" principle is even more troublesome. For it has been held that a statutory classification is subject to the "compelling interest" test if the result of the classification may be to affect a "fundamental right," regardless of the basis of the classification. [*Skinner*; Reynolds v. Sims (1964); *Harper*]. . . . [This rule] has reappeared today in the Court's cryptic suggestion that the "compelling interest" test is applicable merely because the result of the classification may be to deny the appellees "food, shelter, and other necessities of life," as well as in the Court's statement that "[s]ince the classification here touches on the fundamental right of interstate movement, its constitutionality must be judged by the stricter standard of *whether* it promotes a *compelling* state interest."

I think this branch of the "compelling interest" doctrine ... is unfortunate because it creates an exception which threatens to swallow the standard equal protection rule. Virtually every state statute affects important rights. ... This branch of the doctrine is also unnecessary. When the right affected is one assured by the Federal Constitution, any infringement can be dealt with under the Due Process Clause. But when a statute affects only matters not mentioned in the Federal Constitution and is not arbitrary or irrational, I ... know of nothing which entitles this Court to pick out particular human activities, characterize them as "fundamental," and give them added protection under an unusually stringent equal protection test. ...

... If the issue is regarded purely as one of equal protection, ... this nonracial classification should be judged by ordinary equal protection standards. ... In light of [the] undeniable relation of residence requirements to valid legislative aims, it cannot be said that the requirements are "arbitrary" or "lacking in rational justification." ...

III

The next issue ... is whether a one-year welfare residence requirement amounts to an undue burden upon the right of interstate travel [and thus a denial of due process. The decisive question is] whether the governmental interests served by residence requirements outweigh the burden imposed upon the right to travel. In my view, a number of considerations militate in favor of constitutionality. ... This is not ... an instance in which legislatures have acted without mature deliberation.

... Today's decision, it seems to me, reflects to an unusual degree the current notion that this Court possesses a peculiar wisdom all its own whose capacity to lead this Nation out of its present troubles is contained only by the limits of judicial ingenuity in contriving new constitutional principles to meet each problem as it arises. For anyone who, like myself, believes that it is an essential function of this Court to maintain the constitutional divisions between state and federal authority and among the three branches of the Federal Government, today's decision is a step in the wrong direction. This resurgence of the expansive view of "equal protection" carries the seeds of more judicial interference with the state and federal legislative process, much more indeed than does the judicial application of "due process" according to traditional concepts (see my dissenting opinion in Duncan v. Louisiana (1968)), about which some members of this Court have expressed fears as to its potentialities for setting us judges "at large." I consider it particularly unfortunate that this judicial roadblock to the powers of Congress in this field should occur at the very threshold of the current discussions regarding the "federalizing" of these aspects of welfare relief.

Editors' Notes

(1) **Query:** What is the difference between a "fundamental right" and a mere "right"? Does the fact that the constitutional text mentions a right make it fundamental? If not, what does? More specifically, in *Shapiro*, Justice Brennan stressed the existence of a "fundamental right" to travel. Where did he find that right? In the plain words of the text? In its structure? In the structure of the political system? In the purpose(s) of the text or the broader constitution? In political theory? In judicially created doctrine? Which of these are legitimate sources of constitutional rights, fundamental or otherwise?

(2) **Query:** Justice Stewart's opinion posed much the same question: The "Court," he said emphatically, "simply recognizes ... an established constitutional right. ..." How does the Court "recognize" such a right?

(3) **Query:** Compare Crandall v. Nevada (1868; reprinted above, p. 543), cited in *Shapiro,* where the Court in part based the right to travel on "the right to come to the seat of [national] government to assert any claim he may have upon that government." Did that formulation anticipate the theme of paragraph 2 of *Carolene Products?* John Hart Ely would base the right to travel or relocate on paragraph 3: "a dissenting member for whom the 'voice' option [paragraph 2] seems unavailing should have the option of exiting and relocating in a community whose values he or she finds more compatible." *Democracy and Distrust* (Cambridge: Harvard University Press, 1980), p. 179.

(4) **Query:** What sort of approach(es) to constitutional interpretation did Chief Justice Warren use in his dissent? Justice Harlan? How, if at all, did their visions of WHAT is "the Constitution" differ from each other's and from Brennan's?

(5) **Query:** Compare Harlan's dissenting remarks here, "The criterion of wealth was apparently added to the list of 'suspects' as an alternative justification for the rationale in Harper v. Virginia Board of Elections" (1966; reprinted above, p. 225), with the Court's subsequent claim in San Antonio v. Rodriguez (1973; reprinted above, p. 1002) that it had never held wealth to be a suspect classification. And contrast Brennan's remark here about "food, shelter, and other necessities of life." Was he intimating the existence of a fundamental constitutional right to the means of subsistence?

(6) Problems of the right to travel, residency requirements, and state benefits reserved to state citizens raise the question of the meaning of national citizenship under the opening clause of the Fourteenth Amendment ("All persons born or naturalized in the United States ... are citizens of the United States and of the State wherein they reside") and Article IV, § 2 ("The citizens of each State shall be entitled to all privileges and immunities of citizens in the several States"). For discussions, see: C. Herman Pritchett, *Constitutional Law of the Federal System* (Englewood Cliffs, NJ: Prentice–Hall, 1984), pp. 83–86; and Laurence H. Tribe, *American Constitutional Law* (2d ed.; Mineola, NY: Foundation Press, 1988), §§ 6–34 to 6–35.

(7) *Shapiro* concerned only the right to travel within the United States. For decisions on foreign travel, see Haig v. Agee (1981), upholding revocation

of a citizen's passport for reasons of national security, and Regan v. Wald (1984) sustaining the Treasury Department's authority under the Trading with the Enemy Act to ban travel to Cuba.

D. Welfare?

"In the area of economics and social welfare, a State does not violate the Equal Protection Clause merely because the classifications made by its laws are imperfect."—Justice STEWART

"[C]oncentration must be placed upon the character of the classification in question, the relative importance to individuals in the class discriminated against of the governmental benefits that they do not receive, and the asserted state interests in support of the classification."—Justice MARSHALL

DANDRIDGE v. WILLIAMS

397 U.S. 471, 90 S.Ct. 1153, 25 L.Ed.2d 491 (1970).

Under the joint federal-state program of Aid to Families with Dependent Children (AFDC), Maryland provided a sliding scale of payments to poor families. The exact amount depended on the number of children in the family and an administrative determination of the help the family needed to achieve a minimum standard of living. In no case, however, could the welfare payment exceed $250 a month. Linda Williams and others sued in a federal district court, attacking the regulations setting a maximum to the grant as violating the basic federal statute and denying members of large families equal protection. The district court agreed on both issues and Maryland appealed to the Supreme Court.

Mr. Justice **STEWART** delivered the opinion of the Court. ...

I

[Stewart concluded that Maryland's policy did not conflict with federal statutory provisions.]

II

... The District Court ... held that the regulation "is invalid on its face for overreaching"—that it violates the Equal Protection Clause "[b]ecause it cuts too broad a swath on an indiscriminate basis as applied to the entire group of AFDC eligibles to which it purports to apply. ..."

If this were a case involving government action claimed to violate the First Amendment guarantee of free speech, a finding of "overreaching" would be significant and might be crucial. For when otherwise valid governmental regulation sweeps so broadly as to impinge upon activity protected by the First Amendment, its very overbreadth may make it unconstitutional. See, *e.g.*, Shelton v. Tucker [1960]. But ... here we deal with state regulation in the social and economic field, not affecting freedoms guaranteed by the Bill of Rights, and claimed to violate the Fourteenth Amendment only because the regulation results in some disparity in grants of welfare payments to the largest AFDC families.[1] For this Court to approve the invalidation of state economic or social regulation as "overreaching" would be far too reminiscent of an era when the Court thought the Fourteenth Amendment gave it power to strike down state laws "because they may be unwise, improvident, or out of harmony with a particular school of thought." Williamson v. Lee Optical [1955]. That era long ago passed into history. Ferguson v. Skrupa [1963].

In the area of economics and social welfare, a State does not violate the Equal Protection Clause merely because the classifications made by its laws are imperfect. If the classification has some "reasonable basis," it does not offend the Constitution simply because the classification "is not made with mathematical nicety or because in practice it results in some inequality." Lindsley v. Natural Carbonic Gas Co. [1911]. ... "A statutory discrimination will not be set aside if any state of facts reasonably may be conceived to justify it." McGowan v. Maryland [1961].

To be sure, the cases ... enunciating this fundamental standard ... have in the main involved state regulation of business or industry. The administration of public welfare assistance, by contrast, involves the most basic economic needs of impoverished human beings. We recognize the dramatically real factual difference between the cited cases and this one, but we can find no basis for applying a different constitutional standard. ...

Under this long-established meaning of the Equal Protection Clause, it is clear that the Maryland maximum grant regulation is constitutionally valid. ... By combining a limit on the recipient's grant with permission to retain money earned, without reduction in the amount of the grant, Maryland provides an incentive to seek gainful employment. And by keying the maximum family AFDC grants to the minimum wage a steadily employed head of a household receives, the State maintains some semblance of an equitable balance between families on welfare and those supported by an employed breadwinner.

It is true that in some AFDC families there may be no person who is employable. It is also true that with respect to AFDC families whose determined standard of need is below the regulatory maximum, ... the employment incentive is absent. But the Equal Protection Clause does not require that a State must choose between attacking every aspect of a

---

1. Cf. Shapiro v. Thompson [1969], where, by contrast, the Court found state interference with the constitutionally protected freedom of interstate travel. [Footnote by the Court.]

problem or not attacking the problem at all. It is enough that the State's action be rationally based and free from invidious discrimination. The regulation before us meets that test.

We do not decide today that the Maryland regulation is wise, that it best fulfills the relevant social and economic objectives that Maryland might ideally espouse, or that a more just and humane system could not be devised. ... [T]he intractable economic, social, and even philosophical problems presented by public welfare assistance programs are not the business of this Court. The Constitution may impose certain procedural safeguards upon systems of welfare administration, Goldberg v. Kelly [1970]. But [it] does not empower this Court to second-guess state officials charged with the difficult responsibility of allocating limited public welfare funds among the myriad of potential recipients. ...

[*Reversed.*]

Mr. Justice **BLACK,** with whom the Chief Justice [**BURGER**] joins, concurring. ...

Mr. Justice **HARLAN,** concurring. ...

Mr. Justice **DOUGLAS,** dissenting. ...

On the basis of the inconsistency of the Maryland maximum grant regulation with the [federal statute], I would affirm the judgment below.

Mr. Justice **MARSHALL,** whom Mr. Justice **BRENNAN** joins, dissenting.

For the reason stated by Mr. Justice Douglas ... I believe that the Court has erroneously concluded that Maryland's maximum grant regulation is consistent with the federal statute. ... More important in the long run ... is the Court's emasculation of the Equal Protection Clause as a constitutional principle applicable to the area of social welfare administration. ...

The Maryland AFDC program in its basic structure operates uniformly with regard to all needy children by taking into account the basic subsistence needs of all eligible individuals in the formulation of the standards of need for families of various sizes. However, superimposed upon this uniform system is the maximum grant regulation, the operative effect of which is to create two classes of needy children and two classes of eligible families: those small families and their members who receive payments to cover their subsistence needs and those large families who do not. ...

... [A]s a general principle, individuals should not be afforded different treatment by the State unless there is a relevant distinction between them. ... Consequently, the State may not, in the provision of important services or the distribution of governmental payments, supply benefits to some individuals while denying them to others who are similarly situated. See, *e.g.*, Griffin v. County School Board of Prince Edward County (1964).

In the instant case, the only distinction between those children with respect to whom assistance is granted and those children who are denied such assistance is the size of the family into which the child permits himself to be born. The class of individuals with respect to whom payments are actually made (the first four or five eligible dependent children in a family), is grossly underinclusive in terms of the class that the AFDC program was designed to assist, namely, *all* needy dependent children. Such underinclusiveness ... [compels] the State to come forward with a persuasive justification for the classification.

The Court never undertakes to inquire for such a justification; rather it avoids the task by focusing upon the abstract dichotomy between two different approaches to equal protection problems. ... Under the so-called "traditional test," a classification is said to be permissible ... unless it is "without any reasonable basis." On the other hand, if the classification affects a "fundamental right," then the state interest in perpetuating the classification must be "compelling" in order to be sustained.

This case simply defies easy characterization in terms of one or the other of these "tests." The cases relied on by the Court in which a "mere rationality" test was actually used are most accurately described as involving the application of equal protection reasoning to the regulation of business interests. The extremes to which the Court has gone in dreaming up rational bases for state regulation in that area may in many instances be ascribed to a healthy revulsion from the Court's earlier excesses in using the Constitution to protect interests that have more than enough power to protect themselves in the legislative halls. This case, involving the literally vital interests of a powerless minority—poor families without breadwinners—is far removed from the area of business regulation, as the Court concedes. Why then is the standard used in those cases imposed here? We are told no more than that this case falls in "the area of economics and social welfare." ...

In my view, equal protection analysis of this case is not appreciably advanced by the a priori definition of a "right," fundamental or otherwise. Rather, concentration must be placed upon the character of the classification in question, the relative importance to individuals in the class discriminated against of the governmental benefits that they do not receive, and the asserted state interests in support of the classification. ...[1]

It is the individual interests here at stake that, as the Court concedes, most clearly distinguished this case from the "business regula-

---

1. This is essentially what this Court has done in applying equal protection concepts in numerous cases, though the various aspects of the approach appear with a greater or lesser degree of clarity in particular cases. See, *e.g.*, McLaughlin v. Florida [1964]; Carrington v. Rash (1965); Douglas v. California (1963); Skinner v. Oklahoma [1942]. ... [Footnote by Justice Marshall.]

tion" equal protection cases. AFDC support to needy dependent children provides the stuff that sustains those children's lives: food, clothing, shelter. And this Court has already recognized several times that when a benefit, even a "gratuitous" benefit, is necessary to sustain life, stricter constitutional standards, both procedural and substantive, are applied to the deprivation of that benefit.[2]

Nor is the distinction upon which the deprivation is here based—the distinction between large and small families—one that readily commends itself as a basis for determining which children are to have support approximating subsistence and which are not. Indeed, governmental discrimination between children on the basis of a factor over which they have no control—the number of their brothers and sisters—bears some resemblance to the classification between legitimate and illegitimate children which we condemned as a violation of the Equal Protection Clause in Levy v. Louisiana (1968).

The asserted state interests in the maintenance of the maximum grant regulation, on the other hand, are hardly clear. ... Maryland has urged that [that] regulation serves to maintain a rough equality between [minimum] wage earning families and AFDC families, thereby increasing the political support for—or perhaps reducing the opposition to—the AFDC program. ... The only question presented here is whether, having once undertaken such a program, the State may arbitrarily select from among the concededly eligible those to whom it will provide benefits. And it is too late to argue that political expediency will sustain discrimination not otherwise supportable. Cf. Cooper v. Aaron (1958).

... [I]t cannot suffice merely to invoke the spectre of the past and to recite from Lindsley and Williamson to decide the case. Appellees are not a gas company or an optical dispenser; they are needy dependent children and families who are discriminated against by the State. The basis of that discrimination—the classification of individuals into large and small families—is too arbitrary and too unconnected to the asserted rationale, the impact on those discriminated against—the denial of even a subsistence existence—too great, and the supposed interests served too contrived and attenuated to meet the requirements of the Constitution. ...

Editors' Notes

(1) **Query:** Would a close reading of the equal protection clause help settle this case? A close reading of the Fourteenth Amendment? Of the entire constitutional text? An analysis of the political system? (Recall Justice Harlan's reference in Shapiro, above at p. 1019, to the federal nature of that system.) What about a careful analysis of the political theories that underpin the constitutional structure?

---

2. [Cases such as Goldberg v. Kelly (1970) and Shapiro v. Thompson (1969)] ... suggest that whether or not there is a constitutional "right" to subsistence ... deprivations of benefits necessary for subsistence will receive closer constitutional scrutiny, under both the Due Process and Equal Protection Clauses, than will deprivations of less essential forms of government entitlements. [Footnote by Justice Marshall.]

(2) **Query:** Did Stewart try to identify a "fundamental right" or a "suspect classification" that might have triggered strict scrutiny? What fundamental right might have been involved?

(3) **Query:** Are there any bases in the constitutional text besides equal protection for recognizing a right to welfare? In the Ninth Amendment? The Preamble? The Declaration of Independence? See Charles L. Black, Jr., "Further Reflections on the Constitutional Justice of Livelihood," 86 *Colum.L.Rev.* 1103 (1986). In democratic theory? More specifically in a theory of *reinforcing representative democracy*? See Frank I. Michelman, "Welfare Rights in a Constitutional Democracy," 1979 *Wash.U.L.Q.* 659. In constitutionalism?

(4) Compare the spectrum or continuum for classifications and rights that Marshall's dissent here suggests with the fuller statement of that position he articulated in his dissent in San Antonio v. Rodriguez (1973; reprinted above, p. 1002).

(5) Lindsey v. Normet (1972) refused to find constitutional protection for a right to decent housing. For the Court, Justice White, echoing Harlan's dissent in *Shapiro*, wrote: "[T]he Constitution does not provide judicial remedies for every social and economic ill. ... Absent constitutional mandate, the assurance of adequate housing and the definition of landlord-tenant relationships are legislative, not judicial, functions. ..."

(6) In *Dandridge* Stewart referred to procedural safeguards surrounding governmental welfare programs, citing Goldberg v. Kelly (1970), the leading case. It ruled that the interest of a person in continued receipt of welfare benefits was a "statutory entitlement" that constituted "property" within the meaning of the Due Process Clause and therefore that before a state could terminate welfare payments it had to accord the person affected a hearing. For a discussion of later cases, see Laurence H. Tribe, *American Constitutional Law* (2d ed.; Mineola, NY: Foundation Press, 1988), ch. 10. See also "Symposium: The Legacy of Goldberg v. Kelly: A Twenty Year Perspective," 56 *Brooklyn L.Rev.* 729 (1990).

————

E. Education?

"It is not the province of this Court to create substantive constitutional rights in the name of guaranteeing equal protection of the laws. Thus the key to discovering whether education is 'fundamental' ... lies in assessing whether there is a right to education explicitly or implicitly guaranteed by the Constitution."

SAN ANTONIO SCHOOL DISTRICT v. RODRIGUEZ
411 U.S. 1, 93 S.Ct. 1278, 36 L.Ed.2d 16 (1973).

This case, upholding Texas' system of financing public education against challenges that it involved an unconstitutional wealth-based classification and that it impinged upon a fundamental right to education, is reprinted above, p. 1002.

"Public education is not a 'right' granted to individuals by the Constitution. But neither is it merely some governmental 'benefit' indistinguishable from other forms of social welfare legislation."

PLYLER v. DOE

457 U.S. 202, 102 S.Ct. 2382, 72 L.Ed.2d 786 (1982).

This case, invalidating as a denial of equal protection a Texas statute withholding state funds for education of children of illegal aliens and denying enrollment to such children, is reprinted below, p. 1040.

F.   Marriage

"The Fourteenth Amendment requires that the freedom of choice to marry not be restricted by invidious racial discriminations."

LOVING v. VIRGINIA

388 U.S. 1, 87 S.Ct. 1817, 18 L.Ed.2d 1010 (1967).

This decision, striking down Virginia's statute forbidding interracial marriage, is reprinted above, at p. 926.

"When a statutory classification significantly interferes with the exercise of a fundamental right, it cannot be upheld unless it is supported by sufficiently important state interests and is closely tailored to effectuate only those interests."—Justice MARSHALL

"The Equal Protection Clause deals not with substantive rights or freedoms but with invidiously discriminatory classifications."—Justice STEWART

"[T]here is a right of marital and familial privacy which places some substantive limits on the regulatory power of government. But the Court has yet to hold that all regulation touching upon marriage implicates a 'fundamental right' triggering the most exacting judicial scrutiny."—Justice POWELL

"I think that under the Equal Protection Clause the statute need pass only the 'rational basis test,' and that under the Due Process Clause it need only be shown that it bears a rational relation to a constitutionally permissible objective."—Justice REHNQUIST

ZABLOCKI v. REDHAIL

434 U.S. 374, 98 S.Ct. 673, 54 L.Ed.2d 618 (1978).

Wisconsin Statutes, §§ 245.10(1), (4), (5) (1973), provided that no one "having minor issue not in his custody and which he is under obligation to support by any court order or judgment" could remarry without obtaining the permission of a court, which could not grant permission unless the petitioner showed that he had met his obligations to support the offspring covered by the order and that such children were not likely to become "public charges." Invoking these provisions, Thomas Zablocki, a county clerk, denied Roger Redhail a marriage license. Redhail then filed suit in a U.S. district court, which held that the law denied equal protection, and Wisconsin appealed to the U.S. Supreme Court.

Mr. Justice **MARSHALL** delivered the opinion of the Court. ...

II

In evaluating §§ 245.10(1), (4), (5) under the Equal Protection Clause, "we must first determine what burden of justification the classification created thereby must meet, by looking to the nature of the classification and the individual interests affected." Memorial Hospital v. Maricopa County (1974). Since our past decisions make clear that the right to marry is of fundamental importance, and since the classification at issue here significantly interferes with the exercise of that right, we believe that "critical examination" of the state interests advanced in support of the classification is required. Massachusetts Board of Retirement v. Murgia (1976).

The leading decision of this Court on the right to marry is Loving v. Virginia (1967). ...:

> The freedom to marry has long been recognized as one of the vital personal rights essential to the orderly pursuit of happiness by free men.
> ...

Although *Loving* arose in the context of racial discrimination, prior and subsequent decisions of this Court confirm that the right to marry is of fundamental importance for all individuals. ... In Meyer v. Nebraska (1923), the Court recognized that the right "to marry, establish a home and bring up children" is a central part of the liberty protected by the Due Process Clause, and in *Skinner*, marriage was described as "fundamental to the very existence and survival of the race." More recent decisions have established that the right to marry is part of the fundamental "right of privacy" implicit in the Fourteenth Amendment's Due Process Clause. ... [Griswold v. Connecticut (1965).]

Cases subsequent to *Griswold* and *Loving* have routinely categorized the decision to marry as among the personal decisions protected by the right of privacy. See generally Whalen v. Roe (1977). For example ... in Carey v. Population Services International (1977), we declared:

> While the outer limits of [the right of personal privacy] have not been marked by the Court, it is clear that among the decisions that an individual may make without unjustified government interference are personal decisions relating to marriage, *Loving*; procreation, *Skinner*; contraception, Eisenstadt v. Baird [1972] (White, J., concurring in result); family relationships, Prince v. Massachusetts (1944); and child rearing and education, Pierce v. Society of Sisters (1925); *Meyer*. ...

It is not surprising that the decision to marry has been placed on the same level of importance as decisions relating to procreation, childbirth, child rearing, and family relationships. As the facts of this case illustrate, it would make little sense to recognize a right of privacy with respect to other matters of family life and not with respect to the decision to enter the relationship that is the foundation of the family in our society. The woman whom appellee desired to marry had a fundamental right to seek an abortion of their expected child, see Roe v. Wade (1973), or to bring the child into life to suffer the myriad social, if not economic, disabilities that the status of illegitimacy brings. Surely, a decision to marry and raise the child in a traditional family setting must receive equivalent protection. And, if appellee's right to procreate means anything at all, it must imply some right to enter the only relationship in which the State of Wisconsin allows sexual relations legally to take place.

By reaffirming the fundamental character of the right to marry, we do not mean to suggest that every state regulation which relates in any way to the incidents of or prerequisites for marriage must be subjected to rigorous scrutiny. To the contrary, reasonable regulations that do not significantly interfere with decisions to enter into the marital relationship may legitimately be imposed. The statutory classification at issue here, however, clearly does interfere directly and substantially with the right to marry.

Under the challenged statute, no Wisconsin resident in the affected class may marry in Wisconsin or elsewhere without a court order, and marriages contracted in violation of the statute are both void and punishable as criminal offenses. Some of those in the affected class, like appellee, will never be able to obtain the necessary court order, because they either lack the financial means to meet their support obligations or cannot prove that their children will not become public charges. These persons are absolutely prevented from getting married. Many others, able in theory to satisfy the statute's requirements, will be sufficiently burdened by having to do so that they will in effect be coerced into forgoing their right to marry. And even those who can be persuaded to meet the statute's requirements suffer a serious intrusion into their freedom of choice in an area in which we have held such freedom to be fundamental.

III

When a statutory classification significantly interferes with the exercise of a fundamental right, it cannot be upheld unless it is supported by sufficiently important state interests and is closely tailored to effectuate only those interests. See, *e.g.*, *Carey; Memorial Hospital;* San Antonio v. Rodriguez (1973); Bullock v. Carter (1972). Appellant asserts that two interests are served by the challenged statute: ... opportunity to counsel the applicant as to the necessity of fulfilling his prior support obligations [is created]; and the welfare of the out-of-custody children is protected. We may accept for present purposes that these are legitimate and substantial interests. ... The statute ..., however, does not expressly require or provide for any counseling whatsoever. ... Even assuming that counseling does take place—a fact as to which there is no evidence in the record—this interest obviously cannot support the withholding of court permission to marry once counseling is completed.

With regard to safeguarding the welfare of the out-of-custody children, appellant's brief does not make clear the connection between the State's interest and the statute's requirements. At [oral] argument, appellant's counsel suggested that ... the statute provides incentive for the applicant to make support payments to his children. This "collection device" rationale cannot justify the statute's broad infringement on the right to marry.

First, with respect to individuals who are unable to meet the statutory requirements, the statute merely prevents the applicant from getting married, without delivering any money at all into the hands of the applicant's prior children. More importantly, ... the State already has numerous other means for exacting compliance with support obligations, means that are at least as effective as the instant statute's and yet do not impinge upon the right to marry. ...

There is also some suggestion that § 245.10 protects the ability of marriage applicants to meet support obligations to prior children by preventing the applicants from incurring new support obligations. But the challenged provisions of § 245.10 are grossly underinclusive with respect to this purpose, since they do not limit in any way new financial commitments by the applicant other than those arising out of the contemplated marriage. The statutory classification is substantially overinclusive as well [, given] the possibility that the new spouse will actually better the applicant's financial situation, by contributing income from a job or otherwise. ... And, although it is true that the applicant will incur support obligations to any children born during the contemplated marriage, preventing the marriage may only result in the children being born out of wedlock, as in fact occurred in appellee's case. Since the support obligation is the same whether the child is born in or out of wedlock, the net result of preventing the marriage is simply more illegitimate children. ...

Affirmed.

Mr. Chief Justice **BURGER,** concurring. ...

Mr. Justice **STEWART,** concurring in the judgment.

... The Equal Protection Clause deals not with substantive rights or freedoms but with invidiously discriminatory classifications. *San Antonio* (concurring opinion). The paradigm of its violation is, of course, classification by race.

Like almost any law, the Wisconsin statute now before us affects some people and does not affect others. But to say that it thereby creates "classifications" in the equal protection sense strikes me as little short of fantasy. The problem in this case is not one of discriminatory classifications, but of unwarranted encroachment upon a constitutionally protected freedom. I think that the Wisconsin statute is unconstitutional because it exceeds the bounds of permissible state regulation of marriage, and invades the sphere of liberty protected by the Due Process Clause of the Fourteenth Amendment. ...

In an opinion of the Court half a century ago, Mr. Justice Holmes described an equal protection claim as "the usual last resort of constitutional arguments." Buck v. Bell [1927]. Today equal protection doctrine has become the Court's chief instrument for invalidating state laws. Yet, in a case like this one, the doctrine is no more than substantive due process by another name.

Although the Court purports to examine the bases for legislative classifications and to compare the treatment of legislatively defined groups, it actually erects substantive limitations on what States may do. Thus, the effect of the Court's decision in this case is not to require Wisconsin to draw its legislative classifications with greater precision or to afford similar treatment to similarly situated persons. Rather, the message of the Court's opinion is that Wisconsin may not use its control over marriage to achieve the objectives of the state statute. Such restrictions on basic governmental power are at the heart of substantive due process.

The Court is understandably reluctant to rely on substantive due process. But to embrace the essence of that doctrine under the guise of equal protection serves no purpose but obfuscation. ... To conceal this appropriate inquiry invites mechanical or thoughtless application of misfocused doctrine. To bring it into the open forces a healthy and responsible recognition of the nature and purpose of the extreme power we wield when, in invalidating a state law in the name of the Constitution, we invalidate *pro tanto* the process of representative democracy in one of the sovereign States of the Union.

Mr. Justice **POWELL,** concurring in the judgment. ...

On several occasions, the Court has acknowledged the importance of the marriage relationship to the maintenance of values essential to organized society. Our decisions indicate that the guarantee of personal privacy or autonomy secured against unjustifiable governmental interference by the Due Process Clause "has some extension to activities relating to marriage," *Loving*. ... Thus, it is fair to say that there is a right of marital and familial privacy which places some substantive limits on the regulatory power of government. But the Court has yet to hold that all regulation touching upon marriage implicates a "fundamental right" triggering the most exacting judicial scrutiny. ...

In my view, analysis must start from the recognition of domestic relations as "an area that has long been regarded as a virtually exclusive province of the States." *Sosna v. Iowa* (1975). ... A "compelling state purpose" inquiry would cast doubt on the network of restrictions that the States have fashioned to govern marriage and divorce.

State power over domestic relations is not without constitutional limits. The Due Process Clause requires a showing of justification "when the government intrudes on choices concerning family living arrangements" in a manner which is contrary to deeply rooted traditions. *Moore v. East Cleveland* (1977) (plurality opinion). Due process constraints also limit the extent to which the State may monopolize the process of ordering certain human relationships while excluding the truly indigent from that process. *Boddie v. Connecticut* (1971). Furthermore, under the Equal Protection Clause the means chosen by the State in this case must bear " 'a fair and substantial relation' " to the object of the legislation. *Reed v. Reed* (1971); *Craig v. Boren* (1976) (Powell, J., concurring).

The Wisconsin measure in this case does not pass muster under either due process or equal protection standards. ...

Mr. Justice **STEVENS,** concurring in the judgment. ...

Mr. Justice **REHNQUIST,** dissenting.

I substantially agree with my Brother Powell's reasons for rejecting the Court's conclusion that marriage is the sort of "fundamental right" which must invariably trigger the strictest judicial scrutiny. I disagree with his imposition of an "intermediate" standard of review. ... I would view this legislative judgment in the light of the traditional presumption of validity. I think that under the Equal Protection Clause the statute need pass only the "rational basis test," *Dandridge v. Williams* (1970), and that under the Due Process Clause it need only be shown that it bears a rational relation to a constitutionally permissible objective. *Williamson v. Lee Optical Co.* (1955); *Ferguson v. Skrupa* (1963) (Harlan, J., concurring). The statute so viewed is a permissible exercise of the State's power to regulate family life and to assure the support of minor children, despite its possible imprecision in ... extreme cases. ...

... "The broad legislative classification must be judged by reference to characteristics typical of the affected classes rather than by focusing on selected, atypical examples." [*Califano v. Jobst* (1977).] ... I conclude that the statute, despite its imperfections, is sufficiently rational to satisfy the demands of the Fourteenth Amendment. ...

Editors' Notes

(1) **Query:** With the possible exception of Rehnquist, all of the justices who wrote in this case agreed that "the Constitution" protects a "fundamental right" to marry. What different approaches to constitutional interpretation led the justices to find such a right? To what extent were the reasons various justices offered convincing?

(2) **Query:** To what degree was Stewart's criticism of the Court's use of the equal protection clause to protect fundamental rights valid? Did the justices in *Zablocki* and in earlier rulings such as Skinner v. Oklahoma (1942; reprinted above, p. 1014) and Shapiro v. Thompson (1969; reprinted above, p. 1019) decide the cases because of denials of equal protection or because of violations of substantive rights protect by the due process clause? If the meanings of these clauses overlap, what would that "fact" tell us about HOW to interpret "the Constitution"?

(3) **Query:** Did Marshall subject the statute to strict scrutiny, to intermediate scrutiny, or to some scrutiny along the lines of the spectrum of standards that he articulated in *Dandridge* and *San Antonio*? Did Powell adopt, at least with respect to a supposed fundamental right to marry, Marshall's argument about continua as expressed in those earlier cases? Or was Powell proposing intermediate scrutiny as in Craig v. Boren (1976; reprinted above, p. 992)?

(4) In Turner v. Safley (1987), the Court followed *Zablocki* and unanimously invalidated a prison regulation that restricted inmates' right to marry to those circumstances in which the superintendent found compelling reasons to grant permission.

III. A NEW MODEL? REASONABLENESS "WITH BITE" AND WITHOUT PRESUMPTION?

"If the State is to deny a discrete group of innocent children the free public education that it offers to other children residing within its borders, that denial must be justified by a showing that it furthers some substantial state interest."—Justice BRENNAN

"[T]hese cases demonstrate the wisdom ... of employing an approach that allows for varying levels of scrutiny depending upon 'the constitutional and societal importance of the interest adversely affected and the recognized invidiousness of the basis upon which the particular classification is drawn.' "—Justice MARSHALL

"Our review in cases such as these is properly heightened."—Justice POWELL

"[I]t simply is not 'irrational' for a state to conclude that it does not have the same responsibility to provide benefits for persons whose very presence in the state ... is illegal as it does to provide for persons lawfully present."—Chief Justice BURGER

PLYLER v. DOE

457 U.S. 202, 102 S.Ct. 2382, 72 L.Ed.2d 786 (1982).

Faced with an increasing number of illegal aliens crossing from Mexico, Texas in 1975 added § 21.031 to its Educational Code, withholding from local school boards state funds for the education of children who were "not legally admitted" into the United States. Sec. 21.031 further authorized local boards to deny enrollment to children of illegal aliens. A series of class actions filed in U.S. district courts challenged the statute as a denial of equal protection. Those courts and the Court of Appeals for the Fifth Circuit agreed. Texas appealed.

Justice **BRENNAN** delivered the opinion of the Court. ...

II

... Appellants argue ... that undocumented aliens ... are not "persons within the jurisdiction" of ... Texas, and that therefore they have no right to the equal protection of Texas law. We reject this argument. ... [E]ven aliens whose presence in this country is unlawful have long been recognized as "persons" guaranteed due process of law by the Fifth and Fourteenth Amendments. Yick Wo v. Hopkins (1886). Indeed, we have clearly held that the Fifth Amendment protects aliens whose presence in this country is unlawful from invidious discrimination by the Federal Government.[1] Mathews v. Diaz (1976). ...

There is simply no support for appellant's suggestion that "due process" is somehow of greater stature than "equal protection" and therefore available to a larger class of persons. To the contrary, each aspect of the Fourteenth Amendment reflects an elementary limitation on state power. To permit a State to employ the phrase "within its jurisdiction" in order to identify subclasses of persons whom it would define as beyond its jurisdiction ... would undermine the principal purpose for which the Equal Protection Clause was incorporated. ... [It] was intended to work nothing less than the abolition of all caste-based and invidious class-based legislation. That objective is fundamentally at odds with the power the State asserts here. ...

III ...

... A legislature must have substantial latitude to establish classifications that roughly approximate the nature of the problem perceived,

---

1. It would be incongruous to hold that the United States ... is barred from invidious discrimination with respect to unlawful aliens, while exempting the States from a similar limitation. ... [Footnote by the Court.]

that accommodate competing concerns both public and private, and that account for limitations on the practical ability of the State to remedy every ill. In applying the Equal Protection Clause to most forms of state action, we thus seek only the assurance that the classification ... bears some fair relationship to a legitimate public purpose.

But we would not be faithful to our obligations under the Fourteenth Amendment if we applied so deferential a standard to every classification. The Equal Protection Clause was intended as a restriction on state legislative action inconsistent with elemental constitutional premises. Thus we have treated as presumptively invidious those classifications that disadvantage a "suspect class," [2] or that impinge upon the exercise of a "fundamental right. ..." [3] In addition, we have recognized that certain forms of legislative classification, while not facially invidious, nonetheless give rise to recurring constitutional difficulties; in these limited circumstances we have sought the assurance that the classification reflects a reasoned judgment consistent with the ideal of equal protection by inquiring whether it may fairly be viewed as furthering a substantial interest of the state. We turn to a consideration of the standard appropriate for the evaluation of § 21.031.

A

Sheer incapability or lax enforcement of the laws barring entry into this country, coupled with the failure to establish an effective bar to the employment of undocumented aliens, has resulted in the creation of a substantial "shadow population" of illegal immigrants ... within our borders ... [raising] the specter of a permanent caste ... [whose existence] presents most difficult problems for a Nation that prides itself on adherence to principles of equality under law.[4]

---

2. Several formulations might explain our treatment of certain classifications as "suspect." Some ... are more likely than others to reflect deep-seated prejudice ... [and are] easily recognized as incompatible with the constitutional understanding that each person is to be judged individually and to be entitled to equal justice under the law. Classifications treated as suspect tend to be irrelevant to any proper legislative goal. See McLaughlin v. Florida (1964); Hirabayashi v. United States (1943). Finally, certain groups ... have historically been "relegated to such a position of political powerlessness as to command extraordinary protection from the majoritarian political process." San Antonio v. Rodriguez (1973); see United States v. Carolene Products (1938). ... Legislation imposing special disabilities upon groups disfavored by virtue of circumstances beyond their control suggests the kind of "class or caste" treatment that the Fourteenth Amendment was designed to abolish. [Footnote by the Court.]

3. In determining whether a class-based denial of a particular right is deserving of strict scrutiny ... we look to the Constitution to see if the right infringed has its source, explicitly or implicitly therein. But we have also recognized the fundamentality of participation in state "elections on an equal basis with other citizens in the jurisdiction," Dunn v. Blumstein (1972), even though "the right to vote, *per se,* is not a constitutionally protected right." *San Antonio.* With respect to suffrage, we have explained the need for strict scrutiny as arising from the significance of the franchise as the guardian of all other rights. See Harper v. Virginia (1966); Reynolds v. Sims (1964); Yick Wo v. Hopkins (1886). [Footnote by the Court.]

4. We reject the claim that "illegal aliens" are a "suspect class." ... [Footnote by the Court.]

The children who are plaintiffs in these cases are special members of this underclass. Persuasive arguments support the view that a State may withhold its beneficence from those whose very presence within the United States is the product of their own unlawful conduct. These arguments do not apply with the same force to classifications imposing disabilities on the minor *children* of such illegal entrants. ... Even if the State found it expedient to control the conduct of adults by acting against their children, legislation directing the onus of a parent's misconduct against his children does not comport with fundamental conceptions of justice.

> [V]isiting ... condemnation on the head of an infant is illogical and unjust. Moreover, imposing disabilities on the ... child is contrary to the basic concept of our system that legal burdens should bear some relationship to individual responsibility or wrongdoing. Obviously, no child is responsible for his birth and penalizing the ... child is an ineffectual—as well as unjust—way of deterring the parent. Weber v. Aetna Casualty & Surety Co. (1972).

Of course, undocumented status is not irrelevant to any proper legislative goal. Nor is [it] an absolutely immutable characteristic since it is the product of conscious, indeed unlawful, action. But § 21.031 is directed against children, and imposes its discriminatory burden on the basis of a legal characteristic over which children can have little control. It is thus difficult to conceive of a rational justification for penalizing these children for their presence within the United States. Yet that appears to be precisely the effect of § 21.031.

Public education is not a "right" granted to individuals by the Constitution. San Antonio v. Rodriguez (1973). But neither is it merely some governmental "benefit" indistinguishable from other forms of social welfare legislation. Both the importance of education in maintaining our basic institutions, and the lasting impact of its deprivation on the child, mark the distinction. ... [E]ducation provides the basic tools by which individuals might lead economically productive lives to the benefit of us all. In sum, education has a fundamental role in maintaining the fabric of our society. We cannot ignore the significant social costs borne by our Nation when select groups are denied the means to absorb the values and skills upon which our social order rests. ... The inestimable toll of that deprivation on the social, economic, intellectual, and psychological well-being of the individual, and the obstacle it poses to individual achievement, makes it most difficult to reconcile the cost or the principle of a status-based denial of basic education with the framework of equality embodied in the Equal Protection Class. ...

B

These well-settled principles allow us to determine the proper level of deference to be afforded § 21.031. Undocumented aliens cannot be treated as a suspect class because their presence in this country in violation of federal law is not a "constitutional irrelevancy." Nor is education a fundamental right; a State need not justify by compelling necessity every variation in the manner in which education is provided to its population. *San Antonio.* But more is involved in these cases. ... In determining the rationality of § 21.031, we may appropriately take into account its costs to the Nation and to the innocent children who are its victims. In light of these countervailing costs, the discrimination contained in § 21.031 can hardly be considered rational unless it furthers some substantial goal of the State.

IV

... [I]n the State's view, Congress' apparent disapproval of the presence of these children within the United States ... provides authority for [Texas's] decision to impose upon them special disabilities. ... [W]e agree that the courts must be attentive to congressional policy; the exercise of congressional power might well affect the State's prerogatives to afford differential treatment to a particular class of aliens. But we are unable to find in the congressional immigration scheme any statement of policy that might weigh significantly in arriving at an equal protection balance concerning the State's authority to deprive these children of an education. ...

V

Appellants argue that the classification ... furthers an interest in the "preservation of the state's limited resources for the education of its lawful residents." Of course, a concern for preservation of resources standing alone can hardly justify the classification used in allocating those resources. Graham v. Richardson (1971). Apart from the asserted state prerogative to act against undocumented status ... we discern three colorable state interests that might support § 21.031.

First, appellants ... suggest that the State may ... protect itself from an influx of illegal immigrants. While a State might have an interest in mitigating the potentially harsh economic effects of sudden shifts in population, ... [t]here is no evidence in the record suggesting that illegal entrants impose any significant burden on the State's economy. ... [E]ven making the doubtful assumption that the net impact of illegal aliens on the economy is negative, we think it clear that "[c]harging tuition to undocumented children constitutes a ludicrously ineffectual attempt to stem the tide of illegal immigration," at least when compared with the alternative of prohibiting the employment of illegal aliens.

Second, while ... a State may "not ... reduce expenditures for education by barring [some arbitrarily chosen class of] children from its schools," Shapiro v. Thompson (1969), appellants suggest that undocumented children are appropriately singled out for exclusion because of the special burdens they impose on the State's ability to provide high-quality public education. But the record in no way supports the claim that exclusion of undocumented children is likely to improve the overall quality of education in the State. ... Of course, even if improvement in the quality of education were a likely result of barring some *number* of children from the schools of the State, the State must support its selection of *this* group as the appropriate target for exclusion. In terms of educational cost and need, however, undocumented children are "basically indistinguishable" from legally resident alien children.

Finally, appellants suggest that undocumented children are appropriately singled out because their unlawful presence within the United States renders them less likely than other children to remain within the boundaries of the State, and to put their education to productive social or political use within the State. ... The State has no assurance that any child, citizen or not, will employ the education provided by the State within the confines of the State's borders. ... It is difficult to understand precisely what the State hopes to achieve by promoting the creation and perpetuation of a subclass of illiterates within our boundaries, surely adding to the problems and costs of unemployment, welfare, and crime. It is thus clear that whatever savings might be achieved by denying these children an education, they are wholly insubstantial in relation to the costs involved to these children, the State, and the Nation.

VI

If the State is to deny a discrete group of innocent children the free public education that it offers to other children residing within its borders, that denial must be justified by a showing that it furthers some substantial state interest. No such showing was made here.

Affirmed.

Justice **MARSHALL**, concurring. ...

While I join the Court's opinion, I do so without in any way retreating from my [dissenting] opinion in *San Antonio.* I continue to believe that an individual's interest in education is fundamental. ... Furthermore, I believe that the facts of these cases demonstrate the wisdom of rejecting a rigidified approach to equal protection analysis, and of employing an approach that allows for varying levels of scrutiny depending upon "the constitutional and societal importance of the interest adversely affected and the recognized invidiousness of the basis upon which the particular classification is drawn."

Justice **BLACKMUN**, concurring. ...

... I write separately ... because in my view the nature of the interest at stake is crucial to the proper resolution of these cases. ...

[T]he Court's experience has demonstrated that the *San Antonio* formulation does not settle every issue of "fundamental rights" arising under the Equal Protection Clause. Only a pedant would insist that there are *no* meaningful distinctions among the multitude of social and political interests regulated by the States, and *San Antonio* does not stand for quite so absolute a proposition. ...

Justice **POWELL,** concurring.   ...

Our review in cases such as these is properly heightened. [Trimble v. Gordon (1977).] Cf. Craig v. Boren (1976). The classification at issue deprives a group of children of the opportunity for education afforded all other children simply because they have been assigned a legal status due to a violation of law by their parents. These children thus have been singled out for a lifelong penalty and stigma. A legislative classification that threatens the creation of an underclass of future citizens and residents cannot be reconciled with one of the fundamental purposes of the Fourteenth Amendment. In these unique circumstances, the Court properly may require that the State's interests be substantial and that the means bear a "fair and substantial relation" to these interests. See Lalli v. Lalli (1978). ...

Chief Justice **BURGER,** with whom Justice **WHITE,** Justice **REHN-QUIST,** and Justice **O'CONNOR** join, dissenting.

Were it our business to set the Nation's social policy, I would agree without hesitation that it is senseless for an enlightened society to deprive any children—including illegal aliens—of an elementary education. ... However, the Constitution does not constitute us as "Platonic Guardians" nor does it vest in this Court the authority to strike down laws because they do not meet our standards of desirable social policy, "wisdom," or "common sense." See TVA v. Hill (1978). We trespass on the assigned function of the political branches under our structure of limited and separated powers when we assume a policymaking role as the Court does today. ...

The dispositive issue ... is whether, for purposes of allocating its finite resources, a state has a legitimate reason to differentiate between persons who are lawfully within the state and those who are unlawfully there. The distinction ... Texas has drawn—based not only upon its own legitimate interests but on classifications established by the Federal Government in its immigration laws and policies—is not unconstitutional.

A ...

The Court first suggests that these illegal alien children, although not a suspect class, are entitled to special solicitude under the Equal Protection Clause because they lack "control" over or "responsibility" for their unlawful entry into this country. Similarly, the Court appears to take the position that § 21.031 is presumptively "irrational" because it has the effect of imposing "penalties" on "innocent" children. However, the Equal Protection Clause does not preclude legislators from classifying among persons on the basis of factors over which individuals ... lack "control." ... The Equal Protection Clause protects against arbitrary and irrational classifications, and invidious discrimination stemming from prejudice and hostility; it is not an all-encompassing "equalizer" designed to eradicate every distinction for which persons are not "responsible." ...

The second strand of the Court's analysis rests on the premise that, although public education is not a constitutionally guaranteed right, "neither is it merely some governmental 'benefit' indistinguishable from other forms of social welfare legislation." Whatever meaning or relevance this opaque observation might have in some other context, it simply has no bearing on the issues at hand. ...

The importance of education is beyond dispute. Yet we have held repeatedly that the importance of a governmental service does not elevate it to the status of a "fundamental right" for purposes of equal protection analysis. In *San Antonio,* Justice Powell, speaking for the Court, expressly rejected the proposition that state laws dealing with public education are subject to special scrutiny under the Equal Protection Clause. Moreover, the Court points to no meaningful way to distinguish between education and other governmental benefits in this context. Is the Court suggesting that education is more "fundamental" than food, shelter, or medical care?

The Equal Protection Clause ... does not mandate a constitutional hierarchy of governmental services. ... The fact that the distinction is drawn in legislation affecting access to public education—as opposed to ... other important governmental benefits, such as public assistance, health care, or housing—cannot make a difference in the level of scrutiny applied.

B

... [O]ur inquiry should focus on and be limited to whether the legislative classification at issue bears a rational relationship to a legitimate state purpose. Vance v. Bradley (1979); Dandridge v. Williams (1970). ... [I]t simply is not "irrational" for a state to conclude that it does not have the same responsibility to provide benefits for persons whose very presence in the state ... is illegal as it does to provide for persons lawfully present. ... The Court has failed to offer even a plausible explanation why illegality of residence in this country is not a factor that may legitimately bear upon the bona fides of state residence and entitlement to the benefits of lawful residence. ...

... Today's cases ... present yet another example of unwarranted judicial action which in the long run tends to contribute to the weakening of our political processes. ... While the "specter of a permanent caste" of illegal Mexican residents of the United States is indeed a disturbing one, it is but one segment of a larger problem, which is for the political branches to solve. I find it difficult to believe that Congress would long tolerate such a self-destructive result. ...

Editors' Notes

(1) **Query:** To what extent did Brennan and Burger each follow a *purposive approach* to constitutional interpretation?

(2) **Query:** To what extent did Brennan craft a new doctrinal model to interpret equal protection? Is this model what Prof. Gerald Gunther would call a rational basis test with bite? (See his "In Search of Evolving Doctrine on a Changing Court," 86 *Harv.L.Rev.* 1 [1972], discussed above, p. 983.) Or was Brennan simply refining Marshall's theory of continua as explained in his dissents to San Antonio v. Rodriguez (1973; reprinted above, p. 1002), Dandridge v. Williams (1970; reprinted above, p. 1027), and Harris v. McRae (1980; reprinted below, p. 1271). Or was Brennan silently applying "intermediate scrutiny" as in Craig v. Boren (1976; reprinted above, p. 992)? Or was he merely exercising his well known talent as a builder of coalitions, compromising to weave a majority together? See Mark Tushnet, "The Optimist's Tale," 132 *U.Pa.L.Rev.* 1257 (1984).

(3) **Query:** In footnote 3, Brennan wrote:

In determining whether a class-based denial of a particular right is deserving of strict scrutiny . . . we look to the Constitution to see if the right infringed has its source, explicitly or implicitly therein.

What did Brennan mean by "the Constitution"? Simply the text? Something more? What more?

(4) **Query:** Did Blackmun's concurring opinion suggest he had become sympathetic to if not a convert to Marshall's theory of continua?

(5) **Query:** Are we witnessing the justices combining the questions WHO and HOW along with WHAT? Did they do so thoughtfully and carefully? Consciously?

(6) In November 1994, voters in California adopted Proposition 187, which bars illegal immigrants from receiving public benefits such as public education, non-emergency health care, and social welfare services. Critics of the measure immediately filed lawsuits challenging its constitutionality.

(7) In Kadrmas v. Dickinson Public Schools (1988), the Court through O'Connor held that *San Antonio,* not *Plyler*, controlled the level of scrutiny applicable to North Dakota's program permitting local school boards to charge a fee for transporting students to and from public schools. The Court concluded that neither a classification based on wealth nor education called for any judicial oversight more searching than rational basis scrutiny. O'Connor construed *Plyler* as having applied the intermediate or "heightened" scrutiny ordinarily applied to classifications based upon sex or illegitimacy, but stated that the Court had done so because of the "unique circumstances" of that case. Marshall, joined by Brennan, dissented, citing *Plyler* and his dissent in *San Antonio,* to bolster an argument that classifications based on wealth, especially in the context of education, "have a measure of special constitutional significance." Stevens, joined by Blackmun, also dissented, arguing that the fee for school bus service could not withstand the sort of rational basis scrutiny applied in Cleburne v. Cleburne Living Center (1985; reprinted as the next case).

"[T]he Court of Appeals erred in holding mental retardation a quasi-suspect classification calling for a more

exacting standard of judicial review than is normally accorded economic and social legislation."—Justice WHITE

"[T]he word 'rational'—for me at least—includes elements of legitimacy and neutrality that must always characterize the performance of the sovereign's duty to govern impartially."—Justice STEVENS

"[T]he Court does not label its handiwork heightened scrutiny, and perhaps the method employed must hereafter be called 'second order' rational basis review. ..."—Justice MARSHALL

CLEBURNE v. CLEBURNE LIVING CENTER
473 U.S. 432, 105 S.Ct. 3249, 87 L.Ed.2d 313 (1985).

Cleburne, Texas, acting pursuant to a municipal zoning ordinance requiring special permits for construction of "[h]ospitals for the insane or feeble-minded, or alcoholic [sic] or drug addicts, or penal or correctional institutions," denied Cleburne Living Center (CLC) such a permit for the operation of a group home for the mentally retarded. CLC filed suit in federal district court, alleging the zoning ordinance discriminated against the mentally retarded in violation of the Equal Protection Clause. Applying the rational basis standard, the district court sustained the ordinance both on its face and as applied. On the other hand, the court of appeals held mental retardation was a "quasi-suspect" classification that triggered intermediate or heightened scrutiny and so reversed in both respects. The Supreme Court granted certiorari.

Justice **WHITE** delivered the opinion of the Court. ...

II

The Equal Protection Clause of the Fourteenth Amendment ... is essentially a direction that all persons similarly situated should be treated alike. Plyler v. Doe (1982). Section 5 of the Amendment empowers Congress to enforce this mandate, but absent controlling congressional direction, the courts have themselves devised standards for determining the validity of state legislation or other official action that is challenged as denying equal protection. The general rule is that legislation is presumed to be valid and will be sustained if the classification drawn by the statute is rationally related to a legitimate state interest. ... When social or economic legislation is at issue, the Equal Protection Clause allows the states wide latitude, United States Railroad Retirement Board v. Fritz [1980]; New Orleans v. Dukes [1976], and the Constitution presumes that even improvident decisions will eventually be rectified by the democratic processes.

The general rule gives way, however, when a statute classifies by race, alienage or national origin. These factors are so seldom relevant to the achievement of any legitimate state interest that laws grounded in such considerations are deemed to reflect prejudice and antipathy—a view that those in the burdened class are not as worthy or deserving as others. For these reasons and because such discrimination is unlikely to be soon rectified by legislative means, these laws are subjected to strict scrutiny and will be sustained only if they are suitably tailored to serve a compelling state interest. McLaughlin v. Florida (1964); Graham v. Richardson (1971). Similar oversight by the courts is due when state laws impinge on personal rights protected by the Constitution. Kramer v. Union Free School District (1969); Shapiro v. Thompson (1969); Skinner v. Oklahoma (1942).

Legislative classifications based on gender also call for a heightened standard of review. ... [S]tatutes distributing benefits and burdens between the sexes in different ways very likely reflect outmoded notions of the relative capabilities of men and women. A gender classification fails unless it is substantially related to a sufficiently important governmental interest. Mississippi University for Women v. Hogan (1982); Craig v. Boren (1976). Because illegitimacy is beyond the individual's control and bears "no relation to the individual's ability to participate in and contribute to society," Mathews v. Lucas (1976), official discriminations resting on that characteristic are also subject to somewhat heightened review. ... Mills v. Habluetzel (1982).

We have declined, however, to extend heightened review to differential treatment based on age:

> While the treatment of the aged in this Nation has not been wholly free of discrimination, such persons, unlike, say, those who have been discriminated against on the basis of race or national origin, have not experienced a "history of purposeful unequal treatment" or been subjected to unique disabilities on the basis of stereotyped characteristics not truly indicative of their abilities. Massachusetts Board of Retirement v. Murgia (1976).

The lesson of *Murgia* is that where individuals in the group affected by a law have distinguishing characteristics relevant to interests the state has the authority to implement, the courts have been very reluctant, as they should be in our federal system and with our respect for the separation of powers, to closely scrutinize legislative choices as to whether, how and to what extent those interests should be pursued. In such cases, the Equal Protection Clause requires only a rational means to serve a legitimate end.

III

... [T]he Court of Appeals erred in holding mental retardation a quasi-suspect classification calling for a more exacting standard of judicial review than is normally accorded economic and social legislation. First, it is undeniable ... that those who are mentally retarded have a reduced ability to cope with and function in the everyday world. ... They are thus different, immutably so, in relevant respects, and the states' interest in dealing with and providing for them is plainly a legitimate one. How this large and diversified group is to be treated under the law is a difficult and often a technical matter, very much a task for legislators guided by qualified professionals and not by the perhaps ill-informed opinions of the judiciary. Heightened scrutiny inevitably involves substantive judgments about legislative decisions, and we doubt that the predicate for such judicial oversight is present where the classification deals with mental retardation.

Second, the distinctive legislative response, both national and state, to the plight of those who are mentally retarded demonstrates ... that the lawmakers have been addressing their difficulties in a manner that belies a continuing antipathy or prejudice and a corresponding need for more intrusive oversight by the judiciary. Thus, the federal government has not only outlawed discrimination against the mentally retarded in federally funded programs, but it has also provided the retarded with the right to receive "appropriate treatment, services, and habilitation" in a setting that is "least restrictive of [their] personal liberty." In addition, the government has conditioned federal education funds on a State's assurance that retarded children will enjoy an education that, "to the maximum extent appropriate," is integrated with that of non-mentally retarded children. The government has also facilitated the hiring of the mentally retarded into the federal civil service by exempting them from the requirement of competitive examination. The State of Texas has similarly enacted legislation that acknowledges the special status of the mentally retarded by conferring certain rights upon them, such as "the right to live in the least restrictive setting appropriate to [their] individual needs and abilities," including "the right to live ... in a group home."

Such legislation thus singling out the retarded for special treatment reflects the real and undeniable differences between the retarded and others. That a civilized and decent society expects and approves such legislation indicates that governmental consideration of those differences in the vast majority of situations is not only legitimate but desirable. It may be, as CLC contends, that legislation designed to benefit, rather than disadvantage, the retarded would generally withstand examination under a test of heightened scrutiny. The relevant inquiry, however, is whether heightened scrutiny is constitutionally mandated in the first instance. Even assuming that many of these laws could be shown to be substantially related to an important governmental purpose, merely requiring the legislature to justify its efforts in these terms may lead it to refrain from acting at all. Much recent legislation intended to benefit the retarded also assumes the need for measures that might be perceived to disadvantage them. ... Especially given the wide variation in the abilities and needs of the retarded themselves, governmental bodies must have a certain amount of flexibility and freedom from judicial oversight in shaping and limiting their remedial efforts.

Third, the legislative response ... negates any claim that the mentally retarded are politically powerless in the sense that they have no ability to attract the attention of the lawmakers. Any minority can be said to be powerless to assert direct control over the legislature, but if that were a criterion for higher level scrutiny by the courts, much economic and social legislation would now be suspect.

Fourth, if the large and amorphous class of the mentally retarded were deemed quasi-suspect ..., it would be difficult to find a principled way to distinguish a variety of other groups who have perhaps immutable disabilities setting them off from others, who cannot themselves mandate the desired legislative responses, and who can claim some degree of prejudice from at least part of the public at large. One need mention in this respect only the aging, the disabled, the mentally ill, and the infirm. We are reluctant to set out on that course, and we decline to do so.

Doubtless, there have been and there will continue to be instances of discrimination against the retarded that are in fact invidious, and that are properly subject to judicial correction under constitutional norms. But the appropriate method of reaching such instances is not to create a new quasi-suspect classification and subject all governmental action based on that classification to more searching evaluation. Rather, we should look to the likelihood that governmental action premised on a particular classification is valid as a general matter, not merely to the specifics of the case before us. Because mental retardation is a characteristic that the government may legitimately take into account in a wide range of decisions, and because both state and federal governments have recently committed themselves to assisting the retarded, we will not presume that any given legislative action, even one that disadvantages retarded individuals, is rooted in considerations that the Constitution will not tolerate.

Our refusal to recognize the retarded as a quasi-suspect class does not leave them entirely unprotected from invidious discrimination. To withstand equal protection review, legislation that distinguishes between the mentally retarded and others must be rationally related to a legitimate governmental purpose. This standard, we believe, affords government the latitude necessary both to pursue policies designed to assist the retarded in realizing their full potential, and to freely and efficiently engage in activities that burden the retarded in what is essentially an incidental manner. The State may not rely on a classification whose relationship to an asserted goal is so attenuated as to render the distinction arbitrary or irrational. See Zobel v. Williams (1982); United States Department of Agriculture v. Moreno (1973). Furthermore, some objectives—such as "a bare ... desire to harm a politically unpopular group," Moreno—are not legitimate state interests. Beyond that, the mentally retarded, like others, have and retain their substantive constitutional rights in addition to the right to be treated equally by the law.

IV

We turn to the issue of the validity of the zoning ordinance insofar as it requires a special use permit for homes for the mentally retarded. We inquire first whether requiring a special use permit for the Featherston home in the circumstances here deprives respondents of the equal protection of the laws. If it does, there will be no occasion to decide whether the special use permit provision is facially invalid. ... This is the preferred course of adjudication since it enables courts to avoid making unnecessarily broad constitutional judgments. ...

The constitutional issue is clearly posed. ... May the city require the permit for this facility when other care and multiple dwelling facilities are freely permitted? ... [T]he mentally retarded as a group are indeed different from others not sharing their misfortune. ... But this difference is largely irrelevant unless the Featherston home and those who would occupy it would threaten legitimate interests of the city in a way that other permitted uses such as boarding houses and hospitals would not. [In] our view the record does not reveal any rational basis for believing that the Featherston home would pose any special threat to the city's legitimate interests. ...

The District Court found that the City Council's insistence on the permit rested on several factors. First, the Council was concerned with the negative attitude of the majority of property owners located within 200 feet of the Featherston facility, as well as with the fears of elderly residents of the neighborhood. But mere negative attitudes, or fear, unsubstantiated by factors which are properly cognizable in a zoning proceeding, are not permissible bases for treating a home for the mentally retarded differently from apartment houses, multiple dwellings, and the like. It is plain that the electorate as a whole, whether by referendum or otherwise, could not order city action violative of the Equal Protection Clause, Lucas v. Forty–Fourth General Assembly of Colorado (1964), and the City may not avoid the strictures of that Clause by deferring to the wishes or objections of some fraction of the body politic. "Private biases may be outside the reach of the law, but the law cannot, directly or indirectly, give them effect." Palmore v. Sidoti (1984).

Second, the Council had two objections to the location of the facility. It was concerned that the facility was across the street from a junior high school, and it feared that the students might harass the occupants of the Featherston home. But the school itself is attended by about 30 mentally retarded students, and denying a permit based on such vague, undifferentiated fears is again permitting some portion of the community to validate what would otherwise be an equal protection violation. The other objection to the home's location was that it was located on "a five hundred year flood plain." This concern with the possibility of a flood, however, can hardly be based on a distinction between the Featherston home and, for example, nursing homes, homes for convalescents or the aged, or sanitariums or hospitals, any of which could be located on the Featherston site without obtaining a special use permit. ...

Fourth, the Council was concerned with the size of the home and the number of people that [sic] would occupy it. ... [But] there would be no restrictions on the number of people who could occupy this home as a boarding house, nursing home, family dwelling, fraternity house, or dormitory. The question is whether it is rational to treat the mentally retarded differently. It is true that they suffer disability not shared by others; but why this difference warrants a density regulation that others need not observe is not at all apparent. ...

... [T]he city also urged that the ordinance is aimed at avoiding concentration of population and at lessening congestion of the streets. These concerns [and] ... the expressed worry about fire hazards, the serenity of the neighborhood, and the avoidance of danger to other residents fail rationally to justify singling out a home such as 201 Featherston for the special use permit, yet imposing no such restrictions on the many other uses freely permitted in the neighborhood. The short of it is that requiring the permit in this case appears to us to rest on an irrational prejudice against the mentally retarded. ...

The judgment of the Court of Appeals is affirmed insofar as it invalidates the zoning ordinance as applied to the Featherston home. The judgment is otherwise vacated.

It is so ordered.

Justice **STEVENS**, with whom The Chief Justice [**BURGER**] joins, concurring.

The Court of Appeals disposed of this case as if a critical question to be decided were which of three clearly defined standards of equal protection review should be applied to a legislative classification discriminating against the mentally retarded. In fact, our cases have not delineated three—or even one or two—such well defined standards.[1] Rather, our cases reflect a continuum of judgmental responses to differing classifications which have been explained in opinions by terms ranging from "strict scrutiny" at one extreme to "rational basis" at the other. I have never been persuaded that these so called "standards" adequately explain the decisional process. Cases involving classifications based on alienage, illegal residency, illegitimacy, gender, age, or ... mental retardation, do not fit well into sharply defined classifications.

... In my own approach to these cases, I have always asked myself whether I could find a "rational basis" for the classification at issue. The term "rational," of course, includes a requirement that an impartial lawmaker could logically believe that the classification would serve a legitimate public purpose that transcends the harm to the members of the disadvantaged class. Thus, the word "rational"—for me at least—includes elements of legitimacy and neutrality that must always characterize the performance of the sovereign's duty to govern impartially.

The rational basis test, properly understood, adequately explains why a law that deprives a person of the right to vote because his skin has

---

1. In United States Railroad Retirement Board v. Fritz (1980), after citing 11 cases applying the rational basis standard, the Court stated: "The most arrogant legal scholar would not claim that all of these cases applied a uniform or consistent test under equal protection principles." [Footnote by Justice Stevens.]

a different pigmentation than that of other voters violates the Equal Protection Clause. It would be utterly irrational to limit the franchise on the basis of height or weight; it is equally invalid to limit it on the basis of skin color. None of these attributes has any bearing at all on the citizen's willingness or ability to exercise that civil right. We do not need to apply a special standard, or to apply "strict scrutiny," or even "heightened scrutiny," to decide such cases.

In every equal protection case, we have to ask certain basic questions. What class is harmed by the legislation, and has it been subjected to a "tradition of disfavor" by our laws? What is the public purpose that is being served by the law? What is the characteristic of the disadvantaged class that justifies the disparate treatment? In most cases the answer to these questions will tell us whether the statute has a "rational basis." The answers will result in the virtually automatic invalidation of racial classifications and in the validation of most economic classifications, but they will provide differing results in cases involving classifications based on alienage, gender, or illegitimacy. But that is not because we apply an "intermediate standard of review" in these cases; rather it is because the characteristics of these groups are sometimes relevant and sometimes irrelevant to a valid public purpose, or, more specifically, to the purpose that the challenged laws purportedly intended to serve.

Every law that places the mentally retarded in a special class is not presumptively irrational. The differences between mentally retarded persons and those with greater mental capacity are obviously relevant to certain legislative decisions. ...

... The record convinces me that this permit was required because of the irrational fears of neighboring property owners, rather than for the protection of the mentally retarded persons who would reside in respondent's home. ... I cannot believe that a rational member of this disadvantaged class could ever approve of the discriminatory application of the city's ordinance in this case. Accordingly, I join the opinion of the Court.

Justice **MARSHALL,** with whom Justice **BRENNAN** and Justice **BLACKMUN** join, concurring in the judgment in part and dissenting in part.

The Court holds that all retarded individuals cannot be grouped together as the "feebleminded" and deemed presumptively unfit to live in a community. Underlying this holding is the principle that mental retardation *per se* cannot be a proxy for depriving retarded people of their rights and interests without regard to variations in individual ability. With this holding and principle I agree. The equal protection clause requires attention to the capacities and needs of retarded people as individuals.

... Because I dissent from [the Court's] novel and truncated remedy, and because I cannot accept [its] disclaimer that no "more exacting standard" than ordinary rational basis review is being applied, I write separately.

I

... Cleburne's ordinance is invalidated only after being subjected to precisely the sort of probing inquiry associated with heightened scrutiny. To be sure, the Court does not label its handiwork heightened scrutiny, and perhaps the method employed must hereafter be called "second order" rational basis review. ... But however labelled, the rational basis test invoked today is most assuredly not the rational basis test of Williamson v. Lee Optical (1955) and [its] progeny. ...

The refusal to acknowledge that something more than minimum rationality review is at work here is ... unfortunate in at least two respects. The suggestion that the traditional rational basis test allows this sort of searching inquiry creates precedent for this Court and lower courts to subject economic and commercial classifications to similar and searching "ordinary" rational basis review—a small and regrettable step back toward the days of Lochner v. New York (1905). Moreover, by failing to articulate the factors that justify today's "second order" rational basis review, the Court provides no principled foundation for determining when more searching inquiry is to be invoked. ...

II

I have long believed the level of scrutiny employed in an equal protection case should vary with "the constitutional and societal importance of the interest adversely affected and the recognized invidiousness of the basis upon which the particular classification is drawn." San Antonio v. Rodriguez (1973) (Marshall, J., dissenting). See also Plyler v. Doe (1982) (Marshall, J., concurring); Dandridge v. Williams (1970) (Marshall, J., dissenting). When a zoning ordinance works to exclude the retarded from all residential districts in a community, these two considerations require that the ordinance be convincingly justified as substantially furthering legitimate and important purposes. ...

[An extended application of this framework led Marshall to conclude that] Cleburne's vague generalizations for classifying the "feeble minded" with drug addicts, alcoholics, and the insane, and excluding them where the elderly, the ill, the boarder, and the transient are allowed, are not substantial or important enough to overcome the suspicion that the ordinance rests on impermissible assumptions or outmoded and perhaps invidious stereotypes.

III

... [T]he Court offers several justifications as to why the retarded do not warrant heightened judicial solicitude. These justifications, however, find no support in our heightened scrutiny precedents and cannot withstand logical analysis. ... First, heightened scrutiny is said to be inapplicable where *individuals* in a group have distinguishing characteristics that legislatures properly may take into account in some circumstances. [It] is also purportedly inappropriate when many legislative classifications affecting the *group* are likely to be valid. ...

Our ... precedents belie the claim that a characteristic must virtually always be irrelevant to warrant heightened scrutiny. ... Heightened but not strict scrutiny is considered appropriate in areas such as gender, illegitimacy, or alienage because the Court views the trait as relevant under some circumstances but not others. ...

Potentially discriminatory classifications exist only where some constitutional basis can be found for presuming that equal rights are required. Discrimination, in the Fourteenth Amendment sense, connotes a substantive constitutional judgment that two individuals or groups are entitled to be treated equally with respect to some thing. With regard to economic and commercial matters, no basis for such a conclusion exists, for as Justice Holmes urged the Lochner [v. New York (1905)] Court, the Fourteenth Amendment was not "intended to embody a particular economic theory. ..." As a matter of substantive policy, therefore, government is free to move in any direction, or to change directions, in the economic and commercial sphere. The structure of economic and commercial life is a matter of political compromise, not constitutional principle, and no norm of equality requires that there be as many opticians as optometrists, see *Williamson,* or new businesses as old, see New Orleans v. Dukes [1976].

But the Fourteenth Amendment does prohibit other results under virtually all circumstances, such as castes created by law along racial or ethnic lines, and significantly constrains the range of permissible government choices where gender or illegitimacy, for example, are concerned. Where such constraints ... are present, and where history teaches they have systemically been ignored, a "more searching judicial inquiry" is required. United States v. Carolene Products n. 4 (1938).

That more searching inquiry, be it called heightened scrutiny or "second order" rational basis review, is a method of approaching certain classifications skeptically, with judgment suspended until the facts are in and the evidence considered. ... Heightened scrutiny does not allow courts to second guess reasoned legislative or professional judgments tailored to the unique needs of a group like the retarded, but it does seek to assure that the hostility or thoughtlessness with which there is reason to be concerned has not carried the day. ... [1]

---

1. No single talisman can define those groups likely to be the target of classifications offensive to the Fourteenth Amendment and therefore warranting heightened or strict scrutiny; experience, not abstract logic, must be the primary guide. The "political powerlessness" of a group may be relevant, *Rodriguez,* but that factor is neither necessary, as the gender cases demonstrate, nor sufficient, as the example of minors illustrates. ... Similarly, immutability of the trait at issue may be relevant, but many immutable characteristics, such as height or blindness, are valid bases of governmental action and classifications under a variety of circumstances.

The political powerlessness of a group and the immutability of its defining trait are relevant insofar as they point to a social and cultural isolation that gives the majority little reason to respect or be concerned with that group's interests and needs. Statutes

IV

In light of the scrutiny that should be applied here, Cleburne's ordinance sweeps too broadly to dispel the suspicion that it rests on a bare desire to treat the retarded as outsiders, pariahs who do not belong in the community. The Court, while disclaiming that special scrutiny is necessary or warranted, reaches the same conclusion. Rather than striking the ordinance down, however, the Court invalidates it merely as applied to respondents. I must dissent from the novel proposition that "the preferred course of adjudication" is to leave standing a legislative act resting on "irrational prejudice," thereby forcing individuals in the group discriminated against to continue to run the act's gauntlet.

... [T]he Court's as-applied remedy relegates future retarded applicants to the standardless discretion of low-level officials who have already shown an all too willing readiness to be captured by the "vague, undifferentiated fears" of ignorant or frightened residents. Invalidating on its face the ordinance's special treatment of the "feebleminded," in contrast, would place the responsibility for tailoring and updating Cleburne's unconstitutional ordinance where it belongs: with the legislative arm of the City of Cleburne. ...

To my knowledge, the Court has never before treated an equal protection challenge to a statute on an as applied basis. When statutes rest on impermissibly overbroad generalizations, our cases have invalidated the presumption on its face. We do not ... leave to the courts the task of redrafting the statute through an ongoing and cumbersome process of "as applied" constitutional rulings. ...

Editors' Notes

(1) **Query:** What approach(es) to constitutional interpretation did White follow here? How did his approach(es) differ from Stevens's? From Marshall's?

(2) **Query:** Did *Cleburne* articulate a standard of "rationality with bite"? How did its doctrine relating to levels of scrutiny differ from that of Plyler v. Doe (1982; reprinted above, p. 1040)? Was Marshall correct in suggesting

---

discriminating against the young have not been common nor need be feared because those who do vote and legislate were once themselves young, typically have children of their own, and certainly interact regularly with minors. Their social integration means that minors, unlike discrete and insular minorities, tend to be treated in legislative arenas with full concern and respect, despite their formal and complete exclusion from the electoral process.

The discreteness and insularity warranting a "more searching judicial inquiry," *Carolene Products,* must therefore be viewed from a social and cultural perspective as well as a political one. To this task judges are well suited, for the lessons of history and experience are surely the best guide as to when, and with respect to what interests, society is likely to stigmatize individuals as members of an inferior caste or view them as not belonging to the community. Because prejudice spawns prejudice, and stereotypes produce limitations that confirm the stereotype on which they are based, a history of unequal treatment requires sensitivity to the prospect that its vestiges endure. In separating those groups that are discrete and insular from those that are not, as in many important legal distinctions, "a page of history is worth a volume of logic." New York Trust Co. v. Eisner (1921) (Holmes, J.). [Footnote by Justice Marshall.]

that the Court in fact used a "second order rational basis" standard that amounts to heightened or intermediate scrutiny?

(3) **Query:** Did Stevens's opinion further develop or merely reiterate his argument in Craig v. Boren (1976; reprinted above, p. 992) that "[t]here is only one Equal Protection Clause"? What is the difference between his conception of the proper single standard and Marshall's notion of a spectrum of standards? If they differ, which is more defensible?

(4) **Query:** Stevens defined " 'rational' as including 'elements of legitimacy and neutrality that must always characterize the performance of the sovereign's duty to govern impartially.' " Does this definition conform to any of the usual usages of the word? How could Stevens justify it as the command of 'the Constitution' "?

(5) **Query:** In footnote 1, Marshall said:

No single talisman can define those groups likely to be the target of classifications offensive to the Fourteenth Amendment and therefore warranting heightened or strict scrutiny; experience, not abstract logic, must be the primary guide.

This prescription follows from what approach to constitutional interpretation?

(6) **Query:** To what extent do *Plyler* and *Cleburne* represent efforts to cope simultaneously with questions of WHO and HOW?

E

MAINTAINING CONSTITU-TIONAL DEMOCRACY: PROTECTING FUNDAMENTAL RIGHTS

Building on the general discussion in Chapter 9 of HOW to interpret, Section C of this Part of the book examined problems of freedom of political communication and participation, especially important to democratic theory. We tried, though often with small help from the Supreme Court, to explore *reinforcing representative democracy* as providing an approach to constitutional interpretation. Section D took up a different problem, treating equals equally, a concern that democratic and constitutional theory, though perhaps for different reasons, share. Now we move to a purposive approach lying at the heart of constitutionalism, called *protecting fundamental rights.*[1]

I. FUNDAMENTAL RIGHTS AS AN INTERPRETIVE APPROACH

A. The Standards of Fundamental Rights

For an interpreter who follows a *fundamental-rights approach*, a valid policy must meet not only the procedural rules demanded by representative democracy—that is, be the product of free and open political processes—it must also meet substantive standards. Essentially, it must respect individual rights as explicitly and implicitly guaranteed by the larger constitution as well as the constitutional text. The touchstone for the legitimacy of a public policy is its respect for the individual's "liberty," "autonomy," and "dignity."

The connection between this approach and constitutionalism is both direct and obvious. As we saw in Chapter 3, however, "pure constitutionalists" are much rarer than "pure representative democrats." Constitutional democrats, however, are numerous. These interpreters share much of the concern of representative democrats for open political processes and broad-based political participation. With constitutionalists they also share deep concern for basic rights and a broad definition of "the Constitution." Because they are heavily represented among commentators, judges, and other public officials, we shall pit their arguments rather than those of pure constitutionalists against the opponents of a *fundamental-rights approach*.

B. Criticisms of the Approach

The initial and most critical problem with this interpretive approach lies in the fuzziness of its rules of recognition. How do

---

1. Much of the literature of constitutional interpretation uses "fundamental rights" and "fundamental values" as pretty much equivalent terms; see, for example, John Hart Ely, *Democracy and Distrust* (Cambridge: Harvard University Press, 1980), ch. 3. But the first term is narrower than the second: Rights may be only specific reflections of more abstract values and not all values need be associated with rights. For the sake of clarity, we shall maintain a distinction between the two concepts. The chapters in this Section focus on "fundamental rights"; when we refer to "fundamental values" we shall be speaking more abstractly.

interpreters discover "fundamental rights"? And how do they justi-fy (validate) that "fundamental" status? *Textualists, originalists,* and *doctrinalists,* or example, do not necessarily deny that certain rights are essential; but their usual justification is that the plain words of the document, the Founders' understanding, or an inter-pretive tradition has singled some rights out. A *fundamental-rights approach,* however, need not limit itself to the document's words, the Founders' understandings, or previous interpretations. As Ed-ward S. Corwin summed up the argument, "These rights are not fundamental because they find mention in the written instrument; they find mention there because they are fundamental." [2] That fundamentality, moreover, may fall upon rights that the Founders or previous interpreters had not thought so to hallow.

Although heavily dependent on constitutionalist theory *funda-mental rights* also rests in part on the words of the document, especially those of the Preamble, with its goal of securing "the Blessings of Liberty," the Ninth Amendment, with its protection of unlisted rights, and the Fifth and Fourteenth amendments' protect-ing "life, liberty, and property" against government's acting "with-out due process of law." In addition, it is a peculiar right for which an energetic scholar cannot find favorable mention by members of the founding generation and later authoritative interpreters.

But these clauses in the document are as open-ended as is the guarantee of equal protection. Their interpretation demands a degree of judgment and discretion that democratic theorists and even some constitutional democrats would reserve to elected offi-cials. Thus the indeterminacy of vital rights generates problems of WHO shall interpret as well as HOW to interpret. Beyond worry that wrong decisions will be made about which rights to protect and which not to protect, is concern that the wrong officials will make those inevitably controversial and consequential determinations and interfere with the execution of the people's will as expressed at the ballot box. The fear is that of judicial power running amok. And, as we have several times mentioned in referring to the period 1890–1937 and Chapter 16 will explain in detail, that fear is not the product of paranoid imaginations.

For most of half a century, judges saw the right to acquire, use, and dispose of property, including the "property" one has in his or her own labor, as *the* fundamental right and read the economic theory of laissez faire into the larger constitution. For much of that era, judicial supremacy was a reality, and "substantive due process" was its most powerful instrument. As we have noted before, the term "process" refers to procedure; thus "due process" meant normal legal procedure. Substantive due process, on the other

---

2. "The Basic Doctrine of American Constitutional Law," reprinted in Alpheus Thomas Mason and Gerald Garvey, eds., *American Constitutional History: Essays by Edward S. Corwin* (New York: Harper & Row, 1964), p. 26 (originally published in 12 *Mich.L.Rev.* 247 [1914]).

hand, holds that some forms of liberty are so essential that government may not abridge them by any process (procedure) whatever.
It makes the clauses in the Fifth and Fourteenth amendments
forbidding the federal or state governments to deprive any person
of "life, liberty or property, without due process of law" read:

> Neither the state nor the federal government may take away
> certain liberties no matter what procedures are used.

Substantive due process, as John Hart Ely has remarked, "is a
contradiction in terms—sort of like 'green pastel redness.' ... By
the same token, 'procedural due process' is redundant." [3] But the
justices, having refused in the Slaughter–House Cases (1873; reprinted above, p. 550) to infer much of significance from the
privileges or immunities clause of the Fourteenth Amendment,
needed some tie to the constitutional document to protect what
they thought were basic rights against state infractions. And they
chose the due process clause. Constitutional interpretation seems
stuck with the concept.

Since 1937 and more particularly since *Carolene Products*
(1938; reprinted above, p. 609), the Court has turned its attention
to rights other than those to property and freedom of contract.
Section C of this book analyzed the rights to participate freely in
open political processes that Stone included in paragraph 2 of
footnote 4 of *Carolene Products*, and Section D those to equal
treatment he included under paragraph 3. This Section treats those
rights arguably included in paragraph 1. Each of those rights is no
less consequential than property for the political system, and each is
no less controversial.

Dissenting in *Griswold* against the Court's reading a right to
privacy into "the Constitution," Justice Hugo Black expressed the
basic objection to using the due process clause to employ *fundamental-rights approach* to constitutional interpretation:

> The due process argument ... is based ... on the premise
> that this Court is vested with power to invalidate all state laws
> that it considers to be arbitrary, capricious, unreasonable, or
> oppressive, or this Court's belief that a particular state law has no
> "rational or justifying" purpose, or is offensive to a "sense of
> fairness and justice." If these formulas based on "natural jus-
> tice," or others which mean the same thing, are to prevail, they
> require judges to determine what is or is not constitutional on the
> basis of their own appraisal of what laws are unwise or unneces-
> sary. The power to make such decisions is of course that of a
> legislative body.

Ely echoes Black's assertions and says more generally that, as an
interpretive approach, *fundamental rights* means little more than

---

3. Ely, supra note 1, p. 16.

the imposition of judges' personal values: "the fact that it's done with mirrors shouldn't count as a defense."[4]

C. The Defenders Reply: The Judges

This objection points to a flaw that representative democrats, constitutional democrats, and constitutionalists alike would deem fatal, for the sort of rule of law the American political system values is not the rule of whim, whether executive, legislative, or judicial. But the response of interpreters who favor a *fundamental-rights approach* is that the objection is invalid; this approach does not leave judges free to impose their personal values, or at least any more free than do other interpretive approaches.

Arguments supporting this reply have varied in intellectual power. Justice Benjamin N. Cardozo spoke of grounding notions of fundamentality in the "traditions and [collective] conscience of our people"[5] and in "the very essence of a scheme of ordered liberty."[6] Felix Frankfurter thought that judicial choices, if "deeply rooted in reason," were effectively bounded by "the deposit of history," "the traditions and conscience of our people," and the "decencies of civilized conduct," all of which could be discovered by a "disinterested inquiry pursued in the spirit of science, on a balanced order of facts exactly and fairly stated, on the detached consideration of conflicting claims."[7] Earl Warren's comment about the standards of "cruel and unusual punishments" was part of his concept of primary rights as reflections of "the evolving standards of decency that mark the progress of a maturing society."[8]

In his dissenting opinion in Poe v. Ullman (1961; reprinted above, p. 141), John Marshall Harlan, II, tried his hand at explaining how judges translated "due process" into substantive fundamental rights:

> The best that can be said is that, through the course of this Court's decisions, [due process] has represented the balance which our Nation, built upon postulates of respect for the liberty of the individual, has struck between that liberty and the demands of organized society. If the supplying of content to this Constitutional concept has of necessity been a rational process, it certainly has not been one where judges have felt free to roam where unguided speculation might take them. The balance of which I speak is the balance struck by this country, having regard to what history teaches are the traditions from which it developed as well

4. *Ibid.*, p. 70.

5. Snyder v. Massachusetts (1934).

6. Palko v. Connecticut (1937; reprinted above, p. 128).

7. Rochin v. California (1952; reprinted above, p. 135).

8. Trop v. Dulles (1958; reprinted above, p. 219).

as the traditions from which it broke. ... No formula could serve as a substitute, in this area, for judgment and restraint.

In Rochin v. California (1952; reprinted above, p. 135), Douglas joined Black in condemning "the accordion-like qualities" of substantive due process in particular and the *fundamental-rights approach* (which Black misconstrued as a form of natural law) in general. Later, however, Douglas, to Black's dismay, became a convert to *fundamental rights*, though he tried to anchor decisions in the document and to do so in clauses other than due process. In *Griswold*, for example, he used *structuralism* to find a right of privacy in the "penumbra" of the First, Third, Fourth, and Ninth amendments as well as in self-incrimination clause of the Fifth.

Justice Arthur Goldberg's interpretive strategy was different. Concurring in *Griswold*, he agreed that "the concept of liberty protects those personal rights that are fundamental, and is not confined to the specific terms of the Bill of Rights." His principal textual grounding was the Ninth Amendment, whose "language and history," he claimed, "reveal that the Framers ... believed that there are additional fundamental rights, protected from governmental infringement, which exist alongside those fundamental rights specifically mentioned in the first eight amendments." But, he added, he did not view that amendment as

> an independent source of rights protected from infringement by either the States or the Federal Government. Rather, the Ninth Amendment ... simply shows the intent of the Constitution's authors that other fundamental personal rights should not be denied such protection or disparaged in any other way simply because they are not specifically listed. ...

This usage is novel, but how it solves the problem of judicial discretion is not obvious, unless it represents an *originalist* claim that the framers meant judges to have discretion.

Thurgood Marshall has also tried to find textual moorings firmer than due process for unlisted basic rights. As he explained in his dissent in San Antonio v. Rodriguez (1973; reprinted above, p. 1002):

> The task in every case should be to determine the extent to which constitutionally guaranteed rights are dependent upon interests not mentioned in the Constitution. As the nexus between the specific constitutional guarantee and the nonconstitutional interest draws closer, the nonconstitutional interest becomes more fundamental and the degree of judicial scrutiny applied ... must be adjusted accordingly.

D. The Defenders Reply: The Commentators

Constitutional commentators offer a different and somewhat broader set of responses. On the one hand, they point out that alternative approaches to interpretation suffer from similar problems of indeterminacy. A *textual approach* solves some but hardly all problems and, if anything, supports *fundamental rights* as an interpretive approach. The plain words of the Ninth Amendment specifically say that the listing of some rights does not put others on a lower plane. Thus those who insist on a *textualist approach* face a cruel dilemma: The document tells them to look beyond the document. It is no accident, proponents of *fundamental rights* chortle, that many *textualists* ignore the plain words of the Ninth Amendment. In *Griswold*, for instance, Hugo Black dismissed it as "a recent discovery" even though it had then been in the constitutional document for 173 years.

John Hart Ely is more subtle in trying to outflank the Ninth Amendment. Addressing the interrogative WHO, he claims the amendment is not directed toward judges but toward elected officials. Why its plain words deflect it from judicial concern any more than other clauses of the Bill of Rights, especially the First, which begins "Congress shall make no law," is something Ely finds it difficult to explain. What he does explain very convincingly, however, is that excluding the Ninth Amendment from the judicial ambit enables a theory of democracy to fit "the Constitution" more closely and so supports *reinforcing representative democracy* as *the* proper interpretative approach. But this argument, proponents of *fundamental rights* retort, reasons that because the analytical model does not fit the constitutional text, it is the constitutional text and not the model that is wrong-headed.

Originalism's quest for the Founders' understanding fails on its own terms for it seeks a collective state of mind that may well not have existed and in any event is beyond our power to recapture. Insofar as a *developmental approach* looks at "the Constitution" as changing over time, it is much more likely to find several patterns among which interpreters must choose than to discover a single bright thread. *Structural analysis* is often useful but it, too, requires wide discretion, as does *prudential analysis*. As do all of these approaches, *doctrinal analysis* will probably produce a variety of models from which an interpreter must select.

As we have seen in the chapters in Section C, *reinforcing representative democracy* also requires an interpreter to make important choices, not least of which is to read democratic theory into "the Constitution." Indeed, Laurence H. Tribe argues that that interpretive approach is merely a particular aspect of a fundamental-values approach (as is *fundamental rights*): An interpreter decides that self-government through political participation is *the* primary value of the polity and proceeds from there.[9]

---

9. "The Puzzling Persistence of Process–Based Constitutional Theories," 89 *Yale L.J.* 1063 (1980); reprinted as ch. 2 of his *Constitutional Choices* (Cambridge: Harvard University Press, 1985).

More positively, proponents of a *fundamental-rights approach* assert that the constitutional text as well as the broader constitution are based on two political theories, constitutionalism as well as democracy, and the interpretive approach of *fundamental rights* is necessary to the integrity of interpretation that takes the text seriously.

However one evaluates these arguments and counterarguments, it is essential to recognize that interpretation inevitably involves judgment and judgment inevitably brings power to whoever possesses it. Proponents of *fundamental rights* are correct to underline the wide range of discretion that the other interpretive approaches require, but reading constitutionalist theory into "the Constitution" represents just as great—democratic theorists would say greater—discretion as reading democratic theory into "the Constitution."

II. THE PLAN OF CHAPTERS 16–18

The most logical way to analyze *fundamental rights* as a an approach to constitutional interpretation would seem to be to start with the plain words of the document and analyze the fate of a listed basic right such as freedom of religion, then proceed outward to less textually entrenched rights such as property, to those "implicit" in the document and claiming beatification by tradition, such as marriage, and ultimately to those, such as privacy, that some interpreters believe constitutionalism requires. Unfortunately, American constitutional development has not proceeded so logically. In deciding the first cases—see, for example, Calder v. Bull (1798; reprinted above, p. 121)—judges immediately leaped beyond the text to theories of "free government," constitutionalism, and natural law and natural rights. In the second decade of the nineteenth century, the Court retreated from invocation of those theories, just as, more slowly and less completely, it withdrew from open use of a *fundamental-rights approach*.

When, near the end of the nineteenth century, the Court returned to this sort of analysis, both the justices and commentators couched analyses largely in terms of property or of putative liberties, such as freedom of contract, closely connected to property. The core problem was individual liberty and autonomy but the context was property—how much control over an individual's economic freedom, even to work for starvation wages, could government exert without infringing, even in the name of benevolence, the autonomy that constitutionalism says is the goal of the state?

Because many current concepts and much juridical vocabulary of *fundamental rights* developed in the battle over property, economic liberty, and due process of law—as did many of the scars that still mark the Supreme Court's institutional psyche—understanding past struggles over economic rights is essential to understanding more recent struggles about *fundamental rights* outside the economic sphere. Thus this Section begins with a chapter that focuses on the problems generated for constitutional interpretation when property is—or is not—held to be a basic right. Only then does Chapter 17 proceed to a more textually secure right, that to freedom of religion. Last, Chapter 18 takes up a set of claims to rights relating to privacy and personal liberty, most of which are at least as strongly based in visions of the polity's transcendent structure and underlying political theories as in the constitutional document.

SELECTED BIBLIOGRAPHY

Arkes, Hadley. *The Return of George Sutherland: Restoring a Jurisprudence of Natural Rights* (Princeton: Princeton University Press, 1994).

Barber, Sotirios A. *On What the Constitution Means* (Baltimore: Johns Hopkins University Press, 1984).

————. "The New Right Assault on Moral Inquiry in Constitutional Law," 54 *Geo.Wash.L.Rev.* 253 (1986).

————. "Stanley Fish and the Future of Pragmatism in Legal Theory," 58 *U.Chi.L.Rev.* 1033 (1991).

————. *The Constitution of Judicial Power* (Baltimore: Johns Hopkins University Press, 1993).

Berns, Walter F. *Taking the Constitution Seriously* (New York: Simon & Schuster, 1987).

Brest, Paul. "The Fundamental Rights Controversy," 90 *Yale L.J.* 1063 (1981).

————. "Interpretation and Interest," 34 *Stan.L.Rev.* 765 (1982). (A reply to Fiss, listed below.)

Choper, Jesse H. *Judicial Review and the National Political Process* (Chicago: University of Chicago Press, 1980), espec. chs. 1–2.

Corwin, Edward S. "The Basic Doctrine of American Constitutional Law," 12 *Mich.L.Rev.* 247 (1914); reprinted in Alpheus Thomas Mason and Gerald Garvey, eds., *American Constitutional History: Essays by Edward S. Corwin* (New York: Harper & Row, 1964).

Dworkin, Ronald. *Life's Dominion* (New York: Knopf, 1993).

Ely, John H. *Democracy and Distrust* (Cambridge: Harvard University Press, 1980), espec. ch. 3.

Fish, Stanley. "Almost Pragmatism: Richard Posner's Jurisprudence," 57 *U.Chi.L.Rev.* 1447 (1990).

Fiss, Owen. "Objectivity and Interpretation," 43 *Stan.L.Rev.* 739 (1982).

Flathman, Richard. *The Practice of Rights* (Cambridge: Cambridge University Press, 1976).

Fleming, James E. "Constructing the Substantive Constitution," 72 *Tex.L.Rev.* 211 (1993).

Macedo, Stephen. *Liberal Virtues* (Oxford: Clarendon Press, 1990).

Miller, Arthur S. "Toward a Definition of 'the' Constitution," 8 *U. of Dayton L.Rev.* 633 (1983).

Murphy, Walter F. "Constitutional Interpretation: Text, Values, and Processes," 9 *Reviews in Am. Hist.* 7 (1981).

————. "Constitutions, Constitutionalism, and Democracy," in Douglas Greenberg, Stanley N. Katz, Melanie Beth Oliviero, and Steven C. Wheatley, eds., *Constitutionalism and Democracy* (New York: Oxford University Press, 1993).

Parker, Richard D. "The Past of Constitutional Theory—And Its Future," 42 *Ohio St.L.J.* 223 (1981).

Pennock, J. Roland, and John W. Chapman, eds. *Constitutionalism* (New York: New York University Press, 1979) (*Nomos*, vol. 20).

————. *Human Rights* (New York: New York University Press, 1979) (*Nomos*, vol. 23).

————. *Liberal Democracy* (New York: New York University Press, 1979) (*Nomos*, vol. 25).

Perry, Michael J. *The Constitution in the Courts* (New York: Oxford University Press, 1994).

Posner, Richard A. *The Problems of Jurisprudence* (Cambridge: Harvard University Press, 1990).

Richards, David A.J. "Moral Philosophy and the Search for Fundamental Values in Constitutional Law," 42 *Ohio St.L.J.* 319 (1981).

————. *Conscience and the Constitution: History, Theory, and Law of the Reconstruction Amendments* (Princeton: Princeton University Press, 1993).

Smith, Rogers M. "The Constitution and Autonomy," 60 *Tex.L.Rev.* 175 (1982).

Sunstein, Cass R. *The Partial Constitution* (Cambridge: Harvard University Press, 1993).

Tribe, Laurence H. "The Puzzling Persistence of Process–Based Constitutional Theories," 89 *Yale L.J.* 1063 (1980); reprinted in his *Constitutional Choices* (Cambridge: Harvard University Press, 1985).

_____. *American Constitutional Law* (2d ed.; Mineola, NY: Foundation Press, 1988), chs. 11, 14–15.

_____, and Michael C. Dorf. *On Reading the Constitution* (Cambridge: Harvard University Press, 1991), espec. chs. 3, 5.

Wellington, Harry H. *Interpreting the Constitution* (New Haven: Yale University Press, 1990).

16

The Right to Property: To Individual Autonomy and Back

As we saw in Chapter 3, the framers of the constitutional text believed that legislatures, if checked only by popular election, threatened the institution of private property. Not surprisingly, then, the Philadelphia Convention proposed a document with explicit limitations on state authority to tax, regulate trade, enact bankruptcy laws, coin money, refuse to recognize legal transactions in other states, and impair the obligation of contracts.

The initial constitutional document also ordered that any "direct" federal tax be apportioned among the states according to population; and Article IV protected a form of property in humans by imposing an obligation on each state to hand over persons "held to Service or Labour" who might have fled another state's jurisdiction. The Fifth Amendment later included an additional pair of restrictions on the power of the federal government over property: a ban on depriving persons of property "without due process of law," and a requirement that the government pay "just compensation" when taking private property for public use.[1]

The Federalists' desire to safeguard their own possessions and their belief that commercialism was essential to scientific progress, prosperity, and moderation of religious conflict, all pushed the Founders toward a government that would protect private property, reward acquisitiveness, and foster economic growth (in contradistinction to goals like moral excellence and self-sacrificing civic mindedness). They sought a society that would exemplify the statement in John Locke's *Second Treatise of Civil Government* (1690) that the "great and *chief end*" of society "*is the Preservation of their property.*" (Emphasis in original; reprinted below, p. 1083.)

---

1. In limiting searches and seizures, the Fourth Amendment speaks of "the right of the people to be secure in their persons, houses, papers, and effects. . . ."

I. PROPERTY AS A CIVIL RIGHT

At the outset, we should note four points important to a discussion of property as a fundamental constitutional right. First, the constitutional text does not explicitly recognize rights to own, use, and dispose of property as "basic." That status was quite possibly assumed by the founding generation (see Madison's discussion in *Federalist* No. 10, below at p. 1087); certainly generations of interpreters have made that assumption. Nevertheless, the text does not so bless property rights.

Second, at the close of the eighteenth century, people often used the word "property" in a broader sense than we do, encompassing much more than tangible goods. For Locke, "property" had embraced a man's right "in his own person" to use his labor as he saw fit. In his *Second Treatise*, he spoke of men uniting to form civil society for "the mutual *preservation* of their Lives, Liberties and Estates, which I call by the general name, *Property*." (Reprinted below, p. 1083.) And James Madison said that

> a man has a property in his opinions and the free communication
> of them, ... in his religious opinions, and in the profession and
> practice dictated by them. ... In a word, as a man is said to have
> a right to his property, he may be equally said to have a property
> in his rights.[2]

In this broad sense, a right to property is shorthand for an expanse of personal freedoms that need be only tangentially related, if at all, to economic activity.

The third point is that, for most of America's founding generation, tangible property was first and foremost land. The society was basically agricultural, the population heavily composed of those who worked their own farms, along with artisans ("mechanics"), shopkeepers, and small-scale merchants. Only in the Plantation South was there anything like the huge modern factory, where masses of people worked for an owner. Productive property thus was something that the typical white, male adult could possess and exploit with his own labor. His relationships with other members of the community were usually direct and face to face. In these respects, the change from eighteenth to twentieth century America is radical.

Fourth, then as now, people recognized the exclusive use of some tangible property as essential to survival and the *right* to such use as essential to autonomy. Without a minimal amount of food, water, and clothing a human being soon dies. And to the extent that a person is dependent on another for the necessities of life, that person is not autonomous. He or she cannot make independent decisions about the religious, social, and economic choices life presents, including the choices that confront active citizens of a

---

2. "Property," *National Gazette*, March 29, 1792; reprinted in Marvin Meyers, ed., *The Mind of the Founder* (Indianapolis: Bobbs–Merrill, 1973), pp. 243–244.

representative democracy. Franklin Roosevelt spoke only ancient wisdom when he said that "Necessitous men are not free men."[3] In *Federalist* No. 79, Alexander Hamilton had written that "*a power over a man's subsistence amounts to a power over his will.*" (Emphasis in original.) Jefferson agreed that full citizenship under a "free government" required some economic autonomy:

> Dependence begets subservience and venality, suffocates the germ of virtue, and prepares fit tools for the designs of ambition. ... It is the manners and spirit of a people which preserve a republic in vigour.[4]

A few years earlier, Jefferson had proposed that, to make Virginians truly independent, that state should give to "every person of full age" enough land to total fifty acres and that women should have a right to inherit equal to men.[5]

Psychological expectations change the content of "necessities" across time and culture. Even an agrarian like Jefferson "came to appreciate the political and economic advantage, if not the virtue, of commerce and urban growth. ...."[6] And few people in a modern society are likely to be completely autonomous. Even so, the impersonal interdependence of a middle class American in the 1990s is not the abject personal dependence of a factory worker in the 1890s, or a share cropper in the 1930s, or a migrant agricultural worker, an illegal alien, or a welfare mother.

When the constitutional text was drafted, the connection between private property and political autonomy may have been more apparent than it is today. Because voting then was usually done publicly and orally, employers and creditors could check on employees and debtors to "encourage" them to vote "correctly." Yet studies of electoral behavior show that, despite institutional changes, linkages between individual economic well being and active citizenship remain significant. And notwithstanding such chronic problems as the emergence of what could be a permanent underclass in America, the relative wealth of capitalist economies together with the recent collapse of European Communism and China's movement toward more private ownership indicates a strong positive relation among private property, economic productivity, and relative social contentment. These considerations provide some justification for Madison's statement in *Federalist* No. 10 (reprinted below, p. 1087) that protecting the "different and un-

---

3. "Message to Congress on the State of the Union," Jan. 11, 1944; Samuel I. Rosenman, ed., *The Public Papers and Addresses of Franklin D. Roosevelt* (Harper & Bros., 1950), XIII, 41.

4. *Notes on Virginia* (1782), in Andrew A. Lipscomb, ed., *The Writings of Thomas Jefferson* (Washington, D.C.: The Thomas Jefferson Memorial Association, 1903), II, 229.

5. "The Virginia Constitution: Third Draft of Jefferson," Julian P. Boyd, ed., *The Papers of Thomas Jefferson* (Princeton: Princeton University Press, 1950), I, 358.

6. Stanley N. Katz, "Thomas Jefferson and the Right to Property in Revolutionary America," 19 *J. of Law and Econ.* 467, 487 (1976).

equal faculties of acquiring property" is "the first object of government."

II. THE DEVELOPMENT OF SUBSTANTIVE DUE PROCESS

A. The Transformation of American Law

For the generation of 1787–91, property was probably a natural right, though the constitutional text did not so label it. And, because the right to property included rights to use and increase property, that basic right included a cognate right to contract with other property holders. Thus did the right to contract borrow a measure of moral status from the broader right in which it originated; the obligation to keep one's contracts was a duty flowing from the natural right to property. This duty was no more an absolute than the broader right to property itself, however. Thus property could be regulated, occupied, and even taken by legally competent authority under conditions set forth in the constitutional text and statutes—conditions like those prevailing "in time of war" (Amendment III) or, if taken by the national government, in return for "just compensation" or only after its owner has been accorded "due process of law" (Amendment V).

Although the Founders appreciated the need to regulate property (at p. 1088, below, we find Madison in *Federalist* No. 10 calling such regulation "the principal task of modern Legislation"), paper money, and other debtor relief laws and resulting economic uncertainty in the states under the Articles of Confederation taught the Federalists to distrust state legislatures. Article I, § 10 of the constitutional document reflects this suspicion by providing that "No State shall ... make any Thing but gold and silver Coin a Tender in Payment of Debts ... [or]pass any ... Law ... impairing the Obligation of Contracts." Early judicial opinions—for example, those of Marshall and Johnson in Fletcher v. Peck (1810; reprinted below, p. 1091)—show just how fundamental many members of that age thought property and contract were. Ever solicitous of the needs of investors, Marshall extended the notion of contract from that of agreement between private persons, to land sales by the states. *Fletcher* held that, because the Contract Clause protected those sales, they were irreversible, even when caused by land speculators bribing state legislators. And Johnson, invoking a law higher than that of man, would have held that the Deity himself had to respect the obligation of contracts—though the justice did not mention how he would enforce his writ. The Marshall Court was to extend the notion of contract again in Dartmouth College v. Woodward (1819), this time to include a corporate charter issued by a state.

By the time of the Charles River Bridge Case (1837; reprinted below, p. 1095), the balance of political power in America had changed and with it the attitude of the Supreme Court. Now less solicitous of investors and more concerned with permitting state legislatures to pursue their versions of the public interest, the Court was willing to tolerate more state intervention, usually in the interests of new economic groups of merchants and capitalists as opposed to those of farmers and other landholders. "While the rights of private property are safely guarded," Chief Justice Roger Brooke Taney said for the Court, "we must not forget that the community also have rights, and that the happiness and well being of every citizen depends on their faithful preservation."

Yet Taney was not simply choosing the interests of the community over the rights of the individual, he was also preferring one form of private property over another. He was presiding over a massive transformation—a shift of which he did not fully approve—from the legal economy of an agricultural society to that of a capitalist nation.[7] Morton J. Horwitz has summarized the changes:

> As the spirit of economic development began to take hold of American society in the early years of the nineteenth century ... the idea of property underwent a fundamental transformation—from a static agrarian conception entitling an owner to undisturbed enjoyment, to a dynamic, instrumental, and more abstract view of property that emphasized the newly paramount virtues of productive use and development. By the time of the Civil War, the basic change in legal conceptions about property was completed.[8]

Entrepreneurs and merchants allied with lawyers, Horwitz argues, to encourage state intervention to help the new capitalism. On the one hand, these groups persuaded state legislatures to use tax money and public lands to subsidize mills, canals, and railroads. On the other hand, the new financiers persuaded legislatures to delegate to them the state's power of eminent domain, the authority to seize private property for "public use." That "public use," of

---

7. Taney's opinion for the Court in Dred Scott v. Sandford (1857; reprinted above, p. 195 and cross-referenced below, p. 1100) may appear to be an exception to this pattern because it declared that Congress could not outlaw slavery in the territories consistently with the Fifth Amendment's guarantee of due process. But *Dred Scott* came near the end of Taney's career, long after cases like *Charles River Bridge* (1837), and was enmeshed with the raging debate over slavery and the nature of the Union. There was a clash between different notions of property, but property-in-humans versus property-in-liberty. Despite his personal revulsion against slavery, Taney believed, or professed to believe, that the constitutional text and its founders had recognized that whites had a fundamental right to own black slaves.

8. *The Transformation of American Law, 1780–1860* (Cambridge: Harvard University Press, 1977), p. 31. Horwitz's thesis has not been universally accepted. For sharp critiques, see espec.: A.W.B. Simpson, "The Horwitz Thesis and the History of Contracts," 46 *U.Chi.L.Rev.* 533 (1979); Gary T. Schwartz, "Tort Law and the Economy in Nineteenth Century America: A Reinterpretation," 90 *Yale L.J.* 1717 (1981); Stephen Presser, "Revising the Conservative Tradition," 52 *N.Y.U.L.Rev.* 700 (1977); and Tony Freyer, "Reassessing the Impact of Eminent Domain," 1981 *Wisc.L.Rev.* 1263.

course, would be for "civic improvements" that these developers were constructing for their own private gain.

B. The Grangers, the ABA, and Social Darwinism

The avarice and ruthlessness of the new alliance caused periodic popular reactions, first from Jacksonian democracy, then the Grangers, the Populists, the Progressives, and eventually the New Deal. In part, Chief Justice Taney's defense of states rights was a Jacksonian affirmation of state power—the state police power—to regulate the new corporations. But the great victory came a dozen years after the Civil War, when in Munn v. Illinois (1877; reprinted below, p. 1101) the Grangers won the Court's constitutional approval of state legislative authority to regulate fees that owners of grain elevators could charge farmers to store their grain.

Munn alarmed the business alliance by showing how the state power it had so carefully cultivated could be captured by other forces. The counterattack was swift, effective, and, ironically, "conservative" in tone, urging not continuing legal changes but protecting changes effected by the previous generation—in effect, guarding the newly transformed status quo. Among the first reactions to *Munn* was the founding of the American Bar Association in 1878, an organization that soon became, in Prof. Corwin's words, "a juristic sewing circle for mutual education in the gospel of *laissez faire*." [9] Seeking the reversal of *Munn* the ABA began a campaign to "educate" both lawyers and judges.

The times were propitious. In a series of essays and speeches and his popular book entitled *Social Statics* (1866), Herbert Spencer preached a doctrine of "Social Darwinism" that fit well with economic laissez faire and a constitutional right to own, use, and dispose of private property with minimal governmental regulation. As Darwin taught biological evolution, so Spencer and his followers taught social evolution: Left to themselves, the best of mankind, "the fittest," would survive and prosper. If government intervened beyond keeping public order and protecting private property, the intellectually and morally weak would also survive and impede the march of progress. Life was a dog-eat-dog battle. The kindest and most efficient course for government was to let the economic struggle develop on its own terms—terms, incidentally, that had recently given legal advantages to business over labor, railroads over farmers, and bankers over almost everybody.

Spencer was immensely influential in the last quarter of the nineteenth century and well into the twentieth, exercising, Henry

---

9. *Liberty Against Government* (Baton Rouge: Louisiana State University Press, 1948), p. 138. Corwin relied heavily on what is still among the most important works on the incorporation of laissez faire into American constitutional law: Benjamin R. Twiss, *Lawyers and the Constitution* (Princeton: Princeton University Press, 1942). (Twiss had been Corwin's student at Princeton.)

Steele Commager remarked, "such sovereignty over America as George III had never enjoyed." [10]   Other writers, like Charles W. Eliot of Harvard, Nicholas Murray Butler at Columbia, and, most eloquently of all, William Graham Sumner of Yale, lent academic prestige to the spread of Spencer's good news that competition was "a law of nature," the reward of liberty was progress, and the price of mitigating the economic struggle was "the survival of the unfittest" and the destruction of liberty. [11]

More positively, "the Gospel of Wealth" transformed acquisitiveness into civic duty and religious virtue.   "[T]he acquisition of property is required by love," Mark Hopkins, president of Williams College, wrote in 1868, "because it is a powerful means of benefitting others."   "Godliness is in league with riches," Episcopalian Bishop William Lawrence said at the turn of the century.   "Material prosperity is helping to make the national character sweeter, more joyous, more unselfish, more Christlike."   Earlier, the Rev. Russell H. Conwell, who was to become president of Temple University, had urged young people "get rich, get rich!"   To "make money honestly," he claimed, "is to preach the gospel.   ... Money is power and you ought to be reasonably ambitious to have it.   You ought to because you can do more good with it than without it. ... If you can honestly attain unto riches ... it is your Christian and godly duty to do so." [12]

There were, of course, dissenting voices who warned that the economic theory of laissez faire was self-defeating, the sociology of Social Darwinism fallacious, the theology of wealth a cruel sacrilege, and the effects of all three destructive to the lives of millions of farmers, workers, and their families.   And, as we have mentioned, there were occasional counteralliances, like those of the Populists and the Progressives, who managed to dull some of capitalism's harsher edges.   But, early on, the counteralliances were no match for the Social Darwinists, and it took the Great Depression of 1929 and the New Deal before wide scale and long term regulatory reform could achieve some degree of success.

In the legal sphere, Thomas Cooley's *Treatise on Constitutional Limitations* (1868) and Christopher G. Tiedeman's *Treatise on the Limitations of Police Power in the United States* (1886) were the most influential books of their time.   Cooley anticipated the development of property as *the* fundamental constitutional value, liberty as the primary constitutional right, and substantive due process as the instrument for their accomplishment; but Tiedeman

---

10.   *The American Mind* (New Haven: Yale University Press, 1950), p. 87.

11.   See the excellent analyses in A.J. Beitzinger, *A History of American Political Thought* (New York: Dodd, Mead, 1972), ch. 19; and Alpheus Thomas Mason and Gordon E. Baker, eds., *Free Government in the Making* (4th ed.; New York: Oxford University Press, 1985), ch. 14.

12.   Quoted in Mason and Baker, supra note 11, pp. 522–523.

"deserves credit for [their] crystallization into a fixed and pervading doctrine." [13]

C. The Judges Respond

The conservatives' first great judicial victory came in 1885 when the Court held that corporations were "persons" protected by the Fourteenth Amendment.[14] In 1890 Chicago, Milwaukee, and St. Paul Ry. v. Minnesota gutted *Munn* by ruling that the fairness of rates businesses could charge was ultimately a judicial not a legislative question. In 1895, three landmark decisions solidified laissez faire. United States v. E.C. Knight held that the Sherman Antitrust Act could not reach a sugar manufacturer who produced more than 95 per cent of the sugar sold in the United States because manufacturing was local commerce, beyond the scope of congressional power. Pollock v. Farmers' Loan & Trust Co. held the income tax unconstitutional, in spite of precedents as old as 1796[15] and as recent as 1881.[16] The third case, In re Debs, hit at labor unions by ruling that the President could seek an injunction to prevent a railroad strike and the district judge could summarily punish for contempt of court the labor leader whose union violated the injunction. Later decisions held unions liable for treble damages under the Sherman Act[17] and invalidated both federal and state statutes outlawing so-called "yellow dog" contracts, under which owners made not joining a union a condition of employment.[18]

In 1897, Allgeyer v. Louisiana summed up the Court's new jurisprudence, explaining WHAT "the Constitution" included as well as HOW the judges were interpreting it:

> The liberty mentioned in that [Fourteenth] amendment means not only the right of the citizen to be free from the mere physical restraint of his person ... but the term is deemed to embrace the right of the citizen to be free in the enjoyment of all his faculties; to be free to use them in all lawful ways: to live and work where he will; to earn his livelihood by any lawful calling; to pursue any livelihood or avocation, and for that purpose to enter into all contracts which may be proper, necessary and essential to his carrying out to a successful conclusion the purposes above mentioned.

Of this litany, it was the last right, that of contract, which the Court came to consider paramount. Interestingly, the list did not mention such freedoms as those of speech, press, and religion expressly

---

13. Clyde E. Jacobs, *Law Writers and the Courts* (Berkeley: University of California Press, 1954), p. 62.

14. Santa Clara County v. South Pacific R. Co. (1886).

15. Hylton v. United States (1796).

16. Springer v. United States (1880).

17. For example, Loewe v. Lawlor (1908) (the Danbury Hatters' Case).

18. Adair v. United States (1908); Coppage v. Kansas (1915).

listed in the text. The justices would not begin to protect these until well into the 1920s.

The paradigm case of laissez faire and substantive due process was Lochner v. New York (1905; reprinted below, p. 1110), in which the Court by a 5–4 vote held that a state law limiting bakers to no more than a 60–hour work week was "a mere meddlesome interference" with freedom of contract. As we shall see in the head- and endnotes to the cases reprinted in this chapter, the judicial record was not uniform during the period 1890–1937, but generally the justices used the due process clause of the Fourteenth Amendment to strike down state regulations of business and the Tenth Amendment to strike down federal regulations.

D. The End of Liberty of Contract

The climax came during the years 1935–36, when a majority of the justices opposed the New Deal's efforts to regulate business and labor. As Justice Stone wrote his sister at the close of the 1935 term:

> Our latest exploit was a holding by a divided vote that there was no power in a state to regulate minimum wages for women. Since the court last week said that this could not be done by the national government, as the matter was local, and it is said that it cannot be done by local government even though it is local, we have tied Uncle Sam up in a hard knot.[19]

The knot, of course, did not stay tied. Stinging dissents from Stone and sometimes Brandeis and Cardozo, along with an occasional protest from Charles Evans Hughes, ate at the majority's self-confidence. The crucial event, however, was Roosevelt's stunning victory at the polls in November, 1936, winning in every state except Maine and Vermont. "Looking back," Justice Owen J. Roberts commented fifteen years later, "it is difficult to see how the Court could have resisted the popular urge for uniform standards throughout the country—for what in effect was a unified economy."[20]

By early December 1936, the justices began to capitulate. Roberts changed his mind first on the constitutionality of state regulation of wages (see West Coast Hotel v. Parrish [1937; reprinted below, p. 1123]),[21] then on the reach of the commerce clause,[22]

---

19. Quoted in Alpheus Thomas Mason, *Harlan Fiske Stone* (New York: Viking, 1956), p. 426.

20. *The Court and the Constitution* (Cambridge: Harvard University Press, 1951), p. 61.

21. In 1936 Roberts had provided the fifth vote in Morehead v. New York to invalidate a state law regulating wages and less than a year later the fifth vote in *Parrish* upholding a practically identical law. In a memorandum he left with Frankfurter, Roberts tried to explain his shift. "Mr. Justice Roberts," 104 *U.Pa.L.Rev.* 311 (1955), reprinted in Philip Elman, ed., *Of Law and Men: Papers and Addresses of Felix Frankfurter* (New York:

---

22. See note 22 on page 1079.

and later on the authority of the federal government to use its power to tax not merely for purposes of revenue, but also as a tool for regulating social and economic behavior.[23]   Because these changes began in December, 1936 in the justices' secret conferences, months before they were publicly announced, Roosevelt had no way of knowing that he was winning the war.   In February, 1937, he launched his plan to add one justice to the Court for each member over 70 who did not retire, up to a maximum number of fifteen.   Given the advanced age of many of the justices, Roosevelt would have immediately had six nominations.   Ultimately, the Court-packing bill failed to pass either house of Congress;   but, when the Court's shift became public that spring, it seemed that the justices had retreated under fire.   References to the about-face in *West Coast Hotel* as "the switch in time that saved nine" implied more than an outburst of judicial prudence.

III. PROPERTY, AUTONOMY, AND CONSTITUTIONAL INTERPRETATION

Between 1890 and 1937, a majority of the justices were ready to safeguard constitutionalism against the onslaughts of democracy by discovering fundamental rights in the breadth of "liberty" and the interstices of "due process."   At least partly in reaction to the early expressions of this judicial policy James Bradley Thayer formulated his "doctrine of the clear mistake" in 1893 (reprinted above, p. 602) and Harlan F. Stone later wrote his famous footnote in *Carolene Products* (1938; reprinted above, p. 609).   For similar reasons, Hugo L. Black began proclaiming the necessity of literal interpretation and, though an ardent civil libertarian, at times opposed the Court's finding fundamental rights beyond the explicit provisions of the constitutional document.

For a time after what Corwin called "the constitutional revolution" of 1937,[24] the justices ranked economic freedoms very low in the hierarchy of constitutional values, as we saw in the cases dealing

---

Harcourt, Brace, 1956).   For a full length study of Roberts, see Charles A. Leonard, *A Search for a Judicial Philosophy* (Port Washington, NY: Kennikat Press, 1971).

22. During the war against the New Deal, Roberts joined the majority in several cases (espec. Schecter Poultry Co. v. United States (1935) and Carter v. Carter Coal Co. (1936)) that construed the commerce clause narrowly.   But in the spring of 1937 he provided the fifth vote (in NLRB v. Jones & Laughlin) for a very broad interpretation of the commerce clause, and he later joined even broader interpretations in United States v. Darby (1941) and Wickard v. Filburn (1942).

23. He wrote the opinion for the Court in United States v. Butler (1935), one of narrowest interpretations of federal taxing power in the Court's history; but he later joined in broad interpretations and even wrote the opinion in one, Mulford v. Smith (1939).

24. *Constitutional Revolution, Ltd.* (Claremont: Claremont Colleges Press, 1941); see also Bruce Ackerman, *We the People: Foundations* (Cambridge: Harvard University Press, 1991), who characterizes the New Deal as fundamentally changing the American political system.

with equal protection and business interests in Chapter 14 and shall see again in Ferguson v. Skrupa (1963; reprinted below, p. 1129) and Hawaii Housing Authority v. Midkiff (1984; reprinted below, p. 1131). Yet the connection between property and autonomy remains real. William O. Douglas argued in 1955 that "no right is more precious" than the right to earn a living.[25] Eight years later he added:

> Man's liberty is, of course, often related to his property rights. The home and its privacy are property interests. Ownership of a press is essential to the freedom granted newspapers, magazines, pamphlets, and books. Ownership of a cathedral or church is basic to the exercise of religion by those whose faith brings them together in congregations.[26]

In 1972, Justice Stewart noted for the Court:

> [T]he dichotomy between personal liberties and property rights is a false one. Property does not have rights. People have rights. The right to enjoy property without unlawful deprivation, no less than the right to speak or the right to travel, is in truth a "personal" right, whether the "property" in question be a welfare check, a home, or a savings account. In fact, a fundamental interdependence exists between the personal right to liberty and the personal right to property. Neither could have meaning without the other.[27]

If, then, economic liberty is linked to individual autonomy and protecting individual autonomy is a leading goal of constitutional democracy, the Court's attitude toward property between 1890 and 1937 cannot have been entirely mistaken. And, in recent years several, constitutional theorists have argued for a return to some of the protections that property enjoyed before the revolution of 1937.[28] Indeed, a limited reconsideration of the Court's policy toward property may now be underway, as we shall see in Lucas v. South Carolina Coastal Council (1992; reprinted at p. 1135).[29] There six justices agreed that a state's ban on developing privately held, often flooded, oceanfront land might amount to the state's "taking" of the property for public use, for which the Fifth Amendment would require "just compensation." The dissenters claimed that *Lucas* took a step back toward *Lochner* by suggesting government could not achieve environmental goals that adversely affect

---

25. Barsky v. Board of Regents (1955).

26. *Anatomy of Liberty* (New York: Trident Press, 1963), p. 87.

27. Lynch v. Household Finance Corp. (1972).

28. See Bernard Siegan, *Economic Liberties and the Constitution* (Chicago: University of Chicago Press, 1980); Richard Epstein, *Takings: Private Property and the Power of Eminent Domain* (Cambridge: Harvard University Press, 1985); Stephen Macedo, *The New Right v. The Constitution* (Washington, DC: Cato, 1987).

29. See also Dolan v. City of Tigard (1994), discussed in Editors' Notes to *Lucas*, below at p. 1148.

people who had expected to develop land in ways that were legal, though hazardous, at the time of purchase.

In addition, during the last several decades constitutional commentators have referred to "the new property" [30]—property in such governmental benefits as welfare payments, public jobs, subsidies to farmers, guaranteed loans, and free education. Does constitutionalism require government, in a modern version of Jefferson's scheme to distribute public lands, to guarantee each citizen a sufficient share of this new property to provide a minimal standard of living and so ensure a large degree of autonomy?

Or does constitutionalism's other chief goal, preserving individual dignity, require government to leave citizens alone to struggle to achieve as much autonomy as his or her talents and inner drive permit? To what extent was William O. Douglas speaking "good constitutionalism" when he said "So far as the Bill of Rights is concerned, the individual is on his own when it comes to the pursuit of happiness"? [31] Would guaranteeing a minimal standard of living imply that individuals who accepted such grants were not capable of self-sufficiency?

What about the demands of democratic theory here? Does it require that citizens must have, if not equality of resources, at least access to those necessary for a minimum standard of living so people can exercise their civic rights and responsibilities? Providing such a minimum would, of course, entail some redistribution of property beyond what current tax structures attempt.

If the emphasis were on rights and duties of democratic citizenship, what about access to intangibles? In his dissent in San Antonio v. Rodriguez (1973; reprinted above, p. 1002), Thurgood Marshall argued that intelligent communication, effective organization, and wise use of the ballot all require considerable education. Beyond the high school level, education, in turn, is expensive, if not in direct monetary outlays for tuition, books, food, and housing, at least in opportunity costs. The person attending college or graduate school could be working and earning money—an opportunity that the wealthy can forego more easily than the poor. Does it follow that democratic theory requires government to provide enough free education (and perhaps similar benefits) to enable people to perform *effectively* as citizens? The Court's answer in *San Antonio*, was, of course, no; but was that answer consistent with the full implications of accepting a democratic political system?

---

30. See espec. Charles A. Reich, "The New Property," 73 *Yale L.J.* 733 (1964).

31. "The Bill of Rights Is Not Enough," in Edmund Cahn, ed., *The Great Rights* (New York: Macmillan, 1963), pp. 146–147.

SELECTED BIBLIOGRAPHY

Ackerman, Bruce A. *Property and the Constitution* (New Haven: Yale University Press, 1977).

————. *Social Justice in the Liberal State* (New Haven: Yale University Press, 1980).

————. *We the People: Foundations* (Cambridge: Harvard University Press, 1991).

Brigham, John. *Property and the Politics of Entitlement* (Philadelphia: Temple University Press, 1990).

Corwin, Edward S. *Liberty Against Government* (Baton Rouge: Louisiana State University Press, 1948).

Dworkin, Ronald. *A Matter of Principle* (Cambridge: Harvard University Press, 1985), espec. ch. 12.

Epstein, Richard A. *Takings: Property and the Power of Eminent Domain* (Cambridge: Harvard University Press, 1985).

Faulkner, Robert K. *The Jurisprudence of John Marshall* (Princeton: Princeton University Press, 1968).

Garvey, George E., and Gerald J. Garvey. *Economic Law and Economic Growth* (New York: Praeger, 1990).

Goldwin, Robert A., and William A. Schambra, eds. *How Capitalistic Is the Constitution?* (Washington, DC: American Enterprise Institute, 1982).

Hofstadter, Richard. *Social Darwinism in American Thought* (rev. ed.; Boston: Beacon Press, 1955).

Horwitz, Morton J. *The Transformation of American Law 1780–1860*, (Cambridge: Harvard University Press, 1977).

————. *The Transformation of American Law 1870–1960* (New York: Oxford University Press, 1992).

McCurdy, Charles W. "Justice Field and the Jurisprudence of Government–Business Relations: Some Parameters of Laissez Faire Constitutionalism, 1863–1897," 61 *J. of Am.Hist.* 970 (1975); reprinted in Lawrence M. Friedman and Harry N. Scheiber, eds., *American Law and the Constitutional Order* (Cambridge: Harvard University Press, 1978).

MacPherson, C.B. "Human Rights as Property Rights," *Dissent* (Winter, 1977), pp. 72–77.

Michelman, Frank I. "Welfare Rights in a Constitutional Democracy," 1979 *Wash.U.L.Q.* 659.

Munzer, Stephen R. *A Theory of Property* (New York: Cambridge University Press, 1990).

Nedelsky, Jennifer. *Private Property and the Limits of American Constitutionalism: The Madisonian Framework and Its Legacy* (Chicago: University of Chicago Press, 1990).

Nozick, Robert. *Anarchy, State, and Utopia* (New York: Basic Books, 1974), espec. ch. 7.

Paul, Arnold M. *The Conservative Crisis and the Rule of Law: Attitudes of Bench and Bar, 1887–1895* (Ithaca: Cornell University Press, 1960).

Pennock, J. Roland, and John W. Chapman, eds. *Property* (New York: New York University Press, 1980) (*Nomos*, vol. 22).

Radin, Margaret Jane. *Reinterpreting Property* (Chicago: University of Chicago Press, 1993).

————. "Property and Personhood," 34 *Stan.L.Rev.* 957 (1982).

Rawls, John. *A Theory of Justice* (Cambridge: The Belknap Press of Harvard University Press, 1971), espec. ch. 5.

Reich, Charles A. "The New Property," 73 *Yale L.J.* 733 (1964).

Scheiber, Harry N. "The Road to *Munn*," 5 *Perspectives in Am. Hist.* 329 (1971).

Siegen, Bernard H. *Economic Liberties and the Constitution* (Chicago: University of Chicago Press, 1980).

Treanor, William M. "The Origins and Original Significance of the Just Compensation Clause of the Fifth Amendment," 94 *Yale L.J.* 694 (1985).

Twiss, Benjamin R. *Lawyers and the Constitution* (Princeton: Princeton University Press, 1942).

Van Alstyne, William. "The Recrudescence of Property Rights as the Foremost Principle of Civil Liberties," 43 *Law & Cont. Probs.* 66 (1980).

"The great and *chief end* therefore, of Mens uniting into Commonwealths, and putting themselves under Government, *is the Preservation of their Property.*"

PROPERTY AND THE ENDS OF POLITICAL SOCIETY*
John Locke (1690).

27. Though the Earth, and all inferior Creatures be common to all Men, yet every Man has a *Property* in his own *Person*. This no Body has any Right to but himself. The *Labour* of his Body, and the *Work* of his

---

* John Locke, *The Second Treatise of Civil Government* (1690), chs. V, IX.

Hands, we may say, are properly his. Whatsoever then he removes out of the State that Nature hath provided, and left it in, he hath mixed his *Labour* with, and joined to it something that is his own, and thereby makes it his *Property*. It being by him removed from the common state Nature placed it in, hath by this *labour* something annexed to it, that excludes the common right of other Men. For this *Labour* being the unquestionable Property of the Labourer, no Man but he can have a right to what that is once joined to, at least where there is enough, and as good left in common for others. ...

31. It will perhaps be objected to this, That if gathering the Acorns, or other Fruits of the Earth, & c. makes a right to them, then any one may *ingross* as much as he will. To which I Answer, Not so. The same Law of Nature, that does by this means give us Property, does also *bound* that *Property* too. ... As much as any one can make use of to any advantage of life before it spoils; so much he may by his labour fix a Property in. Whatever is beyond this, is more than his share, and belongs to others. ...

32. But the *chief matter of Property* being now ... the *Earth it self* ... I think it is plain, that *Property* in that too is acquired as the former. *As much Land* as a Man Tills, Plants, Improves, Cultivates, and can use the Product of, so much is his *Property*. He by his Labour does, as it were, inclose it from the Common. Nor will it invalidate his right to say, Every body else has an equal Title to it; and therefore he cannot appropriate, he cannot inclose, without the Consent of all his Fellow–Commoners, all Mankind. ...

33. Nor was this *appropriation* of any parcel of *Land,* by improving it, any prejudice to any other Man, since there was still enough, and as good left; and more than the yet unprovided could use. ... No Body could think himself injur'd by the drinking of another Man, though he took a good Draught, who had a whole River of the same Water left him to quench his thirst. And the Case of Land and Water, where there is enough of both, is perfectly the same. ...

36. The measure of Property, Nature has well set, by the Extent of Mens *Labour, and the Conveniency of Life:* No Mans Labour could subdue, or appropriate all: nor could his Enjoyment consume more than a small part; so that it was impossible for any Man, this way, to intrench upon the right of another, or acquire, to himself, a Property, to the Prejudice of his Neighbour, who would still have room, for as good, and as large a Possession (after the other had taken out his) as before it was appropriated. This *measure* did confine every Man's *Possession,* to a very moderate Proportion. ... And the same *measure* may be allowed still, without prejudice to any Body, as full as the World seems. ... That the same *Rule of Propriety,* (*viz.*) that every Man should have as much as he could make use of, would hold still in the World, without straitening any body, since there is Land enough in the World to suffice double the Inhabitants had not the *Invention of Money,* and the tacit

Agreement of Men to put a value on it, introduced (by Consent) larger Possessions, and a Right to them. ...

46. ... Again if he would give us Nuts for a piece of Metal, pleased with its colour, or exchanged his Sheep for Shells, or Wool for a sparkling Pebble or a Diamond, and keep those by him all his Life, he invaded not the Right of others, he might heap up as much of these durable things as he pleased; the *exceeding of the bounds of his* just *Property* not lying in the largeness of his Possession, but the perishing of any thing uselessly in it. ...

47. And thus *came in the use of Money,* some lasting thing that Men might keep without spoiling, and that by mutual consent Men would take in exchange for the truly useful, but perishable Supports of Life. ...

50. But since Gold and Silver, being little useful to the Life of Man in proportion to Food, Raiment, and Carriage, has its *value* only from the consent of Men, whereof Labour yet makes, in great part, *the measure,* it is plain, that Men have agreed to disproportionate and unequal Possession of the Earth, they having by a tacit and voluntary consent found out a way, how a man may fairly possess more land than he himself can use the product of, by receiving in exchange for the overplus, Gold and Silver, which may be hoarded up without injury to any one, these metals not spoiling or decaying in the hands of the possessor. ...

123. If Man in the State of Nature be so free ..., [i]f he be absolute Lord of his own Person and Possessions, equal to the greatest, and subject to no Body, why will he part with his Freedom? Why will he give up this Empire, and subject himself to the Dominion and Control of any other Power? To which 'tis obvious to Answer, that though in the state of Nature he hath such a right, yet the Enjoyment of it is very uncertain, and constantly exposed to the Invasion of others. For all being Kings as much as he, every Man his Equal, and the greater part no strict Observers of Equity and Justice, the enjoyment of the property he has in this state is very unsafe, very unsecure. This makes him willing to quit a Condition, which however free, is full of fears and continual dangers: And 'tis not without reason, that he seeks out, and is willing to join in Society with others who are already united, or have a mind to unite for the mutual *Preservation* of their Lives, Liberties and Estates, which I call by the general Name *Property.*

124. The great and *chief end* therefore, of Mens uniting into Commonwealths, and putting themselves under Government, *is the Preservation of their Property.* To which in the state of Nature there are many things wanting.

First, There wants an *establish'd,* settled, known *Law,* received and allowed by common consent to be the Standard of Right and Wrong, and the common measure to decide all Controversies between them. For though, the Law of Nature be plain and intelligible to all rational

Creatures; yet Men being biassed by their Interest, as well as ignorant for want of study of it, are not apt to allow of it as a Law binding to them in the application of it to their particular Cases.

125. *Secondly,* In the State of Nature there wants a *known and indifferent Judge,* with Authority to determine all differences according to the established Law. For every one in that state being both Judge and Executioner of the Law of Nature, Men being partial to themselves, Passion and Revenge is very apt to carry them too far, and with too much heat, in their own Cases, as well as negligence and unconcernedness, to make them too remiss, in other Mens.

126. *Thirdly,* In the state of Nature there often wants *Power* to back and support the Sentence when right, and to *give* it due *Execution.* They who by any Injustice offended, will seldom fail, where they are able, by force to make good their Injustice: such resistance many times makes the punishment dangerous, and frequently destructive, to those who attempt it. . . .

128. For in the State of Nature . . . a Man has two Powers. The first is to do whatsoever he thinks fit for the preservation of himself and others within the permission of the *Law of Nature:* by which Law common to them all, he and all the rest of *Mankind are one Community.* . . . And were it not for the corruption, and vitiousness of degenerate Men, there would be no need of any other. . . . The other power a Man has in the State of Nature, is the *power to punish the Crimes* committed against that Law. Both these he gives up, when he joins in a . . . particular Political Society, and incorporates into any Commonwealth, separate from the rest of Mankind. . . .

131. But though Men when they enter into Society, give up the Equality, Liberty, and Executive Power they had in the State of Nature, into the hands of the Society, to be so far disposed of by the Legislative, as the good of the Society shall require; yet it being only with an intention in every one the better to preserve himself his Liberty and Property . . . the power of the Society, or *Legislative* constituted by them, *can never be suppos'd to extend farther than the common good;* but is obliged to secure every ones Property by providing against those three defects above-mentioned, that made the State of Nature so unsafe and uneasy. And so whoever has the Legislative or Supreme Power of any Common-wealth, is bound to govern by establish'd *standing Laws,* promulgated and known to the People, and not by Extemporary Decrees; by *indifferent* and upright *Judges,* who are to decide Controversies by those Laws; And to employ the force of the Community at home, *only in the Execution of such Laws,* or abroad to prevent or redress Foreign Injuries, and secure the Community from Inroads and Invasion. And all this to be directed to no other *end,* but the *Peace, Safety,* and *public good* of the People.

Editors' Note

Query: Recall Taney's opinion for the Court in *Dred Scott* (1857; reprinted above, p. 195). If the founders were Lockean, how should they have logically chosen between Sanford's "right" to property in Dred Scott and Dred Scott's right to liberty? How, then, should Taney have chosen to be faithful to his interpretive standard of original understanding or intent?

"The diversity in the faculties of men from which the rights of property originate, is ... an insuperable obstacle to a uniformity of interests. The protection of these faculties is the first object of Government."

FEDERALIST NO. 10

James Madison (1787).

Among the numerous advantages promised by a well constructed Union, none deserves to be more accurately developed than its tendency to break and control the violence of faction. The friend of popular governments, never finds himself so much alarmed for their character and fate, as when he contemplates their propensity to this dangerous vice. ... The instability, injustice and confusion introduced into the public councils, have in truth been the mortal diseases under which popular governments have every where perished. ...

By a faction I understand a number of citizens, whether amounting to a majority or minority of the whole, who are united and actuated by some common impulse of passion, or of interest, adverse to the rights of other citizens, or to the permanent and aggregate interests of the community. There are two methods of curing the mischiefs of faction: the one, by removing its causes; the other, by controlling its effects. There are again two methods of removing the causes of faction: the one by destroying the liberty which is essential to its existence; the other, by giving to every citizen the same opinions, the same passions, and the same interests.

It could never be more truly said than of the first remedy, that it is worse than the disease. Liberty is to faction, what air is to fire, an aliment without which it instantly expires. But it could not be a less folly to abolish liberty, which is essential to political life, because it nourishes faction, than it would be to wish the annihilation of air, which is essential to animal life, because it imparts to fire its destructive agency.

The second expedient is as impracticable, as the first would be unwise. As long as the reason of man continues fallible, and he is at liberty to exercise it, different opinions will be formed. As long as the connection subsists between his reason and his self-love, his opinions and his passions will have a reciprocal influence on each other. ... The diversity in the faculties of men from which the rights of property originate, is not less an insuperable obstacle to a uniformity of interests. The protection of these faculties is the first object of Government. From the protection of different and unequal faculties of acquiring property, the possession of different degrees and kinds of property immediately results: and from the influence of these on the sentiments and views of the respective proprietors, ensues a division of the society into different interests and parties.

The latent causes of faction are thus sown in the nature of man. ... So strong is this propensity of mankind to fall into mutual animosities, that where no substantial occasion presents itself, the most frivolous and fanciful distinctions have been sufficient to kindle their unfriendly passions, and excite their most violent conflicts. But the most common and durable source of factions, has been the various and unequal distribution of property. Those who hold, and those who are without property, have ever formed distinct interests in society. Those who are creditors, and those who are debtors, fall under a like discrimination. A landed interest, a manufacturing interest, a mercantile interest, a monied interest, with many lesser interests, grow up of necessity in civilized nations, and divide them into different classes, actuated by different sentiments and views. The regulation of these various and interfering interests forms the principal task of modern Legislation. ...

No man is allowed to be a judge in his own cause; because his interest would certainly bias his judgment, and, not improbably, corrupt his integrity. With equal, nay with greater reason, a body of men, are unfit to be both judges and parties, at the same time; yet, what are many of the most important acts of legislation, but so many judicial determinations ... concerning the rights of large bodies of citizens; and what are the different classes of legislators, but advocates and parties to the causes which they determine? Is a law proposed concerning private debts? It is a question to which the creditors are parties on one side, and the debtors on the other. Justice ought to hold the balance between them. Yet the parties are and must be themselves the judges; and the most numerous party, or, in other words, the most powerful faction must be expected to prevail. ... The apportionment of taxes on the various descriptions of property, is an act which seems to require the most exact impartiality; yet, there is perhaps no legislative act in which greater opportunity and temptation are given to a predominant party, to trample on the rules of justice. ...

It is in vain to say, that enlightened statesmen will be able to adjust these clashing interests, and render them all subservient to the public good. Enlightened statesmen will not always be at the helm: Nor, in many cases, can such an adjustment be made at all, without taking into view indirect and remote considerations, which will rarely prevail over the immediate interest which one party may find in disregarding the rights of another, or the good of the whole.

The inference to which we are brought, is, that the *causes* of faction cannot be removed; and that relief is only to be sought in the means of controlling its *effects*. If a faction consists of less than a majority, relief is supplied by the republican principle, which enables the majority to defeat its sinister views by regular vote. ... When a majority is included in a faction, the form of popular government on the other hand enables it to sacrifice to its ruling passion or interest, both the public good and the rights of other citizens. To secure the public good, and private rights, against the danger of such a faction, and at the same time to preserve the spirit and the form of popular government, is then the great object to which our enquiries are directed. ...

By what means is this object attainable? Evidently by one of two only. Either the existence of the same passion or interest in a majority at the same time, must be prevented; or the majority, having such co-existent passion or interest, must be rendered, by their number and local situation, unable to concert and carry into effect schemes of oppression. If the impulse and the opportunity be suffered to coincide, we well know that neither moral nor religious motives can be relied on as an adequate control. ...

... [A] pure Democracy, by which I mean, a Society, consisting of a small number of citizens, who assemble and administer the Government in person, can admit of no cure for the mischiefs of faction. A common passion or interest will, in almost every case, be felt by a majority of the whole ... and there is nothing to check the inducements to sacrifice the weaker party, or an obnoxious individual. Hence it is, that such Democracies have ever been spectacles of turbulence and contention; have ever been found incompatible with personal security, or the rights of property; and have in general been as short in their lives, as they have been violent in their deaths. Theoretic politicians, who have patronized this species of Government, have erroneously supposed, that by reducing mankind to a perfect equality in their political rights, they would, at the same time, be perfectly equalized and assimilated in their possessions, their opinions, and their passions.

A Republic, by which I mean a Government in which the scheme of representation takes place, opens a different prospect, and promises the cure for which we are seeking. ... The two great points of difference between a Democracy and a Republic are, first, the delegation of the Government, in the latter, to a small number of citizens elected by the rest: secondly, the greater number of citizens, and greater sphere of country, over which the latter may be extended.

The effect of the first difference is ... to refine and enlarge the public views, by passing them through the medium of a chosen body of citizens, whose wisdom may best discern the true interest of their country, and whose patriotism and love of justice, will be least likely to sacrifice it to temporary or partial considerations. ... On the other hand, the effect may be inverted. Men of factious tempers, of local prejudices, or of sinister designs, may by intrigue, by corruption or by other means, first obtain the suffrages, and then betray the interests of the people. The question resulting is, whether small or extensive Republics are most favorable to the election of proper guardians of the public weal: and it is clearly decided in favor of the latter by two obvious considerations.

In the first place it is to be remarked that however small the Republic may be, the Representatives must be raised to a certain number, in order to guard against the cabals of a few; and that however large it may be, they must be limited to a certain number, in order to guard against the confusion of a multitude. Hence the number of Representatives in the two cases, not being in proportion to that of the Constituents, and being proportionally greatest in the small Republic, it follows, that if the proportion of fit characters, be not less, in the large than in the small Republic, the former will present a greater option, and consequently a greater probability of a fit choice. In the next place, as each Representative will be chosen by a greater number of citizens in the large than in the small Republic, it will be more difficult for unworthy candidates to practice with success the vicious arts, by which elections are too often carried. ...

The other point of difference is, the greater number of citizens and extent of territory which may be brought within the compass of Republican, than of Democratic Government; and it is this circumstance principally which renders factious combinations less to be dreaded in the former, than in the latter. The smaller the society, the fewer probably will be the distinct parties and interests composing it; the fewer the distinct parties and interests, the more frequently will a majority be found of the same party; and the smaller the number of individuals composing a majority, and the smaller the compass within which they are placed, the more easily will they concert and execute their plans of oppression. Extend the sphere, and you take in a greater variety of parties and interests; you make it less probable that a majority of the whole will have a common motive to invade the rights of other citizens; or if such a common motive exists, it will be more difficult for all who feel it to discover their own strength, and to act in unison with each other. Besides other impediments ... where there is a consciousness of unjust or dishonorable purposes, communication is always checked by distrust, in proportion to the number whose concurrence is necessary.

The influence of factious leaders may kindle a flame within their particular States, but will be unable to spread a general conflagration through the other States. ... A rage for paper money, for an abolition of debts, for an equal division of property, or for any other improper or wicked project, will be less apt to pervade the whole body of the Union than a particular member of it. ...

Editors' Notes

(1) **Query:** To what extent did Madison use a *philosophic* argument? Did he argue from democratic theory, constitutionalism, both, or some other theory? To what extent was Madison's argument *structuralist*? *Purposive*? *Prudential*?

(2) **Query:** Did Madison *argue* or *assume* that citizens had a fundamental (natural?) right to property? Indeed, did his argument depend on any such status for a right to own and use property?

———

> "It may well be doubted, whether the nature of society and of government does not prescribe some limits to the legislative power. ... But Georgia cannot be viewed as a single, unconnected, sovereign power. ... [S]he is a member of the American union; and that union has a constitution ... which imposes limits to the legislatures of the several states."—Chief Justice MARSHALL

> "I do not hesitate to declare, that a state does not possess the power of revoking its own grants. But I do it, on a general principle, on the reason and nature of things; a principle which will impose laws even on the Deity."—Justice JOHNSON

FLETCHER v. PECK
10 U.S. (6 Cranch) 87, 3 L.Ed. 162 (1810).

In 1795, a group of speculators bribed the Georgia legislature to grant them, at less than a penny and a half an acre, the so-called Yazoo Land Tract, some 35 million acres in what is now Mississippi. After a great public outcry, the very next year the newly elected legislature annulled the grant, directing named state officers to come to the capitol

> with the several records, documents, and deeds ... and which records and documents shall then and there be expunged from the faces and indexes of the books of record of the State, and the enrolled law or usurped act shall then be publicly burnt, in order that no trace of so unconstitutional, vile, and fraudulent a transaction, other than the infamy attached to it by this law, shall remain in the public offices. ...

Further, the legislature ordered all county officers responsible for recording deeds to bring deeds resulting from the grant of 1795 to local courts and destroy them.

This case, a friendly suit to untangle what had become a massive legal as well as political mess, was between two private citizens. Robert Fletcher of New Hampshire, who had purchased land in the Yazoo Tract from John Peck of Massachusetts—who, in turn, had bought it from one of the original speculators—asked a U.S. circuit court to order return of the money he had paid Peck because, if the grant of 1795 was invalid, the sale was void. That court, however, sustained the legality of the sale, and Fletcher obtained a writ of error from the U.S. Supreme Court.

MARSHALL, Ch. J., delivered the opinion of the court. ...

The question, whether a law be void for its repugnancy to the constitution, is, at all times, a question of much delicacy, which ought seldom, if ever, to be decided in the affirmative, in a doubtful case. The court, when impelled by duty to render such a judgment, would be unworthy of its station, could it be unmindful of the solemn obligations which that station imposes. But it is not on slight implication and vague conjecture, that the legislature is to be pronounced to have transcended its powers, and its acts to be considered as void. The opposition between the constitution and the law should be such that the judge feels a clear and strong conviction of their incompatibility with each other. ...

If a suit be brought to set aside a conveyance obtained by fraud, and the fraud be clearly proved, the conveyance will be set aside, as between the parties; but the rights of third persons, who are purchasers without notice, for a valuable consideration, cannot be disregarded. Titles which, according to every legal test, are perfect, are acquired with that confidence which is inspired by the opinion that the purchaser is safe. If there be any concealed defect, arising from the conduct of those who had held the property long before he acquired it, of which he had no notice, that concealed defect cannot be set up against him. He has paid his money for a title good at law, he is innocent, whatever may be the guilt of others, and equity will not subject him to the penalties attached to that guilt. All titles would be insecure, and the intercourse between man and man would be very seriously obstructed, if this principle be overturned. ...

Is the power of the legislature competent to the annihilation of such title ...? The principle asserted is, that one legislature is competent to repeal any act which a former legislature was competent to pass; and that one legislature cannot abridge the powers of a succeeding legislature. The correctness of this principle, so far as respects general legislation, can never be controverted. But, if an act be done under a law, a succeeding legislature cannot undo it. The past cannot be recalled by the most absolute power. ... When, then, a law is in its nature a contract, when absolute rights have vested under that contract, a repeal of the law cannot divest those rights; and the act of annulling them, if legitimate, is rendered so by a power applicable to the case of every individual in the community.

It may well be doubted, whether the nature of society and of government does not prescribe some limits to the legislative power; and if any be prescribed, where are they to be found, if the property of an individual, fairly and honestly acquired, may be seized without compensation? To the legislature, all legislative power is granted; but the question, whether the act of transferring the property of an individual to the public, be in the nature of the legislative power, is well worthy of serious reflection. It is the peculiar province of the legislature, to prescribe general rules for the government of society; the application of those rules to individuals in society would seem to be the duty of other departments. How far the power of giving the law may involve every other power, in cases where the constitution is silent, never has been, and perhaps never can be, definitely stated.

The validity of this rescinding act, then, might well be doubted, were Georgia a single sovereign power. But Georgia cannot be viewed as a single, unconnected, sovereign power, on whose legislature no other restrictions are imposed than may be found in its own constitution. She is a part of a large empire; she is a member of the American union; and that union has a constitution, the supremacy of which all acknowledge, and which imposes limits to the legislatures of the several states. ... The constitution of the United States declares that no state shall pass any bill of attainder, *ex post facto* law, or law impairing the obligation of contracts.

Does the case now under consideration come within this prohibitory section of the constitution? In considering this very interesting question, we immediately ask ourselves, what is a contract? Is a grant a contract? A contract is a compact between two or more parties. ... The contract between Georgia and the purchasers was executed by the grant. A contract ... contains obligations binding on the parties. A grant, in its own nature, amounts to an extinguishment of the right of the grantor, and implies a contract not to re-assert that right. A party is, therefore, always estopped by his own grant.

Since, then, in fact, a grant is a contract executed, the obligation of which still continues, and since the constitution uses the general term contract ... it must be construed to comprehend [grants]. ...

If, under a fair construction of the constitution, grants are comprehended under the term contracts, is a grant from the state excluded from the operation of the provision?. ... The words themselves contain no such distinction. They are general, and are applicable to contracts of every description. If contracts made with the state are to be exempted from their operation, the exception must arise from the character of the contracting party, not from the words which are employed.

Whatever respect might have been felt for the state sovereignties, it is not to be disguised, that the framers of the constitution viewed, with some apprehension, the violent acts which might grow out of the feelings of the moment; and that the people of the United States, in adopting that instrument, have manifested a determination to shield themselves and their property from the effects of those sudden and strong passions to which men are exposed. The restrictions on the legislative power of the states are obviously founded in this sentiment; and the constitution of the United States contains what may be deemed a bill of rights for the people of each state. ... What motive, then, for implying, in words which import a general prohibition to impair the obligation of contracts, an exception in favor of the right to impair the obligation of those contracts into which the state may enter?

The state legislatures can pass no *ex post facto* law. An *ex post facto* law is one which renders an act punishable in a manner in which it was not punishable when it was committed. Such a law may inflict penalties on the person, or may inflict pecuniary penalties which swell the public treasury. The legislature is then prohibited from passing a law by which a man's estate, or any part of it, shall be seized for a crime which was not declared, by some previous law, to render him liable to that punishment. Why, then, should violence be done to the natural meaning of words for the purpose of leaving to the legislature the power of seizing, for public use, the estate of an individual, in the form of a law annulling the title by which he holds that estate? The court can perceive no sufficient grounds for making this distinction. This rescinding act would have the effect of an *ex post facto* law. It forfeits the estate of Fletcher for a crime not committed by himself, but by those from whom he purchased. This cannot be effected in the form of an *ex post facto* law, or bill of attainder; why then, is it allowable in the form of a law annulling the original grant? ...

It is, then, the unanimous opinion of the court, that, in this case, the estate having passed into the hands of a purchaser for a valuable consideration, without notice, the state of Georgia was restrained, either by general principles which are common to our free institutions, or by the particular provisions of the constitution of the United States, from passing a law whereby the estate of the plaintiff in the premises so purchased could be constitutionally and legally impaired and rendered null and void. ...

Affirmed.

JOHNSON, J.

In this case, I entertain ... an opinion different from that which has been delivered by the court. I do not hesitate to declare, that a state does not possess the power of revoking its own grants. But I do it, on a general principle, on the reason and nature of things; a principle which will impose laws even on the Deity. ...

The right of jurisdiction is essentially connected to, or rather identified with, the national sovereignty. To part with it, is to commit a species of political suicide. ... But it is not so with the interests or property of a nation. Its possessions nationally are in no wise necessary to its political existence; they are entirely accidental, and may be parted with, in every respect, similarly to those of the individuals who compose the community. When the legislature have once conveyed their interest or property in any subject to the individual, they have lost all control over it; have nothing to act upon; it has passed from them; is vested in the individual; becomes intimately blended with his existence, as essentially so as the blood that circulates through his system. ...

I have thrown out these ideas, that I may have it distinctly understood, that my opinion on this point is not founded on the provision in the constitution of the United States, relative to laws impairing the obligation of contracts. ...

Editors' Notes

(1) **Query:** To what extent did Marshall follow a *philosophic approach*? A *textualist approach*? A *structuralist approach*? Was his argument funda-

mentally different from that of Chase in Calder v. Bull (1798; reprinted above, p. 121)? From the legal positivism that Iredell espoused in *Calder* and Black in *Griswold* (1965; reprinted above, p. 147)? To what extent are these various approaches to interpretation compatible with each other?

(2) **Query:** Johnson rejected *textualism*, but what sort of approach did he follow?

(3) **Query:** What was Marshall's concept of WHAT "the Constitution" included? Johnson's?

(4) Congress and the executive were also deeply involved in the settlement of the Yazoo controversy. During the period 1798–1803, federal commissioners worked out an agreement under which Georgia gave its title to the territory to the United States in exchange for $1,250,000 and assumption of all the claims that resulted from the rescinding act of 1796. It was not, however, until 1814 that Congress passed an act allowing claimants to be repaid, either in cash or land, as they chose.

(5) For excellent accounts of the Yazoo controversy, see: C. Peter Magrath, *Yazoo: Law and Politics in the New Republic* (New York: Norton, 1966); Albert J. Beveridge, *The Life of John Marshall* (Boston: Houghton Mifflin, 1919), III, ch. 10; and George Lee Haskins and Herbert A. Johnson, *Foundations of Power: John Marshall, 1801–15* (New York: Macmillan, 1981), pp. 336–353.

"And what would be the fruits of this doctrine of implied contracts on the part of the states, and of property in a line of travel by a corporation, if it should now be sanctioned by this court?"—Chief Justice TANEY

"I can conceive of no surer plan to arrest all public improvements, founded on private capital and enterprise, than to make the outlay of that capital uncertain, and questionable both as to security, and as to productiveness."—Justice STORY

CHARLES RIVER BRIDGE v. WARREN BRIDGE

36 U.S. (11 Pet.) 420, 9 L.Ed. 773 (1837).

In 1650 Massachusetts Bay Colony gave Harvard College the right to operate a ferry across the Charles River between Boston and Charlestown. The arrangement proved to be unsatisfactory to the college as well as the community; and, in 1785, Massachusetts chartered a corporation to build a toll bridge to replace the ferry. The corporation was to pay Harvard an annual fee of $666.66 until 1856. For decades the bridge operated profitably, earning more than $800,000. Then in 1828 the state chartered a new corporation to build a second bridge. Not only was this structure to be located only a few hundred yards from the old but, as soon as tolls paid off its costs of construction plus 5 per cent, it was to be free to the public.

The Charles River Bridge Co. sued in a state court to invalidate the new charter. Among its claims was that the law of 1828 unconstitutionally impaired the obligation of the grant of 1785 which, according to Fletcher v. Peck (1810; reprinted above, p. 1091) and the Dartmouth College Case (1819), was a contract. The state courts upheld the constitutionality of the new charter, and the Charles River Bridge Co. obtained a writ of error from the U.S. Supreme Court.

The Court first heard argument in March, 1831, but, because of absences and divisions among the justices, several times ordered reargument. Final argument came in 1837, shortly after Roger Brooke Taney, Andrew Jackson's nominee, had replaced John Marshall as Chief Justice. Marshall had wanted to adhere to the doctrine of *Fletcher* and *Dartmouth College,* but Taney had different views.

Mr. Chief Justice **TANEY** delivered the opinion of the court.

The questions involved in this case are of the gravest character, and the court have given to them the most anxious and deliberate consideration. ... [T]he questions which have been raised as to the power of the several states, in relation to the corporations they have chartered, are pregnant with important consequences; not only to the individuals who are concerned in the corporate franchises, but to the communities in which they exist. The court are fully sensible that it is their duty, in exercising the high powers conferred on them by the constitution of the United States, to deal with these great and extensive interests with the utmost caution; guarding, as far as they have the power to do so, the rights of property, and at the same time carefully abstaining from any encroachment on the rights reserved to the states. ...

Much has been said in the argument of the principles of construction by which this law is to be expounded. ... The rule of construction in such cases is well settled, both in England, and by the decisions of our own tribunals. In ... the case of the Stourbridge Canal against Wheely and others, the court say,

> the canal having been made under an act of parliament, the rights of the plaintiffs are derived entirely from that act. This, like many other cases, is a bargain between a company of adventurers and the public, the terms of which are expressed in the statute; and the rule of construction in all such cases, is ... that any ambiguity in the terms of the contract, must operate against the adventurers, and in favour of the public, and the plaintiffs can claim nothing that is not clearly given them by the act. ...

Borrowing, as we have done, our system of jurisprudence from the English law; and having adopted, in every other case, civil and criminal, its rules for the construction of statutes; is there any thing in our local situation, or in the nature of our political institutions, which should lead us to depart from the principle where corporations are concerned? ... We think not. ...

But we are not now left to determine, for the first time, the rules by which public grants are to be construed in this country. The subject has already been considered in this court; and the rule of construction, above stated, fully established. In the case of the United States v. Arredondo [1832], the leading cases upon this subject are collected ... and the principle recognized, that in grants by the public, nothing passes by implication. ...

... [T]he object and end of all government is to promote the happiness and prosperity of the community ... and it can never be assumed, that the government intended to diminish its power of accomplishing the end for which it was created. And in a country like ours, free, active, and enterprising, continually advancing in numbers and wealth; new channels of communication are daily found necessary, both for travel and trade; and are essential to the comfort, convenience, and prosperity of the people. A state ought never to be presumed to surrender this power, because, like the taxing power, the whole community have an interest in preserving it undiminished. And when a corporation alleges, that a state has surrendered for seventy years, its power of improvement and public accommodation, in a great and important line of travel, along which a vast number of its citizens must daily pass; the community have a right to insist ... "that its abandonment ought not to be presumed, in a case, in which the deliberate purpose of the state to abandon it does not appear." The continued existence of a government would be of no great value, if by implications and presumptions, it was disarmed of the powers necessary to accomplish the ends of its creation. ... While the rights of private property are sacredly guarded, we must not forget that the community also have rights, and that the happiness and well being of every citizen depends on their faithful preservation.

Adopting the rule of construction above stated ... we proceed to apply it to the charter of 1785, to the proprietors of the Charles river bridge. ... It confers on them the ordinary faculties of a corporation, for the purpose of building the bridge; and establishes certain rates of toll, which the company are authorized to take. This is the whole grant. There is no exclusive privilege given to them over the waters of Charles river, above or below their bridge. No right to erect another bridge themselves, nor to prevent other persons from erecting one. No engagement from the state, that another shall not be erected; and no undertaking not to sanction competition, nor to make improvements that may diminish the amount of its income. Upon all these subjects the charter is silent. ...

... Can such an agreement be implied? The rule of construction before stated is an answer to the question. ...

Indeed, the practice and usage of almost every state in the Union ... is opposed to the doctrine contended for on the part of the plaintiffs in error. Turnpike roads have been made in succession, on the same line of travel; the later ones interfering materially with the profits of the first. These corporations have, in some instances, been utterly ruined by the introduction of newer and better modes of transportation, and travelling. In some cases, rail roads have rendered the turnpike roads on the same line of travel so entirely useless, that the franchise of the turnpike corporation is not worth preserving. Yet in none of these cases have the corporation supposed that their privileges were invaded, or any contract violated on the part of the state. ... We cannot deal thus with the rights reserved to the states; and by legal intendments and mere technical reasoning, take away from them any portion of that power over their own internal police and improvement, which is so necessary to their well being and prosperity.

And what would be the fruits of this doctrine of implied contracts on the part of the states, and of property in a line of travel by a corporation, if it should now be sanctioned by this court? ... Let it once be understood that such charters carry with them these implied contracts, and give this unknown and undefined property in a line of travelling; and you will soon find the old turnpike corporations awakening from their sleep, and calling upon this court to put down the improvements which have taken their place. The millions of property which have been invested in rail roads and canals, upon lines of travel which had been before occupied by turnpike corporations, will be put in jeopardy. We shall be thrown back to the improvements of the last century ... until ... the old turnpike corporations ... shall consent to permit these states to avail themselves of the lights of modern science, and to partake of the benefit of those improvements which are now adding to the wealth and prosperity, and the convenience and comfort, of every other part of the civilized world. ... This court are not prepared to sanction principles which must lead to such results. ...

[Affirmed.]

Mr. Justice **McLEAN**. ...

... I am in favour of dismissing the bill for want of jurisdiction.

Mr. Justice **STORY,** dissenting. ...

The present ... is not the case of a royal grant, but of a legislative grant, by a public statute. The rules of the common law in relation to royal grants have, therefore, in reality, nothing to do with the case. We are to give this act of incorporation a rational and fair construction, according to the general rules which govern in all cases of the exposition of public statutes. We are to ascertain the legislative intent; and that once ascertained, it is our duty to give it a full and liberal operation. The books are full of cases to this effect. ...

... [W]here the terms of a grant are to impose burdens upon the public, or to create a restraint injurious to the public interests, there is sound reason for interpreting the terms, if ambiguous, in favour of the public. But at the same time ... there is not the slightest reason for saying, even in such a case, that the grant is not to be construed favourably to the grantee, so as to secure him in the enjoyment of what is actually granted. ...

... Our legislatures neither have, nor affect to have any royal prerogatives. There is no provision in the constitution authorizing their grants to be construed differently from the grants of private persons, in regard to the like subject matter. The policy of the common law, which gave the crown so many exclusive privileges, and extraordinary claims ... was founded in a good measure, if not altogether, upon the divine right of kings, or at least upon a sense of their exalted dignity and preeminence over all subjects. ... [Yet t]hey were always construed according to common sense and common reason, upon their language and their intent. ... Is it not at least as important in our free governments, that a citizen should have as much security for his rights and estate derived from the grants of the legislature, as he would have in England? What solid ground is there to say, that the words of a grant in the mouth of a citizen, shall mean one thing, and in the mouth of the legislature shall mean another thing? That in regard to the grant of a citizen, every word shall in case of any question of interpretation or implication be construed against him, and in regard to the grant of the government, every word shall be construed in its favour? ...

But it has been argued ... that if grants of this nature are to be construed liberally ... it will interpose an effectual barrier against all general improvements of the country. ... For my own part, I can conceive of no surer plan to arrest all public improvements, founded on private capital and enterprise, than to make the outlay of that capital uncertain, and questionable both as to security, and as to productiveness. No man will hazard his capital in any enterprise, in which, if there be a loss, it must be borne exclusively by himself; and if there be success, he has not the slightest security of enjoying the rewards of that success for a single moment. ...

Mr. Justice **THOMPSON**.

The opinion delivered by my brother, Mr. Justice Story, I have read over, and deliberately considered. On this full consideration, I concur entirely in all the principles and reasonings contained in it. ...

Editors' Notes

(1) **Query:** To what extent did Taney use a *prudential approach*? Story? To what extent did either argue more from practical consequences than principles embedded in the constitutional text or the larger political system? If either did so to any real degree, was he not making an implicit argument about WHO?

(2) Did Taney express a notion of property as a fundamental right? Did Story?

(3) As the introductory essay to this Chapter explained, Morton J. Horwitz, *The Transformation of American Law, 1780–1860* (Cambridge: Harvard University Press, 1977), argues that, during the first decades of the nineteenth century, the American law of property underwent a dramatic transformation from a static, agrarian conception of a right to quiet enjoyment to one that benefitted venturesome new groups of merchants, industrialists, and entrepre-

neurs—"a dynamic, instrumental, and more abstract view of property that emphasized the newly paramount virtues of productive use and development." (P. 31.) Thus, for Horwitz, *Charles River Bridge* "represented the last great contest in America between two different models of economic development." (P. 134.) Story spoke for the old order, Taney for the new. Horwitz's general thesis has been hotly contested. See the literature cited in fn. 8 to the introductory essay to this chapter.

(4) After the decision, Daniel Webster, who had argued the case for the Charles River Bridge Co., sensed the change that Horwitz was to describe: "The decision of the Court will have completely overturned, in my judgment, a great provision of the Constitution." Quoted in Charles Warren, *The Supreme Court in United States History* (Boston: Little, Brown, 1926), II, p. 25n.

(5) Story felt the same change as Webster and wrote to Justice McLean: "There will not, I fear, ever in our day, be any case in which a law of a State or of Congress will be declared unconstitutional; for the old constitutional doctrines are fast fading away, and a change has come over the public mind from which I augur little good." Quoted in Warren, II, p. 28. During Story's remaining eight years on the bench, the Supreme Court invalidated seven state statutes, though none under the contract clause. (During his previous 26 years on the Court, the justices had held 16 state statutes unconstitutional, a somewhat lower annual average but a much higher mortality rate of laws challenged.) The Court was not to invalidate an act of Congress again until Dred Scott v. Sanford (1857); so during Story's entire tenure, the Court never declared an act of Congress unconstitutional.

(6) For a study tracing the decline of the contracts clause as a bulwark of property rights, see: Benjamin F. Wright, *The Contract Clause of the Constitution* (Cambridge: Harvard University Press, 1938). Despite the general decline of the contracts clause, and the Court's continuing policy of deference to state legislatures in contract clause questions [see Energy Reserves Group v. Kansas Power and Light Co. (1983)], the Court has used the contract clause several times in recent years to invalidate state statutes: United States Trust Co. v. New Jersey (1977); and Allied Structural Steel Co. v. Spannaus (1978). See Bernard Schwartz, "Old Wine in New Bottles? The Renaissance of the Contracts Clause," 1979 *Sup.Ct.Rev.* 95; and C. Herman Pritchett, *Constitutional Civil Liberties* (Englewood Cliffs, NJ: Prentice–Hall, 1984), pp. 284–289.

"[T]he right of property in a slave is distinctly and expressly affirmed in the Constitution."—Chief Justice TANEY

"James Madison ... was solicitous to guard the language of that instrument so as not to convey the idea that there could be property in man."—Justice McLean

DRED SCOTT v. SANDFORD

60 U.S. (19 How.) 393, 15 L.Ed. 691 (1857).

This case, reprinted above at p. 195, held the Missouri Compromise invalid. The majority ruled, *inter alia,* that African Americans could not be citizens of the United States, that slaves were property, and that Congress could not forbid slavery in the territories for such a ban would take away slave owners' rights to their property "without due process of law."

Editors' Note

Dred Scott marks the first time the U.S. Supreme Court invalidated a statute even on partial grounds of "substantive due process." A dozen years later, when a narrow majority held Congress lacked authority to issue paper money (Hepburn v. Griswold [1869]), the Court again used "substantive due process." For a few years thereafter, the justices shelved the doctrine, but the shelf remained accessible to judges and lawyers alike. For a concise history of the birth and early use of this concept, see Edward S. Corwin, *Liberty Against Government* (Baton Rouge: Louisiana State University Press, 1948), ch. 3.

————

"For protection against abuses by legislatures the people must resort to the polls, not to the courts."—Chief Justice WAITE

"The decision of the court in this case gives unrestrained license to legislative will."—Justice FIELD

MUNN v. ILLINOIS

94 U.S. (4 Otto) 113, 24 L.Ed. 77 (1877).

The Grangers were an agrarian reform movement that gathered force in the Midwest after the Civil War in reaction against the new corporations who, the farmers had good reason to believe, were stealing their land for railroad rights-of-way, then overcharging them to haul their goods to market, and again overcharging them to store their crops in grain elevators while awaiting sale. Chicago was, of course, a central market, and a few companies had what amounted to monopolistic control over storage elevators. They unashamedly used that power to charge exorbitant rates and to speculate with other people's property. The new constitutional text that Illinois adopted in 1870 declared grain elevators to be "public warehouses" and authorized the legislature to regulate the business of grain storage. Under this authority, the legislature in 1871 passed a comprehensive regulatory act that, among other things, required a license to operate a grain elevator and fixed charges for storage. Munn and Scott, a particularly unscrupulous firm, were fined $100 for violating the statute. When news of the company's other illegal activities leaked out, the firm went bankrupt. Its successors, however, appealed the judgment, claiming the state had deprived them of property "without due process of law." The operators lost in the Illinois courts but obtained a writ of error from the U.S. Supreme Court.

Mr. Chief Justice **WAITE** delivered the opinion of the court.   ...

Every statute is presumed to be constitutional. The courts ought not to declare one to be unconstitutional, unless it is clearly so. If there is doubt, the expressed will of the legislature should be sustained.

The Constitution contains no definition of the word "deprive," as used in the Fourteenth Amendment. To determine its signification, therefore, it is necessary to ascertain the effect which usage has given it, when employed in the same or a like connection. While this provision of the amendment is new in the Constitution of the United States, as a limitation upon the powers of the States, it is old as a principle of civilized government. It is found in Magna Charta, and, in substance if not in form, in nearly or quite all the constitutions that have been from time to time adopted by the several States of the Union. By the Fifth Amendment, it was introduced into the Constitution of the United States as a limitation upon the powers of the national government, and by the Fourteenth, as a guaranty against any encroachment upon an acknowledged right of citizenship by the legislatures of the States. ...

When one becomes a member of society, he necessarily parts with some rights or privileges which, as an individual not affected by his relations to others, he might retain. ... This does not confer power upon the whole people to control rights which are purely and exclusively private ... but it does authorize the establishment of laws requiring each citizen to so conduct himself, and so use his own property, as not unnecessarily to injure another. This is the very essence of government. ... From this source come the police powers, which as was said by Mr. Chief Justice Taney in the *License Cases* [1847], "are nothing more or less than the powers of government inherent in every sovereignty, ... the power to govern men and things." Under these powers the government regulates the conduct of its citizens one towards another, and the manner in which each shall use his own property, when such regulation becomes necessary for the public good. In their exercise it has been customary in England from time immemorial, and in this country from its first colonization, to regulate ferries, common carriers, hackmen, bakers, millers, wharfingers, innkeepers, & c. and in so doing to fix a maximum of charge to be made for services rendered, accommodations furnished, and articles sold. ... [I]t has never yet been successfully contended that such legislation came within any of the constitutional prohibitions against interference with private property. With the Fifth Amendment in force, Congress, in 1820, conferred power upon the city of Washington "to regulate ... the rates of wharfage at private wharves, ... the sweeping of chimneys, and to fix the rates of fees therefor, ... and the weight and quality of bread," ... and, in 1848, "to make all necessary regulations respecting hackney carriages and the rates of fare of the same, and the rates of hauling by cartmen, wagoners, carmen, and draymen, and the rates of commission of auctioneers." ...

From this it is apparent that, down to the time of the adoption of the Fourteenth Amendment, it was not supposed that statutes regulat-

ing the use, or even the price of the use, of private property necessarily
deprived an owner of his property without due process of law. Under
some circumstances they may, but not under all. The amendment does
not change the law in this particular: it simply prevents the States from
doing that which will operate as such a deprivation.

This brings us to inquire as to the principles upon which this power
of regulation rests. ...

... Looking ... to the common law, from whence came the right
which the Constitution protects, we find that when private property is
"affected with a public interest, it ceases to be *juris privati* only." This
was said by Lord Chief Justice Hale more than two hundred years ago
... and has been accepted without objection as an essential element in
the law of property ever since. Property does become clothed with a
public interest when used in a manner to make it of public consequence,
and affect the community at large. When, therefore, one devotes his
property to a use in which the public has an interest, he, in effect, grants
to the public an interest in that use, and must submit to be controlled by
the public for the common good, to the extent of the interest he has thus
created. He may withdraw his grant by discontinuing the use; but, so
long as he maintains the use, he must submit to the control. ...

... Enough has already been said to show that, when private
property is devoted to a public use, it is subject to public regulation. It
remains only to ascertain whether the warehouses of these plaintiffs in
error ... come within the operation of this principle.

... [I]t appears that "the great producing region of the West and
North-west sends its grain by water and rail to Chicago, where the
greater part of it is shipped by vessel for transportation to the seaboard
by the Great Lakes, and some of it is forwarded by railway to the
Eastern ports. ... The grain warehouses or elevators in Chicago are
immense structures, holding from 300,000 to 1,000,000 bushels at one
time. ... They are located with the river harbor on one side and the
railway tracks on the other; and the grain is run through them from car
to vessel, or boat to car. ... It has been found impossible to preserve
each owner's grain separate, and this has given rise to a system of
inspection and grading, by which the grain of different owners is mixed,
and receipts issued for the number of bushels which are negotiable, and
redeemable in like kind, upon demand. ..."

... [A]lthough in 1874 there were in Chicago fourteen warehouses
adapted to this particular business, and owned by about thirty persons,
nine business firms controlled them, and ... the prices charged and
received for storage were such "as have been from year to year agreed
upon and established by the different elevators or warehouses in the city
of Chicago. ..." Thus it is apparent that all the elevating facilities
through which these vast productions "of seven or eight great States of
the West" must pass on the way "to four or five of the States on the
seashore" may be a "virtual" monopoly.

Under such circumstances it is difficult to see why, if the common carrier, or the miller, or the ferryman, or the innkeeper, or the wharfinger, or the baker, or the cartman, or the hackney-coachman, pursues a public employment and exercises "a sort of public office," these plaintiffs in error do not. They stand ... in the very "gateway of commerce," and take toll from all who pass. Their business most certainly "tends to a common charge, and is become a thing of public interest and use." ... Certainly, if any business can be clothed "with a public interest, and cease to be *juris privati* only," this has been. It may not be made so by the operation of the Constitution of Illinois or this statute, but it is by the facts.

... For our purposes we must assume that, if a state of facts could exist that would justify such legislation, it actually did exist when the statute now under consideration was passed. For us the question is one of power, not of expediency. If no state of circumstances could exist to justify such a statute, then we may declare this one void, because in excess of the legislative power of the State. But if it could, we must presume it did. Of the propriety of legislative interference within the scope of legislative power, the legislature is the exclusive judge.

Neither is it a matter of any moment that no precedent can be found for a statute precisely like this. It is conceded that the business is one of recent origin. ... It presents, therefore, a case for the application of a long-known and well-established principle in social science, and this statute simply extends the law so as to meet this new development of commercial progress. There is no attempt to compel these owners to grant the public an interest in their property, but to declare their obligations, if they use it in this particular manner. ...

It is insisted, however, that the owner of property is entitled to a reasonable compensation for its use, even though it be clothed with a public interest, and that what is reasonable is a judicial and not a legislative question.

As has already been shown, the practice has been otherwise. ... Undoubtedly, in mere private contracts, relating to matters in which the public has no interest, what is reasonable must be ascertained judicially. But this is because the legislature has no control over such a contract. ... Rights of property which have been created by the common law cannot be taken away without due process; but the law itself, as a rule of conduct, may be changed at the will, or even at the whim, of the legislature, unless prevented by constitutional limitations. ...

We know that this is a power which may be abused; but that is no argument against its existence. For protection against abuses by legislatures the people must resort to the polls, not to the courts. ...

Judgment Affirmed.

Mr. Justice **FIELD**.

... The principle upon which the opinion of the majority proceeds is, in my judgment, subversive of the rights of private property. ...

The declaration of the [Illinois] Constitution of 1870, that private buildings used for private purposes shall be deemed public institutions, does not make them so. The receipt and storage of grain in a building erected by private means for that purpose does not constitute the building a public warehouse. There is no magic in the language, though used by a constitutional convention, which can change a private business into a public one. ... A tailor's or a shoemaker's shop would still retain its private character, even though the assembled wisdom of the State should declare ... that such a place was a public workshop. ... One might as well attempt to change the nature of colors, by giving them a new designation. The defendants were no more public warehousemen ... than the merchant who sells his merchandise to the public is a public merchant, or the blacksmith who shoes horses for the public is a public blacksmith; and it is a strange notion that by calling them so they would be brought under legislative control. ...

... When Sir Matthew Hale ... spoke of property as affected by a public interest, ... [he] referred to property dedicated by the owner to public uses, or to property the use of which was granted by the government, or in connection with which special privileges were conferred. Unless the property was thus dedicated, or some right bestowed by the government was held with the property ... the property was not affected by any public interest so as to be taken out of the category of property held in private right. But it is not in any such sense that the terms "clothing property with a public interest" are used in this case. From the nature of the business under consideration ... which, in any sense in which the words can be used, is a private business, in which the public are interested only as they are interested in the storage of other products of the soil, or in articles of manufacture, it is clear that the court intended to declare that, whenever one devotes his property to a business which is useful to the public,—"affects the community at large,"—the legislature can regulate the compensation which the owner may receive for its use, and for his own services in connection with it. ...

If this be sound law, if there be no protection, either in the principles upon which our republican government is founded, or in the prohibitions of the Constitution against such invasion of private rights, all property and all business in the State are held at the mercy of a majority of its legislature. The public has no greater interest in the use of buildings for the storage of grain than it has in the use of buildings for the residences of families ... and, according to the doctrine announced, the legislature may fix the rent of all tenements used for residence, without reference to the cost of their erection. If the owner does not like the rates prescribed, he may cease renting his houses. He has granted to the public, says the court, an interest in the use of the buildings, and "he may withdraw his grant by discontinuing the use; but, so long as he maintains the use, he must submit to the control." ... [T]here is hardly an enterprise or business engaging the attention and labor of any considerable portion of the community, in which the public has not an interest in the sense in which that term is used by the court in its opinion. ...

   ... The provision [of the Fourteenth Amendment] ... places property under the same protection as life and liberty. Except by due process of law, no State can deprive any person of either. The provision has been supposed to secure to every individual the essential conditions for the pursuit of happiness; and for that reason has not been heretofore, and should never be, construed in any narrow or restricted sense.

   No State "shall deprive any person of life, liberty, or property without due process of law. ..." By the term "life" ... something more is meant than mere animal existence. The inhibition against its deprivation extends to all those limbs and faculties by which life is enjoyed. The provision equally prohibits the mutilation of the body by the amputation of an arm or leg, or the putting out of an eye, or the destruction of any other organ of the body through which the soul communicates with the outer world. The deprivation not only of life, but of whatever God has given to every one with life, for its growth and enjoyment, is prohibited ... if its efficacy be not frittered away by judicial decision.

   By the term "liberty" ... something more is meant than mere freedom from physical restraint or the bounds of a prison. It means freedom to go where one may choose, and to act in such manner, not inconsistent with the equal rights of others, as his judgment may dictate for the promotion of his happiness; that is, to pursue such callings and avocations as may be most suitable to develop his capacities, and give to them their highest enjoyment.

   The same liberal construction which is required for the protection of life and liberty, in all particulars in which life and liberty are of any value, should be applied to the protection of private property. ...

   ... The will of the legislature is made the condition upon which the owner shall receive the fruits of his property and the just reward of his labor, industry, and enterprise. "That government," says Story, "can scarcely be deemed to be free where the rights of property are left solely dependent upon the will of a legislative body without any restraint. The fundamental maxims of a free government seem to require that the rights of personal liberty and private property should be held sacred," Wilkinson v. Leland ... [1829]. The decision of the court in this case gives unrestrained license to legislative will. ...

Mr. Justice **STRONG**. ...

   I concur in what [Mr. Justice **FIELD**] has said.

Editors' Notes

   (1) **Query:** This case was as much about WHO as HOW. How would James Bradley Thayer (see his article, reprinted above, p. 602) have analyzed the opinions? Would constitutionalism prescribe a solution here different from that which democratic theory would offer?

(2) **Query:** Was Fields's approach more *textualist* than *philosophic*? Compare his dissent in *Munn* with that in the Slaughter–House Cases (1873; reprinted above, p. 550). To what extent, if any, did the two utilize different approaches to constitutional interpretation?

(3) The doctrine "affected with a public interest" sounds strange to modern ears, but it was widely used in nineteenth century law. See Harry N. Scheiber, "The Road to *Munn*," 5 *Perspectives in Am.Hist.* 329 (1971).

(4) As the introductory essay to this Chapter noted, *Munn* heartened the Grangers but shocked and angered many wealthy economic and political interest groups. *Munn* did not challenge the new conception of dynamic, productive use of property. Rather it built on that concept to legitimate legislative action that imposed *duties* on the sorts of people who had expanded their rights to property, on grounds that these people were performing public functions. By 1895, however, the doctrine of laissez faire had become the dominant constitutional jurisprudence. The justices were to use the Tenth Amendment to strike down federal regulations and the Fourteenth's due process clause to invalidate state statutes. To understand these cases involving substantive due process in the economic sphere and later decisions involving substantive due process in other areas, such as privacy—see, for example, *Griswold* (1965; reprinted above, p. 147) and Roe v. Wade (1973; reprinted below, p. 1258)—one must keep in mind that more than economic interests were in conflict in the earlier cases. There were also clashes between different visions of what society was, what it was becoming, what it should become, and what individual autonomy meant and required in those actual and potential worlds.

"No legislature can bargain away the public health or the public morals."

STONE v. MISSISSIPPI

101 U.S. (11 Otto) 814, 25 L.Ed. 1079 (1880).

In 1867 Mississippi granted a 25–year charter to a lottery company for an initial fee of $5,000 and an annual tax of $1,000. The following year, however, the state adopted a new constitutional text, one clause of which forbade the legislature to authorize lotteries or the sale of lottery tickets. In 1870 the legislature enacted a statute which, in effect, repealed the charter of 1867. In 1874 the state attorney general began legal proceedings against the company, and state courts ruled that it could no longer do business within Mississippi. The company then obtained a writ of error from the U.S. Supreme Court.

Mr. Chief Justice **WAITE** delivered the opinion of the court.   ...

It is now too late to contend that any contract which a State actually enters into when granting a charter to a private corporation is not within the protection of the clause in the Constitution of the United States that prohibits States from passing laws impairing the obligation of contracts.   ...   The doctrines of Dartmouth College v. Woodward

[1819] have become so imbedded in the jurisprudence of the United States as to make them to all intents and purposes a part of the Constitution itself. In this connection, however, it is to be kept in mind that it is not the charter which is protected, but only any contract the charter may contain. If there is no contract, there is nothing in the grant on which the Constitution can act. Consequently, the first inquiry in this class of cases always is, whether a contract has in fact been entered into, and if so, what its obligations are.

In the present case the question is whether the State of Mississippi, in its sovereign capacity, did by the charter now under consideration bind itself irrevocably by a contract. ... There can be no dispute but that ... the legislature of the State chartered a lottery company ... for twenty-five years. ... If the legislature that granted this charter had the power to bind the people of the State and all succeeding legislatures to allow the corporation to continue its corporate business during the whole term of its authorized existence, there is no doubt about the sufficiency of the language employed to effect that object. ... Whether the alleged contract exists, therefore, or not, depends on the authority of the legislature to bind the State and the people of the State in that way.

All agree that the legislature cannot bargain away the police power of a State. ... Many attempts have been made in this court and elsewhere to define the police power, but never with entire success. It is always easier to determine whether a particular case comes within the general scope of the power, than to give an abstract definition of the power itself which will be in all respects accurate. No one denies, however, that it extends to all matters affecting the public health or the public morals. Beer Co. v. Mass. [1878]; Patterson v. Ky. [1878]. Neither can it be denied that lotteries are proper subjects for the exercise of this power. When the government is untrammelled by any claim of vested rights or chartered privileges, no one has ever supposed that lotteries could not lawfully be suppressed, and those who manage them punished severely as violators of the rules of social morality. ...

The question is therefore directly presented, whether ... the legislature of a State can, by the charter of a lottery company, defeat the will of the people, authoritatively expressed, in relation to the further continuance of such business in their midst. We think it cannot. No legislature can bargain away the public health or the public morals. The people themselves cannot do it, much less their servants. ... Government is organized with a view to their preservation, and cannot divest itself of the power to provide for them. For this purpose the largest legislative discretion is allowed, and the discretion cannot be parted with any more than the power itself. *Beer Company*. ...

In *Dartmouth College* ... Chief Justice Marshall ... was careful to say ... "that the framers of the Constitution did not intend to restrain States in the regulation of their civil institutions, adopted for internal government, and that the instrument they have given us is not to be so

construed." The present case, we think, comes within this limitation.
. . .

... [T]he power of governing is a trust committed by the people to the government, no part of which can be granted away. The people, in their sovereign capacity, have established their agencies for the preservation of the public health and the public morals, and the protection of public and private rights. These several agencies can govern according to their discretion, if within the scope of their general authority, while in power; but they cannot give away nor sell the discretion of those that are to come after them, in respect to matters the government of which, from the very nature of things, must "vary with varying circumstances."
. . .

The contracts which the Constitution protects are those that relate to property rights, not governmental. It is not always easy to tell on which side of the line which separates governmental from property rights a particular case is to be put; but in respect to lotteries there can be no difficulty. ... They are species of gambling, and wrong in their influences. They disturb the checks and balances of a well-ordered community. ... Certainly the right to suppress them is governmental, to be exercised at all times by those in power, at their discretion. Any one, therefore, who accepts a lottery charter does so with the implied understanding that the people, in their sovereign capacity, and through their properly constituted agencies, may resume it at any time when the public good shall require, whether it be paid for or not. ...

Judgment affirmed.

Editors' Notes

(1) **Query:** *Stone* raised several issues about WHAT "the Constitution" includes. First, where did the Court find an "implied understanding" that a contract with a state regarding lotteries—or any other subject—can be modified by the state? In the words of the constitutional document? In reasoned inference from those words? In original intent or understanding? In previous decisions? In some theory of democracy or constitutionalism?

(2) **Query:** Second, Waite wrote that the doctrine of *Dartmouth College* had "become so imbedded in the jurisprudence of the United States as to make them to all intents and purposes a part of the Constitution itself." To what extent was Waite claiming that judges could amend the larger constitution by interpreting the constitutional text?

(3) **Query:** Waite also raised interesting questions about democratic theory and limits on valid constitutional change. Not only did he deny that a government could alienate its police power but, he added: "The people themselves cannot do it. ..." How can one square such a denial of popular authority with democratic theory?

(4) In Marshall's time, the contracts clause had been the principal judicial instrument for protecting property rights. *Stone,* however, qualified the doctrine of Fletcher v. Peck (1810; reprinted above, p. 1091) and *Dartmouth College* (1819) that state grants were contracts for constitutional purposes.

Home Building & Loan Ass'n v. Blaisdell (1934; reprinted above, p. 210), further weakened the contract clause as a limitation on state power to modify contracts between private citizens. More than forty years after *Blaisdell,* the Court suddenly struck down two state statutes and reminded the world that the "Contract Clause remains part of the Constitution. It is not a dead letter." U.S. Trust v. New Jersey (1977); Allied Structural Steel v. Spannaus (1978). See the literature cited in Editors' Note 6 to *Charles River Bridge* (1837).

"Statutes of the nature of that under review ... are mere meddlesome interferences with the rights of the individual. ..."—Justice PECKHAM

"[T]he rule is universal that a legislative enactment ... is never to be ... held invalid unless it be, beyond question, plainly and palpably in excess of legislative power."—Justice HARLAN

"[A] constitution is not intended to embody a particular economic theory. ..."—Justice HOLMES

LOCHNER v. NEW YORK

198 U.S. 45, 25 S.Ct. 539, 49 L.Ed. 937 (1905).

Mr. Justice **PECKHAM** ... delivered the opinion of the Court.

The indictment ... charges that the plaintiff in error violated ... the labor law of the State of New York, in that he wrongfully and unlawfully required and permitted an employé working for him to work more than sixty hours in one week. ... The mandate of the statute that "no employé shall be required or permitted to work," is the substantial equivalent of an enactment that "no employé shall contract or agree to work," more than ten hours per day, and as there is no provision for special emergencies the statute is mandatory in all cases. It is not an act merely fixing the number of hours which shall constitute a legal day's work, but an absolute prohibition upon the employer, permitting, under any circumstances, more than ten hours work to be done in his establishment. The employé may desire to earn the extra money ... but this statute forbids the employer from permitting the employé to earn it.

The statute necessarily interferes with the right of contract between the employer and employés, concerning the number of hours in which the latter may labor in the bakery of the employer. The general right to make a contract in relation to his business is part of the liberty of the individual protected by the Fourteenth Amendment of the Federal Constitution. Allgeyer v. Louisiana [1897]. Under that provision no State can deprive any person of life, liberty or property without due process of law. The right to purchase or to sell labor is part of the liberty protected by this amendment, unless there are circumstances which exclude the right. There are, however, certain powers, existing in the sovereignty of each State in the Union, somewhat vaguely termed police powers, the exact description and limitation of which have not been attempted by the courts. Those powers ... relate to the safety, health, morals and general welfare of the public. Both property and liberty are held on such reasonable conditions as may be imposed by the governing power of the State in the exercise of those powers, and with such conditions the Fourteenth Amendment was not designed to interfere. Mugler v. Kansas [1887]; In re Kemmler [1890]; Crowley v. Christensen [1890]; In re Converse [1891].

The State, therefore, has power to prevent the individual from making certain kinds of contracts. ... Contracts in violation of a statute, either of the Federal or state government, or a contract to let one's property for immoral purposes, or to do any other unlawful act, could obtain no protection from the Federal Constitution, as coming under the liberty of person or of free contract. Therefore, when the State ... in the assumed exercise of its police powers, has passed an act which seriously limits the right to labor or the right of contract in regard to their means of livelihood between persons ... it becomes of great importance to determine which shall prevail—the right of the individual to labor for such time as he may choose, or the right of the State to prevent the individual from laboring ... beyond a certain time prescribed by the State.

This court has recognized the existence and upheld the exercise of the police powers of the States in many cases. ... It must, of course, be conceded that there is a limit to the valid exercise of the police power by the State. ... Otherwise the Fourteenth Amendment would have no efficacy and the legislatures of the States would have unbounded power. ... The claim of the police power would be a mere pretext—become another and delusive name for the supreme sovereignty of the State to be exercised free from constitutional restraint. ... In every case that comes before this court, therefore, where legislation of this character is concerned ... the question necessarily arises: Is this a fair, reasonable and appropriate exercise of the police power of the State ...? Of course the liberty of contract relating to labor includes both parties to it. The one has as much right to purchase as the other to sell labor.

This is not a question of substituting the judgment of the court for that of the legislature. If the act be within the power of the State it is valid, although the judgment of the court might be totally opposed to the enactment of such a law. But the question would still remain: Is it within the police power of the State? and that question must be answered by the court.

It is a question of which of two powers or rights shall prevail—the power of the State to legislate or the right of the individual to liberty of person and freedom of contract. ...

... There is no reasonable ground for interfering with the liberty of person or the right of free contract, by determining the hours of labor, in the occupation of a baker. There is no contention that bakers as a class are not equal in intelligence and capacity to men in other trades or manual occupations, or that they are not able to assert their rights and care for themselves without the protecting arm of the State, interfering with their independence of judgment and of action. They are in no sense wards of the State. ... [W]e think that a law like the one before us involves neither the safety, the morals nor the welfare of the public, and that the interest of the public is not in the slightest degree affected by such an act. The law must be upheld, if at all, as a law pertaining to the health of the individual engaged in the occupation of a baker. ... Clean and wholesome bread does not depend upon whether the baker works but ten hours per day or only sixty hours a week. The limitation of the hours of labor does not come within the police power on that ground. ...

We think that there can be no fair doubt that the trade of a baker, in and of itself, is not an unhealthy one to that degree which would authorize the legislature to interfere with the right to labor, and with the right of free contract on the part of the individual, either as employer or employé. ... It might be safely affirmed that almost all occupations more or less affect the health. ... But are we all, on that account, at the mercy of legislative majorities? ...

It is also urged ... that it is to the interest of the State that its population should be strong and robust, and therefore any legislation which may be said to tend to make people healthy must be valid as health laws, enacted under the police power. If this be a valid argument ... it follows that the protection of the Federal Constitution from undue interference with liberty of person and freedom of contract is visionary. ... Scarcely any law but might find shelter under such assumptions. ... We do not believe in the soundness of the views which uphold this law. On the contrary, we think that such a law as this, although passed in the assumed exercise of the police power ... is not within the meaning of that power, and is invalid. ... Statutes of the nature of that under review ... are mere meddlesome interferences with the rights of the individual. ...

This interference on the part of the legislatures of the several States with the ordinary trades and occupations of the people seems to be on the increase. ... It is impossible to shut our eyes to the fact that many of the laws of this character, while passed under what is claimed to be the police power for the purpose of protecting the public health or welfare, are, in reality, passed from other motives. ... The purpose of a statute must be determined from the natural and legal effect of the language employed; and whether or not it is repugnant to the Constitution of the United States must be determined from the natural effect of such statutes when put into operation, and not from their proclaimed purpose. ... The court looks beyond the mere letter of the law in such cases. Yick Wo v. Hopkins [1886].

It is manifest to us that ... the real object and purpose were simply to regulate the hours of labor between the master and his employés ...

in a private business, not dangerous in any degree to morals or in any real and substantial degree, to the health of the employés. Under such circumstances the freedom of the master and employé to contract with each other ... cannot be prohibited or interfered with, without violating the Federal Constitution. ...

Reversed.

Mr. Justice **HARLAN,** with whom Mr. Justice **WHITE** and Mr. Justice **DAY** concurred, dissenting. ...

Granting ... that there is a liberty of contract which cannot be violated even under the sanction of direct legislative enactment, but assuming, as according to settled law we may assume, that such liberty of contract is subject to such regulations as the State may reasonably prescribe for the common good and the well-being of society, what are the conditions under which the judiciary may declare such regulations to be in excess of legislative authority and void? Upon this point there is no room for dispute; for, the rule is universal that a legislative enactment, Federal or state, is never to be disregarded or held invalid unless it be, beyond question, plainly and palpably in excess of legislative power. ... If there be doubt as to the validity of the statute, that doubt must therefore be resolved in favor of its validity ... leaving the legislature to meet the responsibility for unwise legislation. If the end which the legislature seeks to accomplish be one to which its power extends, and if the means employed to that end, although not the wisest or best, are yet not plainly and palpably unauthorized by law, then the court cannot interfere. ... [W]hen the validity of a statute is questioned, the burden of proof ... is upon those who assert it to be unconstitutional. McCulloch v. Maryland [1819].

Let these principles be applied to the present case. ...

It is plain that this statute was enacted in order to protect the physical well-being of those who work in bakery and confectionery establishments. ... [T]he statute must be taken as expressing the belief of the people of New York that, as a general rule ... labor in excess of sixty hours during a week in such establishments may endanger the health of those who thus labor. Whether or not this be wise legislation it is not the province of the court to inquire. Under our systems of government the courts are not concerned with the wisdom or policy of legislation. ... I find it impossible ... to say that there is here no real or substantial relation between the means employed by the State and the end sought to be accomplished by its legislation. ... Nor can I say that the statute has no appropriate or direct connection with that protection to health which each State owes to her citizens ... or that it is not promotive of the health of the employés in question ... or that the regulation prescribed by the State is utterly unreasonable and extravagant or wholly arbitrary. ... Still less can I say that the statute is, beyond question, a plain, palpable invasion of rights secured by the fundamental law. ...

Mr. Justice **HOLMES** dissenting. ...

This case is decided upon an economic theory which a large part of the country does not entertain. If it were a question whether I agreed with that theory, I should desire to study it further and long before making up my mind. But I do not conceive that to be my duty, because I strongly believe that my agreement or disagreement has nothing to do with the right of a majority to embody their opinions in law. It is settled by various decisions of this court that state constitutions and state laws may regulate life in many ways which we as legislators might think as injudicious or if you like as tyrannical as this, and which equally with this interfere with the liberty to contract. Sunday laws and usury laws are ancient examples. ... The liberty of the citizen to do as he likes so long as he does not interfere with the liberty of others to do the same, which has been a shibboleth for some well-known writers, is interfered with by school laws, by the Post Office, by every state or municipal institution which takes his money for purposes thought desirable, whether he likes it or not. The Fourteenth Amendment does not enact Mr. Herbert Spencer's *Social Statics*. The other day we sustained the Massachusetts vaccination law. Jacobson v. Massachusetts [1905].

United States and state statutes and decisions cutting down the liberty to contract by way of combination are familiar to this court. Northern Securities Co. v. United States [1904]. Two years ago we upheld the prohibition of sales of stock on margins or for future delivery in the constitution of California. Otis v. Parker [1903]. The decision sustaining an eight hour law for miners is still recent. Holden v. Hardy [1898]. Some of those laws embody convictions or prejudices which judges are likely to share. Some may not. But a constitution is not intended to embody a particular economic theory, whether of paternalism and the organic relation of the citizen to the State or of *laissez faire*. It is made for people of fundamentally differing views, and the accident of our finding certain opinions natural and familiar or novel and even shocking ought not to conclude our judgment upon the question whether statutes embodying them conflict with the Constitution of the United States.

General propositions do not decide concrete cases. The decision will depend on a judgment or intuition more subtle than any articulate major premise. ... Every opinion tends to become a law. I think that the word liberty in the Fourteenth Amendment is perverted when it is held to prevent the natural outcome of a dominant opinion, unless it can be said that a rational and fair man necessarily would admit that the statute proposed would infringe fundamental principles as they have been understood by the traditions of our people and our law. It does not need research to show that no such sweeping condemnation can be passed upon the statute before us. A reasonable man might think it a proper measure on the score of health. Men whom I certainly could not pronounce unreasonable would uphold it as a first instalment of a general regulation of the hours of work. ...

Editors' Notes

(1) **Query:** What sort of approach to constitutional interpretation did Peckham take in *Lochner*? Did he argue or assume that Americans had a fundamental right to own and dispose of "property"? Neither?

(2) **Query:** Holmes claimed that "a constitution is not intended to embody a particular economic theory"? Did he mean that the Founders expected "the Constitution" to accommodate a socialist economy should the American public so demand? Did he mean "intended" in some other sense of that word? What if any provisions of the constitutional text, as currently written, would bar Congress from transforming private property to property held in common by everyone?

(3) **Query:** What about Holmes's related claim that "a constitution . . . is made for people of fundamentally different views"? Was he saying something about the concrete beliefs of those who drafted and ratified the American constitutional text? Was Holmes's proposition compatible with Lincoln's statement that the Union could not survive half slave and half free? Might Holmes have meant that constitutions are made for people with fundamentally different beliefs as long as those people generally agree that certain beliefs shall not be principles for the political and social conduct of others—as long, that is, as the people in question believe more or less in religious, ideological, and cultural *toleration*? But would such people actually be fundamentally different in their politically relevant beliefs? For an indication that the Court itself has found it difficult to live by all that Holmes said in *Lochner* see the dissent of Justice Harlan, II, in Harper v. Virginia (1966; reprinted above, p. 225.)

(4) **Query:** With *Dred Scott* (1857; reprinted above, p. 195) and Korematsu v. United States (1944; reprinted below, p. 1383), *Lochner* is a member of the most infamous trio of cases in American constitutional history. "To Lochner" or "to Lochnerize" has become a term of opprobrium referring to judges' reading their personal preferences about fundamental rights into the Constitution. To what extent are the Court's critics correct when they claim that any discovery of unlisted fundamental rights involves "Lochnering"? And can we be sure that *Lochner* itself is merely a case of "Lochnering"? Has "liberty to contract" no significant support in the American constitutional text or tradition beyond the preferences of the judges and others who pushed it from 1890 to 1937? For a reinterpretation of what was wrong with *Lochner,* see Cass R. Sunstein, *"Lochner's* Legacy," 87 *Colum.L.Rev.* 873 (1987).

"[F]reedom of contract is . . . the general rule and restraint the exception . . . and the exercise of legislative authority to abridge it can be justified only by the existence of exceptional circumstances."—Justice SUTHERLAND

"[I]t is not the function of this Court to hold congressional acts invalid simply because they are passed to carry out economic views which the Court believes to be unwise. . . ."—Chief Justice TAFT

> **"The criterion of constitutionality is not whether we believe the law to be for the public good."—Justice HOLMES**

ADKINS v. CHILDREN'S HOSPITAL

261 U.S. 525, 43 S.Ct. 394, 67 L.Ed. 785 (1923).

Lochner stirred a reaction among liberals much as Munn had among the new alliance for capitalism. The National Consumers League retained a prominent Boston attorney, Louis D. Brandeis, to defend legislation the Progressive movement had managed to get on the statute books to protect workers. The immediate result was an instrument known as the Brandeis Brief, a legal argument that justified such statutes by amassing hard social and economic data to show the nature of the problem and the reasonableness of the regulation rather than by construing abstract constitutional doctrines or explaining away earlier decisions. Brandeis first used this instrument in Muller v. Oregon (1908) and won a unanimous ruling sustaining, "without questioning in any respect the decision in Lochner v. New York," the validity of an Oregon law limiting the hours that women could work in laundries. Bunting v. Oregon (1917)—Brandeis was then on the Supreme Court and a young lawyer named Felix Frankfurter had taken his place as advocate—upheld a law setting maximum hours for both men and women.

Bunting, however, was a temporary high water mark for the constitutionality of progressive legislation. During oral argument in Adams v. Tanner (1917), Chief Justice Edward Douglass White picked up the Brandeis Brief dealing with abuses by private employment agencies and remarked that he could easily compile a document twice as thick that would justify outlawing the legal profession. By a 6–3 vote, the Court then struck down the state statute that forbade private employment agencies to charge job seekers fees for finding them work. The validity of a state minimum wage law for women divided the justices 4–4 in Stettler v. O'Hara. Equal division meant that the lower court's decision, which had held the act constitutional, stood; equal division also meant, however, that Stettler had no authority as a precedent of the Supreme Court.

Another opportunity to settle the issue of regulation of wages arose when a hospital and a female employee obtained an injunction against enforcement of an Act of Congress that had created a board to set minimum wages for women and minors in the District of Columbia. The board appealed to the Supreme Court.

Mr. Justice **SUTHERLAND** delivered the opinion of the Court. . . .

The judicial duty of passing upon the constitutionality of an act of Congress is one of great gravity and delicacy. The statute here in question has successfully borne the scrutiny of the legislative branch of the government, which, by enacting it, has affirmed its validity; and that determination must be given great weight. This Court, by an unbroken line of decisions from Chief Justice Marshall to the present day, has steadily adhered to the rule that every possible presumption is in favor of the validity of an act of Congress until overcome beyond rational doubt. But if by clear and indubitable demonstration a statute be opposed to the Constitution we have no choice but to say so. The Constitution, by its own terms, is the supreme law of the land, emanating from the people, the repository of ultimate sovereignty under our form of government. A congressional statute, on the other hand, is the act of an agency of this sovereign authority and if it conflict with the Constitution must fall; for that which is not supreme must yield to that which is. To hold it invalid (if it be invalid) is a plain exercise of the judicial power—that power vested in courts to enable them to administer justice according to law. From the authority to ascertain and determine the law in a given case, there necessarily results, in case of conflict, the duty to declare and enforce the rule of the supreme law and reject that of an inferior act of legislation which, transcending the Constitution, is of no effect and binding on no one. This is not the exercise of a substantive power to review and nullify acts of Congress, for no such substantive power exists. It is simply a necessary concomitant of the power to hear and dispose of a case or controversy properly before the court, to the determination of which must be brought the test and measure of the law.

That the right to contract about one's affairs is a part of the liberty of the individual protected by this [the Due Process] clause, is settled by the decisions of this Court and is no longer open to question. Allgeyer v. Louisiana [1897]; Coppage v. Kansas [1915]; Adair v. United States [1908]; *Lochner*; *Muller*.

There is, of course, no such thing as absolute freedom of contract. It is subject to a great variety of restraints. But freedom of contract is, nevertheless, the general rule and restraint the exception; and the exercise of legislative authority to abridge it can be justified only by the existence of exceptional circumstances. Whether these circumstances exist in the present case constitutes the question to be answered. ...

In the *Muller Case* the validity of an Oregon statute, forbidding the employment of any female in certain industries more than ten hours during any one day was upheld. The decision proceeded upon the theory that the difference between the sexes may justify a different rule respecting hours of labor in the case of women than in the case of men. It is pointed out that these consist in differences of physical structure, especially in respect of the maternal functions, and also in the fact that historically woman has always been dependent upon man, who has established his control by superior physical strength. ... But the ancient inequality of the sexes, otherwise than physical, ... has continued "with diminishing intensity." In view of the great—not to say revolutionary—changes which have taken place ... in the contractual, political and civil status of women, culminating in the Nineteenth Amendment, it is not unreasonable to say that these differences have now come almost, if not quite, to the vanishing point. ... [Thus] we cannot accept the doctrine that women of mature age, *sui juris,* require or may be subjected to restrictions upon their liberty of contract which could not lawfully be imposed in the case of men under similar circumstances. ...

The essential characteristics of the statute now under consideration, which differentiate it from the laws fixing hours of labor, will be made to appear as we proceed. It is sufficient now to point out that the latter ... deal with incidents of the employment having no necessary effect upon the heart of the contract, that is, the amount of wages to be paid and received. A law forbidding work to continue beyond a given number of hours leaves the parties free to contract about wages and thereby equalize whatever additional burdens may be imposed upon the employer as a result of the restrictions as to hours, by an adjustment in respect to the amount of wages. ... [T]he authority to fix hours of labor cannot be exercised except in respect of those occupations where work of long continued duration is detrimental to health. This Court has been careful in every case where the question has been raised, to place its decision upon this limited authority of the legislature to regulate hours of labor and to disclaim any purpose to uphold the legislation as fixing wages. ... It seems plain that these decisions afford no real support for any form of law establishing minimum wages.

... [This statute] differs from them in every material respect. It is not a law dealing with any business charged with a public interest or with public work, or to meet and tide over a temporary emergency. It has nothing to do with the character, methods or periods of wage payments. It does not prescribe hours of labor or conditions under which labor is to be done. It is not for the protection of persons under legal disability or for the prevention of fraud. It is simply and exclusively a price-fixing law, confined to adult women ... who are legally as capable of contracting for themselves as men. ... The price fixed by the board need have no relation to the capacity or earning power of the employee, the number of hours which may happen to constitute the day's work, the character of the place where the work is to be done, or the circumstances or surroundings of the employment. ... It is based wholly on the opinions of the members of the board and their advisers ... as to what will be necessary to provide a living for a woman, keep her in health and preserve her morals. It applies to any and every occupation in the District, without regard to its nature or the character of the work. ...

The law takes account of the necessities of only one party to the contract. It ignores the necessities of the employer by compelling him to pay not less than a certain sum, not only whether the employee is capable of earning it, but irrespective of the ability of his business to sustain the burden, generously leaving him, of course, the privilege of abandoning his business as an alternative for going on at a loss. ... It therefore undertakes to solve but one-half of the problem. The other half is the establishment of a corresponding standard of efficiency. ... To the extent that the sum fixed exceeds the fair value of the services rendered, it amounts to a compulsory exaction from the employer for the support of a partially indigent person, for whose condition there rests upon him no peculiar responsibility, and therefore, in effect, arbitrarily shifts to his shoulders a burden which, if it belongs to anybody, belongs to society as a whole. ...

... The ethical right of every worker, man or woman, to a living wage may be conceded. ... [B]ut the fallacy of the proposed method of attaining it is that it assumes that every employer is bound at all events to furnish it. The moral requirement implicit in every contract of employment, viz, that the amount to be paid and the service to be rendered shall bear to each other some relation of just equivalence, is completely ignored. ...

We are asked, upon the one hand, to consider the fact that several States have adopted similar statutes, and we are invited, upon the other hand, to give weight to the fact that three times as many States ... have refrained from enacting such legislation. We have also been furnished with a large number of printed opinions approving the policy of the minimum wage, and our own reading has disclosed a large number to the contrary. These are all proper enough for the consideration of the lawmaking bodies, since their tendency is to establish the desirability or undesirability of the legislation; but they reflect no legitimate light upon the question of its validity, and that is what we are called upon to decide. The elucidation of that question cannot be aided by counting heads.

It is said that great benefits have resulted from the operation of such statutes. ... They may be, and quite probably are, due to other causes. We cannot close our eyes to the notorious fact that earnings everywhere in all occupations have greatly increased. ... No real test of the economic value of the law can be had during periods of maximum employment. ...

Finally, it may be said that if, in the interest of the public welfare, the police power may be invoked to justify the fixing of a minimum wage, it may, when the public welfare is thought to require it, be invoked to justify a maximum wage. The power to fix high wages connotes, by like course of reasoning, the power to fix low wages. ...

... To sustain the individual freedom of action contemplated by the Constitution, is not to strike down the common good but to exalt it; for surely the good of society as a whole cannot be better served than by the preservation against arbitrary restraint of the liberties of its constituent members. ...

Affirmed.

Mr. Justice **BRANDEIS** took no part in the consideration or decision of these cases.

Mr. Chief Justice **TAFT,** dissenting. ...

The boundary of the police power beyond which its exercise becomes an invasion of the guaranty of liberty under the Fifth and Fourteenth Amendments to the Constitution is not easy to mark. Our Court has been laboriously engaged in pricking out a line in successive cases. We must be careful ... to follow that line as well as we can and not to depart from it by suggesting a distinction that is formal rather than real.

... [I]t is a disputable question in the field of political economy how far a statutory requirement of maximum hours or minimum wages may be a useful remedy. ... But it is not the function of this Court to hold congressional acts invalid simply because they are passed to carry out economic views which the Court believes to be unwise or unsound. The right of the legislature under the Fifth and Fourteenth Amendments to limit the hours of employment on the score of the health of the employee, it seems to me, has been firmly established. ...

... It is impossible for me to reconcile the *Bunting Case* and the *Lochner Case* and I have always supposed that the *Lochner Case* was thus overruled *sub silentio*. Yet the opinion of the Court herein in support of its conclusion quotes from the opinion in the *Lochner Case* as one which has been sometimes distinguished but never overruled. Certainly there was no attempt to distinguish it in the *Bunting Case*.

However, the opinion herein does not overrule the *Bunting Case* in express terms, and therefore I assume that the conclusion in this case rests on the distinction between a minimum of wages and a maximum of hours in the limiting of liberty to contract. ... In absolute freedom of contract the one term is as important as the other, for both enter equally into the consideration given and received, a restriction as to one is not any greater in essence than the other, and is of the same kind. One is the multiplier and the other the multiplicand.

If it be said that long hours of labor have a more direct effect upon the health of the employee than the low wage, there is very respectable authority from close observers, disclosed in the record and in the literature on the subject quoted at length in the briefs, that they are equally harmful in this regard. Congress took this view and we can not say it was not warranted in so doing.

With deference to the very able opinion of the Court ... it appears to me to exaggerate the importance of the wage term of the contract of employment as more inviolate than its other terms. Its conclusion seems influenced by the fear that the concession of the power to impose a minimum wage must carry with it a concession of the power to fix a maximum wage. This, I submit, is a *non sequitur*. A line of distinction like the one under discussion in this case is, as the opinion elsewhere admits, a matter of degree and practical experience and not of pure logic. Certainly the wide difference between prescribing a minimum wage and a maximum wage could as a matter of degree and experience be easily affirmed.

I am authorized to say that Mr. Justice **SANFORD** concurs in this opinion.

Mr. Justice **HOLMES,** dissenting. ...

... [T]he power of Congress seems absolutely free from doubt. The end, to remove conditions leading to ill health, immorality and the deterioration of the race, no one would deny to be within the scope of constitutional legislation. The means are means that have the approval of Congress, of many States, and of those governments from which we have learned our greatest lessons. When so many intelligent persons, who have studied the matter more than any of us can, have thought that the means are effective and are worth the price, it seems to me impossible to deny that the belief reasonably may be held by reasonable men. ... [I]n the present instance the only objection that can be urged is found within the vague contours of the Fifth Amendment, prohibiting the depriving any person of liberty or property without due process of law. ...

The earlier decisions upon the same words in the Fourteenth Amendment began within our memory and went no farther than an unpretentious assertion of the liberty to follow the ordinary callings. Later that innocuous generality was expanded into the dogma, Liberty of Contract. Contract is not specially mentioned in the text that we have to construe. It is merely an example of doing what you want to do, embodied in the word liberty. But pretty much all law consists in forbidding men to do some things that they want to do, and contract is no more exempt from law than other acts. Without enumerating all the restrictive laws that have been upheld I will mention a few that seem to me to have interfered with liberty of contract quite as seriously and directly as the one before us. Usury laws prohibit contracts by which a man receives more than so much interest for the money that he lends. Statutes of frauds restrict many contracts to certain forms. Some Sunday laws prohibit practically all contracts during one-seventh of our whole life. Insurance rates may be regulated. ...

I confess that I do not understand the principle on which the power to fix a minimum for the wages of women can be denied by those who admit the power to fix a maximum for their hours of work. ... The bargain is equally affected whichever half you regulate. Muller v. Oregon, I take it, is as good law today as it was in 1908. It will need more than the Nineteenth Amendment to convince me that there are no differences between men and women, or that legislation cannot take those differences into account. I should not hesitate to take them into account if I thought it necessary to sustain this act. Quong Wing v. Kirkendall [1912]. But after *Bunting*, I had supposed that it was not necessary, and that *Lochner* would be allowed a deserved repose.

The criterion of constitutionality is not whether we believe the law to be for the public good. We certainly cannot be prepared to deny that a reasonable man reasonably might have that belief in view of the legislation of Great Britain, Victoria and a number of the States of this Union. The belief is fortified by a very remarkable collection of documents submitted on behalf of the appellants, material here, I conceive, only as showing that the belief reasonably may be held. ...

Editors' Notes

(1) **Query:** What did Sutherland's "Constitution" include? How did he justify the Court's protecting "freedom of contract," a phrase the text does not mention, as a fundamental right? How can one distinguish between the nature of that fundamental right and those guarded, for example, by Skinner v. Oklahoma (1942; reprinted above, p. 1014), Shapiro v. Thompson (1969; reprinted above, p. 1019). Those guarded by *Griswold* (1965; reprinted above, p. 147) or Roe v. Wade (1973; reprinted below, p. 1259).

(2) **Query:** In the third sentence of *Adkins* reprinted here, Sutherland said:

This Court ... has steadily adhered to the rule that every possible presumption in favor of the validity of an act of Congress until overcome beyond rational doubt.

Two paragraphs later, however, he added:

[F]reedom of contract is ... the general rule and restraint the exception; and the exercise of legislative authority to abridge it can be justified only by the existence of exceptional circumstances.

Can these two sentences be reconciled? If so, what answer to the interrogative WHO does that reconciliation offer?

(3) Sutherland also said that the Court had no "substantive power to review and nullify acts of Congress. ... It is simply a necessary concomitant of the power to hear and dispose of a case or controversy properly before the court, to the determination of which must be brought the test and measure of the law." Here he was distinguishing the American version of judicial review from that of the Austrian Constitutional Court, which later became the model for similar institutions in Europe. Those tribunals usually do not decide cases but answer general questions about the validity of statutes. See also Massachusetts v. Mellon (1923) which would repeat this distinction.

(4) For the genesis of the Brandeis Brief, see: Clement E. Vose, "The National Consumers' League and the Brandeis Brief," 1 *Midw. J. of Pol.Sci.* 267 (1957); and Alpheus Thomas Mason, *Brandeis: A Free Man's Life* (New York: Viking, 1946), ch. 16.

(5) As Sutherland's opinion in *Adkins* and his dissents in the Minnesota Moratorium Case (1934; reprinted above, p. 210) and West Coast Hotel v. Parrish (1937; reprinted below, p. 1123) indicate, he had a rather consistent jurisprudence. For two studies of his constitutional philosophy, see: Joel Francis Paschal, *Mr. Justice Sutherland: A Man Against the State* (Princeton: Princeton University Press, 1951); and Hadley Arkes, *The Return of George Sutherland: Restoring a Jurisprudence of Natural Rights* (Princeton: Princeton University Press, 1994).

––––––––

"The Constitution does not speak of freedom of contract. It speaks of liberty and prohibits the deprivation of liberty without due process of law."—Chief Justice HUGHES

"The suggestion that the only check upon the exercise of the judicial power ... is the judge's own faculty of self-restraint, is both ill considered and mischievous."—Justice SUTHERLAND

WEST COAST HOTEL v. PARRISH

300 U.S. 379, 57 S.Ct. 578, 81 L.Ed. 703 (1937).

Lochner and *Adkins* stood as barriers against state and federal regulation of economic affairs; but other decisions—most recently before West Coast Hotel v. Parrish, Nebbia v. New York (1934)—indicated a more tolerant judicial attitude. The Court had also been giving mixed signals about federal regulations of the economy. Hammer v. Dagenhart (1918) invalidated a statute curtailing shipment in interstate commerce of goods produced by child labor. As in the Sugar Trust Case (1895), the majority held that neither mining nor manufacturing was commerce. The Court ignored the "necessary and proper clause" and gave a misleading paraphrase of the Tenth Amendment:

> In interpreting the Constitution it must never be forgotten that the nation is made up of States to which are entrusted the powers of local government. And to them and to the people the powers not expressly [sic] delegated to the national government are reserved.

Hammer, however, was an extreme decision. During the 1920s the Court, though seldom warmly receptive, sustained most federal statutes attacked as exceeding the commerce power. Then the New Deal's rash of regulation revived judicial hostility. During 1935 and 1936, the Court struck down much of the legislation Franklin Roosevelt had pushed through Congress. The usual explanation was that, in attempting to regulate conditions of labor, the federal government was exceeding its authority under the commerce clause and invading power the Tenth Amendment reserved to the states.

In the spring of 1936, Morehead v. New York held, 5–4, that a state law establishing minimum wages and maximum hours violated liberty of contract. In the fall, Roosevelt won in a landslide election. Three weeks before the election, the justices denied a rehearing in *Morehead.* Six weeks after, they heard argument in West Coast Hotel v. Parrish, a challenge to a statute from the state of Washington that was almost identical to the one in *Morehead.* At the conference, Owen J. Roberts, who had supplied the fifth vote in *Morehead,* now voted to sustain Washington's statute. Chief Justice Hughes, who had dissented in *Morehead,* assigned himself the task of writing the opinion of the Court. His work was not finished until March, and by then Roosevelt's campaign for his Court-packing bill was well under way.

Mr. Chief Justice **HUGHES** delivered the opinion of the Court. ...

The appellant conducts a hotel. The appellee Elsie Parrish was employed as a chambermaid and (with her husband) brought this suit to recover the difference between the wages paid her and the minimum wage fixed pursuant to the state law. The minimum wage was $14.50 per week of 48 hours. The appellant challenged the act as repugnant to the due process clause of the Fourteenth Amendment. ... The Supreme

Court of the State, reversing the trial court, sustained the statute. ...
This case is here on appeal.

The appellant relies upon the decision of this Court in Adkins v.
Children's Hospital. ... [C]ounsel for the appellees attempted to distinguish the *Adkins* case. ... That effort at distinction is obviously futile.
...

... The Supreme Court of Washington has ... decided that the
statute is a reasonable exercise of the police power. ... In reaching that
conclusion the state court has invoked principles long established by this
Court in the application of the Fourteenth Amendment. The state court
has refused to regard ... *Adkins* ... as determinative and has pointed to
our decisions both before and since that case as justifying its position.
We are of the opinion that this ruling ... demands ... reexamination of
the *Adkins* case. The importance of the question, in which many States
have similar laws are concerned, the close division by which the decision
in the *Adkins* case was reached, and the economic conditions which have
supervened, and in the light of which the reasonableness of the exercise
of the protective power of the State must be considered, make it not only
appropriate, but ... imperative, that ... the subject receive fresh
consideration. ...

The principle which must control our decision is not in doubt. ...
In each case the violation alleged by those attacking minimum wage
regulation for women is deprivation of freedom of contract. What is this
freedom? The Constitution does not speak of freedom of contract. It
speaks of liberty and prohibits the deprivation of liberty without due
process of law. In prohibiting that deprivation the Constitution does not
recognize an absolute and uncontrollable liberty. Liberty in each of its
phases has its history and connotation. But the liberty safeguarded is
liberty in a social organization which requires the protection of law
against the evils which menace the health, safety, morals and welfare of
the people. Liberty under the Constitution is thus necessarily subject to
the restraints of due process, and regulation which is reasonable in
relation to its subject and is adopted in the interests of the community is
due process.

This essential limitation of liberty in general governs freedom of
contract in particular. More than twenty-five years ago we set forth the
applicable principles ...: " ... [f]reedom of contract is a qualified and
not an absolute right. There is no absolute freedom to do as one wills or
to contract as one chooses. ... Liberty implies the absence of arbitrary
restraint, not immunity from reasonable regulations and prohibitions
imposed in the interests of the community." Chicago, B. & Q. R. Co. v.
McGuire [1911].

This power under the Constitution to restrict freedom of contract
has had many illustrations. ... Thus statutes have been sustained
limiting employment in underground mines and smelters to eight hours
[per] day; in forbidding the payment of seamen's wages in advance; in
prohibiting contracts limiting liability for injuries to employees; in

limiting hours of work of employees in manufacturing establishments; and in maintaining workmen's compensation laws. ... [T]he legislature has necessarily a wide field of discretion in order that there may be suitable protection of health and safety, and that peace and good order may be promoted through regulations designed to insure wholesome conditions of work and freedom from oppression. ...

The point that has been strongly stressed that adult employees should be deemed competent to make their own contracts was decisively met nearly forty years ago in Holden v. Hardy [1898] where we pointed out the inequality in the footing of the parties. ... And we added that the fact "that both parties are of full age and competent to contract does not necessarily deprive the State of the power to interfere where the parties do not stand upon an equality, or where the public health demands that one party to the contract shall be protected against himself." "The State still retains an interest in his welfare, however reckless he may be. ... [W]hen the individual health, safety and welfare are sacrificed or neglected, the State must suffer."

... [T]his established principle is peculiarly applicable in relation to the employment of women in whose protection the State has a special interest. That phase of the subject received elaborate consideration in Muller v. Oregon (1908), where the constitutional authority of the State to limit the working hours of women was sustained. We emphasized the consideration that "woman's physical structure and the performance of maternal functions place her at a disadvantage in the struggle for subsistence" and that her physical well being "becomes an object of public interest and care in order to preserve the strength and vigor of the race." We emphasized the need of protecting women against oppression despite her possession of contractual rights. ...

This array of precedents and the principles they applied were thought by the dissenting Justices in the Adkins case to demand that the minimum wage statute be sustained. The validity of the distinction made by the Court between a minimum wage and a maximum of hours in limiting liberty of contract was especially challenged. ... That challenge persists and is without any satisfactory answer. As Chief Justice Taft observed [dissenting in Adkins]: " ... One is the multiplier and the other the multiplicand." ...

The minimum wage ... under the Washington statute is fixed after full consideration by representatives of employers, employees and the public. It may be assumed that the minimum wage is fixed in consideration of the services that are performed in the particular occupations under normal conditions. ... The statement of Mr. Justice Holmes in the Adkins case is pertinent: "This statute does not compel anybody to pay anything. It simply forbids employment at rates below those fixed as the minimum requirement of health and right living. It is safe to assume that women will not be employed at even the lowest wages allowed unless they earn them, or unless the employer's business can sustain the burden. ..."

We think that ... the *Adkins* case was a departure from the true application of the principles governing the regulation by the State of the relation of employer and employed. Those principles have been reenforced by our subsequent decisions. Thus in Radice v. New York [1924] we sustained the New York statute which restricted the employment of women in restaurants at night. ... In Nebbia v. New York [1934] dealing with ... the general subject of the regulation of the use of private property and of the making of private contracts ... we again declared that if such laws "have a reasonable relation to a proper legislative purpose, and are neither arbitrary nor discriminatory, the requirements of due process are satisfied" ... that the legislature is primarily the judge of the necessity of such an enactment, that every possible presumption is in favor of its validity. ...

... [We] find it impossible to reconcile that ruling [*Adkins*] with these well-considered declarations. What can be closer to the public interest than the health of women and their protection from unscrupulous and overreaching employers? And if the protection of women is a legitimate end of the exercise of state power, how can it be said that the requirement of the payment of a minimum wage fairly fixed in order to meet the very necessities of existence is not an admissible means to that end? ...

... [A]doption of similar requirements by many States evidences a deep seated conviction both as to the presence of the evil and as to the means adapted to check it. Legislative response to that conviction cannot be regarded as arbitrary or capricious, and that is all we have to decide. ...

... Adkins v. Children's Hospital should be, and it is, overruled. The judgment of the Supreme Court of the State of Washington is

Affirmed.

Mr. Justice **SUTHERLAND**, dissenting:

Mr. Justice **VAN DEVANTER**, Mr. Justice **McREYNOLDS,** Mr. Justice **BUTLER** and I think the judgment of the court below should be reversed. ...

Under our form of government, where the written Constitution, by its own terms, is the supreme law, some agency, of necessity, must have the power to say the final word as to the validity of a statute assailed as unconstitutional. The Constitution makes it clear that the power has been intrusted to this court when the question arises in a controversy within its jurisdiction; and so long as the power remains there, its exercise cannot be avoided without betrayal of the trust.

It has been pointed out many times ... that this judicial duty is one of gravity and delicacy; and that rational doubts must be resolved in favor of the constitutionality of the statute. But whose doubts, and by whom resolved? Undoubtedly it is the duty of a member of the court, in the process of reaching a right conclusion, to give due weight to the opposing views of his associates; but in the end, the question ... is not whether such views seem sound to those who entertain them, but whether they convince him that the statute is constitutional or engender in his mind a rational doubt upon that issue. The oath which he takes as a judge is not a composite oath, but an individual one. And in passing upon the validity of a statute, he discharges a duty imposed upon *him,* which cannot be consummated justly by an automatic acceptance of the views of others which have neither convinced, nor created a reasonable doubt in, his mind. If upon a question so important he thus surrender his deliberate judgment, he stands forsworn. He cannot subordinate his convictions to that extent and keep faith with his oath or retain his judicial and moral independence.

The suggestion that the only check upon the exercise of the judicial power ... is the judge's own faculty of self-restraint, is both ill considered and mischievous. Self-restraint belongs in the domain of will and not of judgment. The check upon the judge is that imposed by his oath of office, by the Constitution and by his own conscientious and informed convictions; and since he has the duty to make up his own mind and adjudge accordingly, it is hard to see how there could be any other restraint. ...

It is urged that the question involved should now receive fresh consideration, among other reasons, because of "the economic conditions which have supervened"; but the meaning of the Constitution does not change with the ebb and flow of economic events. We frequently are told in more general words that the Constitution must be construed in the light of the present. If by that it is meant that the Constitution is made up of living words that apply to every new condition which they include, the statement is quite true. But to say ... that the words of the Constitution mean today what they did not mean when written— that is, that they do not apply to a situation now to which they would have applied then—is to rob that instrument of the essential element which continues it in force as the people have made it until they, and not their official agents, have made it otherwise. ...

The judicial function is that of interpretation; it does not include the power of amendment under the guise of interpretation. To miss the point of difference between the two is to miss all that the phrase "supreme law of the land" stands for. ... If the Constitution, intelligently and reasonably construed in the light of these principles, stands in the way of desirable legislation, the ... remedy in that situation—and the only true remedy—is to amend the Constitution. ...

The people by their Constitution created three separate, distinct, independent and coequal departments of government. The governmental structure rests, and was intended to rest, not upon any one or upon any two, but upon all three of these fundamental pillars. It seems unnecessary to repeat ... that the powers of these departments are different and are to be exercised independently. ... Each is answerable to its creator ... not to another agent. The view, therefore, of the

Executive and of Congress that an act is constitutional is persuasive in a high degree; but it is not controlling.

... [T]he Washington statute ... is in every substantial respect identical with the statute involved in the *Adkins* case. ... And if the *Adkins* case was properly decided, as we ... think it was, it necessarily follows that the Washington statute is invalid.

In support of minimum-wage legislation it has been urged ... that great benefits will result in favor of underpaid labor. ... But with these speculations we have nothing to do. We are concerned only with the question of constitutionality. ...

Editors' Notes

(1) **Query:** To what extent was Hughes's approach to constitutional interpretation *textualist*? *Doctrinalist*? What about Sutherland's? Did either depend heavily on democratic theory? Constitutionalism?

(2) **Query:** Would Hugo Black (see, for example, his dissent in *Griswold*, above p. 147) have joined Sutherland when he wrote:

> the meaning of the Constitution does not change with the ebb and flow of economic events. We frequently are told in more general words that the Constitution must be construed in the light of the present. If by that it is meant that the Constitution is made up of living words that apply to every new condition which they include, the statement is quite true. But to say ... that the words of the Constitution mean today what they did not mean when written ... is to rob that instrument of the essential element which continues it in force as the people have made it until they, and not their official agents, have made it otherwise.

But Black wrote for the Court in Ferguson v. Skrupa (1963; reprinted below, p. 1129), which upheld even broader governmental authority over business affairs than had *Parrish*. Did Sutherland really believe that the drafters and ratifiers of the constitutional text of 1787–88 or of the Fourteenth Amendment were disciples of *laissez faire*? Or even that they anticipated modern industrial and finance capitalism?

(3) For *Parrish*'s effect on the fate of Roosevelt's "Court-packing plan" and the entire doctrine of "freedom of contract," see the introductory essay to this Chapter. Within weeks, the Court began to lift the other barrier to governmental regulation of economic relations, the Tenth Amendment as a restriction on federal control over commerce. The first decisions, NLRB v. Jones & Laughlin, Corp., NLRB v. Fruehauf Trailer Co., and NLRB v. Friedman–Harry Marks, sustained the Wagner Act's regulation of labor relations in a large steel conglomerate, a medium sized truck factory, and a small clothing plant. Not until National League of Cities v. Usery (1976; reprinted above, p. 565) did the justices again invalidate a federal statute as exceeding congressional control over commerce.

(4) Sutherland's comment about "self-restraint" referred to Stone's dissent in United States v. Butler (1936). There, in his most eloquent protest against how far afield of the Constitution he felt the majority was roaming to

invalidate the New Deal, Stone—in an opinion in which Brandeis and Cardozo joined and FDR loved to quote—wrote:

> The power of courts to declare a statute unconstitutional is subject to two guiding principles of decision. . . . One is that courts are concerned only with the power to enact statutes, not with their wisdom. The other is that while unconstitutional exercise of power by the executive and legislative branches of government is subject to judicial restraint, the only check upon our own exercise of power is our own sense of self-restraint. For the removal of unwise laws from the statute books appeal lies not to the courts but to the ballot and to the processes of democratic government. . . .
>
> A tortured construction of the Constitution is not to be justified by recourse to extreme examples . . . which might occur if courts could not prevent [them]. Courts are not the only agency of government that must be assumed to have the capacity to govern.

For analyses of Sutherland's jurisprudence, see Editors' Note 5 to *Adkins* (1923; at p. 1122).

"The day is gone when this Court uses the Due Process Clause of the Fourteenth Amendment to strike down state laws, regulatory of business and industrial conditions, because they may be unwise, improvident, or out of harmony with a particular school of thought."

WILLIAMSON v. LEE OPTICAL CO.

348 U.S. 483, 75 S.Ct. 461, 99 L.Ed. 563 (1955).

Oklahoma enacted a complex statute regulating visual care, reducing drastically the scope of optician's lawful activities and correspondingly enlarging those phases of visual care that could be performed only by ophthalmologists or optometrists. Lee Optical Co. claimed that, by taking away the company's business, the statute deprived it of property without due process and denied it equal protection of the laws. The Supreme Court rejected both arguments in the opinion reprinted above, p. 908.

"Whether the legislature takes for its textbook Adam Smith, Herbert Spencer, Lord Keynes, or some other is no concern of ours."

FERGUSON v. SKRUPA

372 U.S. 726, 83 S.Ct. 1028, 10 L.Ed.2d 93 (1963).

Kansas law forbade anyone to engage in "debt adjusting"—defined as consolidating the debts of another and, for a fee, arranging to have them paid off—except as part of the licensed practice of law. Skrupa, a "credit adviser," attacked the statute in a special federal three-judge district court, claiming that Kansas had deprived him of his property—his right to carry on a legitimate business—without due process. That court agreed and enjoined enforcement of the act. Kansas appealed to the Supreme Court.

Mr. Justice **BLACK** delivered the opinion of the Court. . . .

. . . Under the system of government created by our Constitution, it is up to legislatures, not courts, to decide on the wisdom and utility of legislation. There was a time when the Due Process Clause was used by this Court to strike down laws which were thought unreasonable, that is, unwise or incompatible with some particular economic or social philosophy. In this manner the Due Process Clause was used, for example, to nullify laws prescribing maximum hours for work in bakeries, Lochner v. New York (1905), outlawing "yellow dog" contracts, Coppage v. Kansas (1915), setting minimum wages for women, Adkins v. Children's Hospital (1923), and fixing the weight of loaves of bread, Jay Burns Baking Co. v. Bryan (1924). This intrusion by the judiciary into the realm of legislative value judgments was strongly objected to at the time, particularly by Mr. Justice Holmes and Mr. Justice Brandeis. Dissenting from the Court's invalidating a state statute which regulated the resale price of theatre and other tickets, Mr. Justice Holmes said, "I think the proper course is to recognize that a state legislature can do whatever it sees fit to do unless it is restrained by some express prohibition in the Constitution of the United States or of the State, and that Courts should be careful not to extend such prohibitions beyond their obvious meaning by reading into them conceptions of public policy that the particular Court may happen to entertain." . . .

The doctrine that prevailed in *Lochner, Coppage, Adkins, Burns,* and like cases—that due process authorizes courts to hold laws unconstitutional when they believe the legislature has acted unwisely—has long since been discarded. We have returned to the original constitutional proposition that courts do not substitute their social and economic beliefs for the judgment of legislative bodies, who are elected to pass laws. As this Court stated in a unanimous opinion in 1941, "We are not concerned . . . with the wisdom, need, or appropriateness of the legislation." Olsen v. Nebraska (1941). Legislative bodies have broad scope to experiment with economic problems, and this Court does not sit to "subject the State to an intolerable supervision hostile to the basic principles of our Government and wholly beyond the protection which the general clause of the Fourteenth Amendment was intended to secure." It is now settled that States "have power to legislate against what are found to be injurious practices in their internal commercial and business affairs, so long as their laws do not run afoul of some specific federal constitutional prohibition, or of some valid federal law."

. . . We conclude that the Kansas Legislature was free to decide for itself that legislation was needed to deal with the business of debt adjusting. Unquestionably, there are arguments showing that the busi-

ness of debt adjusting has social utility, but such arguments are properly addressed to the legislature, not to us. We refuse to sit as a "super-legislature to weigh the wisdom of legislation," and we emphatically refuse to go back to the time when courts used the Due Process Clause "to strike down state laws, regulatory of business and industrial conditions, because they may be unwise, improvident, or out of harmony with a particular school of thought." [Williamson v. Lee Optical (1955).] ...
Whether the legislature takes for its textbook Adam Smith, Herbert Spencer, Lord Keynes, or some other is no concern of ours. ...

Reversed.

Mr. Justice **HARLAN** concurs in this judgment on the ground that this state measure bears a rational relationship to a constitutionally permissible objective. See Williamson v. Lee Optical [1955].

Editors' Note

(1) **Query:** What sort of approach to constitutional interpretation did Black follow?

(2) **Query:** Would the Court have been so tolerant if Kansas had taken Karl Marx for "its textbook"?

(3) **Query:** Justice Black confidently announced in *Ferguson* in 1963 that the Court had "long since" discarded substantive due process in the economic field. Two years later in *Griswold* (reprinted above, p. 147), he contended that the Court was adopting another form of the same doctrine, and he protested bitterly. Can one convincingly distinguish between the kind of reasoning in *Lochner* (reprinted above, p. 1110) and *Griswold*?

(4) **Query:** Note Black's bow to *originalism* at p. 1130: "We have returned to the original constitutional proposition that courts do not substitute their social and economic beliefs for the judgment of legislative bodies. ..."
Did he offer any evidence to support this claim? Do cases like Fletcher v. Peck (1810; reprinted above, p. 1091) bolster or undermine his assertion?

"[T]he Court has made it clear that it will not substitute its judgment for a legislature's judgment as to what constitutes [taking of private property for] a public use 'unless the use be palpably without reasonable foundation.'"

HAWAII HOUSING AUTHORITY v. MIDKIFF
467 U.S. 229, 104 S.Ct. 2321, 81 L.Ed.2d 186 (1984).

In the mid–1960s, an investigation by the Hawaiian legislature showed that 72 people held more than 90 per cent of the privately owned land in the state. They leased land to those who wished to build their own homes. Claiming that this concentration of ownership was inflating real estate prices and contributing to public unrest, the legislature passed the Land Reform Act of 1967, which authorized the Hawaiian Housing Authority, when asked by people leasing the land on which they lived, to condemn large tracts of land occupied by single family homes, pay the land owner(s) a fair price as determined either by negotiation between the lessors and the lessees or by arbitration, and resell the land to the home owners at the purchase price, with the proviso that no person could so purchase more than one lot.

In 1977, the HHA began condemnation procedures under the Land Reform Act and ordered Frank E. Midkiff and others to negotiate with some of their lessees over the value of land they were leasing. When those negotiations broke down, the HHA ordered arbitration. Midkiff et al. refused and sued in a federal district court for an injunction against enforcement of the Act. The district judge upheld the statute as constitutional, but the Court of Appeals for the Ninth Circuit reversed, saying the Act was "a naked attempt on the part of Hawaii to take the private property of A and transfer it to B solely for B's private use and benefit." Hawaii then appealed to the Supreme Court.

Justice **O'CONNOR** delivered the opinion of the Court. . . .

III . . .

A

The starting point for our analysis of the Act's constitutionality is the Court's decision in Berman v. Parker (1954) . . . [which] held constitutional the District of Columbia Redevelopment Act of 1945. That Act provided both for the comprehensive use of the eminent domain power to redevelop slum areas and for the possible sale or lease of the condemned lands to private interests. In discussing whether the takings authorized by that Act were for a "public use," the Court stated

> We deal . . . with what traditionally has been known as the police power.
> . . . The definition is essentially the product of legislative determinations addressed to the purposes of government, purposes neither abstractly nor historically capable of complete definition. Subject to specific constitutional limitations, when the legislature has spoken, the public interest has been declared in terms well-nigh conclusive. In such cases the legislature, not the judiciary, is the main guardian of the public needs to be served by social legislation, whether it be Congress legislating concerning the District of Columbia . . . or the States legislating concerning local affairs. . . . This principle admits of no exception merely because the power of eminent domain is involved. . . .

The Court explicitly recognized the breadth of the principle it was announcing, noting:

> Once the object is within the authority of Congress, the right to realize it through the exercise of eminent domain is clear. For the power of eminent domain is merely the means to the end. . . . Once the object is within the authority of Congress, the means by which it will be attained is also for Congress to determine. Here one of the means chosen is the use of private enterprise for redevelopment of the area. Appellants argue that this makes the project a taking from one businessman for the benefit of another businessman. But the means of executing the project are for Congress and Congress alone to determine, once the public purpose has been established.

The "public use" requirement is thus coterminous with the scope of a sovereign's police powers.

There is, of course, a role for courts to play in reviewing a legislature's judgment of what constitutes a public use. ... But the Court in *Berman* made clear that it is "an extremely narrow" one. ... In short, the Court has made clear that it will not substitute its judgment for a legislature's judgment as to what constitutes a public use "unless the use be palpably without reasonable foundation." United States v. Gettysburg Electric R. Co. (1896).

To be sure, the Court's cases have repeatedly stated that "one person's property may not be taken for the benefit of another private person without a justifying public purpose, even though compensation be paid." Thompson v. Consolidated Gas Corp. (1937). ... [W]here the exercise of the eminent domain power is rationally related to a conceivable public purpose, the Court has never held a compensated taking to be proscribed by the Public Use Clause. See *Berman;* Block v. Hirsh (1921).

On this basis, we have no trouble concluding that the Hawaii Act is constitutional. The people of Hawaii have attempted, much as the settlers of the original 13 Colonies did,[1] to reduce the perceived social and economic evils of a land oligopoly traceable to their monarchs. ... Regulating oligopoly and the evils associated with it is a classic exercise of a State's police powers. See Exxon Corp. v. Maryland (1978); Block v. Hirsh. We cannot disapprove of Hawaii's exercise of this power.

Nor can we condemn as irrational the Act's approach to correcting the land oligopoly problem. The Act presumes that when a sufficiently large number of persons declare that they are willing but unable to buy lots at fair prices the land market is malfunctioning. When such a malfunction is signalled, the Act authorizes HHA to condemn lots in the relevant tract. The Act limits the number of lots any one tenant can purchase and authorizes HHA to use public funds to ensure that the market dilution goals will be achieved. This is a comprehensive and rational approach to identifying and correcting market failure.

Of course, this Act, like any other, may not be successful in achieving its intended goals. ... When the legislature's purpose is legitimate and its means are not irrational, our cases make clear that empirical debates over the wisdom of takings—no less than debates over the wisdom of other kinds of socioeconomic legislation—are not to be carried out in the federal courts. ... Therefore, the Hawaii statute must pass the scrutiny of the Public Use Clause.

B

The Court of Appeals read ... our "public use" cases, especially *Berman,* as requiring that government possess and use property at some

---

1. After the American Revolution, the colonists in several states took steps to eradicate the feudal incidents with which large proprietors had encumbered land in the colonies. ... [Footnote by the Court.]

point during a taking. Since Hawaiian lessees retain possession of the property for private use throughout the condemnation process, the court found that the Act exacted takings for private use. Second, it determined that these cases involved only "the review of ... *congressional* determination[s] that there was a public use, *not* the review of ... state legislative determination[s]." Because state legislative determinations are involved in the instant cases, the Court of Appeals decided that more rigorous judicial scrutiny of the public use determinations was appropriate. ...

The mere fact that property taken outright by eminent domain is transferred in the first instance to private beneficiaries does not condemn that taking as having only a private purpose. The Court long ago rejected any literal requirement that condemned property be put into use for the general public. "It is not essential that the entire community, nor even any considerable portion, ... directly enjoy or participate in any improvement in order [for it] to constitute a public use." Rindge Co. v. Los Angeles [1923]. ... As the unique way titles were held in Hawaii skewed the land market, exercise of the power of eminent domain was justified. The Act advances its purposes without the State taking actual possession of the land. In such cases, government does not itself have to use property to legitimate the taking; it is only the taking's purpose, and not its mechanics, that must pass scrutiny under the Public Use Clause.

Similarly, the fact that a state legislature, and not the Congress, made the public use determination does not mean that judicial deference is less appropriate.[2] Judicial deference is required because, in our system of government, legislatures are better able to assess what public purposes should be advanced by an exercise of the taking power. State legislatures are as capable as Congress of making such determinations within their respective spheres of authority. See *Berman.* Thus, if a legislature, state or federal, determines there are substantial reasons for an exercise of the taking power, courts must defer to its determination that the taking will serve a public use. ...

[*Reversed.*]

Justice **MARSHALL** took no part in the consideration or decision of these cases.

Editors' Notes

(1) **Query:** In footnote 2 Justice O'Connor argued that the Court should accord state legislatures the same deference as Congress because the

---

2. It is worth noting that the Fourteenth Amendment does not itself contain an independent "public use" requirement. Rather, that requirement is made binding on the states only by the incorporation of the Fifth Amendment's Eminent Domain Clause through the Fourteenth Amendment's Due Process Clause. See Chicago, Burlington & Quincy R. Co. v. Chicago (1897). It would be ironic to find that state legislation is subject to greater scrutiny under the incorporated "public use" requirement than is congressional legislation under the express mandate of the Fifth Amendment. [Footnote by the Court.]

Fourteenth Amendment "incorporated" the Fifth's eminent domain clause and so provided the same constitutional text to interpret. To what extent is this argument based on a *textual approach*? Whether arguing from plain words or not, is O'Connor persuasive about equal deference? To what extent do considerations of federalism—and of WHO interprets, state or national officials—come into play? What did James Bradley Thayer say about the comparative deference judges owe to Congress and state legislatures? See his article, reprinted above at p. 602. More generally, what would democratic theory say? Constitutionalism? Is O'Connor more persuasive in the body of her opinion when she addresses the functional capabilities of courts and legislatures? For an analysis of the underlying problems, see Charles L. Black, *Structure and Relationship in Constitutional Law* (Baton Rouge: Louisiana State University Press, 1969), ch. 3.

(2) **Query:** Does *Hawaii Housing Authority*, leave room for any judicially enforceable limit to a state's authority to redistribute private property as long as it provides just compensation to the former owners? For other important decisions in accord with *HHA,* see: Penn Central v. New York (1978) and a case from the Supreme Court of Michigan, Poletown v. Detroit (1981).

"[T]o win its case South Carolina must do more than proffer the legislature's declaration that the uses Lucas desires are inconsistent with the public interest."—Justice SCALIA

"The Takings Clause does not require a static body of state property law. ..."—Justice KENNEDY

"Rather than invoking these traditional rules, the Court decides the State has the burden to convince the courts that its legislative judgments are correct."—Justice BLACKMUN

"The Court's holding today effectively freezes the State's common law, denying the legislature much of its traditional power to revise the law governing the rights and uses of property."—Justice STEVENS

LUCAS v. SOUTH CAROLINA COASTAL COUNCIL

505 U.S. ____, 112 S.Ct. 2886, 120 L.Ed.2d 798 (1992).

To cope with erosion of its coastline, South Carolina in 1977 enacted legislation requiring owners in areas near beaches and sand dunes to obtain a permit to build on the land. At about that time, David Lucas began purchasing and developing land for residential use on the Isle of Palms, a thin barrier island northeast of Charleston. In 1986 he bought an additional pair of lots. Despite the fact that in recent decades tides and storms had often flooded and several times carried part of that land away and later rebuilt it, Lucas's plan to develop and sell the lots for homesites was still within the law. Then, in 1988, the state adopted the Beachfront Management Act, under which lots so situated were too close to the ocean for residential use and so, Lucas asserted, became commercially worthless. He sued in a state court, claiming the state had, in effect, "taken" his property and thus owed him "just compensation." The trial judge agreed but the state supreme court reversed. Lucas sought and obtained certiorari from the U.S. Supreme Court.

Justice **SCALIA** delivered the opinion of the Court. . . .

III

A

Prior to Justice Holmes's exposition in Pennsylvania Coal Co. v. Mahon (1922), it was generally thought that the Takings Clause reached only a "direct appropriation" of property, or the functional equivalent of a "practical ouster of [the owner's] possession." Transportation Co. v. Chicago (1879). Justice Holmes recognized in *Mahon*, however, that if the protection against physical appropriations of private property was to be meaningfully enforced, the government's power to redefine the range of interests included in the ownership of property was necessarily constrained by constitutional limits. . . . If, instead, the uses of private property were subject to unbridled, uncompensated qualification under the police power, "the natural tendency of human nature [would be] to extend the qualification more and more until at last private property disappeared." . . . These considerations gave birth in that case to the oft-cited maxim that, "while property may be regulated to a certain extent, if regulation goes too far it will be recognized as a taking." . . .

Nevertheless, our decision in *Mahon* offered little insight into when, and under what circumstances, a given regulation would be seen as going "too far". . . . In 70–odd years of succeeding "regulatory takings" jurisprudence, we have generally eschewed any " 'set formula' " for determining how far is too far, preferring to "engag[e] in . . . essentially *ad hoc*, factual inquiries," Penn Central v. New York City (1978) (quoting Goldblatt v. Hempstead [1962]). We have, however, described at least two discrete categories of regulatory action as compensable without case-specific inquiry into the public interest advanced in support of the restraint. The first encompasses regulations that compel the property owner to suffer a physical "invasion" of his property. In general (at least with regard to permanent invasions), no matter how minute the intrusion, and no matter how weighty the public purpose behind it, we have required compensation. . . .

The second situation in which we have found categorical treatment appropriate is where regulation denies all economically beneficial or productive use of land. See Nollan v. California Coastal Comm'n (1987); Keystone Bituminous Coal Ass'n v. DeBenedictis (1987); Hodel v. Va. Surface & M. & R. Ass'n (1981).[1]

---

1. We will not attempt to respond to all of Justice Blackmun's mistaken citations of case precedent. Characteristic of its nature is his assertion that the cases we discuss here stand merely for the proposition "that proof that a regulation does *not* deny an owner

As we have said on numerous occasions, the Fifth Amendment is violated when land-use regulation "does not substantially advance legitimate state interests or denies an owner economically viable use of his land."

We have never set forth the justification for this rule. Perhaps it is simply, as Justice Brennan suggested, that total deprivation of beneficial use is . . . the equivalent of a physical appropriation. See San Diego Gas & Electric v. San Diego (Brennan, J., dissenting). "For what is the land but the profits thereof?" 1 E[dward] Coke, *Institutes*, ch. 1. Surely, at least, in the extraordinary circumstance when no productive or economically beneficial use of land is permitted, it is less realistic to indulge our usual assumption that the legislature is simply "adjusting the benefits and burdens of economic life" in a manner that secures an "average reciprocity of advantage" to everyone concerned. And the functional basis for permitting the government, by regulation, to affect property values without compensation—that "Government hardly could go on if to some extent values incident to property could not be diminished without paying for every such change in the general law," does not apply to the relatively rare situations where the government has deprived a landowner of all economically beneficial uses.

On the other side of the balance, affirmatively supporting a compensation requirement, is the fact that regulations that leave the owner of land without economically beneficial or productive options for its use . . . carry with them a heightened risk that private property is being pressed into some form of public service under the guise of mitigating serious public harm. . . . As Justice Brennan explained: "From the government's point of view, the benefits flowing to the public from preservation of open space through regulation may be equally great as from creating a wildlife refuge through formal condemnation. . . ." *San Diego Gas & Elec.* (dissenting). . . .

We think, in short, that there are good reasons for our frequently expressed belief that when the owner of real property has been called upon to sacrifice all economically beneficial uses in the name of the common good, that is, to leave his property economically idle, he has suffered a taking. . . .

B . . .

. . . [M]any of our prior opinions have suggested that "harmful or noxious uses" of property may be proscribed by government regulation without the requirement of compensation. For a number of reasons, however, we think the South Carolina Supreme Court was too quick to

___

economic use of his property is sufficient to defeat a facial taking challenge" and not for the point that "*denial* of such use is sufficient to establish a taking claim regardless of any other consideration." The cases say, repeatedly and unmistakably, that " '[t]he test to be applied in considering [a] facial [takings] challenge is fairly straightforward.' " A statute regulating the uses that can be made of property effects a taking if it "*denies an owner economically viable use of the land.*" Keystone. . . . [Footnote by the Court, no. 6 in the original.]

conclude that that principle decides the present case. The "harmful or noxious uses" principle was the Court's early attempt to describe in theoretical terms why government may, consistent with the Takings Clause, affect property values by regulation without incurring an obligation to compensate—a reality we nowadays acknowledge explicitly with respect to the full scope of the State's police power. ... We made this very point in *Penn Central,* where, in the course of sustaining New York City's landmarks preservation program against a takings challenge, we rejected the petitioner's suggestion that *Mugler* and the cases following it were premised on, and thus limited by, some objective conception of "noxiousness." ... These cases are better understood as resting ... rather on the ground that the restrictions were reasonably related to the implementation of a policy—not unlike historic preservation—expected to produce a widespread public benefit and applicable to all similarly situated property. ...

When it is understood that "prevention of harmful use" was merely our early formulation of the police power justification necessary to sustain (without compensation) any regulatory diminution in value; and that the distinction between regulation that "prevents harmful use" and that which "confers benefits" is difficult, if not impossible, to discern on an objective, value-free basis; it becomes self-evident that noxious-use logic cannot serve as a touchstone to distinguish regulatory "takings"—which require compensation—from regulatory deprivations that do not require compensation. A *fortiori* the legislature's recitation of a noxious-use justification cannot be the basis for departing from our categorical rule that total regulatory takings must be compensated. If it were, departure would virtually always be allowed. ...

Where the State seeks to sustain regulation that deprives land of all economically beneficial use, we think it may resist compensation only if the logically antecedent inquiry into the nature of the owner's estate shows that the proscribed use interests were not part of his title to begin with. ... It seems to us that the property owner necessarily expects the uses of his property to be restricted, from time to time, by various measures newly enacted by the State in legitimate exercise of its police powers. ... *Pennsylvania Coal.* And in the case of personal property, by reason of the State's traditionally high degree of control over commercial dealings, he ought to be aware of the possibility that new regulation might even render his property economically worthless (at least if the property's only economically productive use is sale or manufacture for sale), see Andrus v. Allard (1979) (prohibition on sale of eagle feathers). In the case of land, however, we think the notion pressed by the Council that title is somehow held subject to the "implied limitation" that the State may subsequently eliminate all economically valuable use is inconsistent with the historical compact recorded in the Takings Clause that has become part of our constitutional culture.

Where "permanent physical occupation" of land is concerned, we have refused to allow the government to decree it anew (without compensation), no matter how weighty the asserted "public interests" involved ... though we assuredly would permit the government to assert a permanent easement that was a preexisting limitation upon the landowner's title. ... We believe similar treatment must be accorded confiscatory regulations, *i.e.*, regulations that prohibit all economically beneficial use of land: Any limitation so severe cannot be newly legislated or decreed (without compensation), but must inhere in the title itself. ...

The "total taking" inquiry we require today will ordinarily entail ... analysis of, among other things, the degree of harm to public lands and resources, or adjacent private property, posed by the claimant's proposed activities, the social value of the claimant's activities and their suitability to the locality in question, and the relative ease with which the alleged harm can be avoided through measures taken by the claimant and the government (or adjacent private landowners) alike. The fact that a particular use has long been engaged in by similarly situated owners ordinarily imports a lack of any common-law prohibition (though changed circumstances or new knowledge may make what was previously permissible no longer so). So also does the fact that other landowners, similarly situated, are permitted to continue the use denied to the claimant.

It seems unlikely that common-law principles would have prevented the erection of any habitable or productive improvements on petitioner's land; they rarely support prohibition of the "essential use" of land, Curtin v. Benson (1911). The question, however, is one of state law to be dealt with on remand. We emphasize that to win its case South Carolina must do more than proffer the legislature's declaration that the uses Lucas desires are inconsistent with the public interest, or the conclusory assertion that they violate a common-law maxim such as *sic utere tuo ut alienum non laedas* [use your property so as not to injure that of another]. ... [A] "State, by *ipse dixit*, may not transform private property into public property without compensation. ..." Webb's Fabulous Pharmacies, Inc. v. Beckwith (1980). Instead, as it would be required to do if it sought to restrain Lucas in a common-law action for public nuisance, South Carolina must identify background principles of nuisance and property law that prohibit the uses he now intends in the circumstances in which the property is presently found. Only on this showing can the State fairly claim that, in proscribing all such beneficial uses, the Beachfront Management Act is taking nothing. ...

The judgment is reversed and the cause remanded for proceedings not inconsistent with this opinion.

Justice **KENNEDY**, concurring in the judgment. ...

... The Takings Clause, while conferring substantial protection on property owners, does not eliminate the police power of the State. ... Where a taking is alleged from regulations which deprive the property of all value, the test must be whether the deprivation is contrary to reasonable, investment-backed expectations. ... [R]easonable expectations must be understood in light of the whole of our legal tradition. The common law of nuisance is too narrow a confine for the exercise of regulatory power in a complex and interdependent society. The State should not be prevented from enacting new regulatory initiatives in response to changing conditions, and courts must consider all reasonable expectations whatever their source. The Takings Clause does not require a static body of state property law. ... I agree with the Court that nuisance prevention accords with the most common expectations of property owners who face regulation, but I do not believe this can be the sole source of state authority to impose severe restrictions. ...

The Supreme Court of South Carolina erred ... by reciting the general purposes for which the state regulations were enacted without a determination that they were in accord with the owner's reasonable expectations and therefore sufficient to support a severe restriction on specific parcels of property. ...

Justice **BLACKMUN**, dissenting. ...

I ...

C

The South Carolina Supreme Court found that the Beach Management Act did not take petitioner's property without compensation. The decision rested on two premises that until today were unassailable—that the State has the power to prevent any use of property it finds to be harmful to its citizens, and that a state statute is entitled to a presumption of constitutionality. ...

If the state legislature is correct that the prohibition on building in front of the setback line prevents serious harm, then, under this Court's prior cases, the Act is constitutional. "Long ago it was recognized that all property in this country is held under the implied obligation that the owner's use of it shall not be injurious to the community, and the Takings Clause did not transform that principle to one that requires compensation whenever the State asserts its power to enforce it." Keystone Bituminous Coal Ass'n v. DeBenedictis (1987). The Court consistently has upheld regulations imposed to arrest a significant threat to the common welfare, whatever their economic effect on the owner. See *e.g.*, Goldblatt v. Hempstead (1962); Euclid v. Ambler (1926); Gorieb v. Fox (1927); Mugler v. Kansas (1887). ...

Petitioner never challenged the legislature's findings that a building ban was necessary to protect property and life. ... Nothing in the record undermines the General Assembly's assessment that prohibitions on building in front of the setback line are necessary to protect people and property from storms, high tides, and beach erosion. ... [T]hat legislative determination cannot be disregarded in the absence of such evidence. ...

II ...

... The Court creates its new taking jurisprudence based on the trial court's finding that the property had lost all economic value. This finding is almost certainly erroneous. Petitioner still can enjoy other attributes of ownership, such as the right to exclude others, "one of the most essential sticks in the bundle of rights that are commonly characterized as property." ... Petitioner can picnic, swim, camp in a tent, or live on the property in a movable trailer. ... Petitioner also retains the right to alienate the land, which would have value for neighbors and for those prepared to enjoy proximity to the ocean without a house. ...

III ...

... [A] decision to defer to legislative judgments in the absence of a challenge from petitioner comports with one of this Court's oldest maxims: "the existence of facts supporting the legislative judgment is to be presumed." United States v. Carolene Products (1938). Indeed, we have said the legislature's judgment is "well-nigh conclusive." Berman v. Parker (1954). ... Accordingly, this Court always has required plaintiffs challenging the constitutionality of an ordinance to provide "some factual foundation of record" that contravenes the legislative findings. In the absence of such proof, "the presumption of constitutionality must prevail." ...

Rather than invoking these traditional rules, the Court decides the State has the burden to convince the courts that its legislative judgments are correct. Despite Lucas' complete failure to contest the legislature's findings of serious harm to life and property if a permanent structure is built, the Court decides that the legislative findings are not sufficient to justify the use prohibition. ... The Court offers no justification for its sudden hostility toward state legislators, and I doubt that it could.

IV

The Court ... also takes the opportunity to create a new scheme for regulations that eliminate all economic value. From now on, there is a categorical rule finding these regulations to be a taking unless the use they prohibit is a background common-law nuisance or property principle. ...

A

I first question the Court's rationale in creating a category that obviates a "case-specific inquiry into the public interest advanced" ... if all economic value has been lost. If one fact about the Court's taking jurisprudence can be stated without contradiction, it is that "the particular circumstances of each case" determine whether a specific restriction will be rendered invalid by the government's failure to pay compensation. United States v. Central Eureka Mining (1958). This is so because although we have articulated certain factors to be considered, including the economic impact on the property owner, the ultimate conclusion "necessarily requires a weighing of private and public interests." Agins [v. Tiburon (1980)]. ... [T]he Court's prior decisions "uniformly reject the proposition that diminution in property value, standing alone, can establish a 'taking.' " *Penn Central.*

... More than a century ago, the Court explicitly upheld the right of States to prohibit uses of property injurious to public health, safety, or welfare without paying comper.sation: "A prohibition simply upon the use of property for purposes that are declared, by valid legislation, to be injurious to the health, morals, or safety of the community, cannot, in any just sense, be deemed a taking or an appropriation of property." Mugler v. Kansas (1887). On this basis, the Court upheld an ordinance effectively prohibiting operation of a previously lawful brewery, although the "establishments will become of no value as property." ...

Mugler was only the beginning in a long line of cases. In Powell v. Pennsylvania (1888), the Court upheld legislation prohibiting the manufacture of oleomargarine, despite the owner's allegation that " ... the value of his property employed therein would be entirely lost". ... In Hadacheck v. Sebastian (1915), the Court upheld an ordinance prohibiting a brickyard, although the owner had made excavations on the land that prevented it from being utilized for any purpose but a brickyard. ... In Miller v. Schoene (1928), the Court held that the Fifth Amendment did not require Virginia to pay compensation to the owner of cedar trees ordered destroyed to prevent a disease from spreading to nearby apple orchards. ... Again, in Omnia Commercial Co. v. United States (1923), the Court stated that "destruction of, or injury to, property is frequently accomplished without a 'taking' in the constitutional sense."

More recently, in *Goldblatt*, the Court upheld a town regulation that barred continued operation of an existing sand and gravel operation in order to protect public safety. ... And in *Keystone*, the Court summarized over 100 years of precedent: "the Court has repeatedly upheld regulations that destroy or adversely affect real property interests." ...

The Court recognizes that "our prior opinions have suggested that harmful or noxious uses' of property may be proscribed by government regulation without the requirement of compensation," ... but seeks to reconcile them with its categorical rule by claiming that the Court never has upheld a regulation when the owner alleged the loss of all economic value. Even if the Court's factual premise were correct, its understanding of the Court's cases is distorted. In none of the cases did the Court suggest that the right of a State to prohibit certain activities without paying compensation turned on the availability of some residual valuable use. Instead, the cases depended on whether the government interest was sufficient to prohibit the activity, given the significant private cost.

These cases rest on the principle that the State has full power to prohibit an owner's use of property if it is harmful to the public. "Since no individual has a right to use his property so as to create a nuisance or otherwise harm others, the State has not taken anything when it asserts its power to enjoin the nuisance-like activity." *Keystone.* It would make no sense under this theory to suggest that an owner has a constitutionally protected right to harm others, if only he makes the proper showing of economic loss.   ...

B

Ultimately even the Court cannot embrace the full implications of its *per se* rule: it eventually agrees that there cannot be a categorical rule for a taking based on economic value that wholly disregards the public need asserted. Instead, the Court decides that it will permit a State to regulate all economic value only if the State prohibits uses that would not be permitted under "background principles of nuisance and property law."   ...

Until today, the Court explicitly had rejected the contention that the government's power to act without paying compensation turns on whether the prohibited activity is a common-law nuisance. The brewery closed in *Mugler* itself was not a common-law nuisance, and the Court specifically stated that it was the role of the legislature to determine what measures would be appropriate for the protection of public health and safety. ... In upholding the state action in *Miller*, the Court found it unnecessary to "weigh with nicety the question whether the infected cedars constitute a nuisance according to common law; or whether they may be so declared by statute." ... See also *Goldblatt*; *Hadacheck*. Instead the Court has relied in the past, as the South Carolina Court has done here, on legislative judgments of what constitutes a harm.

The Court rejects the notion that the State always can prohibit uses it deems a harm to the public without granting compensation because "the distinction between 'harm-preventing' and 'benefit-conferring' regulation is often in the eye of the beholder." ... The threshold inquiry for imposition of the Court's new rule, "deprivation of all economically valuable use," itself cannot be determined objectively. As the Court admits, whether the owner has been deprived of all economic value of his property will depend on how "property" is defined. ...

Even more perplexing, however, is the Court's reliance on common-law principles of nuisance in its quest for a value-free taking jurisprudence. In determining what is a nuisance at common law, state courts make exactly the decision that the Court finds so troubling when made by the South Carolina General Assembly today: they determine whether the use is harmful. Common-law public and private nuisance law is simply a determination whether a particular use causes harm. ... See Prosser, Private Action for Public Nuisance, 52 *Va.L.Rev.* 997 (1966) ("Nuisance is a French word which means nothing more than harm"). There is nothing magical in the reasoning of judges long dead. They determined a harm in the same way as state judges and legislatures do today. If judges in the 18th and 19th centuries can distinguish a harm from a benefit, why not judges in the 20th century, and if judges can, why not legislators? There simply is no reason to believe that new interpretations of the hoary common law nuisance doctrine will be particularly "objective" or "value-free." ...

C

Finally, the Court justifies its new rule that the legislature may not deprive a property owner of the only economically valuable use of his land, even if the legislature finds it to be a harmful use, because such action is not part of the "long recognized" "understandings of our citizens." ... These "understandings" permit such regulation only if the use is a nuisance under the common law. Any other course is "inconsistent with the historical compact recorded in the Takings Clause." ... It is not clear from the Court's opinion where our "historical compact" or "citizens' understanding" comes from, but it does not appear to be history.

The principle that the State should compensate individuals for property taken for public use was not widely established America at the time of the Revolution.

> "The colonists ... inherited ... a concept of property which permitted extensive regulation of the use of that property for the public benefit—regulation that could even go so far as to deny all productive use of the property to the owner if, as Coke himself stated, the regulation 'extends to the public benefit ... for this is for the public, and every one hath benefit by it.' " F. Bosselman, D. Callies & J. Banta, *The Taking Issue* 80–81 (1973). ...

Although, prior to the adoption of the Bill of Rights, America was replete with land use regulations describing which activities were considered noxious and forbidden, ... the Fifth Amendment's Taking Clause originally did not extend to regulations of property, whatever the effect. ... Most state courts agreed with this narrow interpretation of a taking. ... Even when courts began to consider that regulation in some situations could constitute a taking, they continued to uphold bans on particular uses without paying compensation, notwithstanding the economic impact, under the rationale that no one can obtain a vested right to injure or endanger the public. ...

Nor does history indicate any common-law limit on the State's power to regulate harmful uses even to the point of destroying all economic value. Nothing in the discussions in Congress concerning the Taking Clause indicates that the Clause was limited by the common-law nuisance doctrine. Common law courts themselves rejected such an understanding. They regularly recognized that it is "for the legislature to interpose, and by positive enactment to prohibit a use of property which would be injurious to the public." ...

In short, I find no clear and accepted "historical compact" or "understanding of our citizens" justifying the Court's new taking doctrine. Instead, the Court seems to treat history as a grab-bag of principles, to be adopted where they support the Court's theory, and ignored where they do not. ...

Justice **STEVENS**, dissenting. ...

II

... [T]he Court starts from the premise that this Court has adopted a "categorical rule that total regulatory takings must be compensated," ... and then sets itself to the task of identifying the exceptional cases in which a State may be relieved of this categorical obligation. ... The test the Court announces is that the regulation must do no more than duplicate the result that could have been achieved under a State's nuisance law. ... [T]he Court is doubly in error. The categorical rule the Court establishes is an unsound and unwise addition to the law and the Court's formulation of the exception to that rule is too rigid and too narrow.

The Categorical Rule

As the Court recognizes, *Pennsylvania Coal* provides no support for its—or, indeed, any—categorical rule. To the contrary, Justice Holmes recognized that such absolute rules ill fit the inquiry into "regulatory takings." ... Holmes regarded economic injury to be merely one factor to be weighed: "One fact for consideration in determining such limits is the extent of the diminution [of value]. So the question depends upon the particular facts." ...

Nor does the Court's new categorical rule find support in decisions following *Mahon*. Although in dicta we have sometimes recited that a law "effects a taking if [it] ... denies an owner economically viable use of his land," Agins v. Tiburon (1980), our rulings have rejected such an absolute position. ... [A]s we stated in *Keystone*, " 'Although a comparison of values before and after' a regulatory action 'is relevant, ... it is by no means conclusive.' "

In addition to lacking support in past decisions, the Court's new rule is wholly arbitrary. A landowner whose property is diminished in value 95% recovers nothing, while an owner whose property is diminished 100% recovers the land's full value. ...

Moreover, because of the elastic nature of property rights, the Court's new rule will also prove unsound in practice. In response to the rule, courts may define "property" broadly and only rarely find regulations to effect total takings. This is the approach the Court itself adopts in its revisionist reading of venerable precedents. We are told that—notwithstanding the Court's findings to the contrary in each case—the brewery in *Mugler*, the brickyard in *Hadacheck,* and the gravel pit in *Goldblatt* all could be put to "other uses" and that, therefore, those cases did not involve total regulatory takings. ...

On the other hand, developers and investors may market specialized estates to take advantage of the Court's new rule. The smaller the estate, the more likely that a regulatory change will effect a total taking. Thus, an investor may, for example, purchase the right to build a multifamily home on a specific lot, with the result that a zoning regulation

that allows only single-family homes would render the investor's property interest "valueless." ...

Finally, the Court's justification for its new categorical rule is
remarkably thin. The Court mentions in passing three arguments in
support of its rule; none is convincing. First, the Court suggests that
"total deprivation of feasible use is, from the landowner's point of view,
the equivalent of a physical appropriation." ... This argument proves
too much. From the "landowner's point of view," a regulation that
diminishes a lot's value by 50% is as well "the equivalent" of the
condemnation of half of the lot. ... Second, the Court emphasizes that
because total takings are "relatively rare" its new rule will not adversely
affect the government's ability to "go on." ... This argument proves
too little. ... The Court's suggestion only begs the question of why
regulations of this particular class should always be found to effect
takings.

Finally, the Court suggests that "regulations that leave the owner
... without economically beneficial ... use ... carry with them a
heightened risk that private property is being pressed into some form of
public service." ... I agree that the risks of such singling out are of
central concern in takings law. However, such risks do not justify a per
se rule for total regulatory takings. ... What matters in such cases is
not the degree of diminution of value, but rather the specificity of the
expropriating act. ...

The Nuisance Exception

Like many bright-line rules, the categorical rule established in this
case is only "categorical" for a page or two. ... No sooner does the
Court state that "total regulatory takings must be compensated," ...
than it quickly establishes an exception to that rule.

The exception provides that a regulation that renders property
valueless is not a taking if it prohibits uses of property that were not
"previously permissible under relevant property and nuisance principles." ... The Court thus rejects the basic holding in *Mugler*. There
we held that a state-wide statute that prohibited the owner of a brewery
from making alcoholic beverages did not effect a taking, even though the
use of the property had been perfectly lawful and caused no public harm
before the statute was enacted. We squarely rejected the rule the Court
adopts today. ...

Under our reasoning in *Mugler*, a state's decision to prohibit or to
regulate certain uses of property is not a compensable taking just
because the particular uses were previously lawful. Under the Court's
opinion today, however, if a state should decide to prohibit the manufacture of asbestos, cigarettes, or concealable firearms, for example, it must
be prepared to pay for the adverse economic consequences of its decision.
One must wonder if Government will be able to "go on" effectively if it
must risk compensation "for every such change in the general law." ...

The Court's holding today effectively freezes the State's common law, denying the legislature much of its traditional power to revise the law governing the rights and uses of property. Until today, I had thought that we had long abandoned this approach to constitutional law. More than a century ago we recognized that "the great office of statutes is to remedy defects in the common law as they are developed, and to adapt it to the changes of time and circumstances." Munn v. Illinois (1877). ...

Arresting the development of the common law is not only a departure from our prior decisions; it is also profoundly unwise. The human condition is one of constant learning and evolution—both moral and practical. Legislatures implement that new learning; in doing so they must often revise the definition of property and the rights of property owners. ...

Statement of Justice **SOUTER**.

I would dismiss the writ of certiorari ... as having been granted improvidently. ...

Editor's Notes

(1) **Query:** Compare the answer to the interrogative WHO that *Hawaii Housing* offered with that of *Lucas*. Which is more congruent with democratic theory? With constitutionalism? O'Connor was the author of the Court's opinion in *Hawaii Housing* yet she joined Scalia's opinion for the Court in *Lucas*. To what extent was she inconsistent?

(2) **Query:** Scalia has been the usual defender of decisions made by public officials. See, *e.g.*, his dissent in Planned Parenthood v. Casey (1992; reprinted below, p. 1281), decided the same day as *Lucas*. In *Casey*, he would have left to elected officials settlement of conflicts between advocates of a woman's right to control her body and advocates of a fetus's right to life. Why then in *Lucas* did he insist that judges, not elected officials, should decide sharply contested questions about protection of the environment against real-estate development? How could he reconcile his opinions in *Casey* and *Lucas*?

(3) **Query:** Scalia has also been the great exponent of an *originalist approach* to constitutional interpretation. Why in *Lucas* was he so uninterested in the background and early history of the Takings Clause? To what extent did he follow a *textualist approach*? A *doctrinal approach*? Was he following a *philosophic approach* in seeking justice for Lucas's plan to sell land that had several times recently been washed away? Was Scalia concerned to maintain a tradition, perhaps, a tradition of unfettered private development of land? But was there such a tradition in the United States? Would any of these approaches have permitted the Court to avoid controversial value judgments?

(4) For other instances of Scalia's use of the Takings Clause to review the substance of economic "regulations," see his opinion for the Court in Nollan v. Cal. Coastal Comm'n (1987) and his dissent in Pennell v. San Jose (1988). See also his debate with Prof. Richard A. Epstein over governmental regulation of the economy. Epstein argued that courts should return to the role that

Lochner had marked. Scalia claimed that judges would better serve the system by allowing legislators to make most decisions:

> In the long run, and perhaps even in the short run, the reinforcement of mistaken and unconstitutional perceptions of the role of the courts in our system far outweighs whatever evils may have accrued from undue judicial abstention in the economic field. ["Economic Affairs as Human Affairs," in *Scalia v. Epstein: Two Views on Judicial Activism* (Washington, DC: Cato, 1985), p. 4.]

(5) Dolan v. City of Tigard (1994) held that a city had offended the Takings Clause by placing certain conditions on a permit to enlarge a plumbing supply store and pave its parking lot. Because the new development would increase downtown traffic and flooding problems along a creek adjacent to the property, the city had said Dolan could have a permit only by dedicating portions of the property to a public drainage system and a bicycle path. By a 5–4 majority, the Court held that: (1) the City's goals were permissible and (2) it might be "reasonable" to suppose problems of flooding and traffic were linked to the conditions imposed on Dolan; but (3) the city had to offer evidence, not merely an assertion, of a connection between those conditions and the problems the new construction would create.

(6) **Query:** Like *Lucas*, *Dolan* placed the burden of proof on local authorities. In neither case was a majority of the justices willing to accord a presumption of constitutionality to the government's decision. In dissent, Stevens accused the Court of "resurrect[ing] ... a species of substantive due process analysis that it firmly rejected decades ago." For the majority, Rehnquist responded: "We see no reason why the Takings Clause of the Fifth Amendment, as much a part of the Bill of Rights as the First Amendment or the Fourth Amendment, should be relegated to the status of a poor relation." Is there a *constitutional* reason for according property rights less judicial protection than First Amendment rights? If so, what sort of reason is it? A *textualist* reason? An *originalist* reason? A reason that reflects some assumptions about the nature of democracy, constitutionalism, or justice? What might a defender of *Lucas* and *Dolan* say in response? Was the Court (re)extending the concept of "fundamental rights" to include rights to property? What objections would a democratic theorist raise to such an inclusion? A constitutionalist?

17

Autonomy and the Fundamental Right to Religious Freedom

From the problems of property we turn to what should be a much simpler issue for American constitutional interpretation, religious freedom. Here is a right that, like freedom of speech and press, provides an ideal case for fundamentality. First of all, the plain words of the document are very plain indeed: "Congress shall make no law respecting an establishment of religion or prohibiting the free exercise thereof. ..."[1] If property, protected only against infringement "without due process of law," is fundamental, then religious liberty must be also. Even John Hart Ely, an opponent of a *fundamental-rights approach* and the arch advocate of *reinforcing representative democracy*, concedes that the text's clear command requires an active judicial role in protecting the substantive right to religious liberty.[2]

The document's words, at least as far as "free exercise" is concerned, are congruent with the political theories of democracy and constitutionalism. The latter's exaltation of individual autonomy and dignity demands that government leave matters of religion to the citizen's own conscience. For democratic theory, the issue is not so evident; but one can make a powerful *structuralist* argument, as do some of the opinions we read—most strikingly, West Virginia v. Barnette (1943; reprinted below, p. 1174)—that free expression of religious views is merely a subset of general free expression. In fact, much of constitutional law regarding freedom of communication comes from litigation brought by Jehovah's Witnesses to protect their free exercise of religion. (See, for instance, Cantwell v. Connecticut [1940; reprinted below, p. 1161].)

---

1. As earlier chapters have pointed out, see espec. Chapter 5, p. 133, "incorporation" of some of the Bill of Rights into the Fourteenth Amendment has made the First Amendment binding on the states.

2. *Democracy and Distrust* (Cambridge: Harvard University Press, 1980), p. 94. In part, Ely derives this exception to his general rule from the document's plain words; in part, however, he also finds it in a mild form of *originalism*: "[P]art of the explanation of the Free Exercise Clause has to be that for the framers religion was an important substantive value they wanted to put significantly beyond the reach of at least the federal legislature."

Threads of political tradition weave smoothly with these other sources of constitutional law. Americans frequently congratulate themselves on having separated church and state and established religious toleration as integral elements of their cultural heritage. Many early colonists came to the new world to escape persecution; and, although religious bigotry has been an ugly part of the American past and remains an even uglier part of its present, the ideal has been and remains religious freedom. Furthermore, as a practical matter, the existence of a dozen large denominations and thousands of smaller ones usually makes it politically inexpedient for elected politicians openly to prefer one religion over another or, again openly, to trample on religious freedoms.

We have, then, a general, if somewhat scarred, pattern: The language of the constitutional text, constitutionalist and democratic theory, tradition, and political expediency all respect religious liberty as a "fundamental right." Thus there would seem to be no serious problem here for constitutional interpretation, at least for those people who follow an approach that sees the basic purpose of interpretation as protecting such rights.

I. THE INTERPRETIVE PROBLEMS

A. What Constitutes Establishment?

As is so often the case, however, those seemingly clear words, theories, and traditions may blur when they confront specific problems and pluralistic checks may not function effectively. The text of the First Amendment and the aura that surrounds it set bounds on current controversies but by no means eliminate them.

When, for instance, does government "establish" a religion? Only when it makes one religion that of the state, as governments typically did in the eighteenth century when the Bill of Rights was adopted? Or when it gives real but less favorable treatment to one religion or only to some religions?

What about government's aiding all religions? Does it violate the ban to allow any sect that wishes to offer religious instruction in public schools for students who freely opt to attend? Eight justices said yes, one said no.[3] Does allowing "released time" for public school students to attend religious instruction off school property but during school hours constitute establishment? Six justices said no, three said yes.[4] Does purchasing books on non-religious subjects for children attending public and private, including sectarian, schools? Six justices said no, three said yes.[5] Does supplying instructional material and equipment to public and private, includ-

---

3. McCullom v. Board (1948).

4. Zorach v. Clauson (1952).

5. Board of Educ. v. Allen (1968).

ing sectarian, schools? The Court unanimously said yes, but divided four different ways in explaining its response.[6] Does providing free buses for children attending religious as well as public schools? Five justices said no, four said yes.[7] Do grants to private colleges, including those with religious affiliations? Five justices said no, four said yes.[8] Does exempting religious institutions from taxation and donations to churches from donors' taxable incomes? Seven justices said no, one said yes.[9] Does a state's allowing parents of children in private, including religious, schools tax deductions for part of the tuition? Five justices said no, four said yes.[10] Does a city's building a creche at Christmas? Five justices said no, four said yes.[11] Does inviting a clergyman to offer a nondenominational prayer at a public school graduation? Five justices said yes, four said no.[12]

B. Free Exercise and the Police Power

Perhaps failures of constitutional interpretation here are inevitable: However far apart one might keep church and state, it is impossible completely to separate religion and politics; they both compete for people's minds and loyalties. "Justice," one of the Preamble's stated goals, is as much a moral as a political construct, one freighted with millennia of theological disputation.

The meaning of the "free exercise" clause is equally clouded. May government force a religious pacifist to take up a gun and serve in the armed forces? Eight justices said yes in Gillette v. United States (1971; reprinted below, p. 1216). May government outlaw a religiously ordained practice of polygamy and even forbid believers to vote? All nine justices said yes in Davis v. Beason (1890; reprinted below, p. 1159). May it forbid religious rituals involving snake handling?[13] Hallucinogenic drugs as part of a religious ceremony?[14] May it force Jehovah's Witnesses, who believe that blood transfusions violate the Biblical ban against drinking blood, to submit to such a procedure when needed to save their own lives? To save their children's lives?[15] What if a sect preaches the necessi-

---

6. Meek v. Pittinger (1975).

7. Everson v. Ewing Township (1947).

8. Roemer v. Maryland (1976).

9. Walz v. Tax Comm. (1970).

10. Mueller v. Allen (1983).

11. Lynch v. Donnelly (1984).

12. Lee v. Weisman (1992; reprinted above p. 167).

13. In Pack v. Tennessee (1976), the U.S. Supreme Court denied certiorari to review a decision by the Supreme Court of Tennessee upholding an injunction against snake handling as a public nuisance.

14. Department of Human Resources v. Smith (1990; reprinted below, p. 1200).

15. Earlier American decisions tended to grant hospitals' requests for court orders to give transfusions to save lives. See, for example, Application of Georgetown College (U.S.

ty of killing its opponents? May government take action against it? Where is the fundamental right here?

C. Tensions Between Clauses

When we consider the two clauses as a unit, problems multiply. At first glance the pair seem directed toward the common goal of religious freedom, the first by forbidding government to tax or otherwise regulate its citizens in order to support religions of which they do not approve, the second by allowing citizens to practice or not practice their religious beliefs, according to their own individual consciences. As the Court has admitted, however, either clause, "if expanded to a logical extreme, would tend to clash with the other." [16] Even under circumstances far short of logical extremes, the two may send out conflicting messages, as several cases reprinted in this chapter demonstrate. (See espec. Thomas v. Review Board [1981; reprinted below, p. 1193].) To require a pacifist to serve in the armed forces may violate his right to free exercise; to give him an exemption because of his religious beliefs might "establish" his religion. "The problem," C. Herman Pritchett has said, "is that too much coercion may deny free exercise, while exemption from coercion in response to religious objections may be favoritism amounting to establishment." [17]

II. POSSIBLE SOLUTIONS: APPROACHES
TO INTERPRETATION

A. Textualism

If *protecting fundamental rights* does not of itself provide an interpretive key, perhaps others approaches would help. Some, however, may offer so much assistance as to drown the problem

---

Court of Appeals for the DC Cir., 1964); John F. Kennedy Memorial Hosp. v. Heston (S.C. of NJ, 1971). But there is a growing movement among judges not to intervene. See the discussion by the Supreme Court of New Jersey in In re Karen Quinlan (1976). See also Norman L. Cantor, "A Person's Decision to Decline Life–Saving Medical Treatment," 26 *Rutgers L.Rev.* 228 (1973). The older rule that courts will intervene to allow hospitals to administer life-saving care to children seems to be giving way, at least where the question of quality of life of the child is at stake, as with retarded children suffering from illnesses that are incurable or curable only after long and expensive treatment, to an attitude that parents should have ultimate authority. But, in the most famous case since In re Quinlan, Missouri required "clear and convincing evidence" that a comatose adult who had no medically predictable chance of recovering consciousness have earlier indicated a desire for termination of life support. The U.S. Supreme Court upheld the state's regulations against a challenge by the patient's parents. Cruzan v. Missouri (1990; reprinted below, p. 1338).

16. *Walz.* Concurring in Abington Sch. Dist. v. Schempp (1963), Justice Brennan visualized a more harmonious relationship between the two clauses. For a similar argument, see Leo Pfeffer, "Freedom and/or Separation," 64 *Minn.L.Rev.* 561 (1980). See also Thomas v. Rev. Bd. (1981; reprinted below, p. 1193), espec. Justice Rehnquist's dis. op.

17. *The American Constitution* (3rd ed.; New York: McGraw–Hill, 1977), p. 391.

rather than solve it. *Textualism*, for example, presents a very simple solution. The First Amendment guarantees "free exercise" of religion, not merely "free belief" in religion, and it specifies "no law," not merely "no unreasonable law"; and we are back in the debates we earlier read between Frankfurter and Black and Harlan and Black. If we read the document literally, all regulations that impinge on the practice of religion must be invalid. But can "free exercise" of religion confer a right to inflict on others harmful consequences of that exercise? An exemption from civic duties that all other citizens must bear? Or an obligation to obey general laws?

Worse, this potential clash between the words of the establishment and free exercise clauses often becomes actual, as with the military draft or when government provides chaplains for people in the armed forces. Not to furnish the means for these people to practice their religion could mean denying them free exercise; bringing clergy to them—or them to clergy—would remove the denial, but it would also help religion, perhaps to the extent of violating the ban against establishment.

B. Originalism

Neither "original understanding" nor "intent of the framers" provides much additional nourishment. The amendment Madison introduced was quite different from that which Congress approved and the states ratified:

> The civil rights of none shall be abridged on account of religious belief or worship, nor shall any national religion be established, nor shall the full and equal rights of conscience be in any manner, or on any pretext, infringed.

But even this proposal was full of ambiguity. It did not address any of the problems about what "worship" would include: Use of peyote? Snake handling? Human sacrifice?[18] And Congress's changing Madison's proposals does not tell us much about the meaning of the words actually adopted.

At times, the Court has sought to find constitutional meaning in a letter Jefferson wrote in 1802[19] and from the Statute on Religious Liberty that he had drafted for Virginia in 1779. In the letter he asserted that the amendment erected "a wall of separation between

---

18. Another of Madison's proposals would have made some of the awkward business of incorporation through the Fourteenth Amendment unnecessary:

No State shall violate the equal rights of conscience, or the freedom of the press, or the trial by jury in criminal cases.

Because several states continued to have established churches, Congress did not propose this amendment.

19. Jefferson's reply to the Committee of the Danbury Baptists Association, January 1, 1802; Andrew A. Lipscomb, ed., *The Writings of Thomas Jefferson* (Washington, DC: Jefferson Memorial Association, 1903), XVI, 282.

church and State." The Statute, widely reprinted in the United States and Europe, read:

> Whereas Almighty God hath created the mind free. ... *Be it enacted by the General Assembly*, that no man shall be compelled to frequent or support any religious worship, place or ministry whatsoever, nor shall be enforced, restrained, molested, or burthened in his body or goods, nor shall otherwise suffer on account of his religious opinions or belief; but that all men shall be free to profess, and by argument to maintain, their opinion in matters of religion, and the same shall in no wise diminish, enlarge or affect their civil capacities.

Even accepting the Court's unsubstantiated assertion in Reynolds v. United States (1878) that this statute provided the model for those who edited Madison's draft, voted for the revised version in Congress, and ratified it in the state legislatures, does not solve modern problems. As do the words of the amendment, the statute expresses general principles with which few Americans would disagree but around whose application there is sharp dispute. "It is remarkable," a commentator has noted,[20] that, Justice Scalia, the justice who most vocally proclaims "original understanding" to be the key to constitutional interpretation, never once mentioned Jefferson, Madison, or any other person usually connected with the adoption of the First Amendment in writing the opinion of the Court upholding a state's criminalizing use of peyote by Native Americans in their religious ceremonies. (Department of Human Resources v. Smith [1990; reprinted below, p. 1200].)

C. Doctrinalism and Developmentalism

These two approaches offer no help at all in illuminating whatever original understanding or intent there was, for the initial cases reached the Supreme Court nearly a century after adoption of the First Amendment. They may, however, illuminate the nature of the "fundamental right" at stake. And astute commentators might organize the wisdom of the Court as an institution into a coherent, perhaps developing, doctrine. The judicial heritage surrounding free exercise, however, could be charitably described as a mixed bag. Rehnquist's dissent in Thomas v. Review Board (1981; reprinted below, p. 1193) was a caustic indictment of constitutional interpretation in this area. The justices have followed a tortuous course which, the Court has admitted, "sacrifices clarity and predictability for flexibility. ..."[21] For example, in establishment cases the justices have abandoned Jefferson's "wall of separation" in favor of a new metaphor, equally unanchored in the text: "a blurred,

---

20. Michael W. McConnell, "Free Exercise Revisionism and the *Smith* Decision," 57 *U.Chi.L.Rev.* 1109, 1117 (1990).

21. Committee for Public Educ. v. Regan (1980).

indistinct and variable barrier, depending on all the circumstances of a particular relationship." [22]

D. Balancing

Balancing offers its usual attractions and drawbacks. It seems to explain the justices' meanderings, but accounting for cacophony hardly makes a strong argument for *balancing*'s use as an approach to future interpretation. The typical failures of this approach—lack of relative weights among interests. as well as among constitutional clauses and absence of any indication about how the judicial "scale" is calibrated—are especially evident in the Court's work here.

E. Structuralism

One or another variety of a *structural approach* might hold out greater promise. In 1961 Prof. Philip B. Kurland suggested a form of *textual structuralism*: The two clauses of the First Amendment should be read as unit, forbidding government's using religion as a standard for action or inaction.[23] Justice Harlan adopted this approach, though without converting the Court to its gospel.[24] But, as C. Herman Pritchett has commented,

> the Kurland–Harlan position, while attractive in its simplicity, would prevent any accommodation of religious claims such as the Court approved in releasing the Amish from school attendance laws [25] and would render invalid the exemption granted by Congress in 1965 to the Amish—who believe that any form of insurance shows a lack of faith in God—from the social security system.[26]

III. ANOTHER SOLUTION: A MARRIAGE OF FUNDAMENTAL RIGHTS, STRUCTURALISM, AND PHILOSOPHY

There is something important in what Kurland and Harlan argued, but they were using *structuralism* at a low level of abstraction, looking at the *structure* of part of the text (the First Amendment) rather than to the document as a whole, to the larger political system, or to that system and its underlying political theories. It is not likely that an interpreter can resolve the tensions between the two clauses without first justifying constitutional protection for

---

22. Lemon v. Kurtzman (1971).

23. "Of Church and State and the Supreme Court," 29 *U.Chi.L.Rev.* 1 (1961).

24. See his separate opinions in Board of Educ. v. Allen (1968) and *Walz*.

25. Wisconsin v. Yoder (1972; reprinted below, p. 1187).

26. *Constitutional Civil Liberties* (Englewood Cliffs, NJ: Prentice–Hall, 1984), p. 155. For another critique of the Kurland–Harlan position, see John H. Garvey, "Freedom and Equality in the Religion Clauses," 1981 *Sup.Ct.Rev.* 193, 218–221.

religious freedom as a fundamental right and then establishing the place of that right within a larger structure. For the twin guarantees of religious liberty not only have internal tensions, on occasion they also conflict with other very important rights and values. The Flag Salute Cases of 1940 and 1943 (reprinted below at pp. 1165 and 1174) provided, Felix Frankfurter said, "an illustration of what the Greeks thousands of years ago recognized as a tragic issue, namely, the clash of rights, not the clash of wrongs." [27] The state thought it had a compelling public interest in promoting national loyalty; the children (or at least their parents) thought that saluting the flag violated the First Commandment's ban against worshipping "graven images."

Similar tragedies have played on the Court's dramatic stage: The refusal of the Amish to educate their children beyond grammar school lest their religious faith be corrupted by secular, materialistic values pitted against the authority of the state to educate all citizens (Wisconsin v. Yoder [1972; reprinted below, p. 1187) and perhaps against the right of the children to make meaningful choices about their own lives; the consciences of those whose religious beliefs allow them to fight only in "just wars"—which includes all Roman Catholics who closely follow their Church's teaching—pitted against the authority of Congress to raise armies (Gillette v. United States [1971; reprinted below, p. 1216); or the belief of some Christian Fundamentalists that God has forbidden racial intermarriage, and therefore they must require social separation of the races within their private schools pitted against the authority of the government to eradicate all vestiges of racial discrimination (Bob Jones University v. United States [1983; reprinted below, p. 1230).

The so-called "strict scrutiny test" is the one the Court often, though seldom unanimously, applies to such problems: When legislation utilizes a "suspect classification," such as race, or touches on a "fundamental right," such as to freedom of speech or religion, the law, to be valid, must protect a "compelling" governmental interest and be "closely tailored" to achieve that goal. But the meanings of terms like "compelling" and "closely tailored" are not self-evident, They rest on practical judgments, perhaps on some sort of *balancing*. Indeed, Justice O'Connor, among others, has claimed the "strict scrutiny test" is a form of *balancing*. (See her concurrences in Roberts v. United States Jaycees [1984]; reprinted above, p. 818 and *Smith* [1990]; reprinted below, p. 1200.) To the extent that she is right, does this test make *balancing* a more useful interpretive approach or contaminate the "strict scrutiny test" itself?

What a systematic, intellectually defensible approach of *protecting fundamental rights* needs is a general scheme under which to justify religious freedom as fundamental right and within which to order the larger values religious liberty reflects. Only under such a

---

27. Felix Frankfurter to Harlan F. Stone, May 27, 1940; reprinted below, at p. 1167.

scheme can choices among competing values be principled rather than *ad hoc*. To discover, or perhaps to construct, such a hierarchical scheme requires more than *structural analysis* of a text. It also requires a concern for deeper constitutional *purposes*, which is why we have classified *protecting fundamental rights* as a *purposive approach*.

But finding *purposes* and ranking them (for they too are likely to exist in tension with each other) are no easier tasks than applying terms like "compelling" and "fundamental" or discerning a larger structure in a text and/or political system. Logically required for each operation is a *philosophic approach*, one sufficiently sophisticated to deal with the myriad of conceptual, textual, and practical problems that religious liberty poses for a free, poly-religious society. We shall see a similar need when, in Chapter 18, we move to rights like privacy and personhood not explicitly mentioned in the constitutional text. Looking back at earlier chapters, we can see the same need reflected in efforts to solve most problems of constitutional interpretation. We return to a point Chapter 9 made: A *philosophic approach* offers a path strewn with booby-traps and buried mines, but the only choice interpreters have is to follow it blindly or to grope along it as clear mindedly as their resources permit.

SELECTED BIBLIOGRAPHY

Berman, Harold J. *Faith and Order: The Reconciliation of Law and Religion* (Atlanta: Scholars Press, 1993).

Berns, Walter. *The First Amendment and the Future of American Democracy* (New York: Basic Books, 1976).

Carter, Lief. *An Introduction to Constitutional Interpretation: Cases in Law and Religion* (New York: Longmans, 1991).

Carter, Stephen L. *The Culture of Disbelief* (New York: Basic Books, 1993).

Eisgruber, Christopher L. and Lawrence G. Sager. "The Vulnerability of Conscience: The Constitutional Basis for Protecting Religious Conduct," 61 *U.Chi.L.Rev.* 1245 (1994).

Greenawalt, Kent. *Religious Convictions and Political Choice* (New York: Oxford University Press, 1988).

Greene, Abner S. "The Political Balance of the Religion Clauses," 102 *Yale L.J.* 1611 (1993).

Howe, Mark DeWolfe. *The Garden and the Wilderness: Religion and Government in American Constitutional History* (Chicago: University of Chicago Press, 1965).

Hunter, James D., and Os Guinness, eds. *Articles of Faith, Articles of Peace* (Washington, DC: The Brookings Institution, 1990).

Kurland, Philip. *Religion and the Law* (Chicago: Aldine, 1962).

Manwaring, David R. *Render unto Caesar: The Flag–Salute Controversy* (Chicago: University of Chicago Press, 1962).

Marty, Martin E. *A Nation of Believers* (Chicago: University of Chicago Press, 1976).

McConnell, Michael W. "The Origins and Historical Understanding of Free Exercise of Religion," 103 *Harv.L.Rev.* 1409 (1990).

———. "Free Exercise Revisionism and the *Smith* Decision," 57 *U.Chi.L.Rev.* 1109 (1990).

———. "Religious Freedom at a Crossroads," 59 *U.Chi.L.Rev.* 115 (1992).

Morgan, Richard E. *The Supreme Court and Religion* (New York: The Free Press, 1972)

Note. "Toward a Constitutional Definition of Religion," 91 *Harv. L.Rev.* 1056 (1978).

Pfeffer, Leo. *God, Caesar, and the Constitution* (Boston: Beacon Press, 1975).

Pritchett, C. Herman. *Constitutional Civil Liberties* (Englewood Cliffs, NJ: Prentice–Hall, 1984), ch. 7.

Richards, David A.J. *Toleration and the Constitution* (New York: Oxford University Press, 1986).

Roberts, Bernard. "The Common Law Sovereignty of Religious Lawfinders and the Free Exercise Clause," 101 *Yale L.J.* 211 (1991).

Sandoz, Ellis. *A Government of Laws: Political Theory, Religion, and the American Founding* (Baton Rouge: Louisiana State University Press, 1990).

Smith, Michael E. "The Special Place of Religion in the Constitution," 1983 *Sup.Ct.Rev.* 83.

Sorauf, Frank J. *The Wall of Separation* (Princeton: Princeton University Press, 1976).

Sullivan, Kathleen M. "Religion and Liberal Democracy," 59 *U.Chi. L.Rev.* 195 (1992).

Swanson, Wayne R. *The Christ Child Goes to Court* (Philadelphia: Temple University Press, 1990).

Tribe, Laurence H. *American Constitutional Law* (2d ed.; Mineola, NY: Foundation Press, 1988), ch. 14.

"However free the exercise of religion may be, it must be subordinate to the criminal laws of the country...."

DAVIS v. BEASON

133 U.S. 333, 10 S.Ct. 299, 33 L.Ed. 637 (1890).

As part of a continuing campaign against Mormons—most of whom had migrated to Utah under Brigham Young—Congress forbade polygamy in the territories. Reynolds v. United States (1878) unanimously sustained this statute, as applied to the Territory of Utah, against Mormons' claims that it interfered with their free exercise of religion. Branding polygamy "odious" to western culture, the Court said:

> Congress was deprived of all legislative power over mere opinion, but was left free to reach actions which were in violation of social duties or subversive of good order. ... Laws are made for the government of actions, and while they cannot interfere with mere religious belief and opinions, they may with practices. Suppose one believed that human sacrifices were a necessary part of worship, would it be seriously contended that the civil government under which he lived could not interfere to prevent a sacrifice?

> Later, the Territory of Idaho limited the right to vote to adult males of sound mind who had not been convicted of treason, bribery, or other felony and who would swear not only that they were not themselves practicing polygamy but also that they were not members of an organization that "advises, counsels, or encourages" anyone "to commit the crime of bigamy or polygamy." Samuel Davis, a Mormon, was convicted for conspiring with others to swear falsely to this oath. He appealed to the Supreme Court.

Mr. Justice **FIELD**, after stating the case, delivered the opinion of the Court.

... Bigamy and polygamy are crimes by the laws of all civilized and Christian countries. They are crimes by the laws of the United States, and they are crimes by the laws of Idaho. They tend to destroy the purity of the marriage relation, to disturb the peace of families, to degrade woman and to debase man. Few crimes are more pernicious to the best interests of society and receive more general or more deserved punishment. To extend exemption from punishment for such crimes would be to shock the moral judgment of the community. To call their advocacy a tenet of religion is to offend the common sense of mankind. . . .

The term "religion" has reference to one's views of his relations to his Creator, and to the obligations they impose of reverence for his being and character, and of obedience to his will. It is often confounded with the *cultus* or form of worship of a particular sect, but is distinguishable from the latter. The first amendment to the Constitution ... was intended to allow every one under the jurisdiction of the United States to entertain such notions respecting his relations to his Maker and the duties they impose as may be approved by his judgment and conscience, and to exhibit his sentiments in such form of worship as he may think proper, not injurious to the equal rights of others, and to prohibit legislation for the support of any religious tenets, or the modes of worship of any sect. ... It was never intended or supposed that the amendment could be invoked as a protection against legislation for the punishment of acts inimical to the peace, good order and morals of society. With man's relations to his Maker and the obligations he may think they impose, and the manner in which an expression shall be made by him of his belief on those subjects, no interference can be permitted, provided always the laws of society, designed to secure its peace and prosperity, and the morals of its people, are not interfered with. However free the exercise of religion may be, it must be subordinate to the criminal laws of the country, passed with reference to actions regarded by general consent as properly the subjects of punitive legislation. There have been sects which denied as a part of their religious tenets that there should be any marriage tie, and advocated promiscuous intercourse of the sexes as prompted by the passions of its members. And history discloses the fact that the necessity of human sacrifices, on special occasions, has been a tenet of many sects. Should a sect of either of these kinds ever find its way into this country, swift punishment would follow the carrying into effect of its doctrines, and no heed would be given to the pretence that, as religious beliefs, their supporters could be protected in their exercise by the Constitution of the United States. Probably never before in the history of this country has it been seriously contended that the whole punitive power of the government for acts, recognized by the general consent of the Christian world in modern times as proper matters for prohibitory legislation, must be suspended in order that the tenets of a religious sect encouraging crime may be carried out without hindrance. ...

... Whilst legislation for the establishment of a religion is forbidden, and its free exercise permitted, it does not follow that everything which may be so called can be tolerated. Crime is not the less odious because sanctioned by what any particular sect may designate as religion. ...

Editors' Notes

(1) **Query:** What was Field's conception of WHAT "the Constitution" includes? What approach to constitutional interpretation did he follow?

(2) **Query:** *Davis* raises two questions, which apparently did not occur to Field, who considered himself a great defender of constitutional rights: (i) What did it leave of a constitutionalist right to free exercise, as contrasted with a democratic right to participate in the political processes and to share in the community's judgment about what is or is not objectionable? Or, in terms of *Carolene Products,* what protections did Field leave to "discrete and insular" religious minorities against the prejudices of hostile majorities? And (ii) What democratic rights did Mormons have under this law? Once it was in place, they lost the right to vote. How could they retrieve that right?

(3) Even after the Mormons fled to Utah, laws against the practice of their religion followed them. In 1882 Congress denied the right to vote to any citizen in the territories (Utah was not yet a state) who practiced polygamy. Five years later, Congress annulled the Mormon Church's corporate charter and declared most of its property forfeit. The Supreme Court affirmed in The Late Corporation of the Church of Jesus Christ of Latter Day Saints v. United States (1890). Referring to polygamy as a "barbarous practice" and a "nefarious" doctrine "contrary to the spirit of Christianity," the justices, speaking through Justice Brewer, Field's nephew, ruled the government's action constitutional. They abruptly dismissed as a "sophistical plea" the Mormons' claim to freedom of religion: "No doubt the Thugs of India imagined that their belief in the right of assassination was a religious belief; but their thinking did not make it so."

In 1890 the Mormon Church abandoned the teaching and practice of polygamy, but some fundamentalist groups have refused to accept the change; and occasional legal problems still arise. As recently as 1946, the Supreme Court sustained the conviction under the Mann Act, outlawing transporting women across state lines for "immoral" purposes, of a Mormon who traveled on a vacation with several of his wives. Cleveland v. United States.

For scholarly studies of the Mormons' travails, see Klaus J. Hansen, *Mormonism and the American Experience* (Chicago: University of Chicago Press, 1981); and Marvin S. Hill and James B. Allen, eds., *Mormonism and American Culture* (New York: Harper & Row, 1972).

(4) In keeping with its general jurisprudence, the Court has pretty much given up the role of Grand Inquisitor and no longer equates "the spirit of Christianity" as a criterion for judging rights protected under the First Amendment. See, for example, Thomas v. Review Bd. (1981; reprinted below, p. 1193): "[R]eligious beliefs need not be acceptable, logical, consistent, or comprehensible to others in order to merit First Amendment protection. ... Courts are not arbiters of scriptural interpretation."

"The essential characteristic of these liberties is, that under their shield many types of life, character, opinion and belief can develop unmolested and unobstructed."

CANTWELL v. CONNECTICUT
310 U.S. 296, 60 S.Ct. 900, 84 L.Ed. 1213 (1940).

On Palm Sunday, 1938, Newton Cantwell and his two sons Jesse and Russell, all Jehovah's Witnesses, went from house to house and also stopped people in the street in a heavily Catholic neighborhood in New Haven, offering to play a phonograph record and to sell religious literature. The message on the record and in some of the literature not only explained the Witnesses' beliefs but also attacked the Catholic Church as "the Whore of Babylon." The Cantwells were arrested and convicted on the third and fifth counts of charges lodged against them. The third count alleged violation of a statute forbidding solicitation of funds for any "religious, charitable or philanthropic cause" without the prior approval of the secretary of the public welfare council. The fifth count alleged incitement to breach of peace in that Jesse Cantwell played his record for two men who became angry at its attack on Catholicism and threatened to punch him. At that point Jesse retreated without further discussion. The state supreme court sustained the convictions, and the Cantwells appealed to the U.S. Supreme Court.

Mr. Justice **ROBERTS** delivered the opinion of the Court. ...

First. We hold that the statute, as construed and applied to the appellants, deprives them of their liberty without due process of law in contravention of the Fourteenth Amendment. The fundamental concept of liberty embodied in that Amendment embraces the liberties guaranteed by the First Amendment. The First Amendment declares that Congress shall make no law respecting an establishment of religion or prohibiting the free exercise thereof. ... The constitutional inhibition of legislation on the subject of religion has a double aspect. On the one hand, it forestalls compulsion by law of the acceptance of any creed or the practice of any form of worship. Freedom of conscience and freedom to adhere to such religious organization or form of worship as the individual may choose cannot be restricted by law. On the other hand, it safeguards the free exercise of the chosen form of religion. Thus the Amendment embraces two concepts,—freedom to believe and freedom to act. The first is absolute but, in the nature of things, the second cannot be. Conduct remains subject to regulation for the protection of society. The freedom to act must have appropriate definition to preserve the enforcement of that protection. In every case the power to regulate must be so exercised as not, in attaining a permissible end, unduly to infringe the protected freedom. No one would contest the proposition that a state may not, by statute, wholly deny the right to preach or to disseminate religious views. ... It is equally clear that a state may by general and nondiscriminatory legislation regulate the times, the places, and the manner of soliciting upon its streets, and of holding meetings thereon; and may in other respects safeguard the peace, good order and comfort of the community, without unconstitutionally invading the liberties protected by the Fourteenth Amendment. ...

The general regulation, in the public interest, of solicitation, which does not involve any religious test and does not unreasonably obstruct or delay the collection of funds, is not open to any constitutional objection, even though the collection be for a religious purpose. ...

It will be noted, however, that [this] Act requires an application to the secretary of the public welfare council of the State; that he is empowered to determine whether the cause is a religious one, and that the issue of a certificate depends upon his affirmative action. If he finds that the cause is not that of religion, to solicit for it becomes a crime. He is not to issue a certificate as a matter of course. His decision to issue or refuse it involves appraisal of facts, the exercise of judgment, and the formation of an opinion. He is authorized to withhold his approval if he determines that the cause is not a religious one. Such a censorship of religion as the means of determining its right to survive is a denial of liberty protected by the First Amendment and included in the liberty which is within the protection of the Fourteenth. ...

... [A]vailability of a judicial remedy for abuses in the system of licensing still leaves that system one of previous restraint which, in the field of free speech and press, we have held inadmissible. A statute authorizing previous restraint upon the exercise of the guaranteed freedom by judicial decision after trial is as obnoxious to the Constitution as one providing for like restraint by administrative action.

Nothing we have said is intended even remotely to imply that, under the cloak of religion, persons may, with impunity, commit frauds upon the public. ... Without doubt a state may protect its citizens from fraudulent solicitation by requiring a stranger in the community, before permitting him publicly to solicit funds for any purpose, to establish his identity and his authority to act for the cause which he purports to represent. The state is likewise free to regulate the time and manner of solicitation generally, in the interest of public safety, peace, comfort or convenience. But to condition the solicitation of aid for the perpetuation of religious views or systems upon a license, the grant of which rests in the exercise of a determination by state authority as to what is a religious cause, is to lay a forbidden burden upon the exercise of liberty protected by the Constitution.

Second. We hold that, in the circumstances disclosed, the conviction of Jesse Cantwell on the fifth count must be set aside. Decision as to the lawfulness of the conviction demands the weighing of two conflicting interests. The fundamental law declares the interest of the United States that the free exercise of religion be not prohibited and that freedom to communicate information and opinion be not abridged. The state of Connecticut has an obvious interest in the preservation and protection of peace and good order within her borders. We must determine whether the alleged protection of the State's interest, means to which end would, in the absence of limitation by the federal Constitution, lie wholly within the State's discretion, has been pressed, in this instance, to a point where it has come into fatal collision with the overriding interest protected by the federal compact. ...

The offense known as breach of the peace embraces a great variety of conduct destroying or menacing public order and tranquillity. It includes not only violent acts but acts and words likely to produce violence in others. No one would have the hardihood to suggest that the principle of freedom of speech sanctions incitement to riot or that religious liberty connotes the privilege to exhort others to physical attack upon those belonging to another sect. When clear and present danger of riot, disorder, interference with traffic upon the public streets, or other immediate threat to public safety, peace, or order, appears, the power of the state to prevent or punish is obvious. Equally obvious is it that a state may not unduly suppress free communication of views, religious or other, under the guise of conserving desirable conditions.　...

The record played by Cantwell embodies a general attack on all organized religious systems as instruments of Satan and injurious to man; it then singles out the Roman Catholic Church for strictures couched in terms which naturally would offend not only persons of that persuasion, but all others who respect the honestly held religious faith of their fellows.　The hearers were in fact highly offended.　...

We find in the instant case no assault or threatening of bodily harm, no truculent bearing, no intentional discourtesy, no personal abuse.　On the contrary, we find only an effort to persuade a willing listener to buy a book or to contribute money in the interest of what Cantwell, however misguided others may think him, conceived to be true religion.　In the realm of religious faith, and in that of political belief, sharp differences arise.　... To persuade others to his own point of view, the pleader ...,　at times, resorts to exaggeration, to vilification of men who have been, or are, prominent in church or state, and even to false statement.　But the people of this nation have ordained in the light of history, that, in spite of the probability of excesses and abuses, these liberties are, in the long view, essential to enlightened opinion and right conduct on the part of the citizens of a democracy.　...

Although the contents of the record not unnaturally aroused animosity, we think that, in the absence of a statute narrowly drawn to define and punish specific conduct as constituting a clear and present danger to a substantial interest of the State, the petitioner's communication, considered in the light of the constitutional guaranties, raised no such clear and present menace to public peace and order as to render him liable to conviction of the common law offense in question.　...

Reversed.

Editors' Notes

(1) **Query:** In Barenblatt v. United States (1959; reprinted above, p. 803), the justices debated whether Roberts' opinion in *Cantwell* used a *balancing approach.* To what extent did he do so? To what extent was he groping toward the "strict scrutiny test"? To what extent did he treat free exercise as a "fundamental right"?

(2) *Cantwell* is the leading case interpreting the First and Fourteenth amendments to limit governmental authority to regulate dissemination of information on public streets to "time, place, and manner." This case and its descendants bar government's restricting the content of the information a speaker/writer wishes to communicate. For analyses of this "two-track" framework, see Laurence H. Tribe, *American Constitutional Law* (2d ed.; Mineola, NY: Foundation Press, 1988), ch. 12; John Hart Ely, *Democracy and Distrust* (Cambridge: Harvard University Press, 1980), ch. 5; and John Rawls, *Political Liberalism* (New York: Columbia University Press, 1993), Lecture VIII.

"Where all the effective means of inducing political changes are left free from interference, education in the abandonment of foolish legislation is itself a training in liberty."—Justice FRANKFURTER

"I am not persuaded that we should refrain from passing upon the legislative judgment 'as long as the remedial channels of the democratic process remain open and unobstructed.' This seems to me no more than the surrender of the constitutional protection of the liberty of small minorities to the popular will."—Justice STONE

MINERSVILLE SCHOOL DISTRICT v. GOBITIS

310 U.S. 586, 60 S.Ct. 1010, 84 L.Ed. 1375 (1940).

Minersville, Pennsylvania, had a long established *custom* of opening each day at public schools with a flag saluting ceremony. In October, 1935, Lillian and William Gobitis, two children of the Jehovah's Witnesses' faith, refused to salute the flag because the ceremony violated their religious scruples: The First Commandment forbids worshipping "a graven image." After unsuccessfully negotiating with the students' father, the local school superintendent asked the state attorney general if the school board could require the flag salute. The attorney general said it could, and Minersville's school board adopted a resolution ordering the ceremony and providing that failure to participate would constitute "an act of insubordination and shall be dealt with accordingly."

Immediately after, the superintendent expelled the Gobitis children. Mr. Gobitis sought help from the Witnesses' national headquarters; and, almost eighteen months later, the Witnesses' national legal counsel filed suit for Gobitis in a federal district court, claiming that requiring the salute violated the First and Fourteenth Amendments and asking for an injunction against its enforcement. The district court agreed, and the court of appeals affirmed. The board then obtained certiorari from the Supreme Court.

The Saturday after oral argument, the justices met in conference to discuss and vote on the case. According to Justice Frank Murphy's notes, Chief Justice Hughes opened the debate:

It is the requirement of the [salute] that is objected to. We can't say this requirement is contrary to state law. . . . [T]he question here is one of the free exercise of religion.

Religious scruples or belief will not give a citizen immunity from payment of taxes or instruction in military science. As Justice Cardozo has said, "The right of private judgment has never yet been exalted above the powers and the compulsion of the agencies of government." *

---

* We have slightly edited Murphy's notes to quote exactly from Cardozo's concur. op. in Hamilton v. Regents (1934), upholding compulsory military training at a state university against a pacifist's claim of free exercise. Hughes often brought into the conference either copies of the U.S. Reports or quotations from them. Murphy actually wrote "etc." to

Consider the nature of the requirement. If the requirement is aimed at religion, then it lies outside the sphere of regulation because the [First] Amendment prohibits such regulation. So I must first inquire—is it a reasonable regulation that the state asks? On the proper needs of a social order a state can require not devotions, not family prayers or religious observances ... but if the state acts in its proper sphere the scruples of the individual cannot avoid the proper state power.

So let's look at it. The pledge of allegiance. The gesture is objected to as a token of loyalty to the flag. As I see it the state can insist on inculcation of loyalty. It would be extraordinary if this country and the state could not provide for the respect for the flag of our land. It has nothing to do with religion—indeed it has to do with freedom of religion.

Who is entitled to a judgment on the general effect of what is required? Almost anything the state might do may be [an] offense to many people. If the legislature has judgment there is room for the belief to the effect that judgment would be good.

I come up to this case like a skittish horse to a brass band. ... There is nothing that I have more profound belief in than religious freedom so I must bring myself to view this case on the question of state power. There is no [il]legitimate impingement on religious belief here. What is required of those who salute the flag is a legitimate object [of state power]. We have no jurisdiction as to the wisdom of this. We have to deal with state power and consider whether this is a proper exercise or not. I don't want to be dogmatic about this, but I simply cannot believe that the state has not the power to inculcate this social objective.

According to Justice Douglas' recollection, no one disputed Hughes at the Conference; the vote was 7–0 to sustain the constitutionality of requiring the salute. Two justices, Harlan Fiske Stone and Hugo L. Black, passed, i.e., did not vote. Hughes assigned the task of writing the opinion of the Court to Felix Frankfurter, who had been anxious, for several reasons, to do that job. After he circulated his opinion, all but two members of the Court joined in it. McReynolds decided to note simply that he concurred in the result, and Stone hesitated. Eventually he told his brethren that he was deeply troubled and circulated the draft of a dissent. A week before the Court announced its decision, Frankfurter sent a message to Stone:

May 27, 1940

Dear Stone:

Were No. 690 [Minersville School District v. Gobitis] an ordinary case I should let the opinion speak for itself. But that you should entertain doubts has naturally stirred me to an anxious re-examination of my own views, even though I can assure you that nothing has weighed as much on my conscience, since I have come on this Court, as has this case. ... After all, the vulgar intrusion of law in the

_____

summarize what Hughes quoted from Cardozo. Again, we warn that Murphy took notes, not a verbatim record.—**Eds.**

domain of conscience is for me a very sensitive area. For various reasons ... a good part of my mature life has thrown whatever weight it has had against foolish and harsh manifestations of coercion and for the amplest expression of dissident views, however absurd or offensive these may have been to my own notions of rationality and decency. ...

But no one has more clearly in his mind than you, that even when it comes to these ultimate civil liberties ... we are not in the domain of absolutes. Here, also, we have an illustration of what the Greeks thousands of years ago recognized as a tragic issue, namely, the clash of rights, not the clash of wrongs. For resolving such clash we have no calculus. But there is for me, and I know also for you, a great make-weight for dealing with this problem, namely, that we are not the primary resolvers of the clash. We are not exercising an independent judgment; we are sitting in judgment upon the judgment of the legislature. I am aware of the important distinction which you so skillfully adumbrated in your footnote 4 (particularly the second paragraph of it) in the *Carolene Products Co.* case. I agree with that distinction; I regard it as basic. I have taken over that distinction in its central aspect ... in the present opinion by insisting on the importance of keeping open all those channels of free expression by which undesirable legislation may be removed, and keeping unobstructed all forms of protests against what are deemed invasions of conscience. ...

What weighs with me strongly in this case is my anxiety that ... we do not exercise our judicial power unduly, and as though we ourselves were legislators by holding too tight a rein on the organs of popular government. In other words, I want to avoid the mistake comparable to that made by those whom we criticized when dealing with the control of property. I hope I am aware of the different interests that are compendiously summarized by opposing "liberty" to "property." But I also know that the generalizations implied in these summaries are also inaccurate and hardly correspond to the complicated realities of an advanced society. I cannot rid myself of the notion that it is not fantastic, although I think foolish and perhaps worse, for school authorities to believe ... that to allow exemption to some of the children goes far towards disrupting the whole patriotic exercise. ...

For time and circumstances are surely not irrelevant considerations in resolving the conflicts that we do have to resolve in this particular case. ... [T]his case would have a tail of implications as to legislative power that is certainly debatable and might easily be invoked far beyond the size of the immediate kite, were it to deny the very minimum exaction, however foolish as to the Gobitis children, of expression of faith in the heritage and purposes of our country.

For my intention ... was to use this opinion as a vehicle for preaching the true democratic faith of not relying on the Court for the impossible task of assuring a vigorous, mature, self-protecting and tolerant democracy by bringing the responsibility for a combination of firmness and toleration directly home where it belongs—to the people and their representatives themselves.

I have tried in this opinion really to act on what will, as a matter of history, be a lodestar for due regard between legislative and judicial powers, to wit, your dissent in the *Butler* case.* ... The duty of compulsion [in the flag salute requirement] being as minimal as it is for an act, the normal legislative authorization of which certainly cannot be denied, and all channels of affirmative free expression being open to both children and parents, I cannot resist the conviction that we ought to let the legislative judgment stand and put the responsibility for its exercise where it belongs. ...

Faithfully yours,
Felix Frankfurter

Stone remained unconvinced, and the judgment came down on June 3, 1940, as the Nazi army, which had just swept across Holland and Belgium, was in the process of crushing France.

Mr. Justice **FRANKFURTER** delivered the opinion of the Court. ...

Centuries of strife over the erection of particular dogmas as exclusive or all-comprehending faiths led to the inclusion of a guarantee for religious freedom in the Bill of Rights. The First Amendment, and the Fourteenth through its absorption of the First, sought to guard against repetition of those bitter religious struggles by prohibiting the establishment of a state religion and by securing to every sect the free exercise of its faith. ...

Certainly the affirmative pursuit of one's convictions about the ultimate mystery of the universe and man's relation to it is placed beyond the reach of law. Government may not interfere with organized or individual expression of belief or disbelief. Propagation of belief—or even of disbelief in the supernatural—is protected, whether in church or chapel, mosque or synagogue, tabernacle or meeting-house. Likewise the Constitution assures generous immunity to the individual from imposition of penalties for offending, in the course of his own religious activities, the religious views of others, be they a minority or those who are dominant in government. Cantwell v. Connecticut [1940].

But the manifold character of man's relations may bring his conception of religious duty into conflict with the secular interests of his fellowmen. When does the constitutional guarantee compel exemption from doing what society thinks necessary for the promotion of some great common end, or from a penalty for conduct which appears dangerous to the general good? To state the problem is to recall the truth that no single principle can answer all of life's complexities. The right to freedom of religious belief, however dissident and however obnoxious to

---

* The relevant part of Stone's dissent in United States v. Butler (1936), in which he urged judges to remember that they were not the sole protectors of liberty, is quoted in Eds.' Note (3) to West Coast Hotel v. Parrish (1937; reprinted above, p. 1123).—**Eds.**

the cherished beliefs of others ... is itself the denial of an absolute. But to affirm that the freedom to follow conscience has itself no limits in the life of a society would deny that very plurality of principles which, as a matter of history, underlies protection of religious toleration. ... Our present task then ... is to reconcile two rights in order to prevent either from destroying the other. But, because in safeguarding conscience we are dealing with interests so subtle and so dear, every possible leeway should be given to the claims of religious faith.

   ... The religious liberty which the Constitution protects has never excluded legislation of general scope not directed against doctrinal loyalties of particular sects. Judicial nullification of legislation cannot be justified by attributing to the framers of the Bill of Rights views for which there is no historic warrant. Conscientious scruples have not, in the course of the long struggle for religious toleration, relieved the individual from obedience to a general law not aimed at the promotion or restriction of religious beliefs. The mere possession of religious convictions which contradict the relevant concerns of a political society does not relieve the citizen from the discharge of political responsibilities. The necessity for this adjustment has again and again been recognized. In a number of situations the exertion of political authority has been sustained, while basic considerations of religious freedom have been left inviolate. Reynolds v. United States [1878]; Davis v. Beason [1890]; Selective Draft Law Cases [1918]; Hamilton v. University of California [1934]. In all these cases the general laws in question ... were manifestations of specific powers of government deemed by the legislature essential to secure and maintain that orderly, tranquil, and free society without which religious toleration itself is unattainable. ... We are dealing with an interest inferior to none in the hierarchy of legal values. National unity is the basis of national security. To deny the legislature the right to select appropriate means for its attainment presents a totally different order of problem from that of the propriety of subordinating the possible ugliness of littered streets to the free expression of opinion through distribution of handbills. Compare Schneider v. Irvington [1939].

   Situations like the present are phases of the profoundest problem confronting a democracy—the problem which Lincoln cast in memorable dilemma: "Must a government of necessity be too *strong* for the liberties of its people, or too *weak* to maintain its own existence?" No mere textual reading or logical talisman can solve the dilemma. And when the issue demands judicial determination, it is not the personal notion of judges of what wise adjustment requires which must prevail. ...

   ... [S]pecific activities of government presuppose the existence of an organized political society. The ultimate foundation of a free society is the binding tie of cohesive sentiment. Such a sentiment is fostered by all those agencies of the mind and spirit which may serve to gather up the traditions of a people, transmit them from generation to generation, and thereby create that continuity of a treasured common life which constitutes a civilization. "We live by symbols." The flag is the symbol of our national unity, transcending all internal differences, however large, within the framework of the Constitution. ...

The case before us must be viewed as though the legislature of Pennsylvania had itself formally directed the flag-salute for the children of Minersville. ... The precise issue ... is whether the legislatures of the various states and the authorities in a thousand counties and school districts of this country are barred from determining the appropriateness of various means to evoke that unifying sentiment without which there can ultimately be no liberties, civil or religious. To stigmatize legislative judgment in providing for this universal gesture of respect for the symbol of our national life in the setting of the common school as a lawless inroad on that freedom of conscience which the Constitution protects, would amount to no less than the pronouncement of pedagogical and psychological dogma in a field where courts possess no marked and certainly no controlling competence. The influences which help toward a common feeling for the common country are manifold. Some may seem harsh and others no doubt are foolish. Surely, however, the end is legitimate. And the effective means for its attainment are still so uncertain and so unauthenticated by science as to preclude us from putting the widely prevalent belief in flag-saluting beyond the pale of legislative power. ...

The wisdom of training children in patriotic impulses by those compulsions which necessarily pervade so much of the educational process is not for our independent judgment. ... [T]he courtroom is not the arena for debating issues of educational policy. ... So to hold would in effect make us the school board for the country. That authority has not been given to this Court, nor should we assume it. ...

... Except where the transgression of constitutional liberty is too plain for argument, personal freedom is best maintained—so long as the remedial channels of the democratic process remain open and unobstructed—when it is ingrained in a people's habits and not enforced against popular policy by the coercion of adjudicated law. That the flag-salute is an allowable portion of a school program for those who do not invoke conscientious scruples is surely not debatable. But for us to insist that ... exceptional immunity must be given to dissidents, is to maintain that there is no basis for a legislative judgment that such an exemption might introduce elements of difficulty into the school discipline, might cast doubts in the minds of the other children which would themselves weaken the effect of the exercise.

The preciousness of the family relation, the authority and independence which give dignity to parenthood, indeed the enjoyment of all freedom, presuppose the kind of ordered society which is summarized by our flag. A society which is dedicated to the preservation of these ultimate values of civilization may in self-protection utilize the educational process for inculcating those almost unconscious feelings which bind men together in a comprehending loyalty, whatever may be their

lesser differences and difficulties. That is to say, the process may be
utilized so long as men's right to believe as they please, to win others to
their way of belief, and their right to assemble in their chosen places of
worship for the devotional ceremonies of their faith, are all fully respected.

Judicial review, itself a limitation on popular government, is a
fundamental part of our constitutional scheme. But to the legislature
no less than to courts is committed the guardianship of deeply-cherished
liberties. See Missouri, K. & T.R. Co. v. May [1904]. Where all the
effective means of inducing political changes are left free from interference, education in the abandonment of foolish legislation is itself a
training in liberty. To fight out the wise use of legislative authority in
the forum of public opinion and before legislative assemblies rather than
to transfer such a contest to the judicial arena, serves to vindicate the
self-confidence of a free people.

Reversed.

Mr. Justice **McREYNOLDS** concurs in the result.

Mr. Justice **STONE,** dissenting. ...

The law which is ... sustained is unique in the history of Anglo–
American legislation. It does more than suppress freedom of speech and
more than prohibit the free exercise of religion. ... For by this law the
state seeks to coerce these children to express a sentiment which ...
they do not entertain, and which violates their deepest religious convictions. ...

Concededly the constitutional guaranties of personal liberty are not
always absolutes. Government has a right to survive and powers
conferred upon it are not necessarily set at naught by the express
prohibitions of the Bill of Rights. ... But it is a long step, and one
which I am unable to take, to the position that government may, as a
supposed educational measure and as a means of disciplining the young,
compel public affirmations which violate their religious conscience.

The very fact that we have constitutional guaranties of civil liberties
and the specificity of their command where freedom of speech and of
religion are concerned require some accommodation of the powers which
government normally exercises ... to the constitutional demand that
those liberties be protected against the action of government itself. The
state concededly has power to require and control the education of its
citizens, but it cannot by a general law compelling attendance at public
schools preclude attendance at a private school adequate in its instruction, where the parent seeks to secure for the child the benefits of
religious instruction not provided by the public school. Pierce v. Society
of Sisters [1925]. And only recently we have held that the state's
authority to control its public streets by generally applicable regulations
is not an absolute to which free speech must yield, and cannot be made
the medium of its suppression, Hague v. Committee of Industrial Organi-

zation [1939], any more than can its authority to penalize littering of the streets by a general law be used to suppress the distribution of handbills as a means of communicating ideas to their recipients. Schneider v. Irvington [1939].

... [W]here there are competing demands of the interests of government and of liberty under the Constitution, and where the performance of governmental functions is brought into conflict with specific constitutional restrictions, there must, when that is possible, be reasonable accommodation between them so as to preserve the essentials of both and ... it is the function of courts to determine whether such accommodation is reasonably possible. ... [E]ven if we believe that such compulsions will contribute to national unity, there are other ways to teach loyalty and patriotism ... than by compelling the pupil to affirm that which he does not believe and by commanding a form of affirmance which violates his religious convictions. ...

... The very essence of the liberty which [the Bill of Rights] guarantee is the freedom of the individual from compulsion as to what he shall think and what he shall say, at least where the compulsion is to bear false witness to his religion. If these guaranties are to have any meaning they must, I think, be deemed to withhold from the state any authority to compel belief or the expression of it where that expression violates religious convictions. ...

History teaches us that there have been but few infringements of personal liberty by the state which have not been justified ... in the name of righteousness and the public good, and few which have not been directed, as they are now, at politically helpless minorities. The framers were not unaware that under the system which they created most governmental curtailments of personal liberty would have the support of a legislative judgment that the public interest would be better served by its curtailment than by its constitutional protection. I cannot conceive that in prescribing ... the freedom of the mind and spirit secured by the explicit guaranties of freedom of speech and religion, they intended or rightly could have left any latitude for a legislative judgment that the compulsory expression of belief which violates religious convictions would better serve the public interest than their protection. The Constitution may well elicit expressions of loyalty to it and to the government which it created, but it does not command such expressions or otherwise give any indication that compulsory expressions of loyalty play any such part in our scheme of government as to override the constitutional protection of freedom of speech and religion. And while such expressions of loyalty, when voluntarily given, may promote national unity, it is quite another matter to say that their compulsory expression by children in violation of their own and their parents' religious convictions can be regarded as playing so important a part in our national unity as to leave school boards free to exact it despite the constitutional guaranty of freedom of religion. The very terms of the Bill of Rights preclude, it seems to me, any reconciliation of such compulsions with the constitutional guaranties by a legislative declaration that they are more important to the public welfare than the Bill of Rights. ...

... I am not persuaded that we should refrain from passing upon the legislative judgment "as long as the remedial channels of the democratic process remain open and unobstructed." This seems to me no more than the surrender of the constitutional protection of the liberty of small minorities to the popular will. We have previously pointed to the importance of a searching judicial inquiry into the legislative judgment in situations where prejudice against discrete and insular minorities may tend to curtail the operation of those political processes ordinarily to be relied on to protect minorities. See United States v. Carolene Products Co. [1938]. And until now we have not hesitated similarly to scrutinize legislation restricting the civil liberty of racial and religious minorities although no political process was affected. Meyer v. Nebraska [1923]; *Pierce.* Here we have such a small minority entertaining in good faith a religious belief, which is such a departure from the usual course of human conduct, that most persons are disposed to regard it with little toleration or concern. In such circumstances careful scrutiny of legislative efforts to secure conformity of belief and opinion by a compulsory affirmation of the desired belief, is especially needful if civil rights are to receive any protection. Tested by this standard, I am not prepared to say that the right of this small and helpless minority ... to refrain from an expression obnoxious to their religion, is to be overborne by the interest of the state in maintaining discipline in the schools.

The Constitution expresses more than the conviction of the people that democratic processes must be preserved at all costs. It is also an expression of faith and a command that freedom of mind and spirit must be preserved, which government must obey, if it is to adhere to that justice and moderation without which no free government can exist. For this reason it would seem that legislation which operates to repress the religious freedom of small minorities, which is admittedly within the scope of the protection of the Bill of Rights, must at least be subject to the same judicial scrutiny as legislation which we have recently held to infringe the constitutional liberty of religious and racial minorities. ...

Editors' Notes

(1) **Query:** Frankfurter told Stone he was following *Carolene Products* (1938; reprinted above, p. 609). To what extent did he do so? Was he following the approach called *reinforcing representative democracy*? If he was, why did Stone dissent? Does this case point to a basic tension in *Carolene Products'* jurisprudence? To what extent does *Gobitis* pit *reinforcing representative democracy* against *protecting fundamental rights*?

(2) **Query:** Neither Frankfurter nor Stone relied on *textualism*. Why not?

(3) Frankfurter said that the "case before us must be viewed as though the legislature of Pennsylvania had itself formally directed the flag-salute. ..." Does that claim comport with the facts of the case? What difference for

constitutional interpretation would it have made had Frankfurter said the "case before us concerns an administrative regulation adopted by a local school board"? See Richard Danzig, "How Questions Begot Answers in Felix Frankfurter's First Flag Salute Opinion," 1977 *Sup.Ct.Rev.* 257. For a general discussion of different deference due to various levels of government, see Charles L. Black, *Structure and Relationship in Constitutional Law* (Baton Rouge: Louisiana State University Press, 1969), ch. 3.

"The very purpose of a Bill of Rights was to withdraw certain subjects from the vicissitudes of political controversy."—Justice JACKSON

"Reliance for the most precious interests of civilization ... must be found outside of their vindication in courts of law."—Justice Frankfurter

WEST VIRGINIA v. BARNETTE

319 U.S. 624, 63 S.Ct. 1178, 87 L.Ed. 1628 (1943).

Justices Black, Douglas, and Murphy had joined the majority in *Gobitis* with uneasy feelings. A series of later events increased their doubts. First, many commentators in law reviews, educational journals, and even newspapers were highly critical of the decision. Second, during the next few years there was increased persecution of the Witnesses by local officials and private citizens. Third, Black, Douglas, and Murphy began to part with Frankfurter on personal and, more importantly, on jurisprudential grounds. They had come to believe in the necessity of the Court's playing a positive role in protecting the Bill of Rights and saw Frankfurter, as Douglas said two decades later, as "deeply and passionately devoted to the British system, to the supremacy of the legislative branch." In 1942, when the Court sustained a local licensing tax applied to Witnesses who were trying to distribute religious pamphlets, Black, Douglas, and Murphy noted in dissent: "This is but another step in the direction which ... [*Gobitis*] took against the same religious minority and is a logical extension of the principles upon which that decision rested. Since we joined in the opinion in the Gobitis Case, we think it is appropriate to state that we now believe that it was also wrongly decided." Jones v. Opelika (1942).

These defections meant that there would be at least four votes to overturn *Gobitis* if the issue ever came before the Court again. Moreover, two other members of the majority in *Gobitis,* Hughes and McReynolds, retired and were replaced by Robert H. Jackson and Wiley Rutledge, both of whom were rumored to favor overruling. Hayden Covington, national counsel for the Witnesses, decided to present the Court with an opportunity to reconsider. His choice for a test case was West Virginia, whose state board of education, following *Gobitis,* had required a ceremony similar to Minersville's. A special three-judge district court noted the changes of heart and personnel on the U.S. Supreme Court and enjoined enforcement of West Virginia's policy. The state appealed to the Supreme Court.

Mr. Justice **JACKSON** delivered the opinion of the Court. . . .

The freedom asserted by these appellees does not bring them into collision with rights asserted by any other individual. It is such conflicts which most frequently require intervention of the State to determine where the rights of one end and those of another begin. But the refusal of these persons to participate in the ceremony does not interfere with or deny rights of others to do so. Nor is there any question in this case that their behavior is peaceable and orderly. The sole conflict is between authority and rights of the individual. The State asserts power to condition access to public education on making a prescribed sign and profession and at the same time to coerce attendance by punishing both parent and child. The latter stand on a right of self-determination in matters that touch individual opinion and personal attitude. . . .

There is no doubt that, in connection with the pledges, the flag salute is a form of utterance. Symbolism is a primitive but effective way of communicating ideas. . . . Causes and nations, political parties, lodges and ecclesiastical groups seek to knit the loyalty of their followings to a flag or banner, a color or design. The State announces rank, function, and authority through crowns and maces, uniforms and black robes; the church speaks through the Cross, the Crucifix, the altar and shrine, and clerical raiment. Symbols of State often convey political ideas just as religious symbols come to convey theological ones. . . .

It is also to be noted that the compulsory flag salute and pledge requires affirmation of a belief and an attitude of mind. . . . It is now a commonplace that censorship or suppression of expression of opinion is tolerated by our Constitution only when the expression presents a clear and present danger of action of a kind the State is empowered to prevent and punish. It would seem that involuntary affirmation could be commanded only on even more immediate and urgent grounds than silence. . . . To sustain the compulsory flag salute we are required to say that a Bill of Rights which guards the individual's right to speak his own mind, left it open to public authorities to compel him to utter what is not in his mind. . . .

The *Gobitis* opinion reasoned that this is a field "where courts possess no marked and certainly no controlling competence," that it is committed to the legislatures as well as the courts to guard cherished liberties and that it is constitutionally appropriate to "fight out the wise use of legislative authority in the forum of public opinion and before legislative assemblies rather than to transfer such a contest to the judicial arena," since all the "effective means of inducing political changes are left free."

. . . [*Gobitis* also] reasoned that "national unity is the basis of national security," that the authorities have "the right to select appropriate means for its attainment," and hence reaches the conclusion that such compulsory measures toward "national unity" are constitutional. Upon the verity of this assumption depends our answer in this case.

Struggles to coerce uniformity of sentiment in support of some end thought essential to their time and country have been waged by many good as well as by evil men. Nationalism is a relatively recent phenomenon but at other times and places the ends have been racial or territorial security, support of a dynasty or regime, and particular plans for saving souls. ... Probably no deeper division of our people could proceed from any provocation than from finding it necessary to choose what doctrine and whose program public educational officials shall compel youth to unite in embracing. ... Those who begin coercive elimination of dissent soon find themselves exterminating dissenters. Compulsory unification of opinion achieves only the unanimity of the graveyard.

It seems trite but necessary to say that the First Amendment to our Constitution was designed to avoid these ends by avoiding these beginnings. ... We set up government by consent of the governed, and the Bill of Rights denies those in power to coerce that consent. Authority here is to be controlled by public opinion, not public opinion by authority.

The very purpose of a Bill of Rights was to withdraw certain subjects from the vicissitudes of political controversy, to place them beyond the reach of majorities and officials and to establish them as legal principles to be applied by the courts. One's right to life, liberty, and property, to free speech, a free press, freedom of worship and assembly, and other fundamental rights may not be submitted to vote; they depend on the outcome of no elections.

In weighing arguments of the parties it is important to distinguish between the due process clause of the Fourteenth Amendment as an instrument for transmitting the principles of the First Amendment and those cases in which it is applied for its own sake. The test of legislation which collides with the Fourteenth Amendment, because it also collides with the principles of the First, is much more definite than the test when only the Fourteenth is involved. Much of the vagueness of the due process clause disappears when the specific prohibitions of the First become its standard. The right of a State to regulate, for example, a public utility may well include, so far as the due process test is concerned, power to impose all of the restrictions which a legislature may have a "rational basis" for adopting. But freedoms of speech and of press, of assembly, and of worship may not be infringed on such slender grounds. They are susceptible of restriction only to prevent grave and immediate danger to interests which the state may lawfully protect. ...

Nor does our duty to apply the Bill of Rights to assertions of official authority depend upon our possession of marked competence in the field where the invasion of rights occurs. True, the task of translating the majestic generalities of the Bill of Rights, conceived as part of the pattern of liberal government in the eighteenth century, into concrete restraints on officials dealing with the problems of the twentieth century, is one to disturb self-confidence. ... But we act in these matters not by authority of our competence but by force of our commissions. We cannot, because of modest estimates of our competence in such specialties as public education, withhold the judgment that history authenticates as the function of this Court when liberty is infringed.

... [F]reedom to differ is not limited to things that do not matter much. That would be a mere shadow of freedom. The test of its substance is the right to differ as to things that touch the heart of the existing order. If there is any fixed star in our constitutional constellation, it is that no official, high or petty, can prescribe what shall be orthodox in politics, nationalism, religion, or other matters of opinion or force citizens to confess by word or act their faith therein. ...

The decision of this Court in *Gobitis* and the holdings of those few *per curiam* decisions which preceded and foreshadowed it are overruled, and the judgment enjoining enforcement of the West Virginia Regulation is

Affirmed.

Mr. Justice **BLACK** and Mr. Justice **DOUGLAS** concurring. ...

Mr. Justice **ROBERTS** and Mr. Justice **REED** adhere to the views expressed by the Court in *Gobitis*. ...

Mr. Justice **FRANKFURTER,** dissenting.

One who belongs to the most vilified and persecuted minority in history is not likely to be insensible to the freedoms guaranteed by our Constitution. Were my purely personal attitude relevant I should wholeheartedly associate myself with the general libertarian views in the Court's opinion, representing as they do the thought and action of a lifetime. But as judges we are neither Jew nor Gentile, neither Catholic nor agnostic. We owe equal attachment to the Constitution and are equally bound by our judicial obligations whether we derive our citizenship from the earliest or the latest immigrants to these shores. As a member of this Court I am not justified in writing my private notions of policy into the Constitution, no matter how deeply I may cherish them or how mischievous I may deem their disregard. The duty of a judge ... is not that of the ordinary person. It can never be emphasized too much that one's own opinion about the wisdom or evil of a law should be excluded altogether when one is doing one's duty on the bench. The only opinion of our own even looking in that direction that is material is our opinion whether legislators could in reason have enacted such a law. In the light of all the circumstances, including the history of this question in this Court, it would require more daring than I possess to deny that reasonable legislators could have taken the action which is before us for review. ...

The admonition that judicial self-restraint alone limits arbitrary exercise of our authority is relevant every time we are asked to nullify legislation. The Constitution does not give us greater veto power when dealing with one phase of "liberty" than with another. ... In neither situation is our function comparable to that of a legislature or are we free to act as though we were a super-legislature. Judicial self-restraint is equally necessary whenever an exercise of political or legislative power is challenged. There is no warrant in the constitutional basis of this Court's authority for attributing different roles to it depending upon the nature of the challenge to the legislation. Our power does not vary according to the particular provision of the Bill of Rights which is invoked. The right not to have property taken without just compensation has, so far as the scope of judicial power is concerned, the same constitutional dignity as the right to be protected against unreasonable searches and seizures, and the latter has no less claim than freedom of the press or freedom of speech or religious freedom. In no instance is this Court the primary protector of the particular liberty that is invoked. . . .

    . . . [R]esponsibility for legislation lies with legislatures, answerable as they are directly to the people, and this Court's only and very narrow function is to determine whether within the broad grant of authority vested in legislatures they have exercised a judgment for which reasonable justification can be offered. . . . The reason why from the beginning even the narrow judicial authority to nullify legislation has been viewed with a jealous eye is that it serves to prevent the full play of the democratic process. The fact that it may be an undemocratic aspect of our scheme of government does not call for its rejection or its disuse. But it is the best of reasons, as this Court has frequently recognized, for the greatest caution in its use. . . .

    . . . If the avowed or intrinsic legislative purpose is either to promote or to discourage some religious community or creed, it is clearly within the constitutional restrictions . . . and cannot stand. But it by no means follows that legislative power is wanting whenever a general non-discriminatory civil regulation in fact touches conscientious scruples or religious beliefs. . . . Regard for such scruples or beliefs undoubtedly presents one of the most reasonable claims for the exertion of legislative accommodation. . . . But the real question is, who is to make such accommodations, the courts or the legislature?

    This is no dry, technical matter. It cuts deep into one's conception of the democratic process—it concerns no less the practical differences between the means for making these accommodations that are open to courts and to legislatures. A court can only strike down. It can only say "This or that law is void." It cannot modify or qualify, it cannot make exceptions to a general requirement. And it strikes down not merely for a day. At least the finding of unconstitutionality ought not to have ephemeral significance unless the Constitution is to be reduced to the fugitive importance of mere legislation. When we are dealing with the Constitution of the United States, and more particularly with the great safeguards of the Bill of Rights, we are dealing with principles of liberty and justice "so rooted in the traditions and conscience of our people as to be ranked as fundamental"—something without which "a fair and enlightened system of justice would be impossible." Palko v. Connecticut [1937]. If the function of this Court is to be essentially no different from that of a legislature ... then indeed judges should not have life tenure and they should be made directly responsible to the electorate. ...

The subjection of dissidents to the general requirement of saluting the flag, as a measure conducive to the training of children in good citizenship, is very far from being the first instance of exacting obedience to general laws that have offended deep religious scruples. Compulsory vaccination, food inspection regulations, the obligation to bear arms, testimonial duties, compulsory medical treatment—these are but illustrations of conduct that has often been compelled in the enforcement of legislation of general applicability even though the religious consciences of particular individuals rebelled at the exaction.

Law is concerned with external behavior and not with the inner life of man. It rests in large measure upon compulsion. Socrates lives in history partly because he gave his life for the conviction that duty of obedience to secular law does not presuppose consent to its enactment or belief in its virtue. The consent upon which free government rests is the consent that comes from sharing in the process of making and unmaking laws. The state is not shut out from a domain because the individual conscience may deny the state's claim. The individual conscience may profess what faith it chooses. ... [B]ut it cannot thereby restrict community action through political organs in matters of community concern, so long as the action is not asserted in a discriminatory way either openly or by stealth. One may have the right to practice one's religion and at the same time owe the duty of formal obedience to laws that run counter to one's beliefs. ...

One's conception of the Constitution cannot be severed from one's conception of a judge's function in applying it. The Court has no reason for existence if it merely reflects the pressures of the day. Our system is built on the faith that men set apart for this special function, freed from the influences of immediacy and from the deflections of worldly ambition, will become able to take a view of longer range than the period of responsibility entrusted to Congress and legislatures. We are dealing with matters as to which legislators and voters have conflicting views. Are we as judges to impose our strong convictions on where wisdom lies? ...

Of course patriotism can not be enforced by the flag salute. But neither can the liberal spirit be enforced by judicial invalidation of illiberal legislation. Our constant preoccupation with the constitutionality of legislation rather than with its wisdom tends to preoccupation of the American mind with a false value. The tendency of focussing attention on constitutionality is to make constitutionality synonymous with wisdom, to regard a law as all right if it is constitutional. Such an attitude is a great enemy of liberalism. Particularly in legislation affecting freedom of thought and freedom of speech much which should offend a free-spirited society is constitutional. Reliance for the most precious interests of civilization, therefore, must be found outside of their vindication in courts of law. Only a persistent positive translation of the faith of a free society into the convictions and habits and actions of a community is the ultimate reliance against unabated temptations to fetter the human spirit.

Editors' Notes

(1) **Query:** Are there basic differences between Stone's dissent in *Gobitis* and Jackson's opinion for the Court in *Barnette?* To what extent did Jackson use a *fundamental rights approach* to constitutional interpretation and to what extent did he use *reinforcing representative democracy?* To what extent are the two *approaches* compatible?

(2) **Query:** Did Frankfurter's interpretive approach in *Barnette* differ from that in *Gobitis?* Douglas claimed that Frankfurter confused the British and American political systems: What was Frankfurter's conception of the American constitutional system? How did it require him to approach constitutional interpretation?

(3) For the background and aftermath of the Flag Salute Cases, see Alpheus Thomas Mason, *Harlan Fiske Stone* (New York: Viking, 1956), ch. 31; and David R. Manwaring, *Render unto Caesar* (Chicago: University of Chicago Press, 1962).

(4) New Hampshire had the motto "Live Free or Die" on its license plates. A pair of Jehovah's Witnesses who found this creed offensive to their pacifist religious beliefs covered up the motto. After being twice convicted in state courts for defacing a license, they obtained an injunction from a federal court against further enforcement of the statute. Starting from *Barnette* 's proposition that "the right of freedom of thought protected by the First Amendment against state action includes both the right to speak freely and the right to refrain from speaking at all," the Supreme Court, 5–4, affirmed. Wooley v. Maynard (1977).

————

"[I]f the State regulates conduct by enacting a general law within its power, the purpose and effect of which is to advance the State's secular goals, the statute is valid despite its indirect burden on religious observance unless the State may accomplish its purpose by means which do not impose such a burden."—Chief Justice WARREN

"If the 'free exercise' of religion were subject to reasonable regulations ... rational men, representing a predominantly Christian civilization, might think these Sunday laws did not unreasonably interfere with anyone's free exercise of religion."—Justice DOUGLAS

"The Court in such cases is not confined to the narrow inquiry whether the challenged law is rationally related to some legitimate legislative end."—Justice BRENNAN

BRAUNFELD v. BROWN

366 U.S. 599, 81 S.Ct. 1144, 6 L.Ed.2d 563 (1961).

This case presented one of a series of challenges to state laws requiring certain businesses to be closed on Sundays. A special three-judge federal district court had dismissed a suit brought by Jewish merchants, and they appealed to the Supreme Court.

Mr. Chief Justice **WARREN** announced the judgment of the Court and an opinion in which Mr. Justice **BLACK,** Mr. Justice **CLARK,** and Mr. Justice **WHITTAKER** concur. . . .

Appellants contend that the enforcement against them of the Pennsylvania statute will prohibit the free exercise of their religion because, due to the statute's compulsion to close on Sunday, appellants will suffer substantial economic loss, to the benefit of their non-Sabbatarian competitors, if appellants also continue their Sabbath observance by closing their businesses on Saturday; that this result will either compel appellants to give up their Sabbath observance, a basic tenet of the Orthodox Jewish faith, or will put appellants at a serious economic disadvantage if they continue to adhere to their Sabbath. Appellants also assert that the statute will operate so as to hinder the Orthodox Jewish faith in gaining new adherents. . . .

In McGowan v. Maryland [1961] we noted the significance that this Court has attributed to the development of religious freedom in Virginia in determining the scope of the First Amendment's protection. We observed that when Virginia passed its Declaration of Rights in 1776, providing that "all men are equally entitled to the free exercise of religion," Virginia repealed its laws which in any way penalized "maintaining any opinions in matters of religion, forbearing to repair to church, or the exercising any mode of worship whatsoever." But Virginia retained its laws prohibiting Sunday labor. We also took cognizance, in *McGowan,* of the evolution of Sunday Closing Laws from wholly religious sanctions to legislation concerned with the establishment of a day of community tranquility, respite and recreation. . . .

Concededly, appellants . . . will be burdened economically by the State's day of rest mandate; and appellants point out that their religion requires them to refrain from work on Saturday as well. Our inquiry then is whether . . . the First and Fourteenth Amendments forbid application of the Sunday Closing Law to appellants.

Certain aspects of religious exercise cannot, in any way, be restricted or burdened by either federal or state legislation. Compulsion by law of the acceptance of any creed or the practice of any form of worship is strictly forbidden. The freedom to hold religious beliefs and opinions is absolute. Cantwell v. Connecticut [1940]; Reynolds v. United States [1878]. Thus, in West Va. v. Barnette [1945], this Court held that state action compelling school children to salute the flag, on pain of expulsion from public school, was contrary to the First and Fourteenth Amendments when applied to those students whose religious beliefs forbade saluting a flag. But this is not the case at bar; the statute before us does not make criminal the holding of any religious belief or opinion, nor does it force anyone to embrace any religious belief or to say or believe anything in conflict with his religious tenets.

However, the freedom to act, even when the action is in accord with one's religious convictions, is not totally free from legislative restrictions. *Cantwell.* ... [L]egislative power may reach people's actions when they are found to be in violation of important social duties or subversive of good order, even when the actions are demanded by one's religion. ... Thus, in *Reynolds*, this Court upheld the polygamy conviction of a member of the Mormon faith despite the fact that an accepted doctrine of his church then imposed upon its male members the *duty* to practice polygamy. And, in Prince v. Massachusetts [1944], this Court upheld a statute making it a crime for a girl under eighteen years of age to sell any newspapers, periodicals or merchandise in public places despite the fact that a child of the Jehovah's Witnesses faith believed that it was her religious *duty* to perform this work. ...

... [T]he statute at bar does not make unlawful any religious practices of appellants; the Sunday law simply regulates a secular activity and, as applied to appellants, operates so as to make the practice of their religious beliefs more expensive. Furthermore, the law's effect does not inconvenience all members of the Orthodox Jewish faith but only those who believe it necessary to work on Sunday. And even these are not faced with as serious a choice as forsaking their religious practices or subjecting themselves to criminal prosecution. Fully recognizing that the alternatives open to appellants and others similarly situated ... may well result in some financial sacrifice in order to observe their religious beliefs, still the option is wholly different than when the legislation attempts to make a religious practice itself unlawful.

To strike down, without the most critical scrutiny, legislation which imposes only an indirect burden on the exercise of religion ... would radically restrict the operating latitude of the legislature. Statutes which tax income and limit the amount which may be deducted for religious contributions impose an indirect economic burden on the observance of the religion of the citizen whose religion requires him to donate a greater amount to his church; statutes which require the courts to be closed on Saturday and Sunday impose a similar indirect burden on the observance of the religion of the trial lawyer whose religion requires him to rest on a weekday. The list of legislation of this nature is nearly limitless.

Needless to say, when entering the area of religious freedom, we must be fully cognizant of the particular protection that the Constitution has accorded it. Abhorrence of religious persecution and intolerance is a basic part of our heritage. But we are a cosmopolitan nation made up of people of almost every conceivable religious preference. ... Consequently, it cannot be expected, much less required, that legislators enact no law regulating conduct that may in some way result in an economic disadvantage to some religious sects and not to others because of the special practices of the various religions. We do not believe that such an effect is an absolute test for determining whether the legislation violates the freedom of religion protected by the First Amendment.

Of course, to hold unassailable all legislation regulating conduct which imposes solely an indirect burden on the observance of religion would be a gross oversimplification. If the purpose or effect of a law is to impede the observance of one or all religions or is to discriminate invidiously between religions, that law is constitutionally invalid even though the burden may be characterized as being only indirect. But if the State regulates conduct by enacting a general law within its power, the purpose and effect of which is to advance the State's secular goals, the statute is valid despite its indirect burden on religious observance unless the State may accomplish its purpose by means which do not impose such a burden. ...

As we pointed out in *McGowan*, we cannot find a State without power to provide a weekly respite from all labor and, at the same time, to set one day of the week apart from the others as a day of rest ... a day which all members of the family and community have the opportunity to spend and enjoy together, a day on which people may visit friends and relatives who are not available during working days. ... Also, in *McGowan*, we examined several suggested alternative means by which ... the State might accomplish its secular goals without even remotely or incidentally affecting religious freedom. We found there that a State might well find that those alternatives would not accomplish bringing about a general day of rest. ...

However, appellants advance yet another means at the State's disposal which they would find unobjectionable. They contend that the State should cut an exception from the Sunday labor proscription for those people who, because of religious conviction, observe a day of rest other than Sunday. ... A number of States provide such an exemption, and this may well be the wiser solution to the problem. But our concern is not with the wisdom of legislation but with its constitutional limitation. Thus, reason and experience teach that to permit the exemption might well undermine the State's goal of providing a day that, as best possible, eliminates the atmosphere of commercial noise and activity. Although not dispositive of the issue, enforcement problems would be more difficult since there would be two or more days to police rather than one and it would be more difficult to observe whether violations

were occurring. ... For all of these reasons, we cannot say that the
Pennsylvania statute before us is invalid, either on its face or as applied.

Mr. Justice **HARLAN** concurs in the judgment. Mr. Justice **BREN-
NAN** and Mr. Justice **STEWART** concur in our disposition of
appellants' claims under the Establishment Clause and the Equal
Protection Clause. Mr. Justice **FRANKFURTER** and Mr. Justice
HARLAN have rejected appellants' claim under the Free Exercise
Clause in a separate opinion.* ...

Mr. Justice **DOUGLAS,** dissenting.

The question is not whether one day out of seven can be imposed by
a State as a day of rest. The question is not whether Sunday can by
force of custom and habit be retained as a day of rest. The question is
whether a State can impose criminal sanctions on those who ... worship
on a different day or do not share the religious scruples of the majority.
If the "free exercise" of religion were subject to reasonable regulations,
as it is under some constitutions, or if all laws "respecting the establishment of religion" were not proscribed, I could understand how rational
men, representing a predominantly Christian civilization, might think
these Sunday laws did not unreasonably interfere with anyone's free
exercise of religion. ...

But that is not the premise from which we start. ... The First
Amendment commands government to have no interest in theology or
ritual; it admonishes government to be interested in allowing religious
freedom to flourish—whether the result is to produce Catholics, Jews, or
Protestants, or turn the people toward the path of Buddha, or to end in a
predominantly Moslem nation, or to produce in the long run atheists or
agnostics. On matters of this kind government must be neutral. ...
Certainly the "free exercise" clause does not require that everyone
embrace the theology of some church or of some faith, or observe the
religious practices of any majority or minority sect. ...

Mr. Justice **BRENNAN,** concurring and dissenting. ...

The Court has demonstrated that public need for a weekly surcease
from worldly labor. ... I would approach this case differently, from the
point of view of the individuals whose liberty is—concededly—curtailed
by these enactments. For the values of the First Amendment, as
embodied in the Fourteenth, look primarily towards the preservation of
personal liberty, rather than towards the fulfillment of collective goals.
...

The first question to be resolved ... concerns the appropriate
standard of constitutional adjudication in cases in which a statute is
assertedly in conflict with the First Amendment. ... The Court in such
cases is not confined to the narrow inquiry whether the challenged law is
rationally related to some legitimate legislative end. Nor is the case
decided by a finding that the State's interest is substantial and impor-

---

* In a companion case, McGowan v. Maryland (1961).—**Eds.**

tant, as well as rationally justifiable. This canon of adjudication was
clearly stated by Mr. Justice Jackson, speaking for the Court in *Barnette*:

> ... The test of legislation which collides with the Fourteenth
> Amendment, because it also collides with the principles of the First, is
> much more definite than the test when only the Fourteenth is involved.
> ... The right of a State to regulate, for example, a public utility may
> well include ... power to impose all of the restrictions which a legisla-
> ture may have a 'rational basis' for adopting. But freedoms of speech
> and of press, of assembly, and of worship may not be infringed on such
> slender grounds. They are susceptible of restriction only to prevent
> grave and immediate danger to interests which the State may lawfully
> protect. ...

This exacting standard has been consistently applied by this Court
as the test of legislation under all clauses of the First Amendment. ...
For religious freedom ... has classically been one of the highest values
of our society. ... The honored place of religious freedom in our
constitutional hierarchy, ... foreshadowed by a prescient footnote in
Carolene Products, must now be taken to be settled. Or at least so it
appeared until today. For in this case the Court seems to say, without
so much as a deferential nod towards that high place which we have
accorded religious freedom in the past, that any substantial state interest will justify encroachments on religious practice, at least if those
encroachments are cloaked in the guise of some nonreligious public
purpose.

Admittedly, these laws do not compel overt affirmation of a repugnant belief, as in *Barnette*, nor do they prohibit outright any of appellants' religious practices, as did the federal law upheld in *Reynolds*. But
their effect is that appellants may not simultaneously practice their
religion and their trade, without being hampered by a substantial
competitive disadvantage. Their effect is that no one may at one and
the same time be an Orthodox Jew and compete effectively with his
Sunday-observing fellow tradesmen. This clog upon the exercise of
religion, this state-imposed burden on Orthodox Judaism, has exactly the
same economic effect as a tax levied upon the sale of religious literature.
And yet, such a tax, when applied in the form of an excise or license fee,
was held invalid in Follett v. McCormick [1944]. ...

What, then, is the compelling state interest which impels the Commonwealth of Pennsylvania to impede appellants' freedom of worship?
What overbalancing need is so weighty in the constitutional scale that it
justifies this substantial, though indirect, limitation of appellants' freedom? It is not the desire to stamp out a practice deeply abhorred by
society, such as polygamy, as in *Reynolds*, for the custom of resting one
day a week is universally honored, as the Court has amply shown. Nor
is it the State's traditional protection of children, as in Prince v.
Massachusetts, for appellants are reasoning and fully autonomous
adults. It is not even the interest in seeking that everyone rests one day
a week, for appellants' religion requires that they take such a rest. It is
the mere convenience of having everyone rest on the same day. ...

It is true, I suppose, that the granting of such an exemption would make Sundays a little noisier, and the task of police and prosecutor a little more difficult. It is also true that a majority—21—of the 34 States which have general Sunday regulations have exemptions of this kind. We are not told that those States are significantly noisier, or that their police are significantly more burdened, than Pennsylvania's. ...

In fine, the Court, in my view, has exalted administrative convenience to a constitutional level high enough to justify making one religion economically disadvantageous. ... The Court forgets, I think, a warning uttered during the congressional discussion of the First Amendment itself: "... the rights of conscience are, in their nature, of peculiar delicacy, and will little bear the gentlest touch of governmental hand. ..."

Mr. Justice **STEWART**, dissenting. ...

Editors' Notes

(1) **Query:** Did Warren use an approach of *protecting fundamental rights?* Did he use a version of the "strict scrutiny test"? Did he regard freedom of religion as a "fundamental right" What about Douglas? Brennan? Where would *reinforcing representative democracy* lead an interpreter in this case?

(2) Sherbert v. Verner (1963) to some extent undercut the substantive holding in *Braunfeld*. In an opinion written by Brennan, the Court held, with Warren joining the majority, that a denial of unemployment benefits to a Seventh Day Adventist who refused to take any job that required her to work on Saturdays violated free exercise. Despite the vote of 7–2, Brennan had difficulty in mustering a majority behind his opinion. See Bernard Schwartz, *Super Chief* (New York: New York University Press, 1983), pp. 468–470. Stewart concurred separately, expressing concern about the Court's creating a conflict between the establishment and free exercise clauses. For further analysis of this problem, see Rehnquist's dis. op. in Thomas v. Review Bd. (1981; reprinted below, p. 1193).

(3) For the background and aftermath of *Braunfeld* and its companion cases, see Candida Lund, "Religion and Commerce," in C. Herman Pritchett and Alan F. Westin, eds., *The Third Branch of Government* (New York: Harcourt, Brace & World, 1963); for a comparative study of Sunday Closing laws in Canada and the United States, see Jerome A. Barron, "Sunday in North America," 79 *Harv.L.Rev.* 42 (1965). Ireland, 97 per cent Catholic, has an exemption for Jews in its Sunday closing law. Christian merchants challenged the exemption as a denial of equal protection, but the Supreme Court sustained the statute after rejecting Warren's reasoning in *Braunfeld* and agreeing with that of Brennan in *Sherbert*. Quinn's Supermarket v. Attorney General (1972).

"[A] State's interest in universal education ... is not totally free from a balancing process when it impinges

on fundamental rights and interests.   ...."—Chief Justice BURGER

"It is the student's judgment, not his parents', that is essential if we are to give full meaning to what we have said about the Bill of Rights."—Justice DOUGLAS

WISCONSIN v. YODER

406 U.S. 205, 92 S.Ct. 1526, 32 L.Ed.2d 15 (1972).

Wisconsin prosecuted three Old Order Amish parents who kept their teenage children at home, in violation of a state law requiring education of children up to age sixteen. The Amish explained that they believe in the religious necessity of living a simple farm life in harmony with nature. They are willing to send their children to grammar school but consider it morally dangerous to expose teenagers to the culture and values of secular society. The trial court convicted the parents, but Wisconsin's Supreme Court reversed, holding that compulsory attendance violated the right of the Old Order Amish to free exercise of religion. The state obtained certiorari from the U.S. Supreme Court.

Mr. Chief Justice **BURGER** delivered the opinion of the Court. ...

I

There is no doubt as to the power of a State ... to impose reasonable regulations for the control and duration of basic education. See, e.g., Pierce v. Society of Sisters [1925]. Providing public schools ranks at the very apex of the function of a State. Yet even this paramount responsibility was, in *Pierce,* made to yield to the right of parents to provide an equivalent education in a privately operated system. ... As that case suggests, the values of parental direction of the religious upbringing and education of their children in their early and formative years have a high place in our society. ... Thus, a State's interest in universal education ... is not totally free from a balancing process when it impinges on fundamental rights and interests, such as those specifically protected by the Free Exercise Clause of the First Amendment, and the traditional interest of parents with respect to the religious upbringing of their children so long as they, in the words of *Pierce,* "prepare [them] for additional obligations."

 ... [F]or Wisconsin to compel school attendance beyond the eighth grade against a claim that such attendance interferes with the practice of a legitimate religious belief, it must appear either that the State does not deny the free exercise of religious belief by its requirement, or that there is a state interest of sufficient magnitude to override the interest claiming protection under the Free Exercise Clause. Long before there was general acknowledgment of the need for universal formal education, the Religion Clauses had specifically and firmly fixed the right to free exercise of religious beliefs, and buttressing this fundamental right was an equally firm, even if less explicit, prohibition against the establishment of any religion by government. ...

The essence of all that has been said and written on the subject is that only those interests of the highest order and those not otherwise served can overbalance legitimate claims to the free exercise of religion. We can accept it as settled, therefore, that, however strong the State's interest in universal compulsory education, it is by no means absolute to the exclusion of all other interests. E.g. Sherbert v. Verner (1963); McGowan v. Maryland (1961) (separate opinion of Frankfurter, J.); Prince v. Massachusetts (1944).

II

... In evaluating those claims we must be careful to determine whether the Amish religious faith and their mode of life are ... inseparable and interdependent. A way of life, however virtuous and admirable, may not be interposed as a barrier to reasonable state regulation of education if it is based on purely secular considerations; to have the protection of the Religion Clauses, the claims must be rooted in religious belief. Although a determination of what is a "religious" belief or practice entitled to constitutional protection may present a most delicate question, the very concept of ordered liberty precludes allowing every person to make his own standards on matters of conduct in which society as a whole has important interests. Thus, if the Amish asserted their claims because of their subjective evaluation and rejection of the contemporary secular values accepted by the majority, much as Thoreau rejected the social values of his time and isolated himself at Walden Pond, their claims would not rest on a religious basis. Thoreau's choice was philosophical and personal rather than religious, and such belief does not rise to the demands of the Religion Clauses.

... [W]e see that the record in this case abundantly supports the claim that the traditional way of life of the Amish is not merely a matter of personal preference, but one of deep religious conviction, shared by an organized group, and intimately related to daily living. ... Moreover, for the Old Order Amish, religion is not simply a matter of theocratic belief. As the expert witnesses explained, the Old Order Amish religion pervades and determines virtually their entire way of life. ...

... The conclusion is inescapable that secondary schooling, by exposing Amish children to worldly influences in terms of attitudes, goals, and values contrary to beliefs, and by substantially interfering with the religious development of the Amish child and his integration into the way of life of the Amish faith community at the crucial adolescent stage of development, contravenes the basic religious tenets and practice of the Amish faith, both as to the parent and the child. ...

III ...

Wisconsin ... argues that "actions," even though religiously grounded, are outside the protection of the First Amendment. But our decisions have rejected the idea that religiously grounded conduct is always outside the protection of the Free Exercise Clause. It is true that activities of individuals, even when religiously based, are often subject to regulation by the States. ... See, e.g., Gillette v. United States [1971]; Braunfeld v. Brown [1961]; *Prince*; Reynolds v. United States [1878]. But to agree that religiously grounded conduct must often be subject to the broad police power of the State is not to deny that there are areas of conduct protected by the Free Exercise Clause of the First Amendment and thus beyond the power of the State to control. ...

Nor can this case be disposed of on the grounds that Wisconsin's requirement for school attendance to age 16 applies uniformly ... or that it is motivated by legitimate secular concerns. A regulation neutral on its face may, in its application, nonetheless offend the constitutional requirement for governmental neutrality if it unduly burdens the free exercise of religion. *Sherbert.* ...

We turn, then, to the State's broader contention that its interest in its system of compulsory education is so compelling that even the established religious practices of the Amish must give way. ... The State advances two primary arguments. ... [S]ome degree of education is necessary to prepare citizens to participate effectively and intelligently in our open political system. ... Further, education prepares individuals to be self-reliant and self-sufficient participants in society. We accept these propositions.

However, the evidence adduced by the Amish ... is persuasively to the effect that an additional one or two years of formal high school for Amish children in place of their long-established program of informal vocational education would do little to serve those interests. ... It is one thing to say that compulsory education for a year or two beyond the eighth grade may be necessary when its goal is the preparation of the child for life in modern society as the majority live, but it is quite another if the goal of education be viewed as the preparation of the child for life in the separated agrarian community that is the keystone of the Amish faith. See Meyer v. Nebraska [1923].

We must not forget that in the Middle Ages important values of the civilization of the Western World were preserved by members of religious orders who isolated themselves from all worldly influences against great obstacles. There can be no assumption that today's majority is "right" and the Amish and others like them are "wrong." ... The State, however, supports its interest ... because of the possibility that some such children will choose to leave the Amish community, and that if this occurs they will be ill-equipped for life. ... However, on this record, that argument is highly speculative. ...

Insofar as the State's claim rests on the view that a brief additional period of formal education is imperative to enable the Amish to participate effectively and intelligently in our democratic process, it must fall. The Amish alternative to formal secondary school education has enabled them to function effectively in their day-to-day life ... for more than 200 years in this country. In itself this is strong evidence that they are capable of fulfilling the social and political responsibilities of citizenship without compelled attendance beyond the eighth grade at the price of jeopardizing their free exercise of religious belief. ...

IV

Finally, the State, on authority of *Prince*, argues that a decision exempting Amish children from the State's requirement fails to recognize the substantive right of the Amish child to a secondary education, and fails to give due regard to the power of the State as *parens patriae* to extend the benefit of secondary education to children regardless of the wishes of their parents. Taken at its broadest sweep, the Court's language in *Prince* might be read to give support to the State's position. However, the Court was not confronted in *Prince* with a situation comparable to that of the Amish as revealed in this record. ... The Court later took great care to confine *Prince* to a narrow scope in *Sherbert*. This case, of course, is not one in which any harm to the physical or mental health of the child or to the public safety, peace, order, or welfare has been demonstrated or may be properly inferred. The record is to the contrary. ...

Contrary to the suggestion of the dissenting opinion of Mr. Justice Douglas, our holding today in no degree depends on the assertion of the religious interest of the child as contrasted with that of the parents. It is the parents who are subject to prosecution here for failing to cause their children to attend school, and it is their right of free exercise, not that of their children, that must determine Wisconsin's power to impose criminal penalties on the parent. ... The children are not parties to this litigation. ...

Our holding in no way determines the proper resolution of possible competing interests of parents, children, and the State in an appropriate state court proceeding. ...

V ...

Nothing we hold is intended to undermine the general applicability of the State's compulsory school-attendance statutes or to limit the power of the State to promulgate reasonable standards that, while not impairing the free exercise of religion, provide for continuing agricultural vocational education under parental and church guidance by the Old Order Amish or others similarly situated. ...

Affirmed.

Mr. Justice **POWELL** and Mr. Justice **REHNQUIST** took no part in the consideration or decision of this case.

Mr. Justice **STEWART**, with whom Mr. Justice **BRENNAN** joins, concurring. ...

Mr. Justice **WHITE**, with whom Mr. Justice **BRENNAN** and Mr. Justice **STEWART** join, concurring. ...

Mr. Justice **DOUGLAS** dissenting in part.

I

... The Court's analysis assumes that the only interests at stake in the case are those of the Amish parents on the one hand, and those of the State on the other. The difficulty with this approach is that ... the parents are seeking to vindicate not only their own free exercise claims, but also those of their high-school-age children. ...

First, respondents' motion to dismiss in the trial court expressly asserts, not only the religious liberty of the adults, but also that of the children. ... If the parents in this case are allowed a religious exemption, the inevitable effect is to impose the parents' notions of religious duty upon their children. Where the child is mature enough to express potentially conflicting desires, it would be an invasion of the child's rights to permit such an imposition without canvassing his views. ... As the child has no other effective forum, it is in this litigation that his rights should be considered. And, if an Amish child desires to attend high school, and is mature enough to have that desire respected, the State may well be able to override the parents' religiously motivated objections.

Religion is an individual experience. It is not necessary, nor even appropriate, for every Amish child to express his views on the subject in a prosecution of a single adult. Crucial, however, are the views of the child whose parent is the subject of the suit. ...

II ...

These children are "persons" within the meaning of the Bill of Rights. We have so held over and over again. ... On this important and vital matter of education, I think the children should be entitled to be heard. While the parents ... normally speak for the entire family, the education of the child is a matter on which the child will often have decided views. He may want to be a pianist or an astronaut or an oceanographer. To do so he will have to break from the Amish tradition.[1] It is the future of the student, not the future of the parents, that

---

1. A significant number of Amish children do leave the Old Order. Professor Hostetler notes that "[t]he loss of members is very limited in some Amish districts and considerable in others." J. Hostetler, *Amish Society* 226 (1968). In one Pennsylvania church, he observed a defection rate of 30%. ... Rates up to 50% have been reported by others. ... [Footnote by Justice Douglas.]

is imperiled by today's decision. If a parent keeps his child out of school beyond the grade school, then the child will be forever barred from entry into the new and amazing world of diversity that we have today. ...

III ...

The Court rightly rejects the notion that actions, even though religiously grounded, are always outside the protection of the Free Exercise Clause of the First Amendment. In so ruling, the Court departs from the teaching of *Reynolds*. ... What we do today, at least in this respect, opens the way to give organized religion a broader base than it has ever enjoyed; and it even promises that in time *Reynolds* will be overruled.

In another way, however, the Court retreats when in reference to Henry Thoreau it says his "choice was philosophical and personal rather than religious, and such belief does not rise to the demands of the Religion Clauses." That is contrary to what we held in United States v. Seeger [1965] where we were concerned with the meaning of the words "religious training and belief" in the Selective Service Act, which were the basis of many conscientious objector claims. We said:

> Within that phrase would come all sincere religious beliefs which are based upon a power or being, or upon a faith, to which all else is subordinate or upon which all else is ultimately dependent. The test might be stated in these words: A sincere and meaningful belief which occupies in the life of its possessor a place parallel to that filled by the God of those admittedly qualifying for the exemption comes within the statutory definition. ...

Welsh v. United States [1970] was in the same vein. ...

I adhere to these exalted views of "religion" and see no acceptable alternative to them now that we have become a Nation of many religions and sects, representing all of the diversities of the human race. ...

Editors' Notes

(1) **Query**: Chief Justice Burger claimed to have used a *balancing approach* here. What strengths and weaknesses of *balancing* are evident in his opinion? (One should reread Douglas' opinion before trying to answer.) Burger also said that religious liberty was a "fundamental right"? Why then did he not use some form of the "strict scrutiny test"? Or, to return to an oft-repeated question, to what extent is "strict scrutiny" a form of *balancing*?

(2) **Query**: Because the Amish forbid acceptance of insurance benefits—caring for one another, they reason, is a religious duty—some members have refused to pay social security taxes. Respecting this view, Congress in 1965 exempted from the social security tax on the self-employed anyone who is

> a member of a recognized religious sect or division thereof and is an adherent of established tenets or teachings of such sect or division opposed to acceptance of the benefits of any public or private insurance. ... 26 U.S.C. § 1402(g).

Does this exemption constitute a preference for some religions over others? For religion over non-religion?

(3) United States v. Lee (1982) unanimously held that the Amish must pay social security taxes on employers and employees. The Court conceded that the tax conflicted with the religious beliefs of the Amish but ruled that the government's interest in uniform collection of taxes was compelling.

———

"The state may justify an inroad on religious liberty by showing that it is the least restrictive means of achieving some compelling state interest."—Chief Justice BURGER

"Where ... a State has enacted a general statute, the purpose and effect of which is to effectuate the State's secular goals, the Free Exercise Clause does not ... require the State to conform that statute to the dictates of the religious conscience of any group."—Justice Rehnquist.

THOMAS v. REVIEW BOARD

450 U.S. 707, 101 S.Ct. 1425, 67 L.Ed.2d 624 (1981).

Eddie Thomas, a foundry worker in Indiana, was transferred from making steel sheeting to producing gun turrets for tanks. He felt that, as a Jehovah's Witness and a pacifist, he could not engage in such work and requested another transfer. The company refused, and Thomas quit his job. When he applied for unemployment benefits, the state administrative review board ruled that Indiana law did not cover those who left work for personal, even religious reasons. The state supreme court affirmed the ruling and expressed doubts about the religious grounding of Thomas' decision to leave his job. He obtained certiorari from the U.S. Supreme Court.

Mr. Chief Justice **BURGER** delivered the opinion of the Court. ...

II

Only beliefs rooted in religion are protected by the Free Exercise clause, which, by its terms, gives special protection to the exercise of religion. Sherbert v. Verner [1963]; Wisconsin v. Yoder (1972). The determination of what is a "religious" belief or practice is more often than not a difficult and delicate task. ... However, the resolution of that question is not to turn upon a judicial perception of the particular belief or practice in question; religious beliefs need not be acceptable, logical, consistent, or comprehensible to others in order to merit First Amendment protection.

In support of his claim for benefits, Thomas testified:

"Q. And then when it comes to actually producing the tank itself, hammering it out; that you will not do." ...

"A. That's right, that's right when ... I'm daily faced with the knowledge that these are tanks. ... I really could not, you know, conscientiously continue to work with armaments. It would be against all of the
... religious principles that ... I have come to learn. ..."

Based upon this and other testimony, the referee held that Thomas
"quit due to his religious convictions." The Review Board adopted that
finding. ...

The Indiana Supreme Court apparently took a different view of the
record. It concluded that "although the claimant's reasons for quitting
were described as religious, it was unclear what his belief was, and what
the religious basis of his belief was." In that court's view, Thomas had
made a merely "personal philosophical choice rather than a religious
choice." In reaching its conclusion, the Indiana court seems to have
placed considerable reliance on the facts that Thomas was "struggling"
with his beliefs and that he was not able to "articulate" his belief
precisely. It noted, for example, that Thomas admitted before the
referee that he would not object to

working for United States Steel or Inland Steel ... produc[ing] the raw
product necessary for the production of any kind of tank ... [because I]
would not be a direct party to whoever they shipped it to [and] would
not be ... chargeable in ... conscience. ...

The court found this position inconsistent with Thomas' stated opposition to participation in the production of armaments. But, Thomas'
statements reveal no more than that he found work in the roll foundry
sufficiently insulated from producing weapons of war. We see, therefore, that Thomas drew a line, and it is not for us to say that the line he
drew was an unreasonable one. Courts should not undertake to dissect
religious beliefs because the believer admits that he is "struggling" with
his position or because his beliefs are not articulated with the clarity and
precision that a more sophisticated person might employ.

The Indiana court also appears to have given significant weight to
the fact that another Jehovah's Witness had no scruples about working
on tank turrets. ... Intrafaith differences of that kind are not uncommon among followers of a particular creed, and the judicial process is
singularly ill equipped to resolve such differences in relation to the
Religion Clauses. One can, of course, imagine an asserted claim so
bizarre, so clearly nonreligious in motivation, as not to be entitled to
protection under the Free Exercise Clause; but that is not the case here,
and the guarantee of free exercise is not limited to beliefs which are
shared by all of the members of a religious sect. ... [I]t is not within
the judicial function and judicial competence to inquire whether the
petitioner or his fellow worker more correctly perceived the commands of
their common faith. Courts are not arbiters of scriptural interpretation.
... On this record, it is clear that Thomas terminated his employment
for religious reasons.

III

A

More than 30 years ago, the Court held that a person may not be compelled to choose between the exercise of a First Amendment right and participation in an otherwise available public program. A state may not

> exclude individual Catholics, Lutherans, Mohammedans, Baptists, Jews, Methodists, Non-believers, Presbyterians, or the members of any other faith, because of their faith, or lack of it, from receiving the benefits of public welfare legislation. Everson v. Bd. of Educ. (1947).

Later, in *Sherbert,* the Court examined South Carolina's attempt to deny unemployment compensation benefits to a Sabbatarian who declined to work on Saturday. In sustaining her right to receive benefits, the Court held:

> The ruling ... forces her to choose between following the precepts of her religion and forfeiting benefits, on the one hand, and abandoning one of the precepts of her religion in order to accept work, on the other hand. Governmental imposition of such a burden puts the same kind of burden upon the free exercise of religion as would a fine imposed against [her] for her Saturday worship. ...

The respondent Review Board argues, and the Indiana Supreme Court held, that the burden upon religion here is only the indirect consequence of public welfare legislation that the state clearly has authority to enact. ... Indiana requires applicants for unemployment compensation to show that they left work for "good cause in connection with the work." ... A similar argument was made and rejected in *Sherbert,* however. It is true that, as in *Sherbert,* the Indiana law does not *compel* a violation of conscience. But, "this is only the beginning, not the end, of our inquiry." In a variety of ways we have said that "a regulation neutral on its face may, in its application, nonetheless offend the constitutional requirement for governmental neutrality if it unduly burdens the free exercise of religion." *Yoder.*

Here, as in *Sherbert,* the employee was put to a choice between fidelity to religious belief or cessation of work; the coercive impact on Thomas is indistinguishable from *Sherbert.* ... Where the state conditions receipt of an important benefit upon conduct proscribed by a religious faith, or where it denies such a benefit because of conduct mandated by religious belief, thereby putting substantial pressure on an adherent to modify his behavior and to violate his beliefs, a burden upon religion exists. While the compulsion may be indirect, the infringement upon free exercise is nonetheless substantial. ...

B

The mere fact that the petitioner's religious practice is burdened by a governmental program does not mean that an exemption accommodating his practice must be granted. The state may justify an inroad on religious liberty by showing that it is the least restrictive means of achieving some compelling state interest. However, it is still true that "[t]he essence of all that has been said and written on the subject is that only those interests of the highest order can overbalance legitimate claims to the free exercise of religion." *Yoder.*

The purposes urged to sustain the disqualifying provision of the Indiana unemployment compensation scheme are two-fold: (1) to avoid the widespread unemployment and the consequent burden on the fund resulting if people were permitted to leave jobs for "personal" reasons; and (2) to avoid a detailed probing by employers into job applicants' religious beliefs. These are by no means unimportant considerations. When the focus of the inquiry is properly narrowed, however, we must conclude that the interests advanced by the state do not justify the burden placed on free exercise of religion.

There is no evidence in the record to indicate that the number of people who find themselves in the predicament of choosing between benefits and religious beliefs is large enough to create "widespread unemployment," or even to seriously affect unemployment—and no such claim was advanced by the Review Board. Similarly, although detailed inquiry by employers into applicants' religious beliefs is undesirable, there is no evidence in the record to indicate that such inquiries will occur in Indiana, or that they have occurred in any of the states that extend benefits to people in the petitioner's position. Nor is there any reason to believe that the number of people terminating employment for religious reasons will be so great as to motivate employers to make such inquiries.

Neither of the interests advanced is sufficiently compelling to justify the burden upon Thomas' religious liberty. Accordingly, Thomas is entitled to receive benefits unless, as the state contends and the Indiana court held, such payment would violate the Establishment Clause.

IV

The respondent contends that to compel benefit payments to Thomas involves the state in fostering a religious faith. There is, in a sense, a "benefit" to Thomas deriving from his religious beliefs, but this manifests no more than the tension between the two Religious Clauses which the Court resolved in *Sherbert:*

> In holding as we do, plainly we are not fostering the 'establishment' of the Seventh Day Adventist religion in South Carolina, for the extension of unemployment benefits to Sabbatarians in common with Sunday worshippers reflects nothing more than the governmental obligation of neutrality in the face of religious differences, and does not represent that involvement of religious with secular institutions which it is the object of the Establishment Clause to forestall. . . .

Reversed.

Justice **BLACKMUN** joins Parts ... **II** and **III** of the Court's opinion. As to Part **IV** thereof, he concurs in the result.

Justice **REHNQUIST**, dissenting. ...

I

The Court correctly acknowledges that there is a "tension" between the Free Exercise and Establishment Clauses. ... Although the relationship of the two clauses has been the subject of much commentary, the "tension" is of fairly recent vintage, unknown at the time of the framing and adoption of the First Amendment. The causes of the tension, it seems to me, are three-fold. First, the growth of social welfare legislation during the latter part of the 20th century has greatly magnified the potential for conflict between the two clauses, since such legislation touches the individual at so many points in his life. Second, the decision by this Court that the First Amendment was "incorporated" into the Fourteenth Amendment and thereby made applicable against the States, Stromberg v. California (1931); Cantwell v. Connecticut (1940), similarly multiplied the number of instances in which the "tension" might arise. The third, and perhaps most important, cause of the tension is our overly expansive interpretation of *both* clauses. By broadly construing both clauses, the Court has constantly narrowed the channel between the Scylla and Charybdis through which any state or federal action must pass in order to survive constitutional scrutiny.

None of these developments could have been foreseen by those who framed and adopted the First Amendment. ...

II

The decision today illustrates how far astray the Court has gone in interpreting the Free Exercise and Establishment Clauses. ... Although the Court ... recognizes the "tension" between the two clauses, it does little to help resolve that tension or to offer meaningful guidance to other courts which must decide cases like this on a day-by-day basis. Instead, it simply asserts that there is no Establishment Clause violation here and leaves tension between the two Religion Clauses to be resolved on a case-by-case basis. ... I believe that the "tension" is largely of this Court's own making, and would diminish almost to the vanishing point if the clauses were properly interpreted.

Just as it did in *Sherbert*, the Court today reads the Free Exercise Clause more broadly than is warranted. As to the proper interpretation of the Free Exercise Clause, I would accept the decision of Braunfeld v. Brown (1961), and the dissent in *Sherbert*. In *Braunfeld,* we held that Sunday Closing laws do not violate the First Amendment rights of Sabbatarians. Chief Justice Warren explained that the statute did not make unlawful any religious practices of appellants; it simply made the practice of their religious beliefs more expensive. ... Likewise in this case, it cannot be said that the State discriminated against Thomas on the basis of his religious beliefs or that he was denied benefits *because* he was a Jehovah's Witness. Where, as here, a State has enacted a general statute, the purpose and effect of which is to advance the State's secular goals, the Free Exercise Clause does not in my view require the State to conform that statute to the dictates of religious conscience of any group. . . .

The Court's treatment of the Establishment Clause is equally unsatisfying. . . . I would agree that the Establishment Clause, properly interpreted, would not be violated if Indiana voluntarily chose to grant unemployment benefits to those persons who left their jobs for religious reasons. But I also believe that the decision below is inconsistent with many of our prior Establishment Clause cases. Those cases, if faithfully applied, would require us to hold that such voluntary action by a State *did* violate the Establishment Clause.

. . . In *Everson*, the Court stated that the Establishment Clause bespeaks a "government . . . stripped of all power . . . to support, or otherwise assist any or all religions . . .," and no State "can pass laws which aid one religion [or] all religions." In Torcaso v. Watkins (1961), the Court asserted that the government cannot "constitutionally pass laws or impose requirements which aid all religions as against non-believers." And in Sch. Dist. of Abington Township v. Schempp (1963), the Court adopted Justice Rutledge's words in *Everson* that the Establishment Clause forbids "every form of public aid or support for religion." See also Engel v. Vitale (1962).

In recent years the Court has moved away from the mechanistic "no-aid-to-religion" approach to the Establishment Clause and has stated a three-part test to determine the constitutionality of governmental aid to religion. See Lemon v. Kurtzman (1971); Comm. for Public Educ. & Religious Liberty v. Nyquist (1973). First, the statute must serve a secular legislative purpose. Second, it must have a "primary effect" that neither advances nor inhibits religion. And third, the State and its administration must avoid excessive entanglement with religion. Walz v. Tax Comm'n (1970).

It is not surprising that the Court today makes no attempt to apply those principles to the facts of this case. If Indiana were to legislate what the Court today requires—an unemployment compensation law which permitted benefits to be granted to those persons who quit their jobs for religious reasons—the statute would "plainly" violate the Establishment Clause as interpreted in such cases as *Lemon* and *Nyquist*. First, although the unemployment statute as a whole would be enacted to serve a secular legislative purpose, the proviso would clearly serve only a religious purpose. It would grant financial benefits for the sole purpose of accommodating religious beliefs. Second, there can be little doubt that the primary effect on the proviso would be to "advance" religion by facilitating the exercise of religious belief. Third, any statute including such a proviso would surely "entangle" the State in religion. . . . By granting financial benefits to persons solely on the basis of their religious beliefs, the State must necessarily inquire whether the claimant's belief is "religious" and whether it is sincerely held. Otherwise any dissatisfied employee may leave his job without cause and claim that he did so because his own particular beliefs required it.

It is unclear from the Court's opinion whether it has temporarily retreated from its expansive view of the Establishment Clause, or wholly abandoned it. I would welcome the latter. ...

... I believe that Justice Stewart, dissenting in *Schempp*, accurately stated the reach of the Establishment Clause. He explained that the Establishment Clause is limited to "government support of proselytizing activities of religious sects by throwing the weight of secular authorities behind the dissemination of religious tenets." ... Conversely, governmental assistance which does not have the effect of "inducing" religious belief, but instead merely "accommodates" or implements an independent religious choice does not impermissibly involve the government in religious choices. ... I would think that in this case, as in *Sherbert*, had the state voluntarily chosen to pay unemployment compensation benefits to persons who left their jobs for religious reasons, such aid would be constitutionally permissible because it redounds directly to the benefit of the individual. ...

Editors' Notes

(1) **Query:** As in *Yoder* (1972; reprinted above, p. 1187) Burger referred to religious liberty as a "fundamental right"; in *Yoder* he followed a *balancing approach* while here he used "strict scrutiny." What accounts for this difference?

(2) **Query:** What approach(es) to constitutional interpretation did Rehnquist follow? To what extent did he and/or Burger use a *structuralist approach*? What kind of *structuralism*? What does Rehnquist's admission that the Founders could not have seen the changes in American society and constitutional interpretation imply for the value of an *originalist approach*? (One might re-ask this question after reading Justice Scalia's opinion for the Court in the Peyote Case, the very next reading.)

"[W]e cannot afford the luxury of deeming presumptively invalid, as applied to the religious objector, every regulation of conduct that does not protect an interest of the highest order."—Justice SCALIA

"The compelling interest test reflects the First Amendment's mandate of preserving religious liberty to the fullest extent possible in a pluralistic society. ... [To] deem this command a 'luxury' is to denigrate '[t]he very purpose of a Bill of Rights.' "—Justice O'CONNOR

"I do not believe the Founders thought their dearly bought freedom from religious persecution a 'luxury,'

**but an essential element of liberty. ...."—Justice
BLACKMUN**

EMPLOYMENT DIVISION, DEPARTMENT OF HUMAN RE-
SOURCES OF OREGON v. SMITH

494 U.S. 872, 110 S.Ct. 1595, 108 L.Ed.2d 876 (1990).

A private employer fired Alfred Smith and Galen Black, members of the
Native American Church, for using peyote for sacramental purposes at religious ceremonies. Both men then claimed unemployment benefits from
Oregon; the state denied the requests, saying the two had been discharged
for misconduct. They sued in a state court, alleging that the denial had
interfered with their free exercise of religion. Oregon's Supreme Court upheld
their claims. The state obtained certiorari from the U.S. Supreme Court,
which, in *Smith I* (1988), remanded the case for a determination whether use
of peyote for religious purposes violated Oregon's law. On remand, the state
Supreme Court held that relevant statutes did forbid such use and thus
violated the First Amendment's guarantee of free exercise. Oregon again
obtained certiorari.

Justice **SCALIA** delivered the opinion of the Court. ...

II

Respondents' claim for relief rests on our decisions in Sherbert v.
Verner [1963], Thomas v. Review Bd. [1981], and Hobbie v. Unemployment Appeals Comm'n (1987), in which we held that a State could not
condition the availability of unemployment insurance on an individual's
willingness to forgo conduct required by his religion. ...

A

The Free Exercise Clause of the First Amendment, which has been
made applicable to the States by incorporation into the Fourteenth
Amendment ... means, first and foremost, the right to believe and
profess whatever religious doctrine one desires. Thus, the First Amendment obviously excludes all "governmental regulation of religious beliefs
as such." *Sherbert.* The government may not compel affirmation of
religious belief, see Torcaso v. Watkins (1961), punish the expression of
religious doctrines it believes to be false, United States v. Ballard (1944),
impose special disabilities on the basis of religious views or religious
status, see McDaniel v. Paty (1978); Fowler v. Rhode Island (1953); or
lend its power to one or the other side in controversies over religious
authority or dogma, see Presbyterian Church v. Hull Church (1969);
Kedroff v. St. Nicholas Cathedral (1952); Serbian Eastern Orthodox
Diocese v. Milivojevich (1976).

But the "exercise of religion" often involves not only belief and
profession but the performance of (or abstention from) physical acts.
... [A] state would be "prohibiting the free exercise [of religion]" if it
sought to ban such acts or abstentions only when they are engaged in for

religious reasons, or only because of the religious belief that they display. It would doubtless be unconstitutional, for example, to ban the casting of "statues that are to be used for worship purposes," or to prohibit bowing down before a golden calf. . . .

. . . [But w]e have never held that an individual's religious beliefs excuse him from compliance with an otherwise valid law prohibiting conduct that the State is free to regulate. On the contrary, the record of more than a century of our free exercise jurisprudence contradicts that proposition. As described succinctly by Justice Frankfurter in Minersville v. Gobitis (1940): "Conscientious scruples have not, in the course of the long struggle for religious toleration, relieved the individual from obedience to a general law not aimed at the promotion or restriction of religious beliefs. The mere possession of religious convictions . . . does not relieve the citizen from the discharge of political responsibilities." We first had occasion to assert that principle in Reynolds v. United States (1879), where we rejected the claim that criminal laws against polygamy could not be constitutionally applied to those whose religion commanded the practice. "Laws," we said, "are made for the government of actions, and while they cannot interfere with mere religious belief and opinions, they may with practices. . . . Can a man excuse his practices to the contrary because of his religious belief? To permit this would be to make the professed doctrines of religious belief superior to the law of the land, and in effect to permit every citizen to become a law unto himself."

Subsequent decisions have consistently held that the right of free exercise does not relieve an individual of the obligation to comply with a "valid and neutral law of general applicability on the ground that the law proscribes (or prescribes) conduct that his religion prescribes (or proscribes)." United States v. Lee (1982) (Stevens, J., concurring); see *Minersville.* . . .

The only decisions in which we have held that the First Amendment bars application of a neutral, generally applicable law to religiously motivated action have involved not the Free Exercise Clause alone, but the Free Exercise Clause in conjunction with other constitutional protections, such as freedom of speech and of the press, see *Cantwell* . . . ; Murdock v. Penn. (1943) (invalidating a flat tax on solicitation as applied to the dissemination of religious ideas); Follett v. McCormick (1944) (same), or the right of parents, acknowledged in Pierce v. Society of Sisters (1925). To direct the education of their children, see Wisc. v. Yoder (1972). . . . Some of our cases prohibiting compelled expression, decided exclusively upon free speech grounds, have also involved freedom of religion, cf. Wooley v. Maynard (1977) (invalidating compelled display of a license plate slogan that offended individual religious beliefs); West Va. v. Barnette (1943) (invalidating compulsory flag salute statute challenged by religious objectors). . . .

The present case does not present such a hybrid situation. . . . "Our cases do not at their farthest reach support the proposition that a stance of conscientious opposition relieves an objector from any colliding duty fixed by a democratic government." *Gillette.*

B

Respondents argue that ... the claim for a religious exemption must be evaluated under the balancing test set forth in *Sherbert*[:] ... governmental actions that substantially burden a religious practice must be justified by a compelling governmental interest. Applying that test we have, on three occasions, invalidated state unemployment compensation rules that conditioned the availability of benefits upon an applicant's willingness to work under conditions forbidden by his religion. We have never invalidated any governmental action on the basis of the *Sherbert* test except the denial of unemployment compensation. Although we have sometimes purported to apply the *Sherbert* test in contexts other than that, we have always found the test satisfied, see *Lee*; *Gillette.* In recent years we have abstained from applying the *Sherbert* test (outside the unemployment compensation field) at all. In Bowen v. Roy (1986), we declined to apply *Sherbert* analysis to a federal statutory scheme that required benefit applicants and recipients to provide their Social Security numbers. The plaintiffs in that case asserted that it would violate their religious beliefs to obtain and provide a Social Security number for their daughter. We held the statute's application to the plaintiffs valid regardless of whether it was necessary to effectuate a compelling interest. In Lyng v. Northwest Indian Cemetery (1988), we declined to apply *Sherbert* analysis to the Government's logging and road construction activities on lands used for religious purposes by several Native American Tribes, even though it was undisputed that the activities "could have devastating effects on traditional Indian religious practices." In Goldman v. Weinberger (1986), we rejected application of the *Sherbert* test to military dress regulations that forbade the wearing of yarmulkes. In O'Lone v. Estate of Shabazz (1987), we sustained, without mentioning the *Sherbert* test, a prison's refusal to excuse inmates from work requirements to attend worship services.

Even if we were inclined to breathe into *Sherbert* some life beyond the unemployment compensation field, we would not apply it to require exemptions from a generally applicable criminal law. ... Whether or not the decisions are that limited, they at least have nothing to do with an across-the-board criminal prohibition on a particular form of conduct. Although ... we have sometimes used the *Sherbert* test to analyze free exercise challenges to such laws, see *Lee, Gillette,* we have never applied the test to invalidate one. We conclude today that the sounder approach, and the approach in accord with the vast majority of our precedents, is to hold the test inapplicable to such challenges. ... To make an individual's obligation to obey such a law contingent upon the law's coincidence with his religious beliefs, except where the State's interest is "compelling" ... contradicts both constitutional tradition and common sense.

The "compelling government interest" requirement seems benign, because it is familiar. ... But using it as the standard that must be met before the government may accord different treatment on the basis of race, see, e.g., Palmore v. Sidoti (1984), or before the government may regulate the content of speech, see, e.g., Sable Communications v. FCC (1989), is not remotely comparable to using it for the purpose asserted here. What it produces in those other fields—equality of treatment, and an unrestricted flow of contending speech—are constitutional norms; what it would produce here—a private right to ignore generally applicable laws—is a constitutional anomaly.[1]

Nor is it possible to limit the impact of respondents' proposal by requiring a "compelling state interest" only when the conduct prohibited is "central" to the individual's religion. It is no more appropriate for judges to determine the "centrality" of religious beliefs before applying a "compelling interest" test in the free exercise field, than it would be for them to determine the "importance" of ideas before applying the "compelling interest" test in the free speech field. ... Repeatedly and in many different contexts, we have warned that courts must not presume to determine the place of a particular belief in a religion or the plausibility of a religious claim. See, e.g., *Thomas*; Presbyterian Church v. Hull Church; Jones v. Wolf (1979); *Ballard*.

If the "compelling interest" test is to be applied at all, then, it must be applied across the board, to all actions thought to be religiously commanded. Moreover, if "compelling interest" really means what it says (and watering it down here would subvert its rigor in the other fields where it is applied), many laws will not meet the test. Any society adopting such a system would be courting anarchy, but that danger increases in direct proportion to the society's diversity of religious beliefs, and its determination to coerce or suppress none of them. Precisely because "we are a cosmopolitan nation made up of people of almost every conceivable religious preference," *Braunfeld*, and precisely because we value and protect that religious divergence, we cannot afford the luxury of deeming presumptively invalid, as applied to the religious

---

1. Justice O'Connor suggests that "[t]here is nothing talismanic about neutral laws of general applicability," and that all laws burdening religious practices should be subject to compelling-interest scrutiny because "the First Amendment unequivocally makes freedom of religion, like freedom from race discrimination and freedom of speech, a 'constitutional norm,' not an 'anomaly.' " But this comparison with other fields supports, rather than undermines, the conclusion we draw today. Just as we subject to the most exacting scrutiny laws that make classifications based on race, see *Palmore*, or on the content of speech, see *Sable Communications*, so too we strictly scrutinize governmental classifications based on religion, see *McDaniel*; see also *Torcaso*. But we have held that race-neutral laws that have the effect of disproportionately disadvantaging a particular racial group do not thereby become subject to compelling-interest analysis under the Equal Protection Clause, see Washington v. Davis (1976) (police employment examination); and we have held that generally applicable laws unconcerned with regulating speech that have the effect of interfering with speech do not thereby become subject to compelling-interest analysis under the First Amendment, see Citizen Publishing Co. v. United States (1969) (antitrust laws). Our conclusion that generally applicable, religion-neutral laws that have the effect of burdening a particular religious practice need not be justified by a compelling governmental interest is the only approach compatible with these precedents. [Footnote by the Court.]

objector, every regulation of conduct that does not protect an interest of the highest order. The rule respondents favor would open the prospect of constitutionally required religious exemptions from civic obligations of almost every conceivable kind. ...

Values that are protected against government interference through enshrinement in the Bill of Rights are not thereby banished from the political process. Just as a society that believes in the negative protection accorded to the press by the First Amendment is likely to enact laws that affirmatively foster the dissemination of the printed word, so also a society that believes in the negative protection accorded to religious belief can be expected to be solicitous of that value in its legislation as well. It is therefore not surprising that a number of States have made an exception to their drug laws for sacramental peyote use. ... [Justice Scalia cited statutes from Arizona, Colorado, and New Mexico—**Eds.**] But to say that a nondiscriminatory religious-practice exemption is permitted, or even that it is desirable, is not to say that it is constitutionally required. ... It may fairly be said that leaving accommodation to the political process will place at a relative disadvantage those religious practices that are not widely engaged in; but that unavoidable consequence of democratic government must be preferred to a system in which each conscience is a law unto itself or in which judges weight the social importance of all laws against the centrality of all religious beliefs.

Because respondents' ingestion of peyote was prohibited under Oregon law, and because that prohibition is constitutional, Oregon may, consistent with the Free Exercise Clause, deny respondents unemployment compensation when their dismissal results from use of the drug. ...

Justice **O'CONNOR**, with whom Justice **BRENNAN,** Justice **MARSHALL**, and Justice **BLACKMUN** join as to Parts **I** and **II**, concurring in the judgment. ... *

II

The Court today extracts from our long history of free exercise precedents the single categorical rule that "if prohibiting the exercise of religion ... is ... merely the incidental effect of a generally applicable and otherwise valid provision, the First Amendment has not been offended." Indeed, the Court holds that where the law is a generally applicable criminal prohibition, our usual free exercise jurisprudence does not even apply. To reach this sweeping result, however, the Court must not only give a strained reading of the First Amendment but must also disregard our consistent application of free exercise doctrine to cases involving generally applicable regulations that burden religious conduct.

---

* Although Justice Brennan, Justice Marshall, and Justice Blackmun join Parts I and II of this opinion, they do not concur in the judgment. [Footnote by Justice O'Connor.]

A

[T]he "free exercise" of religion often, if not invariably, requires the performance of (or abstention from) certain acts. "[B]elief and action cannot be neatly confined in logic-tight compartments." *Yoder*. Because the First Amendment does not distinguish between religious belief and religious conduct, conduct motivated by sincere religious belief, like the belief itself, must therefore be at least presumptively protected by the Free Exercise Clause.

The Court today, however, interprets the Clause to permit the government to prohibit, without justification, conduct mandated by an individual's religious beliefs, so long as that prohibition is generally applicable. But a law that prohibits certain conduct—conduct that happens to be an act of worship for someone—manifestly does prohibit that person's free exercise of his religion. ... The Court responds that generally applicable laws are "one large step" removed from laws aimed at specific religious practices. The First Amendment, however, does not distinguish between laws that are generally applicable and laws that target particular religious practices. ... Our free exercise cases have all concerned generally applicable laws that had the effect of significantly burdening a religious practice. ...

To say that a person's right to free exercise has been burdened, of course, does not mean that he has an absolute right to engage in the conduct. ... [W]e have recognized that the freedom to act, unlike the freedom to believe, cannot be absolute. See, e.g., *Cantwell*; *Reynolds*. Instead, we have respected both the First Amendment's express textual mandate and the governmental interest in regulation of conduct by requiring the Government to justify any substantial burden on religiously motivated conduct by a compelling state interest and by means narrowly tailored to achieve that interest. The compelling interest test effectuates the First Amendment's command that religious liberty is an independent liberty, that it occupies a preferred position, and that the Court will not permit encroachments upon this liberty, whether direct or indirect, unless required by clear and compelling governmental interests "of the highest order," *Yoder*. ...

The Court attempts to support its narrow reading of the Clause by claiming that "[w]e have never held that an individual's religious beliefs excuse him from compliance with an otherwise valid law prohibiting conduct that the State is free to regulate." But as the Court later notes, as it must, in cases such as *Cantwell* and *Yoder* we have in fact interpreted the Free Exercise Clause to forbid application of a generally applicable prohibition to religiously motivated conduct. Indeed, in *Yoder* we expressly rejected the interpretation the Court now adopts:

> "... [T]o agree that religiously grounded conduct must often be subject to the broad police power of the State is not to deny that there are areas of conduct protected by the Free Exercise Clause of the First Amendment and thus beyond the power of the State to control, *even under regulations of general applicability*." ...

"... A regulation neutral on its face may, in its application, nonetheless offend the constitutional requirement for government neutrality if it unduly burdens the free exercise of religion." (Emphasis added; citations omitted.)

The Court endeavors to escape from our decisions in *Cantwell* and *Yoder* by labeling them "hybrid" decisions, but there is no denying that both cases expressly relied on the Free Exercise Clause, and that we have consistently regarded those cases as part of the mainstream of our free exercise jurisprudence. Moreover, in each of the other cases cited by the Court to support its categorical rule, we rejected the particular constitutional claims before us only after carefully weighing the competing interests. That we rejected the free exercise claims in those cases hardly calls into question the applicability of First Amendment doctrine in the first place. ...

B ...

... A State that makes criminal an individual's religiously motivated conduct burdens that individual's free exercise of religion in the severest manner possible, for it "results in the choice to the individual of either abandoning his religious principle or facing criminal prosecution." *Braunfeld*. I would have thought it beyond argument that such laws implicate free exercise concerns. ...

Legislatures, of course, have always been "left free to reach actions which were in violation of social duties or subversive of good order." *Reynolds*; see also *Yoder*; *Braunfeld*. Yet because of the close relationship between conduct and religious belief, "[i]n every case the power to regulate must be so exercised as not, in attaining a permissible end, unduly to infringe the protected freedom." *Cantwell*. Once ... a government regulation or criminal prohibition burdens the free exercise of religion, we have consistently asked the Government to demonstrate that unbending application of its regulation to the religious objector "is essential to accomplish an overriding governmental interest," *Lee*, or represents "the least restrictive means of achieving some compelling state interest," *Thomas*. ... Even if, as an empirical matter, a government's criminal laws might usually serve a compelling interest in health, safety, or public order, the First Amendment at least requires a case-by-case determination of the question, sensitive to the facts of each particular claim. ... [W]e cannot assume, merely because a law carries criminal sanctions and is generally applicable, that the First Amendment never requires the State to grant a limited exemption for religiously motivated conduct.

Moreover, we have not "rejected" or "declined to apply" the compelling interest test in our recent cases. Recent cases have instead affirmed that test as a fundamental part of our First Amendment doctrine. ... The cases cited by the Court signal no retreat from our consistent adherence to the compelling interest test. In both *Roy* and *Lyng*, for example, we expressly distinguished *Sherbert* on the ground that the First Amendment does not "require the Government *itself* to behave in ways that the individual believes will further his or her spiritual development. ...." This distinction makes sense because "the Free Exercise Clause is written in terms of what the government cannot do to the individual, not in terms of what the individual can exact from the government." *Sherbert* (Douglas, J., concurring). ...

Similarly, the other cases cited by the Court for the proposition that we have rejected application of the *Sherbert* test outside the unemployment compensation field, are distinguishable because they arose in the narrow, specialized contexts in which we have not traditionally required the government to justify a burden on religious conduct by articulating a compelling interest. See *Goldman* ("Our review of military regulations challenged on First Amendment grounds is far more deferential than constitutional review of similar laws or regulations designed for civilian society"); O'Lone v. Estate of Shabazz (1987) ("[P]rison regulations alleged to infringe constitutional rights are judged under a 'reasonableness' test less restrictive than that ordinarily applied to allege infringements of fundamental constitutional rights"). That we did not apply the compelling interest test in these cases says nothing about whether the test should continue to apply in paradigm free exercise cases such as the one presented here.

The Court today gives no convincing reason to depart from settled First Amendment jurisprudence. There is nothing talismanic about neutral laws of general applicability or general criminal prohibitions, for laws neutral toward religion can coerce a person to violate his religious conscience or intrude upon his religious duties just as effectively as laws aimed at religion. Although the Court suggests that the compelling interest test, as applied to generally applicable laws, would result in a "constitutional anomaly," the First Amendment unequivocally makes freedom of religion, like freedom from race discrimination and freedom of speech, a "constitutional nor[m]," not an "anomaly." ... As the language of the Clause itself makes clear, an individual's free exercise of religion is a preferred constitutional activity. A law that makes criminal such an activity therefore triggers constitutional concern—and heightened judicial scrutiny—even if it does not target the particular religious conduct at issue. Our free speech cases similarly recognize that neutral regulations that affect free speech values are subject to a balancing, rather than categorical, approach. ...

Finally, the Court today suggests that the disfavoring of minority religions is an "unavoidable consequence" under our system of government and that accommodation of such religions must be left to the political process. In my view, however, the First Amendment was enacted precisely to protect the rights of those whose religious practices are not shared by the majority and may be viewed with hostility. The history of our free exercise doctrine amply demonstrates the harsh impact majoritarian rule has had on unpopular or emerging religious groups such as the Jehovah's Witnesses and the Amish. Indeed, the words of Justice Jackson in West Va. v. Barnette (overruling Minersville School District v. Gobitis [1940]) are apt:

> "The very purpose of a Bill of Rights was to withdraw certain subjects from the vicissitudes of political controversy, to place them beyond the reach of majorities and officials and to establish them as legal principles to be applied by the courts. One's right to life, liberty, and property, to free speech, a free press, freedom of worship and assembly, and other fundamental rights may not be submitted to vote; they depend on the outcome of no elections."

The compelling interest test reflects the First Amendment's mandate of preserving religious liberty to the fullest extent possible in a pluralistic society. For the Court to deem this command a "luxury" is to denigrate "[t]he very purpose of a Bill of Rights."

III

The Court's holding today not only misreads settled First Amendment precedent; it appears to be unnecessary to this case. I would reach the same result applying our established free exercise jurisprudence. . . . [Justice O'Connor went on to argue that drug abuse was a grave problem and the state had a compelling interest in curbing trafficking in such substances.—**Eds.**]

Justice **BLACKMUN**, with whom Justice **BRENNAN** and Justice **MARSHALL** join, dissenting.

This Court over the years painstakingly has developed a consistent and exacting standard to test the constitutionality of a state statute that burdens the free exercise of religion. Such a statute may stand only if the law in general, and the State's refusal to allow a religious exemption in particular, are justified by a compelling interest that cannot be served by less restrictive means.

. . . I thought this was a settled and inviolate principle of this Court's First Amendment jurisprudence. The majority, however, perfunctorily dismisses it as a "constitutional anomaly." . . . [T]he majority is able to arrive at this view only by mischaracterizing this Court's precedents. The Court discards leading free exercise cases such as *Cantwell* and *Yoder*, as "hybrid." The Court views traditional free exercise analysis as somehow inapplicable to criminal prohibitions (as opposed to conditions on the receipt of benefits), and to state laws of general applicability (as opposed, presumably, to laws that expressly single out religious practices). . . . In short, it effectuates a wholesale overturning of settled law. . . .

This distorted view of our precedents leads the majority to conclude that strict scrutiny of a state law burdening the free exercise of religion is a "luxury" . . . and that the repression of minority religions is an "unavoidable consequence of democratic government." I do not believe the Founders thought their dearly bought freedom from religious persecution a "luxury," but an essential element of liberty—and they could not have thought religious intolerance "unavoidable," for they drafted the Religion Clauses precisely in order to avoid that intolerance. ...

I

... It is not the State's broad interest in fighting the critical "war on drugs" that must be weighed against respondents' claim, but the State's narrow interest in refusing to make an exception for the religious, ceremonial use of peyote. ... Failure to reduce the competing interests to the same plane of generality tends to distort the weighing process in the State's favor. See ... [Roscoe] Pound, A Survey of Social Interests, 57 *Harv.L.Rev.* 1, 2 (1943) ("When it comes to weighing or valuing claims or demands with respect to other claims or demands, we must be careful to compare them on the same plane ... [or else] we may decide the question in advance in our very way of putting it"). ...

The State's interest in enforcing its prohibition, in order to be sufficiently compelling to outweigh a free exercise claim, cannot be merely abstract or symbolic. The State cannot plausibly assert that unbending application of a criminal prohibition is essential to fulfill any compelling interest, if it does not, in fact, attempt to enforce that prohibition. In this case, the State actually has not evinced any concrete interest in enforcing its drug laws against religious users of peyote. Oregon has never sought to prosecute respondents, and does not claim that it has made significant enforcement efforts against other religious users of peyote. The State's asserted interest thus amounts only to the symbolic preservation of an unenforced prohibition. But a government interest in "symbolism, even symbolism for so worthy a cause as the abolition of unlawful drugs," (Treasury Employees v. Von Raab (1989) Scalia, J., dissenting), cannot suffice to abrogate the constitutional rights of individuals.

Similarly, this Court's prior decisions have not allowed a government to rely on mere speculation about potential harms, but have demanded evidentiary support for a refusal to allow a religious exception. ... In this case, the State's justification for refusing to recognize an exception to its criminal laws for religious peyote use is entirely speculative. The State ... [offers] no evidence that the religious use of peyote has ever harmed anyone. The factual findings of other courts cast doubt on the State's assumption that religious use of peyote is harmful. ... The Federal Government, which created the classifications of unlawful drugs from which Oregon's drug laws are derived, apparently does not find peyote so dangerous as to preclude an exemption for religious use.

The carefully circumscribed ritual context in which respondents used peyote is far removed from the irresponsible and unrestricted recreational use of unlawful drugs.[1] The Native American Church's

---

1. In this respect, respondents' use of peyote seems closely analogous to the sacramental use of wine by the Roman Catholic Church. During Prohibition, the Federal Government exempted such use of wine from its general ban on possession and use of alcohol.

internal restrictions on, and supervision of, its members' use of peyote substantially obviate the State's health and safety concerns. . . . The State also seeks to support its refusal to make an exception for religious use of peyote by invoking its interest in abolishing drug trafficking. There is, however, practically no illegal traffic in peyote. . . .

Finally, the State argues that granting an exception for religious peyote use would erode its interest in the uniform, fair, and certain enforcement of its drug laws. The State fears that, if it grants an exemption for religious peyote use, a flood of other claims to religious exemptions will follow. . . . The State's apprehension of a flood of other religious claims is purely speculative. Almost half the States, and the Federal Government, have maintained an exemption for religious peyote use for many years, and apparently have not found themselves over-whelmed by claims to other religious exemptions. Allowing an exemption for religious peyote use would not necessarily oblige the State to grant a similar exemption to other religious groups. . . . Though the State must treat all religions equally . . . this obligation is fulfilled by the uniform application of the "compelling interest" test to all free exercise claims, not by reaching uniform results as to all claims. A showing that religious peyote use does not unduly interfere with the State's interests . . . does not mean that an exemption limited to peyote use is tanta-mount to an establishment of religion. . . .

II

Finally . . . I do not think this means that the courts must turn a blind eye to the severe impact of a State's restrictions on the adherents of a minority religion. . . . Respondents believe, and their sincerity has never been at issue, that the peyote plant embodies their deity, and eating it is an act of worship and communion. Without peyote, they could not enact the essential ritual of their religion. . . .

. . . This potentially devastating impact must be viewed in light of the federal policy—reached in reaction to many years of religious perse-cution and intolerance—of protecting the religious freedom of Native Americans. See American Indian Religious Freedom Act. . . . Congress recognized that certain substances, such as peyote, "have religious significance because they are sacred, they have power, they heal, they are necessary to the exercise of the rites of the religion, they are necessary to the cultural integrity of the tribe, and, therefore, religious survival." H. R. Rep. No. 95–1308, p. 2 (1978). . . .

Editors' Notes

(1) **Query:** *Smith* intermeshed fascinating questions of HOW and WHAT. Scalia seemed to be using a *doctrinal approach* to constitutional interpretation, yet the dissenters accused him of distorting the Court's jurisprudence. Who

---

However compelling the Government's then general interest in prohibiting the use of alcohol may have been, it could not plausibly have asserted an interest sufficiently compelling to outweigh Catholics' right to take communion. [Footnote by Justice Black-mun.]

had the better of the *doctrinal* argument? What other approaches did Scalia follow? To what extent was he faithful to the constitutional text? Did his approach or that of O'Connor and/or Blackmun display greater fidelity to the document?

(2) **Query:** After quoting from *Gobitis*, the First Flag Salute Case (1940; reprinted above, p. 1165), Scalia said:

> Values that are protected against government interference through enshrinement in the Bill of Rights are not thereby banished from the political process. ... It may fairly be said that leaving accommodation to the political process will place at a relative disadvantage those religious practices that are not widely engaged in; but that unavoidable consequence of democratic government must be preferred to a system in which each conscience is a law unto itself or in which judges weight the social importance of all laws against the centrality of all religious beliefs.

West Va. v. Barnette (1943; reprinted above, p. 1174), of course, overruled *Gobitis*. As O'Connor and Blackmun noted, in *Barnette* Jackson said for the Court—over eloquent objections from Frankfurter—that "The very purpose of a Bill of Rights was to withdraw certain subjects from the vicissitudes of political controversy, to place them beyond the reach of majorities and officials and to establish them as legal principles to be applied by the courts."

Consider the constitutional text: Is it the command of the Bill of Rights to remove "certain subjects from the vicissitudes of political controversy"? Consider the broader constitution: Which statement, Jackson's or Scalia's, more accurately describes the way the American constitutional system has operated? What are the implications of any answer to this question for relationships between the constitutional text and the larger constitution?

(3) **Query:** To what extent did Scalia rely on democratic theory? (To the extent that he was, he was following a *philosophical approach*.) Was he relying on democratic theory so heavily as to read it into "the Constitution"? Did he do so to the exclusion of constitutionalism? Can one legitimately lodge against Scalia the criticism that Douglas levied against Frankfurter, that he confused the British and American constitutional systems?

(4) **Query:** Scalia, like all of the justices, was quite familiar with the earlier controversy over the flag salute. Thus his quoting from *Gobitis* and ignoring *Barnette* raised interesting questions: Why did he cite Frankfurter's opinion in *Gobitis* and why did a majority of his colleagues go along? Before answering, reconsider Chapter 2's discussion of stare decisis. Was Scalia trying to convey a not very subtle message?

(5) **Query:** "It is remarkable," Michael W. McConnell has said, "Free Exercise Revisionism and the *Smith* Decision," 57 *U.Chi.L.Rev.* 1109, 1117 (1990), that Scalia, the arch advocate of an *originalist approach* to constitutional interpretation, offers not a shred of historical evidence to support his argument. Why not? Does that failure say anything about the worth of an *originalist approach*?

Similarly, Bernard Roberts, "The Common Law Sovereignty of Religious Lawfinders and the Free Exercise Clause," 101 *Yale L.J.* 211, 212 (1991), has noted that Scalia, who in Michael H. v. Gerald D. (1989; reprinted above, p.

158) and Lee v. Weisman (1992; reprinted above, p. 167) spoke so eloquently about the important role of tradition in constitutional interpretation, made no mention of the great tradition surrounding the First Amendment's guarantee of religious freedom. Why not?

(6) **Query:** To what extent did O'Connor and Blackmun implicitly rely on constitutionalism and thus read that normative theory into the "constitution"? In their separate opinions, O'Connor and Blackmun urged the Court to use a version of strict scrutiny/compelling interest to judge the validity of laws that touch on the exercise of religion. They treated this test as a form of "balancing." We repeat an oft-asked question: To what extent were they correct? Is a *balancing approach* compatible with constitutionalism?

(7) Three years after *Smith*, but before passage of the Religious Freedom Restoration Act of 1993 (reprinted immediately below), Church of Lukumi v. Hialeah (1993) offered the Court an opportunity to rethink its language in *Smith*. Followers of Lukumi sacrificed animals in their religious rituals and attacked the validity of ordinances that restricted killing animals even for religious purposes. All of the justices thought that, as applied against this sect, the ordinances were unconstitutional. The justices could agree, however, only on part of the reasoning behind such a result and produced four separate opinions. Justice Kennedy wrote an opinion that, on some points, commanded a majority. He made scant mention of *Smith*, and, in a section endorsed by only three other justices, wrote that,

> if the object of the law is to infringe upon or restrict practices because of their religious motivation, the law is not neutral, see *Smith*, and it is invalid unless justified by a compelling interest and is narrowly tailored to advance that interest.

A paragraph later, Kennedy added that, although to be valid a law restricting religious practice must be neutral, "Facial neutrality is not determinative." Scalia wrote a brief concurrence, saying the ordinances were not generally applicable but applied specifically to religious activity and thus were not neutral.

"Government may substantially burden a person's exercise of religion only if it demonstrates that application of the burden to the person——(1) is in furtherance of a compelling governmental interest; and (2) is the least restrictive means of furthering that compelling governmental interest."—Pub. L. 103–141

THE RELIGIOUS FREEDOM RESTORATION ACT OF 1993
42 U.S. Code 2000bb–2000bb4, 107 Stat. 1488, Pub. Law. 103–141.

Insofar as *Smith* presented a clash between democratic theory and constitutionalism, it is ironic that the protection of the constitutionalist value of religious liberty would come not from the institution most usually associated with constitutionalism, an independent judiciary, but from popularly elected politicians. Reacting against *Smith*, several states, including Oregon, quickly decriminalized religious use of peyote by Native Americans. Then Congress offered its own capacious interpretation of the First Amendment by passing the Religious Freedom Restoration Act of 1993, which President William J. Clinton signed into law.

Sec. 2. CONGRESSIONAL FINDINGS AND DECLARATION OF PURPOSES

(a) *FINDINGS.*——The Congress finds that——

(1) the framers of the Constitution, recognizing free exercise of religion as an unalienable right, secured its protection in the First Amendment to the Constitution;

(2) laws "neutral" toward religion may burden religious exercise as surely as laws intended to interfere with religious exercise;

(3) governments should not substantially burden religious exercise without compelling justification;

(4) in Employment Division v. Smith (1990) the Supreme Court virtually eliminated the requirement that the government justify burdens on religious exercise imposed by laws neutral toward religion; and

(5) the compelling interest test as set forth in prior Federal court rulings is a workable test for striking sensible balances between religious liberty and competing prior governmental interests.

(b) *PURPOSES.*——The purposes of this Act are——

(1) to restore the compelling interest test as set forth in Sherbert v. Verner (1963) and Wisconsin v Yoder (1972) and to guarantee its application in all cases where free exercise of religion is substantially burdened; and

(2) to provide a claim or defense to persons whose religious exercise is substantially burdened by government.

Sec. 3. FREE EXERCISE OF RELIGION PROTECTED.

(a) *IN GENERAL.*——Government shall not substantially burden a person's exercise of religion, even if the burden results from a rule of general applicability, except as provided in subsection (b).

(b) *EXCEPTION.*——Government may substantially burden a person's exercise of religion only if it demonstrates that the burden to the person——

"(1) is in furtherance of a compelling governmental interest"; and

"(2) is the least restrictive means of furthering that compelling governmental interest."

(c) *JUDICIAL RELIEF.*——A person whose religious exercise has been burdened in violation of this section may assert that violation as a claim or defense in a judicial proceeding and obtain appropriate relief against a government. Standing to assert a claim or defense under this section shall be governed by the general rules of standing under article III of the Constitution. ...

Sec. 5. DEFINITIONS.

As used in this Act——

(1) the term "government" includes a branch, department, agency, instrumentality, and official (or other person acting under color of law) of the United States, a State, or a subdivision of a State ...

(3) the term "demonstrates" means meets the burdens of going forward with the evidence and of persuasion; and

(4) the term "exercise of religion" means the exercise of religion under the First Amendment to the Constitution.

Sec. 6. APPLICABILITY.

(a) *IN GENERAL.*——This Act applies to all Federal and State law, and the implementation of that law, whether statutory or otherwise, and whether adopted before or after the enactment of this Act.

(b) *RULE OF CONSTRUCTION.*——Federal statutory law adopted after the date of enactment of this Act is subject to this Act unless such law explicitly excludes such application by reference to this Act.

(c) *RELIGIOUS BELIEF UNAFFECTED.*——Nothing in this Act shall be construed to authorize any government to burden any religious belief.

Sec. 7. ESTABLISHMENT CLAUSE UNAFFECTED.

Nothing in this Act shall be construed to affect, interpret, or in any way address that portion of the First Amendment prohibiting laws respecting the establishment of religion. ...

Editors' Notes

(1) **Query:** The Religious Freedom Act is sweeping in its coverage. But what specifically, if anything, does it tell federal judges to do? State judges? Does it merely announce congressional and presidential endorsement of the strict scrutiny/compelling interest test? Does it also instruct judges, state and federal, to interpret federal statutes as respecting that test? Does it define "the Constitution"? Does it try require judges, state and federal, to interpret the constitutional text in a particular way?

(2) **Query:** To the extent the answer to the last question is yes, the Act raises interesting questions of WHO shall interpret. Does such a congressional declaration bind federal judges when considering the validity of a federal statute? If Congress can legitimately instruct judges to hold its laws to a tougher test than the U.S. Supreme Court believes appropriate, can Congress also legitimately instruct judges to hold federal statutes to a weaker test? If not, why not?

(3) **Query:** Query 2 leads back to the "ratchet theory" expounded in Katzenbach v. Morgan (1966; reprinted above, p. 327). In essence, this theory holds that, because § 5 of the Fourteenth Amendment grants Congress "power to enforce, by appropriate legislation, the provisions" of the rest of the amendment, Congress can add to but not subtract from the rights of individuals the Supreme Court has interpreted the amendment to protect. Now: given that the First Amendment applies to the states through the Fourteenth Amendment, does Congress have authority to instruct judges, state and federal, on what test to apply where *state* legislation is being challenged as violating religious freedom?

CONSCIENTIOUS OBJECTION

Compulsory military service presents the most dramatic clash between claims of Caesar and God. Despite the First Amendment's bold proclamation, the United States was slow to recognize claims of conscience when pitted against perceptions of national security. During the early years, it was the states, not bound by the First Amendment, who insisted on the primacy of Caesar's call to join the militia. The first national draft came during the Civil War, and Congress showed itself equally insensitive. One should note that the basic authority of Congress to raise an army by conscription was controversial. On his deathbed in 1864, Chief Justice Roger Brooke Taney wrote an unpublished opinion denying such authority. And the first ruling by the Supreme Court did not come until 1918, in the Selective Draft Law Cases. The opinion stated a conclusion rather than reasoned toward a reconciliation of Article I's grant of authority "to raise and support armies" and the Thirteenth Amendment's prohibition of "involuntary servitude."

During World War I, the draft act exempted any member of a "well-recognized religious sect or organization [then] organized and existing and whose existing creed or principles [forbade] its members to participate in war in any form. ..." The Secretary of War interpreted the statute to include "personal scruples against war," but the history of the administration of the act was often ungenerous. Between the two world wars, over eloquent dissents by Holmes, Hughes, and Stone, the Supreme Court several times interpreted the naturalization act to deny citizenship to aliens who were conscientious objectors.[1] In 1946, however, the Court reinterpreted this statute to eliminate the ban.[2]

During World War II, Congress again allowed conscientious exemption from the draft, dropping the requirement that an objector had to belong to a recognized religion. It was sufficient that his objection be based on "religious training and belief." In 1948, Congress further

---

1. United States v. Schwimmer (1929); United States v. Macintosh (1931); and United States v. Bland (1931).

2. Girouard v. United States (1946).

modified the law to define "religious training and belief" as "an individual's belief in a relation to a Supreme Being involving duties superior to those arising from any human relation, but [not including] essentially political, sociological, or philosophical views or a merely personal moral code." During the war in Vietnam, the Court avoided the constitutional question whether Congress had violated the First Amendment by giving preference to religion over non-religion by interpreting the statute to include a "sincere and meaningful belief which occupies in the life of its possessor a place parallel to that filled by the God of" theologically motivated objectors.[3] In vain, Justice Harlan protested that the Court had "performed a lobotomy and completely transformed the statute. . . ."

The Court's surgery could not avoid all constitutional problems. Some religious sects, such as the Quakers, oppose war in any form. Roman Catholicism, however, teaches that citizens may participate in wars, but only in "just wars," raising yet another possibility of a complex clash among basic values: On the one hand, the fundamental rights to free exercise of religion and freedom from governmental preference among religions, and on the other hand, the fundamental necessity of national security.[4]

"The incidental burdens felt by persons in petitioners' position are strictly justified by substantial governmental interests that relate directly to the very impacts questioned."—Justice MARSHALL

"The implied First Amendment right of 'conscience' is certainly as high as the 'right of association'. . . ."— Justice DOUGLAS

GILLETTE v. UNITED STATES; NEGRE v. LARSEN
401 U.S. 437, 91 S.Ct. 828, 28 L.Ed.2d 168 (1971).

Sec. 6(j) of the Selective Service Act of 1967 provided:

Nothing contained in this title . . . shall be construed to require any person to be subject to combatant training and service in the armed forces . . . who, by reasons of religious training and belief, is conscientiously opposed to participation in war in any form.

---

3. United States v. Seeger (1965); Welsh v. United States (1970).

4. Among the more useful studies of the problems of conscientious objection are: James Finn, ed., *A Conflict of Loyalties: The Case for Selective Conscientious Objection* (New York: Pegasus, 1968); Lillian Schlissel, *Conscience in America: A Documentary History of Conscientious Objection in America* (New York: Dutton, 1968); Paul Ramsey, *The Just War* (New York: Scribner's, 1968); John A. Rohr, *Prophets without Honor: Public Policy and the Selective Conscientious Objector* (Nashville: Abington Press, 1974). It is no accident that three of these four books were published during the peak of the war in Vietnam.

Guy Gillette claimed a draft exemption under § 6(j) not because he was "opposed to participation in war in any form," but because he was opposed to participation in wars, such as that in Vietnam, that violated his conscience. (United States v. Seeger [1965] had interpreted "religious training and belief" to include general considerations of conscience not connected to formal religion.) His draft board denied the exemption, and Gillette refused to report for induction. He was convicted in a U.S. district court for this refusal, and the court of appeals affirmed. He sought and obtained certiorari from the U.S. Supreme Court.

Louis Negre, a Catholic, claimed status as a conscientious objector after his induction in the army, basing his claim on his religion's tenet that to fight in an unjust war is to participate in murder. The Army rejected his application, and he began habeas corpus proceedings in a U.S. district court. The judge denied his petition, and the court of appeals affirmed. The Supreme Court granted certiorari and consolidated Negre's case with Gillette's.

Mr. Justice **MARSHALL** delivered the opinion of the Court. ...

... Petitioners contend that Congress interferes with free exercise of religion by failing to relieve objectors to a particular war from military service, when the objection is religious or conscientious in nature. While the two religious clauses—pertaining to "free exercise" and "establishment" of religion—overlap and interact in many ways, it is best to focus first on petitioners' other contention, that § 6(j) is a law respecting the establishment of religion. For despite free exercise overtones, the gist of the constitutional complaint is that § 6(j) impermissibly discriminates among types of religious belief and affiliation.

... [P]etitioners ask how their claims to relief from military service can be permitted to fail, while other "religious" claims are upheld by the Act. It is a fact that § 6(j), properly construed, has this effect. Yet we cannot conclude in mechanical fashion, or at all, that the section works an establishment of religion.

An attack founded on disparate treatment of "religious" claims invokes what is perhaps the central purpose of the Establishment Clause—the purpose of ensuring governmental neutrality in matters of religion. See Epperson v. Arkansas (1968); Everson v. Bd. of Educ. (1947). ... And as a general matter it is surely true that the Establishment Clause prohibits government from abandoning secular purposes in order to put an imprimatur on one religion, or on religion as such, or to favor the adherents of any sect or religious organization. See Engel v. Vitale (1962); Torcaso v. Watkins (1961). The metaphor of a "wall" or impassable barrier between Church and State, taken too literally, may mislead constitutional analysis, see Walz v. Tax Comm'n [1970]; Zorach v. Clauson (1952), but the Establishment Clause stands at least for the proposition that when Government activities touch on the religious sphere, they must be secular in purpose, evenhanded in operation, and neutral in primary impact. Abington Sch. Dist. v. Schempp [1963].

A

The critical weakness of petitioners' establishment claim arises from the fact that § 6(j), on its face, simply does not discriminate on the basis of religious affiliation or religious belief, apart of course from beliefs concerning war. The section says that anyone who is conscientiously opposed to all war shall be relieved of military service. The specified objection must have a grounding in "religious training and belief," but no particular sectarian affiliation or theological position is required. ... Congress has framed the conscientious objector exemption in broad terms compatible with "its long-established policy of not picking and choosing among religious beliefs." United States v. Seeger [1965]. ... [Sec.] 6(j) does not single out any religious organization or religious creed for special treatment. ...

Properly phrased, petitioners' contention is that the special statutory status accorded conscientious objection to all war, but not objection to a particular war, works a de facto discrimination among religions. ... [T]his contention of de facto religious discrimination, rendering § 6(j) fatally underinclusive, cannot simply be brushed aside. The question of governmental neutrality is not concluded by the observation that § 6(j) on its face makes no discrimination between religions, for the Establishment Clause forbids subtle departures from neutrality, "religious gerrymanders," as well as obvious abuses. Still a claimant alleging "gerrymander" must be able to show the absence of a neutral, secular basis for the lines government has drawn. For the reasons that follow, we believe that petitioners have failed to make the requisite showing with respect to § 6(j).

Section 6(j) serves a number of valid purposes having nothing to do with a design to foster or favor any sect, religion, or cluster of religions. There are considerations of a pragmatic nature, such as the hopelessness of converting a sincere conscientious objector into an effective fighting man, but no doubt the section reflects as well the view that "in the forum of conscience, duty to a moral power higher than the State has always been maintained." United States v. Macintosh [1931] (Hughes, C.J., dissenting). See Seeger. We have noted that the legislative materials show congressional concern for the hard choice that conscription would impose on conscientious objectors to war, as well as respect for the value of conscientious action and for the principle of supremacy of conscience.

... The point is that these affirmative purposes are neutral in the sense of the Establishment Clause. Quite apart from the question whether the Free Exercise Clause might require some sort of exemption, it is hardly impermissible for Congress to attempt to accommodate free exercise values, in line with "our happy tradition" of "avoiding unnecessary clashes with the dictates of conscience." Macintosh. "Neutrality" in matters of religion is not inconsistent with "benevolence" by way of exemptions from onerous duties, Walz, so long as an exemption is tailored broadly enough that it reflects valid secular purposes. In the draft area for 30 years the exempting provision has focused on individual conscientious belief, not on sectarian affiliation. The relevant individual belief is simply objection to all war, not adherence to any extraneous theological viewpoint. And while the objection must have roots in conscience and personality that are "religious" in nature, this requirement has never been construed to elevate conventional piety or religiosity of any kind above the imperatives of a personal faith. ...

B

We conclude not only that the affirmative purposes underlying § 6(j) are neutral and secular, but also that valid neutral reasons exist for limiting the exemption to objectors to all war, and that the section therefore cannot be said to reflect a religious preference. Apart from the Government's need for manpower, perhaps the central interest involved in the administration of conscription laws is the interest in maintaining a fair system for determining "who serves when not all serve." When the Government exacts so much, the importance of fair, evenhanded, and uniform decisionmaking is obviously intensified. ...

A virtually limitless variety of beliefs are subsumable under the rubric, "objection to a particular war." All the factors that might go into nonconscientious dissent from policy, also might appear as the concrete basis of an objection that has roots as well in conscience and religion. Indeed, over the realm of possible situations, opposition to a particular war may more likely be political and nonconscientious, than otherwise. ... The difficulties of sorting the two, with a sure hand, are considerable. Moreover, the belief that a particular war at a particular time is unjust is by its nature changeable and subject to nullification by changing events. ...

To view the problem of fairness and evenhanded decisionmaking, in the present context, as merely a commonplace chore of weeding out "spurious claims," is to minimize substantial difficulties of real concern to a responsible legislative body. ...

Ours is a Nation of enormous heterogeneity in respect of political views, moral codes, and religious persuasions. It does not bespeak an establishing of religion for Congress to forgo the enterprise of distinguishing those whose dissent has some conscientious basis from those who simply dissent. ... There is even a danger of unintended religious discrimination—a danger that a claim's chances of success would be greater the more familiar or salient the claim's connection with conventional religiosity could be made to appear. ... While the danger of erratic decisionmaking unfortunately exists in any system of conscription that takes individual differences into account, no doubt the dangers would be enhanced if a conscientious objection of indeterminate scope were honored in theory. ...

Tacit at least in the Government's view of the instant cases is the contention that the limits of § 6(j) serve an overriding interest in protecting the integrity of democratic decisionmaking against claims to individual noncompliance. ...

... [I]t is not inconsistent with orderly democratic government for individuals to be exempted by law, on account of special characteristics, from general duties of a burdensome nature. But real dangers ... might arise if an exemption were made available that in its nature could not be administered fairly and uniformly over the run of relevant fact situations. Should it be thought that those who go to war are chosen unfairly or capriciously, then a mood of bitterness and cynicism might corrode the spirit of public service and the values of willing performance of a citizen's duties that are the very heart of free government.

III

Petitioners' remaining contention is that Congress interferes with the free exercise of religion by conscripting persons who oppose a particular war on grounds of conscience and religion. ... [O]ur analysis of § 6(j) for Establishment Clause purposes has revealed governmental interests of a kind and weight sufficient to justify under the Free Exercise Clause the impact of the conscription laws on those who object to particular wars.

Our cases do not at their farthest reach support the proposition that a stance of conscientious opposition relieves an objector from any colliding duty fixed by a democratic government. See Cantwell v. Connecticut (1940); Jacobson v. Massachusetts (1905). To be sure, the Free Exercise Clause bars "governmental regulation of religious *beliefs* as such," Sherbert v. Verner (1963), or interference with the dissemination of religious ideas. See Fowler v. Rhode Island (1953); Follett v. McCormick (1944); Murdock v. Pennsylvania (1943). It prohibits misuse of secular governmental programs "to impede the observance of one or all religions or ... to discriminate invidiously between religions, ... even though the burden may be characterized as being only indirect." Braunfeld v. Brown [1961]. And even as to neutral prohibitory or regulatory laws having secular aims, the Free Exercise Clause may condemn certain applications clashing with imperatives of religion and conscience, when the burden on First Amendment values is not justifiable in terms of the Government's valid aims. See *id., Sherbert.* However, the impact of conscription on objectors to particular wars is far from unjustified. The conscription laws, applied to such persons as to others, are not designed to interfere with any religious ritual or practice, and do not work a penalty against any theological position. The incidental burdens felt by persons in petitioners' position are strictly justified by substantial governmental interests that relate directly to the very impacts questioned. And more broadly, of course, there is the Government's interest in procuring the manpower necessary for military purposes, pursuant to the constitutional grant of power to Congress to raise and support armies. ...

Affirmed.

Mr. Justice **BLACK** concurs in the Court's judgment and in [portions] of the opinion of the Court.

Mr. Justice **DOUGLAS,** dissenting in Gillette v. United States. ...

The question, Can a conscientious objector, whether his objection be rooted in "religion" or in moral values, be required to kill? has never been answered by the Court. Hamilton v. Regents [1934] did no more than hold that the Fourteenth Amendment did not require a State to make its university available to one who would not take military training. *Macintosh* denied naturalization to a person who "would not promise in advance to bear arms in defense of the United States unless he believed the war to be morally justified." The question of compelling a man to kill against his conscience was not squarely involved. Most of the talk in the majority opinion concerned "serving in the armed forces of the Nation in time of war." Such service can, of course, take place in noncombatant roles. The ruling was that such service is "dependent upon the will of Congress and not upon the scruples of the individual, except as Congress provides." The dicta of the Court in the *Macintosh* case squint towards the denial of Gillette's claim, though as I have said, the issue was not squarely presented.

Yet if dicta are to be our guide, my choice is the dicta of Chief Justice Hughes who, dissenting in *Macintosh,* spoke as well for Justices Holmes, Brandeis, and Stone:

> Nor is there ground, in my opinion, for the exclusion of Professor Macintosh because his conscientious scruples have particular reference to wars believed to be unjust. ... Among the most eminent statesmen here and abroad have been those who condemned the action of their country in entering into wars they thought to be unjustified. Agreements for the renunciation of war presuppose a preponderant public sentiment against wars of aggression. If ... the mere holding of religious or conscientious scruples against all wars should not disqualify a citizen from holding office in this country, or an applicant otherwise qualified from being admitted to citizenship, there would seem to be no reason why a reservation of religious or conscientious objection to participation in wars believed to be unjust should constitute such a disqualification. ...

I think the Hughes view is the constitutional view. It is true that the First Amendment speaks of the free exercise of religion, not of the free exercise of conscience or belief. Yet conscience and belief are the main ingredients of First Amendment rights. They are the bedrock of free speech as well as religion. The implied First Amendment right of "conscience" is certainly as high as the "right of association" which we recognized in Shelton v. Tucker [1960]. ...

But the constitutional infirmity in the present Act seems obvious once "conscience" is the guide. As Chief Justice Hughes said in *Macintosh*:

> But, in the forum of conscience, duty to a moral power higher than the State has always been maintained. The reservation of that supreme

obligation, as a matter of principle, would unquestionably be made by many of our conscientious and law-abiding citizens. The essence of religion is belief in a relation to God involving duties superior to those arising from any human relation.

The law as written is a species of those which show an invidious discrimination in favor of religious persons and against others with like scruples. Mr. Justice Black once said: "The First Amendment has lost much if the religious follower and the atheist are no longer to be judicially regarded as entitled to equal justice under law." *Zorach* (dissenting). We said as much in our recent decision in *Epperson*, where we struck down as unconstitutional a state law prohibiting the teaching of the doctrine of evolution in the public schools:

> Government in our democracy, state and national, must be neutral in matters of religious theory, doctrine, and practice. It may not be hostile to any religion or to the advocacy of no-religion; and it may not aid, foster, or promote one religion or religious theory against another or even against the militant opposite. The First Amendment mandates governmental neutrality between religion and religion, and between religion and nonreligion. ...

While there is no Equal Protection Clause in the Fifth Amendment, our decisions are clear that invidious classifications violate due process. Bolling v. Sharpe [1954]. ... A classification of "conscience" based on a "religion" and a "conscience" based on more generalized, philosophical grounds is equally invidious by reason of our First Amendment standards.

I had assumed that the welfare of the single human soul was the ultimate test of the vitality of the First Amendment. ...

Mr. Justice **DOUGLAS**, dissenting in Negre v. Larsen. ...

Under the doctrines of the Catholic Church a person has a moral duty to take part in wars declared by his government so long as they comply with the tests of his church for just wars. Conversely, a Catholic has a moral duty not to participate in unjust wars. ... The Fifth Commandment, "Thou shall not kill," provides a basis for the distinction. ... In the 16th century Francisco Victoria, Dominican master of the University of Salamanca, ... elaborated on the distinction. "If a subject is convinced of the injustice of a war, he ought not to serve in it, even on the command of his prince. This is clear, for no one can authorize the killing of an innocent person." ... Well over 400 years later, today, the Baltimore Catechism makes an exception to the Fifth Commandment for a "soldier fighting a just war."

No one can tell a Catholic that this or that war is either just or unjust. This is a personal decision that an individual must make on the basis of his own conscience after studying the facts. Like the distinction between just and unjust wars, the duty to obey conscience is not a new doctrine in the Catholic Church. When told to stop preaching by the Sanhedrin, to which they were subordinate by law, "Peter and the apostles answered and said, 'We must obey God rather than men.'"

That duty has not changed. Pope Paul VI has expressed it as follows: "On his part, man perceives and acknowledges the imperatives of the divine law through the mediation of conscience. In all his activity a man is bound to follow his conscience, in order that he may come to God, the end and purpose of life." ...

... The full impact of the horrors of modern war were emphasized in the *Pastoral Constitution* announced by Vatican II:

> The development of armaments by modern science has immeasurably magnified the horrors and wickedness of war. Warfare conducted with these weapons can inflict immense and indiscriminate havoc which goes far beyond the bounds of legitimate defense. Indeed, if the kind of weapons now stocked in the arsenals of the great powers were to be employed to the fullest, the result would be the almost complete reciprocal slaughter of one side by the other, not to speak of the widespread devastation that would follow in the world and the deadly after-effects resulting from the use of such arms. ...

> [I]t is one thing to wage a war of self-defense; it is quite another to seek to impose domination on another nation. ...

The *Pastoral Constitution* announced that "[e]very act of war directed to the indiscriminate destruction of whole cities or vast areas with their inhabitants is a crime against God and man which merits firm and unequivocal condemnation." ...

For the reasons I have stated in my dissent in the *Gillette* case ... I would reverse the judgment.

Editors' Notes

(1) **Query:** To what extent did the Court in *Gillette* treat religious freedom as a fundamental right? Did the Court require government to show the draft act's exemptions were "narrowly tailored" to justify the intrusion on free exercise?

(2) **Query**: To what extent did either Marshall or Douglas follow a *structuralist approach* to constitutional interpretation? Did these two cases present serious problems of equal protection? Do the establishment and free exercise clauses function as guarantees of equal protection as far as religious matters are concerned? If so, can interpreters address the first two without considering the third? Do all variations on the strict-scrutiny/compelling-interest test require judges to treat classifications by religion as suspect? Given Justice Marshall's views about race as a suspect classification, would he have been likely to vote to sustain draft legislation, apparently neutral on its face, that imposed heavier burdens on African Americans than on Caucasians?

(3) **Query**: But was the problem here wider than it first appears? Is it possible for a person affiliated with the Judeo–Christian ethic or who considers him/herself to be a humanitarian (or a "secular humanist") *not* to be at least a selective conscientious objector? To what extent did the fear that we are all selective CO's cause Marshall and his colleagues to put such heavy emphasis on problems of administration, a consideration that the Court has repeatedly said in equal protection cases is not compelling when it affects a fundamental

right or employs a suspect classification? (See, for example, Brennan's plurality opinion in Frontiero v. Richardson [1973; reprinted above, p. 986], which Marshall joined.) Do we have here another shift of the question to WHO shall interpret, with the Court giving way to Congress and the President on matters falling under the war powers?

————

"[W]e support the right of selective conscientious objection as a moral conclusion which can be validly drawn from the classical moral teaching of just-war theory."

STATEMENT BY THE ADMINISTRATIVE BOARD OF THE UNITED STATES CATHOLIC CONFERENCE
(1980).

The Military Service Act authorizes the President to order males between the ages of 18 and 26 to register for possible military service. In 1980, President Jimmy Carter ordered registration to begin again, the first time since conscription had ended at the close of the war in Vietnam. This decision was controversial—see Rostker v. Goldberg (1981) for a challenge to the MSA's exclusion of females. Among the reactions it provoked was a declaration by the Administrative Board of the organization of Roman Catholic Bishops in the United States.

... The questions of registration and conscription for military service are part of the broader political-moral issue of war and peace in the nuclear age. But registration and conscription bear so directly on the moral decision making of citizens that they require specific attention. ...

We recognize, of course, that the questions of registration and conscription arise, as Vatican II [the Second Vatican Council] said, "because war has not been rooted out of human affairs." In the face of the sad truth of this statement, our response as teachers in the church must be the same as that of all popes of this century. We call in season and out of season for the international community to turn from war and to do the works of peace. The primary obligation of the nuclear age is to banish resort to force from the daily affairs of nations and peoples. From Pius XII to John Paul II the cry of the church and the prayer of all believers is a reiteration of the words of Paul VI: "No more war, war never again!" This must remain our primary response to war today.

Only in the context of this statement can we consider the question of what is the legitimate role of governments and the responsibilities of citizens regarding military conscription. We see registration, conscription and participation in military service as moral questions as well as political issues. Our perspective on these issues is shaped by Catholic moral teaching on the role of the state and the rights and responsibilities of citizens when both citizen and state are confronted by questions of war and peace.

With Vatican II we recognize that "as long as the danger of war remains and there is no competent and sufficiently powerful authority at the international level, governments cannot be denied the right to legitimate defense once every means of peaceful settlement has been exhausted." ... To this right there corresponds the duty each citizen has to contribute to the common good of society, including, as an essential element, the defense of society. Both the right of the state and the responsibility of the citizen are governed by moral principles which seek to protect the welfare of society and to preserve inviolate the conscience of the citizen.

The moral right of the state to use force is severely limited both in terms of the reasons for which force is employed and the means to be used. While acknowledging the duty of the state to defend society and its correlative right to use force in certain circumstances, we also affirm the Catholic teaching that the state's decision to use force should always be morally scrutinized by citizens asked to support the decision or to participate in war. From the perspective of the citizen, the moral scrutiny of every use of force can produce a posture of responsible participation in the government's decision, or conscientious objection to some reasons for using force, some methods of using force or even some specific branches of the service because of the missions they may be asked to perform. ...

In light of these general principles, we are led to the following specific positions:

1. *Registration:* We acknowledge the right of the state to register citizens for the purpose of military conscription, both in peacetime and in times of national emergency. ...

2. *Military Conscription:* We are opposed to any re-institution of military conscription except in the case of a national defense emergency. ...

3. *Conscientious Objection:* We regard this question in all its dimensions as a central element in Catholic teaching on the morality of war. First, we support the right of conscientious objection, as a valid moral position, derived from the Gospel and Catholic teaching, and recognized as well in U.S. civil law. The legal protection provided conscientious objectors is a commendable part of our political system which must be preserved in any policy of conscription.

Second, we support the right of selective conscientious objection as a moral conclusion which can be validly derived from the classical moral teaching of just-war theory. The position of selective conscientious objection has not yet found expression in our legal system, but a means should be found to give this legitimate moral position a secure legal status. The experience of the Vietnam War highlighted the moral and political significance of precisely this question. We are sure of the moral validity of selective conscientious objection; we would welcome a dialogue with legislators, lawyers, ethicists and other religious leaders about how to transpose this moral position into effective legal language. ...

Editors' Notes

(1) This statement was by no means the first time American Catholic bishops had proclaimed a moral right to selective conscientious objection. In November 1968, for example, when the war in Vietnam was near its peak, the Conference issued a pastoral letter, "Human Life in Our Day," affirming a moral right to conscientious objection and calling on Congress to modify the Selective Service Act not only to allow selective conscientious objectors to refuse "to serve in wars they consider unjust" but also to decline to serve "in branches of service (e.g., the strategic nuclear forces) which would subject them to the performance of actions contrary to deeply held moral convictions about indiscriminate killing."

(2) By 1982, some Catholic bishops' opposition to war, and more particularly to threats of use or even possession of nuclear arms, had moved far beyond earlier statements. Seventeen bishops signed a letter questioning whether any nuclear conflict could qualify as a "just war." Archbishop John Quinn of San Francisco wrote: "The teaching of the church is clear. Nuclear weapons and the arms race must be condemned as immoral." As more and more clergy of all faiths questioned the morality of serving in forces that had nuclear weapons, Archbishop Raymond Hunthausen of Seattle announced he was refusing to pay part of his income tax as a protest against American nuclear armaments. Then in May 1983, American Catholic bishops, speaking as a group, issued a Pastoral Document on War and Peace subtitled "The Challenge of Peace." In it, the bishops stressed that all human beings were members of the same family, reiterated their endorsement of selective conscientious objection, and reminded their people that "no state may demand blind obedience." Disobedience by the military of immoral orders, the bishops claimed, was "not an act of cowardice or treason but one of courage and patriotism." What was new in the pastoral was an institutional attack on the morality of nuclear deterrence as a national policy. Such a doctrine, the bishops said, was moral only as a stop-gap measure to keep the peace while proceeding with disarmament.

(3) The Gulf War: In the summer of 1990, Iraq, one of the largest producers of oil in the world, invaded and then annexed Kuwait, another of the great sources of oil. After the Iraqi leader, Saddam Hussein, continued to ignore resolutions of the United Nations ordering withdrawal, a coalition of nations began a large military build up in Saudi Arabia and the Persian Gulf. These forces were principally but not exclusively American. In January, 1991, they began heavy air attacks against Iraqi targets then launched a ground offensive that swiftly decimated Hussein's troops.

President George Bush and his advisers were skilled at weaving together an international coalition, but inept in justifying intervention to the American people. At various times, they described the reason for use of force as "saving jobs," preventing Hussein from obtaining a choke hold on the world's oil, and righting the horrible wrong of invasion and annexation of a "free" nation. The fact that Kuwait's authoritarian government did not recognize that its citizens had either democratic or constitutionalist rights did not strengthen a claim for justice. As we saw in Chapter 11, the Gulf War Resolution, authorizing use of American troops, passed Congress by a slim margin. (For text, see p. 461.) And many religious leaders, Protestant and a well as Catholic, protested that the impending conflict did not fit into the category of a "just war."

Because the United States had moved to an all-volunteer military, there were no new constitutional challenges along the lines of *Gillette*. Nevertheless, some 2,500 people in the armed services claimed the status conscientious objectors because they believed the war to be unjust. The Pentagon released some of these people but court martialed and imprisoned others. No appeal from these convictions reached the Supreme Court.

"The withholding of educational benefits involves only an incidental burden upon appellee's free exercise of religion—if, indeed, any burden exists at all."—Justice BRENNAN

"Where Government places a price on the free exercise of one's religious scruples it crosses the forbidden line."—Justice DOUGLAS

JOHNSON v. ROBISON

415 U.S. 361, 94 S.Ct. 1160, 39 L.Ed.2d 389 (1974).

The Veterans' Readjustment Act of 1966 (the GI Bill) limited its benefits to those who had served on active duty in the armed forces. William Robison, a conscientious objector who had completed two years of alternate, non-military service required by the draft act, instituted a class action for himself and other COs against the Veterans Administration, seeking a declaratory judgment that, so limited, the GI Bill violated the First Amendment's free exercise clause and the Fifth Amendment's implicit guarantee of equal protection. The district court sustained the statute under the First Amendment, but held it invidiously discriminated, contrary to the Fifth Amendment. The Veterans Administration appealed directly to the Supreme Court.

Mr. Justice **BRENNAN** delivered the opinion of the Court. . . .

Unlike many state and federal statutes that come before us, Congress in this statute has responsibly revealed its express legislative objectives in § 1651 of the Act and no other objective is claimed:

> The Congress of the United States hereby declares that the education program created by this chapter is for the purpose of (1) enhancing and making more attractive service in the Armed Forces of the United States, (2) extending the benefits of a higher education to qualified and deserving young persons who might not otherwise be able to afford such an education, (3) providing vocational readjustment and

restoring lost educational opportunities to those service men and women whose careers have been interrupted or impeded by reason of active duty after January 31, 1955, and (4) aiding such persons in attaining the vocational and educational status which they might normally have aspired to and obtained had they not served their country.

Legislation to further these objectives is plainly within Congress' Art. I, § 8, power "to raise and support Armies." Our task is therefore narrowed to the determination of whether there is some ground of difference having a fair and substantial relation to at least one of the stated purposes justifying the different treatment accorded veterans who served on active duty in the Armed Forces, and conscientious objectors who performed alternative civilian service.

The District Court reasoned that objectives (2), (3), and (4) of § 1651 are basically variations on a single theme reflecting a congressional purpose to "eliminate the educational gaps between persons who served their country and those who did not." ...

The error in this rationale is that it states too broadly the congressional objective reflected in (2), (3), and (4) of § 1651. The wording of those sections, in conjunction with the attendant legislative history, makes clear that Congress' purpose in enacting the Veterans' Readjustment Benefits Act of 1966 was ... primarily ... to compensate for the disruption that military service causes to civilian lives. ... Indeed ... "the very name of the statute—the Veterans' Readjustment Benefits Act—emphasizes congressional concern with the veteran's need for assistance in readjusting to civilian life."

Of course, merely labeling the class of beneficiaries under the Act as those having served on active duty in the Armed Services cannot rationalize a statutory discrimination against conscientious objectors who have performed alternative civilian service, if, in fact, the lives of the latter were equally disrupted and equally in need of readjustment. See Richardson v. Belcher (1971). ...

First, the disruption caused by military service is quantitatively greater than that caused by alternative civilian service. A conscientious objector performing alternative service is obligated to work for two years. Service in the Armed Forces, on the other hand, involves a six-year commitment. While active duty may be limited to two years, the military veteran remains subject to an Active Reserve and then Standby Reserve obligation after release from active duty. This additional military service obligation was emphasized by Congress as a significant reason for providing veterans' readjustment benefits. ...

Second, the disruptions suffered by military veterans and alternative service performers are qualitatively different. Military veterans suffer a far greater loss of personal freedom during their service careers. Uprooted from civilian life, the military veteran becomes part of the military establishment, subject to its discipline and potentially hazardous duty. ... Congress' reliance upon these differences between military and civilian service is highlighted by the inclusion of Class I-A-O conscientious objectors, who serve in the military in noncombatant roles, within the class of beneficiaries entitled to educational benefits under the Act.

These quantitative and qualitative distinctions, expressly recognized by Congress, form a rational basis for Congress' classification limiting educational benefits to military service veterans as a means of helping them readjust to civilian life; alternative service performers are not required to leave civilian life to perform their service.

The statutory classification also bears a rational relationship to objective (1) of § 1651, that of "enhancing and making more attractive service in the Armed Forces of the United States." By providing educational benefits to *all* military veterans who serve on active duty Congress expressed its judgment that such benefits would make military service more attractive to enlistees and draftees alike. Appellee concedes ... that this objective is rationally promoted by providing educational benefits to those who *enlist*. But, appellee argues, there is no rational basis for extending educational benefits to *draftees* who serve in the military and not to draftees who perform civilian alternative service, since neither group is induced by educational benefits to enlist. ...

The two groups of draftees are, in fact, not similarly circumstanced. To be sure, a draftee, by definition, does not find educational benefits sufficient incentive to enlist. But, military service with educational benefits is obviously more attractive to a draftee than military service without educational benefits. ... Furthermore, once drafted, educational benefits may help make military service more palatable to a draftee and thus reduce a draftee's unwillingness to be a soldier. ...

Finally, appellee ... contends that the Act's denial of benefits to alternative service conscientious objectors interferes with his free exercise of religion by increasing the price he must pay for adherence to his religious beliefs. That contention must be rejected in light of our decision in Gillette v. United States (1971). ...

... The withholding of educational benefits involves only an incidental burden upon appellee's free exercise of religion—if, indeed, any burden exists at all. ... Appellee and his class were not included in the class of beneficiaries, not because of any legislative design to interfere with their free exercise of religion, but because to do so would not rationally promote the Act's purposes. Thus, in light of *Gillette,* the Government's substantial interest in raising and supporting armies, Art. I, § 8, is "a kind and weight" clearly sufficient to sustain the challenged legislation, for the burden upon appellee's free exercise of religion—the denial of the economic value of veterans' educational benefits under the Act—is not nearly of the same order or magnitude as the infringement upon free exercise of religion suffered by petitioners in *Gillette.* See also Wisconsin v. Yoder (1972).

Reversed.

Mr. Justice **DOUGLAS,** dissenting. ...

... [T]he discrimination against a man with religious scruples seems apparent. ... Full benefits are available to occupants of safe desk jobs and the thousands of veterans who performed civilian type duties at home and for whom the rigors of the "war" were far from "totally disruptive," to use the Government's phrase. The benefits are provided, though the draftee did not serve overseas but lived with his family in a civilian community and worked from nine until five as a file clerk on a military base or attended college courses in his off-duty hours. No condition of hazardous duty was attached to the educational assistance program. ...

But the line drawn in the Act is between Class I–O conscientious objectors who performed alternative civilian service and all other draftees. Such conscientious objectors get no educational benefits whatsoever. ... Those who would die at the stake for their religious scruples may not constitutionally be penalized for the Government by the exaction of penalties because of their free exercise of religion. Where Government places a price on the free exercise of one's religious scruples it crosses the forbidden line. The issue of "coercive effects" ... is irrelevant. Government, as I read the Constitution and the Bill of Rights, may not place a penalty on anyone for asserting his religious scruples. ...

Editors' Note

Query: Several times Brennan spoke of a "rational basis" for Congress's distinction. Is that the test that the Court has applied when fundamental rights (or suspect classifications) have been involved? What sort of approach to constitutional interpretation was Brennan using? Douglas? Why did the Court not use some version of strict scrutiny/compelling interest here?

"[T]he Government has a fundamental, overriding interest in eradicating racial discrimination in education ... [that] substantially outweighs whatever burden denial of tax benefits places on petitioners' exercise of their religious beliefs."—Chief Justice BURGER

"[T]his Court should not legislate for Congress."—Justice REHNQUIST

BOB JONES UNIVERSITY v. UNITED STATES
461 U.S. 574, 103 S.Ct. 2017, 76 L.Ed.2d 157 (1983).

In 1970 a special three-judge district court enjoined the Internal Revenue Service from according tax-exempt status to private schools in Mississippi that discriminated because of race in admitting students (Green v. Connally). The Supreme Court affirmed per curiam, without opinion (Coit v. Green [1971]).

Following those decisions, IRS issued Revenue Bulletin 71–447 denying tax exempt status to all private schools practicing racial discrimination. This ruling denied exemption to the finances of the schools themselves under § 501(c)(3) of the Internal Revenue Code, making them liable to federal taxes, and also excluded donations by private individuals from tax deductions under § 170 of the Code. Neither section of the Code mentioned racial discrimination as a basis for denying exemption, but IRS and the three-judge district court reasoned that racial discrimination was so directly contrary to public policy as, even in the absence of explicit statutory language, to exclude its practitioners from claiming to be charitable organizations aiding the public welfare.

Bob Jones University, located in Greenville, SC, is a non-denominational, fundamentalist Christian institution whose purposes are both religious and educational. Its rules require all faculty to be devout Christians, and the Bible (as the University's administrators interprets it) to provide the guiding principles of education. The school's regulations carefully prescribe codes of conduct for students. Until 1975, BJU was open only to whites, but after the Court of Appeals for the Fourth Circuit held that a federal statute enacted pursuant to the Thirteenth Amendment outlawed racial exclusion practiced even by private schools—the Supreme Court affirmed in Runyon v. McCrary (1976)—BJU began to admit unmarried blacks, but with certain restrictions:

There is to be no interracial dating

    1. Students who are partners in an interracial marriage will be expelled.

    2. Students who are members of or affiliated with any group or organization which holds as one of its goals or advocates interracial marriage will be expelled.

    3. Students who date outside their own race will be expelled.

    4. Students who espouse, promote, or encourage others to violate the University's dating rules and regulations will be expelled.

This policy was based on a belief that God forbids racial intermarriage.

In 1970 IRS informed BJU it was losing its status as a tax exempt institution. The University then began a long series of legal actions that in 1980 resulted in a decision by the Court of Appeals for the Fourth Circuit that the University had no statutory or constitutional right to a tax exemption. BJU sought and obtained certiorari. Before oral argument, the Reagan administration announced that it agreed with Bob Jones University's interpretation of the Revenue Code, but the Supreme Court refused to dismiss the case. Instead, it appointed William T. Coleman, a prominent black attorney and former cabinet official under Richard M. Nixon, to argue the case as amicus curiae.

Chief Justice **BURGER** delivered the opinion of the Court. ...

II ...

B

    We are bound to approach these questions with full awareness that determinations of public benefit and public policy are sensitive matters with serious implications for the institutions affected; a declaration that a given institution is not "charitable" should be made only where there can be no doubt that the activity involved is contrary to a fundamental public policy. But there can no longer be any doubt that racial discrimination in education violates deeply and widely accepted views of elementary justice. Prior to 1954, public education in many places still was conducted under the pall of Plessy v. Ferguson, (1896); racial segregation in primary and secondary education prevailed in many parts of the country. This Court's decision in Brown v. Bd. of Educ. (1954) signalled an end to that era. Over the past quarter of a century, every pronouncement of this Court and myriad Acts of Congress and Executive Orders attest a firm national policy to prohibit racial segregation and discrimination in public education.

An unbroken line of cases following *Brown* establishes beyond doubt this Court's view that racial discrimination in education violates a most fundamental national public policy, as well as rights of individuals. ... Congress, in Titles IV and VI of the Civil Rights Act of 1964, clearly expressed its agreement that racial discrimination in education violates a fundamental public policy. Other sections of that Act, and numerous enactments since then, testify to the public policy against racial discrimination. See, e.g., the Voting Rights Act of 1965; Title VIII of the Civil Rights Act of 1968; the Emergency School Aid Act of 1972 (repealed effective Sept. 30, 1979; replaced by similar provisions in the Emergency School Aid Act of 1978). The Executive Branch has consistently placed its support behind eradication of racial discrimination. ...

Few social or political issues in our history have been more vigorously debated and more extensively ventilated than the issue of racial discrimination, particularly in education. Given the stress and anguish of the history of efforts to escape from the shackles of the "separate but equal" doctrine of *Plessy*, it cannot be said that educational institutions that, for whatever reasons, practice racial discrimination, are institutions exercising "beneficial and stabilizing influences in community life," Walz v. Tax Comm'n (1970), or should be encouraged by having all taxpayers share in their support by way of special tax status.

There can thus be no question that the interpretation of § 170 and § 501(c)(3) announced by the IRS in 1970 was correct. ... It would be wholly incompatible with the concepts underlying tax exemption to grant the benefit of tax-exempt status to racially discriminatory educational entities, which "exer[t] a pervasive influence on the entire educational process." Norwood v. Harrison [1973]. Whatever may be the rationale for such private schools' policies, and however sincere the rationale may be, racial discrimination in education is contrary to public policy. Racially discriminatory educational institutions cannot be viewed as conferring a public benefit within the "charitable" concept discussed earlier, or within the Congressional intent underlying § 170 and § 501(c)(3). ...

D

The actions of Congress since 1970 leave no doubt that the IRS reached the correct conclusion in exercising its authority. ... [F]or a dozen years Congress has been made aware—acutely aware—of the IRS rulings of 1970 and 1971. ... Failure of Congress to modify the IRS rulings of 1970 and 1971, of which Congress was, by its own studies and by public discourse, constantly reminded; and Congress' awareness of the denial of tax-exempt status for racially discriminatory schools when enacting other and related legislation make out an unusually strong case of legislative acquiescence in and ratification by implication of the 1970 and 1971 rulings.

Ordinarily, and quite appropriately, courts are slow to attribute significance to the failure of Congress to act on particular legislation. Here, however, we do not have an ordinary claim of legislative acquiescence. Only one month after the IRS announced its position in 1970, Congress held its first hearings on this precise issue. ... Exhaustive hearings have been held on the issue at various times since then. These include hearings in February 1982, after we granted review in this case.
...

... [T]he non-action here is significant. During the past 12 years there have been no fewer than 13 bills introduced to overturn the IRS interpretation of § 501(c)(3). Not one of these bills has emerged from any committee, although Congress has enacted numerous other amendments to § 501 during this same period. ... It is hardly conceivable that Congress ... was not abundantly aware of what was going on. In view of its prolonged and acute awareness of so important an issue, Congress' failure to act on the bills proposed on this subject provides added support for concluding that Congress acquiesced in the IRS rulings of 1970 and 1971. ...

The evidence of Congressional approval of the policy embodied in [the] Revenue Ruling goes well beyond the failure of Congress to act on legislative proposals. Congress affirmatively manifested its acquiescence in the IRS policy when it enacted the present § 501(i) of the Code. ... That provision denies tax-exempt status to social clubs whose charters or policy statements provide for "discrimination against any person on the basis of race, color, or religion." Both the House and Senate committee reports on that bill articulated the national policy against granting tax exemptions to racially discriminatory private clubs. Even more significant is the fact that both reports focus on this Court's affirmance of Green v. Connally [1971] as having established that "discrimination on account of race is inconsistent with an *educational institution's* tax exempt status." (Emphasis added.) ...

III

Petitioners contend that, even if the Commissioner's policy is valid as to nonreligious private schools, that policy cannot constitutionally be applied to schools that engage in racial discrimination on the basis of sincerely held religious beliefs. As to such schools, it is argued that the IRS construction of § 170 and § 501(c)(3) violates their free exercise rights under the Religion Clauses of the First Amendment. This contention presents claims not heretofore considered by this Court in precisely this context.

This Court has long held the Free Exercise Clause of the First Amendment an absolute prohibition against governmental regulation of religious beliefs, Wisconsin v. Yoder (1972); Sherbert v. Verner (1963); Cantwell v. Connecticut (1940). As interpreted by this Court, moreover, the Free Exercise Clause provides substantial protection for lawful conduct grounded in religious belief, see Yoder, Thomas v. Review Bd. (1981). However, "[n]ot all burdens on religion are unconstitutional. ... The state may justify a limitation on religious liberty by showing that it is essential to accomplish an overriding governmental interest." United States v. Lee (1982).

On occasion this Court has found certain governmental interests so compelling as to allow even regulations prohibiting religiously based conduct. In Prince v. Massachusetts (1944), for example, the Court held that neutrally cast child labor laws prohibiting sale of printed materials on public streets could be applied to prohibit children from dispensing religious literature. ... See also Reynolds v. United States (1878); Lee; Gillette v. United States (1971). Denial of tax benefits will inevitably have a substantial impact on the operation of private religious schools, but will not prevent those schools from observing their religious tenets.

The governmental interest at stake here is compelling. ... [T]he Government has a fundamental, overriding interest in eradicating racial discrimination in education. ... That governmental interest substantially outweighs whatever burden denial of tax benefits places on petitioners' exercise of their religious beliefs. The interests asserted by petitioners cannot be accommodated with that compelling governmental interest, see Lee, and no "less restrictive means," see Thomas, are available to achieve the governmental interest.[1] ...

[Affirmed.]

Justice **POWELL,** concurring in part and concurring in the judgment. ...

Justice **REHNQUIST**, dissenting. ...

I have no disagreement with the Court's finding that there is a strong national policy in this country opposed to racial discrimination. I agree with the Court that Congress has the power to further this policy

---

1. Bob Jones University also contends that denial of tax exemption violates the Establishment Clause by preferring religions whose tenets do not require racial discrimination over those which believe racial intermixing is forbidden. ... [A] regulation does not violate the Establishment Clause merely because it "happens to coincide or harmonize with the tenets of some or all religions." McGowan v. Maryland (1961). See Harris v. McRae (1980). The IRS policy at issue here is founded on a "neutral, secular basis," Gillette, and does not violate the Establishment Clause. ... [Footnote by the Court.]

by denying § 501(c)(3) status to organizations that practice racial discrimination. But as of yet Congress has failed to do so. Whatever the reasons for the failure, this Court should not legislate for Congress. ...

Editors' Notes

(1) **Query:** We return to a now familiar pair of questions: (a) Did Burger use an approach of *protecting fundamental rights* or did he follow a *balancing approach*? Is it necessary to choose between the two? Why or why not?

(2) **Query:** All the justices identified hostility toward racial discrimination as a prominent national public policy. Granted the correctness of this claim, was there also a prominent national public policy to the effect that people should be able, when neither public money nor violation of ordinary criminal law is involved, to practice their religion as their consciences direct? Did Burger make a convincing case that racial equality is a more important constitutional value than freedom of conscience? What shape would such an argument, to be convincing, take?

(3) **Query:** Can one make the case that public money is involved in Bob Jones' claim to be tax exempt? Even so, would that "fact" give constitutional preference to the value of racial equality over the value of freedom of conscience? See Mayer G. Freed and Daniel D. Polsby, "Race, Religion, and Public Policy: Bob Jones University v. United States," 1983 *Sup.Ct.Rev.* 1; also Paul B. Stephan III, "Bob Jones University v. United States: Public Policy in Search of Tax Policy," *ibid.* 33.

(4) Allen v. Wright (1984) held 5–3 that a group of African–American parents lacked standing to challenge IRS's decision to give tax immune status to private schools practicing racial discrimination. In effect, the parents were claiming that the Reagan administration was not enforcing the law as interpreted by *Bob Jones*. Speaking through O'Connor, the Court held the "abstract stigmatic injury" the parents asserted their children suffered was insufficient to confer standing. Brennan, Blackmun, and Stevens dissented; Marshall did not participate.

18

Individual Autonomy: Privacy, Personhood, and Personal Liberty

Most readers of this book would agree that the rights to worship or not worship as one chooses, to express oneself freely, and to secure enough personal property to achieve a meaningful degree of independence from the state and fellow citizens are all essential to individual autonomy and dignity. It is equally essential that a human being have control over his or her own bodily integrity as well as over a certain amount of surrounding physical and psychological space into which no one may enter uninvited. Some commentators have referred to this cluster of rights as relating to "personhood," "privacy," or "personal liberty." Laurence H. Tribe described the underlying thought:

> The very idea of a fundamental right of personhood rests on the conviction that, even though one's identity is constantly and profoundly shaped by ... one's social environment, the "personhood" resulting from this process is sufficiently "one's own" to be deemed fundamental in confrontation with the one entity that retains a monopoly over legitimate violence—the government. Thus active coercion by government to alter a person's being, or deliberate neglect by government which permits a being to suffer, are conceived as qualitatively different from the passive, incremental coercion that shapes all life. ...[1]

Whatever name one puts on this concept, it is intrinsic to any operative notion of constitutionalism and underlies the American constitutional order. "The right to be let alone," William O. Douglas once said, "is indeed the beginning of all freedom."[2]

Closely allied is the notion of "equal concern and respect" from government,[3] an equal "respect that is owed to persons

---

1. *American Constitutional Law* (2d ed.; Mineola, NY: Foundation Press, 1988), pp. 1305–06.

2. PUC v. Pollack, dis. op., (1952).

3. Ronald Dworkin, *Taking Rights Seriously* (Cambridge: Harvard University Press, 1977), p. 180, and chs. 6 and 12 generally. See also his "Foundations of Liberal Equality," in *The Tanner Lectures on Human Values*, XI (Salt Lake City: University of Utah Press, 1990).

irrespective of their social position."[4] It is, constitutionalists argue, precisely these basic rights to equal dignity and personal liberty that limited government protects—*government* to protect each person against encroachments by foreign nations or fellow citizens, *limited* government to prevent public officials from invading that private sphere.

One might think that the words of the Preamble, stating the systems's objectives as including "the Blessings of Liberty," would have been at least one of the principal textual anchors for unlisted rights to personal liberty. Judges, however, rarely cite that language, though elected officials often do, if only for rhetorical rather than substantive purposes. To protect general rights to personal freedom, judges have usually sought textual justification in the due process clauses of the Fifth and Fourteenth amendments. On rare occasions, they have utilized the Ninth's command that the "enumeration in the Constitution, of certain rights, shall not be construed to deny or disparage others retained by the people." A *textualist* might find this fact strange, but the document does "command" interpreters to search for unlisted rights: According to the rules of English syntax and grammar, the language of the Ninth Amendment, like that of the First, is not declarative but imperative in mood.

I. WHAT IS THE CONSTITUTION?

If few Americans would deny the importance of rights to privacy, personhood, and personal liberty, they still might disagree sharply about the source and scope of those rights as well as about who has authority to declare and define them—in sum, about the WHAT and WHO as well as the HOW of constitutional interpretation. One might plausibly argue that these rights originate in the constitutional text—in the document's plain words, in its clear implications, in its "architectural scheme," in its "penumbras," in the ways the larger political system has developed, or in a theory of constitutionalism that undergirds both the document and the system. Or one might argue, as William H. Rehnquist did in "The Notion of a Living Constitution" (reprinted above, p. 243), that the source of these rights, except when they are specifically listed in the document, lies in the people's will made binding on society through formal enactments by popularly elected officials.

There are still those who look for the source of these rights in a higher law than the constitutional text or even the broader constitution. Jefferson, after all, saw man's "unalienable rights" as having been "endowed" by the "Creator," a notion Lincoln echoed. In the 1950s, as Justice William O. Douglas began to abandon the

---

4. John Rawls, *A Theory of Justice* (Cambridge: Harvard University Press, 1971), p. 511. See also his *Political Liberalism* (New York: Columbia University Press, 1993).

positivism that he had once shared with Hugo Black, Douglas made a series of off-the-bench statements that laid bare some of the theological underpinnings of his jurisprudence. "In our scheme of things," he wrote in 1954, "the rights of men are unalienable. They come from the Creator, not from a president, a legislator, or a court."[5] "Man," he reiterated in 1958, "is a child of God, entitled to dignified treatment."[6] Then, in 1963, two years before Griswold v. Connecticut (1965; reprinted above, p. 147) and its announcement that a right to privacy hovered in the "penumbras" of the Bill of Rights, he spoke even more emphatically:

> Men do not acquire rights from the government; one man does not give another rights. Man gets his rights from the Creator. They come to him because of the divine spark in every human being.[7]

More recently, other justices have returned to Jefferson's constitutionalist conception of natural rights as expressed in the Declaration of Independence. Dissenting in Meachum v. Fano (1976), Justice John Paul Stevens wrote:

> I had thought it self-evident that all men were endowed by their Creator with liberty as one of the cardinal unalienable rights. It is that basic freedom which the Due Process Clause protects, rather than the particular rights or privileges conferred by specific laws or regulations.

A year later, writing for the Court, Justice Brennan said that the family's right to privacy "has its source . . . not in state law, but in intrinsic human rights."[8] In 1986 and 1990, Stevens repeated his reliance on the Declaration as a source of constitutional meaning;[9] and, before going to the Supreme Court, Clarence Thomas wrote that a " 'plain reading of the Constitution . . .' puts the fitly spoken words of the Declaration of Independence in the center of the frame formed by the Constitution."[10]

All these sorts of arguments, from Jefferson's natural rights to Douglas's theology and to Rehnquist's positivism, are still very much alive. As we have seen throughout this book, the choices interpreters make here are as crucial as they are controversial. And, despite

---

5. *An Almanac of Liberty* (Garden City, NY: Doubleday, 1954), p. 5.

6. *The Right of the People* (Garden City, NY: Doubleday, 1958), p. 145.

7. *The Anatomy of Liberty* (New York: Trident Press, 1963), p. 2. For Douglas's change from positivism to natural rights, see Kenneth L. Karst, "The Return of the Natural–Law–Due–Process Formula," 16 *U.C.L.A.L.Rev.* 716 (1969).

8. Smith v. Organization of Foster Families (1977). See also William J. Brennan, Jr., "The Constitution of the United States: Contemporary Ratification," 27 *S.Tex.L.J.* 433 (1986; reprinted above, p. 236).

9. Dissenting in Bowers v. Hardwick (1986; reprinted below, p. 1322), and Cruzan v. Director, Missouri Dept. of Health (1990; reprinted below p. 1338).

10. "Toward a 'Plain Reading' of the Constitution—The Declaration of Independence in Constitutional Interpretation," 30 *How.L.J.* 983 (1987). Thomas's first few terms on the Court indicate, however, that if he believes "the Constitution" protects natural rights, he does not believe judges have much of a role in making that protection effective.

disagreements over sources, interpreters have tended to find a plethora of unlisted rights in notions of a constitution broader than the document. Commentators, executives, legislators, and judges have often viewed the constitutional text as mapping only the "core of a much wider region of private rights, which, though not reduced to black and white, are as fully entitled to the protection of government as if defined in the minutest detail." [11]

This attitude goes back to the early days of the Republic. Justice Chase in Calder v. Bull (1798; reprinted above, p. 121) and Marshall and Johnson in Fletcher v. Peck (1810; reprinted above, p. 1091) exemplify what could be called a traditional constitutionalist view. Justices like James Iredell in *Calder*, Hugo Black in Griswold v. Connecticut (1965; reprinted above, p. 147), and Antonin Scalia in Planned Parenthood v. Casey (1992; reprinted below, p. 1281) have challenged this approach to constitutional interpretation, but the debate within the Court, though acerbic, has typically focused on whether this or that unlisted right is constitutionally protected, not on whether *any* unlisted rights deserve such status. [12]

The issue of incorporation of the Bill of Rights in the Fourteenth Amendment (see above, pp. 133–35) has concerned not only whether some listed rights are more or less fundamental than others, but also whether some unlisted rights are so fundamental as to be "of the very essence of a scheme of ordered liberty" (Palko v. Connecticut [1937; reprinted above, p. 128) or "deeply rooted in this Nation's history and tradition" (Moore v. East Cleveland [1977 (plurality opinion); reprinted below, p. 1314]). Over the years, the Court has recognized at least the following unlisted rights as fundamental:

> (1) To retain American citizenship, despite even criminal activities, until explicitly and voluntarily renouncing it; [13]

> (2) To receive equal protection, not only from the states but also from the federal government. [14]

> (3) To vote, subject only to reasonable restrictions to prevent fraud, and to cast a ballot equal in weight to those of other citizens; [15]

---

11. Edward S. Corwin, "The Basic Doctrine of American Constitutional Law," 12 *Mich.L.Rev.* 247 (1912); reprinted in Alpheus Thomas Mason and Gerald Garvey, eds., *American Constitutional History* (New York: Harper & Row, 1964).

12. Speaking for the Court in San Antonio v. Rodriguez (1973; reprinted above, p. 1002), Justice Powell spoke of fundamental rights as those "explicitly or implicitly guaranteed by the Constitution." (See Justice Marshall's response, at p. 1008.) Putting aside questions of what "the Constitution" and "implicitly guaranteed" mean in this context, Powell in his opinion for the plurality in Moore v. East Cleveland (1977; reprinted below, p. 1314) unequivocally endorsed the fundamentality of some unlisted constitutional rights.

13. Afroyim v. Rusk (1967).

14. See the cases in Chapters 14 and 15.

15. See the cases in Chapter 13.

(4) To enjoy a presumption of innocence and to demand proof beyond a reasonable doubt before being convicted of crime; [16]

(5) To use the federal courts and other governmental institutions and to urge others to use these processes to protect their interests; [17]

(6) To associate with others; [18]

(7) To enjoy a zone of privacy; [19]

(8) To travel within the United States; [20]

(9) To marry or not to marry [21] and to make one's own choice about having children; [22]

(10) To educate one's children as long as one meets certain minimum standards set by the state; [23]

(11) To choose and follow a profession; [24]

(12) To attend and report on criminal trials. [25]

(13) To refuse unwanted medical treatment, including artificial nutrition and hydration, even if doing so may result in one's death. [26]

In 1986, however, the Court declined to recognize a fundamental right of homosexuals to intimate association [27] and in 1989 of a biological father's right to a relationship with his child whose mother was married to another man at the time the child was conceived and born. [28] More generally, the Court has rejected the idea that "the Constitution" grants unlisted "positive liberties" to basic governmental services, such as protection from an abusive

---

16. In re Winship (1970); Estelle v. Williams (1976); Taylor v. Kentucky (1978); Sandstrom v. Montana (1979); Jackson v. Virginia (1979). Schall v. Martin (1984), however, upheld pretrial detention for juveniles who, in the opinion of the juvenile judge, present a serious risk of committing an offense before trial.

17. Slaughter–House Cases (1873; reprinted above, p. 550); NAACP v. Button (1963; reprinted above, p. 811).

18. De Jonge v. Oregon (1937); NAACP v. Alabama (1958; reprinted above, p. 798).

19. Griswold v. Connecticut (1965; reprinted above, p. 147). Palmer v. Hudson (1984), however, held that prisoners have no right to privacy even in their cells.

20. Crandall v. Nevada (1868; reprinted above, p. 543); Shapiro v. Thompson (1969; reprinted above, p. 1019).

21. Loving v. Virginia (1967; reprinted above p. 926) and Zablocki v. Redhail (1978; reprinted above, p. 1034).

22. *Griswold*; Eisenstadt v. Baird (1972); Carey v. Population Services (1977); Roe v. Wade (1973; reprinted below, p. 1258); and Planned Parenthood v. Casey (1992; reprinted below, p. 1281).

23. Pierce v. Society of Sisters (1925; reprinted below, p. 1251).

24. For example: Allgeyer v. Louisiana (1897); Meyer v. Nebraska (1923; reprinted below, p. 1247); Gibson v. Berryhill (1973).

25. Richmond Newspapers v. Virginia (1980; reprinted above, p. 642).

26. Cruzan v. Director, Missouri Dept. of Health (1990; reprinted below, p. 1338).

27. Bowers v. Hardwick (1986; reprinted below, p. 1322).

28. Michael H. v. Gerald D. (1989; reprinted above, p. 158).

parent, proclaiming instead that "the Constitution" is a charter of "negative liberties."[29]

In recent years, Justice Scalia in particular has sought to cabin the Court's recognition of unlisted rights, arguing that "no 'substantive due process' claim can be maintained unless the claimant demonstrates that the State has deprived him of a right historically and traditionally protected against State interference," and insisting that these rights—as well as the "tradition" in which they are rooted—must be defined quite specifically and narrowly.[30] So far, only Chief Justice Rehnquist has unequivocally endorsed Scalia's theory, but there are indications that Justice Clarence Thomas might embrace it should occasion arise.[31] Scalia's other colleagues have protested that his jurisprudence is both narrow and novel, and that, had the Court historically operated on such a concept of WHAT "the Constitution" is, judges would not have recognized many of the unlisted rights they in fact have. As Justice Brennan said about Scalia's opinion in *Michael H.*: "The document that the plurality construes today is unfamiliar to me. It is not the living charter that I have taken to be our Constitution; it is instead a stagnant, archaic, hide-bound document steeped in the prejudices and superstitions of a time long past."

II. WHO SHALL INTERPRET?

Protecting privacy, personhood, and personal liberty frequently involves a paradox. For government, even limited government, to safeguard this cluster of rights leaves them less than absolute and to some degree restricts their orbit. Privacy, even of the home, cannot mean that a householder may conduct criminal activities in the basement of his or her castle.[32] One's right to personal liberty has to stop short of a right to drive an automobile on a public highway after consuming intoxicating quantities of alcohol or ingesting other hallucinogens. "In this world as it is," Lord Devlin has written, "no man can be free unless he lives under the protection of a free society."[33] And the price of protecting liberty includes some restraints on liberty. These ideas are encapsulated in the notion of "ordered liberty."[34]

---

29. DeShaney v. Winnebago County Dept. of Social Services (1989; reprinted below, p. 1350).

30. *Cruzan*, concur. op., citing his plurality opinion in Michael H. v. Gerald D. (1989; reprinted above p. 158).

31. See, however, the discussion, at p. 1238 above, of Thomas's early belief in natural rights.

32. Whether acts legitimate within the privacy of one's home would be criminal if performed outside the home is another question. See Stanley v. Georgia (1969).

33. Patrick Devlin, *The Enforcement of Morals* (London: Oxford University Press, 1965), p. 100.

34. See Palko v. Connecticut (1937; reprinted above, p. 128) and Poe v. Ullman (1961 [Harlan, J., dissenting]; reprinted above, p. 141).

"Some restraints" means choices about the breadth, depth, and shape of the private sphere as well as the dimensions of the public sphere. In the context of constitutional interpretation, this requirement returns us to the critical question of WHO shall interpret—who may legitimately make these sorts of fundamental choices.

James Bradley Thayer's "doctrine of the clear mistake" (reprinted above, p. 602) would solve the problem for judges by virtual abdication where congressional authority is involved.[35] In effect, he concluded that, for the national government, constitutional interpretation is basically a task for Congress and the President. The proper judicial role is only to determine if those branches of government have acted rationally in their choices. The practical results of this doctrine would be two-fold: First, private citizens would have little judicial defense against congressional or presidential action, though they could appeal to the courts against state decisions. Second, most of the responsibility for constitutional interpretation would fall on senators, congressmen, and presidents. And, if they were to assume that burden in a responsible manner, they would have to seek a more substantive theory to justify their interpretations: Thus Thayer's doctrine only allocates interpretive authority, it does not prescribe HOW to exercise it.

Broader theories of representative democracy like John Hart Ely's [36] justify judges' taking an active role in defining and enforcing only political participation, equality of government's treatment of people under its jurisdiction, and such rights as are specifically listed in the constitutional document. Elected officials would define all other rights. Thus the protection, even the existence, of most unlisted rights would depend on changing public moods to a degree unacceptable to many constitutional democrats.

And here, of course, we are revisiting a familiar battlefield. Public officials and commentators who stress constitutionalism in a hybrid system of constitutional democracy tend to accept, as did Gouverneur Morris, the judiciary as "that fortress of the Constitution" and judges as its "noble guards," [37] and so to endorse a creative judicial role in defining the nature and scope of unlisted rights. As with the question of WHAT is "the Constitution," some jurists like James Wilson, William H. Rehnquist, and Antonin Scalia, not to mention Hugo Black, have challenged judges' authority to carry on such tasks; but the Supreme Court has tended to accept, if

---

35. Thayer himself would have allowed judges great discretion when determining the constitutionality of state action. Justice Frankfurter, however, would have extended Thayer's theory to federal judicial review of state authority. See, *e.g.*, his opinion for the Court in Minersville School Dist. v. Gobitis (1940; reprinted above, p. 1165); and his dissent in West Virginia v. Barnette (1943; reprinted above, p. 1174) against the Court's overruling *Gobitis*.

36. *Democracy and Distrust* (Cambridge: Harvard University Press, 1980). See also Cass R. Sunstein, *The Partial Constitution* (Cambridge: Harvard University Press, 1993).

37. Senate Debates on the Judiciary Act of 1802; reprinted above, p. 291.

not to explicate and justify, a role for itself as the principal (though hardly exclusive) constitutional interpreter. (Recall the analyses of the interrogative WHO shall interpret in Chapters 7 and 8.)

Still, the debate goes on, though in truncated form. Dissenting in an abortion case, Akron v. Akron Center for Reproductive Health (1983), Justice O'Connor quoted Lewis Powell, author of the majority opinion in *Akron*, quoting Oliver Wendell Holmes:

> In determining whether the State imposes an "undue burden" [on a woman's right to choose an abortion], we must keep in mind that when we are concerned with extremely sensitive issues, such as the one involved here, "the appropriate forum for their resolution in a democracy is the legislature. We should not forget that 'legislatures are ultimate guardians of the liberties and welfare of the people in quite as great a degree as the courts.'"

III. HOW TO INTERPRET?

HOW one interprets is critical to this enterprise, and is bound up with one's conception of WHAT is "the Constitution." A positivist theory of constitutional meaning based on plain words of the amended text of 1787–88, even if augmented by an inquiry into original intent or understanding, would impose on interpreters a form of intellectual schizophrenia. As we have often remarked, the Ninth Amendment orders interpreters not to act as narrow positivists. And that command carries out Madison's precise purpose in drafting that amendment—though it is dangerous to generalize from *his* purpose to that of a majority of those who supported the amendment.

The specific *purposive approach* around which this block of three chapters is organized, that of *protecting fundamental rights*, addresses the problem of HOW by stressing that one of the, if not *the*, central purposes of a constitutional democracy is to defend certain basic rights of individual human beings against government as well as against fellow citizens. This *approach* is to some extent *textualist*, drawing not only on the Preamble and the Ninth Amendment but also on the Bill of Rights, later amendments such as the Thirteenth and Fourteenth, as well as on protections in Article I against bills of attainder and ex post facto laws and in Article VI against religious oaths.

Moreover, *protecting fundamental rights* is to some extent a *philosophic approach*, relying on concepts of human dignity and equality and perhaps, insofar as it harks back to the Declaration of Independence, to a theory of natural rights as well. In any event, it is congruent with democratic theory and constitutionalism, though much more with the latter than the former in that it prescribes a special role for judges in defending minorities against policies that may have overwhelming and thoughtful public approval.[38]

Protecting fundamental rights also links to a *doctrinal approach* in that, at least since Calder v. Bull (1798; reprinted above, p. 121), judges have been asserting a judicial duty to protect certain basic rights, including some whose textual grounding is only through the word "liberty." In addition, because doctrines of natural rights were popular within the founding generation, *protecting fundamental rights* also links to *originalism*. Curiously, however, many current originalists, such as Antonin Scalia, deny the constitutional relevance of natural rights.

Like other conceptions of HOW to interpret, *protecting fundamental rights* offers neither definitive answers to many critical questions, nor have its defenders been able to supply absolutely persuasive justifications for its use. It may be true, as Justice Louis D. Brandeis once claimed, that the term "liberty" encompasses "all fundamental rights," [39] but so saying tells us precious little about what those rights include and how far they stretch.

As articulated by judges and commentators, this quest has been open-ended. Formulations such as a "disinterested inquiry pursued in the spirit of science" [40] into "history and tradition," [41] deciding whether an asserted right is "implicit in the concept of ordered liberty" or "deeply rooted in this Nation's history and tradition," [42] or "reasoned judgment," [43] do little to straighten what an eighteenth century critic called "the Crooked Cord of a Judge's Discretion in matters of the greatest moment and value." [44] As Justice White protested in dissent in Moore v. East Cleveland (1977; reprinted below, p. 1314): "What the deeply rooted traditions of the country are is arguable; which of them deserve the protection of the Due Process Clause is even more debatable." Indeed, Justice Scalia has gone so far as to suggest that the answers to questions like these are "neither set forth in the Constitution nor known to the nine Justices of this Court any better than they are known to nine people picked at random from the Kansas City telephone directory." [45]

Serious reservations about judges' performing such creative interpretation need not be rooted in democratic theory; they may

---

38. Because of this special judicial responsibility, *protecting fundamental rights* also addresses the question WHO interprets.

39. Whitney v. California, concur. op. (1927; reprinted above, p. 651).

40. Rochin v. California (1952; reprinted above, p. 135).

41. Griswold v. Connecticut, Harlan, J., concur. op. (1965; reprinted above, p. 147).

42. Palko v. Connecticut (1937; reprinted above, p. 128); Moore v. East Cleveland (1977 [plurality opinion]; reprinted below, p. 1314).

43. Planned Parenthood v. Casey (1992 [joint opinion]; reprinted below, p. 1281).

44. Quoted in Morton J. Horwitz, *The Transformation of American Law, 1780–1860* (Cambridge: Harvard University Press, 1977), p. 13.

45. Cruzan v. Director, Missouri Dept. of Health, concur. op. (1990; reprinted below, p. 1338).

also stem from constitutionalism itself. In a pluralistic society such as that of the United States, disagreements with the practical wisdom and moral values that inform judges' choices are inevitable. It would hardly be irrational to be disturbed by judges' finding within "the Constitution" a right of a woman to choose an abortion (Roe v. Wade [1973; reprinted below, p. 1258]) or not finding a right to a decent reputation (Paul v. Davis [1976]).

Faced with the awesome responsibility of deciding WHAT is included in the substantive liberties protected by the Fourteenth Amendment, the joint opinion of Justices O'Connor, Kennedy, and Souter in Planned Parenthood v. Casey (1992; reprinted below, p. 1281) acknowledged that it was "tempting" to suppose that such liberty "encompasses no more than those rights already guaranteed to the individual against federal interference by the express provisions of the first eight amendments" (Black's view) or that the Due Process Clause "protects only those practices, defined at the most specific level, that were protected against government interference by other rules of law when the Fourteenth Amendment was ratified" (Scalia's view). The joint opinion, however, resisted both of these temptations, stating instead: "The inescapable fact is that adjudication of substantive due process claims may call upon the Court in interpreting the Constitution to exercise that same capacity which by tradition courts always have exercised: reasoned judgment." Scalia angrily retorted: "The Court's temptation is in the quite opposite and more natural direction—toward systematically eliminating checks upon its own power, and it succumbs." He asserted that "reasoned judgment" was no more than "philosophical predilection and moral intuition." He insisted that constitutional interpretation should be a matter of studying relatively uncontroversial "historical facts," not a matter of making highly controversial "value judgments."

If, however, definiteness were the sole criterion for choosing among theories of constitutional interpretation, all but the most banal would fail. More important, discarding the protection of unlisted fundamental rights would mean discarding much of constitutionalism itself. The difficulties outlined here and in the cases that follow present constitutional interpretation with a challenge: HOW to identify rights essential to autonomy and dignity, protect those rights without harming the rights of others, and accomplish both goals without allowing the "crooked cord" of judicial discretion to become a noose around society's neck.

SELECTED BIBLIOGRAPHY

Ball, Milner S. *The Promise of American Law* (Athens: University of Georgia Press, 1981).

Barber, Sotirios A. *On What the Constitution Means* (Baltimore: Johns Hopkins University Press, 1984), espec. chs. 4–6.

————. *The Constitution of Judicial Power* (Baltimore: Johns Hopkins University Press, 1993).

Benedict, Michael Les. "To Secure These Rights: Rights, Democracy, and Judicial Review in the Anglo–American Constitutional Heritage," 42 *Ohio St.L.J.* 69 (1982).

Bobbitt, Philip. *Constitutional Interpretation* (Cambridge, MA: Basil Blackwell, 1991).

Brest, Paul. "The Fundamental Rights Controversy," 90 *Yale L.J.* 1063 (1981).

Choper, Jesse H. *Judicial Review and the National Political Process* (Chicago: University of Chicago Press, 1980), espec. chs. 1–2.

Corwin, Edward S. "The Basic Doctrine of American Constitutional Law," 12 *Mich.L.Rev.* 247 (1914); reprinted in Alpheus Thomas Mason and Gerald Garvey, eds., *American Constitutional History: Essays by Edward S. Corwin* (New York: Harper & Row, 1964).

Craven, J. Braxton, Jr. "Personhood: The Right to be Let Alone," 1976 *Duke L.J.* 699.

Dworkin, Ronald. *Life's Dominion* (New York: Knopf, 1993).

Ely, John H. *Democracy and Distrust* (Cambridge: Harvard University Press, 1980), espec. ch. 3.

Fleming, James E. "Constructing the Substantive Constitution," 72 *Tex.L.Rev.* 211 (1993).

————. "Securing Deliberative Autonomy," 48 *Stan.L.Rev.* ____ (forthcoming 1995).

Fried, Charles. "Privacy," 77 *Yale L.J.* 475 (1968).

————. *Order and Law: Arguing the Reagan Revolution—A Firsthand Account* (New York: Simon & Schuster, 1991).

Glendon, Mary Ann. *Rights Talk: The Impoverishment of Political Discourse* (New York: Free Press, 1991).

————. *Abortion and Divorce in Western Law* (Cambridge: Harvard University Press, 1987).

Karst, Kenneth L. "The Freedom of Intimate Association," 89 *Yale L.J.* 624 (1980).

McCorvey, Norma, with Andy Meisler. *I Am Roe: My Life, Roe v. Wade, and Freedom of Choice* (New York: HarperCollins, 1994).

O'Brien, David M. *Privacy, Law, and Public Policy* (New York: Praeger, 1979).

Pennock, J. Roland, and John W. Chapman, eds. *Privacy* (New York: Atherton, 1971).

Perry, Michael J. *Morality, Politics, and Law* (New York: Oxford University Press, 1988).

Posner, Richard A. *Sex and Reason* (Cambridge: Harvard University Press, 1992).

Richards, David A.J. *Toleration and the Constitution* (New York: Oxford University Press, 1986).

————. *Conscience and the Constitution* (Princeton: Princeton University Press, 1993).

Rubenfeld, Jed. "The Right of Privacy," 102 *Harv.L.Rev.* 737 (1989).

Smith, Rogers M. "The Constitution and Autonomy," 60 *Tex.L.Rev.* 175 (1982).

Sullivan, Kathleen. "Foreword: The Justices of Rules and Standards," 106 *Harv.L.Rev.* 24 (1992).

Sunstein, Cass R., *The Partial Constitution* (Cambridge: Harvard University Press, 1993).

Tribe, Laurence H. and Michael C. Dorf. *On Reading the Constitution* (Cambridge: Harvard University Press, 1991).

West, Robin. "Foreword: Taking Freedom Seriously," 104 *Harv. L.Rev.* 43 (1990).

Wilkinson, J. Harvie, III, and G. Edward White. "Constitutional Protection for Personal Lifestyles," 62 *Corn.L.Rev.* 563 (1977).

I. PERSONAL LIBERTY: ANTECEDENTS FROM THE ERA OF LOCHNER V. NEW YORK

"[T]he individual has certain fundamental rights which must be respected."—Justice McREYNOLDS

"[The law] appears to me to present a question upon which men reasonably might differ and therefore I am unable to say that the Constitution of the United States prevents the experiment being tried."—Justice HOLMES

MEYER v. NEBRASKA

262 U.S. 390, 43 S.Ct. 625, 67 L.Ed. 1042 (1923).

As part of a general xenophobia that pulsed in America during the first and second decades of this century and more particularly of anti-German feeling engendered by World War I, Nebraska in 1919 enacted a statute forbidding teaching in, or the teaching of, a modern language other than English to pupils who had not successfully completed eight years of schooling. Meyer, a parochial school instructor, was convicted for violating this act by teaching German to a ten-year-old boy. After the state supreme court sustained his conviction, Meyer sought and obtained review by the U.S. Supreme Court.

Mr. Justice **McREYNOLDS** delivered the opinion of the Court. ...

The problem for our determination is whether the statute as construed and applied unreasonably infringes the liberty guaranteed to the plaintiff in error by the Fourteenth Amendment. "No State shall ... deprive any person of life, liberty, or property, without due process of law."

While this Court has not attempted to define with exactness the liberty thus guaranteed, the term has received much consideration and some of the included things have been definitely stated. Without doubt, it denotes not merely freedom from bodily restraint but also the right of the individual to contract, to engage in any of the common occupations of life, to acquire useful knowledge, to marry, establish a home and bring up children, to worship God according to the dictates of his own conscience, and generally to enjoy those privileges long recognized at common law as essential to the orderly pursuit of happiness by free men. Slaughter–House Cases [1873]; Yick Wo v. Hopkins [1886]; Minnesota v. Barber [1890]; Allgeyer v. Louisiana [1897]; Lochner v. New York [1905]; Twining v. New Jersey [1908]; Truax v. Raich [1915]; Adams v. Tanner [1917]; Truax v. Corrigan [1921]; Adkins v. Children's Hospital [1923]. The established doctrine is that this liberty may not be interfered with, under the guise of protecting the public interest, by legislative action which is arbitrary or without reasonable relation to some purpose within the competency of the State to effect. Determination by the legislature of what constitutes proper exercise of police power is not final or conclusive but is subject to supervision by the courts. Lawton v. Steele [1894].

The American people have always regarded education and acquisition of knowledge as matters of supreme importance which should be diligently promoted. ... Corresponding to the right of control, it is the natural duty of the parent to give his children education suitable to their station in life; and nearly all the States, including Nebraska, enforce this obligation by compulsory laws.

Practically, education of the young is only possible in schools conducted by especially qualified persons who devote themselves thereto. The calling always has been regarded as useful and honorable, essential, indeed, to the public welfare. Mere knowledge of the German language cannot reasonably be regarded as harmful. Heretofore it has been commonly looked upon as helpful and desirable. Plaintiff in error taught this language in school as part of his occupation. His right thus to teach and the right of parents to engage him so to instruct their children, we think, are within the liberty of the Amendment. ...

That the State may do much, go very far, indeed, in order to improve the quality of its citizens, physically, mentally and morally, is clear; but the individual has certain fundamental rights which must be respected. The protection of the Constitution extends to all, to those who speak other languages as well as to those born with English on the tongue. Perhaps it would be highly advantageous if all had ready understanding of our ordinary speech, but this cannot be coerced by methods which conflict with the Constitution—a desirable end cannot be promoted by prohibited means. . . .

The desire of the legislature to foster a homogeneous people with American ideals prepared readily to understand current discussions of civic matters is easy to appreciate. Unfortunate experiences during the late war and aversion toward every characteristic of truculent adversaries were certainly enough to quicken that aspiration. But the means adopted, we think, exceed the limitations upon the power of the State and conflict with rights assured to plaintiff in error. The interference is plain enough and no adequate reason therefor in time of peace and domestic tranquility has been shown.

The power of the State to compel attendance at some school and to make reasonable regulations for all schools, including a requirement that they shall give instructions in English, is not questioned. Nor has challenge been made of the State's power to prescribe a curriculum for institutions which it supports. *Adams* pointed out that mere abuse incident to an occupation ordinarily useful is not enough to justify its abolition, although regulation may be entirely proper. No emergency has arisen which renders knowledge by a child of some language other than English so clearly harmful as to justify its inhibition with the consequent infringement of rights long freely enjoyed. We are constrained to conclude that the statute as applied is arbitrary and without reasonable relation to any end within the competency of the State.

As the statute undertakes to interfere only with teaching which involves a modern language, leaving complete freedom as to other matters, there seems no adequate foundation for the suggestion that the purpose was to protect the child's health by limiting his mental activities. It is well known that proficiency in a foreign language seldom comes to one not instructed at an early age, and experience shows that this is not injurious to the health, morals or understanding of the ordinary child. . . .

Reversed.

Mr. Justice **HOLMES,** dissenting.

We all agree . . . that it is desirable that all the citizens of the United States should speak a common tongue, and therefore that the end aimed at by the statute is a lawful and proper one. The only question is whether the means adopted deprive teachers of the liberty secured to them by the Fourteenth Amendment. . . . I cannot bring my mind to believe that in some circumstances and circumstances existing it

is said in Nebraska, the statute might not be regarded as a reasonable or even necessary method of reaching the desired result. The part of the act with which we are concerned deals with the teaching of young children. Youth is the time when familiarity with a language is established and if there are sections in the State where a child would hear only Polish or French or German spoken at home I am not prepared to say that it is unreasonable to provide that in his early years he shall hear and speak only English at school. But if it is reasonable it is not an undue restriction of the liberty either of teacher or scholar. No one would doubt that a teacher might be forbidden to teach many things, and the only criterion of his liberty under the Constitution that I can think of is "whether, considering the end in view, the statute passes the bounds of reason and assumes the character of a merely arbitrary fiat." Purity Extract & Tonic Co. v. Lynch [1912]. Hebe v. Shaw [1919]. Jacob Ruppert v. Caffey [1920]. I think I appreciate the objection to the law but it appears to me to present a question upon which men reasonably might differ and therefore I am unable to say that the Constitution of the United States prevents the experiment being tried.
. . .

Mr. Justice **SUTHERLAND** concurs in this opinion.

Editors' Notes

(1) **Query:** Chapter 9 and the introductory essay to this Part of the book as well as the three individual chapters have spoken of a particular *purposive approach* to constitutional interpretation, *protecting fundamental rights*. *Meyer* is usually cited as a classic example of such an approach. Did Justice McReynolds intimate if not articulate a general theory for deciding what liberty is included in the constitutional text and, more specifically, in the Fourteenth Amendment? To what extent did McReynolds take a *doctrinal approach*, simply calling the roll of earlier decisions, and to what extent did he follow the path of *protecting fundamental rights*?

(2) **Query**: What specific constitutional right(s) did the Court recognize in *Meyer*? The parents' "right to contract" with the teacher? The teacher's "right to teach"? The parents' right, and corresponding "natural duty," to control the upbringing and education of their children? All of the above? At what level of generality did McReynolds conceive the right(s) recognized in *Meyer*? Quite specifically or quite broadly? Reconsider this question after reading Pierce v. Society of Sisters (1925; the next case) and after rereading Michael H. v. Gerald D. (1989; reprinted above, p. 158).

(3) **Query:** McReynolds spoke of the "privileges long recognized at common law as essential to the orderly pursuit of happiness by free men." What was the constitutional relevance of such long recognition "at common law"?

(4) **Query:** What approach(es) did Justice Holmes follow? How did his jurisprudence, as he explained it here and in his dissent in Lochner v. New York (1905; reprinted above, p. 1110), differ from Stone's jurisprudence outlined in *Carolene Products* (1938; reprinted above, p. 609)? From Thayer's jurisprudence (reprinted above, p. 602)?

(5) Holmes's dissent surprised many people. He was still groping his way toward a distinction between judicial deference to governmental regulation of economic affairs and to governmental regulation of ideas. Brandeis, the son of German-speaking immigrants, did not join Holmes's dissent, but the only immigrant on the Court, Sutherland, did. He was an ardent defender of economic laissez faire and the author of the Court's opinion in Adkins v. Childrens Hospital (1923; reprinted above, p. 1116). How can one reconcile Holmes's dissent in *Meyer* with Sutherland's opinion in *Adkins*?

(6) Like Sutherland, McReynolds was one of the justices most closely associated with economic laissez faire; after 1937, the Court spent a good deal of time undoing the constitutional jurisprudence that he and his brethren had constructed. In the plurality opinion in Moore v. East Cleveland (1977; reprinted below, p. 1314), Justice Powell cited *Meyer* and Pierce v. Society of Sisters (1925; the next case below) to support a decision defending rights of the extended family against a municipal zoning ordinance. Quoting Harlan's dissent in Poe v. Ullman (1961; reprinted above, p. 141) to the effect that the American constitutional tradition is a "living thing" and that a decision "which builds on what has survived is likely to be sound," Powell added a footnote:

> This explains why *Meyer* and *Pierce* have survived and enjoyed frequent reaffirmation, while other substantive due process cases of the same era have been repudiated—including a number written, as were *Meyer* and *Pierce,* by Mr. Justice McReynolds.

Perhaps another reason why *Meyer* and *Pierce* have survived is that the Court has retrospectively reconstrued them as involving rights protected by the letter and spirit of the First Amendment, not merely the "liberty of contract" that the Court protected in the era of *Lochner*. See, *e.g.*, Griswold v. Connecticut (1965; reprinted above, p. 147).

(7) For the background of *Meyer,* see Orville H. Zabel, *God and Caesar in Nebraska* (Lincoln: University of Nebraska Press, 1955).

(8) Bartels v. Iowa (1923) consolidated several rulings the same day as *Meyer,* invalidating similar laws from Iowa and Ohio. *Pierce*, reprinted as the next principal case, struck down an Oregon law that required parents to send their children between the ages of 8 and 16 to *public* schools.

"The child is not the mere creature of the state. ..."

PIERCE v. SOCIETY OF SISTERS

268 U.S. 510, 45 S.Ct. 571, 69 L.Ed. 1070 (1925).

In 1922 Oregon enacted a law that required parents to send all their children between the ages of 8 and 16, with limited exceptions, to public schools. The Society of Sisters of Holy Names, a Catholic religious order that operated several parochial schools in Oregon, and the Hill Military Academy, a private school, brought suit in a federal district court for an injunction against enforcement of the act. The state defended the statute as a reasonable means of insuring that its citizens would be educated and as a means of insuring separation of church and state. The district court granted the writ and Oregon appealed.

Mr. Justice **McREYNOLDS** delivered the opinion of the Court. ...

Under the doctrine of Meyer v. Nebraska [1923], we think it entirely plain that the Act of 1922 unreasonably interferes with the liberty of parents and guardians to direct the upbringing and education of children under their control. As often heretofore pointed out, rights guaranteed by the Constitution may not be abridged by legislation which has no reasonable relation to some purpose within the competency of the state. The fundamental theory upon which all governments in this Union repose excludes any general power of the state to standardize its children by forcing them to accept instruction from public teachers only. The child is not the mere creature of the state; those who nurture him and direct his destiny have the right, coupled with the high duty, to recognize and prepare him for additional obligations.

Appellees are corporations, and therefore, it is said, they cannot claim for themselves the liberty which the 14th Amendment guarantees. Accepted in the proper sense, this is true. But they have business and property for which they claim protection. These are threatened with destruction through the unwarranted compulsion which appellants are exercising over present and prospective patrons of their schools. And this court has gone very far to protect against loss threatened by such action. Truax v. Raich [1915]; Truax v. Corrigan [1921]; Terrace v. Thompson [1923]. ...

[Affirmed.]

Editors' Notes

(1) **Query:** Did McReynolds offer more than a *doctrinal* justification for *Pierce*? Did he move any closer toward an articulation of a justification for an approach of *protecting fundamental rights*? What constitutional right(s) did the Court recognize here? How, if at all, did they differ from those in *Meyer*? Did McReynolds conceive of those rights at a different level of generality in the two opinions? Reconsider this question after rereading Michael H. v. Gerald D. (1989; reprinted above, p. 158).

(2) Did McReynolds base the decision on the rights of parents to educate their children? The suit was brought by private corporations. How could a corporation obtain "standing to sue" if the rights it asserted were those of people not party to the case?

(3) The decision in *Pierce* was apparently unanimous. Neither Holmes nor Sutherland repeated objections like those they voiced in *Meyer*. They may not have changed their minds but simply followed a common practice in those times of not dissenting a second time except on issues justices deemed of extraordinary constitutional importance.

(4) Like *Meyer*, *Pierce* illustrates the intertwining of economic and other kinds of personal liberty. Since the Court repudiated special judicial protection for economic liberties under the Due Process Clause in West Coast Hotel

v. Parrish (1937; reprinted above, p. 1123), it generally has sought to distinguish economic liberties from other personal liberties. See, *e.g.*, Griswold v. Connecticut (1965; reprinted above, p. 147). To what extent is that distinction constitutionally viable? Why should other personal rights deserve greater judicial solicitude than economic rights? Think back on the cases in Chapter 16. Are not certain distinctions *among* various sorts of economic rights constitutionally relevant?

(5) **Query:** "The child is not the mere creature of the state," *Pierce* said. Did McReynolds imply the child *is* the mere creature of her or his parents? Consider *Pierce* in relation to the Amish school case, Wisconsin v. Yoder (1972; reprinted above, p. 1187), espec. Douglas's separate opinion.

II. THE RIGHT TO CITIZENSHIP: THE RIGHT TO HAVE RIGHTS

"Citizenship is not a license that expires upon misbehavior. ..."

TROP v. DULLES
356 U.S. 86, 78 S.Ct. 590, 2 L.Ed.2d 630 (1958).

This case, invalidating a federal statute that revoked American citizenship for desertion in time of war, is reprinted above, p. 219. There was no opinion for the Court; it was not until Afroyim v. Rusk (1967) that a majority of the Court held that the government could not strip a person of citizenship. "The very nature of our free government," the majority said, "makes it completely incongruous to have a rule of law under which a group of citizens temporarily in office can deprive another group of citizens of their citizenship."

Notwithstanding this general pronouncement, the Court has continued to rule that the federal government can revoke the citizenship of a person who was naturalized if he or she obtained that citizenship through fraud. See, for example, Fedorenko v. United States (1981).

III. THE RIGHT TO BODILY INTEGRITY

"There are manifold restraints to which every person is necessarily subject for the common good."

JACOBSON v. MASSACHUSETTS
197 U.S. 11, 25 S.Ct. 358, 49 L.Ed. 643 (1905).

This case, upholding a local ordinance requiring vaccinations against Smallpox, is reprinted above, p. 125.

"It is better ..., if instead of waiting to execute degenerate offspring for crime, or to let them starve for their
imbecility, society can prevent those who are manifestly
unfit from continuing their kind. ..."

BUCK v. BELL

274 U.S. 200, 47 S.Ct. 584, 71 L.Ed. 1000 (1927).

Mr. Justice **HOLMES** delivered the opinion of the Court. ...

Carrie Buck is a feeble minded white woman who was committed to
the State mental hospital. She was the daughter of a feeble minded
mother in the same institution, and the mother of an illegitimate feeble
minded child. She was eighteen years old at the time of the trial of her
case in the Circuit Court, in the latter part of 1924. An Act of Virginia
recites that the health of the patient and the welfare of society may be
promoted in certain cases by the sterilization of mental defectives, under
careful safeguard, & c.; that the sterilization may be effected in males by
vasectomy and in females by salpingectomy, without serious pain or
substantial danger to life; that the Commonwealth is supporting in
various institutions many defective persons who if now discharged would
become a menace but if incapable of procreating might be discharged
with safety and become self-supporting with benefit to themselves and to
society; and that experience has shown that heredity plays an important
part in the transmission of insanity, imbecility, & c. The statute then
enacts that whenever the superintendent of certain institutions ... shall
be of opinion that it is for the best interests of the patients and of society
that an inmate under his care should be sexually sterilized, he may have
the operation performed upon any patient afflicted with hereditary forms
of insanity, imbecility, etc., on complying with the very careful provisions
by which the act protects the patients from possible abuse. ...

The attack[, however,] is not upon the procedure but upon the
substantive law. It seems to be contended that in no circumstances
could such an order be justified. It certainly is contended that the order
cannot be justified upon the existing grounds. The judgment finds the
facts that have been recited and that Carrie Buck "is the probable
potential parent of socially inadequate offspring, likewise afflicted, that
she may be sexually sterilized without detriment to her general health
and that her welfare and that of society will be promoted by her
sterilization," and thereupon makes the order. In view of the general
declarations of the legislature and the specific findings of the Court,
obviously we cannot say as matter of law that the grounds do not exist,
and if they exist they justify the result. We have seen more than once
that the public welfare may call upon the best citizens for their lives. It
would be strange if it could not call upon those who already sap the
strength of the State for these lesser sacrifices, often not felt to be such
by those concerned, in order to prevent our being swamped with incom-
petence. It is better for all the world, if instead of waiting to execute
degenerate offspring for crime, or to let them starve for their imbecility,

society can prevent those who are manifestly unfit from continuing their kind. The principle that sustains compulsory vaccination is broad enough to cover cutting the Fallopian tubes. Jacobson v. Massachusetts [1905]. Three generations of imbeciles are enough.

But, it is said, however it might be if this reasoning were applied generally, it fails when it is confined to the small number who are in the institutions named and is not applied to the multitudes outside. It is the usual last resort of constitutional arguments to point out shortcomings of this sort. But the answer is that the law does all that is needed when it does all that it can, indicates a policy, applies it to all within the lines, and seeks to bring within the lines all similarly situated so far and so fast as its means allow. Of course so far as the operations enable those who otherwise must be kept confined to be returned to the world, and thus open the asylum to others, the equality aimed at will be more nearly reached.

Judgment affirmed.

Mr. Justice **BUTLER** dissents.

Editors' Notes

(1) Justice Holmes said Carrie Buck's daughter was "feeble minded." In fact, she "would [not] be considered mentally deficient by today's standards." Stephen J. Gould, *The Mismeasure of Man* (New York: Norton, 1981), p. 336. See also Paul A. Lombardo, "Three Generations, No Imbeciles: New Light on *Buck v. Bell*," 60 *N.Y.U.L.Rev.* 30 (1985).

(2) **Query:** Holmes obviously followed a doctrinal approach here: "The principle that sustains compulsory vaccination is broad enough to cover cutting the Fallopian tubes." Does his claim hold? By Holmes's reasoning, would that principle also sustain compulsory abortion? Compulsory childbearing?

(3) **Query**: Did Holmes also (silently?) employ other approach(es) to constitutional interpretation? Did he give any hint that he thought *protecting fundamental rights* was a judicial duty? How would a democratic theorist judge Holmes's reasoning? A constitutionalist? What sort of political theory, if any, did Holmes see "the Constitution" embodying?

(4) **Query:** Why were there no dissenting opinions in *Buck* from McReynolds, who was so eloquent in Meyer v. Nebraska (1923; reprinted above, p. 1247) in defense of the rights "to marry, establish a home and bring up children," or Sutherland, the great exponent in Adkins v. Children's Hospital (1923; reprinted above, p. 1116) of individual autonomy in the economic sphere? Only Butler dissented and he did so without opinion. Commentators usually attribute his opposition to his Catholicism. See the discussion in David J. Danelski, *A Supreme Court Justice Is Appointed* (New York: Random House, 1964), pp. 189–190.

(5) Holmes had given his personal views on eugenics a dozen years before *Buck*:

I believe that the wholesale social regeneration which so many now seem to expect, if it can be helped by conscious, co-ordinated human effort, cannot be affected appreciably by tinkering with the institutions of property, but only by taking in hand life and trying to build a race. That would be my starting point for an ideal for the law. [Quoted in Walter Berns, "Buck v. Bell: Due Process of Law?" 6 *West.Pol.Q.* 762 (1953).]

At the time of the litigation, Holmes wrote to a friend that he "took pleasure" in sustaining Virginia's law. James B. Peabody, ed., *The Holmes–Einstein Letters* (New York: St. Martin's, 1964), p. 267. Berns presents an interesting analysis of *Buck,* showing that it was a friendly suit designed to test the constitutionality of Virginia's law rather than a genuine conflict. See also Clement E. Vose, *Constitutional Change: Amendment Politics and Supreme Court Litigation Since 1900* (Lexington, MA: Lexington Books, 1972); and Elliot A. Brown, "Cases Histories, Interest Group Litigation, and Mr. Justice Holmes," 24 *Emory L.J.* 1037 (1975).

(6) **Query:** To what extent did Skinner v. Oklahoma (1942; reprinted above, p. 1014) modify *Buck*?

(7) Congress has passed a series of statutes to protect mental patients, mentally retarded persons, and disabled adults as well as children. See, *e.g.,* the Developmental Disabilities Assistance and Bill of Rights Act of 1975 (42 U.S.C. § 6010) and the Americans with Disabilities Act of 1990 (42 U.S.C. § 12101).

(8) In Cleburne v. Cleburne Living Center (1985; reprinted above, p. 1048), the Court held that classifications based on mental retardation are neither suspect nor "quasi-suspect" and therefore do not warrant heightened judicial scrutiny. The Court reasoned that recent federal and state legislation attempting to ameliorate the condition of the mentally retarded "belie[d] a continuing antipathy or prejudice" against such persons.

(9) In the Matter of Lee Ann Grady (1981) presented the Supreme Court of New Jersey with a variation on *Buck.* In *Grady,* the parents and physician of a 19–year old woman suffering from Down's Syndrome—her IQ was below 40—sought to have her sterilized. The hospital refused and the family sued. The state supreme court held that the constitutional right to privacy (see Griswold v. Connecticut [1965; reprinted above, p. 147]; and Roe v. Wade [1973; reprinted below, p. 1258]) included a right to sterilization, but that the decision to exercise that right for a mentally retarded person would have to be made by a judge, not by parents or guardians. The judge, the court said, must weigh many factors, including the risks of pregnancy, the dangers to the retarded person's health of a pregnancy and of sterilization, the feasibility of less drastic means of contraception, and a showing that those who sought the sterilization were seeking it for the good of the retarded person and not for their own or the public's convenience. See George J. Annas, "Sterilization of the Mentally Retarded," 11 *The Hastings Center Report* 18 (August, 1981), and literature cited.

(10) In *Buck,* Holmes disparagingly referred to arguments under the Equal Protection Clause as "the usual last resort of constitutional arguments." Recall the equal protection cases reprinted in Chapters 14 and 15. Do they

suggest that, although the Clause enjoys a higher status now than it did in 1927, some justices still share Holmes's view?   If so, who?

"We are dealing here with legislation which involves one of the basic civil rights of man. ... **[S]trict scrutiny of the classification which a state makes in a sterilization law is essential, lest** ... **invidious discriminations are made against groups or types of individuals in violation of the constitutional guaranty of just and equal laws."**

SKINNER v. OKLAHOMA
316 U.S. 535, 62 S.Ct. 1110, 86 L.Ed. 1655 (1942).

This case, which invalidated a state statute requiring some habitual criminals to be sterilized, is reprinted above, p. 1014.

"This is conduct that shocks the conscience."

ROCHIN v. CALIFORNIA
342 U.S. 165, 72 S.Ct. 205, 96 L.Ed. 183 (1952).

This decision, holding that use by police of a stomach pump to regain evidence that a suspect had swallowed, violated the due process clause of the Fourteenth Amendment, is reprinted above, p. 135.

IV.   THE RIGHT TO PRIVACY

"[S]pecific guarantees in the Bill of Rights have penumbras, formed by emanations from those guarantees that help give them life and substance."

GRISWOLD v. CONNECTICUT
381 U.S. 479, 85 S.Ct. 1678, 14 L.Ed.2d 510 (1965).

This ruling, striking down a Connecticut statute that made it a crime to use or to aid, abet, or counsel use of "any drug, medicinal article or instrument for the purpose of preventing conception," is reprinted above, p. 147.

"The right of privacy ... **is broad enough to encompass a woman's decision whether or not to terminate her pregnancy."—Justice BLACKMUN**

"I find nothing in the language or history of the Constitution to support the Court's judgment."—Justice WHITE

"While the Court's opinion quotes from the dissent of Mr. Justice Holmes in *Lochner*, the result it reaches is more closely attuned to the majority opinion of Mr. Justice Peckham in that case."—Justice REHNQUIST

ROE v. WADE
410 U.S. 113, 93 S.Ct. 705, 35 L.Ed.2d 147 (1973).

Mr. Justice **BLACKMUN** delivered the opinion of the Court.   ...

We forthwith acknowledge our awareness of the sensitive and emotional nature of the abortion controversy, of the vigorous opposing views, even among physicians, and of the deep and seemingly absolute convictions that the subject inspires.   One's philosophy, one's experiences, one's exposure to the raw edges of human existence, one's religious training, one's attitudes toward life and family and their values, and the moral standards one establishes and seeks to observe, are all likely to influence and to color one's thinking and conclusions about abortion.   In addition, population growth, pollution, poverty, and racial overtones tend to complicate and not to simplify the problem.

Our task, of course, is to resolve the issue by constitutional measurement free of emotion and of predilection.   We seek earnestly to do this, and, because we do, we have inquired into, and in this opinion place some emphasis upon, medical and medical-legal history and what that history reveals about man's attitudes toward the abortive procedure over the centuries.   We bear in mind, too, Mr. Justice Holmes' admonition in his now vindicated dissent in Lochner v. New York (1905).

> [The Constitution] is made for people of fundamentally differing views, and the accident of our finding certain opinions natural and familiar or novel and even shocking ought not to conclude our judgment upon the question whether statutes embodying them conflict with the Constitution of the United States.

I

The Texas statutes ... make it a crime to "procure an abortion," as therein defined, or to attempt one, except with respect to "an abortion procured or attempted by medical advice for the purpose of saving the life of the mother."   Similar statutes are in existence in a majority of the States.   ...

VI

It perhaps is not generally appreciated that the restrictive criminal abortion laws in effect in a majority of States today are of relatively recent vintage.   Those laws ... are not of ancient or even of common

law origin. Instead, they derive from statutory changes effected, for the
most part, in the latter half of the 19th century. ...

[Justice Blackmun devoted 18 pages to surveying the history of
abortion under eight subheadings: ancient attitudes; the Hippocratic
Oath; the common law; the English statutory law; the American law;
the position of the American Medical Association; the position of the
American Public Health Association; and the position of the American
Bar Association. We reprint here only portions from his discussion of
the common law and the American law.—**Eds.**]

3. *The common law.* It is undisputed that at the common law,
abortion performed before "quickening"—the first recognizable movement of the fetus in utero, appearing usually from the 16th to the 18th
week of pregnancy—was not an indictable offense. ... There was
agreement ... that prior to this point the fetus was to be regarded as
part of the mother and its destruction, therefore, was not homicide. ...

Whether abortion of a quick fetus was a felony at common law, or
even a lesser crime, is still disputed. [Although Coke and Blackstone
took the position that abortion of a quick fetus was not murder but a
lesser offense.] ... A recent view of the common law precedents argues,
however, that ... even post-quickening abortion was never established
as a common law crime. This is of some importance because while most
American courts ruled ... that abortion of an unquickened fetus was not
criminal under their received common law, others followed Coke in
stating that abortion of a quick fetus was a "misprision," a term they
translated to mean "misdemeanor." That their reliance on Coke on this
aspect of the law was uncritical and, apparently in all the reported cases,
dictum ... makes it now appear doubtful that abortion was ever firmly
established as a common law crime even with respect to the destruction
of a quick fetus. ...

5. *The American law.* In this country the law in effect in all but a
few States until mid–19th century was the pre-existing English common
law. ... It was not until after the War Between the States that
legislation began generally to replace the common law. Most of these
initial statutes dealt severely with abortion after quickening but were
lenient with it before quickening. ...

Gradually, in the middle and late 19th century the quickening
distinction disappeared from the statutory law of most States and the
degree of the offense and the penalties were increased. By the end of
the 1950's a large majority of the States banned abortion, however and
whenever performed, unless done to save or preserve the life of the
mother. ... In the past several years, however, a trend toward liberali-
zation of abortion statutes has resulted in adoption, by about one-third
of the States, of less stringent laws. ...

It is thus apparent that at common law, at the time of the adoption
of our Constitution, and throughout the major portion of the 19th
century, abortion was viewed with less disfavor than under most Ameri-

can statutes currently in effect. Phrasing it another way, a woman enjoyed a substantially broader right to terminate a pregnancy than she does in most States today. ...

VII

Three reasons have been advanced to explain historically the enactment of criminal abortion laws in the 19th century and to justify their continued existence. It has been argued occasionally that these laws were the product of a Victorian social concern to discourage illicit sexual conduct. Texas, however, does not advance this justification ... and it appears that no court or commentator has taken the argument seriously. ...

A second reason is concerned with abortion as a medical procedure. When most criminal abortion laws were first enacted, the procedure was a hazardous one for the woman. This was particularly true prior to the development of antisepsis. ... Abortion mortality was high. Even after 1900, and perhaps until as late as the development of antibiotics in the 1940's, standard modern techniques such as dilation and curettage were not nearly so safe as they are today. Thus it has been argued that a State's real concern in enacting a criminal abortion law was to protect the pregnant woman, that is, to restrain her from submitting to a procedure that placed her life in serious jeopardy.

Modern medical techniques have altered this situation. ... Mortality rates for women undergoing early abortions, where the procedure is legal, appear to be as low as or lower than the rates for normal childbirth. Consequently, any interest of the State in protecting the woman from an inherently hazardous procedure ... has largely disappeared. Of course, important state interests in the area of health and medical standards do remain. The State has a legitimate interest in seeing to it that abortion, like any other medical procedure, is performed under circumstances that insure maximum safety for the patient. ... The prevalence of high mortality rates at illegal "abortion mills" strengthens, rather than weakens, the State's interest in regulating the conditions under which abortions are performed. Moreover, the risk to the woman increases as her pregnancy continues. Thus the State retains a definite interest in protecting the woman's own health and safety when an abortion is proposed at a late stage of pregnancy.

The third reason is the State's interest—some phrase it in terms of duty—in protecting prenatal life. Some of the argument for this justification rests on the theory that a new human life is present from the moment of conception. The State's interest and general obligation to protect life then extends, it is argued, to prenatal life. Only when the life of the pregnant mother herself is at stake, balanced against the life she carries within her, should the interest of the embryo or fetus not prevail. Logically, of course, a legitimate state interest in this area need not stand or fall on acceptance of the belief that life begins at conception or at some other point prior to live birth. In assessing the State's interest, recognition may be given to the less rigid claim that as long as at least potential life is involved, the State may assert interests beyond the protection of the pregnant woman alone. ...

VIII

The Constitution does not explicitly mention any right of privacy. In a line of decisions, however, ... the Court has recognized that a right of personal privacy, or a guarantee of certain areas or zones of privacy, does exist under the Constitution. In varying contexts the Court or individual Justices have indeed found at least the roots of that right in the First Amendment, Stanley v. Georgia (1969); in the Fourth and Fifth Amendments, Terry v. Ohio (1968), Katz v. United States (1967), Boyd v. United States (1867), see Olmstead v. United States (1928) (Brandeis, J., dissenting); in the penumbras of the Bill of Rights, Griswold v. Connecticut (1965); in the Ninth Amendment, id. (Goldberg, J., concurring); or in the concept of ordered liberty guaranteed by the first section of the Fourteenth Amendment, see Meyer v. Nebraska (1923). These decisions make it clear that only personal rights that can be deemed "fundamental" or "implicit in the concept of ordered liberty," Palko v. Connecticut (1937), are included in this guarantee of personal privacy. They also make it clear that the right has some extension to activities relating to marriage, Loving v. Virginia (1967); procreation, Skinner v. Oklahoma (1942); contraception, Eisenstadt v. Baird [1972]; family relationships, Prince v. Massachusetts (1944); and child rearing and education, Pierce v. Society of Sisters (1925), *Meyer.*

This right of privacy, whether it be found in the Fourteenth Amendment's concept of personal liberty and restrictions upon state action, as we feel it is, or, as the District Court determined, in the Ninth Amendment's reservation of rights to the people, is broad enough to encompass a woman's decision whether or not to terminate her pregnancy. The detriment that the State would impose upon the pregnant woman by denying this choice altogether is apparent. Specific and direct harm medically diagnosable even in early pregnancy may be involved. Maternity, or additional offspring, may force upon the woman a distressful life and future. Psychological harm may be imminent. Mental and physical health may be taxed by child care. There is also the distress, for all concerned, associated with the unwanted child, and there is the problem of bringing a child into a family already unable, psychologically and otherwise, to care for it. In other cases ... the additional difficulties and continuing stigma of unwed motherhood may be involved. All these are factors the woman and her responsible physician necessarily will consider in consultation.

... [A]ppellant and some amici argue that the woman's right is absolute. ... With this we do not agree. ... The Court's decisions recognizing a right of privacy also acknowledge that some state recognizing a right of privacy also acknowledge that some state regulation in areas protected by that right is appropriate. ... [A] state may properly assert important interests in safe-guarding health, in maintaining medi-

cal standards, and in protecting potential life. At some point in pregnancy, these respective interests become sufficiently compelling to sustain regulation of the factors that govern the abortion decision. ... We
therefore conclude that the right of personal privacy includes the abortion decision, but that this right is not unqualified and must be considered against important state interests in regulation. ...

Where certain "fundamental rights" are involved, the Court has
held that regulation limiting these rights may be justified only by a
"compelling state interest," Kramer v. Union Free School District
(1969); Shapiro v. Thompson (1969); Sherbert v. Verner (1963), and
that legislative enactments must be narrowly drawn to express only the
legitimate state interests at stake. *Griswold*; Aptheker v. Secretary of
State (1964); Cantwell v. Connecticut (1940). ...

IX ...

A

The appellee and certain amici argue that the fetus is a "person"
within the language and meaning of the Fourteenth Amendment. ... If
this suggestion of personhood is established, the appellant's case, of
course, collapses, for the fetus' right to life is then guaranteed specifically by the amendment. ... On the other hand, the appellee conceded on
reargument that no case could be cited that holds that a fetus is a person
within the meaning of the Fourteenth Amendment.

The Constitution does not define "person" in so many words. Sec. I
of the Fourteenth Amendment contains three references to "person".
... "Person" is used in other places in the Constitution. ... But in
nearly all these instances, the use of the word is such that it has
application only post-natally. None indicates, with any assurance, that
it has any possible pre-natal application.

All this, together with our observation ... that throughout the
major portion of the 19th century prevailing legal abortion practices
were far freer than they are today, persuades us that the word "person,"
as used in the Fourteenth Amendment, does not include the unborn.
... This conclusion, however, does not of itself fully answer the contentions raised by Texas, and we pass on to other considerations.

B

The pregnant woman cannot be isolated in her privacy. She carries
an embryo and, later, a fetus. ... The situation therefore is inherently
different from marital intimacy, or bedroom possession of obscene material, or marriage, or procreation, or education. ... [I]t is reasonable and
appropriate for a State to decide that at some point in time another
interest, that of health of the mother or that of potential human life,
becomes significantly involved. The woman's privacy is no longer sole
and any right of privacy she possesses must be measured accordingly.

Texas urges that, apart from the Fourteenth Amendment, life begins at conception and is present throughout pregnancy, and that, therefore, the State has a compelling interest in protecting that life from and after conception. We need not resolve the difficult question of when life begins. When those trained in the respective disciplines of medicine, philosophy, and theology are unable to arrive at any consensus, the judiciary, at this point in the development of man's knowledge, is not in a position to speculate as to the answer. It should be sufficient to note briefly the wide divergence of thinking on this most sensitive and difficult question. There has always been strong support for the view that life does not begin until live birth. ...

In the areas other than criminal abortion the law has been reluctant to endorse any theory that life, as we recognize it, begins before live birth or to accord legal rights to the unborn except in narrowly defined situations and except when the rights are contingent upon live birth. ... In most States recovery is said to be permitted only if the fetus was viable or at least quick when the injuries were sustained, though few courts have squarely so held. In a recent development, generally opposed by the commentators, some States permit the parents of a stillborn child to maintain an action for wrongful death because of prenatal injuries. Such an action, however, would appear to be one to vindicate the parents' interest and is thus consistent with the view that the fetus, at most, represents only the potentiality of life. Similarly, unborn children have been recognized as acquiring rights or interests by way of inheritance or other devolution of property, and have been represented by guardians ad litem. Perfection of the interests involved, again, has generally been contingent upon live birth. In short, the unborn have never been recognized in the law as persons in the whole sense.

X

In view of all this, we do not agree that, by adopting one theory of life, Texas may override the rights of the pregnant woman. ... With respect to the State's important and legitimate interest in the health of the mother, the "compelling" point, in the light of present medical knowledge, is at approximately the end of the first trimester. This is so because of the now established medical fact ... that until the end of the first trimester mortality in abortion may be less than mortality in normal childbirth. It follows that, from and after this point, a state may regulate the abortion procedure to the extent that the regulation reasonably relates to the preservation and protection of maternal health. ...

This means, on the one hand, that, for the period of pregnancy prior to this "compelling" point, the attending physician, in consultation with his patient, is free to determine, without regulation by the State, that in his judgment the patient's pregnancy should be terminated. If that decision is reached, the judgment may be effectuated by an abortion free of interference by the State.

With respect to the State's important and legitimate interest in potential life, the "compelling" point is at viability. This is so because the fetus then presumably has the capability of meaningful life outside the mother's womb. State regulation protective of fetal life after viability thus has both logical and biological justifications. If the State is interested in protecting fetal life after viability, it may go so far as to proscribe abortion during that period except when it is necessary to preserve the life or health of the mother.

Measured against these standards, Art. 1196 of the Texas Penal Code ... sweeps too broadly. The statute makes no distinction between abortions performed early in pregnancy and those performed later, and it limits to a single reason, "saving" the mother's life, the legal justification for the procedure. The statute, therefore, cannot survive the constitutional attack made upon it here. ...

This holding, we feel, is consistent with the relative weights of the respective interests involved, with the lessons and examples of medical and legal history, with the lenity of the common law, and with the demands of the profound problems of the present day. The decision leaves the State free to place increasing restrictions on abortion as the period of pregnancy lengthens, so long as those restrictions are tailored to the recognized state interests. The decision vindicates the right of the physician to administer medical treatment according to his professional judgment up to the points where important state interests provide compelling justifications for intervention. Up to those points, the abortion decision in all its aspects is inherently, and primarily, a medical decision, and basic responsibility for it must rest with the physician. If an individual practitioner abuses the privilege of exercising proper medical judgment, the usual remedies, judicial and intra-professional, are available. ...

Mr. Chief Justice **BURGER,** concurring. ...

Mr. Justice **DOUGLAS,** concurring. ...

Mr. Justice **STEWART,** concurring. ...

Mr. Justice **WHITE,** with whom Mr. Justice **REHNQUIST** joins, dissenting. ...

... I find nothing in the language or history of the Constitution to support the Court's judgment. The Court simply fashions and announces a new constitutional right for pregnant mothers and, with scarcely any reason or authority for its action, invests that right with sufficient substance to override most existing state abortion statutes. The upshot is that the people and the legislatures of the 50 States are constitutionally disentitled to weigh the relative importance of the continued existence and development of the fetus on the one hand against a spectrum of possible impacts on the mother on the other hand. As an exercise of raw judicial power, the Court perhaps has authority to do what it does today; but in my view its judgment is an improvident and extravagant exercise of the power of judicial review that the Constitution extends to this Court.

The Court apparently values the convenience of the pregnant mother more than the continued existence and development of the life or potential life which she carries. Whether or not I might agree with that marshalling of values, I can in no event join the Court's judgment because I find no constitutional warrant for imposing such an order of priorities on the people and legislatures of the States. In a sensitive area such as this, involving as it does issues over which reasonable men may easily and heatedly differ, I cannot accept the Court's exercise of its clear power of choice by interposing a constitutional barrier to state efforts to protect human life and by investing mothers and doctors with the constitutionally protected right to exterminate it. This issue, for the most part, should be left with the people and to the political processes the people have devised to govern their affairs. ...

Mr. Justice **REHNQUIST**, dissenting. ...

... I have difficulty in concluding, as the Court does, that the right of "privacy" is involved in this case. Texas ... bars the performance of a medical abortion by a licensed physician on a plaintiff such as Roe. A transaction resulting in an operation such as this is not "private" in the ordinary usage of that word. Nor is the "privacy" which the Court finds here even a distant relative of the freedom from searches and seizures protected by the Fourth Amendment to the Constitution which the Court has referred to as embodying a right to privacy. ...

If the Court means by the term "privacy" no more than that the claim of a person to be free from unwanted state regulation of consensual transactions may be a form of "liberty" protected by the Fourteenth Amendment, there is no doubt that similar claims have been upheld in our earlier decisions on the basis of that liberty. I agree ... that the "liberty," against deprivation of which without due process the Fourteenth Amendment protects, embraces more than the rights found in the Bill of Rights. But that liberty is not guaranteed absolutely against deprivation, but only against deprivation without due process of law. The test traditionally applied in the area of social and economic legislation is whether or not a law such as that challenged has a rational relation to a valid state objective. Williamson v. Lee Optical Co. (1955). If the Texas statute were to prohibit an abortion even where the mother's life is in jeopardy, I have little doubt that such a statute would lack a rational relation to a valid state objective under the test stated in *Williamson*. ... But the Court's sweeping invalidation of any restrictions on abortion during the first trimester is impossible to justify under that standard, and the conscious weighing of competing factors which the Court's opinion apparently substitutes for the established test is far more appropriate to a legislative judgment than to a judicial one. ...

While the Court's opinion quotes from the dissent of Mr. Justice Holmes in *Lochner,* the result it reaches is more closely attuned to the majority opinion of Mr. Justice Peckham in that case. As in *Lochner* and similar cases applying substantive due process standards, . . . adoption of the compelling state interest standard will inevitably require this Court to examine the legislative policies and pass on the wisdom of these policies in the very process of deciding whether a particular state interest put forward may or may not be "compelling." The decision here to break the term of pregnancy into three distinct terms and to outline the permissible restrictions the State may impose in each one, for example, partakes more of judicial legislation than it does of a determination of the intent of the drafters of the Fourteenth Amendment.

The fact that a majority of the States, reflecting, after all, the majority sentiment in those States, have had restrictions on abortions for at least a century, it seems to me, is a strong indication that the asserted right to an abortion is not "so rooted in the traditions and conscience of our people as to be ranked as fundamental," Snyder v. Massachusetts (1934). Even today, when society's views on abortion are changing, the very existence of the debate is evidence that the "right" to an abortion is not so universally accepted. . . .

To reach its result the Court necessarily has had to find within the scope of the Fourteenth Amendment a right that was apparently completely unknown to the drafters of the Amendment. . . . By the time of the adoption of the Fourteenth Amendment in 1868 there were at least 36 laws enacted by state or territorial legislatures limiting abortion. While many States have amended or updated their laws, 21 of the laws on the books in 1868 remain in effect today. Indeed, the Texas statute struck down today was, as the majority notes, first enacted in 1857 and "has remained substantially unchanged to the present time." . . .

There apparently was no question concerning the validity of this provision or of any of the other state statutes when the Fourteenth Amendment was adopted. The only conclusion possible from this history is that the drafters did not intend to have the Fourteenth Amendment withdraw from the States the power to legislate with respect to this matter. . . .

Editors' Notes

(1) **Query:** To what extent did Justice Blackmun follow an approach of *protecting fundamental rights*? Is the Court's ruling that a fetus is not, in the legal sense, a "person" compatible with such an approach? To what extent did Blackmun also follow a *developmental approach*? A *doctrinal approach*? A *balancing approach*? Any other(s)?

(2) **Query:** How strongly does a *textualist approach* support Blackmun's claim that a right to privacy is "found in the Fourteenth Amendment's concept of personal liberty and restrictions upon state action"? If one finds such a right in the amendment's words, does it follow that a woman must have a right to an abortion? However firm the textual base, did this conclusion follow from

cases like Meyer v. Nebraska (1923; reprinted above, p. 1247) and Griswold v. Connecticut (1965; reprinted above, p. 147)? What justification(s) did Blackmun offer for dividing a pregnancy—and the strength of a woman's right to privacy in her decision to have an abortion—into trimesters?

(3) **Query:** What approach to constitutional interpretation did White take? Rehnquist? To what extent did either rely on a *originalist approach*? An approach of *protecting fundamental rights*?

(4) **Query:** How is the history of the law of abortion that Blackmun chronicled in Part VI of his opinion relevant to his reasoning? Rehnquist claimed that to "reach its result the Court necessarily has had to find within the scope of the Fourteenth Amendment a right that was apparently completely unknown to the drafters of the Amendment." Would that fact, if it is a fact, meet and rebut Blackmun's argument? In Michael H. v. Gerald D. n.6 (1989; reprinted above, p. 158), Scalia wrote: "In *Roe,* we spent about a fifth of our opinion negating the proposition that there was a longstanding tradition of laws proscribing abortion." Did Scalia grasp Blackmun's point? Incidentally, Blackmun's recital of the history of the common law on abortion has been challenged as inaccurate and misleading. See, for example, John Keown, *Abortion, Doctors, and the Law* (New York: Cambridge University Press, 1988).

(5) **Query:** In a widely cited critique of *Roe*, John Hart Ely wrote:

What is frightening about *Roe* is that [this] super-protected right is not inferable from the language of the Constitution, the framers' thinking respecting the specific problem in issue, any general value derivable from the provisions they included, or the nation's governmental structure. Nor is it explainable in terms of the unusual political impotence of the group judicially protected vis-à-vis the interest that legislatively prevailed over it. ... And that, I believe, ... is a charge that can responsibly be leveled at no other decision [since 1937]. ... The Court continues to disavow the philosophy of Lochner v. New York. Yet ... it is impossible candidly to regard *Roe* as the product of anything else. ["The Wages of Crying Wolf: A Comment on *Roe v. Wade*," 82 *Yale L.J.* 920, 935–36, 939 (1973).]

Was Ely correct that *Roe* cannot be justified on the basis of any of the sources of constitutional rights that he listed? Does his litany exhaust the legitimate sources from which to derive constitutional meaning? Was he correct in claiming *Roe* "Lochnered"? How can we intelligently distinguish *Roe*'s reasoning and approach from those of *Lochner*? Those in Brown v. Board (1954; reprinted above, p. 912) from either?

(6) **Query:** Judge Robert H. Bork has written about *Roe*: "Unfortunately, in the entire opinion there is not one line of explanation, not one sentence that qualifies as a legal argument." *The Tempting of America* (New York: The Free Press, 1990), p. 112. On what conception of constitutional interpretation (both WHAT is "the Constitution" and HOW to interpret it) did Bork's critique rest? How persuasive is that critique? In what ways does it differ from those of White, Rehnquist, and Ely?

(7) **Query:** To what extent has the debate surrounding *Roe* been a dispute about WHO shall interpret? See, for example, the arguments about

one form of a "Human Life Amendment," S. 158 (1981; reprinted above, p. 336). Borrowing from James Bradley Thayer, "The Origin and Scope of the American Doctrine of Constitutional Law" (1893; reprinted above, p. 602), some observers (on both the political right and left) have contended that, when the Court decided *Roe,* many state legislatures were liberalizing their laws restricting abortion. *Roe,* however, cut short those political processes and polarized the controversy. See, *e.g.,* Mary Ann Glendon, *Abortion and Divorce in Western Law* (Cambridge: Harvard University Press, 1987); Gerald N. Rosenberg, *The Hollow Hope* (Chicago: University of Chicago Press, 1991); Cass R. Sunstein, *The Partial Constitution* (Cambridge: Harvard University Press, 1993); Laurence H. Tribe, *Abortion: The Clash of Absolutes* (New York: Norton, 1990); and Justice Scalia's opinion in Planned Parenthood v. Casey (1992; reprinted below, p. 1281). Ruth Bader Ginsburg's comments to this effect in her Madison Lecture at New York University School of Law were the subject of much controversy while her nomination to the Supreme Court was pending. See her "Speaking in a Judicial Voice," 67 *N.Y.U.L.Rev.* 1185 (1993). Did *Roe* actually debilitate or galvanize the political processes?

(8) The Papers of Justice Thurgood Marshall reveal that Blackmun's first draft of an opinion of the Court in *Roe* would have invalidated Texas's statute on the ground that its exception for abortions "for the purpose of saving the life of the mother" was unconstitutionally vague: It did not give physicians sufficient notice of what the statute prohibited and permitted. (Library of Congress, Manuscripts Division, Case File 99.) The draft opinion did not reach the question whether the Due Process Clause or the Ninth Amendment embraced a woman's right to choose an abortion. Would such reasoning have been more satisfactory—whether from the standpoint of constitutional interpretation or political prudence—than the course the Court ultimately took? Marshall's papers also reveal that Blackmun's second draft chose the end of the first trimester rather than viability as the crucial line for accommodating the interests involved. Instead, Marshall urged drawing the line at viability. After a long discussion, Blackmun's trimester framework appeared in the opinion.

(9) On same day as *Roe* came down, the Court also decided Doe v. Bolton. Again speaking through Blackmun, the Court stressed that *Roe* "sets forth our conclusion that a woman does not have an absolute constitutional right to an abortion of her demand." Nevertheless, the justices also emphasized that a woman had a limited right which the state could not "unconstitutionally" burden and held as unconstitutional burdens Georgia's requirements that (a) abortion be performed only in accredited hospitals; (b) the procedure be approved by a special committee of physicians; (c) two other physicians concur in the attending physician's recommendation for an abortion; and (d) the patient be a state resident.

(10) These rulings, of course, are among the most controversial of this century. They were followed by a spate of additional decisions as well as efforts to overturn them by constitutional amendment—see the *Hearings* on S. 158—to limit their effect by restricting use of federal money—see Harris v. McRae (1980; reprinted as the next case)—and to outflank them by new legislation and regulations. For the latter, see, *e.g.,* Tribe, *Abortion*; Walter Dellinger and Eugene Sperling, "Abortion and the Supreme Court: The Retreat from *Roe v. Wade,*" 138 *U.Pa.L.Rev.* 83 (1989); and Lee Epstein and Joseph F. Koblyka, *The Supreme Court & Legal Change: Abortion and the*

Death Penalty (Chapel Hill: University of North Carolina Press, 1992), espec. chs. 1–2, 5–7. The leading decisions between *Roe* and *Casey* were:

(a) Akron v. Akron Center for Reproductive Health (1983) (*Akron I*), reaffirmed *Roe* 6–3; O'Connor, who had replaced Stewart, a member of the majority in *Roe*, dissented. *Akron I* struck down five provisions of an ordinance: (1) requiring all abortions after the first trimester be "performed in a hospital," thus preventing late abortions in out-patient clinics; (2) prohibiting abortions on unmarried minors under 15, without consent from one of her parents or an order from a court; (3) demanding, for "truly informed consent," a pregnant woman seeking an abortion be "orally informed by her attending physician" (rather than by other professional counsellors) that:

(i) "the unborn child is a human life from the moment of conception," (ii) physical and emotional complications may result from an abortion, and (iii) governmental and private agencies were ready to assist a pregnant woman with respect to birth control, childbirth, and adoption;

(4) mandating a 24–hour waiting period between signing a consent form and aborting a fetus; and (5) requiring physicians who perform abortions to "insure that the remains of the unborn child are disposed of in a humane and sanitary manner."

(b) Thornburgh v. American College of Obstetricians and Gynecologists (1986), reaffirmed *Roe* 5–4 (Burger, one of the majority in *Roe* dissented) and invalidated, among other provisions: (1) requirements for "informed consent" and "printed information" like those struck down in *Akron I*, on the ground that they were "designed not to inform the woman's consent but rather to persuade her to withhold it altogether"; (2) reporting regulations, because they "raise the specter of public exposure and harassment of women who choose to exercise their personal, intensely private, right"; and (3) requiring physicians performing post-viability abortions to use the technique that provides the best opportunity for the "unborn child" to remain alive unless it "would present a significantly greater risk to the life or health of the pregnant woman," on the ground that it "fails to require that maternal health be the physician's paramount consideration."

(c) Webster v. Reproductive Health Services (1989) marked a significant turning point, upholding, with Chief Justice Rehnquist writing the plurality opinion, a state law that prohibited the use of public facilities or employees "to perform or assist in an abortion not necessary to save the life of the mother" and required physicians to conduct viability tests prior to performing an abortion on a woman whom they have reason to believe is 20 or more weeks pregnant. Four justices (certainly Rehnquist, White, and Scalia and possibly Kennedy) apparently wished to overrule *Roe,* and four justices (Brennan, Marshall, Blackmun, and Stevens) definitely wished to reaffirm it, leaving O'Connor as the swing vote. Justice Marshall's Papers suggest that the Court nearly overruled *Roe,* but O'Connor declined to join the relevant parts of Rehnquist's opinion, instead merely concurring in the judgment and stating that a "fundamental rule of judicial restraint" required the Court to avoid reconsidering *Roe*. Scalia attacked O'Connor for refusing to overrule *Roe*. Her view regarding judicial restraint, he said, "cannot be taken seriously." "It . . . appears that the mansion of constitutionalized abortion-law, constructed overnight in Roe v. Wade, must be disassembled door-jamb by door-jamb, and never entirely brought down, no matter how wrong it may be."

    (d) Ohio v. Akron Center for Reproductive Health (1990) (*Akron II*) rejected, 6–3, a facial challenge to a state law that prohibited unemancipated minors from obtaining abortions without notice to one of the minor's parents or a court order. A companion case, Hodgson v. Minnesota (1990), invalidated a state provision requiring *both* parents of an unemancipated minor to be notified 48 hours before she underwent an abortion, but upheld such a requirement *combined with* an alternative "judicial bypass."

    (e) Planned Parenthood v. Casey (1992; reprinted below, p. 1281), partially overruled *Akron I* and *Thornburgh*.

    (11) *Roe* and its progeny have sired a vast number of legal, ethical, and theological analyses. Some of this material is collected in U.S. Senate, Subcommittee on the Separation of Powers, *Hearings on S. 158,* 97th Cong., 1st Sess. (1981), 2 vols. See also, in addition to the works cited in the earlier Editors Notes to *Roe*:

James T. Burtchaell, *Rachel Weeping* (Kansas City: Andrews & McMeel, 1981);

Marshall Cohen et al., eds., *The Rights and Wrongs of Abortion* (Princeton: Princeton University Press, 1974);

Ronald Dworkin, *Life's Dominion* (New York: Knopf, 1993);

Joel Feinberg, ed., *The Problem of Abortion* (Belmont, CA: Wadsworth, 1973);

Wolfgang Friedman, "Interferences with Human Life: Jurisprudential Reflections," 70 *Colum.L.Rev.* 1058 (1970);

David J. Garrow, *Liberty and Sexuality: The Right to Privacy and the Making of Roe v. Wade* (New York: Macmillan, 1994).

Bernard N. Nathanson, *Aborting America* (New York: Doubleday, 1979);

John T. Noonan, Jr., "Abortion: The Case for a Constitutional Amendment," *New Oxford Rev.* (Jan., 1978), p. 4;

Paul Ramsey, *Ethics at the Edges of Life* (New Haven: Yale University Press, 1978), chs. 1–3;

Donald H. Regan, "Rewriting *Roe v. Wade*," 77 *Mich.L.Rev.* 1569 (1979);

Jed Rubenfeld, "The Right of Privacy," 102 *Harv.L.Rev.* 737 (1989);

Sacred Congregation for the Doctrine of the Faith, "Declaration on Procured Abortion," *L'Osservatore Romano* (English language ed.), Dec. 5, 1974;

Gilbert Y. Steiner, ed., *The Abortion Dispute and the American System* (Washington, DC: The Brookings Institution, 1983);

Judith Jarvis Thomson, "A Defense of Abortion," 1 *Phil. & Pub. Aff.* 47 (1971); (and the response by John Finnis: "The Rights and Wrongs of Abortion," 2 *ibid.* 117 [1973]);

Laurence H. Tribe, *American Constitutional Law* (2d ed; Mineola, NY: Foundation Press, 1988), § 15-10.

(12) For feminist analyses of a woman's right to choose an abortion as against the right of the unborn to life, see:

Kristin Luker, *Abortion and the Politics of Motherhood* (Berkeley: University of California Press, 1984);

Linda C. McClain, "The Poverty of Privacy?" 3 *Colum.J. Gender & L.* 119 (1992); and

Rosalind Pollack Petchesky, *Abortion and Women's Choice* (rev. ed.; Boston: Northeastern University Press, 1990).

See also resources cited in the Eds.' Note 14 to *Casey* (below, p. 1311).

(13) Walter F. Murphy and Joseph Tanenhaus, *Comparative Constitutional Law* (New York: St. Martin's, 1977), ch. 12, reprints cases from Canada and West Germany as well as the United States and includes a long bibliography. For a fictionalized account of American justices' struggling over the legal, political, and moral issues surrounding the constitutionality of laws restricting abortion, see Walter F. Murphy, *The Vicar of Christ* (New York: Macmillan, 1979), Part II, ch. 9.

"[I]t simply does not follow that a woman's freedom of choice carries with it a constitutional entitlement to the financial resources to avail herself of the full range of protected choices."—Justice STEWART

"The fundamental flaw in the Court's due process analysis ... is its failure to acknowledge that the discriminatory distribution of the benefits of governmental largesse can discourage the exercise of fundamental liberties just as effectively as can an outright denial of those rights through criminal and regulatory sanctions."—Justice BRENNAN

"I do not believe that legislation that imposes a crushing burden on indigent women can be treated with the same deference given to legislation distinguishing among business interests. ..."—Justice MARSHALL

"When the sovereign provides a special benefit or a special protection for a class of persons, it must define the membership in the class by neutral criteria. ..."— Justice STEVENS

HARRIS v. McRAE
448 U.S. 297, 100 S.Ct. 2671, 65 L.Ed.2d 784 (1980).

Through the Medicaid Program, enacted in 1965 as Title XIX of the Social Security Act, Congress had provided for federal assistance to states that set up programs to help pay the costs for medical care of the poor. Thus, following *Roe*, federal money became available to the states to pay for poor women to have abortions. Between 1976 and 1980, however, Congress each year attached a rider—known as "the Hyde Amendment"—to the appropriations bill limiting the circumstances under which federal money could be spent to subsidize abortions. The terms of those limitations varied from year to year; in fiscal 1980, the rider allowed federal funding only when the pregnancy was the result of rape or threatened the life of the mother.

Maher v. Roe (1977) upheld Connecticut's limiting state financing of abortions to those "medically necessary," but did not discuss the Hyde Amendment. A year earlier, Cora McRae, a pregnant woman otherwise eligible for benefits under Medicaid, had filed suit in a federal district court, alleging violation of her rights under the First, Fourth, Fifth, and Ninth amendments. The suit was later joined by other pregnant women and interested parties. The district court invalidated the Hyde Amendment, and the government appealed directly to the Supreme Court.

Mr. Justice **STEWART** delivered the opinion of the Court. . . .

III

It is well settled that, quite apart from the guarantee of equal protection, if a law "impinges upon a fundamental right explicitly or implicitly secured by the Constitution [it] is presumptively unconstitutional." Mobile v. Bolden [1980] (plurality opinion). Accordingly, before turning to the equal protection issue in this case, we examine whether the Hyde Amendment violates any substantive rights secured by the Constitution.

A

We address first the appellees' argument that the Hyde Amendment, by restricting the availability of certain medically necessary abortions under Medicaid, impinges on the "liberty" protected by the Due Process Clause as recognized in Roe v. Wade [1973] and its progeny. . . . The constitutional underpinning of *Wade* was a recognition that the "liberty" protected by the Due Process Clause of the Fourteenth Amendment includes not only the freedoms explicitly mentioned in the Bill of Rights, but also a freedom of personal choice in certain matters of marriage and family life. This implicit constitutional liberty, the Court in *Wade* held, includes the freedom of a woman to decide whether to terminate a pregnancy. . . .

In Maher v. Roe [1977], the Court was presented with the question whether the scope of personal constitutional freedom recognized in *Wade* included an entitlement to Medicaid payments for abortions that are not medically necessary. At issue in *Maher* was a Connecticut welfare regulation under which Medicaid recipients received payments for medical services incident to childbirth, but not for medical services incident to nontherapeutic abortions. ...

... The doctrine of [Roe v.] *Wade*, the Court held in *Maher*, ... did not translate into a constitutional obligation of Connecticut to subsidize abortions. [T]he Court cited the "basic difference between direct state interference with a protected activity and state encouragement of an alternative activity consonant with legislative policy. Constitutional concerns are greatest when the State attempts to impose its will by force of law; the State's power to encourage actions deemed to be in the public interest is necessarily far broader." ...

The Hyde Amendment, like the Connecticut welfare regulation at issue in *Maher*, places no governmental obstacle in the path of a woman who chooses to terminate her pregnancy, but rather, by means of unequal subsidization of abortion and other medical services, encourages alternative activity deemed in the public interest. The present case does differ factually from *Maher* insofar as that case involved a failure to fund nontherapeutic abortions, whereas the Hyde Amendment withholds funding of certain medically necessary abortions. Accordingly, the appellees argue that because the Hyde Amendment affects a significant interest not present or asserted in *Maher*—the interest of a woman in protecting her health during pregnancy—and because that interest lies at the core of the personal constitutional freedom recognized in *Wade*, the present case is constitutionally different from *Maher*. ...

... [R]egardless of whether the freedom of a woman to choose to terminate her pregnancy for health reasons lies at the core or the periphery of the due process liberty recognized in *Wade*, it simply does not follow that a woman's freedom of choice carries with it a constitutional entitlement to the financial resources to avail herself of the full range of protected choices. ... The financial constraints that restrict an indigent woman's ability to enjoy the full range of constitutionally protected freedom of choice are the product not of governmental restrictions on access to abortions, but rather of her indigency. ... [T]he Hyde Amendment leaves an indigent woman with at least the same range of choice in deciding whether to obtain a medically necessary abortion as she would have had if Congress had chosen to subsidize no health care costs at all. ...

... To translate the limitation on governmental power implicit in the Due Process Clause into an affirmative funding obligation would require Congress to subsidize the medically necessary abortion of an indigent woman even if Congress had not enacted a Medicaid program to subsidize other medically necessary services. Nothing in the Due Process Clause supports such in extraordinary result. Whether freedom of choice that is constitutionally protected warrants federal subsidization is a question for Congress to answer, not a matter of constitutional entitlement. Accordingly, we conclude that the Hyde Amendment does not impinge on the due process liberty recognized in *Wade*.

B

The appellees also argue that the Hyde Amendment contravenes rights secured by the Religion Clauses of the First Amendment. ... [They argue that it] violates the Establishment Clause because it incorporates into law the doctrines of the Roman Catholic Church concerning the sinfulness of abortion and the time at which life commences. Moreover, insofar as a woman's decision to seek a medically necessary abortion may be a product of her religious beliefs under certain Protestant and Jewish tenets, the appellees assert that the funding limitations of the Hyde Amendment impinge on the freedom of religion guaranteed by the Free Exercise Clause.

... [T]he Hyde Amendment does not run afoul of the Establishment Clause. Although neither a State nor the Federal Government can constitutionally "pass laws which aid one religion, aid all religions, or prefer one religion over another," Everson v. Bd of Ed. [1947], it does not follow that a statute violates the Establishment Clause because it "happens to coincide or harmonize with the tenets of some or all religions." McGowan v. Maryland [1961]. That the Judeo–Christian religions oppose stealing does not mean that a State or the Federal Government may not consistent with the Establishment Clause enact law prohibiting larceny. The Hyde Amendment ... is as much a reflection of "traditionalist" values toward abortion, as it is an embodiment of the views of any particular religion. ...

[The Court also rejected the argument that the Hyde Amendment violates the Free Exercise Clause.—**Eds.**]

C

It remains to be determined whether the Hyde Amendment violates the equal protection component of the Fifth Amendment. This challenge is premised on the fact that, although federal reimbursement is available under Medicaid for medically necessary services generally, the Hyde Amendment does not permit federal reimbursement of all medically necessary abortions. ...

The guarantee of equal protection ... is not a source of substantive rights or liberties, but rather a right to be free from invidious discrimination in statutory classifications and other governmental activity. It is well-settled that where a statutory classification does not itself impinge on a right or liberty protected by the Constitution, the validity of classification must be sustained unless "the classification rests on grounds wholly irrelevant to the achievement of [any legitimate governmental] objective." McGowan. This presumption of constitutional validity, however, disappears if a statutory classification is predicated on criteria that are, in a constitutional sense, "suspect," the principal example of which is a classification based on race, e.g., Brown v. Bd of Ed. [1954].

... [W]e have already concluded that the Hyde Amendment violates no constitutionally protected substantive rights. We now conclude as well that it is not predicated on a constitutionally suspect classification. ... Here, as in *Maher,* the principal impact of the Hyde Amendment falls on the indigent. But that fact does not itself render the funding restriction constitutionally invalid, for this Court has held repeatedly that poverty, standing alone, is not a suspect classification. ...

The remaining question then is whether the Hyde Amendment is rationally related to a legitimate governmental objective. ... In *Wade,* the Court recognized that the State has "an important and legitimate interest in protecting the potentiality of human life." ... Moreover, in *Maher,* the Court held that Connecticut's decision to fund the costs associated with childbirth but not those associated with nontherapeutic abortions was a rational means of advancing the legitimate state interest in protecting potential life by encouraging childbirth.

It follows that the Hyde Amendment, by encouraging childbirth except in the most urgent circumstances, is rationally related to the legitimate governmental objective of protecting potential life. By subsidizing the medical expenses of indigent women who carry their pregnancies to term while not subsidizing the comparable expenses of women who undergo abortions (except those whose lives are threatened), Congress has established incentives that make childbirth a more attractive alternative than abortion for persons eligible for Medicaid. ... Nor is it irrational that Congress has authorized federal reimbursement for medically necessary services generally, but not for certain medically necessary abortions. Abortion is inherently different from other medical procedures, because no other procedure involves the purposeful termination of a potential life. ... [I]t is not the mission of this Court or any other to decide whether the balance of competing interests reflected in the Hyde Amendment is wise social policy. If that were our mission, not every Justice who has subscribed to the judgment of the Court today could have done so. But we cannot, in the name of the Constitution, overturn duly enacted statutes simply "because they may be unwise, improvident or out of harmony with a particular school of thought." Williamson v. Lee Optical Co. [1955]. Rather, "when an issue involves policy choices as sensitive as those implicated [here] ... the appropriate forum for their resolution in a democracy is the legislature." *Maher.* ...

[Reversed.]

Mr. Justice **WHITE,** concurring. ...

Mr. Justice **BRENNAN,** with whom Mr. Justice **MARSHALL** and Mr. Justice **BLACKMUN** join, dissenting.

I agree entirely with my Brother Stevens. ... I write separately to express my continuing disagreement with the Court's mischaracterization of the nature of the fundamental right recognized in *Wade,* and its misconception of the manner in which that right is infringed by federal and state legislation withdrawing all funding for medically necessary abortions. ...

... *Wade* and its progeny established that the pregnant woman has a right to be free from state interference with her choice to have an abortion. ... The proposition for which these cases stand thus is not that the State is under an affirmative obligation to ensure access to abortions for all who may desire them; it is that the State must refrain from wielding its enormous power and influence in a manner that might burden the pregnant woman's freedom to choose whether to have an abortion. The Hyde Amendment[ ] ... plainly intrudes upon this constitutionally protected decision, for both by design and in effect it serves to coerce indigent pregnant women to bear children that they would otherwise elect not to have.

When viewed in the context of the Medicaid program to which it is appended, it is obvious that the Hyde Amendment is nothing less than an attempt by Congress to circumvent the dictates of the Constitution and achieve indirectly what *Wade* said it could not do directly. ... [It] is a transparent attempt by the Legislative Branch to impose the political majority's judgment of the morally acceptable and socially desirable preference on a sensitive and intimate decision that the Constitution entrusts to the individual. Worse yet, the Hyde Amendment does not foist that majoritarian viewpoint with equal measure upon everyone in our Nation, rich and poor alike; rather, it imposes that viewpoint only upon that segment of our society which, because of its position of political powerlessness, is least able to defend its privacy rights from the encroachments of state-mandated morality. The instant legislation thus calls for more exacting judicial review than in most other cases. ...

... [W]hat the Court fails to appreciate is that it is not simply the woman's indigency that interferes with her freedom of choice, but the combination of her own poverty and the government's unequal subsidization of abortion and childbirth. A poor woman in the early stages of pregnancy confronts two alternatives: she may elect either to carry the fetus to term or to have an abortion. In the abstract, of course, this choice is hers alone. ...

... [But] as a practical matter, many poverty-stricken women will choose to carry their pregnancy to term simply because the government provides funds for the associated medical services, even though these same women would have chosen to have an abortion if the government had also paid for that option, or indeed if the government had stayed out of the picture altogether and had defrayed the costs of neither procedure.

The fundamental flaw in the Court's due process analysis, then, is its failure to acknowledge that the discriminatory distribution of the benefits of governmental largesse can discourage the exercise of fundamental liberties just as effectively as can an outright denial of those rights through criminal and regulatory sanctions. Implicit in the Court's reasoning is the notion that as long as the government is not obligated to provide its citizens with certain benefits or privileges, it may condition the grant of such benefits on the recipient's relinquishment of his constitutional rights.

... [W]e have heretofore never hesitated to invalidate any scheme of granting or withholding financial benefits that incidentally or intentionally burdens one manner of exercising a constitutionally protected choice. ...

Mr. Justice **MARSHALL** dissenting. ...

... The Court's decision today marks a retreat from *Wade* and represents a cruel blow to the most powerless members of our society. ...

The Court resolves the equal protection issue in this case through a relentlessly formalistic catechism. ... I continue to believe that the rigid "two-tiered" approach is inappropriate and that the Constitution requires a more exacting standard of review than mere rationality in cases such as this one. Further, in my judgment the Hyde Amendment cannot pass constitutional muster even under the rational-basis standard of review.

This case is perhaps the most dramatic illustration to date of the deficiencies in the Court's obsolete "two-tiered" approach to the Equal Protection Clause. ... Heightened scrutiny of legislative classifications [is] designed to protect groups "saddled with such disabilities or subjected to such a history of purposeful unequal treatment, or relegated to such a position of political powerlessness as to command extraordinary protection from the majoritarian political process." *San Antonio.* And while it is now clear that traditional "strict scrutiny" is unavailable to protect the poor against classifications that disfavor them, *Dandridge,* I do not believe that legislation that imposes a crushing burden on indigent women can be treated with the same deference given to legislation distinguishing among business interests ["more than able to protect themselves in the political process."]

The Hyde Amendment ... distinguishes between medically necessary abortions and other medically necessary expenses. ... [S]uch classifications must be assessed by weighing " 'the importance of the governmental benefits denied, the character of the class, and the asserted state interests.' " Under that approach, the Hyde Amendment is clearly invalid.

As in *Maher,* the governmental benefits at issue here are "of absolutely vital importance in the lives of the recipients." An indigent woman denied governmental funding for a medically necessary abortion is confronted with two grotesque choices. First, she may seek to obtain "an illegal abortion that poses a serious threat to her health and even her life." Alternatively, she may attempt to bear the child, a course that may both significantly threaten her health and eliminate any chance she might have had "to control the direction of her own life."

The class burdened by the Hyde Amendment consists of indigent women, a substantial proportion of whom are members of minority races. ... In my view, the fact that the burden of the Hyde Amendment falls exclusively on financially destitute women suggests "a special condition, which tends seriously to curtail the operation of those political processes ordinarily to be relied upon to protect minorities, and which may call for a correspondingly more searching judicial inquiry." United States v. Carolene Products Co., n. 4 (1938). For this reason, I continue to believe that "a showing that state action has a devastating impact on the lives of minority racial groups must be relevant" for purposes of equal protection analysis. Jefferson v. Hackney (1972) (Marshall, J., dissenting).

... [T]he asserted state interest in protecting potential life is insufficient to "outweigh the deprivation or serious discouragement of a vital constitutional right of especial importance to poor and minority women." ... The governmental interest in the present case is substantially weaker than in *Maher,* for under the Hyde Amendment funding is refused even in cases in which normal childbirth will not result. ... I am unable to see how even a minimally rational legislature could conclude that the interest in fetal life outweighs the brutal effect of the Hyde Amendment on indigent women. ...

... The Court treats this case as though it were controlled by *Maher.* To the contrary, this case is the mirror image of *Maher.* The result in *Maher* turned on the fact that the legislation there under consideration discouraged only nontherapeutic, or medically unnecessary, abortions. In the Court's view, denial of Medicaid funding for nontherapeutic abortions was not a denial of equal protection because Medicaid funds were available only for medically necessary procedures. Thus the plaintiffs were seeking benefits which were not available to others similarly situated ... [But respondents here] are protesting their exclusion from a benefit that is available to all others similarly situated. This, it need hardly be said, is a crucial difference for equal protection purposes.

Under Title XIX and the Hyde Amendment, funding is available for essentially all necessary medical treatment for the poor. Respondents have met the statutory requirements for eligibility, but they are excluded because the treatment that is medically necessary involves the exercise of a fundamental right, the right to choose an abortion. ... In such circumstances the Hyde Amendment must be invalidated because it does not meet even the rational-basis standard of review. ...

Mr. Justice **BLACKMUN,** dissenting. ...

Mr. Justice **STEVENS,** dissenting.

"The federal sovereign, like the States, must govern impartially. ..." Hampton v. Mow Sun Wong (1976). When the sovereign provides a special benefit or a special protection for a class of persons, it must define the membership in the class by neutral criteria; it may not make special exceptions for reasons that are constitutionally insufficient.

... Individuals who satisfy two neutral statutory criteria—financial need and medical need—are entitled to equal access to [the pool of benefits under Title XIX]. The question is whether certain persons who satisfy those criteria may be denied access to benefits solely because they must exercise the constitutional right to have an abortion in order to obtain the medical care they need. Our prior cases plainly dictate the answer to that question. ...

If a woman has a constitutional right to place a higher value on avoiding either serious harm to her own health or perhaps an abnormal childbirth than on protecting potential life, the exercise of that right cannot provide the basis for the denial of a benefit to which she would otherwise be entitled. ... The Court focuses exclusively on the "legitimate interest in protecting the potential life of the fetus." ... [But] *Wade* squarely held that the States may not protect that interest when a conflict with the interest in a pregnant woman's health exists. ...

Nor can it be argued that the exclusion of this type of medically necessary treatment of the indigent can be justified on fiscal grounds. ... [T]he cost of an abortion is only a small fraction of the costs associated with childbirth. Thus, the decision to tolerate harm to indigent persons who need an abortion in order to avoid "serious and long-lasting health damage" is one that is financed by draining money out of the pool that is used to fund all other necessary medical procedures. Unlike most invidious classifications, this discrimination harms not only its direct victims but also the remainder of the class of needy persons that the pool was designed to benefit. ...

... In my judgment, these amendments constitute an unjustifiable, and indeed blatant, violation of the sovereign's duty to govern impartially. ...

Editors' Notes

(1) **Query:** There is a striking similarity between Stewart's reasoning in Harris v. McRae and Harlan's dissenting opinion in Griffin v. Illinois (1956), the grandparent of modern cases involving wealth as a classification. There the Court invalidated as a denial of equal protection a state law that required indigent prisoners to pay for transcripts of their trials in order to appeal their convictions. Harlan wrote: "Nor is this a case where the State's own action has prevented a defendant from appealing. All that Illinois has done is to fail to alleviate the consequences of the differences [in wealth] that exist wholly apart from any state action." Is there a difference relevant to constitutional interpretation between requiring an indigent prisoner to pay for a transcript as a condition for appealing a conviction and requiring an indigent pregnant woman whose life is not threatened by her pregnancy and whose pregnancy was not caused by rape to pay for an abortion if she chooses one?

(2) **Query:** To what extent did Stewart follow a *balancing approach*?

(3) **Query:** How convincing as a matter of constitutional interpretation— as opposed to wise or just public policy—is Brennan's argument that it violates equal protection for the government to subsidize a live birth but not an abortion? Did the Hyde Amendment impose an "unconstitutional condition," that is, did it condition indigent women's receipt of governmental benefits

upon their relinquishment of their constitutional right to choose an abortion? See the discussion of the doctrine of "unconstitutional conditions" in the Editors' Notes following Rust v. Sullivan (1991; reprinted above, p. 749).

(4) **Query:** All the justices who wrote in this case implicitly said or implied that "equal protection of the law" means "equal treatment" in the bestowal of benefits. How would a textualist like Hugo Black have responded to these opinions?

(5) For recent analyses of the problems that *McRae* raised, see, *e.g.*, Ronald Dworkin, *Life's Dominion* (New York: Knopf, 1993); Catharine A. MacKinnon, "Reflections on Sex Equality Under Law," 100 *Yale L.J.* 1281 (1991); Michael W. McConnell, "The Selective Funding Problem: Abortions and Religious Schools," 104 *Harv.L.Rev.* 989 (1991); Cass R. Sunstein, *The Partial Constitution* (Cambridge: Harvard University Press, 1993); Laurence H. Tribe, *Abortion: The Clash of Absolutes* (New York: Norton, 1990).

(6) Despite much opposition to the Hyde Amendment, Congress has continued to enact versions of it since the Supreme Court decided *McRae.*

––––––––

"The condition that federal funds will be used only to further the purposes of a grant does not violate constitutional rights."

RUST v. SULLIVAN

500 U.S. 173, 111 S.Ct. 1759, 114 L.Ed.2d 233 (1991).

This case upheld an administrative regulation prohibiting organizations that accepted federal funding to advise people on family planning to use that money to "encourage, promote or advise abortion as a method of family planning." The opinions are reprinted above, p. 749.

––––––––

"[S]ubstantive due process claims may call upon the Court in interpreting the Constitution to exercise that same capacity which by tradition courts always have exercised: reasoned judgment."—Justices O'CONNOR, KENNEDY, and SOUTER

"The societal costs of overruling *Roe* at this late date would be enormous."—Justice STEVENS

"A woman's right to reproductive choice is one of those fundamental liberties. Accordingly, that liberty need not seek refuge at the ballot box."—Justice BLACKMUN

"[A]uthentic principles of stare decisis do not require that any portion of the reasoning in *Roe* be kept intact."—Chief Justice REHNQUIST

"The emptiness of the 'reasoned judgment' that produced *Roe* is displayed in plain view by the fact that, after more than 19 years of effort ... the best the Court can do to explain how it is that the word 'liberty' *must* be thought to include the right to destroy human fetuses is to rattle off a collection of adjectives that simply ... conceal a political choice."—Justice SCALIA

PLANNED PARENTHOOD v. CASEY

505 U.S. ___, 112 S.Ct. 2791, 120 L.Ed.2d 674 (1992).

Roe v. Wade (1973; reprinted above, p. 1258) marked the beginning, not the end, of struggle over abortion. Hundreds of lawsuits attacked the constitutionality both of old laws and the wave of new regulations many state legislatures enacted to try to channel *Roe*'s impact. The Court's initial reaction was almost uniformly hostile to *any* regulation of the right *Roe* defined. Later, as new justices replaced members of the majority in *Roe,* the Court upheld several state regulations. Still, the justices did not overrule *Roe.*

Ronald Reagan's and later George Bush's staffs tried to select justices who would cut *Roe's* life short. Indeed, on six occasions during the Reagan and Bush administrations, the United States asked the Court to overrule *Roe*— a course some justices found appealing. Not only did White and Rehnquist remain convinced that *Roe* was wrong, but two of the younger justices seemed to agree. Dissenting in Akron v. Akron Center (1983), Sandra Day O'Connor declared that the logic of *Roe*'s trimester framework was "on a collision course with itself." Concurring in Webster v. Reproductive Health Services (1989), Antonin Scalia explicitly said *Roe* should be overruled. Supposedly the other three new justices, Anthony M. Kennedy, David Souter, and Clarence Thomas, shared those views, though to varying degrees. In 1989, in his dissenting opinion in *Webster*, Harry Blackmun, the author of *Roe*, went so far as to predict the ruling's early demise.

In this case from Pennsylvania, five abortion clinics and a physician who performed abortions filed suit in federal district court attacking the constitutionality of state regulations amended in 1988 and 1989. This statute required that, unless a medical emergency were present: (1) a woman seeking an abortion be provided with certain information so she could give "informed consent," then wait 24 hours before having an abortion; (2) a minor obtain the consent of one parent or the approval of a judge; (3) a married woman, under most circumstances, sign a statement saying she had notified her husband of her intended abortion; (4) those performing abortions file certain reports. The district court invalidated all these provisions, but the Court of Appeals reversed, except for the requirement to inform the husband. The Supreme Court granted certiorari.

Justice **O'CONNOR**, Justice **KENNEDY**, and Justice **SOUTER** announced the judgment of the Court and delivered the opinion of the Court with respect to Parts **I**, **II**, **III**, **V-A**, **V-C**, and **VI**, an opinion with respect to Part **V-E**, in which Justice **STEVENS** joins, and an opinion with respect to Parts **IV**, **V-B**, and **V-D**.

I

Liberty finds no refuge in a jurisprudence of doubt. Yet 19 years after our holding that the Constitution protects a woman's right to terminate her pregnancy in its early stages, Roe v. Wade (1973), that definition of liberty is still questioned. Joining the respondents as *amicus curiae*, the United States, as it has done in five other cases in the last decade, again asks us to overrule *Roe*. ... [W]e acknowledge that our decisions after *Roe* cast doubt upon the meaning and reach of its holding. ... State and federal courts as well as legislatures throughout the Union must have guidance as they seek to address this subject in conformance with the Constitution. ... After considering the fundamental constitutional questions resolved by *Roe*, principles of institutional integrity, and the rule of stare decisis, we are led to conclude this: the essential holding of *Roe* should be retained and once again reaffirmed.

... *Roe*'s essential holding ... has three parts. First is a recognition of the right of the woman to choose to have an abortion before viability and to obtain it without undue interference from the State. Before viability, the State's interests are not strong enough to support a prohibition of abortion or the imposition of a substantial obstacle to the woman's effective right to elect the procedure. Second is a confirmation of the State's power to restrict abortions after fetal viability, if the law contains exceptions for pregnancies which endanger a woman's life or health. And third is the principle that the State has legitimate interests from the outset of the pregnancy in protecting the health of the woman and the life of the fetus that may become a child. ...

II

Constitutional protection of the woman's decision to terminate her pregnancy derives from the Due Process Clause of the Fourteenth Amendment. It declares that no State shall "deprive any person of life, liberty, or property, without due process of law." The controlling word in the case before us is "liberty." Although a literal reading of the Clause might suggest that it governs only the procedures by which a State may deprive persons of liberty, ... at least since Mugler v. Kansas (1887), the Clause has been understood to contain a substantive component as well. ...

The most familiar of the substantive liberties protected by the Fourteenth Amendment are those recognized by the Bill of Rights. We have held that the Due Process Clause of the Fourteenth Amendment incorporates most of the Bill of Rights against the States. It is tempting, as a means of curbing the discretion of federal judges, to suppose that liberty encompasses no more than those rights already guaranteed to the individual against federal interference by the express provisions of the first eight amendments to the Constitution. See Adamson v. California (1947) (Black, J., dissenting). But of course this Court has never accepted that view.

It is also tempting, for the same reason, to suppose that the Due Process Clause protects only those practices, defined at the most specific level, that were protected against government interference by other rules of law when the Fourteenth Amendment was ratified. See Michael H. v. Gerald D. n.6 (1989) (opinion of Scalia, J.). But such a view would be inconsistent with our law. It is a promise of the Constitution that there is a realm of personal liberty which the government may not enter. We have vindicated this principle before. Marriage is mentioned nowhere in the Bill of Rights and interracial marriage was illegal in most States in the 19th century, but the Court was no doubt correct in finding it to be an aspect of liberty protected against state interference by the substantive component of the Due Process Clause in Loving v. Virginia (1967). Similar examples may be found in Turner v. Safley (1987); in Carey v. Population Services Int'l (1977); in Griswold v. Connecticut (1965) ...; in Pierce v. Society of Sisters (1925); and in Meyer v. Nebraska (1923).

Neither the Bill of Rights nor the specific practices of States at the time of the adoption of the Fourteenth Amendment marks the outer limits of the substantive sphere of liberty which the Fourteenth Amendment protects. See U.S. Const., Amend. 9. As the second Justice Harlan recognized:

> "[T]he full scope of the liberty guaranteed by the Due Process Clause cannot be found in or limited by the precise terms of the specific guarantees elsewhere provided in the Constitution. This 'liberty' is not a series of isolated points. ... It is a rational continuum which ... includes a freedom from all substantial arbitrary impositions and purposeless restraints ... and which also recognizes ... that certain interests require particularly careful scrutiny of the state needs asserted to justify their abridgment." Poe v. Ullman [1961] (Harlan, J., dissenting).

... [T]he Court adopted his position four Terms later in *Griswold* ... [which] held that the Constitution does not permit a State to forbid a married couple to use contraceptives. That same freedom was later guaranteed, under the Equal Protection Clause, for unmarried couples. See Eisenstadt v. Baird (1972). Constitutional protection was extended to the sale and distribution of contraceptives in *Carey*. It is settled now, as it was when the Court heard arguments in *Roe*, that the Constitution places limits on a State's right to interfere with a person's most basic decisions about family and parenthood ... as well as bodily integrity. ...

The inescapable fact is that adjudication of substantive due process claims may call upon the Court in interpreting the Constitution to exercise that same capacity which by tradition courts always have exercised: reasoned judgment. Its boundaries are not susceptible of expression as a simple rule. That does not mean we are free to invalidate state policy choices with which we disagree; yet neither does it permit us to shrink from the duties of our office. As Justice Harlan observed:

> "Due process has not been reduced to any formula; its content cannot be determined by reference to any code. The best that can be said is that ... it has represented the balance which our Nation, built upon postulates of respect for the liberty of the individual, has struck between that liberty and the demands of organized society. If the supplying of content to this Constitutional concept has of necessity been a rational process, it certainly has not been one where judges have felt free to roam where unguided speculation might take them. The balance of which I speak is the balance struck by this country, having regard to what history teaches are the traditions from which it developed as well as the traditions from which it broke. That tradition is a living thing. A decision of this Court which radically departs from it could not long survive, while a decision which builds on what has survived is likely to be sound. No formula could serve as a substitute, in this area, for judgment and restraint." *Poe* (Harlan, J., dissenting).

See also Rochin v. California [1952] (Frankfurter, J., writing for the Court) ("To believe that this judicial exercise of judgment could be avoided by freezing 'due process of law' at some fixed stage of time or thought is to suggest that the most important aspect of constitutional adjudication is a function for inanimate machines and not for judges").

Men and women of good conscience can disagree ... about the profound moral and spiritual implications of terminating a pregnancy, even in its earliest stage. Some of us as individuals find abortion offensive to our most basic principles of morality, but that cannot control our decision. Our obligation is to define the liberty of all, not to mandate our own moral code. The underlying constitutional issue is whether the State can resolve these philosophic questions in such a definitive way that a woman lacks all choice in the matter, except perhaps in those rare circumstances in which the pregnancy is itself a danger to her own life or health, or is the result of rape or incest.

It is conventional constitutional doctrine that where reasonable people disagree the government can adopt one position or the other. See, *e.g.*, Ferguson v. Skrupa (1963); Williamson v. Lee Optical (1955). That theorem, however, assumes a state of affairs in which the choice does not intrude upon a protected liberty. ...

Our law affords constitutional protection to personal decisions relating to marriage, procreation, contraception, family relationships, child rearing, and education. Our cases recognize "the right of the *individual,* married or single, to be free from unwarranted governmental intrusion into matters so fundamentally affecting a person as the decision whether to bear or beget a child." *Eisenstadt* (emphasis in original). ... These matters, involving the most intimate and personal choices a person may make in a lifetime, choices central to personal dignity and autonomy, are central to the liberty protected by the Fourteenth Amendment. At the heart of liberty is the right to define one's own concept of existence, of meaning, of the universe, and of the mystery of human life. Beliefs about these matters could not define the attributes of personhood were they formed under compulsion of the State.

These considerations begin our analysis of the woman's interest in terminating her pregnancy but cannot end it, for [abortion] is more than a philosophic exercise. Abortion is a unique act ... fraught with consequences for others: for the woman who must live with the implications of her decision; for the persons who perform and assist in the procedure; for the spouse, family, and society which must confront the knowledge that these procedures exist, procedures some deem nothing short of an act of violence against innocent human life; and, depending on one's beliefs, for the life or potential life that is aborted. Though abortion is conduct, it does not follow that the State is entitled to proscribe it in all instances. That is because the liberty of the woman is at stake in a sense unique to the human condition and so unique to the law. The mother who carries a child to full term is subject to anxieties, to physical constraints, to pain that only she must bear. That these sacrifices have from the beginning of the human race been endured by woman with a pride that ennobles her in the eyes of others and gives to the infant a bond of love cannot alone be grounds for the State to insist she make the sacrifice. Her suffering is too intimate and personal for the State to insist, without more, upon its own vision of the woman's role, however dominant that vision has been in the course of our history and our culture. The destiny of the woman must be shaped to a large extent on her own conception of her spiritual imperatives and her place in society.

It should be recognized, moreover, that in some critical respects the abortion decision is of the same character as the decision to use contraception, to which *Griswold, Eisenstadt,* and *Carey* afford constitutional protection. We have no doubt as to the correctness of those decisions. They support the reasoning in *Roe* relating to the woman's liberty because they involve personal decisions concerning not only the meaning of procreation but also human responsibility and respect for it. ...

While we appreciate the weight of the arguments made on behalf of the State ... [which] conclude that *Roe* should be overruled, the reservations any of us may have in reaffirming the central holding of *Roe* are outweighed by the explication of individual liberty we have given combined with the force of stare decisis. We now turn to that doctrine.

III

A

... [I]t is common wisdom that the rule of stare decisis is not an "inexorable command". ... Rather, when this Court reexamines a prior holding, its judgment is customarily informed by a series of prudential and pragmatic considerations designed to test the consistency of overruling a prior decision with the ideal of the rule of law, and to gauge the respective costs of reaffirming and overruling a prior case. Thus, for example, we may ask whether the rule has proved to be intolerable simply in defying practical workability ...; whether the rule is subject to a kind of reliance that would lend a special hardship to the consequences of overruling and add inequity to the cost of repudiation ...; whether related principles of law have so far developed as to have left the old rule no more than a remnant of abandoned doctrine ...; or whether facts have so changed or come to be seen so differently, as to have robbed the old rule of significant application or justification. ...

1. Although *Roe* has engendered opposition, it has in no sense proven "unworkable," see Garcia v. San Antonio Metropolitan Transit Authority (1985). ... [T]he required determinations fall within judicial competence.

2. The inquiry into reliance counts the cost of a rule's repudiation as it would fall on those who have relied reasonably on the rule's continued application. Since the classic case for weighing reliance heavily in favor of following the earlier rule occurs in the commercial context, where advance planning of great precision is most obviously a necessity, it is no cause for surprise that some would find no reliance worthy of consideration in support of *Roe.* ...

To eliminate the issue of reliance that easily, however, one would need to limit cognizable reliance to specific instances of sexual activity. But to do this would be simply to refuse to face the fact that for two decades of economic and social developments, people have organized intimate relationships and made choices that define their views of themselves and their places in society, in reliance on the availability of abortion in the event that contraception should fail. The ability of women to participate equally in the economic and social life of the Nation has been facilitated by their ability to control their reproductive lives. See, *e.g.,* R. Petchesky, *Abortion and Woman's Choice* 109, 133, n.7 (rev. ed. 1990). The Constitution serves human values, and while the effect of reliance on *Roe* cannot be exactly measured, neither can the certain cost of overruling *Roe* for people who have ordered their thinking and living around that case be dismissed.

3. No evolution of legal principle has left *Roe* 's doctrinal footings weaker than they were in 1973. ... *Roe* stands at an intersection of two lines of decisions. ... The *Roe* Court itself placed its holding in the succession of cases most prominently exemplified by *Griswold.* When it is so seen, *Roe* is clearly in no jeopardy, since subsequent constitutional developments have neither disturbed, nor do they threaten to diminish, the scope of recognized protection accorded to the liberty relating to intimate relationships, the family, and decisions about whether or not to beget or bear a child. See, *e.g., Carey*; Moore v. East Cleveland (1977).

Roe, however, may be seen not only as an exemplar of *Griswold* liberty but as a rule (whether or not mistaken) of personal autonomy and bodily integrity, with doctrinal affinity to cases recognizing limits on governmental power to mandate medical treatment or to bar its rejection. If so, our cases since *Roe* accord with *Roe*'s view that a State's interest in the protection of life falls short of justifying any plenary override of individual liberty claims. Cruzan v. Director, Missouri Dept. of Health (1990); see also, *e.g.*, *Rochin*; Jacobson v. Massachusetts (1905).

Finally, one could classify *Roe* as *sui generis*. If the case is so viewed, then there clearly has been no erosion of its central determination. The original holding resting on the concurrence of seven Members of the Court in 1973 was expressly affirmed by a majority of six in 1983, see Akron v. Akron Center for Reproductive Health, Inc. (1983) (*Akron I*), and by a majority of five in 1986, see Thornburgh v. American College of Obstetricians and Gynecologists (1986). ... More recently, in Webster v. Reproductive Health Services (1989), although two of the present authors questioned the trimester framework in a way consistent with our judgment today (Rehnquist C. J., joined by White, and Kennedy, JJ.); (O'Connor, J., concurring in part and concurring in judgment), a majority of the Court either decided to reaffirm or declined to address the constitutional validity of the central holding of *Roe*.

Nor will courts building upon *Roe* be likely to hand down erroneous decisions as a consequence. Even on the assumption that the central holding of *Roe* was in error, that error would go only to the strength of the state interest in fetal protection, not to the recognition afforded by the Constitution to the woman's liberty. The latter aspect of the decision fits comfortably within the framework of the Court's prior decisions including Skinner v. Oklahoma (1942), *Griswold*, Loving v. Virginia (1967), and *Eisenstadt*. ...

The soundness of this prong of the *Roe* analysis is apparent from a consideration of the alternative. If indeed the woman's interest in deciding whether to bear and beget a child had not been recognized as in *Roe*, the State might as readily restrict a woman's right to choose to carry a pregnancy to term as to terminate it, to further asserted state interests in population control, or eugenics, for example. Yet *Roe* has been sensibly relied upon to counter any such suggestions. ...

4. ... [T]ime has overtaken some of *Roe*'s factual assumptions: advances in maternal health care allow for abortions safe to the mother later in pregnancy than was true in 1973, see *Akron I*, and advances in neonatal care have advanced viability to a point somewhat earlier. But these facts go only to the scheme of time limits on the realization of competing interests, and the divergences from the factual premises of 1973 have no bearing on the validity of *Roe*'s central holding. ... The soundness or unsoundness of that constitutional judgment in no sense turns on whether viability occurs at approximately 28 weeks, as was usual at the time of *Roe*, at 23 to 24 weeks, as it sometimes does today, or at some moment even slightly earlier in pregnancy. ... Whenever it may occur, the attainment of viability may continue to serve as the critical fact. ...

5. The sum of the precedential inquiry to this point shows *Roe*'s underpinnings unweakened in any way affecting its central holding. While it has engendered disapproval, it has not been unworkable. An entire generation has come of age free to assume *Roe*'s concept of liberty in defining the capacity of women to act in society, and to make reproductive decisions; no erosion of principle going to liberty or personal autonomy has left *Roe*'s central holding a doctrinal remnant; *Roe* portends no developments at odds with other precedent for the analysis of personal liberty; and no changes of fact have rendered viability more or less appropriate as the point at which the balance of interests tips. . . .

B

[S]tare decisis analysis could . . . stop at the point we have reached. But the sustained and widespread debate *Roe* has provoked calls for some comparison between that case and others of comparable dimension that have responded to national controversies. . . .

The first example is that line of cases identified with Lochner v. New York (1905), which imposed substantive limitations on legislation limiting economic autonomy in favor of health and welfare regulation. . . . The *Lochner* decisions were exemplified by Adkins v. Children's Hospital (1923), in which this Court held it to be an infringement of constitutionally protected liberty of contract to require the employers of adult women to satisfy minimum wage standards. Fourteen years later, West Coast Hotel Co. v. Parrish (1937) signalled the demise of *Lochner* by overruling *Adkins*. In the meantime, the Depression had come and, with it, the lesson that seemed unmistakable to most people by 1937, that the interpretation of contractual freedom protected in *Adkins* rested on fundamentally false factual assumptions about the capacity of a relatively unregulated market to satisfy minimal levels of human welfare. See *West Coast Hotel*. . . .

The second comparison that 20th century history invites is with the cases employing the separate-but-equal rule. . . . They began with Plessy v. Ferguson (1896) . . . [which held] "the underlying fallacy of the plaintiff's argument to consist in the assumption that the enforced separation of the two races stamps the colored race with a badge of inferiority. If this be so, it is not by reason of anything found in the act, but solely because the colored race chooses to put that construction upon it." . . . But this understanding of the facts and the rule it was stated to justify were repudiated in Brown v. Bd. of Ed. (1954). . . .

The Court in *Brown* . . . observ[ed] that whatever may have been the understanding in *Plessy*'s time of the power of segregation to stigmatize those who were segregated with a "badge of inferiority," it was clear by 1954 that legally sanctioned segregation had just such an effect. . . . While we think *Plessy* was wrong the day it was decided, we must also recognize that the *Plessy* Court's explanation for its decision was so clearly at odds with the facts apparent to the Court in 1954 that the decision to reexamine *Plessy* was on this ground alone not only justified but required.

West Coast Hotel and *Brown* each rested on facts, or an understanding of facts, changed from those which furnished the claimed justifications for the earlier constitutional resolutions. ... In constitutional adjudication as elsewhere in life, changed circumstances may impose new obligations, and the thoughtful part of the Nation could accept each decision to overrule a prior case as a response to the Court's constitutional duty.

... Because neither the factual underpinnings of *Roe*'s central holding nor our understanding of it has changed ... the Court could not pretend to be reexamining the prior law with any justification beyond a present doctrinal disposition to come out differently from the Court of 1973. To overrule prior law for no other reason than that would run counter to the view repeated in our cases that a decision to overrule should rest on some special reason over and above the belief that a prior case was wrongly decided.. See, *e.g.*, Mitchell v. W.T. Grant (1974) (Stewart, J., dissenting). ("A basic change in the law upon a ground no firmer than a change in our membership invites the popular misconception that this institution is little different from the two political branches of the Government. No misconception could do more lasting injury to this Court and to the system of law which it is our abiding mission to serve.")

C

... Our analysis would not be complete ... without explaining why overruling *Roe*'s central holding ... would seriously weaken the Court's capacity to exercise the judicial power and to function as the Supreme Court of a Nation dedicated to the rule of law. ... The root of American governmental power is revealed most clearly in the instance of the power conferred by the Constitution upon the Judiciary of the United States and specifically upon this Court. As Americans of each succeeding generation are rightly told, the Court cannot buy support for its decisions by spending money and, except to a minor degree, it cannot independently coerce obedience to its decrees. The Court's power lies, rather, in its legitimacy, a product of substance and perception that shows itself in the people's acceptance of the Judiciary as fit to determine what the Nation's law means and to declare what it demands.

... The Court must take care to speak and act in ways that allow people to accept its decisions ... as grounded truly in principle, not as compromises with social and political pressures. ... Thus, the Court's legitimacy depends on making legally principled decisions under circumstances in which their principled character is sufficiently plausible to be accepted by the Nation. The need for principled action to be perceived as such is implicated to some degree whenever this, or any other appellate court, overrules a prior case. ... People understand that some of the Constitution's language is hard to fathom and that the Court's

Justices are sometimes able to perceive significant facts or to understand principles of law that eluded their predecessors. ... [T]he country can accept some correction of error without necessarily questioning the legitimacy of the Court.

In two circumstances, however, the Court would almost certainly fail to receive the benefit of the doubt in overruling prior cases. There is, first, a point beyond which frequent overruling would overtax the country's belief in the Court's good faith. ... There is a limit to the amount of error that can plausibly be imputed to prior courts. If that limit should be exceeded, disturbance of prior rulings would be taken as evidence that justifiable reexamination of principle had given way to drives for particular results in the short term. The legitimacy of the Court would fade with the frequency of its vacillation.

That first circumstance can be described as hypothetical; the second is to the point here and now. Where, in the performance of its judicial duties, the Court decides a case in such a way as to resolve the sort of intensely divisive controversy reflected in *Roe* and those rare, comparable cases, its decision has a dimension that the resolution of the normal case does not carry. It is the dimension present whenever the Court's interpretation of the Constitution calls the contending sides of a national controversy to end their national division by accepting a common mandate rooted in the Constitution.

... [W]hen the Court does act in this way, its decision requires an equally rare precedential force to counter the inevitable efforts to overturn it and to thwart its implementation. ... [O]nly the most convincing justification under accepted standards of precedent could suffice to demonstrate that a later decision overruling the first was anything but a surrender to political pressure, and an unjustified repudiation of the principle on which the Court staked its authority in the first instance. ... Cf. Brown v. Bd. of Ed. (1955) (*Brown II*). ...

The country's loss of confidence in the judiciary would be underscored by an equally certain and equally reasonable condemnation for another failing in overruling unnecessarily and under pressure. Some cost will be paid by anyone who approves or implements a constitutional decision where it is unpopular, or who refuses to work to undermine the decision or to force its reversal. The price may be criticism or ostracism, or it may be violence. An extra price will be paid by those who themselves disapprove of the decision's results when viewed outside of constitutional terms, but who nevertheless struggle to accept it, because they respect the rule of law. To all those who will be so tested by following, the Court implicitly undertakes to remain steadfast, lest in the end a price be paid for nothing. The promise of constancy, once given, binds its maker for as long as the power to stand by the decision survives and the understanding of the issue has not changed so fundamentally as to render the commitment obsolete. From the obligation of this promise this Court cannot and should not assume any exemption when duty requires it to decide a case in conformance with the Constitution. A willing breach of it would be nothing less than a breach of faith, and no Court that broke its faith with the people could sensibly expect credit for principle in the decision by which it did that.

It is true that diminished legitimacy may be restored, but only slowly. Unlike the political branches, a Court thus weakened could not seek to regain its position with a new mandate from the voters. ... Like the character of an individual, the legitimacy of the Court must be earned over time. So, indeed, must be the character of a Nation of people who aspire to live according to the rule of law. Their belief in themselves as such a people is not readily separable from their understanding of the Court invested with the authority to decide their constitutional cases and speak before all others for their constitutional ideals. If the Court's legitimacy should be undermined, then, so would the country be in its very ability to see itself through its constitutional ideals. The Court's concern with legitimacy is not for the sake of the Court but for the sake of the Nation to which it is responsible.

The Court's duty in the present case is clear. ... A decision to overrule *Roe*'s essential holding under the existing circumstances would address error, if error there was, at the cost of both profound and unnecessary damage to the Court's legitimacy, and to the Nation's commitment to the rule of law. It is therefore imperative to adhere to the essence of *Roe*'s original decision, and we do so today.

IV

... [I]t follows that it is a constitutional liberty of the woman to have some freedom to terminate her pregnancy. ... The woman's liberty is not so unlimited, however, that from the outset the State cannot show its concern for the life of the unborn, and at a later point in fetal development the State's interest in life has sufficient force so that the right of the woman to terminate the pregnancy can be restricted.

That brings us, of course, to the point where much criticism has been directed at *Roe*, a criticism that always inheres when the Court draws a specific rule from what in the Constitution is but a general standard. We conclude, however, that the urgent claims of the woman to retain the ultimate control over her destiny and her body, claims implicit in the meaning of liberty, require us to perform that function. Liberty must not be extinguished for want of a line that is clear. ...

We conclude the line should be drawn at viability, so that before that time the woman has a right to choose to terminate her pregnancy. We adhere to this principle for two reasons. First ... is the doctrine of stare decisis. Any judicial act of line-drawing may seem somewhat arbitrary, but *Roe* was a reasoned statement, elaborated with great care. We have twice reaffirmed it in the face of great opposition. See *Thornburgh*; *Akron I*. Although we must overrule those parts of *Thornburgh* and *Akron I* which ... are inconsistent with *Roe*'s statement that the State has a legitimate interest in promoting the life or potential life of the unborn, the central premise of those cases represents an unbroken commitment by this Court to the essential holding of *Roe*. It is that premise which we reaffirm today.

The second reason is that the concept of viability, as we noted in *Roe*, is the time at which there is a realistic possibility of maintaining and nourishing a life outside the womb, so that the independent existence of the second life can in reason and all fairness be the object of state protection that now overrides the rights of the woman. ... [T]here is no line other than viability which is more workable. ... The viability line also has, as a practical matter, an element of fairness. In some broad sense it might be said that a woman who fails to act before viability has consented to the State's intervention on behalf of the developing child.

The woman's right to terminate her pregnancy before viability is the most central principle of *Roe*. ... On the other side of the equation is the interest of the State in the protection of potential life. ... That portion of the decision in *Roe* has been given too little acknowledgement and implementation by the Court in its subsequent cases. Those cases decided that any regulation touching upon the abortion decision must survive strict scrutiny, to be sustained only if drawn in narrow terms to further a compelling state interest. See, *e.g.*, *Akron I*. Not all of the cases decided under that formulation can be reconciled with the holding in *Roe* itself that the State has legitimate interests in the health of the woman and in protecting the potential life within her. In resolving this tension, we choose to rely upon *Roe*, as against the later cases.

Roe established a trimester framework. ... Under this elaborate but rigid construct, almost no regulation at all is permitted during the first trimester of pregnancy; regulations designed to protect the woman's health, but not to further the State's interest in potential life, are permitted during the second trimester; and during the third trimester, when the fetus is viable, prohibitions are permitted provided the life or health of the mother is not at stake. ...

Though the woman has a right to choose to terminate or continue her pregnancy before viability, it does not at all follow that the State is prohibited from taking steps to ensure that this choice is thoughtful and informed. Even in the earliest stages of pregnancy, the State may enact rules and regulations designed to encourage her to know that there are philosophic and social arguments of great weight that can be brought to bear in favor of continuing the pregnancy to full term and that there are procedures and institutions to allow adoption of unwanted children as well as a certain degree of state assistance if the mother chooses to raise the child herself. ... It follows that States are free to enact laws to provide a reasonable framework for a woman to make a decision that has such profound and lasting meaning. This, too, we find consistent with *Roe*'s central premises, and indeed the inevitable consequence of our holding that the State has an interest in protecting the life of the unborn. We reject the trimester framework, which we do not consider to be part of the essential holding of *Roe*. ...

As our jurisprudence relating to all liberties save perhaps abortion has recognized, not every law which makes a right more difficult to exercise is, *ipso facto*, an infringement of that right. ... The fact that a law which serves a valid purpose, one not designed to strike at the right itself, has the incidental effect of making it more difficult or more expensive to procure an abortion cannot be enough to invalidate it. Only where state regulation imposes an undue burden on a woman's ability to make this decision does the power of the State reach into the heart of the liberty protected by the Due Process Clause. ...

... [D]espite the protestations contained in the original *Roe* opinion to the effect that the Court was not recognizing an absolute right, the Court's experience applying the trimester framework has led to the striking down of some abortion regulations which in no real sense deprived women of the ultimate decision. Those decisions went too far. ... Not all governmental intrusion is of necessity unwarranted; and that brings us to the other basic flaw in the trimester framework: even in *Roe*'s terms, in practice it undervalues the State's interest in the potential life within the woman. ...

The very notion that the State has a substantial interest in potential life leads to the conclusion that not all regulations must be deemed unwarranted. Not all burdens on the right to decide whether to terminate a pregnancy will be undue. ... In our view, the undue burden standard is the appropriate means of reconciling the State's interest with the woman's constitutionally protected liberty. The concept of an undue burden has been utilized by the Court as well as individual members of the Court, including two of us, in ways that could be considered inconsistent. ... Because we set forth a standard ... to which we intend to adhere, it is important to clarify what [it means]. ...

A finding of an undue burden is shorthand for the conclusion that a state regulation has the purpose or effect of placing a substantial obstacle in the path of a woman seeking an abortion of a nonviable fetus. A statute with this purpose is invalid because the means chosen by the State to further the interest in potential life must be calculated to inform the woman's free choice, not hinder it. ...

Some guiding principles should emerge. What is at stake is the woman's right to make the ultimate decision, not a right to be insulated from all others in doing so. Regulations which do no more than create a structural mechanism by which the State, or the parent or guardian of a minor, may express profound respect for the life of the unborn are permitted, if they are not a substantial obstacle to the woman's exercise of the right to choose. Unless it has that effect on her right of choice, a state measure designed to persuade her to choose childbirth over abortion will be upheld if reasonably related to that goal. Regulations designed to foster the health of a woman seeking an abortion are valid if they do not constitute an undue burden.

Even when jurists reason from shared premises, some disagreement is inevitable. ... We do not expect it to be otherwise with respect to the undue burden standard. We give this summary:

(a) ... An undue burden exists, and therefore a provision of law is invalid, if its purpose or effect is to place a substantial obstacle in the path of a woman seeking an abortion before the fetus attains viability.

(b) We reject the rigid trimester framework of *Roe*. To promote the State's profound interest in potential life, throughout pregnancy the State may take measures to ensure that the woman's choice is informed, and measures designed to advance this interest will not be invalidated as long as their purpose is to persuade the woman to choose childbirth over abortion. These measures must not be an undue burden on the right.

(c) As with any medical procedure, the State may enact regulations to further the health or safety of a woman seeking an abortion. Unnecessary health regulations that have the purpose or effect of presenting a substantial obstacle to a woman seeking an abortion impose an undue burden on the right.

(d) ... Regardless of whether exceptions are made for particular circumstances, a State may not prohibit any woman from making the ultimate decision to terminate her pregnancy before viability.

(e) We also reaffirm *Roe* 's holding that "subsequent to viability, the State in promoting its interest in the potentiality of human life may, if it chooses, regulate, and even proscribe, abortion except where it is necessary ... for the preservation of the life or health of the mother."

These principles control our assessment of the Pennsylvania statute, and we now turn to the issue of the validity of its challenged provisions.

V ...

[The joint opinion stated that the reasoning just offered led to the following conclusions:

(1) The statute's definition of "medical emergencies," which would allow a woman to omit the 24–hour waiting period, was not so restrictive as to impose an undue burden.

(2) The requirement of "informed consent"—that at least 24 hours before performing an abortion a physician must inform a woman seeking an abortion of the nature of the procedure, the health risks of abortion and of childbirth, and provide her with certain medical information—did not constitute an undue burden.

(3) The requirement that a minor child obtain the consent of at least one parent—or if she could show that obtaining such consent was not feasible, the permission of a court—was also valid for the same reason.

(4) The requirement that hospitals, clinics, and physicians keep certain records about abortions was also valid for the same reason.

(5) The requirement that a wife notify her husband did impose an undue burden and was therefore unconstitutional.

On each of these five points, the plurality picked up enough votes from other justices to make **Part V** of their opinion that of the Court.—**Eds.**]

VI

Our Constitution is a covenant running from the first generation of Americans to us and then to future generations. It is a coherent succession. Each generation must learn anew that the Constitution's written terms embody ideas and aspirations that must survive more ages than one. We accept our responsibility not to retreat from interpreting the full meaning of the covenant in light of all of our precedents. We invoke it once again to define the freedom guaranteed by the Constitution's own promise, the promise of liberty. . . .

Justice **STEVENS**, concurring in part and dissenting in part.

The portions of the Court's opinion that I have joined are more important than those with which I disagree. . . .

I

The Court is unquestionably correct in concluding that the doctrine of stare decisis has controlling significance in a case of this kind, notwithstanding an individual justice's concerns about the merits.[1] The central holding of *Roe* has been a "part of our law" for almost two decades. It was a natural sequel to the protection of individual liberty established in *Griswold*. The societal costs of overruling *Roe* at this late date would be enormous. *Roe* is an integral part of a correct understanding of both the concept of liberty and the basic equality of men and women. . . .

I also accept . . . *Roe*'s explanation of why the State's obligation to protect the life or health of the mother must take precedence over any duty to the unborn. The Court in *Roe* carefully considered, and rejected, the State's argument "that the fetus is a 'person' within the language and meaning of the Fourteenth Amendment." . . . From this holding, there was no dissent; indeed, no member of the Court has ever questioned this fundamental proposition. Thus, as a matter of federal constitutional law, a developing organism that is not yet a "person" does not have what is sometimes described as a "right to life."[2] This has

---

1. It is sometimes useful to view the issue of stare decisis from a historical perspective. In the last nineteen years, fifteen Justices have confronted the basic issue presented in Roe. Of those, eleven have voted as the majority does today. . . . Only four—all of whom happen to be on the Court today—have reached the opposite conclusion. [Footnote by Justice Stevens.]

2. Professor Dworkin has made this comment on the issue:

"The suggestion that states are free to declare a fetus a person . . . assumes that a state can curtail some persons' constitutional rights by adding new persons to the constitutional population. The constitutional rights of one citizen are of course very much affected by who or what else also has constitutional rights, because the rights of others may compete or conflict with his. So any power to increase the constitutional population by unilateral decision would be, in effect, a power to decrease rights the national Constitution grants to others.

been and, by the Court's holding today, remains a fundamental premise of our constitutional law governing reproductive autonomy.

II

My disagreement with the joint opinion begins with its understanding of the trimester framework. ... First, ... to be legitimate, the State's interest must be secular; consistent with the First Amendment the State may not promote a theological or sectarian interest. Moreover ... the state interest in potential human life is not an interest *in loco parentis,* for the fetus is not a person. Identifying the State's interests—which the States rarely articulate with any precision—makes clear that the interest in protecting potential life is not grounded in the Constitution. It is, instead, an indirect interest supported by both humanitarian and pragmatic concerns. ... The State may also have a broader interest in expanding the population. ...

In counterpoise is the woman's constitutional interest in liberty. One aspect of this liberty is a right to bodily integrity, a right to control one's person. See *e.g., Rochin; Skinner.* This right is neutral on the question of abortion: The Constitution would be equally offended by an absolute requirement that all women undergo abortions as by an absolute prohibition on abortions. ...

The woman's constitutional liberty interest also involves her freedom to decide matters of the highest privacy and the most personal nature. Cf. Whalen v. Roe (1977). ... The authority to make such traumatic and yet empowering decisions is an element of basic human dignity. ... [A] woman's decision to terminate her pregnancy is nothing less than a matter of conscience. ...

Weighing the State's interest in potential life and the woman's liberty interest, I agree ... that the State may " 'expres[s] a preference for normal childbirth,' " that the State may take steps to ensure that a woman's choice "is thoughtful and informed," and that "States are free to enact laws to provide a reasonable framework for a woman to make a decision that has such profound and lasting meaning." Serious questions arise, however, when a State attempts to "persuade the woman to choose childbirth over abortion." Decisional autonomy must limit the State's power to inject into a woman's most personal deliberations its own views of what is best. The State may promote its preferences by funding childbirth, by creating and maintaining alternatives to abortion, and by espousing the virtues of family; but it must respect the individual's freedom to make such judgments. ...

... Under these principles, §§ 3205(a)(2)(i)-(iii) of the Pennsylvania statute are unconstitutional. Those sections require a physician or

---

"... If a fetus is not part of the constitutional population ... then states have no power to overrule that ... arrangement by themselves declaring that fetuses have rights competitive with the constitutional rights of pregnant women." Dworkin, Unenumerated Rights: Whether and How *Roe* Should be Overruled, 59 *U.Chi.L.Rev.* 381, 400–401 (1992). [Footnote by Justice Stevens.]

counselor to provide the woman with a range of materials clearly designed to persuade her to choose not to undergo the abortion. While the State is free to produce and disseminate such material, the State may not inject such information into the woman's deliberations just as she is weighing such an important choice.

Under this same analysis, §§ 3205(a)(1)(i) and (iii) of the Pennsylvania statute are constitutional. Those sections, which require the physician to inform a woman of the nature and risks of the abortion procedure and the medical risks of carrying to term, are neutral requirements comparable to those imposed in other medical procedures. Those sections indicate no effort by the State to influence the woman's choice in any way. If anything, such requirements *enhance*, rather than skew, the woman's decisionmaking.

III

The [requirement of a] 24–hour waiting period raises even more serious concerns. ... [I]t may be argued that ... delay ... furthers the State's interest in ensuring that the woman's decision is informed and thoughtful. But there is no evidence that the mandated delay benefits women or that it is necessary to enable the physician to convey any relevant information to the patient. The mandatory delay thus appears to rest on outmoded and unacceptable assumptions about the decisionmaking capacity of women. ... Just as we have left behind the belief that a woman must consult her husband before undertaking serious matters, so we must reject the notion that a woman is less capable of deciding matters of gravity. Cf. Reed v. Reed (1971).

In the alternative, the delay requirement may be premised on the belief that the decision to terminate a pregnancy is presumptively wrong. This premise is illegitimate. ... No person undertakes such a decision lightly—and States may not presume that a woman has failed to reflect adequately merely because her conclusion differs from the State's preference. A woman who has, in the privacy of her thoughts and conscience, weighed the options and made her decision cannot be forced to reconsider all, simply because the State believes she has come to the wrong conclusion.

Part of the constitutional liberty to choose is the equal dignity to which each of us is entitled. A woman who decides to terminate her pregnancy is entitled to the same respect as a woman who decides to carry the fetus to term. The mandatory waiting period denies women that equal respect. ...

... [W]hile I disagree with Parts **IV**, **V-B**, and **V-D** of the joint opinion, I join the remainder of the Court's opinion.*

---

* Part **V–B** upheld the statute's requirement of informed consent, and **V–D** upheld the provision regarding parental consent.—**Eds.**

Justice **BLACKMUN**, concurring in part, concurring in the judgment in
part, and dissenting in part.

I join parts **I**, **II**, **III**, **V-A**, **V-C**, and **VI** of the joint opinion of
Justices O'Connor, Kennedy, and Souter.**

Three years ago, in *Webster*, four Members of this Court appeared
poised to "cast into darkness the hopes and visions of every woman in
this country" who had come to believe that the Constitution guaranteed
her the right to reproductive choice. (Blackmun, J., dissenting). All
that remained between the promise of *Roe* and the darkness of the
plurality was a single, flickering flame. Decisions since *Webster* gave
little reason to hope that this flame would cast much light. But now,
just when so many expected the darkness to fall, the flame has grown
bright.

... I remain steadfast in my belief that the right to reproductive
choice is entitled to the full protection afforded by this Court before
Webster. And I fear for the darkness as four Justices anxiously await the
single vote necessary to extinguish the light.

I

Make no mistake, the joint opinion is an act of personal courage and
constitutional principle. ... What has happened today should serve as a
model for future Justices and a warning to all who have tried to turn
this Court into yet another political branch. ...

II

Today, no less than yesterday, the Constitution and decisions of this
Court require that a State's abortion restrictions be subjected to the
strictest of judicial scrutiny. ... Under this standard, the Pennsylvania
statute's provisions requiring content-based counseling, a 24–hour delay,
informed parental consent, and reporting of abortion-related information
must be invalidated.

A

The Court today reaffirms the long recognized rights of privacy and
bodily integrity. ... State restrictions on abortion violate a woman's
right of privacy in two ways. First, compelled continuation of a pregnancy infringes upon a woman's right to bodily integrity. ... Further,
... it deprives a woman of the right to make her own decision about
reproduction and family planning—critical life choices that this Court
long has deemed central to the right to privacy. ... Because motherhood has a dramatic impact on a woman's educational prospects, employment opportunities, and self-determination, restrictive abortion laws
deprive her of basic control over her life. ...

** Part **V–A** involved the definition of "medical emergency," and **V–C** required a
pregnant woman to notify her spouse before undergoing an abortion.—**Eds.**

A State's restrictions ... also implicate constitutional guarantees of gender equality. ... By restricting the right to terminate pregnancies, the State conscripts women's bodies into its service, forcing women to continue their pregnancies, suffer the pains of childbirth, and in most instances, provide years of maternal care. The State does not compensate women for their services; instead, it assumes that they owe this duty as a matter of course. This assumption—that women can simply be forced to accept the "natural" status and incidents of motherhood—appears to rest upon a conception of women's role that has triggered the protection of the Equal Protection Clause. See, *e.g.*, Mississippi Univ. for Women v. Hogan (1982); Craig v. Boren (1976).[1] The joint opinion recognizes that these assumptions about women's place in society "are no longer consistent with our understanding of the family, the individual, or the Constitution."

III

... If there is much reason to applaud the advances made by the joint opinion today, there is far more to fear from The Chief Justice's opinion. ... [His] criticism of *Roe* follows from his stunted conception of individual liberty. While recognizing that the Due Process Clause protects more than simple physical liberty, he then goes on to construe this Court's personal-liberty cases as establishing only a laundry list of particular rights, rather than a principled account of how these particular rights are grounded in a more general right of privacy. This constricted view is reinforced by The Chief Justice's exclusive reliance on tradition as a source of fundamental rights. ... [P]eople using contraceptives seem the next likely candidate for his list of outcasts.

Even more shocking ... is [The Chief Justice's] complete omission of any discussion of the effects that compelled childbirth and motherhood have on women's lives. ... [H]is view of the State's compelling interest in maternal health has less to do with health than it does with compelling women to be maternal. Nor does The Chief Justice give any serious consideration to the doctrine of stare decisis. ... The Chief Justice's narrow conception of individual liberty and stare decisis leads him to propose the same standard of review proposed by the plurality in *Webster*. ...[2]

---

1. A growing number of commentators are recognizing this point. See, *e.g.*, L. Tribe, *American Constitutional Law* § 15–10 (2d. ed. 1988); Siegel, "Reasoning from the Body: A Historical Perspective on Abortion Regulation and Questions of Equal Protection," 44 *Stan.L.Rev.* 161 (1992); Sunstein, "Neutrality in Constitutional Law," 92 *Colum.L.Rev.* 1 (1992); MacKinnon, "Reflections on Sex Equality Under Law," 100 *Yale L.J.* 1281 (1991); cf. Rubenfeld, "The Right of Privacy," 102 *Harv.L.Rev.* 737 (1989) (similar analysis under the rubric of privacy). [Footnote by Justice Blackmun.]

2. Justice Scalia urges the Court to "get out of this area" and leave questions regarding abortion entirely to the States. Putting aside the fact that what he advocates is nothing short of an abdication by the Court of its constitutional responsibilities, Justice Scalia is uncharacteristically naive if he thinks that overruling *Roe* and holding that restrictions on a woman's right to an abortion are subject only to rational-basis review will enable the Court henceforth to avoid reviewing abortion-related issues. State efforts to regulate and prohibit abortion in a post-*Roe* world undoubtedly would raise a host of distinct and

But, we are reassured, there is always the protection of the democratic process. While there is much to be praised about our democracy, our country since its founding has recognized that there are certain fundamental liberties that are not to be left to the whims of an election. A woman's right to reproductive choice is one of those fundamental liberties. Accordingly, that liberty need not seek refuge at the ballot box.

IV

In one sense, the Court's approach is worlds apart from that of The Chief Justice and Justice Scalia. And yet, in another sense, the distance between the two approaches is short—the distance is but a single vote. I am 83 years old. I cannot remain on this Court forever, and when I do step down, the confirmation process for my successor well may focus on the issue before us today. That, I regret, may be exactly where the choice between the two worlds will be made.***

Chief Justice **REHNQUIST**, with whom Justice **WHITE**, Justice **SCA-LIA**, and Justice **THOMAS** join, concurring in the judgment in part and dissenting in part.

The joint opinion, following its newly-minted variation on stare decisis, retains the outer shell of *Roe*, but beats a wholesale retreat from the substance of that case. We believe that *Roe* was wrongly decided, and that it can and should be overruled consistently with our traditional approach to stare decisis in constitutional cases. We would adopt the approach of the plurality in *Webster* and uphold the challenged provisions of the Pennsylvania statute in their entirety. ...

II

... Instead of claiming that *Roe* was correct as a matter of original constitutional interpretation, the [joint] opinion ... contains an elaborate discussion of stare decisis ... [which] appears to be almost entirely dicta, because the joint opinion does not apply that principle in dealing with *Roe*. *Roe* decided that a woman had a fundamental right to an abortion. The joint opinion rejects that view. *Roe* decided that abortion regulations were to be subjected to "strict scrutiny" and could be

---

important constitutional questions meriting review by this Court. For example, does the Eighth Amendment impose any limits on the degree or kind of punishment a State can inflict upon physicians who perform, or women who undergo, abortions? What effect would differences among States in their approaches to abortion have on a woman's right to engage in interstate travel? Does the First Amendment permit States that choose not to criminalize abortion to ban all advertising providing information about where and how to obtain abortions? [Footnote by Justice Blackmun.]

*** When *Casey* was decided, George Bush was still in the White House and, allegedly, was choosing judges who were opposed to *Roe*. Whatever the truth of these rumors, Blackmun did not retire until William J. Clinton was President. To replace Blackmun, Clinton nominated Stephen Breyer, who did not appear to be opposed to *Roe*. Clinton's first nominee, Ruth Bader Ginsburg, had criticized *Roe*—see the citations in Editors' Note 14, below at p. 1311—but had said she believed that a woman had a constitutional right to an abortion.—**Eds.**

justified only in the light of "compelling state interests." The joint opinion rejects that view. *Roe* analyzed abortion regulation under a rigid trimester framework, a framework which has guided this Court's decisionmaking for 19 years. The joint opinion rejects that framework.

... *Roe* continues to exist, but only in the way a storefront on a western movie set exists: a mere facade to give the illusion of reality. Decisions following *Roe*, such as *Akron I* and *Thornburgh*, are frankly overruled in part under the "undue burden" standard. ... [A]uthentic principles of stare decisis do not require that any portion of the reasoning in *Roe* be kept intact. ... Erroneous decisions in such constitutional cases are uniquely durable, because correction through legislative action, save for constitutional amendment, is impossible. It is therefore our duty to reconsider constitutional interpretations that "depart from a proper understanding" of the Constitution. *Garcia.* ...

The joint opinion ... points to the reliance interests involved in this context in its effort to explain why precedent must be followed for precedent's sake. ... [But] any traditional notion of reliance is not applicable here. ... The joint opinion thus turns to what can only be described as an unconventional—and unconvincing—notion of reliance, a view based on the surmise that the availability of abortion since *Roe* has led to "two decades of economic and social developments" that would be undercut if the error of *Roe* were recognized. The joint opinion's assertion of this fact is undeveloped and totally conclusory. In fact, one cannot be sure to what economic and social developments the opinion is referring. Surely it is dubious to suggest that women have reached their "places in society" in reliance upon *Roe*, rather than as a result of their determination to obtain higher education and compete with men in the job market, and of society's increasing recognition of their ability to fill positions that were previously thought to be reserved only for men.

... [T]he joint opinion's argument is based solely on generalized assertions about the national psyche, on a belief that the people of this country have grown accustomed to the *Roe* decision over the last 19 years and have "ordered their thinking and living around" it. ... However, the simple fact that a generation or more had grown used to [*Lochner* and *Plessy*] did not prevent the Court from correcting its errors in those cases, nor should it prevent us from correctly interpreting the Constitution here. See *Brown; West Coast Hotel.* ...

The joint opinion picks out and discusses two prior Court rulings [*Lochner* and *Plessy*] that it believes are of the "intensely divisive" variety, and concludes that they are of comparable dimension to *Roe*. It appears to us very odd indeed that the joint opinion chooses as benchmarks two cases in which the Court chose *not* to adhere to erroneous constitutional precedent, but instead enhanced its stature by acknowledging and correcting its error, apparently in violation of the joint opinion's "legitimacy" principle. See *West Coast Hotel; Brown.* ...

The joint opinion agrees that the Court's stature would have been seriously damaged if in *Brown* and *West Cost Hotel* it had dug in its heels and refused to apply normal principles of stare decisis to the earlier decisions. But the opinion contends that the Court was entitled to overrule *Plessy* and *Lochner* in those cases ... only because both the Nation and the Court had learned new lessons in the interim. This is at best a feebly supported, post hoc rationalization for those decisions. ...

When the Court finally recognized its error in *West Coast Hotel,* it did not engage in the post hoc rationalization that the joint opinion attributes to it today; it did not state that *Lochner* had been based on an economic view that had fallen into disfavor, and that it therefore should be overruled. Chief Justice Hughes in his opinion for the Court simply recognized what Justice Holmes had previously recognized in his *Lochner* dissent, that "the Constitution does not speak of freedom of contract." ... Although the Court did acknowledge in the last paragraph of its opinion the state of affairs during the then-current Depression, the theme of the opinion is that the Court had been mistaken as a matter of constitutional law when it embraced "freedom of contract" 32 years previously.

The joint opinion also agrees that the Court acted properly in rejecting the doctrine of "separate but equal" in *Brown.* ... [It] concludes that such repudiation was justified only because of newly discovered evidence that segregation had the effect of treating one race as inferior to another. But [t]he Court in *Brown* simply recognized, as Justice Harlan had recognized beforehand [dissenting in *Plessy*], that the Fourteenth Amendment does not permit racial segregation. ...

The sum of the joint opinion's labors ... is this: *Roe* stands as a sort of judicial Potemkin Village, which may be pointed out to passers by as a monument to the importance of adhering to precedent. But behind the facade, an entirely new method of analysis, without any roots in constitutional law, is imported to decide the constitutionality of state laws regulating abortion. Neither stare decisis nor "legitimacy" is truly served by such an effort.

... [W]e think that the correct analysis is that set forth by the plurality opinion in *Webster.* A woman's interest in having an abortion is a form of liberty protected by the Due Process Clause, but States may regulate abortion procedures in ways rationally related to a legitimate state interest. Williamson v. Lee Optical (1955). ... [W]e therefore would hold that each of the challenged provisions of the Pennsylvania statute is consistent with the Constitution. ...

Justice **SCALIA**, with whom The Chief Justice [**REHNQUIST**], Justice **WHITE**, and Justice **THOMAS** join, concurring in the judgment in part and dissenting in part. ...

... The issue is whether ["the power of a woman to abort her unborn child"] is a liberty protected by the Constitution of the United States. I am sure it is not. I reach that conclusion not because of anything so exalted as my views concerning the "concept of existence, of meaning, of the universe, and of the mystery of human life." Rather, I reach it for the same reason I reach the conclusion that bigamy is not constitutionally protected—because of two simple facts: (1) the Constitution says absolutely nothing about it, and (2) the longstanding traditions of American society have permitted it to be legally proscribed.[1]

The Court destroys the proposition, evidently meant to represent my position, that "liberty" includes "only those practices, defined at the most specific level, that were protected against government interference by other rules of law when the Fourteenth Amendment was ratified." That is not, however, what *Michael H.* says; it merely observes that, in defining "liberty," we may not disregard a specific, "relevant tradition protecting, or denying protection to, the asserted right." ... The Court's statement that it is "tempting" to acknowledge the authoritativeness of tradition in order to "cur[b] the discretion of federal judges," is of course rhetoric rather than reality; no government official is "tempted" to place restraints upon his own freedom of action, which is why Lord Acton did not say "Power tends to purify." The Court's temptation is in the quite opposite and more natural direction—towards systematically eliminating checks upon its own power; and it succumbs.

... [A]pplying the rational basis test, I would uphold the Pennsylvania statute in its entirety. I must, however, respond to a few of the more outrageous arguments in today's opinion. ...

"The inescapable fact is that adjudication of substantive due process claims may call upon the Court in interpreting the Constitution to exercise that same capacity which by tradition courts always have exercised: reasoned judgment."

Assuming that the question before us is to be resolved at such a level of philosophical abstraction, in such isolation from the traditions of American society, as by simply applying "reasoned judgment," I do not see how that could possibly have produced the answer the Court arrived at in *Roe*. ..."[R]easoned judgment" does not begin by begging the question, as *Roe* and subsequent cases unquestionably did by assuming that what the State is protecting is the mere "potentiality of human life." The whole argument of abortion opponents is that what the Court calls the fetus and what others call the unborn child *is a human life*. Thus, whatever answer *Roe* came up with after conducting its "balancing" is bound to be wrong, unless it is correct that the human fetus is in

---

1. The Court's suggestion that adherence to tradition would require us to uphold laws against interracial marriage is entirely wrong. Any tradition in that case was contradicted *by a text*—an Equal Protection Clause that explicitly establishes racial equality as a constitutional value. See *Loving*. The enterprise launched in *Roe*, by contrast, sought to establish—in the teeth of a clear, contrary tradition—a value found nowhere in the constitutional text.

There is, of course, no comparable tradition barring recognition of a "liberty interest" in carrying one's child to term free from state efforts to kill it. For that reason, it does not follow that the Constitution does not protect childbirth simply because it does not protect abortion. The Court's contention that the only way to protect childbirth is to protect abortion shows the utter bankruptcy of constitutional analysis deprived of tradition as a validating factor. ... [Footnote by Justice Scalia.]

some critical sense merely potentially human. There is of course no way to determine that as a legal matter; it is in fact a value judgment. Some societies have considered newborn children not yet human, or the incompetent elderly no longer so.

... [I]n their exhaustive discussion of all the factors that go into the determination of when stare decisis should be observed ... they never mention "how wrong was the decision on its face?" ... *Roe* was plainly wrong—even on the Court's methodology of "reasoned judgment," and even more so (of course) if the proper criteria of text and tradition are applied.

The emptiness of the "reasoned judgment" that produced *Roe* is displayed in plain view by the fact that, after more than 19 years of effort by some of the brightest (and most determined) legal minds in the country, after more than 10 cases upholding abortion rights in this Court, and after dozens upon dozens of amicus briefs submitted in this and other cases, the best the Court can do to explain how it is that the word "liberty" *must* be thought to include the right to destroy human fetuses is to rattle off a collection of adjectives that simply decorate a value judgment and conceal a political choice. ... The right to abort, we are told, inheres in "liberty" because it is among "a person's most basic decisions," ... it involves "intimate relationships," and notions of "personal autonomy and bodily integrity." ... But it is obvious to anyone applying "reasoned judgment" that the same adjectives can be applied to many forms of conduct that this Court (including one of the Justices in today's majority), see *Bowers*, has held are *not* entitled to constitutional protection—because, like abortion, they are forms of conduct that have long been criminalized in American society. Those adjectives might be applied, for example, to homosexual sodomy, polygamy, adult incest, and suicide, ... all of which can constitutionally be proscribed because it is our unquestionable constitutional tradition that they are proscribable. It is not reasoned judgment that supports the Court's decision; only personal predilection. ...

"Liberty finds no refuge in a jurisprudence of doubt."

One might have feared to encounter this august and sonorous phrase in an opinion defending the real *Roe*, rather than the revised version fabricated today by the authors of the joint opinion. The shortcomings of *Roe* did not include lack of clarity: Virtually all regulation of abortion before the third trimester was invalid. But to come across this phrase in the joint opinion—which calls upon federal district judges to apply an "undue burden" standard as doubtful in application as it is unprincipled in origin—is really more than one should have to bear. ... [T]he standard is inherently manipulable and will prove hopelessly unworkable in practice. ...

... The joint opinion is flatly wrong in asserting that "our jurisprudence relating to all liberties save perhaps abortion has recognized" the permissibility of laws that do not impose an "undue burden." ... I agree, indeed I have forcefully urged, that a law of general applicability which places only an incidental burden on a fundamental right does not infringe that right, see R.A.V. v. St. Paul (1992); Employment Div'n v. Smith (1990), but that principle does not establish the quite different (and quite dangerous) proposition that a law which *directly* regulates a fundamental right will not be found to violate the Constitution unless it imposes an "undue burden." It is that, of course, which is at issue here. ... The "undue burden" standard is ... a unique concept created specially for this case, to preserve some judicial foothold in this ill-gotten territory. In claiming otherwise, the three Justices show their willingness to place all constitutional rights at risk in an effort to preserve what they deem the "central holding in *Roe*." ...

... Reason finds no refuge in this jurisprudence of confusion.

"While we appreciate the weight of the arguments ... that *Roe* should be overruled, the reservations any of us may have in reaffirming the central holding of *Roe* are outweighed by the explication of individual liberty we have given combined with the force of stare decisis."

The Court's reliance upon stare decisis can best be described as contrived. ... It seems to me that stare decisis ought to be applied even to the doctrine of stare decisis, and I confess never to have heard of this new, keep-what-you-want-and-throw-away-the-rest version. I wonder whether, as applied to Marbury v. Madison (1803), for example, the new version of stare decisis would be satisfied if we allowed courts to review the constitutionality of only those statutes that (like the one in *Marbury*) pertain to the jurisdiction of the courts. ...

"Where, in the performance of its judicial duties, the Court decides a case in such a way as to resolve the sort of intensely divisive controversy reflected in *Roe* ..., its decision has a dimension that the resolution of the normal case does not carry. It is the dimension present whenever the Court's interpretation of the Constitution calls the contending sides of a national controversy to end their national division by accepting a common mandate rooted in the Constitution."

The Court's description of the place of *Roe* in the social history of the United States is unrecognizable. Not only did *Roe* not, as the Court suggests, *resolve* the deeply divisive issue of abortion; it did more than anything else to nourish it, by elevating it to the national level where it is infinitely more difficult to resolve. National politics were not plagued by abortion protests, national abortion lobbying, or abortion marches on Congress, before *Roe* was decided. Profound disagreement existed among our citizens over the issue ... but that disagreement was being worked out at the state level. ... [T]he division of sentiment within each State was not as closely balanced as it was among the population of the Nation as a whole, meaning not only that more people would be satisfied with the results of state-by-state resolution, but also that those

results would be more stable. Pre-*Roe*, moreover, political compromise
was possible.

Roe's mandate for abortion-on-demand destroyed the compromises
of the past, rendered compromise impossible for the future, and required
the entire issue to be resolved uniformly, at the national level. At the
same time, *Roe* created a vast new class of abortion consumers and
abortion proponents by eliminating the moral opprobrium that had
attached to the act. ("If the Constitution *guarantees* abortion, how can
it be bad?"—not an accurate line of thought, but a natural one.) ... But
to portray *Roe* as the statesmanlike "settlement" of a divisive issue, a
jurisprudential Peace of Westphalia that is worth preserving, is nothing
less than Orwellian. *Roe* fanned into life an issue that has inflamed our
national politics in general, and has obscured with its smoke the selection of Justices to this Court in particular, ever since. And by keeping
us in the abortion-umpiring business, it is the perpetuation of that
disruption, rather than of any *pax Roeana*, that the Court's new majority
decrees.

> **"To overrule under fire ... would subvert the
> Court's legitimacy. ..."**

> **"To all those who will be ... tested by following, the
> Court implicitly undertakes to remain steadfast. ...
> The promise of constancy, once given, binds its maker
> for as long as the power to stand by the decision survives
> and ... the commitment [is not] obsolete. ..."**

> **"[The American people's] belief in themselves as ...
> a people [who aspire to live according to the rule of law]
> is not readily separable from their understanding of the
> Court invested with the authority to decide their consti-
> tutional cases and speak before all others for their con-
> stitutional ideals. If the Court's legitimacy should be
> undermined, then, so would the country be in its very
> ability to see itself through its constitutional ideals."**

The Imperial Judiciary lives. It is instructive to compare this
Nietzschean vision of us unelected, life-tenured judges ... with the
somewhat more modest role envisioned for these lawyers by the Founders.

> "The judiciary ... has ... no direction either of the strength or of the
> wealth of the society, and can take no active resolution whatever. It
> may truly be said to have neither FORCE nor WILL but merely
> judgment. ..." *The Federalist* No. 78.

Or, again, to compare this ecstasy of a Supreme Court in which there is,
especially on controversial matters, no shadow of change or hint of
alteration ... with the more democratic views of a more humble man:

> "The candid citizen must confess that if the policy of the Government
> upon vital questions affecting the whole people is to be irrevocably fixed
> by decisions of the Supreme Court, ... the people will have ceased to be

their own rulers, having to that extent practically resigned their Government into the hands of that eminent tribunal." A. Lincoln, First Inaugural Address (Mar. 4, 1861).

It is particularly difficult, in the circumstances of the present decision, to sit still for the Court's lengthy lecture upon the virtues of "constancy," of "remaining steadfast," of adhering to "principle." ...
The only principle the Court "adheres" to, it seems to me, is the principle that the Court must be seen as standing by *Roe*. That is not a principle of law ... but a principle of *Realpolitik*—and a wrong one at that.

... I am appalled by [ ] the Court's suggestion that the decision whether to stand by an erroneous constitutional decision must be strongly influenced—*against* overruling, no less—by the substantial and continuing public opposition the decision has generated. ... In my history-book, the Court was covered with dishonor and deprived of legitimacy by Dred Scott v. Sandford (1857), an erroneous (and widely opposed) opinion that it did not abandon, rather than by *West Coast Hotel* (1937), which produced the famous "switch in time" from the Court's erroneous (and widely opposed) constitutional opposition to the social measures of the New Deal. (Both *Dred Scott* and one line of the cases resisting the New Deal rested upon the concept of "substantive due process" that the Court praises and employs today. Indeed, *Dred Scott* was "very possibly the first application of substantive due process in the Supreme Court, the original precedent for *Lochner* and *Roe*." D. Currie, *The Constitution in the Supreme Court* 271 (1985).)

But whether it would "subvert the Court's legitimacy" or not, the notion that we would decide a case differently from the way we otherwise would have in order to show that we can stand firm against public disapproval is frightening. It is a bad enough idea, even in the head of someone like me, who believes that the text of the Constitution, and our traditions, say what they say and there is no fiddling with them. But when it is in the mind of a Court that believes the Constitution has an evolving meaning; that the Ninth Amendment's reference to "other" rights is not a disclaimer, but a charter for action; and that the function of this Court is to "speak before all others for [the people's] constitutional ideals" unrestrained by meaningful text or tradition—then the notion that the Court must adhere to a decision for as long as the decision faces "great opposition" and the Court is "under fire" acquires a character of almost czarist arrogance. ...

Of course ... we have been subjected to what the Court calls "political pressure" by *both* sides of this issue. Maybe today's decision *not* to overrule *Roe* will be seen as buckling to pressure from *that* direction. Instead of engaging in the hopeless task of predicting public perception ... the Justices should do what is *legally* right by asking two questions: (1) Was *Roe* correctly decided? (2) Has *Roe* succeeded in producing a settled body of law? If the answer to both questions is no, *Roe* should undoubtedly be overruled.

... How upsetting it is, that so many of our citizens (good people, not lawless ones, on both sides ...) think that we Justices should properly take into account their views, as though we were engaged not in ascertaining an objective law but in determining some kind of social consensus. The Court would profit, I think, from giving less attention to the *fact* of this distressing phenomenon, and more attention to the *cause* of it. That cause permeates today's opinion: a new mode of constitutional adjudication that relies not upon text and traditional practice to determine the law, but upon what the Court calls "reasoned judgment," which turns out to be nothing but philosophical predilection and moral intuition. All manner of "liberties," the Court tells us, inhere in the Constitution and are enforceable by this Court—not just those mentioned in the text or established in the traditions of our society. Why even the Ninth Amendment ... is, despite our contrary understanding for almost 200 years, a literally boundless source of additional, unnamed, unhinted-at "rights," definable and enforceable by us, through "reasoned judgment."

What makes all this relevant to the bothersome application of "political pressure" against the Court are the twin facts that the American people love democracy and the American people are not fools. As long as this Court thought (and the people thought) that we Justices were doing essentially lawyers' work up here—reading text and discerning our society's traditional understanding of that text—the public pretty much left us alone. Texts and traditions are facts to study, not convictions to demonstrate about. But if in reality our process of constitutional adjudication consists primarily of making *value judgments;* if we can ignore a long and clear tradition clarifying an ambiguous text, [if] ... our pronouncement of constitutional law rests primarily on value judgments, then a free and intelligent people's attitude towards us can be expected to be (*ought* to be) quite different. The people know that their value judgments are quite as good as those taught in any law school—maybe better. If, indeed, the "liberties" protected by the Constitution are, as the Court says, undefined and unbounded, then the people *should* demonstrate, to protest that we do not implement *their* values instead of *ours.* Not only that, but confirmation hearings for new Justices *should* deteriorate into question-and-answer sessions in which Senators go through a list of their constituents' most favored and most disfavored alleged constitutional rights, and seek the nominee's commitment to support or oppose them. Value judgments, after all, should be voted on, not dictated; and if our Constitution has somehow accidently committed them to the Supreme Court, at least we can have a sort of plebiscite each time a new nominee to that body is put forward. Justice Blackmun not only regards this prospect with equanimity, he solicits it.
...

We should get out of this area, where we have no right to be, and where we do neither ourselves nor the country any good by remaining.

Editors' Notes

(1) In the *U.S. Reports*, the full opinions in this case take up more than a hundred pages studded with personal invective and strained efforts to strike quotable phrases—indications both of the importance of the issues and the intensity of the justices' reactions. Although *Casey* displayed within its heated corners many critical problems of constitutional interpretation, it is improbable that it will be hailed as a model of a logically neat debate. In part the reason lies in the justices' efforts to carry on several arguments simultaneously: (1) the correctness of *Roe*; (2) the meaning and application of stare decisis; (3) how often the Court should look over its marble shoulder to see what the public is thinking about its work; and (4) the relevance and authority of competing demands of constitutionalist and democratic theories.

(2) **Query:** To what extent was the disagreement between the five justices who voted to reaffirm the central holding of *Roe* and the four who voted to overrule it a disagreement about WHAT is "the Constitution"? What more than the text does "the Constitution" include? To what extent does that text contain an exhaustive list of rights? To what extent is it a scheme of general principles? How did each justice respond, implicitly or explicitly, to these issues?

(3) **Query:** To what extent was the disagreement about WHO shall interpret? What roles did democratic and constitutionalist theories play in the opinion of each of the justices?

(4) **Query:** To what extent did the joint opinion follow a *doctrinal approach*? A *textualist approach*? A *developmental approach*? The *approach* we have labelled *protecting fundamental rights*? A *prudential approach*? A *philosophic approach*?

(5) **Query:** What about Scalia? To what extent did he follow these approaches? He criticized the joint opinion for using a *philosophic approach*. To what extent did he do so as well? What about his claim that "the text and tradition" were the lodestars of constitutional interpretation? He claimed the Equal Protection Clause "explicitly establishes racial equality as a constitutional value." Where? Did he reach outside "the text and tradition" to justify his conclusion? Does the *text* of the Equal Protection Clause any less explicitly endorse sexual than racial equality? Does the *text* of the Due Process Clause any less explicitly endorse liberty of procreative autonomy and bodily integrity than liberty to marry or educate one's children? Is there a constitutional difference between a woman's right to marry and to abort the fetus she is carrying?

(6) **Query:** The joint opinion spoke of the "accepted standards of precedent." What are they? Only a week before publishing this opinion in *Casey*, two of the three authors had joined Scalia's opinion for the Court in R.A.V. v. St. Paul (1992; reprinted above, p. 686), which rewrote a great deal of the law of the First Amendment. Ten days earlier, O'Connor, joined by the other two, had authored the opinion for the Court in New York v. United States (1992; reprinted above, p. 585), which cut back on a recent ruling, Garcia v. SAMTA (1985; reprinted above, p. 576). Under these circumstances, how seriously should we take the joint opinion's panegyric to stare decisis and stability?

(7) **Query:** Why did the joint opinion stress the pressure on the Court to reverse *Roe* rather than the pressure on the Court to affirm it? Which arguments about stare decisis and overruling are more persuasive, those of the joint opinion or those of Rehnquist and Scalia?

(8) **Query:** The joint opinion characterized "reasoned judgment" as "that same capacity which by tradition courts always have exercised" in interpreting the Constitution, whereas Scalia referred to it as "a new mode of constitutional adjudication," which "turns out to be nothing but philosophical predilection and moral intuition." Recall the debates among Douglas, Harlan, and Black in Griswold v. Connecticut (1965; reprinted above, p. 147) and earlier between Frankfurter and Black in Rochin v. California (1952; reprinted above, p. 135). Who had the better argument on this subquestion of HOW? Is Scalia's distinction between studying historical "facts" and making "value judgments" sustainable in constitutional interpretation? To what extent does all constitutional interpretation involve value judgments?

(9) **Query:** Stevens explicitly said and the joint opinion implied that *Roe* was "the natural sequel" to *Griswold* and the later cases dealing with birth control. Even assuming that *Roe* did not contradict *Griswold*, to what extent did *Roe* logically follow from *Griswold*? Is there a constitutionally relevant difference between using contraceptives and aborting a fetus?

(10) **Query:** How does the joint opinion's notion of "undue burden" under the due process clause differ from the "intermediate scrutiny" we saw in the cases on equal protection in Chapter 15? Was Stevens correct in referring to the new test as a form of *balancing*?

(11) **Query:** "The whole argument of abortion opponents," Scalia said

is that what the Court calls the fetus and what others call the unborn child *is a human life.* Thus, whatever answer *Roe* came up with after conducting its "balancing" is bound to be wrong, unless it is correct that the human fetus is in some critical sense merely potentially human. There is of course no way to determine that as a legal matter; it is in fact a value judgment.

How accurately did Scalia describe the substantive difference between those who think *Roe* was rightly and wrongly decided? Suppose his description exactly fit the situation: What would that fact tell us about constitutional interpretation? About *approaches* to constitutional interpretation? Did Scalia himself *explicitly* contend that the fetus is a child? Was he attacking Stevens's claim that none of the fifteen justices who had been on the Court when the issue was raised had held that a fetus was, for purposes of the Fourteenth Amendment, a person?

(12) **Query:** Scalia likened *Roe* to *Dred Scott.* On the other hand, the joint opinion intimated that *Roe* was like *Brown.* To what extent is either (or each) analogy persuasive?

(13) **Query:** Did the joint opinion in *Casey* provide a stronger constitutional justification for a woman's right to choose an abortion than did *Roe*? Simply a fuller explication of the same basic rationale? What role(s) did "a right to privacy" play in *Roe* and *Casey*? Notions of autonomy and bodily integrity? To what extent did *Casey* replace the physician, whose role the Court emphasized in *Roe*, with the state as the guarantor of women's

responsible decisionmaking? See Linda C. McClain, "The Poverty of Privacy?" 3 *Colum.J.Gender & L.* 119 (1992).

(14) **Query:** Do arguments from the Equal Protection Clause, such as those invoked by Blackmun and alluded to by Stevens and the joint opinion, provide a firmer basis for a right to abortion than do arguments from autonomy or bodily integrity under the Due Process Clauses? See, in addition to the material Blackmun cited, two articles by Ruth Bader Ginsburg, "Some Thoughts on Autonomy and Equality in Relation to *Roe v. Wade*," 63 *No.Car.L.R.* 375 (1985), and "Speaking in a Judicial Voice," 67 *N.Y.U.L.Rev.* 1185 (1993). To what extent do arguments about sexual equality meet objections (such as those advanced by Bork and Ely) to the Court's protecting "unenumerated" fundamental rights through the Due Process Clauses? (See the Eds.' Notes following Roe v. Wade (1973; reprinted above, p. 1258.)) The rights of husbands also raise questions of equal protection; see below, Eds.' Note 19.

(15) **Query:** What was the relevance of Scalia's discussion of the Ninth Amendment? Did the joint opinion, as published, rely on the Ninth Amendment, actually or potentially treating it as "a literally boundless source of additional, unnamed, unhinted-at 'rights,' " as Scalia charged? If the joint opinion did not so treat the Ninth Amendment, why would Scalia have inserted this discussion?

(16) **Query:** Scalia spoke of the Court's being tempted "towards systematically eliminating checks upon its own power; and it succumbs." To what extent do the cases since Calder v. Bull (1798; p. 121) and Marbury v. Madison (1803; p. 298) through McCulloch v. Maryland (1819; p. 530), *Dred Scott* (1857; p. 195), Lochner v. New York (1905; p. 1110), West Coast Hotel v. Parrish (1937; p. 1123), Brown v. Board (1954; p. 912), Reynolds v. Sims (1964; p. 777), Garcia v. SAMTA (1985; p. 576), and *Roe* support or undermine Scalia's claim?

(17) Both the joint opinion and Scalia spoke about how the American public perceived the Court and expected the justices to decide cases. Students of public opinion have produced a large body of relevant professional literature, yet neither opinion cited a single source for its speculations. The reason may be that the detailed studies do not support either side. It seems that most people who are knowledgeable about the Court's work understand that the justices do more than interpret "the law"; furthermore, a majority of those people think the justices *should* do more. See among other studies: David Adamany, "Legitimacy, Realigning Elections, and the Supreme Court," 1973 *Wis.L.Rev.* 790; Adamany and Joel Grossman, "Support for the Supreme Court as a National Policymaker," 5 *Law & Pol.Q.* 405 (1983); Gregory A. Caldeira, "Neither the Purse Nor the Sword: Public Confidence in the U.S. Supreme Court," 80 *Am.Pol.Sci.Rev.* 1209 (1986); Robert A. Dahl, "Decision–Making in a Democracy: The Supreme Court as National Policy Maker," 6 *J. of Pub.L.* 279 (1957); Thomas R. Marshall, *Public Opinion and the Supreme Court* (Boston: Unwin Hyman, 1989); Walter F. Murphy, Joseph Tanenhaus, and Daniel L. Kastner, *Public Evaluations of Constitutional Courts* (Los Angeles: Sage, 1973); and several articles by Murphy and Tanenhaus: "Public Opinion and the Supreme Court," in Joel Grossman and Tanenhaus, eds., *Frontiers of Judicial Research* (New York: Wiley, 1969); "Constitutional Courts

and Political Representation," in Michael N. Danielson and Murphy, eds., *Modern American Democracy* (New York: Holt, Rinehart & Winston, 1969); "Patterns of Public Support for the Supreme Court: A Panel Study," 43 *J. of Pols.* 24 (1981); and "Publicity, Public Opinion, and the Courts," 84 *Nw. U.L.Rev.* 985 (1990). For more recent work, see: William Mishler and Reginald Sheehan, "The Supreme Court as a Countermajoritarian Institution? The Impact of Public Opinion on Supreme Court Decisions," 87 *Am.Pol.Sci.Rev.* 87 (1993); the critique by Helmut Norpoth and Jeffrey Segal, "Popular Influence on Supreme Court Decisions," 88 *ibid.* 711 (1994); and the response by Mishner and Sheehan, 88 *ibid.* 716 (1994).

(18) Blackmun said that *Casey* should stand as "a warning to all who have tried to turn this Court into yet another political branch." He was referring to the efforts of various groups—and probably especially to the efforts of those who opposed *Roe*—to change judicial minds. Reagan and Bush vetted potential judges to select candidates who would try to overturn *Roe*. Did such a vetting make the Court any more "political" than George Washington's efforts to select only deserving Federalists, Thomas Jefferson's to select Republicans who would vote against John Marshall, Lincoln's to choose men who would oppose slavery and secession, and Franklin Roosevelt's to find judges who thought laissez-faire economics were not embedded in "the Constitution"? Would presidents be foolish not to try to pick judges who basically agreed with their own constitutional interpretations? Did the (successful) attempts of businessmen in the late nineteenth century to "educate" judges (and to "educate" public officials who chose judges) to write laissez faire into the constitutional text politicize the Court less than the interest groups struggling about abortion? The NAACP's (successful) attempts to push judges to reverse *Plessy*? Conservative Republicans' and Southern Democrats' (only partly successful) attempts to get the Court to change its mind during the McCarthy era about rights to free speech and association? Segregationists' (only partly successful) attempts to fight Brown v. Board (1954) in Congress, in every state legislature and governor's office in the South, and in state and federal courts as well as to put the NAACP out of business (see NAACP v. Alabama [1958; reprinted above, p. 798])? From 1954 until 1968, "Impeach Earl Warren" was the slogan of some interest groups all over the country. Demonstrators followed him from city to city protesting against a raft of decisions, including *Brown*.

In sum, the controversy over abortion is hardly a new phenomenon in American constitutional history. The Supreme Court has been, as Chief Justice William Howard Taft said, a "stormy petrel" in American politics. For attempts by presidents to use their nominating power to guide the Court, see: Walter F. Murphy, "Reagan's Judicial Strategy," in Larry Berman, ed., *Looking Back on the Reagan Presidency* (Baltimore: Johns Hopkins University Press, 1990); for the Court's frequent involvement in struggles among public officials and interest groups, see Murphy, *Congress and the Court* (Chicago: University of Chicago Press, 1962).

Query: Given this long, almost continuous history of efforts by public officials and private citizens to influence the Court, to what extent was Blackmun indulging, perhaps unwittingly, in self-serving rhetoric and to what extent was he stating an important truth? To what extent did Scalia agree with Blackmun's claim?

(19) In invalidating as an undue burden the requirement that a married woman seeking an abortion notify her husband, the joint opinion accepted the district court's finding that for "the great many women who are victims of abuse inflicted by their husbands, or whose children are the victims of such abuse, a spousal notice requirement enables the husband to wield an effective veto over his wife's decision." Observing that our understanding of the family, the individual, and "the Constitution" has changed since Bradwell v. Illinois (1873) said that "a woman had no legal existence separate from her husband, who was regarded as her head and representative in the social state," the joint opinion concluded: "A State may not give to a man the kind of dominion over his wife that parents exercise over their children."

Query: Need, however, such a requirement of notification impute a secondary status to wives? Might it not represent an effort to protect the right of the husband, as the putative father, to express an opinion about whether the wife should terminate the pregnancy? To what extent did the justices in the majority implicitly deny that husbands have a right to a voice in that decision? To what extent would such a denial accord equal protection of the laws?

(20) Since *Casey,* lower federal courts have struck down several restrictive abortion statutes. The Fifth Circuit held Louisiana's law banning all abortions except in cases of rape, incest, or threat to a pregnant woman's life "clearly unconstitutional under *Casey.*" Sojourner T. v. Edwards (1992). Similarly, the Ninth Circuit invalidated Guam's law outlawing abortions except for ectopic pregnancy or when two physicians practicing independently determine that the pregnancy would endanger the life of the pregnant woman or "gravely impair" her health. Guam Society of Obstetricians & Gynecologists v. Ada (1992). The Supreme Court denied certiorari in both of these cases.

(21) In *Casey* the joint opinion left open the possibility that evidence in a future case may show that a 24-hour waiting period in fact imposes an undue burden upon pregnant women who are seeking an abortion. The Court, however, denied certiorari in a case that upheld Mississippi's 24-hour waiting period against a challenge that it constituted an undue burden. See Barnes v. Moore (U.S.C.A., 5th Cir.1992).

(22) In recent years, some people who believe that the fetus is human and therefore abortion is homicide have formed organizations such as Operation Rescue, Rescue America, and Lambs of Christ, which have obstructed access to and otherwise disrupted activities at facilities that perform abortions. In many cases, defenders of the right to abortion have obtained injunctions prohibiting or limiting such activities as constituting trespass or nuisance under state law, or as denying pregnant women their civil rights in violation of federal law. In Bray v. Alexandria Women's Health Clinic (1993), the Supreme Court held that a Reconstruction-era civil rights law Congress originally enacted in part to protect blacks from the Ku Klux Klan, 42 U.S.C. § 1985 (3), did not give federal courts jurisdiction to enjoin such blockades and mass demonstrations. Speaking through Scalia, the Court reasoned that Operation Rescue's goal of preventing abortion did not qualify as an "invidiously discriminatory animus" against women within the meaning of the statute. With the strong support of President Clinton, Congress enacted the Freedom of Access to Clinic Entrances Act (1994), which prohibits force, threat of force,

or physical obstruction to block access to clinics providing abortions or services related to reproductive health. Furthermore, Madsen v. Women's Health Center (1994), with Rehnquist writing the opinion, upheld, against a challenge under the First Amendment, the core of a state injunction imposing a 36 foot "buffer zone" around a clinic to keep protestors away from the entrance and banning excessive noise during the clinic's operating hours. Scalia, joined by Kennedy and Thomas, bitterly dissented.

V. THE RIGHT TO FAMILY INTEGRITY

"The freedom to marry has long been recognized as one of the vital personal rights essential to the orderly pursuit of happiness by free men."

LOVING v. VIRGINIA
388 U.S. 1, 87 S.Ct. 1817, 18 L.Ed.2d 1010 (1967).

This case, invalidating a state law prohibiting interracial marriage on the grounds that it denied both equal protection and due process, is reprinted above, p. 926.

"[T]he Constitution protects the sanctity of the family precisely because the institution of the family is deeply rooted in this Nation's history and tradition."—Justice POWELL

"The Judiciary ... is most vulnerable and comes nearest to illegitimacy when it deals with judge-made constitutional law having little or no cognizable roots in the language or even the design of the Constitution."—Justice WHITE

MOORE v. EAST CLEVELAND
431 U.S. 494, 97 S.Ct. 1932, 52 L.Ed.2d 531 (1977).

An ordinance of East Cleveland, Ohio, limited occupancy of each dwelling unit to members of a single family, with "family" defined essentially as parents and their children. (The ordinance, however, permitted grandparents to live with their children and their children's children, provided that all of the grandchildren were siblings rather than cousins.) The ordinance also provided an administrative procedure to request variances. Without following this procedure, Inez Moore shared her home with her son and two grandsons who were cousins rather than brothers. She was convicted for violating the ordinance and state appellate courts affirmed her conviction. She then appealed to the U.S. Supreme Court.

Mr. Justice **POWELL** announced the judgment of the Court and delivered an opinion in which Mr. Justice **BRENNAN,** Mr. Justice **MARSHALL,** and Mr. Justice **BLACKMUN** joined. ...

II

The city argues that our decision in Village of Belle Terre v. Boraas (1974) requires us to sustain the ordinance attacked here. Belle Terre, like East Cleveland, imposed limits on the types of groups that could occupy a single dwelling unit. Applying the constitutional standard announced in this Court's leading land-use case, Euclid v. Ambler (1926), we sustained the Belle Terre ordinance on the ground that it bore a rational relationship to permissible state objectives.

But one overriding factor sets this case apart from *Belle Terre*. The ordinance there affected only *unrelated* individuals. It expressly allowed all who were related by "blood, adoption, or marriage" to live together, and in sustaining the ordinance we were careful to note that it promoted "family needs" and "family values." ... East Cleveland, in contrast, has chosen to regulate the occupancy of its housing by slicing deeply into the family itself. This is no mere incidental result of the ordinance. On its face it selects certain categories of relatives who may live together and declares that others may not. ...

When a city undertakes such intrusive regulation of the family, neither *Belle Terre* nor *Euclid* governs; the usual judicial deference to the legislature is inappropriate. "This Court has long recognized that freedom of personal choice in matters of marriage and family life is one of the liberties protected by the Due Process Clause of the Fourteenth Amendment." Cleveland Bd. of Ed. v. LaFleur (1974). A host of cases, tracing their lineage to Meyer v. Nebraska (1923) and Pierce v. Society of Sisters (1925), have consistently acknowledged a "private realm of family life which the state cannot enter." Prince v. Massachusetts (1944). See, *e.g.*, Roe v. Wade (1973); Wisconsin v. Yoder (1972); Stanley v. Illinois (1972); Ginsberg v. New York (1968); Griswold v. Connecticut (1965); Poe v. Ullman (1961) (Harlan, J., dissenting); cf. Loving v. Virginia (1967); May v. Anderson (1953); Skinner v. Oklahoma (1942). Of course, the family is not beyond regulation. See *Prince*. But when the government intrudes on choices concerning family living arrangements, this Court must examine carefully the importance of the governmental interests advanced and the extent to which they are served by the challenged regulation. See *Poe* (Harlan, J., dissenting).

When thus examined, this ordinance cannot survive. The city seeks to justify it as a means of preventing overcrowding, minimizing traffic and parking congestion, and avoiding an undue financial burden on East

Cleveland's school system. Although these are legitimate goals, the ordinance before us serves them marginally, at best. ...

III

The city would distinguish the cases based on *Meyer* and *Pierce*. It ... suggests that any constitutional right to live together as a family extends only to the nuclear family—essentially a couple and its dependent children. To be sure, these cases did not expressly consider the family relationship presented here. ... But unless we close our eyes to the basic reasons why certain rights associated with the family have been accorded shelter under the Fourteenth Amendment's Due Process Clause, we cannot avoid applying the force and rationale of these precedents to the family choice involved in this case.

Understanding those reasons requires careful attention to this Court's function under the Due Process Clause. Mr. Justice Harlan described it eloquently:

> "Due process has not been reduced to any formula; its content cannot be determined by reference to any code. The best that can be said is that ... it has represented the balance which our Nation, built upon postulates of respect for the liberty of the individual, has struck between that liberty and the demands of organized society. If the supplying of content to this Constitutional concept has of necessity been a rational process, it certainly has not been one where judges have felt free to roam where unguided speculation might take them. The balance ... is the balance struck by this country, having regard to what history teaches are the traditions from which it developed as well as the traditions from which it broke. That tradition is a living thing. A decision of this Court which radically departs from it could not long survive, while a decision which builds on what has survived is likely to be sound. No formula could serve as a substitute, in this area, for judgment and restraint.
>
> ... [T]he full scope of the liberty guaranteed by the Due Process Clause cannot be found in or limited by the precise terms of the specific guarantees elsewhere provided in the Constitution. This 'liberty' is not a series of isolated points pricked out in terms of the taking of property; the freedom of speech, press, and religion; the right to keep and bear arms; the freedom from unreasonable searches and seizures; and so on. It is a rational continuum which, broadly speaking, includes a freedom from all substantial arbitrary impositions and purposeless restraints, ... and which also recognizes, what a reasonable and sensitive judgment must, that certain interests require particularly careful scrutiny of the state needs asserted to justify their abridgment." *Poe* (dissenting opinion).

Substantive due process has at times been a treacherous field for this Court. There *are* risks when the judicial branch gives enhanced protection to certain substantive liberties without the guidance of the more specific provisions of the Bill of Rights. As the history of the *Lochner* era demonstrates, there is reason for concern lest the only limits to such judicial intervention become the predilections of those who happen at the time to be Members of this Court. That history counsels caution and restraint. But it does not counsel abandonment, nor does it require what the city urges here: cutting off any protection of family rights at the first convenient, if arbitrary boundary—the boundary of the nuclear family.

Appropriate limits on substantive due process come not from drawing arbitrary lines but rather from careful "respect for the teachings of history [and] solid recognition of the basic values that underlie our society." *Griswold* (Harlan, J., concurring). Our decisions establish that the Constitution protects the sanctity of the family precisely because the institution of the family is deeply rooted in this Nation's history and tradition. It is through the family that we inculcate and pass down many of our most cherished values, moral and cultural.

Ours is by no means a tradition limited to respect for the bonds uniting the members of the nuclear family. The tradition of uncles, aunts, cousins, and especially grandparents sharing a household along with parents and children has roots equally venerable and equally deserving of constitutional recognition. ... Even if conditions of modern society have brought about a decline in extended family households, they have not erased the accumulated wisdom of civilization, gained over the centuries and honored throughout our history, that supports a larger conception of the family. ...

Whether or not such a household is established because of personal tragedy, the choice of relatives in this degree of kinship to live together may not lightly be denied by the State. *Pierce* struck down an Oregon law requiring all children to attend the State's public schools, holding that the Constitution "excludes any general power of the State to standardize its children by forcing them to accept instruction from public teachers only." By the same token the Constitution prevents East Cleveland from standardizing its children—and its adults—by forcing all to live in certain narrowly defined family patterns.

Reversed.

Mr. Justice **BRENNAN,** with whom Mr. Justice **MARSHALL** joins, concurring. ...

Mr. Justice **STEVENS** concurring in the judgment.

... [T]he critical question ... is whether East Cleveland's housing ordinance is a permissible restriction on appellant's right to use her own property as she sees fit. ...

There appears to be no precedent for an ordinance which excludes any of an owner's relatives from the group of persons who may occupy his residence on a permanent basis. Nor does there appear to be any justification for such a restriction on an owner's use of his property. The city has failed totally to explain the need for a rule which would allow a homeowner to have two grandchildren live with her if they are brothers, but not if they are cousins. Since this ordinance has not been shown to have any "substantial relation to the public health, safety, morals or general welfare" of the city of East Cleveland, and since it cuts so deeply into a fundamental right normally associated with the owner-ship of residential property—that of an owner to decide who may reside on his or her property—it must fall under the limited standard of review of zoning decisions which this Court preserved in *Euclid*. Under that standard, East Cleveland's unprecedented ordinance constitutes a taking of property without due process and without just compensation. ...

Mr. Chief Justice **BURGER,** dissenting [on procedural grounds]. ...

Mr. Justice **STEWART,** with whom Mr. Justice **REHNQUIST** joins, dissenting. ...

The *Belle Terre* decision ... disposes of the appellant's contentions to the extent they focus not on her blood relationships with her sons and grandsons but on more general notions about the "privacy of the home." ... To suggest that the biological fact of common ancestry necessarily gives related persons constitutional rights of association superior to those of unrelated persons is to misunderstand the nature of the associa-tional freedoms that the Constitution has been understood to protect. Freedom of association has been constitutionally recognized because it is often indispensable to effectuation of explicit First Amendment guaran-tees. See NAACP v. Alabama [1958]; ... NAACP v. Button [1963]. ...

The "association" in this case is not for any purpose relating to the promotion of speech, assembly, the press, or religion. And wherever the outer boundaries of constitutional protection of freedom of association may eventually turn out to be, they surely do not extend to those who assert no interest other than the gratification, convenience, and economy of sharing the same residence. ...

... When the Court has found that the Fourteenth Amendment placed a substantive limitation on a State's power to regulate, it has been in those rare cases in which the personal interests at issue have been deemed " 'implicit in the concept of ordered liberty.' " The inter-est that the appellant may have in permanently sharing a single kitchen and a suite of contiguous rooms with some of her relatives simply does not rise to that level. To equate this interest with the fundamental decisions to marry and to bear and raise children is to extend the limited substantive contours of the Due Process Clause beyond recognition. ...

... I do not think East Cleveland's definition of "family" offends the Constitution. The city has undisputed power to ordain single-family residential occupancy. *Belle Terre*; *Euclid*. And that power plainly carries with it the power to say what a "family" is. Here the city has defined "family" to include not only father, mother, and dependent children, but several other close relatives as well. The definition is rationally designed to carry out the legitimate governmental purposes identified in the *Belle Terre* opinion. ...

Mr. Justice **WHITE**, dissenting. ...

The emphasis of the Due Process Clause is on "process." ... Although the Court regularly proceeds on the assumption that the Due Process Clause has more than a procedural dimension, we must always bear in mind that the substantive content of the Clause is suggested neither by its language nor by preconstitutional history; that content is nothing more than the accumulated product of judicial interpretation. ... This is not to suggest ... that any of these cases should be overruled, or that the process by which they were decided was illegitimate or even unacceptable, but only to underline Mr. Justice Black's constant reminder to his colleagues that the Court has no license to invalidate legislation which it thinks merely arbitrary or unreasonable. ...

... That the Court has ample precedent for the creation of new constitutional rights should not lead it to repeat the process at will. The Judiciary, including this Court, is the most vulnerable and comes nearest to illegitimacy when it deals with judge-made constitutional law having little or no cognizable roots in the language or even the design of the Constitution. Realizing that the present construction of the Due Process Clause represents a major judicial gloss on its terms, as well as on the anticipation of the Framers, and that much of the underpinning for the broad, substantive application of the Clause disappeared in the conflict between the Executive and the Judiciary in the 1930's and 1940's, the Court should be extremely reluctant to breathe still further substantive content into the Due Process Clause so as to strike down legislation adopted by a State or city to promote its welfare. Whenever the Judiciary does so, it unavoidably pre-empts for itself another part of the governance of the country without express constitutional authority. ...

... Under our cases, the Due Process Clause extends substantial protection to various phases of family life, but none requires that the claim made here be sustained. I cannot believe that the interest in residing with more than one set of grandchildren is one that calls for any kind of heightened protection under the Due Process Clause. ... The present claim is hardly one of which it could be said that "neither liberty nor justice would exist if it were sacrificed." *Palko.*

Mr. Justice Powell would apparently construe the Due Process Clause to protect from all but quite important state regulatory interests any right or privilege that in his estimate is deeply rooted in the country's traditions. For me, this suggests a far too expansive charter for this Court. ... What the deeply rooted traditions of the country are is arguable; which of them deserve the protection of the Due Process Clause is even more debatable. The suggested view would broaden enormously the horizons of the Clause; and, if the interest involved here is any measure of what the States would be forbidden to regulate, the courts would be substantively weighing and very likely invalidating a wide range of measures that Congress and state legislatures think appropriate to respond to a changing economic and social order.

Mrs. Moore's interest in having the offspring of more than one dependent son live with her qualifies as a liberty protected by the Due Process Clause; but, because of the nature of that particular interest, the demands of the Clause are satisfied once the Court is assured that the challenged proscription is the product of a duly enacted or promulgated statute, ordinance, or regulation and that it is not wholly lacking in purpose or utility. ...

Editors' Notes

(1) Thurgood Marshall's papers reveal that, at the justices' conference on *Moore*, the Court initially voted to uphold the ordinance. Potter Stewart drafted what was to be the opinion of the Court and Powell circulated a dissent. Then, after reflecting on home owners' property rights, Stevens changed his vote. Stewart's opinion became a dissent and Powell's the opinion of the plurality. (Library of Congress, Manuscripts Division, the Papers of Justice Thurgood Marshall, Case File 194.)

(2) **Query:** Speaking for the Court in Palko v. Connecticut (1937; reprinted above, p. 128), Cardozo framed the inquiry under the Due Process Clause of the Fourteenth Amendment as being whether an asserted fundamental right was "implicit in the concept of ordered liberty." In *Moore*, Powell for the plurality formulated the inquiry as being whether it is "deeply rooted in this Nation's history and tradition." To what extent are these formulations similar? To what extent do they reflect different conceptions of WHAT is "the Constitution"? To what extent in *Moore* did differences between Powell and White about HOW to interpret "the Constitution" depend on different views about WHAT is "the Constitution" and WHO shall interpret it?

(3) **Query:** At root, how different was Powell's approach to constitutional interpretation from White's? Suppose Powell had argued that whatever "unenumerated" rights are "deeply rooted in this Nation's history and tradition" do have "cognizable roots" in "the design of the Constitution." Would that reformulation have fundamentally changed his reasoning? Would it have met White's objections? To what extent did Stevens avoid White's objections to Powell's reasoning?

(4) Compare the tone of White's statement that "[t]he Judiciary ... is most vulnerable and comes nearest to illegitimacy when it deals with judge-made constitutional law having little or no cognizable roots in the language or even the design of the Constitution" with the Court's claim in the Little Rock Case (Cooper v. Aaron [1958; reprinted above, p. 375]) that "the federal judiciary is supreme in the exposition of the law of the Constitution."

(5) **Query:** Stewart saw the right of association as limited to democratic purposes. What claims, if any, does constitutionalism have here? In Roberts v. United States Jaycees (1984; reprinted above, p. 818), the Court stated that it has long recognized not only "freedom of expressive association" for democratic purposes but also "freedom of intimate association," citing cases such as Meyer v. Nebraska (1923; reprinted above, p. 1247), Pierce v. Society of Sisters (1925; reprinted above, p. 1251), Griswold v. Connecticut (1965;

reprinted above, p. 147), and *Moore.* The term "freedom of intimate association" derives from Kenneth L. Karst, "The Freedom of Intimate Association," 89 *Yale L.J.* 624 (1980).

(6) For the status of the family as a unit in American constitutional law and politics, see: Robert A. Burt, "The Constitution of the Family," 1979 *Sup.Ct.Rev.* 329; James S. Fishkin, *Justice, Equal Opportunity, and the Family* (New Haven: Yale University Press, 1983); Bruce C. Hafen, "The Constitutional Status of Marriage, Kinship, and Sexual Privacy," 81 *Mich.L.Rev.* 463 (1983); Stanley N. Katz, "Legal History and Family History," 21 *Bost.Coll. L.Rev.* 1025 (1980); Martha Minow, ed., *Family Matters* (New York: Norton, 1992); Note, "Developments in the Law—The Constitution and the Family," 93 *Harv.L.Rev.* 1156 (1980); Laurence H. Tribe, *American Constitutional Law* (2d ed.; Mineola, NY: Foundation Press, 1988), pp. 1414–20. See also Susan Moller Okin, *Justice, Gender, and the Family* (New York: Basic Books, 1989).

(7) Questions of state power and family integrity have frequently arisen in the context of disputes about a woman's right to have an abortion. Planned Parenthood of Central Missouri v. Danforth (1976) invalidated a state requirement that a married woman obtain her husband's consent before obtaining an abortion, and Bellotti v. Baird (1976) struck down a state requirement that unmarried, minor females get parental consent. On the other hand, H.L. v. Matheson (1981) upheld Utah's requirement that, before performing an abortion on an unmarried minor, a doctor notify "if possible" her parents or guardian. Taking the statute as on its face not applying to females who were "mature and emancipated," the Court said that " 'constitutional interpretation has consistently recognized the parents' claim to authority in their own household to direct the rearing of their children is basic in the structure of our society.' " (Quoting Ginsberg v. New York [1968].) The majority, speaking through Chief Justice Burger, found the statute served the important state interests of furthering "family integrity and protecting adolescents." Brennan, Marshall, and Blackmun dissented. They did not dispute the importance of the family as a traditional value, but warned that many families did not fit the ideal and that parental reaction, especially when the pregnancy was the result of incest, might result in physical and emotional abuse, withdrawal of financial support, or force the daughter either to have an abortion from an unlicensed person or bear the fetus to term. See also the cases briefly noted in Eds.' Notes to Roe v. Wade (1973; reprinted above, p. 1258), and Planned Parenthood v. Casey (1992; reprinted above, p. 1281), which invalidated a requirement that a married woman notify her husband.

"When a statutory classification significantly interferes with the exercise of a fundamental right, it cannot be upheld unless it is supported by sufficiently important state interests and is closely tailored to effectuate only those interests."

ZABLOCKI v. REDHAIL
434 U.S. 374, 98 S.Ct. 673, 54 L.Ed.2d 618 (1978).

This decision, striking down a state law that prohibited people who had fallen behind in court-ordered child support to remarry, is reprinted above, p. 1034.

"Though the dissent has no basis for the level of generality it would select, we do: We refer to the most specific level at which a relevant tradition protecting, or denying protection to, the asserted right can be identified."—Justice SCALIA

"The document that the plurality construes today is unfamiliar to me. It is not the living charter that I have taken to be our Constitution; it is instead a stagnant, archaic, hide-bound document steeped in the prejudices and superstitions of a time long past."—Justice BRENNAN

MICHAEL H. v. GERALD D.

491 U.S. 110, 109 S.Ct. 2333, 105 L.Ed.2d 91 (1989).

This decision upheld a state decision that the biological father of a child, conceived when the mother was married to another man, had no constitutionally protected "liberty interest" that would support his asking a court to protect his relationship with his child. The opinions are reprinted above, p. 158.

VI. THE RIGHT TO INTIMATE SEXUAL CHOICE

"The Court is most vulnerable and comes nearest to illegitimacy when it deals with judge-made constitutional law having little or no cognizable roots in the language or design of the Constitution."—Justice WHITE

"[T]his case is about 'the most comprehensive of rights and the right most valued by civilized men,' namely, 'the right to be let alone.' "—Justice BLACKMUN

BOWERS v. HARDWICK

478 U.S. 186, 106 S.Ct. 2841, 92 L.Ed.2d 140 (1986).

In 1982, police charged Michael Hardwick with engaging in oral sex in his own bedroom with a consenting, adult male. Georgia Code Ann. § 16–6–2 (1984) provides, in pertinent part:

> (a) "A person commits the offense of sodomy when he performs or submits to any sexual act involving the sex organs of one person and the mouth or anus of another. ... [and] (b) A person convicted of the offense of sodomy shall be punished by imprisonment for not less than one nor more than 20 years. ..."

The district attorney decided not to prosecute. Hardwick then brought suit in federal district court, seeking an injunction forbidding Georgia to enforce the statute. He asserted that, as a practicing homosexual, he was in imminent danger of arrest for violating this statute—a threat which deprived him of the liberty guaranteed by the due process clause of the Fourteenth Amendment.

The district court dismissed the suit, but a divided panel of the Court of Appeals for the Eleventh Circuit reversed, holding that the Georgia statute violated Hardwick's fundamental rights because his homosexual activity was a private and intimate association beyond the reach of state regulation. The judges invoked the Ninth Amendment as well as the Due Process Clause. Georgia then obtained review from the U.S. Supreme Court.

Justice **WHITE** delivered the opinion of the Court. ...

This case does not require a judgment on whether laws against sodomy between consenting adults in general, or between homosexuals in particular, are wise or desirable. It raises no question about the right or propriety of state legislative decisions to repeal their laws that criminalize homosexual sodomy, or of state-court decisions invalidating those laws on state constitutional grounds. The issue presented is whether the Federal Constitution confers a fundamental right upon homosexuals to engage in sodomy and hence invalidates the laws of [many] States. ... [1] The case also calls for some judgment about the limits of the Court's role in carrying out its constitutional mandate.

We first register our disagreement ... that the Court's prior cases have construed the Constitution to confer a right of privacy that extends to homosexual sodomy. ... The reach of this line of cases was sketched in Carey v. Population Services Int'l (1977). Pierce v. Society of Sisters (1925) and Meyer v. Nebraska (1923) were described as dealing with child rearing and education; Prince v. Massachusetts (1944) with family relationships; Skinner v. Oklahoma (1942) with procreation; Loving v. Virginia (1967) with marriage; Griswold v. Connecticut (1965) and Eisenstadt v. Baird (1972) with contraception; and Roe v. Wade (1973) with abortion. ...

... [W]e think it evident that none of the rights announced in those cases bears any resemblance to the claimed constitutional right of

---

1. ... The only claim properly before the Court ... is Hardwick's challenge to the Georgia statute as applied to consensual homosexual sodomy. We express no opinion on the constitutionality of the Georgia statute as applied to other acts of sodomy. [Footnote by the Court (moved by Editors).]

homosexuals to engage in acts of sodomy. . . . No connection between family, marriage, or procreation on the one hand and homosexual activity on the other has been demonstrated. . . . Moreover, any claim that these cases nevertheless stand for the proposition that any kind of private sexual conduct between consenting adults is constitutionally insulated from state proscription is unsupportable. Indeed, the Court's opinion in *Carey* twice asserted that the privacy right, which the *Griswold* line of cases found to be one of the protections provided by the Due Process Clause, did not reach so far.

Precedent aside, however, respondent would have us announce . . . a fundamental right to engage in homosexual sodomy. This we are quite unwilling to do. It is true that despite the language of the Due Process Clauses of the Fifth and Fourteenth Amendments, which appears to focus only on the processes by which life, liberty, or property is taken, the cases are legion in which those Clauses have been interpreted to have substantive content. . . . Among such cases are those recognizing rights that have little or no textual support in the constitutional language. *Meyer, Prince,* and *Pierce* fall in this category, as do the privacy cases from *Griswold* to *Carey*.

Striving to assure itself and the public that announcing rights not readily identifiable in the Constitution's text involves much more than the imposition of the Justices' own choice of values on the States and the Federal Government, the Court has sought to identify the nature of the rights qualifying for heightened judicial protection. In Palko v. Connecticut (1937), it was said that this category includes those fundamental liberties that are "implicit in the concept of ordered liberty," such that "neither liberty nor justice would exist if [they] were sacrificed." A different description of fundamental liberties appeared in Moore v. East Cleveland (1977) (opinion of Powell, J.), where they are characterized as those liberties that are "deeply rooted in this Nation's history and tradition." See also *Griswold*.

It is obvious to us that neither of these formulations would extend a fundamental right to homosexuals to engage in acts of consensual sodomy. Proscriptions against that conduct have ancient roots. Sodomy was a criminal offense at common law and was forbidden by the laws of the original 13 States when they ratified the Bill of Rights. In 1868, when the Fourteenth Amendment was ratified, all but 5 of the 37 States in the Union had criminal sodomy laws. In fact, until 1961, all 50 States outlawed sodomy, and today, 24 States and the District of Columbia continue to provide criminal penalties for sodomy performed in private and between consenting adults. Against this background, to claim that a right to engage in such conduct is "deeply rooted in this Nation's history and tradition" or "implicit in the concept of ordered liberty" is, at best, facetious.

Nor are we inclined to take a more expansive view of our authority to discover new fundamental rights imbedded in the Due Process Clause. The Court is most vulnerable and comes nearest to illegitimacy when it

deals with judge-made constitutional law having little or no cognizable roots in the language or design of the Constitution. That this is so was painfully demonstrated by the face-off between the Executive and the Court in the 1930's, which resulted in the repudiation of much of the substantive gloss that the Court had placed on the Due Process Clauses of the Fifth and Fourteenth Amendments. There should be, therefore, great resistance to expand the substantive reach of those Clauses, particularly if it requires redefining the category of rights deemed to be fundamental. Otherwise, the Judiciary necessarily takes to itself further authority to govern the country without express constitutional authority.
. . .

Respondent, however, asserts that the result should be different where the homosexual conduct occurs in the privacy of the home. He relies on Stanley v. Georgia (1969), where the Court held that the First Amendment prevents conviction for possessing and reading obscene material in the privacy of one's home. . . .

Stanley did protect conduct that would not have been protected outside the home, and it partially prevented the enforcement of state obscenity laws; but the decision was firmly grounded in the First Amendment. The right pressed upon us here has no similar support in the text of the Constitution, and it does not qualify for recognition under the prevailing principles for construing the Fourteenth Amendment. Its limits are also difficult to discern. Plainly enough, otherwise illegal conduct is not always immunized whenever it occurs in the home. Victimless crimes, such as the possession and use of illegal drugs, do not escape the law where they are committed at home. *Stanley* itself recognized that its holding offered no protection for the possession in the home of drugs, firearms, or stolen goods. And if respondent's submission is limited to the voluntary sexual conduct between consenting adults, it would be difficult, except by fiat, to limit the claimed right to homosexual conduct while leaving exposed to prosecution adultery, incest, and other sexual crimes even though they are committed in the home. We are unwilling to start down that road.

Even if the conduct at issue here is not a fundamental right, respondent asserts that there must be a rational basis for the law and that there is none in this case other than the presumed belief of a majority of the electorate in Georgia that homosexual sodomy is immoral and unacceptable. This is said to be an inadequate rationale to support the law. The law, however, is constantly based on notions of morality, and if all laws representing essentially moral choices are to be invalidated under the Due Process Clause, the courts will be very busy indeed. Even respondent makes no such claim, but insists that majority sentiments about the morality of homosexuality should be declared inadequate. We do not agree, and are unpersuaded that the sodomy laws of some 25 States should be invalidated on this basis.

Reversed.

Chief Justice **BURGER**, concurring. ...

... [T]he proscriptions against sodomy have very "ancient roots." Decisions of individuals relating to homosexual conduct have been subject to state intervention throughout the history of Western civilization. Condemnation of those practices is firmly rooted in Judeao–Christian moral and ethical standards. Homosexual sodomy was a capital crime under Roman law. During the English Reformation ... the first English statute criminalizing sodomy was passed. Blackstone described "the infamous crime against nature" as an offense of "deeper malignity" than rape, a heinous act "the very mention of which is a disgrace to human nature," and "a crime not fit to be named." 4 W. Blackstone, *Commentaries* at 215. The common law of England, including its prohibition of sodomy, became the received law of Georgia and the other Colonies. In 1816 the Georgia Legislature passed the statute at issue here, and that statute has been continuously in force in one form or another since that time. To hold that the act of homosexual sodomy is somehow protected as a fundamental right would be to cast aside millennia of moral teaching. ...

Justice **POWELL**, concurring.

... I agree with the Court that there is no fundamental right—*i.e.*, no substantive right under the Due Process Clause—such as that claimed by respondent Hardwick. ... This is not to suggest, however, that respondent may not be protected by the Eighth Amendment. ... The Georgia statute ... authorizes a court to imprison a person for up to 20 years for a single private, consensual act of sodomy. In my view, a prison sentence for such conduct—certainly a sentence of long duration—would create a serious Eighth Amendment issue. ...

In this case, however, respondent has not been tried, much less convicted and sentenced. Moreover, respondent has not raised the Eighth Amendment issue below. For these reasons this constitutional argument is not before us.

Justice **BLACKMUN**, with whom Justice **BRENNAN**, Justice **MAR-SHALL**, and Justice **STEVENS** join, dissenting.

This case is no more about "a fundamental right to engage in homosexual sodomy" ... than *Stanley* was about a fundamental right to watch obscene movies, or Katz v. United States (1967) was about a fundamental right to place interstate bets from a telephone booth. Rather, this case is about "the most comprehensive of rights and the right most valued by civilized men," namely, "the right to be let alone." Olmstead v. United States (1928) (Brandeis, J., dissenting).

The statute ... denies individuals the right to decide for themselves whether to engage in particular forms of private, consensual sexual activity. The Court concludes that § 16–6–2 is valid essentially because "the laws of ... many States ... still make such conduct illegal and have done so for a very long time." But the fact that the moral judgments expressed by statutes like § 16–6–2 may be " 'natural and familiar ... ought not to conclude our judgment upon the question whether statutes embodying them conflict with the Constitution of the United States.' " *Roe*, quoting Lochner v. New York (1905) (Holmes, J., dissenting). Like Justice Holmes, I believe that "[it] is revolting to have no better reason for a rule of law than that so it was laid down in the time of Henry IV. It is still more revolting if the grounds upon which it was laid down have vanished long since, and the rule simply persists from blind imitation of the past." Holmes, The Path of the Law, 10 *Harv.L.Rev.* 457, 469 (1897). I believe we must analyze respondent Hardwick's claim in the light of the values that underlie the constitutional right to privacy. If that right means anything, it means that, before Georgia can prosecute its citizens for making choices about the most intimate aspects of their lives, it must do more than assert that the choice they have made is an " 'abominable crime not fit to be named among Christians.' "

I

... A fair reading of the statute and of the complaint clearly reveals that the majority has distorted the question this case presents. First, the Court's almost obsessive focus on homosexual activity is particularly hard to justify in light of the broad language Georgia has used. Unlike the Court, the Georgia Legislature has not proceeded on the assumption that homosexuals are so different from other citizens that their lives may be controlled in a way that would not be tolerated if it limited the choices of those other citizens. Rather, Georgia has provided that "[a] person commits the offense of sodomy when he performs or submits to any sexual act involving the sex organs of one person to the mouth or anus of another." "The sex or status of the persons who engage in the act is irrelevant. ... one person and the mouth or anus of another." ... [T]o the extent I can discern a legislative purpose for Georgia's 1968 enactment of § 16–6–2, that purpose seems to have been to broaden the coverage of the law to reach heterosexual as well as homosexual activity. I therefore see no basis for the Court's decision to treat this case as an "as applied" challenge to § 16–6–2, or for Georgia's attempt ... to defend § 16–6–2 solely on the grounds that it prohibits homosexual activity. Michael Hardwick's ... claim that § 16–6–2 involves an unconstitutional intrusion into his privacy and his right of intimate association does not depend in any way on his sexual orientation.

Second, I disagree with the Court's refusal to consider whether § 16–6–2 runs afoul of the Eighth or Ninth Amendments or the Equal Protection Clause of the Fourteenth Amendment. Respondent's complaint expressly invoked the Ninth Amendment, and he relied heavily before this Court on *Griswold*, which identifies that Amendment as one of the specific constitutional provisions giving "life and substance" to our understanding of privacy. ... [N]either the Eighth Amendment nor the Equal Protection Clause is so clearly irrelevant that a claim resting on either provision should be peremptorily dismissed.[1] The Court's cramped reading of the issue before it makes for a short opinion, but it does little to make for a persuasive one.

II

"Our cases long have recognized that the Constitution embodies a promise that a certain private sphere of individual liberty will be kept largely beyond the reach of government." Thornburgh v. American College of Obstetricians & Gynecologists (1986). In construing the right to privacy, the Court has proceeded along two somewhat distinct, albeit complementary, lines. First, it has recognized a privacy interest with reference to certain decisions that are properly for the individual to make. *E.g., Roe; Pierce.* Second, it has recognized a privacy interest with reference to certain places without regard for the particular activities in which the individuals who occupy them are engaged. *E.g.,* United States v. Karo (1984); Payton v. New York (1980); Rios v. United States (1960). The case before us implicates both the decisional and the spatial aspects of the right to privacy.

A

... While ... [our earlier] cases may be characterized by their connection to protection of the family, the Court's conclusion that they extend no further than this boundary ignores the warning in *Moore* (plurality opinion), against "[closing] our eyes to the basic reasons why certain rights associated with the family have been accorded shelter under the Fourteenth Amendment's Due Process Clause." We protect those rights not because they contribute, in some direct and material way, to the general public welfare, but because they form so central a

---

1. In Robinson v. California (1962), the Court held that the Eighth Amendment barred convicting a defendant due to his "status" as a narcotics addict, since that condition was "apparently an illness which may be contracted innocently or involuntarily." ...

Despite historical views of homosexuality, it is no longer viewed by mental health professionals as a "disease" or disorder. But, obviously, neither is it simply a matter of deliberate personal election. Homosexual orientation may well form part of the very fiber of an individual's personality. Consequently, under Justice White's analysis in Powell [v. Texas (1968)], the Eighth Amendment may pose a constitutional barrier to sending an individual to prison for acting on that attraction regardless of the circumstances. An individual's ability to make constitutionally protected "decisions concerning sexual relations," *Carey* (Powell, J., concurring in part and concurring in judgment), is rendered empty indeed if he or she is given no real choice but a life without any physical intimacy.

With respect to the Equal Protection Clause's applicability to § 16–6–2, I note that Georgia's exclusive stress before this Court on its interest in prosecuting homosexual activity despite the gender-neutral terms of the statute may raise serious questions of discriminatory enforcement, questions that cannot be disposed of before this Court on a motion to dismiss. See Yick Wo v. Hopkins (1886). The legislature having decided that the sex of the participants is irrelevant to the legality of the acts, I do not see why the State can defend § 16–6–2 on the ground that individuals singled out for prosecution are of the same sex as their partners. Thus ... a claim under the Equal Protection Clause may well be available without having to reach the more controversial question whether homosexuals are a suspect class. See, *e.g.,* Rowland v. Mad River Local School Dist. (1985) (Brennan, J., dissenting from denial of cert.); Note, "The Constitutional Status of Sexual Orientation: Homosexuality as a Suspect Classification," 98 *Harv.L.Rev.* 1285 (1985). [Footnote by Justice Blackmun.]

part of an individual's life. "[The] concept of privacy embodies the 'moral fact that a person belongs to himself and not others nor to society as a whole.'" *Thornburgh* (Stevens, J., concurring), quoting Fried, Correspondence, 6 *Phil. & Pub. Affrs* 288–289 (1977). And so we protect the decision whether to marry precisely because marriage "is an association that promotes a way of life, not causes; a harmony in living, not political faiths; a bilateral loyalty, not commercial or social projects." *Griswold.* We protect the decision whether to have a child because parenthood alters so dramatically an individual's self-definition, not because of demographic considerations or the Bible's command to be fruitful and multiply. And we protect the family because it contributes so powerfully to the happiness of individuals, not because of a preference for stereotypical households. Cf. *Moore* (plurality opinion). The Court recognized in *Roberts* [v. U.S. Jaycees (1984)] that the "ability independently to define one's identity that is central to any concept of liberty" cannot truly be exercised in a vacuum; we all depend on the "emotional enrichment from close ties with others."

Only the most willful blindness could obscure the fact that sexual intimacy is "a sensitive, key relationship of human existence, central to family life, community welfare, and the development of human personality," Paris Adult Theatre I v. Slaton (1973); see also *Carey.* The fact that individuals define themselves in a significant way through their intimate sexual relationships with others suggests, in a Nation as diverse as ours, that there may be many "right" ways of conducting those relationships, and that much of the richness of a relationship will come from the freedom an individual has to choose the form and nature of these intensely personal bonds. See Karst, The Freedom of Intimate Association, 89 *Yale L.J.* 624, 637 (1980); cf. *Eisenstadt; Roe.*

In a variety of circumstances we have recognized that a necessary corollary of giving individuals freedom to choose how to conduct their lives is acceptance of the fact that different individuals will make different choices. For example, in holding that the clearly important state interest in public education should give way to a competing claim by the Amish to the effect that extended formal schooling threatened their way of life, the Court declared: "There can be no assumption that today's majority is 'right' and the Amish and others like them are 'wrong.' A way of life that is odd or even erratic but interferes with no rights or interests of others is not to be condemned because it is different." Wisconsin v. Yoder (1972). The Court claims that its decision today merely refuses to recognize a fundamental right to engage in homosexual sodomy; what the Court really has refused to recognize is the fundamental interest all individuals have in controlling the nature of their intimate associations with others.

B

The behavior for which Hardwick faces prosecution occurred in his own home, a place to which the Fourth Amendment attaches special significance. The Court's treatment of this aspect of the case is symptomatic of its overall refusal to consider the broad principles that have informed our treatment of privacy in specific cases. Just as the right to privacy is more than the mere aggregation of a number of entitlements to engage in specific behavior, so too, protecting the physical integrity of the home is more than merely a means of protecting specific activities that often take place there. ...

The Court's interpretation of the pivotal case of *Stanley* is entirely unconvincing. ... According to the majority here, *Stanley* relied entirely on the First Amendment, and thus ... sheds no light on cases not involving printed materials. But ... the *Stanley* Court anchored its holding in the Fourth Amendment's special protection for the individual in his home. ...

The central place that *Stanley* gives Justice Brandeis' dissent in *Olmstead,* a case raising *no* First Amendment claim, shows that *Stanley* rested as much on the Court's understanding of the Fourth Amendment as it did on the First. Indeed, in *Paris Adult Theatre I,* the Court suggested that reliance on the Fourth Amendment not only supported the Court's outcome in *Stanley* but actually was *necessary* to it. ... "The right of the people to be secure in their ... houses," expressly guaranteed by the Fourth Amendment, is perhaps the most "textual" of the various constitutional provisions that inform our understanding of the right to privacy, and thus I cannot agree with the Court's statement that "[the] right pressed upon us here has no ... support in the text of the Constitution." Indeed, the right of an individual to conduct intimate relationships in the intimacy of his or her own home seems to me to be the heart of the Constitution's protection of privacy.

III

The Court's failure to comprehend the magnitude of the liberty interests at stake in this case leads it to slight the question whether ... [Georgia] has justified [its] infringement on these interests. ... [2]

The core of petitioner's defense of § 16–6–2 ... is that respondent and others who engage in the conduct prohibited by § 16–6–2 interfere with Georgia's exercise of the " 'right of the Nation and of the States to maintain a decent society,' " *Paris Adult Theatre I,* quoting Jacobellis v. Ohio (1964) (Warren, C. J., dissenting). Essentially, petitioner argues,

---

2. ... [I]t does seem to me that a court could find simple, analytically sound distinctions between certain private, consensual sexual conduct, on the one hand, and adultery and incest (the only two vaguely specific "sexual crimes" to which the majority points), on the other. ... A State might define the contractual commitment necessary to become eligible for [mutual] benefits to include a commitment of fidelity and then punish individuals for breaching that contract. Moreover, a State might conclude that adultery is likely to injure third persons, in particular, spouses and children of persons who engage in extramarital affairs. With respect to incest, a court might well agree with respondent that the nature of familial relationships renders true consent to incestuous activity sufficiently problematical that a blanket prohibition of such activity is warranted. Notably, the Court makes no effort to explain why it has chosen to group private, consensual homosexual activity with adultery and incest rather than with private, consensual heterosexual activity by unmarried persons or, indeed, with oral or anal sex within marriage. [Footnote by Justice Blackmun.]

and the Court agrees, that the fact that the acts described in § 16–6–2 "for hundreds of years, if not thousands, have been uniformly condemned as immoral" is a sufficient reason to permit a State to ban them today.

I cannot agree that either the length of time a majority has held its convictions or the passions with which it defends them can withdraw legislation from this Court's scrutiny. See, *e.g., Roe; Loving;* Brown v. Bd. of Ed. (1954).[3] As Justice Jackson wrote so eloquently for the Court in West Virginia Bd. of Ed. v. Barnette (1943), "we apply the limitations of the Constitution with no fear that freedom to be intellectually and spiritually diverse or even contrary will disintegrate the social organization. ... [Freedom] to differ is not limited to things that do not matter much. That would be a mere shadow of freedom. The test of its substance is the right to differ as to things that touch the heart of the existing order." It is precisely because the issue raised by this case touches the heart of what makes individuals what they are that we should be especially sensitive to the rights of those whose choices upset the majority.

The assertion that "traditional Judeo–Christian values proscribe" the conduct involved cannot provide an adequate justification for § 16–6–2. That certain, but by no means all, religious groups condemn the behavior at issue gives the State no license to impose their judgments on the entire citizenry. The legitimacy of secular legislation depends instead on whether the State can advance some justification for its law beyond its conformity to religious doctrine. See, *e.g.,* McGowan v. Maryland (1961); Stone v. Graham (1980). Thus, far from buttressing his case, petitioner's invocation of Leviticus, Romans, St. Thomas Aquinas, and sodomy's heretical status during the Middle Ages undermines his suggestion that § 16–6–2 represents a legitimate use of secular coercive power. A State can no more punish private behavior because of religious intolerance than it can punish such behavior because of racial animus. "The Constitution cannot control such prejudices, but neither can it tolerate them. Private biases may be outside the reach of the law, but the law cannot, directly or indirectly, give them effect." Palmore v. Sidoti (1984). No matter how uncomfortable a certain group may make the majority of this Court, we have held that "[mere] public intolerance or animosity cannot constitutionally justify the deprivation of a person's physical liberty." O'Connor v. Donaldson (1975). See also Cleburne v. Cleburne Living Center, Inc. (1985).

---

3. The parallel between *Loving* and this case is almost uncanny. There, too, the State relied on a religious justification for its law. ... There, too, defenders of the challenged statute relied heavily on the fact that when the Fourteenth Amendment was ratified, most of the States had similar prohibitions. There, too, at the time the case came before the Court, many of the States still had criminal statutes concerning the conduct at issue. Yet the Court held, not only that the invidious racism of Virginia's law violated the Equal Protection Clause, but also that the law deprived the Lovings of due process by denying them the "freedom of choice to marry" that had "long been recognized as one of the vital personal rights essential to the orderly pursuit of happiness by free men." [Footnote by Justice Blackmun.]

Nor can § 16–6–2 be justified as a "morally neutral" exercise of Georgia's power to "protect the public environment," *Paris Adult Theatre I*. Certainly, some private behavior can affect the fabric of society as a whole. Reasonable people may differ about whether particular sexual acts are moral or immoral, but "we have ample evidence for believing that people will not abandon morality, will not think any better of murder, cruelty and dishonesty, merely because some private sexual practice which they abominate is not punished by the law." H. L. A. Hart, Immorality and Treason, reprinted in *The Law as Literature* 220, 225 (L. Blom–Cooper ed. 1961). Petitioner and the Court fail to see the difference between laws that protect public sensibilities and those that enforce private morality. Statutes banning public sexual activity are entirely consistent with protecting the individual's liberty interest in decisions concerning sexual relations: the same recognition that those decisions are intensely private which justifies protecting them from governmental interference can justify protecting individuals from unwilling exposure to the sexual activities of others. But the mere fact that intimate behavior may be punished when it takes place in public cannot dictate how States can regulate intimate behavior that occurs in intimate places. ...

This case involves no real interference with the rights of others, for the mere knowledge that other individuals do not adhere to one's value system cannot be a legally cognizable interest, cf. Diamond v. Charles (1986), let alone an interest that can justify invading the houses, hearts, and minds of citizens who choose to live their lives differently.

IV

It took but three years for the Court to see the error in its analysis in Minersville v. Gobitis (1940), and to recognize that the threat to national cohesion posed by a refusal to salute the flag was vastly outweighed by the threat to those same values posed by compelling such a salute. See West Virginia v. Barnette (1943). I can only hope that here, too, the Court soon will reconsider its analysis and conclude that depriving individuals of the right to choose for themselves how to conduct their intimate relationships poses a far greater threat to the values most deeply rooted in our Nation's history than tolerance of nonconformity could ever do. Because I think the Court today betrays those values, I dissent.

Justice **STEVENS**, with whom Justice **BRENNAN** and Justice **MARSHALL** join, dissenting.

Like the statute that is challenged in this case, the rationale of the Court's opinion applies equally to the prohibited conduct regardless of whether the parties who engage in it are married or unmarried, or are of the same or different sexes. ... The history of the Georgia statute before us clearly reveals this traditional prohibition of heterosexual, as well as homosexual, sodomy. Indeed, at one point in the 20th century, Georgia's law was construed to permit certain sexual conduct between homosexual women even though such conduct was prohibited between heterosexuals. The history of the statutes cited by the majority as proof for the proposition that sodomy is not constitutionally protected, similarly reveals a prohibition on heterosexual, as well as homosexual, sodomy.[1]

Because the Georgia statute expresses the traditional view that sodomy is an immoral kind of conduct regardless of the identity of the persons who engage in it, I believe that a proper analysis of its constitutionality requires consideration of two questions: First, may a State totally prohibit the described conduct by means of a neutral law applying without exception to all persons subject to its jurisdiction? If not, may the State save the statute by announcing that it will only enforce the law against homosexuals? ...

I

Our prior cases make two propositions abundantly clear. First, the fact that the governing majority in a State has traditionally viewed a particular practice as immoral is not a sufficient reason for upholding a law prohibiting the practice; neither history nor tradition could save a law prohibiting miscegenation from constitutional attack.[2] Second, individual decisions by married persons, concerning the intimacies of their physical relationship, even when not intended to produce offspring, are a form of "liberty" protected by the Due Process Clause of the Fourteenth Amendment. *Griswold.* Moreover, this protection extends to intimate choices by unmarried as well as married persons. *Carey; Eisenstadt.*

In consideration of claims of this kind, the Court has emphasized the individual interest in privacy, but its decisions have actually been animated by an even more fundamental concern. As I wrote some years ago:

> "These cases ... [deal] with the individual's right to make certain unusually important decisions that will affect his own, or his family's, destiny. The Court has referred to such decisions as implicating 'basic values,' as being 'fundamental,' and as being dignified by history and tradition. The ... Court's language in these cases brings to mind the origins of the American heritage of freedom—the abiding interest in individual liberty that makes certain state intrusions on the citizen's right to decide how he will live his own life intolerable. Guided by history, our tradition of respect for the dignity of individual choice in matters of conscience ... federal judges have accepted the responsibility for recognition and protection of these rights in appropriate cases." Fitzgerald v. Porter Memorial Hospital (7th Cir.1975), cert. denied (1976).

Society has every right to encourage its individual members to follow particular traditions in expressing affection for one another and in

---

1. A review of the statutes cited by the majority discloses that, in 1791, in 1868, and today, the vast majority of sodomy statutes do not differentiate between homosexual and heterosexual sodomy. [Footnote by Justice Stevens.]

2. See *Loving.* Interestingly, miscegenation was once treated as a crime similar to sodomy. [Footnote by Justice Stevens.]

gratifying their personal desires. It, of course, may prohibit an individual from imposing his will on another to satisfy his own selfish interests. It also may prevent an individual from interfering with, or violating, a legally sanctioned and protected relationship, such as marriage. And it may explain the relative advantages and disadvantages of different forms of intimate expression. But when individual married couples are isolated from observation by others, the way in which they voluntarily choose to conduct their intimate relations is a matter for them—not the State—to decide. The essential "liberty" that animated the development of the law in cases like *Griswold, Eisenstadt,* and *Carey* surely embraces the right to engage in nonreproductive, sexual conduct that others may consider offensive or immoral.

... [O]ur prior cases thus establish that a State may not prohibit sodomy within "the sacred precincts of marital bedrooms," *Griswold,* or, indeed, between unmarried heterosexual adults. *Eisenstadt.* In all events, it is perfectly clear that the State of Georgia may not totally prohibit the conduct proscribed by § 16–6–2.

II

If the Georgia statute cannot be enforced as it is written ... the State must assume the burden of justifying a selective application of its law. Either the persons to whom Georgia seeks to apply its statute do not have the same interest in "liberty" that others have, or there must be a reason why the State may be permitted to apply a generally applicable law to certain persons that it does not apply to others. The first possibility is plainly unacceptable. Although the meaning of the principle that "all men are created equal" is not always clear, it surely must mean that every free citizen has the same interest in "liberty" that the members of the majority share. From the standpoint of the individual, the homosexual and the heterosexual have the same interest in deciding how he will live his own life. ...

The second possibility is similarly unacceptable. A policy of selective application must be supported by a neutral and legitimate interest—something more substantial than a habitual dislike for, or ignorance about, the disfavored group. Neither the State nor the Court has identified any such interest in this case. The Court has posited as a justification for the Georgia statute "the presumed belief of a majority of the electorate in Georgia that homosexual sodomy is immoral and unacceptable." But the Georgia electorate has expressed no such belief—instead, its representatives enacted a law that presumably reflects the belief that all sodomy is immoral and unacceptable. Unless the Court is prepared to conclude that such a law is constitutional, it may not rely on the work product of the Georgia Legislature to support its holding. For the Georgia statute does not single out homosexuals as a separate class meriting special disfavored treatment. ...

Editors' Notes

(1) **Query:** To what extent was the disagreement between Justices White and Blackmun a disagreement about WHAT "the Constitution" is? That is, a disagreement about the level of generality at which we should conceive the constitutional right of privacy? Did White's opinion anticipate Scalia's interpretive method for cabining substantive due process outlined in footnote 6 of Michael H. v. Gerald D. (1989; reprinted above, p. 158)? Was Michael Hardwick urging the Court to "discover new fundamental rights," or asking it to extend a fundamental right of heterosexuals to homosexuals?

(2) **Query:** What approaches to constitutional interpretation did White follow? Burger? Blackmun? Stevens?

(3) **Query:** What was White's (and Burger's) conception of constitutionally relevant "tradition"? Was it merely a notion of historical practices, like Scalia's in Michael H. (1989; reprinted above, p. 158), or was it a notion of tradition as a "living thing," like Harlan's in his dissenting opinion in Poe v. Ullman (1961; reprinted above, p. 141)?

(4) **Query:** Do the "traditions" that White and Burger invoked condemn homosexual sodomy or simply sodomy? Did the majority's analyses imply that a statute criminalizing sodomy between married heterosexuals would be constitutional? Would Griswold's principles imply that such a statute would be unconstitutional? In Bowers itself, Georgia conceded at oral argument that such a statute would be unconstitutional. What would White and Burger have said?

(5) **Query:** Stevens said that "Although the meaning of the principle that 'all men are created equal' is not always clear, it surely must mean that every free citizen has the same interest in 'liberty' that the members of the majority share." The words "all men are created equal" do not, of course, appear in the constitutional text of 1787–88 as amended, but in the Declaration of Independence. (Cf. his remark, dissenting in Meachum v. Fano [1976]: "I had thought it self-evident that all men were endowed by their Creator with liberty as one of the cardinal unalienable rights.") Was Stevens implying that the Declaration is part of the larger constitution? Or was he merely using it as an interpretive tool to pry loose the meaning of "liberty"? What difference does it make for constitutional interpretation if the answer is the one or the other?

(6) The Papers of Justice Thurgood Marshall indicate that in Bowers, Powell initially voted to affirm the decision below on the basis of the Eighth Amendment's prohibition of cruel and unusual punishment but subsequently changed his vote. (The Library of Congress, Manuscripts Division, Case File 393.) For a critique of Bowers based on the Eighth Amendment, see Kendall Thomas, "Beyond the Privacy Principle," 92 Colum.L.Rev. 1431 (1992).

Several years later, after he had retired, Powell publicly remarked, "I think I probably made a mistake" in voting with the majority in Bowers. See Linda Greenhouse, "When Second Thoughts In Case Come Too Late," N.Y. Times, Nov. 5, 1990, p. A14. He had come to believe the majority opinion in Bowers "was inconsistent in a general way" with Roe v. Wade (1973; reprinted above, p. 1258). To what extent were Powell's second thoughts about a conflict between Bowers and Roe correct? Concretely put, does a right to terminate pregnancy before viability imply a right to engage in homosexual intercourse? Phrased at another level of abstraction, does a right to privacy and bodily integrity that encompasses a woman's right to terminate pregnancy also include a right to engage in homosexual intercourse?

(7) **Query:** Did *Bowers* leave open the possibility of challenges to discrimination against homosexuals under the Equal Protection Clause? Or did it imply that discrimination on the basis of sexual orientation does not violate that clause? Should the Court recognize sexual orientation as a suspect (or semi-suspect) classification under the Equal Protection Clause? For contrasting approaches, see Padula v. Webster (D.C.Cir.1987), and Watkins v. U.S. Army (9th Cir.1988), withdrawn but affirmed en banc (1989). See also Cass R. Sunstein, "Sexual Orientation and the Constitution: A Note on the Relationship Between Due Process and Equal Protection," 55 *U.Chi.L.Rev.* 1161 (1988).

(8) **Query:** In constitutional interpretation, critics of controversial decisions often liken them to infamous, earlier decisions. Dissenting in *Watkins,* Judge Reinhardt argued that "history will view Bowers v. Hardwick much as it views Plessy v. Ferguson. ... And I am confident that, in the long run, *Bowers,* like *Plessy,* will be overruled by a wiser and more enlightened Court." In *Democracy and Distrust* (Cambridge: Harvard University Press, 1980), p. 163, John Hart Ely also anticipated this analogy. Advocates for the rights of homosexuals have also likened *Bowers* to *Plessy.* See Greenhouse, above, Eds.' Note 6. What do they mean by this analogy? Is it persuasive?

(9) **Query:** Some scholars have contended that discrimination on the basis of sexual orientation is a form of discrimination on the basis of sex: Andrew M. M. Koppelman, "Why Discrimination Against Lesbians and Gay Men Is Sex Discrimination," 69 *N.Y.U.L.Rev.* 197 (1994); Sylvia A. Law, "Homosexuality and the Social Meaning of Gender," 1988 *Wis.L.Rev.* 187. So has the Supreme Court of Hawaii: Baehr v. Lewin (1993). Is this argument more persuasive, as a matter of constitutional interpretation, than the argument that courts should recognize sexual orientation as a semi-suspect classification?

(10) Some state constitutions explicitly provide for a right of privacy, and some state courts have construed their state constitutions to invalidate criminal sodomy statutes notwithstanding the Supreme Court's interpretation of the U.S. Constitution in *Bowers.* For example, in Commonwealth of Kentucky v. Wasson (1992), the Supreme Court of Kentucky, criticizing *Bowers* "as a misdirected application of the theory of original intent" in light of precedents such as Loving v. Virginia (1967; reprinted above, p. 926), interpreted its state constitution's privacy and equal protection guarantees to prohibit a criminal statute proscribing consensual homosexual sodomy.

(11) **Query:** Is *Bowers* likely to be overruled soon? White, the author of the opinion of the Court, has retired. His replacement, Ruth Bader Ginsburg, while a judge on the Court of Appeals for the District of Columbia Circuit, voted with the en banc majority denying a rehearing in a 1984 case that rejected a discharged homosexual sailor's argument that the military's ban on homosexuals violated his constitutional right to privacy and denied him equal protection. See Dronenburg v. Zech (en banc). She wrote separately from Judge Robert Bork's more conservative opinion, stating simply: "I am of the

view that the Supreme Court's disposition in Doe [v. Commonwealth's Attorney (1976)] controls our judgment in this case." (*Doe* had affirmed, without argument or opinion, a lower federal court's upholding a Virginia law that made it a crime, even for consenting adults acting in private, to engage in homosexual relations.) Nonetheless, some observers have predicted that Ginsburg might vote to overrule *Bowers.* Senator Jesse Helms of North Carolina, one of only three senators to vote against her confirmation, claimed that she was "likely to uphold the homosexual agenda." Linda Greenhouse, "Senate, 96–3, Easily Affirms Judge Ginsburg as a Justice," *N.Y. Times*, Aug. 4, 1993, p. B8.

(12) In November 1992, the voters of Colorado adopted an amendment to their state constitution forbidding both state and local governments to enact laws protecting gay men and lesbians from discrimination. At the same time, the voters of Oregon narrowly rejected a referendum that condemned homosexual life styles as "abnormal" and "perverse." In July 1993, the Supreme Court of Colorado invalidated the initiative on the ground that it denied a defined group of citizens—homosexuals—the fundamental right to participate equally in the political process. Evans v. Romer (1993).

(13) During his 1992 presidential campaign, William J. Clinton promised that he would lift the ban on homosexuals in the military. After a hard-fought battle with the Joint Chiefs of Staff and Senator Sam Nunn, Chair of the Senate Armed Services Committee, all of whom strongly opposed lifting the ban, Clinton compromised on a "don't ask, don't tell, don't pursue" policy. Essentially it allows homosexuals to serve in the military as long as they are silent about their sexual orientation. In 1994, however, the Court of Appeals for the Ninth Circuit gave broad hints that the new policy would not pass constitutional muster. The case, Meinhold v. United States, began under older regulations. The Navy had discharged a petty officer for admitting to a reporter in 1992 that he was gay. The judges said that, although they would defer to the Navy's judgment that homosexual conduct harmed morale, discharging a person merely because he admitted to being a homosexual without evidence of homosexual actions would raise serious constitutional questions. The court avoided those issues by interpreting the Navy's older regulations to require more than mere admission of homosexual orientation. The United States did not appeal that decision. As this edition went to press a federal district court held that the new policy violated freedom of speech and denied equal protection. The United States indicated that it would appeal this decision.

VII. THE RIGHT TO DIE

"[W]e assume that the United States Constitution would grant a competent person a constitutionally protected

right to refuse lifesaving hydration and nutrition."—
Chief Justice REHNQUIST

"[T]he point at which life becomes 'worthless,' and the
point at which the means necessary to preserve it become 'extraordinary' or 'inappropriate,' are neither set
forth in the Constitution nor known to the nine Justices
of this Court any better than they are known to nine
people picked at random from the Kansas City telephone
directory. ..."—Justice SCALIA

"[F]reedom from unwanted medical attention is unquestionably among those principles 'so rooted in the traditions and conscience of our people as to be ranked as
fundamental.' "—Justice BRENNAN

"Choices about death touch the core of liberty. Our
duty, and the concomitant freedom, to come to terms
with ... our own mortality are undoubtedly 'so rooted in
the traditions and conscience of our people as to be
ranked as fundamental,' and indeed are essential incidents of the unalienable rights to life and liberty endowed us by our Creator."—Justice STEVENS

CRUZAN v. DIRECTOR, MISSOURI DEPT. OF HEALTH
497 U.S. 261, 110 S.Ct. 2841, 111 L.Ed.2d 224 (1990).

In 1983, Nancy Beth Cruzan, then 25 years old, suffered severe injuries in
an automobile accident. After she went into a persistent vegetative state and
it became apparent that she had virtually no chance of recovering her
cognitive faculties, her parents asked the hospital to terminate the artificial
nutrition and hydration procedures that were keeping her alive. The hospital
refused to honor the request without authorization by a court. The parents
then sought and received authorization from a state judge. He found that a
person in Cruzan's condition had a fundamental right under the state and
federal Constitutions to refuse or direct the withdrawal of "death prolonging
procedures." The judge also found that her "expressed thoughts at age
twenty-five in somewhat serious conversations with a friend that if sick or
injured she would not wish to continue her life unless she could live at least
halfway normally suggests that given her present condition she would not wish
to continue on with her nutrition and hydration." Cruzan had not, however,
executed a living will nor had she designated anyone to make health-care
decisions for her in the event that she became incompetent. The Missouri
Supreme Court reversed, finding no clear and convincing evidence of her
desire to have life-sustaining treatment withdrawn under such circumstances,
and therefore concluding that her parents lacked authority to effectuate such a
request.

Chief Justice **REHNQUIST** delivered the opinion of the Court.

... This is the first case in which we have been squarely presented
with the issue of whether the United States Constitution grants what is

in common parlance referred to as a "right to die." ... The Fourteenth Amendment provides that no State shall "deprive any person of life, liberty, or property, without due process of law." The principle that a competent person has a constitutionally protected liberty interest in refusing unwanted medical treatment may be inferred from our prior decisions. [*E.g.*,] Jacobson v. Massachusetts (1905). ...

Just this Term ... we recognized that prisoners possess "a significant liberty interest in avoiding the unwanted administration of antipsychotic drugs under the Due Process Clause of the Fourteenth Amendment." Washington v. Harper (1990). ... But determining that a person has a "liberty interest" under the Due Process Clause does not end the inquiry;[1] "whether respondent's constitutional rights have been violated must be determined by balancing his liberty interests against the relevant state interests." Youngberg v. Romeo (1982).

Petitioners insist that under the general holdings of our cases, the forced administration of life-sustaining medical treatment, and even of artificially-delivered food and water essential to life, would implicate a competent person's liberty interest. Although we think the logic of the cases ... would embrace such a liberty interest, the dramatic consequences involved in refusal of such treatment would inform the inquiry as to whether the deprivation of that interest is constitutionally permissible. But for purposes of this case, we assume that the United States Constitution would grant a competent person a constitutionally protected right to refuse lifesaving hydration and nutrition.

Petitioners go on to assert that an incompetent person should possess the same right in this respect as is possessed by a competent person. ... The difficulty with [that] claim is that in a sense it begs the question: an incompetent person is not able to make an informed and voluntary choice to exercise a hypothetical right to refuse treatment or any other right. Such a "right" must be exercised for her, if at all, by some sort of surrogate. Here, Missouri has in effect recognized that under certain circumstances a surrogate may act for the patient ... but it has established a procedural safeguard to assure that the action of the surrogate conforms as best it may to the wishes expressed by the patient while competent. Missouri requires that evidence of the incompetent's wishes as to the withdrawal of treatment be proved by clear and convincing evidence. The question, then, is whether the United States Constitution forbids the establishment of this procedural requirement by the State. We hold that it does not.

Whether or not Missouri's clear and convincing evidence requirement comports with the United States Constitution depends in part on what interests the State may properly seek to protect in this situation. Missouri relies on its interest in the protection and preservation of

---

1. Although many state courts have held that a right to refuse treatment is encompassed by a generalized constitutional right of privacy, we have never so held. We believe this issue is more properly analyzed in terms of a Fourteenth Amendment liberty interest. See Bowers v. Hardwick (1986). [Footnote by the Court.]

human life, and there can be no gainsaying this interest. As a general matter, the States—indeed, all civilized nations—demonstrate their commitment to life by treating homicide as serious crime. Moreover, the majority of States in this country have laws imposing criminal penalties on one who assists another to commit suicide. We do not think a State is required to remain neutral in the face of an informed and voluntary decision by a physically-able adult to starve to death.

But in the context presented here, a State has more particular interests at stake. The choice between life and death is a deeply personal decision of obvious and overwhelming finality. We believe Missouri may legitimately seek to safeguard the personal element of this choice through the imposition of heightened evidentiary requirements. It cannot be disputed that the Due Process Clause protects an interest in life as well as an interest in refusing life-sustaining medical treatment. Not all incompetent patients will have loved ones available to serve as surrogate decisionmakers. And even where family members are present, "[t]here will, of course, be some unfortunate situations in which family members will not act to protect a patient." In re Jobes (N.J. 1987). A State is entitled to guard against potential abuses in such situations. Similarly, a State is entitled to consider that a judicial proceeding to make a determination regarding an incompetent's wishes may very well not be an adversarial one, with the added guarantee of accurate factfinding that the adversary process brings with it. See Ohio v. Akron Center for Reproductive Health (1990). Finally, we think a State may properly decline to make judgments about the "quality" of life that a particular individual may enjoy, and simply assert an unqualified interest in the preservation of human life to be weighed against the constitutionally protected interests of the individual.

In our view, Missouri has permissibly sought to advance these interests through the adoption of a "clear and convincing" standard of proof to govern such proceedings. ...

We think it self-evident that the interests at stake in the instant proceedings are more substantial, both on an individual and societal level, than those involved in a run-of-the-mine civil dispute. ... The more stringent the burden of proof a party must bear, the more that party bears the risk of an erroneous decision. We believe that Missouri may permissibly place an increased risk of an erroneous decision on those seeking to terminate an incompetent individual's life-sustaining treatment. An erroneous decision not to terminate results in a maintenance of the status quo; the possibility of subsequent developments such as advancements in medical science, the discovery of new evidence regarding the patient's intent, changes in the law, or simply the unexpected death of the patient despite the administration of life-sustaining treatment, at least create the potential that a wrong decision will eventually be corrected or its impact mitigated. An erroneous decision to withdraw life-sustaining treatment, however, is not susceptible of correction. ...

In sum, we conclude that a State may apply a clear and convincing evidence standard in proceedings where a guardian seeks to discontinue nutrition and hydration of a person diagnosed to be in a persistent vegetative state. ...

The Supreme Court of Missouri held that ... the testimony adduced at trial did not amount to clear and convincing proof of the patient's desire to have hydration and nutrition withdrawn. ... The testimony adduced ... consisted primarily of Nancy Cruzan's statements made to a housemate about a year before her accident that she would not want to live should she face life as a "vegetable," and other observations to the same effect. The observations did not deal in terms with withdrawal of medical treatment or of hydration and nutrition. We cannot say that the Supreme Court of Missouri committed constitutional error in reaching the conclusion that it did.

Petitioners alternatively contend that Missouri must accept the "substituted judgment" of close family members even in the absence of substantial proof that their views reflect the views of the patient. They rely primarily upon our decisions in Michael H. v. Gerald D. (1989), and Parham v. J. R. (1979). But we do not think these cases support their claim. ...

No doubt is engendered by anything in this record but that Nancy Cruzan's mother and father are loving and caring parents. If the State were required by the United States Constitution to repose a right of "substituted judgment" with anyone, the Cruzans would surely qualify. But we do not think the Due Process Clause requires the State to repose judgment on these matters with anyone but the patient herself. Close family members may have a strong feeling—a feeling not at all ignoble or unworthy, but not entirely disinterested, either—that they do not wish to witness the continuation of the life of a loved one which they regard as hopeless, meaningless, and even degrading. But there is no automatic assurance that the view of close family members will necessarily be the same as the patient's would have been had she been ... competent. All of the reasons previously discussed for allowing Missouri to require clear and convincing evidence of the patient's wishes lead us to conclude that the State may choose to defer only to those wishes, rather than confide the decision to close family members.[2] ...

Affirmed.

Justice **O'CONNOR**, concurring.

I agree that a protected liberty interest in refusing unwanted medical treatment may be inferred from our prior decisions, and that the refusal of artificially delivered food and water is encompassed within

---

2. We are not faced in this case with the question of whether a State might be required to defer to the decision of a surrogate if competent and probative evidence established that the patient herself had expressed a desire that the decision to terminate life-sustaining treatment be made for her by that individual. [Footnote by the Court.]

that liberty interest. I write separately to clarify why I believe this to be so.

As the Court notes, the liberty interest in refusing medical treatment flows from decisions involving the State's invasions into the body. Because our notions of liberty are inextricably entwined with our idea of physical freedom and self-determination, the Court has often deemed state incursions into the body repugnant to the interests protected by the Due Process Clause. See, *e.g.*, Rochin v. California (1952). ... The State's imposition of medical treatment on an unwilling competent adult necessarily involves some form of restraint and intrusion. ... Artificial feeding cannot readily be distinguished from other forms of medical treatment. ... Requiring a competent adult to endure such procedures against her will burdens the patient's liberty, dignity, and freedom to determine the course of her own treatment. Accordingly, the liberty guaranteed by the Due Process Clause must protect, if it protects anything, an individual's deeply personal decision to reject medical treatment, including the artificial delivery of food and water.

... Today's decision ... does not preclude a future determination that the Constitution requires the States to implement the decisions of a patient's duly appointed surrogate. Nor does it prevent States from developing other approaches for protecting an incompetent individual's liberty interest in refusing medical treatment. ... [N]o national consensus has yet emerged on the best solution for this difficult and sensitive problem. Today we decide only that one State's practice does not violate the Constitution; the more challenging task of crafting appropriate procedures for safeguarding incompetents' liberty interests is entrusted to the "laboratory" of the States, New State Ice Co. v. Liebmann (1932) (Brandeis, J., dissenting), in the first instance.

Justice **SCALIA**, concurring. ...

While I agree with the Court's analysis today, and therefore join in its opinion, I would have preferred that we announce, clearly and promptly, that the federal courts have no business in this field; that American law has always accorded the State the power to prevent, by force if necessary, suicide—including suicide by refusing to take appropriate measures necessary to preserve one's life; that the point at which life becomes "worthless," and the point at which the means necessary to preserve it become "extraordinary" or "inappropriate," are neither set forth in the Constitution nor known to the nine Justices of this Court any better than they are known to nine people picked at random from the Kansas City telephone directory; and hence, that even when it is demonstrated by clear and convincing evidence that a patient no longer wishes certain measures to be taken to preserve her life, it is up to the citizens of Missouri to decide, through their elected representatives, whether that wish will be honored. ...

The text of the Due Process Clause does not protect individuals against deprivations of liberty *simpliciter*. It protects them against deprivations of liberty "without due process of law." To determine that such a deprivation would not occur if Nancy Cruzan were forced to take nourishment against her will, it is unnecessary to reopen the historically recurrent debate over whether "due process" includes substantive restrictions. It is at least true that no "substantive due process" claim can be maintained unless the claimant demonstrates that the State has deprived him of a right historically and traditionally protected against State interference. *Michael H.* (plurality opinion); *Bowers;* Moore [v. East Cleveland (1977)] (plurality opinion). That cannot possibly be established here.

At common law in England, a suicide—defined as one who "deliberately puts an end to his own existence, or commits any unlawful malicious act, the consequence of which is his own death," 4 W. Blackstone, *Commentaries* 189—was criminally liable. ... Case law at the time of the Fourteenth Amendment generally held that assisting suicide was a criminal offense. See Marzen et al., Suicide: A Constitutional Right?, 24 *Duquesne L.Rev.* 1 (1985). ... And most States that did not explicitly prohibit assisted suicide in 1868 recognized, when the issue arose in the 50 years following the Fourteenth Amendment's ratification, that assisted and (in some cases) attempted suicide was unlawful. Thus, "there is no significant support for the claim that a right to suicide is so rooted in our tradition that it may be deemed 'fundamental' or 'implicit in the concept of ordered liberty.'" *Id.*

Petitioners rely on three distinctions to separate Nancy Cruzan's case from ordinary suicide: (1) that she is permanently incapacitated and in pain; (2) that she would bring on her death not by any affirmative act but by merely declining treatment that provides nourishment; and (3) that preventing her from effectuating her presumed wish to die requires violation of her bodily integrity. None of these suffices.
...

What I have said above is not meant to suggest that I would think it desirable, if we were sure that Nancy Cruzan wanted to die, to keep her alive by the means at issue here. I assert only that the Constitution has nothing to say about the subject. ... Are there, then, no reasonable and humane limits that ought not to be exceeded in requiring an individual to preserve his own life? There obviously are, but they are not set forth in the Due Process Clause. What assures us that those limits will not be exceeded is the same constitutional guarantee that is the source of most of our protection. ... Our salvation is the Equal Protection Clause, which requires the democratic majority to accept for themselves and their loved ones what they impose on you and me. This Court need not, and has no authority to, inject itself into every field of human activity where irrationality and oppression may theoretically occur, and if it tries to do so it will destroy itself.

Justice **BRENNAN**, with whom Justice **MARSHALL** and Justice **BLACKMUN** join, dissenting.

... Because I believe that Nancy Cruzan has a fundamental right to be free of unwanted artificial nutrition and hydration, which right is not outweighed by any interests of the State, and because I find that the improperly biased procedural obstacles imposed by the Missouri Supreme Court impermissibly burden that right, I respectfully dissent. Nancy Cruzan is entitled to choose to die with dignity. ... [F]reedom from unwanted medical attention is unquestionably among those principles "so rooted in the traditions and conscience of our people as to be ranked as fundamental." Snyder v. Massachusetts (1934). ...

No material distinction can be drawn between the treatment to which Nancy Cruzan continues to be subject—artificial nutrition and hydration—and any other medical treatment. ... Nor does the fact that Nancy Cruzan is now incompetent deprive her of her fundamental rights. ... As the majority recognizes, the question is not whether an incompetent has constitutional rights, but how such rights may be exercised. ...

Although the right to be free of unwanted medical intervention, like other constitutionally protected interests, may not be absolute, no State interest could outweigh the rights of an individual in Nancy Cruzan's position. Whatever a State's possible interests in mandating life-support treatment under other circumstances, there is no good to be obtained here by Missouri's insistence that Nancy Cruzan remain on life-support systems if it is indeed her wish not to do so. Missouri does not claim, nor could it, that society as a whole will be benefited by Nancy's receiving medical treatment. No third party's situation will be improved and no harm to others will be averted.[1]

The only state interest asserted here is a general interest in the preservation of life. But the State has no legitimate general interest in someone's life, completely abstracted from the interest of the person living that life, that could outweigh the person's choice to avoid medical treatment. "[T]he regulation of constitutionally protected decisions ... must be predicated on legitimate state concerns *other than* disagreement with the choice the individual has made. ... Otherwise, the interest in liberty protected by the Due Process Clause would be a nullity." Hodgson v. Minnesota (1990) (Opinion of Stevens, J.) (emphasis added). Thus, the State's general interest in life must accede to Nancy Cruzan's particularized and intense interest in self-determination in her choice of medical treatment. ...

This is not to say that the State has no legitimate interests to assert here. As the majority recognizes, Missouri has a *parens patriae* interest

---

1. Were such interests at stake, however, I would find that the Due Process Clause places limits on what invasive medical procedures could be forced on an unwilling comatose patient in pursuit of the interests of a third party. If Missouri were correct that its interests outweigh Nancy's interest in avoiding medical procedures as long as she is free of pain and physical discomfort, it is not apparent why a State could not choose to remove one of her kidneys without consent on the ground that society would be better off if the recipient of that kidney were saved from renal poisoning. ... Indeed, why could the State not perform medical experiments on her body, experiments that might save countless lives, and would cause her no greater burden than she already bears by being fed through the gastrostomy tube? This would be too brave a new world for me and, I submit, for our Constitution. [Footnote by Justice Brennan.]

in providing Nancy Cruzan, now incompetent, with as accurate as possible a determination of how she would exercise her rights under these circumstances. Second, if and when it is determined that Nancy Cruzan would want to continue treatment, the State may legitimately assert an interest in providing that treatment. But until Nancy's wishes have been determined, the only state interest that may be asserted is an interest in safeguarding the accuracy of that determination.

Accuracy, therefore, must be our touchstone. Missouri may constitutionally impose only those procedural requirements that serve to enhance the accuracy of a determination of Nancy Cruzan's wishes or are at least consistent with an accurate determination. The Missouri "safeguard" that the Court upholds today does not meet that standard. ... Missouri's rule of decision imposes a markedly asymmetrical evidentiary burden. Only evidence of specific statements of treatment choice made by the patient when competent is admissible to support a finding that the patient, now in a persistent vegetative state, would wish to avoid further medical treatment. Moreover, this evidence must be clear and convincing. No proof is required to support a finding that the incompetent person would wish to continue treatment. ...

... The new medical technology can reclaim those who would have been irretrievably lost a few decades ago and restore them to active lives. For Nancy Cruzan, it failed, and for others with wasting incurable disease it may be doomed to failure. In these unfortunate situations, the bodies and preferences and memories of the victims do not escheat to the State; nor does our Constitution permit the State or any other government to commandeer them. No singularity of feeling exists upon which such a government might confidently rely as *parens patriae*. ... Yet Missouri and this Court have displaced Nancy's own assessment of the processes associated with dying. They have discarded evidence of her will, ignored her values, and deprived her of the right to a decision as closely approximating her own choice as humanly possible. They have done so disingenuously in her name, and openly in Missouri's own. That Missouri and this Court may truly be motivated only by concern for incompetent patients makes no matter. As one of our most prominent jurists warned us decades ago: "Experience should teach us to be most on our guard to protect liberty when the government's purposes are beneficent. ... The greatest dangers to liberty lurk in insidious encroachment by men of zeal, well meaning but without understanding." Olmstead v. United States (1928) (Brandeis, J., dissenting).

Justice **STEVENS**, dissenting.

Our Constitution is born of the proposition that all legitimate governments must secure the equal right of every person to "Life, Liberty, and the pursuit of Happiness." In the ordinary case we quite naturally assume that these three ends are compatible, mutually enhancing, and perhaps even coincident. The Court would make an exception here. It permits the State's abstract, undifferentiated interest in the preservation of life to overwhelm the best interests of Nancy Beth

Cruzan, interests which would, according to an undisputed finding, be served by allowing her guardians to exercise her constitutional right to discontinue medical treatment. ... [T]he Constitution requires the State to care for Nancy Cruzan's life in a way that gives appropriate respect to her own best interests.

... Choices about death touch the core of liberty. Our duty, and the concomitant freedom, to come to terms with the conditions of our own mortality are undoubtedly "so rooted in the traditions and conscience of our people as to be ranked as fundamental," Snyder v. Massachusetts (1934), and indeed are essential incidents of the unalienable rights to life and liberty endowed us by our Creator. See Meachum v. Fano (1976) (Stevens, J., dissenting).

The more precise constitutional significance of death is difficult to describe; not much may be said with confidence about death unless it is said from faith, and that alone is reason enough to protect the freedom to conform choices about death to individual conscience. ...

These considerations cast into stark relief the injustice, and unconstitutionality, of Missouri's treatment of Nancy Beth Cruzan. Nancy Cruzan's death, when it comes, cannot be an historic act of heroism; it will inevitably be the consequence of her tragic accident. But Nancy Cruzan's interest in life, no less than that of any other person, includes an interest in how she will be thought of after her death by those whose opinions mattered to her. There can be no doubt that her life made her dear to her family, and to others. How she dies will affect how that life is remembered. The trial court's order authorizing Nancy's parents to cease their daughter's treatment would have permitted the family that cares for Nancy to bring to a close her tragedy and her death. Missouri's objection to that order subordinates Nancy's body, her family, and the lasting significance of her life to the State's own interests. The decision we review thereby interferes with constitutional interests of the highest order. ...

It seems to me that the Court errs insofar as it characterizes this case as involving "judgments about the 'quality' of life that a particular individual may enjoy." Nancy Cruzan is obviously "alive" in a physiological sense. But for patients like Nancy Cruzan, who have no consciousness and no chance of recovery, there is a serious question as to whether the mere persistence of their bodies is "life" as that word is commonly understood, or as it is used in both the Constitution and the Declaration of Independence. The State's unflagging determination to perpetuate Nancy Cruzan's physical existence is comprehensible only as an effort to define life's meaning, not as an attempt to preserve its sanctity. ...

In short, there is no reasonable ground for believing that Nancy Beth Cruzan has any personal interest in the perpetuation of what the State has decided is her life. ... It is not within the province of secular government to circumscribe the liberties of the people by regulations designed wholly for the purpose of establishing a sectarian definition of life. See Webster v. Reproductive Services (1989) (Stevens, J., dissenting).

My disagreement with the Court is thus unrelated to its endorsement of the clear and convincing standard of proof for cases of this kind. Indeed, I agree that the controlling facts must be established with unmistakable clarity. The critical question, however, is not how to prove the controlling facts but rather what proven facts should be controlling. In my view, the constitutional answer is clear: the best interests of the individual, especially when buttressed by the interests of all related third parties, must prevail over any general state policy that simply ignores those interests. Indeed, the only apparent secular basis for the State's interest in life is the policy's persuasive impact upon people other than Nancy and her family. ... The failure of Missouri's policy to heed the interests of a dying individual with respect to matters so private is ample evidence of the policy's illegitimacy.

Only because Missouri has arrogated to itself the power to define life, and only because the Court permits this usurpation, are Nancy Cruzan's life and liberty put into disquieting conflict. If Nancy Cruzan's life were defined by reference to her own interests ... then her constitutionally protected interest in freedom from unwanted treatment would not come into conflict with her constitutionally protected interest in life. Conversely, if there were any evidence that Nancy Cruzan herself defined life to encompass every form of biological persistence by a human being ... then once again there would be no conflict between life and liberty. The opposition of life and liberty in this case are thus not the result of Nancy Cruzan's tragic accident, but are instead the artificial consequence of Missouri's effort, and this Court's willingness, to abstract Nancy Cruzan's life from Nancy Cruzan's person.

... [T]his Court cannot defer to any State policy that drives a theoretical wedge between a person's life, on the one hand, and that person's liberty or happiness, on the other. The consequence of such a theory is to deny the personhood of those whose lives are defined by the State's interests rather than their own. This consequence may be acceptable in theology or in speculative philosophy, see Meyer [v. Nebraska (1923)], but it is radically inconsistent with the foundation of all legitimate government. Our Constitution presupposes a respect for the personhood of every individual, and nowhere is strict adherence to that principle more essential than in the Judicial Branch. See, e.g., Thornburgh v. American College of Obstetricians and Gynecologists (1986) (Stevens, J., concurring). ...

Editors' Notes

(1) **Query**: Did the Court recognize a constitutional right to die? What is the meaning and significance of the Court's distinction, in footnote 1, between a "generalized constitutional right of privacy" and a "liberty interest"? Did Rehnquist's opinion of the Court hold or imply that states are constitutionally obligated to honor competent persons' advance directives regarding extraordinary medical procedures?

(2) **Query**: How consistent with the interpretive method Scalia outlined in footnote 6 of Michael H. v. Gerald D. (1989; reprinted above, p. 158) was his concurrence in *Cruzan*? Did he imply in *Cruzan* that states are not constitutionally obligated to honor advance directives? What was the relevance of his references to historical practices concerning suicide? Assuming that such practices were relevant, would it matter for purposes of constitutional interpretation that suicide and attempt to commit suicide are no longer crimes in any state? See Note, "Developments in the Law: Medical Technology and the Law," 103 *Harv.L.Rev.* 1519, 1664 n.153 (1990). Did Scalia's method provide a useful criterion to determine the traditions from which this country "broke," to use Harlan's term in his dissent in Poe v. Ullman [1961; reprinted above, p. 141]?

(3) **Query**: Rehnquist and Scalia assumed that the states have an interest in preserving human life for its own sake, even when doing so runs against what some citizens, including judges, see as the best interests of the persons whose lives are preserved. What is the basis for this assumption? Does the constitutional text offer any guidance? Tradition? The political theories that underlie "the Constitution"? For critiques, see not only Stevens's dissent but also Ronald Dworkin, *Life's Dominion* (New York: Knopf, 1993), ch. 7.

(4) **Query:** What was Scalia's conception of the relationship between the Due Process Clause and the Equal Protection Clause? In what senses did he believe that use of the Due Process Clause will lead to destruction of the Court, and that recourse to the Equal Protection Clause will lead to "[o]ur salvation"? How persuasive is this claim?

(5) Before *Cruzan*, the critical case was In re Karen Quinlan, decided by the Supreme Court of New Jersey in 1976. The facts in the two cases were quite similar. New Jersey's justices appointed the young woman's father as guardian with authority to terminate the life-support system if physicians determined there was no reasonable chance of her emerging from the coma. The court excused the hospital from all civil liability, then added: "we do not intend to be understood as implying that a proceeding for judicial declaratory relief is necessarily required for the implementation of comparable decisions in the field of medical practice."

Quinlan is especially interesting in light of the comments by several justices in *Cruzan* hinting at a link between opposition to abortion and a requirement that doctors keep human beings alive regardless of the prospects of recovery. The Catholic bishops of New Jersey had filed an *amicus curiae* brief endorsing Mr. Quinlan's suit to discontinue life-support for his daughter. Furthermore, in 1957, speaking before a group of physicians, Pope Pius XII had carefully distinguished between taking human life and keeping a person alive by extraordinary means when recovery was not a reasonable prospect. The first, he said, was morally impermissible, the second was not morally required. ("The Prolongation of Life," 4 *The Pope Speaks* 393 [1958].) On the other hand, shortly after *Quinlan*, two Catholic theologians debated each other in *L'Osservatore Romano*, the Vatican's unofficial official newspaper, about the decision's moral correctness. For a brief bibliography on the intertwined moral and constitutional issues, as well as citations to some earlier cases, see Walter F. Murphy and Joseph Tanenhaus, *Comparative Constitutional Law* (New York: St. Martin's, 1977), pp. 448–50.

(6) As it turned out, Nancy Cruzan was allowed to die. After the Supreme Court's decision, her parents petitioned the lower court, offering new evidence of her intent: three more friends had come forward and stated that she had told them that she would not want to live as a vegetable. Missouri's Attorney General then decided not to oppose the parents' petition, and the lower court granted it. Soon after the hospital withdrew feeding and hydration, she died.

(7) At present, almost all states recognize advance directives such as living wills, health-care proxies, or both. See Alan Meisel, *The Right to Die* (New York: Wiley, 1993 Cum. Supp.), p. xviii. In 1991, the voters of the state of Washington narrowly defeated a referendum that would have legalized euthanasia. In 1992, voters in California also narrowly rejected such legislation. In 1994, voters in Oregon adopted a measure legalizing physician-assisted suicide in certain circumstances. Lawsuits challenging its constitutionality immediately followed. Similar measures are likely to be considered in the future. Furthermore, in 1994, a federal district court held unconstitutional a Washington law that prohibited physician-assisted suicide by mentally competent, terminally ill adults. Compassion in Dying v. Washington. The Court of Appeals for the Ninth Circuit, however, reversed that decision.

(8) For analyses of "the right to die," see not only Dworkin, *Life's Dominion*, but also John H. Garvey, "Freedom and Choice in Constitutional Law," 94 *Harv.L.Rev.* 1756 (1981); Yale Kamisar, "When Is There a Constitutional 'Right to Die'?," 25 *Ga.L.Rev.* 1203 (1991); Thomas W. Mayo, "Constitutionalizing the 'Right to Die,'" 49 *Md.L.Rev.* 103 (1990); Alan Meisel, *The Right to Die* (New York: Wiley, 1989); and Nancy K. Rhoden, "Litigating Life and Death," 102 *Harv.L.Rev.* 375 (1988).

VIII. THE RIGHT TO POSITIVE LIBERTIES

"[T]he Due Process Clauses generally confer no affirmative right to governmental aid, even where such aid may be necessary to secure life, liberty, or property interests of which the government itself may not deprive the individual"—Chief Justice REHNQUIST

"[I]naction can be every bit as abusive of power as action . . . [and] oppression can result when a State undertakes a vital duty and then ignores it."—Justice BRENNAN

"Faced with the choice, I would adopt a 'sympathetic' reading, one which comports with dictates of fundamental justice and recognizes that compassion need not be

exiled from the province of judging."—Justice BLACK-MUN

DESHANEY v. WINNEBAGO COUNTY DEPT. OF SOCIAL SERVICES

489 U.S. 189, 109 S.Ct. 998, 103 L.Ed.2d 249 (1989).

Chief Justice **REHNQUIST** delivered the opinion of the Court.   ...

I

The facts of this case are undeniably tragic. Petitioner Joshua DeShaney was born in 1979. In 1980, a Wyoming court granted his parents a divorce and awarded custody of Joshua to his father, Randy DeShaney, ... [who] shortly thereafter moved to ... Winnebago County, Wisconsin, taking the infant Joshua with him. There he entered into a second marriage, which also ended in divorce.

The Winnebago County authorities first learned that Joshua DeShaney might be a victim of child abuse in January 1982, when his father's second wife complained to the police, at the time of their divorce, that he had previously "hit the boy causing marks and [was] a prime case for child abuse." The Winnebago County Department of Social Services (DSS) interviewed the father, but he denied the accusations, and DSS did not pursue them further. In January 1983, Joshua was admitted to a local hospital with multiple bruises and abrasions. The examining physician suspected child abuse and notified DSS, which immediately obtained an order from a Wisconsin juvenile court placing Joshua in the temporary custody of the hospital. Three days later, the county convened an ad hoc "Child Protection Team"—consisting of a pediatrician, a psychologist, a police detective, the county's lawyer, several DSS caseworkers, and various hospital personnel—to consider Joshua's situation. At this meeting, the Team decided that there was insufficient evidence of child abuse to retain Joshua in the custody of the court.   ...

Based on the recommendation of the Child Protection Team, the juvenile court dismissed the child protection case and returned Joshua to the custody of his father. A month later, emergency room personnel called the DSS caseworker handling Joshua's case to report that he had once again been treated for suspicious injuries. The caseworker concluded that there was no basis for action. For the next six months, the caseworker made monthly visits to the DeShaney home, during which she observed a number of suspicious injuries on Joshua's head; she also noticed that he had not been enrolled in school, and that the girlfriend had not moved out. The caseworker dutifully recorded these incidents in her files, along with her continuing suspicions that someone in the DeShaney household was physically abusing Joshua, but she did nothing more. In November 1983, the emergency room notified DSS that Joshua had been treated once again for injuries that they believed to be caused by child abuse. On the caseworker's next two visits to the

DeShaney home, she was told that Joshua was too ill to see her. Still DSS took no action.

In March 1984, Randy DeShaney beat 4–year-old Joshua so severely that he fell into a life-threatening coma. ... Joshua did not die, but he suffered brain damage so severe that he is expected to spend the rest of his life confined to an institution for the profoundly retarded. Randy DeShaney was subsequently tried and convicted of child abuse.

Joshua and his mother brought this action under 42 U.S.C. § 1983 in the United States District Court for the Eastern District of Wisconsin against respondents Winnebago County, DSS, and various individual employees of DSS. The complaint alleged that respondents had deprived Joshua of his liberty without due process of law, in violation of his rights under the Fourteenth Amendment, by failing to intervene to protect him against a risk of violence at his father's hands of which they knew or should have known. The District Court granted summary judgment for respondents. The Court of Appeals for the Seventh Circuit affirmed. ... We now affirm.

II

The Due Process Clause of the Fourteenth Amendment provides that "no State shall ... deprive any person of life, liberty, or property, without due process of law." Petitioners contend that the State deprived Joshua of his liberty interest in "freedom from ... unjustified intrusions on personal security," see Ingraham v. Wright (1977), by failing to provide him with adequate protection against his father's violence. The claim is one invoking the substantive rather than the procedural component of the Due Process Clause ...: the State ... was categorically obligated to protect him in these circumstances.

But nothing in the language of the Due Process Clause itself requires the State to protect the life, liberty, and property of its citizens against invasion by private actors. The Clause is phrased as a limitation on the State's power to act, not as a guarantee of certain minimal levels of safety and security. ... Nor does history support such an expansive reading of the constitutional text. ... Its purpose was to protect the people from the State, not to ensure that the State protected them from each other. The Framers were content to leave the extent of governmental obligation in the latter area to the democratic political processes.

Consistent with these principles, our cases have recognized that the Due Process Clauses generally confer no affirmative right to governmental aid, even where such aid may be necessary to secure life, liberty, or property interests of which the government itself may not deprive the individual. See, e.g., Harris v. McRae (1980) (no obligation to fund abortions or other medical services); Lindsey v. Normet (1972) (no obligation to provide adequate housing). ... If the Due Process Clause does not require the State to provide its citizens with particular protective services, it follows that the State cannot be held liable under the Clause for injuries that could have been averted had it chosen to provide them.[1] As a general matter, then, we conclude that a State's failure to protect an individual against private violence simply does not constitute a violation of the Due Process Clause.

Petitioners contend, however, that even if the Due Process Clause imposes no affirmative obligation on the State to provide the general public with adequate protective services, such a duty may arise out of certain "special relationships" created or assumed by the State with respect to particular individuals. Petitioners argue that such a "special relationship" existed here because the State knew that Joshua faced a special danger of abuse at his father's hands, and specifically proclaimed, by word and by deed, its intention to protect him against that danger. Having actually undertaken to protect Joshua from this danger—which petitioners concede the State played no part in creating—the State acquired an affirmative "duty," enforceable through the Due Process Clause, to do so in a reasonably competent fashion. Its failure to discharge that duty, so the argument goes, was an abuse of governmental power that so "shocks the conscience," Rochin v. California (1952), as to constitute a substantive due process violation.

We reject this argument. It is true that in certain limited circumstances the Constitution imposes upon the State affirmative duties of care and protection with respect to particular individuals. In Estelle v. Gamble (1976), we recognized that the Eighth Amendment's prohibition against cruel and unusual punishment, made applicable to the States through the Fourteenth Amendment's Due Process Clause, requires the State to provide adequate medical care to incarcerated prisoners. ...

In Youngberg v. Romeo (1982), we [held] that the substantive component of the Fourteenth Amendment's Due Process Clause requires the State to provide involuntarily committed mental patients with such services as are necessary to ensure their "reasonable safety" from themselves and others (dicta indicating that the State is also obligated to provide such individuals with "adequate food, shelter, clothing, and medical care"). ...

But these cases afford petitioners no help. Taken together, they stand only for the proposition that when the State takes a person into its custody and holds him there against his will, the Constitution imposes upon it a corresponding duty to assume some responsibility for his safety and general well-being. ... In the substantive due process analysis, it is the State's affirmative act of restraining the individual's freedom to act on his own behalf—through incarceration, institutionalization, or other similar restraint of personal liberty—which is the "deprivation of liberty" triggering the protections of the Due Process Clause, not its failure to act to protect his liberty interests against harms inflicted by other means.

---

1. The State may not, of course, selectively deny its protective services to certain disfavored minorities without violating the Equal Protection Clause. See Yick Wo v. Hopkins (1886). But no such argument has been made here. [Footnote by the Court.]

The *Estelle-Youngberg* analysis simply has no applicability in the present case. Petitioners concede that the harms Joshua suffered did not occur while he was in the State's custody, but while he was in the custody of his natural father, who was in no sense a state actor.[2] While the State may have been aware of the dangers that Joshua faced in the free world, it played no part in their creation, nor did it do anything to render him any more vulnerable to them. That the State once took temporary custody of Joshua does not alter the analysis, for when it returned him to his father's custody, it placed him in no worse position than that in which he would have been had it not acted at all; the State does not become the permanent guarantor of an individual's safety by having once offered him shelter. Under these circumstances, the State had no constitutional duty to protect Joshua.

It may well be that, by voluntarily undertaking to protect Joshua against a danger it concededly played no part in creating, the State acquired a duty under state tort law to provide him with adequate protection against that danger. ... But the claim here is based on the Due Process Clause of the Fourteenth Amendment, which ... does not transform every tort committed by a state actor into a constitutional violation. ... Because, as explained above, the State had no constitutional duty to protect Joshua against his father's violence, its failure to do so—though calamitous in hindsight—simply does not constitute a violation of the Due Process Clause.

Judges and lawyers, like other humans, are moved by natural sympathy in a case like this to find a way for Joshua and his mother to receive adequate compensation for the grievous harm inflicted upon them. But before yielding to that impulse, it is well to remember once again that the harm was inflicted not by the State of Wisconsin, but by Joshua's father. The most that can be said of the state functionaries in this case is that they stood by and did nothing when suspicious circumstances dictated a more active role for them. In defense of them it must also be said that had they moved too soon to take custody of the son away from the father, they would likely have been met with charges of improperly intruding into the parent-child relationship, charges based on the same Due Process Clause that forms the basis for the present charge of failure to provide adequate protection.

The people of Wisconsin may well prefer a system of liability which would place upon the State and its officials the responsibility for failure to act in situations such as the present one. They may create such a system, if they do not have it already, by changing the tort law of the State in accordance with the regular lawmaking process. But they

---

2. Had the State by the affirmative exercise of its power removed Joshua from free society and placed him in a foster home operated by its agents, we might have a situation sufficiently analogous to incarceration or institutionalization to give rise to an affirmative duty to protect. Indeed, several Courts of Appeals have held, by analogy to *Estelle and Youngberg*, that the State may be held liable under the Due Process Clause for failing to protect children in foster homes from mistreatment at the hands of their foster parents. We express no view on the validity of this analogy, however. ... [Footnote by the Court.]

should not have it thrust upon them by this Court's expansion of the Due Process Clause of the Fourteenth Amendment.

Affirmed.

Justice **BRENNAN**, with whom Justice **MARSHALL** and Justice **BLACKMUN** join, dissenting. . . .

It may well be . . . that the Due Process Clause as construed by our prior cases creates no general right to basic governmental services. That, however, is not the question presented here. . . . No one, in short, has asked the Court to proclaim that, as a general matter, the Constitution safeguards positive as well as negative liberties. . . . In a constitutional setting that distinguishes sharply between action and inaction, one's characterization of the misconduct alleged under § 1983 may effectively decide the case. Thus, by leading off with a discussion (and rejection) of the idea that the Constitution imposes on the States an affirmative duty to take basic care of their citizens, the Court foreshadows—perhaps even preordains—its conclusion that no duty existed even on the specific facts before us. . . .

The Court's baseline is the absence of positive rights in the Constitution and a concomitant suspicion of any claim that seems to depend on such rights. From this perspective, the DeShaneys' claim is first and foremost about inaction (the failure, here, of respondents to take steps to protect Joshua), and only tangentially about action (the establishment of a state program specifically designed to help children like Joshua). And from this perspective, holding these Wisconsin officials liable where the only difference between this case and one involving a general claim to protective services is Wisconsin's establishment and operation of a program to protect children—would seem to punish an effort that we should seek to promote.

I would begin from the opposite direction. I would focus first on the action that Wisconsin *has* taken with respect to Joshua and children like him, rather than on the actions that the State failed to take. Such a method is not new to this Court. Both *Estelle* and *Youngberg* began by emphasizing that the States had confined J. W. Gamble to prison and Nicholas Romeo to a psychiatric hospital. This initial action rendered these people helpless to help themselves or to seek help from persons unconnected to the government. . . .

. . . I would read *Youngberg* and *Estelle* to stand for the much more generous proposition that, if a State cuts off private sources of aid and then refuses aid itself, it cannot wash its hands of the harm that results from its inaction. . . .

Wisconsin has established a child-welfare system specifically designed to help children like Joshua. Wisconsin law places upon the local departments of social services such as respondent (DSS or Department) a duty to investigate reported instances of child abuse. While other governmental bodies and private persons are largely responsible for the reporting of possible cases of child abuse, Wisconsin law channels all such reports to the local departments of social services for evaluation and, if necessary, further action. Even when it is the sheriff's office or police department that receives a report of suspected child abuse, that report is referred to local social services departments for action; the only exception to this occurs when the reporter fears for the child's immediate safety. In this way, Wisconsin law invites—indeed, directs—citizens and other governmental entities to depend on local departments of social services such as respondent to protect children from abuse. ...

In these circumstances, a private citizen, or even a person working in a government agency other than DSS, would doubtless feel that her job was done as soon as she had reported her suspicions of child abuse to DSS. Through its child-welfare program, in other words, the State of Wisconsin has relieved ordinary citizens and governmental bodies other than the Department of any sense of obligation to do anything more than report their suspicions of child abuse to DSS. If DSS ignores or dismisses these suspicions, no one will step in to fill the gap. Wisconsin's child-protection program thus effectively confined Joshua DeShaney within the walls of Randy DeShaney's violent home until such time as DSS took action to remove him. Conceivably, then, children like Joshua are made worse off by the existence of this program when the persons and entities charged with carrying it out fail to do their jobs.

It simply belies reality, therefore, to contend that the State "stood by and did nothing" with respect to Joshua. Through its child-protection program, the State actively intervened in Joshua's life and, by virtue of this intervention, acquired ever more certain knowledge that Joshua was in grave danger. ...

As the Court today reminds us, "the Due Process Clause of the Fourteenth Amendment was intended to prevent government 'from abusing [its] power, or employing it as an instrument of oppression.' " My disagreement with the Court arises from its failure to see that inaction can be every bit as abusive of power as action, that oppression can result when a State undertakes a vital duty and then ignores it. Today's opinion construes the Due Process Clause to permit a State to displace private sources of protection and then, at the critical moment, to shrug its shoulders and turn away from the harm that it has promised to try to prevent. Because I cannot agree that our Constitution is indifferent to such indifference, I respectfully dissent.

Justice **BLACKMUN**, dissenting.

Today, the Court purports to be the dispassionate oracle of the law, unmoved by "natural sympathy." But, in this pretense, the Court itself retreats into a sterile formalism which prevents it from recognizing either the facts of the case before it or the legal norms that should apply to those facts. As Justice Brennan demonstrates, the facts here involve not mere passivity, but active state intervention in the life of Joshua DeShaney—intervention that triggered a fundamental duty to aid the boy once the State learned of the severe danger to which he was exposed.

The Court fails to recognize this duty because it attempts to draw a sharp and rigid line between action and inaction. But such formalistic reasoning has no place in the interpretation of the broad and stirring Clauses of the Fourteenth Amendment. Indeed, I submit that these Clauses were designed, at least in part, to undo the formalistic legal reasoning that infected antebellum jurisprudence, which the late Professor Robert Cover analyzed so effectively in his significant work entitled *Justice Accused* (1975).

Like the antebellum judges who denied relief to fugitive slaves, the Court today claims that its decision, however harsh, is compelled by existing legal doctrine. On the contrary, the question presented by this case is an open one, and our Fourteenth Amendment precedents may be read more broadly or narrowly depending upon how one chooses to read them. Faced with the choice, I would adopt a "sympathetic" reading, one which comports with dictates of fundamental justice and recognizes that compassion need not be exiled from the province of judging. ...

Poor Joshua! Victim of repeated attacks by an irresponsible, bullying, cowardly, and intemperate father, and abandoned by respondents who placed him in a dangerous predicament and who knew or learned what was going on, and yet did essentially nothing except, as the Court revealingly observes, "dutifully recorded these incidents in [their] files." It is a sad commentary upon American life, and constitutional principles—so full of late of patriotic fervor and proud proclamations about "liberty and justice for all," that this child, Joshua DeShaney, now is assigned to live out the remainder of his life profoundly retarded. Joshua and his mother, as petitioners here, deserve—but now are denied by this Court—the opportunity to have the facts of their case considered in the light of the constitutional protection that 42 U.S. C. § 1983 is meant to provide.

Editors' Notes

(1) **Query:** To what extent is the disagreement between Rehnquist and Brennan a disagreement about WHAT "the Constitution" the Court should interpret includes and what its functions are? Is the constitutional text merely a charter of "negative liberties" or does it also protect "positive liberties"? That is, does it simply protect the people from oppression by the government, or does it also impose affirmative obligations upon government to provide basic services, such as police protection, necessary to life, liberty, and property?

(2) "State action" is a concept that has bedeviled constitutional interpretation since ratification of the Fourteenth Amendment. As Brennan mentioned, and the Court has sometimes held, "inaction" can deprive citizens of their rights as effectively as "action" and thus may violate either the Fourteenth or Fifteenth Amendment. For an analysis of the literature and cases, see Gerald Gunther, *Constitutional Law* (12th ed.; Westbury, NY: Foundation Press, 1991), pp. 891–925.

V

Constitutional Democracy in the Crucible of Crisis

Chapter 19: Constitutional Interpretation and Emergency Powers

The essays, cases, speeches, debates, notes, and queries in this book have stressed the necessity, importance, and complexity of constitutional interpretation. As practiced in the United States over the past two centuries, this enterprise, despite recurrent failures, has enjoyed a great measure of success. The country prospers; there is a greater degree of both constitutionalism and democracy in the system than there was in 1787. Not since the Civil War has there been a widespread, fundamental challenge to the very nature of the political system. Still, no one who experienced the domestic crises of the New Deal in the 1930s, of the Red Scare during the Cold War, or of the Civil Rights Movement during the 1950s and '60s can claim to have lived in times of constitutional calm. And there is no assurance that this enterprise will continue to be successful in preserving constitutional democracy.

There are additional kinds of crisis, those brought on by war or terrorism. Looking back with the omniscience of hindsight, it is easy to judge that dire threats to national security have been rare; but honesty would compel us to acknowledge that had we lived in other times, our perceptions of those events might have been different. And, the world in which we now live is rife with war and rumors of war, of terrorism and threats of terrorism. It is likely that, when future crises occur, decision makers will act even more swiftly in self-defense but not necessarily more wisely than have their predecessors.

A precipitate response, of course, generates its own kind of crisis, a crisis of legitimacy for the entire political system and its ideals, as Korematsu v. United States (1944; reprinted below p. 1383)[1] so dreadfully illustrates. Perhaps the most difficult problem that will confront future constitutional interpreters is that of how to save both the country and its constitution.

---

1. See also the analysis of this case in Chapter 4.

19

Constitutional Interpretation and Emergency Powers

Most of the problems of constitutional interpretation discussed in previous chapters take on added urgency in emergencies. Severe crises often demand immediate action, and fastidious regard for constitutional rights or democratic processes may endanger the nation's survival. "It is in vain," Madison wrote in *Federalist* No. 41,

> to oppose constitutional barriers to the impulse of self-preservation. It is worse than in vain; because it plants in the Constitution itself necessary usurpations of power, every precedent of which is a germ of unnecessary and multiplied repetitions.

Hamilton was even more blunt. "These powers," he wrote in *Federalist* No. 23 about national defense, "ought to exist without limitation, *because it is impossible to foresee or define the extent and variety of the means which may be necessary* to *satisfy them.*" (Italics in original.) He continued:

> The circumstances that endanger the safety of nations are infinite, and for this reason no constitutional shackles can wisely be imposed on the power to which the care of it is committed. This power ought to be co-extensive with all the possible combinations of such circumstances; and ought to be under the direction of the same councils which are appointed to preside over the common defense.

Despite Jefferson's opposition to the Alien and Sedition Acts (see the Kentucky Resolutions, reprinted above p. 354), his general views on emergency powers were rather close to those of Hamilton. Because of his insistence on "strict construction" of the constitutional text, Jefferson did not advocate a broad view of governmental powers to cope with emergencies; rather, he argued for duty to a higher authority:

> A strict observance of the written laws is doubtless *one* of the high duties of a good citizen, but it is not *the highest*. The laws of necessity, of self-preservation, of saving our country when in danger, are of higher obligation.[1]

---

1. Letter to J.B. Colvin, Sept. 20, 1810; reprinted below, p. 1367.

Lincoln was equally candid in justifying his use of military tribunals to try civilians:

> Was it possible to lose the nation, and yet preserve the constitution? By general law life *and* limb must be protected; yet often a limb must be amputated to save a life; but a life is never wisely given to save a limb. I felt that measures, otherwise unconstitutional, might become lawful, by becoming indispensable to the preservation of the constitution, through the preservation of the nation.[2]

A defender of Jefferson and Lincoln could argue that they acted on a proposition derived from structural considerations: Preserving the broader constitutional system can justify temporary violations of the document's specific terms. A critic might reply that this proposition suggests that "the Constitution" constitutes us as a people only in good times and thus is less than essential to our public life. Such was the Supreme Court's reaction in Ex parte Milligan (1866; reprinted below, p. 1376) to Lincoln's war-time suspension of habeas corpus. The Court declared the President could not authorize military tribunals to try civilians in areas where actual hostilities had not closed civilian courts. Having prudently found ways to avoid the issue during the war [see Ex parte Vallandigham (1864)], the Court now courageously affirmed: "The Constitution of the United States is a law for rulers and people, equally in war and in peace, and covers with the shield of its protection all classes of men, at all times, and under all circumstances."

I.   PRESERVING "THE CONSTITUTION" AND THE NATION

In practice, emergencies seem to confront judges and other officials with three general alternatives. They can (1) avoid at least the appearance of unconstitutional action by pretending to ignore the document; (2) formally suspend some (perhaps all?) of the text's guarantees; or (3) interpret that text or the broader constitution to accommodate claims of national security with those of individual rights or democratic processes.

A.   Ignoring the Constitutional Text

When public officials believe they have "good" reason to violate the exact terms of the constitutional text, they may well ask: WHY interpret? Or even When should we interpret? To ignore the document may be more prudent than to try to interpret in an open and formal way, at least for the time being. Such was Jefferson's decision in 1803 when he purchased the Louisiana Territory despite

---

2. To A.G. Hodges, April 4, 1864; Roy P. Basler, ed., *The Collected Works of Abraham Lincoln* (New Brunswick: Rutgers University Press, 1953), VII, 281.

his belief that the national government lacked authority to acquire
new lands. "It appears to me," Thomas Paine wrote him, "to be
one of those cases with which the Constitution has nothing to do"[3]
—in effect, speaking to the question of WHAT and limiting "the
Constitution's" reach. Jefferson's solution was different, though he
also spoke to the question of WHAT more than he realized. Per-
ceiving a grave danger to national security in foreign control of the
mouth of the Mississippi—the Napoleonic wars were raging in
Europe, and the territory had been traded between France and
Spain—and presented with an opportunity to remove that peril as
well as to acquire an empire at a bargain price, he signed the treaty
and urged his supporters in the Senate to consent to it "with as
little debate as possible, & particularly so far as respects the
constitutional difficulty." He then explained his reasoning:

> Our peculiar security is in possession of a written Constitution.
> Let us not make it a blank paper by construction. I say the same
> as to the opinion of those who consider the grant of the treaty
> making power as boundless. If it is, we have no Constitution.
> ... Let us go on then perfecting it, by adding, by way of
> amendment to the Constitution, those powers which time & trial
> show are still wanting.[4]

Ignoring both the constitutional text as well as the larger
constitution may be a more frequent occurrence than Americans
imagine. Especially during the years of Richard Nixon's presidency
but also under earlier presidents, the CIA, FBI, and IRS often spied
on, harassed, and sometimes silenced political dissidents. Most
notorious was the FBI's obsession with Rev. Martin Luther King, Jr.
Recognizing the minister's popular appeal, J. Edgar Hoover, the
FBI's director, reasoned that if King abandoned his advocacy of non-
violence and brotherly love, he could start a revolution. The
Bureau then began a campaign to discredit the African–American
leader. "No holds were barred," the official in charge of the
operation admitted. Agents followed King, tapped his telephone,
and bugged his hotel rooms. They even threatened to make public
allegedly damaging tapes unless he committed suicide.[5] Walter
Sullivan, then Assistant Director of the FBI, conceded that the
campaign had not been "an isolated phenomenon ... this was the
practice of the Bureau down through the years." He added:

---

3. Quoted in Dumas Malone, *Jefferson the President: First Term, 1801–1805* (Boston:
Little, Brown, 1970), p. 318.

4. To Senator Wilson Cary Nicholas, Sept. 7, 1803; reprinted in Paul L. Ford, ed., *The
Works of Thomas Jefferson* (New York: Putnam's, 1905), X, 10–11n. As noted below,
Jefferson wrote out several drafts of a constitutional amendment, but never formally
proposed such a change.

5. See the 7 volumes of *Hearings* and 6 volumes of the *Final Report* of the Church
Committee: U.S. Senate, Select Committee to Study Governmental Operations with
Respect to Intelligence Activities, 94th Cong., 2d sess. (1975–76); Book III of the *Final
Report* contains a 106-page summary of the FBI's efforts to "get" Dr. King.

> [N]ever once did I hear anybody, including myself, raise the
> question, is this course of action which we have agreed upon
> lawful, is it legal, is it ethical or moral?   We never gave any
> thought to this realm of reasoning.   ... [6]

Nor, of course, did anyone give adequate thought to the query: "Is
it constitutional?"

The Bureau's campaign against King should remind us of the
claim of Chapter 1 that one of the primary reasons for constitutional
interpretation is to reaffirm commitment to the constitutional document.   The kindest thing to be said about the Bureau is that its
leadership no longer regarded the constitutional text as expressing
an effective set of means to achieve the nation's proclaimed goal of
"domestic Tranquility"—hence the Bureau's violation of the document's provisions in the name of domestic peace.   Although one
might admire the purity of Jefferson's motives and his resolve—on
which he failed to act—to seek a constitutional amendment to ratify
what he thought was a necessary but unconstitutional act,[7] his
decision to ignore the constitutional text set a dangerous precedent.

B.   Suspending the Constitutional Text

Another solution involves formally suspending some provisions
of the constitutional text during emergencies.   The document itself
provides for suspension of several safeguards for individual rights.[8]
The most important, Article I, § 9, reads:

> The privilege of the writ of habeas corpus shall not be
> suspended, unless when in cases of rebellion or invasion the
> public safety may require it.

Because habeas corpus is an order from a judge to the civilian or
military official who has custody of a prisoner to bring the prisoner
before the judge and justify his detention, its suspension allows
arbitrary arrest and imprisonment—practices, if maintained over a
long period, incompatible with any constitutional democracy,
though perhaps necessary for short periods of emergency.

Suspension of the writ raises several constitutional questions.
(See Ex parte Merryman [1861; reprinted below, p. 1369]; Lincoln's Message to Congress of July 4, 1861 [reprinted below, p.
1373], and Ex parte Milligan [1866; reprinted below, p. 1376]).
First are questions of WHAT, of purposes and inclusion.   In speaking of emergency powers, Jefferson and Lincoln saw the document

---

6. Quoted in Church Committee, *Final Report*, supra note 5, III, 135.

7. Ford reprints several of Jefferson's drafts of a possible constitutional amendment;
supra note 4, X, 3–12.

8. See, for example, the Third Amendment, allowing quartering of troops in civilian
homes during wartime, "in a manner prescribed by law"; and the Fifth Amendment,
suspending the right to indictment by grand jury of members of the militia "when in actual
service in time of war or public danger," and allowing government to take, "with just
compensation," private property for public use.

as mostly prescribing means to achieve the goals the Preamble set out. This conception makes it easier to justify deviations from the specific terms of the text either to save the nation or to aggrandize power. For both presidents, "the Constitution" meant pretty much only the text. Widening the conception of "the Constitution" would widen the focus of debate to what the text plus underlying political theories, previous interpretations, and historic practices and traditions would allow. Debate within that broader arena might restrict the sort of options legitimately open to government.[9]

Second are questions of WHO. Does the location in Article I of this authority mean that only Congress (subject to the usual presidential veto) can authorize suspension? Or is that textual location a mere accident of drafting, which leaves it to the President, alone if necessary, to suspend the writ in order to "take care that the laws be faithfully executed" and to "protect and defend the Constitution," as required by Article II?

What role, if any, do the constitutional text and the broader constitution leave to judges in deciding when the elected branches can suspend judicial power to protect individual rights? If the proper institution suspends the writ, may judges legitimately inquire whether "the public safety" in fact requires that action? It is worth noting that the Basic Law of the Federal Republic of Germany has elaborate provisions for suspension of constitutional guarantees and processes but with the provisos that the constitutional text cannot be amended during such time [10] nor the jurisdiction of the Constitutional Court suspended without the consent of the justices themselves.[11]

After problems of WHO come questions of HOW interpreters— legislative, executive, or judicial—decide when suspension is legitimate. What are the standards? Indeed, are there any standards beyond a decision maker's (mis)perception of peril during hectic moments of crisis? And if an initial suspension was legitimate, HOW does one determine the length of time it remains valid?

The effects of suspending habeas corpus may be immense. With the writ suspended, a President who enjoyed the support of Congress could punish any person for any offense before a court martial, without normal due process. Although such actions would, of course, be unconstitutional, they would remain effective because no judicial remedy would be available.

Further questions arise. In an emergency, might some federal official (the President, say, pursuant to power delegated by a pliant Congress) suspend all constitutional limitations on his power, in-

---

9. See John E. Finn, *Constitutions in Crisis: Political Violence and the Rule of Law* (Oxford: Oxford University Press, 1991), espec. ch. 1.

10. Art. 115e.

11. Art. 115g.

cluding elections? The history of such actions in other constitutional democracies—Weimar Germany before the rise of Hitler, for
example—does not radiate happy omens. Yet it is hardly impossible for a crisis brought on, say, by a major war, massive terrorism,
huge natural calamity, to overwhelm the usual governmental processes.

Some observers have suggested that a total suspension of
constitutional limitations and safeguards may on occasion be unavoidable. But one of these scholars, John E. Finn, has attached a
significant limitation: The government could not legitimately suspend its commitment to constitutionalism. That is, the government
must continue to observe such basic requirements as respect for the
worth and dignity of each citizen, though it may, as a temporary
measure, suspend any or all of the document's specific limitations
and procedures.[12]

C. Interpreting the Constitutional Text

Some observers interpret the constitutional document as granting powers sufficiently broad to deal with any emergency. During
the First World War, Charles Evans Hughes claimed that "we have a
fighting constitution" and the power to wage war "is a power to
wage war successfully." [13] Even Justice Sutherland, the prophet of a
constitutional text forever fixed in meaning said:

> The provisions of the federal Constitution, undoubtedly, are
> pliable in the sense that in appropriate cases they have the
> capacity of bringing within their grasp every new condition. But
> their *meaning* is changeless; it is only their *application* which is
> extensible. (Minnesota Moratorium Case [1934; reprinted above,
> p. 210].)

That the founding generation contemplated emergencies is
clear. Not only do we have Madison and Hamilton's argument in
the Federalist, but the Preamble lists "the common defence" and
"domestic Tranquility" among the nation's fundamental objectives;
and Article I specifically gives Congress authority to establish armed
forces, punish piracy (an ancient form of terrorism), declare war,
and call out the militia to repel invasions or insurrections. Moreover, Article IV guarantees each state a republican form of government and imposes on the federal government additional obligations
to repel invasions of the states and put down insurrections there.
These provisions, Justice Frankfurter wrote in Korematsu v. United

---

12. Finn, supra note 9, pp. 21–44. For a quite different analysis, but one receptive to
the notion that a temporary "constitutional dictatorship" may be the least of evils in the
real world, see Carl J. Friedrich, *Constitutional Government and Democracy* (4th ed.;
Waltham, MA: Blaisdell, 1968), ch. 25.

13. "War Powers under the Constitution," 42 *Am.Bar Ass'n Rep.* 232, 238 (1917).
Hughes had resigned from the Court in 1916 to run against Woodrow Wilson in the
presidential election of that year. He returned to the Court as Chief Justice in 1930.

States (1944; reprinted below, p. 1383), "are as much part of the Constitution as provisions looking to a nation at peace."

Thus some interpreters have claimed that the constitutional text provides means for meeting emergencies. Yet the document can hardly be adequate to *any* emergency, for we can imagine catastrophes that would make it physically impossible to honor constitutional provisions, even when those provisions are stretched to the limits of interpretive flexibility. During the Second World War, the British, facing an enemy 20 miles away across the English Channel, thought it necessary to suspend national elections until peacetime. Because the requirement for parliamentary elections at least every five years was formally embodied only in a statute (though it was certainly deeply grounded in tradition), constitutional interpretation was easier than it would have been in the United States. How flexible can an interpreter render the President's "Term of four Years," for example?

The hard fact is that, in times of severe crisis, official interpreters have been more concerned with governmental policies relating to security than with fidelity to the words of the constitutional text. *Milligan* thus sounded a hymn to constitutional means *after* the Civil War. When the bullets were flying, the justices were careful not to oppose Lincoln's court martialing civilians. So, too, *during* World War II, the justices agonized over Hirabayashi v. United States (1943) and Korematsu v. United States (1944; reprinted below, p. 1383); but, in the name of "military necessity," they upheld the government's harsh and discriminatory treatment of American citizens of Japanese ancestry. *After* the war, when confronted with a case concerning martial law in Hawaii during a time when the military had excellent reasons to fear invasion, the Court leaped to the defense of civil liberties.[14]

This pattern of interpretation led Clinton Rossiter to conclude that we have two constitutions, one for peace and one for national emergencies.[15] We would prefer to say that, in times of national emergency, the constitutional text and the broader constitution may significantly deviate. When interpreters "accommodate" the claims of necessity against the plain words of the document, the winner has typically, though not always, been emergency powers.[16] When the crisis has passed, the claim of necessity sometimes turns out to have been justified, as during the Civil War, with guerrillas in the border states and Indiana. More often, however, the claim of necessity turns out to have been fraudulent, as it was in the persecution of "seditious" subversives and "alien enemies" during

---

14. Duncan v. Kahanamoku (1946).

15. *The Supreme Court and the Commander in Chief*, expanded ed. with Richard P. Longaker (Ithaca: Cornell University Press, 1976).

16. United States v. United States District Court (1972; reprinted below, p. 1391) is one of the most significant exceptions.

the administration of John Adams, the deportation of foreigners after World War I, in *Korematsu* during World War II, the exposure of "communist sympathizers" during the McCarthy era, and the persecution of the "radicals" who opposed Richard Nixon from 1968 until 1974.

II. *INTER ARMES SILENT LEGES?*

America's record of constitutional violations in the name of survival can hardly be squared with a constitutional system that would enshrine human dignity and the life of reason as national ideals. A century after *Milligan* Earl Warren preached for the Court a sermon whose message has often been ignored:

> "[N]ational defense" cannot be deemed an end in itself. . . . Implicit in the term . . . is the notion of defending those values and ideas which set this Nation apart. . . . It would indeed be ironic if, in the name of national defense, we would sanction the subversion of one of those liberties . . . which makes the defense of the Nation worthwhile.[17]

The usual response is that America's record is better than that of other nations, our delinquencies have been few and temporary, and the system has survived to right its wrongs. In addition, the argument goes, good democrats must trust their elected officials to use emergency powers in the public interest, not to perpetuate their hold on office. This argument has its virtues.

Yet democrats need only remember *Korematsu* to temper their optimism that the political process will protect hated minorities. Jefferson's comment on the partisan prosecutions of the Adams administration remains in point: "In questions of power then let no more be heard of confidence in man, but bind him down from mischief by the chains of the Constitution."[18] Lest constitutionalists grow smug, they need to recall that textual guarantees, under the oversight of an independent judiciary, did no more to protect the Nisei against concentration camps than did democratic political processes.

The nation's record in emergencies indicates that constitutional forms fare poorly when people are divided by racial and ideological hatreds and when they face bullets or economic ruin. One obvious lesson is that constitutional maintenance is a much greater task than judges can handle on their own. If applying the law of "the Constitution" (or even inventing that law) is a duty of judges, achieving and maintaining racial toleration, economic health, social peace, and other conditions that favor constitutionalism seem tasks primarily for elected politicians.

---

17. United States v. Robel (1967).

18. Kentucky Resolutions (1798; reprinted above, p. 354).

Yet politicians, too, have limited power in a political culture accustomed to constitutional democracy. Because officials are answerable to their constituents, policies that maintain constitutionalism will eventually fail unless the public wants those policies to succeed—or unless these officials can persuade the public to want those policies. This generalization also applies to decisions upon which the political system's survival depends. Maintaining "the Constitution" thus proves to be a complex task in which everyone has a part—a task that judges share with elected politicians and ordinary citizens.

SELECTED BIBLIOGRAPHY

Barber, Sotirios A. *On What the Constitution Means* (Baltimore: Johns Hopkins University Press, 1984), ch. 4.

Bessette, Joseph M., and Jeffrey Tulis, *The Presidency in the Constitutional Order* (Baton Rouge: Louisiana State University Press, 1981).

Corwin, Edward S. *The Presidency: Office and Powers* (4th ed.; New York: New York University Press, 1957), ch. 6.

————. *Of Presidential Prerogative* (Whittier, CA: Whittier College, 1954).

Fairman, Charles. *The Law of Martial Rule* (2d. ed.; Chicago: University of Chicago Press, 1943).

Finn, John E. *Constitutions in Crisis: Political Violence and the Rule of Law* (Oxford: Oxford University Press, 1991), ch. 1.

Friedrich, Carl J. *Constitutional Government and Democracy* (4th ed.; Waltham, MA: Blaisdell, 1968), ch. 25.

Genovese, Michael A. *The Supreme Court, the Constitution, and Presidential Power* (Lanham, MD: University Press of America, 1980).

Pritchett, C. Herman. *Constitutional Law of the Federal System* (Englewood Cliffs, NJ: Prentice–Hall, 1984). ch. 17.

Pyle, Christopher H., and Richard M. Pious, *The President, Congress, and the Constitution* (New York: The Free Press, 1984), chs. 4–5.

Rossiter, Clinton. *Constitutional Dictatorship* (Princeton: Princeton University Press, 1948).

————. *The Supreme Court and the Commander in Chief*, expanded ed., with Richard P. Longaker (Ithaca: Cornell University Press, 1976).

Winterton, George.   "The Concept of Extra–Constitutional Executive Power in Domestic Affairs," 7 *Hastings Con.L.Q.* 7 (1979).

"To lose our country by a scrupulous adherence to written law, would be to lose the law itself, with life, liberty, property and all those who are enjoying them with us; thus absurdly sacrificing the end to the means."

THOMAS JEFFERSON TO J.B. COLVIN*
(1810).

As the introductory essay to this chapter points out, as President, Jefferson believed that the federal government lacked constitutional authority to acquire foreign lands. On the other hand, he saw ownership of the Louisiana Territory as critical to national security. His solution to the dilemma was to pretend to ignore rather than to interpret the constitutional text, that is, to purchase the territory without trying to justify the purchase as constitutional. This strategy succeeded partly because many officials did not share Jefferson's belief that the document precluded acquisition of foreign territory. Even in retirement, however, he remained troubled by the larger question of fidelity to law in time of crisis.

Monticello, September 20, 1810

SIR . . .

The question you propose, whether circumstances do not sometimes occur, which make it a duty in officers of high trust, to assume authorities beyond the law, is easy of solution in principle, but sometimes embarrassing in practice. A strict observance of the written laws is doubtless *one* of the high duties of a good citizen, but it is not *the highest.* The laws of necessity, of self-preservation, of saving our country when in danger, are of higher obligation. To lose our country by a scrupulous adherence to written law, would be to lose the law itself, with life, liberty, property and all those who are enjoying them with us; thus absurdly sacrificing the end to the means. When, in the battle of Germantown, General Washington's army was annoyed from Chew's house, he did not hesitate to plant his cannon against it, although the property of a citizen. When he besieged Yorktown, he leveled the suburbs, feeling that the laws of property must be postponed to the safety of the nation. While the army was before York, the Governor of Virginia took horses, carriages, provisions and even men by force, to enable that army to stay together till it could master the public enemy; and he was justified. A ship at sea in distress for provisions, meets

* Andrew A. Lipscomb, ed., *The Writings of Thomas Jefferson* (Washington, D.C.: The Thomas Jefferson Memorial Ass'n, 1903), XII, 418–422.

another having abundance, yet refusing a supply; the law of self-preservation authorizes the distressed to take a supply by force. In all these cases, the unwritten laws of necessity, of self-preservation, and of the public safety, control the written laws of *meum* and *tuum*. ...

... After the affair of the *Chesapeake*,* we thought war a very possible result. Our magazines were illy provided with some necessary articles, nor had any appropriations been made for their purchase. We ventured, however, to provide them, and to place our country in safety; and stating the case to Congress, they sanctioned the act.

To proceed to the conspiracy of [Aaron] Burr, and particularly to General Wilkinson's situation in New Orleans. In judging this case, we are bound to consider the state of the information, correct and incorrect, which he then possessed. He expected Burr and his band from above, a British fleet from below, and he knew there was a formidable conspiracy within the city. Under these circumstances, was he justifiable, 1st, in seizing notorious conspirators? On this there can be but two opinions: one, of the guilty and their accomplices; the other, that of all honest men. 2d. In sending them to the seat of government, when the written law gave them a right to trial in the territory? The danger of their rescue, of their continuing their machinations, the tardiness and weakness of the law, apathy of the judges, active patronage of the whole tribe of lawyers, unknown disposition of the juries, an hourly expectation of the enemy, salvation of the city, and of the Union itself, which would have been convulsed to its centre, had that conspiracy succeeded; all these constituted a law of necessity and self-preservation, and rendered the *salus populi* supreme over the written law. The officer who is called to act on this superior ground, does indeed risk himself on the justice of the controlling powers of the Constitution, and his station makes it his duty to incur that risk. But those controlling powers, and his fellow citizens generally, are bound to judge according to the circumstances under which he acted. They are not to transfer the information of this place or moment to the time and place of his action; but to put themselves into his situation. We knew here that there never was danger of a British fleet from below, and that Burr's band was crushed before it reached the Mississippi. But General Wilkinson's information was very different, and he could act on no other.**

From these examples and principles you may see what I think on the question proposed. They do not go to the case of persons charged

---

* In 1807, just off Norfolk, a British warship attacked and disabled the American frigate *Chesapeake,* boarded her, and took off seamen whom the British alleged had earlier deserted from the royal navy. The circumstances of the attack—the British ship had come close aboard under the pretense of asking the *Chesapeake* to accept mail—as well as the kidnapping of American seamen and the death of others during the attack—provoked loud demands for war.—**Eds.**

** The situation was more complex than Jefferson knew. Modern research in the Spanish archives in Madrid has shown that General Wilkinson was on the payroll of the Spanish government, who wanted Burr's expedition stopped before he took over territory that Spain then claimed. Thus Wilkinson probably well knew that the "information" he was sending to Jefferson was false.—**Eds.**

with petty duties, where consequences are trifling, and time allowed for a legal course, nor to authorize them to take such cases out of the written law. In these, the example of overleaping the law is of greater evil than a strict adherence to its imperfect provisions. It is incumbent on those only who accept of great charges, to risk themselves on great occasions, when the safety of the nation, or some of its very high interests are at stake. An officer is bound to obey orders; yet he would be a bad one who should do it in cases for which they were not intended, and which involved the most important consequences. The line of discrimination between cases may be difficult; but the good officer is bound to draw it at his own peril, and throw himself on the justice of his country and the rectitude of his motives. ...

"He certainly does not faithfully execute the laws, if he takes upon himself legislative power, by suspending the writ of habeas corpus, and the judicial power also, by arresting and imprisoning a person without due process of law."

EX PARTE MERRYMAN

17 Fed.Cases 144 (C.C.Md., 1861).

At 2 a.m. on May 25, 1861, Union troops entered the home of John Merryman outside Baltimore—which had recently experienced pro-Southern riots—arrested him for helping destroy several railroad bridges, and brought him to Fort McHenry. Merryman was a prominent local citizen, a state legislator, a member of a state unit of cavalry, and strongly Confederate in his sympathies. The military allowed him to see his attorney, who filed the next day in the U.S. circuit court (then the name of the federal courts that conducted trials in serious cases) in Baltimore for habeas corpus. As was also then required by law, Supreme Court justices "rode circuit"—presided at circuit court. Baltimore fell within the jurisdiction of Chief Justice Roger Brooke Taney. He issued the writ, ordering General George Cadwalader, commanding Fort McHenry, to come to court with Merryman on May 27 and justify the detention.

The General did not appear, but sent a letter explaining that Merryman was guilty of treasonous acts and also that the President had authorized him (Cadwalader) to suspend the writ of habeas corpus. Furious, Taney issued a writ of attachment (arrest) against the General. On May 28, the marshal returned to court and explained he had tried to serve the writ but had been denied entrance to the fort. Taney then inquired why the marshal had not summoned a posse, and the marshal explained that such a remedy was likely to be ineffective against federal troops. Still frustrated, the Chief Justice ruled that the President had no authority to suspend the writ and thus could not authorize anyone else to do so.*

TANEY, Circuit Justice. . . .

As the case comes before me . . . I understand that the president not only claims the right to suspend the writ of habeas corpus himself, at his discretion, but to delegate that discretionary power to a military officer, and to leave it to him to determine whether he will or will not obey judicial process that may be served upon him. No official notice has been given to the courts of justice, or to the public, by proclamation or otherwise, that the president claimed this power. . . . And I certainly listened to it with some surprise, for I had supposed it to be one of those points of constitutional law upon which there was no difference of opinion, and that it was admitted on all hands, that the privilege of the writ could not be suspended, except by act of congress. . . .

The clause of the constitution, which authorizes the suspension of the privilege of the writ of habeas corpus, is in the 9th section of the first article. This article is devoted to the legislative department of the United States, and has not the slightest reference to the executive department. It begins by providing "that all legislative powers therein granted, shall be vested in a congress of the United States, which shall consist of a senate and house of representatives." And after prescribing the manner in which these two branches of the legislative department shall be chosen, it proceeds to enumerate specifically the legislative powers which it thereby grants [and legislative powers which it expressly prohibits]; and at the conclusion of this specification, a clause is inserted giving congress "the power to make all laws which shall be necessary and proper for carrying into execution the foregoing powers, and all other powers vested by this constitution in the government of the United States, or in any department or officer thereof." . . .

It is true, that . . . congress is, of necessity, the judge of whether the public safety does or does not require it [suspension of the writ of habeas corpus]; and their judgment is conclusive. But the introduction of these words is a standing admonition to the legislative body of the danger of suspending it, and of the extreme caution they should exercise, before they give the government of the United States such power over the liberty of a citizen.

It is the second article of the constitution that provides for the organization of the executive department, enumerates the powers conferred on it, and prescribes its duties. And if the high power over the liberty of the citizen now claimed, was intended to be conferred on the president, it would undoubtedly be found in plain words in this article; but there is not a word in it that can furnish the slightest ground to justify the exercise of the power. . . .

---

* When he had been Attorney General, Taney had drafted Andrew Jackson's veto of the bank bill (reprinted above, p. 313), which asserted an independent presidential power to interpret "the Constitution."—**Eds.**

The only power, therefore, which the president possesses, where the "life, liberty or property" of a private citizen is concerned, is the power and duty prescribed in the third section of the second article, which requires "that he shall take care that the laws shall be faithfully executed." He is not authorized to execute them himself, or through agents or officers, civil or military, appointed by himself, but he is to take care that they be faithfully carried into execution, as they are expounded and adjudged by the co-ordinate branch of the government to which that duty is assigned by the constitution. It is thus made his duty to come in aid of the judicial authority, if it shall be resisted by a force too strong to be overcome without the assistance of the executive arm; but in exercising this power he acts in subordination to judicial authority, assisting it to execute its process and enforce its judgments.

With such provisions in the constitution, expressed in language too clear to be misunderstood by any one, I can see no ground whatever for supposing that the president, in any emergency, or in any state of things, can authorize the suspension of the privileges of the writ of habeas corpus, or the arrest of a citizen, except in aid of the judicial power. He certainly does not faithfully execute the laws, if he takes upon himself legislative power, by suspending the writ of habeas corpus, and the judicial power also, by arresting and imprisoning a person without due process of law.

Nor can any argument be drawn from the nature of sovereignty, or the necessity of government, for self-defence in times of tumult and danger. The government of the United States is one of delegated and limited powers; it derives its existence and authority altogether from the constitution, and neither of its branches, executive, legislative or judicial, can exercise any of the powers of government beyond those specified and granted; for the tenth article of the amendments to the constitution, in express terms, provides that "the powers not delegated to the United States by the constitution, nor prohibited by it to the states, are reserved to the states, respectively, or to the people." . . .

. . . Chief Justice Marshall, in delivering the opinion of the supreme court in the case of Ex parte Bollman and Swartwout [1807] uses this decisive language . . .: "If at any time, the public safety should require the suspension of the powers vested by this act in the courts of the United States, it is for the legislature to say so. That question depends on political considerations, on which the legislature is to decide; until the legislative will be expressed, this court can only see its duty, and must obey the laws." I can add nothing to these clear and emphatic words of my great predecessor.

But the documents before me show, that the military authority in this case has gone far beyond the mere suspension of the privilege of the writ of habeas corpus. It has, by force of arms, thrust aside the judicial authorities and officers to whom the constitution has confided the power and duty of interpreting and administering the laws, and substituted a military government in its place, to be administered and executed by military officers. For, at the time these proceedings were had against John Merryman, the district judge of Maryland, the commissioner appointed under the act of congress, the district attorney and the marshal, all resided in the city of Baltimore, a few miles only from the home of the prisoner. Up to that time, there had never been the slightest resistance or obstruction to the process of any court or judicial officer of the United States, in Maryland, except by the military authority. And if a military officer, or any other person, had reason to believe that the prisoner had committed any offence against the laws of the United States, it was his duty to give information of the fact and the evidence to support it, to the district attorney. ...

The constitution provides ... that "no person shall be deprived of life, liberty or property, without due process of law." It declares that "the right of the people to be secure in their persons, houses, papers and effects, against unreasonable searches and seizures, shall not be violated; and no warrant shall issue, but upon probable cause, supported by oath or affirmation, and particularly describing the place to be searched, and the persons or things to be seized." It provides that the party accused shall be entitled to a speedy trial in a court of justice.

These great and fundamental laws, which congress itself could not suspend, have been disregarded and suspended, like the writ of habeas corpus, by a military order, supported by force of arms. Such is the case now before me, and I can only say that if the authority which the constitution has confided to the judiciary department and judicial officers, may thus, upon any pretext or under any circumstances, be usurped by the military power, at its discretion, the people of the United States are no longer living under a government of laws, but every citizen holds life, liberty and property at the will and pleasure of the army officer in whose military district he may happen to be found.

In such a case, my duty was too plain to be mistaken. I have exercised all the power which the constitution and laws confer upon me, but that power has been resisted by a force too strong for me to overcome. It is possible that the officer who has incurred this grave responsibility may have misunderstood his instructions, and exceeded the authority intended to be given him; I shall, therefore, order all the proceedings in this case, with my opinion, to be filed and recorded in the circuit court of the United States for the district of Maryland, and direct the clerk to transmit a copy, under seal, to the president of the United States. It will then remain for that high officer, in fulfillment of his constitutional obligation to "take care that the laws be faithfully executed," to determine what measures he will take to cause the civil process of the United States to be respected and enforced.

Editors' Notes

(1) **Query:** Note how Taney addressed the question WHO and the President's authority to interpret: "[H]e is to take care that [the laws] be faithfully carried into execution, as they are expounded and adjudged by the

co-ordinate branch of the government to which that duty is assigned by the constitution." (P. 1371.) Compare Andrew Jackson's veto message, which Taney had drafted when he was Attorney General, at p. 313. Which argument is more convincing?

(2) **Query:** What approach to constitutional interpretation did Taney follow here? Obviously he followed a *textualist approach*, but did he utilize others as well?

(3) Lincoln's administration did not acknowledge that Taney's ruling had imposed any obligation, but it quietly transferred jurisdiction of the case to the regular civilian courts. A grand jury indicted Merryman for conspiracy to commit treason. He was released on bail and never tried.

(4) For the background and aftermath of *Merryman,* see Carl B. Swisher, *The Taney Period, 1836–1864* (New York: Macmillan, 1974), chs. 33 and 35, vol. 5 of *History of the Supreme Court of the United States.*

"[A]re all the laws, *but one,* to go unexecuted, and the government itself go to pieces, lest that one be violated?"

LINCOLN'S MESSAGE TO CONGRESS

(July 4, 1861).*

Lincoln received Taney's opinion in *Merryman,* but he did not respond directly. Instead, he took up the issue of emergency powers in a more general way in a special message to Congress six weeks later.

Fellow-citizens of the Senate and House of Representatives:

Having been convened on an extraordinary occasion, as authorized by the Constitution, your attention is not called to any ordinary subject of legislation. At the beginning of the present Presidential term, four months ago, the functions of the Federal Government were found to be generally suspended within the several States of South Carolina, Georgia, Alabama, Mississippi, Louisiana, and Florida, excepting only those of the Post Office Department.

Within these States, all the Forts, Arsenals, Dock-yards, Custom-houses, and the like, including the movable and stationary property in, and about them, had been seized, and were held in open hostility to this Government, excepting only Forts Pickens, Taylor, and Jefferson, on, and near the Florida coast, and Fort Sumter, in Charleston harbor, South Carolina. The Forts thus seized had been put in improved condition; new ones had been built; and armed forces had been organized, and were organizing, all avowedly with the same hostile purpose.

---

* From *The Collected Works of Abraham Lincoln,* edited by Roy P. Basler, IV, 421ff. Copyright © 1953, by the Abraham Lincoln Association. Reprinted by permission of Rutgers University Press.

The Forts remaining in the possession of the Federal government, in, and near, these States, were either besieged or menaced by warlike preparations; and especially Fort Sumter was nearly surrounded by well-protected hostile batteries, with guns equal in quality to the best of its own, and outnumbering the latter as perhaps ten to one. A disproportionate share, of the Federal muskets and rifles, had somehow found their way into these States, and had been seized, to be used against the government. Accumulations of the public revenue, lying within them, had been seized for the same object. The Navy was scattered in distant seas; leaving but a very small part of it within the immediate reach of the government. Officers of the Federal Army and Navy, had resigned in great numbers; and, of those resigning, a large proportion had taken up arms against the government. Simultaneously, and in connection, with all this, the purpose to sever the Federal Union, was openly avowed. In accordance with this purpose, an ordinance had been adopted in each of these States, declaring the States, respectively, to be separated from the National Union. A formula for instituting a combined government of these states had been promulgated; and this illegal organization, in the character of confederate States was already invoking recognition, aid, and intervention, from Foreign Powers.

Finding this condition of things, and believing it to be an imperative duty upon the incoming Executive, to prevent, if possible, the consummation of such attempt to destroy the Federal Union, a choice of means to that end became indispensable. This choice was made; and was declared in the Inaugural address. The policy chosen looked to the exhaustion of all peaceful measures, before a resort to any stronger ones. It sought only to hold the public places and property, not already wrested from the Government, and to collect the revenue; relying for the rest, on time, discussion, and the ballot-box. It promised a continuance of the mails, at government expense, to the very people who were resisting the government; and it gave repeated pledges against any disturbance to any of the people, or any of their rights. Of all that which a president might constitutionally, and justifiably, do in such a case, everything was foreborne, without which, it was believed possible to keep the government on foot. ...

... By the affair at Fort Sumter, with its surrounding circumstances, that point [of conflict] was reached. Then, and thereby, the assailants of the Government, began the conflict of arms, without a gun in sight, or in expectancy, to return their fire, save only the few in the Fort, sent to that harbor, years before, for their own protection, and still ready to give that protection, in whatever was lawful. In this act, discarding all else, they have forced upon the country, the distinct issue: "Immediate dissolution, or blood."

And this issue embraces more than the fate of these United States. It presents to the whole family of man, the question, whether a constitutional republic, or a democracy—a government of the people, by the same people—can, or cannot, maintain its territorial integrity, against its own domestic foes. It presents the question, whether discontented individuals, too few in numbers to control administration, according to organic law, in any case, can always ... break up their Government, and thus practically put an end to free government upon the earth. It forces us to ask: "Is there, in all republics, this inherent, and fatal weakness?" "Must a government, of necessity, be too *strong* for the liberties of its own people, or too *weak* to maintain its own existence?"

So viewing the issue, no choice was left but to call out the war power of the Government; and so to resist force, employed for its destruction, by force, for its preservation. ...

Soon after the first call for militia, it was considered a duty to authorize the Commanding General, in proper cases, according to his discretion, to suspend the privilege of the writ of habeas corpus; or, in other words, to arrest, and detain, without resort to the ordinary processes and forms of law, such individuals as he might deem dangerous to the public safety. This authority has purposely been exercised but very sparingly. Nevertheless, the legality and propriety of what has been done under it, are questioned; and the attention of the country has been called to the proposition that one who is sworn to "take care that the laws be faithfully executed," should not himself violate them. Of course some consideration was given to the questions of power, and propriety, before this matter was acted upon. The whole of the laws which were required to be faithfully executed, were being resisted, and failing of execution, in nearly one-third of the States. Must they be allowed to finally fail of execution, even had it been perfectly clear, that by the use of the means necessary to their execution, some single law, made in such extreme tenderness of the citizen's liberty, that practically, it relieves more of the guilty, than of the innocent, should, to a very limited extent, be violated? To state the question more directly, are all the laws, *but one,* to go unexecuted, and the government itself go to pieces, lest that one be violated? Even in such a case, would not the official oath be broken, if the government should be overthrown, when it was believed that disregarding the single law, would tend to preserve it? But it was not believed that this question was presented. It was not believed that any law was violated. The provision of the Constitution that "The privilege of the writ of habeas corpus, shall not be suspended unless when, in cases of rebellion or invasion, the public safety may require it," is equivalent to a provision—is a provision—that such privilege may be suspended when, in cases of rebellion, or invasion, the public safety *does* require it. It was decided that we have a case of rebellion, and that the public safety does require the qualified suspension of the privilege of the writ which was authorized to be made. Now it is insisted that Congress, and not the Executive, is vested with this power. But the Constitution itself, is silent as to which, or who, is to exercise the power; and as the provision was plainly made for a dangerous emergency, it cannot be believed the framers of the instrument intended, that in every case, the danger should run its course, until

Congress could be called together; the very assembling of which might be prevented, as was intended in this case, by the rebellion.

No more extended argument is now offered; as an opinion, at some length, will probably be presented by the Attorney General. Whether there shall be any legislation upon the subject, and if any, what, is submitted entirely to the better judgment of Congress. ...

Editors' Notes

(1) **Query:** Compare Lincoln's response to WHO here with that in his first inaugural (reprinted above, p. 314). How consistent was he?

(2) **Query:** What approach to constitutional interpretation did Lincoln follow in his message of July 4, 1861? What was his conception of "the Constitution" he was interpreting? How did that conception compare with Taney's in *Merryman*? With Taney's in *Dred Scott* (1857; reprinted above, p. 195)?

(3) In August 1861, Congress gave retrospective approval to Lincoln's suspension of habeas corpus. At that time, however, Congress failed to authorize future presidential suspensions. Lincoln again acted on his own in September, 1862. In March, 1863, Congress finally authorized the President to use his own judgment in suspending habeas corpus (12 Stat. 755). But Congress also imposed certain restrictions on presidential suspensions of the writ within states loyal to the Union. See the discussion in the concur. op. of Chief Justice Chase in Ex parte Milligan (1866; reprinted immediately below). For a detailed analysis, see Charles Fairman, *Reconstruction and Reunion, 1864–1868* vol. VI, Part 1, *History of the Supreme Court of the United States* (New York: Macmillan, 1971), chs. 4–5.

"The Constitution of the United States is a law for rulers and people, equally in war and in peace. ..."

EX PARTE MILLIGAN

71 U.S. (4 Wall.) 2, 18 L.Ed. 281 (1866).

Early in the Civil War, Lambdin P. Milligan, a citizen of Indiana, had been a "Peace Democrat"—one who believed the South should be allowed to leave the Union in peace. Later he became a "major general" in "the Sons of Liberty," a group who planned to raid military prisons in the Midwest and release thousands of Confederate prisoners of war. In October, 1864, before the raids could begin, federal troops arrested Milligan. He was tried by a military commission and sentenced to be hanged. Lincoln had suspended habeas corpus in the area, but Milligan's counsel applied to the nearest federal circuit court for the writ. The two judges—one was Justice David Davis, who had been among Lincoln's managers during the presidential campaign of 1864—certified the case to the Supreme Court.

Mr. Justice **DAVIS** delivered the opinion of the Court.   ...

The importance of the main question presented by this record cannot be overstated, for it involves the very framework of the government and the fundamental principles of American liberty. During the late wicked Rebellion the temper of the times did not allow that calmness in deliberation and discussion so necessary to a correct conclusion of a purely judicial question. Then, considerations of safety were mingled with the exercise of power, and feelings and interests prevailed which are happily terminated. Now that the public safety is assured, this question, as well as all others, can be discussed and decided without passion.   ...

... Milligan, not a resident of one of the rebellious states, or a prisoner of war, but a citizen of Indiana for twenty years past, and never in the military or naval service, is, while at his home, arrested by the military ... imprisoned and ... tried, convicted, and sentenced to be hanged by a military commission, organized under the direction of the military commander of the military district of Indiana. Had this tribunal the legal power and authority to try and punish this man?

No graver question was ever considered by this court, nor one which more nearly concerns the rights of the whole people; for it is the birthright of every American citizen when charged with crime, to be tried and punished according to law.   ... The decision of this question does not depend on argument or judicial precedents.   ... These precedents inform us of the extent of the struggle to preserve liberty and to relieve those in civil life from military trials. The founders of our government were familiar with the history of that struggle; and secured in a written Constitution every right which the people had wrested from power during a contest of ages.   ...

... The Constitution of the United States is a law for rulers and people, equally in war and in peace, and covers with the shield of its protection all classes of men, at all times, and under all circumstances. No doctrine, involving more pernicious consequences, was ever invented by the wit of man than that any of its provisions can be suspended during any of the great exigencies of government. Such a doctrine leads directly to anarchy or despotism, but the theory of necessity on which it is based is false; for the government, within the Constitution, has all the powers granted to it which are necessary to preserve its existence, as has been happily proved by the result of the great effort to throw off its just authority.   ...

Every trial involves the exercise of judicial power; and from what source did the Military Commission that tried him derive their authority? Certainly no part of the judicial power of the country was conferred on them; because the Constitution expressly vests it "in one Supreme Court and such inferior courts as the Congress may from time to time ordain and establish," and it is not pretended that the commission was a court ordained and established by Congress. They cannot justify on the mandate of the President; because he is controlled by law, and has his

appropriate sphere of duty, which is to execute, not to make, the laws.
. . .

But it is said that the jurisdiction is complete under the "laws and usages of war." It can serve no useful purpose to inquire what those laws and usages are. . . . [T]hey can never be applied to citizens in states which have upheld the authority of the government, and where the courts are open and their process unobstructed. This court has judicial knowledge that in Indiana the Federal authority was always unopposed, and its courts always open . . .; and no usage of war could sanction a military trial there for any offense whatever of a citizen in civil life in nowise connected with the military service. Congress could grant no such power; and to the honor of our national legislature . . . it has never been provoked by the state of the country even to attempt its exercise. One of the plainest constitutional provisions was, therefore, infringed when Milligan was tried by a court not ordained and established by Congress, and not composed of judges appointed during good behavior. . . .

Another guarantee of freedom was broken when Milligan was denied a trial by jury. The great minds of the country have differed on the correct interpretation to be given to various provisions of the Federal Constitution . . . but until recently no one ever doubted that the right of trial by jury was fortified in the organic law against the power of attack. It is now assailed; but if ideas can be expressed in words, and language has any meaning, this right . . . is preserved to every one accused of crime who is not attached to the Army or Navy or Militia in actual service. . . .

. . . This privilege is a vital principle, underlying the whole administration of criminal justice; it is not held by sufferance, and cannot be frittered away on any plea of state or political necessity. When peace prevails . . . there is no difficulty in preserving the safeguards of liberty; . . . but if society is disturbed by civil commotion—if the passions of men are aroused and the restraints of law weakened, if not disregarded— these safeguards need, and should receive, the watchful care of those entrusted with the guardianship of the Constitution and laws. In no other way can we transmit to posterity unimpaired the blessings of liberty, consecrated by the sacrifices of the Revolution.

It is claimed that martial law covers with its broad mantle the proceedings of this Military Commission. The proposition is this: That in a time of war the commander of an armed force . . . has the power, within the lines of his military district, to suspend all civil rights and their remedies, and subject citizens as well as soldiers to the rule of his will; and in the exercise of his lawful authority cannot be restrained, except by his superior officer or the President of the United States.

If this position is sound . . . then when war exists, foreign or domestic, and the country is subdivided into military departments for mere convenience, the commander of one of them can, if he chooses . . . with the approval of the Executive, substitute military force for and to the exclusion of the laws, and punish all persons, as he thinks right and proper, without fixed or certain rules. The statement of this proposition shows its importance; for, if true, republican government is a failure, and there is an end of liberty regulated by law. ... Civil liberty and this kind of martial law cannot endure together. ... [O]ne or the other must perish.

This nation ... cannot always remain at peace, and has no right to expect that it will always have wise and humane rulers. ... Wicked men, ambitious of power, with hatred of liberty and contempt of law, may fill the place once occupied by Washington and Lincoln; and if this is conceded, and the calamities of war again befall us, the dangers to human liberty are frightful to contemplate. If our fathers had failed to provide for just such a contingency, they would have been false to the trust reposed in them. ...

... [T]here are occasions when martial rule can be properly applied. If, in foreign invasion or civil war, the courts are actually closed, and it is impossible to administer criminal justice according to law, then, in the theater of actual military operations, where war really prevails, there is a necessity to furnish a substitute for the civil authority. ... As necessity creates the rule, so it limits its duration; for, if this government is continued after the courts are reinstated, it is a gross usurpation of power. Martial rule can never exist where the courts are open, and in the proper and unobstructed exercise of their jurisdiction. It is also confined to the locality of actual war. ...

It is proper to say, although Milligan's trial and conviction by a military commission was illegal, yet, if guilty of the crimes imputed to him, and his guilt had been ascertained by an established court and impartial jury, he deserved severe punishment. ...

Mr. Chief Justice **CHASE**. ...

The act of Congress of March 3rd, 1863, comprises all the legislation which seems to require consideration in this connection. The constitutionality of this act has not been questioned and is not doubted. The first section authorized the suspension, during the Rebellion, of the writ of *habeas corpus* throughout the United States by the President. The two next sections limited this authority in important respects.

The second section required that lists of all persons, being citizens of states in which the administration of the laws had continued unimpaired in the Federal courts, who were then held or might thereafter be held as prisoners of the United States, under the authority of the President, otherwise than as prisoners of war, should be furnished to the judges of the Circuit and District Courts. The lists transmitted to the judges were to contain the names of all persons, residing within their respective jurisdictions, charged with violation of national law. And it was required, in cases where the grand jury in attendance upon any of these courts should terminate its session without proceeding by indictment or otherwise against any prisoner named in the list, that the judge of the court should forthwith make an order that such prisoner desiring a discharge, should be brought before him or the court to be discharged ... [or] to be further dealt with according to law. Every officer of the United States having custody of such prisoners was required to obey and execute the judge's order. ...

The third section provided, in case lists of persons other than prisoners of war then held in confinement, or thereafter arrested, should not be furnished within twenty days after the passage of the act, or, in cases of subsequent arrest, within twenty days after the time of arrest, that any citizen after the termination of a session of the grand jury without indictment or presentment, might, by petition alleging the facts and verified by oath, obtain the judge's order of discharge in favor of any person so imprisoned, on the terms and conditions prescribed in the second section. ...

It was under this act that Milligan petitioned the Circuit Court for the District of Indiana for discharge from imprisonment. The holding of the Circuit and District Courts of the United States in Indiana had been uninterrupted. The administration of the laws in the Federal courts had remained unimpaired. Milligan was imprisoned under the authority of the President, and was not a prisoner of war. No list of prisoners had been furnished to the judges ... as required by the law. A grand jury had attended the Circuit Courts of the Indiana district, while Milligan was there imprisoned, and had closed its session without finding any indictment or presentment or otherwise proceeding against the prisoner. His case was thus brought within the precise letter and intent of the act of Congress. ...

The first question, therefore—Ought the writ to issue? must be answered in the affirmative. And it is equally clear that he was entitled to the discharge prayed for.

It must be borne in mind that the prayer of the petition was not for an absolute discharge, but to be delivered from military custody and imprisonment, and if found probably guilty of any offence, to be turned over to the proper tribunal for inquiry and punishment; or, if not found thus probably guilty, to be discharged altogether. And the express terms of the act of Congress required this action of the court. ... An affirmative answer must, therefore, be given to the second question, namely: Ought Milligan to be discharged according to the prayer of the petition?

That the third question, namely: Had the military commission in Indiana, under the facts stated, jurisdiction to try and sentence Milligan? must be answered negatively is an unavoidable inference from affirmative answers to the other two.

But the opinion ... [of the Court] goes further and ... asserts not only that the military commission held in Indiana was not authorized by Congress but that it was not in the power of Congress to authorize it. ... We cannot agree. ... We think that Congress had power, though not exercised, to authorize the military commission which was held in Indiana. ... The Constitution itself provides for military government as well as for civil government. ...

Where peace exists the laws of peace must prevail. ... [W]hen the nation is involved in war, and some portions of the country are invaded, and all are exposed to invasion, it is within the power of Congress to determine in what states or districts such great and imminent public danger exists as justifies the authorization of military tribunals for the trial of crimes and offenses against the discipline or security of the army or against the public safety. ... [Indiana] was a military district, was the theater of military operations, had been actually invaded, and was constantly threatened with invasion. It appears, also, that a powerful secret association, composed of citizens and others, existed within the state, under military organization, conspiring against the draft, and plotting insurrection, the liberation of the prisoners of war at various depots, the seizure of the state and national arsenals, armed cooperation with the enemy, and war against the national government.

We cannot doubt that, in such a time of public danger, Congress had power, under the Constitution, to provide for the organization of a military commission, and for trial by that commission of persons engaged in this conspiracy. The fact that the Federal courts were open was regarded by Congress as a sufficient reason for not exercising the power; but that fact could not deprive Congress of the right to exercise it. Those courts might be open and undisturbed in the execution of their functions, and yet wholly incompetent to avert threatened danger, or to punish, with adequate promptitude and certainty, the guilty conspirators. ...

We have no apprehension that this power, under our American system of government, in which all official authority is derived from the people, and exercised under direct responsibility to the people, is more likely to be abused than the power to regulate commerce, or the power to borrow money. And we are unwilling to give our assent by silence to expressions of opinion which seem to us calculated, though not intended, to cripple the constitutional powers of the government, and to augment the public dangers in times of invasion and rebellion.

Mr. Justice **WAYNE,** Mr. Justice **SWAYNE,** and Mr. Justice **MILLER** concur with me in these views.

Editors' Notes

(1) **Query:** How did Davis and Chase differ on the question of WHO shall interpret? On WHAT "the Constitution" to be interpreted included? On HOW to approach constitutional interpretation?

(2) Milligan's execution had been stayed pending the outcome of his appeal, and President Johnson commuted his sentence to life imprisonment before the Supreme Court heard the case. After the Court's decision, Milligan was released and never tried. In 1868 he sued the commanding general and

won a nominal award. See Charles Warren, *The Supreme Court in United States History* (Rev. ed.; Boston: Little Brown, 1926), II, 427n. The most authoritative accounts of constitutional problems during the Civil War and Reconstruction are: Harold Hyman, *A More Perfect Union* (New York: Knopf, 1973); Carl B. Swisher, *The Taney Period, 1836–1864* vol. 5 of *History of the Supreme Court of the United States* (New York: Macmillan, 1974), chs. 32–37; and Charles Fairman, *Reconstruction and Reunion, 1864–1888* vol. 6, Part 1, *History of the Supreme Court of the United States* (New York: Macmillan, 1974), chs. 1–13.

(3) In 1863–64, the Court had almost become embroiled in a similar controversy. Clement L. Vallandigham, a prominent Ohio politician and "supreme commander" of the Sons of Liberty, the organization in which Milligan was a "major general," had been arrested by the military for sedition. He was convicted and sentenced to imprisonment until the end of the war. He then unsuccessfully petitioned the U.S. circuit court for writ of habeas corpus. Before the Supreme Court could hear the appeal, Lincoln commuted the sentence to banishment and had Vallandigham released behind Confederate lines. The justices were not anxious to take on the President during the middle of the war, and they held that they were without jurisdiction in the case. Ex parte Vallandigham (1864).

(4) *Milligan* triggered a direct confrontation with Congress. Radical Republicans had enacted a series of Reconstruction Acts that provided for military tribunals to try Southern civilians, and Radical leaders saw *Milligan* as a menace to their entire program. "That decision," Thaddeus Stevens thundered, "although in terms perhaps not as infamous as the *Dred Scott* decision, is yet far more dangerous in its operations upon the lives and liberties of the loyal men of this country. . . . That decision has unsheathed the dagger of the assassin. . . ." Congressman John Bingham, one of the principal architects of the Fourteenth Amendment, stated that, if the Court persisted in its error, Congress would "defy judicial usurpation" and propose a constitutional amendment for "the abolition of the tribunal itself." The opponents of Reconstruction saw *Milligan* as an opportunity; and a case, Ex parte McCardle (1869; reprinted above, p. 467) quickly appeared on the docket.

(5) In Ex parte Quirin (1942), the Supreme Court unanimously sustained the authority of the federal government to try by military commission eight German saboteurs who had landed in the United States by submarine. After the war, the Court refused to intervene to stop trials of Axis leaders by special military courts. In re Yamashita (1946) and Hirota v. MacArthur (1948). See also Johnson v. Eisentrager (1950).

(6) After the attack on Pearl Harbor in 1941, the governor of Hawaii (then a territory) suspended habeas corpus and placed the islands under martial law. The President approved the governor's action and authorized the commanding general in the area to exercise all normal executive and judicial powers. The local U.S. district judge, however, ruled that the courts were open and that, on the basis of *Milligan,* he would issue writs. The general forbade the judge to do so, and the judge held the general in contempt of court and fined him $5,000. An emissary from the Department of Justice had to negotiate a compromise that eventually led to a pair of cases being taken to the Supreme Court. The justices decided the cases after the war and ruled in

favor of the judge.   But the Court avoided the constitutional issue and held that the governor had exceeded his statutory authority.   Duncan v. Kahanamoku (1946).

———

" '[W]e cannot reject as unfounded the judgment of the military authorities and of Congress that there were disloyal members of that population.   ...' "   Justice BLACK

"To talk about a military order that expresses an allowable judgment of war needs ... as 'an unconstitutional order' is to suffuse a part of the Constitution with an atmosphere of unconstitutionality."—Justice FRANKFURTER

"A military judgment based upon such racial and sociological considerations is not entitled to the great weight ordinarily given the judgments based upon strictly military considerations."—Justice MURPHY

"[I]f we cannot confine military expedients by the Constitution, neither would I distort the Constitution to approve all that the military may deem expedient."—Justice JACKSON

KOREMATSU v. UNITED STATES
323 U.S. 214, 65 S.Ct. 193, 89 L.Ed. 194 (1944).

Chapter 4, pp. 87–101, provides a detailed background of this case: Several months after the attack on Pearl Harbor, Congress made it a crime for certain persons to enter or remain in zones designated by the President. Pursuant to this authority, the Commanding General of the west coast region ordered all persons, including American citizens, of Japanese ancestry to report to relocation centers for internment in concentration camps.   (German and Italian aliens were not, as groups, affected by the order.)   Fred Korematsu, an American citizen of Japanese descent, defied this order, was arrested, and convicted.   He obtained certiorari from the Supreme Court.

Mr. Justice **BLACK** delivered the opinion of the Court.   ...

It should be noted ... that all legal restrictions which curtail the civil rights of a single racial group are immediately suspect.   That is not to say that all such restrictions are unconstitutional.   It is to say that courts must subject them to the most rigid scrutiny.   Pressing public necessity may sometimes justify the existence of such restrictions; racial antagonism never can.   ...

In light of the principles we announced in Hirabayashi [v. United States (1943)], we are unable to conclude that it was beyond the war power of Congress and the Executive to exclude those of Japanese ancestry from the West Coast war area. ... True, exclusion from ... one's home ... is a far greater deprivation than constant confinement to the home from 8 P.M. to 6 A.M. ... But exclusion from a threatened area, no less than curfew, has a definite and close relationship to the prevention of espionage and sabotage. The military authorities, charged with the primary responsibility of defending our shores, concluded that curfew provided inadequate protection and ordered exclusion. They did so ... in accordance with congressional authority to the military to say who should, and who should not, remain in the threatened areas. ...

Here, as in *Hirabayashi*, "we cannot reject as unfounded the judgment of the military authorities and of Congress that there were disloyal members of that population. ..." ... It was because we could not reject the finding of the military authorities that it was impossible to bring about an immediate segregation of the disloyal from the loyal that we sustained the validity of the curfew order as applying to the whole group. In the instant case, temporary exclusion of the entire group was rested by the military on the same ground. ...

... That there were members of the group who retained loyalties to Japan has been confirmed by investigations made subsequent to the exclusion. Approximately five thousand American citizens of Japanese ancestry refused to swear unqualified allegiance to the United States and to renounce allegiance to the Japanese Emperor, and several thousand evacuees requested repatriation to Japan.

We uphold the exclusion order as of the time it was made and when the petitioner violated it. ... [W]e are not unmindful of the hardships imposed by it upon a large group of American citizens. ... But hardships are part of war, and war is an aggregation of hardships. Compulsory exclusion of large groups of citizens from their homes, except under circumstances of direst emergency and peril, is inconsistent with our basic governmental institutions. But when under conditions of modern warfare our shores are threatened by hostile forces, the power to protect must be commensurate with the threatened danger. ...

We are thus being asked to pass at this time upon the whole subsequent detention program in both assembly and relocation centers, although the only issues framed at the trial related to petitioner's remaining in the prohibited area in violation of the exclusion order. Had petitioner here left the prohibited area and gone to an assembly center we cannot say either as a matter of fact or law, that his presence in that center would have resulted in his detention in a relocation center.* Some who did report to the assembly center were not sent to relocation centers, but were released upon condition that they remain outside the prohibited zone until the military orders were modified or lifted. ...

---

* In its brief, the Department of Justice conceded that, had Korematsu obeyed the army's order, he would have been placed in a detention camp.—**Eds.**

Since the petitioner has not been convicted of failing to report or to remain in an assembly or relocation center, we cannot in this case determine the validity of those separate provisions of the order. ... Some of the members of the Court are of the view that evacuation and detention in an assembly center were inseparable. ... The power to exclude includes the power to do it by force if necessary. And any forcible measure must necessarily entail some degree of detention or restraint whatever method of removal is selected. But whichever view is taken, it results in holding that the order under which petitioner was convicted was valid.

... Our task would be simple were this a case involving the imprisonment of a loyal citizen in a concentration camp because of racial prejudice. Regardless of the true nature of the assembly and relocation centers—and we deem it unjustifiable to call them concentration camps with all the ugly connotations that term implies—we are dealing specifically with nothing but an exclusion order. To cast this case into outlines of racial prejudice, without reference to the real military dangers which were presented, merely confuses the issue. Korematsu was not excluded from the Military Area because of hostility to him or his race. He *was* excluded because we are at war with the Japanese Empire, because the properly constituted military authorities feared an invasion of our West Coast and felt constrained to take proper security measures, because they decided that the military urgency of the situation demanded that all citizens of Japanese ancestry be segregated from the West Coast temporarily, and finally, because Congress, reposing its confidence in this time of war in our military leaders—as inevitably it must—determined that they should have the power to do just this. There was evidence of disloyalty on the part of some, the military authorities considered that the need for action was great, and time was short. We cannot—by availing ourselves of the calm perspective of hindsight—now say that at that time these actions were unjustified.

Affirmed.

Mr. Justice **FRANKFURTER,** concurring. ...

The provisions of the Constitution which confer on the Congress and the President powers to ... wage war are as much part of the Constitution as provisions looking to a nation at peace. ... Therefore the validity of action under the war power must be judged wholly in the context of war. That action is not to be stigmatized as lawless because like action in times of peace would be lawless. To talk about a military order that expresses an allowable judgment of war needs by those entrusted with the duty of conducting war as "an unconstitutional order" is to suffuse a part of the Constitution with an atmosphere of unconstitutionality. The respective spheres of action of military authorities and of judges are of course very different. But within their sphere, military authorities are no more outside the bounds of obedience to the Constitution than are judges within theirs. ... If a military order ... does not transcend the means appropriate for conducting war, such action by the military is as constitutional as would be any authorized action by the Interstate Commerce Commission within the limits of the constitutional power to regulate commerce. ... To find that the Constitution does not forbid the military measures now complained of does not carry with it approval of that which Congress and the Executive did. That is their business, not ours.

Mr. Justice **ROBERTS:**

... [T]he indisputable facts exhibit a clear violation of Constitutional rights. ... [E]xclusion was but a part of an over-all plan for forcible detention. ... The two conflicting orders, one of which commanded him to stay and the other which commanded him to go, were nothing but a cleverly devised trap to accomplish the real purpose of the [military] authority, which was to lock him up in a concentration camp. ... Why should we set up a figmentary and artificial situation instead of addressing ourselves to the actualities of the case? ...

Mr. Justice **MURPHY,** dissenting:

This exclusion ... goes over "the very brink of constitutional power" and falls into the ugly abyss of racism. In dealing with matters relating to the prosecution and progress of a war, we must accord great respect ... to the judgments of the military authorities. ... At the same time, however, it is essential that there be limits to military discretion. ...

The judicial test of whether the Government, on a plea of military necessity, can validly deprive an individual of any of his constitutional rights is whether the deprivation is reasonably related to a public danger that is so "immediate, imminent, and impending" as not to admit of delay and not to permit the intervention of ordinary constitutional processes to alleviate the danger. ... Civilian Exclusion Order No. 34 ... clearly does not meet that test. Being an obvious racial discrimination, the order deprives all those within its scope of the equal protection of the laws as guaranteed by the Fifth Amendment. It further deprives these individuals of their constitutional rights to live and work where they will, to establish a home where they choose and to move about freely. In excommunicating them without benefit of hearings, this order also deprives them of all their constitutional rights to procedural due process. Yet no reasonable relation to an "immediate, imminent, and impending" public danger is evident to support this racial restriction. ...

It must be conceded that the military and naval situation in the spring of 1942 was such as to generate a very real fear of invasion of the Pacific Coast, accompanied by fears of sabotage and espionage in that area. The military command was therefore justified in adopting all reasonable means necessary to combat these dangers. In adjudging the military action taken in light of the then apparent dangers, we must not erect too high or too meticulous standards; it is necessary only that the

action have some reasonable relation to the removal of the dangers. . . .
But the exclusion . . . of all persons with Japanese blood in their veins
has no such reasonable relation . . . because the exclusion order necessarily must rely for its reasonableness upon the assumption that *all*
persons of Japanese ancestry may have a dangerous tendency to commit
sabotage and espionage and to aid our Japanese enemy in other ways.
. . .

That this forced exclusion was the result in good measure of this
erroneous assumption of racial guilt rather than bona fide military
necessity is evidenced by the Commanding General's Final Report on the
evacuation from the Pacific Coast area. In it he refers to all individuals
of Japanese descent as "subversive," as belonging to "an enemy race"
whose "racial strains are undiluted," and as constituting "over 112,000
potential enemies . . . at large today" along the Pacific Coast. In
support of this blanket condemnation of all persons of Japanese descent,
however, no reliable evidence is cited. . . .

Justification . . . is sought instead, mainly upon questionable racial
and sociological grounds not ordinarily within the realm of expert
military judgment, supplemented by certain semi-military conclusions
drawn from an unwarranted use of circumstantial evidence. Individuals
of Japanese ancestry are condemned because they are said to be "a large,
unassimilated, tightly knit racial group, bound to an enemy nation by
strong ties of race, culture, custom and religion." They are claimed to
be given to "emperor worshipping ceremonies" and to "dual citizenship." Japanese language schools and allegedly pro-Japanese organizations are cited as evidence of possible group disloyalty, together with
facts as to certain persons being educated and residing at length in
Japan. It is intimated that many of these individuals deliberately
resided "adjacent to strategic points," thus enabling them "to carry into
execution a tremendous program of sabotage on a mass scale should any
considerable number of them have been inclined to do so."

The need for protective custody is also asserted. The report refers
without identity to "numerous incidents of violence" as well as to other
admittedly unverified or cumulative incidents. From this, plus certain
other events not shown to have been connected with the Japanese
Americans, it is concluded that the "situation was fraught with danger
to the Japanese population itself" and that the general public "was
ready to take matters into its own hands." Finally, it is intimated,
though not directly charged or proved, that persons of Japanese ancestry
were responsible for three minor isolated shellings and bombings of the
Pacific Coast area, as well as for unidentified radio transmissions and
night signalling. The main reasons . . . appear . . . to be largely an
accumulation of much of the misinformation, half-truths and insinua-
tions that for years have been directed against Japanese Americans by
people with racial and economic prejudices—the same people who have
been among the foremost advocates of the evacuation. A military
judgment based upon such racial and sociological considerations is not

entitled to the great weight ordinarily given the judgments based upon strictly military considerations. Especially is this so when every charge relative to race, religion, culture, geographical location, and legal and economic status has been substantially discredited by independent studies made by experts in these matters. ...

I dissent, therefore, from this legalization of racism. Racial discrimination in any form and in any degree has no justifiable part whatever in our democratic way of life. It is unattractive in any setting but it is utterly revolting among a free people who have embraced the principles set forth in the Constitution of the United States. ...

Mr. Justice **JACKSON,** dissenting.

Now if any fundamental assumption underlies our system, it is that guilt is personal and not inheritable. ... But here is an attempt to make an otherwise innocent act a crime merely because this prisoner is the son of parents as to whom he had no choice, and belongs to a race from which there is no way to resign. ...

... [T]he "law" which this prisoner is convicted of disregarding is not found in an act of Congress, but in a military order. Neither the Act of Congress nor the Executive Order of the President, nor both together, would afford a basis for the conviction. ... And it is said that if the military commander had reasonable military grounds for promulgating the orders, they are constitutional and become law, and the Court is required to enforce them. ...

It would be impracticable and dangerous idealism to expect or insist that each specific military command in an area of probable operations will conform to conventional tests of constitutionality. ... The armed services must protect a society, not merely its Constitution. The very essence of the military job is to marshal physical force, to remove every obstacle to its effectiveness, to give it every strategic advantage. Defense measures will not, and often should not, be held within the limits that bind civil authority in peace. ...

But if we cannot confine military expedients by the Constitution, neither would I distort the Constitution to approve all that the military may deem expedient. ... I cannot say ... that the orders of General DeWitt were not reasonably expedient military precautions, nor could I say that they were. But even if they were permissible military procedures, I deny that it follows that they are constitutional. If, as the Court holds, it does follow, then we may as well say that any military order will be constitutional and have done with it. ...

Much is said of the danger to liberty from the Army program. ... But a judicial construction of the due process clause that will sustain this order is a far more subtle blow to liberty. ... A military order, however unconstitutional, is not apt to last longer than the military emergency. Even during that period a succeeding commander may revoke it all. But once a judicial opinion rationalizes such an order to show that it conforms to the Constitution, or rather rationalizes the Constitution to show that the Constitution sanctions such an order, the Court for all time has validated the principle of racial discrimination in criminal procedure and of transplanting American citizens. The principle then lies about like a loaded weapon ready for the hand of any authority that can bring forward a plausible claim of an urgent need. ... All who observe the work of courts are familiar with what Judge Cardozo described as "the tendency of a principle to expand itself to the limit of its logic." A military commander may overstep the bounds of constitutionality, and it is an incident. But if we review and approve, that passing incident becomes the doctrine of the Constitution. There it has a generative power of its own, and all that it creates will be in its own image. Nothing better illustrates this danger than does the Court's opinion in this case. It argues that we are bound to uphold the conviction of Korematsu because we upheld one in *Hirabayashi*. ...

In that case we were urged to consider only the curfew feature. ... We yielded, and the Chief Justice guarded the opinion as carefully as language will do. He said: "... We decide only the issue as we have defined it—we decide only that the *curfew order* as applied, and at the time it was applied, was within the boundaries of the war power." ... Now the principle of racial discrimination is pushed from support of mild measures to very harsh ones, and from temporary deprivations to indeterminate ones. And the precedent which it is said requires us to do so is *Hirabayashi*. The Court is now saying that in *Hirabayashi* we did decide the very things we there said we were not deciding. Because we said that these citizens could be made to stay in their homes during the hours of dark, it is said we must require them to leave home entirely; and if that, we are told they may also be taken into custody for deportation; and if that, it is argued they may also be held for some undetermined time in detention camps. How far the principle of this case would be extended before plausible reasons would play out, I do not know.

I should hold that a civil court cannot be made to enforce an order which violates constitutional limitations even if it is a reasonable exercise of military authority. The courts can exercise only the judicial power, can apply only law, and must abide by the Constitution, or they cease to be civil courts and become instruments of military policy.

... I would not lead people to rely on this Court for a review that seems to me wholly delusive. ... If the people ever let command of the war power fall into irresponsible and unscrupulous hands, the courts wield no power equal to its restraint. The chief restraint upon those who command the physical forces of the country ... must be their responsibility to the political judgments of their contemporaries and to the moral judgments of history.

My duties as a justice ... do not require me to make a military judgment as to whether General DeWitt's evacuation and detention program was a reasonable military necessity. I do not suggest that the courts should have attempted to interfere with the Army in carrying out its task. But I do not think they may be asked to execute a military expedient that has no place in law under the Constitution. I would reverse the judgment and discharge the prisoner.

Editors' Notes

(1) **Query:** How did Black's and Frankfurter's conceptions of WHAT "the Constitution" includes differ? What were Murphy's and Jackson's conceptions?

(2) **Query:** To what extent was Black's opinion consistent with his usual approach to interpretation? How did he and Frankfurter differ in justifying the decision to uphold Korematsu's conviction? Compare these two opinions with those by the same justices in Rochin v. California (1952; reprinted above, p. 135). What approaches did Murphy and Jackson follow?

(3) **Query:** Implicitly and sometimes explicitly, Black, Frankfurter, Murphy, and Jackson each addressed the question WHO. What were their answers and how did they justify those answers? To what extent did they address one another's arguments?

(4) **Query:** Jackson's dissent has been called "an essay in judicial nihilism." To what extent is that charge accurate?

(5) **Query:** Compare the way in which the Court scrutinized the military's claim of necessity in *Korematsu*, decided in 1944, when the war was still going on in both Europe and Asia, with its much tougher attitude in 1946, when, a year after the end of the war, it decided Duncan v. Kahanamoku, discussed in Eds.' Note 6 to Ex parte Milligan, above, p. 1382. How can one reasonably account for this difference? What does that difference tell us about the basic questions around which this book is organized?

(6) In 1983, Korematsu asked the U.S. District Court in San Francisco, the jurisdiction in which he had been tried, to vacate his conviction, on grounds that the government's claims of danger from Nisei had been false. The Department of Justice filed a brief that, according to the district judge, was "tantamount to a confession of error." The judge granted Korematsu's request and the conviction was expunged from his record.

(7) In 1948, in a minor spasm of guilt, Congress passed the Japanese–Americans Evacuation Claims Act, allowing Nisei to file for "loss of real or personal property," not compensated by insurance, resulting from the evacuation. 50 U.S.C. App. § 1981ff. The government eventually paid out about $37 million of the $148 million claimed. The Federal Reserve Bank in San Francisco estimated the actual losses at $400 million. See Commission on Wartime Relocation and Internment of Civilians, *Report: Personal Justice Denied* (Washington, D.C.: Government Printing Office, 1982), ch. 4. In 1988, Congress carried out the Relocation Commission's recommendation and passed additional legislation awarding $20,000 (tax free) to each living internee. (P.L. 100–383, 102 Stat. 903.)

(8) In addition to the *Report* cited in Note 7, the best studies of the relocation program's origins, effects, and constitutional as well as human problems are: Morton Grodzins, *Americans Betrayed* (Chicago: University of Chicago Press, 1949); Jacobus tenBroek et al., *Prejudice, War, and the Constitution* (Berkeley: University of California Press, 1954); Alpheus Thomas

Mason, *Harlan Fiske Stone* (New York: Viking, 1956), ch. 40; J. Woodford Howard, *Mr. Justice Murphy* (Princeton: Princeton University Press, 1968), chs. 12–13; and Peter Irons, *Justice at War* (New York: Oxford University Press, 1983).

"Even though 'theater of war' be an expanding concept, we cannot with faithfulness to our constitutional system hold that the Commander in Chief of the Armed Forces has the ultimate power as such to take possession of private property in order to keep labor disputes from stopping production."

YOUNGSTOWN SHEET & TUBE CO. v. SAWYER
343 U.S. 579, 72 S.Ct. 863, 96 L.Ed. 1153 (1952).

This case, involving the authority of the President, acting without congressional authorization, to seize and operate steel mills to prevent a strike that would have crippled production of ammunition during the Korean War, is reprinted above at p. 443.

"We cannot accept the Government's argument that internal security matters are too subtle and complex for judicial evaluation."

UNITED STATES v. UNITED STATES DISTRICT COURT
407 U.S. 297, 92 S.Ct. 2125, 32 L.Ed.2d 752 (1972).

The United States charged three people with conspiring to destroy government property and one of the three with dynamiting a CIA office. During pretrial proceedings, the defendants asked the judge to order the government to produce information gathered against them by electronic surveillance to determine if the government's case was "tainted" by illegally obtained evidence. The Nixon administration conceded that it had used wiretaps without obtaining a warrant as required by Title III of the Omnibus Crime Control and Safe Streets Act, but asserted that the President's "inherent power" to protect national security was sufficient authority for such, even though the source of danger was domestic not foreign.

The district judge held that the wiretaps, without a warrant, violated the Fourth Amendment. The Court of Appeals for the Sixth Circuit agreed, and the government sought and obtained certiorari.

Mr. Justice **POWELL** delivered the opinion of the Court. . . .

The issue before us . . . involves the delicate question of the President's power . . . to authorize electronic surveillance in internal security matters without prior judicial approval. Successive Presidents for more than one-quarter of a century have authorized such surveillance ... without guidance from the Congress or a definitive decision of this Court. This case brings the issue here for the first time. Its resolution is a matter of national concern, requiring sensitivity both to the Government's right to protect itself from unlawful subversion and attack and to the citizen's right to be secure in his privacy against unreasonable Government intrusion. ...

I

Title III of the Omnibus Crime Control and Safe Streets Act, 18 U.S.C. §§ 2510–2520, authorizes the use of electronic surveillance for classes of crimes carefully specified. ... Such surveillance is subject to prior court order. Section 2518 sets forth the detailed and particularized application necessary to obtain such an order as well as carefully circumscribed conditions for its use. The Act represents a comprehensive attempt by Congress to promote more effective control of crime while protecting the privacy of individual thought and expression. Much of Title III was drawn to meet the constitutional requirements for electronic surveillance enunciated by this Court in Berger v. New York (1967) and Katz v. United States (1967).

Together with the elaborate surveillance requirements in Title III, there is the following proviso, 18 U.S.C. § 2511(3):

> Nothing contained in this chapter or in section 605 of the Communications Act of 1934 shall limit the constitutional power of the President to take such measures as he deems necessary to protect the Nation against actual or potential attack or other hostile acts of a foreign power, to obtain foreign intelligence information deemed essential to the security of the United States, or to protect national security information against foreign intelligence activities. *Nor shall anything contained in this chapter be deemed to limit the constitutional power of the President to take such measures as he deems necessary to protect the United States against the overthrow of the Government by force or other unlawful means, or against any other clear and present danger to the structure or existence of the Government.* ... (Emphasis supplied.)

The Government relies on § 2511(3). It argues that "in excepting national security surveillances from the Act's warrant requirement Congress recognized the President's authority to conduct such surveillances without prior judicial approval." The section thus is viewed as a recognition or affirmance of a constitutional authority in the President to conduct warrantless domestic security surveillance such as that involved in this case.

We think the language of § 2511(3), as well as the legislative history of the statute, refutes this interpretation. ... At most, this [language] is an implicit recognition that the President does have certain powers in the specified areas. Few would doubt this. ... But so far as the use of the President's electronic surveillance power is concerned, the language is essentially neutral.

Section 2511(3) certainly confers no power. . . . It merely provides that the Act shall not be interpreted to limit or disturb such power as the President may have under the Constitution. In short, Congress simply left presidential powers where it found them. The language of subsection (3), here involved, is to be contrasted with the language of the exceptions set forth in the preceding subsection. Rather than stating that warrantless presidential uses of electronic surveillance "shall not be unlawful" and thus employing the standard language of exception, subsection (3) merely disclaims any intention "to limit the constitutional power of the President."

The express grant of authority to conduct surveillances is found in § 2516, which authorizes the Attorney General to make application to a federal judge when surveillance may provide evidence of certain offenses. These offenses are described with meticulous care and specificity.

Where the Act authorizes surveillance, the procedure to be followed is specified in § 2518. Subsection (1) thereof requires application to a judge of competent jurisdiction for a prior order of approval, and states in detail the information required in such application. Subsection (3) prescribes the necessary elements of probable cause which the judge must find before issuing an order authorizing an interception. Subsection (4) sets forth the required contents of such an order. Subsection (5) sets strict time limits on an order. Provision is made in subsection (7) for "an emergency situation" found to exist by the Attorney General (or by the principal prosecuting attorney of a State) "with respect to conspiratorial activities threatening the national security interest." In such a situation, emergency surveillance may be conducted "if an application for an order approving the interception is made . . . within forty-eight hours." If such an order is not obtained, or the application therefor is denied, the interception is deemed to be a violation of the Act.

In view of these and other interrelated provisions delineating permissible interceptions of particular criminal activity upon carefully specified conditions, it would have been incongruous for Congress to have legislated with respect to the important and complex area of national security in a single brief and nebulous paragraph. This would not comport with the sensitivity of the problem involved or with the extraordinary care Congress exercised in drafting other sections of the Act. We therefore think the conclusion inescapable that Congress only intended to make clear that the Act simply did not legislate with respect to national security surveillances.

The legislative history of § 2511(3) supports this interpretation. . . .

II

It is important at the outset to emphasize the limited nature of the question before the Court. This case raises no constitutional challenge to electronic surveillance as specifically authorized by Title III of the [Act]. Nor is there any question or doubt as to the necessity of obtaining a warrant in the surveillance of crimes unrelated to the national security interest. *Katz*; *Berger*. Further, the instant case requires no judgment on the scope of the President's surveillance power with respect to the activities of foreign powers, within or without his country. ... There is no evidence of any involvement, directly or indirectly, of a foreign power.

Our present inquiry, though important, is therefore a narrow one. It addresses a question left open by *Katz*: "Whether safeguards other than prior authorization by a magistrate would satisfy the Fourth Amendment in a situation involving the national security. ..."

... We begin the inquiry by noting that the President of the United States has the fundamental duty, under Art. II, § 1, of the Constitution, to "preserve, protect, and defend the Constitution of the United States." Implicit in that duty is the power to protect our Government against those who would subvert or overthrow it by unlawful means. In the discharge of this duty, the President ... may find it necessary to employ electronic surveillance to obtain intelligence information on the plans of those who plot unlawful acts against the Government. The use of such surveillance in internal security cases has been sanctioned more or less continuously by various Presidents and Attorneys General since July 1946. ... *

... The covertness and complexity of potential unlawful conduct against the Government and the necessary dependency of many conspirators upon the telephone make electronic surveillance an effective investigatory instrument in certain circumstances. The marked acceleration in technological developments and sophistication in their use have resulted in new techniques for the planning, commission, and concealment of criminal activities. It would be contrary to the public interest for Government to deny to itself the prudent and lawful employment of those very techniques which are employed against the Government and its law-abiding citizens.

It has been said that "[t]he most basic function of any government is to provide for the security of the individual and of his property." Miranda v. Arizona (1966) (White, J., dissenting). And unless Government safeguards its own capacity to function and to preserve the security of its people, society itself could become so disordered that all rights and liberties would be endangered. ...

But a recognition of these elementary truths does not make the employment by Government of electronic surveillance a welcome development. ... There is ... a deep-seated uneasiness and apprehension that this capability will be used to intrude upon cherished privacy of law-abiding citizens. We look to the Bill of Rights to safeguard this privacy. Though physical entry of the home is the chief evil against which the wording of the Fourth Amendment is directed, its broader spirit now shields private speech from unreasonable surveillance. *Katz*; *Berger*;

---

* In fact at least since 1940.—**Eds.**

Silverman v. United States (1961). Our decision in *Katz* refused to lock the Fourth Amendment into instances of actual physical trespass. Rather, the Amendment governs "not only the seizure of tangible items, but extends as well to the recording of oral statements ... without any 'technical trespass under ... local property law.' " That decision implicitly recognized that the broad and unsuspected governmental incursions into conversational privacy which electronic surveillance entails necessitate the application of Fourth Amendment safeguards.

National security cases, moreover, often reflect a convergence of First and Fourth Amendment values not present in cases of "ordinary" crime. Though the investigative duty of the executive may be stronger in such cases, so also is there greater jeopardy to constitutionally protected speech. ... History abundantly documents the tendency of Government—however benevolent and benign its motives—to view with suspicion those who most fervently dispute its policies. Fourth Amendment protections become the more necessary when the targets of official surveillance may be those suspected of unorthodoxy in their political beliefs. The danger to political dissent is acute where the Government attempts to act under so vague a concept as the power to protect "domestic security." Given the difficulty of defining the domestic security interest, the danger of abuse in acting to protect that interest becomes apparent. ... The price of lawful public dissent must not be a dread of subjection to an unchecked surveillance power. Nor must the fear of unauthorized official eavesdropping deter vigorous citizen dissent and discussion of Government action in private conversation. For private dissent, no less than open public discourse, is essential to our free society.

III

As the Fourth Amendment is not absolute in its terms, our task is to examine and balance the basic values at stake in this case: the duty of Government to protect the domestic security, and the potential danger posed by unreasonable surveillance to individual privacy and free expression. If the legitimate need of Government to safeguard domestic security requires the use of electronic surveillance, the question is whether the needs of citizens for privacy and free expression may not be better protected by requiring a warrant before such surveillance is undertaken. We must also ask whether a warrant requirement would unduly frustrate the efforts of Government to protect itself from acts of subversion and overthrow directed against it.

Though the Fourth Amendment speaks broadly of "unreasonable searches and seizures," the definition of "reasonableness" turns, at least in part, on the more specific commands of the warrant clause. ... [That clause] has been "a valued part of our constitutional law for decades. ... It is not an inconvenience to be somehow 'weighed' against the claims of police efficiency. It is, or should be, an important working part of our machinery of government." ...

These Fourth Amendment freedoms cannot properly be guaranteed if domestic security surveillances may be conducted solely within the discretion of the executive branch. The Fourth Amendment does not contemplate the executive officers of Government as neutral and disinterested magistrates. Their duty and responsibility is to enforce the laws, to investigate, and to prosecute. *Katz*. But those charged with this investigative and prosecutorial duty should not be the sole judges of when to utilize constitutionally sensitive means in pursuing their tasks. The historical judgment, which the Fourth Amendment accepts, is that unreviewed executive discretion may yield too readily to pressures to obtain incriminating evidence and overlook potential invasions of privacy and protected speech.

It may well be that, in the instant case, the Government's surveillance ... was a reasonable one which readily would have gained prior judicial approval. ... The Fourth Amendment contemplates a prior judicial judgment, not the risk that executive discretion may be reasonably exercised. This judicial role accords with our basic constitutional doctrine that individual freedoms will best be preserved through a separation of powers and division of functions among the different branches and levels of Government. The independent check upon executive discretion is not satisfied, as the Government argues, by "extremely limited" post-surveillance judicial review. Indeed, post-surveillance review would never reach the surveillances which failed to result in prosecutions. Prior review by a neutral and detached magistrate is the time-tested means of effectuating Fourth Amendment rights. Beck v. Ohio (1964).

It is true that there have been some exceptions to the warrant requirement. But those exceptions are few in number and carefully delineated, *Katz*; in general, they serve the legitimate needs of law enforcement officers to protect their own well-being and preserve evidence from destruction. ...

The Government argues that ... the requirement of prior judicial review would obstruct the President in the discharge of his constitutional duty to protect domestic security. We are told further that these surveillances are directed primarily to the collecting and maintaining of intelligence with respect to subversive forces, and are not an attempt to gather evidence for specific criminal prosecutions. It is said that this type of surveillance should not be subject to traditional warrant requirements which were established to govern investigation of criminal activity. ...

As a final reason for exemption from a warrant requirement, the Government believes that disclosure to a magistrate of all or even a significant portion of the information involved in domestic security surveillances "would create serious potential dangers to the national security and to the lives of informants and agents. ..." These contentions in behalf of a complete exemption from the warrant requirement, when urged on behalf of the President and the national security in its

domestic implications, merit the most careful consideration. We certainly do not reject them lightly, especially at a time of worldwide ferment.
. . .

But we do not think a case has been made for the requested departure from Fourth Amendment standards. The circumstances described do not justify complete exemption of domestic security surveillance from prior judicial scrutiny. Official surveillance, whether its purpose be criminal investigation or ongoing intelligence gathering, risks infringement of constitutionally protected privacy of speech. Security surveillances are especially sensitive because of the inherent vagueness of the domestic security concept, the necessarily broad and continuing nature of intelligence gathering, and the temptation to utilize such surveillances to oversee political dissent. We recognize . . . the constitutional basis of the President's domestic security role, but we think it must be exercised in a manner compatible with the Fourth Amendment. In this case we hold that this requires an appropriate prior warrant procedure.

We cannot accept the Government's argument that internal security matters are too subtle and complex for judicial evaluation. Courts regularly deal with the most difficult issues of our society. There is no reason to believe that federal judges will be insensitive to or uncomprehending of the issues involved in domestic security cases. . . .

Nor do we believe prior judicial approval will fracture the secrecy essential to official intelligence gathering. The investigation of criminal activity has long involved imparting sensitive information to judicial officers who have respected the confidentialities involved. . . . Title III of the [Act] already has imposed this responsibility on the judiciary in connection with such crimes as espionage, sabotage, and treason, each of which may involve domestic as well as foreign security threats. Moreover, a warrant application involves no public or adversary proceedings: it is an ex parte request before a magistrate or judge. . . .

Thus, we conclude that the Government's concerns do not justify departure in this case from the customary Fourth Amendment requirement of judicial approval prior to initiation of a search or surveillance. Although some added burden will be imposed upon the Attorney General, this inconvenience is justified in a free society to protect constitutional values. . . .

IV

We emphasize . . . the scope of our decision. . . . [T]his case involves only the domestic aspects of national security. We have not addressed, and express no opinion as to, the issues which may be involved with respect to activities of foreign powers or their agents. . . .

The judgment of the Court of Appeals is hereby

Affirmed.

The Chief Justice [**BURGER**] concurs in the result.

Mr. Justice **REHNQUIST** took no part in the consideration or decision of this case.

Mr. Justice **DOUGLAS**, concurring. . . .

Mr. Justice **WHITE** concurring in the judgment. . . .

Editors' Notes

(1) **Query:** In Part **III** of his opinion Powell said that the Court must "balance the basic values at stake." Did he carry through this task in a way that meets Chapter 9's criticisms of a *balancing approach* to interpretation? What relative weights did Powell assign to the values in conflict here? How did he justify this relative weighing?

(2) **Query:** What was Powell's conception of WHAT "the Constitution" includes? How did he link that conception (or how can we link it) to the approach to constitutional interpretation he followed?

(3) **Query:** How did Powell answer the question WHO?

(4) Laird v. Tatum (1972), decided after *U.S. District Court,* involved a class action for an injunction against Army intelligence surveillance of people accused of no crime but suspected of political radicalism. Plaintiffs claimed that this intimate watch on their lives had "a chilling effect" on freedoms protected by the First Amendment. By a 5–4 vote, the Court held that the plaintiffs lacked "standing to sue"—that is, they had not shown real injury to a specifically guaranteed legal right.

Epilogue

As the Convention was breaking up in September, 1787, George Washington, in "the midst of hurry" to leave Philadelphia, sent the Marquis de LaFayette a copy of the new constitutional text. Unsure of what the nation's reaction would be, Washington commented that the document "is now a Child of Fortune, to be fostered by some and buffeted by others."[1] Gouverneur Morris, chairman of the Convention's Committee on Style, which had been largely responsible for putting the text into its final form, was more optimistic about acceptance, but still concerned for the infant's future. When told by a friend that "you have made a good constitution," he allegedly replied: "That depends on how it is construed."[2]

Washington and Morris accurately foretold the history of their offspring. More than two centuries after ratification, "the Constitution" continues to be a "Child of Fortune," and constitutional interpretation remains vital in shaping the child's development. Constitutional interpretation has even played a role in the survival of the nation the document purports to constitute. We read in Chapter 7 Lincoln's First Inaugural claim that "in contemplation . . . of the Constitution, the Union of these States is perpetual." In many less dramatic but still important ways, the interpretive enterprise has helped mold American life. To a large extent, constitutional interpretation determines divisions of authority between Congress and the President and the nation and the states as well as the scope of such (supposed) rights as those to speak, assemble, vote, worship or not worship, control our own bodies, to possess and use property, and to a fair trial if accused of crime.

Constitutional interpretation thus involves clarifying the nation's goals and shaping its culture. Many, perhaps most, people would consider these sorts of actions to be political, a term journalists, judges, and even politicians themselves frequently equate with petty partisanship. But the word need not be so disdainfully defined. Politics, Aristotle wrote, "is most truly the master art,"[3] focusing on the best order for a state and its citizens. By that

---

1. Letter of Sept. 18, 1787, reprinted in Michael Kammen, ed., *The Origins of the American Constitution: A Documentary History* (New York: Penguin, 1987), p. 55.

2. Quoted in Edward S. Corwin, "The Constitution as Instrument and Symbol," 30 *Am.Pol.Sci.Rev.* 1071 (1936); reprinted in Richard Loss, ed., *Corwin on the Constitution* (Ithaca: Cornell University Press, 1981), I, 168, 170.

3. *Nicomachean Ethics*, 1094 [a]–1094 [b]; see also 1099[b] and 1102[a].

definition, the one we utilize, constitutional interpretation is eminently political. It is concerned with determining the goals of a nation and the means that nation considers proper to achieve those goals, that is, allocations of costs and benefits, rights and duties.

As a political undertaking, constitutional interpretation, like the document itself and the traditions, political theories, practices, and earlier interpretations that embed it, is inherently normative. We can speak intelligibly of principles being applied neutrally, that is, uniformly and even-handedly across problems, interests, and parties. But principles are not themselves neutral. We cannot, therefore, speak of any constitution as embodying or constitutional interpretation as involving the definition or application of "neutral principles." [4] Every constitution, like every constitutional text, envisions a particular kind of society and hallows certain values, duties, and rights. Even procedures, whether specified in the basic document or enshrined in practice, designate, at least for that society, certain modes of decision as legitimate and thereby exclude others as illegitimate.

Concerned with such enormous political problems, constitutional interpretation is unavoidably complex. Often couched in arcane jargon, muddled by awkward syntax, and studded with citations to earlier efforts to resolve problems, the enterprise labors to accommodate legal doctrines with evolving reality, the words of a text with unwritten (and perhaps unstable) understandings, grubby customs with high ideals, practical prudence with lofty goals. When Friedrich Nietzsche wrote that "All things are enlinked, enlaced, and enamoured,"[5] he seemed to have been describing the world of constitutional interpretation.

Because of its importance and complexity, that world is commonly characterized by dispute. Its analyses and their implications for human lives are usually contested as well as contestable. Especially in a multi-cultural society, interpretive voices that speak to basic values arouse angry dissent as well as enthusiastic agreement. And the fervor escalates as the stakes increase in significance and the textual bases for interpretations become less determinate.

These contests deeply affect the public and they are open to the public. Justice Brennan spoke common sense when he said "The Constitution is fundamentally a public text." [6] In a constitutional democracy, a constitutional document must be publicly proposed, publicly debated, and publicly accepted. On the other hand, the broader constitution often moves, as Jefferson would have put it, "by silent foot." Sometimes proponents and opponents of a pro-

---

4. See espec. Arthur S. Miller and Ronald F. Howell, "The Myth of Neutrality in Constitutional Adjudication," 27 *U.Chi.L.Rev.* 661 (1960).

5. "The Drunken Song," § 10, *Thus Spake Zarathustra;* in *The Philosophy of Nietzsche* (New York: Modern Library, 1927), p. 363.

6. "The Constitution of the United States: Contemporary Ratification," reprinted above, p. 236.

posed text might not openly debate its fundamental assumptions and broadest implications because they do not perceive these assumptions and implications. Basic practices may develop slowly, sometimes unnoticed even by the practitioners themselves; traditions typically grow by accretion, gradually building up over decades, their progress seldom marked by dramatic events. Nevertheless, the effects of these parts of the constitution may reach as far and as deeply as do the words of the text. Thus, in a constitutional democracy, constitutional interpretation must also be public, required both by the public nature of the document and by the equally public, though often less consciously articulated, broader constitution.

The question recurs: WHO shall do this public interpretation? One message of this book has been that, in the United States, judges do not have a monopoly on constitutional interpretation. They share that function with other governmental officials, academic commentators, journalists, and ordinary citizens. Nor does interpretation, by whomever performed, always settle disputes once and for all. More typically, it operates like a series of intense, sometimes fierce, debates within and among sets of interpreters.[7] Examples abound: the campaign over the Bank of the United States opened in the First Congress and produced, *inter alia,* McCulloch v. Maryland in 1819 and Andrew Jackson's veto of the Bank bill in 1832; the fury over slavery in the territories that the Missouri Compromise of 1820 and the Kansas–Nebraska Act of 1854 tried to calm and *Dred Scott* (1857) fueled; the battle the Court fought for laissez-faire that started in the late nineteenth century and ended only in 1937; the ongoing crusade that Brown v. Board of Education (1954) began and the Civil Rights Act of 1964 joined; and the vituperative, sometimes violent, struggle over abortion that Roe v. Wade (1973) supposedly settled.

Furthermore, American judges typically approach interpretation in a piecemeal, case-by-case, fashion,[8] seldom in the systematic way academic commentators try to do. That is, the justices usually engage in "constitutional adjudication":[9] They claim to interpret "the Constitution" only for the purpose of settling specific cases. The cramped nature of the judicial forum may be functional for a system that aspires to be both democratic and constitutionalist, but the narrow, *ad hoc,* quality of constitutional adjudication underlines the need for other officials as well as private citizens to continue a more wide-ranging debate about WHAT "the Constitution" includes, how it should function, and what it means.

---

7. See, for example, Louis Fisher, *Constitutional Dialogues: Interpretation as a Political Process* (Princeton: Princeton University Press, 1988).

8. There have been, of course, numerous exceptions among the justices, for example: John Marshall, William J. Brennan, Jr., and Antonin Scalia.

9. Thus Harry H. Wellington's apt subtitle: *Interpreting the Constitution: The Supreme Court and the Process of Adjudication* (New Haven: Yale University Press, 1990).

Because constitutional interpretation not only affects contested issues of immediate public policy but also addresses many of a people's basic values, the enterprise inevitably—and profoundly—affects what the nation and its people will become. James Wilson told Pennsylvania's ratifying convention that "We are representatives, sir, not merely of the present age, but of future times...." [10] What Wilson said of the constitution's makers holds for the constitution's interpreters, then and now. Which brings us back to Gouverneur Morris's point: whether we have a good constitution "depends on how it is construed." It is our point also.

---

10. Jonathan Elliot, ed., *The Debates in the Several State Conventions on the Adoption of the Federal Constitution* (2d ed.; Washington: 1836), II, 431.

APPENDIX A

WHEN May a Litigant Invoke "the Constitution"?

In the United States, participants in political debates regularly invoke "the Constitution" as an authoritative ground for political arguments. Even if we restrict the interrogative WHEN to legislative or executive officials, the answer is sweeping, for much governmental work inevitably involves constitutional interpretation. Moreover, as the American political system has developed, for better or worse (see Part III concerning the interrogative, WHO are the Authoritative Interpreters?), judges have taken a special role as constitutional interpreters. And NAACP v. Alabama (1958; reprinted above, p. 798) held that the First and Fourteenth amendments protect the rights of individuals and groups to use the courts to try to redress what they see as political wrongs.

The narrower question of this Appendix is: WHEN may a *litigant,* a person suing or being sued in a court, invoke "the Constitution" as legally protecting his or her interests? To answer that sort of query we must focus on the rules that judges, especially justices of the U.S. Supreme Court, have created to regulate access to their authority to interpret "the Constitution."

Besides its rather narrow original jurisdiction to hear cases in the first instance, the Supreme Court combines three appellate functions that might conceivably have been separated among different courts or, in some respects, not given to courts at all: (1) It serves as the nation's *highest court of appeals,* with the capacity to assure substantive uniformity and procedural consistency in the judicial application of federal law. (2) It operates as the ultimate *judicial* interpreter of federal legislation, deciding, if litigation arises, what Congress meant to say in its efforts to formulate public policy. And (3) it has assumed the role of final *court* of constitutional review, ascertaining the conformity of many, though not all, legally contested governmental actions with the justices' interpretations of "the Constitution." Here, as in earlier chapters, we remind readers that not all public policies can be challenged in courts and that the justices will not automatically pass judgment on all policies that can be so challenged.

Although these three functions may overlap to a greater or lesser extent depending on the case, the first two functions occupy the largest portion of the Court's workload and often do not concern constitutional interpretation. The third role, however, involves the Court in the most, and the most heated, public controversies about the legitimacy of specific public polices as well as the reach of its own authority. And it is access to this third function that the Court has sought most assiduously to control through devices connected to the interrogative WHEN.

Two forces—one of practical political power and the other of normative political theory—combine to require judges to pay a marked degree of deference to the decisions of elected officials. Nevertheless, it is important to understand that the rules judges have constructed around the jurisdictional clauses of the constitutional document and congressional statutes insure that whatever the correct response to the issue of deference may be, decisions about how to respond or whether to respond at all remain firmly under the control of judges.

One can compare judicial power to diplomacy in international relations. Judges share power with legislative and executive officials who not only react to pressures from the electorate but also have their own—often strongly held—ideas about what "the Constitution" means and what policies the nation needs. Furthermore, those officials may have weapons—the power to spend or not spend money, to nominate or confirm new judges, or propose amendments to the constitutional text, for example—with which to combat the Court.[1]

Nowhere are the prudential aspects of judicial power more evident than in deciding whether to interpret "the Constitution." Once the justices choose to interpret it, they frequently confront serious clashes among the logical imperatives of: (1) "the Constitution" simply as a text containing a body of legal rules, (2) "the Constitution" as the expression of normative political theories, and (3) "the Constitution" as a means of coping with the compelling demands of practical government. Sometimes it may be wiser—and more often it may seem wiser—to leave resolution of these competing demands to other officials.

The Supreme Court's procedures allow it some control over timing, even of decisions on controversies it has agreed to hear. The justices can carry a case over for argument in the next term or even two terms, announce their decision many months after oral argument, remand the case to the trial court for clarification of the record, or decide the dispute on procedural rather than substantive grounds. The justices have a rule, not always followed, of deciding constitutional questions only if no other course is open.

There are other, more complex, means of control. But to understand those, one must know something of the sinuosities of federal jurisdiction and judicial organization.

---

1. For a discussion, see Walter F. Murphy, *Elements of Judicial Strategy* (Chicago: University of Chicago Press, 1964), espec. ch. 2.

I. FEDERAL JURISDICTION

A. General

Most succinctly, the term "jurisdiction," means the authority to say what the law is. Obviously, that is an enormous power, but it is not unlimited. Chapter 4 noted that judges lack a self-starter and have only limited jurisdiction to hear and decide cases. Article III of the constitutional document, as modified by the Eleventh Amendment, provides an outline of federal jurisdiction. The two organizing factors are the nature of the controversy and the status of the parties to the dispute:

1. *Nature of the Controversy.* The case must involve:

    a. Interpretation of the U.S. Constitution or a federal statute or treaty;

    b. Admiralty or maritime law.

2. *Status of the Parties.* One of the parties must be:

    c. The United States government or any of its offices or officers;

    d. A diplomatic or consular representative of a foreign nation;

    e. A state government suing:

        (i) Another state;

        (ii) A citizen of another state;

        (iii) A foreign government or its subjects;

    f. A citizen of one state suing a citizen of another state;

    g. An American citizen suing a foreign government or a citizen of a foreign nation;

    h. A citizen of one state suing a citizen of his own state where both claim land under grants of different states.

Any one of elements (a) through (h) raises a federal question, which (subject to congressional regulations and judge-made rules) federal courts may decide.

B. Mandatory Jurisdiction

Article III says that "the judicial power shall extend" to all of these kinds of cases "in law and equity." This sentence is imperative in mood, and Justice Story in Martin v. Hunter's Lessee (1816; reprinted above, at p. 359) and some later commentators[2] have claimed that Congress was obliged to establish lower federal courts and confer jurisdiction upon them. Nevertheless, the working principle of federal judges has been that, except for the original jurisdiction of the Supreme Court, the authority to hear cases flows

---

2. Julius Goebel, *History of the Supreme Court of the United States: Antecedents and Beginnings to 1801* (New York: Macmillan, 1971), pp. 246–47. The late Judge Henry J. Friendly disagreed: *Federal Jurisdiction* (New York: Columbia University Press, 1973), p. 2.

to federal courts not directly from Article III but indirectly through congressional statutes.[3]

In creating national courts, Congress did not give federal judges anything like full authority over these sorts of cases until after the Civil War, and even today it has not completely filled in Article III's outline. Moreover, Congress has granted federal courts *exclusive* jurisdiction in only a few areas—either geographic (such as the District of Columbia) or topical (such as interpretation of congressional statutes regulating bankruptcy, patents, taxes, and most aspects of federal criminal law). A private citizen who initiates a lawsuit raising a federal question typically has a choice of beginning in a state or federal court.

C. Law and Equity

The phrase "in law and equity" refers to different kinds of litigation. The principal difference between courts of law and equity lies in the nature of the remedies they offer. *Law* mainly provides *compensatory* justice. For private litigants, monetary damages will be the usual remedy, jail sentences or fines if the government secures a criminal conviction. *Equity,* on the other hand, provides *preventive* justice. It can order a defendant not to act, to cease acting, or to undo the effects of previous action. Its most common remedy is the injunction, an order directed to a named person or persons, possibly including public officials, forbidding them from certain behavior. Sometimes an injunction is quite simple, as when it prohibits an official from enforcing a particular statute. Sometimes, it can be complicated, as when it in effect requires state officials to redraw the lines of electoral districts to conform to the doctrine of "one person, one vote."

In the Judiciary Act of 1789, Congress accomplished a sweeping innovation by establishing one set of federal courts to function both as courts of law and equity.[4] This dual capacity not only requires fewer judges, it also allows litigants to combine proceedings—for example, to file a single suit for an injunction to prevent further injury as well as for money to compensate for past injury. Most states have copied this reform, though many only in this century.

D. Cases and Controversies

Article III limits federal jurisdiction to "cases" and "controversies." These are words of art, technical terms that refer to a real dispute (as distinguished from a friendly quarrel or an academic debate) between two parties in which one has injured a legally

---

3. See espec. Cary v. Curtis (1845): "[T]he organization of the judicial power, definition and distribution of the subjects of jurisdiction in the federal tribunals, and the modes of their actions and authority, have been, and of right must be, the work of the legislature."

4. Recall Brutus's fear during the debates on ratification that Article III's delegation of both these kinds of jurisdiction to the Supreme Court would give that tribunal almost unlimited power. ("Letters of Brutus," No. 11, [1788]; reprinted above, p. 281.)

protected right of the other or is threatening that right with immediate injury. Repeatedly, the Court has said that federal judges may not answer hypothetical questions or make decisions that will have no practical effect. The requirement that there be a "case" or "controversy" is the reason that justices give for refusing to render advisory opinions.

II. THE ORGANIZATION OF FEDERAL COURTS

Federal jurisdiction is divided into two kinds: *original,* authority to hear and decide cases as a court of first instance, that is, to hold trials; and *appellate,* authority to review decisions of lower courts. Article III specifies that the Supreme Court shall have original jurisdiction in cases involving foreign diplomats and those to which a state is a party. "In all other cases before mentioned, the Supreme Court shall have appellate jurisdiction, both as to law and fact, with such exceptions, and under such regulations as the Congress shall make."

A. Legislative Courts

There is an important difference between courts Congress has established under Article III and those it has created under powers given under Article I—for example, to govern territories. The latter are "special" or "legislative" courts.[5] They have limited jurisdiction, and their judges may serve for specific terms rather than during "good behavior." The best known legislative tribunals are the Tax Court, which hears appeals from the Internal Revenue Service, and the Court of Military Appeals, which reviews courts martial. Congress has specified that litigants may, under certain circumstances, ask "regular" federal courts to review decisions of these legislative tribunals.

B. Constitutional Courts

In Europe the term "constitutional courts" refers to special tribunals whose jurisdiction is pretty much limited to constitutional interpretation. (Other courts usually lack authority to interpret and apply "the Constitution" in cases that come before them.) On the other hand, in the United States the term constitutional courts refers to the tribunals Congress has created under Article III. Judges who staff these courts must be nominated by the President, confirmed by the Senate, and can be removed only by impeachment and conviction. Their jurisdiction is limited to the kinds of cases and controversies described above. Congress has vested most federal jurisdiction in three layers of courts: district courts, courts of appeals, and the Supreme Court.

---

5. See John Marshall's opinion for the Court in American Ins. Co. v. Canter (1828); and discussion in Paul M. Bator, et al., *Hart and Wechsler's The Federal Courts and the Federal System* (3d ed.; Westbury, NY: The Foundation Press, 1988), pp. 425–478; and Martin H. Redish, *Federal Jurisdiction* (Indianapolis: Bobbs–Merrill, 1980), ch. 2.

1. *District Courts.* Most federal civil and criminal cases begin at this level. There are currently 91 such courts in the United States, at least one in each state, the District of Columbia, and Puerto Rico. Usually a single judge presides, though several dozen may be attached to the courts. Here trials are held and juries deliberate. About 200,000 cases a year are filed in these courts. Many of these, however, are settled between the parties without trial and, in criminal cases, by "plea bargains" between defendants and U.S. Attorneys. Nevertheless, dockets are typically crowded and civil suits may take several years to come to trial.

In a nontechnical sense, district courts also sit as appellate tribunals when they hear petitions for habeas corpus from prisoners convicted in state courts. Normally, a person convicted in a state court who wishes to appeal must first utilize the review provided by state law. Afterward, the prisoner may ask the U.S. Supreme Court to take the case. If this effort fails, there is yet another chance: a petition to a federal district court for habeas corpus, alleging a federal constitutional flaw in the state trial.

The district judge must then examine the record and pass on the merits of the case. These petitions are usually frivolous, but occasionally a judge finds serious error and frees the prisoner. The losing side in the district court may appeal to the appropriate U.S. court of appeals, and the loser there may seek review by the Supreme Court.[6]

Some cases reprinted in this book have been appeals from three-judge district courts. These are special tribunals convened to hear a particular controversy; they have no life beyond the case that called them into existence. To prevent a single federal judge from issuing an injunction against enforcement of a state statute, Congress in 1911 required such suits to be heard by a three-judge district court, at least one of whose members had to be a judge from the court of appeals. In 1937, Congress imposed a similar requirement on suits against enforcement of federal statutes; and other regulations authorized such tribunals in other kinds of disputes, such as those under the Sherman AntiTrust Act.

Three-judge courts caused a great strain on judicial energies. In 1976 Congress eliminated these tribunals except for a few situations such as apportionment cases or enforcement of the Civil Rights Acts of 1964 and 1965. As in the past, the loser in these courts can obtain review by direct appeal to the Supreme Court.

2. *Courts of Appeal.* Litigants who lose in federal district courts have one appeal as a matter of right. Congress has divided the areas served by district courts into twelve circuits, each headed

---

6. Under Chief Justice Rehnquist, the Court has severely restricted the access of state prisoners to federal courts through habeas corpus. For a sharply critical analysis, see Larry W. Yackle, *Reclaiming the Federal Courts* (Cambridge: Harvard University Press, 1994).

by a court of appeals. One of these circuits includes only the District of Columbia, but the others, which are numbered, sweep across the country in a fashion that reflects bargains among legislators as much as fully rational divisions of territory.

Until the 1890s, justices of the Supreme Court "rode circuit" during part of the year and sat as trial judges. They still carry the title of circuit judges, and each is assigned to at least one circuit. Some justices try to visit their assigned areas but rarely can they hear cases there. Justices, however, may sit as circuit judges in their own chambers in Washington to hear cases that require immediate action. Usually these involve petitions to "stay" (delay the effect of) lower court orders until the full Supreme Court can decide the cases.

Currently, 150 judges staff the circuit courts.[7] Only six are assigned to the First Circuit but 25 to the Ninth, indicating wide disparities in caseloads. Normally three judges, assigned by the chief judge of the circuit, hear each case, though in rare instances the entire court sits *en banc*. Almost all cases are appeals from district courts, though the Court of Appeals for the District of Columbia also reviews orders of some federal administrative agencies.

3. *The Supreme Court.* The Supreme Court sits at the apex of a twin system of courts. The justices have appellate jurisdiction over all cases from U.S. courts of appeals and some legislative tribunals, as well as those decisions of the highest state courts involving federal questions.

Jurisdiction over state courts, however, does not extend to interpreting state law. Federal courts take state laws to mean what the highest state court says they mean. Even, for example, if a state repeats verbatim the wording of a provision of the U.S. constitutional text, federal courts will take the state document to mean what the highest state court says it means rather than what the U.S. Supreme Court has said the same provision of the federal text means. If no state court has yet interpreted a state statute or constitutional provision, federal judges either will not decide the issue until state courts have had an opportunity to interpret it or, if an immediate ruling is necessary, will follow state interpretations of similar acts or clauses. This deference, however, does not in any way imply that the justices will not exercise their own judgment about the conformity of state enactments with "the Constitution," statutes, or treaties of the United States.

The Supreme Court also has some original jurisdiction. Most of these cases concern disputes between states over such matters as boundaries and allocations of water resources. The Court usually

---

7. The number of federal district and circuit judges increases dramatically if one counts the retired jurists who take "senior status," that is, formally retire but make themselves available to sit to help with burgeoning dockets.

appoints a "special master" to hold hearings, collect evidence, and present recommendations. The final decision, however, belongs to the justices themselves.

C. The Appellate Jurisdiction of the Supreme Court

Cases come to the Court for review in one of three ways: *certification, appeal,* or *certiorari.*

1. *Certification.* Under this seldom used procedure, a court of appeals or the Court of Claims "certifies" to the Supreme Court that a case poses an issue of such difficulty that the lower court needs instruction. Only questions of law, not of fact, can be certified. The Supreme Court may, however, require a court of appeals (though not the Court of Claims) to send the record of the case up so that the justices can decide the basic dispute rather than merely answer a legal question out of context.

2. *Appeal.* At one time, the Court was obliged to hear a wide range of cases that losing litigants would ask it to review. That form of appellate jurisdiction was called "mandatory." The losing litigant had a choice but, supposedly, the justices did not. At least since the 1940s, however, the Court had been treating the decision to hear an appeal as a matter of discretion. And, in recent decades, most especially in 1988,[8] Congress has whittled away at "mandatory jurisdiction" replacing it with "discretionary jurisdiction," that is, leaving it to the justices to decide whether they should hear such cases—what in fact the Court had been doing. Essentially, for purposes of constitutional interpretation, a losing litigant may invoke the Court's mandatory jurisdiction only when a state court has invalidated a federal statute or treaty or a federal court has invalidated a state statute.

3. *Certiorari.* Petitions for a writ of certiorari form the main avenue to the Court's appellate jurisdiction. Unless their circumstances fit the now constricted categories of appeals, losers in courts of appeals or the highest state courts, providing they raise federal questions, who want the Supreme Court to review their cases must petition for certiorari. The Court has been receiving more than 4,000 such petitions each year and has been granting less than 150.

Chapter 4 described in more detail the way the Court handles requests. Granting or denying the writ is completely within the Court's discretion. It takes a vote of only four justices to grant, although a majority of the justices may later "DIG" the writ—that is, "dismiss" it as "improvidently granted." Denial of "cert" means that the lower court's decision stands; but, because of the wide variety of reasons that might be involved, the Court's refusal to review is not a decision on the merits and has no value as a precedent.

---

8. Pub. L. 100–352 (1988), amending 28 *U.S. Code* §§ 1251ff, espec. § 1254.

Rule 10 of the Supreme Court Rules explicitly states that "certiorari is not a matter of right, but of judicial discretion, and will be granted only where there are special and important reasons therefor." That Rule then outlines *some* of the circumstances the justices consider important in evaluating petitions:

(a) When a United States court of appeals has rendered a decision in conflict with the decision of another United States court of appeals on the same matter; or has decided a federal question in a way in conflict with a state court of last resort; or has so far departed from the accepted and usual course of judicial proceedings, or so far sanctioned such a departure by a lower court, as to call for an exercise of this Court's power of supervision.

(b) When a state court of last resort has decided a federal question in a way in conflict with the decision of another state court of last resort or of a United States court of appeals.

(c) When a state court or a United States court of appeals has decided an important question of federal law which has not been, but should be, settled by this Court, or has decided a federal question in a way in conflict with applicable decisions of this Court.

These considerations are hardly exhaustive. Furthermore, several studies[9] have demonstrated that the justices often ignore these factors and seem quite concerned with others.

---

9. See espec. Joseph Tanenhaus et al., "The Supreme Court's Certiorari Jurisdiction: Cue Theory," in Glendon A. Schubert, ed., *Judicial Decision–Making* (New York: The Free Press, 1963); S. Sidney Ulmer et al., "The Decision to Grant or Deny Certiorari," 6 *Law & Soc.Rev.* 637 (1972); and the spate of articles by Fowler Harper and co-authors that appeared in the *U.Pa.L.Rev.* from 1950–55. See also the literature cited in the notes to Chapters 1 and 4; and Melinda Gann Hall, "Docket Control as an Influence on Judicial Voting," 10 *Justice Sys. J.* 243 (1985); H. W. Perry, *Deciding to Decide: Agenda Setting in the United States Supreme Court* (Cambridge: Harvard University Press, 1991); and Doris Marie Provine, *Case Selection in the United States Supreme Court* (Chicago: University of Chicago Press, 1980).

*

APPENDIX B

Table of U.S. Supreme Court Justices

The table shows the positions on the Court as numbered columns, so that lines of succession can be followed. The first column represents the Chief Justice. Each justice's political party affiliation and state are provided. In instances where a justice serves until a year prior to the year in which a successor takes office, the justice's final year of service is given in italics in the numbered column representing his or her position on the Court.

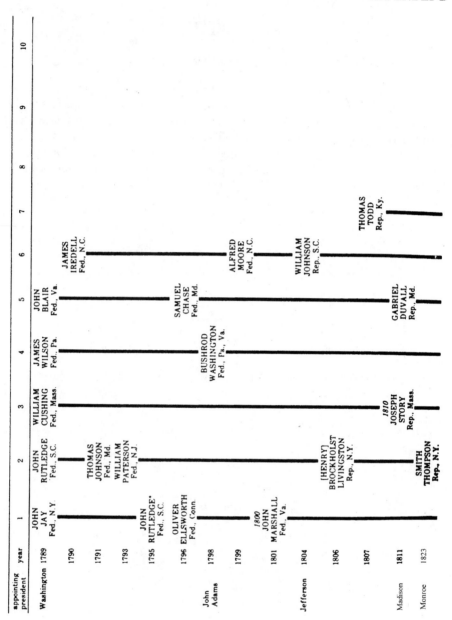

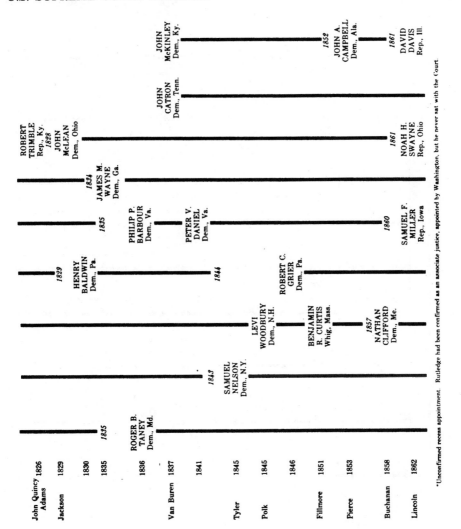

*Unconfirmed recess appointment. Rutledge had been confirmed as an associate justice, appointed by Washington, but he never sat with the Court.

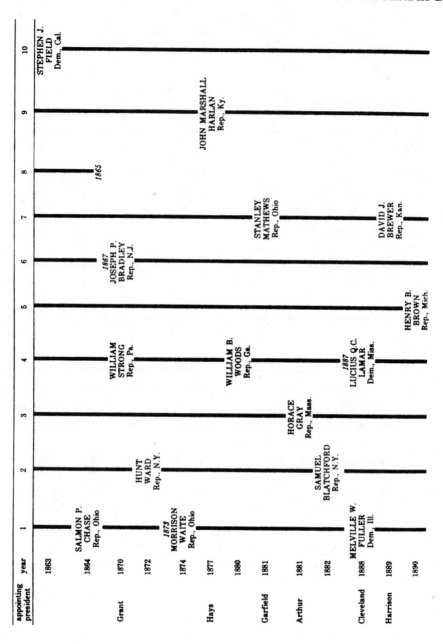

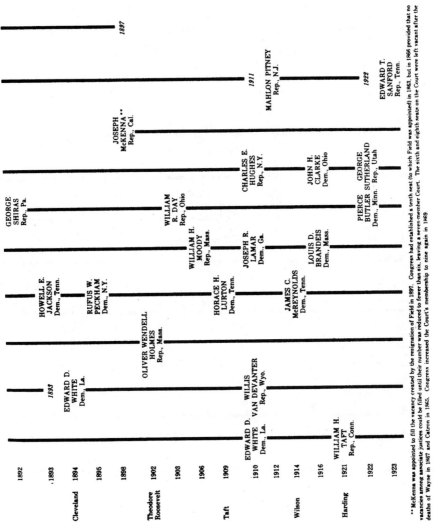

** McKenna was appointed to fill the vacancy created by the resignation of Field in 1897. Congress had established a tenth seat (to which Field was appointed) in 1863, but in 1866 provided that no vacancies among associate justices could be filled until their number was reduced to fewer than six, leaving a seven-member Court. The sixth and eighth seats on the Court were left vacant after the death of Wayne in 1867 and Catron in 1865. Congress increased the Court's membership to nine again in 1869

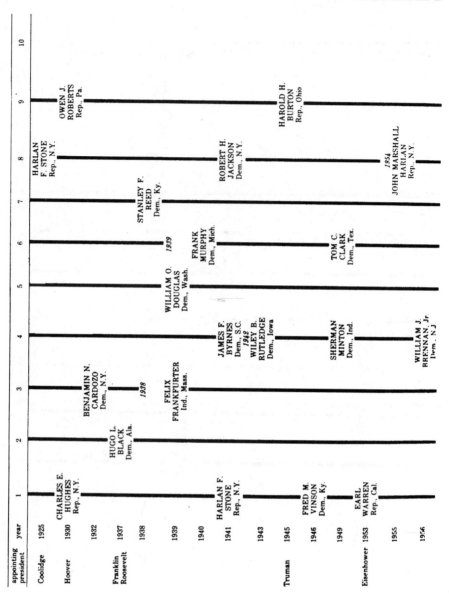

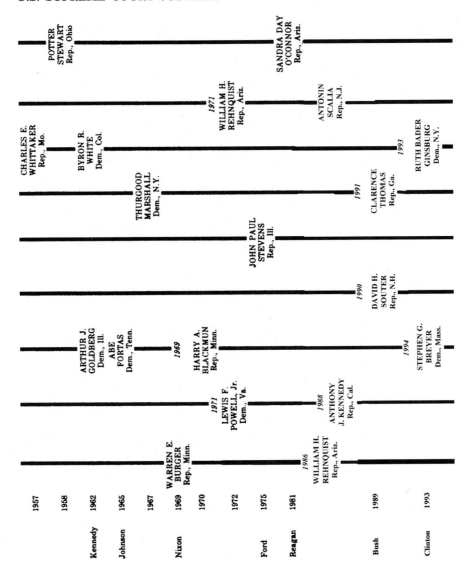

APPENDIX C

The Constitution of the United States of America

We the People of the United States, in Order to form a more perfect Union, establish Justice, insure domestic Tranquility, provide for the common defence, promote the general Welfare, and secure the Blessings of Liberty to ourselves and our Posterity, do ordain and establish this Constitution for the United States of America.

Article I

SECTION 1

All legislative Powers herein granted shall be vested in a Congress of the United States, which shall consist of a Senate and House of Representatives.

SECTION 2

The House of Representatives shall be composed of Members chosen every second Year by the People of the several States, and the Electors in each State shall have the Qualifications requisite for Electors of the most numerous Branch of the State Legislature.

No Person shall be a Representative who shall not have attained to the Age of twenty five Years, and been seven Years a Citizen of the United States, and who shall not, when elected, be an Inhabitant of that State in which he shall be chosen.

Representatives and direct Taxes shall be apportioned among the several States which may be included within this Union, according to their respective Numbers, which shall be determined by adding to the whole Number of free Persons, including those bound to Service for a Term of Years, and excluding Indians not taxed, three fifths of all other Persons. The actual Enumeration shall be made within three Years after the first Meeting of the Congress of the United States, and within every subsequent Term of ten Years, in such Manner as they shall by Law direct. The Number of Representatives shall not exceed one for every thirty Thousand, but each State shall have at Least one Representative; and until such enumeration shall be made, the State of New Hampshire shall be entitled to chuse three, Massachusetts eight, Rhode Island and Providence Plantations one, Connecticut five, New–York six, New Jersey four, Pennsylvania eight, Delaware one, Maryland six, Virginia ten, North Carolina five, South Carolina five, and Georgia three.

When vacancies happen in the Representation from any State, the Executive Authority thereof shall issue Writs of Election to fill such Vacancies.

The House of Representatives shall chuse their Speaker and other Officers; and shall have the sole Power of Impeachment.

SECTION 3

The Senate of the United States shall be composed of two Senators from each State, chosen by the Legislature thereof, for six Years; and each Senator shall have one Vote.

Immediately after they shall be assembled in Consequence of the first Election, they shall be divided as equally as may be into three Classes. The Seats of the Senators of the first Class shall be vacated at the Expiration of the second Year, of the second Class at the Expiration of the fourth Year, and of the third Class at the Expiration of the sixth Year, so that one third may be chosen every second Year; and if Vacancies happen by Resignation, or otherwise, during the Recess of the Legislature of any State, the Executive thereof may make temporary Appointments until the next Meeting of the Legislature, which shall then fill such Vacancies.

No Person shall be a Senator who shall not have attained to the Age of thirty Years, and been nine Years a Citizen of the United States, and who shall not, when elected, be an Inhabitant of that State for which he shall be chosen.

The Vice President of the United States shall be President of the Senate, but shall have no Vote, unless they be equally divided.

The Senate shall chuse their other Officers, and also a President pro tempore, in the Absence of the Vice President, or when he shall exercise the Office of President of the United States.

The Senate shall have the sole Power to try all Impeachments. When sitting for that Purpose, they shall be on Oath or Affirmation. When the President of the United States is tried the Chief Justice shall preside: And no Person shall be convicted without the Concurrence of two thirds of the Members present.

Judgment in Cases of Impeachment shall not extend further than to removal from Office, and disqualification to hold and enjoy any Office of honor, Trust or Profit under the United States: but the Party convicted shall nevertheless be liable and subject to Indictment, Trial, Judgment and Punishment, according to Law.

SECTION 4

The Times, Places and Manner of holding Elections for Senators and Representatives, shall be prescribed in each State by the Legislature thereof; but the Congress may at any time by Law make or alter such Regulations, except as to the Places of chusing Senators.

The Congress shall assemble at least once in every Year, and such Meeting shall be on the first Monday in December, unless they shall by Law appoint a different Day.

SECTION 5

Each House shall be the Judge of the Elections, Returns and Qualifications of its own Members, and a Majority of each shall constitute a Quorum to do Business; but a smaller Number may adjourn from day to day, and may be authorized to compel the Attendance of absent Members, in such Manner, and under such Penalties as each House may provide.

Each House may determine the Rules of its Proceedings, punish its Members for disorderly Behaviour, and, with the Concurrence of two thirds, expel a Member.

Each House shall keep a Journal of its Proceedings, and from time to time publish the same, excepting such Parts as may in their Judgment require Secrecy; and the Yeas and Nays of the Members of either House on any question shall, at the Desire of one fifth of those Present, be entered on the Journal.

Neither House, during the Session of Congress, shall, without the Consent of the other, adjourn for more than three days, nor to any other Place than that in which the two Houses shall be sitting.

SECTION 6

The Senators and Representatives shall receive a Compensation for their Services, to be ascertained by Law, and paid out of the Treasury of the United States. They shall in all Cases, except Treason, Felony and Breach of the Peace, be privileged from Arrest during their Attendance at the Session of their respective Houses, and in going to and returning from the same; and for any Speech or Debate in either House, they shall not be questioned in any other Place.

No Senator or Representative shall, during the Time for which he was elected, be appointed to any civil Office under the Authority of the United States, which shall have been created, or the Emoluments whereof shall have been encreased during such time; and no Person holding any Office under the United States, shall be a Member of either House during his Continuance in Office.

SECTION 7

All Bills for raising Revenue shall originate in the House of Representatives; but the Senate may propose or concur with amendments as on other Bills.

Every Bill which shall have passed the House of Representatives and the Senate, shall, before it become a Law, be presented to the President of the United States; If he approve he shall sign it, but if not he shall return it, with his Objections to that House in which it shall have originated, who shall enter the Objections at large on their Journal, and proceed to reconsider it. If after such Reconsideration two thirds of that House shall agree to pass the Bill, it shall be sent, together with the Objections, to the other House, by which it shall likewise be reconsidered, and if approved by two thirds of that House, it shall become a Law. But in all such Cases the Votes of both Houses shall be determined by Yeas and Nays, and the Names of the Persons voting for and against the Bill shall be entered on the Journal of each House respectively. If any Bill shall not be returned by the President within ten Days (Sunday excepted) after it shall have been presented to him, the Same shall be a Law, in like Manner as if he had signed it, unless the Congress by their Adjournment prevent its Return, in which Case it shall not be a Law.

Every Order, Resolution, or Vote to which the Concurrence of the Senate and House of Representatives may be necessary (except on a question of Adjournment) shall be presented to the President of the United States; and before the Same shall take Effect, shall be approved by him, or being disapproved by him, shall be repassed by two thirds of the Senate and House of Representatives, according to the Rules and Limitations prescribed in the Case of a Bill.

SECTION 8

The Congress shall have Power To lay and collect Taxes, Duties, Imposts and Excises, to pay the Debts and provide for the common Defence and general Welfare of the United States; but all Duties, Imposts and Excises shall be uniform throughout the United States;

To borrow Money on the credit of the United States;

To regulate Commerce with foreign Nations, and among the several States, and with the Indian Tribes;

To establish an uniform Rule of Naturalization, and uniform Laws on the subject of Bankruptcies throughout the United States;

To coin Money, regulate the Value thereof, and of foreign Coin, and fix the Standard of Weights and Measures;

To provide for the Punishment of counterfeiting the Securities and current Coin of the United States;

To establish Post Offices and post Roads;

To promote the Progress of Science and useful Arts, by securing for limited Times to Authors and Inventors the exclusive Right to their respective Writings and Discoveries;

To constitute Tribunals inferior to the supreme Court;

To define and punish Piracies and Felonies committed on the high Seas, and Offences against the Law of Nations;

To declare War, grant Letters of Marque and Reprisal, and make Rules concerning Captures on Land and Water;

To raise and support Armies, but no Appropriation of Money to that Use shall be for a longer Term than two Years;

To provide and maintain a Navy;

To make Rules for the Government and Regulation of the land and naval Forces;

To provide for calling forth the Militia to execute the Laws of the Union, suppress Insurrections and repel Invasions;

To provide for organizing, arming, and disciplining, the Militia, and for governing such Part of them as may be employed in the Service of the United States, reserving to the States respectively, the Appointment of the Officers, and the Authority of training the Militia according to the discipline prescribed by Congress;

To exercise exclusive Legislation in all Cases whatsoever, over such District (not exceeding ten Miles square) as may, by Cession of particular States, and the Acceptance of Congress, become the Seat of the Government of the United States, and to exercise like Authority over all Places purchased by the Consent of the Legislature of the State in which the Same shall be, for the Erection of Forts, Magazines, Arsenals, dock-Yards, and other needful Buildings;—And

To make all Laws which shall be necessary and proper for carrying into Execution the foregoing Powers, and all other Powers vested by this Constitution in the Government of the United States, or in any Department or Officer thereof.

SECTION 9

The Migration or Importation of such Persons as any of the States now existing shall think proper to admit, shall not be prohibited by the Congress prior to the Year one thousand eight hundred and eight, but a Tax or duty may be imposed on such Importation, not exceeding ten dollars for each Person.

The Privilege of the Writ of Habeas Corpus shall not be suspended, unless when in Cases of Rebellion or Invasion the public Safety may require it.

No Bill of Attainder or ex post facto Law shall be passed.

No Capitation, or other direct, Tax shall be laid, unless in Proportion to the Census or Enumeration herein before directed to be taken.

No Tax or Duty shall be laid on Articles exported from any State.

No Preference shall be given by any Regulation of Commerce or Revenue to the Ports of one State over those of another; nor shall Vessels bound to, or from, one State, be obliged to enter, clear or pay Duties in another.

No Money shall be drawn from the Treasury, but in Consequence of Appropriations made by Law; and a regular Statement and Account of the Receipts and Expenditures of all public Money shall be published from time to time.

No Title of Nobility shall be granted by the United States: And no Person holding any Office of Profit or Trust under them, shall, without the Consent of the Congress, accept of any present, Emolument, Office, or Title, of any kind whatever, from any King, Prince or foreign State.

SECTION 10

No State shall enter into any Treaty, Alliance, or Confederation; grant Letters of Marque and Reprisal; coin Money; emit Bills of Credit; make any Thing but gold and silver Coin a Tender in Payment of Debts; pass any Bill of Attainder, ex post facto Law, or Law impairing the Obligation of Contracts, or grant any Title of Nobility.

No State shall, without the Consent of the Congress, lay any Imposts or Duties on Imports or Exports, except what may be absolutely necessary for executing its inspection Laws: and the net Produce of all Duties and Imposts, laid by any State on Imports or Exports, shall be for the Use of the Treasury of the United States; and all such Laws shall be subject to the Revision and Controul of the Congress.

No State shall, without the Consent of Congress, lay any Duty of Tonnage, keep Troops, or Ships of War in time of Peace, enter into any Agreement or Compact with another State, or with a foreign Power, or engage in War, unless actually invaded, or in such imminent Danger as will not admit of delay.

Article II

SECTION 1

The executive Power shall be vested in a President of the United States of America. He shall hold his Office during the Term of four Years, and, together with the Vice President, chosen for the same Term, be elected, as follows

Each State shall appoint, in such Manner as the Legislature thereof may direct, a Number of Electors, equal to the whole Number of Senators and Representatives to which the State may be entitled in the Congress: but no Senator or Representative, or Person holding an Office of Trust or Profit under the United States, shall be appointed an Elector.

The Electors shall meet in their respective States, and vote by Ballot for two Persons, of whom one at least shall not be an Inhabitant of the same State with themselves. And they shall make a List of all the Persons voted for, and of the Number of Votes for each; which List they shall sign and certify, and transmit sealed to the Seat of the Government of the United States, directed to the President of the Senate. The President of the Senate shall, in the Presence of the Senate and House of Representatives, open all the

Certificates, and the Votes shall then be counted. The Person having the greatest Number of Votes shall be the President, if such Number be a Majority of the whole Number of Electors appointed; and if there be more than one who have such Majority, and have an equal Number of Votes, then the House of Representatives shall immediately chuse by Ballot one of them for President; and if no Person have a Majority, then from the five highest on the List the said House shall in like Manner chuse the President. But in chusing the President, the Votes shall be taken by States, the Representation from each State having one Vote; a quorum for this Purpose shall consist of a Member or Members from two thirds of the States, and a Majority of all the States shall be necessary to a Choice. In every Case, after the Choice of the President, the Person having the greatest Number of Votes of the Electors shall be the Vice President. But if there should remain two or more who have equal Votes, the Senate shall chuse from them by Ballot the Vice President.

The Congress may determine the Time of chusing the Electors, and the Day on which they shall give their Votes; which Day shall be the same throughout the United States.

No Person except a natural born Citizen, or a Citizen of the United States, at the time of the Adoption of this Constitution, shall be eligible to the Office of President; neither shall any Person be eligible to that Office who shall not have attained to the Age of thirty five Years, and been fourteen Years a Resident within the United States.

In Case of the Removal of the President from Office, or of his Death, Resignation, or Inability to discharge the Powers and Duties of the said Office, the Same shall devolve on the Vice President, and the Congress may by Law provide for the Case of Removal, Death, Resignation or Inability, both of the President and Vice President, declaring what Officer shall then act as President, and such Officer shall act accordingly, until the Disability be removed, or a President shall be elected.

The President shall, at stated Times, receive for his Services, a Compensation, which shall neither be encreased nor diminished during the Period for which he shall have been elected, and he shall not receive within that Period any other Emolument from the United States, or any of them.

Before he enter on the Execution of his Office, he shall take the following Oath or Affirmation:—"I do solemnly swear (or affirm) that I will faithfully execute the Office of President of the United States, and will to the best of my Ability, preserve, protect and defend the Constitution of the United States."

SECTION 2

The President shall be Commander in Chief of the Army and Navy of the United States, and of the Militia of the several States, when called into the actual Service of the United States; he may require the Opinion, in writing, of the principal Officer in each of the executive Departments, upon any Subject relating to the Duties of their respective Offices, and he shall have Power to grant Reprieves and Pardons for Offences against the United States, except in Cases of Impeachment.

He shall have Power, by and with the Advice and Consent of the Senate, to make Treaties, provided two thirds of the Senators present concur; and he shall nominate, and by and with the Advice and Consent of the Senate, shall appoint Ambassadors, other public Ministers and Consuls, Judges of the supreme Court, and all other Officers of the United States, whose Appointments are not herein otherwise provided for, and which shall be established by Law: but the Congress may by Law vest the Appointment of such inferior Officers, as they think proper, in the President alone, in the Courts of Law, or in the Heads of Departments.

The President shall have Power to fill up all Vacancies that may happen during the Recess of the Senate, by granting Commissions which shall expire at the End of their next Session.

SECTION 3

He shall from time to time give to the Congress Information of the State of the Union, and recommend to their Consideration such Measures as he shall judge necessary and expedient; he may, on extraordinary Occasions, convene both Houses, or either of them, and in Case of Disagreement between them, with Respect to the Time of Adjournment, he may adjourn them to such Time as he shall think proper; he shall receive Ambassadors and other public Ministers; he shall take Care that the Laws be faithfully executed, and shall Commission all the Officers of the United States.

SECTION 4

The President, Vice President and all Civil Officers of the United States, shall be removed from Office on Impeachment for, and Conviction of, Treason, Bribery, or other high Crimes and Misdemeanors.

Article III

SECTION 1

The judicial Power of the United States, shall be vested in one supreme Court, and in such inferior Courts as the Congress may from time to time ordain and establish. The Judges, both of the supreme and inferior Courts, shall hold their Offices during good Behaviour, and shall, at stated Times, receive for their Services, a Compensation, which shall not be diminished during their Continuance in Office.

SECTION 2

The judicial Power shall extend to all Cases, in Law and Equity, arising under this Constitution, the Laws of the United States, and Treaties made, or which shall be made, under their Authority;—to all Cases affecting Ambassadors, other public Ministers and Consuls;—to all Cases of admiralty and maritime Jurisdiction;—to Controversies to which the United States shall be a Party;—to Controversies between two or more States;—between a State and Citizens of another State;—between Citizens of different States;—between Citizens of the same State claiming Lands under Grants of different States, and between a State, or the Citizens thereof, and foreign States, Citizens or Subjects.

In all Cases affecting Ambassadors, other public Ministers and Consuls, and those in which a State shall be Party, the Supreme Court shall have original Jurisdiction. In all the other Cases before mentioned, the supreme Court shall have appellate Jurisdiction, both as to Law and Fact, with such Exceptions, and under such Regulations as the Congress shall make.

The Trial of all Crimes, except in Cases of Impeachment, shall be by Jury; and such Trial shall be held in the State where the said Crimes shall have been committed; but when not committed within any State, the Trial shall be at such Place or Places as the Congress may by Law have directed.

SECTION 3

Treason against the United States, shall consist only in levying War against them, or in adhering to their Enemies, giving them Aid and Comfort. No Person shall be convicted of Treason unless on the Testimony of two Witnesses to the same overt Act, or on Confession in open Court.

The Congress shall have Power to declare the Punishment of Treason, but no Attainder of Treason shall work Corruption of Blood, or Forfeiture except during the Life of the Person attainted.

Article IV

SECTION 1

Full Faith and Credit shall be given in each State to the public Acts, Records, and judicial Proceedings of every other State. And the Congress may by general Laws prescribe the Manner in which such Acts, Records and Proceedings shall be proved, and the Effect thereof.

SECTION 2

The Citizens of each State shall be entitled to all Privileges and Immunities of Citizens in the several States.

A Person charged in any State with Treason, Felony, or other Crime, who shall flee from Justice, and be found in another State, shall on Demand of the executive Authority of the State from which he fled, be delivered up, to be removed to the State having Jurisdiction of the Crime.

No Person held to Service or Labour in one State, under the Laws thereof, escaping into another, shall, in Consequence of any Law or Regulation therein, be discharged from such Service or Labour, but shall be delivered up on Claim of the Party to whom such Service or Labour may be due.

SECTION 3

New States may be admitted by the Congress into this Union; but no new State shall be formed or erected within the Jurisdiction of any other State; nor any State be formed by the Junction of two or more States, or Parts of States, without the Consent of the Legislatures of the States concerned as well as of the Congress.

The Congress shall have Power to dispose of and make all needful Rules and Regulations respecting the Territory or other Property belonging to the United States; and nothing in this Constitution shall be so construed as to Prejudice any Claims of the United States, or of any particular State.

SECTION 4

The United States shall guarantee to every State in this Union a Republican Form of Government, and shall protect each of them against Invasion; and on Application of the Legislature, or of the Executive (when the Legislature cannot be convened) against domestic Violence.

Article V

The Congress, whenever two thirds of both Houses shall deem it necessary, shall propose Amendments to this Constitution, or, on the Application of the Legislatures of two thirds of the several States, shall call a Convention for proposing Amendments, which, in either Case, shall be valid to all Intents and Purposes, as Part of this Constitution, when ratified by the Legislatures of three fourths of the several States, or by Conventions in three fourths thereof, as the one or the other Mode of Ratification may be proposed by the Congress; Provided that no Amendment which may be made prior to the Year One thousand eight hundred and eight shall in any Manner affect the first and fourth Clauses in the Ninth Section of the first Article; and that no State, without its Consent, shall be deprived of its equal Suffrage in the Senate.

Article VI

All Debts contracted and Engagements entered into, before the Adoption of this Constitution, shall be as valid against the United States under this Constitution, as under the Confederation.

This Constitution, and the Laws of the United States which shall be made in Pursuance thereof; and all Treaties made, or which shall be made, under the Authority of the United States, shall be the supreme Law of the Land; and the Judges in every State shall be bound thereby, any Thing in the Constitution or Laws of any State to the Contrary notwithstanding.

The Senators and Representatives before mentioned, and the Members of the several State Legislatures, and all executive and judicial Officers, both of the United States and of the several States, shall be bound by Oath or Affirmation, to support this Constitution; but no religious Test shall ever be required as a Qualification to any Office or public Trust under the United States.

Article VII

The Ratification of the Conventions of nine States, shall be sufficient for the Establishment of this Constitution between the States so ratifying the Same.

. . .

Articles in Addition to, and Amendment of, the Constitution of the United States of America, Proposed by Congress, and Ratified by the Several States, Pursuant to the Fifth Article of the Original Constitution

Amendment I [1791]

Congress shall make no law respecting an establishment of religion, or prohibiting the free exercise thereof; or abridging the freedom of speech, or of the press; or the right of the people peaceably to assemble, and to petition the Government for a redress of grievances.

Amendment II [1791]

A well regulated Militia, being necessary to the security of a free State, the right of the people to keep and bear Arms, shall not be infringed.

Amendment III [1791]

No Soldier shall, in time of peace be quartered in any house, without the consent of the Owner, nor in time of war, but in a manner to be prescribed by law.

Amendment IV [1791]

The right of the people to be secure in their persons, houses, papers, and effects, against unreasonable searches and seizures, shall not be violated, and no Warrants shall issue, but upon probable cause, supported by Oath or affirmation, and particularly describing the place to be searched, and the persons or things to be seized.

Amendment V [1791]

No person shall be held to answer for a capital, or otherwise infamous crime, unless on a presentment or indictment of a Grand Jury, except in cases arising in the land or naval forces, or in the Militia, when in actual service in time of War or public danger; nor shall any person be subject for the same offence to be twice put in jeopardy of life or limb; nor shall be compelled in any criminal case to be a witness against himself, nor be deprived of life, liberty, or property, without due process of law; nor shall private property be taken for public use, without just compensation.

Amendment VI [1791]

In all criminal prosecutions, the accused shall enjoy the right to a speedy and public trial, by an impartial jury of the State and district wherein the crime shall have been committed, which district shall have been previously ascertained by law, and to be informed of the nature and cause of the accusation; to be confronted with the witnesses against him; to have compulsory process for obtaining Witnesses in his favor, and to have the Assistance of Counsel for his defence.

Amendment VII [1791]

In Suits at common law, where the value in controversy shall exceed twenty dollars, the right of trial by jury shall be preserved, and no fact tried by a jury, shall be otherwise re-examined in any Court of the United States, than according to the rules of the common law.

Amendment VIII [1791]

Excessive bail shall not be required, nor excessive fines imposed, nor cruel and unusual punishments inflicted.

Amendment IX [1791]

The enumeration in the Constitution, of certain rights, shall not be construed to deny or disparage others retained by the people.

Amendment X [1791]

The powers not delegated to the United States by the Constitution, nor prohibited by it to the States, are reserved to the States respectively, or to the people.

Amendment XI [1798]

The Judicial power of the United States shall not be construed to extend to any suit in law or equity, commenced or prosecuted against one of the United States by Citizens of another State, or by Citizens or Subjects of any Foreign State.

Amendment XII [1804]

The Electors shall meet in their respective states and vote by ballot for President and Vice–President, one of whom, at least, shall not be an inhabitant of the same state with themselves; they shall name in their ballots the person voted for as President, and in distinct ballots the person voted for as Vice–President, and they shall make distinct lists of all persons voted for as President, and of all persons voted for as Vice–President, and of the number of votes for each, which lists they shall sign and certify, and transmit sealed to the seat of the government of the United States, directed to the President of the Senate;—The President of the Senate shall, in the presence of the Senate and House of Representatives, open all the certificates and the votes shall then be counted;—The person having the greatest number of votes for President, shall be the President, if such number be a majority of the whole number of Electors appointed; and if no person have such majority, then from the persons having the highest numbers not exceeding three on the list of those voted for as President, the House of Representatives shall choose immediately, by ballot, the President. But in choosing the President, the votes shall be taken by states, the representation from each state having one vote; a quorum for this purpose shall consist of a member or members from two-thirds of the states, and a majority of all the states shall be necessary to a choice. And if the House of Representatives shall not choose a President whenever the right of choice shall devolve upon them, before the fourth day of March next following, then the Vice–President shall act as President, as in the case of the death or other constitutional disability of the President—The person having the greatest number of votes as Vice–President, shall be the Vice–President, if such number be a majority of the whole number of Electors appointed, and if no person have a majority, then from the two highest numbers on the list, the Senate shall choose the Vice–President; a quorum for the purpose shall consist of two-thirds of the whole number of Senators, and a majority of the whole number shall be necessary to a choice. But no person constitutionally ineligible to the office of President shall be eligible to that of Vice–President of the United States.

Amendment XIII [1865]

SECTION 1

Neither slavery nor involuntary servitude, except as a punishment for crime whereof the party shall have been duly convicted, shall exist within the United States, or any place subject to their jurisdiction.

SECTION 2

Congress shall have power to enforce this article by appropriate legislation.

Amendment XIV [1868]

SECTION 1

All persons born or naturalized in the United States and subject to the jurisdiction thereof, are citizens of the United States and of the State wherein they reside. No State shall make or enforce any law which shall abridge the privileges or immunities of citizens of the United States; nor shall any State deprive any person of life, liberty, or property, without due process of law; nor deny to any person within its jurisdiction the equal protection of the laws.

SECTION 2

Representatives shall be apportioned among the several States according to their respective numbers, counting the whole number of persons in each State, excluding Indians not taxed. But when the right to vote at any election for the choice of electors for President and Vice President of the United States, Representatives in Congress, the Executive and Judicial officers of a State, or the members of the Legislature thereof, is denied to any of the male inhabitants of such State, being twenty-one years of age, and citizens of the United States, or in any way abridged, except for participation in rebellion, or other crime, the basis of representation therein shall be reduced in the proportion which the number of such male citizens shall bear to the whole number of male citizens twenty-one years of age in such State.

SECTION 3

No person shall be a Senator or Representative in Congress, or elector of President and Vice President, or hold any office, civil or military, under the United States, or under any State, who, having previously taken an oath, as a member of Congress, or as an officer of the United States, or as a member of any State legislature, or as an executive or judicial officer of any State, to support the Constitution of the United States, shall have engaged in insurrection or rebellion against the same, or given aid or comfort to the enemies thereof. But Congress may by a vote of two-thirds of each House, remove such disability.

SECTION 4

The validity of the public debt of the United States, authorized by law, including debts incurred for payment of pensions and bounties for services in suppressing insurrection or rebellion, shall not be questioned. But neither the United States nor any State shall assume or pay any debt or obligation incurred in aid of insurrection or rebellion against the United States, or any claim for the loss of emancipation of any slave; but all such debts, obligations and claims shall be held illegal and void.

SECTION 5

The Congress shall have power to enforce, by appropriate legislation, the provisions of this article.

Amendment XV [1870]

SECTION 1

The right of citizens of the United States to vote shall not be denied or abridged by the United States or by any State on account of race, color, or previous condition of servitude.

SECTION 2

The Congress shall have power to enforce this article by appropriate legislation.

Amendment XVI [1913]

The Congress shall have power to lay and collect taxes on incomes, from whatever source derived, without apportionment among the several States, and without regard to any census or enumeration.

Amendment XVII [1913]

The Senate of the United States shall be composed of two Senators from each State, elected by the people thereof, for six years; and each Senator shall have one vote. The electors in each State shall have the qualifications requisite for electors of the most numerous branch of the State legislatures.

When vacancies happen in the representation of any State in the Senate, the executive authority of such State shall issue writs of election to fill such vacancies: *Provided,* That the legislature of any State may empower the executive thereof to make temporary appointments until the people fill the vacancies by election as the legislature may direct.

This amendment shall not be so construed as to affect the election or term of any Senator chosen before it becomes valid as part of the Constitution.

Amendment XVIII [1919]

SECTION 1

After one year from the ratification of this article the manufacture, sale, or transportation of intoxicating liquors within, the importation thereof into, or the exportation thereof from the United States and all territory subject to the jurisdiction thereof for beverage purposes is hereby prohibited.

SECTION 2

The Congress and the several States shall have concurrent power to enforce this article by appropriate legislation.

SECTION 3

This article shall be inoperative unless it shall have been ratified as an amendment to the Constitution by the legislatures of the several States, as provided in the Constitution, within seven years from the date of the submission hereof to the States by the Congress.

Amendment XIX [1920]

The right of citizens of the United States to vote shall not be denied or abridged by the United States or by any State on account of sex.

Congress shall have power to enforce this article by appropriate legislation.

Amendment XX [1933]

SECTION 1

The terms of the President and Vice President shall end at noon on the 20th day of January, and the terms of Senators and Representatives at noon on the 3d day of January, of the years in which such terms would have ended if this article had not been ratified; and the terms of their successors shall then begin.

SECTION 2

The Congress shall assemble at least once in every year, and such meeting shall begin at noon on the 3d day of January, unless they shall by law appoint a different day.

SECTION 3

If, at the time fixed for the beginning of the term of the President, the President elect shall have died, the Vice President elect shall become President. If a President shall not have been chosen before the time fixed for the beginning of his term, or if the President elect shall have failed to qualify, then the Vice President elect shall act as President until a President shall have qualified; and the Congress may by law provide for the case wherein neither a President elect nor a Vice President elect shall have qualified, declaring who shall then act as President, or the manner in which one who is to act shall be selected, and such person shall act accordingly until a President or Vice President shall have qualified.

SECTION 4

The Congress may by law provide for the case of the death of any of the persons from whom the House of Representatives may choose a President whenever the right of choice shall have devolved upon them, and for the case of the death of any of the persons from whom the Senate may choose a Vice President whenever the right of choice shall have devolved upon them.

SECTION 5

Sections 1 and 2 shall take effect on the 15th day of October following the ratification of this article.

SECTION 6

This article shall be inoperative unless it shall have been ratified as an amendment to the Constitution by the legislatures of three-fourths of the several States within seven years from the date of its submission.

Amendment XXI [1933]

SECTION 1

The eighteenth article of amendment to the Constitution of the United States is hereby repealed.

SECTION 2

The transportation or importation into any State, Territory, or possession of the United States for delivery or use therein of intoxicating liquors, in violation of the laws thereof, is hereby prohibited.

SECTION 3

This article shall be inoperative unless it shall have been ratified as an amendment to the Constitution by conventions in the several States, as provided in the Constitution, within seven years from the date of the submission hereof to the States by the Congress.

Amendment XXII [1951]

SECTION 1

No person shall be elected to the office of the President more than twice, and no person who has held the office of President, or acted as President, for more than two years of a term to which some other person was elected President shall be elected to the office of the President more than once. But this Article shall not apply to any person holding the office of President when this Article was proposed by the Congress, and shall not prevent any person who may be holding the office of President, or acting as President, during the term within which this Article becomes operative from holding the office of President or acting as President during the remainder of such term.

SECTION 2

This article shall be inoperative unless it shall have been ratified as an amendment to the Constitution by the legislatures of three-fourths of the several States within seven years from the date of its submission to the States by the Congress.

Amendment XXIII [1961]

SECTION 1

The District constituting the seat of Government of the United States shall appoint in such manner as the Congress may direct:

A number of electors of President and Vice President equal to the whole number of Senators and Representatives in Congress to which the District would be entitled if it were a State, but in no event more than the least populous State; they shall be in addition to those appointed by the States, but they shall be considered, for the purposes of the election of President and Vice President, to be electors appointed by a State; and they shall meet in the District and perform such duties as provided by the twelfth article of amendment.

SECTION 2

The Congress shall have power to enforce this article by appropriate legislation.

Amendment XXIV [1964]

SECTION 1

The right of citizens of the United States to vote in any primary or other election for President or Vice President, for electors for President or Vice President, or for Senator or Representative in Congress, shall not be denied or abridged by the United States or any State by reason of failure to pay any poll tax or other tax.

SECTION 2

The Congress shall have power to enforce this article by appropriate legislation.

Amendment XXV [1967]

SECTION 1

In case of the removal of the President from office or of his death or resignation, the Vice President shall become President.

SECTION 2

Whenever there is a vacancy in the office of the Vice President, the President shall nominate a Vice President who shall take office upon confirmation by a majority vote of both Houses of Congress.

SECTION 3

Whenever the President transmits to the President pro tempore of the Senate and the Speaker of the House of Representatives his written declaration that he is unable to discharge the powers and duties of his office, and until he transmits to them a written declaration to the contrary, such powers and duties shall be discharged by the Vice President as Acting President.

SECTION 4

Whenever the Vice President and a majority of either the principal officers of the executive departments or of such other body as Congress may by law provide, transmit to the President pro tempore of the Senate and the Speaker of the House of Representatives their written declaration that the President is unable to discharge the powers and duties of his office, the Vice President shall immediately assume the powers and duties of the office as Acting President.

Thereafter, when the President transmits to the President pro tempore of the Senate and the Speaker of the House of Representatives his written declaration that no inability exists, he shall resume the powers and duties of his office unless the Vice President and a majority of either the principal officers of the executive department or of such other body as Congress may by law provide, transmit within four days to the President pro tempore of the Senate and the Speaker of the House of Representatives their written declaration that the President is unable to discharge the powers and duties of his office. Thereupon Congress shall decide the issue, assembling within forty-eight hours for that purpose if not in session. If the Congress, within twenty-one days after receipt of the latter written declaration, or, if Congress is not in session, within twenty-one days after Congress is required to assemble, determines by two-thirds vote of both Houses that the President is unable to discharge the powers and duties of his office, the Vice President shall continue to discharge the same as Acting President; otherwise, the President shall resume the powers and duties of his office.

Amendment XXVI [1971]

SECTION 1

The right of citizens of the United States, who are eighteen years of age or older, to vote shall not be denied or abridged by the United States or by any State on account of age.

SECTION 2

The Congress shall have power to enforce this article by appropriate legislation.

Amendment XXVII [1992][1]

No law, varying the compensation for the services of the Senators and Representatives, shall take effect, until an election of Representatives shall have intervened.

---

1. The First Congress proposed this amendment in 1789 as one of the Bill of Rights. By 1792, after the first ten amendments had been ratified, only six states had endorsed this proposal. In 1873 a seventh state added its approval. Interest in the amendment arose again in 1978. By 1992, 32 more states ratified, bringing the number to 39, one more than the three-fourths prescribed by Article V. As Chapter 6 indicated, the validity of the amendment raises serious question because its process of ratification stretched over 203 years. Nevertheless, in May 1992, the Archivist of the United States announced that he was certifying to Congress that the amendment had been duly ratified.

TABLE OF CASES

Principal cases are in italic type. Non-principal cases are in roman type. References are to Pages. If a case is cited more than once in a principal case, generally only the first citation is listed.

1441

*

INDEX

References are to Pages

†

1-56662-240-9